TROPICAL
FLOWERING
PLANTS

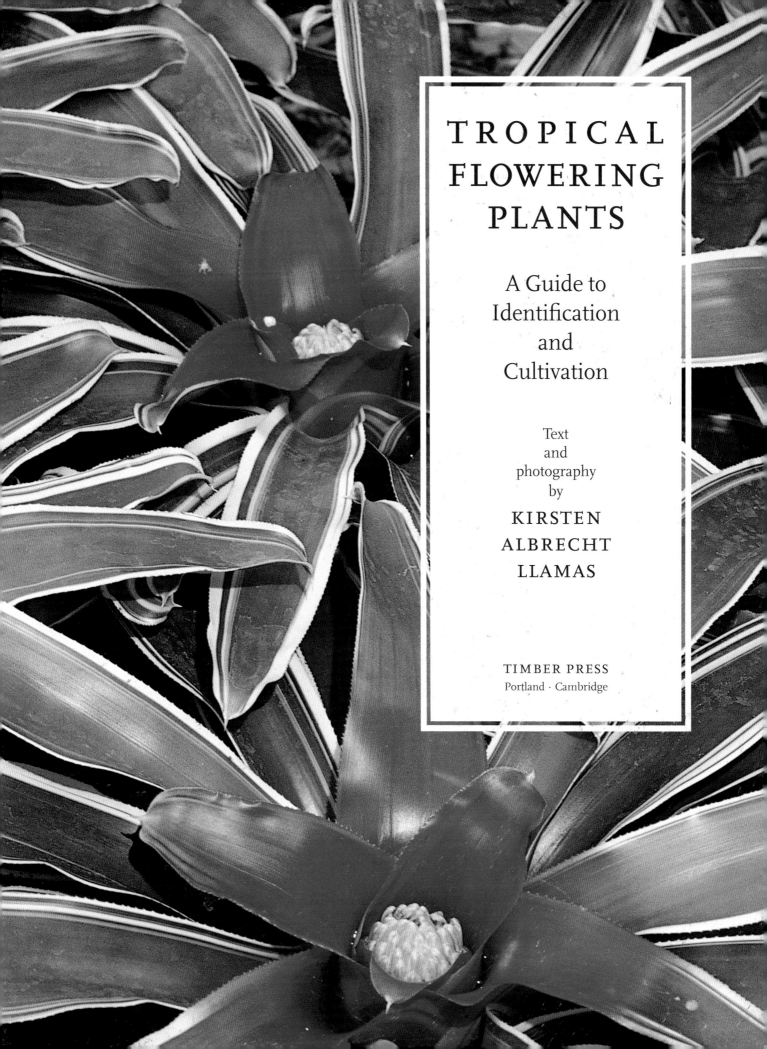

TROPICAL
FLOWERING
PLANTS

A Guide to
Identification
and
Cultivation

Text
and
photography
by

KIRSTEN
ALBRECHT
LLAMAS

TIMBER PRESS
Portland · Cambridge

Half title: *Plumeria* hybrids. Title page: *Neoregelia carolinae* 'Meyendorfii'.
Page 27: *Etlingera elatior*, red form.

Published in 2003 by

Timber Press, Inc.
The Haseltine Building
133 S.W. Second Avenue, Suite 450
Portland, Oregon 97204, U.S.A.

Timber Press
2 Station Road
Swavesey
Cambridge CB4 5QJ, U.K.

Designed by Susan Applegate
Printed in Hong Kong

Library of Congress Cataloging-in-Publication Data

Llamas, Kirsten Albrecht.
    Tropical flowering plants: a guide to identification / text
and photography by Kirsten Albrecht Llamas.
        p. cm.
    Includes bibliographical references and index.
    ISBN 0-88192-585-3
    1. Tropical plants. 2. Tropical plants—Identification. 3. Tropical
plants—Pictorial works. I. Title.

SB407 .L59 2003
635'.9523'0222—dc21   2002075651

To
my husband, Roberto

our daughters,
Marcela Teresa Llamas Losh
Tania Cecilia Llamas Cornelison
Sasha Lenora Llamas

our grandson,
Liam Joseph Losh

and to my mother and father,
Josephine Eleanor Farmer Albrecht
Herbert Otto Albrecht
(1899–1977)

CONTENTS

11 Foreword *by*
   Richard A. Howard
12 Preface
15 Acknowledgments
19 Introduction
25 USDA Hardiness
   Zone Map

27 Plant Descriptions
28 ACANTHACEAE
28   *Acanthus*
28   *Aphelandra*
29   *Asystasia*
29   *Barleria*
30   *Crossandra*
31   *Dyschoriste*
31   *Eranthemum*
32   *Fittonia*
32   *Graptophyllum*
32   *Hypoestes*
32   *Justicia*
34   *Mackaya*
34   *Megaskepasma*
34   *Odontonema*
35   *Pachystachys*
35   *Pseuderanthemum*
36   *Ruellia*
38   *Ruspolia*
38   *Ruttya*
38   ×*Ruttyruspolia*
38   *Sanchezia*
39   *Schaueria*
39   *Strobilanthes*
39   *Thunbergia*

41 ADOXACEAE
41   *Sambucus*
42 AGAPANTHACEAE
42   *Agapanthus*
42 AGAVACEAE
42   *Agave*
47   *Furcraea*
47   *Yucca*
48 AIZOACEAE
49   *Aptenia*
49   *Carpobrotus*
49   *Glottiphyllum*
49   *Lampranthus*
50   *Trichodiadema*
50 ALISMATACEAE
50   *Hydrocleys*
50   *Sagittaria*
51 ALLIACEAE
51   *Tulbaghia*
51 ALSTROEMERIACEAE
51   *Alstroemeria*
52 AMARANTHACEAE
52   *Alternanthera*
52   *Celosia*
52   *Iresine*
53 AMARYLLIDACEAE
53   ×*Amarcrinum*
53   *Amaryllis*
53   *Clivia*
54   *Crinum*
55   *Eucharis*
56   *Eucrosia*
56   *Habranthus*
56   *Haemanthus*

56   *Hippeastrum*
57   *Hymenocallis*
57   *Proiphys*
58   *Rhodophiala*
58   *Scadoxus*
58 ANACARDIACEAE
58   *Mangifera*
59   *Schinus*
60   *Spondias*
60 ANNONACEAE
60   *Annona*
61   *Artabotrys*
61   *Cananga*
61   *Polyalthia*
62   *Rollinia*
62 APOCYNACEAE
62   *Adenium*
63   *Allamanda*
64   *Alstonia*
64   *Beaumontia*
65   *Carissa*
65   *Catharanthus*
65   *Chonemorpha*
65   *Kopsia*
65   *Mandevilla*
66   *Nerium*
66   *Ochrosia*
67   *Odontadenia*
67   *Pachypodium*
68   *Pentalinon*
68   *Plumeria*
69   *Prestonia*
70   *Stemmadenia*
70   *Strophanthus*

70   *Tabernaemontana*
72   *Thevetia*
72   *Trachelospermum*
72   *Wrightia*
72 APOCYNACEAE
   formerly ASCLEPIADACEAE
73   *Asclepias*
73   *Calotropis*
73   *Cryptostegia*
74   *Hoya*
74   *Orbea*
75   *Stapelia*
75   *Stephanotis*
75 AQUIFOLIACEAE
75   *Ilex*
76 ARACEAE
76   *Aglaonema*
77   *Alocasia*
78   *Amorphophallus*
80   *Anthurium*
81   *Caladium*
81   *Colocasia*
82   *Cyrtosperma*
82   *Dieffenbachia*
82   *Dracontium*
82   *Epipremnum*
83   *Gonatopus*
83   *Homalomena*
84   *Monstera*
84   *Philodendron*
85   *Pistia*
86   *Pothoidium*
86   *Spathicarpa*
86   *Spathiphyllum*

6

87	*Syngonium*	119	*Syagrus*	142	*Saritaea*	169	*Casuarina*
87	*Xanthosoma*	120	*Thrinax*	142	*Spathodea*	170	CECROPIACEAE
87	*Zantedeschia*	120	*Veitchia*	142	*Tabebuia*	170	*Cecropia*
88	ARALIACEAE	121	*Washingtonia*	145	*Tecoma*	170	CISTACEAE
88	*Osmoxylon*	122	*Wodyetia*	146	*Tecomanthe*	171	*Cistus*
88	*Schefflera*	123	*Zombia*	146	BIXACEAE	171	CLUSIACEAE
89	ARECACEAE	123	ARISTOLOCHIACEAE	146	*Bixa*	172	*Clusia*
90	*Acoelorrhaphe*	123	*Aristolochia*	147	BORAGINACEAE	172	*Mammea*
90	*Adonidia*	124	ASPHODELACEAE	147	*Cordia*	173	*Mesua*
90	*Aiphanes*	124	*Aloe*	148	*Echium*	173	COCHLOSPERMACEAE
91	*Allagoptera*	128	*Bulbine*	150	*Wigandia*	173	*Cochlospermum*
91	*Archontophoenix*	128	ASTERACEAE	150	BRASSICACEAE	173	COLCHICACEAE
92	*Areca*	128	*Cheirolophus*	150	*Capparis*	174	*Gloriosa*
92	*Astrocaryum*	128	*Coreopsis*	150	*Cleome*	174	COMBRETACEAE
92	*Attalea*	129	*Dahlia*	151	*Crateva*	174	*Bucida*
93	*Beccariophoenix*	129	*Montanoa*	151	BROMELIACEAE	175	*Calopyxis*
94	*Bentinckia*	129	*Pericallis*	152	*Aechmea*	175	*Combretum*
94	*Bismarckia*	129	*Phymaspermum*	155	*Alcantarea*	175	*Quisqualis*
94	*Borassus*	130	*Podachaenium*	155	*Ananas*	176	COMMELINACEAE
95	*Brahea*	130	*Pseudogynoxys*	156	*Androlepis*	176	*Cochliostema*
96	*Butia*	130	*Senecio*	156	*Billbergia*	176	*Dichorisandra*
96	*Carpentaria*	131	*Sphagneticola*	157	*Bromelia*	176	*Tradescantia*
97	*Caryota*	131	*Tagetes*	157	*Cryptanthus*	177	CONVOLVULACEAE
98	*Chamaedorea*	131	*Tithonia*	158	*Guzmania*	177	*Argyreia*
98	*Chambeyronia*	132	BALSAMINACEAE	158	*Hohenbergia*	177	*Evolvulus*
99	*Coccothrinax*	132	*Impatiens*	159	*Navia*	177	*Ipomoea*
100	*Cocos*	133	BEGONIACEAE	159	*Neoregelia*	179	*Jacquemontia*
101	*Copernicia*	133	*Begonia*	160	*Orthophytum*	179	*Merremia*
102	*Corypha*	134	BERBERIDACEAE	160	*Pepinia*	179	*Poranopsis*
102	*Cyrtostachys*	134	*Nandina*	161	*Pitcairnia*	179	CRASSULACEAE
103	*Dictyosperma*	134	BIGNONIACEAE	161	*Portea*	180	*Aeonium*
104	*Dypsis*	134	*Adenocalymna*	161	*Quesnelia*	180	*Crassula*
105	*Elaeis*	134	*Campsis*	161	*Tillandsia*	180	*Kalanchoe*
106	*Hyophorbe*	135	*Catalpa*	162	*Vriesea*	182	*Sedum*
106	*Hyphaene*	135	×*Chitalpa*	163	CACTACEAE	182	CUCURBITACEAE
107	*Latania*	135	*Clytostoma*	163	Cactus Intergeneric	183	*Gurania*
107	*Licuala*	135	*Crescentia*		Hybrids	183	*Luffa*
108	*Livistona*	136	*Cydista*	164	*Cereus*	183	*Momordica*
108	*Lodoicea*	136	*Delostoma*	164	*Consolea*	183	CYCLANTHACEAE
109	*Phoenix*	136	*Distictis*	165	*Epiphyllum*	183	*Carludovica*
112	*Pritchardia*	137	*Dolichandrone*	165	*Hylocereus*	184	*Dicranopygium*
113	*Pseudophoenix*	137	*Jacaranda*	165	*Opuntia*	184	DILLENIACEAE
114	*Ptychosperma*	139	*Kigelia*	166	*Pereskia*	184	*Dillenia*
114	*Raphia*	139	*Macfadyena*	167	*Schlumbergera*	184	*Hibbertia*
115	*Ravenea*	139	*Mansoa*	167	CANELLACEAE	185	DIOSCOREACEAE
115	*Reinhardtia*	140	*Markhamia*	167	*Canella*	185	*Dioscorea*
115	*Rhapis*	140	*Newbouldia*	167	CANNACEAE	185	EBENACEAE
116	*Roystonea*	140	*Pandorea*	168	*Canna*	185	*Diospyros*
117	*Sabal*	140	*Parmentiera*	168	CAPRIFOLIACEAE	186	ERICACEAE
118	*Schippia*	141	*Podranea*	169	*Lonicera*	186	*Rhododendron*,
118	*Serenoa*	141	*Pyrostegia*	169	CASUARINACEAE		Vireya Group

186 EUPHORBIACEAE
186 *Acalypha*
187 *Aleurites*
187 *Antidesma*
188 *Breynia*
188 *Cnidoscolus*
188 *Codiaeum*
189 *Dalechampia*
189 *Elaeophorbia*
189 *Euphorbia*
193 *Jatropha*
194 *Macaranga*
194 *Manihot*
194 *Phyllanthus*
195 *Ricinus*
195 FABACEAE
195 FABACEAE, Subfamily
    CAESALPINIOIDEAE
195 *Amherstia*
196 *Bauhinia*
199 *Brownea*
200 *Caesalpinia*
201 *Cassia*
203 *Colvillea*
203 *Delonix*
205 *Moullava*
205 *Parkinsonia*
205 *Peltophorum*
206 *Saraca*
207 *Schotia*
207 *Senna*
209 *Tamarindus*
210 FABACEAE, Subfamily
    MIMOSOIDEAE
210 *Acacia*
211 *Adenanthera*
211 *Albizia*
212 *Archidendron*
213 *Calliandra*
213 *Ebenopsis*
214 *Inga*
214 *Lysiloma*
214 *Mimosa*
214 FABACEAE, Subfamily
    PAPILIONOIDEAE
215 *Brya*
216 *Butea*
216 *Cajanus*
216 *Chadsia*
217 *Clitoria*
217 *Crotalaria*

217 *Erythrina*
220 *Gliricidia*
220 *Hebestigma*
221 *Kennedia*
221 *Lonchocarpus*
221 *Millettia*
221 *Mucuna*
221 *Periandra*
222 *Poitea*
222 *Sesbania*
222 *Sophora*
222 *Spartium*
223 *Strongylodon*
223 *Tipuana*
223 *Uraria*
223 *Vigna*
224 FLACOURTIACEAE
224 *Banara*
224 *Casearia*
224 *Oncoba*
225 *Samyda*
225 GELSEMIACEAE
225 *Gelsemium*
225 GENTIANACEAE
225 *Fagraea*
226 GERANIACEAE
226 *Geranium*
226 *Pelargonium*
227 GESNERIACEAE
227 *Episcia*
227 *Gloxinia*
227 *Streptocarpus*
227 GOODENIACEAE
228 *Scaevola*
228 HAEMODORACEAE
228 *Anigozanthos*
228 HAMAMELIDACEAE
228 *Loropetalum*
229 HELICONIACEAE
229 *Heliconia*
234 HEMEROCALLIDACEAE
234 *Hemerocallis*
234 HYACINTHACEAE
234 *Eucomis*
234 HYPOXIDACEAE
234 *Molineria*
235 IRIDACEAE
235 *Aristea*
235 *Chasmanthe*
235 *Crocosmia*
235 *Dietes*

236 *Neomarica*
236 *Trimezia*
236 *Watsonia*
236 LAMIACEAE
237 *Leonotis*
237 *Orthosiphon*
237 *Plectranthus*
238 *Salvia*
238 *Scutellaria*
238 LAMIACEAE,
    formerly VERBENACEAE
238 *Clerodendrum*
241 *Congea*
241 *Cornutia*
242 *Gmelina*
242 *Holmskioldia*
242 *Oxera*
243 *Vitex*
243 LAURACEAE
243 *Persea*
243 LECYTHIDACEAE
244 *Barringtonia*
244 *Couroupita*
244 *Gustavia*
245 LEEACEAE
245 *Leea*
245 LINACEAE
245 *Reinwardtia*
246 LOMANDRACEAE
246 *Cordyline*
246 LYTHRACEAE
246 *Cuphea*
247 *Duabanga*
247 *Ginoria*
247 *Lagerstroemia*
249 *Lawsonia*
249 *Punica*
249 MAGNOLIACEAE
249 *Magnolia*
250 *Michelia*
250 MALPIGHIACEAE
250 *Bunchosia*
251 *Byrsonima*
251 *Callaeum*
252 *Galphimia*
252 *Hiptage*
252 *Malpighia*
253 *Stigmaphyllon*
253 *Tristellateia*
253 MALVACEAE
253 *Abelmoschus*

254 *Abutilon*
254 *Alyogyne*
254 *Anisodontea*
255 *Gossypium*
255 *Hibiscus*
258 *Kosteletzkya*
258 *Malva*
258 *Malvaviscus*
259 *Pavonia*
259 *Sida*
259 *Thespesia*
260 *Wercklea*
260 MALVACEAE, formerly
    BOMBACACEAE
260 *Adansonia*
260 *Bombax*
261 *Ceiba*
263 *Ochroma*
264 *Pachira*
265 *Pseudobombax*
265 *Quararibea*
266 MALVACEAE, formerly
    STERCULIACEAE
266 *Abroma*
266 *Brachychiton*
267 *Dombeya*
268 *Helicteres*
268 *Kleinhovia*
268 *Pterospermum*
269 *Sterculia*
269 *Theobroma*
269 MALVACEAE,
    formerly TILIACEAE
270 *Berrya*
270 *Grewia*
270 *Luehea*
270 MARANTACEAE
271 *Calathea*
271 *Maranta*
272 MELASTOMATACEAE
272 *Dissotis*
272 *Heterocentron*
272 *Medinilla*
273 *Melastoma*
274 *Sonerila*
274 *Tetrazygia*
274 *Tibouchina*
276 MELIACEAE
276 *Melia*
276 MENYANTHACEAE
276 *Nymphoides*

276 MORACEAE
277 Artocarpus
277 Dorstenia
277 Ficus
278 Morus
279 MORINGACEAE
279 Moringa
279 MUNTINGIACEAE
279 Dicraspidia
279 Muntingia
279 MUSACEAE
280 Musa
281 MYRSINACEAE
281 Ardisia
282 MYRTACEAE
282 Acca
282 Agonis
283 Callistemon
283 Calyptranthes
283 Chamelaucium
284 Corymbia
284 Eucalyptus
285 Eugenia
286 Leptospermum
286 Lophostemon
286 Melaleuca
288 Metrosideros
288 Myrcianthes
289 Myrciaria
289 Pimenta
289 Psidium
290 Syzygium
291 NELUMBONACEAE
291 Nelumbo
291 NYCTAGINACEAE
291 Bougainvillea
293 NYMPHAEACEAE
293 Nymphaea
294 Victoria
295 OCHNACEAE
295 Ochna
295 Ouratea
296 OLEACEAE
296 Jasminum
296 Ligustrum
297 ONAGRACEAE
297 Fuchsia
297 Hauya
297 Ludwigia
298 Oenothera
298 ORCHIDACEAE

298 ×Ascocenda
298 ×Brassocattleya
298 Calanthe
299 Cattleya
300 Cymbidium
300 Dendrobium
301 ×Doritaenopsis
301 Encyclia
301 Epidendrum
301 Haemaria
301 Lycaste
302 Miltonia
302 Oncidium
302 Paphiopedilum
303 Phaius
303 Phalaenopsis
303 Psychopsis
303 Renanthera
304 Sobralia
304 ×Sophrolaeliocattleya
304 Spathoglottis
304 Stanhopea
305 Vanda
305 Zeuxine
306 OXALIDACEAE
306 Averrhoa
306 Oxalis
306 PANDANACEAE
307 Freycinetia
307 Pandanus
308 PAPAVERACEAE
308 Argemone
309 Eschscholzia
309 Romneya
309 PASSIFLORACEAE
309 Passiflora
311 PAULOWNIACEAE
311 Paulownia
312 PEDALIACEAE
312 Uncarina
312 PHYTOLACCACEAE
312 Phytolacca
312 PIPERACEAE
313 Piper
313 PITTOSPORACEAE
313 Hymenosporum
314 Pittosporum
314 PLANTAGINACEAE
314 Angelonia
314 Digitalis
314 Globularia

314 Isoplexis
315 Otacanthus
315 Russelia
315 PLUMBAGINACEAE
316 Limonium
316 Plumbago
316 POLYGALACEAE
316 Polygala
317 Securidaca
317 POLYGONACEAE
317 Antigonon
318 Coccoloba
318 Muehlenbeckia
318 Ruprechtia
318 Triplaris
319 PONTEDERIACEAE
319 Eichhornia
319 Pontederia
319 PORTULACACEAE
319 Portulaca
320 PROTEACEAE
320 Alloxylon
320 Banksia
321 Grevillea
322 Leucadendron
322 Leucospermum
323 Protea
323 Stenocarpus
324 ROSACEAE
324 Osteomeles
324 Rhaphiolepis
324 RUBIACEAE
325 Burchellia
325 Catesbaea
325 Coffea
325 Gardenia
326 Hamelia
327 Hoffmannia
328 Ixora
329 Manettia
329 Mussaenda
330 Nauclea
330 Pentas
330 Pogonopus
331 Portlandia
332 Posoqueria
332 Psychotria
332 Richardia
332 Rondeletia
333 Warszewiczia
333 RUSCACEAE

333 Beaucarnea
335 Dasylirion
335 Dracaena
336 Liriope
337 Sansevieria
338 RUTACEAE
338 Calodendrum
339 Citrus
339 Correa
339 Erythrochiton
340 Limonia
340 Murraya
340 Pamburus
340 Ravenia
341 Swinglea
341 SAPINDACEAE
341 Aesculus
341 Blighia
341 Dimocarpus
342 Dodonaea
342 Harpullia
343 Koelreuteria
343 Litchi
343 Majidea
343 SAPOTACEAE
343 Manilkara
344 Mimusops
344 Pouteria
344 Synsepalum
345 SCHLEGELIACEAE
345 Schlegelia
345 SCROPHULARIACEAE
345 Buddleja
346 Leucophyllum
346 SOLANACEAE
346 Acnistus
346 Brugmansia
348 Brunfelsia
350 Cestrum
351 Datura
351 Goetzea
351 Iochroma
351 Lycianthes
352 Solandra
352 Solanum
353 Streptosolen
354 STRELITZIACEAE
354 Ravenala
355 Strelitzia
355 TACCACEAE
355 Tacca

356 THEOPHRASTACEAE
356 *Clavija*
356 *Jacquinia*
357 THYMELAEACEAE
357 *Dais*
357 *Drimyspermum*
357 *Gnidia*
357 *Phaleria*
357 TURNERACEAE
357 *Turnera*
358 VELLOZIACEAE
358 *Vellozia*
358 VERBENACEAE
358 *Duranta*
359 *Lantana*
359 *Petrea*

360 *Stachytarpheta*
360 VIOLACEAE
361 *Hybanthus*
361 ZINGIBERACEAE
361 *Alpinia*
363 *Burbidgea*
363 *Costus*
365 *Curcuma*
367 *Dimerocostus*
368 *Etlingera*
368 *Globba*
369 *Hedychium*
370 *Kaempferia*
371 *Monocostus*
371 *Riedelia*
371 *Siphonochilus*

372 *Tapeinochilos*
372 *Zingiber*
373 ZYGOPHYLLACEAE
373 *Bulnesia*
373 *Guaiacum*

375 APPENDIX 1. Invasive and Potentially Invasive Species
376 APPENDIX 2. Rare, Endangered, and Threatened Species
377 APPENDIX 3. Plants for Coastal Landscaping
379 APPENDIX 4. Xerophytic Plants
381 Glossary
390 Bibliography
393 List of Web Sites
395 Index of Scientific and Common Names

FOREWORD

THIS BOOK is a unique publication combining an outstanding collection of more than 1500 color photographs of tropical and subtropical flowering plants with descriptions of the families, genera, species, and cultivars, including country or area of origin, general maintenance, propagation, and horticultural use. No other single volume is available with such appropriate application.

The descriptions are arranged alphabetically by family, genus, and species. The family groups are based on *Plant Systematics, A Phylogenetic Approach* (Judd et al. 2002). This textbook, recognizing and incorporating many of the latest studies in molecular biology, has redefined many families of flowering plants, the angiosperms, so that *Tropical Flowering Plants: A Guide to Identification and Cultivation* becomes the first volume in the field of horticulture to recognize the modern status of plant systematics.

For the treatments of genera and species Mrs. Llamas has consulted specialists in the United States and elsewhere and has followed their published work and frequently shared their currently unpublished work in progress. Synonyms and misapplied names are also listed, greatly increasing the reference value of this book.

Many cultivars are illustrated and described in the text. In the literature of horticulture, cultivar names are indexed by name, author, or bibliographic citation only by the relatively small number of International Cultivar Registration Authorities (ICRAs) for cultivar names. Few of the cultivars treated in this book are represented by ICRAs. Thus, the cultivar names given in this volume will have increasing value in the future as the place of publication, with a colored illustration, aiding the work of the Horticultural Taxonomic Group, at the Royal Horticultural Society Wisley Garden, Woking, Surrey, United Kingdom.

The common names given in this publication are those used primarily in English- and Spanish-speaking areas. The cultural information was derived from the personal experience of the author and that shared by practitioners in other areas. The volume has immediate value to the gardener or home owner who is considering the investment of time and money in the addition of new but unusual or unknown plants to existing plantings.

RICHARD A. HOWARD
Professor emeritus at Harvard University
Former director of Arnold Arboretum

PREFACE

THE NATURAL FUNCTION of tropical flowers, with their luminous colors and ingenious designs, is to lure pollinators within the boundless green of the rain forest or during a brief rainy season in arid regions. We humans respond to the aesthetics and exotic allure of their fecund natural beauty. Nurseries vie for new and exotic species to quench the collectors' thirst. The floral business imports flowers from around the globe. In the United States, tropical plants are grown outdoors year-round in Hawaii, California, Florida, and along the Gulf Coast. They are grown indoors, at least in winter, from Maine to Alaska. They appear on the pages of glossy magazines, in ads, television studio sets, homes, and work places. It is evident that the pleasure derived from having tropical plants around us is a passion shared by many.

The wild habitat of tropical species is disappearing at an alarming rate. It is calculated that literally thousands of species have become extinct without our ever having had a glimpse of them, and untold thousands more seem likely to be exterminated within the next few decades. Only a relative few species make it into cultivation because of their aesthetic, medicinal, or utilitarian value. Others with unknown value are lost every day to the saw, bulldozer, and fire.

This volume illuminates many species saved through cultivation. Tropical gardens and conservatories not only exhibit but also protect plants as zoos protect animal species. It is hoped that this volume will help impart a deeper appreciation for tropical species through plants in cultivation and, by extension, the need to preserve their wild habitat. Gardeners help maintain diversity by seeking out, growing, and sharing unusual species.

When I began to study tropical botany in the 1950s, the books on tropical plants were usually densely scientific.

Illustrations, if present at all, were black-and-white drawings or stylistic color paintings. For a young Northerner freshly transplanted to the subtropics, it made learning about this intriguing flora especially challenging. Dry herbarium specimens did not relate very well to the verdant green that surrounded me. Available collections were limited. Little was available on tropical plants from distant regions.

As a lifelong photographer as well as a budding botanist, I decided to create my own photo collection of the plants that caught my eye. The process of discovering an exciting species, taking its photo, finding its name, and labeling the photo made a species indelible in my memory. In 1992 after Hurricane Andrew cut a large swath across South Florida, resulting in loss of trees and cooling greenness, my photographic perspective on tropical plants took on new meaning. Stress often incites a plant to bloom. Previously out-of-reach flowers on tall trees burst forth on mangled limbs at camera level.

To file my burgeoning collection I had to identify the plants correctly, but popular literature proved contradictory and untrustworthy. During the same period diagnostic technology using DNA was providing fresh insight into plant relationships, which resulted in massive rearrangement of plant families and numerous name changes. Thus, this volume evolved out of the need for a reliable broad reference for plants in cultivation.

As the photos and accompanying information in the database grew, it became clear that the information would be valuable to others as well. As the photographer as well as the writer, I have had firsthand experience with each plant and control over the accuracy of their descriptions. References were challenged and cross-checked.

This book is intended to be concise, detailed enough for

students and professionals, and written in language that can be understood by the average plant enthusiast. Above all, I want the reader to enjoy tropical plants and perhaps search for something a little out of the ordinary for a container on the porch or a special place in the garden.

The vast majority of the world's plant species come from the tropics, and no single volume could possibly cover even a fraction of the tropicals in cultivation. This book includes a selection of plants that demonstrate the great diversity of species in cultivation. It offers information about their native habitats and growing conditions which, in turn, suggests how they will best thrive in cultivation. Cultivated plants more commonly encountered in the garden and nurseries are presented along with rare and tantalizing plants for jaded readers. Woody plants are covered in greatest depth. A diverse selection from the very large herbaceous families provides essential information for distinguishing these groups. Particular attention has been given to the rarely published but magnificent ginger family, Zingiberaceae.

The criterion for selecting species to be included in this volume is their ability to thrive in zone 9 (with average lows between 20° and 30°F) or higher. Species with a broad temperature tolerance may also grow in temperate regions. Selections are included from moist tropical regions and seasonally moist/dry climates as well as cool montane and arid regions. A few technically nontropical species have been included that are commonly grown and thrive in tropical regions. Most annuals and species grown primarily as foliage plants are excluded.

In temperate regions many tropical species can be grown indoors in containers in winter and moved outdoors in spring. Some fast-growers are planted as summer annuals. Species from higher altitudes, deciduous shrubs, and winter-dormant herbs are often grown as perennials outdoors in mild areas with a blanket of mulch to protect the roots from freezing.

Maximum effort has been given to determining the currently accepted name for each species. Specialists in the various families have been consulted—sometimes prodded unmercifully—for details. Live scans and/or vouchers have been sent out for verification as needed. In a few cases where information is insufficient to support an identification, out-dated, or still under investigation, the best determination is given with the caveat that the identification is tentative. Uncertain determinations are clearly stated in an effort to counter any subsequent propagation of unverified names as fact in the popular literature.

Though some may dream of stability for scientific plant names, systematics is an evolving science. Naming a plant is not like giving a name to a newborn child, but rather like adopting an orphan and trying to determine its family roots and relationships after the fact. Names are based on the current understanding of the relationships among plant groups and evolutionary hierarchy. A number of different botanists may independently collect the same or very similar species, and each may have given them names based upon what information they can find. It takes considerable research, often involving international herbaria, to track down and compare collections to see which is a previously named species and which a new one. With each new study and technique, specimens are reviewed, and any new information often results in a name being revised. Inevitably, some experts will disagree on classification. The current studies using DNA have initiated a complete reevaluation of all previously named genera.

Botanical reorganization is one thing, but the most difficult task has been weeding out names that have been applied illegitimately in the trade, commonly without any regard for registration. Invalid names have become indelibly embedded in the popular literature and psyche of gardeners. For lack of understanding of what must seem like a constant stream of changes on the botanical side, the trade holds tenaciously to familiar names no matter how wrong or out of date they may be.

Growers often protect hybrid ancestry and origin for short-term commercial competition or fail to keep accurate records. This has led to considerable confusion and misinformation that distorts and quickly devalues the work of the grower. This is especially unfortunate in view of the drastic loss of biodiversity in wild habitat and the growing imperative to establish records of surviving species in cultivation and their hybrids. The Web address for the International Cultivar Registration Authorities (ICRAs), which provides information on registration of cultivar names, is given at the end of this book in the list of Web sites.

This volume is arranged alphabetically by family. This positions photos of related genera in close proximity for easy comparison. Leaf and floral size, morphology, gross size, and habit for each species are based on my original measurements with comparative figures included to show the range of natural variability. One or two field marks, or distinctive characteristics, are provided to help differentiate similar species. Botanical terminology is often used for brevity, but terms are explained in nearby family and genus headings. A glossary is also provided. Every effort has been made to enlighten while keeping this volume simple to use and pleasant to browse.

Information provided will help differentiate plants

with benign behavior from potential pests. Lists of invasive and weedy species are at the end of this book. As far as is known, only Florida actually prohibits certain species from distribution and this information is included as cautionary to other regions; however, it must be noted that a pest in one region or type of climate may be quite benign in another. Institutions such as state universities in Hawaii, Texas, and California provide lists of invasive plants in their regions on the Web. A list of Web sites can be found at the end of this book.

Be forewarned that state and county lists of restricted species do not always deter unscrupulous or unimaginative landscapers from selling undesirable species to the unwary. Anything from expensive builder-homes to subdivisions are landscaped primarily with mass-produced plants designed to sell property but without regard to how they will look in several years. Weedy species are fast-growing and cheap to produce, which means that a landscape company makes a return trip for maintenance, taking another bite out of your wallet. Checking for weedy species and size characteristics in this volume in advance will save considerable expense and regret in the future.

In our rapidly aging society, drastically reducing garden maintenance is a sound investment in the future both physically and financially. Elders can literally be driven from their homes by the cost of maintenance. Foresighted selection of plants by mature size, gradually reducing grassy areas with xeric plants, and generous mulching can make a garden practical enough to withstand extended vacations and inflation on a retirement income. Plants adapted to local growing conditions are more pest resistant and easier to maintain, reducing or eliminating the need for fertilizers and toxic chemicals. Increasing property taxes are partially related to the cost of controlling unwisely selected trees near power lines and streets.

Most small birds and butterflies are gourmands and will flock to a garden given a wide selection of local and introduced plant species. Many cultivated species are familiar to migratory birds and butterflies in distant parts of their ranges. Certain birds will visit flowering plants but not a feeder. For example, hummingbirds in South Florida are rarely interested in feeders but strongly fancy orchid trees (*Bauhinia* species), aloes, and other flowering species foreign to their ranges. It is noteworthy that the threatened swallow-tailed kite prefers a restricted species, Australian pine (*Casuarina equisetifolia*), to native Florida pine (*Pinus elliottii*) for nest building and will leave an area when Australian pines are removed. Stands of these trees, isolated from areas where they can become invasive, should be left for the benefit of this magnificent bird. The native-exotic dilemma is not black and white.

Though butterflies may dine on a wide range of introduced and local species, they are dependent upon certain host species for their larvae. Host plants will be periodically defoliated, but the larvae generally do no lasting harm to established plants. Including larval food plants (and not spraying them with pesticides) will keep the garden aflutter with butterflies. Species with special appeal to birds and butterflies are noted in this volume. Other species provide cover and nesting places. Choose a selection of species that bloom in all the seasons for year-round food for wildlife.

The latest horticultural advice strongly discourages the use of toxic chemicals in the garden. Healthy plants usually adapt to periodic infestations. Birds and insect predators of plant pests are killed by spraying. The use of pesticides is only a temporary solution because it produces pests with greater resistance to these chemicals. Pesticides also are toxic to humans, especially children, and pets. Choosing resistant plants and thinning to allow air to circulate reduces the likelihood and severity of infestations.

Temperate climate immigrants to the tropics at first may long for temperate species but usually find they demand too much care, pesticide, and fungicide, or fail to thrive in tropical conditions. Though the tropics are inhospitable to dogwoods and apples, this volume provides many beguiling substitutes.

As the backbone of the landscape, using xeric species that require little or no added moisture once established reduces the need for irrigation and saves precious water. Keep thirsty species well mulched and within easy reach of a sprinkler, and plant xeric species around the perimeter. Reduce grassy areas to the minimum. It is unnecessary to irrigate the entire property. Avoid planting moisture-loving herbs and annuals near the roots of trees that need a seasonally dry dormant period. An efficient garden is a less perishable garden but no less beautiful with the choices provided in this book.

ACKNOWLEDGMENTS

DURING THE CURRENT era of dynamic changes in plant systematics a book such as this one could not have been accomplished without the assistance of numerous experts who provided information about arrangements and current names of plant genera and families. The generosity of authorities who contributed information based upon their lifetimes of experience is overwhelming. I am deeply honored and gratified.

Some more recent updates in this volume were provided through personal communications and, as far as possible, are noted in the text. Personal contributions, however, are by no means limited to individual notations.

Who knows if this project would have come to fruition but for the persuasive and unflagging support of my good friend, the preeminent pied piper of tropical flowers, Larry Schokman. Larry is director of the Kampong of the National Tropical Botanical Garden near Miami, in Coconut Grove, Florida. The Kampong is the former home and garden of America's plant collector extraordinaire, David Fairchild, who introduced winter wheat and many other important food crops. More than a few of the flowering plants and fruits in this book were photographed there. Larry's war chest of anecdotes fleshes out many of the descriptions. His obvious delight in what he does captivates everyone he encounters.

It has been my great privilege to have three distinguished authorities on tropical flora and systematics review the manuscript. A list of their qualifications would go far beyond the space allotted. I pay them tribute and thank them fervently for their time and suggestions. I have felt a heavy responsibility to produce a book worthy of their confidence.

Richard Howard, professor emeritus at Harvard University, former director of the Arnold Arboretum, and principal author of the *Flora of the Lesser Antilles* among many other technical works, provided his experience and invaluable guidance under the most difficult of personal circumstances. I am especially grateful to Dick for writing the foreword for this book. He is a highly esteemed authority on tropical flora and I am honored by his support.

Derek Burch, with an unusually broad perspective as both a botanist and horticultural consultant with wide-ranging experience in the field and laboratory, helped sort out numerous identification problems and was especially helpful with the horticultural information. His British exactitude on the fine points of the English language, botanical terminology, and editing experience have been invaluable.

Walter Judd, an extraordinarily busy professor at the University of Florida and the lead author of the state-of-the-art textbook on plant systematics, astounded me by actually offering to read the manuscript. The arrangement of plant families and genera in this book is based on his text, which uses DNA analysis to determine natural order. Walt provided guidance and helped me extract key characteristics on many new and redistributed groups.

Numerous authorities gave generously of their expertise on plant families in the manuscript. I particularly want to thank Dieter Wasshausen (Smithsonian Herbarium, Washington, D.C.), who went out of his way, quite literally, to help with identifications on troublesome Acanthaceae. Peter Gibbs (University of St. Andrews, Scotland) provided extensive background analysis and interesting discussion on his ongoing research on the extraordinary *Ceiba/Chorisia* species. Peter Boyce and Simon Mayo (both of the Royal Botanic Gardens, Kew, England)

and Tom Croat (Missouri Botanical Garden, St. Louis) took time during a busy meeting to look over slides of the Araceae, answered numerous follow-up questions, and Tom and Peter later reviewed the whole section. Chuck Hubbuch (former director of plant collections at Fairchild Tropical Garden, Coral Gables, Florida, now curator of horticulture, Jacksonville Zoo, Florida) looked over the section on palms and fielded frequent questions concerning the garden collections. While working on his Ph.D. thesis at the University of Florida or on his way to a sale towing a trailer of gorgeous gingers, Tom Wood provided extensive unpublished technical detail and checked the identifications on the Zingiberaceae. I am especially fortunate that, before his death, noted *Heliconia* authority Fred Berry reviewed the collection of *Heliconia* photos and provided firsthand information.

Special thanks go to Shirley Graham (Kent State University, Ohio) who assisted with Lythraceae identifications including vouchers on highly ornamental but still unsettled species of *Lagerstroemia*. It would have been impossible to unravel unfamiliar species of Agavaceae without the very generous and friendly guidance of Mary Irish (former director of public horticulture, Desert Botanical Garden, Phoenix). Lúcia Lohmann (Missouri Botanical Garden) took precious time from her Ph.D. studies at the University of Missouri, St. Louis, to confirm *Tabebuia* vouchers and provide diagnostics on other species of Bignoniaceae. Harry Luther (director, Bromeliad Identification Center, Marie Selby Garden, Sarasota, Florida) and Donna Atwood (formerly of Marie Selby Garden) helped with Bromeliaceae and Gesneriaceae identifications and provided valuable reference material. Roger Hammer (naturalist and director of Castellow Hammock Park, Homestead, Florida) knows the location of practically every weed and benign ornamental in South Florida and is a respected authority on local species. His own garden is a showplace of local and introduced species working together in harmony, confirmed by the plethora of butterflies and birds dancing among the blossoms. Many unusual species were photographed there.

Alan Meerow (curator ARS-SHRS, USDA, Chapman Field, Miami) was consulted on identifications of bulbous herbs. Editor and author of recent authoritative succulent volumes Urs Eggli (Sukkulenten-Sammlung, Zürich, Switzerland) and co-author Bernard Descoings (Museum of Natural History, France) helped with Crassulaceae identifications. Richard Olmstead (University of Washington) provided the updated list of revisions for Lamiales.

I gratefully acknowledge the help provided by Richard Wunderlin (University of South Florida Tampa). Dick fielded questions on Florida native and naturalized species as well as identifications of *Bauhinia* species. The late Ed Anderson (Desert Botanical Garden, Phoenix) helped with desert Cactaceae identifications. Myron Kimnach (former director Huntington Botanical Gardens, California, and editor of the U.S. *Cactus and Succulent Journal*) helped with identifications of tropical Cactaceae; Steve Hammer (Bolus Herbarium, Cape Town, South Africa) provided identifications on Aizoaceae. Identifications of *Tibouchina* and other species of Melastomataceae were graciously provided by Frank Almeda (California Academy of Sciences) and Jacinto Regalado (Field Museum of Natural History, Chicago). Suzanne Mace (Mesemb Study Group, England) put me in contact with various succulent authorities; Nat Deleon and Moira Prince (Bromeliad Society, Miami) provided expertise and subject matter for Bromeliaceae; Reto Nyffeler (University of Zürich) helped with Crassulaceae; Allen Paton (Royal Botanic Gardens, Kew, England) helped with Lamiaceae; George Staples (Bishop Museum, Hawaii) provided information on cultivated species in Hawaii.

Some individuals contributed details on difficult genera. Scott Armbruster (Norwegian University of Science and Technology and University of Alaska) provided identification and enlightenment concerning the enigmatic flowers of *Dalechampia*. Dave Bogler (Fairchild Tropical Garden, Coral Gables, Florida and Florida International University) helped with *Agave* and *Beaucarnea*. Willem Meijer (University of Kentucky) shared his yet unpublished work on *Berrya*. Gwilym Lewis (Royal Botanic Gardens, Kew, England) was kind enough to identify vouchers of difficult *Caesalpinia* and *Peltophorum* species and confirmed the identification of the illusive *Periandra*. Barry Hammel (Missouri Botanical Garden, St. Louis) provided information on Cyclanthaceae; Gideon Smith (director of research, National Botanical Institute, Pretoria, South Africa) kindly checked *Aloe* identifications; Tom Daniel (California Academy of Science) on *Justicia* and *Crossandra*; Paul Fryxell (University of Texas, Austin), *Abelmoschus* and *Hibiscus*; Thomas Elias (curator, U.S. National Arboretum), *Hamelia* and the interesting history of ×*Chitalpa*; Paul Franz (North Carolina State University) pointed out the right direction toward the identification of *Periandra*. Wilbert Hetterscheid (National Herbarium, Leiden, Netherlands) checked identifications of questionable *Amorphophallus*; Kenneth Hill (Royal Botanical Gardens, Sydney) helped with identifications of *Corymbia* and *Eucalyptus*; Alan Paton (Royal Botanic Gardens, Kew, England), *Plectranthus*; Hugh Iltis (University of Wisconsin), *Crateva*; Mattias Iwarsson (Uppsala University Botanical Garden, Sweden), *Leonotis*; Anthonius "Toon" Leeuwenberg (National Herbarium, Wageningen, Netherlands), *Tabernaemontana*; Beat Leuenberger (Botanical Garden and Museum, Free University, Berlin-Dahlem), *Pereskia*; David Middleton (Harvard University), *Alstonia*; Harvey Ballard (Ohio University), *Hybanthus*; John Mood provided help on *Zingiber* and reviewed the list of ornamentals in Hawaii; Tim Anderson, *Begonia*; David Orr (director, Waimea Arboretum, Hawaii), *Erythrina* and *Hauya* species; Kent Perkins (University of Florida), *Orthosiphon*; Chris Puttock (Bishop Museum, Hawaii), *Gardenia*; Sandra Atkins (Royal Botanic Gardens, Kew, England), *Vitex*; Andrea Schwarzbach (Kent State University, Ohio), *Argemone*; Ruth Evans Kiew (Singapore Botanical Garden), *Musella*; Cornelius Berg (University of Bergen, Norway), *Dorstenia*; Mario Blanco (University of Florida), *Aristolochia*; and Dean Wheeler (Agresults) lent his expertise on cultivation of pineapples, *Ananas*.

Jim Solomon (curator of the herbarium, Missouri Botanical Garden) and John Wiersema (taxonomist, USDA, ARS, Systematic Botany and Mycology Laboratory, Beltsville, Maryland) directed me to authorities and references and provided generous assistance concerning information on their respective Web sites.

I owe special gratitude to the late Monroe Birdsey, my taxonomy professor at the University of Miami and latter-day mentor. He will be remembered for his great fondness for bad puns and unusual plants, in which order I am not certain. The word play was intended to impress unfamiliar Latin and Greek names on budding botanists (Polygonaceae will forever be the "family of the departed parrot" to me). His eccentric individualism, incorrigible mispronunciations, and malapropos left indelible marks for better or worse. Many photos were made in his private jungle, especially those of his beloved aroids and water-lilies.

I particularly want to salute the staff at Fairchild Tropical Garden, Coral Gables, Florida, who collect and nurture new and exciting species. Without their often unheralded efforts—and those of similar folks at other botanical gardens—these lovely plants would not be available for us to enjoy. For their exceptional patience and assistance I want to thank Craig Allen, David Bar-Zvi, Mary Collins, Don Evans, Jack Fisher, Dena Garvue, Marilyn Griffiths, Gerald "Stinger" Guala, Benoit Jonckheere, Mike McLaughlin and his trusty cherry picker, Ken Neugent, board member and collector Lester Pan-

coast, Scott Zona, and the late Bert Zuckerman. Special thanks go to Susan Knorr and Nick Cockshutt of the publications department who were among the first to encourage my efforts.

The botanical garden and conservatory at Balboa Park is located in San Diego and includes numerous succulent species from arid regions of the Americas, Africa, and Australia. Horticulturist Kathy Puplava has been most helpful providing information on plants in that collection. Bart O'Brien of Rancho Santa Ana Botanical Garden in Claremont, California, provided information on the introduction of ×*Chitalpa*. Quail Botanical Garden in Encinitas, California, has an excellent collection of threatened Canary Islands plants as well as many succulents and xerophytes.

It would be impossible to acknowledge all the members and presenters at the Miami Chapter of the Tropical Flowering Tree Society for tips from their firsthand horticultural experience covering hundreds of tropical species. Members pride themselves on introducing new and unusual species. Their motto is "Color the Horizon," promoting and planting ornamental flowering plants in public landscaping. I especially want to thank Mark Stebbins for his generosity in sharing his research on identifications; Bob McMillan for information on plant diseases and pests; and propagation expert and migratory species, Crafton Clift, a storehouse of revelations on untold numbers of plants and grafting. Photos were made at the homes and nurseries of many members including Tropical Colors Nursery, Luc and Carol Vannoorbeeck, Homestead, Florida, specialists in *Hibiscus* and *Plumeria*; Tropical Paradise Nursery, Joe Fondeur, Davie, Florida, home of the ravishing *Warszewiczia* and other uncommon beauties; Bloomin' Good Nursery, Dolores Fugina, Homestead, Florida, specializing in unusual flowering trees; Ernesto's Nursery, Ernesto Rodriguez and Dimitris Petropoulos, Miami, Florida, renowned for its pampered *Amherstia* and other rarities; Darlene Mann, home to a fast-growing *Ochroma*; Rob and Cindy Bobson, Biospheric Engineering, Homestead, Florida; Paradise Found, Lee Cicchella, Davie, Florida, ardent Bombacaceae hybridizer; Jesse Durko's Nursery, Davie, Florida; Richard Lyon's Nursery, Perrine, Florida; Maurice Kong, whose garden is a demonstration of how to grow hundreds of unusual tropical fruit trees within the confines and regulations of a subdivision lot; and Willis Harding and the neighborhood park he filled with stunning *Ceiba/Chorisia* hybrids in northwestern Miami-Dade County, Florida.

I always enjoy the ebullient Aussie repartee of Mike

Ferrero, curator of palms and flowering trees at Nong Nooch Tropical Garden, Thailand. He has generously shared his experience, grapevine of authorities in Australia, and references on Asian species. Wilhelmina "Willy" Wasik, plant recorder, spent an afternoon with me digging through old plant records of the USDA Subtropical Horticulture Research Station and National Germplasm Repository, Chapman Field, Miami, for information on *Dombeya burgessiae* 'Seminole' revealing for the first time its full identity. Steve Jankalski shared his trials and tribulations with the often obscure history of *Euphorbia* cultivars.

Information and photos were gathered from innumerable sources including public and private gardens. For graciously giving permission to photograph the collections, I would like to thank Terrence Walters, executive director of the Montgomery Botanical Center, Coral Gables, Florida, which specializes in the study of cycads and palms; the late Frank Smathers and Four Fillies Farm, Coral Gables, Florida, his home garden and mango collection; and Eric Eimstad of the Parrot Jungle and Gardens, Pinecrest, Florida. Numerous tropical fruits and flowers were photographed at Miami-Dade County Fruit and Spice Park, where Chris Rollins is director.

For photo subjects and/or information, I would also like to acknowledge Alberts and Merkel Brothers Nursery, Boynton Beach, Florida; Rio Grande Botanical Garden, Albuquerque, New Mexico; Black Olive Nursery, Ft. Lauderdale, Florida; Bosque del Apache, New Mexico; the Deepwood Estate Conservatory, Salem, Oregon; Desert Botanical Garden, Phoenix, Arizona; Gifford Arboretum, University of Miami, Coral Gables, Florida; Huntington Botanical Garden, San Marino, California; Logee's Greenhouse, Danielson, Connecticut; Longwood Gardens, Kennett Square, Pennsylvania; Medellin Botanical Garden, Colombia; the Ospina family at El Ranchito, Medellin, Colombia, for their renowned orchid collection; Plantation Spice Nursery, Goulds, Florida; Rainbow Gardens, Vista, California; Silver Krome Nursery, Homestead, Florida; Bob Smoley's Gardenworld, Gibsonia, Pennsylvania; Tan Kiat, Singapore Botanic Gardens; Georgia Tasker, garden editor of the *Miami Herald*; Stokes Tropicals, New Iberia, Louisiana; USDA Subtropical Horticulture Research Station, Chapman Field, Miami-Dade County, Florida; and the Victorian garden at the Del Coronado Hotel, San Diego, California.

I greatly appreciate the gracious home owners who opened their garden gates, delighted to exchange information and allow me to photograph their prized tropical specimens.

Enduring gratitude goes to my dear husband, Roberto, for his unqualified love, trust, and steadfast support. No institution would have granted such unfettered freedom over so many years, and without such freedom this book would not have been possible. His personal contribution goes far beyond Spanish consultant, sharp-eyed flower scout, equipment bearer, and abiding companion on many a photo safari.

INTRODUCTION

OVER MANY YEARS of researching identifications of plants, I have been impressed by the value of good photographs in my quests. While photos do not always serve as definitive identification of very similar species, their value in quickly narrowing down the possibilities is immeasurable. While keys are standard in botany, they can be time-consuming or bewildering to all but the experts and often useless for plants in cultivation.

Because detail is paramount, a good botanical photo should maintain high photographic quality including proper exposure. Plants should appear in natural position without artiness or artifice, and the photographs should reveal as many unique characteristics of each species as possible. This does not, however, preclude the photographer from translating the aesthetic beauty of even the most humble blossom. That this collection of photos is successful can be measured by the frequency with which experts have been able to make valid identifications based upon scanned photos—of great importance when one is working with experts from around the globe.

Ideally one would prefer a number of photos for each plant but this would be at the expense of the number of species that could be published. For readers of this volume, a broader understanding of a particular plant group can be found by perusing information on related species as well as the genera and family headings.

Scientific Names

Every attempt has been made to locate the current accepted name for each species. A number of on-line databases made this task easier. Where the literature is out of date or insufficient evidence is available to support an identification, a specialist working with a particular group has been consulted. Live scans and specimens, where necessary, of the photographed plant have been provided for verification.

Scientific names are not simply tags but imply relationships and the hierarchy among family groups. If new information about a species indicates its previous placement in a group was incorrect, the name must be changed in agreement with the *International Code of Botanical Nomenclature*. Outdated or incorrect names are listed as synonyms and may be of value when referring to older publications. In scientific works, author's names—the person who published the name of a species—follow the scientific name in roman type. They are not used here for brevity. Authors' names, however, are readily available on the Web sites listed at the back of this book.

Common Names

Common names are often treated disdainfully by scientists because they are highly variable from region to region and not universally recognized. Some less familiar species have not acquired a common name in English. To some, however, common names feel more comfortable, less formal than words with Roman and Greek roots. They might seem easier to remember or pronounce. This is, however, just a lack of familiarity considering how we routinely rattle off medical Latin or Greek—cardiologist, dentist, rubella, influenza—and myriad foreign-language proper names such as Philadelphia or Los Angeles. If we can say Massachusetts, then *Megaskepasma* shouldn't stick in the throat.

Thanks to the busy nursery trade in tropical plants, many cultivated species have acquired universal names in English. Since birds have standardized common names in English, there is no reason that plants couldn't have them also. As a first step toward standardization, this volume lists the preferred common name first. Inaccurate names and those likely to produce confusion have usually been excluded with a few exceptions where usage is common or no other choice is available. Many tropical species in cultivation come from Latin America, so widely recognized common names in Spanish have been provided after the English names wherever possible. Names from other countries of origin are sometimes added at the end. These may be colorful in themselves or they might be handy for travelers who wish to look up an interesting species in its home territory.

Names that originated in horticulture but have no botanical merit are listed as "hort." This is indicated in some references as "of gardens." When a grower or nursery is not sure of or cannot find the correct scientific name, it is tempting to invent a name or mistakenly apply one that belongs to a similar species. Growers should use a common name until a botanist positively identifies a species. When a grower has produced a cultivar or hybrid, he or she must register the name to conserve it and preserve his or her rights over someone who might come up with a similar cross later. A committee is currently working on registration of cultivars and hybrids. At this time, it covers many but not all plant groups. Registration information is provided on the Web site listed at the end of this book.

Origin

The origin or native range of each species is provided. Origins were cross-checked against information from herbaria and actual collection sites listed on on-line databases. Though a plant may be listed as having a native range in a particular region, this does not imply that a particular species is native to all parts of that region. The misapplication of the term *native* often leads to confusion. Plants are only native within the confines of a particular habitat within a region such as seaside forest, wetlands, seasonally moist/dry hardwood forest, low/high elevation, desert, savanna, grasslands, and so forth. Some species, often rare, may have their habitat restricted to a specific locale. Knowing the native range, in combination with growing conditions, indicates where and under what conditions a plant is likely to thrive in cultivation. Origin is also important for identifying species.

Habit

A general description of each species is followed by a range of size. The first figure is the average size of species seen in cultivation. The second figure includes information from reliable sources that suggests the potential mature size of a species in its native habitat or under optimum conditions. This does not indicate that an individual plant will necessarily reach this size or that it might not grow larger under certain circumstances. A plus sign indicates an indeterminate growth potential, such as a vine, a rare plant with little experience in cultivation to rely on, or when a larger size seems probable under optimum circumstances. Health, climate, genetics, and growing conditions influence the growth potential of individual plants. In hurricane-prone areas, few large trees reach their full potential.

Landscapers and gardeners are advised to seriously consider potential size and spread when deciding where to locate large trees in the vicinity of buildings, streets, or power lines. Some trees grow extremely rapidly in the tropics, reaching 30 feet or more in as little as 3–5 years. If possible, move species with inappropriate growth potential while young and replace them with compact species. Inappropriately sized landscape trees usually are at the mercy of unskilled maintenance crews who destroy their shape and health, chopping off branches and flowers in an attempt to fit an oversized plant into a bad location. Also, consider the spread of roots. A carefully planned landscape remains elegant for years and has considerable influence on maintenance costs, future home value, utility bills, and security in windstorms.

Hardiness Zones

A USDA hardiness zone map is provided to indicate the general range within which a plant is likely to thrive. Most plants in this volume originate in tropical or subtropical regions. All thrive in zone 9 (average winter lows between 20° and 30°F) or higher. Some tropical plants, especially those from higher altitudes, may tolerate brief freezing temperatures, while ultra-tropical species, often from moist lowlands, may need extra protection from even mild chills. The total number of days above or below average temperatures annually plays a significant role in a particular species's ability to thrive and bloom. Conditions may vary from one side of a hill to the other, on the north or south, windy or leeward sides of a structure, or from the coast to a few miles inland. Sheltering trees or proximity to a warming body of water will raise local temperature a few degrees over those of surrounding areas. The southwestern states and Hawaii are notorious for their myriad microclimates. Wise selections take advantage of local conditions.

Though efforts have been made to produce more precise climate maps, there are so many local variables and so many species that any climate map must be taken only as a general guide. Within reasonable limits, the best way to determine if a newly introduced species will thrive in a particular location is to compare species from the same or similar regions known to thrive in the area. Many avid gardeners pride themselves on their ability to push zone limits though this is generally not a low-maintenance approach. The simplest device is to keep tender plants in containers that can be moved as necessary.

Evergreen, Deciduous, Seasonally Dormant

Deciduous trees, shrubs, and perennials become dormant seasonally and lose all their leaves. In the tropics this is usually in response to dry and/or cooler seasons. Some herbaceous tropical species die back to the ground in dry seasons and others stop growing and blooming but retain all or some foliage. These species are listed as seasonally dormant. The roots or rhizomes of seasonally dormant tropicals may survive in mild temperate areas in the ground if protected from freezing temperatures by a thick layer of mulch; otherwise, it is best to dig them up and overwinter indoors.

Evergreen trees also shed leaves but gradually or partially while remaining mostly green. They may or may not become semidormant seasonally. In temperate areas the term *evergreen* is often applied loosely to conifers (gymnosperms), though some other temperate species such as hollies remain evergreen in winter.

Semideciduous species may lose their leaves in dry or chilly conditions or behave as perennials in mild temperate areas but usually remain evergreen in warmer and/or moister conditions.

Bloom Season

Time of flowering is listed by season rather than by month to be applicable in both the Northern and Southern Hemispheres. Gardeners can mark their calendars by the date some species bloom, while others may vary considerably from year to year and location to location. Many factors determine when, how prolifically, or if a plant will bloom at all. Some species bloom during a dry season or when the rainy season begins regardless of the time of year. In areas with 2 dry seasons, for instance, jacarandas often bloom twice a year. Artificial irrigation during the dry season will disrupt this cycle and often results in poorer or no bloom. Many plants will not thrive or may even die if kept excessively moist when dormant.

Poinsettias and holiday cactus are sensitive to decreasing periods of light; they begin to bloom when daylight hours shorten and will fail to bloom when darkness is interrupted by artificial light. Other species rely on increasing hours of daylight in spring, moisture, and/or warmth to initiate bloom. Some herbs, such as alpinias, which bloom on second-year growth, usually do not flower in areas where the tops are killed back annually although they produce plentiful new foliage each year.

Moisture

Moisture requirement is an important consideration in deciding the conditions where a particular species will thrive. A preference for species from a radically different climate than the local one must be balanced against cost of special maintenance and the time one is prepared to provide, how reliable the source of water is, and other requirements.

The level of moisture needed by a species is predetermined by the conditions to which a plant is adapted in its native habitat. This may be a narrow range. Other species may be quite adaptable. The amount of irrigation needed is influenced by how long the soil remains moist, which in turn depends on other conditions such as heat or cold, rate of evaporation, and soil porosity. Mulch and other organic matter greatly reduce the loss of moisture from the soil among other benefits. All plants except those that require dry conditions benefit from at least 5 inches of mulch covering the root area to just beyond the edge of the canopy with a clear area around the trunk. Excess water is just as bad for a plant as not enough. This volume presents general guidelines. Advice on particular groups of plants can often be found in specialty books or through local plant societies.

"Moist" conditions refer to soil that remains slightly damp at all time around the plant roots. Candidates suitable for moist conditions are often tender plants of rainforest understory that grow in filtered light. They require frequent irrigation and additional misting when the humidity is low. Though these plants like moisture, their roots should not remain wet and the soil should drain off any excess water quickly. The soil should contain considerable organic matter such as peat moss or humus that maintains even moisture between applications of water or rain. Top-dress the soil with mulch or humus to slow evaporation.

"Regular moisture" indicates a plant needs watering at regular intervals so that soil around the finer roots never dries out although the soil surface may become almost dry. Plants in this group usually tolerate somewhat more sunlight or wind as long as the moisture level is adjusted accordingly. They tolerate somewhat longer intervals between watering depending on local conditions including temperatures.

"Moderate moisture" is used for a plant that can tolerate extended intervals between waterings but whose roots should never become completely dry during active growth. Such plants tolerate brief periods without irrigation when the weather is cool and growth is slow. They are often xerophytic in areas with seasonally dry winters. In Mediterranean-type climates with hot, dry summers, irrigation will more likely be needed in summer than winter.

"Dry" conditions apply to plants that usually do not require supplementary irrigation except during extended hot, dry periods. In seasonally moist climates these species often thrive without additional irrigation if provided porous soils that drain off very rapidly. They should not have large amounts of organic materials around the roots. Most of these plants thrive in Mediterranean-type climates such as southern California and parts of Hawaii.

"Arid" plants tolerate bone-dry conditions for long periods in the wild, often depending on brief seasonal showers to bloom. Arid-growing plants differ from dry-growing plants by having special adaptations for storing moisture and preventing evaporation. In cultivation, however, even arid-growing plants may need weekly irrigation in extreme heat and/or drought. If soil becomes completely dry, it will be resistant to rewetting—like a dry sponge—and it may take several applications, or several hours of trickle irrigation, to moisten the soil down to the root system. Arid conditions are typical of the desert Southwest, higher elevations, and down wind of the mountains in Hawaii.

"Seasonally moist/dry" conditions suit plants from forests with distinct wet and dry seasons. These plants grow actively in rainy months but slow or become dormant in dry seasons. Such conditions are typical of regions with monsoons such as Southeast Asia as well as areas of the Americas. These species require regular moisture during active growth, usually summer, but little when dormant.

All moisture recommendations apply to plants in containers as well as in the ground; however, the porosity of a container, its size, and the potting medium must be taken into consideration. Containers have a significant influence on the frequency with which moisture will need to be applied. Plastic pots are not porous and permit less evaporation than with clay pots. Adjusting the type of container and potting soil mix to suit the watering schedule is usually more practical than attempting to water individual plants on different schedules. This is especially important where container-grown plants are kept outdoors, exposed to rain. Moisture should be reduced in cooler seasons when a plant slows its growth or goes dormant; more is needed in hot or windy conditions. Good drainage will save many plants from heavy-handed watering or those times when it rains for days on end.

Anyone who takes long trips or is inclined to forget to water should select species that can tolerate brief to moderate dry spells. Look for xeric (or xerophytic) plants, which tolerate local climate and growing conditions and thrive without supplemental care once established. Such plants will not tolerate any set of conditions or every location. The term is sometimes erroneously used to indicate "native" species though introduced species often meet the requirements perfectly. Remember that native species are local species from specific habitats. A pinelands species is not native to seaside communities or grassy lowlands although it comes from the general region and growing conditions will vary. A species will only be xeric in cultivated situations that resemble its natural habitat. Conversely, any species will thrive as if xeric under local conditions that resemble its natural growing conditions.

Soil

Certain species will adapt to a variety of soils. Others are quite particular. Those that do not adapt well to local soil either need a specially prepared hole or should be grown in containers. The information provided in this volume is based on observations of species in cultivation, usually in the ground, and by people growing them successfully.

Except for aquatic plants, water should drain quickly, allowing air to reach the roots. The coarser the soil particles, the faster water will drain away. Fine particles, particularly clay and marl, retain moisture a long time and need coarser particles for aeration. Sand has a larger grain size that drains quickly and is used to break up fine soil. Coarser materials are added when moisture must drain particularly rapidly. Organic materials open the soil to air and retain moisture like a sponge. Organic and inorganic materials can easily be adjusted to fit the moisture requirements for each plant. Potting soil products are usually not suitable to use alone and need to be amended according to local conditions. Larry Schokman's favorite advice to gardeners (Larry is director of the Kampong of the National Tropical Botanical Garden) is this: "Never plant a ten-dollar tree in a ten-cent hole."

Mulch

Larry's other recipe for success is to "mulch, mulch, mulch." A doughnut-shaped layer of mulch, to at least 5 inches deep, should be maintained over the root area of all but arid plants, leaving a foot of clear space around the trunk to avoid rot. It is impossible to overstate the beneficial properties of mulch. Try it in a small area if you need proof. Many gardeners are finding extensive lawns expensive to maintain, often reaching a crisis during a drought with water restrictions. Reduce lawn areas by gradually extending beds of xeric plants and extend mulched areas at least to the drip line of large trees. Fresh chipped garden debris is fine, no need for bins and laborious turning. Yard maintenance companies are usually happy to dump a load of chips instead of hauling it to overflowing dumps. Decorative mulches have been found to contain harmful chemicals and have already lost most nutrients. Cypress mulch, from a threatened species, should be avoided. Mulch from invasive species should never be used unless treated to kill seeds.

As mulch breaks down it releases nutrients into the soil slowly and the need for additional fertilizers is greatly reduced or sometimes unnecessary. In poor soil mulch gradually builds up layers of topsoil. Some home owners laboriously fertilize their lawn and in a few weeks time throw it all away with the clippings.

Among the greatest attributes of mulch is that of maintaining even moisture. Irrigation can often be reduced from 2 or 3 times a week to once or even less. Mulch is especially important during a drought to prevent rapid drying of the soil. Mulched areas can be edged with cut limbs or decorative borders. Small plants such as bromeliads and aroids can be planted over the top of the mulch if desired.

Mulch discourages weeds and serves as a barrier to protect trunks from string trimmer wounds that invite infection. It may discourage nematodes and helps maintain plant health. Thirsty, heavy feeders such as bananas and heliconias need far less water and fertilizer in deeply mulched beds, and mulch protects tender roots in winter. The only time organic mulch is not advised is for arid species. The ground should be covered with river gravel or other rocks with neutral pH.

Sun

The hours of sun a plant receives each day and its intensity are specific for each species and greatly influence the quality and quantity of bloom and plant health. Select plants for the garden by the light conditions in the places they will be planted. A successful gardener looks to see which conditions can be controlled and which can't and selects plants accordingly. The position of the house or large tree on a property may determine which side of the house to plant particular species. If a property lacks shade, first consider some larger trees that partially filter the light. After a few years more sensitive plants can be added.

"Full sun" indicates direct sunlight at least 6 hours a day. The plant must be positioned away from the shade of larger plants and structures. This might be almost impossible to achieve in gardens on the east or west sides of buildings, which are shaded for half the day, or where fog commonly filters the sun for part of the morning.

"Part sun" indicates at least 3 hours of direct sun preferably in the morning. Such conditions are typical of plants that grow under a deciduous tree with small leaves and a high canopy that provides shade in summer at midday. These plants usually tolerate more sun in winter when the light is less intense. This conveniently coincides with the time deciduous trees lose their leaves.

"Bright filtered light" indicates light that is diffused (but not heavily shaded) throughout the sunniest hours of the day. A tree with a canopy of small leaves provides this type of light to understory plants. A patio with 30–50% shade screen should provide similar light.

"Bright broken light" is similar to bright filtered light but bright sunlight breaks through the canopy intermittently. This light is similar to that under a tall large-leafed tree during the hottest part of the day. A slat house sometimes simulates these conditions. Plants requiring bright broken light tolerate bright early morning and late afternoon sun.

"Shade" refers only to indirect or strongly diffused light. The term is rarely used in this volume because it is interpreted variously by different people. Few flowering plants bloom in even bright shady conditions. Nonflowering plants such as ferns are usually best for shady locations. Too much shade is usually indicated by plants leaning strongly toward the light source, often developing long weak stems.

Too much sun, especially if it occurs suddenly, results in burned leaves and possibly death. Move a plant gradually over 2–3 weeks from low to higher light intensity to allow it to adjust. However, do not expect a plant that naturally grows in filtered light to adjust to full sun. If a shading tree has to be trimmed, spread an old sheet or doubled piece of screening (never plastic) over the plant temporarily. Better yet, trim trees when the sun is weaker in winter or early spring.

Flower and Leaf Descriptions

Descriptions of flowers and leaves in the popular literature are commonly derived from other references, which themselves derived information from another reference leading to the common perpetuation of mistakes. A wag once referred to this phenomenon as the "fossilization of misinformation." Descriptions in this volume are original, taken from the plants themselves, and not derivative. Be aware, however, that plants can exhibit considerable natural variation and the figures given here should be used as a general guide. *Berrya cubense* has large leaves on one Caribbean island and small leaves on another. *Tabebuia impetiginosa* grows from Mexico to Argentina and has developed considerable variation in local regions. Each of these species was given a variety of names by collectors until scientists compared the important floral characteristics and realized they were variations of the same species.

Measurements were taken from the actual plant photographed and, except in the case of very unusual plants, these were averaged with other individuals of the same species in different locations and growing conditions. The leaves of a young plant may be larger or smaller than of a mature plant. Leaves are often different at the bottom of the canopy or in the shade, and leaves on suckers may differ radically from ordinary branches.

Flowers also vary; one that is freshly opened is often smaller and differently colored than when it reaches it peak. Easily discernable floral characteristics are used to distinguish individual species in this volume. Internal and microscopic details are rarely used except where they are particularly unique. A few fairly obvious field marks or characteristics are provided to distinguish similar species. This should not discourage anyone from admiring the amazing intricacies of flowers with a hand lens. General botanical information is provided in the headings. Counting petals, sepals, and stamens is not a difficult exercise in the field and often provides easy clues to distinguish genera and families.

Color is often subject to individual interpretation. Some would call a school bus orange and others would say yellow when according to the laws of physics it is actually yellow-orange. Natural colors are never "pure." They are blended tones of several colors. Complementary colors (red/green, blue/orange, yellow/violet) darken leaves and flowers when they overlay one another. Purple overlaying yellow, as in *Allamanda* 'Cherries Jubilee', may look brownish or bronze. A green leaf with a red back may appear dark green, purple, or almost black.

Overlying hairs often change the perception of the underlying color. The white hairs on *Heliconia mutisiana* cause the red bracts to appear pink when dry, but the red color is more apparent when wet. Indirect light, artificial, or morning and evening light as well as humidity have an effect on our perception of color saturation and hue. Juxtaposition with contrasting colors alters our color judgment.

To be as accurate as possible, one needs a color standard. Fortunately, an almost universally available and uniform standard is a box of 64 Crayola™ crayons. Disregard any colors named for flowers such as fuchsia or rose or other imprecise names. The solid crayon itself represents the deepest shade and the mark of the crayon on white paper is comparable to lighter hues.

Photography Equipment

All photos in this volume were taken with a Nikon™ 35-mm camera on professional Kodak Ektachrome™ 100 ISO transparency film, which provides natural, unexaggerated color values. Only macro and wide-angle lenses were used. Telephoto lenses were avoided because they usually introduce awkward angles backlit by the bright sky. Close-ups sometimes necessitated the use of a stepladder or, on rare occasions, a cherry picker. With few exceptions, flowers were photographed in their natural conditions and position. Occasionally a hand-held fill-flash was used to illuminate the undersides of plants or in shady locations. A tripod was not used because frequent breezes make one useless at slower speeds. My earliest photos depended more on the macro lens, but in natural settings I soon found that a wide-angle lens provided more depth of focus and more surrounding information, such as leaves, in the photo.

Finding Plants

The plants in this book were not difficult to find. They were photographed within a short radius of major metropolitan areas within the continental United States, primarily southern Florida and California. Many of these species also occur in Hawaii and international gardens throughout the tropics, and can be found growing under glass in temperate conservatories. Botanical gardens do not have static collections and from time to time new species replace old ones. If a particular species is of special interest, be sure to check the season when it is likely to be in bloom and then check with the gardens you plan to visit. Many gardens have Web sites with e-mail addresses for questions.

For those interested in growing unusual species, a wide selection can be found in this volume. Some of these are interesting to specialty enthusiasts, students, and academics. Uncommon and often rare species are sold at nurseries specializing in unusual species and at local plant societies. Others are offered periodically at distribution sales by some botanical gardens. On-line searches by botanical name will often reveal sources of seed and plants. The Internet is also a good way to locate plant societies, nurseries, and tropical gardens. Magazines specializing in tropical species can usually be found on the Web or at garden bookstores.

USDA HARDINESS ZONE MAP

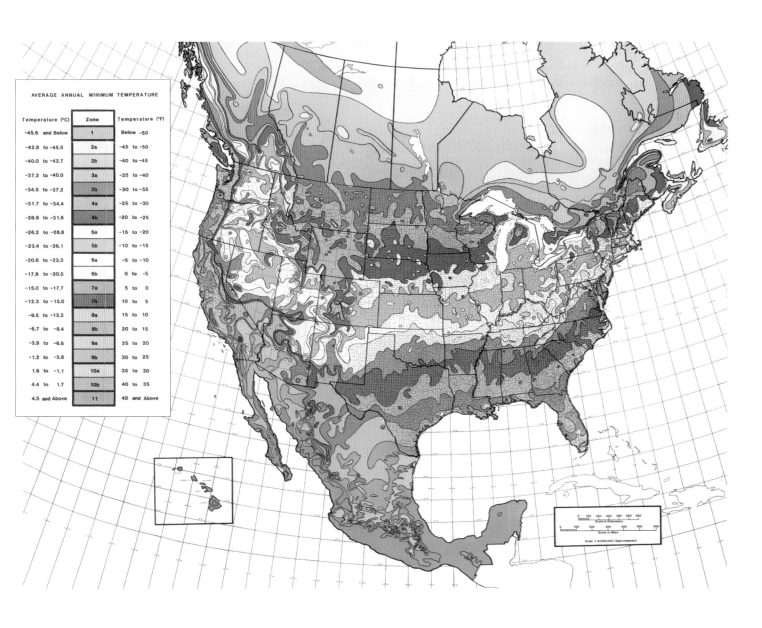

PLANT
DESCRIPTIONS

ACANTHACEAE

ACANTHUS FAMILY,
CLOCK-VINE FAMILY

Acanthaceae includes approximately 256 genera of perennial herbs, shrubs, and climbers, which are widely distributed in warm temperate and tropical regions. Leaves are in opposite pairs, often at right angles to the pair above and below (decussate), and stems are often 4-angled. Flowers are bisexual and bilaterally symmetrical. The sepals and petals are fused at their bases. Upper and lower petals are sometimes elongated into lips. Bracts are often more showy than the tubular or funnel-shaped flowers. The fruit is a dry capsule that, in certain species, opens explosively (dehiscent) to scatter the seed. The shrubby species described here can be used to create informal natural beds in the English perennial garden style or may be lightly clipped as specimen plants or hedges. Most are suitable for containers. For those that require even moisture, a thick layer of mulch greatly reduces the amount of irrigation needed.

Acanthus

Acanthus includes approximately 30 species of evergreen subshrubs and perennial herbs mostly from the Mediterranean region. Stylized acanthus leaves have been used for ornamentation since the Classical Greeks designed the capitals of the Corinthian columns. Flowers have a well-developed lobed lower lip while the other petals are reduced to stubs. The leaves are deeply lobed, toothed, and often spiny. With rare exception, they are arranged in basal whorls. Usually a tall inflorescence spike develops from the center of the leaf whorl or, in the case of *A. montanus*, at the ends of the branches.

Acanthus mollis

OAK-LEAFED BEAR'S BREECHES
Mediterranean region. Evergreen perennial herb to 2 ft.; zones 7–10. Blooms spring, summer. Regular moisture when hot, less when cool. Fertile, well-drained soil. Bright broken light to full sun in milder climates. Flowers: lip greenish white; sepals small, sharply toothed; clasped between leaflike, mauve and green bracts; evenly distributed in whorls of 4 along the erect 3- to 5-ft. spike. Leaves: broad, deeply lobed, glossy; margins softly toothed; arranged in basal whorls to 3–5 ft. wide. *A clump-forming species. Commonly cultivated in mild temperate regions and thrives in southern California. Crosses of this species with* A. spinosus *are distinguished by their sharply toothed leaf margins.*

Acanthus montanus

MOUNTAIN THISTLE
Tropical western Africa. Evergreen perennial herb, 2–5 ft.; zones 9–11. Blooms warm months. Moderate moisture when hot, less when cool. Fertile, well-drained soil. Part sun or bright broken light. Flowers: lip pale pink with purple veins; bracts green, leaflike, spiny; in a compact spike at the ends of upturned, sprawling (decumbent) branches. Leaves: ovate to obovate, deeply lobed, tips tapering (acuminate), 8–10 in. long; margins sharply toothed; cauline (on a stem). *A sprawling or clambering species of montane forest understory. This species lacks the typical basal whorl of leaves. Unusual in cultivation.*

Aphelandra

Aphelandra includes approximately 170 species of evergreen shrubs from tropical America. Flowers are short-lived, the bracts showy and long-lasting. Each pair of leaves is arranged at right angles to the pairs above and below (decussate). In erect species, this sometimes results in a pyramidal shape. Many species are sensitive to chilly temperatures and may suffer leaf damage. If not actually frozen, however, they will recover. Cut back damaged foliage in spring. Aphelandras are pollinated by hummingbirds and insects. Some species commonly grown by nurseries such as zebra plant, *A. squarrosa*, have generally reached their prime at the time of sale and fail to thrive outdoors.

Aphelandra hartwegiana

Panama (Darién Province). Evergreen shrub to 6 ft.+; zones 10–11. Blooms summer, fall. Seasonally moist, moderate moisture when cool. Fertile, well-drained soil. Part sun or bright broken light. Flowers: tubular, yellow, with 2 elongated lips; bracts red-orange, shell-like, overlapping (imbricate); in erect, terminal spikes, 8–24 in. tall. Leaves: elliptic, to 10 in. long, tip tapering (acuminate); blade tapers down the petiole (decurrent). *This recently introduced species is easy to grow and very attractive. Locally self-seeding.*

Acanthus mollis

Acanthus mollis, flowers

Acanthus montanus

Aphelandra sinclairiana

CORAL APHELANDRA,
SINCLAIR'S APHELANDRA

Central America. Evergreen shrub, 6–10 ft.; zones 10–11. Blooms warm months. Regular moisture and humidity. Average to fertile, well-drained soil. Bright filtered light. Flowers: tubular, pink, 2-lipped, short-lived, opening a few at a time; bracts ornamental, orange, shell-like, long-lasting; inflorescences to 8 in. long, in clusters at the ends of the branches; bracteoles needlelike, hidden in the axils of the leaves. Leaves: elliptic, tips narrowing abruptly (cuspidate). *Needs protection from chills. Shoots are inclined to become leggy. Cut back in spring.*

Asystasia

Asystasia includes approximately 70 species of perennial herbs and subshrubs from tropical Africa, India, and Asia. *Asystasia gangetica* has become widely naturalized and is invasive in many coastal areas of the tropics. It is quite variable and possibly represents a hybrid gene pool (Wasshausen, pers. comm.). It is often encountered as a weed in lawns. In established beds, these pretty weeds can be kept under control by mulching. The funnel-shaped flowers are arranged along one side of the inflorescence stalk (secund). Bracts are small and not showy.

Asystasia gangetica

COROMANDEL, GANGES PRIMROSE

Synonym: *A. coromandeliana*. Exact origin obscure (probably India to Malaysia, eastern Africa); widely naturalized. Perennial, clambering herb, 1.5–3 ft.; zones 9–11. Blooms warm months. Moderate moisture, tolerates dry periods. Average, well-drained soil. Full to part sun. Flowers: funnel-shaped, lobes flaring, lip slightly 2-lobed, opening white or yellow, becoming purplish, 1–2 in. wide; calyx cup small, lobes linear. Leaves: cordate to ovate, 1–2 in. long. *A creeping to clambering herb reminiscent of petunias. Highly variable. A weed in lawns and coastal areas. Coromandel is named for the southeastern coast of India.*

Asystasia travancorica (hort.)

Unknown in the wild. Perennial herb, 1–3 ft.; zones 9–11. Blooms warm months. Moderate moisture. Average, well-drained soil. Full to part sun. Flowers: funnel-shaped, deep purple to white, with cream-colored throat; borne on erect, terminal spikes. Leaves: lanceolate to ovate, to about 1 in. long; margins entire or slightly toothed. *Name of no botanical authority. A variable plant, possibly a hybrid or cultigen (Wasshausen, pers. comm.) with characteristics similar to* A. gangetica.

Barleria

Barleria includes approximately 250 species of shrubs primarily from the Old World tropics. A number of species are commonly cultivated. Flowers are showy and funnel-shaped. Bracts are relatively inconspicuous. Bracteoles and calyx are often spined. Barlerias benefit from light trimming for compact shape. Removing old flower heads encourages repeat flushes of bloom.

Barleria albostellata

Southeastern Africa. Evergreen shrub to 4 ft.; zones 9–10. Blooms late winter, spring, early summer. Regular moisture when hot, less when cool. Average to fertile, well-drained soil. Full sun. Flowers: trumpet-shaped with flaring lobes, white, opening 1 or 2 at a time; bracts leaflike, green, with silvery hairs, turning blackish with age; in compact spikes. Leaves: ovate, 5–6 in. long, covered with soft, silvery gray hairs. *The silvery foliage is a landscaping asset at any time of year, an exceptional foil for deep blue to purple flowers or foliage. Remove old spikes. Prune after blooming. Unusual in cultivation.*

Aphelandra hartwegiana

Aphelandra sinclairiana

Asystasia gangetica

Asystasia travancorica

Barleria albostellata

Barleria cristata

BLUE-BELL, PHILIPPINE VIOLET
India, Southeast Asia. Semideciduous shrub to 5 ft.; zones 8–11. Blooms spring, fall, or summer in temperate end of range. Regular moisture when hot, less when cool. Fertile, well-drained soil. Full to part sun. Flowers: trumpet-shaped, blue-violet, pink, or white, throat streaked with white, to 2 in. long, lip 2-lobed; bracts 2, sharply bristled. Leaves: ovate, to 4 in. long, roughly hairy. *This species thrives as a root-hardy perennial along the Gulf Coast. Nematodes tend to limit growth in frost-free parts of Florida.*

Barleria lupulina

HOP-HEADED BARLERIA
Madagascar, possibly Mauritius; naturalized in the Caribbean. Evergreen shrub to 3 ft.; zones 10–11. Blooms warm months. Moderate moisture to fairly dry. Open, well-drained soil. Full to part sun. Flowers: trumpet-shaped, golden-yellow, upper lobes spreading fanlike; bracts shell-shaped, green with red markings and sharp bristles near the base; in ovoid spikes. Leaves: lanceolate to almost linear, to 4 in. long, midvein pink; margins minutely toothed; with paired spines in the leaf axils. *This adaptable and xeric barleria will endure a gardener's extended vacations. It is salt tolerant to the dunes (Burch, pers. comm.). Trim after bloom.*

Barleria oenotheroides

Synonym: *B. micans* (misapplied). Southern Mexico to Colombia. Evergreen shrub to about 4 ft.; zones 10–11. Blooms intermittently, primarily fall and winter. Moderate moisture. Average, well-drained soil. Full to part sun. Flowers: trumpet-shaped, lemon-yellow, 4 upper lobes spreading fanlike, lip narrow; bracts flaring, sharply angled and prickled; inflorescence to 12 in. tall. Leaves: ovate, 6–12 in. long, hairy (tomentose), blade tapers down the petiole (decurrent). *Branches tend to sprawl with upturned ends (decumbent) developing into large clumps. This is the only indigenous New World barleria and has been commonly, but mistakenly, referred to as B. micans, an African*

species not known in cultivation (Wasshausen, pers. comm.).

Barleria repens

CREEPING BARLERIA,
CORAL-CREEPER
Synonym: *B. querimbensis*. South Africa. Evergreen creeping subshrub under 1 ft.; zones 9–10. Blooms warm months. Regular moisture to wet. Fertile, well-drained soil. Full sun to bright filtered light. Flowers: funnel-shaped, pinkish orange, lobes to 2 in. wide; bracts inconspicuous; solitary in the leaf axils. Leaves: ovate, to 0.5 in. long, petiole very short (subsessile). *Thrives in fountain-spray or as ground cover. Flowers are dispersed. Almost ever-blooming. Though listed as invasive in Hawaii, it is not known to be a problem in Florida or Puerto Rico (Burch, pers. comm.).*

Crossandra

Crossandra includes about 50 species of evergreen perennial herbs and shrubs from India, Arabia, Madagascar, and tropical Africa. The upper lobes are spreading, fanlike. The common name, firecracker, alludes to the way the mature dry capsules pop when touched with a damp finger, explosively dispersing their seed—much to the delight of children. Birds and small animals eagerly dig up seeds, making it prudent to start with seedlings. Crossandras are a bit finicky about regular moisture and are inclined to drop leaves if stressed by heat or cold. Because new growth initiates at the ends of the branches, plants that suffer leaf loss should be cut back to the main stems in spring to avoid rangy regrowth. Remove old spikes to stimulate frequent bloom.

Crossandra infundibuliformis

FIRECRACKER PLANT
Synonyms: *C. undulifolia, Justicia infundibuliformis*. Southern India, Sri Lanka, central Africa. Evergreen shrub or subshrub, 1–3 ft.; zones 10–11. Blooms warm months. Regular moisture. Average to fertile, well-drained soil. Full to part sun, morning sun for good bloom. Flowers: salverform, tubular at the base, lobes 5, fanlike, yellow to orange; bracts covered with long hairs (to-

mentose), bract veins not reticulated; inflorescence on a 4- to 6-in. stalk (peduncle). Leaves: elliptic, glossy dark green, 3–5 in. long, blade tapering down the petiole (decurrent); tips obtusely pointed. 'Lutea' is distinguished by its erect, shrubby habit and yellow flowers. 'Mona Walhead' is low and spreading with orange flowers.

Barleria cristata

Barleria lupulina

Barleria oenotheroides

Barleria repens

Crossandra infundibuliformis 'Lutea'

Crossandra infundibuliformis 'Mona Walhead'

Crossandra nilotica

RED FIRECRACKER PLANT

Tropical Africa. Evergreen shrub, 1–2 ft.; zones 10–11. Blooms intermittently in warm months. Regular moisture. Average to fertile, well-drained soil. Bright filtered light, morning sun. Flowers: salverform, lobes fan-shaped, about 1 in. wide, ruby-red, brick-red to mauve. Bracts long haired, reticulated; inflorescence a spike, stalk (peduncle) to 6 in. long. Leaves: elliptic, dull green, 3–4 in. long, blade tapers down the petiole (decurrent), tip abruptly narrows to a point (cuspidate). *The petals are slightly smaller and more deeply lobed than those of* C. infundibuliformis. *Cultivated plants possibly include hybrids of that species.*

Dyschoriste

Dyschoriste includes approximately 65 species of annual and perennial herbs and evergreen shrubs, which are widely distributed in the tropics. One or 2 species are occasionally found in cultivation. The species are poorly defined. *Dyschoriste* species is misrepresented in the trade as dwarf barleria or dwarf Philippine violet. It is only distantly related to *Barleria cristata*, commonly known as Philippine violet. The fact that neither species is from the Philippines is another story.

Dyschoriste hygrophyllodes

BRIDAL-FLOWER

Synonym: *Calophanes hygrophyllodes*. Brazil. Evergreen subshrub, 4–6 ft.; zones 9–11. Blooms spring, summer. Regular moisture. Average, well-drained soil. Full to part sun. Flowers: trumpet-shaped, purple with darker purple markings in the throat; solitary or in small clusters in the leaf axils. Leaves: ovate to suborbicular, to 1 in. long; petioles short. *Dense, spreading shrub. Suitable for informal hedges. Note differing spelling of species and synonym.*

Dyschoriste species

FOXTAIL VIOLET

Origin obscure (possibly Old World tropics). Evergreen shrub, 1–2 ft.; zones 10–11. Blooms intermit-tently winter, spring, summer. Moderate moisture. Average, well-drained soil. Full to part sun. Flowers: funnel-shaped, lips elongated, to about 1 in. wide, violet with darker streaks in the throat; solitary. Leaves: ovate to obovate, about 1 in. long; sessile; densely clustered on woody, trailing to decumbent branches. *An unnamed species with bushy, foxtail-like sprawling branches. Especially attractive spilling over rocks and walls. Prune to shape. Suitable for hanging baskets and as ground cover.*

Eranthemum

Eranthemum includes approximately 30 species of shrubs and subshrubs from tropical Asia. The flowers have a slight bilateral symmetry but may appear radially symmetrical. They are small and massed in showy clusters. Bracts are relatively small. A few unnamed but attractive species or cultivars are circulating in the trade.

Eranthemum nigrum

Solomon Islands. Evergreen shrub, 4–5 ft.; zones 10–11. Blooms warm months. Regular moisture. Fertile, well-drained soil. Full to part sun. Flowers: trumpet-shaped, white, throat spotted with magenta; in many-flowered clusters. Leaves: elliptic, 3–5 in. long, eggplant-purple, glossy or dull, tip narrowing abruptly to a point (cuspidate); margins smooth. *Unusual in cultivation. The deep purple foliage is distinctive and offers excellent contrast for the landscape.*

Eranthemum pulchellum

BLUE SAGE

Synonyms: *E. nervosum, Pseuderanthemum pulchellum*. India. Ever-green shrub, 3–5 ft.; zones 10–11. Blooms winter, spring. Regular moisture. Fertile, well-drained soil. Part sun to bright broken light. Flowers: trumpet-shaped, blue-violet, lobes almost radially symmetrical; bracts green with conspicuous white veins; in spikes clustered near the ends of the branches. Leaves: elliptic, 4–8 in. long, base tapering, dull green, rough (scabrous); margins faintly scalloped (crenulate). *Thrives in bright understory. Has a naturally rounded, compact shape. The white-veined bracts and axillary inflorescences distinguish this species from* E. wattii.

Eranthemum wattii

India. Evergreen shrub, 3–4 ft.; zones 10–11. Blooms winter, spring. Regular moisture when hot, less when cool. Fertile, well-drained

Crossandra nilotica

Dyschoriste species

Dyschoriste hygrophyllodes

Eranthemum nigrum

Eranthemum pulchellum

soil. Full to part sun. Flowers: trumpet-shaped, blue-violet, lobes spreading; bracts completely green; in erect, terminal spikes. Leaves: elliptic, to 4 in. long, dull green, rough (scabrous). *An open, erect shrub. The inflorescence has larger but fewer flowers than E. pulchellum. Note the terminal inflorescences in the photo.*

Fittonia

Fittonia includes a single species of perennial herb from South America. Its natural environment is the moist rainforest understory. It is grown for its colorful, variegated foliage. *Fittonia verschaffeltii* var. *verschaffeltii* has red leaf veins. *Fittonia verschaffeltii* var. *argyroneura*, with white leaf veins, was formerly given species status. Both varieties are highly sensitive to cold and are commonly kept in containers or baskets that can be moved indoors when nights are chilly.

Fittonia verschaffeltii

MOSAIC-PLANT, NERVE-PLANT
Peru. Evergreen subshrub under 1 ft.; zone 11. Blooms summer. Regular moisture. Fertile, humus-rich, well-drained soil. Medium filtered light. Flowers: small, trumpet-shaped, white, lower lip 3-lobed, opening a few at a time; bracts hairy; spikes erect, 4-angled. Leaves: ovate, 2–3 in. long, olive-green; veins reticulated, red. *A creeping species suitable for hanging baskets and beds in warm locations. Var.* argyroneura *has white veins.*

Graptophyllum

Graptophyllum includes a single species of evergreen shrub from the northeastern Australia–New Guinea region of the South Pacific. It has been cultivated for a long time in Southeast Asia. The species is easily recognized by the brightly splashed foliage and is waggishly referred to as the Rorschach-test plant. The crimson buds add an extra flourish of color in spring. The plant is at its best and the foliage most attractive in the filtered light of a high tree canopy. Leaf color does not develop fully in deeper shade and the surface becomes dull in drying sun or low humidity.

The variegated foliage adds a color accent to landscaping at any time of year.

Graptophyllum pictum

CARICATURE PLANT, GRAPTOFILO
Exact origin obscure (New Guinea region); naturalized in Southeast Asia. Evergreen shrub, 4–6 ft.; zones 10–11. Blooms spring, early summer. Regular moisture and humidity. Fertile, well-drained soil. Part sun to bright filtered light. Flowers: trumpet-shaped, crimson, buds club-shaped, showy, dropping shortly after opening. Leaves: broadly ovate, to 7 in. long, bright green splashed white, selections variously overlaid with splashes of blackish or greenish purple; area around veins and petioles red, blade puckered; margins undulate. *Selections are defined primarily by the leaf markings.*

Hypoestes

Hypoestes includes approximately 40 species of subshrubs and perennial herbs from the Old World tropics. The brightly marked foliage is festive any time of year. Bracts are small, enclosing the calyx. *Hypoestes verticillaris* is a source of 2 anti-cancer drugs.

Hypoestes phyllostachya

POLKA-DOT PLANT, FRECKLE-FACE
Synonym: *H. sanguinolenta* (misapplied). Madagascar. Evergreen subshrub to about 1 ft.; zones 10–11. Blooms late summer to winter. Regular moisture. Fertile, well-drained soil. Morning sun to medium filtered light. Flowers: small, 2-lipped, upper lip 3-lobed, lavender to magenta; in spikes to 6 in. tall. Leaves: ovate, to 2 in. long, downy, dark green spotted with pink, tip acuminate. *Commonly*

grown as an annual. Adds color in subdued light where many flowering plants will not bloom. Suitable for containers. Cultivars variously colored. Persuasion Series has leaves somewhat smaller and more heavily spotted pink, white, or magenta.

Justicia

Justicia includes approximately 420 species of perennial herbs and shrubs from tropical America. These species were once segregated into a number of genera, which may still be encountered in older references. Many *Justicia* species have not been thoroughly studied. Bracts are sometimes showy. Flowers have an interesting adaptation for cross-pollination. They have a tubular base and 2 elongated, slender lips. The stamens bearing the pollen are pressed against the upper lip. The

Eranthemum wattii

Fittonia verschaffeltii var. *verschaffeltii*

Graptophyllum pictum 'Tricolor'

Hypoestes phyllostachya Persuasion Series

Justicia aurea

lower lip provides an inviting perch for visiting insects, dipping as they alight and drawing down the upper lip with the stamens thereby planting a dollop of pollen on the visitor's back. When the insect visits the next flower, it passes the pollen along by the same device. Justicias should never be allowed to become completely dry. A generous blanket of mulch helps maintain even moisture around the roots and helps reduce the frequency of irrigation.

Justicia aurea

Synonym: *Jacobinia aurea*. Mexico, Central America. Evergreen shrub, 4–6 ft.; zones 10–11. Blooms fall, winter, spring. Regular moisture. Fertile, well-drained soil. Bright filtered light. Flowers: tubular, 2-lipped, lemon-yellow; in a spirelike spike; bracts bright green. Leaves: lanceolate to broadly ovate, to 12 in. long. Stems: 4-angled, more or less covered with soft hairs (pubescent). *An erect, stately shrub. Somewhat sensitive to chills. Benefits from the shelter of closely planted shrubs and trees on cool nights. Watch for snails.*

Justicia betonica

WHITE SHRIMP-PLANT
Tropical Asia, South Pacific islands. Evergreen shrub to 4 ft.; zones 9–11. Blooms most of the year. Moderate moisture. Average to fertile, well-drained soil. Full to part sun. Flowers: small, 2-lipped, pink; bracts white with contrasting dark green veins. Leaves: ovate; margins with minute teeth. *Forgiving and pest resistant, this spreading shrub tolerates a wide range of conditions, though its appearance suffers if neglected. Prune for shape and control.*

Justicia brandegeana

SHRIMP-PLANT, FALSE HOPS, COLA DE CAMARÓN
Synonym: *Beloperone guttata*. Mexico. Evergreen shrub to 2 ft.; zones 10–11. Blooms winter, spring. Regular moisture and humidity. Fertile, well-drained soil. Bright filtered light. Flowers: tubular, 2-lipped, white, throat streaked with burgundy; bracts ovate, softly hairy (pubescent) in graduated shades of russet-red to orange; inflorescence curved, resembling shrimp-tails.

Leaves: ovate, to 2 in. long; variegated selections splashed with white. *This old-fashioned houseplant has numerous color variations. Sometimes grown as an annual in temperate climates. 'Yellow Queen' is called yellow shrimp plant and is often confused with Pachystachys lutea.*

Justicia candicans

Synonym: *Jacobinia candicans*. Northern Mexico. Evergreen shrub, 3–4 ft.; zones 9–11. Blooms warm months. Regular to moderate moisture. Moderately fertile, well-drained soil. Full to part sun. Flowers: tubular, 2-lipped, lower lip 3-lobed, pink, throat pink with white chevron markings and fine white hairs (pubescent); in clusters in the leaf axils. Leaves: ovate, tip cuspidate, 2–3 in. long. *The naturally compact, rounded shape is suitable as an almost carefree hedge. Unusual in cultivation but highly recommended. Easily propagated by cuttings or seed. Somewhat resembles Justicia carnea but the flowers are distributed along the leaf axils and the leaves are smaller. The species name refers to the white streaks in the flower throat.*

Justicia carnea

KING'S CROWN, FLAMINGO-FLOWER, BRAZILIAN PLUME
Synonym: *Jacobinia carnea*. Colombia, Venezuela to Brazil. Evergreen shrub to 6 ft.; zones 10–11. Blooms late winter to early summer. Regular moisture and humidity. Fertile, well-drained soil. Morning sun, with protection from midday sun. Flowers: tubular, 2-lipped, the long upper lip held erect, pink; inflorescence terminal; bracts inconspicuous. Leaves: broadly ovate, medium green, purple below, to almost black in some selections; margins undulate, to 10 in. long. *Flowers resemble little flamingos. Cold-sensitive. Suitable as an understory shrub or in containers which can be repositioned as the seasons change. Selections have deep pink to white flowers.*

Justicia fulvicoma

COMMON SHRIMP-PLANT
Synonyms: *Beloperone flavicoma, J. comosa*. Mexico to Honduras. Ever-

Justicia betonica

Justicia brandegeana

Justicia candicans

Justicia carnea

Justicia flavicoma, with monarch butterfly

green shrub to 2 ft.; zones 9–10. Blooms winter, spring. Moderate moisture. Average to fertile, well-drained soil. Full to part sun. Flowers: tubular, 2-lipped, red, orange, or yellow; bracts russet to yellow; inflorescence erect. Leaves: ovate, blade narrowly decurrent, 2–3 in. long. *This sprawling shrub can become rangy in summer. Prune back after flowering. Distinguished from J. brandegeana by the erect inflorescences. Cultivars come in numerous color combinations.*

Justicia spicigera

MEXICAN INDIGO, MOHINTLI
Synonyms: *Jacobinia mohintli, Jacobinia spicigera.* Mexico to Colombia. Evergreen shrub to 6 ft.; zones 9–11. Blooms intermittently in warm months. Moderate moisture. Average to fertile, well-drained soil. Full sun to bright filtered light. Flowers: tubular, 2-lipped, the lower lip rolled like a butterfly's tongue, orange to yellow; inflorescence erect, flowers arranged along one side (secund). Leaves: elliptic, to 6 in. long, dull to glossy; margins minutely fringed (fimbriate). *Drooping branches will take root at nodes producing large clumps. Prune to control. In Mexico, the leaves are boiled to make* mohintli, *a blue dye. Also used in folk medicine.*

Mackaya

Mackaya includes a single species of evergreen shrub from eastern South Africa. It grows along wooded riverbanks in an otherwise semiarid region. Dainty mackaya thrives in the woodland understory. It blooms well in light conditions that are lower than those of most flowering shrubs. It is uncommon in cultivation but highly recommended. Mulch well to maintain even moisture and reduce the frequency of irrigation.

Mackaya bella

MACKAYA, FOREST BELL-BUSH
Synonym: *Asystasia bella.* South Africa. Evergreen shrub to 6 ft.; zones 9–11. Blooms spring, sporadically summer, fall. Regular moisture. Fertile, well-drained soil. Bright filtered light to bright shade. Flowers: bell-shaped, pale lavender

to white, throat lined with fine purple veins. Leaves: elliptic, to 5 in. long, tip narrowing abruptly to a point (cuspidate), glossy; margins wavy (sinuate), irregularly toothed; petioles short.

Megaskepasma

Megaskepasma includes a single species of shrub from Venezuela. The shrub's name may look intimidating but it is highly descriptive: the genus name means "large covering" and the species name means "red bracts." Surprisingly underutilized, this plant's medium

size and dense, upright habit make it suitable for informal privacy screening or hedging with minimal maintenance. Mulching helps maintain even moisture and reduce the frequency of irrigation. The species is not known to produce seed in cultivation and is usually propagated from root suckers.

Megaskepasma erythrochlamys

RED CLOAK
Venezuela. Evergreen shrub, 8–12 ft.; zones 9–11. Blooms intermittently in warm months. Regular

moisture when hot, less when cool. Average, well-drained deep soil. Full to part sun. Flowers: tubular, 2-lipped, white to pink, short-lived, opening a few at a time; bracts showy, magenta, long-lasting; in erect, terminal spikes to 1 ft. tall. Leaves: elliptic to ovate, to 10 in. long. *Often inaccurately referred to as "Brazilian" red cloak.*

Odontonema

Odontonema includes approximately 26 species of perennial herbs and shrubs from tropical America. The genus name means

Justicia spicigera

Mackaya bella

Megaskepasma erythrochlamys

Odontonema callistachyum, lavender form

"tooth threads," alluding to the minutely toothed filaments. The flower spikes or racemes are at the ends of the branches. These species are very attractive to hummingbirds and butterflies.

Odontonema callistachyum

FIRE-SPIKE

Synonyms: *Justicia callistachya, O. geminatum.* Mexico, Central America. Semideciduous shrub, 4–10 ft.; zones 9–11. Blooms winter, spring. Moderate moisture. Average, well-drained soil. Full to part sun. Flowers: tubular, lavender to deep magenta; in ascending branched or unbranched panicles; floral stalk (rachis) downy (pubescent). Leaves: elliptic to oblong, 6–12 in. long, minutely downy; margins wavy (undulate). *A somewhat lax, spreading shrub. It is sometimes grown as a root-hardy perennial in mild temperate regions. The 2 color forms are unnamed selections.*

Odontonema cuspidatum

SCARLET FIRE-SPIKE,
CARDINAL'S CREST

Synonyms: *Justicia coccinea, O. strictum* (misapplied). Central America. Semideciduous shrub to 6 ft.; zones 9–11. Blooms primarily spring, fall. Moderate moisture. Average, well-drained soil. Full to part sun. Flowers: tubular, lobes small, red to scarlet; in erect, sometimes branched panicles. Leaves: oblong, to 6 in. long, glossy; margins wavy (sinuate). *The inflorescence is sometimes crested (fasciated). This could be the result of a plant pathogen or a natural variant. Fire-spike is grown as a root-hardy perennial in mild temperate regions. It is commonly, but incorrectly, referred to as O. strictum (syn. O. tubaeforme), a distinct species (Wasshausen, pers. comm.).*

Pachystachys

Pachystachys includes approximately 12 species of evergreen shrubs from tropical America. The genus name means "thick spike," alluding to the dense inflorescences. The species listed are stressed by cold, excess heat, and irregular irrigation, which commonly results in loss of leaves. *Pachystachys lutea* is a common

landscaping plant, but it quickly becomes rangy without regular irrigation and maintenance. Should the leaves fall, new growth starts at the branch tips and the interior remains bare. Damaged plants should be pruned close to the main stem so that new leaves can fill in nicely.

Pachystachys coccinea

CARDINAL'S GUARD

Synonyms: *Jacobinia coccinea, Justicia coccinea.* Northern South America, West Indies. Evergreen shrub, 5–6 ft.; zones 10–11. Blooms spring, summer. Regular moisture and humidity. Fertile, well-drained soil. Bright filtered light. Flowers: tubular, 2-lipped, red; in torchlike terminal spikes to 10 in. high; bracts green. Leaves: elliptic to ovate, to 8 in. long, dark green. *Close planting with other shrubs provides some protection from chills. Suitable for large containers, which are very attractive on the patio or flanking an entrance.*

Pachystachys lutea

YELLOW CANDLES

Synonyms: *Beloperone* 'Super Goldy' (hort.), *Justicia lutea.* Costa Rica to Venezuela and Peru. Evergreen shrub, 3–4 ft.; zones 10–11. Blooms warm months. Regular moisture. Fertile, well-drained soil. Full to part sun. Flowers: tubular, 2-lipped, white, less conspicuous than the yellow bracts; spikes stiffly erect. Leaves: ovate, to 8 in. long. *A common bedding plant. Very striking juxtaposed with purple foliage or flowers. The preferred common name is yellow candles. Justicia brandegeana 'Yellow Queen' has more shrimplike, curved inflorescences.*

Pseuderanthemum

Pseuderanthemum includes approximately 60 species of perennial herbs, subshrubs, and shrubs, which are widely distributed in the tropics. In addition to those listed here, a number of poorly defined varieties or species are occasionally found in nurseries. Flowers are small, usually in clusters at the ends of the branches. These species have 5 petals, but the 2 upper petals typically overlap, appearing 4-petaled. Foliage is sometimes variegated.

Odontonema callistachyum, magenta form

Odontonema cuspidatum

Odontonema cuspidatum, crested form

Pachystachys coccinea

Pachystachys lutea

Pseuderanthemum carruthersii

FALSE ERANTHEMUM

Synonym: *P. atropurpureum*. Vanuatu (New Hebrides), New Caledonia. Evergreen shrub to 3 ft.; zones 10–11. Blooms warm months. Regular moisture. Fertile, well-drained soil. Full to part sun. Flowers: salverform, lobes white, flecked with magenta around the throat. Leaves: ovate, green and white; margins unevenly wavy (sinuate). *Salt tolerant. Recommended for coastal locations and waterfront balconies. Var. atropurpureum leaves have mottled silver-gray to purplish variegation. Leaves of var. reticulatum, golden net-bush, are yellow when young developing green reticulations.*

Pseuderanthemum sinuatum (hort.)

Garden origin. Evergreen subshrub, 2–3 ft.+; zones 10–11. Blooms warm months. Regular moisture. Fertile, well-drained soil. Full to part sun. Flowers: white with purple-spotted lip, solitary. Leaves: lanceolate, to 4 in. long; margins wavy (sinuate). Stems: reddish. *This plant has no recognized botanical name and is unknown in the wild. It may be a hybrid of* Pseuderanthemum bicolor, *a species with wider, purple leaves (Wasshausen, pers. comm.).*

Ruellia

Ruellia includes approximately 150 species of shrubs and herbs, which are widely distributed in tropical and warm temperate regions. The species have been rearranged several times by different authors. Several are common in cultivation. Flowers are showy, the bracts inconspicuous. Floral color tends to be variable even within local wild populations. Many of the species listed thrive in coastal conditions but are not more than minimally salt tolerant. Cut plants back in early spring.

Ruellia brevifolia

RED SPRAY RUELLIA

Synonyms: *R. amoena, R. graecizans*. Tropical South America. Evergreen perennial herb or subshrub, 1–2 ft.; zones 10–11. Blooms pri-

marily winter, spring. Moist to wet. Fertile, humus-rich soil. Bright filtered light. Flowers: tubular and somewhat inflated, to 2 in. long, lobes short, not flared, red; anthers resemble little white teeth at the upper rim of the throat. Leaves: elliptic, to 5 in. long, glossy, purple below. *An understory plant of moist locations. It will grow in fountain spray. Self-propagating in favorable conditions such as under nursery benches.*

Ruellia chartacea

RED SHRIMP-PLANT

Synonyms: *Aphelandra colorata, R. colorata*. Ecuador to Colombia and Brazil. Evergreen shrub, 3–4 ft.; zones 10–11. Blooms winter, spring, occasionally at other times. Regular moisture. Fertile, well-drained soil. Bright filtered light. Flowers: tubular, golden to pinkish orange; bracts showy, scarlet, long-lasting, to 3 in. long; spikes loosely arranged. Leaves: ovate, tip narrowing abruptly to a point (cuspidate), veins often reddish. *Common name a mystery as inflorescences do not resemble shrimps. Sensitive to cold and dry winds. Watch for infestations of sucking insects, especially in warm weather. Prune any winter damage after chance of cold spells passes.*

Ruellia macrantha

CHRISTMAS PRIDE

Brazil. Evergreen shrub to 4 ft.; zone 10. Blooms winter, early spring. Moderate but regular moisture, mist when hot or dry. Fertile, well-drained soil; acid pH. Full to part sun. Flowers: funnel-shaped, pink with darker veins, 2–3 in. long; solitary in the leaf axils. Leaves: ovate-lanceolate, to 5 in. long. *Does best in mild conditions, quickly declining in heat. Allow room for spread and good air circulation. For holiday bloom do not prune after midsummer.*

Ruellia makoyana

TRAILING VELVET-PLANT, MONKEY-PLANT

Brazil. Evergreen subshrub to 2 ft.; zone 10. Blooms fall, winter. Regular moisture and humidity, mist when hot or dry. Fertile, well-drained soil; acid pH. Bright broken

light. Flowers: trumpet-shaped, to 2 in. long, magenta-pink; solitary in the leaf axils. Leaves: ovate to elliptic, 2–3 in. long, dull, dark green,

veins white, undersides purplish. *A trailing, understory plant. Prefers mild temperatures. Suitable as a ground cover or container plant.*

Pseuderanthemum carruthersii

Pseuderanthemum carruthersii var. reticulatum

Pseuderanthemum sinuatum

Ruellia brevifolia

Ruellia chartacea

Ruellia macrantha

Ruellia multisetosa

Synonym: *Suessenguthia multisetosa*. Bolivia. Evergreen sprawling or clambering shrub, 10–15 ft.; zones 9–11. Blooms spring. Regular moisture. Fertile, well-drained soil. Full sun to bright filtered light. Flowers: trumpet-shaped, to 3 in. long, pink; calyx, bracts, and bracteoles with long hairs. Leaves: ovate, tip and base acuminate. Young stems green. *The species will be circumscribed within the genus Suessenguthia but was not officially transferred at the time of writing (Wasshausen, pers. comm.). A plant of mid-elevation streambanks.*

Ruellia pereducta

Belize, Guatemala, Yucatan. Evergreen shrub, 3–5 ft.; zones 10–11. Blooms warm months, primarily early summer. Regular moisture. Average, well-drained soil. Bright filtered light to part sun. Flowers: trumpet-shaped, tube to 3 in. long, red-violet; on a long pedicel; in racemes in the leaf axils, flowers opening a few at a time; bracts leaflike, lanceolate, 1–2 in. long. Leaves: ovate-cordate, 3–8 in. long, tips aristate, dark green, leathery; margins serrate. Stems: 4-angled when young, canelike when mature. *An erect shrub of forest understory and streambanks; unbranched, developing leafless canelike stems. Blooms best in bright light.*

Ruellia rosea

BRAZILIAN TORCH
Synonym: *R. elegans* (hort.). Brazil.

Evergreen perennial herb to 2 ft.; zones 10–11. Blooms warm months. Regular moisture. Fertile, well-drained soil. Bright filtered light. Flowers: trumpet-shaped with flaring lobes, red, under 1 in. wide. Leaves: elliptic to ovate, to 3 in. long. *Bright accent plant. Densely spreading ground cover in native Brazil. Should never be allowed to dry out.*

Ruellia speciosa

Synonym: *R. affinis*. Brazil (Bahia). Evergreen scrambling shrub to 10 ft.; zone 11. Blooms warm months. Moderate but regular moisture. Fertile, well-drained soil. Bright broken light. Flowers: trumpet-shaped, to 6 in. long, translucent red-orange; bracts inconspicuous. Leaves: elliptic, 2–4 in. long, dark green, tip obtusely pointed to

rounded. *Not technically a vine though long shoots can be trained on a support. Resplendent in bloom. Size ideal for framing entries or arches. Somewhat cold-sensitive. Growing in containers facilitates moving into protected areas seasonally. Unusual in cultivation but highly desirable.*

Ruellia squarrosa

PURPLE AND WHITE RUELLIA
Synonym: *Dipteracanthus squarrosus*. Mexico. Evergreen subshrub to about 1 ft.; zones 9–11. Blooms warm months. Regular moisture. Fertile, well-drained soil. Full to part sun. Flowers: trumpet-shaped, purple with 2 more or less white ridges on each unlobed petal; sessile in the leaf axil; solitary. Leaves: ovate, 2–3 in. long, softly hairy (pubescent); margins serrate. *This low, spreading ruellia is an excellent*

ground cover in sunny locations. It will not bloom without direct sun for several hours. The solitary flowers are a good field mark.*

Ruellia tweediana

MEXICAN BLUE-BELLS,
SPANISH LADIES
Synonyms: *R. brittoniana* (misapplied), *R. coerulea*, *R. malacosperma*. South America; naturalized in the eastern United States. Evergreen subshrub, 2–3 ft.; zones 8–11. Blooms warm months. Seasonally wet, moderate. Sandy, well-drained soil. Full sun, morning sun. Flowers: funnel-shaped, blue-violet, pink, or white, throat sometimes red, petal tips shallowly 2-lobed; peduncle 2–4 in. long. Leaves: narrowly to broadly lanceolate, to 7 in. long. Stems sometimes black. *It has not been resolved if R. mala-*

Ruellia makoyana

Ruellia multisetosa

Ruellia pereducta

Ruellia rosea

Ruellia speciosa

Ruellia squarrosa

cosperma *from North America, R. tweediana, and R. brittoniana are variations of the same species, natural hybrids, or very close relatives (Wasshausen, pers. comm.). The form referred to as* R. malacosperma *has broader, lanceolate leaves and white flowers in cultivation. The considerable variation may also be due to hybridization with R. ciliatiflora which overlaps the territory of these species.* 'Compacta Katie' *is a dwarf selection commonly grown as a ground cover. The leaves are densely compacted on stems with short internodes. Self-seeding and weedy in favorable conditions.*

Ruspolia

Ruspolia includes approximately 4 species of shrubs from tropical Africa. The plant listed is unusual in cultivation and unknown in the wild. Despite being offered in the trade as *Eranthemum* 'Twilight', it more closely resembles *Ruspolia* taxonomically, although the flowers are not red or reddish, which is more typical of this genus (Wasshausen, pers. comm.). It could possibly be an intergeneric hybrid, in which case it would require a name change.

Ruspolia 'Twilight'

Synonym: *Eranthemum* 'Twilight' (hort.). Garden origin. Evergreen shrub to 3 ft.; zones 10–11. Blooms winter, spring, intermittently at other times. Regular moisture. Fertile, well-drained soil. Full to part sun. Flowers: trumpet-shaped, lavender, in many-flowered spikes. Leaves: ovate to elliptic, to 4 in. long, slightly rough, scaly (scabrous).

Ruttya

Ruttya includes approximately 3 species of shrubs from tropical Africa. *Ruttya fruticosa* is occasionally cultivated. It has distinctive, blisterlike (bullate) black spots on the lip.

Ruttya fruticosa

Eastern Africa. Evergreen spreading shrub to 3 ft.; zones 9–11. Blooms warm months. Regular moisture. Fertile, well-drained soil. Full to part sun. Flowers: 2-lipped, orange;

glossy black, bullate spot on lower lip. Leaves: elliptic, to 3 in. long. *This lax, spreading shrub can be pruned for a habit that is more compact if preferred. Sometimes grown as a root-hardy perennial in mild temperate regions.* 'Scholesei' *has yellow flowers.*

×Ruttyruspolia

×*Ruttyruspolia* is an intergeneric hybrid of *Ruttya* and *Ruspolia*.

×Ruttyruspolia 'Phyllis van Heeden'

Zimbabwe, possibly a natural hybrid, *Ruttya ovata* × *Ruspolia hypocrateriformis* var. *australis*. Evergreen shrub, 3–4 ft.; zones 10–11. Blooms late spring, summer. Regular moisture. Fertile, well-drained soil. Bright broken or filtered light. Flowers: salverform, pink, throat speck-led with magenta; in many-flowered cymes. Leaves: ovate, 3–5 in. long, leathery. *Scant reliable information is available on this identification. Very attractive as a hedge or shrub for understory locations.*

Sanchezia

Sanchezia includes approximately 20 species of shrubs from Central and South America. The genus is named for Spanish botanist Jóse Sánchez so should be pronounced SAN-cheh-see-ah. The species listed are often cultivated for their vividly marked foliage. Popular literature includes a confusing variety of names for these species. *Sanchezia parvibracteata* (meaning "small bracted") has small green bracts that clasp only the base of one to a few flowers. *Sanchezia speciosa* has large russet-red bracts

that partially enclose a cluster of buds and flowers. Evidently, hybrids between these species are in cultivation. Chilly temperatures burn the leaf edges. Prune plants when danger of cold is past. Plants will recover if they are not actually frozen. Though grown primarily as foliage plants, better selections have very attractive flowers. Make cuttings from plants with both attractive foliage and flowers.

Sanchezia parvibracteata

SMALL-BRACTED SANCHEZIA
Synonyms: *S. glaucophylla* (hort.), *S. nobilis* (misapplied). Colombia, Ecuador, Peru. Evergreen shrub, 6–8 ft.; zones 10–11. Blooms warm months. Regular moisture. Fertile, well-drained soil. Full sun to bright broken light. Flowers: tubular, bright yellow, lobes small, rolled

Ruellia tweediana

Ruellia tweediana 'Compacta Katie'

Ruspolia 'Twilight'

Ruttya fruticosa

Ruttya fruticosa 'Scholesei'

back tightly (reflexed); bracts small, pointed, green with red streaks, enclosing the base of 1 or 2 flowers; calyx yellow, faintly streaked red. Leaves: elliptic, to 8 in. long, glossy green with cream-colored veins, blade quilted. *'Ellen' is an exceptionally well-marked selection (Burch, pers. comm.).*

Sanchezia speciosa
LARGE-BRACTED SANCHEZIA
Synonym: *S. spectabilis* (hort.). Ecuador, Peru; widely distributed in the Caribbean and Central America. Evergreen shrub to 10 ft.; zones 10–11. Blooms warm months. Regular moisture. Fertile, well-drained soil. Full sun to bright broken light. Flowers: tubular, bright yellow, lobes small, tightly rolled back (reflexed); bracts shell-like, russet-red, 1–1.5 in. long; each encloses a cluster of buds and flowers up to half their length, completely hiding the calyx. Leaves: elliptic, 4–10 in. long, glossy green with yellow to cream veins, more or less quilted.

Schaueria
Schaueria includes approximately 8 herbs and shrubs from Brazil. They have distinctive, brushlike (filamentous) calyces, bracts, and bracteoles. *Schaueria flavicoma* is unusual in cultivation. A compact shrub, it provides interesting texture and color contrast especially with plants having dark green or purple foliage. The leaves are naturally yellowish green, but the addition of microelements and organic matter is recommended in alkaline soil.

Schaueria flavicoma
Synonyms: *Chaetothylax rothschuhii* (misapplied), *S. calicotricha.* Brazil. Evergreen shrub to 3 ft.; zones 10–11. Blooms late spring, early summer. Regular moisture when hot, less when cool. Fertile, well-drained soil; neutral to slightly acid pH. Full sun to bright filtered light. Flowers: tubular, 2-lipped, the lower lip divided into 3 lobes, white; bracts, bracteoles, and calyx greenish yellow, brushlike. Leaves: ovate to lanceolate, to 4 in. long, yellowish green.

Strobilanthes
Strobilanthes includes approximately 250 species of perennial herbs and subshrubs from Asia. The opposite leaves are usually unequal in size. *Strobilanthes dyerianus* has stunningly marked foliage with a metallic sheen reminiscent of the intricate mosaics of ancient Persia. It is often grown as a container plant in temperate climates.

Strobilanthes dyerianus
PERSIAN SHIELD
Myanmar (Burma). Evergreen shrub, 2–3 ft.; zones 10–11. Blooms fall and intermittently. Regular moisture. Fertile, well-drained soil. Part sun, bright filtered light. Flowers: small, white or blue, in small spikes. Leaves: ovate to lanceolate, to 8 in. long, tapering gradually to a point (acuminate), quilted; in opposite pairs that are unequal in length, silvery white, younger leaves purple, veins dark green; margins finely toothed.

Thunbergia
Thunbergia includes approximately 90 species of shrubs and climbers primarily from Africa and India. A number of them are great favorites in tropical landscaping. A few species are grown in containers or as annuals in temperate regions. *Thunbergia* belongs to a subfamily of Acanthaceae easily recognized by the pair of clamshell-like bracts that embrace the base of the trumpet- or bell-shaped flowers. The calyx is small, the sepals linear or scalelike, hidden inside the bracts. The typically ovate to lanceolate leaves have a few large marginal teeth or lobes. When only 2 lobes are present the leaves appear diamond-shaped (rhombic).

Thunbergia alata
BLACK-EYED SUSAN
Tropical Africa; widely naturalized. Perennial climber to 10 ft.+; zones 9–11. Blooms most of the year. Moderate moisture. Average, well-drained soil. Full to part sun. Flowers: yellow to orange, rarely white, throat usually with a maroon spot. Leaves: ovate to somewhat deltoid, to 3 in. long; margins toothed; petiole winged. *Grown as an annual in*

temperate climates. Heavily self-seeding. Listed as invasive in Hawaii. Sometimes confused with T. gregorii, *which always lacks the throat spot and has conspicuously hairy bracts.*

Thunbergia battiscombei
Tropical Africa. Evergreen climber to 20 ft.+; zones 10–11. Blooms warm months. Moderate moisture. Fertile, well-drained soil. Full sun.

×*Ruttyruspolia* 'Phyllis van Heeden'

Sanchezia parvibracteata

Sanchezia speciosa

Schaueria flavicoma

Strobilanthes dyerianus

Thunbergia alata

Flowers: trumpet-shaped, 2 in. long, velvety purple lobes to 1.5 in. wide, throat yellow with scattered hairs; bracts leaflike. Leaves: broadly ovate to cordate, 3–4 in. long, often slightly oblique, leathery; petiole long; margins occasionally with widely spaced teeth. *Flowers similar to T. erecta, a shrubby species.*

Thunbergia erecta

KING'S MANTLE, BUSH CLOCK-VINE, MANTO DE REY

Tropical western Africa. Evergreen shrub to 8 ft.; zones 10–11. Blooms almost all year. Moderate moisture. Fertile, well-drained soil. Full sun. Flowers: solitary in the leaf axils, funnel-shaped, 2–3 in. long, tube white outside, curved like a cornucopia, throat yellow, lobes deep purple, semipendent; bracts light green. Leaves: ovate, 1–2 in. long, dark green; margins undulate,

toothed. *'Alba' has creamy white flowers with yellow throats. 'Blue Moon' may be a sport, the older leaves much larger than the type species; the flowers are also larger and blue-violet. Excellent as a hedge because flowers are on old growth, not likely to be pruned away.*

Thunbergia fragrans

WHITE THUNBERGIA

Sri Lanka, India. Perennial climber to 10 ft.+; zones 10–11. Blooms warm months. Moderate moisture. Average, well-drained soil. Full to part sun. Flowers: trumpet-shaped, to 2 in. long, white, lobes ruffled. Leaves: broadly lanceolate; margins sparsely toothed (dentate). *A self-seeding twining vine. The name indicates fragrance though a scent is not evident. Naturalized near the coast in South Florida—a pretty volunteer but not a serious pest.*

Thunbergia grandiflora

SKY-VINE, BENGAL CLOCK-VINE, FAUSTO

India; naturalized in Old World tropics. Evergreen climber to 100 ft.+; zones 9–11. Blooms spring. Seasonally moist/moderate. Fertile, sandy, well-drained soil; acid pH. Full sun. Flowers: funnel-shaped, to 3 in. long, violet-blue, rarely white, throat white and yellow; bracts green, sometimes streaked maroon; racemes terminal, pendent. Leaves: ovate, 4–8 in. long, thin, base cordate; margins coarsely toothed near base. *Aggressive clambering vine. Sterile in cultivation. Outstanding hung from porch eaves or over a wall, such as the one in the photo, an oolite-limestone wall in Miami, Florida. Micronutrients recommended in alkaline soil. T. laurifolia is distinguished by stiff, narrowly lanceolate leaves with attenuate bases and blue-lavender flowers.*

Thunbergia gregorii

ORANGE CLOCK-VINE, GOLDEN GLORY-CLIMBER

Synonym: *T. gibsonii.* Tropical eastern Africa. Evergreen perennial climber to 10 ft.+; zones 9–11. Blooms warm months. Moderate moisture. Average, well-drained soil. Full sun. Flowers: funnel-shaped, yellow-orange; bracts and flower stalks densely covered with hairs (pilose); no throat spot. Leaves: ovate, pubescent; margins with widely spaced teeth. *The conspicuously hairy bracts are a good field mark. This creeper or climber is used as a ground cover or to cover a fence. Tolerates hot, exposed locations. Grown as an annual in mild temperate climates. Self-seeding.*

Thunbergia kirkii

Tropical eastern Africa. Evergreen, erect shrub to 3 ft.; zones 10–11. Blooms intermittently. Seasonally

Thunbergia battiscombei

Thunbergia erecta

Thunbergia erecta 'Blue Moon'

Thunbergia fragrans

Thunbergia grandiflora

moist/dry. Average, well-drained soil. Full sun. Flowers: bell-shaped, 1–1.5 in. long, lobes oblong, upper lobe reflexed, light blue-violet, throat with yellow spot and purple streaks; solitary or in pairs in the leaf axils; bracts green. Leaves: diamond-shaped (rhomboid), to 3 in. long; petiole short; margins somewhat wavy (undulate), with one large tooth midway on each side plus occasional smaller teeth. Stems: grass-green, strongly 4-angled, stiffly erect, somewhat bamboolike. *Blooms after a dry period so water sparingly in dry seasons. Unusual in cultivation.*

Thunbergia mysorensis
MUNZERABAD CREEPER
Southern India (Nilghiri Mountains). Evergreen woody climber to 20 ft.+; zones 9–11. Blooms inter-mittently in warm months. Moist when hot, less when cool. Average to fertile, well-drained soil. Full to part sun. Flowers: hoodlike, mahogany-red outside, golden-yellow inside; bracts also mahogany-red; racemes pendent. Leaves: narrowly elliptic, to 6 in. long, glossy. *This twining mountain plant prefers cool evening temperatures but is tolerant of daytime heat. Nectar-feeding birds and butterflies are attracted to the beads of honeydew spilling over the floral lip.*

Thunbergia togoensis
TOGO THUNBERGIA
Togo, western central Africa. Evergreen shrubby climber; zones 9–11. Blooms warm months. Moderate moisture when hot, less when cool. Fertile, well-drained soil. Full to part sun. Flowers: funnel-shaped, to 4 in. long, lobes rounded, deep purple, throat yellow; bracts reticulated, green and white, hairy; in clusters in the leaf axils. Leaves: broadly ovate to suborbicular, to 6 in. long, bases of pairs overlapping, dark green; margins with a few large teeth; petiole short. *This dramatic climbing shrub is unusual in cultivation but highly recommended. The large, opposite leaves overlap at the base, clasping the stem.*

ADOXACEAE
ELDERBERRY FAMILY, VIBURNUM FAMILY
Adoxaceae includes 4 genera of perennial herbs and shrubs from temperate and tropical America. *Viburnum* and *Sambucus* species are occasionally cultivated. Leaves are trifoliolate or pinnately compound. Flowers are bisexual and radially symmetrical. The fruit is a small drupe.

Sambucus
Sambucus includes 9–25 species of shrubs from temperate to tropical regions. This genus was formerly included in Caprifoliaceae. Some authors prefer to place it in Sambucaceae. Stems are pithy in the center. Leaves are irregularly pinnate. Flowers are small, bisexual, and radially symmetrical. They have 3–5 sepals and petals. The fruits of some species are excellent in pies, somewhat resembling the flavor of blueberries. The fruits are also made into jellies and wine. Some species are toxic or unpleasantly scented.

Sambucus canadensis
ELDERBERRY, ELDER, SAUCO
Canada to Florida, Gulf Coast, Mexico, Central America. Semideciduous shrub, 6–12 ft.; zones 8–10. Blooms spring, summer. Moderate moisture. Most soils. Full to part sun. Flowers: small, white, in many-flowered panicles; fruit purple-black. Leaves: irregularly pinnate; leaflets 5–9, lanceolate to elliptic, 3–4 in. long; margins serrate. *Infrequently cultivated in the United States but commonly found in disturbed areas and along streams. It is grown as a dooryard shrub in Haiti (Judd, pers. comm.) and around graveyards in the West Indies (Howard, pers. comm.).*

Thunbergia grandiflora

Thunbergia gregorii

Thunbergia kirkii

Thunbergia mysorensis

Thunbergia togoensis

Sambucus canadensis

AGAPANTHACEAE

AGAPANTHUS FAMILY

Agapanthaceae includes a single genus of bulbous herbs from South Africa. *Agapanthus* was previously included in Alliaceae or Liliaceae.

Agapanthus

Agapanthus includes approximately 9 species of clump-forming bulbous herbs from South Africa. Some are evergreen, others deciduous in dry seasons. Leaves are strap-shaped and grasslike. *Agapanthus praecox* is commonly grown in the United States. It thrives in Mediterranean-type climates with hot, dry summers, cool evenings, with most moisture in winter. In areas with moist, humid summers, it is not as consistent or prolific a bloomer, but excellent drainage will help encourage bloom. It is propagated by division of bulbs. *Agapanthus praecox* is commonly misidentified as *A. africanus* (syn. *A. minor*), a smaller species with hemispherical rather than almost spherical heads of flowers. Distinguishing the species is somewhat complicated by the fact that *A. praecox* also comes in dwarf forms. A good field mark is the long-exserted anthers in *A. praecox* and the included anthers in *A. africanus*.

Agapanthus praecox

AFRICAN LILY, LILY-OF-THE-NILE, AGAPANTO

South Africa. Perennial bulbous herb, 3–4 ft.; zones 9–11. Blooms late spring, early summer. Moderate moisture. Poor, gritty, well-drained soil; slightly acid pH. Full sun. Flowers: trumpet-shaped, blue-violet, often with darker stripes; anthers exserted; in globular heads of 30 or more; on wiry scapes, 3–4 ft. high. Leaves: strap-shaped, stiff, 3–4 ft. long. *A durable and exceptionally attractive bulb plant. Grown in abundance in southern California. A number of cultivars are available.* 'Albus' has white flowers.

AGAVACEAE

CENTURY-PLANT FAMILY, AGAVE FAMILY

Agavaceae includes 9 genera of more or less succulent herbs and trees from North and Central America and the West Indies, with greatest diversity in Mexico and the southwestern United States. Several inadequately studied species are found in the West Indies, perhaps cultigens dating to pre-Columbian Indians (H. Gentry 1982). This family formerly included *Dracaena*, which is now segregated into Ruscaceae, and *Cordyline*, now in Laxmanniaceae (here described under Lomandraceae). Agaves are utilitarian and have been widely distributed, many becoming naturalized in favorable conditions. Some are salt tolerant, growing on cliffs overlooking the ocean. Hardiness is difficult to predict and depends upon the origin of individual selections. Smaller species are suitable for containers. Cultivated plants should be irrigated deeply once a week during hot months in arid climates. Many agaves tolerate humid climates with few requirements other than excellent drainage. The soil should be gritty, open, with only a small amount of humus. Mulch with rocks or gravel. Moisture-retaining mulch leads to rot. Agaves are pollinated by bats, birds, and moths. Many attract hummingbirds.

Agave

Agave includes approximately 250 species of herbs and trees from tropical and temperate North America. This genus presents identification problems due in part to difficulties of preserving specimens in herbaria and infrequent bloom of plants. A number are quite variable, probably cultigens, the result of centuries of cultivation. Indian migration is associated with distribution beyond the ancient habitat in central Mexico. Agaves are cultivated as barrier hedges, for sisal fiber, food, alcoholic and nonalcoholic beverages, and more recently for birth-control steroids (H. Gentry 1982). Most agaves are monocarpic—multiannuals that bloom once after 5–35 or more years from the terminal growing point and then die. Some produce inflorescence stalks to 30 ft. tall. A few species are polycarpic—trunk-forming perennials that produce flowers annually from the leaf axils and do not die after blooming. The leaves are more or less lance- or sword-shaped, fleshy and/or fibrous, in basal whorls or at the end of a stem. Margins are usually sharply toothed, with a long terminal spine. The upper leaf surface is frequently concave, guttering dew and infrequent rainfall toward the rhizomes. Agaves reproduce from seeds, suckers from the plant base (cespitose), and bulbils that develop in the inflorescences. The agave snout-weevil is a serious pest which attacks plants of flowering age and favors fleshy species. Propagate agaves from uninfected individuals.

Agapanthus praecox

Agapanthus praecox

Agave americana

CENTURY-PLANT, AMERICAN ALOE, MAGUEY, PITA

Synonyms: *A. complicata, A. expansa, A. picta.* Northeastern Mexico, Texas; widely distributed. Succulent multiannual, 6–10 ft.; zones 9–11. Blooms at maturity. Semiarid to seasonally moist/dry. Average, gritty, well-drained soil. Full sun. Flowers: funnel-shaped, to 4 in. long, light yellow and green; panicle stalk slender, to 25 ft. tall. Leaves: lanceolate, fleshy, guttered or flat, spreading irregularly, sometimes twisted, waxy gray to green; margins sharply toothed. Suckering (cespitose). Produces large clumps. *Older leaves often droop near the tips, a good field mark. An extremely variable species with numerous variegated markings and formerly segregated into separate species and varieties. Variegated forms were formerly clumped into var. picta, but these forms are now considered cultivars.*

Agave angustifolia

Synonym: *A. vivipara.* Mexico to Panama; widely distributed. Succulent multiannual, 2–6 ft.; zones 9–11. Blooms at maturity. Arid to seasonally moist/dry. Average, gritty, well-drained soil. Full to part sun. Flowers: trumpet-shaped, greenish yellow; panicle stalk to 15 ft.; bracts purple, triangular. Leaves: sword-shaped, rigid, fibrous, not fleshy, light green to waxy gray-green; margins straight, teeth small, hooked. Suckering (cespitose), with hemispherical habit. *The most recent treatment revises this species to* A. vivipara *(Eggli 2002). Var.* marginata, *now revised to a cultivar, 'Variegata', is more commonly cultivated. It has cream stripes along the margins and cultivated forms are usually smaller than the all-green type species.*

Agave attenuata

FOXTAIL AGAVE, SPINELESS CENTURY-PLANT

Synonym: *A. glaucescens* (incorrectly). West-central Mexico. Succulent polycarpic tree or shrub to 6 ft.; zones 10–11. Blooms winter. Moderate moisture. Average, gritty, well-drained soil. Full sun, or broken light in hot, arid conditions. Flowers: small, tubular, yellowish green; spike densely flowered, 6–10 ft. tall. Leaves: ovate, 1–1.5 ft. long, tips acuminate, waxy yellowish to gray-

Agave americana, variegated form

Agave ghiesbreghtii

Agave angustifolia var. *marginata*

ish green, softly fleshy, almost flat, arching outward; unarmed. Branches reclining or ascending. Trunk-forming, flowering yearly. *The inflorescence stalk develops a swanlike arch with groups of flowering spikes commonly arrayed in the same direction. Of moderate elevation in mountain pine forest understory. Requires light filtration and weekly irrigation in hot, arid climates (Irish and Irish 2000).*

Agave decipiens
FALSE SISAL

Synonym: *A. laxifolia*. Florida Keys. Succulent multiannual tree, 10–12 ft.; zones 9–11. Blooms at maturity. Seasonally moist/dry. Average, gritty, well-drained soil. Full sun. Flowers: greenish yellow; in panicles to 20 ft. Leaves: lanceolate, to 6 ft. long, rigid, fleshy, bright green, narrowing just above the base, upper surface deeply guttered (concave); margins wavy with small, widely spaced teeth; needlelike spine at the tip. Trunk: 3–9 ft. *Probably a cultigen related to* A. delamateri, *a species that was grown by Indians for food and fiber (Eggli 2002). Produces copious fruit, bulbils, and offsets.*

Agave desmettiana

Synonym: *A. miradorensis*. Only known in cultivation, possibly originating in Cuba. Succulent multiannual, 3–4 ft.; zones 9–11. Blooms at maturity. Semiarid to seasonally moist/dry. Average, gritty, well-drained soil. Full to part sun. Flowers: yellow, in compact cymes; inflorescence stalk stout, blue-gray, to 15 ft. tall. Leaves: broad, narrowing toward the base, to 3 ft. long, apex arching slightly outward, fleshy, surface scaly, mottled blue-gray; margins smooth or with tiny black teeth. Usually solitary. *The vaselike shape, small to medium size, tiny or absent marginal teeth, and bluish color are good field marks. Produces numerous bulbils. The pictured plant produced an anomalous but spectacular fountainlike spike. It also exhibits minor variations suggesting a possible hybrid (Irish, pers. comm.).*

Agave filifera

Central Mexico. Succulent multiannual, 12–14 in.; zones 9–11.

Blooms at maturity. Semiarid. Average, gritty, well-drained soil. Full sun. Flowers: trumpet-shaped, tepals yellow-green; stamen filaments reddish, long-exserted; inflorescence spike 7–8 ft. tall. Leaves: lance-shaped, bud imprints white, upper surface guttered (concave); margins unarmed, with white fibrous strands peeling away from the edges; terminal spine weak. Clump-forming (cespitose). *Of rocky montane outcroppings. This agave belongs to the larger-sized of 2, probably artificial, subgenera of agaves with white bud-imprinted leaves and marginal fibers (H. Gentry 1982). Numerous cultivars.*

Agave ghiesbreghtii

Synonyms: *A. huehueteca, A. purpusorum, A. roezliana*. Southern Mexico, Guatemala. Succulent multiannual to 2 ft.; zones 9–11. Blooms at maturity. Moderate moisture to dry. Average, gritty, well-drained soil. Full sun. Flowers: tubular, purplish green; in slender spikes. Leaves: in basal whorls, broadly sword-shaped, narrowing just above the base, dark green, stiff, slightly incurving, upper surface slightly guttered; margins horny, teeth widely spaced, brown. Clump-forming (cespitose). *A small stemless agave suitable for containers.*

Agave lechuguilla
SHIN-DAGGER, LECHUGUILLA ("LITTLE LETTUCE")

Synonyms: *A. heteracantha, A. multilineata, A. poselgeri*. Western Texas into northern Mexico. Succulent multiannual to 2 ft.; zones 9–11. Blooms at maturity. Arid. Average, gritty, well-drained soil. Full sun. Flowers: tubular, yellow, often streaked red; arranged on a blue-gray, unbranched spike, 8–12 ft. tall. Leaves: sword-shaped, to 2 ft. long, deeply guttered, dark green to yellowish green, in basal rosettes; margins with weak, downward-angled spines. Stemless. *Soap and a fiber called* ixtle *are made from this small*

Agave attenuata

Agave decipiens

Agave attenuata, flowers

Agave desmettiana

Agave desmettiana, flowers

agave. *Often confused with* A. lo-*phantha, which has nearly flat leaves. Intergraded hybrids are common.*

Agave neglecta
BLUE AGAVE
West-central Florida (Tampa area). Succulent multiannual to 6 ft.+;

zones 9–11. Blooms at maturity. Seasonally moist/dry. Average, gritty, well-drained soil. Full sun. Flowers: tubular, greenish yellow, to 2 in. long; panicle 25–30 ft. tall, producing many bulbils. Leaves: lanceolate, straight to arching, narrowing above the base, 4–6 ft. long,

somewhat blue-gray; margins straight with fine, sharp teeth when young, gradually lost with age; tip spine gray to 1 in. long. Trunk: short. Suckering. *Originally found around Tampa in localized coastal areas associated with early Indian settlement. Probably of cultivated ori-*

gin, *possibly related to* A. weberi *or* A. desmettiana *(H. Gentry 1982).*

Agave parryi
MESCAL AGAVE
Synonym: *A. patonii.* Northern Mexico (Durango, Chihuahua), eastern Arizona. Succulent multi-

Agave desmettiana, inflorescence

Agave filifera

Agave filifera, flowers

Agave ghiesbreghtii, with inflorescence

Agave lechuguilla, flowers

Agave lechuguilla, with inflorescence

Agave neglecta

annual, 1–2 ft.; zones 7–11. Blooms after 20–30 years. Dry. Average, gritty, well-drained soil. Full sun. Flowers: yellow, buds reddish; flower stalk to 15 ft.+ tall. Leaves: lanceolate to obovate, to 1 ft. long, fleshy, light waxy gray to gray-green, ends broad, flat to slightly guttered; marginal teeth evenly spaced, red-brown. Suckering (cespitose). *A compact species. Very slow-growing. Requires weekly deep irrigation in hot, arid conditions. An alcoholic beverage, mescal, is sometimes made from this agave. Var. truncata is a smaller version of the type species from the southeastern area of the species range. It has a cup-shaped, compact habit. Excellent for containers.*

Agave pygmae

Synonyms: *A. seemanniana, A. seemannii* (hort.). Southern Mexico to northern Honduras. Succulent multiannual, 6–10 in. high; zones 9–11. Blooms at maturity. Semi-arid. Average, gritty, well-drained soil. Full sun, or part shade in hot, arid conditions. Flowers: yellow; in panicles, to 10 ft. Leaves: broadly obovate to spathulate, narrow at the base, to 1 ft. long, bluish green; margins undulate, mammillate, edges near tip folded upward, teeth red-brown. Solitary or in small clumps (cespitose). *A variable species. More compact in dry conditions. Suitable for containers. The most recent treatment revises this species to A. seemanniana (Eggli 2002).*

Agave sisalana
SISAL, HEMP

Only in cultivation, originating in south-central Mexico; distributed pantropically. Succulent multiannual to 6 ft.; zones 9–11. Blooms at maturity. Moderate moisture to seasonally moist/dry. Gritty, well-drained soil. Full to part sun. Flowers: sterile; panicle to 25 ft., producing numerous bulbils. Leaves: sword-shaped, to 4 ft. long, green to gray-green; margins usually smooth or with few widely spaced, tiny teeth, terminal spine short. *A variable cultigen. Invasive in some areas. Cold-sensitive. Characteristics are the stiffly symmetrical shape and slender leaves with mostly unarmed margins. 'Variegata' has a white stripe down the midline of the leaves. Agave tequilana has bluish leaves with narrow white margins.*

Agave sobolifera

Synonym: *A. morrisii* (incorrectly). Jamaica, Hispaniola, Cayman Islands. Succulent multiannual to 6 ft.; zones 10–11. Blooms at maturity. Seasonally moist/dry. Average, gritty, well-drained soil. Full sun. Flowers: bright orange-yellow; inflorescence stalk to 12 ft.; fruit turbinate; bearing numerous bulbils. Leaves: broadly lanceolate to spathulate, to 6 ft. long, tips bending outward (recurved), medium green, guttered; margins undulate, with large sharp teeth on prominences. Solitary. *Though exceptionally attractive, this species is unusual in cultivation in the United States as are most West Indian Agave species.*

Agave stricta
RABO DE LEÓN ("LION'S TAIL")

Synonyms: *A. echinoides, A. striata* var. *stricta.* South-central Mexico. Succulent multiannual to 2 ft.; zones 10–11. Blooms at maturity. Dry. Average, gritty, well-drained soil. Full sun, or part shade in arid conditions. Flowers: funnel-

Agave parryi var. *truncata*

Agave pygmae

Agave stricta

shaped, to 2 in. long, purplish red; spike crooked, to 8 ft. tall. Leaves: 15–20 in. long, diamond-shaped in cross section, curved inward, scaly to the touch; margins thin, faintly toothed. Trunk: 3–6 ft., often branching. Forms dense, grasslike clumps (cespitose). *Suitable for rock gardens and containers.*

Agave victoriae-reginae

Synonyms: *A. consideranti, A. ferdinandi-regis,* Northern Mexico, endangered in the wild. Succulent multiannual under 2 ft.; zones 10–11. Blooms at maturity. Seasonally moist/dry. Average, gritty, well-drained soil. Full sun. Flowers: white; spike dense, to 12 ft. Leaves: thickly wedge-shaped, 1–1.5 ft. long, rigid, medium dull green with white angular bud imprinting, rounded or keeled on the underside, tips rounded; margins white, unarmed; terminal spines 1–3. Usually stemless, solitary. *Compact and variably and strikingly marked. Excellent for containers and beds.*

Furcraea

Furcraea includes approximately 20 species of monocarpic herbs from tropical America, with greatest numbers in northern South America. Plants resemble agaves, but the drooping, bell-like flowers are distinctive. Leaves are lance- or sword-shaped and in basal whorls or on stems (cauline). Margins are usually edged with sharp teeth. Flowers have 6 greenish or creamy tepals, tubular bases, and ovate

lobes. The flowers are in panicles on tall stalks.

Furcraea macdougalii

Southern Mexico (Oaxaca). Arborescent succulent, 10–20 ft.; zones 10–11. Blooms at maturity. Moderate moisture to seasonally dry. Gritty, well-drained soil. Full sun.

Flowers: tepals 6, bases fused, lobes bell-like, creamy; inflorescence stalk to 20 ft. Leaves: narrowly sword-shaped, to 7 ft. long, 2 in. wide at base, stiffly erect, deeply guttered, rough; margins with widely spaced, hooked teeth. *Eventually develops a trunk covered with old, dry leaf bases. Propagated from bulbils.*

Yucca

Yucca includes approximately 40 species of perennial shrubs and trees from Central and North America. Leaves are thin and fibrous, not succulent, with wedge-shaped bases. They are in whorls, either basal or along thick stems (cauline). Leaf margins are

Agave sisalana

Furcraea macdougalii, young plant

Agave victoriae-reginae

Agave sobolifera

Furcraea species, flowers

smooth, usually with a sharp terminal spine (*Beaucarnea* and *Dracaena* lack sharp terminal spines). Flowers have 6 cream to greenish, often purple-tinged, tepals. Yuccas bloom annually (polycarpic) in contrast to most *Agave* species, which die after blooming (monocarpic). Most yuccas are endemic to semiarid conditions.

Yucca aloifolia thrives in moist and dry climates in open soil. It is salt tolerant to the beach. Flowers are eaten in salads or sweetened and dried. Snipping off lower spines helps prevent injury. Indians pounded the leaves until only a few fibers were left attached to the spine, which they then used like needle and thread.

Certain yuccas have symbiotic relationships with particular yucca moths (*Tegeticula* species). The moth gathers sticky clumps of pollen (pollinia) from the flowers, then flies to another flower, lays her eggs in the ovary wall with specially adapted appendages, and stuffs the pollinia into the deeply recessed stigma. This pollinates the flower and provides food for the developing larvae. Although the larvae eat developing seeds throughout the summer, many seeds remain uneaten to germinate. The larvae eventually fall with the seed capsule and pupate in the ground near the yucca. In spring they hatch into moths, mate, and repeat the cycle (Armstrong 1999b).

Yucca aloifolia

SPANISH BAYONET, DAGGER-PLANT
Synonyms: *Y. gloriosa, Y. yucatana*. Southern United States, Mexico, West Indies. Evergreen shrub, 10–15 ft.; zones 8–11. Blooms spring. Dry or seasonally moist/dry. Gritty, well-drained soil. Full sun. Flowers: bell-shaped (campanulate), creamy white, often streaked purple; inflorescence a conical panicle to 2 ft. Leaves: sword-shaped, terminal spines needlelike; in dense whorls around the stem, to 2 ft. long. Old dry leaves persistent, drooping against the stem. Little branched. *Larger plants eventually recline of their own weight, sending up shoots and producing clumps. 'Marginata' has creamy white leaf margins.*

Yucca rostrata

BEAKED YUCCA
Northern Mexico, Arizona, New Mexico, Texas. Evergreen tree to 15 ft.; zones 8–11. Blooms spring, summer. Dry. Average, gritty, well-drained soil. Full to part sun. Flowers: bell-shaped, white; inflorescence terminal, to 2 ft. Leaves: linear, light gray, to about 18 in. long; margins more or less white, with peeling strands of fiber. *Develops a trunk with age. Suitable for containers when young. The species name alludes to the beak-shaped seeds. Some authorities consider Y. thompsoniana to be a smaller, hardier form of this species.*

AIZOACEAE

ICE-PLANT FAMILY,
CARPET-WEED FAMILY
Aizoaceae includes approximately 125 genera of succulent herbs and subshrubs, which are widely distributed in subtropical areas with winter rainfall, with greatest diversity in southwestern Africa. Some are adapted for survival in extremely arid regions where they receive moisture only in the form of ocean mist. Enthusiasts still refer to them as "mesembs," from the old family name Mesembryanthemaceae. Leaves are simple, fleshy, and unarmed. Some have extraordinary adaptations for storing water and resisting evaporation. Flowers have a usually 4- or 5-parted perianth. The showier, primarily African species, have numerous, often vibrantly colored petal-like stamens (staminodes). The species range from very small individuals to matlike colonies. Some are fire resistant. They are commonly planted in California to control slope and beach erosion. It

Yucca aloifolia

Yucca rostrata

Aptenia cordifolia

Carpobrotus deliciosus

Carpobrotus edulis

has been discovered, however, that fleshy leafed species, heavy with stored water, may themselves cause slides on steep slopes. These are xeric species and are very drought tolerant. Occasional supplemental moisture is recommended in extreme hot, dry conditions primarily for appearance. Many are very salt tolerant. Plants were photographed in southern California and New Mexico.

Aptenia

Aptenia includes 2 species of creeping, succulent mat-forming herbs or subshrubs from South Africa. Leaves are small and fleshy; the stems trailing to mounding. Flowers are solitary or in groups of 2 or 3. These species are suitable for hanging baskets and ground covers. They are very attractive cascading over walls and terraces. Aptenias thrive in Mediterranean-type, coastal and dry climates, and are drought tolerant. Water in very hot, dry conditions, never when cool. Plant in sandy, open soil and full sun. Cuttings can be propagated directly in the ground. Aptenias have become weedy in some areas such as in California, the Andes, and the Florida Keys.

Aptenia cordifolia

BABY SUN-ROSE, ROSA DEL SOL
Synonym: *Mesembryanthemum cordifolium*. Southern Africa; widely naturalized. Succulent creeper; zones 9–11. Blooms spring, summer. Moderate moisture when hot, dry when cool. Average, gritty, well-drained soil. Full sun. Flowers: rotate, to 0.5 in. wide, magenta to scarlet, center white to yellow. Leaves: fleshy, heart-shaped (cordate), 0.5 in. long, covered with felty, papillose hairs. *Called sunroses because the flowers open only when the sun shines. May become a pest in favorable conditions. A variegated form has white leaf margins.*

Carpobrotus

Carpobrotus includes approximately 30 species of fleshy leafed, mat-forming subshrubs from Africa and Australia. A number have become naturalized in southern Europe and North and South America. Leaves are cylindrical, more or less 3-angled (triquetrous), often with a frosty (pruinose) surface. Flowers are solitary. Fruits are fleshy, sometimes edible. For more than a century, *Carpobrotus* species have been grown in California for erosion control and dune stabilization, sometimes becoming invasive in coastal areas. Water occasionally in hot, dry conditions, never when cool.

Carpobrotus deliciosus

ICE-PLANT, SOUR FIG,
HIGO MARINO ("MARINE FIG")
Synonym: *Mesembryanthemum deliciosus*. South Africa. Succulent creeper; zones 8–11. Blooms late winter to early summer. Moderate moisture when hot, dry when cool. Average, gritty, well-drained soil. Full sun. Flowers: staminodes brilliant magenta to golden, merging with fertile stamens in center; solitary, 2–3 in. wide; fruit round, edible. Leaves: cylinder-shaped, fleshy, 3-angled, to 4 in. long, 0.5 in. thick, slightly curved like a banana. *Self-seeding, sometimes weedy*.

Carpobrotus edulis

ICE-PLANT, HOTTENTOT FIG,
HIGO MARINO ("MARINE FIG")
Synonym: *Mesembryanthemum edulis*. South Africa (Cape Province). Succulent creeper; zones 8–11. Blooms spring, summer. Moderate moisture when hot, dry when cool. Average, gritty, well-drained soil. Full sun. Flowers: staminodes light yellow to pinkish yellow; solitary, 2–3 in. wide; fruit top-shaped (turbinate). Leaves: flattened, keeled to 3-angled, to 5 in. long, 0.7 in. wide, curved, fleshy, frosty green.

Glottiphyllum

Glottiphyllum includes approximately 16 species of creeping perennials from South Africa. They resemble *Carpobrotus* species, but as the name indicates, the fleshy leaves are tongue-shaped rather than 3-sided. Leaves are densely ranked along opposite sides of the stems (distichous). These creeping to mounding plants form thick, heavy mats sometimes to 2 ft. thick or more. Water once or twice a week in very hot, dry conditions to maintain fresh appearance. Avoid watering when cool to reduce the chance of fungal infections.

Glottiphyllum linguiforme

TONGUE-LEAF ICE-PLANT
South Africa (West Cape). Succulent creeper; zones 9–11. Blooms primarily spring, fall. Moderate moisture when hot, dry when cool. Average, gritty, well-drained soil. Full sun. Flowers: staminodes light yellow; solitary, to 2 in. wide; fruit top-shaped (turbinate). Leaves: fleshy, tongue-shaped, to 6 in. long, 1.5 in. wide, surface frosty green, tip rounded.

Lampranthus

Lampranthus includes approximately 180 species of creeping, perennial subshrubs from South Africa plus 1 from Australia. They are among the more commonly cultivated members of the ice-plant family in the United States. Brilliant mats are frequently seen "glowing" beside the freeways and on coastal dunes in California. Some species are hardy, thriving on plateaus in the Southwest. One or 2 species thrive as far north as the Great Lakes region. Leaves are fleshy, cylindrical (terete), and often 3-angled (triquetrous). Ice-plants get their name from the frosty (pruinose) appearance caused by waxy scales on the surface of the leaves. This coating helps prevent desiccation in arid conditions. Flowers open only when the sun shines, displaying often vividly colored petal-like staminodes. The flowers make stunning accents in rock gardens, cascading down the sides of garden stairs and over walls or as ground cover in dry locations or at seaside.

Lampranthus aureus

TRAILING ICE-PLANT
Synonym: *Mesembryanthemum aureum*. South Africa. Succulent creeper to 6 in.; zones 6–11. Blooms spring, summer. Moderate moisture when hot, dry when cool. Average, gritty, well-drained soil. Full sun. Flowers: rotate, to 2 in. wide, staminodes red-orange to amber; stamens golden. Leaves: cylindrical to somewhat 3-angled, 2–3 in. long, fleshy, frosty green. Stems: tough, woody. *The color of the flowers and leaves varies according to the available moisture. Plants form thick mats that are heat, frost, and drought resistant. Among the hardier species. Photographed at Bosque del Apache, at the edge of the Sonoran desert in New Mexico.*

Lampranthus deltoides

Synonyms: *Oscularia caulescens, Oscularia deltoides, Mesembryanthemum deltoides*. South Africa (Cape Province). Succulent creeper, 3–6 in.; zones 9–11. Blooms spring, summer. Moderate moisture when hot, dry when cool. Average, gritty, well-drained soil. Full sun. Flowers: staminodes lavender-pink, stalkless (sessile), 0.5–1 in. wide, plastic in appearance; stamens pressed together; solitary. Leaves: succulent,

Glottiphyllum linguiforme

Lampranthus aureus

short, strongly 3-angled, blue-green. *A delicate, ground-hugging to mounding plant. The erect leaves with their blunt triangular tips are often densely arranged like a mosaic. Suitable for rock gardens and flat containers.*

Lampranthus zeyheri
TRAILING ICE-PLANT
Synonym: *Mesembryanthemum zeyheri.* South Africa (Cape Province). Succulent creeper; zones 9–11. Blooms spring. Moderate moisture when hot, dry when cool. Average, gritty, well-drained soil. Full sun. Flowers: staminodes magenta, stamens golden, to 2 in. wide; flower stalks (peduncles) to about 4 in. long. Leaves: small, terete, 3-angled, 1–2 in. long, frosty, gray-green. Stems: reddish. *Forms dense mounds. The long-stalked flowers, small leaves, and spring bloom help distinguish this species.*

Trichodiadema
Trichodiadema includes approximately 30 species of creeping perennials or subshrubs from Ethiopia to southern Africa. They are succulent, mat-forming plants, often with bulblike roots. Leaves are tiny, club-shaped, with a little crown of frosty (pruinose) glandular hairs (papillae) at the tips. The genus name aptly describes these crowns as "hairy diadems." Flowers are solitary on very short stalks (subsessile). These species are suitable for growing in hanging baskets or as ground covers. Cuttings root directly in the ground.

Trichodiadema bulbosum
PINK ICE-PLANT, CARPET-WEED
Synonym: *Mesembryanthemum bulbosum.* South Africa. Succulent creeper; zones 9–11. Blooms most of the year. Moderate moisture when hot, dry when cool. Average, gritty, well-drained soil. Full to part sun. Flowers: staminodes linear, loosely arranged, violet-pink toward the tips, white near the center, under 1 in. wide; stamens spreading. Leaves: small, club-shaped to cylindrical, to 1 in. long; hairs short, silvery. *Fast-growing, forming spreading mats. Excellent in rock gardens, terraces, and hanging baskets where*

the plants cascade freely. Differs from Lampranthus deltoides, which has stiff plastic-looking pink flowers and thick, triangular leaves.

ALISMATACEAE
WATER PLANTAIN FAMILY
Alismataceae includes approximately 16 genera of aquatic herbs, which are widely distributed in tropical and temperate regions. This family was assumed to be primitive because of the numerous stamens, but current thought is that the group is more highly evolved (Judd et al. 1999). The plants have tuberous roots or rhizomes and a latex sap. The shape of the leaf varies considerably if growing underwater, floating, or above the surface (emergent). Flowers are bisexual, or unisexual with male and female flowers on the same plant (monoecious) or on separate plants (dioecious). Young plants are produced at the ends of stolons and can be used for propagation. They can be grown in pond margins or in submerged containers half-filled with loam. A layer of gravel is spread on top to keep the soil from floating. Adjust containers with blocks so the water just covers the container. In temperate regions store tubers indoors in winter. Because they are potentially invasive, these species should be grown only in artificial, free-standing ponds, never in bodies of water connected to wetlands or streams.

Hydrocleys
Hydrocleys includes approximately 9 species of tuberous aquatic herbs from South America and the Lesser Antilles. Some authors place *Hydrocleys* in Limnocharitaceae, but these species are awaiting further analysis. Leaves are emergent (held above the water) or sometimes floating. Flowers are bisexual. They have 3 showy petals and are emergent.

Hydrocleys nymphoides
WATER-POPPY
Synonym: *Limnocharis humboldtii.* South America (east of the Andes), Lesser Antilles, Puerto Rico. Semideciduous herb to 4 ft.; zones 9–11. Blooms late summer, fall. Aquatic.

Free-floating or rooted in pond muck. Full to part sun. Flowers: cup-shaped, to 2 in. wide, petals overlapping, lemon-yellow. Leaves: ovate to suborbicular, 4–5 in. wide, base cordate; floating or emergent. *Each flower lasts a day with more opening in succession.*

Sagittaria
Sagittaria includes approximately 20 species of aquatic herbs which are widely distributed. Most of the plant is above the water surface (emergent), the roots in shallow water-edge muck. The tubers of some species, called *wapato,* were

Lampranthus zeyheri

Lampranthus deltoides

Trichodiadema bulbosum

a food staple of American Indians. Cultivation by Indians probably accounts for their wide distribution. Leaves can be quite variable on the same plant making identification difficult. Submerged leaves are usually linear; floating or emergent leaves have broad blades. The genus name alludes to the commonly sagittate leaf (from Sagittarius the Goat), a triangular blade with hornlike, backward-projecting lobes at the base. A few species have spear-shaped leaves. Flowers are unisexual, with male and female flowers on the same plant (monoecious).

Sagittaria lancifolia
BULL-TONGUE ARROWHEAD
Mild temperate and tropical wetlands of the Americas. Aquatic per-

ennial herb, 3–6 ft.; zones 9–11. Blooms warm months. Wet. Fertile loam or pond muck. Full sun. Flowers: unisexual; petals 3, white; on a branched inflorescence stalk to 6 ft. Leaves: lanceolate to elliptic, petioles and blades erect, 2–3 ft. long.

Sagittaria montevidensis
SPOTTED ARROWHEAD
Southern South America; naturalized in the eastern United States. Aquatic perennial herb, 1–2 ft.; zones 9–11. Blooms warm months. Wet. Fertile loam or pond muck. Full sun. Flowers: unisexual; petals 3, white with a large burgundy or green spot on each petal. Leaves: emergent blades triangular with backward-projecting lobes at the base (sagittate); submerged blades linear.

Hydrocleys nymphoides

Sagittaria montevidensis

Sagittaria lancifolia

Tulbaghia violacea

ALLIACEAE
ONION FAMILY
Alliaceae includes 19 genera of usually bulbous perennial herbs, which are widely distributed in tropical and temperate regions. This group is closely related to the amaryllis family, Amaryllidaceae. It includes pungent culinary herbs such as onions, garlic, chives, shallots, and leeks. The characteristic aroma emanates from sulfur compounds. Several species are grown for their ornamental flowers as well. Leaves are narrowly strap-shaped to linear. Flowers are funnel-shaped, with petals fused into a tube at the base. They are clustered in umbels and subtended by a dry, spathelike bract and borne at the end of a leafless stalk (scape).

Tulbaghia
Tulbaghia includes approximately 22 tropical and southern African herbs. The genus is distinguished from other genera in the family by having rhizomes instead of bulbs. Flowers have 6 petals and are radially symmetrical with a corona in the throat. They are in small clusters at the end of an erect scape. These species are often grown as a ground cover in dry regions. They are suitable for containers.

Tulbaghia violacea
SOCIETY GARLIC, SWEET GARLIC, AJO ORNAMENTAL
Northeastern South Africa . Evergreen or seasonally dormant herb to 2 ft.; zones 7–10. Blooms warm months. Moderate moisture, dry when dormant. Fertile, well-drained soil. Full to part sun. Flowers: small, funnel-shaped, lavender; on a scape to 2 ft. tall; sweet-scented. Leaves: linear, to 12 in. high, gray-green, garlic-scented, some selections cream-striped. *These dainty, grasslike mounding plants thrive in dry climates such as California. Young shoots are sometimes used like garlic chives in food. Plants become dormant in cold or dry conditions.*

ALSTROEMERIACEAE
ALSTROEMERIA FAMILY
Alstroemeriaceae includes 5 genera of rhizomatous and tuberous herbs from the Andes and Central Amer-

ica. They are plants of montane tropical regions, generally preferring moderate temperatures. Leaves are on a stem (cauline). Secondary veins run parallel to the midvein. A twist in the petiole inverts the leaf blade (resupinate; see photo of *Alstroemeria psittacina*). Flowers have 3 petal-like sepals and 3 petals. The sepals are larger than the petals. They develop from the apex of the leafy stem, helping to distinguish this family from the amaryllis family, Amaryllidaceae, which bears flowers on separate, leafless stalks (scapes).

Alstroemeria
Alstroemeria includes approximately 50 species of seasonally dormant perennial herbs from South America. They are found primarily in cool montane regions. When plants are dormant, the fleshy roots should be protected from freezing with a thick layer of mulch. Where they are not hardy, tubers can be stored indoors in winter. Alstroemerias prefer even moisture during active growth. Taper off watering after plants flower until they become dormant and then withhold watering until new growth begins the next season. Growing alstroemerias for the cut-flower trade is an important industry, especially in Andean countries and Europe. The sap may be irritating to the skin.

Alstroemeria caryophyllaea
Brazil (Rio State). Seasonally dormant herb to 2 ft.; zones 8–9. Blooms late winter, spring. Seasonally moist/dry. Average, well-drained soil. Full to part sun. Flowers: bilaterally symmetrical; petals slender, not overlapping (valvate), narrowing to a short tube at the base, white with blood red tips, opening a few at a time; inflorescence terminal on the leaf stalk. Leaves: narrowly lanceolate, inverted (resupinate) blade, to 4 in. long; in whorls around the stems.

Alstroemeria hybrids
PERUVIAN LILY, LILY-OF-THE-INCAS
Garden origin. Seasonally dormant perennial herbs to 2 ft.; zones 8–9. Bloom summer, fall. Seasonally

moist/dry. Average, well-drained soil. Part sun to bright filtered light. Flowers: funnel-shaped, lobes flaring, tepals variously tinted, 2–3 in. wide; inflorescence a 3- to 6-flowered umbel. Leaves: lanceolate, to 4 in. long, blade inverted, gray-green. *These hybrids of mountain heritage prefer mild temperatures. A wide range of colors has been developed by the floral industry. Parents include A. pelegrina, A. ligtu, A. haemantha, and A. aurea.*

Alstroemeria psittacina
PERUVIAN LILY, CHRISTMAS BELL
Synonym: *A. inodora.* Brazil. Seasonally dormant perennial herb to 3 ft.; zones 8–10. Blooms spring, summer. Seasonally moist/dry. Average, well-drained soil. Part sun to bright filtered light. Flowers: funnel-shaped, lobes more or less flaring,

Alstroemeria caryophyllaea

Alstroemeria psittacina

green to greenish white, throat streaked with red or maroon; inflorescences 4- to 6-flowered umbels, on wiry stems. Leaves: lanceolate to linear, 4–6 in. long, blade inverted (resupinate). *The green-and-red flowers open at Christmas time in the Southern Hemisphere. Self-seeding. Difficult to eradicate once introduced. A. pulchella is similar and possibly synonymous with this species.*

AMARANTHACEAE
AMARANTH FAMILY
Amaranthaceae includes approximately 170 genera of annual and perennial herbs and subshrubs, which are widely distributed in temperate and tropical regions. Current evidence leans toward including most genera of Chenopodiaceae in this group (Judd, pers.

Alstroemeria hybrid

Alternanthera brasiliana

comm.). If so defined, this family would include spinach (*Spinacia*) and beets (*Beta*). Inca wheat (or amaranth), *Amaranthus caudatus,* is a high-protein cereal grain originally cultivated by the Incas and now found in health-food stores. *Calalou,* a name applied generally to stewed greens in the Caribbean, is a calcium-rich, spinachlike dish of tender young leaves and shoots. Some species are common weeds including pigweed and tumbleweed and some are serious respiratory allergens. Leaves are simple, often red or ruddy, sometimes fleshy. Flowers are small, bisexual or unisexual, often with papery tepals. They are arranged in dense spikes or heads.

Alternanthera
Alternanthera includes approximately 200 species of annual and perennial herbs from mild temperate and tropical America. Alternantheras often have colorful foliage and are grown as bedding plants. Flowers are small, bisexual or unisexual, with usually chaffy sepals arranged in spikes or heads. They lack true petals though the sepals are sometimes petal-like.

Alternanthera brasiliana
PURPLE-LEAFED CHAFF-FLOWER, WHITE BUTTONS, BOUTON BLANC
Exact origin obscure; widely distributed in tropical America, West Indies. Perennial herb to 2 ft.; zones 10–11. Blooms all year. Moderate moisture. Average, well-drained soil. Full sun. Flowers: small; bracts papery, white; in small, compact heads. Leaves: ovate, to about 2 in. long, purple. *A low-growing bedding plant providing contrast in the garden. It is especially effective when combined with golden-yellow foliage or flowers. Self-seeding and sometimes weedy.*

Celosia
Celosia includes approximately 50 species of perennial or annual herbs, which are widely distributed in tropical and temperate regions. Flowers lack true petals. The papery bracts and sepals are small, in many-flowered inflorescences. Cultivars of *C. argentea* are grown as

annuals or for cut flowers. Some commercial varieties are called "cockscombs." Because they are polyploid hybrids (chromosomes more than the normal count), they exhibit great morphological diversity. They are divided into 4 horticultural groups: flowers of the Spicata Group are in spikes; those of the Cristata Group have fasciated crests; those of the Childsii Group have rounded heads; and flowers of the Plumosa Group are feathery or plumed.

Celosia argentea
SILVER AND RED FOX TAIL, LAGOS SPINACH
Synonym: *C. cristata.* Pantropical. Annual or short-lived perennial herb, 3–6 ft.; zones 9–11. Blooms warm months. Moderate moisture when hot, drier when cool. Average, well-drained soil. Full sun. Flowers: minute; bracts papery; densely arranged in spikes at the end of a slender stalk and opening from base to tip (indeterminate). Leaves: lanceolate, slender, to 3 in. long. *Var.* argentea *is a member of the Spicata Group with red-violet bracts which become silvery with age. Clump-forming. Suitable for the tropical perennial garden. Painted buntings love the seed (Hammer, pers. comm.). Self-seeding.*

Iresine
Iresine includes approximately 80 species of annual and perennial herbs and subshrubs primarily from tropical America and Australia. They are distinguished from related genera by their branched panicles rather than spikes. Leaves are simple and opposite. A few species are cultivated as houseplants for their colorful foliage.

Iresine diffusa
BLOODLEAF
Synonym: *I. lindenii.* Only known in cultivation, probably originating in South America. Evergreen perennial herb or subshrub to 3 ft.; zones 9–11. Blooms spring. Moist when hot, moderate moisture when cool. Fertile, well-drained soil. Part sun to bright filtered light. Flowers: very small, whitish, in spreading panicles. Leaves: ovate, 2–3 in. long,

tips tapering (acuminate), blood red with fine, lighter veins. *Sometimes referred to as forma* lindenii. *Commonly confused with* I. herbstii *from Brazil, which has broad, green or purple, kidney-shaped leaves with indented (retuse) tips and broader markings around the veins.*

AMARYLLIDACEAE
AMARYLLIS FAMILY

Amaryllidaceae includes approximately 50 genera of seasonally dormant and evergreen herbs widely distributed from mild temperate to tropical regions. Some genera are frequently, but incorrectly, referred to as lilies. Of several distinctions from the family Liliaceae, perhaps the most readily recognized are the slight bilateral symmetry of the flower, a bent floral neck, and the

stamens clustered near the lower tepals. Lilies have evenly radiating tepals and stamens and come primarily from temperate regions. The plants are poisonous. Leaves are strap-shaped to orbicular, usually in opposite ranks (distichous), deciduous, often basal. The bulbs or rhizomes have contractile roots. Flowers are bisexual with 6 tepals and usually 6 stamens, and are produced on separate stalks (scapes). Some species have a corona (annulus) around the throat . The inflorescence is a cyme or flowers are solitary. Thin spathelike bracts are sometimes located below the flowers. The fruit is a capsule or berry.

×*Amarcrinum*

×*Amarcrinum* is an intergeneric hybrid of *Amaryllis* and *Crinum*.

×*Amarcrinum memoria-corsii*
CRINODONNA

Synonym: ×*A. howardii.* Garden origin, *Amaryllis belladonna* × *Crinum moorei.* Evergreen perennial herb to 30 in.; zones 9–11. Blooms late summer. Regular moisture when warm, less when cool. Fertile, well-drained soil. Full to part sun. Flowers: trumpet-shaped, 2 in. wide, 4 in. long, pink; scape not hollow, to 2 ft. tall. Leaves: evergreen, straplike, to 2 ft. tall. *The flowers resemble* Amaryllis belladonna *but can be distinguished by the evergreen leaves while in bloom. Photographed at Longwood Gardens, Kennett Square, Pennsylvania.*

Amaryllis

Amaryllis includes a single species of seasonally dormant herb from South Africa. The bulbs were introduced into California by early settlers and are still widely cultivated in that state. Irrigate plants freely in spring as soon as new leaves begin to emerge and gradually reduce as they wither. Continue to withhold water until the next growing season. Do not plant near moisture-loving species. The bulb is quite drought resistant. Remove leaves after they dry. The flowers will emerge while the leaves are completely dormant (whence the origin of the name "naked ladies") near the end of summer (if leafy, see ×*Amarcrinum*). In cold climates lift the bulbs after flowering and store them in a dry place. Propagate by division of the bulbs and plant in

early spring with the bulb neck above ground level. It takes 2 years to flower from seed. *Amaryllis* is pollinated by birds and insects. *Hippeastrum*, a mostly New World genus, is commonly, but incorrectly, referred to as amaryllis. *Amaryllis* is distinguished from *Hippeastrum* by the solid flower stalk (scape) and lack of leaves while in bloom.

Amaryllis belladonna
BELLADONNA, NAKED LADIES, AZUCENA

Synonym: *Brunsvigia rosea.* South Africa (Southwest Cape). Seasonally dormant bulbous herb, 18–30 in.; zones 8–11. Blooms late summer. Moist during active growth, dry when dormant. Gritty, well-drained soil. Full sun to lightly filtered midday sun in hot, dry conditions. Flowers: trumpet-shaped, 2 in. wide; 4–5 in. long, deep pink to white; scape solid, to 2 ft., bearing up to 12 flowers. Leaves: straplike, to 2 ft., fleshy. Belladonna *means "beautiful lady." This species should not to be confused with* Atropa belladonna *of the potato family, Solanaceae, from which the drug belladonna (atropine) is derived.*

Clivia

Clivia includes 4 species of evergreen herbs from South Africa. They usually have bulblike swollen leaf bases and solid flower stalks (scapes). Clivias flower most reliably in undersized pots. They may fail to bloom if the shallow root system is disturbed. Divide only when clumps are overgrown by removing a large section without disturbing the rest. Do not separate clumps into individual plants. Plants take 2–3 years to reach blooming size from seed. Clivias are prone to fungal, viral, and bacterial diseases especially if too moist in winter. Snails and slugs can be a problem. Sap may be irritating to the skin. Handle plants with gloves.

Clivia miniata
BUSH-LILY, FIRE-LILY

Synonym: *Vellota miniata.* Eastern South Africa, Swaziland. Evergreen herb to 2 ft.; zones 10–11. Blooms late winter to spring. Seasonally

Iresine diffusa

Celosia argentea var. *argentea*

×*Amarcrinum memoria-corsii*

Amaryllis belladonna

moist/dry. Fertile, well-drained soil. Part sun or filtered midday sun. Flowers: funnel-shaped, orange, in clusters of 15–20. Leaves: broadly strap-shaped, 3 in. wide, 18 in. long; in opposite ranks. *Var. flava has yellow flowers. These plants prefer Mediterranean-type climates.*

Crinum

Crinum includes approximately 130 species of evergreen or seasonally dormant herbs from mild temperate and tropical regions. They are commonly, but inaccurately, referred to as crinum lilies. Some species develop a trunklike pseudostem, which is actually an extension (or neck) of the bulb. Leaves may be broadly sword-shaped or straplike, sometimes with minute teeth (easier to feel than see) along the margins. Flowers are funnel-shaped, the base united into a slender, usually green, stalklike tube. The lobes are free, linear and flaring or broad and funnel- or cup-shaped. They are in clusters at the end of a solid stalk which arises from the side of the pseudostem. *Crinum asiaticum* is grown in conditions as harsh as highway medians and tolerates seasonally dry periods. Some species bloom repeatedly over months, others only for a short time. A number are salt tolerant.

Crinum asiaticum

GIANT CRINUM, POISON-BULB
Synonym: *C. procerum*. Tropical Asia. Evergreen bulbous herb to 6 ft.+; zones 10–11. Blooms warm months. Moderate moisture. Average, well-drained soil. Full to part sun. Flowers: lightly fragrant, base tubular, lobes linear, white to purple on back; filaments violet; several inflorescences may be produced at the same time on long stalks. Leaves: broadly sword-shaped, 4–6 in. wide, flat (not channeled) to 4 ft. long; margins undulate. Pseudostem: to 5 ft. tall. *Common landscape plant. Salt tolerant. Var.* sinicum *(syn.* C. pedunculatum*) is distinguished by white filaments and channeled leaves.* 'Queen Emma' *is a purple form of* C. angustum, *believed to be a hybrid of* C. asiaticum *or its variety* sinicum × C. scabrum *(Meerow, pers. comm.).*

Crinum bulbispermum

VAAL RIVER LILY
South Africa. Seasonally dormant bulbous herb to 3 ft.; zones 9–11. Blooms late spring, summer. Regular moisture. Average to fertile, well-drained soil. Full to part sun. Flowers: funnel-shaped, lobes purple or white with purple streaks, tube green, to 6 in. long, curved. Leaves: strap-shaped, 2–3 ft. long, keeled; margins toothed.

Crinum 'Ellen Bosanquet'

Garden hybrid, possibly *C. moorei* × *C. scabrum*. Seasonally dormant bulbous herb to 2 ft.; zones 10–11. Blooms spring. Regular moisture. Average to fertile, well-drained soil.

Full to part sun. Flowers: trumpet-shaped, lobes pink to burgundy, slightly nodding (deflexed), tube green, curved, to 6 in. long. Leaves: sword-shaped, 3–4 ft. long, 2 in. wide, somewhat keeled, lax; margins smooth. *Mark site to protect dormant plant from injury.*

Crinum jagus

Synonym: *C. giganteum*. Tropical western Africa. Evergreen bulbous herb to 2 ft.; zones 10–11. Blooms intermittently in warm months. Regular moisture. Average to fertile, well-drained soil. Full to part sun. Flowers: lobes cup-shaped, white, tube green, slender, to 10 in. long; stalk shorter than leaves. Leaves: strap-shaped, 18–24 in. long, keeled, ascending to almost erect.

Crinum kirkii

Eastern Africa. Evergreen bulbous herb to 3 ft.; zones 10–11. Blooms summer. Moderate moisture when hot, less when cool. Fertile, well-drained soil. Full to part sun. Flowers: faintly fragrant, trumpet-shaped, pendent, lobes white, keel pink, to 8 in. long, tube to 6 in. long, green; scape purplish, taller than leaves. Leaves: strap-shaped, slightly keeled, to 2.5 ft.; margins minutely toothed. *Salt tolerant. Forms clumps. Photographed bayside at the Kampong, Coconut Grove, Florida.*

Crinum scabrum

MILK AND WINE CRINUM
Synonym: *C. zeylanicum* (misapplied). Tropical western Africa; widely distributed in the Caribbean

Clivia miniata

Clivia miniata, tulip-flowered cultivar

Crinum asiaticum

Crinum asiaticum, purple selection

Crinum jagus

and Central America. Semideciduous bulbous herb to 2 ft.; zones 9–11. Blooms spring. Regular moisture during active growth, less when dormant. Fertile, well-drained soil. Full to part sun. Flowers: funnel-shaped, ascending, lobes white to pinkish with a central magenta stripe, tube green, bent; cymes of 10 or more flowers; scape to 2 ft., slightly taller than leaves. Leaves: strap-shaped, lax, light green, 2 ft. long, 2 in. wide; margins undulate, minutely toothed. Cluster-forming. *Bloom brief but floriferous. Leaves may remain green but limp in winter. Mark site to protect dormant plant from damage.*

Eucharis

Eucharis includes approximately 17 species of bulbous herbs from the Andes to Central America. They are commonly known as Amazon lilies and come from moist river valleys and rain forests. The genus name means "elegant" but is commonly taken to refer to the Christian Last Supper sacrament, the Eucharist, since the plants are frequently in flower around Easter. They also bloom intermittently in summer and fall. Leaves are basal, often broad. Flowers have a distinctive corona (annulus). These "tropical daffodils" can be grown in containers. They are very attractive to slugs, snails, and grasshoppers.

Eucharis amazonica

AMAZON LILY, AZUCENA
Peru (eastern slope of the Andes). Evergreen bulbous herb, 12–18 in.; zones 10–11. Blooms intermittently in warm months. Moist to wet during active growth, less when dormant. Fertile, well-drained soil. Bright filtered light. Flowers: nodding, to 2.5 in. wide, slightly fragrant, basal tube slender, lobes flaring, white, throat encircled by corona streaked with pale green; in few-flowered umbels. Leaves: broadly obovate, 1.5–2 ft. long, 8 in. wide; base tapering down petiole. *A sterile triploid cultigen which has been cultivated for centuries. Forms large clumps in moist areas.* Eucharis moorei *is a fertile diploid species found on both slopes of the Andes.*

Crinum bulbispermum

Crinum kirkii

Crinum 'Ellen Bosanquet'

Crinum scabrum

Eucharis amazonica

Eucharis ulei
AMAZON LILY

Synonym: *Urceolina ulei.* Peru, western watershed of the Amazon River. Evergreen bulbous herb to 12 in.; zones 10–11. Blooms late winter, spring, intermittently. Moist to wet when warm, less when cool . Fertile, well-drained soil. Part sun to bright filtered light. Flowers: lightly fragrant, nodding, to 1.5 in. wide, basal tube slender, green, lobes flaring, white; anthers attached to a corona streaked with white and yellow; borne in umbels, a few flowers opening at a time. Leaves: lanceolate, streaked lengthwise. *Smaller in all aspects than the more commonly cultivated E. amazonica.*

Eucrosia

Eucrosia includes approximately 7 species of evergreen herbs from moist forests of western Ecuador and Peru. They are unusual in cultivation. Only one pair of leaves develops from the bulb. The perianth is vase-shaped and relatively small. The long stamens and pistil extend well beyond the corolla (exserted).

Eucrosia aurantiaca
QUEEN-LILY

Synonym: *Callipsyche aurantiaca.* Ecuador, Peru. Evergreen bulbous herb, 12–18 in.; zones 10–11. Blooms winter. Moist when warm, drier when cool. Fertile, well-drained soil. Bright filtered light. Flowers: vase-shaped, yellow to pink, sepals green-tipped; stamens and pistil 3–4 in. long, extending well beyond the perianth (exserted); umbels few-flowered; stalk to 30 in. Leaves: paired, broadly ovate, to 16 in. long, 8 in. wide.

Habranthus

Habranthus includes approximately 10 species of bulbous herbs from mild temperate and tropical South America. *Habranthus robustus* and *H. ×floryi* (*H. robustus* × ?) are commonly confused with *Zephyranthes grandiflora* and bulbs are commonly intermixed. *Habranthus* flowers are distinguished by slight bilateral symmetry and the floral tube is bent at an angle rather than erect. These sprightly, somewhat crocuslike flowers can be tucked into open spots in a sunny bed. Dividing the bulbs yearly stimulates bloom. They are suitable for containers.

Habranthus robustus

Synonym: *Zephyranthes robusta.* Brazil. Seasonally dormant bulbous herb, 6–8 in.; zones 9–11. Blooms intermittently in warm months. Moist when hot, less when cool. Humus-rich, well-drained soil. Full sun. Flowers: bell-shaped, held obliquely, tepals white with pink veins and edges. Leaves: strap-shaped, grasslike, 6–8 in. long; upper surface concave (guttered).

Haemanthus

Haemanthus includes approximately 20 species of bulbous perennial herbs from South Africa and Namibia. Individual flowers are small and massed in dense clusters surrounded by a whorl of bracts at the top of a short flower stalk. The showy stamens appear brushlike. A characteristic of this genus is the single pair of leaves, which are strap- or lance-shaped. Species with more than one pair of leaves previously included in this genus are now segregated into *Scadoxus*.

Haemanthus albiflos
WHITE PAINTBRUSH

Synonym: *H. albomaculatus.* Eastern South Africa, Swaziland. Seasonally dormant bulbous herb under 1 ft.; zones 10–11. Blooms summer, fall. Moist during active growth, dry when dormant. Humus-rich, well-drained soil. Part sun to bright filtered light. Flowers: perianth small, white, completely enclosed inside a cup-shaped, greenish white whorl of bracts (involucre); stamens white, exserted, brushlike. Leaves: one pair, broadly elliptic, sometimes white-spotted, 8–10 in. long, downy (pubescent); margins fringed with tiny hairlike projections (ciliate).

Hippeastrum

Hippeastrum includes approximately 70 species of evergreen or seasonally dormant herbs from tropical America, plus 1 from Africa. They are commonly but incorrectly referred to as "amaryllis," a distinct genus (see *Amaryllis*). Leaves are strap-shaped. Flowers are funnel-shaped with a tubular base and spreading lobes. They are on a hollow stalk (scape) that develops directly from the bulb. Papery bracts subtend the flowers.

Eucharis ulei

Eucrosia aurantiaca

Habranthus robustus (or possibly *H. ×floryi*)

Haemanthus albiflos

Hippeastrum 'Apple Blossom'

Hippeastrum evansiae

Hippeastrums prefer well-drained, neutral or slightly alkaline soil. They are commonly grown in containers and often forced into early bloom in winter. Use pots only slightly larger than the base of the bulb, and plant with the upper third of the bulb above soil level. Taper off water gradually when the leaves begin to wither to allow the bulbs to develop for the next season. In mild climates plants thrive outdoors in full sun or slightly filtered light.

Hippeastrum evansiae
HIPPEASTRUM, KNIGHT'S STAR, AZUCENA
Bolivia. Seasonally dormant bulbous herb to 14 in.; zones 10–11. Blooms late winter, spring. Evenly moist during active growth, dry when dormant. Gritty, well-drained soil. Part sun to bright filtered light. Flowers: pale yellow to greenish yellow, pinkish near the base, 3–4 in. wide, held horizontally, 1–4 per scape; bracts at base of flowers, pointed, becoming papery. Leaves: strap-shaped, 8–12 in. long.

Hippeastrum hybrids
HYBRID HIPPEASTRUM, KNIGHT'S STAR, AZUCENA
Garden hybrids. Seasonally dormant bulbous herb to 16 in.; zones 10–11. Blooms winter, spring. Moist during active growth, dry when dormant. Gritty, well-drained soil. Part sun to bright filtered light. Flowers: funnel-shaped with recurved lobes, to 6 in. wide, held more or less horizontally. Leaves: strap-shaped, to 14 in. long. *A large floral industry, notably in the Netherlands, produces a variety of cultivars. 'Apple Blossom' has white upper and side tepals with dark pink veins, and the lower petal is mostly white.*

Hippeastrum puniceum
BARBADOS LILY, LIS ROUGE
Synonym: *H. equestre*. Puerto Rico, Lesser Antilles, northern South America. Seasonally dormant bulbous herb to 1.5 ft.; zones 10–11. Blooms spring. Moist during active growth, dry when dormant. Gritty, well-drained soil. Part sun to bright filtered light. Flowers: trumpet-shaped, slightly nodding, to 5 in. wide, terracotta orange, red, or

pink, throat greenish yellow; in clusters of 2–4; scape about the same height as the leaves. Leaves: strap-shaped, 2 in. wide, 14 in. long. *Ancestor of many hybrids. Variable over its extensive range.*

Hymenocallis
Hymenocallis includes approximately 50 species of evergreen or seasonally dormant bulbous herbs, which are widely distributed in moist tropical and temperate regions. They are often referred to as spider-lilies because of the weblike corona connecting the bases of the 6 stamens. Leaves are strap-shaped or with broad blades tapering into petioles. The tepals are white or greenish white, often linear. Plant bulbs 8–10 in. deep or plants produce foliage but no flowers. Many are semiaquatic. Spider-lilies are often salt tolerant, some species thriving directly on the beach.

Hymenocallis caribaea
SPIDER-LILY, LIRIO DE CINTA
Synonym: *Pancratium caribaeum*. West Indies. Evergreen bulbous herb, 2–3 ft.; zones 10–11. Blooms late winter, early spring. Moist, humid when hot, less when cool. Fertile, well-drained soil. Full sun. Flowers: lobes linear, white, somewhat recurved, tube green; staminal corona funnel-shaped. Leaves: strap-shaped, to 2 ft. long. *Salt tolerant.*

Hymenocallis littoralis
SPIDER-LILY
Mexico to Colombia, Florida. Semideciduous perennial herb to 2 ft.; zones 10–11. Blooms spring. Moist when hot, less when cool. Fertile, well-drained soil to beach sand. Full sun. Flowers: white, tube green at the base; lobes narrowly linear, lax; corona funnel-shaped. Leaves: elliptic, to 2 ft. long; petiole short. *Very salt tolerant. The species name means "of the seashore."*

Hymenocallis tubiflora
SPIDER-LILY
Trinidad, northeastern South America. Evergreen bulbous herb to 2 ft.; zones 10–11. Blooms late winter, early spring. Moist when hot, less

when cool. Fertile, well-drained soil. Full sun. Flowers: tube green, lobes linear, white, twisted and drooping; staminal corona funnel-shaped. Leaves: blade broadly elliptic, tapering onto a long petiole, to 1.5 ft. long.

Proiphys
Proiphys includes 3 species of seasonally dormant herbs from Australia. The genus name alludes to the premature germination of the seeds while they are still on the plant (viviparous). The flowers somewhat resemble white agapanthus but are easily distinguished by the corona in the throat and the broad, corrugated leaves. Unlike *Agapanthus*, this tender genus of tropical understory is sensitive to chilly temperatures and needs protection from strong sunlight. The

species are suitable for containers. They are unusual in cultivation.

Proiphys amboinensis
CARDWELL LILY
Synonyms: *Eurycles sylvestris, Pancratium amboinense*. Northeastern Australia (Queensland). Seasonally dormant bulbous herb to 18 in.; zones 10–11. Blooms late spring, early summer. Moist when hot, dry when cool. Fertile, well-drained soil. Bright filtered light. Flowers: funnel-shaped, white; inflorescence of 10 or more flowers; stamen filaments fused into a corona in the throat; on a scape 12–18 in. tall. Leaves: broadly kidney-shaped (reniform) to ovate, curved into a funnel shape when young, surface corrugated, to 12 in. wide. *The seed germinates in the fruit while still on the plant. Bulbs are slow to multiply.*

Hippeastrum puniceum

Hymenocallis caribaea

Hymenocallis littoralis

Hymenocallis tubiflora

Rhodophiala

Rhodophiala includes approximately 31 species of bulbous perennial herbs from southern South America. The flowers are funnel-shaped to tubular and bilaterally symmetrical. They have 6 tepals and 6 stamens. A bilobed spathe-like bract is located at the base of the inflorescence. The inflorescence is born at the end of a hollow stalk (scape) that develops directly from the bulb.

Rhodophiala bifida

Synonym: *Hippeastrum bifidum*. Argentina, Uruguay. Seasonally dormant perennial herb to 2 ft.; zone 9. Blooms late summer, fall. Regular moisture when warm, dry when cool. Average to fertile, well-drained soil. Full to part sun. Flow-

Proiphys amboinensis

ers: funnel-shaped, slightly ascending, lobes burgundy-red, streaked white, corona in throat, tubular base slender, green bract bilobed; scape green, to 2 ft. tall. Leaves: basal, lorate, to 2 ft. long, lax. *Resembles certain* Crinum *species but is distinguished by the corona and bilobed bract.*

Scadoxus

Scadoxus includes approximately 9 species of perennial bulbous herbs from tropical Africa and Arabia. Numerous leaves are arranged in a basal whorl distinguishing these species from *Haemanthus* species, which have one pair of leaves. Petals are linear. Filaments are long and showy. Flowers emerge before the leaves. Like many bulbous plants, these have a short but spec-

Rhodophiala bifida

tacular blooming season. Plant the large bulbs so their shoulders are even with the ground surface. Suitable for containers.

Scadoxus multiflorus subsp. katherinae

CATHERINE'S WHEEL, BLOOD-LILY
Synonym: *Haemanthus katherinae*. Eastern South Africa, Swaziland. Seasonally dormant bulbous herb to 18 in.; zones 10–11. Blooms late spring, early summer. Moist during active growth, dry when dormant. Fertile, well-drained soil. Part sun to bright filtered light. Flowers: in globular heads of radiating red filaments to 7 in. diameter; scape 14–18 in. tall. Leaves: strap-shaped, in a basal whorl. *Grow in pots only slightly larger than the bulb.*

Scadoxus puniceus

RED PAINTBRUSH,
ROYAL PAINTBRUSH
Synonyms: *Haemanthus natalensis*, *Haemanthus puniceus*. South Africa. Seasonally dormant herb to 18 in.; zones 10–11. Blooms spring. Moist during active growth, dry when dormant. Humus-rich, well-drained soil. Part sun to bright filtered light. Flowers: perianth small; stamens, showy, red; in dense, brushlike umbels; surrounded by an involucre of green bracts; scape 12–18 in. tall. Leaves: spear-shaped; margins deeply undulate; in basal rosettes. *The species name alludes to the color of pomegranate flowers in the genus* Punica.

Scadoxus multiflorus subsp. *katherinae*

Scadoxus puniceus

ANACARDIACEAE

POISON IVY FAMILY,
MANGO FAMILY
Anacardiaceae includes approximately 70 genera of trees, shrubs, and vines distributed throughout the tropics with some in temperate regions. This family includes cashew, *Anacardium*; mango *Mangifera*; pistachio, *Pistacia*; sumac, *Rhus*; and poison ivy, *Toxicodendron*. These species secrete a clear, resinous sap that may cause a mild to severe allergic reaction in susceptible individuals. Leaves may be simple, pinnately compound, or trifoliolate. Flowers are small, usually unisexual, on sometimes showy inflorescences. The fruit is typically a fleshy, one-seeded drupe.

Mangifera

Mangifera includes approximately 30 species of trees from India and Indomalaysia to Australia. Mango, *M. indica*, has been cultivated for thousands of years and is widely distributed in the tropics. It has more than 300 cultivars. South Florida is the principal center of U.S. cultivation. A midsummer festival at Fairchild Tropical Garden is devoted to mango tasting and horticulture. Those who have sampled only commercial fruit, typically the rather mediocre 'Tommy Atkins', might wonder at the passion, but this seductive fruit is surely the "apple" of the Garden of Eden. The fruit must ripen on the tree and many superior varieties do not ship well. The resinous, stringy 'Turpentine' and spotted 'Haden' are early cultivars which still have devoted fans. Newer selections may be mellow to spicy, and/or fiberless.

Mango trees require well-drained soil and distinct wet/dry seasons. The latest horticultural technique is to remove the vertical leads, keeping the trees under 12 ft. to induce prolific fruiting on the lateral branches (Campbell, pers. comm.). Mangoes are susceptible to anthracnose, a fungal disease that causes black spots on the leaves and fruit. Certain varieties are more resistant, but blemished fruits are edible. Persons allergic to poison ivy should be cautious about handling mangos. Many peo-

Mangifera indica, tree in flower

Schinus molle, with fruit

Mangifera indica, tree with fruit

Mangifera indica 'Haden' (white speckled) and 'Dupuis' (yellow)

ple with mild sensitivity find they can eat the flesh but must avoid touching the skin. Selections are propagated by grafting. Mangoes are pollinated by bats and bees.

Mangifera indica
MANGO

Exact origin obscure (probably India, Myanmar [Burma]); widely cultivated. Evergreen tree to 50 ft.; zones 10–11. Blooms winter or dry season. Seasonally moist/dry. Fertile, well-drained soil. Full sun. Flowers: small, cream to pinkish, musky-scented; in large panicles; fruit bilaterally symmetrical, round to ovoid or much elongated, yellow, red, purple, or green when ripe, 3–8 in. long; on long, pendent stalks (peduncles). Leaves: elliptic-oblong, 6–10 in. long; veins yellow, lateral veins parallel, margins undulate. *A cultigen. Crown rounded. Many fruit normally abort prematurely. Each stalk can carry only 1 or 2 heavy fruits to maturity.*

Schinus

Schinus includes approximately 28 species of trees and shrubs from tropical and subtropical regions of the Americas. Leaves are usually pinnately compound. Male and female flowers are on separate trees (dioecious). *Schinus molle*, California pepper, has willowlike weeping branches. It was reputedly introduced into California at Mission San Luis Ray in the 1830s. A few old trees have attained impressive girth. This species is frequently grown in Mediterranean-type climates for erosion control. It is an alternative host of black citrus scale and should not be planted in citrus-growing regions. *Schinus terebinthifolius*, Brazilian pepper, Florida holly, or pepper-berry, is among the most egregiously invasive species in Florida, where it is prohibited, and in Hawaii. In California it is a pest along waterways though the dry climate slows its spread in upland areas. Sawdust and pollen of this poison-ivy relative may cause a skin rash or aggravate respiratory problems. Removal of existing trees before fruit set is strongly recommended as seed is dispersed by birds. The red or pink berries of either species are sold mixed with black and white pepper, *Piper nigrum* (white pepper is the same as black with the skin removed), as gourmet pepper. This mixture has no special culinary attribute and may cause serious allergic reaction in sensitive individuals.

Schinus molle
PEPPER-TREE, CALIFORNIA PEPPER, PERUVIAN MASTIC, MUELLE, PIMIENTO FALSO

Eastern slope of the Andes. Evergreen tree, 15–40 ft.; zones 9–11. Blooms fall, winter. Moderate moisture to dry. Average, well-drained soil. Full sun. Flowers: creamy white, tiny; panicles pendent; berries the size of peppercorns, pink, resinously aromatic. Leaves: pinnate, 6–12 in. long, pendent; leaflets 15–29, lanceolate, asymmetrical, rubbery, light green; petiole to 1 ft. long. Bark: light tan, shredding. *Pendent leaves hang from stiff branches, rather willowlike. Heat and drought tolerant. Var. areira has tiny leaf tip spurs (mucronate).*

Schinus terebinthifolius

BRAZILIAN PEPPER, PEPPER-BERRY, FLORIDA HOLLY, CHRISTMAS BERRY, AREIRA

Brazil. Evergreen shrub or small tree, 20–25 ft.; zones 9–11. Blooms fall, winter. Wet to dry. Most soils. Full sun to part shade. Flowers: tiny, white; berries red, size of pep-

percorns, in clusters from the leaf axils. Leaves: pinnate; leaflets usually 7, ovate, veins light; margins serrate; rachis and petiole reddish; resinous scent. *A fast-growing tree. Quickly produces impenetrable thickets excluding all other species. Migratory birds, notably robins, binge on the fruit, distributing seeds in their droppings. Highly invasive. Prohibited in Florida. Learn to recognize the leaves and pull seedlings immediately. The species name alludes to the turpentine-like aroma.*

Spondias

Spondias includes approximately 10 species of mostly deciduous trees, which are widely distributed in the tropics. The trees have been cultivated for millennia by the Mayan Indians. Flowers are small, produced in subsessile clusters at the

nodes on bare branches before the new leaves develop. The fruits of *S. purpurea* are sweet, subacidic, somewhat plumlike. Juice of the rounder golden fruits of *S. dulces* is popular in the Caribbean as a breakfast drink somewhat like orange juice (Howard, pers. comm.).

Spondias purpurea

PURPLE MOMBIN, SPANISH PLUM, CIRUELA ESPAÑOLA, JOCOTE
Synonym: *S. cirouella*. Mexico, Central America; widely distributed in the American tropics. Deciduous tree, 25–75 ft.; zones 10–11. Blooms spring. Seasonally moist/dry. Average, well-drained soil. Full to part sun. Flowers: small, red; in clusters on short stalks at the branch nodes; fruit oblong, to 2 in. long, edible, yellow to purple.

Leaves: pinnate, arranged in spirals, leaflets 5–25. Bark: light gray, twigs reddish. *The tiny flowers are a curiosity growing on bare branches. Fruit somewhat plumlike in appearance and taste.*

ANNONACEAE

ANNONA FAMILY
Annonaceae includes approximately 128 genera of evergreen trees, shrubs, and climbers distributed throughout the tropics. The family is considered evolutionarily primitive, related to the magnolia family, Magnoliaceae. Certain species are grown as shade trees or for their tasty fruits. Leaves are simple. Flowers are bisexual and radially symmetrical. They are not particularly showy, but some are prized for their fragrance. The compound fruit is a syncarp (several fleshy fruits fused together like a pineapple) or an aggregate on a short rachis (tightly clustered but separate like a blackberry).

Annona

Annona includes approximately 100 species of evergreen or semideciduous shrubs and trees. They come from lowland moist forests but are cultivated to moderate altitude in South America. The compound fruits are either aggregates or syncarps. Soursop, sweetsop, sugar-apple, and cherimoya are very popular fruits in Latin America. Nothing is quite so refreshing on a hot day as an ice-cold *batido de guanábana* (soursop smoothie). These species are too cold-sensitive for commercial growth in the continental United States but are often grown for local consumption in South Florida. Plants grown from seed vary in quality. Grafts are recommended. Pond apple, *A. glabra*, is an invasive pest in Australia.

Annona montana 'Fairchild'

MOUNTAIN SOURSOP, FAIRCHILD'S ANNONA
Bolivia. Evergreen tree to 20 ft.; zones 10–11. Blooms late winter, spring. Moderate moisture. Fertile, well-drained soil. Full to part sun. Flowers: yellow; fruit a syncarp, ovoid, silvery green; the outlines of the carpel segments form a reticu-

Schinus terebinthifolius, with fruit

Spondias purpurea, flowers

Annona montana 'Fairchild', fruit

Spondias purpurea, unripe fruit

Annona muricata, fruit

lated network with flower remnants in the center of the segments. Leaves: elliptic, to 6 in. long. *It has been suggested that this selection could be a hybrid of* A. montana *and* A. squamosa *(Schokman, pers. comm.). The fruit is fibrous but the juice tasty.* Annona montana *is used as rootstock for other cultivated annonas.*

Annona muricata

SOURSOP, GUANÁBANA, CATUCHE
Caribbean region; widely distributed. Evergreen tree, 10–20 ft.; zones 10–11. Blooms late winter, spring. Moderate moisture. Fertile, well-drained soil. Full to part sun. Flowers: yellow-green, solitary; fruit a syncarp, irregularly ovoid, to 10 in. long, dark green; with protruding flower remnants in the segments. Leaves: oblong, 4–6 in. long. *Cold-sensitive but grows to*

fruiting size in coastal South Florida. The pulp is sweetened and made into refreshing drinks and ice cream. Flowers attractive to butterflies.

Annona squamosa

SWEETSOP, CUSTARD-APPLE,
SUGAR-APPLE, ANÓN
Caribbean region; widely cultivated. Evergreen tree to 20 ft.; zones 10–11. Blooms summer. Moderate moisture. Fertile, well-drained soil. Full to part sun. Flowers: yellow-green, solitary; fruit a waxy syncarp, heart-shaped, 5–6 in. wide, fleshy, light green, overlapping edges of the carpel segments separate at maturity. Leaves: elliptic, to 5 in. long. *Cold-sensitive but grows to fruiting size in coastal South Florida. The sweet pulp is made into refreshing drinks and ice cream.* 'Kampong Mauve' *is a sweet, mauve-colored selection.*

Annona squamosa, fruit

Annona squamosa 'Kampong Mauve', fruit

Artabotrys hexapetalus, flower

Cananga odorata

Artabotrys

Artabotrys includes approximately 100 species of shrubby climbers from Southeast Asia. The flowers are not especially showy but highly fragrant. Natural scents are much appreciated in tropical Asia, where it is a common practice to tuck a scented flower in the pocket. Thais adorn arbors with *A. hexapetalus*, climbing ylang-ylang, to welcome guests. *Artabotrys* oils are sometimes blended with those of *Cananga*, tree ylang-ylang, in perfume production.

Artabotrys hexapetalus

CLIMBING YLANG-YLANG,
TAIL-GRAPE, COQ DU LEVANT
Synonyms: *Annona odoratissimus*, *Annona uncinatus*. Sri Lanka, India, Southeast Asia, southern China; widely naturalized. Evergreen climber to 15 ft.; zones 10–11. Blooms spring, summer. Moist and humid. Fertile, well-drained soil. Full sun to bright filtered light. Flowers: creamy yellow, solitary or in pairs, with one of the pair modified into a hook adapted for climbing; sweet, banana-like fragrance; fruit an aggregate in grapelike clusters. Leaves: elliptic to lanceolate, rubbery, glossy, to 6 in. long, in opposite ranks (distichous). *This heavy, shrubby climber is cultivated for its fragrance. It requires a sturdy arbor.*

Cananga

Cananga includes 2 species of trees from Southeast Asia to Australia. The yellow-green flowers on pendent branches are renowned for their intense fragrance. The French introduced *C. odorata*, the ylang-ylang tree, to Madagascar and the Comoro Islands for commercial production of aromatic oils used in perfumery. The tree also has minor uses in woodworking and as food flavoring. Be cautioned of the intensity of the perfume when choosing a planting site. While pleasing in occasional whiffs on a tropical evening breeze, the fragrance can become strident in large doses. Ylang-ylang can be induced to bloom for an extended period with the application of substantial layers of mulch to maintain even mois-

ture (Schokman, pers. comm.). It otherwise requires little care. Insect pests are generally of minor consequence to healthy trees.

Cananga odorata

YLANG-YLANG, ILANG-ILANG,
FLOR DE ILÁN, CANANG ODORANT
Synonyms: *Unona odorata*, *Uvaria odorata*. Southeast Asia to northern Australia; widely cultivated. Evergreen tree, 25–30 ft., rarely more; zones 10–11. Blooms warm months. Seasonally moist, less when cool. Fertile, well-drained soil. Full to part sun. Flowers: petals linear, ribbony, greenish yellow, twisted, extremely fragrant; in the leaf axils of the pendent branches; fruit an aggregate, dark green, oblong, to 2 in. Leaves: oblong, to 10 in.; margins scalloped (crenulate), with turned-up edges, undulate; in opposite ranks (distichous). *An erect tree with little spread.* 'Fruticosa' *is a dwarf selection, 6–10 ft. high.*

Polyalthia

Polyalthia includes approximately 100 species of shrubs and trees primarily from India and Southeast Asia. Asoka or Asok (pronounced ah-SHO-ka or AH-shock) is a third-century-B.C. king of Magadha (northeastern India) who was instrumental in disseminating Buddhism in southern Asia, and stone pillars with inscriptions were erected in his honor. These pillar-like trees with sweeping foliage are planted around temples. In the landscape they add a unique dimension with their somewhat conifer shape ideal for tall screening or stepped up a slope. Occasional branches from the base are usually removed. An unrelated tree, *Saraca*, is also referred to as Asoka.

Polyalthia longifolia

MAST-TREE, ASOKA
Synonym: *Uvaria longifolia*. India; widely distributed in Southeast Asia and the Pacific. Evergreen tree to 25 ft.; zones 10–11. Blooms warm months. Seasonally moist/dry. Fertile, well-drained soil. Full sun. Flowers: inconspicuous, petals 5, triangular, yellow-green, leathery; in pendent, many-flow-

ered racemes, not fragrant; fruits red to black in aggregates of 4–8. Leaves: lanceolate, to 8 in. long, pendent, glossy dark green with lighter midvein and undersides; margins upturned, undulate.

Rollinia

Rollinia includes approximately 60 species of shrubs and trees from tropical America. They closely resemble *Annona* species and some were formerly included in that genus. Flowers are bisexual and radially symmetrical. They have 3 minute petals and 3 petal-like sepals with wings or spurs on the outside. Stamens and pistils are numerous.

Rollinia deliciosa

BIRIBÁ, FRUTA DE CONDESSA
Synonym: *Annona deliciosa*. Brazil. Evergreen tree; zones 10–11. Blooms late winter, early spring. Moderate moisture. Fertile, well-drained soil. Full to part sun. Flowers: inconspicuous; fruit an ovoid aggregate, 6–12 in. long, fleshy, greenish yellow when ripe with pointed segments. Leaves: elliptic-oblong, to 10 in. long. *Fruit with lemony sweet, gelatinous flesh (Whitman 2001).*

APOCYNACEAE

OLEANDER FAMILY
Apocynaceae includes approximately 355 genera of herbs, shrubs, trees, and climbers distributed worldwide, with greatest diversity in the tropics. Characteristics include a milky latex sap and complex flowers. Recent revisions include the genera traditionally segregated into Asclepiadaceae in this family. For the convenience of readers more familiar with this arrangement, these species are kept together here as a subgroup of Apocynaceae. The family is very important pharmaceutically. Many, though not all, species are poisonous. An exception is *Carissa*. Most are suitable for coastal planting and are at least modestly salt tolerant. Leaves are simple, entire, opposite or whorled. Traditional members of Apocynaceae can be recognized by the radially symmetrical, trumpet-shaped corollas,

commonly with lobes twisted like a propeller. The fruit is a capsule, schizocarp, nutlet, berry, or drupe, commonly in pairs (see photo of *Ochrosia*).

Adenium

Adenium includes a single species of deciduous pachycaulous tree from arid regions of eastern Africa and the Arabian peninsula. The various forms were once segregated into several species based upon range and presence or lack of a caudex (a swollen intersection of the trunk base and root). They are now classified as subspecies. The subspecies readily hybridize, but individuals are self-sterile. Plants in cultivation are mostly hybrids, but only a few cultivar names have valid descriptions. The succulent, spineless trunks of these highly prized little trees store water for the dry season. The leaves fold when dry to decrease evaporation. Caudices are commonly exposed in cultivation to display their gnarled contortions. Adeniums start to bloom toward the end of the dry season and continue through summer. In the wild, they may attain 15 ft.

Grow adeniums in fast-draining, neutral to slightly acid soil. In moist climates add plenty of grit to the soil and grow in raised beds or undersized, tight containers. Top-dress with neutral pH river gravel, not alkaline pea-rock. Organic mulch causes rot. Use dilute liquid or slow-release fertilizer. Water deeply twice weekly when leafing out. Adeniums tolerate cool tem-

peratures if dry but not frost. Cuttings are not favored as a means of propagation because they do not produce well-developed caudices. A horsetail hair is used as a slender propagation tool (Eggli 2001). Special selections are grafted.

Adenium obesum

DESERT-ROSE, IMPALA-LILY, KUDU-LILY
Synonyms: *A. multiflorum*, *A. coetanum*, *A. arabicum*. Arabia, eastern Africa. Deciduous succulent tree, 3–15 ft.; zones 9–11. Blooms warm

Polyalthia longifolia

Polyalthia longifolia, flowers

Rollinia deliciosa, immature fruit

Adenium obesum subsp. *obesum*

months. Semi-arid or seasonally moist/dry. Average, gritty, exceptionally well-drained soil; neutral to slightly acid pH. Full sun. Flowers: funnel-shaped; pink, white, or a combination; fringed corona in throat. Leaves: dark green, obovate, 2–3 in. long. Caudex: if present, normally subterranean. Bark: light gray. *Subsp.* obesum *differs from subsp.* swazicum *(endemic to Swaziland and KwaZulu-Natal) by the more or less pubescent calyx and exserted anthers. Recognized cultivars of subsp.* obesum *are 'Crimson Picotee' (red and white), 'Red Everbloomer' (red), and 'Tom Grumbley' (pure white). Described cultivars of subsp.* swazicum *are 'Boyce Thompson' and 'Perpetual Pink' (Eggli 2001).*

Allamanda

Allamanda includes approximately 8 species of shrubs and shrubby climbers from tropical America. Several are among the most commonly cultivated summer-blooming plants. Cultivar names, of dubious merit, vary from country to country. Allamandas thrive in moist, coastal regions but are only slightly salt tolerant at best. Some are night fragrant. Prune them in early spring to keep shrubby or tie to a support for climbing. Plant in deep, humus-rich soil. Cool night temperatures, lack of water in summer, or spider mite infestation induce leaf loss and sparse appearance. Propagate from cuttings of better selections. Allamandas are superb when landscaped with complementary dark purple foliage plants.

Allamanda blanchetii

PURPLE ALLAMANDA, ALAMANDA MORADA
Synonym: *A. violacea.* Brazil. Evergreen clambering shrub, 5–10 ft.; zones 10–11. Blooms summer, fall. Regular moisture when hot, moderate moisture when cool. Fertile, well-drained soil. Full sun. Flowers: bell-shaped, ascending, mauvepurple, throat dark red, lobes 1.5 in. wide, 3 in. long, pedicel yellow. Leaves: elliptic, 3–4 in. long, lightgreen, with short, stiff hairs (hispid); petiole very short (subsessile); usually in whorls of 4. Stems: bristly (hispid), red-tinged.

Allamanda cathartica

YELLOW ALLAMANDA, GOLDEN TRUMPET, ALAMANDA, CANARIO
Brazil to northeastern South America. Evergreen climber, 10–20 ft.; zones 10–11. Blooms warm months. Moist when hot, moderate moisture when cool. Fertile, well-drained soil. Full sun. Flowers: trumpet-shaped, bright yellow, lobes 3–5 in. wide, white spot at notch between the lobes, throat streaked with orange; buds and outer floral tube bronze. Leaves: elliptic, 4–5 in. long, glossy, tips obtuse, hairs on underside of midrib and on stems; in whorls of 3–6. *The type seems to be a more vigorous climber than cultivars. Large-flowered cultivar names include 'Williamsii' and 'Hendersonii', but no verifiable descriptions have been found. Double-flowered sports, though very attractive, are unusual in cultivation.*

Allamanda 'Cherries Jubilee'

GIANT PURPLE ALLAMANDA, ALAMANDA MORADA GRANDE
Garden origin, unknown parentage. Evergreen climbing shrub, 5–10 ft.; zones 10–11. Blooms warm months. Regular moisture when hot, less when cool. Fertile, well-drained soil. Full sun. Flowers: bellshaped, lobes to 6 in. wide, purplish pink, throat dark red, tube

Adenium obesum subsp. *swazicum*

Allamanda blanchetii

Allamanda cathartica

Allamanda cathartica, double

Allamanda 'Cherries Jubilee'

mauve, yellow to bronze toward the base; calyx and pedicel downy (pubescent). Leaves: ovate, to 6 in. long, pointed, dull light-green, covered with short, stiff hairs or scales; mostly in whorls of 3; sessile. *A spectacular, clambering plant with large flowers. Commonly but incorrectly listed as a cultivar of* A. cathartica.

Allamanda schottii

SHRUB ALLAMANDA

Synonyms: *A. cathartica* var. *schottii*, *A. neriifolia*. Brazil to northeastern South America. Evergreen shrub to 4 ft.; zones 9–11. Blooms warm months. Moist when hot, moderate moisture when cool. Fertile, well-drained soil. Full sun. Flowers: bright yellow, lobes pointed, throat streaked with orange, floral tube and buds bronze. Leaves: elliptic, 2–3 in. long; in whorls of 4. *This shrubby, spreading allamanda is somewhat hardier than A. cathartica and has smaller leaves and flowers. For compact growth, prune lightly after bloom.*

Alstonia

Alstonia includes approximately 45 species of trees and shrubs from Southeast Asia, Indomalaysia, Africa, and Australia. Some are large timber trees which develop great buttressed trunks with age. They have a milky sap. Leaves are in whorls of 3–9. Flowers are small, white to greenish, and in clusters. Capsules are long and slender, splitting at maturity to release seeds with 2 hairs attached. *Alstonia scholaris* is called scholar-tree because its white wood is used as makeshift writing tablets. The moniker devil-tree refers to the leaves and inflorescences often arranged in tiered whorls of approximately 6, but is most aptly applied to those species with devilishly invasive tendencies.

Alstonia scholaris

SCHOLAR-TREE, DEVIL-TREE, MILK-WOOD, PULAI

Synonym: *Echites scholaris*. Southeast Asia, New Guinea, Australia; widely naturalized. Evergreen tree to 75 ft.+; zones 10–11. Blooms fall. Moderate moisture. Average, well-drained soil. Full to part sun. Flow-

ers: small, white, downy, fragrant at night; throat with tufted corona; in headlike cymes at the ends of 3- to 6-in. spokelike stalks; capsules slender, to 2 ft. long. Leaves: oblanceolate, 6–10 in. long with about 50 parallel veins; in whorls of 5–9; blade decurrent on the short petiole. *Develops a rounded canopy and buttressed trunk with age. Self-seeding.*

Alstonia venenata

India. Evergreen shrub, 6–8 ft.; zones 10–11. Blooms spring. Moderate moisture to seasonally moist/dry. Average, well-drained soil. Full to part sun. Flowers: salverform, white, tube slender, to 2 in. long, lobes spreading, twisted like a propeller, in axillary clusters. Leaves: narrowly lanceolate to oblanceolate, 6–8 in. long, 1 in.

wide; veins lighter green, lateral veins perpendicular to the midrib; tip tapering; base decurrent; in whorls of 4; margins undulate.

Beaumontia

Beaumontia includes approximately 9 species of woody climbers (lianas) from India and Southeast Asia. They are spectacular tropical vines with funnel-shaped flowers resembling large Easter lilies and arranged in great clusters dripping from stout stems. Leaves are simple. Flowering vines like these are underutilized in landscaping. Simple or elaborate arbors can be devised to create a peaceful sanctuary or to shade a table or west-facing porch in the Mediterranean style. Vines are particularly useful for landscaping where space is limited.

Beaumontia grandiflora

HERALD'S TRUMPET,
NEPAL TRUMPET-FLOWER,
EASTER LILY VINE

Synonym: *Echites grandiflorus*. Himalayan foothills from India to Vietnam. Evergreen woody climber to 30 ft.+; zones 10–11. Blooms late winter, early spring. Seasonally moist/dry. Average to fertile, well-drained soil. Full sun. Flowers: corolla white, funnel-shaped, lobes flaring, 7–8 in. long, fragrant; calyx covered with rust-colored hairs. Leaves: oblong to ovate, 4–10 in. long, glossy dark green, rust-colored hairs on the underside when young. *A spectacular and vigorous vine.* Beaumontia multiflora *is often mistaken for this species. It has much shorter, bell-shaped white flowers.*

Allamanda schottii

Alstonia scholaris

Alstonia venenata

Beaumontia grandiflora

Carissa macrocarpa

Catharanthus roseus cultivar

Carissa

Carissa includes approximately 37 species of evergreen shrubs and climbers from the Old World tropics. They commonly have forked spines in the leaf axils. Cultivated species are moderately salt tolerant. Plum-sized fruits are red to black with a milky sap. The fleshier forms are edible, tasting somewhat like raspberries and cream. Shrubby forms may be utilized as barrier hedges. Spreading forms are useful as a deterrent to graffiti scribblers when planted in front of walls and around the bases of traffic signs. Clambering varieties can infiltrate tree canopies and become difficult to control. Be forewarned that climbing forms are used to fence out elephants in Africa. Many cultivars are available. Selecting an appropriate mature size and habit will greatly reduce maintenance. Prune lower branches before they root at the nodes and develop into thickets. *Carissa* sometimes contracts a fungal disease that may cause an isolated branch or the whole plant to turn brown and die.

Carissa macrocarpa

CARISSA, NATAL PLUM, AMATUNGULU (SOUTH AFRICA)
Synonym: *C. grandiflora*. Eastern coastal South Africa. Evergreen shrub or climber, 3–25 ft.; zones 9–11. Blooms intermittently in warm months. Regular moisture, tolerates dry periods. Average, well-drained soil. Full to part sun. Flowers: salverform, to 2 in. wide, white, lobes twisted like a propeller. Leaves: ovate, 1–2 in. long, glossy dark green, stiff, tips sharply pointed. Heavily armed with forked spines in the leaf axils. *Cultivars are quite variable. Choose size and habit to suit location. Though this is the only species name encountered in cultivation, it is likely that at least some selections are actually hybrids or different species.*

Catharanthus

Catharanthus includes approximately 6 species of shrubs, subshrubs, and annual herbs from Madagascar, Sri Lanka, and India. *Catharanthus roseus* and its many cultivars are ubiquitous bedding plants. This species is widely naturalized in the tropics. The petal lobes have a characteristic propeller twist and the throat has a spot, or "eye," of color around it. Though once grouped with *Vinca*, *Catharanthus* has a number of distinctive characteristics. Vincristine and vinblastin, pharmaceutical alkaloids derived from this genus, were among the first potent antileukemia drugs. The need to preserve species diversity for yet undiscovered pharmaceutical and chemical properties such as this is but one example of why conservation of wild habitat is essential to humans.

Catharanthus roseus

MADAGASCAR PERIWINKLE, OLD MAID, VINCA
Synonyms: *Lochnera rosea, Vinca rosea*. Madagascar; widely naturalized. Evergreen subshrub, 12–18 in.; zones 9–11. Blooms warm months. Moderate moisture, tolerates brief dry periods. Average, well-drained soil. Full to part sun. Flowers: salverform, tube slender, white, pink, or salmon with a red eye around the small opening of the throat. Leaves: ovate, dark green, glossy, midvein lighter. *Many cultivars, including compact forms, are familiar garden plants. They thrive in coastal locations. Also grown as annuals in temperate climates. Self-seeding.*

Chonemorpha

Chonemorpha includes approximately 13 species of woody climbers (lianas) from India and Indomalaysia. Leaves are simple. Flowers are fragrant, bisexual, and radially symmetrical. Fruits are long hairy follicles. The woody fibers are used to weave fishing nets in native regions.

Chonemorpha fragrans

FRANGIPANI-VINE
Synonyms: *C. macrophylla, Trachelospermum grandiflorum* (hort.). India to Malaysia. Evergreen climber to 20 ft.+; zones 10–11. Blooms spring, summer. Regular moisture when hot, moderate moisture when cool. Fertile, well-drained soil; acid pH. Full to part sun. Flowers: salverform, lobes twisted, white, throat yellow. Leaves: broadly ovate, 14 in. long, 8 in. wide, downy (pubescent) below. *Grown for the fragrant flowers. Needs a sturdy support. Water early or avoid wetting flowers if possible. Water-droplet lenses magnify the sunlight, causing brown spots.*

Kopsia

Kopsia includes approximately 25 species of trees and shrubs from Indomalaysia. They produce alkaloids that are important pharmaceutically. Fruits are fleshy drupes with hard pits, somewhat resembling plums.

Kopsia fruticosa

SHRUB VINCA
Synonyms: *Cerbera fruticosa, K. vinciflora*. India, Malay Peninsula.

Evergreen shrub or small tree, 8–12 ft.; zones 10–11. Blooms spring, summer. Moderate moisture in summer, less in winter. Average, well-drained soil. Full to part sun. Flowers: salverform, lobes spreading, to 2 in. wide, pink with a dark red eye around the small throat opening, fading to white with age. Leaves: broadly elliptic, to 6 in. long, glossy. *This free-flowering small tree is suitable for containers. The flowers resemble Madagascar periwinkle,* Catharanthus. *The species name means "shrubby."*

Kopsia pruniformis

Southeast Asia. Evergreen shrub to 8 ft.; zones 10–11. Blooms warm months. Moderate moisture in summer, less in winter. Average, well-drained soil. Full to part sun. Flowers: salverform, white; tube slightly inflated below the white lobes, in many-flowered clusters (cymes); fruit a small plumlike drupe, 1.5 in. long, blue-black, waxy (glaucous). Leaves: elliptic to lanceolate, 4–6 in. long, tip tapering (acuminate), glossy; sap milky. Unusual in cultivation. Suitable for borders and hedges.

Mandevilla

Mandevilla includes approximately 125 species of shrubs and climbers from Central and South America, most abundant in the eastern mountain ranges of Brazil and the Andes. Cultivars are complex hybrids of obscure ancestry and should not be listed with species

Chonemorpha fragrans

Kopsia fruticosa

Kopsia pruniformis

names. Mandevillas thrive in seaside locations and areas with mild temperatures. Sensitive to heat and cold, mandevillas are often grown as spring or fall annuals. Growing plants in containers provides some control over temperature fluctuations as the plants can be moved into shaded locations when hot. Containers are also recommended where nematodes are a problem such as in South Florida.

Mandevilla boliviensis

WHITE MANDEVILLA, WHITE DIPLADENIA
Synonyms: *Dipladenia boliviensis*, *M. cereola*. Bolivia, Ecuador. Evergreen climber to 12 ft.; zones 10–11. Blooms spring, summer, fall. Moderate moisture. Fertile, well-drained soil; neutral to slightly acid pH. Full to part sun, filtered light in hot weather. Flowers: trumpet-shaped, to 2 in. wide, white, throat yellow. Leaves: elliptic, to 4 in. long, glossy. *Thrives in seaside locations.*

Mandevilla hybrids

MANDEVILLA, ROSE-DIPLADENIA
Garden origin. Evergreen climbers to 10 ft.; zones 10–11. Blooms spring, summer. Evenly moist in warm months, moderate moisture in cool. Fertile, well-drained soil; neutral to slightly acid pH. Full to part sun, filtered light in hot weather. Flowers: funnel-shaped, 2–3 in. wide, pale to deep pink, often with a yellow throat. Leaves: elliptic, slightly downy or smooth, 4–6 in. long. *More easily maintained in containers in many areas. The ancestry of these hybrids probably involves* M. sanderi *(syn.* M. ×amoena) *and/or* M. splendens.

Nerium

Nerium includes a single species of shrub from the Mediterranean eastward to southern China. It has innumerable cultivars. They thrive in California and other regions with dry, hot summers and are widely used in landscaping. The flowers range from funnel-shaped to flaring, single to double, in a wide assortment of colors. A characteristic star-shaped, frilly corona (annulus) in the throat is a good field mark.

The paired fruits are elongated capsules. Tufts attached to the seeds act like parachutes, aiding in dispersal. All parts of the plant contain a heart poison, which is toxic if ingested or inhaled in smoke. Oleanders are not as reliable growers in Florida and similar climates (Burch, pers. comm.). They do not like excess moisture in summer and are susceptible to local pests including scale insects, orange and black oleander caterpillars, and nematodes. Oleander is a poor choice for formal, sheared hedges. Because new leaves are produced only on new growth, the base soon becoming bare sticks. If overgrown, cut short, letting new growth develop near the ground. Oleander is suitable for coastal locations. *Thevetia peruviana* is incorrectly and confusingly referred to as yellow oleander.

Nerium oleander

OLEANDER, ROSE-BAY, ADELFA
Synonyms: *N. indicum*, *N. odoratum*. Mediterranean region; widely distributed. Evergreen shrub, 10–20 ft.; zones 8–11. Blooms spring, summer. Moderate moisture to fairly dry. Average, well-drained soil. Full sun. Flowers: funnel-shaped, 1–2 in. wide. Leaves: narrowly lanceolate, grayish green, to 7 in. long. *Oleander is heat and drought resistant. Often used in public landscaping in California and for screening. Produces large clumps.*

Ochrosia

Ochrosia includes approximately 30 species of trees and shrubs from the Seychelles, Mascarene Islands (in the Indian Ocean off eastern Africa), Southeast Asia, Indomalaysia, and Australia. *Ochrosia elliptica*, twin plum, is commonly culti-

vated in the tropics. It is salt tolerant and has a dense, rounded habit. The paired, pointed red fruits are very ornamental. This species is sometimes invasive in coastal areas. It is apparently not a problem inland. The glossy foliage is handsome in a container on a sunny porch.

Ochrosia elliptica

TWIN PLUM, KOPSIA, POKOSOLA
Synonym: *O. parviflora* (misapplied). New Caledonia to Australia. Evergreen shrub, 10–25 ft.; zones 10–11. Blooms fall, winter. Moderate moisture. Average, sandy, well-drained soil. Full to part sun. Flowers: salverform, to 1 in. long, 0.5 in. wide, white; fruit glossy red, to 2 in. long, ovoid, tips pointed, in subsessile pairs. Leaves: obovate, 6–7 in. long, glossy bright green, leathery, tip obtuse; margins somewhat un-

Mandevilla boliviensis

Mandevilla 'Janelle Rosy Pink'

Mandevilla 'Pink Leah'

Nerium oleander

Nerium oleander, double flower

Nerium oleander 'Luteum'

dulate; in whorls, densely clustered at the ends of the branches.

Odontadenia

Odontadenia includes approximately 30 species of shrubs and woody climbers from tropical America. They are uncommon in cultivation in the United States. Crushed leaves are reportedly used as an insect repellant in South America.

Odontadenia macrantha

Synonyms: *O. grandiflora, O. speciosa.* Costa Rica to Peru, Brazil. Evergreen woody climber to 20 ft.+; zones 10–11. Blooms all summer. Moderate moisture. Average to fertile, well-drained soil. Full sun. Flowers: funnel-shaped, 3–4 in. wide, scented, lemon-yellow, throat with orange, starlike streaks and a small corona. Leaves: oblong to ovate, 7–10 in. long, dark green, leathery. *A fragrant, vigorous climber. Grow over a sturdy arbor to shade a porch or picnic table.*

Pachypodium

Pachypodium includes approximately 16 species of trees and shrubs of semiarid regions: 5 in Namibia and 11 in Madagascar. The genus name means "thick-footed," alluding to the water-storing, pachycaulous trunk or underground stem (caudex). Plants become dormant during the dry season. Water deeply once a week when in active growth. Branching takes place only after flowers are produced. The trunk and branches are covered with spines in clusters of 2 or 3 (*Adenium* and *Plumeria* are spineless). In moist, humid climates, pachypodiums do well in fast-draining pumice or limestone grit. In nature, they grow in limestone outcroppings and granite crevices. Containers should be tight and undersized. The expanding caudex should be raised above the rim of the pot occasionally to prevent the container from bursting. Use slow-release low-nitrogen fertilizers only during active growth. Though these plants come from semiarid regions, cultivated plants, especially those in containers, benefit from deep weekly irrigation dur-

ing extended hot, dry periods. Madagascar species are threatened in the wild.

Pachypodium baronii

Northern Madagascar. Deciduous pachycaulous tree to 8 ft.; zones 9–11. Blooms spring, summer. Semiarid. Gritty, very porous soil. Full sun. Flowers: salverform, petals red, lobes spreading, not overlapping, to 1.5 in. wide, corona yellow, tube to 1 in. long; on a peduncle to 8 in. long. Leaves: obovate, 6–10 in. long, glossy. Trunk: bottle-shaped, no caudex, bark gray, spines conical, paired. *The only Pachypodium with red flowers. Var. windsori has broader overlapping red petals with yellow streaks and a swollen caudex.*

Pachypodium lamerei
CLUBFOOT

Southern Madagascar; widely cultivated. Deciduous pachycaulous tree to 18 ft.; zones 9–11. Blooms warm months. Semiarid. Gritty, very porous soil. Full sun. Flowers: funnel-shaped, to 6 in. long, white, fragrant. Leaves: elliptic, 8–10 in. long, glossy dark green, hairy below, in whorls at branch tips; margins revolute. Trunk: bottle- or barrel-shaped, spines in clusters of 3 in a spiral pattern around the trunk. *The most common Pachypodium cultivated. Branching occurs only after flowering. Often produces sports with crests or variegated leaves. Var. ramosum differs by having leaves that are glabrous (smooth) below.*

Pachypodium lealii

Synonym: *P. saundersii.* Southern Angola, Namibia, Zimbabwe, northern South Africa. Deciduous

Ochrosia elliptica, fruit

Pachypodium lamerei var. *ramosum*

Odontadenia macrantha

Pachypodium baronii var. *baronii,* young plant

Pachypodium lamerei var. *lamerei,* flowers

pachycaulous tree to 18 ft.; zones 9–11. Blooms warm months. Semi-arid. Gritty, very porous soil. Full sun. Flowers: funnel-shaped, white, tinged red on the outside; calyx reddish, cup-shaped with toothlike lobes. Leaves: oblong, 1–2 in. long; margins rolled upward, undulate, 1.5–2 in., spines in clusters of 3, needlelike. Caudex massive when mature. *Subsp.* lealii *has hairy leaves. Resembles* Adenium *when young but that genus lacks spines.*

Pachypodium rosulatum

Synonym: *P. cactipes*. Madagascar. Deciduous pachycaulous tree to 6 ft.; zones 9–11. Blooms warm months. Semiarid. Gritty, very porous soil. Full sun. Flowers: trumpet-shaped, bright yellow; on a branched stalk to 15 in. long. Leaves: oblong, to 6 in. long, midrib white, undersides of leaves and young shoots white felty; margins rolled upward. Trunk: covered with paired spines. The mature caudex may swell to 3 ft. diameter. *The 4 varieties of this species come from diverse habitats.*

Pachypodium rutenbergianum

Southern Madagascar. Deciduous succulent tree to 15 ft.; zones 10–11. Blooms winter, spring. Semiarid. Gritty, very porous soil. Full sun. Flowers: trumpet-shaped, lobes twisted, white; in clusters at the ends of thick branches. Leaves: lanceolate, to 6 in. long. Trunk: light gray, branching from the top, covered with short spines when young. *Blooms while leafless.*

Pentalinon

Pentalinon includes 2 shrubby climbers from Florida, the West Indies, and South and Central America. *Pentalinon lutea* is cultivated in the United States. It is quite variable over its extensive range. The selection in cultivation allegedly originated in Brazil. The naturally yellow-green foliage is not mineral deficient. Landscaping with strongly contrasting dark green or purple foliage can perk up the chartreuse coloration. The plant is salt tolerant and suitable for coastal locations and poor soil. "Wild alla-

manda" and "yellow mandevilla" are unfortunate misnomers that tend to confuse this species with 2 related ones.

Pentalinon luteum

SUNDIAL

Synonyms: *Urechites lutea, Urechites pinetorum*. Central and South America, West Indies, Florida. Evergreen climber to 10 ft.; zones 10–11. Blooms warm months. Moderate moisture. Average to poor, well-drained soil. Full to part sun. Flowers: trumpet-shaped, yellow, to 3 in. long. Leaves: ovate, to 2 in. long, yellowish green, glossy to pubescent. *Confusingly referred to in the trade as yellow mandevilla. A form native to South Florida rock pinelands is called wild allamanda, a relatively small vine.* Pests include oleander caterpillars.

Plumeria

Plumeria includes approximately 45 species of trees and shrubs from tropical America. Plumerias were widely disseminated by missionary priests and commonly planted around graveyards. They hybridize readily, making attempts to identify cultivated plants and even some wild populations dubious. Plumerias have thick, pachycaulous, brittle, spineless stems which do not branch until after flowering or pruning. Leaves are simple, in clusters near the ends of the branches. Petioles are short. Flowers are trumpet-shaped to salverform, with 4–7, usually 5, more or less spreading lobes. They are redolent of coconut, buttered popcorn, citrus, or peaches. Fruits are T-shaped twin capsules.

Plumeria alba, with white flowers, is distinguished by having

Pachypodium rosulatum var. *rosulatum*

Pachypodium rutenbergianum

Pachypodium lealii subsp. *saundersii*

Pentalinon luteum

Plumeria 'Lei Rainbow'

leaves no more than 0.5 in. wide (Howard et al. 1988b). *Plumeria obtusa*, also with white flowers, is a variable species with isolated populations in the Caribbean and has broader, oblong leaves. Hybrids of this species and *P. rubra* tend to have pastel floral colors. *Plumeria rubra*, probably a cultigen, is involved in the ancestry of the most widely distributed hybrids. It is loosely characterized by acuminate leaf tips, red petioles, and red or white flowers with overlapping petals. *Plumeria rubra* f. *tricolor* flowers are multicolored; f. *lutea* flowers are yellow.

Plumerias thrive in dry climates and in coastal areas. Irrigation or fertilization before or during the flowering season inhibits bloom. Feed with high-phosphate, low-nitrogen fertilizer only after new leaves appear. A rust fungus spots the leaves in humid conditions but does not require treatment as the leaves fall naturally shortly after the time the infection usually appears (Vannoorbeeck, pers. comm.). Plumerias are easily propagated from cuttings allowed to dry out for a few days or even weeks before planting.

Plumeria hybrids

PLUMERIA, FRANGIPANI, TEMPLE-TREE, FLOR DE MAYO, FRANCHIPÁN
Garden origin. Deciduous shrubs or trees, 6–25 ft.; zones 10–11. Bloom spring, summer, occasionally at other times. Moderate moisture, seasonally dry . Poor to average, open, well-drained soil. Full to part sun. Flowers: funnel-shaped or salverform, lobes twisted like propellors, open to overlapping, white with yellow throat to multihued. Leaves: lanceolate, obovate to oblong, 7–14 in. long, tips obtuse, blunt, or acuminate; petioles short. *Loosely referred to as P. rubra cultivars. Cultivated plants by this name are undoubtedly complex hybrids and a species name is inappropriate. The Salsa Group refers to unnamed selections collected in Mexico.*

Plumeria obtusa

PLUMERIA, FRANGIPANI, FLOR DE MAYO, AMAPOLA, ATAPAIMA
Synonyms: *P. bahamensis, P. inaguensis*. Bahamas, Greater Antilles, Central America. Briefly deciduous shrub, 6–15 ft.; zones 10–11. Blooms warm months. Moderate, seasonally dry. Poor to average, open, well-drained soil. Full sun. Flowers: salverform, petals narrowly obovate, not overlapping, white with a yellow throat, citrus-scented. Leaves: oblong to obovate, 7–12 in. long, 1.5–3 in. wide, leathery, tip blunt or indented (emarginate); petioles short; margins revolute. *Heat tolerant. Excellent for coastal landscaping. Spreading habit. Var.* sericifolia *has fine hair on the undersides of the leaves and on the petioles.*

Plumeria pudica

Panama, Colombia, Venezuela. Semideciduous shrub, 6–15 ft.; zones 10–11. Blooms warm months. Seasonally moist/dry. Poor to average, open, well-drained soil. Full sun. Flowers: funnel-shaped white, throat yellow. Leaves: oblong, to 7 in. long, with a pair of large lobes near the pointed tip; petioles short; margins upturned, deeply undulate. *Evergreen when winters are mild. The lobed leaves are a distinctive field mark. Unusual in cultivation.*

Plumeria stenopetala

PLUMERIA, FRANGIPANI, FLOR DE MAYO
Hispaniola. Deciduous tree to 12 ft.; zones 10–11. Blooms spring, summer. Seasonally moist/dry. Poor to fertile, open, well-drained soil. Full to part sun. Flowers: fun-nel-shaped, white with a yellow throat, petal lobes narrowly elliptic, tips acuminate. Leaves: elliptic to lanceolate, to 10 in. long, 1.5 in. wide, tip acuminate. *Unusual in cultivation.*

Prestonia

Prestonia includes approximately 60 species of shrubby climbers from tropical America. This genus is a source of valuable alkaloid pharmaceuticals. There are small nectar glands in the leaf axils. The flowers have a short corona around the throat, somewhat reminiscent of narcissus. The species listed here is a dainty climber of modest proportions and easy culture.

Prestonia mollis

Synonym: *P. glabrata*. Amazon headwaters of Peru and Ecuador. Evergreen climber, 10–15 ft.+;

Plumeria 'Maui Beauty'

Plumeria Salsa Group

Plumeria 'Singapore Dwarf Petite Pink'

Plumeria obtusa var. *obtusa*

Plumeria pudica

Plumeria stenopetala

zones 10–11. Blooms winter, spring. Seasonally moist/moderate. Fertile, well-drained soil. Full sun. Flowers: salverform, lobes spreading, twisted, yellow, corona around the throat. Leaves: broadly ovate, to 8 in. long, glossy dark green; palmipinnate venation; petiole to 1 in., streaked red. Bark: corky. *A striking climber from rain forests and streambanks of the Amazon interior. Rare in cultivation but highly recommended.*

Stemmadenia

Stemmadenia includes approximately 10 species of shrubs and trees from tropical America. Some species were formerly included in *Tabernaemontana* but can be distinguished by the larger calyx and corolla lobes. Fruits are ovoid and paired.

Stemmadenia litoralis

MILKY-WAY TREE, COJÓN, LECHOSO
Synonyms: *S. bella*, *Tabernaemontana litoralis*. Mexico, Central America, Colombia. Evergreen shrub or tree, 15–20 ft.+; zones 9–11. Blooms primarily late spring, early summer, or after dry spells. Moderate moisture. Average, well-drained soil; neutral to acid pH. Full sun. Flowers: salverform, tube to 4 in. long, fragrant, throat yellow inside, lobes twisted; fruit ovoid, in pairs, yellow, 2 in. diameter. Leaves: elliptic, 5–8 in. long, tips cuspidate, glossy dark green; margins slightly undulate. *Flowers open one to a few at a time. Of coastal forests. Sap milky.* Cojón *is Spanish for the paired, testicle-like fruits.*

Strophanthus

Strophanthus includes approximately 38 shrubs and climbers from the Old World tropics. The genus is typical of Indonesian rain forests. Seeds of *S. hispidus*, *S. gratus*, and other species are an important source of a cortisone precursor and strophanthin, a pharmaceutical drug used to treat high blood pressure. The native habitat is seriously threatened by logging. The flowers of certain species have strongly twisted or unusually elongated petal tips. Though unusual in cultivation, these plants are highly ornamental and easy to grow. Propagated from cuttings.

Strophanthus boivinii

Synonym: *Roupellia boivinii*. Madagascar. Semideciduous shrub to 15 ft.; zones 10–11. Blooms spring, early summer. Seasonally moist/moderate. Average, well-drained soil. Full to part sun. Flowers: salverform, lobes slender, twisted, honey-brown with a white corona around the mouth of the narrow throat; calyx small, green. Leaves: lanceolate, to 10 in. long, glossy dark green, occasionally forked at the tip. *This dense, spreading shrub is deciduous in dry conditions. Withhold water in late winter for strong bloom. Moist conditions encourage a prolonged but less prolific bloom.*

Strophanthus gratus

CLIMBING OLEANDER, ESTROFANTO
Synonym: *Roupellia grata*. Western and central Africa. Semideciduous climber to 25 ft.; zones 10–11. Blooms warm months. Seasonally moist/moderate. Fertile, well-drained soil. Full or morning sun. Flowers: salverform, petals pink to white, corona dark pink, fringed, throat yellow. Leaves: ovate to obovate, rubbery, glossy dark green. *A vigorous climber but may be kept shrubby by pruning. Flower-spotting sometimes caused by water droplet lenses in sunlight. Water early to allow the flowers to dry if possible.*

Strophanthus preussii

MEDUSA FLOWER
Western and central Africa. Semideciduous climber, 15–20 ft.; zones 10–11. Blooms spring, summer. Seasonally moist/moderate. Average to fertile, well-drained soil. Full to part sun. Flowers: salverform, cream-colored petals, tips greatly elongated, dangling, twisted, sticky maroon strands to 8 in. or more long, throat and corona ruddy-brown. Leaves: ovate, 4–6 in. long, dark glossy green; petiole short, ruddy. *A clambering shrub. Can be kept shrubby by pruning. Tolerates heat well. Deciduous in dry conditions. An Asian species,* S. divaricatus, *has green striped corona and shorter petal threads.*

Tabernaemontana

Tabernaemontana includes approximately 100 species of trees and shrubs, which are widely distributed in the tropics. *Ervatamia* and *Conopharyngia* are now included in this genus. Many species have rather similar white flowers with lobes twisted like a propeller. Many in cultivation are poorly differentiated. The genus name is a Latin translation of Bergzabern, a German physician. The preferred common name for some fragrant species is jessamine, in an effort to avoid confusion with true jasmines, *Jasminum*, in a different family, Oleaceae (Morton 1974). This distinction is important for landscaping because, unlike often weedy or invasive jasmines, this genus is not known to be self-seeding in cultivation. They are also excellent substitutes for acid-loving gardenias where the soil is alkaline (sweet) and are pest and disease resistant. Some are somewhat sensitive to cold temperatures and drought.

Prestonia mollis

Stemmadenia litoralis

Strophanthus boivinii

Strophanthus gratus

Strophanthus preussii

Shrub forms make excellent hedges and take pruning well.

Tabernaemontana arborea

WILD ORANGE JESSAMINE

Synonyms: *Peschiera arborea, T. schippii*. Mexico, Guatemala. Evergreen tree, 35–50 ft.+; zones 10–11. Blooms spring. Moderate moisture. Average, well-drained soil. Full sun. Flowers: salverform, lobes twisted, white, throat more or less yellowish; in many-flowered clusters, not fragrant at least during the day. Leaves: oblanceolate, to 6 in. long, glossy. *Potentially large, spreading shade tree of tropical forests and streamsides. Unusual in cultivation but highly recommended.*

Tabernaemontana australis

PINWHEEL FLOWER,
PINWHEEL JESSAMINE

Synonym: *Peschiera australis*. Brazil.

Evergreen shrub or small tree to 15 ft.; zones 10–11. Blooms spring. Moderate moisture in summer, less in winter. Average to fertile, well-drained soil. Full to part sun. Flowers: salverform, small, fragrant, petal lobes twisted like a propeller, creamy white. Leaves: ovate, 4–6 in. long, glossy dark green. *Australis means "southern," alluding to the Southern Hemisphere, and does not necessarily indicate an association with Australia.*

Tabernaemontana divaricata

CREPE JESSAMINE, BUTTERFLY GARDENIA, CEYLON JESSAMINE, FLEUR D'AMOUR

Synonyms: *Ervatamia coronaria, Nerium divaricatum, T. coronaria*. India to northern Thailand and southwestern China. Evergreen shrub to 6 ft.; zones 10–11. Blooms intermittently in spring, summer.

Regular moisture in summer, less in winter, never dry. Fertile, well-drained soil. Full to part sun. Flowers: salverform, lobes broadly obovate, twisted like a propeller, white, throat yellow; fragrant at night. Leaves: ovate, to 5 in. long, tip acuminate; margins undulate. *Suitable for large containers. Cold-sensitive. Fragrant wood used for incense, resins. 'Flore Pleno' has a double corolla. Tabernaemontana corymbosa has pointed petals.*

Tabernaemontana pachysiphon

GIANT PINWHEEL FLOWER

Synonyms: *Conopharyngia pachysiphon, T. holstii*. Tropical eastern Africa. Evergreen shrub or tree, 10–40 ft.; zones 10–11. Blooms almost all year. Regular moisture, never dry. Fertile, open, well-drained soil. Part sun to bright, fil-

tered light. Flowers: salverform, tube to 4 in. long, white, lobes twisted, slender, edges ruffled, throat yellow, silky hairs inside; fragrance sweet, vanilla-like. Leaves: elliptic, to 8 in. long, dark green. *This large-flowered species has arching, clambering limbs. Blooms sparsely but almost constantly. Mulch well to maintain moisture.*

Tabernaemontana pandacaqui

Synonyms: *Ervatamia floribunda, T. orientalis*. Southeast Asia, Indomalaysia, Philippines, Fiji, Vanuatu, New Guinea, Australia. Evergreen spreading shrub or small tree to 20 ft.; zones 9–11. Blooms summer. Regular moisture in summer, moderate in winter. Fertile, well-drained soil. Full to part sun. Flowers: salverform, white, petal margins fringed, faintly scented; in small

Tabernaemontana arborea

Tabernaemontana australis

Tabernaemontana divaricata

Tabernaemontana divaricata 'Flore Pleno'

Tabernaemontana pachysiphon

Tabernaemontana pandacaqui

Tabernaemontana pandacaqui, fruit

clusters, a few flowers opening at a time; capsules ovoid with pointed ends, in pairs, red-orange. Leaves: ovate to elliptic, 4–8 in. long; margins smooth.

Thevetia

Thevetia includes approximately 8 species of shrubs and trees from tropical America. The pharmaceutical drug thevetin is used to treat heart ailments. Species included here are at their best in Mediterranean-type climates such as southern California.

Thevetia ahouai

BROADLEAF THEVETIA, CASCABEL
Synonyms: *Cerbera ahouai*, *T. nitida*. Mexico to Colombia, Venezuela. Evergreen shrub, 5–10 ft.; zones 10–11. Blooms spring. Moderate moisture. Average to fertile, well-drained soil. Full to part sun. Flowers: salverform, creamy white, lobes strongly twisted, tube 2–3 in. long; edges ruffled; in cymes, a few opening at a time. Leaves: obovate, to 7 in. long, 2 in. wide, dark glossy green, leathery; petiole short (subsessile). *Unusual in cultivation.*

Thevetia peruviana

LUCKY-NUT, BE-STILL TREE, CASCABEL
Synonyms: *Cascabela thevetia*, *Cerbera peruviana*, *T. neriifolia*. Tropical America. Evergreen shrub, 10–20 ft.; zones 9–11. Blooms warm months. Moderate moisture, seasonally dry. Average, sandy, well-drained soil. Full sun. Flowers: bell-shaped, to 2 in. long, peach to yellow, rarely white; in few-flowered clusters. Leaves: oblong-linear, to 6 in. long, 1 in. wide, stiff, glossy; spirally arranged at the ends of the branches. *Xeric. Thrives in hot, dry climates and at seaside. "Lucky-nut" alludes to the raised, crosslike seams of the nut. "Yellow oleander" (*adelfa amarilla* in Spanish) is a confusing misnomer. True oleander is Nerium.*

Thevetia thevetioides

GIANT THEVETIA, GIANT LUCKY-NUT, CASCABEL GRANDE
Synonyms: *Cascabela thevetioides*, *Cerbera thevetioides*. Mexico. Evergreen shrub to 15 ft.; zones 9–11. Blooms spring, summer. Moderate

moisture, seasonally dry. Sandy, well-drained soil. Full sun. Flowers: funnel-shaped, bright yellow to peach, 3–4 in. long, in large clusters. Leaves: linear, to 5 in. long, glossy dark green; margins revolute; in whorls at the ends of the branches. *This large, xeric shrub thrives in Mediterranean-type climates with hot, dry summers. Excellent for coastal locations. A more prolific bloomer than* T. peruviana.

Trachelospermum

Trachelospermum includes approximately 20 species of shrubs and climbers from the Old World. *Trachelospermum jasminoides*, Confederate jessamine, is widely cultivated in mild temperate climates as well as the subtropics. The common name alludes to the plant's popularity in the southeastern states, but it is Chinese in origin. The preferred common name for fragrant jasminelike species is jessamine, in an effort to avoid confusion with true jasmines, *Jasminum*, in a different family, Oleaceae (Morton 1974). *Trachelospermum* species can be distinguished from true jasmines by the twisted, propeller-like petals in contrast to the flat petals of *Jasminum* species. They will grow in filtered light, but 4 or 5 hours of direct sun are necessary for vigorous bloom. They are pest and disease resistant.

Trachelospermum jasminoides

CHINESE STAR-JESSAMINE, CONFEDERATE JESSAMINE, LUO SHI
Synonym: *Rhynchospermum jasminoides*. Southern China, Vietnam. Semideciduous climber, 10–20 ft.; zones 7–11. Blooms warm months. Moderate moisture. Average, well-drained soil; acid pH. Full to part sun. Flowers: salverform, nutmeg-scented, white, lobes obovate, twisted, tips blunt; margins revolute. Leaves: ovate to lanceolate, glossy dark green, downy below when young. *Cultivars come in variegated, bronze, and narrow-leafed forms. They thrive in coastal locations. Add micronutrients in alkaline soil. Often used as a ground cover. Aggressive once established. Prune sharply after flowering to control.*

Small-leafed Confederate jessamine, *T. asiaticum*, *has cream or yellow flowers and hairy stems.*

Wrightia

Wrightia includes approximately 24 species of trees from tropical Old World forests. Several large tree species are cut for timber and woodworking. They are rare in cultivation in the United States but commonly used for landscaping in Southeast Asia.

Wrightia arborea

Synonyms: *Holarrhena tomentosa* (misapplied), *W. tomentosa*. Southern China, India, Sri Lanka, Southeast Asia, Malaysia. Deciduous tree, 30–75 ft.; zones 10–11. Blooms late spring, early summer. Seasonally moist/dry. Average, well-drained soil. Full to part sun. Flowers: salverform, lobes to 2 in.

wide, peach, rarely yellow or white, corona apricot-orange, felty (tomentose), petal tips revolute; opening a few at a time. Leaves: ovate, 6–8 in. long, glossy dark green, in opposite ranks. Bark: gray-tan, peeling. *A rounded-crown forest tree. The white wood is used for carving. Unusual in the United States but elegantly used in the sculptured gardens at Noong Nooch Botanical Garden in Thailand. Highly recommended as a shade or street tree. Pest resistant.*

APOCYNACEAE

Formerly Asclepiadaceae

MILKWEED SUBFAMILY
This subgroup within the family Apocynaceae includes approximately 240 genera of herbs, shrubs, and climbers, which are widely distributed in tropical and temperate regions. Leaves are simple, entire,

Thevetia ahouai

Thevetia peruviana var. *aurantiaca*

Thevetia thevetioides

Trachelospermum jasminoides

often reduced, and opposite or whorled. This group lacks the characteristic salverform or funnel-shaped corolla of the traditional Apocynaceae genera. Flowers are highly modified. The pollen grains are usually clumped in sticky masses called pollinia (orchids also have pollinia). Upon close inspection, the flower structures are quite marvelous, if not bizarre. The milky sap may be irritating to some people. Milkweeds, familiar wildflowers of the United States, belong in this group. The fruits are paired papery follicles. Silky tufts are attached to the seeds, which are easily carried away in the wind. Most species in this group attract monarch and viceroy butterflies.

Asclepias

Asclepias includes approximately 100 species of herbs, which are widely distributed in temperate and tropical regions. Flowers are rotate (wheel-shaped). The modified stamens and carpels (gynostegium) are descriptively referred to as hoods and horns. Pollen grains are stuck together in clumps (pollinia). Visiting insects depart with a knapsack of pollen rather than a mere dusting. Glands can be found at the base of the leaf midvein. *Asclepias curassavica* is widely cultivated and has become naturalized in the eastern United States. It is a problem in pastures because it is poisonous to livestock. As a larval food, the species helps support the eastern population of monarch butterflies. This should not be surprising since the species is native to the winter territory of the threatened western population of monarchs. *Asclepias physocarpa* was once cultivated in Hawaii for possible commercial use of the silky fiber attached to its seeds and has become naturalized there. The fibers can be used as a downlike stuffing that is lighter than *Ceiba* kapok.

Asclepias curassavica

MEXICAN MILKWEED, BUTTERFLY WEED, BATAL, FLOR DE SEDA ("SILK-FLOWER")
Tropical America; widely naturalized .Short-lived perennial herb to 2 ft.; zones 8–11. Blooms warm months. Moderate moisture. Sandy, well-drained soil. Full to part sun. Flowers: rotate, fleshy, scarlet, selections orange and yellow or all yellow. Leaves: lanceolate, to 4 in. long. *A larval food of the monarch butterfly. Of woodlands, open fields, and coastal areas, but not salt tolerant. Poisonous to livestock. Grown as an annual in temperate regions.*

Asclepias physocarpa

BALLOON COTTON-BUSH, SWAN MILKWEED
Synonym: *Gomphocarpus physocarpus.* Southeast Africa; widely naturalized. Shrubby perennial herb to 6 ft.+; zones 9–11. Blooms warm months. Moderate moisture. Sandy, well-drained soil. Full sun. Flowers: small, hoods (gynostegium) white; capsule a pale green inflated sphere, covered with bristly hairs (setose), to 3 in. diameter; seeds with silky tufts attached. Leaves: lanceolate-linear, 3–4 in. long. *Coastal. The species name alludes to the "bladderlike fruit," a good field mark.*

Calotropis

Calotropis includes 3 species of shrubs or trees from India and Africa. They are sometimes cultivated for their strong fiber and for the downlike silky hairs attached to the seeds and used as stuffing material. They have become naturalized in some areas where they were introduced. Biochemicals are produced from the milky, poisonous latex. The highly modified stigma and stamens (gynostegium) suggest an elaborate crownlike structure in the center of the flower. The globular fruit has a spongy pericarp (Howard, pers. comm.). These xeric plants thrive in hot, dry locations but also do well in humid climates with excellent drainage. Plants are salt tolerant to the dunes.

Calotropis gigantea

CROWN-FLOWER, BOWSTRING HEMP, LECHOSO
Synonym: *Asclepias gigantea.* China to India, Sri Lanka, Indonesia. Evergreen spreading shrub to 15 ft.; zones 10–11. Blooms intermittently in warm months. Moderate moisture to seasonally dry. Gritty, well-drained soil. Full sun. Flowers: rotate, to 1.5 in. wide, lavender. Leaves: obovate, to 8 in. long, woolly, veins light. Stems: covered with white woolly hairs. *Suitable for large containers. Attractive to monarch butterflies. Calotropis procera, widely naturalized in the tropics, is distinguished by its white petals with dark purple tips.*

Cryptostegia

Cryptostegia includes 2 species of shrubby climbers from Africa, India, and Madagascar. These species were sometimes listed as subspecies of *C. grandiflora.* They are distinguished by the characteristics of the corona in the throat. These old-fashioned plants are currently enjoying a small revival. They can be supported on trellises or maintained as spreading shrubs with light pruning. Rubber vines are very salt tolerant and thrive near the beach. They are invasive in Australia. *Cryptostegia* and other latex-producing species were cultivated as a rubber substitute after the rubber supply was cut off by the Japanese occupation of Southeast Asia and Indonesia during World War II. *Hevea* (in Euphorbiaceae), Pará rubber, a native of the Amazon, was cultivated primarily in Asia during the early part of the 20th century (Howard, pers. comm.).

Cryptostegia grandiflora

RUBBER-VINE
Madagascar. Evergreen shrubby, twining climber; zones 10–11. Blooms spring, early summer. Moderate moisture. Average, well-drained soil. Full sun. Flowers: bell-shaped, 2–3 in. long, violet, corona lobes forked and filamentous.

Wrightia arborea

Asclepias curassavica

Asclepias physocarpa, capsule

Calotropis gigantea

Leaves: elliptic, 4–6 in. long, stiff, glossy dark green, veins light green.

Cryptostegia madagascariensis

MADAGASCAR RUBBER-VINE

Synonym: *C. grandiflora* subsp. *madagascariensis*. Madagascar, Seychelles, possibly Mauritius. Evergreen shrubby, twining vine; zones 10–11. Blooms spring, early summer. Moderate moisture. Average, well-drained soil. Full sun. Flowers: bell-shaped, to 2 in. long, violet to deep reddish violet, corona lobes smooth, not forked. Leaves: elliptic, 4–6 in. long, stiff, glossy dark green.

Hoya

Hoya includes 200–230 species of climbers, epiphytes, and shrubs from India, Southeast Asia, Malaysia, Indonesia, and the western Pacific Islands. Collectively known as wax flowers, they are more or less succulent and often xeric. Leaves are waxy and often fleshy. Flowers are star-shaped, waxy or hairy, and in clusters. Plants are easily propagated from cuttings. A number of species are commonly grown as houseplants, in hanging baskets, or in trees in mild climates. Most need plenty of filtered light to bloom well.

Hoya multiflora

SHOOTING-STAR HOYA

Synonym: *Centrostemma multiflorum*. Malaysia, Indonesia, Philippines. Evergreen semiepiphytic shrub or climber; zones 9–11. Blooms intermittently in warm months. Regular moisture and humidity, less when cool. Open, fast-draining bark mix. Bright filtered light. Flowers: star-shaped, perianth lobes reflexed, white, tips greenish yellow, gynostegium orange or purple; in cometlike, semipendent clusters on long stalks, fragrant. Leaves: elliptic, 4–7 in. long, rubbery, glossy green. *An elegant plant with dark green foliage.*

Hoya pottsii

Synonyms: *H. angustifolia*, *H. obscurinervia*. Southern China to northern India. Succulent climber to 10 ft.+; zones 10–11. Blooms in-

termittently in warm months. Regular moisture and humidity, drier when cool. Open, fast-draining bark mix. Full sun to bright filtered light. Flowers: star-shaped, small, cream, gynostegium mauve-purple in center; faintly fragrant; in spherical clusters, to 3 in. wide. Leaves: ovate, to 3 in. long, waxy. *Flowers are clustered along the stems in long garlands.*

Hoya purpureofusca

Indonesia. Evergreen epiphytic vine to 15 ft.; zones 10–11. Blooms intermittently in warm months. Regular moisture and humidity, less when cool. Open, fast-draining bark mix. Full sun to bright filtered light. Flowers: calyx fused, star-shaped, magenta and pink with white margins, hairy, petals smaller, white; in pendent clusters on a long stalk. Leaves: ovate, to 5 in. long, waxy.

Orbea

Orbea includes approximately 20 species of herbs from South Africa. They are endemic to semiarid regions. These species resemble and are closely related to *Stapelia* but differ by the depression in the center of the flower. *Orbea variegata* was among the first South African plants introduced into cultivation in Europe as a great curiosity. Leaves are rudimentary and short-lived, produced at the tips of the fleshy stems, or are sometimes absent. Plants like gritty, open soil. A clump will produce a succession of flowers during warm months. They are easily propagated by division. Orbeas are pollinated by flies attracted by the carrion scent. Plants are suitable for rock gardens and small containers.

Orbea variegata

LITTLE CARRION-FLOWER

Synonym: *Stapelia variegata*. South Africa (Cape Province). Succulent herb, 4–6 in.; zones 9–11. Blooms spring, intermittently in warm months. Moderate moisture to dry. Gritty, well-drained soil. Full sun. Flowers: corolla fused at base into a cup with 5 star-shaped, spreading lobes, to 1.5 in. wide, greenish cream with purple-maroon spots,

corrugated, malodorous; on short stalks, resting on the ground. Leaves: rudimentary, short-lived.

Stems: fleshy, with soft raised nubs along 4 lengthwise ridges, reddish, decumbent.

Cryptostegia grandiflora

Cryptostegia madagascariensis

Hoya multiflora

Hoya pottsii

Hoya purpureofusca

Orbea variegata

Stapelia

Stapelia includes approximately 100 species of succulent perennial herbs from semiarid tropical and subtropical regions of Africa and India. Leaves are rudimentary and short-lived, produced around the tips of the stems, or sometimes lacking. The flowers are star- or bell-shaped, usually solitary, the corolla corrugated and hairy. A small double corona is in the center. Flowers emerge at the bases of the short stems and rest on the ground. The stems are spineless and soft. Stapelias like gritty, open soil and will mound over rocks. Some do well in moist regions if provided excellent drainage. A clump can produce a succession of flowers during warm months. They are easily propagated by division. Stapelias are pollinated by flies attracted by the carrion odor. These fascinating, easy-to-grow, xeric plants are an excellent addition to a rock garden.

Stapelia gigantea

GIANT STARFISH FLOWER, CARRION-FLOWER
Synonym: *S. nobilis*. South Africa, Tanzania, Mozambique. Succulent herb to 12 in.; zones 9–11. Blooms intermittently in warm months. Moderate moisture to fairly dry. Open, well-drained soil. Full sun. Flowers: corolla star-shaped, lobes spreading with a shallow central cup, solitary, 10–12 in. wide, red with pale yellow corrugations lined with long red hairs, malodorous. Leaves: rudimentary, short-lived. Stems: fleshy, 4-ridged, with soft, upright hooks along the ridges, 8–12 in. high. *A pale yellow form was previously referred to as var.* pallida. *'Schwankart' is a commonly grown, almost odorless selection.*

Stapelia grandiflora

STARFISH FLOWER, CARRION-FLOWER
Synonym: *S. ambigua*. South Africa. Succulent herb to 12 in.; zones 9–11. Blooms intermittently in warm months. Moderate moisture to fairly dry. Open, well-drained soil. Full sun. Flowers: corolla spreading, lobes star-shaped, to 6 in. wide, solitary, spreading, almost flat, blood red with transverse cor-

rugations and purplish hairs, undersides red to greenish, malodorous. Leaves: short-lived, rudimentary. Stems: fleshy, 4-angled lengthwise with soft, upright hooks along the ridges, 6–10 in. high. *Flowers are smaller than those of* S. gigantea.

Stapelia leendertziae

ZULU GIANT
Synonym: *S. wilmaniae*. Northeastern South Africa. Succulent herb to 12 in.; zones 9–11. Blooms intermittently in warm months. Moderate moisture to fairly dry. Open, well-drained soil. Full sun. Flowers: corolla deeply bell-shaped, lobes short, pointed, covered with fleshy corrugations inside, eggplant-purple, to 5 in. deep, 3 in. wide, malodorous; produced at the base of the stem and resting on the ground. Leaves: rudimentary, short-lived. Stems: fleshy, 4 lengthwise ridges covered with soft, raised nubs, 6–10 in. high.

Stephanotis

Stephanotis includes approximately 5 twining climbers from the Old World. Leaves are simple and smooth. *Stephanotis floribunda* is an old-fashioned, sweet-scented garden vine whose flowers are used in bridal bouquets. They are moth-pollinated at night in their native habitat. *Stephanotis* roots are heat-sensitive, and vines should be grown on arbors or fences with their "heads in the sun and their feet in a shady spot." Light filtration from a high canopy is ideal in hot weather. Propagate from seed or

cuttings. Not aggressive. Growing in containers is recommended where nematodes are a problem.

Stephanotis floribunda

BRIDAL-WREATH, MADAGASCAR JESSAMINE, FLORADORA, ESTEFANOTE, FLOR DE NOVIA
Synonym: *Marsdenia floribunda*. Madagascar. Evergreen twining climber, 15–20 ft.; zones 10–11. Blooms intermittently in warm months. Seasonally moist in summer, dry in winter. Sandy, well-drained soil. Slightly filtered midday sun. Flowers: salverform, white, tube 2–3 in. long, sometimes tinged red, lobes short, flaring, fragrant; in clusters of 4–8. Leaves: ovate to elliptic, rubbery, slightly dull dark green.

AQUIFOLIACEAE

HOLLY FAMILY
Aquifoliaceae includes a single

Stapelia gigantea

genus of trees and shrubs, which are widely distributed. Hollies are common landscape trees in temperate zones. Tropical species are equally attractive, with dark green foliage and ornamental berries, but are underutilized in landscaping. Leaf extracts of certain species are used in beverages; Paraguayan tea (*mate* in Spanish) is a high-caffeine drink made from *Ilex paraguariensis*. Leaves are simple, entire, usually evergreen, leathery, and usually in whorls. Flowers are unisexual, with male and female flowers on different plants (dioecious). Petals and sepals are 4–6, sometimes 8. The corolla is sometimes absent.

Ilex

Ilex includes approximately 400 species of trees and shrubs, which are widely distributed. Leaves are simple with more or less sharply toothed margins. Female and male

Stapelia gigantea, light form

Stapelia grandiflora

Stapelia leendertziae

Stephanotis floribunda

flowers are usually on different trees (dioecious). Female trees bear small red, yellow, or black berries. Holly is associated with holiday decoration in temperate regions, retaining red berries into winter. Tropical species fruit at different times but should not be overlooked. *Ilex cassine*, a native of coastal South Florida and Cuba, is highly recommended as an attractive, subtropical landscape plant and can handle seasonally wet locations but also thrives in drier conditions. Plant several individuals to ensure a few berry-bearing female trees. Grafting is another means to ensure trees with berries. Florida holly, *Schinus terebinthifolius* (in Anacardiaceae), is an invasive relative of poison ivy and not a true holly.

Ilex cassine

DAHOON HOLLY

Cuba, Florida. Evergreen tree to 30 ft.+; zones 7–11. Blooms late summer, fall. Seasonally moist to wet/dry. Average soil. Full to part sun. Flowers: unisexual, small, white; berries red. Leaves: oblong, 3–4 in. long, dark green; margins with widely spaced, soft prickles. *Highly recommended for lowland landscaping. Tolerates periodic flooding with fresh or brackish water. While narrowly erect in coastal forests, it has a more spreading crown when grown in open locations. Contains high amounts of caffeine, a heart stimulant that can be toxic if ingested in concentrated form.*

ARACEAE

AROID FAMILY, ARUM FAMILY

Araceae includes approximately 108 terrestrial, epiphytic, and climbing herbs plus a few aquatics, which are widely distributed in tropical and temperate regions. The flowers are greatly reduced and crowded onto a cylindrical spadix, usually surrounded by a bractlike, often showy, spathe. Some temperate species are familiarly known as Jack-in-the-pulpit. Tubers of some species are eaten as starchy vegetables in the tropics after cooking. Fully ripe compound fruits of *Monstera deliciosa* are edible fresh, a sweet-tart blend the texture of bananas with a fragrance of coconut

and pineapple, a ready-made piña colada. Leaves are usually simple, often lobed or variegated. Some species produce adventitious roots for climbing. Flowers are bisexual, or unisexual with male and female flowers on the same plant (monoecious) or occasionally on separate plants (dioecious). The fruit is usually a red or yellow berry or syncarp. The sap often contains oxalates, which can cause a burning inflammation of the skin or serious swelling of mucous membranes if eaten. Sodium bicarbonate (baking soda) as a paste or in water is an excellent first aid to neutralize the burn. Other poisonous compounds are often present.

Aglaonema

Aglaonema includes approximately 21 species of evergreen herbs from tropical Asia. They are clump-forming terrestrial plants. In Asia they are thought to bring good fortune. Aglaonemas have a wide range of leaf variegation within local populations. These variations were once listed as varieties; however, botanists have determined that these natural variations are too widespread to qualify as varieties (Boyce, pers. comm.). Fanciers converted the former varietal names into cultivar names where the use of Latin made them invalid. These selections are properly listed as common names until a valid cultivar name has been registered. Aglaonema leaves have stem-sheathing petioles that often impart a white translucence to the stem. This helps distinguish these species from *Dieffenbachia* species with canelike stems. The inflorescences are slender and fairly inconspicuous. Usually weak-stemmed, they gradually recline from their own weight, sending up new shoots from the nodes, soon forming large clumps outdoors. In moist locations, they thrive with little care in plentiful mulch under trees. Aglaonemas are commonly grown in containers.

Aglaonema commutatum

SILVER QUEEN AGLAONEMA, CHINESE EVERGREEN

Synonym: *A. commutatum* 'Silver Queen' (hort.) .Southeast Asia, Su-

lawesi (Celebes). Evergreen herb, 2–3 ft.; zones 10–11. Blooms intermittently in warm months. Regular moisture and humidity. Fertile, sandy, humus-rich, well-drained soil. Medium to bright filtered light. Flowers: unisexual; spathe white. Leaves: elliptic, to 12 in. long, blade mottled green and white in regular patterns. *Clump-forming medium ground cover in bright understory to medium shade. Because this is the type form, cultivar names like 'Silver Queen' are inappropriately applied (Boyce, pers. comm.).*

Aglaonema costatum

FOX'S AGLAONEMA, CHINESE EVERGREEN

Synonyms: *A. costatum* var. *foxii*, *A. costatum* 'Foxii' (hort.). India, Southeast Asia, Malaysia. Evergreen herb, 1–1.5 ft.; zones 10–11. Blooms intermittently in warm

months. Regular moisture and humidity. Fertile, sandy, humus-rich, well-drained soil. Medium to bright filtered light. Flowers: unisexual; spathe white to greenish. Leaves: ovate, to 8 in. long, blade dark green with white spots or solid green, midvein usually white. *Habit low and spreading.*

Aglaonema 'Peacock'

CHINESE EVERGREEN

Garden origin. Evergreen herb, 2–3 ft.; zones 10–11. Blooms intermittently in warm months. Regular moisture and humidity. Fertile, sandy, humus-rich, well-drained soil. Medium to bright filtered light. Flowers: unisexual; spadix white; spathe white. Leaves: ovate, to 8 in. long; blade irregularly mottled dark, medium, and light green; midvein light green. *Striking leaves resemble certain* Dieffenbachia *species.*

Ilex cassine

Aglaonema costatum

Aglaonema commutatum

Aglaonema 'Peacock'

Alocasia

Alocasia includes approximately 70 species of medium to large herbs from tropical rain forests of Southeast Asia, Indomalaysia, and the Philippines to northeastern Australia. Plants are evergreen or seasonally dormant during dry months. A number of cultivars are grown for their showy foliage. The petiole is sometimes attached to the underside of the blade (peltate) in juvenile leaves but is often attached to the blade margin in adult leaves. Flowers are unisexual, with male flowers located above a ring of sterile flowers separating them from the female flowers, which are on the lower spadix and are enclosed by the base of the spathe. The spadix has a sterile apex (appendix). *Alocasia macrorrhizos*, giant taro or dasheen, is a food staple in the islands of the South Pacific. The starchy rhizomes must be cooked before they are edible.

Alocasia ×amazonica

Garden hybrid, *A. sanderiana* × *A. longiloba* var. *grandis*. Evergreen herb; zones 10–11. Blooms warm months. Regular moisture and humidity. Fertile, sandy, humus-rich, well-drained soil. Medium to bright filtered light. Flowers: unisexual. Leaves: sagittate, 1–2 ft. long, to 1 ft. wide, basal lobes large and pointed, dark green; veins white, widely spaced; margins white with large teeth; peltate.

Alocasia cuprea

GIANT CALADIUM

Malaysia, Borneo. Evergreen herb to 4 ft.; zones 10–11. Blooms warm months. Regular moisture and humidity. Fertile, sandy, humus-rich, well-drained soil. Medium to bright filtered light. Flowers: unisexual. Leaves: broadly ovate, basal lobes almost continuous, the sinus shallow, silvery green with darker depressed veins, undersides purple.

Alocasia longiloba

Synonym: *A. lowii*. Borneo. Evergreen herb to 2.5 ft.; zones 10–11. Blooms warm months. Regular moisture and humidity. Fertile, sandy, humus-rich, well-drained soil. Medium to bright filtered light. Flowers: unisexual. Leaves: sagittate, to 2 ft. long, basal lobes long and pointed, blade silvery dark green with feathery white veins; margins undulate; peltate.

Alocasia macrorrhizos

GIANT TARO, GIANT ALOCASIA, ELEPHANT-EAR

Synonyms: *A. alba*, *Colocasia indica*. Origin obscure (probably tropical Asia and Pacific Islands where it is widely distributed). Evergreen herb to 15 ft.; zones 10–11. Blooms warm months. Regular moisture and humidity. Fertile, sandy, humus-rich, well-drained soil. Part sun to bright filtered light. Flowers: unisexual. Leaves: broadly sagittate, green or variegated white, gray, and green, blade 2–5 ft. long, not peltate. Sometimes develops a trunklike stem. *The starchy rhizome is a staple in Asia (similar to* Colocasia esculenta). 'New Guinea Gold' *has dark green blades with golden-yellow veins and stems.*

Alocasia macrorrhizos, inflorescence

Alocasia macrorrhizos 'New Guinea Gold'

Alocasia ×*amazonica*

Alocasia cuprea

Alocasia longiloba

Alocasia macrorrhizos 'Variegata'

Alocasia micholitziana
GREEN-VELVET ALOCASIA
Synonyms: *A.* 'Green Velvet'
(hort.), *A. micholitzii*. Philippines.
Evergreen herb to 1.5 ft.; zones
10–11. Blooms warm months.
Moderate moisture and humidity.
Fertile, humus-rich, well-drained
soil. Bright filtered light to bright
shade. Flowers: unisexual; spathe
and spadix greenish white, inconspicuous. Leaves: sagittate, velvety
dark green, larger veins greenish
white, smaller veins inconspicuous; margins sinuate. *Because this
is the type form, a cultivar name is inappropriate (Boyce, pers. comm.).
The velvety, strongly marked foliage
provides striking contrast in understory locations.*

Alocasia plumbea
Synonyms: *A. indica* var. *metallica*,
A. macrorrhizos var. *rubra*. India to
Indonesia (Java). Evergreen herb,
5–8 ft.; zones 10–11. Blooms warm
months. Regular moisture and humidity. Fertile, sandy, humus-rich,
well-drained soil. Medium to bright
filtered light. Flowers: unisexual;
spadix white; spathe canoe-shaped,
white, tinted purple on the back.
Leaves: sagittate, lobes long, silvery
green above, rumpled; underside
purple; petioles purple.

Alocasia portei
Synonym: *Schizocasia portei*. Sri
Lanka, Thailand, Philippines. Evergreen treelike herb to 10 ft.+; zone
11. Blooms warm months. Regular
moisture and humidity. Fertile,
sandy, humus-rich, well-drained
soil. Medium to bright filtered light.
Flowers: unisexual; spadix 12–16
in. long; spathe funnel-shaped,
creamy white to green, enclosing
the base of the spadix, erect, then
drooping with the weight of the
golden-yellow fruits. Leaves: sagittate, to 6 ft. long, deeply lobed,
metallic green; margins wavy; petiole streaked purple. *Develops a
thick, trunklike stalk. The lilylike inflorescences develop at the base of the
leaves. Cold-sensitive.*

Alocasia zebrina
Philippines. Evergreen herb, 3–4
ft.; zones 10–11. Blooms warm
months. Regular moisture and

humidity. Fertile, sandy, humus-
rich, well-drained soil. Medium to
bright filtered light. Flowers: unisexual; spadix white; spathe canoe-
shaped, green. Leaves: blade
broadly sagittate, to 1 ft. long; petiole reticulated with green to brown
markings, to 2 ft. long.

Amorphophallus
Amorphophallus includes approximately 180 species of seasonally
dormant herbs from Southeast
Asia, the western Pacific Islands,
and Africa. Titan-arum, *A. titanum*,
is one of the great curiosities of the
plant world with its large, spectacular inflorescence. Once rare in cultivation, it is now displayed at a
number of botanical gardens. The
inflorescence emerges in spring,
before the leaves, from a large underground corm. As the flowers

mature, the spathe slowly unfurls
its maroon Elizabethan collar. The
female flowers, hidden inside, at
the base of the spadix, open first
emitting a pungent, fetid aroma
that attracts carrion beetles and
lasts from a few hours to a day.
When the female flowers are no
longer receptive, male flowers
above them open, avoiding self-
pollination. Most of the upper part
of the spadix is a giant hollow appendix. After flowering the inflorescence collapses and one immense
umbrella-like leaf emerges from the
tuber. The blade has 3 main lobes
that are much subdivided; the petiole is up to 15 ft. tall depending on
the size of the tuber. The plant
again becomes dormant in late
summer (or the dry season). In the
wild, it grows on limestone outcroppings in seasonally moist/dry

woodlands. Despite their notoriously malodorous moments, *Amorphophallus* species have an exotic
allure that draws an enthusiastic
following—from little boys to refined ladies with dainty hankies
pressed to their noses. In temperate climates, the resting tubers are
stored indoors in winter.

Amorphophallus bulbifer
Synonym: *Arum bulbiferum*. India,
Myanmar (Burma), Sub-Himalayan
Asia. Seasonally dormant herb;
zones 9–11. Blooms spring. Seasonally moist/dry when dormant.
Fertile, well-drained soil; alkaline
pH. Bright filtered light. Flowers:
spadix creamy white; spathe upright; margins revolute, pink with
gray speckles to 16 in. high; on a 6-
in. spotted pedicel. Leaf: blade 3-
lobed, much subdivided. *A fairly*

Alocasia micholitziana

Alocasia plumbea

Alocasia plumbea, inflorescence

Alocasia portei, infructescence

Alocasia zebrina, inflorescence

common amorphophallus redolent of overripe fruit when female flowers are receptive (Allen, pers. comm.).

Amorphophallus gigas

GIANT ARUM, LEOPARD-PALM
Indonesia (Sumatra). Seasonally dormant herb to 15 ft.; zone 11. Blooms summer. Moist and humid during active growth, dry when dormant. Fertile, well-drained soil; alkaline pH. Part sun, bright filtered light. Flowers: unisexual, malodorous; spadix purple-maroon, apex pointed, 2–3 ft.; spathe funnel-shaped, brown-black; on a very tall green stalk with white spots, to 10 ft.+. Leaf: solitary, blade 3-parted, deeply lobed or divided; petiole to 10 ft., white spotted.

Amorphophallus lambii

Malaysia, Borneo. Seasonally dormant herb to 9 ft.; zone 11. Blooms spring. Moist and humid during active growth, dry when dormant. Fertile, well-drained soil; alkaline pH. Part sun, bright filtered light. Flowers: unisexual; spadix slender, maroon, to 12 in. high; spathe vase-shaped, green with faint maroon veins. Leaf: solitary, deeply lobed, 3–4 ft. long; petiole purple. *Differs from A. tinekeae in the minutia of the flowers (Hetterscheid, pers. comm.).*

Amorphophallus paeonii-folius

VOODOO LILY, ELEPHANT-YAM, TALINGO POTATO
Synonyms: A. campanulatus, Hydro-sme gigantiflorus. India to New Guinea. Seasonally dormant perennial herb, 4–6 ft.; zones 8–11. Blooms spring. Moist and humid during active growth, dry when dormant. Fertile, well-drained soil. Bright filtered light. Flowers: unisexual; spadix reddish brown, appendix crumpled as if under-inflated; spathe funnel-shaped, gray with white spots, green near the base, partly enfolding the spadix; stalkless. Leaves: 1 or 2, blade 3-lobed, deeply divided, 3–5 ft.; petiole white spotted.

Amorphophallus prainii

Indonesia (Sumatra), Malaysia. Seasonally dormant tuberous herb to 3 ft.+; zones 10–11. Blooms spring. Evenly moist and humid during active growth, dry when dormant. Fertile, well-drained soil; alkaline pH. Bright filtered light. Flowers: yellow on lower spadix; spadix appendix creamy white, pointed, rumpled; spathe cuplike, rim revolute, creamy white with purplish streaks. Leaves: basal, usually solitary, blade much dissected; petiole spotted. *Tubers are* eaten in Malaysia after cooking and other preparation.

Amorphophallus titanum

TITAN-ARUM
Synonym: A. selebicus. Indonesia (Sumatra). Seasonally dormant herb to 15 ft.; zone 11. Blooms spring, early summer. Evenly moist and humid during active growth, little when dormant. Fertile, well-drained soil; alkaline pH. Bright filtered light. Flowers: unisexual, enclosed by spathe, female flowers malodorous when receptive; ap-

Amorphophallus gigas, inflorescence

Amorphophallus titanum

Amorphophallus bulbifer, inflorescence

Amorphophallus lambii

Amorphophallus paeoniifolius

Amorphophallus prainii

pendix conical, creamy tan, inflated; spathe green, deeply furrowed, enclosing the spadix until the maroon-purple collar unfurls at maturity, rim golden. Leaf: solitary, umbrella-like, blade 3-lobed, deeply divided; petiole erect to 12 ft., reticulated green and white. *Photo of "Mr. Stinky's" second bloom, inflorescence over 6.5 ft. tall, May 2001, at Fairchild Tropical Garden.*

Anthurium

Anthurium includes approximately 1000 species of creeping, climbing, semiepiphytic to epiphytic herbs from tropical America. This group is widely cultivated and frequently hybridized. Most cultivated plants of *A. andraeanum* and *A. scherzerianum* are mass-produced clones of uncertain ancestry. Forms without verifiable ancestry should be referred to respectively as *A. ×cultorum* and *A. ×hortulanum* (Birdsey, pers. comm.). Leaves are usually entire, sometimes hastate or deeply divided. "Bird's-nest" type anthuriums are a distinctive subgroup with rosettes of large, oblanceolate basal leaves and very short petioles. Flowers are bisexual, sometimes scented. In air-conditioned or heated buildings with insufficient humidity, move container plants outside in mild weather and mist as often as possible. In warm climates, grow plants outdoors in sandy, humus-rich loam.

Anthurium bakeri

Southern Mexico, Guatemala. Evergreen epiphytic herb; zones 10–11. Blooms warm months. Regular moisture and humidity. Fertile, humus-rich, well-drained soil. Bright to medium filtered light. Flowers: bisexual; spadix creamy; spathe narrow, greenish yellow, reflexed; berries red on a pendent stalk. Leaves: strap-shaped, 20–30 in. long, to 2 in. wide, lax, leathery. *Grow this cascading epiphyte in a strong basket or attached to a tree limb.*

Anthurium bonplandii var. guayanum

BIRD'S-NEST ANTHURIUM
Venezuela (Guiana Highlands). Evergreen semiepiphytic herb to 6

ft.; zones 10–11. Blooms warm months. Regular moisture and humidity. Soil-less or in bark orchid medium. Bright filtered light. Flowers: bisexual; spadix purple, slender, to 10 in. long; spathe spear-shaped, reflexed; berries red. Leaves: broadly oblanceolate, guttered; petioles short; in basal whorls; margins entire, undulate. *Support with rocks or in a heavy pot without soil. The funnel-shaped foliage gutters fine debris and water to the vellum-covered aerial roots at the base. Use liquid or slow-release fertilizers. Slow-growing.*

Anthurium clarinervium

Southern Mexico. Evergreen climbing herb; zones 10–11. Blooms warm months. Evenly moist and humid. Fertile, humus-rich, well-drained soil. Bright filtered light.

Flowers: bisexual; spadix and spathe slender, light green, recurved; fruit yellow. Leaves: broadly cordate, to 16 in. long, basal lobes overlapping, silvery dark green with light veins.

Anthurium ×cultorum

FLAMINGO-FLOWER, ANTURIO
Synonyms: *A. andraeanum* (hort.), *A. ×ferrierense*. Garden hybrids, *A. andraeanum × ?*. Evergreen semiclimbing herbs; zones 10–11. Blooms intermittently when nights are cool. Regular moisture and humidity. Fertile, humus-rich, well-drained soil. Bright filtered light. Flowers: bisexual; spadix red, yellow, orange, or white; spathe cordate, glossy with a hammered-metal (bullate) texture, red, deep red, scarlet, or white. Leaves: cordate, more or less elongated de-

pending on ancestry. *Plants in cultivation are mostly complex hybrids involving* A. andraeanum, *which originated in mountainous regions of Colombia and Ecuador. They do not bloom reliably where night temperatures are warm.*

Anthurium ×hortulanum

PIGTAIL-ANTHURIUM, TAIL-FLOWER, ANTURIO
Garden origin, *A. scherzerianum × ?*. Evergreen herb under 1 ft.; zones 10–11. Blooms when nights are cool. Regular moisture and humidity. Fertile, sandy, humus-rich, well-drained soil. Bright filtered light. Flowers: bisexual; spadix slender, twisted, orange to scarlet; spathe scarlet to red, recurved. Leaves: lanceolate to long cordate. *A mass-produced hybrid involving* A. scherzerianum *(commonly misspelled*

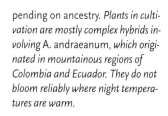

Anthurium bakeri

Anthurium bonplandii var. guayanum

Anthurium clarinervium

Anthurium ×cultorum, red form

Anthurium ×cultorum, white form

Anthurium 'Midori'

scherzeranum), a Costa Rican species from montane cloud-forests. Not a dependable bloomer where night temperatures are warm.

Anthurium hybrids

ANTHURIUM HYBRIDS, ANTURIO
Garden hybrids. Evergreen semi-climbing herbs; zones 10–11. Blooms intermittently when nights are cool. Regular moisture and humidity. Fertile, sandy, humus-rich, well-drained soil. Bright filtered light. Flowers: bisexual; spadix variously colored depending on ancestry; spathe in various shapes and colors depending on ancestry. Leaves: mostly hastate. *These hybrids may involve* A. andraeanum. *'Midori' is known as green goddess anthurium. 'Obake' has a multicolored, hastate spathe. 'Trinidad' is a better bloomer in areas with warm*

night temperatures than many hybrids.

Caladium

Caladium includes approximately 12 species of seasonally dormant herbs from South America and the West Indies. Many selections are cultivated for their brightly marked leaves. The leaves are ovate or hastate. Markings range from scattered spots to mottled color zones. Flowers are unisexual, the female flowers below, male above on the same inflorescence (monoecious). The sheathing spathe enfolds the spadix and is constricted below the middle. Cultivated plants of uncertain ancestry involving *C. bicolor* should be referred to collectively as *C. ×hortulanum* (Birdsey, pers. comm.). The genus has been revised several times, but the standing of various

forms and taxa is still unsettled. In temperate zones the ovoid tubers are lifted and stored indoors in winter. The sap may be irritating.

Caladium ×hortulanum

CALADIUM, ANGEL-WINGS, ELEPHANT-EAR
Synonym: *C. bicolor* (hort.). Garden origin. Seasonally dormant herbs to about 2 ft.; zones 10–11. Blooms warm months. Regular moisture and humidity during active growth, dry when dormant. Fertile, well-drained soil; slightly acid pH. Full sun to part shade. Flowers: unisexual; spadix green or white; spathe greenish white or variously spotted, constricted near the middle. Leaves: hastate to lanceolate, green variously marked red and white, usually peltate. *Excellent for color in shady spots where many flowering*

plants will not bloom but also adapts to full sun with adequate moisture.

Caladium lindenii

CALADIUM, ANGEL-WINGS
Colombia. Seasonally dormant herb, 1–2 ft.; zones 10–11. Blooms spring. Regular moisture and humidity during active growth, dry when dormant. Fertile, well-drained soil; slightly acid pH. Full sun to part shade. Flowers: unisexual; spadix green; spathe white. Leaves: sagittate; veins white, midvein hairy; petiole attached to margin, not peltate.

Colocasia

Colocasia includes approximately 6 species of evergreen and seasonally dormant herbs from tropical America, India, Southeast Asia, and peninsular Malaysia. The number of species has not been firmly established. Plants range from small and stemless to treelike (arborescent). Petioles are attached to the lower surface of the blade (peltate), which helps distinguish these species from *Alocasia*, but some *Alocasia* species have peltate leaves at least when young. The starchy tubers and young leaves of taro, *C. esculenta*, are important food staples in Asia and the Pacific Islands. The tubers must be properly prepared and cooked before eating. These humble tubers have arrived on mainland U.S. supermarket shelves as overpriced "exotic" chips. Taro starch is used in plastic grocery bags to improve biodegradability. Numerous selections are cultivated for their fancy foliage. Distributed with prehistoric human interisland migrations, taro preceded rice as the basic staple in tropical Asia and Oceania. It is a variable cultigen. Wild populations are probably reintroductions.

Colocasia esculenta

TARO, ELEPHANT-EAR, DASHEEN
Synonyms: *Colocasia antiquorum*, *Caladium esculentum*. Exact origin obscure (probably mainland and maritime Southeast Asia); widely cultivated. Semiaquatic herb to 4 ft.; zones 8–11. Blooms intermittently in warm months. Evenly moist and humid or aquatic. Fer-

Anthurium 'Obake'

Anthurium 'Trinidad'

Anthurium ×hortulanum

Caladium ×hortulanum

Caladium lindenii

Colocasia esculenta 'Black Knight'

tile, well-drained soil; slightly acid pH. Full sun. Flowers: unisexual; spathe greenish white, inflated at the base; inflorescence on a short stalk (stipe). Leaves: hastate, blade tilted forward (deflexed), peltate. *The large tubers are edible when cooked. Confine to containers and enclosed water gardens. Do not plant in open bodies of water where they can become invasive.*

Cyrtosperma

Cyrtosperma includes approximately 12 species of evergreen herbs from Malaysia, Indonesia, the Philippines, and New Guinea. Species range from creepers to treelike (arborescent) or climbing. Leaves are simple, sagittate or hastate, and sometimes divided. Petioles and the underside of the main leaf veins are usually covered with prickles. Flowers are bisexual. The spathe is hooded, purple to white, sometimes narrowly elongated. These are plants of moist rain forest and wetlands. They are quite cold-sensitive.

Cyrtosperma johnstonii

Indomalaysia to the South Pacific islands. Evergreen climbing herb; zone 11. Blooms intermittently. Moist to wet, humid. Fertile, humus-rich soil. Bright filtered light. Flowers: bisexual. Leaves: hastate, basal lobes pointed, green with red veins; petiole and underside of veins prickled. *Suitable for growing in shallow ponds. Unusual in cultivation.*

Dieffenbachia

Dieffenbachia includes at least 50 (but probably many more) species of evergreen herbs from Central and northern South America and the West Indies. They have canelike, unbranched stems. Many fancy-leafed cultivars exist, generally of uncertain ancestry, with bold green-and-white markings. The lower half of the petiole sheathes the stem. Older leaves are shed revealing an erect, canelike stalk (this helps distinguish them from aglaonemas). If stems become tall and ungainly, the cane can be cut and rooted. Flowers are unisexual. The lower half of the spathe is fused to the female section of the spadix. The upper half is hooded, reflexing when the male flowers mature. A short sterile zone separates the fertile flowers.

These are herbs of moist woodlands, streambanks, and marshes. Dieffenbachias are suitable for containers. Though sometimes listed as very cold-sensitive, they thrive outdoors in South Florida in protected locations as long as moisture is reduced in cool weather. Dieffenbachias may have acquired the name dumb-cane because ingesting any part causes severe swelling of the throat and irritation of the digestive tract (but not unique to this genus). This reaction is due to oxalate crystals in the sap. First aid is baking soda (bicarbonate of soda) sprinkled directly on the skin or drunk dissolved in a glass of water.

Dieffenbachia cultivars
DIEFFENBACHIA, DUMB-CANE
Selections or hybrids of unknown ancestry. Evergreen herbs to about 4 ft.; zones 10–11. Bloom spring. Regular moisture and humidity when warm, drier when cool. Fertile, well-drained soil. Bright filtered light. Flowers: unisexual; spathe greenish to white. Leaves: elliptic, variously mottled white, cream, and light and dark green; margins usually green. *Cultivars have various leaf patterns. They are sometimes used as foliage in florists' arrangements.*

Dracontium

Dracontium includes approximately 23 seasonally dormant herbs from Costa Rica to the western Amazon basin and Surinam. The inflorescence emerges before the leaves from underground corms. It has usually only a single 3-lobed leaf, which is umbrella-like and much subdivided. The petiole is prickly. Dracontiums are unusual in cultivation but much prized by collectors of strange and unusual species. They superficially resemble the Old World genus *Amorphophallus*, but *Dracontium* has bisexual flowers and the spadix lacks an appendix. Flowers are malodorous during the short time they are receptive. The spathes are stalkless and usually dark in color. These species grow naturally in woodland understory in layers of well-rotted leaf mold. The location of the corm should be marked to avoid stepping on the inflorescence when it emerges in spring.

Dracontium soconuscum

Synonym: *D. dressleri*. Brazil. Seasonally dormant herb, 6–7 ft.; zones 10–11. Blooms spring. Moderate moisture in warm months, dry in cool. Fertile, humus-rich, well-drained soil. Moderate shade. Flowers: bisexual; spadix short, thick, dark brown; spathe cup-shaped, hooded, dark brown, velvety on the outside, lustrous inside. Leaves: 3-lobed, deeply divided and subdivided, to 3 ft. wide; on an erect petiole, 3–5 ft.+ tall, becoming larger as the corm grows.

Epipremnum

Epipremnum includes approximately 18 species of mostly climb-

Colocasia esculenta 'Imperialis'

Cyrtosperma johnstonii

Dieffenbachia 'Star Bright'

Dracontium soconuscum

Dieffenbachia 'Tropic Marianne'

ing herbs from Indomalaysia to Fiji and Australia. *Epipremnum aureum* is frequently grown indoors and often included in live arrangements. Like *E. pinnatum*, it produces juvenile and adult leaf forms. It rarely produces flowers, probably because it multiplies so successfully vegetatively. The common houseplant is the juvenile form with small, heart-shaped leaves. When plants are confined to containers, the leaves do not develop the adult configuration. Outdoors the adult leaves soon grow larger, eventually becoming deeply cut along the margins. *Epipremnum aureum* has been through several name revisions and is usually sold as *E. pinnatum* 'Aureum'. The 2 species are considered distinct by current authorities (Boyce, pers. comm.). The leaves of *E. aureum* are variegated with bold yellow streaks; those of *E. pinnatum* are all green. They are arranged in opposite ranks that spiral around the stem (spirally distichous). Both species are highly invasive and controlled in Florida. Cuttings should not be planted or discarded outdoors. The aptly named devil's ivy quickly takes over trees, which can break from the weight, and is difficult to eradicate once established.

Epipremnum aureum
DEVIL'S IVY, HUNTER'S ROBE, VARIEGATED POTHOS
Synonyms: *E. pinnatum* 'Aureum', *Pothos aureus*, *Scindapsus aureus*. Solomon Islands. Evergreen climbing to semiepiphytic herb; zones 10–11. Blooms rarely. Seasonally moist/moderate. Most soils to semiepiphytic. Full sun to shade. Leaves: juvenile form cordate, dull to glossy green, sometimes streaked yellow, 2–10 in. long; margins entire; adult form irregularly cut (pinnatifid) and boldly streaked yellow, to 1–2 ft. long. *Current revision segregates* E. pinnatum *as a distinct species (Boyce, pers. comm.). Aggressive wherever cultivated. Controlled in South Florida.*

Epipremnum pinnatum
DEVIL'S IVY, POTHOS
Synonym: *Rhaphidophora pinnata*. Indomalaysia, New Guinea, Aus-

tralia. Evergreen climbing to semi-epiphytic herb; zones 10–11. Blooms rarely. Seasonally moist/moderate. Most soils to semiepiphytic. Full sun to shade. Leaves: juvenile form cordate, 2–10 in. long, glossy green; adult form deeply and fairly regularly lobed or cut (pinnatifid), occasionally with small perforations, to 2 ft. long. *Current revision distinguishes this species from* E. aureum *(Boyce, pers. comm.).*

Gonatopus
Gonatopus includes approximately 5 species of seasonally dormant herbs from southeastern Africa. Their natural habitat is seasonally moist/dry deciduous forest understory. Leaves are usually 3-lobed, the lobes pinnately divided. Flowers are unisexual, the female flowers located at the base of the spadix and separated from the male flowers above by a ring of sterile flowers.

Gonatopus boivinii
Tanzania, tropical eastern Africa. Seasonally dormant herb, 4–6 ft.; zones 10–11. Blooms spring. Moist during active growth, little when dormant. Average, well-drained soil. Bright filtered light. Flowers: unisexual; spadix creamy white;

spathe mottled gray and white, reflexed. Leaves: 3-lobed, the lobes pinnately divided; leaflets ovate to elliptic; margins with a few isolated teeth. Stems: mottled gray and white "snakeskin"; another form has bright green stems. *This species, with pinnately arranged leaflets, is easily mistaken for a woody shrub. Tends to become weedy in amenable conditions.*

Homalomena
Homalomena includes approximately 135 species of evergreen perennial herbs from tropical Asia and the Pacific Islands, plus about 12 species from tropical America. A few are occasionally cultivated. Homalomenas sometimes have an anise (licorice-like) scent. Leaves of the Asian species are smooth, unarmed, and extremely variable in shape, even on the same plant, while leaves of the American species usually have hairs and prickles. The petioles have sheathing bases. The stem is very short or sometimes subterranean. The spathe is cylindrical, almost enclosing the spadix.

Epipremnum aureum, juvenile form

Gonatopus boivinii

Epipremnum aureum, adult form

Epipremnum pinnatum

Homalomena rubescens

Indonesia (Java), Myanmar (Burma) to northeastern India. Evergreen herb to 5 ft.; zones 10–11. Blooms intermittently in warm months. Regular moisture and humidity. Fertile, sandy, humus-rich, well-drained soil. Bright filtered light. Flowers: unisexual, female flowers reddish, male flowers white; spathe crimson; inflorescence solitary. Leaves: elongated cordate, to 14 in. long, dark glossy green, lighter below; veins reddish; petioles reddish, to 2 ft. long. *The striking red spathe may be hidden by foliage. A few leaves may be removed for better display.*

Monstera

Monstera includes approximately 40 semiepiphytic herbs from tropical America. They come from wet and seasonally moist/dry habitats. The juvenile leaves are simple to lobed. Adult leaves often develop deeply cut margins and/or large perforations within the blade. Plants in containers usually retain the juvenile form. At one time different species names were mistakenly given to juvenile and adult forms. Monsteras are strong climbers, sending down aerial roots from the nodes. Climbing is a light-seeking adaptation that also serves to raise these plants above seasonal flood waters. The fibrous stems are tough and survive cold and even light frost though the leaf edges may turn brown. Propagated from stem sections that include 3 or 4 nodes with a few roots attached.

Monstera adansonii

SWISS CHEESE PLANT, TARO-VINE
Synonym: *M. pertusa* (misapplied). Central America to Brazil, Lesser Antilles. Evergreen climber; zones 10–11. Blooms intermittently in warm months. Seasonally moist and humid, drier when cool. Average to fertile, well-drained soil. Bright broken or filtered light. Flowers: bisexual; spadix white; spathe white, hooded, falling when flowers mature, 6–8 in. tall. Leaves: broadly oblong, to 3 ft. long, tilted forward (deflexed); blade with irregular, elongated perforations which occasionally break through the otherwise entire margin.

Monstera deliciosa

MONSTERA, CERIMAN, BALAZOS ("BULLET HOLES")
Mexico, Central America. Evergreen creeping or climbing herb; zones 9–11. Blooms warm months. Seasonally moist/dry. Humus-rich, well-drained soil. Part sun to bright filtered light. Flowers: bisexual; spadix thick, white; spathe creamy white, hooded, to 1 ft. high. Leaves: ovate, to 3 ft. long, glossy, tilted forward (deflexed); juvenile leaves cordate with entire margins; adult leaf margins deeply cut, with oval perforations 2–3 in. long through the blade; petiole to 5 ft. long. *Compound edible fruits take a year to ripen. The felty "caps" fall away easily when individual segments are ripe enough to eat. Allow the rest to ripen at room temperature. Flavor of pineapple and banana.*

Monstera tuberculatum

Mexico. Evergreen climbing herb to 50 ft.+; zones 10–11. Blooms warm months. Regular moisture and humidity. Fertile, humus-rich soil. Part sun to bright filtered light. Flowers: bisexual; spadix thick, tubercled; spathe creamy white; on a long, pendent stalk. Leaves: elliptic to ovate, sides unequal (oblique), base cordate, tip acuminate; margins deeply undulate and twisted. *Distinguished by the pendent, upside-down inflorescence and unlobed adult leaves.*

Philodendron

Philodendron includes 700 or more species of herbs and climbers from tropical America. The genus name means "tree-loving," alluding to the often climbing habit. A number of philodendrons are cultivated as foliage plants both indoors and out. Many hybrids are available though ancestry is generally unrecorded. Juvenile leaves are more or less heart-shaped (cordate). Adult leaves are entire or variously lobed. Male and female flowers are on the same plant (monoecious), with female flowers segregated at the base of the spadix and male flowers at the tip. A boatlike spathe completely encloses the spadix, which opens only 1 or 2 days for pollination when the flowers are receptive. The spathe is constricted near the base. Hybrids usually do not produce inflorescences. Philodendrons are suitable for containers with a post for climbing.

Homalomena rubescens

Monstera adansonii

Monstera deliciosa

Monstera tuberculatum

Philodendron 'Autumn'

Philodendron bipinnatifidum

Philodendron 'Autumn'

PHILODENDRON, FILODENDRO
Garden hybrid. Evergreen climbing herb; zones 10–11. Blooms unknown or rare. Regular moisture and humidity. Fertile, well-drained soil. Bright to medium filtered light. Leaves: elliptic, young leaves copper; petioles reddish.

Philodendron bipinnatifidum

SELLOUM
Synonyms: *P. selloum, P. lundii.* Southeastern Brazil. Evergreen herb to 8 ft.; zones 10–11. Blooms occasionally. Regular moisture. Fertile, sandy, humus-rich, well-drained soil. Full sun to bright filtered light. Flowers: unisexual; spathe white. Leaves: ovate, to 3 ft. long, deeply lobed, with irregular secondary lobes (bipinnatifid), dark green; margins deeply ruffled (sinuate); petioles short. Stems: erect, to trailing (decumbent) in older plants. *Mounding habit. Slow growing but produces a sprawling stem with age. These sun-tolerant species are used like shrubs in the landscape. Chills or dry wind may cause the leaf edges to brown.*

Philodendron ×evansii

IMPERIAL PHILODENDRON
Garden hybrid, *P. speciosum* × *P. bipinnatifidum.* Evergreen herb to 8 ft.; zones 10–11. Blooms intermittently in warm months. Regular moisture. Fertile, sandy, humus-rich, well-drained soil. Full sun to part shade. Flowers: unisexual; spathe hoodlike, white with purple-pink margins; at the base of the leaves. Leaves: to 3 ft. long, blades deeply lobed; margins sinuate; petioles short. Stems: short, erect, to trailing in older plants (decumbent). *Rounded habit. A few lower leaves may be removed to expose the attractive inflorescence. Chills and dry wind may cause the leaf edges to brown.*

Philodendron goeldii

Amazon headwaters of Brazil, Peru, Venezuela, Colombia. Evergreen climbing to semiepiphytic herb; zones 10–11. Blooms intermittently. Regular moisture. Fertile, sandy, humus-rich, well-drained soil. Part sun to bright filtered light.

Flowers: unisexual. Leaves: rachis curved, attached centrally to the petiole (pedatisect) to which radiating leaflets are attached.

Philodendron hastatum

Synonym: *P. glaucophyllum* (hort.). Brazil (Rio State). Evergreen climbing herb; zones 10–11. Blooms intermittently. Regular moisture. Fertile, sandy, humus-rich, well-drained soil. Part sun to bright filtered light. Flowers: unisexual. Leaves: sagittate, glossy gray-green, basal lobes and tip rounded.

Philodendron hybrid

ARROW-HEAD PHILODENDRON
Synonym: *P. williamsii* (misapplied). Garden hybrid. Evergreen climbing herb to 8 ft.+; zones 10–11. Bloom rare or unknown. Regular moisture. Fertile, sandy, well-drained soil. Part sun to part shade. Leaves: narrowly sagittate, to 2 ft.+ long, tilted forward (deflexed), dark green; margins wavy (sinuate); petioles to 3 ft. long. *This plant is sold in the trade as* P. williamsii; *however, that species, from Esposito Santo, Brazil, has broader, shorter leaves. Authorities suggest this is a hybrid (Mayo, pers. comm.).*

Philodendron speciosum

ARROW-HEAD PHILODENDRON
Brazil. Evergreen herb to 6 ft.; zones 10–11. Blooms warm months. Regular moisture. Fertile, sandy, humus-rich, well-drained soil. Part sun to part shade. Flowers: unisexual. Leaves: sagittate, tilted forward (deflexed); margins toothed, wavy (sinuate), to 2 ft.+ long; petioles 3–4 ft. long. Stems: erect, to trailing in older plants. *A compact philodendron used in the landscape like a rounded shrub. Chills or dry wind may cause the leaf edges to brown.*

Pistia

Pistia includes a single species of stemless aquatic herb. Its exact origin is obscure. It is widely distributed in the tropics. A number of names have been applied based upon various leaf characteristics. Authorities now consider all to be forms of the same species. They are free-floating, stalkless plants of quiet freshwater. The plants remain afloat by air bubbles trapped among the leaf hairs. New plants develop at the ends of stolons creating large rafts. The hairy spathe, situated in the center of the leaf cup, is only about 1 in. high. The inflorescence is divided into 2 chambers, male flowers in the upper chamber, female flowers below. The roots are fibrous and free-floating.

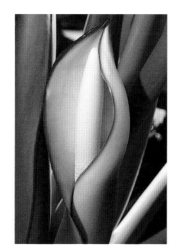

Philodendron ×evansii

Philodendron goeldii

Philodendron hastatum

Philodendron hybrid

Philodendron speciosum

Pistia is sometimes used in water gardens. Though widely distributed in Florida since the earliest botanical surveys by John Bartrum, it is nevertheless treated as if it were introduced (Howard, pers. comm.) and cultivation and distribution are prohibited in Florida. It clogs canals and wetlands. For control, it is suitable as domestic forage. Endangered manatees in Florida feed on it. It has been investigated for the production of alternative fuel because of its capacity to generate methane gas as it rots. The plants are used to purify water in the Far East because they absorb large amounts of heavy metals and other impurities.

Pistia stratiotes
WATER-LETTUCE, WATER-BONNET, NILE CABBAGE, SHELL-FLOWER, LECHUGA DE AGUA

Pantropical. Evergreen herb, 8–12 in. wide; zones 10–11. Blooms warm months. Aquatic. Free-floating. Full to part sun. Flowers: unisexual; spathe 1–2 in., 2-chambered, greenish white, located in the center of the foliage cup. Leaves: wedge-shaped, spongy, fluted, ends truncate; covered with air-trapping hairs, gray-green; margins smooth to undulate, recurved; in cuplike rosettes that close at night. *Forms large, free-floating colonies or rafts in freshwater. Cultivation prohibited or strongly discouraged in warm regions. Genus and species names allude to the watery environment.*

Pothoidium
Pothoidium includes a single species of climbing, semiepiphytic herb from Southeast Asia, Indomalaysia, and the Philippines. It grows in tropical rainforest understory. The petiole is flattened and is separated from the blade by a joint. The leaves are somewhat palmlike, arranged in opposite ranks on pendent or trailing branches. Flowers are often bisexual but are apparently functionally unisexual. Small inflorescences are arranged on a long, sometimes branching stalk. Spathes are often absent. These climbers can be grown over a wall, from a tree, or on a support.

Pothoidium lobbianum
Southeast Asia, Indomalaysia, Philippines. Evergreen climbing herb; zones 10–11. Blooms warm months. Regular moisture and humidity. Fertile, humus-rich, well-drained soil. Bright filtered light to part shade. Flowers: bisexual but functionally unisexual; inflorescence small, on a branched stalk; berries red. Leaves: oblong, arranged in opposite ranks (distichous) on pendent, slender branches; petiole flattened, bladelike.

Spathicarpa
Spathicarpa includes approximately 6 species of small seasonally dormant or evergreen herbs from tropical and subtropical eastern Brazil, Paraguay, and Uruguay. One species is occasionally cultivated in shaded locations. Leaves develop from a thick subterranean tuber or rhizome. The blades are simple and hastate. Flowers are unisexual. The spadix is fused down the center of a leaflike spathe.

Spathicarpa sagittifolia
CATERPILLAR PLANT

Brazil, Paraguay, Argentina. Evergreen herb, 10–15 in.; zones 10–11. Blooms most of the year. Evenly moist. Fertile, well-drained, humus-rich soil. Medium filtered light.

Flowers: reduced, on a spadix fused along the midline of the spathe; spathe leaflike, elliptic to lanceolate, on a stalk 8–10 in. long. Leaves: cordate or with short hastate lobes. *A low understory plant. Suitable for containers.*

Spathiphyllum
Spathiphyllum includes approximately 60 species of evergreen short-stemmed herbs from Central and northern South America as well as Sulawesi, New Guinea, and the Philippines. Leaves are simple and unlobed. Flowers are bisexual with scalelike tepals that appear as green hatch marks around the flow-

Pistia stratiotes

Pothoidium lobbianum

Pistia stratiotes, inflorescence

Spathicarpa sagittifolia

ers on the spadix. A short stalk (or stipe) is located between the base of the spadix and the attachment of the spathe. The spathe is erect or reflexed. Spathiphyllums are mass-produced commercially through tissue culture. Cultivated plants represent complex hybrids of unknown ancestry, which are nearly indistinguishable except for size. 'Mauna Loa' and 'Clevelandii' are among the largest named forms. Some are delicately fragrant when flowers mature. All are well suited to bright shady areas where many flowering plants will not bloom.

Spathiphyllum floribundum
PEACE-LILY, SNOW-FLOWER, ESPATIFILO
Synonym: *Anthurium floribundum*. Colombia. Evergreen herb to 2 ft.; zones 10–11. Blooms late spring, early summer. Evenly moist. Fertile, sandy, well-drained soil. Bright filtered light to moderate shade. Flowers: bisexual, white; spadix cross-hatched with scalelike green tepals; spathe white, more or less reflexed. Leaves: ovate to oblong, to 8 in. long or more, dull green; midvein lighter.

Syngonium
Syngonium includes approximately 38 species of climbing herbs from tropical America. They climb by adventitious roots at the nodes. Juvenile leaves are simple, elliptic to sagittate, sometimes variegated with white. Adult leaves may be simple, oblong to cordate or pedatisect with 3–15 lobes or pinnately divided. Container-grown plants usually do not develop adult leaf forms. Flowers are unisexual, with male and female flowers separated on the spadix by a ring of sterile flowers corresponding to a constriction below the middle of the spathe. The inflated base surrounds the female flowers. The inflorescences develop from the axils of the adult leaves. Syngoniums are invasive outdoors and difficult to eradicate once escaped.

Syngonium neglectum
Synonym: *S. auritum* var. *neglectum*. Mexico to northern South America. Evergreen climbing herb;

zones 10–11. Blooms intermittently. Evenly moist. Average to fertile, humus-rich, well-drained soil. Part sun to filtered light. Flowers: unisexual; spadix thick, white, taller than the spathe; spathe hoodlike, white, streaked red to brown inside. Leaves: hastate. *Uncommon in cultivation.*

Syngonium podophyllum
ARROWHEAD VINE
Mexico to northern South America. Evergreen climbing herb; zones 10–11. Blooms rarely in cultivation. Evenly moist. Average to fertile, well-drained soil. Part sun to filtered light. Flowers: unisexual. Leaves: juvenile leaves simple, hastate, green or variegated with white, adult leaves pedatisect, the lateral lobes 3-parted. *Invasive. A controlled species in South Florida. Cultivation outdoors strongly discouraged. Difficult to eradicate because every broken piece of stem sprouts. Commonly but incorrectly referred to as* Nephthytis *or African evergreen.*

Xanthosoma
Xanthosoma includes 57–70 species of evergreen herbs from tropical America. They are often used in landscaping shrubs. Some species are arborescent with trunklike stems. Leaves are simple "elephant-ears," with large sagittate or hastate basal lobes, or sometimes deeply divided. The petiole is usually attached to the margin of the blade as in *Alocasia*. Flowers are unisexual, with male and female flowers segregated on the spadix (monoecious). Some species are commercially cultivated for their starchy tubers, which may be white, orange, or purple. These potato-like vegetables are sold in mainland U.S. supermarkets, along with taro, as "gourmet" chips. In the Caribbean the leaves are also stewed as "calalou," a catch-all name roughly equivalent to cooked "greens" (also see *Amaranthaceae*). Malanga is common in Latin American cuisine and in the Far East. It must be cooked before eating. The sap is extremely irritating. Handle raw tubers with rubber gloves. The burning can be neutralized with baking soda (bicarbonate of soda). Plants may become pests in cultivation.

Xanthosoma maffafa
MALANGA, COCOYAM, YAUTÍA, TANIA
Exact origin obscure (probably northern South America, West Indies); widely cultivated. Evergreen herb, 6–10 ft.; zones 10–11. Blooms intermittently. Regular moisture. Fertile, well-drained soil. Full to part sun. Flowers: unisexual; spadix taller than the spathe; spathe white, vaselike, constricted below, to 10 in. high. Leaves: broad, sagittate, 2–4 ft.+ long; margins undulate. Cultivars bluish or white-veined. *Commonly confused with* X. sagittifolium. *These similar species are cultivated together and hybridize.* Xanthosoma maffafa *can be distinguished by the gap in the blade membrane on either side of the sinus where the petiole is attached (Boyce, pers. comm.).*

Zantedeschia
Zantedeschia includes approximately 6 species of seasonally dormant stemless herbs from southern Africa. Inflorescences are often used in flower arrangements and bridal bouquets. Leaves are simple, often with hastate basal lobes. Spathes are funnel-shaped on long stalks and in cultivars range from white to almost black or multihued. Callas overwinter outdoors in mild temperate zones if the dormant rhizome is protected from freezing. In colder climates the rhizomes are lifted and stored indoors in winter. Grow in sandy loam well fortified with humus and keep moist to wet from spring until late summer, then taper off water to begin dormancy. Callas may remain evergreen in tropical areas if kept continuously moist. They are a good choice for

Spathiphyllum floribundum

Syngonium neglectum

Syngonium podophyllum

Xanthosoma maffafa

low boggy spots in the garden. In their native South Africa, they spring up in drainage ditches. Can be grown in a container with an outer container partly filled with water. Change water often. In tropical America, they have become weeds in some wetlands. Birds eat the fruit. Though often called calla-lilies, these plants are not related to lilies.

Zantedeschia aethiopica

CALLA, CALLA-LILY, LILY-OF-THE-NILE, WHITE ARUM-LILY
Synonyms: *Calla aethiopica, Z. aethiopica* var. *minor*. Southern Africa; widely naturalized. Seasonally dormant to evergreen herb, 2–2.5 ft.; zones 8–11. Blooms summer. Seasonally moist/dry. Fertile, humus-rich soil. Full to part sun. Flowers: unisexual; spadix yellow; spathe funnel-shaped, erect, white to greenish, covered with felty hairs. Leaves: lanceolate, green, not spotted; petioles long. *Thrives in seasonally moist regions.*

Zantedeschia elliottiana

YELLOW CALLA, YELLOW CALLA-LILY, GOLDEN ARUM-LILY
Only known in cultivation. Seasonally dormant perennial herb, 2–3 ft.; zones 7–11. Blooms summer. Seasonally moist/dry. Fertile, well-drained soil. Full to part sun. Flowers: unisexual; spathe funnel-shaped, erect; on a tall stalk; spadix golden-yellow; fruit a yellow berry. Leaves: ovate to sagittate, held stiffly erect, dark green, spotted white, to 18 in. tall. *Probably a cultigen. Thrives in seasonally moist tropics and subtropics where nights are cool. Hybrids of* Z. pentlandii *are also yellow.*

ARALIACEAE

ARALIA FAMILY, GINSENG FAMILY
Araliaceae includes 47–84 genera of shrubs, trees, woody climbers (lianas), epiphytes, and rarely herbs, which are widely distributed but most diverse in Indonesia and the Americas. This family could also be more broadly circumscribed in the family Apiaceae (Judd, pers. comm.). *Hedera* and *Polyscias* are frequently cultivated as foliage plants in temperate and tropical climates. Some species are armed with prickles. Leaves are leathery, often deeply divided or compound and spirally arranged. Juvenile leaves sometimes differ from adult leaves (dimorphic). Flowers are reduced and bisexual, or unisexual with male and female flowers on the same plant (monoecious) or on different plants (dioecious).

Osmoxylon

Osmoxylon includes approximately 50 species from Malaysia, Taiwan, and the western Pacific Islands. These unarmed tropical evergreens are unusual in cultivation though they are very attractive foliage plants. The leaves are simple or palmately lobed, the bases often fringed. Plants are suitable for containers and Japanese-style landscaping.

Osmoxylon lineare

Synonym: *Boerlagiodendron lineare*. Micronesia. Evergreen shrub, 2–3 ft.+; zones 10–11. Blooms warm months. Regular moisture. Average to fertile, well-drained soil. Part sun or bright filtered light. Flowers: reduced, russet, in flat-topped terminal clusters (umbels); fruit whitish. Leaves: palmatifid, 5 narrow lobes cut almost to the petiole; margins with widely spaced teeth. *A spreading shrub. Said to be somewhat salt tolerant. Suitable for containers. Unusual in cultivation.*

Schefflera

Schefflera includes approximately 650 species of shrubs, trees, and climbers, which are widely distributed but most abundant in the Americas, mainland and maritime Southeast Asia, and Oceania. Only a few species are widely cultivated, primarily as foliage plants. Leaves are usually palmately compound,

Zantedeschia aethiopica

Osmoxylon lineare

Schefflera arboricola, fruit

Zantedeschia elliottiana

Schefflera actinophylla

the leaflets on short stalks (petiolules). Flowers are reduced and not individually ornamental, but large inflorescences are showy. Inflorescences are mostly umbels or spikes. *Schefflera actinophylla* is a commonly grown, self-seeding pest that is prohibited in Florida. The seeds are distributed by birds, especially exotic wild parrots.

Schefflera actinophylla
SCHEFFLERA, QUEENSLAND UMBRELLA-TREE, OCTOPUS-TREE, CHEFLERA
Synonym: *Brassaia actinophylla*. New Guinea, Indonesia, Australia; widely distributed. Evergreen tree to 35 ft.; zones 10–11. Blooms summer. Moderate moisture. Average, well-drained soil. Full to part sun. Flowers: reduced, dark-red; inflorescence with long spokelike branches. Leaves: palmately compound; leaflets about 12, obovate,

Schefflera arboricola, variegated leaf

Schefflera elegantissima

to 1 ft. long; margins undulate; petioles to 16 in. *This erect, fast-growing tree is slightly salt tolerant. Seeds often start epiphytically in other trees and palms, quickly overwhelming the host. Invasive in Hawaii. Prohibited in South Florida. Removal strongly recommended.*

Schefflera arboricola
DWARF UMBRELLA-TREE, DWARF SCHEFFLERA, ARBORICOLA
Synonym: *Heptapleurum arboricolum*. Taiwan, southern China. Evergreen shrub, 8–12 ft.; zones 10–11. Blooms winter. Moderate moisture. Average, well-drained soil. Full to part sun. Flowers: reduced; fruit an orange berry turning purple-black. Leaves: palmately compound; about 10 leaflets, 4–6 in. long. *These shrubs are popular hedge plants. So far, this species does not seem to be invasive. The variegated form has irregular cream markings on the leaflets.*

Schefflera elegantissima
ELEGANT SCHEFFLERA, FALSE ARALIA
Synonyms: *Aralia elegantissima*, *Dizygotheca elegantissima*. New Caledonia. Evergreen shrub or small tree, 6–20 ft.+; zones 10–11. Blooms fall. Moderate moisture.

Average, well-drained soil. Bright broken light, part sun. Flowers: in terminal umbels. Leaves: palmate; leaflets 7–11, lanceolate, black to dark green, midvein light green, juvenile leaflets 6–10 in. long; margins widely toothed; petioles white spotted; adult form with larger leaflets. *An erect foliage plant, sparsely branching, primarily from the base. Bloom rarely seen in cultivation. Suitable for containers.*

ARECACEAE
PALM FAMILY
Arecaceae (Palmae) includes approximately 200 genera of evergreen solitary or clustering trees or stemless shrubs, rarely climbers, from tropical and mild temperate regions. The architecture of palms is elegant and diverse. Though unfamiliar to many, inflorescences and fruit are often highly ornamental. Leaves are compound, some with pinnate (featherlike) leaflets arranged along a midrib (rachis), and sometimes with an elongated petiole base (crownshaft) that sheathes the top of the trunk. Other palms have palmately compound leaves, with the leaflets spreading fanlike and radiating from a disklike structure (hastula) at the end of the petiole. Costapal-

mate leaves are also fan-shaped but somewhat folded lengthwise, the sides arching, with the bases congested on a short rachis. Fishtail palms are the only bipinnately leafed palms, with a branched rachis and wedge-shaped leaflets. Palm leaflets may be partially fused along their edges or completely free, juvenile leaflets are often more fused than adults. Flowers are small, in many-flowered panicles. The inflorescence is subtended by a spathelike bract.

The apical meristem at the apex of the trunk or stalk is the only growing point. It cannot be cut back without killing the individual stem, making it very important to select palms of appropriate mature height. Palms are susceptible to a variety of diseases and pests. Lethal yellowing disease has devastated susceptible species where it occurs. Palms often develop nutritional deficiencies in alkaline soils and need supplemental micronutrients. Photos of the trunks and leaf scar patterns are provided here because they are often ornamental and excellent field marks that are easily observed at eye level. Palms were photographed primarily at Fairchild Tropical Garden and the Montgomery Botanical Center.

Palm Glade at Fairchild Tropical Garden, Coral Gables, Florida, from the viewpoint of an anhinga

Acoelorrhaphe

Acoelorrhaphe includes a single species of densely clustering palm from the western Caribbean, Belize, Cuba, the Bahamas, and South Florida. Adapted to marshy, brackish conditions, this palm can be cultivated in upland areas with adequate irrigation. Leaves are fan-shaped, the side leaflets shorter than those in the center. They are held stiffly, often so congested that some are turned on edge. Petiole margins are lined with hooked teeth. Old leaf stalks should not be added to mulch as the persistent teeth can snag long after they dry. Natural stands are characteristic of the southern marshes of Everglades National Park in Florida. In some countries, once vast stands have been cleared for farming. In alkaline soils, these palms require added organics and micronutrients.

Acoelorrhaphe wrightii

EVERGLADES PALM, PAUROTIS-PALM
Synonyms: *Copernicia wrightii, Paurotis wrightii, Serenoa arborescens.* South Florida, Bahamas, Cuba, Yucatan to Central America. Clustering palm, 25–35 ft.; zones 9–11. Blooms intermittently in warm, wet months. Seasonally moist to wet, or brackish. Deep, humus-rich soil; acid pH. Full sun. Flowers: bisexual; inflorescence stalk erect, 3–4 ft. long, becoming pendent with weight of orange to black fruit; bracts 3, papery. Leaves: palmate, gray-green below, persistent; leaflet tips free halfway to the petiole; petiole armed with sharp, hooked teeth, base not divided. *Distinguished by the very dense clumps and congested, disorderly arrangement of the fan-shaped leaves.*

Adonidia

Adonidia includes a single species of solitary palm from the Philippines. Leaves are pinnate. Flowers are unisexual, with male and female flowers on the same tree (monoecious). This popular palm was included in *Veitchia* for a long time but has now been returned to *Adonidia* because of a number of characteristics that differ from *Veitchia* (Zona, pers. comm.). One biological distinction, unfortunately, is susceptibility to lethal yellowing disease. This palm bears fruit from fall to spring. It is called Christmas palm for the baublelike fruits that appear over many months, not just the Christmas season.

Adonidia merrillii

MANILA PALM, CHRISTMAS PALM
Synonym: *Veitchia merrillii.* Philippines. Solitary palm, 20–50 ft.; zones 10–11. Blooms intermittently in warm, wet months. Moderate moisture. Average to fertile, well-drained soil. Full sun to bright broken light. Flowers: unisexual; inflorescence stalk white; fruit plum-shaped, crimson-red; bracts 2, one inside the other, short-lived, papery. Leaves: pinnate, arched; leaflets near the base in several ranks with long reins, becoming one-ranked toward the ends, held obliquely in a V; tips jagged; crownshaft long, gray-green. Stems: base spreading, leaf scar rings closely spaced or up to 2 in. apart depending on light exposure. *A cold-sensitive, fast-growing, and somewhat salt-tolerant palm. Because it is highly susceptible to lethal yellowing disease, it is short-lived in affected areas.*

Aiphanes

Aiphanes includes approximately 38 species of solitary palms from the West Indies and South America. All Caribbean species are now grouped as *A. minima.* These striking palms

Acoelorrhaphe wrightii

Aiphanes minima

are heavily armed with needlelike gray or black spines which have flattened, triangular bases. The spines ring the trunk and line the leaf rachis and petioles. The pinnate leaflets are in one rank. They have blunt, jagged tips. Male and female flowers are on the same plant (monoecious) with male flowers toward the end of the inflorescence and female flowers toward the base. Fruits are red.

Aiphanes minima
COYURE, GRIGRI
Synonym: *A. corallina*. Martinique,

southeastern Antilles, endangered in the wild. Solitary palm to 20 ft.; zones 10–11. Blooms intermittently in warm, wet months. Regular moisture and humidity. Deep, humus-rich, well-drained soil. Part sun to medium shade. Flowers: unisexual; fruit red. Leaves: pinnate; leaflets wedge-shaped, spiny. Stems: armed with long spines. *Of moist tropical forests. A very attractive palm for isolated locations where the spines do not present a danger to people or animals.*

Allagoptera
Allagoptera includes approximately 5 species of mostly clustering palms from Brazil and Paraguay. Leaves are pinnate. Male and female flowers are on the same plant (monoecious). *Allagoptera arenaria*, native to sandy coastal scrub and beaches, is extremely salt tolerant. It gathers sand, building up dunes around the stem, and may be useful to slow erosion. The species name comes from *arena*, the Spanish word for sand. On firm ground, this palm attains moderate height. Inland species are not salt tolerant.

Allagoptera arenaria
SEASHORE-PALM
Synonym: *Cocos arenaria*. Southern coastal Brazil. Clustering palm, 6–15 ft.; zones 10–11. Blooms intermittently in warm, wet months. Moderate moisture to fairly dry. Poor to average, sandy, well-drained soil. Full sun. Flowers: unisexual; infructescence resembles an ear of corn. Leaves: pinnate, dull green; leaflets in clusters of 3, lax, sharp-tipped, in whorls around the rachis. Stems: covered with spiraling, interlaced leaf bases. *Palmate leaf in photo center belongs to neighboring* Thrinax.

Archontophoenix
Archontophoenix includes approximately 6 species of solitary palms from Queensland, Australia. They grow from moist coastal forests to inland mountain slopes. Leaves are pinnate and arching. Petioles are twisted, turning the leaves on edge. These palms have long, slender green crownshafts. Male and female flowers are on the same tree (monoecious).

Archontophoenix alexandrae
ALEXANDRA PALM, KING-PALM
Synonym: *Ptychosperma alexandrae*. Northeastern Australia. Solitary palm to 75 ft.; zones 9–11. Blooms intermittently in warm, wet months. Regular moisture and humidity. Fertile, well-drained soil. Full to part sun. Flowers: unisexual, each female flower bracketed by 2 male flowers; inflorescence lax,

Acoelorrhaphe wrightii, infructescence

Adonidia merrillii

Aiphanes minima, fruit and spiny trunk

Allagoptera arenaria

Archontophoenix alexandrae

Allagoptera arenaria, fruit

stalk white, enclosed by 2 papery bracts; fruit red. Leaves: pinnate, silvery gray below; leaflet tips sharp; petiole twisted. Stems: slender, rings closely spaced, slightly stepped. Trunk: base spreading. *A graceful, slender palm. The crownshaft is longer and slimmer than Dictyosperma. Protected in Australia.*

Areca

Areca includes approximately 60 species of solitary and clustering palms from Southeast Asia, Malaysia, India, and New Guinea. The origin of some species is obscured by centuries of cultivation. Leaves are pinnate. Male and female flowers are on the same plant (monoecious). These palms, from tropical rainforest understory, are sensitive to cold. In the United States, they grow outdoors only in Hawaii and protected areas of South Florida. In Southeast Asia, the nut of *A. catechu* is sometimes chewed with *Piper betle* leaves and lime (calcium oxide) as a mild narcotic. The mixture stains saliva red. This practice fed legends of island cannibals and bequeathed Bloody Mary her name in the musical *South Pacific*. The nut, chewed by itself, is sometimes used as a toothbrush (Schokman, pers. comm.).

Areca catechu

BETEL-NUT PALM, ARECA-NUT, PINANG, BONGA

Origin obscure; cultivated from Southeast Asia to New Guinea. Solitary palm, 30–100 ft.; zone 11. Blooms intermittently in warm, wet months. Moist and humid. Fertile, well-drained soil. Bright broken light. Flowers: unisexual, mostly male, a few female flowers near the base of the inflorescence, fragrant; inflorescence resembles an upturned whisk broom; fruit orange. Leaves: pinnate, leaflets fused almost to the edge of the leaf; crownshaft slender, green. *Cultivated for millennia. Possibly a cultigen. Wild populations unknown. Flowers are used to make perfume. Cold-sensitive.*

Astrocaryum

Astrocaryum includes approximately 50 species of solitary palms from tropical America. They grow in moist forest understory. Leaves are pinnate. Male and female flowers are on the same plant (monoecious). Some species are utilized for oil or fiber. The genus name probably alludes to the starlike fibers arranged around the pore openings at the end of the fruit where the embryonic root emerges (Hubbuch, pers. comm.). These armed species are not commonly cultivated though they make formidable barrier fences.

Astrocaryum mexicanum

STAR-NUT PALM

Mexico to Honduras. Solitary palm to 8 ft.; zones 9–11. Blooms intermittently in warm, wet months. Regular moisture and humidity. Fertile, well-drained soil. Full to part sun or bright broken light. Flowers: unisexual, small, brown and white; inflorescence compact, branched; fruit ovoid, woody, to 2 in. long; bracts one, spiny. Leaves: pinnate, in one rank, dull green; leaflets unevenly divided; petiole and rachis spiny. Stems: heavily armed with long spines.

Attalea

Attalea includes approximately 30–71 species of solitary palms from tropical America. Some authors divide these species among *Attalea* (22 species), *Orbignya* (20), *Scheelea* (28), and *Maximiliana* (1) based upon minor differences of floral anatomy. They are combined here because they are very closely related and intermediate forms are recognized (Zona, pers. comm.). Leaves are pinnate, relatively long, and shaggy, in 1 or 2 ranks. Old leaves are semipersistent, remaining attached to the stem for a long time. Male and female flowers are

Archontophoenix alexandrae, inflorescence

Areca catechu, stem and inflorescence

Astrocaryum mexicanum, inflorescence

Areca catechu

Astrocaryum mexicanum

on the same plant (monoecious). These palms are generally massive, slow-growing trees of both dry and seasonally moist forest. They require plenty of space to spread. The oil is used for fuel by indigenous peoples and the seeds are eaten by wild and domestic animals alike.

Attalea butyracea

Synonyms: *A. zonensis, Scheelea liebmanii, Scheelea phalerata.* Mexico. Solitary palm to 50 ft.+; zones 9–11. Blooms intermittently. Regular moisture and humidity. Fertile, well-drained soil. Full sun. Flowers: unisexual. Leaves: ascending. Stems: stocky, leaf scar rings undulating, smooth.

Attalea cohune

AMERICAN OIL-PALM, COHUNE PALM

Synonym: *Orbignya cohune.* Central America. Solitary palm, 40–50 ft.+; zones 9–11. Blooms intermittently. Regular moisture and humidity. Fertile, well-drained soil. Full sun. Flowers: unisexual. Leaves: pinnate, to 25 ft. long even on relatively young trees, tips lax, bases long and broad, persistent for many years. Stems: thick, leaf scar rings undulating.

Beccariophoenix

Beccariophoenix includes a single species of solitary palm from mountainous regions of eastern Madagascar. It is related to the coconut palm, *Cocos*. The seeds of both genera have 3 openings (pores). Flowers are unisexual. Leaves are pinnate, almost as broad as they are long. The leaflets of juvenile leaves are coherent toward the leaflet tips but free close to the rachis, leaving slits, or "windows." This very attractive understory palm is endangered in the wild and rare in cultivation. Young palms suitable for containers.

Beccariophoenix madagascariensis

WINDOW-PALM

Madagascar, endangered in the wild. Solitary palm to 30 ft.; zones 10–11. Blooms intermittently in warm, wet months. Moderate moisture. Fertile, well-drained soil. Bright filtered light. Flowers: unisexual: Leaves: pinnate, about as wide as long, juvenile leaflets fused

Attalea butyracea, stem detail

Attalea cohune, infructescence

Attalea butyracea, center

Attalea cohune

at the tips, producing a pattern of slitlike openings, or "windows." *Only juvenile leaves have windows. Mature leaflets are completely free. Reinhardtia also has leaves with coherent leaflet tips and openings near the rachis.*

Bentinckia

Bentinckia includes just 2 species of solitary palms, one from India and the other from the Nicobar Islands (located in the Indian Ocean between Sri Lanka and the Malay Peninsula). These slender, graceful palms grow at moderate elevations. They are rare in cultivation. Leaves are pinnate. Male and female flowers are on the same tree (monoecious). The genus was named for Captain John Bentinck who invented a boom used to stretch a triangular sail.

Bentinckia nicobarica

BENTINCKIA PALM
Synonym: *Orania nicobarica.* Nicobar Islands (Indian Ocean). Solitary palm, 25–50 ft.+; zones 10–11. Blooms intermittently in warm, wet months. Regular moisture and humidity. Fertile, well-drained soil. Full sun. Flowers: unisexual; fruit red becoming black. Leaves: pinnate, to 6 ft. long; crownshaft dark green; petioles twisted. Stems: slender, green with a white, waxy (glaucous) coating, leaf scar rings widely spaced. *A slender palm with a somewhat sparse crown of leaves, which are twisted on edge. Salt tolerance unknown; it has withstood occasional salt-bearing tropical storms in South Florida as it might in its native habitat.*

Bismarckia

Bismarckia includes a single species of solitary palm from western Madagascar. This stocky, stiffly erect, blue-gray palm of open savanna is adapted to seasonally moist/dry climate. It thrives in alkaline soil and has become an important landscaping palm in South Florida but also thrives in California clay. Leaves are costapalmate. Male and female flowers are on separate trees (dioecious) and must be planted in proximity for seed production. *Bismarckia* has proven highly resistant to pests and lethal

yellowing disease but is easily confused with *Latania*, which is susceptible to lethal yellowing. The deep tap root is sensitive to disturbance and these palms must be root-pruned for successful transplanting. They are moderately salt and drought tolerant.

Bismarckia nobilis

BISMARCK PALM
Western Madagascar. Solitary palm, 30–60 ft.; zones 9–11. Blooms intermittently in warm, wet months. Seasonally moist and humid, dry. Average to fertile, well-drained soil. Full sun. Flowers: unisexual; male inflorescence stalk black, pendent; fruit blue-green becoming dark brown, ovate to 2 in. long. Leaves: costapalmate, arching from the rachis, blue-gray to grayish green; leaflets coherent at the base; petioles waxy, with clumps of rust-colored, stiff hairs; edges sharply toothed, bases split. Trunk: erect, stout, to 18 in. diameter.

Borassus

Borassus includes approximately 7 species of solitary palms from tropical Africa and Southeast Asia to New Guinea. Leaves are costapalmate. Male and female flowers are on different trees (dioecious). *Borassus aethiopium* and *B. flabellifer*, the palmyra palm, are highly utilitarian to indigenous peoples. The timber is salt-water resistant; leaves are used for thatch, fiber, and paper; coconut-like seeds are eaten; and the sap is made into palm sugar (jaggery), alcohol, and vinegar. These palms do not bear fruit until they are mature after 30 years or more. The sprouting shoot first grows downward for several feet before turning up, so the planting hole should be deep, the soil open. *Borassus aethiopium* is threatened in the wild.

Borassus aethiopium

BORASSUS PALM,
AFRICAN FAN-PALM
Eastern Africa, threatened in the wild. Solitary palm to 80 ft.; zones 9–11. Blooms intermittently in warm, wet months. Moderate moisture. Deep, sandy, well-drained soil. Full sun. Flowers:

unisexual; fruit 4–5 in. diameter, resembling a small coconut. Leaves: costapalmate, semipersistent, bases divided. Stems: gray with fairly closely spaced rings, base swollen. *Salt tolerant. In dry seasons,*

irrigate deeply once a week. If roots have reached the water table, irrigation is unnecessary. This large, sturdy palm is a protected species. The pair of palms photographed at Fairchild Tropical Garden survived being top-

Beccariophoenix madagascariensis, juvenile leaves

Bentinckia nicobarica, stem detail

Bentinckia nicobarica

pled and reset after Hurricane Andrew in 1992.

Brahea

Brahea includes approximately 16 species of small to medium palms from Mexico. Leaves are costapalmate. Flowers are bisexual. The flower stalk is very long and pendent, up to 10 ft. or more, reaching the ground in some species. Hesper-palms are desert palms and are often cultivated in southern California and Mexico. They generally do not thrive in moist climates. The nuts are sometimes eaten by local people and are sometimes cultivated for the oil.

Brahea armata

BLUE HESPER-PALM,
MEXICAN FAN-PALM

Synonym: *Erythea armata*. Mexico (Baja California, eastern Gulf of Baja). Solitary palm to 40 ft.; zones

Bismarckia nobilis, costapalmate leaf detail

Bismarckia nobilis, male inflorescence

Borassus aethiopium, fruit

Borassus aethiopium, trunk

Bismarckia nobilis, female tree with fruit

Borassus aethiopium, female and male

10–11. Blooms warm months. Semiarid. Average to poor, gritty, well-drained soil; alkaline pH. Full sun. Flowers: bisexual, purplish; inflorescence pendent, long, often to the ground; fruit round, speckled. Leaves: costapalmate, suborbicular, to 3 ft. wide, 6–8 ft. long, rigid, waxy blue-green; leaflets partly fused; petiole stiff, edges armed with sharp, recurved yellow teeth, bases semipersistent. Stems: erect, stocky, to 3 ft. diameter, base spreading; surface vertically fissured. *A slow-growing palm of coastal areas. Photographed at Balboa Park.*

Butia

Butia includes 8–12 species of solitary palms from subtropical South America. Several of previously segregated varieties and species are now considered forms of *B. capitata*. Leaves are pinnate. Male and female flowers are on the same plant (monoecious). These palms are commonly cultivated in Florida and southern South America. They are hardy, slightly salt tolerant, and drought resistant once established. The genus is very closely related to *Syagrus* with which it is occasionally hybridized. Do not confuse the spelling of this genus name with *Butea* in the legume family, Fabaceae.

Butia capitata

JELLY-PALM, WINE-PALM, PINDO PALM

Synonyms: *Butia bonnetii, Cocos capitata*. Southern Brazil, Uruguay, Argentina. Solitary palm to 20 ft.; zones 7–11. Blooms intermittently in warm, wet months. Seasonally moist/moderately dry. Average, well-drained soil. Full sun. Flowers: unisexual; inflorescence erect, brushlike, gold to purplish brown; spathe woody; fruit yellow. Leaves: pinnate, gray-green, arched and held obliquely in a V; leaflet tips pointed or split; petiole edges roughly fibrous to jagged, bases persistent. *The fruit is used to make jelly and wine. Persistent old leaves* are usually removed in cultivation. Grown in the United States as far north as coastal Georgia.

Carpentaria

Carpentaria includes a single species of solitary palm from the

Butia capitata, inflorescence

Butia capitata, infructescence

Brahea armata

Butia capitata

coast of the Gulf of Carpentaria in northeastern Australia. Leaves are pinnate and drooping. Male and female flowers are on the same tree (monoecious). This palm is tall and fairly slender with a long, green crownshaft, a light gray stem, and widely spaced leaf scar rings. It is very elegant and fast-growing. Do not confuse the spelling of this genus name with that of *Carpenteria* in the hydrangea family, Hydrangeaceae.

Carpentaria acuminata
CARPENTARIA PALM
Northeastern Australia. Solitary palm to 60 ft.+; zones 9–11. Blooms intermittently in warm, wet months. Regular moisture and humidity. Fertile, well-drained soil. Full sun. Flowers: unisexual, white, fragrant; inflorescence white, located at the base of the crownshaft; fruit ovoid, red; bracts 2. Leaves:

pinnate, 8–10 ft. long, softly arching; leaflets held in a slightly oblique V, tips lax, terminal leaflets fused; crownshaft somewhat swollen near the base. Stems: to 8 in. diameter, light gray, leaf scar rings narrow and widely spaced.

Caryota
Caryota includes approximately 12 species of solitary and clustering palms from Southeast Asia to Australia. Some species may represent a hybrid gene pool and their botany is not definitive. This is the only palm genus with bipinnate leaves (the rachis is branched). The leaflets are fan-, wedge-, or fishtail-shaped and pleated with jagged ends. Male and female flowers are on the same tree (monoecious). Growth is monocarpic. At maturity these palms begin producing inflorescences sequentially from top to bottom over several years. When

the lowest inflorescence has matured, the entire stem dies. Clustering forms produce new shoots from the base, but solitary forms require timely replacement as the palm approaches maturity. *Caryota mitis* and *C. monostachya* are the only clustering species. They may be thinned to expose the trunk architecture. Of the cultivated solitary species, nurseries often arbitrarily refer to short species as *C. cumingii* and to taller ones as *C. urens*. Other solitary species include *C. no*, *C. nymphiana*, and *C. obtusa*. Young palms are suitable for containers.

Caryota mitis
CLUSTERING FISHTAIL-PALM
Synonym: *C. sobolifera*. India, Indonesia, Philippines. Clustering palm to 10 ft.; zones 10–11. Blooms sequentially at maturity. Regular moisture and humidity. Fertile, well-drained soil. Full to part

sun or bright filtered light. Flowers: unisexual; inflorescence moplike with many pendent branches. Leaves: bipinnate; leaflets fanlike. Stems: green, with black coarsely woven fibers left behind when the petiole bases split. *The only other*

Caryota mitis, leaves

Carpentaria acuminata

Caryota mitis

clustering fishtail palm, C. mono-stachya, *has very short stems.*

Chamaedorea

Chamaedorea includes approximately 100 species of solitary and clustering palms from Mexico to South America. It is a diverse and variable group of small palms, which are often difficult to identify. Hybrids may occur in cultivation. Male and female flowers are on separate plants (dioecious), though some cultivated individuals appear to be self-fertile. Leaves are pinnate, the leaflet margins often partly or wholly coherent. These reedlike or bamboolike understory palms generally prefer bright broken light or bright shade with plenty of air movement, though some do quite well in full sun. The tall clustering types are highly recommended for screening in narrow spaces with minimal footing. They can be very effective as privacy hedges and to hide ugly walls or deter graffiti. They grow relatively quickly from seed but even faster by division. If stems become too tall, the longest canes can be selectively thinned and the shorter ones will fill in. Save the cut canes for natural plant stakes. With specimen plants, the dry crownshafts and lower leaves may be removed to expose the bamboolike structure. Plants are suitable for containers. Mockingbirds like the fruit.

Caryota species, infructescence

Chamaedorea metallica, female inflorescence

Chamaedorea metallica

Mexico, endangered in the wild. Solitary palm, 3–15 ft.; zones 10–11. Blooms intermittently in warm, wet months. Regular moisture and humidity. Average to fertile, well-drained soil. Bright filtered light. Flowers: unisexual; female inflorescence a spike, fruit black; male inflorescence branched. Leaves: pinnate; leaflets 6–10, mostly fused, dark green, often with a silvery or bronze sheen, clustered at the end of the stem. Stems: slender, flexible, nodes circled by stubby aerial roots. Roots will develop if stems touch the ground. *Attractive in small groupings. When this palm gets too tall and leggy, the top can be air-layered and repotted. The base will die.*

Chamaedorea seifrizii

BAMBOO PALM, REED-PALM
Synonyms: *C. donnell-smithii, C. erumpens.* Honduras, Guatemala, endangered in the wild. Clustering palm to 12 ft.+; zones 10–11. Blooms intermittently in warm, wet months. Seasonally moist/dry. Average to fertile, well-drained soil. Full sun to bright filtered light. Flowers: unisexual; fruit olive-sized, waxy green ripening to glossy black, rachis orange. Leaves: pinnate; leaflets in 12–24 staggered pairs, a few of the distal pairs fused. Stems: to 1 in. diameter, partly enclosed by papery leaf bases, leaf scar rings widely spaced, reedlike. *A variable and adaptable clustering palm. Forms are now grouped together as a single species (Zona, pers. comm.). Tolerates dry periods. At least some plants in cultivation appear to be self-fertile.*

Chambeyronia

Chambeyronia includes 2 species of solitary palms from New Caledonia in Melanesia. Leaves are pinnate. Petiole bases expand into a long crownshaft. New leaves open russet-red. Male and female flowers are on the same plant (monoecious). These are tall, slender palms with spreading bases. They are tender when young but more cold tolerant as they mature. They are unusual in cultivation.

Chambeyronia macrocarpa

New Caledonia (New Hebrides). Solitary palm, 50–60 ft.; zones 10–11. Blooms intermittently in warm, wet months. Regular moisture and humidity. Fertile, well-drained soil. Full sun, bright filtered light when young. Flowers: unisexual, pink; fruit small, scarlet. Leaves: pinnate, slightly drooping, crownshaft long, dark green; young leaves russet-red. Stems: slender with prominent, closely spaced leaf scar rings. *This sparsely leafed palm comes from moist tropical forest up to 3000 ft. elevation. Shelter young*

342

Chamaedorea seifrizii

Chamaedorea seifrizii, fruit

plants from cold. A slow-growing palm producing only a few, but striking, new leaves each year.

Coccothrinax

Coccothrinax includes 14–50 species of mostly solitary, small palms from the West Indies. This group is typical of the Caribbean flora, especially areas with limestone soils, including 2 species in South Florida. Leaves are palmate with a raised hastula. Flowers may be bisexual, or unisexual with male and female flowers on the same plant (monoecious). The inflorescence is creamy white, the fruit black (*Thrinax* has white fruit).

These palms tolerate brief freezing temperatures with minimal damage. Stems and leaf bases are enmeshed in finely to coarsely woven or tangled fibers distinctive to each species. When the old fiber comes loose, it can be used as a natural medium for potted epiphytes. Orchids and bromeliads thrive attached directly to the stem. These palms require only minimal care. They are resistant to lethal yellowing disease.

Coccothrinax argentata

FLORIDA SILVER PALM, SILVER-TOP Synonym: *Thrinax garberi*. Southern peninsular Florida, Florida Keys, Bahamas. Solitary palm, 2–20 ft.; zones 9–11. Blooms intermittently in warm, wet months. Seasonally moist/dry. Average, well-drained soil; alkaline pH. Full sun to bright broken light. Flowers: unisexual. Leaves: palmate, light green above, silvery below; leaflets narrow, free almost to the hastula, tips lax; petiole thin, base not divided, spineless. *A slow-growing palm endemic to oolite limestone strands and pine forests of southern Florida. Small on the mainland; rarely to 20–30 ft. in the Florida Keys and the Bahamas. Salt tolerant. Difficult to transplant successfully.*

Coccothrinax argentea

SILVER PALM, YURAGUANA (DOMINICAN REPUBLIC), LATANIER BALAI (HAITI) Hispaniola. Solitary palm to 30 ft.; zones 9–11. Blooms intermittently in warm, wet months. Seasonally moist/dry. Average, well-drained soil; alkaline pH. Full to part sun. Flowers: unisexual. Leaves: palmate, dark green above, slightly silvery below. *A slender palm, typically taller and faster growing than C. argentata, leaflets broader and not as silvery below. A salt-tolerant coastal palm.*

Coccothrinax barbadensis

Synonyms: *C. dussiana, Thrinax barbadensis*. Barbados. Solitary palm to 40 ft.; zones 9–11. Blooms intermittently in warm, wet months. Seasonally moist/dry. Average, well-drained soil; alkaline pH. Full sun to bright filtered light. Flowers: bisexual, inflorescence creamy white. Leaves: palmate, younger leaves often completely circular, 3–5 ft. wide; older leaves subcircular, 2–3 ft. wide; leaflets partly fused, drooping, underside somewhat silvery; hastula yellowish, hornlike; bases wrapped in gauzy fiber. Stems: 8–10 in. thick, base

Chambeyronia macrocarpa, juvenile

Coccothrinax argentata

Coccothrinax argentea

Coccothrinax barbadensis

develops a boss of aerial roots. *Relatively fast-growing. Leaves below the tree canopy may be quite large, a light gathering adaptation. Heavily self-seeding, often producing dense clumps of individual palms. Salt tolerant.*

Coccothrinax crinita subsp. crinita

OLD MAN PALM

Cuba, threatened in the wild. Solitary palm to 15 ft.; zones 10–11. Blooms intermittently in warm, wet months. Seasonally moist/dry. Average, well-drained soil; alkaline pH. Full to part sun. Flowers: unisexual; inflorescence creamy white. Leaves: palmate, subcircular; leaflets broad, partly fused, hastula yellow-green. Stems: thickly matted with tangled, straw-colored fibers. *This subspecies is easily recognized by the abundant tangle of fiber among* the leaf bases. *The older fibers are sometimes blown away in tropical storms.* Subsp. brevicrinis *has short fibers.*

Cocos

Cocos includes a single species of solitary palm but several varieties originating in the southwestern Pacific region. Humans distributed coconuts during migrations, and the seeds are capable of floating considerable distances on their own. Leaves are pinnate. Male and female flowers are on the same plant (monoecious). The oil, husk (coir), nut-shell, and leaves have countless uses. Coconut is used mainly in sweets in the United States. Coconut "water" is the clear liquid endosperm inside the seed. Coconut "milk" is extracted by grating the nut-meat, adding hot water, and straining out the milky fluid. In the tropics, coconut milk is added to rice, soups, and curries.

In the 1960s lethal yellowing disease, an untreatable plant malady, devastated commercial plantations of 'Panama Tall' and 'Jamaica Tall' and other susceptible palms as it swept through the Caribbean. 'Malayan Dwarf' proved highly resistant; it has golden-yellow to peach-colored seeds. When crossed with 'Panama Tall', it yields the 80% disease-resistant 'Maypan', which has golden to green seeds. Obtain certified first-generation 'Maypan' hybrids. Second-generation, open-pollinated seeds, taken from a generous neighbor's resistant tree, will have lower resistance to lethal yellowing. Seeds are easy to sprout. Lay seed in its husk on its side, cover it halfway with humus-rich soil, and keep it moist.

Cocos nucifera 'Malayan Dwarf'

GOLDEN COCONUT,
MALAYAN DWARF COCONUT,
COCOTERO AMARILLO

Exact origin obscure (southwestern Pacific). Solitary palm to 60 ft.; zones 10–11. Blooms continuously in warm, wet months. Moist to moderately dry. Sandy, well-drained soil. Full sun. Flowers: unisexual; bracts 2, one small, the other canoelike, woody, and persistent; fruit rounded, golden to peach-colored. Leaves: pinnate, to 10 ft. long, drooping. Stems: erect, base spreading. *Moderately salt tolerant. Highly resistant to lethal yellowing disease. 'Malayan Dwarf' is not truly dwarf. It just starts bearing fruit when the stem is about 6 ft. tall. 'Maypan' is a hybrid of 'Malayan Dwarf' and 'Panama Tall' and the seeds may be golden or green.*

Coccothrinax barbadensis, inflorescence

Coccothrinax barbadensis, leaf hastula detail

Coccothrinax crinita subsp. *crinita*

Cocos nucifera 'Maypan'

Cocos nucifera 'Panama Tall'

COCONUT PALM, COCOTERO

Exact origin obscure (probably eastern Africa to the Pacific Islands). Solitary palm to 60 ft.; zones 10–11. Blooms continuously in warm, wet months. Moist to moderately dry. Sandy, well-drained soil. Full sun. Flowers: unisexual; bracts 2, one small, the other canoelike, woody and persistent, fruit 3-angled, green. Leaves: pinnate, to 10 ft. long, drooping. Stems: gracefully swayed. *This palm is the epitome of tropical island flora, growing right on the sand dunes. It has mostly succumbed in areas with lethal yellowing disease.*

Copernicia

Copernicia includes 25–30 species of usually solitary palms from the Caribbean and South America. Leaves are palmate, the petioles often sharply toothed. Flowers are bisexual, on long, branched stalks that stick out horizontally between and below the leaves. These stately palms are disease resistant and exceptionally handsome. They are underutilized in cultivation but highly recommended.

Copernicia baileyana

BAILEY PALM

Cuba, West Indies. Solitary palm to 50 ft. or more; zones 10–11. Blooms continuously in warm, wet months. Moderate moisture to fairly dry. Fertile, well-drained soil. Full sun. Flowers: bisexual; inflorescences emerging laterally between the leaves. Leaves: palmate, stiff, clustered at the crown; leaflets mostly fused, free only at the tips; petioles short, waxy, toothed, persisting for a relatively short time. Stems: columnar, concrete gray, leaf scar rings almost imperceptible, vascular bundle scars dot the surface; aerial roots protrude near base. *This is a majestic, slow-growing palm of dry savanna and open woodlands with a clean, straight trunk.*

Cocos nucifera 'Malayan Dwarf', mature fruit

Unusual but highly recommended for landscaping.

Copernicia hospita

Cuba. Solitary palm to 25 ft.; zones 10–11. Blooms continuously in

Copernicia baileyana, trunk detail

Cocos nucifera 'Panama Tall'

Copernicia baileyana

warm, wet months. Moderate moisture to fairly dry. Fertile, well-drained soil. Full sun. Flowers: bisexual; inflorescence stalks very long, drooping, emerging from between the leaves. Leaves: palmate, waxy gray-green; petioles toothed, bases long,

Copernicia hospita, trunk detail

persistent for several years. Leaf scar rings on older trees are raised, undulating, and ridged with traces of fiber. *The erect stem is not as stocky as C. baileyana and is often partly covered by persistent leaf bases.*

Copernicia macroglossa
PETTICOAT PALM
Synonym: *C. torreana.* Cuba. Solitary palm to 25 ft.; zones 10–11. Blooms almost constantly in warm, wet months. Moderate moisture to fairly dry. Fertile, well-drained soil. Full sun. Flowers: bisexual, creamy white; inflorescences protrude from between the leaves. Leaves: palmate, rigid, arranged spirally around the crown; leaflets with sharp teeth on outer segments, persistent; petioles very short (subsessile). *The almost stalkless leaves create a dense, tidy skirt completely hiding the stem in young palms, though dry leaves are sometimes lost*

in windstorms or spoiled by overly fastidious landscapers. Old leaves provide hiding places for birds.

Corypha
Corypha includes 6–8 species of solitary palms from tropical Asia to Australia. Leaves are costapalmate. Male and female flowers are on the same plant (monoecious). Coryphas flower only once before dying (monocarpic) but certainly go out with a flourish. *Corypha umbraculifera*, the talipot palm, reaches maturity after 30–40 years. It then produces a towering inflorescence, 20 ft. or more above the crown, the largest in nature, and about a quarter million seeds. The bloom may last for several months. A close relative, the gebang palm, *C. utan* (syn. *C. elata*), is native from Southeast Asia to Australia and has narrower leaves.

Corypha umbraculifera
TALIPOT PALM, TALIPOTE
Southern India, Sri Lanka. Solitary monocarpic palm to 75 ft. or more; zones 10–11. Blooms at maturity. Moderate moisture to seasonally wet, humid. Fertile, well-drained soil. Full sun. Flowers: unisexual; inflorescence erect, much branched, to 20 ft. Leaves: costapalmate, undulating, to 15 ft. long, 12 ft. wide; leaflets broad, partly fused, tips blunt; petiole toothed, bases semipersistent. Leaf scar rings on the stem are closely spaced. *A slow-growing palm of open areas and floodplains. Rare in cultivation in the United States.*

Cyrtostachys
Cyrtostachys includes approximately 8 species of solitary and clustering palms from Malaysia to New Guinea. Leaves are pinnate with long, slender crownshafts. The

Copernicia hospita

Copernicia macroglossa

crownshaft of *C. renda* may be green, striped red and green, red, or orange. The red form is more commonly cultivated, though rarer color selections merit attention. Male and female flowers are on the same plant (monoecious). This very ornamental palm is much admired by collectors, but its sensitivity to cold has kept it from becoming more common in cultivation outdoors in the continental United States. It is suitable for containers.

Cyrtostachys glauca

Papua New Guinea. Clustering palm to 30 ft., generally smaller in cultivation; zones 10–11. Bloom intermittently in warm, wet months. Moist to wet, humid. Fertile, well-drained soil. Full to part sun. Flowers: unisexual; fruit black. Leaves: pinnate, slender crownshafts gray-green; lower petiole gray-green (glaucous). Stems: slender.

Cyrtostachys renda

SEALING-WAX PALM, MAHARAJAH PALM

Synonym: *C. lakka.* Malaysia, Indonesia (Sumatra), Borneo. Clustering palm, 10–30 ft.; zone 11. Blooms intermittently in warm, wet months. Moist to wet, humid. Fertile soil. Full sun to bright filtered light. Flowers: unisexual; fruit black. Leaves: pinnate, crownshafts and lower petiole bright green to glossy red. Stems: slender. *A highly ornamental, slow-growing palm of tropical rain forest and wetlands. Cold-sensitive and often grown in warm greenhouses or in containers that can be moved indoors when chilly.*

Dictyosperma

Dictyosperma includes a single species of solitary palm from the Mascarene Islands (in the Indian Ocean off eastern Africa). Leaves are pinnate with long crownshafts. A twist of the petiole turns the blades on edge. Flowers are unisexual, the male and female flowers on the same plant (monoecious). This palm is endangered in the wild but often cultivated.

Cyrtostachys renda

Cyrtostachys renda, red crownshaft detail

Dictyosperma album

PRINCESS-PALM, HURRICANE PALM

Synonym: *Areca alba.* Mascarene Islands (Mauritius and Reunion), endangered in the wild. Solitary palm to 30 ft.; zones 9–11. Blooms intermittently in warm, wet

Corypha umbraculifera

Cyrtostachys glauca

months. Moderate moisture and humidity. Fertile, well-drained soil. Full to part sun. Flowers: unisexual; bracts thin, double, one inside the other; inflorescence stalk branched. Leaves: pinnate; crownshaft long, green; petioles twisted, turning the ends of the leaves on edge. Stems: base spreading, leaf scar rings closely spaced, cut by vertical fissures. *Crownshaft reddish brown in var.* rubrum.

Dictyosperma album, inflorescence

Dypsis decaryi, infructescence

Dypsis

Dypsis includes approximately 150 species of solitary and clustering palms from Madagascar and the neighboring Comoro Islands. This genus now circumscribes species formerly segregated into *Chrysalidocarpus*, *Neodypsis*, *Neophloga*, and *Phloga*. Leaves are pinnate. Male and female flowers are on the same plant (monoecious). These species are often cold-sensitive.

Dypsis decaryi
TRIANGLE-PALM
Synonym: *Neodypsis decaryi*. Madagascar. Solitary palm to 35 ft.; zones 10–11. Blooms intermittently in warm, wet months. Moderate moisture to seasonally moist/dry. Fertile, deep, well-drained soil. Full sun. Flowers: unisexual, yellow-green; fruit round, blue-green, waxy (glaucous), on obliquely erect, yellowish green branched stalks. Leaves: pinnate, 10 ft.+ long, ascending and arching in an acute V; leaflets linear, bluish gray, lower leaflets much elongated (reins); petiole covered with stiff purplish-maroon hairs, bases broad, in 3 ranks, persistent. Stems: stocky, to 20 in. diameter. *The 3 ranks of leaves are an excellent field mark. Fairly common in cultivation.*

Dypsis leptocheilos
TEDDY-BEAR PALM
Synonym: *Neodypsis leptocheilos*. Madagascar. Solitary, erect palm to 35 ft.; zones 10–11. Blooms intermittently in warm wet months. Regular moisture to wet. Fertile, deep soil. Full sun. Flowers: unisexual. Leaves: pinnate; leaflets narrow, lax at the tips; crownshaft covered with stiff brown hairs. Stems: thickly covered with white wax when young, leaf scar rings chocolate brown. *A*

Dictyosperma album

Dypsis decaryi

striking, erect palm. Unusual in cultivation. This swamp native thrives in
wet conditions and in upland locations with adequate moisture. Cold-
sensitive. For protected sites.

Dypsis lutescens

YELLOW BUTTERFLY PALM,
BAMBOO PALM
Synonyms: *Areca lutescens* (misapplied), *Chrysalidocarpus lutescens*.
Madagascar. Clustering palm,
15–30 ft.; zones 9–11. Blooms intermittently late spring, summer.
Moderate moisture to seasonally
moist in summer, drier in winter.
Average, well-drained soil. Full to
part sun. Flowers: unisexual, fruit
purple-black. Leaves: pinnate, yellow-green, arching; leaflets many,
narrow, held in a V. Stems: bamboolike. *This common palm is still
often referred to as areca palm because it was long ago mistakenly attached to that genus. Some mis-*

*nomers die hard. The leaves have a
naturally yellowish hue. The dense
clusters can be thinned to expose the
canelike stems.*

Elaeis

Elaeis includes 2 species of solitary
palms, one from Africa and the
other from tropical America.
Leaves are pinnate. Male and female flowers are on separate inflorescences on the same tree (monoecious). These palms ultimately
become very large and need considerable room for spread. Local
people use palm oil from the seed
for lighting and cooking fuel. The
palms are grown in plantations in
Africa where the rain forest has
been dozed. The nuts are harvested
as a commercial crop. In the
United States, this highly saturated
oil (the most serious contributor to
blood vessel blockage) can be
found in some margarines, pre-

pared and packaged foods, cooking
oils, soaps, and cosmetics. *Elaeis
oleifera*, from northern South America to Costa Rica, is known as the
American oil-palm, palmiche, or
coquito ("little coconut").

Dypsis leptocheilos, trunk detail

Elaeis guineensis

AFRICAN OIL-PALM,
PALMA AFRICANA
Synonyms: *E. madagascariensis*, *E.
melanococca*. Tropical Africa; widely
cultivated and naturalized. Solitary

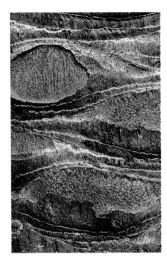

Elaeis guineensis, trunk detail

Dypsis leptocheilos

Dypsis lutescens

palm, 40–80 ft.; zones 10–11. Blooms intermittently in warm, wet months. Moist and humid. Fertile, well-drained or wet soil. Full sun. Flowers: unisexual, female flowers in clustered inflorescences, male flowers in spikes; spathes 2, papery. Leaves: pinnate; leaflets dull green, lax; petiole bases broad with sharp-edged, semipersistent bases. Stems: gray, leaf scar rings undulate, base spreading. *A stocky palm of rain forest and moist riverbanks. The crown is rounded, green leaves filling the upper hemisphere, dry ones filling in the lower half.*

Hyophorbe

Hyophorbe includes 5 species of solitary palms from the Mascarene Islands (in the Indian Ocean off eastern Africa). Leaves are pinnate with long crownshafts. Male and female flowers are on the same plant (monoecious). The species are un-common in general cultivation, though they are very popular among palm enthusiasts. Trunks of *H. lagenicaulis* and *H. verschaffeltii* are notable for their distinctively swelling profiles. The lesser-known species have straight trunks. The species here are very ornamental, adaptable, and salt tolerant. They are endangered in the wild.

Hyophorbe lagenicaulis
BOTTLE-PALM

Mascarene Islands, endangered in the wild. Solitary palm to 35 ft.; zones 10–11. Blooms intermittently in warm, wet months. Seasonally moist/dry. Average, well-drained soil. Full to part sun. Flowers: unisexual, fragrant; inflorescence large, branching; fruit ovoid, to 2 in. long. Leaves: pinnate, sturdy, rigid; crownshaft blue-green, waxy. Stems: swelling below the crownshaft, developing a bottle shape with age. *The stocky, bulging trunk and relatively few leaves are distinctive. Drought tolerant.*

Hyophorbe verschaffeltii
SPINDLE PALM

Mascarene Islands, endangered in the wild. Solitary palm to 35 ft.; zones 10–11. Blooms intermittently in warm, wet months. Seasonally moist/dry. Average, well-drained soil. Full to part sun. Flowers: unisexual. Leaves: pinnate, erect; crownshaft abruptly swelling at the base, bluish gray, purplish at the lower edge, waxy. Stems: waxy gray, spindle-shaped when mature. *Drought tolerant. Sugar cane beetle is a serious threat to this palm in the Caribbean. It is also susceptible to lethal yellowing disease.*

Hyphaene

Hyphaene includes 5 species of solitary palms from Africa, Mada-gascar, the Arabian Peninsula, and India. Some species are difficult to distinguish. Leaves are costapalmate. Male and female flowers are on different trees (dioecious). The fruits are used for animal feed and oil, the leaves for thatch and bas-

Hyophorbe lagenicaulis, infructescence

Elaeis guineensis

Hyophorbe lagenicaulis

ketry. These palms are probably called gingerbread palms because of the gingerbread-colored fruits. The moist, mealy flesh (pericarp) clinging to fibers surrounding the seed is, at best, a subsistence food.

Hyphaene compressa

GINGERBREAD PALM, DOUM
Eastern and southeastern Africa. Solitary palm to 40 ft.+; zones 10–11. Blooms intermittently. Semiarid. Average, well-drained soil. Full sun. Flowers: unisexual. Leaves: costapalmate, arching from the rachis, semipersistent; leaflets held in a V; petiole edges sharply toothed. Stems: cross-hatched with divided leaf bases, often branching (rare in palms). *A slow-growing palm of arid regions but can grow in moist climates with excellent drainage. Salt tolerant. The orange-brown fruit is turbinate or somewhat cupcake-shaped compared to the more rounded fruit of* H. coriacea.

Latania

Latania includes 3 solitary species of palms from the Mascarene Islands (in the Indian Ocean off eastern Africa). Leaves are costapalmate and bluish green. Male and female flowers are on separate trees (dioecious). The palms are salt tolerant and marginally hardy. *Latania loddigesii* is difficult to distinguish from *Bismarckia nobilis*. The stem is not quite as stocky and the crown is somewhat more spreading than rounded. A more definitive distinction is the raised pattern on the seedcoat of *Latania*; *Bismarckia* seeds are smooth. *Latania* is susceptible to lethal yellowing disease and palm bud weevils, while *Bismarckia* is resistant.

Latania loddigesii

BLUE LATAN-PALM
Mauritius, endangered in the wild. Solitary palm, 40–50 ft.; zones 8–11. Blooms in warm, wet months. Seasonally moist/dry. Average, sandy, well-drained soil. Full sun. Flowers: unisexual, male and female on separate trees. Leaves: costapalmate, grayish green. *An erect, moderately salt-tolerant species. Marginally cold tolerant. Requires plentiful moisture when*

hot. Similar to but not as blue-gray as Bismarckia nobilis.

Licuala

Licuala includes approximately 108 species of solitary and clustering palms from Southeast Asia to northern Australia, New Guinea, and Vanuatu (New Hebrides). Leaves are palmate or costapalmate, with leaflets variously fused and divided. Leaves may be almost circular, fan-shaped, or sometimes divided into windmill-like segments. Flowers are bisexual. These are small, striking palms of under-

Hyophorbe verschaffeltii, stem detail

Latania loddigesii, female tree with fruit

Hyophorbe verschaffeltii

Hyphaene compressa

story locations. They are suitable for containers.

Licuala grandis
RUFFLED FAN-PALM
Vanuatu (New Hebrides). Solitary palm to about 10 ft.; zones 10–11. Blooms winter or intermittently. Moist. Fertile, well-drained soil. Bright broken to filtered light. Flowers: bisexual. Leaves: costapalmate, large, undulating; leaflets fused, pleated, subcircular. *A cold-sensitive species of moist, tropical understory. Suitable for containers.*

Licuala peltata
India, Myanmar (Burma). Solitary palm to 15 ft.; zones 10–11. Blooms winter or intermittently. Moist. Fertile, well-drained soil. Bright filtered light. Flowers: bisexual; fruit small, on branches of a pendent stalk. Leaves: costapalmate; leaflets divided into segments like windmill vanes, 2–3 ft. long; margin notched. *The large leaves of the very ornamental subsp.* sumawongii *are 4–5 ft. wide and the leaflet margins are completely fused.*

Livistona
Livistona includes approximately 28 species of solitary palms from northeastern Africa and Saudi Arabia to Southeast Asia, southern Japan, and northern Australia. Leaves are costapalmate. Flowers are unisexual, male and female flowers are on the same tree (monoecious), rarely on separate trees (dioecious), or sometimes bisexual. *Livistona chinensis* is a commonly cultivated landscape palm.

Livistona chinensis
CHINESE FAN-PALM
China, Taiwan, Japan (Ryukyu Islands). Solitary palm, 15–30 ft.; zones 9–11. Blooms fall, winter or intermittently. Moist. Fertile, well-drained soil. Full to part sun. Flowers: bisexual; fruit olive-shaped, pearly gray, becoming speckled, then completely black. Leaves: costapalmate, leaflets partly fused, tips free and drooping; bases semipersistent. Trunk with close-set leaf scar rings. *This erect fan-palm is moderately salt tolerant. It is marginally hardy but with some leaf damage from frost.*

Lodoicea
Lodoicea includes a single species of solitary palm from the Seychelles

Licuala grandis

Licuala peltata

Licuala peltata, infructescence

Licuala peltata subsp. *sumawongii*

in the Indian Ocean. Unlike the co-conut palm, *Cocos nucifera, Lodoicea* has a thin, dense husk that is not buoyant, so this palm is probably not widely dispersed by water. The husked seed resembles 2 fused, elongated coconuts, the largest seed in nature weighing up to 50 lbs. These palms are rare even in botanical gardens. Leaves are costapalmate, large, and very broad, with the sides arching from the slender rachis in a deep V. The leaflet margins are fused almost to the ends. *Lodoicea* bears only 1 or 2 large leaves at a time while young. Male and female flowers, up to 4 in. wide, are on separate plants (dioecious). *Lodoicea maldivica* is an exceptionally slow-growing palm that may take several hundred years to reach full height. Flowering begins after 30–40 years. Trees of both sexes must be grown in proximity for pollination and seed produc-

tion. The seeds take 3–5 years to mature. This palm produces a 10-ft. taproot that requires a deep hole. The seeds were once sold to tourists as curiosities. With so many requirements and so many years to reproduce, this species is, not surprisingly, threatened. Fortunately, preserves have been created in its native habitat.

Lodoicea maldivica

DOUBLE COCONUT, COCO DE MER
Seychelles, threatened in the wild. Solitary palm to 90 ft.; zones 10–11. Blooms intermittently after 30–40 years. Moist. Fertile, sandy, deep, well-drained soil. Full sun. Flowers: unisexual. Leaves: costapalmate, to 12 ft. wide (twice as wide as long); gracefully arching from the rachis; leaflet margins fused to within a few inches of the edge; petiole to 20 ft. long when mature. *Rare in cultivation.*

Phoenix

Phoenix includes approximately 13 species of solitary and clustering palms from southern Asia to the Middle East, Africa, southern Europe, and the Canary Islands.

Livistona chinensis, infructescence   *Livistona chinensis*, stem detail

Leaves are pinnate, the lower leaflets often reduced to sharp spines. Flowers are unisexual, the male and female flowers on separate trees (dioecious). The date-palm, *P. dactylifera*, and its varieties have

Livistona chinensis

Lodoicea maldivica, juvenile

been cultivated for millennia. The fruit has been a food staple in the Mediterranean region since ancient times. It is relatively nonperishable and was carried by travelers as food and for trade, resulting in its wide distribution. The stately V shape of the leafy crown is easily recognized in ancient Egyptian decorative art. *Phoenix* palms readily hybridize.

Phoenix canariensis
CANARY ISLAND DATE-PALM
Canary Islands. Solitary palm to 60 ft.; zones 8–11. Blooms intermittently in warm, wet months. Semi-arid or seasonally moist/dry. Average, sandy, well-drained soil. Full sun. Flowers: unisexual; in clusters protruding obliquely between the leaves; fruit dark red, eaten by small animals and birds. Leaves: pinnate, to 20 ft. long, radiating evenly in a symmetrical crown; lower leaflets reduced to spines; leaves deciduous with persistent flat bases creating a spiral pattern. Trunk: stout, 2–3 ft. thick. *Hardy in mild temperate regions. A large, erect palm which needs plenty of space to spread. Moderately salt tolerant. Susceptible to fusarium wilt.*

Phoenix canariensis, fruit

Phoenix canariensis, stem detail

Phoenix dactylifera, stem detail

Phoenix canariensis

Phoenix dactylifera

Phoenix dactylifera

DATE-PALM, PALMA DATILERA

Exact origin obscure (probably North Africa, Arabia). Solitary or clustering palm to 100 ft.; zones 9–11. Blooms spring, summer. Semiarid. Average, sandy, well-drained soil. Full sun. Flowers: uni-sexual; fruit is the edible date. Leaves: pinnate, ascending in a distinctive V, to 15 ft. long, deciduous, stumps rounded. Stems: erect. *Date-palms will grow in moist climates, but bear fruit only in hot, dry climates. Susceptible to numerous diseases but resistant to fusarium wilt.*

Phoenix reclinata, inflorescence with orange bract

Phoenix reclinata, fruit, with leaves of blue buttonwood, *Conocarpus erectus*

Moderately salt tolerant. Selections are hand-pollinated and propagated from suckers. Suckers are usually removed to maintain solitary habit.

Phoenix reclinata

SENEGAL DATE-PALM

Tropical Africa, Madagascar. Clus-

Phoenix roebelinii, trunk detail

tering palm, 30–40 ft.; zones 9–11. Blooms intermittently in warm, wet months. Seasonally moist/dry. Average, well-drained soil. Full sun. Flowers: unisexual; inflorescence erect; bracts orange to yellow; fruit golden to orange. Leaves: pinnate, 8–10 ft. long, lax, somewhat twisted, lower leaflets in several ranks, the lowest reduced to 6- to 8-in. spines. Stems: gracefully "recline" away from others in the cluster. *This salt-tolerant palm is frequently cultivated. It produces large clumps. The spines can inflict septic wounds, a problem primarily for landscapers. Not recommended close to human activity unless lower leaves are removed. Can become invasive in moist areas.*

Phoenix roebelinii

DWARF DATE-PALM, PYGMY DATE-PALM

Southeast Asia. Solitary or clustering palm to 10 ft.; zones 10–11. Blooms intermittently in warm, wet

Phoenix reclinata

Phoenix roebelinii

Phoenix roebelinii, inflorescences

months. Seasonally moist/dry. Average, well-drained soil. Full sun. Flowers: unisexual; inflorescences white, pendent, at the base of the petioles; fruit black. Leaves: pinnate, 3–5 ft. long, forming a rounded crown; petiole edges spined. Stems: covered with knoblike petiole remnants; narrowing at the base. *The numerous whisklike inflorescences are showy for a short time. Primarily a clustering species, but a solitary selection is more common in cultivation. Suitable for containers.*

Pritchardia

Pritchardia includes 25–36 species of solitary palms from Hawaii and the Tuamotu and Fiji islands. Leaves are palmate. Flowers are bisexual. These island dwellers are adapted to tropical winds and have fair to moderate salt tolerance. *Pritchardia* is the only palm genus native to Hawaii. Rats and other introduced animals that eat the seed and seedlings, as well as humans, have rendered these species endangered or extinct in the wild.

Pritchardia aylmer-robinsonii

HAWAIIAN FAN-PALM, LOULU, WAHANE

Hawaii, endangered in the wild. Solitary palm to about 50 ft.; zones 10–11. Blooms intermittently in warm, wet months. Moist. Fertile, well-drained soil; alkaline pH. Full sun. Flowers: bisexual. Leaves: costapalmate, slightly folded and arching from the rachis; leaflets partly fused, tips lax, bases semi-persistent. Stems: slender, leaf scar rings closely spaced, irregular; base somewhat spreading. *A sparsely leafed small palm. Nuts edible. Leaves formerly used for thatch.*

Pritchardia aylmer-robinsonii

Pseudophoenix lediniana

Pseudophoenix

Pseudophoenix includes 4 species of solitary palms from the Caribbean basin and Florida. Leaves are pinnate, the leaflets in several ranks. Flowers are unisexual, male and female flowers on the same plant (monoecious), or sometimes bisexual. The trunk may be swollen near the base or somewhat bottle-shaped. The crownshaft is relatively short and often bulging.

Pseudophoenix lediniana

Haiti. Solitary palm to 40 ft.; zones 10–11. Blooms intermittently in warm, wet months. Seasonally moist/dry. Average, well-drained soil. Full sun. Flowers: unisexual. Leaves: pinnate; leaflets slender; petioles and crownshaft waxy gray. Trunk: slender to slightly bottle-shaped, leaf scar rings regularly spaced.

Pseudophoenix sargentii

BUCCANEER PALM, SARGENT'S CHERRY PALM, HOG-PALM
Cuba, Hispaniola, Bahamas, Florida Keys, Yucatan, Belize, endangered in the wild. Solitary palm to 10–15 ft.; zones 9–11. Blooms intermittently in warm, wet months. Seasonally moist/dry. Sandy, well-drained soil; alkaline pH. Full sun. Flowers: unisexual; inflorescence much branched; fruit in fused clusters of 2 or 3, yellow turning dark red. Leaves: pinnate; slender leaflets in several ranks; petioles silvery; crownshaft often bulging near the base, waxy. Trunk: irregularly swollen, leaf scar rings closely spaced. *A small palm. Extinct in some parts of its native range. Subsp. saonae is endemic to Navassa Island, Haiti. It has a somewhat stockier trunk.*

Pseudophoenix vinifera

WINE-PALM, CHERRY PALM
Hispaniola, endangered in the wild. Solitary palm to 50 ft.; zones 10–11. Blooms intermittently in warm, wet months. Seasonally moist/dry.

Pseudophoenix lediniana, stem detail

Pseudophoenix sargentii, infructescence

Sandy, well-drained soil; alkaline pH. Full sun. Flowers: unisexual. Leaves: pinnate; rachis, petiole, and crownshaft waxy gray. *A tall palm eventually developing a bulging or bottle-shaped stem. The sap is*

Pseudophoenix sargentii subsp. *saonae*

Pseudophoenix sargentii subsp. *sargentii*

made into wine. The top is cut off, killing the palm, and the sap is allowed to ferment inside the trunk.

Ptychosperma

Ptychosperma includes approximately 28 species of solitary or clustering palms from northeastern Australia, New Guinea, and the Solomon Islands. Leaves are pinnate. Flowers are unisexual, with male and female flowers on the same tree (monoecious). These are relatively fast-growing palms. The branched clusters of red fruit at the base of slender crownshafts are quite ornamental. Trunks are slender with widely spaced leaf scar rings. Species in cultivation readily hybridize and it is impossible to identify open-pollinated seedlings with certainty.

Ptychosperma elegans
SOLITAIRE PALM

Papua New Guinea, Australia (Queensland). Solitary palm to 30 ft.; zones 10–11. Blooms intermittently in warm, wet months. Seasonally moist/dry. Average, well-drained soil. Full to part sun. Flowers: unisexual; fruit red, in clusters below the crownshaft; seedcoat has 5 lengthwise grooves. Leaves: pinnate; leaflet tips blunt. *This graceful, slender palm is self-seeding. Distributed by birds and mammals. Sometimes appears clustering where many fruits sprout together. Species in cultivation readily hybridize. Naturalized in South Florida. The Macarthur palm,* P. macarthurii, *is distinguished by its clustering habit.*

Ptychosperma waitianum
LUCITA WAIT PALM

New Guinea. Solitary palm, 10–15 ft.; zones 10–11. Blooms intermittently in warm, wet months. Regular moisture and humidity. Fertile, well-drained soil. Bright broken or filtered light. Flowers: unisexual; fruit dark red. Leaves: pinnate, leaflets triangular, fishtail-like, young leaves russet-red. *A dainty, understory palm. Does not tolerate extended dry periods. The shape and coloration of the new leaves are very ornamental. Suitable for containers. Named in honor of Lucita Wait, a founder of the International Palm Society.*

Raphia

Raphia includes approximately 28 species of solitary and clustering palms from South America, tropical Africa, and Madagascar. Leaves are pinnate, the leaflets arranged in several ranks. Flowers are unisexual, with male and female flowers on the same tree (monoecious). These palms flower once at maturity and then die (monocarpic). The fruits are sometimes fashioned into ornaments and beads. The epidermis is stripped from the young leaves. This raffia "straw" is used as a natural twine or woven into hats, bags, and baskets, and sometimes employed as light structural support in fine garments. *Raphia regalis* is reputed to produce the longest leaf in the plant world.

Raphia farinifera
RAPHIA-PALM

Synonyms: *R. pedunculata, Sagus farinifera, Sagus ruffia*. Tropical eastern Africa, Madagascar. Solitary palm to 35 ft.; zones 10–11. Blooms intermittently in warm, wet months. Moist to wet, humid. Fertile soil. Full sun. Flowers: unisexual; fruit glossy, ovate, stalks scaly. Leaves: pinnate, very long; leaflets in several ranks, rachis orange; petiole bases persistent. Stems: erect, stout, leaf scar rings fairly closely set, gray with glossy orange areas. *A large palm with long leaves. Uncommon in the United States. The name is derived from raffia, the Malagasy name for this palm and its fiber.*

Pseudophoenix vinifera

Ptychosperma elegans

Ptychosperma waitianum, new red leaf

Ptychosperma waitianum, infructescence

Ptychosperma species, infructescence

Ravenea

Ravenea includes approximately 17 species of solitary palms from Madagascar and the nearby Comoro Islands. Leaves are pinnate. Flowers are unisexual, with male and female flowers on separate trees (dioecious). These handsome, feathery palms are unusual in cultivation. Do not confuse this genus name with travelers' tree, *Ravenala*.

Ravenea rivularis
MAJESTY PALM

Madagascar. Solitary palm, 20–75 ft.; zones 10–11. Blooms intermittently in warm, wet months. Moist to wet. Fertile, well-drained soil. Full sun. Flowers: unisexual. Leaves: pinnate, leaflets long and slender, on one plane. Stems: stocky, leaf scar rings closely set. *The species name means "riverside." This palm grows naturally on streambanks and should be kept moist at all times. Young palms are grown in containers.*

Reinhardtia

Reinhardtia includes approximately 6 species of small, solitary or clustering palms from Mexico, Central America, Colombia, and Hispaniola. The leaflets are fused along the edges except for slitlike openings ("windows") on either side of the rachis near the base. Flowers are unisexual, with male and female flowers on the same plant (monoecious). These palms of moist forest understory thrive in diffused light. They require acidic soil. In areas with alkaline soil, they should be grown in containers.

Reinhardtia latisecta
WINDOW-PALM

Belize. Solitary palm to 10 ft.; zones 10–11. Blooms intermittently in warm, wet months. Moist and humid. Fertile, humus-rich, well-drained soil; acid pH. Bright filtered light. Flowers: unisexual; inflorescence white. Leaves: pinnate, leaflets mostly fused except for small slit openings along both sides of the rachis. *This dainty palm is suitable for containers when young. Photographed at the Kampong, Coconut Grove, Florida.*

Rhapis

Rhapis includes approximately 10 species of clustering palms from China and Southeast Asia. Leaves are palmate with partly fused leaflets. Flowers are unisexual, with male and female flowers on separate plants (dioecious) or on the same plant with bisexual flowers (polygamous). Some species are painstakingly cultivated as houseplants in temperate climates. They grow luxuriantly outdoors in the subtropics and tropics as a hedge or screening plant. *Rhapis* is particularly susceptible to sucking insects indoors.

Rhapis excelsa
LADY-PALM

Southern China. Clustering palm, 6–15 ft.; zones 9–11. Blooms intermittently in warm, wet months. Regular moisture and humidity when hot, moderate moisture

Raphia farinifera

Ravenea rivularis

Raphia farinifera, stem detail

Raphia farinifera, infructescence on root boss

Reinhardtia latisecta

Rhapis excelsa

when cool . Fertile, humus-rich, well-drained soil; alkaline pH. Part sun to medium filtered light. Flowers: unisexual, white; fruit white, waxy. Leaves: palmate, bright green, persistent; leaflets partly fused in windmill-like segments,

tips blunt. Stems: slender, bamboolike. *Excellent understory hedge. Remove persistent dry leaves. This species is fairly cold tolerant. Bright sun or too much or too little moisture will result in dull or brown leaves. 'Akatsuki' is an unusual selection or* hybrid of unknown origin with somewhat smaller, variegated leaves.

Roystonea

Roystonea includes approximately 10 species of solitary palms from the Caribbean basin. Known as royal palms, *Roystonea* species readily hybridize and may be difficult to distinguish with certainty in cultivation. Leaves are pinnate with pointed leaflets in 2 to many ranks. A long green crownshaft tops a concrete-gray pillarlike trunk. Flowers are unisexual, with male and female flowers on the same plant (monoecious). The fruit is small and crimson before turning black. The solitary woody bract is canoeshaped, to 6 ft. long. Leaf scar rings become indistinct with age, and the trunk surface is typically covered with gray-green lichens. The base often develops a boss of aerial roots. Royal palms are native to

fresh and brackish wetlands but also thrive in uplands with adequate moisture. *Roystonea regia* is fairly drought tolerant. The native habitats are threatened. Although these monumental palms are often used to landscape boulevards and formal driveways, the heavy, self-shedding leaves present a hazard where they can fall on people or into traffic. The equally elegant Puerto Rican hat palm, *Sabal causiarum*, or the Bailey palm, *Copernicia baileyana*, would be preferable in these locations. String trimmers easily undercut trunk bases. Keep grass away from the base with a border of mulch.

Roystonea oleracea
CARIBBEAN ROYAL PALM,
PALMA REAL
Synonym: *Areca oleracea*. Southern Caribbean, northern South America. Solitary palm to 120 ft.; zones

Rhapis 'Akatsuki'

Roystonea oleracea, stem detail with leaf remnants and lichens

Roystonea oleracea

Roystonea regia

10–11. Blooms intermittently in warm, wet months. Moist to wet, seasonally dry. Fertile soil. Full sun. Flowers: unisexual, yellow-green; inflorescence at base of the crownshaft. Leaves: pinnate; leaflets slender, in 2 ranks, lax; crownshaft long, bright green. *This species is distinguished from the other royals by leaflets in only 2 ranks. The stem tapers fairly evenly. Many authors characterize the leaves as held above the horizontal, an inconsistent distinction as seen in the photo.*

Roystonea regia

ROYAL PALM, PALMA REAL, CHAGUARAMO, PALMIER ROYAL
Synonym: *R. elata*. South Florida, Cuba, Yucatan to Honduras. Solitary palm to 100 ft.; zones 10–11. Blooms intermittently in warm, wet months. Moist to wet, seasonally dry. Fertile soil. Full sun. Flowers: unisexual, yellow-green; inflores-

cences multiple, at the base of crownshaft. Leaves: pinnate, to 10 ft. long; leaflets narrow, in many ranks; crownshaft long, bright green, bulging at the base. Stems: irregularly bulging, often cone-shaped at the base. Produces a boss of aerial roots around the base. *Photographed at Fairchild Tropical Garden. Wild royal palms can be seen in the southern wetlands of Everglades National Park, Florida. The Florida population of royal palms was formerly segregated into R. elata.*

Sabal

Sabal includes approximately 16 species of solitary, sometimes stemless palms from the southern United States to northern South America. Several species are familiar native palms from Florida to South Carolina—*S. palmetto* is the state tree in both states—and west along the Gulf Coast. Leaves are

costapalmate, arching from the rachis in a V, and semipersistent. Dry leaves form a skirt below the crown. Leaflet margins are partly fused. Petioles are not armed. The leaf bases are forked, clasping the stem. These characteristics help distinguish *S. palmetto* from 2 other native Florida palms: saw palmetto, *Serenoa repens*, and paurotis-palm, *Acoelorrhaphe wrightii*. Flowers are unisexual, with male and female flowers on the same plant (monoecious), or sometimes bisexual. Epiphytic ferns and bromeliads find a congenial home in the old leaf bases. Hospitality becomes self-destructive, however, when *Clusia*, *Ficus*, or *Schefflera* seedlings take root, eventually strangling or shading the palm to death. Sabals grow in open grasslands and pine forest. They are sometimes killed by harvesters of "hearts-of-palm," the apical meristem.

Sabal bermudana

BERMUDA PALMETTO
Bermuda. Solitary palm to 25 ft.; zones 8–11. Blooms intermittently in warm, wet months. Seasonally moist/dry. Average, well-drained soil. Full to part sun. Flowers: bisexual. Leaves: costapalmate, grayish green; leaf bases forked. Stems: leaf scar rings ridged and furrowed. Somewhat salt tolerant.

Sabal causiarum

PUERTO RICAN HAT-PALM
Puerto Rico, Virgin Islands, Hispaniola, endangered in the wild. Solitary palm to 40 ft.; zones 10–11. Blooms intermittently in warm, wet months. Seasonally moist/dry. Average, well-drained soil. Full to part sun. Flowers: bisexual. Leaves: costapalmate, semipersistent; bases forked; densely clustered at the top of the massive trunk. *A stately palm with a columnar, straight gray trunk. Infrequently cultivated in the United States but highly recommended. Equally impressive as royal palms,* Roystonea, *with superior landscaping attributes including much lower moisture requirements and lightweight, semipersistent leaves.*

Sabal palmetto

SABAL PALM, CABBAGE PALM
South Carolina to Florida, Bahamas. Solitary palm, 20–80 ft.; zones 8–11. Blooms intermittently in warm, wet months. Seasonally moist/dry. Average to poor, well-drained soil. Full to part sun. Flowers: unisexual, fragrant; inflorescence stalk much branched,

Sabal bermudana

Sabal bermudana, stem detail

Sabal causiarum, stem detail with vascular remnants and lichens

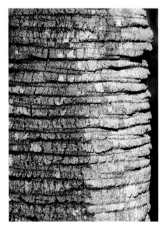

Sabal palmetto, stem detail

Sabal causiarum

Sabal palmetto

yellow-green; fruit ovoid, black. Leaves: costapalmate, arching in a V from the rachis; petiole thick, upper side flat, lower side rounded, unarmed. Stems: thick, erect; leaf bases semipersistent; leaf scar rings narrow, with vertical furrows. *Fairly common throughout Florida in open areas and pinelands, usually taller in the north. Fire resistant. Commonly intermingled with Serenoa repens, saw palmetto, which is distinguished by non-costa-palmate fan-shaped leaves and slender, armed petioles.*

Schippia

Schippia includes a single species of solitary palm from Belize. Leaves are palmate. Flowers are bisexual. This small, slender palm of forest understory resembles *Coccothrinax* with its white inflorescences and fiber-covered leaf bases. It also resembles *Thrinax* with its forked petiole bases. Distinguish *Schippia* by its fruits, about 1 in. diameter, much larger than fruits of either *Coccothrinax* or *Thrinax*, and by the corky texture of the lower trunk which provides insulation against fire.

Schippia concolor

SILVER PIMENTO-PALM
Belize, Central America. Solitary palm to 25 ft.; zones 10–11. Blooms intermittently in warm, wet months. Moderately to seasonally moist. Average, well-drained soil. Part sun to bright broken light. Flowers: bisexual; inflorescence snowy white; fruit white, about 1 in. long. Leaves: palmate; leaflets fused only near the base, arching from the hastula; petiole unarmed, bases forked and surrounded by fiber. Stems: slender, gray, with vertical fissures. *A slender, dainty palm for small spaces.*

Serenoa

Serenoa includes a single species of colony-forming palm endemic to the southeastern United States. Leaves are palmate. Petioles are slender and edged with tiny, sharp teeth. The petiole base is not divided. Flowers are bisexual. This palm is slow-growing but eventually develops a sinuous, semiascending, rarely straight stem. The trunk branches occasionally, often producing offshoots when the terminal apex is killed. These characteristics help distinguish *Serenoa*, saw palmetto, from young *Sabal palmetto* with which it often grows. Saw palmetto is a scrubby spreading species that grows on limestone mainly in coastal pinelands and open grassland. It is adapted to survive periodic fires that clear hardwood growth and maintain the pine-palm habitat. This palm is threatened by development and its current popularity as an herbal remedy. It is difficult to transplant and slow-growing from seed. It is moderately salt tolerant. It provides privacy and excellent screening from street noise on my property. Remove dead leaves to display the graceful trunk and reduce fire hazard.

Schippia concolor

Serenoa repens

Syagrus coronata

Syagrus coronata, stem detail

Syagrus

Syagrus includes approximately 32 species of clustering and solitary palms from South America, principally Brazil, plus a single species from the Lesser Antilles. Leaves are pinnate, the leaflets grouped in small clusters, often in several ranks around the rachis, producing a plumelike effect. These species lack crownshafts and the leaf bases are semipersistent. Flowers are unisexual, with male and female flowers on the same plant (monoecious). The queen-palm, *S. romanzoffiana*, is one of the most commonly cultivated palms. It produces a striking inflorescence resembling a long golden ponytail. Careless landscapers may damage the buds when they remove the old leaves. The seed oil from some species is used in soaps, carnauba wax, and lantern fuel. These species are susceptible to ganoderma, a deadly fungal disease. After infected trees are removed, other palms should not be planted in the same location.

Syagrus coronata
LICURI PALM

Brazil. Solitary palm to 30 ft.; zones 9–11. Blooms intermittently in warm, wet months. Moderate moisture to fairly dry. Average to fertile, well-drained soil. Full sun. Flowers: unisexual. Leaves: pinnate, bases triangular, rachis edges spined; leaflets slender, in many ranks, tips pointed. Stems: persistent leaf bases arranged in a distinctive spiral pattern. *A source of palm oil.*

Syagrus romanzoffiana
QUEEN-PALM

Synonyms: *Arecastrum romanzoffianum, Cocos romanzoffiana*. Argentina, southern Brazil, Paraguay, Uruguay. Solitary palm, 25–50 ft.; zones 9–11. Blooms intermittently in warm, wet months. Moderate moisture. Average to fertile, well-drained soil. Full to part sun. Flowers: unisexual; inflorescence pendent, golden, 3–5 ft. long; fruit golden-yellow to orange, to 1 in.; bract canoe-shaped, woody. Leaves: pinnate, arching; leaflets

Serenoa repens
SAW PALMETTO

Southeastern United States. Clustering palm to 10 ft.; zones 8–11. Blooms intermittently in warm, wet months. Seasonally moist/dry.

Rocky, gritty, well-drained soil. Full to part sun. Flowers: bisexual, fragrant; inflorescence yellow-green, branching; fruit black. Leaves: palmate; petioles slender, edges armed with small sharp teeth.

Starts out creeping but may eventually produce an ascending, rambling trunk. Moderately salt tolerant. Note the older plant with trunk in background of photo.

slender, lax, in clusters of 2–7. Stems: light gray, leaf scar rings widely spaced. *A common landscape palm. Marginally hardy and moderately salt tolerant. Var. australis has a sturdier stem and larger fruits. Squirrels eat the fruit.*

Syagrus sancona

Synonym: *S. tessmanii.* Peru. Solitary palm to 60 ft.; zones 10–11. Blooms intermittently in warm, wet months. Moderate moisture. Fertile, well-drained soil. Full sun. Flowers: unisexual. Leaves: pinnate; leaflets in 3 ranks. Stems: spreading at the base. *Distinguished from* S. romanzoffiana *by the mostly solitary, not clustered leaflet bases, the spreading trunk base, and more closely spaced leaf scar rings.*

Thrinax

Thrinax includes approximately 7 species of solitary palms from the Caribbean basin and the Florida Keys. Leaves are palmate, the leaflets relatively broad and partly fused; they are used for thatching in the West Indies. Flowers are bisexual and wind-pollinated. The inflorescences are creamy white. The fruit is small and white. *Thrinax* can be distinguished from *Coccothrinax* by the forked leaf bases and from *Schippia* by the much smaller white fruit.

Thrinax radiata

CARIBBEAN THATCH-PALM, FLORIDA THATCH-PALM
West Indies, Florida, Honduras. Solitary palm to 30 ft.; zones 10–11. Blooms intermittently in warm, wet months. Seasonally moist/dry. Average to poor, well-drained soil. Full to part sun. Flowers: bisexual; inflorescence white; fruit small, white, under 0.5 in. long. Leaves: palmate; leaflets broad; petiole bases forked, persistent. Stems: covered with old leaf bases and matted fibers. *An erect, relatively fast-growing palm. It tolerates near-freezing temperatures, wind, and salt. Self-seeding. Photographed at Montgomery Botanical Center.*

Veitchia

Veitchia includes approximately 15 species of solitary palms from Vanuatu, New Caledonia, and Melanesia (Fiji). Leaves are pinnate. Flowers are unisexual, with male and

Syagrus romanzoffiana

Syagrus romanzoffiana, inflorescence

Syagrus sancona

Syagrus sancona, infructescence

Syagrus sancona, stem detail

female flowers on the same tree (monoecious). Several species that were previously segregated are now combined. Manila palm, formerly *V. merrillii*, has been placed in its own genus, *Adonidia*. *Veitchia* is resistant to lethal yellowing disease; *Adonidia* is not. Protect young palms from freezing.

Veitchia arecina

Synonyms: *V. macdanielsii, V. montgomeryana*. Vanuatu (New Hebrides). Solitary palm, 25–40 ft.; zones 10–11. Blooms intermittently in warm, wet months. Moderate moisture. Average to fertile, well-drained soil. Full sun. Flowers: unisexual, white, to 1 in. diameter. Leaves: pinnate, leaflet tips droop-

ing. Stems: tall, slender, base often spreading. *Flowers comparatively large for a palm, often cover the ground. Cold-sensitive when young.*

Washingtonia

Washingtonia includes 2 species of solitary palms from Baja California, southern California, and Arizona. They grow along waterways,

Veitchia arecina, inflorescence

Thrinax radiata

Veitchia arecina, flaring base detail

Veitchia arecina

marshes, and beaches in otherwise arid regions. Leaves are costapalmate with drooping tips. The petioles are armed near the base and are not forked. Old leaves are persistent, hanging around the stem in a shaggy skirt. The skirt is often chopped off by landscapers, leaving jagged remnants sticking out in all directions. Left in place, the skirt provides shade and shelter for birds and other wildlife—of particular importance in desert regions. The other petticoat palm, *Copernicia macroglossa*, has a neatly arranged spiral skirt and its leaves lack petioles. Flowers are bisexual. The inflorescence is subtended by one papery bract. The fruit is datelike, consumed mostly by animals. The erect trunk is gray or brown, the leaf scar rings cut by vertical fissures and leaf remnants. These salt-tolerant species can become invasive in coastal wetlands. They interbreed, making it difficult to distinguish the species in cultivation with certainty. With age, *Washingtonia robusta* is taller than *W. filifera* with a more slender stem and a

Washingtonia filifera, trunk detail

spreading base, characteristics often hidden by the skirt. Susceptible to phytophthora bud rot.

Washingtonia filifera

CALIFORNIA WASHINGTON PALM, DESERT FAN-PALM, PETTICOAT PALM, COTTON-PALM

Synonyms: *Brahea filamentosa, W. filamentosa.* Southern California, Mexico (northern Baja California), Arizona. Solitary palm to 60 ft.; zones 9–11. Blooms intermittently. Moderate moisture/seasonally dry. Average, sandy, well-drained soil. Full sun. Flowers: bisexual; inflorescence long, feathery, sticking out laterally between the leaves. Leaves: costapalmate, persistent; leaflets more or less lax; cottony fiber around leaf bases when young; petiole armed. Stems: gray, leaf scar rings vertically fissured.

Washingtonia robusta

MEXICAN WASHINGTONIA, MEXICAN FAN-PALM, PETTICOAT PALM, THREAD-PALM

Mexico (southern Baja California, Sonora). Solitary palm to 80 ft.; zones 9–11. Blooms intermittently. Seasonally moist, moderate to dry. Average, sandy, well-drained soil. Full sun. Flowers: bisexual; inflorescence long, feathery, sticking out between the leaves. Leaves: costapalmate, persistent; leaflets more or less lax at the tips; fiber around young leaf bases; petiole orange-brown, armed. *Widely cultivated. Invasive in wet areas. A controlled species in South Florida.*

Wodyetia

Wodyetia includes a single species of solitary palm from mountainous regions of northeastern Australia. Leaves are pinnate; the leaflets

Washingtonia robusta

Wodyetia bifurcata

whorled around the rachis, foxtail-like. Flowers are unisexual, with male and female flowers on the same tree (monoecious). This distinctive palm has become popular in cultivation. It is erect with minimum spread and fits into most landscapes. It is disease resistant. The genus name (pronounced whoa-d-ET-e-ah) is an Australian aboriginal name. The species name alludes to forked fibers on the seedcoat. This palm likes acid soil. In alkaline soil it needs supplementary chelated iron or leaves become yellowish.

Wodyetia bifurcata
FOXTAIL PALM
Northeastern Australia. Solitary palm, 20–50 ft.; zones 8–11. Blooms summer. Seasonally moist/dry. Deep, sandy, well-drained soil; acid pH. Full sun. Flowers: unisexual. Leaves: pinnate; leaflets slender, in clusters, whorled evenly around the rachis, tips jagged; crownshaft slender, green, covered with white wax. Stems: leaf scar rings distinct and evenly spaced.

Zombia
Zombia includes a single species of clustering palm from Hispaniola. Leaves are palmate. Flowers are bisexual. The fruit is white. This palm is closely related to *Coccothrinax* with which it occasionally hybridizes. The slender stems are wrapped in woven, coarse, straw-colored matting. The fiber tips are bent outward, encircling the trunk with fringes of flat, sharp-tipped spines.

Zombia antillarum
ZOMBIE-PALM
Hispaniola. Clustering palm to 15 ft.; zones 10–11. Blooms spring, summer. Seasonally moist/dry. Average, well-drained soil. Full sun. Flowers: bisexual. Leaves: palmate, bright green; leaflets partly fused, tips more or less lax. *The coarsely woven fiber with evenly spaced, straw-colored spines is distinctive. Habit photo taken at the Montgomery Botanical Center.*

ARISTOLOCHIACEAE
ARISTOLOCHIA FAMILY, DUTCHMAN'S-PIPE FAMILY
Aristolochiaceae includes approximately 7 genera of perennial herbs and climbers, which are widely distributed in most tropical and mild temperate regions except Australia. This group is now considered to consist of nonmonocot paleoherbs, neither monocot nor dicot, more closely related to fossil groups of plants. Leaves are simple, sometimes lobed, palmately veined, and alternately arranged. The corolla is usually rudimentary or sometimes absent. The calyx has a more or less convoluted tube and funnel-shaped lobes. Aristolochias are often cultivated as curiosities and in butterfly gardens. They are larval food for swallowtail butterflies.

Aristolochia
Aristolochia includes approximately 350 species of herbs and herbaceous climbers, which are widely distributed in the tropics and mild temperate regions. The flowers lack true petals and are bilaterally symmetrical. The wondrously bizarre calyx is fused into a curved tube at the base with more or less funnel-shaped, fused lobes. In commonly cultivated species, the reticulated flowers suggest silk paisley handkerchiefs attached to a drain pipe. Common names imaginatively describe the inflated buds as pelicans, ducks, or Dutchmen's pipes. Some species are malodorous. Bees and flies venturing into the throat are trapped by backward-pointing hairs that prevent them from retreating. The insects fall into a swollen tank at the base where they thrash around until they pollinate the flower. Mission accomplished, the hairs wilt, and the insect can escape to pollinate another flower. The name "birthwort" is derived from the fetus-shaped bud of a European species and *wort*, from an Old English word for plant. As function was believed to follow form, an infusion was employed as a folk remedy during child birth. The fruit is a capsule that splits when mature into 6 segments held together by fibers. which resembles a basket. Prune aggressive species radically in fall to control. Of the species listed, only *A. ringens* is a nonaggressive perennial.

Zombia antillarum, infructescence   *Zombia antillarum*, stem detail

Wodyetia bifurcata, infructescence

Zombia antillarum

Aristolochia elegans

CALICO FLOWER, ARISTOLOQUIA
Synonym: *A. littoralis*. Argentina, western South America; widely naturalized. Perennial climber to 50 ft.; zones 7–11. Blooms warm months. Moderate moisture. Average, well-drained soil. Full sun to broken light. Flowers: funnel-shaped, fused lobes hoodlike, reticulated white and maroon, throat greenish white, 6–7 in. wide. Leaves: heart- to kidney-shaped, gray-green, 4–6 in. wide with 5 major veins. *Common in the United States as far north as Georgia. A pest of woodlands in North and Central Florida.*

Aristolochia gigantea

DUCK-FLOWER, ARISTOLOQUIA
Synonym: *A. sylvicola*. Brazil; naturalized in South and Central America. Perennial climber to 50 ft.+; zones 10–11. Blooms spring, summer. Moderate moisture. Average, well-drained soil. Full sun to broken light. Flowers: calyx oblong, edges reflexed, lax, maroon with white reticulations, 6–10 in. wide, throat yellow. Leaves: cordate, gray-green, 4–6 in. wide with 5 major veins. *Aggressive vine. Attractive to atala butterflies. The unopened bud at lower right of photo resembles an upended duck.*

Aristolochia grandiflora

DUTCHMAN'S PIPE, ARISTOLOQUIA
Synonyms: *A. gigas* (hort.), *A. pichinchensis*. Mexico, Central America; naturalized in the West Indies. Perennial climber to 50 ft.+; zones 10–11. Blooms spring, summer. Moderate moisture. Average, well-drained soil. Full sun to broken light. Flowers: calyx fused at base into a tube with a bulbous tank, lobes hoodlike, 8–16 in. wide reticulated maroon and white, a ribbony appendage, 10–20 in. long, dangles from the lower margin, throat maroon, malodorous. Leaves: elongated heart-shaped (cordate), 8–10 in. long. *Aggressive vine. Flowers sometimes very large and referred to as var. sturtevanti, an invalid name.*

Aristolochia ringens

PELICAN-FLOWER, ARISTOLOQUIA
Synonym: *A. globifora*. Brazil. Perennial climber to 10 ft.+; zones 10–11. Blooms winter, spring, summer. Regular moisture. Average, well-drained soil. Full sun to broken light. Flowers: calyx reticulated maroon and white, 2-lobed, the larger, lateral lobe 6–8 in. long, the upper, erect, spoon-shaped; throat lined with stiff white hairs, tube ending in an elongated tank. Leaves: broadly cordate, dull grayish green, paler on underside; about 4–5 in. wide. *Attractive to swallowtail butterflies. Desirable for its moderate growth. Dies back in winter or dry season.*

ASPHODELACEAE

ALOE FAMILY
Asphodelaceae comprises approximately 16 genera of herbs, shrubs, and trees from mostly subtropical, semiarid regions of the Old World. They were once lumped with the diverse genera known as the "lily legions." That group also included century-plants, *Agave*, which are sometimes referred to as American aloes. Leaves are succulent, mostly wedge-shaped, usually guttered, with more or less spined margins. They are arranged in basal rosettes or in whorls at the apex of a stem. Flowers are usually bisexual and radially symmetrical or sometimes asymmetrical. They have 6 tepals in 2 whorls, enclosing 6 stamens and 3 carpels. Bracts subtend the flower. The inflorescence is a spike or raceme on a branched or unbranched stalk arising from leaf axils near the center of the rosette. Aloes are pollinated by insects and nectar-feeding birds.

Aloe

Aloe includes approximately 380 mostly succulent herbs, shrubs, and trees from the Old World, with greatest diversity in southern Africa. The leaves are arranged in basal rosettes or in spiral whorls at the ends of short stems or fibrous trunks. Some species are solitary, others are clump-forming. Aloes flower annually (polycarpic), often over several months—a characteristic that distinguishes them from usually monocarpic agaves. Flowers are bisexual. The corolla is vase-shaped, partly fused, and usually inflated at the base. Flowers are arranged in spikes or racemes, on simple or branched stalks, and open from bottom to top (indeterminate). The colors of the open flowers and stamens often contrast with the color of the closed buds.

Aloes are commonly grown indoors in containers and thrive outdoors in mild, dry regions. In moist

Aristolochia elegans

Aristolochia gigantea

Aristolochia grandiflora

Aristolochia ringens

Aloe camperi

and humid areas, many do well in exceptionally well-drained soil. There is a variety of these xeric plants from which to choose. Some tolerate light frost. Many aloes hybridize and exhibit hybrid vigor, being more vigorous, adaptable, and disease resistant, and blooming over a longer period than the parent species. Aloes are exceptionally attractive to hummingbirds although they are completely alien to these American birds. Many aloe species are endangered in the wild and are protected in South Africa.

Aloe arborescens
CANDELABRA ALOE, TORCH-ALOE
Synonyms: *A. frutescens*, *A. natalensis*. Mozambique, South Africa. Succulent branching shrub to 8 ft.; zones 9–11. Blooms winter. Moderate moisture when hot, dry when cool. Gritty, well-drained soil. Full sun. Flowers: red-orange; inflorescence torchlike. Leaves: succulent, spreading to somewhat incurved; margins with short spines. *This large clustering aloe is prized for its dramatic winter displays. Salt tolerant. Exhibits considerable natural variation and varietal names are no*

longer considered valid. Photographed at Balboa Park.

Aloe camperi
Synonym: *A. eru*. Eritrea, Ethiopia. Succulent shrub to 3 ft.; zones 9–11. Blooms late winter, early spring. Moderate moisture when hot, dry when cool. Gritty, well-drained soil. Full sun. Flowers: tubular, pinkish orange to yellow; inflorescences compact, round-topped; stalk branched. Leaves: spreading, white-spotted; marginal spines short, green to reddish brown. *A short-stemmed, spreading*

aloe. *Sends out off-shoots from the base. Suitable as a bedding plant.*

Aloe capitata
Synonym: *A. cernua*. Madagascar. Succulent shrub, 2–3 ft.; zones 9–11. Blooms winter. Moderate moisture when hot, dry when cool. Gritty, well-drained soil. Full sun. Flowers: light yellow to yellow-orange, lax, with conspicuous reddish pedicels; stalk branched or unbranched; inflorescence a flat-topped, compact spike. Leaves: stiffly erect, wedge-shaped, to 18 in. long; margins lined with reddish brown spines. *An attractive aloe of moderate size. The tight, flat-topped inflorescence is fairly distinctive.*

Aloe ciliaris
CLIMBING ALOE
Synonym: *A. tidmarshi*. South Africa (Eastern Cape). Succulent climber, 6–15 ft.; zones 9–11. Blooms almost all year. Regular moisture when hot, less when cool. Gritty, well-drained soil. Bright broken or filtered light. Flowers: coral-red with green tips; stamens yellow. Leaves: bright green; with long hairs inside the sheathing leaf bases; margins with short, stiff hairs; on a trailing or clambering stem with wide internodes. *The species name alludes to the stiff hairs in place of spines. A semiepiphytic aloe of subtropical forests. Suitable for containers and rock gardens. Prefers moister, shadier conditions than most aloes.*

Aloe cryptopoda var. wickensii
Synonyms: *A. pienaarii*, *A. wickensii*. Northern South Africa. Succulent shrub, 4–5 ft.; zones 9–11. Blooms winter. Moderate moisture when hot, dry when cool. Gritty, well-drained soil. Full sun. Flowers: tubular, russet-red, yellow, or bi-colored; racemes conical to cylindrical; on branched stalks. Leaves: wedge-shaped, incurved, dull gray-green or somewhat reddish when dry; margins with small brown teeth. *A solitary, unbranched aloe. The species name means "hidden foot," alluding to the base of the flower stalks, which are covered by the bracts. The varieties were formerly segregated into separate species. Var.*

Aloe arborescens

Aloe capitata

Aloe ciliaris

Aloe cryptopoda var. *wickensii*

wickensii *(syn. A. wickensii) has yellow flowers. Very similar and closely related to A. lutescens, a clumping species with bi-colored inflorescences and a more northerly distribution (Van Wyk and Smith 1996).*

Aloe distans
JEWELED ALOE
South Africa (Western Cape). Succulent trailing shrub, 2–3 ft.; zones 8–11. Blooms spring, summer. Moderate moisture when hot, dry when cool. Gritty, well-drained soil. Full sun. Flowers: tubular; inflorescences flat-topped, loosely arranged, grayish pink to orange. Leaves: obtusely wedge-shaped, to 6 in. long, dull bluish green, reddish in dry conditions, white spots on lower surface; margins and teeth bright yellow; arranged in whorls on long, creeping stems. *A branching, marginally hardy, coastal species endemic to a limited region. The dense heads of pendent pink flowers are distinctive.*

Aloe ferox
BITTER ALOE, CAPE ALOE
Synonym: *A. supralaevis.* South Africa (Eastern Cape, Free State), Lesotho . Succulent trunk-forming shrub or tree, 3–15 ft.; zones 9–11. Blooms winter. Moderate moisture when hot, dry when cool. Gritty, well-drained soil. Full sun. Flowers: red to orange; spikes tall, cone-shaped, erect; on short, branched stalks. Leaves: tapering, slightly twisted, gray-green to reddish; mar-

gins with small black teeth, lower surface also covered with scattered black prickles. *Species name refers to the "ferocious" prickles. Develops an erect trunk with age. The dried sap, known as Cape aloes, is marketed as a purgative. A yellow-flowered selection from KwaZulu-Natal is some-*

times referred to as A. candelabrum. Aloe ferox *readily hybridizes with other aloes, making identification of plants in cultivation uncertain.*

Aloe kedongensis
Kenya, tropical East Africa. Succulent shrub, 4–5 ft.; zones 9–11.

Blooms winter. Moderate moisture when hot, dry when cool. Gritty, well-drained soil. Full sun. Flowers: tubular, yellow-orange to orange-pink; inflorescence spire-like, erect, to about 12 in. tall. Leaves: lanceolate to about 12 in. long, bluish green with yellowish

Aloe ferox

Aloe maculata

Aloe distans

Aloe marlothii

Aloe mudenensis

teeth along the margins, recurved, densely whorled around a slender stem. *Produces large clumps.*

Aloe maculata

BROADLEAF ALOE, SOAP ALOE

Synonyms: *A. latifolia, A. perfoliata, A. saponaria.* Zimbabwe, South Africa, Botswana. Succulent shrub, 2–3 ft.; zones 9–11. Blooms winter, spring, summer. Moderate moisture when hot, dry when cool. Gritty, well-drained soil. Full sun. Flowers: tubular, pink to yellow, corolla tips sometimes blue; in compact heads with pendent outer flowers, stalk sometimes branched. Leaves: triangular, 6–10 in. long, curved down, tips dry in arid conditions, gray-green to reddish when dry, large white spots (maculata means "spotted"); margins lined with red-brown spines. *A salt-tolerant coastal or inland aloe with flat-topped inflorescences and small, spotted leaves. Older plants develop a short stem. Adaptable. Readily hybridizes. Photographed bayside at the Kampong, Coconut Grove, Florida.*

Aloe marlothii

MOUNTAIN ALOE

Synonym: *A. spectabilis.* Northeastern South Africa to Mozambique. Succulent tree, 4–10 ft.; zones 8–11. Blooms winter. Moderate moisture when hot, dry when cool. Gritty, well-drained soil. Full sun. Flowers: yellow to red-orange; inflorescence stalk branched, the slender spikes spreading radially. Leaves: gray-green, persistent; margins and the leaf undersides covered with short black prickles. *Eventually develops a short stem. Of mountainous regions. Marginally hardy. The spreading inflorescence is distinctive and is often evident in hybrids of this species. A form from KwaZulu-Natal, sometimes referred to as* A. spectabilis, *has almost erect inflorescences.*

Aloe mudenensis

South Africa (KwaZulu-Natal). Succulent shrub to 2 ft.; zones 9–11. Blooms winter. Moderate moisture when hot, dry when cool. Gritty, well-drained soil. Full sun. Flowers: yellow-orange to shrimp pink; inflorescence erect, stalk branched.

Leaves: broad, dull green to reddish in dry conditions, with white streaks; margins spined. *A usually stemless species, but sometimes develops a short, unbranched stem. Endemic to the area around the town of Muden.*

Aloe plicatilis

FAN ALOE

South Africa (Western Cape). Succulent tree to 15 ft.; zones 9–11. Blooms spring. Regular moisture when hot, dry when cool. Sandy, well-drained soil; acid pH. Full sun. Flowers: scarlet, inflorescence rather sparse and small. Leaves: strap-shaped, arranged fanlike in 2 ranks (distichous) at the ends of thick branching stems. *This tree aloe is prized for its distinctive leaves. Of mountainous terrain, it tolerates light frost. Only a rare, stemless species,* A. haemanthefolia, *has a similar leaf shape. Photographed at Quail Botanical Garden.*

Aloe rubroviolacea

Yemen, southern Arabia. Succulent shrub to 3 ft.; zones 7–11. Blooms late spring, early summer. Regular moisture when hot, dry when cool. Gritty, well-drained soil. Full sun. Flowers: red; inflorescence slender, erect; stalk usually not branched.

Leaves: thick, succulent, recurved, tinged purple near the center; margins with hooked teeth. *Blooms later in the year than most cultivated aloes. Mature plants tolerate both light frost and heat.*

Aloe speciosa

TILT-HEAD ALOE

South Africa (Cape Province). Succulent tree, 3–15 ft.; zones 9–11. Blooms winter. Moderate moisture when hot, dry when cool. Gritty, well-drained soil. Full sun. Flowers: buds maroon becoming greenish

white, stamens red; spikes tall, erect, on short, unbranched stalks. Leaves: gray-green tinted reddish; marginal teeth red, soft. *Tolerates light frost. This species and its hybrids are easily recognized by the tilted, heavy rosette on an unbranched stem. Natural hybrids of* A. speciosa *and* A. ferox *are spectacular and exhibit hybrid vigor.*

Aloe vera

ALOE VERA, SÁVILA

Synonym: *A. barbadensis* (hort.). Canary Islands; widely cultivated.

Aloe speciosa

Aloe kedongensis

Aloe plicatilis

Aloe rubroviolacea

Succulent herb to 2 ft.; zones 9–11. Blooms spring. Moderate moisture when hot, dry when cool. Average, gritty, well-drained soil. Full sun. Flowers: greenish yellow; var. *chinensis*, orange; inflorescence stalk to 2 ft. Leaves: erect, gray-green, teeth dull. *The jellylike pulp inside the leaves is widely used in cosmetics and to soothe burns. The outer layer of the leaf produces a bitter, yellow exudate. Similar species may be poisonous. This species accumulated a number of incorrect names and origins, including A. barbadensis, or West Indian aloe, from plants that escaped into the wild from cultivation.*

Bulbine

Bulbine includes 30–50 species of mostly perennial herbs and shrubs from tropical eastern Africa, South Africa, and Australia. Plants are more or less succulent, sometimes with woody or underground stems. One species is occasionally cultivated in the United States. It was reputedly introduced into Florida by the late Brazilian plant collector and landscape architect, Roberto Burle Marx. The linear, grasslike leaves are arranged in basal whorls. Some species are pests in Australia. *Bulbine* is differentiated from the similar *Bulbinella* by fine hairs on the stamen filaments and from closely allied *Aloe* and *Knophofia* by its starlike, 3-parted, not tubular, flowers.

Bulbine frutescens

CAT'S TAIL, BALSEMKOPIVA (SOUTH AFRICA)
Synonym: *B. caulescens*. South Africa (Eastern Cape). Perennial herb to 18 in.; zones 9–11. Blooms warm months. Regular moisture when hot, less when cool. Average, well-drained soil. Full sun. Flowers: small, star-shaped, orange, yellow, or white; inflorescence cone-shaped on slender stalks. Leaves: stemless, grasslike, slightly fleshy; in basal whorls. *A clump-forming species. It thrives in dry climates though it is less verdant than in humid conditions. Attractive to butterflies.*

ASTERACEAE

ASTER FAMILY, COMPOSITE FAMILY
Asteraceae (Compositae) includes approximately 1535 genera of annual and perennial herbs, rarely shrubs and trees, which are distributed throughout the world. It is among the largest, most advanced and diverse plant families. Species are adapted to every type of habitat. Leaves are highly variable, simple or compound, basal or on a stalk (cauline), and usually alternate. The genera are grouped into subfamilies and tribes based on types of inflorescences. The flowers are highly specialized and reduced, organized into heads that collectively fill the functions of one flower. Individual flowers may be unisexual, bisexual, or sterile. The familiar daisy-type inflorescence has sterile ray-flowers, each with a ligule composed of 5 fused petals, which radiate around the outer circumference. The tiny disk-flowers, clustered in the center, bear the stamens and/or pistils and have a tubular corolla. In dandelion-type inflorescences, the flowers are not separated into disk- and ray-flowers, and all are fertile with ligulate corollas. A whorl of leafy bracts surrounds the base of the receptacle. The fruit is an achene with a persistent bristly or scaly calyx (pappus). Seeds are adapted for either wind or animal dispersal. When a dandelion-type inflorescence dries, the pappus, with a seed attached, is the feathery parachute that blows away with a puff.

Cheirolophus

Cheirolophus includes 3 species of perennial herbs from the western Mediterranean and Canary Islands. The inflorescence is a globular head of disk-flowers. Ray-flowers are absent. The heads are on long, unbranched stalks (peduncles). These species are adapted to fairly dry, mild temperate to subtropical climates. The genus is related to *Centaurea*.

Cheirolophus canariensis

Synonym: *Centaurea canariensis*. Canary Islands, endangered in the wild. Perennial herb, 3–4 ft.; zones 8–9. Blooms late spring, early summer. Moderate moisture. Average, well-drained soil. Full sun. Flowers: disk-flowers red-violet, ray-flowers absent; in a rounded head. Leaves: elliptic, to 5 in. long, 1 in. wide, glossy. *Suitable for the perennial garden. Unusual in cultivation. Photographed in the Canary Island collection at Quail Botanical Garden.*

Coreopsis

Coreopsis includes approximately 120 species of herbs and subshrubs from North and Central America and tropical Africa. A number of species are common American wildflowers. Leaves are simple or pinnately lobed (pinnatifid), often softly hairy. Floral heads are daisylike, with white or colored ray-flowers and disk-flowers. The seeds are dispersed by a bristled pappus that readily attaches itself to animal fur and clothing. *Coreopsis* is closely related to the common weed, beggar's ticks (*Bidens*).

Coreopsis leavenworthii

LEAVENWORTH'S TICKSEED
Florida. Perennial herb, 3–4 ft.; zones 8–11. Blooms warm months. Moist to fairly dry. Average soil. Full sun. Flowers: ray-flowers 8, bright yellow, disk-flowers brown to purplish; rotate head to 1 in. wide; stalk branched. Leaves: narrowly oblong to lanceolate, sometimes lobed, hairy. *State flower of Florida. Found in open, wet meadows, disturbed areas, and pinelands over much of the state. Attractive to butterflies.*

Dahlia

Dahlia includes approximately 30 perennial herbs of cool mountainous regions of Mexico, Central America, and Colombia. They are widely grown for their ornamental flowers. The innumerable hybrids

Aloe vera

Bulbine frutescens

Cheirolophus canariensis

Coreopsis leavenworthii

are classed into 11 or more horticultural groups based on the complexity of the floral heads. Leaves are pinnate or pinnately lobed. Some species are cultivated for their edible tuberous roots. Tubers should be protected from freezing or lifted in winter.

Dahlia imperialis
GIANT DAHLIA, DAHLIA GIGANTÓN
Synonym: *D. arborea.* Southern Mexico to Colombia. Perennial herb, 10–15 ft.; zones 8–10. Blooms spring, summer. Moderate moisture. Fertile, well-drained soil, mulch. Full to part sun. Flowers: ray-flowers violet, pink, or white, disk-flowers yellow; heads rotate, to 4 in. wide; arranged in loose panicles. Leaves: pinnate, 8–10 in. long; leaflets ovate, to 2 in. long, downy; margins toothed; petiole base sheathes reddish stalk. *This tall, shrubby dahlia is a parent of many cultivated hybrids. Roots are ground and used as a coffee adulterant similar to chicory.*

Montanoa
Montanoa includes approximately 25 species of trees, shrubs, and vines from mountainous regions of Central America to northwestern South America. They have thick, fibrous stems with pithy centers. Inflorescence heads are rotate. Ray-flowers, usually 8, are white to violet. The seed heads are composed of a spherical involucre of sometimes showy bracts, which develop after the daisylike ray-flowers drop, and are often mistakenly shown in the literature as if they were the flowers. Leaves are entire to lobed, margins more or less toothed. Montanoas are fast-growing, suitable for quick cover, and showy winter bloomers. They are brittle in strong wind. Cut back to the main limbs after bloom for compact growth. *Montanoa hibiscifolia* is listed as invasive in Hawaii.

Montanoa grandiflora
TREE-DAISY, TERESITA
Honduras. Perennial shrub, 10–15 ft.; zones 10–11. Blooms late fall, early winter. Moderate moisture. Average, well-drained soil. Full sun. Flowers: rotate, daisylike, ray-flow-

ers mostly 8, white, disk-flowers yellow; seed heads to 2 in. diameter, spherical, bracts white. Leaves: broadly ovate, to 10 in. long; margins shallowly lobed or toothed. *Seed heads very showy in this species. Attractive to zebra long-wing butterflies.*

Montanoa guatemalensis
Central America. Perennial shrub to 10 ft.; zones 10–11. Blooms fall, winter. Seasonally moist/moderate. Average, well-drained soil. Full sun. Flowers: rotate, daisylike, ray-flowers 5 or 6, white, disk-flowers yellow; heads to 1.5 in. wide; seed heads small, spherical, to 0.5–1 in. diameter, bracts greenish. Leaves: ovate-lanceolate to elliptic, 6–8 in. long; margins entire to shallow toothed, not lobed.

Montanoa hibiscifolia
MEXICAN TREE-DAISY
Southern Mexico to Costa Rica. Perennial shrub, 10–15 ft.; zones 10–11. Blooms late fall, early winter. Moderate moisture. Average, well-drained soil. Full to part sun. Flowers: ray-flowers mostly 8, white, disk-flowers yellow; in lax clusters (corymbs); seed heads to 1 in. diameter; bracts greenish white. Leaves: deeply 5-lobed, downy below, 6–10 in. long; margins with large teeth. *A fast-growing, large shrub. Invasive in Hawaii.*

Pericallis
Pericallis includes approximately 15 perennial herbs and shrubs from

the Canary Islands, Madeira, and the Azores in the eastern Atlantic Ocean. These islands are warmed by the Gulf Stream and have mild temperate to subtropical climates but relatively low precipitation, often in the form of morning mists. *Pericallis* is closely related to *Senecio* and is suitable for cultivation in Mediterranean-type climates. Many Atlantic island species are endangered. Quail Botanical Garden has a collection of Canary Islands flora.

Pericallis webbii
WILD CINERARIA
Synonym: *Senecio webbii.* Canary Islands. Perennial herb to 3 ft.; zones 9–10. Blooms warm months. Moderate moisture. Fertile, well-drained soil. Part sun or bright broken light. Flowers: ray-flowers white to pale

lavender, disk-flowers purple. Leaves: in a basal rosette. Pericallis ×hybrida *(syn.* Cineraria ×hybrida*) is the name of a group of winter-flowering hybrids in red, violet, and blue hues, known in the trade as "florists' cineraria."*

Phymaspermum
Phymaspermum includes approximately 15 shrubs from southern Africa. Floral heads are small and have only disk-flowers in dense, flat-topped clusters (cymes). The genus name refers to the tubercled achene fruits. Plants are suitable for cultivation in semiarid and Mediterranean-type climates.

Phymaspermum acerosa
Synonym: *Athanasia acerosa.* South Africa. Evergreen shrub, 3–4 ft.; zones 9–11. Blooms spring, sum-

Dahlia imperialis

Montanoa grandiflora, seed heads

Montanoa guatemalensis

Montanoa hibiscifolia, flowers and seed heads

Pericallis webbii

mer. Moderate moisture when hot, dry when cool. Average, gritty, well-drained soil. Full sun. Flowers: ray-flowers absent, disk-flowers mustard yellow, small, in compact cymes to 6 in. wide; honey-scented. Leaves: needle-shaped, blue-gray. *A spreading, round-topped shrub. Thrives in hot, semiarid conditions. The species name refers to the needle-shaped leaves.*

Podachaenium

Podachaenium (pronounced poe-duh-KAY-ne-um) includes 2 species of shrubs or small trees from Mexico and Central America. They have large lobed or toothed leaves. The inflorescences are daisylike, with white ray-flowers and yellow disk-flowers. They somewhat resemble *Montanoa* species but have 12 or more ray-flowers and produce substantial woody trunks and larger clusters of small flowers. The genus name means "footed achenes," referring to the long inflorescence stalks. Podachaeniums are quite charming and suitable for dry climates.

Podachaenium eminens
DAISY-TREE
Synonym: *Ferdinanda eminens.* Mexico to Costa Rica. Evergreen shrub or tree to 20 ft.; zones 9–11. Blooms spring, early summer. Fairly dry. Average, gritty, well-drained soil. Full to part sun. Flowers: ray-flowers 12–14, white, disk-flowers yellow, in large panicles. Leaves: broadly ovate, 3-lobed, 6–12 in. long, dull green above with gray, downy hairs below; petiole and branches softly downy (tomentose). *A woody, spreading tree often grown in semiarid regions from southern California to Costa Rica.*

Pseudogynoxys

Pseudogynoxys includes approximately 14 perennial shrubs and herbaceous climbers from tropical South America. The genus is closely related to *Senecio.* Inflorescences are rotate daisylike. Ray-flowers are orange, numbering about 16, and more or less reflexed. They are in branched clusters (corymbs). The receptacle is cup-shaped, which distinguishes this group from *Senecio,* which has a flat receptacle. Mexican flame vine, *P. chenopodioides,* is often used as a striking fence or wall cover in Central America. It produces copious, wind-borne seed and can become weedy. *Pyrostegia venusta* (Bignoniaceae) is also known as flame-vine.

Pseudogynoxys chenopodioides
MEXICAN FLAME-VINE
Synonym: *Senecio confusus.* Mexico to Colombia; widely naturalized. Perennial climber, 10–20 ft.+; zones 9–11. Blooms intermittently in winter, spring. Moderate moisture. Average to poor, well-drained soil. Full to part sun. Flowers: ray-flowers orange to scarlet, disk-flowers golden to orange; heads rotate, 1–1.5 in. wide, in terminal clusters (cymes). Leaves: ovate, 2–3 in. long, green mottled with purple; margins toothed; petiole short. *Heavily self-seeding and potentially weedy.*

Senecio

Senecio includes at least 1500 species of annuals, biennials, and perennial herbs, shrubs, a few trees, and climbers, which are widely distributed. Various *Senecio* species are adapted to diverse habitats, from alpine to coastal, desert to tropical rain forest. The genus includes succulent xerophytes and salt-tolerant species. It is among the largest genera of flowering plants although many species have been segregated into different genera. Leaves are variable. Ray-flowers are short or absent. The receptacle that supports the flower head is disk-shaped.

Senecio cineraria
DUSTY MILLER
Synonyms: *Cineraria maritima, S. candicans.* Mediterranean region. Perennial subshrub to 2.5 ft.; zones 8–10. Blooms warm months. Moderate moisture to fairly dry. Average, well-drained soil. Full sun. Flowers: ray-flowers and disk-flowers yellow, small; in flat-topped clusters (cymes) on branched stalks. Leaves: ovate, more or less lobed in different selections, felty, silver-gray. *Used as a bedding plant. The foliage provides outstanding contrast especially for blues and purples. Thrives in hot, dry climates and coastal locations. Prone to rot in humid climates. Often grown as an*

Phymaspermum acerosa

Podachaenium eminens

Podachaenium eminens, flowers

Pseudogynoxys chenopodioides

Senecio cineraria

annual. *The species name alludes to the cinder-gray leaf color.*

Senecio tamoides

PARLOR-IVY

South Africa. Succulent scrambling climber; zones 9–11. Blooms spring, summer. Moderate moisture to dry. Average, well-drained soil. Full sun. Flowers: ray-flowers 5, yellow, disk-flowers yellow and brown; in cymes. Leaves: ovate, 2–3 in. long, lobed, rubbery; margins finely dentate (toothed). Stems: fleshy, terete, dark green. *Foliage ivylike. Prune lightly for shape.*

Sphagneticola

Sphagneticola includes 4 species of perennial herbs from tropical America and Asia. Ray-flowers and disk-flowers are usually yellow. Inflorescences are rotate, solitary or in small clusters. Wedelia, *S. trilobata*, long grown as a ground cover, has become invasive in wild habitats and is a lawn pest in many areas. It is difficult to eradicate once established.

Sphagneticola trilobata

WEDELIA, CREEPING OXEYE, SINGAPORE DAISY

Synonyms: *Complaya trilobata, Wedelia trilobata.* Tropical and subtropical America; widely naturalized. Perennial trailing herb; zones 9–11. Blooms warm months. Moderate moisture. Average, well-drained soil. Full to part sun. Flowers: rotate, ray-flowers and disk-flowers yellow; solitary. Leaves: 3-lobed or ovate with 2 enlarged lateral teeth, hairy; margins toothed, dark green. *Facetiously referred to as weedelia, this creeping, mounding pest is invasive in Australia, Malaysia, and the Pacific Islands and is a controlled species in South Florida. The species name alludes to the 3-lobed leaves. Cultivation and distribution strongly discouraged.*

Tagetes

Tagetes includes approximately 50 annual and perennial herbs from the southwestern United States to Argentina and 1 from Africa. Among them are marigolds. These aromatic plants have small or ab-sent ray-flowers. The heads may be solitary or in cymes. Some species are sometimes interplanted with vegetables and susceptible ornamentals to repel nematodes. Some are said to be effective controls against mosquito larvae but method of application is unclear (Mabberley 1997).

Tagetes lucida

SWEET-SCENTED MARIGOLD, SWEET MACE, MEXICAN MARIGOLD, YERBA ANÍS

Mexico, Guatemala. Perennial herb or subshrub to 2 ft.; zones 9–11. Blooms warm months. Moderate moisture to fairly dry. Average, well-drained soil. Full sun. Flowers: ray-flowers very short, yellow, disk-flowers yellow; heads globular, peduncles unbranched or sparsely branched. Leaves: linear to oblong, blue-gray, to 1 in. long; margins toothed. Stems: woody. *Anise-scented. Has strong pesticide properties.*

Tithonia

Tithonia includes 10 or 11 species of annual and perennial herbs and shrubs from Mexico and Central America. The floral heads are rotate, solitary or in small clusters on long stalks. *Tithonia diversifolia* is often cultivated as an ornamental in the tropics and becomes naturalized or invasive in wet areas. It is tilled under as "green manure" in Sri Lanka. Tithonias and other sunflower-like species are called *mirasol* ("looks-at-the-sun") in Spanish, referring to the rotation of the floral head toward the sun (heliotropism) throughout the day.

Tithonia diversifolia

MEXICAN BUSH-DAISY, MEXICAN SUNFLOWER, MIRASOL

Mexico, Central America; widely naturalized. Perennial shrub, 6–12 ft.; zones 9–11. Blooms fall, winter, spring, or dry season. Moderate moisture to fairly dry. Average, well-drained soil. Full sun. Flowers: ray-flowers and disk-flowers deep golden-yellow; rotate heads to 5 in. wide, on long stalks. Leaves: ovate, 6–12 in. long, entire to deeply lobed, base tapering toward the petiole, glossy to downy (pubescent). *A fast-growing shrub from hot, dry climates but also thrives in moist and humid conditions with excellent drainage. Used as a quick cover but becomes rangy if not pruned. Cut*

Senecio tamoides

Sphagneticola trilobata

Tagetes lucida

back sharply after bloom. Listed as invasive in Hawaii. Not known to be weedy in South Florida.

BALSAMINACEAE

BALSAM FAMILY,
TOUCH-ME-NOT FAMILY

Balsaminaceae includes only 2 genera but many species of annual and perennial herbs, which are widely distributed in the tropics, with a few in northern temperate regions. They are well represented in India and Asia. Leaves and stems are more or less fleshy. Flowers are bilaterally symmetrical, turned upside down (resupinate), with a petal-like sepal bearing a spurlike nectar tube toward the back of the flower. The fruit is a dry capsule that opens explosively (hence touch-me-not) or a small, berrylike drupe.

Impatiens

Impatiens includes approximately 850 species of annual and perennial herbs and shrubs, with greatest diversity in Southeast Asia and Africa. Hybrids are the most commonly cultivated forms. They have complex and uncertain ancestry. Most are from montane regions and prefer moderate temperatures. Because of their low tolerance for heat and cold, they are commonly grown as mild season annuals. Balsams demand regular moisture. They are not good choices where irrigation is inadequate or where subject to drought restrictions. A thick layer of mulch greatly reduces irrigation requirements. Never plant these or other ground covers with high moisture requirements under flowering trees and shrubs or fruit trees that require a dry season. The excess moisture during dormancy will decrease the bloom or fruit or may permanently harm the tree. Balsams are suitable for containers and hanging baskets. Species *Impatiens* are interesting alternatives to the ubiquitous hybrids. All are susceptible to snails, sucking and chewing insects, damp rot, and mildew.

Impatiens auricoma

Madagascar, Mascarene Islands, Comoro Islands. Perennial herb, 2–3 ft.; zones 10–11. Blooms fall, winter, spring. Regular moisture and humidity. Fertile, humus-rich, well-drained soil. Part sun to bright filtered light. Flowers: yellow-orange, upper petals form a hood, lower petals a 2-lobed lip, spur short. Leaves: ovate to elliptic, to 4 in. long; margins crenulate; petioles with several stalked glands.

Impatiens New Guinea Group hybrids

NEW GUINEA IMPATIENS,
NO-ME-TOQUES

Garden hybrids. Perennial subshrub, 18–24 in.; zones 10–11. Blooms mild seasons. Regular moisture and humidity. Fertile, humus-rich, well-drained soil. Full sun to bright filtered light. Flowers: various colors, to 2 in. wide, spur long. Leaves: lanceolate, tip tapering, dark metallic green with red midvein, sometimes marked with yellow; margins finely toothed. *New Guinea hybrids involve* I. hawkeri *with leaves that are longer and more colorful than those of* I. walleriana *hybrids.*

Impatiens pseudoviola hybrids

Garden hybrid, *I. pseudoviola* × ?. Perennial herbs to 12 in.; zones 10–11. Bloom mild seasons. Regular moisture and humidity. Fertile, humus-rich, well-drained soil. Full to part sun. Flowers: white and magenta-purple, orange, or lavender-pink, spur short. Leaves: ovate, dark green, succulent; margins finely scalloped (serrulate). 'Hawaiian Purple' and 'Hawaiian Orange' are hybrids of unknown ancestry involving *Impatiens pseudoviola*, a mounding species with white or lavender, violet-shaped flowers.

Impatiens sodenii

GIANT IMPATIENS, GIANT TOUCH-ME-NOT, NO-ME-TOQUES GIGANTE
Synonym: *I. oliveri.* Tropical eastern Africa. Perennial subshrub, 3–8 ft.; zones 10–11. Blooms winter, spring. Regular moisture and humidity. Fertile, humus-rich, well-drained soil. Bright filtered light. Flowers: pink to white, to 2 in. wide, spur curved. Leaves: oblanceolate, glossy dark green, in whorls; margins finely toothed (serrulate). Stems: dark green.

Impatiens hybrids

IMPATIENS, BALSAM, BUSY LIZZIE,
SULTANA, NO-ME-TOQUES

Garden hybrids. Perennial herbs, 12–16 in.; zones 10–11. Bloom mild seasons. Regular moisture and humidity. Fertile, humus-rich, well-drained soil. Full sun to bright filtered light. Flowers: many colors, spur straight. Leaves: variable, ovate to elliptic, 1–4 in. long, fleshy; margins scalloped; petioles often with stalked glands. *Many Impatiens hybrids are of uncertain ancestry. They generally involve* I. walleriana *(African origin) and/or* I. balsamina *(Asian origin). New double-flowered selections resemble tuberous begonias.*

Impatiens auricoma 'African Queen'

Impatiens 'Hawaiian Purple' and 'Hawaiian Orange'

Tithonia diversifolia

Impatiens New Guinea Group 'Rosetta'

Impatiens sodenii

BEGONIACEAE

BEGONIA FAMILY

Begoniaceae includes 2 genera of perennial herbs, shrubs, and climbers from the tropics. Flowers are unisexual, with male and female flowers usually on the same plant (monoecious) or occasionally on different plants (dioecious). Leaves are simple, often lobed. Leaves and stems are fleshy. Though often described as preferring neutral to slightly acid pH, many species grow quite vigorously in alkaline soils with a thick bed of mulch.

Begonia

Begonia includes 900–1000 species of fleshy herbs, shrubs, and climbers, which are widely distributed in the tropics. Cool-growing types from the Andes are seasonally dormant. Begonias have been hybridized for centuries and their ancestry is usually obscure. Male flowers have 2–6 unequal tepals and a cluster of bright yellow stamens. Female flowers have 2–5 equal tepals attached to an often 3-winged, inferior ovary. Flowers range from small to showy, usually in shades of pink, red-orange, or white. Inflorescences may be borne on long or short stalks. Some species are delicately scented.

Fanciers group begonias horticulturally by type of growth (fibrous, rhizomatous, or tuberous) and habit (angel-wing, rex, cane, or semperflorens), though hybrids often exhibit a combination of these traits. In containers, begonias are grown in African-violet mix with added sand for good drainage. Use dilute liquid or slow-release fertilizers. In general, begonias like regular moisture and humidity; bright, slightly filtered light; and good air movement. Rhizomatous types are fairly tolerant of seasonal dry spells and chills, though leaves may die back or brown. Propagated from rhizome and leaf cuttings or division. Outdoors begonias usually thrive in understory locations, though a few will take full sun.

Begonia hybrids

Garden hybrids. Perennial rhizomatous herbs, 1–6 ft.; zones 10–11. Bloom variously depending on ancestry. Even moisture; humidity, drier when cool. Fertile, humus-rich, well-drained soil. Bright filtered light. Flowers: usually unisexual, in shades of pink or white. Leaves: suborbicular to obliquely ovate, often with zones of dark red, pink, and green, green and colored veins; often covered with glistening scales and/or hairs; margins sometimes fringed (fimbriate). Stems: often covered with hairs. Begonia ×diurna *is an old French, fibrous-rooted hybrid of B.* coccinea *with canelike stems (also referred to in horticulture as B.* 'Elaine' *or B.* 'Prince D' Liege'). *It thrives outdoors. The tops are killed back by frost but the plants recover if rhizomes are protected from freezing.* 'Merry Christmas' *is a rex/angel-wing type with unusually large flowers.* 'Mirage' *is a spreading rhizomatous type with leaves silver-scaled above and maroon below, and small white flowers. The latter two are suitable for pots and baskets.*

Impatiens hybrids

Begonia 'Merry Christmas', male (left) and female (right) flowers

Begonia ×diurna

Begonia 'Mirage'

Begonia nelumbiifolia
LOTUS-LEAFED BEGONIA,
LILY-PAD BEGONIA

Southern Mexico to Colombia. Perennial rhizomatous herb to 3 ft.; zones 10–11. Blooms late winter, spring. Moderate moisture. Fertile, sandy, humus-rich, well-drained soil. Full to part sun, bright filtered light. Flowers: unisexual, white, sparkling; in many-flowered cymes. Leaves: suborbicular, to 18 in. wide or more; petiole long, with long hairs, attached to the bottom of the blade (peltate); margins serrulate. *A large begonia suitable for outdoor landscaping. It tolerates full sun with adequate moisture. The species name alludes to the lotuslike leaf (Nelumbo). The* rubra *form has crinkled leaves with reddish veins.*

BERBERIDACEAE
BARBERRY FAMILY

Berberidaceae includes approximately 15 genera of herbs and shrubs, which are widely distributed in north temperate and tropical montane regions, primarily the Andes of South America. Plants often have a yellow sap which is toxic. Leaves are simple, sometimes deeply lobed or compound. Flowers are bisexual and radially symmetrical. The 4–6 sepals are free. Petals, or probably, petal-like stamens are free, often in 2 whorls of 4–6. Stamens are 4 to numerous.

Nandina
Nandina includes a single species of shrub from mild temperate areas of China and Japan. It is commonly grown in mild temperate and subtropical regions of the United States. Leaves are tripinnate (subdivided 3 times). Stems are erect, more or less covered with persistent leaf bases. Nandina has a dainty, somewhat bamboolike habit in broken or filtered light. Unfortunately, it is often pruned as a hedge, leaving a clump of graceless, stiff, bare stalks. Nandina is not a satisfactory hedge plant because it branches mainly from the base. It should be allowed to grow naturally. Thin unruly or overly long branches at the base and allow room to spread somewhat. It makes a superb container plant for

the patio. It is weedy in mild temperate regions but is not known to be a pest in South Florida.

Nandina domestica
HEAVENLY BAMBOO

Southern China, Japan. Semideciduous shrub to 5 ft.; zones 7–10. Blooms spring, summer. Regular moisture. Average, well-drained soil. Full to part sun. Flowers: small, white; berries orange. Leaves: tripinnate, turning red in cold temperatures; leaflets ovate to lanceolate, in 3s or irregularly lobed, to 2 in. long, tips acuminate; clustered at the ends of erect branches; persistent petiole bases sheath the stem. *Nandina becomes deciduous when dry or cold. Develops a dainty bamboolike habit with long arching leaves in favorable conditions. Dwarf forms are available. True bamboos (Bambusa) are in the grass family, Poaceae (Gramineae).*

BIGNONIACEAE
TABEBUIA FAMILY,
TRUMPETCREEPER FAMILY

Bignoniaceae includes approximately 110 genera of mostly tropical trees, shrubs, and woody climbers (lianas), with greatest diversity in Central and northern South America. The species are typical of seasonally moist/dry forests. The family includes many extraordinary ornamentals, such as *Jacaranda* and *Tabebuia*. Leaves are usually pinnate, occasionally palmate (as in *Tabebuia*) or simple.

The terminal leaflet(s) of some climbing species are modified into delicately pronged hooklike tendrils. They do not mar surfaces on which they climb (as do vines with adherent aerial roots) and are excellent choices for rough-textured walls which need occasional maintenance because the vines are easily removed. Flowers are funnel- or bell-shaped, bilaterally symmetrical, with a 2-lobed lower lip. The throat often has contrasting colored veins (nectar guides). One or 2 pairs of stamens are pressed against the upper side of the throat, the anthers touching, forming a distinctive gothic arch, facilitating pollination by bees, butterflies, hawkmoths, birds, and bats. The fruit is usually an elongated, podlike capsule that splits open to release winged seeds.

Adenocalymna
Adenocalymna (sometimes spelled *Adenocalymma*) includes approximately 50 species of woody climbers (lianas) from tropical America. They are unusual in cultivation. The stems are 4-angled. Leaves are divided into 3 leaflets, but the terminal leaflet is often modified into a 3-pronged tendril, leaving just 2 apparent leaflets. Flowers are funnel-shaped. The genus name combines *adeno*, meaning "glands," and *calymna*, meaning "calyx," and alludes to the ring of glands dotting the rim of the cuplike calyx.

Adenocalymna comosum
Synonym: *Bignonia comosa*. Brazil. Woody climber, 6–10 ft.+; zones 10–11. Blooms spring, summer. Moderate moisture. Fertile, humus-rich, well-drained soil. Full sun. Flowers: funnel-shaped, deep golden-yellow, to 3 in. long; each calyx lobe with a black glandular dot near the edge. Leaves: trifoliolate; leaflets ovate to lanceolate, 3–4 in. long, dark green, leathery to stiff. *Vaguely resembles* Allamanda *but easily distinguished by the bilateral rather than radial floral symmetry and the pinnate leaves. The species name alludes to the hairy floral tube.*

Campsis
Campsis includes 2 species of deciduous woody climbers from temperate eastern Asia and the eastern United States. *Campsis grandiflora* has long red-orange trumpet-flowers and broadly ovate, toothed leaflets, sparse aerial roots, and smooth midribs; *C. radicans* has more numerous aerial roots and leaflets with hairy midribs. Both species are also grown in the subtropics where they may be confused with the evergreen tropical *Distictis* species. *Campsis* differs from *Distictis* by the aerial roots with adherent pads that develop from the leaf axils and by the much divided pinnate leaves. *Distictis* species have 2–4 leaflets, the terminal leaflet modified into a hooklike tendril with leaflike stipules in the

Begonia nelumbiifolia

Nandina domestica

Adenocalymna comosum

leaf axils. *Bignonia capreolata* has bell-shaped red to scarlet flowers. Planted on an arbor over or near a window, any of these species will attract hummingbirds for close viewing.

Campsis grandiflora

CHINESE TRUMPET-CREEPER
Synonym: *Bignonia chinensis*. Southern China. Deciduous climber; zones 7–9. Blooms summer, fall. Seasonally moist/dry. Average, well-drained soil. Full sun. Flowers: trumpet-shaped, tube 3–4 in. long, orange, throat yellow-orange, lobes scarlet; in loose clusters. Leaves: pinnate; leaflets 7–9, broadly ovate, 2–2.5 in. long; margins coarsely toothed. *Aerial roots are produced at the nodes. A vigorous, suckering vine, difficult to eradicate once introduced. Provide sturdy support or maintain as a shrub by pruning.*

Catalpa

Catalpa includes approximately 11 species of trees, mostly from temperate regions of North America and Asia. A number of these fast-growing species are cultivated. *Catalpa longissima*, a tropical species, is uncommon in cultivation in the United States. It is a medium-sized tree suitable for landscaping. Leaves are simple, arranged in whorls. It flowers diffusely throughout the warm season, intermittently putting on a bigger display.

Catalpa longissima

YOKE-WOOD, FRENCH OAK, INDIAN BEAN, CATAWBA
West Indies. Evergreen tree, 25–50 ft.; zones 10–11. Blooms spring, summer. Seasonally moist/dry. Fertile, well-drained soil. Full sun. Flowers: funnel-shaped, 1–1.5 in.

long, pinkish to white, throat pinkish magenta around the opening with purple veins, lobes reflexed; fruit a cylindrical, pencil-slim capsule to 18 in. long. Leaves: simple, lanceolate to elliptic, 4–6 in. long, in whorls. Bark: medium brown, vertically furrowed, more or less corky. *The species name alludes to the very long, slender capsules.*

×Chitalpa

×*Chitalpa* is an intergeneric hybrid of *Catalpa* and *Chilopsis*. ×*Chitalpa tashkentensis*, a cross made in Tashkent, Uzbekistan, and introduced by the New York Botanical Garden, involves 2 American species: desert willow, *Chilopsis linearis*, a shrub from Texas, southern California, and Mexico, and eastern catalpa, *Catalpa bignonioides*, a large tree from the eastern United States (Elias 1991). This sterile hybrid is unusual in cultivation but highly recommended for dry subtropical areas. In humid climates, it is susceptible to mildew.

×Chitalpa tashkentensis

CHITALPA
Garden hybrid, *Catalpa bignonioides* × *Chilopsis linearis*. Deciduous tree, 20–25 ft.; zones 7–10. Blooms late spring to fall. Moderate moisture/seasonally dry. Average, well-drained soil. Full sun. Flowers: funnel-shaped, pink, lobes ruffled, reflexed, throat yellow with purple nectar guides; buds mauve; in many-flowered clusters. Leaves:

lanceolate; margins smooth, to 7 in. long; turning bright yellow in fall. Bark: gray. *Starts blooming by 3 years and is somewhat hardy. Sterile and must be propagated from cuttings. Two clones exist: 'Pink Dawn', a more spreading tree with a tendency to branch near the base, and 'Morning Cloud', an erect tree with white flowers. Photographed at Balboa Park.*

Clytostoma

Clytostoma includes approximately 9 species of evergreen woody climbers (lianas) from tropical and subtropical South America. Leaves are simple or trifoliolate, the terminal leaflet often modified into a 3-pronged tendril. Flowers are trumpet-shaped and in pairs (somewhat similar *Podranea* and *Cydista* flowers are not paired). *Clytostoma callistegioides* is a popular vine in southern South America and is sometimes cultivated in the United States. It is of modest size and thrives in bright understory.

Clytostoma callistegioides

ARGENTINE TRUMPET-VINE, LOVE-CHARM, PAINTED TRUMPET-VINE
Synonyms: *Bignonia callistegioides*, *Cuspidaria callistegioides*. Argentina to southern Brazil. Evergreen climber to 12 ft.; zones 9–11. Blooms spring, summer. Seasonally moist/dry. Fertile, well-drained soil. Bright filtered light, with some protection from midday sun. Flowers: funnel-shaped, in pairs, lavender-pink, throat creamy white with red-violet veins; calyx with long teeth; fruit round, bristled, seeds circular, winged. Leaves: trifoliolate; leaflets elliptic, to 3 in. long; the terminal leaflet often modified into tendrils or appearing paired or simple. Bristles in the leaf axils. *A vine of modest proportions, nonaggressive. Suitable for an arbor or framing a window or door. Highly recommended.*

Crescentia

Crescentia includes approximately 6 species of trees from tropical America. Flowers and fruit grow directly from the branches and trunk (cauliflorous). The fruits are atypical for this family. Instead of a cap-

Campsis grandiflora

Catalpa longissima

×Chitalpa tashkentensis 'Pink Dawn'

Clytostoma callistegioides

sule that splits open (dehiscent) when ripe and winged seeds, crescentias produce an indehiscent pepo (a large berry with a hard shell) and the seeds are not winged. The round shells of dry fruits are cut into bowls and water-dippers. String is sometimes tied around immature fruit to produce odd shapes as the fruit grows; these fruits are then made into birdhouses and utilitarian objects. Fruits of closely related *Parmentiera* are elongated.

Leaves of *Crescentia alata* are trifoliolate with a leaflike winged petiole shaped like a cross (and given religious significance in the Philippines). Leaves of *C. cujete* are simple and in raised clusters (fascicles) along the branches giving the limbs a distinctive, bushy appearance. Epiphytes are easily grown on the corky bark. Flowers open in the evening and fall in the morning. They emit a musky scent that attracts bat pollinators in the wild.

I fondly remember a calabash (*Crescentia cujete*) growing in an interior patio in Medellin, Colombia, decked out in large green fruits and bristling with long sprays of yellow *Oncidium* orchids. It was a stunning centerpiece.

Crescentia alata

MEXICAN CALABASH, WINGED CALABASH, TECOMATE, JICARA, MORRO
Synonyms: *C. trifolia, Parmentiera alata.* Southern Mexico to Costa Rica. Evergreen tree to 20 ft.; zones 10–11. Blooms warm months. Moderate moisture to fairly dry. Average, well-drained soil. Full to part sun. Flowers: corolla bell-shaped, tube slightly folded on one side, maroon; calyx, cupped, 2-lobed; cauliflorous, with a short stalk; pepo round, green to purple, 4–5 in. diameter. Leaves: trifoliolate, 3–5 in. long; leaflets oblanceolate; petiole winged. *From dry, medium-elevation forest. Mature fruits, smaller than those of* Crescentia cujete, *are often used to make maracas. The species name refers to the winged petioles.*

Crescentia cujete

CALABASH, TOTUMO, TAPARO
Synonyms: *C. acuminata, C. arbo-rea.* Mexico to Colombia, West Indies; widely distributed. Evergreen tree, 20–35 ft.; zones 10–11. Blooms warm months. Seasonally moist to wet, dry. Average, well-drained soil. Full to part sun. Flowers: elongated bell-shaped, tube slightly folded on one side, green and maroon-brown streaked; calyx 2-lobed; cauliflorous; pepo green, round to ovoid, 6–16 in. long, shell hard, pulpy inside. Leaves: simple, oblanceolate, 4–8 in. long; petioles short (subsessile); in fascicles along the branches. Bark: tan, corky. *From moist lowland forests. Somewhat cold-sensitive. The thin shell of the fruit is made into utensils.*

Cydista

Cydista includes approximately 4 species of evergreen climbers from tropical America. They are vigorous lianas characteristic of rainforest habitat (A. Gentry 1993). Stems are more or less 4-angled. Leaves are pinnate, the terminal leaflet often modified into a tendril. Flowers are solitary and the fruit is an elongated, smooth capsule which distinguishes *Cydista* from *Clytostoma*, a small vine with paired flowers and cylindrical, bristly fruit.

Cydista aequinoctialis

BEJUCO COLORADO, VAQUERO BLANCO
Synonym: *Bignonia aequinoctialis.* Mexico, Central America to Brazil, West Indies. Woody climber to 50 ft.+; zones 10–11. Blooms warm months. Regular moisture. Average to fertile, well-drained soil. Full to part sun. Flowers: funnel-shaped, pink, white, or lavender, throat yellowish with magenta veins; capsule long, flattened. Leaves: trifoliolate, the terminal leaflet often modified into a tendril, leaflets ovate, 3–6 in. long, pubescent or glabrous. *An aggressive climber of moist forest. It is sometimes listed as garlic-vine, though this probably indicates confusion with odoriferous* Mansoa *species.*

Delostoma

Delostoma includes approximately 4 species of evergreen shrubs or small trees from Colombia, Ecuador, and Peru. They grow in medium to high intermountain valleys of the Andes and are adapted to cool, dry climate. Leaves are simple, somewhat unusual for this family. The long, very slender trumpet-flowers are in pairs or in few-flowered panicles. *Delostoma integrifolium* (syn. *D. roseum*) is used for public landscaping in Quito, Ecuador, and is said to be cultivated in California though it may be confused with *D. lobbii* (Lohmann, pers. comm.). Highly recommended. Suitable as a flowering hedge. Pollinated by an exceptionally long-beaked hummingbird.

Delostoma lobbii

Synonym: *D. vargasii.* Peru, southern Ecuador. Evergreen shrub or small tree, 6–20 ft.; zones 9–11. Blooms summer. Moderate moisture, seasonally dry. Average, well-drained soil. Full to part sun. Flowers: trumpet-shaped, tube slender, deep magenta to red-orange with white streaks in the throat; anthers white, extending beyond the throat (exserted), to 3 in. long, in upright pairs. Leaves: simple, oblong to elliptic, to 4 in. long, 2 in. wide, softly hairy below, rough to slightly hairy above; margins entire, or sometimes minutely toothed. Delostoma integrifolium *has shorter anthers that do not extend beyond the throat (inserted).*

Distictis

Distictis includes approximately 9 species of evergreen woody climbers (lianas) from Mexico and the West Indies. Leaves are trifoliolate, the terminal leaflet often modified into a slender, 3-pronged tendril that looks like a tiny bird's foot.

Crescentia alata, flowers and fruit

Crescentia cujete, fruit

Cydista aequinoctialis

Delostoma lobbii

The stipules are leaflike in form but can be distinguished by their smaller size and location in the leaf axils. Trumpet-flowers are long and brightly colored. Vines like these with hooked tendrils cling lightly to rough surfaces. They do not mar paint as do vines with adhering aerial roots and can easily be detached if necessary. Tendrils and fewer leaflets distinguish *Distictis* species from *Campsis* species, which have adhering roots and many leaflets. Suitable for arbors and containers.

Distictis buccinatoria

BLOOD-RED TRUMPET-CREEPER, CHERERE

Synonyms: *Bignonia cherere, Phaedranthus buccinatorum.* Mexico. Evergreen climber, 10–30 ft.; zones 9–11. Blooms spring, intermittently in summer. Regular moisture when warm, drier when cool. Fertile, well-drained soil. Full sun. Flowers: trumpet-shaped, 4–5 in. long, orange-pink, throat yellow; stamens slightly exserted. Leaves: leaflets 2–4, the terminal leaflets often modified into 3-pronged tendrils. The leafy stipules are smaller than the true leaves and located in the leaf axils. Stems: 6-angled. *A vigorous climber. Thrives in hot, dry climates and coastal locations. Prune sharply after bloom to control.*

Distictis ×rivers

ROYAL TRUMPET-VINE

Garden hybrid, *D. buccinatoria* × *D. laxiflora.* Evergreen climber, 10–30 ft.; zones 9–11. Blooms late summer, fall. Regular moisture when warm, drier when cool. Fertile, well-drained soil. Full sun. Flowers: trumpet-shaped, 4–5 in. long, pinkish violet, throat yellow-orange; stamens not exserted. Leaves: pinnate, leaflets 2–4, the terminal leaflets often modified into 3-pronged tendrils; stipules leaflike but smaller than the true leaves and located in the leaf axils. *This hybrid thrives in hot, dry climates and coastal locations. Prune sharply after bloom to control.*

Dolichandrone

Dolichandrone includes approximately 9 species of shrubs and trees from New Caledonia in the Pacific Islands to Southeast Asia, Indomalaysia, and eastern Africa. These species are typically found in coastal mangrove forests and are salt tolerant. Flowers are trumpet-shaped, usually white, often fragrant at night, and pollinated by hawkmoths. Plants are suitable for coastal landscaping.

Dolichandrone spathacea

MANGROVE TRUMPET-TREE

Synonyms: *Bignonia spathacea, Spathodea longiflora.* Philippines, Southeast Asia, Indomalaysia to New Guinea. Evergreen tree to 60 ft.; zones 10–11. Blooms intermittently in warm months. Moist to wet. Fertile soil. Full sun. Flowers: trumpet-shaped, to 8 in. long, white, lip large, ruffled; calyx spathelike; solitary. Leaves: pinnate, to 1 ft. long; leaflets 7–9, ovate, to 6 in. long, glossy dark green. *A spreading tree of coastal mangrove forest. Salt tolerant. Uncommon in the United States. A rounded, somewhat spreading tree suitable for landscaping in low areas subject to periodic flooding with fresh or brackish water. The species name alludes to the spathelike calyx.*

Jacaranda

Jacaranda includes approximately 49 species of mostly deciduous trees and shrubs from tropical America. *Jacaranda mimosifolia,* one of the most widely planted tropical trees, is a favorite in southern California and dry areas of Central America, Africa, and Australia. It is not as reliable a bloomer where irrigation or unseasonable moisture interrupts the dry season. Some equally magnificent but lesser-known jacarandas have characteristics which are more amenable to moist climates. Leaves are pinnate or bipinnate, the leaflets fernlike to fairly large. The slender trumpet-flowers have a cornucopia-like curve and are often blue-violet, sometimes purple, pink, or white. The fruit is distinctive, a disk-shaped, woody or papery follicle. A papery, halolike wing encircles the seed. Many *Jacaranda* species bloom with a big display ("big bang") during a dry season. In areas with more than one dry period, such as eastern Africa and Panama, *J. mimosifolia* blooms twice a year. *Jacaranda cuspidifolia* blooms sporadically in moist climates. *Jacaranda arborea, J. caerulea,* and *J. jasminoides* are most reliable in warm, moist/dry climates. The pH of the soil seems to influence flower color like litmus paper, bluer in alkaline soil, pinker in acid.

Jacaranda arborea

JACARANDA, GREEN EBONY, ABEY

Eastern Cuba. Deciduous tree to 30 ft.+; zones 9–11. Blooms spring. Seasonally moist/dry. Average to poor, well-drained soil. Full sun. Flowers: trumpet-shaped, blue-violet, throat white, hairy; inflorescence dense, erect; calyx 5-toothed, buds dark purple; follicle papery. Leaves: bipinnate, to 1 ft. long; pinnae 4–8 pairs; leaflets broadly ovate to 1 in. long, firm, glossy dark green; margins slightly recurved. Trunk: large, sturdy. *A magnificent erect tree. Purportedly the wood is ebonylike. This species is much larger than* Jacaranda caerulea *and distinguished from all species listed here by the firm, dark green rounded leaflets. Rare in cultivation but very highly recommended especially for warm, moist climates.*

Jacaranda caerulea

JACARANDA, GREEN EBONY, BOXWOOD, FERN-TREE

Synonym: *J. sagraeana.* Bahamas, Cuba, northern Dominican Republic. Deciduous tree to 20 ft.; zones 10–11. Blooms spring. Seasonally moist/dry. Average to poor, well-drained soil; alkaline pH. Full sun. Flowers: trumpet-shaped, tube

Distictis buccinatoria

Distictis ×rivers

Dolichandrone spathacea

Jacaranda arborea

curved, 1.5–2 in. long, blue-violet, throat hairy, white; in loose, ascending clusters opening a few at a time; follicle papery. Leaves: bipinnate, with 4–13 pairs of pinnae; leaflets 9–15, rhombic, 0.5–0.75 in. long, soft, dull green, tips obtusely pointed. *A small tree that thrives in coastal limestone. Flowers in loose, ascending to oblique panicles, open a few at a time. Recommended for coastal landscaping. Leaflets larger than* Jacaranda mimosifolia, *not stiff and dark green like* J. arborea.

Jacaranda cuspidifolia

JACARANDA, COROBA,
JACARANDÁ DE MINAS
Southern Brazil to northern Argentina. Deciduous tree to 35 ft.; zones 9–11. Blooms sporadically warm months. Seasonally moist/dry. Average, well-drained soil. Full sun. Flowers: trumpet-shaped, tube curved, 2–3 in. long, blue-violet, lobes slightly toothed, hairy; inflorescence oblique to ascending; fol-

licle papery. Leaves: bipinnate, fern-like, 1.5–3 ft. long; leaflets rhombic, 0.5–1 in. long, tips acutely pointed. *Leaves, leaflets, flowers, and inflorescences more than twice the size of* J. mimosifolia. *From seasonally dry, subtropical hill country. Reaches blooming size in 5–8 years from seed.*

Jacaranda jasminoides

PURPLE JACARANDA
Synonym: *J. tomentosa*. Brazil, Bolivia. Evergreen shrub or small tree to 15 ft.; zones 10–11. Blooms intermittently most of the year. Seasonally moist/dry. Average, well-drained soil. Full to part sun.

Flowers: trumpet-shaped, eggplant-purple, throat darker; in erect panicles; follicle woody. Leaves: bipinnate, with 3–5 pairs of pinnae; leaflets 3–5, ovate, 1–1.5 in. long, dull light green, downy (tomentose). *A distinctive deep purple-flowered jacaranda. The leaflets are larger*

Jacaranda caerulea

Jacaranda cuspidifolia

Jacaranda jasminoides

Jacaranda mimosifolia

and far fewer than the other species listed here. From seasonally moist tropical forests. Unusual in cultivation in the United States. Suitable for use as a natural hedge with light pruning.

Jacaranda mimosifolia
JACARANDA, GUARUPA, ABEY, FLAMBOYÁN AZUL
Synonyms: *J. acutifolia, J. ovalifolia*. Northwestern Argentina, Paraguay, Bolivia. Deciduous tree to 35 ft.; zones 8–10. Blooms spring or dry season. Moderate, seasonally dry. Average, well-drained soil; slightly acid pH best. Full sun. Flowers: trumpet-shaped, blue-violet, throat white, hairy; in lax clusters, capsules woody. Leaves: bipinnate, 10–14 in. long, with 13–31 pairs of pinnae; leaflets narrowly rhombic, 18–20 pairs, to 0.25 in. long; rachis reddish on young growth. *From dry*

savanna (cerrado). Takes 10–15 years to flower from seed. Needs a long, uninterrupted dry season to bloom exuberantly. The floppy clusters of flowers are a distinctive characteristic. Jacaranda 'Alba' is often listed under this species, but its distinctive leaflets and ascending inflorescences suggest a different ancestry.

Kigelia
Kigelia includes a single species of trees from tropical Africa. It grows in savannas and open woodlands. The genus is named for the capital of Rwanda. Plants are grown occasionally for the novelty of the 30-lb. sausagelike fruits, which dangle from the branches on long stalks. More than one roadside stand in South Florida has planted a "world-famous sausage-tree" by the road to waylay passing tourists. The maroon flowers are bell-shaped, open-

ing at night and falling by early morning. They emit a musky scent that attracts bat pollinators in the wild. Self-infertile, the flowers must be cross-pollinated by hand at night to set fruit in cultivation (picture dedicated human pollinator running between trees at night with paintbrush and flashlight in hand). Hawkmoths may occasionally pollinate some flowers in cultivation. The fruit is eaten and seed distributed by baboons.

Kigelia africana
SAUSAGE-TREE
Synonyms: *Crescentia pinnata, K. pinnata*. Tropical Africa to South Africa (KwaZulu-Natal). Semideciduous tree, 25–60 ft.; zones 9–11. Blooms dry season. Seasonally moist/dry. Average, well-drained soil. Full sun. Flowers: bell-shaped, streaked yellowish green and maroon outside, deep maroon inside, on long stalks; fruit cylindrical, up to 18 in. long, concrete-gray. Leaves: pinnate to 16 in. long; leaflets 5–13, ovate, to 5 in. long. Young twigs slightly pubescent. *Flowers open at night and fall by morning. The pulpy fruit is said to be used in folk medicine as a purgative.*

Macfadyena
Macfadyena includes 3 or 4 species of climbers from tropical America. This great imposter is a slender vine that climbs through the canopy of trees. From afar, it has deceived not a few intrepid botanists into believing they had stumbled upon a new and unusual flowering tree. Though the species name *M. unguis-cati* means "cat's claw," the hooklike tendrils more closely resemble the dainty, 3-pronged toes of a canary. *Macfadyena* is self-seeding and occasionally weedy. In southern California, close to its native range, it does an admirable job of disguising chain-link fences.

Macfadyena unguis-cati
CAT'S CLAW, BEJUCO DE MURCIÉLAGO ("BAT VINE"), UÑITAS ("LITTLE CLAWS")
Synonyms: *Bignonia argyreo-vilescens, Doxantha unguis-cati*. Mexico to Argentina, West Indies. Ever-

green climber to 30 ft.; zones 9–11. Blooms intermittently in warm months. Moderate moisture or seasonally moist/dry. Average, well-drained soil. Full to part sun. Flowers: bell-shaped, yellow; throat with orange nectar guides. Leaves: pinnate; leaflets 2 pairs, ovate to elliptic, terminal leaflet often modified into a 3-pronged tendril (visible in photo); juvenile leaves tiny. *Of dry tropical forests. A common weed along the Gulf Coast.* Macfadyena dentate *has serrated leaflets.*

Mansoa
Mansoa includes approximately 15 species of woody climbers from tropical America. Leaves are pinnate, the terminal leaflets often modified into 3-pronged hooks or disk-tipped tendrils. Flowers are trumpet-shaped. Plant extracts are used in folk medicines in Latin America.

Mansoa hymenaea
GARLIC-VINE, BEJUCO DE AJO
Synonyms: *Bignonia hymenaea, M. alboviolaceum*. Mexico, Central America. Woody climber to 20 ft.; zones 10–11. Blooms spring, fall. Seasonally moist/dry. Average, well-drained soil. Full sun. Flowers: trumpet-shaped, to 3 in. long, lobes pink to magenta, throat pink to white; clustered garlandlike at the leaf axils. Leaves: trifoliolate, leaflets elliptic to lanceolate, 2–4 in. long, dull green; terminal leaflet sometimes absent or modified into a tendril. *Glands on the petioles secrete a garlicky aroma. Often confused with apparently odorless Cydista aequinoctialis. Commonly misnamed* M. alliacea *(syn. Adenocalymna alliaceum), a South American species that is rare in the wild and not known in cultivation (A. Gentry 1993).*

Mansoa verrucifera
Mexico (Yucatan peninsula). Evergreen climber to 20 ft.+; zones 10–11. Blooms spring, fall, intermittently when nights are cool. Seasonally moist/dry. Average to fertile, well-drained soil. Full or morning sun. Flowers: funnel-shaped to 3 in. long, deep magenta. Leaves: trifoliolate, leaflets

Jacaranda mimosifolia, inflorescence

Kigelia africana

Macfadyena unguis-cati

Mansoa hymenaea

broadly ovate, terminal leaflet sometimes absent or modified into a hooked tendril. *This stunning vine is rare in cultivation and little is known about its characteristics. The flowers are twice as large and more vivid than M. hymenaea. Photographed at Fairchild Tropical Garden.*

Markhamia

Markhamia includes approximately 12 species of trees from tropical Asia and Africa. *Markhamia lutea* is somewhat unusual in cultivation though this handsome tree is highly recommended. The moderate height and erect habit are excellent for street landscaping. The tree may take up to 10 years to flower from seed, but then it blooms prolifically, typically in spring and intermittently throughout the warm months. Capsules are long, flat, and pointed at the ends. The form of *M. lutea* grown in southern California (where it is known as *M. hildebrandtii*) has denser panicles of flowers with brownish or maroon throats and nectar guides. A form in Florida has all yellow flowers. Both forms are now considered variations of *M. lutea* (Diniz 1988). The bell-bean tree, *M. zanzibarica*, has smaller flowers usually with chocolate-brown lobes and a yellow throat and is rare in cultivation.

Markhamia lutea
NILE TRUMPET

Synonyms: *M. hildebrandtii, M. platycalyx, Spathodea lutea.* Tropical Africa. Tree to 30 ft.; zones 9–11. Blooms spring, summer, sporadically. Moderate moisture. Moderately fertile, well-drained soil. Full sun. Flowers: bell-shaped, golden-yellow, throat and nectar guides sometimes reddish brown; calyx spathelike with lepidote scales; in panicles. Leaves: pinnate, 1.5–2 ft. long, leaflets 7–13, ovate, 4–8 in. long; margins entire to finely toothed. *Of moist tropical woodlands. Golden-yellow flowers with throat more common in California; bright yellow form occasionally grown in Florida.*

Newbouldia

Newbouldia includes a single species of tree from tropical western Africa. It gets its common name, boundary tree, from its frequent use as a living fence to demarcate property lines. In western Africa, it is said to signify "home" or "welcome." Cuttings take root directly in the ground ("quick sticks"). Flowers are in large spires that develop directly on the branches (cauliflorous). The black calyces are a good field mark.

Newbouldia laevis
BOUNDARY TREE

Synonym: *Spathodea laevis.* Cameroon, Senegal, Gabon. Evergreen shrub or tree to 40 ft.; zones 10–11. Blooms late winter, spring. Seasonally moist/dry. Average, well-drained soil. Full sun. Flowers: trumpet-shaped, lavender-pink to purple; buds and spathelike calyx purple-black, in conical panicles, a few to many flowers opening at a time; rachis purple-black; fruit a slender capsule. Leaves: pinnate, leaflets 7, elliptic, to 8 in. long; 1–3 per node. *Plants grown from cuttings tend to be shrublike, branching near the base.*

Pandorea

Pandorea includes approximately 6 species of woody climbers (lianas) from eastern Malaysia, Indonesia, Papua New Guinea, New Caledonia, and Australia. At least a single species and several color selections are cultivated in the United States. A nonaggressive vine, *Pandorea* seems to prefer moderately cool night temperatures. It is especially charming draping from an arbor over an entrance or walk. Sometimes the name is confused with *Podranea.*

Pandorea jasminoides
BOWER-VINE

Synonym: *Tecoma jasminoides.* Northeastern Australia, New Caledonia, Indomalaysia. Woody, twining climber to 15 ft.; zones 9–11. Blooms warm months. Regular moisture. Fertile, humus-rich, well-drained soil. Full sun. Flowers: funnel-shaped, to 4 in. long, white with crimson throat; calyx not inflated. Leaves: pinnate, leaflets ovate, firm, glossy dark green. *'Rosea' is pink with a crimson throat; 'Lady Di',* white with cream throat; *'Alba', all white.*

Parmentiera

Parmentiera includes approximately 9 species of trees from southern Mexico to northwestern Colombia. It is distinguished from *Crescentia* by the elongated fruits. Leaves are trifoliolate with long, winged petioles. Flowers and fruit grow directly from the trunk and branches (cauliflorous). The candle-tree, *P. cereifera*, with fruits that

Mansoa verrucifera

Markhamia lutea

Markhamia lutea, all yellow form

Newbouldia laevis

Pandorea jasminoides

resemble beeswax candles, is sometimes cultivated as a curiosity. In its native range, candle-tree produces fibrous fruits that are eaten by wild and domestic animals. Flowers are musky-scented, opening at night and falling by early morning. They are pollinated by bats in native habitat.

Parmentiera aculeata

COW-OKRA, GUAJALOTE ("TURKEY" IN MEXICO)
Synonym: *P. edulis*. Mexico (Yucatan), Guatemala. Evergreen tree, 15–30 ft.; zones 10–11. Blooms warm months. Moderate moisture to seasonally dry. Average to fertile, well-drained soil. Full to part sun. Flowers: bell-shaped, ridged, streaked green and purple-maroon; fruit green to purple-maroon, resembling a thick okra, to 7 in. long; cauliflorous on trunk and branches. Leaves: trifoliate, 4–5 in. long; leaflets obovate, 1–3 in. long; petiole winged. Branches thorny. *Spreading tree with arching branches. Foliage resembles* Crescentia alata. *The fruit is pineapple-flavored but very fibrous, used mostly for animal feed or in folk medicine. Wood used for carving.*

Parmentiera cereifera

CANDLE-TREE, PALO DE VELAS
Synonym: *Crescentia cereifera*. Central America; widely distributed. Evergreen shrubby tree, 20–45 ft.; zones 9–11. Blooms warm months. Seasonally moist/dry. Fertile, humus-rich, well-drained soil. Full to part sun. Flowers: bell-shaped, greenish white; calyx spathelike, a cup with one lobe; cauliflorous, on a short stalk; fruit a waxy, cylindrical pepo, 8–20+ in. long. Leaves: trifoliolate; leaflets ovate, 2–3 in. long; petiole to 2 in. long, winged. *Of seasonally moist tropical forests. The fruits resemble beeswax candles hanging in clusters directly on the trunk and branches.*

Podranea

Podranea includes 1 or 2 species of shrubby climbers from tropical to subtropical southern Africa and Australia. *Podranea* is sometimes confused with *Pandorea*. Although they are close relatives, they come from different continents. *Podranea*

is distinguished from *Pandorea* by the inflated calyx. Frequently cultivated in the United States. This moderate climber prefers warmth and is frost-sensitive. It is a good choice for walls, fences, and trellises.

Podranea ricasoliana

PINK TRUMPET-VINE, PORT ST. JOHN'S CREEPER, BUBBLE-GUM VINE
Synonyms: *Pandorea ricasoliana*, *Podranea brycei*, *Tecoma ricasoliana*. South Africa; widely distributed in tropics. Evergreen climber to 12 ft.; zones 10–11. Blooms intermittently in warm months. Moist when hot, moderate moisture when cool. Fertile, humus-rich, well-drained soil. Full to part sun. Flowers: bell-shaped, fragrant, bright pink, throat and veins darker pink around the opening; calyx slightly

inflated. Leaves: pinnate; leaflets 5–11, ovate. *A dwarf cultivar is shrubbier than the type with lavender flowers and faint throat markings.*

Pyrostegia

Pyrostegia includes 3 or 4 species of woody climbers (lianas) from tropical South America. One species is often cultivated. Leaves are pinnate. Flowers are long, slender trumpets, in many-flowered clusters. The vine is heavy and very aggressive. Fortunately, it is not known to set seed in the United States. Flame-vine, *P. venusta*, can swallow a house whole and completely envelope trees but is a magnificent winter bloomer if adequately controlled. It should be grown on a sturdy, free-standing support and pruned yearly after blooming. It is very suitable for

shading a picnic table. The unrelated Mexican flame-vine, *Pseudogynoxys*, is in the aster family, Asteraceae.

Pyrostegia venusta

FLAME-VINE
Synonym: *P. ignea*. Southern Brazil, northern Argentina, Bolivia, Paraguay. Evergreen woody climber to 100 ft.+; zones 9–11. Blooms late winter. Moderate moisture/seasonally dry. Average, well-drained soil. Full sun. Flowers: trumpet-shaped, tube slender, to 4 in. long, lobes reflexed, bright orange, occasionally yellow, in dense terminal clusters. Leaves: trifoliolate, one leaflet sometimes modified into a terminal tendril; leaflets ovate, 2–3 in. long, slightly rough or hairy; margins smooth. *Prune back drastically after bloom. Salt tolerant and suit-*

Parmentiera aculeata, fruit

Parmentiera cereifera, fruit

Podranea ricasoliana

Parmentiera cereifera, flower

Pyrostegia venusta

able for coastal locations. Ideally suited to a long, running fence or arbor but isolate from trees and structures onto which it can escape. The species name means "handsome."

Saritaea

Saritaea includes a single species of woody climber from Colombia and Ecuador. It was introduced into Brazil by the late Roberto Burle Marx, a Brazilian landscape architect and plant collector. It is uncommon in cultivation in the United States but highly recommended. *Saritaea* has excellent horticultural attributes including pest resistance and low water consumption. It is not known to produce seed in the United States. This genus is more closely related to *Cydista* than *Arrabidaea* with which it was formerly associated.

Saritaea magnifica

SARITAEA, PURPLE BIGNONIA, CAMPANILLA

Synonyms: *Arrabidaea magnifica*, *Bignonia magnifica*. Northeastern Colombia, Ecuador. Evergreen shrubby climber, 10–20 ft.; zones 10–11. Blooms intermittently in warm months. Moderate moisture/seasonally dry. Fertile, well-drained soil. Full sun. Flowers: funnel-shaped, 3–3.5 in. long, 2 in. wide, lobes magenta, throat white; in few-flowered short panicles. Leaves: trifoliolate; leaflets obovate, leathery with 3 primary veins, the terminal leaflet often absent or modified into a branched tendril.

A climber that is sometimes maintained as a sprawling shrub with pruning. The magenta flowers against the dark foliage are exceptionally pleasing. Highly recommended.

Spathodea

Spathodea includes a single species of tree from tropical Africa. It is evergreen in moist climates but may shed its leaves in dry conditions. Commonly cultivated in its native Africa, it is widely naturalized in Latin America and southern Florida and is listed as invasive in Hawaii, Puerto Rico, and Australia. Flowers are arranged in a crownlike inflorescence the size of a large dinner plate. The corolla emerges through a slit in the claw-shaped brown calyx. The calyx secretes a watery nectar that birds feed upon

Spathodea campanulata, inflorescence

in the wild. While feeding, the birds dust their tails in the pollen of the outer ring of flowers, then fly to the next flower, blithely pollinating as they go. Tulip-trees bloom sporadically in dry conditions or almost continuously in fertile, evenly moist soil. The blooms tend to be carried high on the crown. Infestations of cotton aphids can be heavy but apparently do little harm. The wood has a garlic odor, is resistant to fire, and is brittle in windstorms.

Spathodea campanulata

AFRICAN TULIP-TREE, TULIPÁN AFRICANO, ESPATODEA

Synonyms: *Bignonia tulipifera, S. nilotica*. Tropical Africa; widely distributed. Semideciduous buttressing tree, 40–75 ft.; zones 10–11. Blooms late winter, spring, or sporadically.

Moist to dry. Average to fertile, well-drained soil. Full sun. Flowers: cup-shaped, to 4 in. wide, scarlet with golden rim, occasionally all orange or golden-yellow; calyx spathelike, brown-haired, falcate; capsules woody, dark brown, boat-shaped, to 8 in.; seed flat, winged. Leaves: pinnate, to 18 in. long, leaflets mostly 11–17, to 4 in. long; petioles covered with stiff hairs. Bark: light tan, flaky. *Suitable for coastal planting. Var. lutea has all golden-yellow flowers. Intermediate forms are orange. An East African form with russet-haired twigs and calyces was formerly segregated as S. nilotica.*

Tabebuia

Tabebuia includes approximately 100 species of trees and shrubs from tropical and subtropical

Saritaea magnifica

Spathodea campanulata var. *lutea*

Tabebuia aurea

America. Some, called *roble* ("oak") in Spanish, are important timber trees with exceptionally hard wood. One species, *T. impetiginosa*, is so variable over its vast range that the different forms were originally segregated into at least 6 species. In contrast, several rather similar species are distinguished mostly by the minutia of hairs or scales on the calyx and leaves.

Leaves are palmately compound. Antillean species are characterized by smaller or fewer leaflets or simple leaves. Flowers are trumpet- or bell-shaped, with an enlarged lip and often with contrasting nectar guides in the throat. The cylindrical capsules split open releasing papery-winged seeds.

Technical keys to the species depend heavily on origin and micro-scopic hairs or scales (indumentum), making identification of plants in cultivation difficult. To compound the problem, the species may hybridize in cultivation. Distinctive field marks are used here to assist identification.

Tabebuias are among the most admired flowering tropical trees. In the wild, some species bloom in synchrony during the dry season on briefly deciduous limbs. An effect as dramatic as fall aspens in the Rocky Mountains can be achieved with mass plantings. Irrigation should be withheld during the dry season for a "big bang" bloom. Obtain seed or grafts from selections with excellent flowering characteristics. Coastal and island species are moderately salt tolerant. Fifteen species are threatened in the wild.

Tabebuia aurea
SILVER TRUMPET-TREE
Synonyms: *T. argentea, T. caraiba*. Brazil, Paraguay, Argentina. Semideciduous tree, 20–40 ft.; zones 8–11. Blooms spring. Seasonally moist/dry. Deep, well-drained soil. Full sun. Flowers: trumpet-shaped, to 3 in. long, bright yellow, lobes short, reflexed. Leaves: palmate; leaflets 5–9, oblong to obovate, to 6 in. long, gray-green, roughly scaly (lepidote scales), tips obtuse. Bark: corky, tan-white, furrowed with age. *Common in cultivation. Notoriously shallow-rooted with a highly flexible trunk. Start in a deep hole and stake on 3 sides. Habit is naturally asymmetrical. This gray-leafed form comes from dry highland savanna (cerrado); a green-leafed form is found in lowland forests (A. Gentry 1982).*

Precocious flowering individuals are considered more desirable than those that bloom while leafing out.

Tabebuia bahamensis
BAHAMIAN TRUMPET-TREE
Synonym: *Tecoma bahamensis*. Bahamas, Cuba. Deciduous tree to 15 ft.; zones 10–11. Blooms spring. Seasonally moist/dry. Average, well-drained soil; alkaline pH. Full sun. Flowers: bell-shaped with a flattened throat, to 2 in. long, lip large, crinkled, mauve-pink, throat white; calyx cup 2- to 3-toothed. Leaves: palmate; leaflets 3–5, obovate, to 2.5 in. long, tip emarginate; petioles to 2 in. long. Bark: medium brown, scaly. *An island plant adapted to moderate salt and wind. Unusual in cultivation outside the Bahamas but highly recommended.*

Tabebuia 'Carib Queen'
Garden hybrid (Puerto Rico), *T. heterophylla* × *T. haemantha*. Evergreen tree to 20 ft.+; zones 10–11. Blooms warm months. Seasonally moist/dry. Average to fertile, well-drained soil. Full sun. Flowers: bell-shaped, lip large, frilly, mauve-magenta, throat white; mostly solitary or in few-flowered clusters. Leaves: palmate; leaflets 3–5, obovate, firm, dark green; margins entire. *This hybrid blooms rather sparsely but almost all year with occasional moderate flushes. It thrives in coastal locations but not at seaside.*

Tabebuia chrysotricha
GOLDEN TRUMPET-TREE
Argentina to Brazil. Semideciduous tree, 20–25 ft.; zones 9–11. Blooms late winter, spring. Seasonally moist/dry. Fertile, well-drained soil. Full sun. Flowers: trumpet-shaped, lobes crinkled, to 3 in. long, golden-yellow, throat hairy, veins maroon; in loose clusters; capsule covered with woolly, gold-brown hairs. Leaves: palmate; leaflets 5, obovate, 4–5 in. long, papery, undersides minutely hairy. *A small, open tree. Tabebuia ochracea, from Central America, has thick wool on leaf undersides, calyx, and capsules and shorter light yellow flowers. Tabebuia aurea has stiff, scaly leaflets.*

Tabebuia aurea, flowers

Tabebuia 'Carib Queen'

Tabebuia chrysotricha

Tabebuia bahamensis

Tabebuia chrysotricha, capsule

Tabebuia guayacan

GUAYACAN, CORTEZA, LAPACHO
Synonym: *Tecoma guayacan*. Mexico, Central America, northern South America. Deciduous tree, 25–75 ft.; zones 9–11. Blooms spring, sporadically in summer. Seasonally moist/dry. Average, well-drained soil. Full sun. Flowers: funnel-shaped, 3–4 in. long, lemon-yellow, throat hairy with dark veins; in loose terminal panicles; capsules bumpy. Leaves: palmate, hairless; leaflets 5, broadly oblong to ovate, papery, to 7 in., tips elongated (apiculate); margins smooth. Bark shallow-furrowed. *A "big bang" bloomer commonly cultivated in Costa Rica and Panama. Extremely hard, 2-toned, cabinet-quality wood. Suitable for coastal but not seaside landscaping. Tabebuia ochracea (syn. T. chrysantha) has light yellow floral trumpets and heavy wool on leaf undersides, capsules, and calyx.*

Tabebuia haemantha

BLOOD-RED TRUMPET-TREE, ROBLE CIMARRÓN ("MAROON OAK")
Puerto Rico. Deciduous tree to 20 ft.; zones 10–11. Blooms spring, intermittently in summer. Moderate moisture to seasonally moist/dry. Average, well-drained soil. Full sun. Flowers: trumpet-shaped, ruby-red, paler inside throat, about 2 in. long; calyx olive-green, funnel-shaped, to 0.5 in. long, with 3 small teeth; solitary or in few-flowered clusters. Leaves: palmate; leaflets 3–5, elliptic to oblong, to 5 in. long, dark green, stiff, midvein lighter. *A fairly small, xeric tree. Blooms in flushes 2 or 3 times a year.*

Tabebuia heterophylla

PINK TRUMPET-TREE, PINK POUI
Synonyms: *T. pallida* (misapplied), *T. pentaphylla*, *T. rosea* (misapplied). Antilles. Evergreen tree to 20 ft.; zones 10–11. Blooms intermittently in spring. Seasonally moist/dry. Average, well-drained soil. Full sun. Flowers: funnel-shaped, pink, throat yellow; solitary or in few-flowered clusters. Leaves: palmate; leaflets 1–5 on the same tree, oblong to obovate, 3–6 in. long, tips bluntly rounded, stiff. *Commonly misidentified as T. pallida, a rarely cultivated Antillean tree with simple leaves, or as T. rosea, a potentially large tree with large clusters of flowers. Many sparsely flowering selections in cultivation. Select for good blooming characteristics. A recently introduced thrips is causing leaves of T. heterophylla to curl. It apparently does not do permanent harm in mature plants.*

Tabebuia impetiginosa

PINK TRUMPET TREE, IPE, QUEBRACHO, PAU D'ARCO
Synonyms: *T. avellanedae, T. dugandii, T. ipe, T. palmeri*. Mexico to Argentina. Deciduous tree to 35 ft.+; zones 8–11. Blooms late winter, spring. Seasonally moist/dry. Average, well-drained soil. Full sun. Flowers: trumpet-shaped, tube 2–3 in. long, slender, mauve-pink, rarely white, throat yellow; downy; in unbranched terminal clusters of 30–40+. Leaves: palmate; leaflets 5–7, ovate to oblong, 2–4 in. long, quilted, tip pointed; margins serrated when young. *A highly variable species. Dense clusters of lavender-pink flowers a good field mark. Bark extract used as folk medicine to treat venereal disease and harvested to extermination in large parts of range. Subsp.* heptaphylla *(syn. T. heptaphylla) retains the serrated leaf margins to maturity.*

Tabebuia lepidota

Bahamas, Cuba. Deciduous tree, 10–15 ft.; zones 10–11. Blooms late winter, spring. Seasonally

Tabebuia guayacan

Tabebuia heterophylla, flowers

Tabebuia haemantha

Tabebuia heterophylla

moist/dry. Average, well-drained soil. Full sun. Flowers: funnel-shaped, 4–5 in. long, mauve-pink to white, throat white; solitary. Leaves: simple, ovate, 1–1.5 in. long, stiff, and thick. *Trees in cultivation bloom sparsely on bare or leafing-out branches. Moderately salt tolerant. Suitable for coastal landscaping.*

Tabebuia rosea

PINK POUI, ROBLE BLANCO ("WHITE OAK")
Synonym: *T. pentaphylla* (hort.). Mexico to Venezuela. Briefly deciduous tree to 100 ft.; zones 9–11. Blooms spring. Moderate moisture or seasonally moist/dry. Average, well-drained soil. Full sun. Flowers: funnel-shaped, to 5 in. long, pink to white, throat yellow to white with purple veins, sparsely hairy; in loose clusters of up to 20. Leaves: palmate, lax; leaflets 3–5 with 2 lateral leaflets much shorter than central 1–3, obovate, glabrous; margins entire, tips acuminate. Lower leaves often have fewer leaflets. *The 2 short outer leaflets are a good field mark. A large timber tree of lowland*

forests. Wood made into fine doors and furniture.

Tabebuia umbellata

Synonym: *T. eximia*. Brazil, threatened in the wild. Deciduous tree to 20 ft.; zones 8–11. Blooms late winter. Seasonally moist/dry. Average, well-drained soil. Full to part sun. Flowers: trumpet-shaped, pale yellow, tube somewhat tan, short hairs inside and out, fragrant; calyx cup covered with rust-colored hairs; in somewhat pendent, many-flowered terminal or axillary clusters; capsules smooth. Leaves: palmate, leaflets usually 5; margins smooth. Habit spreading. *Fairly unusual in cultivation. Of wet forest. Marginally hardy. The tree in the photo was given to the Kampong by the late Brazilian landscape architect and collector, Roberto Burle Marx.*

Tecoma

Tecoma includes approximately 12 species of trees and shrubs from Arizona to the Andes in South America, plus a single species from South Africa. The genus is closely related to *Tabebuia*. Leaves are usu-

ally pinnately compound, rarely simple. Flowers are funnel-shaped, yellow, and attractive to hummingbirds. The fruit is a cylindrical capsule containing winged seeds.

Tecoma capensis

CAPE HONEYSUCKLE, COCK-A-DOODLE-DOO
Synonym: *Tecomaria capensis*. South Africa, Mozambique. Evergreen clambering shrub, 6–12 ft.;

Tabebuia impetiginosa, flowers

Tabebuia lepidota

Tabebuia rosea

Tabebuia umbellata

Tabebuia impetiginosa

Tecoma capensis

Tecoma capensis 'Compacta Rosea'

zones 9–10. Blooms primarily fall and spring, or intermittently. Regular moisture when hot, drier when cool. Fertile, sandy, well-drained soil. Full sun. Flowers: slender trumpet-shaped, lobes short, flaring; anthers exserted; in many-flowered clusters. Leaves: pinnate, to 6 in. long; leaflets 5–7; margins toothed. *The only African species, long segregated into its own genus. Inclined to ramble and sucker. Control as a shrub or hedge with occasional trimming. Suitable for coastal landscaping. Cultivars in pastel shades of yellow, orange, and mauve are generally smaller.*

Tecoma castanifolia

CHESTNUT-LEAFED ELDER, CAMPANILLAS AMARILLAS ("YELLOW BELLS")
Synonym: *Tabebuia gaudichaudii* (hort.). Ecuador, Peru. Evergreen tree to 20 ft.+; zones 9–11. Blooms

Tecoma castanifolia

Tecoma stans

late winter, spring, or intermittently. Moderate moisture/seasonally dry. Average, well-drained soil. Full sun. Flowers: funnel-shaped, golden-yellow, throat not streaked; in terminal clusters. Leaves: simple, firm, to 7 in. long; immature leaves sometimes trifoliolate, the center leaflet twice as large as the side leaflets; margins toothed. *The species name alludes to the simple, chestnutlike (Castanea) leaves. Coastal. Unusual but highly recommended for its erect, sturdy habit, dark foliage, and low seed production. Suitable for public landscaping.*

Tecoma ×smithii

ORANGE TRUMPET-BUSH, CAMPANAS ANARANJADAS ("ORANGE BELLS")
Garden hybrid, *T. stans* × *T. capensis*; naturalized in Australia, New Zealand, Singapore. Evergreen shrub, 10–20 ft.; zones 8–11.

Tecoma ×smithii

Tecomanthe dendrophila

Blooms spring, summer, dry seasons. Moderate moisture/seasonally dry. Average, well-drained soil. Full sun. Flowers: trumpet-shaped, yellow-orange; in large clusters. Leaves: pinnate, leaflets 9–15, lanceolate; margins serrate (sawtoothed). *Suitable for coastal landscaping.*

Tecoma stans

YELLOW ELDER, YELLOW BELLS, CAMPANILLAS AMARILLAS, CHIRLOBIRLO
Synonyms: *Stenolobium stans, T. augustatum, T. incisa, T. mollis.* Exact origin obscure (tropical America); widely naturalized. Evergreen shrub or tree, 10–40 ft.; zones 8–11. Blooms primarily spring, fall, and intermittently. Seasonally moist to fairly dry. Average, well-drained soil. Full sun. Flowers: funnel-shaped, yellow, throat with red veins, vanilla-scented. Leaves: pinnate, young leaves sometimes simple; leaflets 3–9, lanceolate, scaly to downy; margins serrate. *Great variability has resulted in numerous synonyms probably due to the species's wide distribution. Brittle, leggy forms of* T. stans *are widely propagated in Florida. Robust, compact forms are more typical in California. Take cuttings from trees with known qualities of strong branches, compact habit, and frequent bloom.*

Tecomanthe

Tecomanthe includes approximately 5 species of twining woody climbers (lianas) from Malaysia, New Guinea, New Zealand, and Australia. The long slender trumpet-shaped flowers are on very short stalks (subsessile) in many-flowered, dense clusters. *Tecomanthe dendrophila* is unusual in cultivation. It is particularly attractive grown as a bower on a sturdy frame over a table or patio. When stems grow horizontally, the flowers hang down below the foliage creating a ceiling of pink several times a year. The vine is also effective climbing on a sturdy deciduous tree where flowers will garland the bare limbs in winter. Flowers develop on the leafless woody second-year growth. A few handfuls of balanced fertilizer every month encourage repeat

bloom. Runners develop from the base. Remove or attach them to the support. Plants are very easy to root from cuttings.

Tecomanthe dendrophila

Synonym: *T. venusta*. Moluccas, New Guinea, Solomon Islands. Evergreen woody climber to 50 ft.+; zones 10–11. Blooms intermittently late summer to spring. Regular moisture. Fertile, well-drained soil. Full sun. Flowers: trumpet-shaped to 4 in. long, lobes slightly flaring; in dense clusters on very short pedicels; buds angular, dark pink, becoming lighter pink when open, throat pale pink to white. Leaves: pinnate; leaflets 5–7, elliptic to obovate, 3–6 in. long, tips mucronate, dull green. Young stems: chocolate brown with white lenticels, second-year bark almost white. *A vigorous, twining vine. The species name means "tree-loving." One of the most spectacular vines but needs some control.*

BIXACEAE

BIXA FAMILY
Bixaceae includes a single genus of small tree from tropical America. Some authors place this species in Cochlospermaceae, but it is distinguished by its simple, unlobed leaves. Flowers are bisexual and radially symmetrical with numerous stamens, 5 sepals, and 5 petals. The inflorescence is a panicle produced at the end of the branch. The fruit is a dry capsule covered with stiff bristles.

Bixa

Bixa includes a single species of tree from tropical America. The inflated capsules, which vary from brilliant crimson to russet-brown, are covered with stiff (setose) hairs. Annatto, the oil-soluble powdery testa covering the seeds, is the "natural yellow coloring" commonly used in margarine, cheese, butter, and yellow- or orange-colored snack foods. Unlike saffron, it is tasteless. It is used throughout Latin America as a food coloring mixed with garlic and herbs, most familiar in yellow rice. A few seeds are briefly heated in hot oil to dissolve the color and then discarded before rice, water, and seasonings are added. In concentrated form, annatto is red-orange. Indigenous peoples of the Amazon region use it for ceremonial body paint. *Bixa* has orange sap, which purportedly has insect-repellant properties.

Bixa orellana

LIPSTICK-TREE, ANNATTO, ACHIOTE
Tropical America; widely cultivated. Evergreen tree, 10–20 ft.; zones 10–11. Blooms fall. Regular moisture. Fertile, well-drained soil. Full sun. Flowers: lavender to pale pink, to 2 in. wide, in terminal clusters; capsule covered with stiff bristles. Leaves: simple, broadly ovate to cordate, 4–6 in. long, tip tapering (acuminate), 3 primary veins reddish; petioles to 4 in. Young twigs rusty brown. *A compact tree that provides winter color. Mildew may be a problem in overly moist locations. The pastel flowers are followed by flamboyant crimson to ruddy capsules. Select for both flower and capsule color. Trees start blooming when quite small.*

BORAGINACEAE

BORAGE FAMILY
Boraginaceae includes approximately 117 genera of trees, shrubs, herbs, and a few woody climbers (lianas) distributed from the tropics to temperate zones. A few species are used as culinary or medicinal herbs, and certain larger tree species are cut for timber. Leaves are usually simple, often narrow, sometimes hairy or scaly (scabrous), sometimes rough enough to be used as fine sandpaper. Flowers are bisexual, or unisexual with male and female flowers on different plants (dioecious). They are radially or bilaterally symmetrical or irregular, wheel-like (rotate), tubular, or funnel-shaped. They usually have 5 sepals and 5 petals.

Cordia

Cordia includes approximately 320 species of trees and shrubs and a few woody vines. A number of shrubby species are used in tropical landscaping. Leaves are covered with single-celled hairs containing silica crystals, which makes them feel sandpapery. Flowers are radially symmetrical, funnel-shaped, fused into a tube at the base. The fruits are usually drupes, berrylike fruits with one pit, or occasionally schizocarps (dry fruits that split into 4 one-seeded segments at maturity). Adhesives are made from the sticky sap of some fruits. These species attract nectar-feeding birds and insects. John James Audubon is said to have named the Geiger tree, *C. sebestena*, in honor of Captain Geiger of Key West. The name geiger is sometimes inappropriately applied to other *Cordia* species. *Cordia glabra* is an invasive pest in Hawaii.

Cordia alliodora

SALMWOOD, ECUADOR LAUREL, LAUREL NEGRO, AJO-AJO
Synonym: *Cerdana alliodora*. Mexico to northern and western South America, West Indies. Evergreen tree, 30–50 ft.; zones 9–11. Blooms summer. Moderate moisture. Fertile, well-drained soil. Full sun. Flowers: small, funnel-shaped, to 0.5 in. long; in round clusters; fruit small, dry, with persistent, purplish-maroon 10-ribbed calyx attached. Leaves: oblong, 4–8 in. long, scabrous, tip acuminate. *A large shade tree. The dry schizocarp is a good field mark. Typically, cordias have fleshy fruit. The species name means "onion-scented" for the odor of the crushed leaves. The light-colored wood is favored for Scandinavian-style furniture and laminates.*

Cordia boissieri

WHITE CORDIA, TEXAS WILD OLIVE, ANCAHUITA
Texas, Mexico. Semideciduous shrub or tree, 10–20 ft.; zones 8–11. Blooms intermittently in warm months. Moderate moisture to fairly dry. Average, well-drained soil. Full sun. Flowers: funnel-

Bixa orellana

Cordia alliodora

Cordia boissieri, flowers

Bixa orellana, capsules

Cordia boissieri

shaped, lobes crinkled, chalk-white, throat yellow turning brownish. Leaves: simple, broadly elliptic, 4–5 in. long, dull gray-green, rough; margins slightly undulate. *Xeric. Pest resistant. Somewhat hardy but becomes deciduous in cold temperatures. Does not like wet locations. Habit varies from a sprawling shrub in desert areas to a small, rounded tree in moist climates. Habit photo shows plant growing in dry conditions at Balboa Park.*

Cordia goeldiana

FREIJO

Brazil (Amazon region). Evergreen tree to 20 ft.+; zones 10–11. Blooms summer. Seasonally moist/dry. Average, well-drained soil. Full sun. Flowers: small, funnel-shaped, white; in large panicles; fruit translucent orange-pink, to 0.5 in. diameter.

eter. Leaves: broadly ovate to obovate, 3–4 in. long, rough; margins widely toothed; petiole to 3 in. Bark: tan, corky, vertically fissured.

Cordia lutea

YELLOW CORDIA

Western Ecuador, Peru, Galapagos Islands. Evergreen shrub, 10–20 ft.; zones 9–11. Blooms warm months. Moderate moisture to seasonally moist/dry. Average, well-drained soil. Full sun. Flowers: funnel-shaped, to 1 in. wide, brilliant yellow; in large clusters. Leaves: ovate, 2–3 in. long, sandpaper rough, dull green; margins finely toothed. *This almost ever-blooming spreading shrub is underutilized. It is marginally hardy, pest resistant, and xeric. It does not like wet locations. Usually propagated by air-layering. Not known to set seed in cultivation.*

Cordia nitida

WEST INDIAN CHERRY, RED MANJACK, GLOSSY CORDIA

West Indies, Costa Rica, Honduras. Evergreen tree, 30–60 ft.; zones 10–11. Blooms summer. Seasonally moist/dry. Average, well-drained soil. Full sun. Flowers: small, white; in many-flowered clusters; fruit a small red drupe, to 0.25 in. diameter. Leaves: obovate, to 4 in. long, glossy dark green, firm. *An erect tree with handsome foliage suitable as a shade tree.*

Cordia sebestena

GEIGER TREE, BROADLEAF CORDIA, ANACONDA, JOAQUIN

West Indies, South America. Evergreen tree, 10–20 ft.; zone 11. Blooms intermittently in warm months. Moderate moisture to dry. Sandy, well-drained soil. Full sun. Flowers: funnel-shaped, orange, lobes spreading; anthers exserted, white; fruit white, waxy, turbinate, 1.5 in. long. Leaves: ovate, base sometimes cordate, 4–8 in. long, rough; margins toothed near the tip. *Salt tolerant. Suitable for warm coastal areas. Though this tender species is claimed as a Florida native, no wild population has ever been documented. Early settlers introduced it into Key West. Black and white larvae of the iridescent tortoise beetle periodically defoliate the tree.*

Cordia superba

Eastern Brazil. Evergreen tree, 10–20 ft.; zones 9–11. Blooms warm months. Moderate moisture.

Fertile, sandy, well-drained soil. Full sun. Flowers: funnel-shaped, snow-white, crinkled, throat white. Leaves: elliptic to obovate, to 6 in. long, dark green, quilted; margins somewhat toothed or notched. *Unusual but highly recommended for humid climates. The contrast between the dark foliage and the pure white flowers is striking. Pest resistant. Compare C. boissieri, which has off-white flowers with yellow-brownish throats.*

Echium

Echium includes 35–40 species of biennial and perennial herbs and shrubs from the Canary Islands, Madeira, the Mediterranean region, and the Near East. The genus name means "spine," but in this case alludes to a viper's sting as certain species were supposed to cure snake bite. The cultivated species are mostly xeric species from the Atlantic islands well adapted to mild dry climates such as coastal California with little rain but frequent morning mists. Leaves are simple and rough (scabrous). Flowers are funnel-shaped. The species listed here generally do not need encouragement to be prolific. In fact, fertilizer and water encourage ranginess and inhibit flowering. Biennial species bloom in the second year and then die. Start new plants annually for yearly bloom. These species are mostly bee pollinated. A number of rare *Echium* species grow at Quail Botanical Garden.

Cordia goeldiana, fruit

Cordia lutea

Cordia nitida, fruit

Cordia sebestena

Cordia superba

Echium candicans, inflorescences

Echium candicans

PRIDE-OF-MADEIRA, MASAROCCO
Synonym: *E. fastuosum*. Madeira Islands. Biennial or perennial shrub to 6 ft.; zones 8–10. Blooms spring. Fairly dry. Average to poor, well-drained soil. Full sun. Flowers: small, funnel-shaped, blue-violet and white or pure white; in spirelike panicles; calyx reddish. Leaves: lanceolate, coarsely hairy, gray-green, clustered near the ends of the branches. Branching from the base. *A xeric, mounding shrub suitable for poor soil and dry climate or seaside locations. Prune sharply after flowering. Supposedly resistant to deer. A pest in New Zealand and Australia.*

Echium decaisnei

Canary Islands.Biennial or perennial shrub to 6 ft.; zones 8–10. Blooms late spring, summer. Moderate moisture to dry. Average to poor, well-drained soil. Full sun. Flowers: small, funnel-shaped, white, throat magenta-pink. Leaves: oblanceolate, 4–5 in. long, clustered at the ends of stout branches. *Unusual in cultivation.*

Echium judaicum

BLUE WEED
Israel. Perennial spreading subshrub to 18 in.; zones 8–11. Blooms spring, summer Fairly dry. Average to poor, well-drained soil. Full to part sun. Flowers: funnel-shaped, blue-violet, in tiny inflorescences at the ends of slender branches. Leaves: ovate to oblong with elongated tips. *Unusual in the United States. A small, attractive bedding plant. Thrives in Mediterranean-type climates.*

Echium nervosum

Madeira Islands. Biennial shrub; zones 8–10. Blooms summer Fairly dry. Average to poor, well-drained soil. Full to part sun. Flowers: small, blue, stamens white, long-exserted; in dense inflorescence to 8 in. long on an unbranched stalk. Leaves: lanceolate, stiff, backward-pointing hairs, in basal rosettes. *Unusual in cultivation. Distinguished from* E. candicans *by the shorter inflorescence on a long stalk. Purportedly pollinated by lizards in native habitat.*

Echium wildpretii

TOWER-OF-JEWELS
Synonym: *E. bourgaeanum*. Canary Islands (Tenerife, La Palma). Biennial or short-lived perennial to 10 ft.; zones 9–10. Blooms summer, early fall.Fairly dry. Average to poor, sandy, well-drained soil. Full to part sun. Flowers: red-mauve, throat darker; stamens red; inflorescence terminal on an unbranched stem;

Echium candicans

Echium decaisnei

Echium decaisnei, flowers

Echium judaicum

Echium nervosum

Echium wildpretii

bracts leaflike, linear, and twisted, hairy, extending well beyond the flowers. Leaves: linear, tips curled, hairy, bluish green; spirally arranged on an erect or reclining, unbranched stalk. *Very striking unbranched plant for rock gardens and coastal locations. Sprawling stems can be staked for display. Does not thrive in wet or fertile situations. Attractive to nectar-feeding birds and insects.*

Wigandia

Wigandia includes 2 or 3 species of trees or shrubs from tropical America. This genus was formerly segregated into its own family, Hydrophyllaceae. Leaves are large and leathery, usually with stinging or irritating hairs. A nonstinging form of *W. urens* is occasionally cultivated. Wigandia provides winter bloom and large, handsome leaves. Accustomed to moderate altitude, it is marginally hardy. It grows naturally in rocky soil. The temperate stinging nettle belongs in the family Urticaceae.

Wigandia urens var. caracasana

WIGANDIA, CARACAS BIG-LEAF
Synonym: *W. caracasana*. Mexico, Central America to Venezuela and Peru. Evergreen shrub or tree, 15–20 ft.; zones 9–11. Blooms late winter, early spring. Moderate moisture. Average, well-drained soil. Full to part sun. Flowers: violet, center white; indeterminate panicles opening over a long period from bottom to top. Leaves: large, broadly ovate, to 14 in. long, dark green, undersides usually with stinging hairs; margins undulate and toothed. Amber hairs on stems. *This cultivated form lacks stinging hairs; the leaves feel somewhat sticky on the underside. A fast-growing plant that tends to become rangy. Prune after bloom for compact growth. Suitable for coastal locations.*

BRASSICACEAE

CRUCIFER FAMILY, CAPER FAMILY
Brassicaceae (Cruciferae) includes approximately 420 genera of herbs, shrubs, and trees, which are widely distributed, with greatest diversity in Asia, the Mediterranean, and North America. Genera tradition-

ally in the caper family, Capparidaceae, are now included in Brassicaceae. Several species are culinary condiments (capers, mustard, horseradish), oils (rapeseed, canola), and vegetables (radishes, cabbage, kale, cauliflower, broccoli, mustard greens, Brussels sprouts, turnips, watercress, kohlrabi). Sulfur compounds impart the typically pungent aroma and piquant flavor. Leaves are simple, sometimes deeply lobed or often compound. Flowers are bisexual, usually radially symmetrical or slightly irregular, and commonly yellow. The 4 sepals and 4 petals of traditional genera form a cross, hence the older name of Cruciferae. The inflorescence is a corymb, spike, or raceme. The fruit is a capsule (members of the former Capparidaceae) or a silique, or silicule (a flattened capsule that splits into 2 halves longitudinally with seeds mounted on a papery septum in the middle).

Capparis

Capparis includes 250–350 species of shrubs and trees, which are widely distributed. Culinary capers are the pickled buds of *C. spinosa*, a Mediterranean shrub. Sometimes the buds of other species are used. Only a few tropical species are cultivated in the United States though they include several very desirable ornamentals. Capers are pest resistant. Some species are armed with small thorns and are useful as barrier hedges. Flowers are attractive to birds and butterflies.

Capparis cynophallophora

JAMAICA CAPER
Synonym: *C. jamaicensis*. Coastal West Indies, South Florida, Florida Keys, Mexico. Evergreen tree or shrub to 20 ft.; zones 10–11. Blooms spring, early summer. Seasonally moist/dry. Poor, sandy, well-drained soil; alkaline pH. Full sun to bright broken light. Flowers: petals 4, white; stamens long, becoming pinkish violet, to 2 in.; fruit a slender, russet capsule, to 10 in. long, seeds have orange arils. Leaves: oblong, 3–4 in. long, firm, glossy, undersides minutely scaly; margins slightly revolute; tip notched (emarginate); petiole

short. Bark: reddish brown. *A spineless tree of coastal woodland understory. Salt tolerant. An excellent low-maintenance hedge. Adapted to porous limestone soils.*

Capparis erythrocarpus

Western Africa from Equatorial Guinea to Angola, Congo. Evergreen clambering shrub to 8 ft.+; zones 10–11. Blooms spring. Moderate moisture. Average, well-drained soil. Full sun to bright broken light. Flowers: petals light green; stamens white, red at the base. Leaves: ovate, to 3 in., glossy dark green, tips acuminate. Stems: dark green and limber when young, brown when mature with small hooked thorns like roses. *A striking green-flowered, clambering shrub. Unusual in cultivation. The tiny thorns cling tenaciously, making an effective barrier hedge.*

Capparis micracantha var. henryi

CAT'S WHISKERS
Synonym: *C. henryi*. Taiwan, Ryukyu Islands, Sulawesi (Celebes). Evergreen shrub to 6 ft.; zones 10–11. Blooms late winter, spring. Moderate moisture. Average, well-drained soil. Full sun to bright broken light. Flowers: petals slightly dimorphic—2 spreading, white, and 2 erect, yellow, turning russet; sepals small, green; stamens to 2 in. long, white. Leaves: broadly ovate, to 6 in. long, glossy dark green. Small thorns on the branches. *Buds sometimes used as a substitute for commercial capers. Often cultivated in Thailand. An effective barrier hedge.*

Cleome

Cleome includes approximately 150 species of perennial and annual herbs widely distributed in the subtropics and tropics. Leaves are pal-

Wigandia urens var. *caracasana*

Capparis cynophallophora

Capparis erythrocarpus

Capparis micracantha var. henryi

mately compound. Inflorescences are usually on slender stalks and borne in large terminal clusters or sometimes solitary. Very attractive to hummingbirds. Bracts are usually present. All parts are pungently scented.

Cleome hassleriana

CLEOME, SPIDER FLOWER
Synonym: *C. spinosa* (misapplied). Southern Brazil, Uruguay, Paraguay, northern Argentina. Annual herb, 4–5 ft.; zones 9–11. Blooms spring to fall. Regular moisture. Fertile, well-drained soil. Full sun. Flowers: petals narrowly stalked, stamens long-exserted; inflorescence 8–10 in. wide. Leaves: palmatifid, 5- to 7-lobed; margins minutely toothed; spines at base of petioles. *Cultivars with red, purple, yellow, or white flowers. Commonly cultivated as a summer annual in temperate climates.*

Crateva

Crateva (formerly spelled *Crataeva*) includes 6–15 species of trees and shrubs, primarily from tropical Asia. The leaves are divided into 3 pointed leaflets (trifoliolate). The petals are spade-shaped, narrowly stalked at the base (clawed), and obtusely pointed at the tips. The stamens are long and showy. Leaves of some species are eaten as vegetables or used in folk medicine. *Crateva religiosa* is often cultivated around Buddhist temples in Asia and the Pacific Islands. In India, old trees are said to be 40 ft. high, with a girth of 6 ft.

Crateva magna

BURMESE DALUR, DALA
Synonyms: *C. hygrophylla*, *C. lophosperma*, *C. nurvala*. Northeastern India, Southeast Asia, Malaysia, Indonesia (Java). Briefly deciduous tree, 30–60 ft.; zones 10–11.

Blooms late summer, fall. Seasonally moist to wet/dry. Fertile, well-drained soil . Full sun. Flowers: petals cream to pinkish, obovate, 6 in. long, base clawed, faintly fragrant; stamens wiry, purple, 4–5 in. long; in clusters; fruit round, rough, tan; pedicel 2–3 in. long. Leaves: trifoliolate; leaflets elliptic, 6–8 in. long, firm; tips acuminate; petioles 3–4 in. long. *Of riverbanks and naturalized around rice paddies in the Far East. This handsome, erect tree is stunning in flower. It is unusual to rare in the United States but highly recommended. Suitable for areas which are occasionally flooded.*

Crateva religiosa

GARLIC-PEAR, TEMPLE-TREE, BRARNA (INDIA), MARSH DALUR (MALAYSIA)
Synonyms: *C. macrocarpa*, *C. membranifolia*, *C. roxburghii*. India, Southeast Asia to northern Australia, Oceania. Deciduous tree,

20–40 ft.; zones 8–11. Blooms spring. Seasonally moist/dry. Average, well-drained soil. Full sun. Flowers: petals ovate, 1–2 in. long, creamy white, base clawed; stamens long, violet; fruit pear-shaped but rarely produced; pedicels long. Leaves: trifoliolate; leaflets lanceolate, to 4 in. long, thin. Bark: gray, white-spotted. *Suggests flowering dogwood in bloom. Flowers precede leaves in spring. From sub-Himalayan to lowland forests especially along rivers. Unusual in mainland United States. In South Florida, this species is slow-growing and relatively small.*

Crateva tapia

SPIDER-FLOWER TREE
Tropical America. Deciduous tree to 25–75 ft.; zones 10–11. Blooms spring. Moderate moisture. Average, well-drained soil. Full sun. Flowers: petals enlarged, creamy white, clawed; stamens purple; in many-flowered clusters; fruit a dark red schizocarp. Leaves: trifoliolate; leaflets obovate, glossy dark green, tips cuspidate. Young branches green. *A very fast growing tree and potentially large. Blooms in 2 or 3 years from large cuttings. Suitable for coastal planting. Flowers and leaves are odorless. Fruit rarely produced in cultivation.*

BROMELIACEAE

BROMELIAD FAMILY, PINEAPPLE FAMILY
Bromeliaceae includes approximately 56 genera of terrestrial to epiphytic herbs of mild temperate

Cleome hassleriana 'Purple Queen'

Crateva magna

Crateva religiosa

Crateva religiosa, flowers

Crateva tapia

and tropical America, plus a single species of *Pitcairnia* from western Africa. The leaves are strap- or sword-shaped, commonly in basal whorls, often guttered, with a water-collecting reservoir ("pitcher" or "tank") in the center, or sometimes in whorls around a stem, or rarely distichous, the bases clasping the stem. They are sometimes strongly patterned or become brightly colored at maturity. The leaf margin is frequently sharply toothed, the tip spined. Flowers are usually small and short-lived, blue-violet, yellow, or white. Floral bracts, sepals, and sometimes the fruits are brightly colored and often long-lasting. The fruit is a berry or capsule.

Individual bromeliad plants die after flowering (monocarpic) after producing new plants ("pups") from offsets. Remove offsets when they are a third the size of the parent. Pot in humus, bark, or chopped coconut fiber with grit for drainage. The roots of epiphytic species are primarily for attachment. Even terrestrial species may rot in wet soil. In warm areas many bromeliads thrive in humus under trees or attached to trees and palms. Mist when dry and keep reservoirs full of water. Bromeliads provide unique niches, moisture, nectar, and food for invertebrates, frogs, lizards, and birds. To deter mosquito larvae and scale insects, spray plants with a mixture of 1 teaspoon each of salad oil and kitchen detergent in a quart of water. Copper sprays are deadly to bromeliads. Most species are easy to grow, some do best in humid climates while others do well where dry.

Aechmea

Aechmea includes approximately 125 species of terrestrial and epiphytic herbs from tropical America, with greatest diversity in Brazil. They are commonly cultivated. The genus name (pronounced ek-MAY-ah) means "spear point" and alludes to the shape of the sepals and floral bracts. Leaves are strap-shaped, usually with a terminal spine, and often with sharp teeth along the margins. The petals are small but the sepals, bracts, and

fruits are often brightly colored and long-lasting. In general, plants with rigid leaves and sharply toothed margins tolerate more direct sunlight and cooler temperatures than soft-leafed, smooth-margined types. The central reservoir should be kept full of water. Mist frequently when humidity is low to keep the appearance fresh. Most aechmeas thrive outdoors in frost-free regions. They can be grown on mulched beds, though never "planted" in the ground. Prop large species with a few rocks or logs until firmly established. Many can be attached to sturdy limbs or the trunks of trees and palms. Smaller species make excellent container plants.

Aechmea blanchetiana
Brazil (Bahia). Terrestrial herb, 3–5 ft.; zones 10–11. Blooms fall, winter. Regular moisture and humidity. Sandy, humus-rich, well-drained soil. Full sun to bright broken light. Flowers: cylindrical, yellow; bracts red; in large, open-branched clusters. Leaves: strap-shaped, streaked copper to red in bright sun. *Produces many pups. Suitable as a medium-sized bedding plant. Thrives in coastal locations but not at seaside.*

Aechmea 'Blue Tango'
Garden hybrid. Semiepiphytic herb to 2 ft.; zones 10–11. Blooms summer, fall. Regular moisture and humidity. Coarse organic material or epiphytic. Part sun to bright filtered light. Flowers: petals tubular, blue-violet; sepals and bracts red-violet; rachis red. Leaves: light green; margins sharply toothed. *'Blue Tango' is a new hybrid with brilliant colors.*

Aechmea burle-marxii
Brazil (Bahia). Semiepiphytic herb, 2–2.5 ft.; zones 10–11. Blooms summer. Regular moisture and humidity. Coarse organic material or epiphytic. Part sun to bright filtered light. Flowers: small, tubular, yellow; bracts salmon-pink, spiny. Leaves: strap-shaped, green- and gray-banded; margins spiny; in rosettes. *Tolerant of cool temperatures but not freezing. Named for landscape architect Roberto Burle Marx.*

Aechmea chantinii hybrids
AMAZON ZEBRA PLANT
South America (Amazon basin). Semiepiphytic herbs to 2 ft.; zones 10–11. Bloom spring, summer. Regular moisture and humidity. Coarse organic material or epiphytic. Part sun to bright filtered light. Flowers: small, tubular, yellow; bracts scarlet. Leaves: strap-shaped, gray-green, yellow, faintly to strongly banded in choice selections; margins spiny; in rosettes. *Many cultivated plants labeled A. chantinii are actually hybrids. 'Little Harve' is a hybrid, possibly involving A. rubens. The species and some of its hybrids are cold-sensitive.*

Aechmea dichlamydea var. trinitensis
Coastal Venezuela and Trinidad. Semiepiphytic herb to 2.5 ft.; zones 10–11. Blooms spring, early summer. Regular moisture and humidity. Coarse organic material or epiphytic. Full sun to filtered light. Flowers: tubular, purple; bracts green becoming purple; flower stalk scarlet. Leaves: light green; margins with small spines. *Long-lasting bloom.*

Aechmea distichantha
Synonym: *Platyaechmea distichantha*. Brazil. Semiepiphytic herb to 1.5 ft.; zones 10–11. Blooms spring. Regular moisture and humidity. Coarse organic material or epiphytic. Bright filtered light. Flowers: small, purple; bracts and flower stalk red. Leaves: strap-shaped, light green; margins with small black spines. *Var. schlumbergeri is larger and more sharply spined than the type species.*

Aechmea blanchetiana

Aechmea 'Blue Tango'

Aechmea burle-marxii

Aechmea 'Little Harve'

Aechmea fasciata
SILVER VASE

Brazil. Semiepiphytic herb to 18 in.; zones 9–11. Blooms spring, summer. Regular moisture and humidity. Coarse organic material or epiphytic. Full to part sun. Flowers: pale pink and blue; bracts pink, sharply toothed; inflorescence long-lasting. Leaves: oblong, with blue-gray and green bands; in vase-like rosettes. *Var. pruinosa is distinguished by the frostlike waxy scales. Thrives in hot to near freezing temperatures. Very attractive in rock gardens. One of the first cultivated bromeliads.*

Aechmea fendleri
Venezuela. Semiepiphytic herb, 2.5–3 ft.; zones 9–11. Blooms spring. Regular moisture and humidity. Coarse organic material or epiphytic. Full to part sun. Flowers: trumpet-shaped, blue-violet; sepals dark violet, peduncles and inflorescence stalk red, with white waxy scales; fruit blue-violet. Leaves: light green, guttered; margins with small, brownish, sharp teeth; arranged in a tight vase shape. *Suitable for outdoor growing in warm climates.*

Aechmea fulgens
CORAL-BERRY

Brazil. Semiepiphytic herb to 12 in.; zones 9–11. Blooms spring, summer. Regular moisture and humidity. Coarse organic material or epiphytic. Part sun to bright broken light. Flowers: small, blue-violet; bracts red; fruit red; inflorescence branches at the base. Leaves: dark green, broad, spineless, in rosettes. *Excellent ground cover under trees or can be attached to tree limbs or trunks. Var. discolor leaves are purple below. 'Variegated' has green and white leaves. The hybrid A. fulgens × A. ramosa is sometimes mistaken for A. fulgens, but is distinguished by the spined leaf margins.*

Aechmea gamosepala
Synonym: *A. thyrsigera.* Brazil. Semiepiphytic herb to 12 in.; zones 10–11. Blooms spring, summer, or fall. Regular moisture and humidity. Coarse organic material or epiphytic. Bright broken light. Flowers: small, blue-violet; bracts pink; fruit ruby- to ruddy-red, long-lasting; inflorescence an unbranched spike. Leaves: broad, spineless, in rosettes; sometimes yellow-striped. *A relatively small bromeliad. Produces clumps suitable for baskets. Flowers short-lived, but fruits last for several weeks. Blooms several times a year.*

Aechmea luddemanniana
Southern Mexico, Guatemala, Honduras. Semiepiphytic herb; zones 10–11. Blooms spring, summer. Regular moisture and humidity. Coarse organic material or epiphytic. Part sun to bright broken light. Flowers: small, blue; bracts black with white scales; berries white, turning purple, then black. Leaves: dark green, in basal rosettes. *The showy season is greatly extended by the colorful berries. Makes dense mounds or can be attached to trunks. Tolerates near-freezing temperatures. 'Rodco' has pink-striped leaves.*

Aechmea mariae-reginae
Synonym: *Pothuava mariae-reginae.* Costa Rica, Central America. Semiepiphytic herb to about 3 ft.; zones 10–11. Blooms spring, early sum-

Aechmea dichlamydea var. *trinitensis*

Aechmea distichantha var. *schlumbergeri*

Aechmea fasciata var. *pruinosa*

Aechmea fendleri

Aechmea fulgens var. *discolor* 'Variegated'

Aechmea fulgens × *Aechmea ramosa*

Aechmea gamosepala

Aechmea luddemanniana 'Rodco'

mer. Regular moisture and humidity. Coarse compost or epiphytic. Bright broken light. Flowers: unisexual, white in dense spikes; primary bracts brilliant pink, reflexed; inflorescence, 3–4 ft. tall. Leaves: medium to dark green; in basal rosettes to 3 ft. wide; margins sharply toothed. *A medium-sized highly ornamental bromeliad. Dioecious. The female inflorescence is shorter, thicker, and more cylindrical than the male.*

Aechmea nudicaulis

Synonyms: *Billbergia nudicaulis, Hohenbergia nudicaulis, Pothuava nudicaulis.* Mexico, West Indies to Brazil. Semiepiphytic herb to 12 in.; zones 9–11. Blooms spring. Moderate moisture and humidity. Coarse organic material or epiphytic. Full sun to bright broken light. Flowers: tubular, yellow;

bracts red, ascending. Leaves: greenish or reddish in strong sun, striped horizontally, covered with waxy scales; deeply guttered; margins sharply toothed; on a short stem. *A small but resilient little bromeliad. Very attractive grouped in a basket.*

Aechmea pineliana

Synonyms: *A. roberto-seidelii, Pothuava pineliana var. minuta.* Brazil. Epiphytic herb, 12–16 in.; zones 10–11. Blooms spring. Regular moisture and humidity. Coarse compost or epiphytic. Full sun. Flowers: small; spike dense, prickly; primary bracts scarlet, sheathing the 1 ft. stalk. Leaves: bronze and reddish; margins with large curved teeth. *Var. minuta is smaller than the type, to about 1 ft. high. A compact, clump-forming bromeliad. Suitable for a basket in a sunny spot.*

Aechmea victoriana

Synonym: *Lamprococcus victorianus.* Brazil. Semiepiphytic herb to 1 ft.; zones 10–11. Blooms spring. Regular moisture. Coarse organic material or epiphytic. Part sun to bright broken light. Flowers: small, violet; spike and floral bracts red, becoming pendent when mature; fruit red. Leaves: strap-shaped, purple below in var. *discolor*; margins smooth, tip spined; in open rosettes. *A small bromeliad that makes an excellent ground cover under high canopy. Can be attached to tree and palm trunks. Tolerant of cold temperatures.*

Aechmea weilbachii

Brazil. Semiepiphytic herb to 1 ft.; zones 10–11. Blooms winter. Regular moisture and humidity. Coarse organic material or epiphytic. Bright broken or filtered light. Flowers: small, violet; sepals, bracts,

and stalk red; inflorescence pendent with short branches. Leaves: strap-shaped, bright green; margins with tiny sharp teeth; in basal rosettes. *Var.* weilbachii *normally has erect inflorescences; forma* pendula *(syn.* A. weilbachii *var.* pendula*) has pendent inflorescences. A small cluster-forming bromeliad. Suitable for baskets. Cold-sensitive.*

Aechmea woronowii

Synonym: *Streptocalyx subnuda.* Colombia. Semiepiphytic herb to 2 ft.; zones 10–11. Blooms late winter, spring. Regular moisture and humidity. Coarse organic material or epiphytic. Bright broken or filtered light. Flowers: small, white; calyx, stalk, and bracts pink. Leaves: strap-shaped, medium green to pinkish, flecked with dark green. *An unusual, but very attractive bromeliad. Suitable for containers.*

Aechmea mariae-reginae, male inflorescence

Aechmea mariae-reginae, female inflorescence

Aechmea nudicaulis

Aechmea pineliana var. *minuta*

Aechmea victoriana var. *discolor*

Aechmea weilbachii forma *pendula*

Aechmea woronowii

Aechmea zebrina

Aechmea zebrina

Synonym: *Platyaechmea zebrina*. Colombia, Ecuador. Semiepiphytic herb to 2.5 ft.; zones 10–11. Blooms spring. Regular moisture and humidity. Coarse organic material or epiphytic. Bright broken or filtered light. Flowers: small, yellow; inflorescence branched, bracts orange. Leaves: strap-shaped, with silvery light green and dark green or purple bands on the undersides; margins sharply toothed, deeply guttered. *An erect, medium-sized bromeliad with well-marked leaves.*

Alcantarea

Alcantarea includes approximately 17 species of monocarpic herbs from southeastern Brazil. Some species were formerly placed in closely related *Vriesea*. *Alcantarea* species can be distinguished by their long, linear petals. Leaves are in basal rosettes. The relatively large flowers open early in the morning and are fragrant.

Alcantarea glaziouana

Synonyms: *Vriesea geniculata*, *Vriesea glaziouana*. Brazil. Terrestrial herb to 3 ft.; zones 10–11. Blooms spring, early summer. Regular moisture. Open, well-drained soil. Bright filtered light. Flowers: creamy white; arranged on a slender red flower stalk to 6 ft.; bracts purplish red. Leaves: sword-shaped, lightly banded; in a spreading basal rosette. *This species differs from* A. imperialis *by the narrow, lightly banded, erect leaves and by the more widely spaced bracts on the inflorescence stalk.*

Alcantarea imperialis

GIANT ALCANTAREA, GIANT VRIESEA
Synonym: *Vriesea imperialis*. Brazil. Terrestrial herb, 3–4 ft.; zones 10–11. Blooms spring, early summer. Regular moisture. Open, well-drained soil. Bright filtered light. Flowers: petals strap-shaped, creamy white; arranged on red stalk to 6 ft.; bracts boat-shaped, reddish, closely spaced along stalk. Leaves: broad, spreading, blue-green, reddish below; in a large basal rosette. *One of the largest bromeliads commonly cultivated, though far larger bromeliads are found in the genus* Puya.

Ananas

Ananas includes approximately 7 species of monocarpic herbs from tropical America. The most widely recognized is the pineapple, *A. co-mosus*, a seedless edible cultigen with numerous selections. Pineapples have been cultivated for millennia by indigenous peoples of the Americas. Their exact origin and ancestry are obscure. They have been distributed throughout the tropics and are an important food crop. In the Philippines, leaf fibers are made into a fine, translucent fabric. Leaf tips and margins of older cultivars, such as 'Spanish Red', have ferocious sharp teeth though almost spineless varieties exist, like 'Smooth Cayenne'. The fruit is a syncarp, a collection of fused fruits topped by a coma (tuft of leaflike bracts).

Pineapples grow from low coastal regions to frost-free higher elevations, wherever sunlight is plentiful. They like regular moisture in hot weather and tolerate almost any fast-draining soil including sand, volcanic ash, and clay. I have grown pineapples between the old leaf bases of *Sabal palmetto*. Since cultivated fruits are sterile, plants are propagated from offsets or by rooting the coma. The coma is cut from the fruit and allowed to dry a week to several months before planting. Pineapples take a year to 18 months to fruit from a coma, 12–16 months from offsets (Wheeler, pers. comm.). After the first plant fruits, multiple offsets are produced. With adequate light and regular moisture, pineapples are very easy to grow.

Ananas bracteatus var. tricolor

VARIEGATED PINEAPPLE,
PIÑA ORNAMENTAL
Only in cultivation. Terrestrial herb, 3–4 ft.; zones 10–11. Blooms spring. Regular moisture when warm, moderate moisture when cool. Sandy, composted, well-drained soil; slightly acid pH. Full sun. Flowers: small, blue, primary bracts pink; fruit bracts conspicuous, pink; coma green- and cream-striped with pink margins and spines. Leaves: sword-shaped, recurved, green- and white-striped; margins white, with hooked, pink teeth. *Fruits are fibrous, inedible.* Ananas comosus *var.* variegatus, *a variety of the edible pineapple, has green leaves with a pink central stripe and the typical brownish fruit.*

Ananas comosus

PINEAPPLE
Only in cultivation. Terrestrial herb, 1–3 ft.; zones 10–11. Blooms spring. Regular moisture when warm, moderate when cool. Sandy, composted, well-drained soil; slightly acid pH. Full sun. Flowers: small, blue, bracts red; coma green, heavily spined. Leaves: sword-shaped, recurved, green to reddish; margins with small hooked, sharp

Alcantarea glaziouana

Alcantarea imperialis

Ananas bracteatus var. *tricolor*

teeth. *'Spanish Red' is an old selection of the common pineapple. Fruits ripen 3–4 months after bloom, sweet-acid, fragrant, and very tasty.*

Ananas nanus

MINIATURE PINEAPPLE, PIÑITA

Northern Brazil to Surinam. Perennial herb, 18–24 in.; zones 10–11. Blooms spring. Regular moisture when warm, moderate moisture when cool. Sandy, composted, well-drained soil; slightly acid pH. Full sun to bright filtered light. Flowers: small; fruit a miniature pineapple, about 2–3 in. high on an erect, 12- to 15-in. stalk, coma to 4 in. Leaves: sword-shaped, 8–12 in. long, slender, more or less covered with waxy white scales, recurved; margins sharply toothed. *Often grown as a curiosity.*

Androlepis

Androlepis includes a single species of monocarpic herb from Central America. It is among the few bromeliads with the male and female flowers on different plants (dioecious). Female plants are rare in cultivation. Male plants are propagated from offsets. The leaves are in basal rosettes, yellow-green in filtered light to mahogany-red in bright sunlight. This clump-forming bromeliad is suitable as a medium bedding plant.

Androlepis skinneri

Synonym: *A. donnell-smithii.* Costa Rica to Panama. Terrestrial herb, 18–24 in.; zones 10–11. Blooms warm months. Regular moisture and humidity. Sandy, humus-rich, well-drained soil; slightly acid pH. Full sun to bright filtered light. Flowers: unisexual; spike white, conical, erect, to 2 ft. tall. Leaves: sword-shaped, 18–24 in. long, outer leaves spreading; margins lined with small sharp teeth; in basal rosettes. *The female inflorescence has a more cylindrical shape on a shorter stalk than the male inflorescence shown here.*

Billbergia

Billbergia includes approximately 63 species of mostly epiphytic herbs from Mexico to South America, with greatest diversity in sea- sonally moist/dry regions of Brazil. Erect, urn-shaped (urceolate) foliage, arching inflorescences, and showy pink bracts often distinguish billbergias. The leaves are usually deeply guttered to channel rain into the deep enclosed reservoir for the dry season. Rosettes of species from moister regions are more spreading and open. Plantlets often develop from branching stolons. Leaves are frequently spotted or banded and a waxy bluish or grayish color. The inflorescences are usually short-lived, lasting a few days to a week, but a cluster of plants may flower several times a year. Flowers are pollinated by hummingbirds. Billbergias are very attractive in a basket or growing up the trunk of a tree. Some species bloom synchronously, a spectacular phenomenon where all the mature plants in a cluster and throughout the area bloom at the same time.

Billbergia 'Catherine Wilson'

Garden origin. Semiepiphytic herb, 12–18 in.; zones 10–11. Blooms winter, spring. Regular moisture. Coarse organic material or epi- phytic. Full sun to bright filtered light. Flowers: greenish white, inflorescence stalk pink; erect to pendent; bracts pink. Leaves: strap-shaped, guttered, dark green with scattered creamy white spots, waxy below; margins sharply toothed; rosettes vase-shaped. *An old cultivar by early bromeliad breeders Bob and Catherine Wilson. Resembles* Billbergia distachia *var.* maculata *from eastern Brazil.*

Billbergia kuhlmannii

Brazil. Semiepiphytic herb to 3 ft.; zones 10–11. Blooms spring. Regu-

Ananas comosus 'Spanish Red', in flower

Billbergia 'Catherine Wilson'

Billbergia kuhlmannii

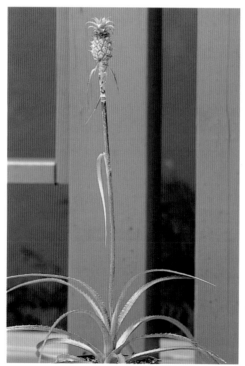

Ananas nanus

Androlepis skinneri, male plant

lar moisture and humidity. Coarse organic material or epiphytic. Full sun to bright filtered light. Flowers: purple, inflorescence stalk covered with waxy gray scales; bracts pink; pendent. Leaves: strap-shaped, guttered; banded gray-green and gray, waxy; margins sharply toothed.

Billbergia pyramidalis
SUMMER-TORCH

Synonyms: *B. bicolor, Bromelia pyramidalis.* Eastern Brazil. Semi-terrestrial herb, 1–1.5 ft.; zones 10–11. Blooms intermittently in warm months. Regular moisture and humidity. Coarse sand and humus. Part sun to bright filtered light. Flowers: petals red with purple tips; inflorescence club-shaped; stalk crimson with waxy scales; bracts crimson to pink. Leaves: strap-shaped, broad, light green; margins with small sharp teeth; in basal rosettes. *Often used for ground cover. The bloom lasts several days but a clump will bloom synchronously 3 or 4 times a year. Var. concolor has all red petals.*

Billbergia viridiflora
Belize, Guatemala. Epiphytic herb to about 1.5 ft.; zones 10–11.

Blooms warm months. Regular moisture and humidity. Coarse humus or epiphytic. Part sun to bright filtered light. Flowers: green; pedicels 3 in. long; inflorescence stalk reddish, to 4 ft.+ long; primary bracts red. Leaves: sword-shaped, arching, green above, undersides waxy, purplish and faintly banded. *Unusual in cultivation. The pendent, fragile inflorescence should be displayed by growing in a hanging basket or from a high limb. The species name means "green flowers."*

Bromelia
Bromelia includes approximately 51 species of mostly terrestrial herbs from tropical America. Some species grow to 6 ft. high and wide and form large clumps, new plants developing at the ends of stolons. A fiber similar to sisal (see *Agave* species) is made from the leaves and has been investigated as a paper substitute. Cultivation of barbed species like *B. pinguin* is not recommended in areas where children and pets might play. The gardener should consider the difficulties of weeding around these well-armed species. Heavy mulching is helpful.

Bromelia humilis
Northern Venezuela, Guyana, Trinidad. Terrestrial herb, 1–2 ft.; zones 9–11. Blooms summer. Seasonally moist/dry. Most well-drained soils. Full sun to bright broken light. Flowers: inconspicuous, white and purple; at the base of the leaves hidden in woolly white hairs. Leaves: sword-shaped, to 1 ft. long, green becoming bright red in the center when in flower; margins with hooked teeth. *The flowers are hidden but the leaf bases turn bright red when in bloom. Low and spreading. Very attractive in rock gardens and beds.*

Bromelia pinguin
BARBED-WIRE FENCE, CORAZÓN DE FUEGO ("HEART-OF-FIRE")

Synonym: *Agallostachys pinguin.* West Indies, Central America, northern Venezuela. Terrestrial herb to 6 ft.; zones 9–11. Blooms spring. Seasonally moist/dry. Most well-drained soils. Full to part sun. Flowers: purple and white; floral and scape bracts white, woolly; congested along a 2- to 3-ft. spike. Leaves: sword-shaped, curved outward, green, turning red at the base when in bloom. *A large, spectacular, spreading bromeliad. Very effective as*

a barrier hedge. The hooked teeth on the leaf margins are as formidable as barbed wire. Mulch deeply (at least 1 ft.) to help control difficult to reach weeds. The yellow fruits are edible and are used in folk medicine (Burch, pers. comm.). Similar B. balansae, from Argentina and Paraguay, has a more spirelike inflorescence on a short stalk.*

Cryptanthus
Cryptanthus includes approximately 53 species of terrestrial herbs from eastern Brazil. The young leaves are held upright at first, then spread almost flat against the ground by the time the flowers appear. New plants are produced in the axils of the old leaves. The leaves of some species have silver-scaled chevron bands resembling hawk feathers. The base color of the leaves may be green, brown, or reddish, striped or banded with contrasting colors. Hybrids are numerous. The genus name means

Bromelia humilis

Billbergia pyramidalis

Billbergia viridiflora

Bromelia pinguin

"hidden flowers," alluding to the small white flowers which are half hidden by their bracts in the reservoir. These species are intriguing when grouped in a large shallow container, rock garden, or among the shallow roots of a tree. They are found in specialty nurseries and the collections of fanciers.

Cryptanthus zonatus
EARTH STAR
Eastern Brazil, extinct in the wild. Terrestrial herb under 1 ft.; zones 10–11. Blooms spring. Regular

moisture and humidity. Sandy, humus-rich, well-drained soil. Bright broken to filtered light. Flowers: white; at the base of the leaves. Leaves: sword-shaped, greenish gray or reddish brown, boldly marked with jagged bands of silvery white scales; margins wavy, spined. *Plants in my garden have survived near-freezing temperatures.*

Guzmania
Guzmania includes approximately 198 species of semiterrestrial herbs from tropical America, with great-

est diversity in montane cloudforests of northwestern South and Central America. Leaves are soft and unarmed which makes them popular for containers. The open to compact inflorescences are nestled in the reservoir or on a stalk surrounded by an involucre of spirally arranged bracts. The flowers are small and tubular. Guzmanias thrive in moist, humid conditions with bright filtered light. Misting is important during dry periods to keep the plants looking fresh. There is a wide variety of ornamental

species with brightly colored leaves or bracts and numerous hybrids. Though commonly regarded as cold- and heat-sensitive, several thrive as understory plants outdoors in my garden in South Florida. In colder regions, containergrown plants may be placed outdoors in the filtered light of a tree in warm weather.

Guzmania lingulata
QUICHE
Colombia, Ecuador. Epiphytic herb to 1.5 ft.; zones 10–11. Blooms spring, summer. Regular moisture and humidity. Coarse organic material or epiphytic. Bright filtered light. Flowers: white; floral bracts yellow; scape bracts red; on a short stalk. Leaves: glossy green, soft; margins smooth. *Var. cardinalis has a fountainlike inflorescence on a moderately tall stalk. 'Fortuna' is a hybrid involving this species.*

Guzmania sanguinea
Costa Rica to Ecuador. Epiphytic herb to 1 ft.; zones 10–11. Blooms spring, summer. Regular moisture and humidity. Coarse organic material or epiphytic. Bright filtered light. Flowers: yellow; bracts green and red; inflorescence stalkless. Leaves: glossy green, becoming red when in bloom, soft, spineless. *A stunning, spreading bromeliad, 1.5–2 ft. diameter. Some selections have brick orange stripes.*

Guzmania wittmackii
Southern Colombia, Ecuador. Epiphytic herb to 18 in.; zones 10–11. Blooms spring. Regular moisture and humidity. Coarse organic material or epiphytic. Bright filtered light. Flowers: white; bracts green and red; inflorescence stalk to 3 ft. Leaves: slender, glossy green, soft; margins smooth. *'Variegated' has green- and white-striped leaves.*

Hohenbergia
Hohenbergia includes approximately 52 species from the West Indies and northern South America. The plants resemble *Aechmea* vegetatively, but the flowers are arranged in whorls rather than in opposite ranks on the stalks. The leaves have sharply toothed margins and termi-

Cryptanthus zonatus 'Silver'

Guzmania lingulata var. cardinalis

Guzmania 'Fortuna'

Guzmania sanguinea

Guzmania wittmackii 'Variegated'

nal spines. More commonly cultivated species are moderately large plants with long flower spikes. It may take up to 3 years for a small offset to reach flowering size, but a large division will flower the next season. Most adapt readily to full sun and can be stuck into crevices or simply supported by a few large rocks with little or no medium. The species listed here are xeric, tolerating near-freezing temperatures and short dry spells.

Hohenbergia rosea

Brazil. Semiepiphytic herb to 2 ft.; zones 10–11. Blooms spring. Moderate moisture. Coarse organic material or epiphytic. Full to part sun. Flowers: purple, floral bracts pink to red; arranged on a thick stalk to 2 ft. Leaves: strap-shaped, mottled dark red; in basal rosettes. *A medium-sized plant.*

Hohenbergia stellata

Trinidad to northeastern Brazil. Semiepiphytic herb to 3 ft.; zones 10–11. Blooms winter, spring, summer. Moderate moisture. Coarse organic material or epiphytic. Full to part sun. Flowers: purple; floral bracts red, sharply pointed; in clusters dispersed along the stalk, 3–5 ft. tall; primary bracts green, drying quickly. Leaves: strap-shaped, stiff, green with red spots; margins sharply toothed; in a vase-shaped basal rosette. *This medium-sized bromeliad produces starlike clusters of red bracts on a long spike. Allow space for a spread of 3–4 ft. Xeric and tough.*

Navia

Navia includes approximately 100 species of epiphytic herbs from northern South America. Unusual in cultivation, *N. arida* is spectacular when in bloom with brightly colored foliage. Plants are produced at intervals on long stolons, which can be secured to a tree or basket, or individual plants can be separated to grow in containers.

Navia arida

Venezuela, Colombia. Semiepiphytic herb to 1 ft.; zones 10–11. Blooms spring, summer. Regular moisture. Coarse organic material or epiphytic. Bright broken light. Flowers: golden-yellow, in central reservoir. Leaves: apple-green becoming golden-yellow and orange near the center when in flower; margins undulate, sharply toothed; in rosettes connected by long stolons. *A striking plant that can develop into an extensive colony interconnected by the long stolons. Individual plants can be removed for container growing. Needs plenty of air circulation such as in a hanging basket.*

Neoregelia

Neoregelia includes approximately 108 species of semiepiphytic herbs from southeastern Brazil and the Amazon basin. Leaves are spreading to almost horizontal with the reservoir fully exposed. Others are more vase-shaped, somewhat enclosing the reservoir. They are much admired for the vivid leaf coloration that develops when plants come into bloom. The strap-shaped, guttering leaves are often very broad, with spined tips. Margins are smooth to sharply toothed. The flowers develop in the water reservoir on a stalkless inflorescence. Neos develop full coloration only with adequate light. Some light filtration from intense midday sun is ideal, but with regular moisture and humidity, many plants will tolerate full sun. Be sure that the reservoir remains full of water and flush it out frequently for a fresh appearance. Mist often when hot or dry. Neos are grown in containers or beds. If grown as an epiphyte, keep the reservoir level. Dilute liquid fertilizer may be applied during active growth for container plants but is unnecessary outdoors. Small animals and birds use the reservoirs as a source of water so avoid toxic chemicals. Amazon species are cold-sensitive. Cultivars are myriad.

Neoregelia carolinae

BLUSHING BROMELIAD
Brazil. Semiepiphytic herb under 1 ft.; zones 10–11. Blooms spring, early summer. Regular moisture and humidity. Coarse organic material or epiphytic. Bright filtered light. Flowers: small, white to lavender; in the central cup. Leaves: soft, variously marked; margins finely toothed; in small rosettes. *Numerous cultivars are dramatically marked.*

Neoregelia concentrica

Brazil. Semiepiphytic herb under 1 ft.; zones 10–11. Blooms spring, early summer. Regular moisture and humidity. Coarse organic mate-

Hohenbergia rosea

Hohenbergia stellata

Navia arida

Neoregelia carolinae 'Meyendorfii'

Neoregelia concentrica

rial or epiphytic. Full to part sun. Flowers: small, white to lavender; inflorescence partly submerged in the reservoir. Leaves: broad, spreading to 2 ft., center violet when in bloom. *Flush the reservoir often to keep the appearance fresh. Cultivars are numerous.*

Neoregelia cruenta

PAINTED FINGERNAILS

Brazil. Semiepiphytic herb under 1 ft.; zones 10–11. Blooms spring, early summer. Regular moisture and humidity. Coarse organic material or epiphytic. Bright broken light. Flowers: lavender, inflorescence partly submerged in the reservoir. Leaves: strap-shaped, olive to bright green with red tips, upper surface concave (guttered); cultivars variously marked; margins finely toothed. *A number of neoregelias are referred to as painted fingernails due to a spot of red at the tips of the leaves. Note the pleasing contrast provided by dark purple foliage of* Alternanthera brasiliana.

Neoregelia hybrids

Garden hybrids. Semiepiphytic herbs, generally under 1 ft.; zones 10–11. Bloom spring, summer. Regular moisture and humidity. Coarse organic material or epiphytic. Bright filtered light. Flowers: small; in the reservoir. Leaves: vivid markings develop as plants come into bloom; margins with small teeth. *Fancy hybrids are usually kept in containers which may be moved indoors when cold. Plentiful light is* necessary for best leaf coloration. Color is often long-lasting.

Orthophytum

Orthophytum includes approximately 30 species of terrestrial herbs from southeastern Brazil. This group has true, nutrient-absorbing roots. They are unusual in cultivation outside collections. *Orthophytum gurkenii* has whorls of bracts clustered on the floral stalk. More typically, the flowers are nestled in the reservoir as in *Neoregelia*. A third type produces plantlets along long stolons.

Orthophytum gurkenii

Southeastern Brazil. Terrestrial herb to 6 ft.+; zones 10–11. Blooms spring, early summer. Regular moisture. Coarse, humus-rich, well-drained soil. Part sun. Flowers: white, protrude from between the whorls of green bracts distributed on the inflorescence stalk. Leaves: sword-shaped, reflexed, dark brown with jagged white, scaly bands. *Unusual in cultivation. The leaves resemble* Cryptanthus zonatus *in coloration and chevron banding.*

Pepinia

Pepinia includes approximately 52 species of mostly terrestrial, monocarpic herbs and a few epiphytes, primarily from the perimeter of the Amazon basin, with a few species in Central America and 1 in Mexico. A number of species currently included in *Pitcairnia* belong in this recently resurrected genus but have not been formally transferred at this time. These plants are usually stemless with basal whorls of leaves. The primary distinction from *Pitcairnia* is that *Pepinia* species have winged seeds (Luther 1995).

Pepinia sanguinea

Synonym: *Pitcairnia sanguinea*. Eastern Colombia. Terrestrial herb, 3–4 ft.; zones 10–11. Blooms spring. Regular moisture. Coarse, well-drained soil. Medium filtered light. Flowers: scarlet, anthers exserted; bracts scarlet, overlapping; develop from base of leaves. Leaves: erect, in 2 forms (dimorphic), outer leaves linear, lacking blades, inner leaves lanceolate; margins serrate with small teeth near the tips; tapering into a petiole-like stalk, green to burgundy. *A recent introduction now being mass propagated through tissue culture. Distinguished from* P. coralina *by the erect habit and serrated leaf margins.*

Neoregelia cruenta

Neoregelia cruenta 'De Rolf'

Neoregelia 'Kahala Dawn'

Neoregelia 'Morado'

Neoregelia 'Royal Burgundy White Margined'

Orthophytum gurkenii

Pitcairnia

Pitcairnia includes approximately 322 species of mostly terrestrial plus a few epiphytic herbs from tropical America with greatest diversity in northwestern South America. This genus includes *P. feliciana* from Guinea in tropical western Africa, the only non-American bromeliad species. Many species with extensive underground stolons are too large for container growing. Several species are cultivated in the ground in frost-free areas. Pitcairnias have grasslike to broad leaves, often with sharp teeth on the margins.

Pitcairnia grafii

Venezuela. Terrestrial herb, 2–3 ft.; zones 10–11. Blooms spring. Regular moisture and humidity. Coarse, well-drained soil. Part sun. Flowers: corolla yellow; calyx red; inflorescence stalk red; loosely arranged. Leaves: strap-shaped; margins sharply toothed. *Suitable for understory planting. Produces large clumps.*

Portea

Portea includes approximately 9 species of terrestrial monocarpic herbs from eastern Brazil. These are generally medium-sized species suitable for outdoor beds in gritty, sandy soil or rock gardens. They are adapted to seasonally moist/dry climates and tolerate full sun. Most species are unusual in cultivation except *P. petropolitana*.

Portea petropolitana

Eastern Brazil. Terrestrial herb to 3 ft.; zones 10–11. Blooms spring, early summer. Regular moisture and humidity. Coarse, well-drained soil. Full sun. Flowers: violet; inflorescence pink-mauve and gray-blue, 3–4 ft. tall. Leaves: strap-shaped, to 2 ft., light green; margins sharply toothed. *A medium-sized, clump-forming bromeliad. Suitable for use as a bedding plant. Var. petropolitana has a shorter, more compact inflorescence than var. extensa.*

Quesnelia

Quesnelia includes approximately 16 species of mostly terrestrial herbs from eastern Brazil. They are found from coastal woodlands to high altitudes. A few species are cultivated occasionally. They are suitable for beds and as container plants. The simple or branched inflorescences are on stalks. The bloom is relatively short-lived but very ornamental. Leaves are strap-shaped, the margins lined with small, sharp teeth.

Quesnelia arvensis

Eastern Brazil. Terrestrial herb, 1–1.5 ft.; zones 10–11. Blooms winter. Regular moisture and humidity. Coarse, humus-rich, well-drained soil. Part sun to bright broken light. Flowers: blue-violet; inflorescence a club-shaped head, bracts red, on a short stalk. Leaves: strap-shaped, medium green, banded with white scales on the underside, 1–1.5 ft. long; margins spined. *Clump-forming. Quesnelia quesneliana has a cylindrical inflorescence on a long stalk.*

Quesnelia marmorata

Eastern Brazil. Terrestrial herb, 1–2 ft.; zones 10–11. Blooms spring. Regular moisture and humidity. Coarse, humus-rich, well-drained soil. Part sun to bright broken light. Flowers: violet; sepals red; stalk and primary bracts pink. Leaves: strap-shaped, medium green, spotted with purple; margins sharply toothed. *Inflorescence has a few short branches. Unusual in cultivation. The species name means "mottled."*

Tillandsia

Tillandsia includes approximately 549 species of epiphytic and terrestrial herbs from tropical and subtropical America plus a number from mild temperate regions. Different species are adapted to a variety of habitats. Rainforest species have basal leaves surrounding a central reservoir similar to most other genera. Tillandsias from dry regions, however, lack the reservoir but have blue-gray scales which absorb moisture from morning mists. The scaly coating also shields the plants from sun and helps reduce evaporation. Leaves are sword-shaped and spineless. The upper surface is guttered or leaves are sometimes cylindrical (terete). They are arranged in basal whorls or on a stem or stolon. The fruits are capsules. Seeds are tufted and wind-dispersed.

Spanish moss, *Tillandsia usneoides*, is widely distributed in humid tropical and mild temperate areas. Live oaks, *Quercus virginiana*, or cypress, *Taxodium* species, draped in

Pepinia sanguinea

Pitcairnia grafii

Quesnelia arvensis

Portea petropolitana var. *extensa*

Quesnelia marmorata

Spanish moss conjure up misty mornings in the bayou, Great Cypress Swamp, or Antebellum mansions of the Old South. Spanish moss is commonly mistaken for a moss rather than a member of the bromeliad family. Swallow-tailed kites and other birds line their nests with these soft plants.

Tillandsia capitata

Mexico to Honduras, Cuba. Semi-epiphytic herb to 1.5 ft.; zones 10–11. Blooms late spring, early summer. Regular moisture and humidity. In bark or on a tree limb. Full to part sun. Flowers: purple; primary bracts red. Leaves: sword-shaped, reddish when in flower. 'Marrón' has yellow bracts.

Tillandsia cyanea

Ecuador. Epiphytic herb under 1 ft.; zones 10–11. Blooms primarily summer or intermittently in warm months. Regular moisture and humidity. In bark or on a tree limb. Full sun to bright filtered light. Flowers: purple, clove-scented, petals spreading, relatively large; bracts imbricate; inflorescence spatula-shaped. Leaves: spear-shaped, to 1 ft. long. *A small plant with relatively large flowers opening one to several at a time over a number of weeks. The bracts turn bright pink at the time of bloom. Stunning in a large basket.*

Tillandsia dyeriana

Ecuador. Epiphytic herb to 1.5 ft.; zone 11. Blooms spring. Regular moisture. In bark. Bright filtered light. Flowers: white; bracts distichous, arching, golden-yellow, turning brick-red during bloom. Leaves: in basal, urn-shaped whorls enclosing the reservoir. *A rainforest species. Cold-sensitive. Best kept in a container that can be moved indoors when cool. Photo includes spotted green and maroon leaves of Neoregelia 'First Prize' in background.*

Tillandsia funckiana

Venezuela. Epiphytic herb to about 6 in.; zones 9–11. Blooms spring. Regular moisture. In bark or on a tree limb. Bright filtered light. Flowers: red-orange; solitary or in small clusters. Leaves: semiterete, 2–3 in. long, blue-gray. *This little species produces spreading colonies. Sometimes mounted on a cut limb, driftwood, or a palm trunk.*

Tillandsia ionantha

Southern Mexico to Costa Rica. Small epiphytic herb; zones 9–11. Blooms fall, winter. Regular moisture. In bark or on a tree trunk.

Bright filtered light. Flowers: purple and white. Leaves: small, spear-shaped, blue-green, covered with gray scales; in basal whorls. *This miniature species develops mounding clumps. Sometimes displayed on a cut limb or tree trunk or in a basket.*

Tillandsia stricta

Venezuela to Argentina. Small epiphytic herb; zones 9–11. Blooms winter, spring. Regular moisture. On branches. Full to part sun. Flowers: violet; floral bracts pink; inflorescence ascending. Leaves: semiterete, blue-gray, covered with gray scales. *A variable and adaptable species due to its wide natural range. Can be attached to a tree or palm trunk or grown in baskets.*

Tillandsia usneoides

SPANISH MOSS, BARBA DE CAPUCHINO ("MONKEY-BEARD") Synonym: *T. filiformis.* Coastal Carolinas to southern South America. Small epiphytic herb; zones 7–11. Blooms winter, spring. Regular moisture. Epiphytic. Full sun to bright broken light. Flowers: blue-green. Leaves: semiterete, blue-gray, covered with gray hairlike scales. *Tiny, threadlike plants produce long chains on filamentous stolons. Colonies of plants drape from tree limbs. Sometimes sold as lining for hanging baskets. Name alludes to Usnea, a lichen.*

Vriesea

Vriesea includes approximately 248 species of mostly epiphytic herbs from tropical America, with greatest diversity in eastern Brazil. These are mostly rainforest plants that prefer plenty of humidity and filtered light. Leaves are smooth, often strongly patterned, a characteristic that makes plants more visible to bats and hawkmoth pollinators. Flowers are generally bell-shaped, white, and often fruit-scented at night. Some are pollinated in the daytime by hummingbirds. Bracts are often imbricate on an erect stalk that develops from the center of the basal whorl of leaves. *Vriesea* is closely related to *Alcantarea*, but the flowers of that genus have linear petals. The name is commonly misspelled vriesia.

Tillandsia capitata 'Marrón'

Tillandsia cyanea

Tillandsia dyeriana

Tillandsia funckiana

Tillandsia ionantha

Tillandsia stricta

Vriesea ensiformis

FLAMING SWORD

Synonym: *V. conferta*. Brazil. Semi-epiphytic herb to 2 ft.; zones 10–11. Blooms spring. Regular moisture and humidity. Coarse compost or epiphytic. Bright filtered light. Flowers: petals yellow; bracts scarlet to partly yellow; imbricate; inflorescence erect, sword-shaped; stalk, 1–2 ft. tall. Leaves: strap-shaped, soft, light green, in basal rosettes. *From tropical rain forest. The species name alludes to the sword-shaped inflorescence.*

CACTACEAE

CACTUS FAMILY

Cactaceae includes approximately 93 genera of succulent herbs, shrubs, and trees from the Americas, with greatest diversity in mild temperate semiarid regions of North America. Some tropical species are climbers and epiphytes. One non-American species, *Rhipsalis baccifera*, comes from western Africa. Stems are usually thickened, succulent water-storing adaptations to arid climates. They may be flattened and jointed or cylindrical and deeply ridged. Spines and barbed hairs (glochids) are on raised pads (areoles), which are actually rudimentary branch tips. Cacti are distinguished from other desert species by the spines clustered in areoles, not evenly distributed, and by the clear not milky sap. Leaves are usually absent, or reduced and ephemeral, with the exception of *Pereskia* species, which have well-developed, persistent simple leaves. Flowers are usually bisexual and solitary with numerous tepals. The fleshy fruits of certain cacti are edible and tasty, with an appearance somewhat like kiwi fruits when cut. *Nopales*, stem segments of *Opuntia* species, are eaten as a vegetable in Mexico after spines are removed. They are also fed to animals. Certain birds and other animals have developed symbiotic relationships with cactus species. Hummingbirds are attracted to the flowers.

Cactus intergeneric hybrids

No formal name exists for this complex group of intergeneric hybrids of garden origin commonly referred to as orchid cacti, a name also applied to *Epiphyllum* species. The hybrids are commonly, though incorrectly, listed as *Epiphyllum* cultivars, even though they usually involve *Disocactus*, *Heliocereus*, *Schlumbergera*, or *Selenicereus*, but rarely *Epiphyllum* species (Anderson 2001). Flowers are large, goblet-shaped, and white or brightly colored. Most are day-bloomers. The clambering, spined stems are succulent, flattened, cylindrical or angular depending on heredity. They are easy to grow, needing only some protection from harsh midday sun and cold. They thrive in a coarse bark mix in dry climates like California but are grown without medium in humid climates. Plants become heavy and should be attached to a sturdy basket or tree limb.

Cactus hybrids

ORCHID-CACTUS

Garden origin. Succulent epiphytes; zones 9–11. Bloom intermittently in warm months. Regular

Tillandsia usneoides

Vriesea ensiformis

Cactus hybrid

Cactus hybrid

moisture. In bark orchid medium or free-growing. Bright filtered light to part sun. Flowers: goblet-shaped, to 8 in. wide, tepals white or brightly colored; solitary. Leafless. Stems: flattened or cylindrical; more or less spiny. *Easily propagated from cuttings. Larger cuttings start to bloom sooner.*

Cereus

Cereus includes 36–40 species of succulent trees or shrubs from eastern South America and the West Indies. This group formerly included genera now segregated into *Hylocereus* (night-blooming cereus) and others. The stems are ribbed lengthwise with areoles clustered along the ridges. Stems may be branched or segmented. The flowers open at night but often last into the morning hours.

Cereus hildmannianus

HEDGE-CACTUS

Synonyms: *C. peruvianus* (misapplied), *C. uruguayensis*. Exact origin obscure (South America); widely distributed. Pachycaulous tree to 20 ft.; zones 9–11. Blooms intermittently in warm months. Moist to arid. Average, well-drained soil. Full sun. Flowers: goblet-shaped, to 7 in. wide, inner tepals ivory white, outer tepals reddish to green. Leafless. Stems: typically 8-ribbed, 8–10 in. diameter. Usually spineless. *Used for fences or as scions for grafting delicate species. Thrives in any well-drained location. Pollinated by bees. Seed bird-dispersed. Invasive in Hawaii. Commonly, but incorrectly, referred to as Cereus peruvianus, which is actually a synonym of C. repandus, a red-flowered species cultivated for its fruit (Anderson 2001).*

Consolea

Consolea includes 9 species of shrubs and trees from the West Indies and Florida Keys. Caribbean species were transferred to this genus from *Opuntia* years ago, but the change went largely unnoticed by taxonomists. Consoleas differ from continental opuntias by their treelike habit, cylindrical trunks, distinctive seeds and pollen, as well as nectaries located at the bases of the stamens (Anderson 2001). Leaves are small, cylindrical, and ephemeral. Flowers are small, cup-shaped, and yellow to orange. Flattened branch segments (cladodes) are paddle-shaped and fleshy, more or less covered with spines and glochids.

Consolea corallicola

SEMAPHORE-CACTUS, SEMAPHORE PRICKLY PEAR

Synonyms: *C. spinosissima* (misapplied), *Opuntia spinosissima*. Florida Keys, nearly extinct in the wild. Succulent tree to 8 ft.+; zones 9–11.

Blooms warm months. Dry. Sandy, well-drained, open soil; alkaline pH. Full sun. Flowers: small, cup-shaped, red-orange. Trunk: cylindrical, erect, long-spined; branches green, segments paddle-shaped, held perpendicular to the stem, narrowly ovate to obovate, long-spined. *Now considered distinct from Consolea spinosissima, a similar species from Jamaica and the Virgin Islands (Anderson 2001). The apt common name refers to the opposite pairs of branches that are held like railway semaphore arms. A new wild population of this endangered species was discovered in Biscayne National Park, Florida. Photographed in the Plant Conservation Collection at Fairchild Tropical Garden.*

Consolea moniliformis

Synonym: *Opuntia moniliformis*. Hispaniola to Puerto Rico. Succulent tree to 12 ft.; zones 9–11. Blooms warm months. Arid. Average, well-drained, open soil. Full sun. Flowers: small, cup-shaped, golden-yellow turning orange. Trunk: long-spined; branches green, segments paddle-shaped, unevenly spined. *An irregularly*

Consolea corallicola

Consolea moniliformis

Cereus hildmannianus

Epiphyllum phyllanthus var. hookeri

Hylocereus escuintlensis

shaped tree. *Thrives in warm, humid climates with adequate drainage.*

Epiphyllum

Epiphyllum includes approximately 19 succulent epiphytes and a few trees from Mexico, Central America, and the Caribbean region. Leaves are absent. Flowers of some species are nocturnal, closing in the early morning, others lasting a day or two. They bloom intermittently when nights are warm. Some are fragrant. Inner tepals are white or cream surrounded by green-, yellow-, or purple-tinted outer tepals. Arboreal species produce rounded trunks with large branches. Limbs start out round becoming 3-sided to flattened as they grow. Margins are scalloped or pointed between the depressed areoles which are usually spineless and lack glochids. Plants tolerate fairly cool temperatures when dormant. Epiphytes are suitable for baskets with a coarse bark medium in dry climates. In moist climates they should be grown bare-root in a basket or with only a little palm fiber to avoid rot. Allow for considerable weight and spread. Epiphyllums need bright filtered light and should be watered often when hot but kept fairly dry when cool. Dilute liquid or slow-release fertilizer during active growth stimulates bloom. Hang night-bloomers near a window where they can be enjoyed with early morning coffee. These species are sometimes mistaken for night-blooming cereus (see *Hylocereus*). They should not be confused with the intergeneric hybrids which are also referred to as orchid cacti.

Epiphyllum phyllanthus var. hookeri

EPIPHYLLUM, ORCHID-CACTUS
Synonyms: *E. hookeri, E. stenopetalum.* Mexico. Succulent epiphytic herb to 6 ft.+; zones 9–11. Blooms intermittently in warm months. Seasonally moist/dry. Bark chips or epiphytic. Bright broken light. Flowers: goblet-shaped, night-blooming, closing in early morning, not fragrant, tepals slender, white, tube long; solitary, from depressed areoles on the stem margins; fruit obovate, dark red, to 1.5 in. long.

Shoots: cylindrical when young, becoming 3-angled, then flat, 2–3 in. wide; margins scalloped; spineless. Branches pendent. *Suspend high in a sturdy basket. Epiphyllum oxypetalum has fragrant creamy white flowers with broader tepals and bronze outer tepals.*

Hylocereus

Hylocereus includes approximately 18 species of sprawling or clambering succulents from tropical America. They grow in forests or open, seasonally dry habitats. A number of species grow in cultivation though they are all usually referred to as *H. undatus*. These species have the largest flowers in the cactus family. The night-blooming flowers are goblet-shaped, the ivory to white inner tepals surrounded by greenish- or purple-tinted outer tepals. Leaflike scales cover the long tube surrounding the ovary. The light-colored, musky-scented flowers attract bats and hawkmoths at night and bees visit in the morning. The stems are 3-angled, succulent to woody, and produce aerial roots. Species are distinguished partly by the relative thickness of the stem, number of spines per areole, and the contour of the margins. *Hylocereus undatus* has a thick, woody stem with scalloped margins and up to 3 spines per areole. The ovoid fruit is crimson with green bracts attached and translucent, tart-sweet white flesh with small black seeds inside.

Hylocereus escuintlensis

Guatemala. Succulent semiepiphytic climber to 20 ft.; zones 10–11. Blooms intermittently in warm months. Seasonally moist/dry. Average soil or epiphytic. Full to part sun. Flowers: goblet-shaped, outer tepals green, purple-tipped, to about 6 in. wide. Stems: 3- to 4-angled, 1.5–2 in. thick, spines short, usually 2 per areole.

Hylocereus undatus

NIGHT-BLOOMING CEREUS, PITAYA, FLOR DE CÁLIZ ("CHALICE FLOWER"), REINA DE LA NOCHE ("QUEEN-OF-THE-NIGHT")
Exact origin obscure (tropical America); widely distributed. Woody climber; zones 9–11. Blooms late spring, early summer. Seasonally moist/dry. Average, well-drained soil. Full to part sun. Flowers: goblet-shaped, fragrant, 8–12 in. long and wide, inner tepals white; outer tepals greenish yellow; stamens numerous, yellow; stigma branched; fruit ovoid, yellow or red, edible. Stems: 3-angled, 3–4 in. thick, woody; margins scalloped, sinuate; spines 1–3 per areole. *Develops into a dense thicket. Requires firm control. Invasive in some areas.*

Opuntia

Opuntia includes more than 181 species of succulent shrubs and trees from the Americas, as well as the Galapagos Islands. It is among the largest, most widely dispersed genera of cacti. It has 10 natural hybrids. Other species readily hybridize in cultivation. This genus has been revised. Groups traditionally included in *Opuntia* are now segregated into *Consolea, Cylindropuntia, Tephrocactus,* and others. Both the stems and branches of opuntias are flattened into paddle-shaped segments (cladodes). Opuntias range from trees with trunks to ground-hugging cushion forms. Leaves are greatly reduced, ephemeral, or absent. Flowers are cup-shaped and usually stalkless (sessile). Opuntias are commonly known as prickly pear cactus, Indian fig, or *tuna* in Spanish. *Nopales*, despined cladodes, and the fruits of certain species are eaten in Mexico and the southwestern United States. A number of opuntias are widely distributed and

Hylocereus undatus

Opuntia engelmannii var. *lindheimeri*

have become naturalized. Some are serious pests. The barbed glochids make them a serious threat to grazing animals. In drought conditions ranchers burn off the glochids to use them for feed. When potting, handle these and other bristly species with barbecue tongs or a rolled-up strap of newspaper and use a long dowel-rod to tamp soil around the roots.

Opuntia engelmannii var. lindheimeri

COW-TONGUE PRICKLY PEAR, DESERT OPUNTIA, TUNA
Synonyms: *O. lindheimeri, O. linguiformis.* Southwestern United States to central Mexico. Succulent sprawling shrub to 10 ft.; zones 9–11. Blooms warm months. Arid. Average, open, well-drained soil. Full sun. Flowers: cup-shaped, orange, turning yellow. Stems: segments ovate, to 1 ft. long; glochids straw-colored, spines straw-colored, 1–2 in. long, 1–6 per areole. *Produces dense clumps.*

Opuntia microdasys

BUNNY-EAR PRICKLY PEAR, NOPAL CEGADOR ("DAZZLING NOPAL")
Synonyms: *O. macrocalyx, Cactus microdasys.* Northern Mexico (Chihuahuan desert). Succulent sprawling shrub to 3 ft.; zones 9–11. Blooms warm months. Arid. Average, open, well-drained soil. Full sun. Flowers: cup-shaped, yellow, buds reddish. Stems: segments ovate, light green; areoles closely spaced; glochids conspicuous, yellow; spines usually absent. *Small plants commonly grown in containers.*

Opuntia rufida

DAZZLING PRICKLY PEAR, NOPAL CEGADOR
Synonyms: *O. herfeldtii, O. lubrica.* Northern Mexico, Texas. Succulent shrub or tree to 6 ft.; zones 9–11. Blooms warm months. Arid. Average, open, well-drained soil. Full sun. Flowers: cup-shaped, yellow to orange. Stems: segments paddle-shaped, gray-green; areoles closely spaced; glochids reddish brown, spines usually absent. *The ruddy coloration of the glochids distinguishes this species from the similar but smaller* O. microdasys. *While*

sometimes translated "blind nopal," the common name cegador *means "blinding" in the sense of dazzling.*

Pereskia

Pereskia includes approximately 17 species of trees and clambering shrubs or climbers from tropical America. These cacti have well-developed leaves and are thought to resemble the ancestors of contemporary genera of desert cacti, which lost their leaves as an adaptation to arid conditions. The stems of pereskias are nonsegmented and woody. Young shoots are often dark green. Spines are in pairs or clusters in the leaf axils in young growth or areoles in older growth. Pereskias lack glochids. These tender plants thrive in coastal locations and other areas with fast-draining soil. They may shed their leaves if chilled. Cool night temperatures damage the stems but, if not frozen, they usually recover from the base. The edible fruits are round, cone-, or pear-shaped berries, often with leaflike scales on the surface. Handle plants with rolled newspaper or tongs.

Pereskia aculeata

BARBADOS GOOSEBERRY, LEMON-VINE, RAMO DE NOVIA
Synonym: *Cactus pereskia.* West Indies, eastern South America; widely cultivated. Evergreen shrubby climber to 25 ft.; zones 10–11. Blooms summer. Moderate moisture or seasonally moist/dry. Average, well-drained soil. Full to part sun. Flowers: rotate, to 1.5 in. wide, white, cream to pinkish with age, waxy, lemon-scented; fruit round, yellowish to orange, juicy. Leaves: obovate, oblong to lanceolate, 2–3 in. long, fleshy. Stems: terete, dark

Opuntia microdasys

Opuntia rufida

Pereskia aculeata

Pereskia grandifolia var. grandifolia

green. Spines dimorphic, 1–3, straight, in the leaf axils of young shoots; in pairs and recurved in the areoles on older canes. *Invasive in some areas. Difficult to eradicate once established. Moderately salt tolerant. Fruits edible, seedy with citrus-like flavor.*

Pereskia bleo

ORANGE ROSE-CACTUS, BLEO, GUAMACHO
Synonyms: *P. corrugata, Rhodocactus bleo*. Panama, Colombia, Venezuela. Semideciduous shrub, 10–20 ft.; zones 10–11. Blooms spring. Seasonally moist/dry. Sandy, well-drained soil. Full to part sun. Flowers: rotate, vivid pinkish orange; solitary, to 3 in. wide; fruit top-shaped (turbinate). Leaves: oblong to oblanceolate, rubbery, 3–7 in. long, tips acuminate; margins undulate; petiole to 2 in. Stems: dark green when young. Spines in clusters of 6. *Somewhat salt tolerant. A more or less clambering shrub, suitable as a barrier hedge. Needs several hours of morning sun to bloom. Young growth lax, may need staking. Becomes woody with age.*

Pereskia grandifolia

ROSE-CACTUS, WAX ROSE, GUAMACHO MORADO
Synonym: *P. grandiflora* (incorrectly). Eastern Brazil. Evergreen shrub, 6–15 ft.; zones 9–11. Blooms spring, summer. Regular moisture. Coarse, sandy, well-drained soil. Full to part sun. Flowers: pink, to 1.5 in. wide; in large clusters, opening a few at a time; fruit yellow, pear-

shaped (turbinate) with leaflike bracts attached. Leaves: lanceolate, 4–6 in. long. Spines slender, black to 2 in. long. *Attractive in rock gardens or as a hedge. Thrives in coastal locations. Needs several hours of sun to bloom. Var.* violacea *has a purple, recurved outer perianth and bracts (Leuenberger, pers. comm.).*

Schlumbergera

Schlumbergera includes approximately 6 species of epiphytes from southeastern Brazil. Three hybrids and hundreds of cultivars of holiday-cactus are available. Species are considered more difficult to grow and are less commonly seen in cultivation. Some species have cylindrical or flattened segments with areoles evenly distributed. The species previously segregated into *Epiphyllanthus* and *Zygocactus* have areoles in depressions along the margins of flattened, more or less toothed or scalloped stems (cladodes). *Schlumbergera truncata* hybrids, known as crab-claw cacti, have more pointed marginal teeth with bristles in the gaps. The flowers have long tubular bases surrounded by several tiers of petal-like scales. *Hatiora* (syn. *Rhipsalidopsis*), also sold as holiday-cactus or Easter cactus, has short floral tubes and a single whorl of tepals. Hybridization and lack of records often make these distinctions tenuous.

Schlumbergera species typically bloom from late fall through winter. Bloom is initiated by decreasing day-length. Grow in fine bark with

coarse sand. Schlumbergeras prefer mild temperatures and bright filtered light. Keep plants evenly moist but not wet during active growth, and fertilize with dilute liquid fertilizer. Reduce moisture and stop fertilizing in fall and keep away from artificial lighting. Resume watering but withhold fertilizer once buds initiate. Avoid moving pots after buds initiate or they will drop. Scale infection is deadly because plants are generally too sensitive for treatment. Purchase from clean sources and discard infected plants.

Schlumbergera hybrids

HOLIDAY-CACTUS, CHRISTMAS CACTUS, ZYGOCACTUS, CACTO DE PASCUA
Garden hybrids. Succulent epiphytic herbs; zones 9–11. Bloom winter. Regular moisture and humidity during active growth, reduce in fall. Fine bark, coarse sand, and humus. Bright filtered light, no artificial light in fall, winter. Flowers: tube long, with 2–3 tiers of petal-like scales, magenta, red, pink, peach, yellow to white; borne at distal ends of the segments. Stems: segments flat, ovate to obovate, 1–2 in. long; margins scalloped or toothed; more or less bristled. Branches pendent. *A variable group of more than 250 hybrids and cultivars.*

CANELLACEAE

CANELLA FAMILY
Canellaceae includes 5 genera of trees and shrubs from tropical America, the West Indies, and

Africa. Leaves are aromatic, simple, and glossy, with smooth margins. Flowers are small, bisexual, and radially symmetrical. Authorities disagree whether the outer whorl of the perianth is composed of bracts or sepals. The fruit is a small berry.

Canella

Canella includes a single species of tree or shrub from South Florida, the West Indies, and South America. Leaves are simple, dark, and glossy. Flowers are small, bisexual, and radially symmetrical, in small clusters at the ends of the branches. The bark is grayish white. All parts have a musky cinnamon scent. This is not the cinnamon of commerce, *Cinnamomum*, an ultra-tropical species with the familiar red-brown bark; however, *Canella* is used in Latin America as a cinnamon substitute and in folk medicine.

Canella winterana

WILD CINNAMON, BAHAMA WHITE WOOD, CANELA, BOIS CANNELLE
Synonyms: *C. alba, Laurus winterana*. South Florida, West Indies to northern South America. Evergreen tree, 20–30 ft.; zones 9–11. Blooms early summer. Moderate moisture. Average, well-drained soil. Full sun to broken light. Flowers: small; sepals suborbicular, bluish green, silvery (glaucous); corolla magenta, about 0.25 in. wide; in terminal clusters; fruit a berry, small, red to purple-black. Leaves: obovate, to 5 in. long, leathery, dark green, glossy above, dull below; margins entire; clustered at ends of the branches. *A dense, small to medium tree with dark foliage. Not commonly cultivated, but recommended.*

CANNACEAE

CANNA FAMILY
Cannaceae includes a single genus of herbs from tropical and mild temperate areas of the Americas. Cannas, often incorrectly referred to as canna lilies, grow in moist areas, sometimes as semiaquatics with their roots periodically submerged. Queensland arrowroot, a food thickener similar to corn starch, is made from the ground rhizome of *Canna indica*, which is grown as a

Pereskia bleo

Schlumbergera hybrid

Canella winterana

crop in Australia and elsewhere. Leaves have broad blades, and the petiole bases clasp the stalk. Flowers are bisexual and asymmetrical. The highly modified floral parts include a petal-like style fused to 1 fertile stamen and 2 sterile, petal-like stamens (staminodes).

Canna

Canna includes 8–50 species of herbs from tropical and subtropical America which are widely distributed. Interbreeding has rendered meaningless the distinctions among hybrid horticultural groups traditionally classified as *C. ×ehemanii, C. ×generalis,* and *C. ×orchiodes* cultivars (Bailey 1976) and are no longer used. Cannas are banana-like, sympodial herbs with underground rhizomes and fibrous roots. The leaves are paddle-shaped, the blades long and wide. The petioles are short and the bases sheath the stem. The lack of a jointed petiole helps distinguish cannas from Zingiberaceae (gingers) and Marantaceae (calatheas), which have jointed petioles. The flowers are asymmetrically funnel-shaped with 3 sepals and 3 fused small petals. The fertile stamen is fused to the petal-like style and the 2 sterile stamens (staminodes) are petal-like. The fruit is a 3-sided tubercled capsule containing very hard, round black seeds.

Cannas are heavy feeders and thrive with a generous application of manure. They require full sun. In colder climates they are grown as annuals or the rhizomes are lifted and stored indoors in winter. In the tropics the rhizomes of certain species are cooked as a starchy vegetable similar to cassava (*yuca*) or potatoes. The seeds have been used by indigenous peoples in blow-pipes (hence the name Indian shot). A story goes that settlers used canna seeds for shot in their blunderbusses; the effectiveness, however, is unrecorded.

Canna hybrids
CANNA

Garden hybrids. Seasonally dormant herbs, 3–6 ft.; zones 8–11. Bloom spring, fall. Seasonally moist to wet, dry while dormant. Fertile soil. Full sun. Flowers: asymmetrically funnel-shaped, variously red, yellow, or orange; capsule rounded, 3-sectioned, covered with tubercles; seeds black, round, very hard. Leaves: paddle-shaped, blade ovate, flat, sometimes reddish or splashed with russet or black dots. *Cannas can be grown in shallow pond margins or in containers in water gardens with water just covering the soil. 'Cleopatra' has bicolored flowers.*

Canna indica
INDIAN SHOT, ARROWROOT CANNA, YUQUILLA ("LITTLE YUCA"), CAÑA COMESTIBLE

Synonym: *C. edulis.* Exact origin obscure (tropical America); widely cultivated and naturalized. Seasonally dormant herb to 6 ft.; zones 8–11. Blooms fall, winter, spring. Seasonally moist to wet, dry while dormant. Fertile soil. Full sun. Flowers: small, red to yellow, lip with red streaks or spots. Leaves: paddle-shaped. *Quite variable with many hybrids. Sometimes grown in shallow ponds. Self-seeding and weedy in amenable conditions.*

Canna 'Cleopatra'

Canna indica, with capsules

Lonicera hildebrandiana

Lonicera japonica

CAPRIFOLIACEAE
HONEYSUCKLE FAMILY

Caprifoliaceae includes approximately 36 genera of trees, shrubs, herbs, and climbers, which are widely distributed, primarily in northern temperate regions. Honeysuckle, *Lonicera,* is often cultivated. Leaves are simple or compound. The organization of these genera is still taxonomically unsettled. Flowers are bisexual and bilaterally symmetrical. The 5 petals are fused at the base, the lobes forming 1 or 2 lips. The genera *Sambucus,* elderberry, and *Viburnum,* distinguished in part by their radially symmetrical flowers and very short styles, have been segregated into Adoxaceae.

Lonicera

Lonicera includes approximately 180 species of primarily deciduous shrubs and climbers from northern temperate regions. A number of species range into the subtropics and tropics in Mexico and Southeast Asia. The many cultivated forms of honeysuckle are well-known for their fragrant 2-lipped flowers. Climbing and scrambling species in cultivation are very difficult to eradicate once they become established. Some species are highly invasive in temperate and tropical regions of the United States. Hybrids with compact, shrubby habits are said to be less aggressive, but caution is advised. Flowers are attractive to hummingbirds.

Lonicera hildebrandiana

GIANT BURMESE HONEYSUCKLE
China, Southeast Asia. Semideciduous climber to 35 ft.+; zones 6–11. Blooms late spring, summer. Moderate moisture. Average, well-drained soil. Full to part sun. Flowers: bilabiate; upper lip to 5 in. long, lobed at the tip, white, turning orange-yellow; fragrant; in pairs or small clusters. Leaves: broadly ovate, to 5 in. long. *An aggressive sprawling or clambering vine. The flowers resemble common species but are exceptionally large.*

Lonicera japonica

JAPANESE HONEYSUCKLE
Eastern Asia. Semideciduous climber to 35 ft.+; zones 4–10. Blooms warm months. Moderate moisture to somewhat dry. Most well-drained soils. Full to part sun. Flowers: white, flushed with pink, turning yellow, fragrant; fruit a berry. Leaves: oblong; tips mucronate, to 3 in. long, downy when young. *Commonly cultivated in California. Highly invasive. Suckers and seedlings difficult to eradicate once established. Prohibited in Florida though some nurseries carry it. Cultivation strongly discouraged and removal of existing plants advised.*

CASUARINACEAE

CASUARINA FAMILY, SHE-OAK FAMILY
Casuarinaceae includes 4 genera of evergreen trees and shrubs from Australia, Southeast Asia, and the South Pacific islands. *Casuarina* has characteristics that resemble both conifers (gymnosperms) and flowering plants (angiosperms) and is related to the oak family (Fagaceae). Roots are nitrogen fixing. Some species are massive trees with dense, oaklike timber used in shipbuilding and woodworking. All introduced species are invasive either by root-suckering or seed.

Casuarina

Casuarina includes approximately 70 species of evergreen trees and shrubs from Australia and Southeast Asia to Polynesia. Casuarinas were planted in Florida as windbreaks around orchards in the early part of the twentieth century. They have produced large monotypical colonies, crowding out all other plants. *Casuarina equisetifolia* is salt tolerant and invades beach areas. *Casuarina glauca*, a dense suckering species, is more often seen inland. Both are prohibited in Florida.

Certain other characteristics have merits that are largely overlooked. *Casuarina* species recover quickly after storms as opposed to native conifers, providing shelter for migratory birds. Conifers are killed when topped and take decades to recover, leaving wildlife without habitat. In South Florida, casuarinas are the preferred nesting site of the magnificent but threatened swallow-tailed kite. Isolated stands which are not an ecological threat should be considered.

Casuarinas have branchlets that resemble segmented pine needles with minute, scalelike leaves in whorls at the nodes. Male and female flowers may be on the same tree (monoecious) or on different trees (dioecious). The female (carpellate) flowers are clustered in heads on the lower branches. The conelike fruit has small openings from which the seed is dispersed. Male (staminate) flowers are in spikes at the ends of the branches near the top of the tree and produce copious pollen. The hard, handsome wood is oaklike with purplish grain. It can be polished to a natural burnished sheen. Selective harvesting for fine cabinet wood should be considered as a control.

Casuarina equisetifolia

AUSTRALIAN PINE, BEEFWOOD,
COMMON IRONWOOD, TOA
Southeast Asia to Australia and Polynesia. Evergreen tree to 100 ft.+; zones 9–11. Blooms late spring. Moist to dry. Most soils. Full sun. Flowers: unisexual (trees monoecious), perianth absent; stigmas numerous, magenta; fruit ovoid, 1 in. long, woody, conelike. Leaves: minute, scalelike, in whorls around the nodes of gray-green, 6–8 in. needlelike, ridged branchlets. *Nonsuckering. Branches spreading. Salt tolerant. Found primarily in coastal areas. The species name alludes to the resemblance of the segmented green branchlets to* Equisetum, *horse-tail.* Casuarina cummingiana *has smaller cones.*

Casuarina glauca

AUSTRALIAN PINE, SWAMP
SHE-OAK, HORSE-TAIL TREE
Coastal northeastern Australia. Evergreen tree to 60 ft.; zones 10–11. Blooms warm months. Wet to moderate. Most soils. Full sun. Flowers: unisexual (trees dioecious) or sterile. Leaves: minute, scalelike, in whorls around the 7- to 10-in. indistinctly ridged branchlets. *Suckering habit, producing large stands. Branches drooping to the ground, dark silvery green. Invasive in freshwater wetlands. Rarely if ever produces cones in Florida. Some theorize*

Casuarina equisetifolia

Casuarina equisetifolia, female flowers

that this species may actually be a sterile hybrid. Another theory is vegetative propagation of only male trees.

CECROPIACEAE

CECROPIA FAMILY

Cecropiaceae includes approximately 6 genera of trees, shrubs, and woody vines (lianas) from tropical America. The family is related to and intermediate between the fig family (Moraceae) and the nettle family (Urticaceae). Leaves are simple or lobed and arranged in whorls. Flowers are reduced and functionally unisexual, and arranged in catkinlike spikes. The fruit is a nut or berry, more or less fused into a syncarp.

Cecropia

Cecropia includes approximately 75 species of trees from tropical America. They are common in moist lowlands and are fast-growing with fibrous hollow stems and branches, which are sometimes inhabited by ants. They may begin life as epiphytes sending down roots like a *Ficus*. They are adapted to wetlands and often produce stilt roots. Leaves are large, shallowly to deeply lobed (palmatifid), often dark green above and silvery gray or white below. The petiole is attached to the underside of the blade (peltate). The inflorescences are compact spikes of greatly reduced flowers. *Cecropia peltata* is the most common species in cultivation and is often escaped. It is listed as invasive in Hawaii. The dry, curled-up leaves fall throughout the year. They are fancied by some for arrangements though they resemble discarded tissues in the garden. The flowers and fruits are highly attractive to parrots and small animals.

Cecropia pachystachya

CECROPIA

Synonym: *C. adenopus.* Southern Brazil, Paraguay (Paraná). Evergreen tree to 35 ft.+; zones 9–11. Blooms warm months. Moderate moisture. Average soil. Full sun. Flowers: unisexual, reduced; in 4- or 5-branched spikes. Leaves: palmatifid, 1.5–2 ft. wide, deeply 9-lobed, bright green above, white tomentose below; margins wavy (undulate); peltate. *Leaves larger and brighter green on the upper side than the commonly cultivated C. peltata. Photographed at the Fruit and Spice Park, Homestead, Florida.*

Cecropia peltata

CECROPIA, TRUMPET-TREE, GUARUMO

Mexico, to northern South America, West Indies. Evergreen tree, 30–50 ft.; zones 9–11. Blooms warm months. Moderate moisture. Average soil. Full sun. Flowers: unisexual, reduced, in branched spikes. Leaves: palmatifid, 1–1.5 ft. wide, deeply 7- to 11-lobed, gray-green, rough above, white tomentose below; margins wavy (undulate); peltate. Trunk: erect with numerous prop roots, bark white. *Umbrella-shaped habit. Dead leaves are a conspicuous and constant litter problem. Seed distributed by birds. Wood used for matches and paper pulp.*

CISTACEAE

ROCK-ROSE FAMILY

Cistaceae includes 7 or 8 genera of perennial herbs and shrubs from mild temperate and subtropical regions, especially abundant in the Mediterranean region. It is related to the hibiscus family, Malvaceae. Leaves are variable, usually opposite, sometimes reduced to scales, often with aromatic oils. Flowers are often solitary or in small clus-

Casuarina glauca

Cecropia peltata

ters (cymes). The calyx consists of 3–5 sepals, with 2 sepals narrower than the rest in an outer ring. Usually 5 petals surround a cluster of numerous stamens.

Cistus

Cistus includes approximately 200 species of herbs and shrubs from the Mediterranean region and the Iberian Peninsula. They are found on limestone or sandy soil. The leaves are often crumpled and felty, usually aromatic. The flowers are showy with a buttonlike, stalkless, gummy stigma surrounded by numerous golden-yellow stamens. The 5 crinkled petals overlap each other. *Cistus* species are said to be drought and fire resistant. This characteristic is under study as a landscaping bonus in fire-prone California. The aromatic resin is used as incense. Each flower is short-lived, but the plants bloom repeatedly in warm months especially if spent flowers are removed. Cut back at the end of the growing season for compact growth. This group is hardy in mild temperate regions. It thrives in dry Mediterranean-type climates.

Cistus ×corbariensis

ROCK-ROSE, JARAS
Garden hybrid (Mediterranean region), *C. populifolius* × *C. salviifolius*. Evergreen shrub to 3 ft.; zones 8–10. Blooms late spring, summer. Moderate moisture to dry. Average, sandy, well-drained soil; alkaline pH. Full to part sun. Flowers: petals white, no spot at base; buds reddish; stamens numerous, short, clustered around the large, buttonlike stigma; in few-flowered clusters. Leaves: ovate, dark green, covered with felty hairs; margins undulate. *A spreading shrub.*

Cistus creticus

WHITE-LEAFED ROCK-ROSE, JARAS
Synonym: *C. incanus* subsp. *creticus*. Mediterranean region. Evergreen shrub to 3 ft.; zones 8–10. Blooms late spring, summer. Moderate moisture to dry. Average, sandy, well-drained soil; alkaline pH. Full to part sun. Flowers: petals magenta to pink, no spot at the base; margins undulate, curled

under; stamens numerous, short, clustered around the buttonlike stigma. Leaves: ovate to obovate, covered with frosty-white hairs. *The species name refers to the island of Crete though the species is apparently widespread.*

Cistus ×dansereaui

ROCK-ROSE, JARAS
Synonym: *C. ×lusitanicus* (hort.). Garden hybrid (Mediterranean region), *C. hirsutus* × *C. ladanifer*. Evergreen shrub to 3 ft.; zones 8–10. Blooms late spring, summer. Moderate moisture to dry. Average, sandy, well-drained soil; alkaline

pH. Full to part sun. Flowers: petals white, with purple spot at base; stamens numerous, short, clustered around the buttonlike stigma. Leaves: lanceolate, glossy dark green, firm, sticky, resinous; margins revolute.

Cistus ×purpureus

ORCHID ROCK-ROSE, JARAS
Garden hybrid (Mediterranean region), *C. ladanifer* × *C. creticus*. Evergreen shrub to 4 ft.; zones 8–10. Blooms late spring, summer. Moderate moisture to dry. Average, sandy, well-drained soil; alkaline pH. Full to part sun. Flowers: petals

magenta, crinkled, dark purple spot at the base of each petal; stamens numerous, short, clustered around a buttonlike stigma. Leaves: lanceolate, to 3 in. long, aromatic when crushed, felty, gray-green; margins undulate.

CLUSIACEAE

CLUSIA FAMILY
Clusiaceae (Guttiferae) includes approximately 40 genera of trees, shrubs, herbs, and woody climbers, which are widely distributed, with greatest diversity in the tropics. These plants have a resinous, clear, black, or colored sap. *Clusia rosea* is

Cistus ×corbariensis

Cistus creticus

Cistus ×purpureus

Cecropia pachystachya, inflorescences

Cistus ×dansereaui

a very salt-tolerant, ornamental tree that has been cultivated for generations in the Florida Keys. Mangosteen, *Garcinia mangostana*, is grown in Southeast Asia and Indomalaysia for its highly esteemed fruit. It is an ultra-tropical, too cold-sensitive to thrive outdoors in the continental United States but is grown in Hawaii and the Florida Keys. Leaves are simple, opposite or whorled, often conspicuously glandular. Flowers are bisexual or unisexual, with few to numerous perianth parts that are sometimes intergraded between sepals and petals. Bracts are often present,

often nearly indistinguishable from the sepals. The fruit of *Mammea americana* is called *mamey* in South America and *sapote* in Cuba. *Sapote* is a Spanish name applied loosely to several edible fruits in different families: *Pouteria sapota* and *Manilkara zapota* (Sapotaceae); *Diospyros digyna* (Ebenaceae), and *Casimiroa edulis* (Rutaceae).

Clusia

Clusia includes approximately 150 species of trees and shrubs, which are widely distributed in tropical America. They sometimes begin their lives as epiphytes: the seed,

deposited in the branches of trees or palms by birds, sends down aerial roots that eventually overwhelm the host tree. Flowers are unisexual with the male and female flowers on the same tree (monoecious) or occasionally on separate trees (dioecious). Only functionally female (carpellate) trees of *C. rosea* are known. Seed is produced asexually (apomixis). *Clusia rosea* is the best-known ornamental. It is probably extinct in the wild in the Florida Keys but is commonly cultivated in beach-front property due to its salt tolerance. The stiff leaves turn white where scratched. This

has given rise to some whimsical uses. Leaves have been used as place-cards at tropical dinners and as makeshift playing cards. The legendary use as a calling-card is the origin of the tongue-in-cheek common name Scotch attorney.

Clusia lanceolata

Brazil, Venezuela. Evergreen shrub or small tree, 6–10 ft.; zones 10–11. Blooms warm months. Moderate moisture. Sandy, well-drained soil. Full to part sun. Flowers: petals white, marked with dark red, to 2 in. wide; fruit woody, size of a Ping-Pong ball, a ring of conspicuous black glands near the stem end, splitting apart when ripe exposing scarlet arils. Leaves: leathery, elliptic, to 6 in. long; margins entire. *A compact tree that starts blooming when quite small. Salt tolerant to the shoreline. Unusual in cultivation.*

Clusia rosea

BALSAM APPLE, PITCH-APPLE, AUTOGRAPH TREE, SCOTCH ATTORNEY, COPEY
Tropical and subtropical America. Evergreen tree, 20–50 ft.; zones 10–11. Blooms warm months. Seasonally moist/dry. Sandy, well-drained soil. Full sun. Flowers: functionally female (carpellate), 3–4 in. wide, petals white and pink; staminodes in a gummy ring; solitary; fruit round, woody, to 3 in. diameter; seeds blue-gray with red arils. Leaves: broadly ovate, to 8 in. wide, thick, stiff; margins entire. *Spreading tree. Xeric and salt tolerant to the shoreline. Suitable for flood-prone areas and erosion control of beaches. A variegated form has white leaf margins.*

Mammea

Mammea includes approximately 50 species of large trees from the Americas, Africa, Madagascar, Indomalaysia, and the Pacific Islands. Leaves are simple and leathery, secreting a yellow latex when broken. Flowers are unisexual or bisexual with both types on the same tree (polygamous). Fruits are large berries with rough, leathery skins. A number of somewhat similar but unrelated fruits are referred to as *sapote* or *sapota* (see Clusiaceae).

Clusia lanceolata

Clusia rosea, flower

Clusia rosea, capsules, leaves

Clusia rosea, habit

Mammea americana

MAMMEE APPLE, MAMEY,
MAMEY SAPOTE

Mexico, Central America, West Indies. Evergreen tree to 60 ft.; zones 10–11. Blooms spring, summer. Seasonally moist/dry. Average, well-drained soil. Full to part sun. Flowers: petals white; stamens numerous; fruit rounded, skin brown, leathery, scaly, flesh juicy, orange, seeds large. Leaves: elliptic to obovate, 4–5 in. long.

Mesua

Mesua includes 3–40 species of evergreen shrubs and trees from India to Indomalaysia. *Mesua ferrea* is unusual in cultivation in the United States but much appreciated as a landscape tree in it native range. Leaves are lanceolate, willowlike, with translucent dots. Flowers have 4 white petals and numerous stamens. The fruit is round and hard-shelled. This species is planted around temples in India.

Mesua ferrea

IRONWOOD, NA

India, Southeast Asia, Malaysia, threatened in the wild. Evergreen tree to 100 ft.; zones 10–11. Blooms spring, summer. Seasonally moist/dry. Average, well-drained soil. Full sun. Flowers: petals 4, white, to 2 in. wide; stamens many, bright yellow; solitary or in pairs; fruit round, tip pointed, dark orange, spotted with glands. Leaves: lanceolate, to 5 in., gray below, new leaves copper-colored. *Crown dense, the willowlike leaves on graceful, pendent branches. A timber tree. Flowers somewhat resemble* Oncoba *though that species has 5 petals. Unusual to rare in cultivation in the United States.*

COCHLOSPERMACEAE

COCHLOSPERMUM FAMILY

Cochlospermaceae includes 2 genera of trees, shrubs, and herbs mostly from tropical America. These genera were formerly included in Bixaceae. The family name alludes to the spirally coiled, shell-like seeds. Leaves are palmately lobed, or if divided, the leaflets lack stalks (petiolules). This family is distinguished from the closely related Bombacaceae (now a subfamily of Malvaceae), which have stalked leaflets, and from *Bixa*, which has simple leaves. The sap is red or yellow.

Cochlospermum

Cochlospermum includes approximately 12 species of trees, shrubs, and herbs, which are widely distributed in the tropics but with greatest diversity in South America. Leaves are usually simple and palmately lobed (palmatifid). *Cochlospermum orinocense* is an exception with palmately compound leaves. Young growth and leaf undersides are downy (pubescent). Flowers are large and showy, bisexual, and radially symmetrical. Stamens are numerous. The genus name refers to the shell-like, spirally twisted seeds attached to long silky hairs in the large capsules. Known as kapok, this fiber is used, as with *Ceiba* species, as stuffing material. *Cochlospermum vitifolium*, a soft-wooded deciduous tree, is sometimes cultivated. It produces large buttercup-like flowers on leafless branches from winter to spring. Fertilize only after leaves are produced. Saplings usually do not branch until they are quite tall. Pruning initiates branching near the base and a more shrubby habit.

Cochlospermum vitifolium

BUTTERCUP TREE, BRAZILIAN ROSE, ROSA AMARILLA, ALGODONILLO ("COTTON-TREE")

Synonym: *Bombax vitifolium*. Mexico, Central and South America. Deciduous tree, 20–35 ft.+; zones 9–11. Blooms winter, spring. Seasonally moist/dry. Average to fertile, sandy, well-drained soil. Full sun. Flowers: bright yellow, sometimes streaked red, 3–4 in. wide; capsule obovate; silky hairs attached to seeds. Leaves: large, to 12 in. wide, 5-lobed, cleft almost to the petiole; margins toothed. Bark: gray-white. *The species name alludes to vaguely grapelike leaves. Fast-growing. In 'Plenum' some of the stamens have converted to petal-like staminodes, resulting in double flowers.*

COLCHICACEAE

COLCHICUM FAMILY,
GLORIOSA FAMILY

Colchicaceae includes approximately 15 genera of rhizomatous or tuberous herbs from South Africa, western Europe, western Asia, and Australia. These species were formerly included in the lily family, Lili-

Mammea americana

Mammea americana, fruit

Mesua ferrea

Cochlospermum vitifolium

Cochlospermum vitifolium 'Plenum'

aceae. The chemical colchicine, derived from *Colchicum* and other species, is used pharmaceutically and in the laboratory. It has been useful in the study of genetics because it delays cell division at metaphase when the chromosomes are densely contracted and more visible under the microscope. Because it interferes with cell division, it is also used to induce polyploidy of plants in tissue culture, sometimes resulting in larger flowers or other changes. Leaves are alternate, usually spirally arranged. Flowers are bisexual with 1 or 2 whorls of free or united tepals.

Gloriosa

Gloriosa includes a single variable species, a climbing tuberous perennial from tropical Africa and Asia. A number of forms were previously segregated into individual species, but all are now considered selections of *G. superba*. Of seasonally wet/dry tropical forests and rivers, gloriosa lilies are remarkable for their climbing habit. *Gloriosa superba* 'Rothschildiana', the largest and most brightly colored selection, is sometimes used in floral bouquets. It has twice the normal quota of chromosomes (4n). Flowers have 6 tepals and 6 stamens. Fruits are capsules with bright red seeds. Leaves are simple with leaf tip (cirrose) tendrils, which are extensions of the leaf midvein and which enable climbing. Gloriosas can be grown on trees or trellises or in hanging baskets. They thrive in coastal locations. Divide tubers when dormant. Plants are poisonous to grazing animals as well as humans.

Gloriosa superba
GLORIOSA LILY, VINE-LILY, ROTHSCHILD'S LILY
Tropical India, Sri Lanka, Africa, Asia. Seasonally dormant climber to 10 ft.; zones 9–11. Blooms warm months. Moist during active growth, dry when dormant. Fertile, well-drained soil. Full to part sun. Flowers: tepals nodding, reflexed, yellow to greenish yellow and marked with red, maroon, or purple; fruit a capsule, seed red. Leaves: lanceolate; cirrose tendrils at the tips. *Of seasonally wet/dry tropical forests and riverbanks. Very salt tolerant. 'Rothschildiana' has more red in the flower than other forms and is polyploid. The fruit in the photo belongs to a nearby Spondias.*

COMBRETACEAE
COMBRETUM FAMILY, WHITE MANGROVE FAMILY
Combretaceae includes approximately 20 genera of trees, shrubs, and woody climbers, which are widely distributed in the tropics and subtropics. Black olive, *Bucida buceras*, and buttonwood, *Conocarpus erectus*, are commonly cultivated landscape trees with inconspicuous flowers. Tropical almond, *Terminalia catappa*, is an invasive pest. *Combretum* includes several species cultivated for their ornamental flowers. The leaves are simple, often with glandular cavities (dolmatia) along the main veins. In the wild, the dolmatia shelter mites, which feed on plant-eating parasites, a mutually beneficial (symbiotic) relationship. Flowers are usually bisexual, infrequently unisexual with male and female flowers on the same tree (monoecious) or on different trees (dioecious). Petals are often absent. A yellow underbark and mucilaginous sap also distinguish this group.

Bucida
Bucida includes approximately 8 species of trees and shrubs from the West Indies, Florida, and Central America. *Bucida buceras*, black olive, is an erect tree commonly cultivated in South Florida. It is native to the Florida Keys. Though an excellent shade tree, it is not recommended for street planting due to the propensity of its small black fruits to stain cars and pavement. *Bucida spinosa* is a smaller, spreading tree that is highly esteemed in the Bahamas for its bonsai shape, storm resistance, and excellent salt tolerance. Leaves are small, densely arranged in whorls at the ends of the branches. The zigzag-branching (divaricate) twigs are a distinctive characteristic. The leaf axils have small spines. Flowers are reduced and inconspicuous.

Bucida spinosa
SPINY BLACK OLIVE, MING TREE (BAHAMAS), BRIAR-TREE
Bahamas. Evergreen tree, 10–20 ft.; zones 10–11. Blooms all year. Seasonally moist/dry. Average to poor, well-drained, calcareous soil. Full sun. Flowers: small, green, petals

Bucida spinosa

absent, in spikes; fruit small, black, one-seeded, in clusters. Leaves: oblanceolate, about 1 in. long, stiff, in almost stalkless (subsessile) fascicles; spines in the leaf axils. *Of coastal woodlands and marshes. Very salt tolerant. Spreading, natural bonsai shape. Not related to the common edible olive,* Olea europaea.

Calopyxis

Calopyxis includes approximately 23 species of climbers from Madagascar. They have bell-shaped flowers and simple leaves. *Calopyxis grandidieri* is a recent collection at Fairchild Tropical Garden. It is rare in cultivation. Flowers are bell-like in loose clusters. Like other islands of the Indian Ocean, Madagascar is relatively isolated. This isolation has played an important role in the development of a unique flora and fauna. Unfortunately, many Mala-

gasy species are threatened due to extensive land clearing for agriculture.

Calopyxis grandidieri

Synonym: *Combretum grandidieri.* Madagascar. Evergreen climber to 15 ft.; zones 10–11. Blooms warm months. Seasonally moist/dry. Average to poor, well-drained, calcareous soil; alkaline pH. Full to part sun. Flowers: bell-shaped, calyx fused, lobes short, greenish yellow to orange-red; in hanging clusters. Leaves: lanceolate, to 2 in. long, tips tapering to a point (acuminate). *Rare in cultivation.*

Combretum

Combretum includes approximately 250 species of trees, shrubs, and woody climbers, which are widely distributed in the tropics with the exception of Australia. The petals

or petal-like calyx are frequently scarlet. Stamens are often brightly colored and extend beyond the perianth (exserted). The flowers are usually in many-flowered racemes or panicles. Leaves are simple. The dry fruits are 4- or 5-angled or winged. Climbing and scrambling species need support.

Combretum coccineum

SCARLET COMB
Madagascar, Mauritius. Evergreen shrubby climber; zones 10–11. Blooms spring, summer. Seasonally moist/dry. Average, well-drained soil. Full to part sun. Flowers: small, scarlet; stamens long-exserted, scarlet; in many-flowered panicles. Leaves: oblong, 4–8 in.; spines hooked. *A scandent, prickly shrub. Salt tolerant. Suitable as a barrier hedge in coastal locations. Prune for shape.*

Combretum grandiflorum

SHOWY COMBRETUM
Tropical western Africa. Evergreen shrubby climber, 10–20 ft.+; zones 10–11. Blooms winter, spring. Moist when hot, less when cool. Average, well-drained soil. Full to part sun. Flowers: cup-shaped, perianth scarlet; anthers yellow, slightly protruding. Leaves: ovate, 4–6 in. long, glossy dark green, midvein purple, tip emarginate; petioles purple. *A spineless species that needs support. Prune occasionally for compactness. The species name means "large-flowered," alluding to the relatively large petal-like calyx.*

Combretum rotundifolium

MONKEY-BRUSH, ESCOBILLA
Synonym: *C. aubletii.* Venezuela, Guyana, Brazil, Peru. Semideciduous climber, 10–20 ft.; zones 10–11. Blooms spring, summer. Seasonally moist/dry. Fertile, well-drained soil; acid pH. Full to part sun. Flowers: small, scarlet; stamens long-exserted, yellow turning orange; spikes terminal. Leaves: ovate, to 5 in. long, opposite to whorled at the ends of the branches. *Inflorescence begins opening first along one side resembling a monkey-sized, red and yellow dustbrush. Pollinated by birds and monkeys. Photo shows a somewhat unusual cluster of several inflorescences.*

Quisqualis

Quisqualis includes approximately 16 species of woody climbers from the Old World tropics. Some authors include these species in *Combretum*. One species, *Q. indica*, is an old favorite in cultivation. The flowers open white at night, turning pink by daybreak and finally magenta as the day progresses. They emit a cloyingly sweet peachy scent that attracts fruit bat pollinators at night in the wild. In amenable conditions, this spiny vine can become aggressive. Reducing moisture and fertility may help keep it under control. An uncommon semidouble selection, 'Flore Pleno', has a second ring of smaller petal lobes.

Quisqualis indica

RANGOON CREEPER, INDIAN JESSAMINE, QUISQUAL
Synonym: *Combretum indicum.*

Gloriosa superba 'Rothschildiana'

Calopyxis grandidieri

Combretum coccineum

Combretum grandiflorum

Combretum rotundifolium

Quisqualis indica

India, Indomalaysia, New Guinea; widely naturalized in the Old World tropics. Evergreen climber to 50 ft.+; zones 10–11. Blooms spring, summer. Moderate moisture. Fertile, well-drained soil. Full sun. Flowers: trumpet-shaped, to 6 in. long, opening white at night, turning pink then magenta; fragrant; in loose clusters. Leaves: elliptic to oblong, to 7 in. long, dull green, papery, roughly hairy. Branches armed with recurved spines. *Sends out long, creeping runners. More easily controlled on an arbor where it can't invade trees.*

COMMELINACEAE

SPIDERWORT FAMILY

Commelinaceae includes approximately 39 genera of rhizomatous, annual or perennial herbs and epiphytes, which are widely distributed in tropical and temperate regions. Familiar species include wandering Jew and oyster-plant and other *Tradescantia* species. *Cochliostema* species have unusually showy flowers. Leaf bases sheath the stem, which is slightly swollen at the nodes. Flowers are short-lived, usually blue or white with 3 petals and 3 sepals. The 3–6 stamens are often fringed. Some of the stamens may be replaced by staminodes (sterile, petal-like stamens). Often a boat-shaped pair of bracts clasps the base of the flowers.

Cochliostema

Cochliostema includes 2 species of epiphytic herbs from Nicaragua to northern South America. They come from tropical rain forests and are sensitive to cold. The genus name alludes to the presence of 3 coiled staminodes (sterile stamens). The fleshy leaves are sword-shaped and arranged in whorls sheathing a short, succulent stalk. Clusters of flowers develop in the leaf axils. Grow in a bark-based orchid mix in a warm, humid environment with medium filtered light but not deep shade. Use dilute liquid fertilizer. Raising the container better displays the stunning blooms located near the base.

Cochliostema odoratissimum

Nicaragua to Ecuador, Venezuela, Guiana. Semiepiphytic herb to 5 ft.+; zone 11. Blooms fall, winter. Evenly moist and humid. Bark epiphyte mix. Filtered light. Flowers: petals blue-violet, fringed; sepals pink; staminodes white, fringed; bracts pink; in clusters in leaf axils. Leaves: broadly sword-shaped, to 16 in. long, fleshy, keeled, dark green, streaked purple above, purple below; in whorls, on a short stem. *Protect from cold. The magnificent, delicately scented plant at Ernesto's Nursery in Miami, Florida, produced more than 30 sequential inflorescences over a 4-month period.*

Cochliostema velutinum

Nicaragua to Ecuador and Brazil. Epiphytic herb to 2 ft.; zone 11. Blooms late winter, spring. Evenly moist and humid. Bark epiphyte mix. Filtered light. Flowers: petals cobalt-blue; sepals lavender; staminodes covered with light blue or white hairs; in clusters in the leaf axils, opening a few at a time. Leaves: sword-shaped, to 3 ft. long, fleshy, light green; margins undulate; in basal whorl. *Plants are stemless. Cold-sensitive.*

Dichorisandra

Dichorisandra includes approximately 25 species of seasonally dormant herbs from tropical America and the West Indies. Despite the misleading use of the name "blue ginger," these species are not related to gingers (Zingiberaceae). Stems are erect and reedlike and have a mucilaginous sap. In mild temperate regions, the rhizomes should be mulched to protect from freezing when dormant. In colder areas, the rhizomes are lifted in winter.

Dichorisandra thyrsiflora

QUEEN-SPIDERWORT, BLUE GINGER

Southeastern Brazil. Evergreen perennial herb to 4–8 ft.; zones 9–11. Blooms late summer, fall. Seasonally moist and humid, dry. Fertile, humus-rich, well-drained soil. Part sun to bright filtered light. Flowers: purple; fruit an orange berry; bracts absent; spike terminal, to 1 ft. tall. Leaves: elliptic, to 12 in. long, sometimes purplish below; bases sheath the stalk and are spirally arranged. *One form has variegated leaves.* Dichorisandra reginae *can be distinguished by the purple-and-white flowers. Attractive to swallowtail butterflies.*

Tradescantia

Tradescantia includes approximately 70 species of fleshy, mostly perennial herbs from tropical and temperate America. Flowers have 3 blue, purple, or white petals. The stamens have long hairs. The flowers last only a day but new flowers, hidden in the boatlike bracts, open sequentially. The leaves are lanceolate to ovate, often variegated. The stems spread rapidly, taking root at the nodes and making these plants useful as ground cover in moist shaded areas. Trailing species known as wandering Jew are commonly grown in hanging baskets. The Andersoniana Group consists of clump-forming hybrids of uncertain ancestry with relatively large flowers.

Tradescantia Andersoniana Group

GIANT SPIDERWORT

Synonyms: *T.* ×*andersoniana, T. andersoniana* × *T. virginiana* (incorrectly). Garden hybrids. Perennial herbs to 18 in.; zones 9–11. Blooms warm months. Regular moisture. Fertile, humus-rich, well-drained soil. Full to part sun. Flowers: petals 3, to 1.5 in. wide, violet, pink, blue or white; stamen filaments have long violet hairs; 2 bracts enclose base of inflorescence. Leaves: strap-shaped, to 18 in. long, fleshy. *A representative hybrid of the group.*

Cochliostema odoratissimum, inflorescence

Cochliostema velutinum

Dichorisandra thyrsiflora

Tradescantia Andersoniana Group

Tradescantia pallida 'Purple Heart'

PURPLE QUEEN

Synonyms: *Setcreasea pallida, Setcreasea purpurea.* Eastern Mexico. Succulent herb to 2 ft.; zones 10–11. Blooms all year. Regular moisture and humidity. Fertile, well-drained soil. Part sun, bright filtered light. Flowers: petals 3, pale pink, bracts 2, elongated. Leaves: lanceolate, eggplant-purple to pink in bright sun, bases clasp the fleshy stalk. *The type species has white flowers and green leaves and bracts. The purple-leafed selection is much more common in cultivation. Suitable as an accent plant in moist locations. Best with a little protection from midday sun. Tolerates dry periods but at the expense of fresh appearance. Leaves may be temporarily spotted by cold and low humidity.*

Tradescantia spathacea

OYSTER-PLANT, RHEO, MOSES-IN-THE-BULRUSHES, PURPLE-LEAFED SPIDERWORT

Synonym: *Rhoeo discolor.* West Indies, Mexico, Guatemala; widely naturalized. Semiepiphytic herb, 1–1.5 ft.; zones 9–11. Blooms all year. Moist to moderate. Average, well-drained soil. Full sun to shade. Flowers: small, white; bracts 2, boat-shaped, purple. Leaves: sword-shaped, to 1 ft. long, fleshy, dark green, undersides purple; cultivars striped or with green undersides; whorled around a fleshy stem. *Infests flower beds, container plants, palm trunks, gutters, and roof tiles. Fast-growing. Removal of seedlings before bloom strongly advised. A restricted species in South Florida. Sterile dwarf cultivars not restricted.*

CONVOLVULACEAE

MORNING-GLORY FAMILY

Convolvulaceae includes approximately 55 genera of mostly annual and perennial climbers plus a number of shrubs and trees which are widely distributed, with greatest diversity in the tropics. Differences among some of the genera are based on minutia of the pistils. Leaves are usually simple, sometimes deeply lobed, rarely compound. Flowers are bisexual, radially symmetrical, and last only for a day. The corolla is funnel-shaped, the 5 petals united into a tube at the base and often united to the edge. Flowers are pleated where the petals join, folded umbrella-like in bud. The stamens are attached to the petals (epipetalous) inside the throat.

Argyreia

Argyreia includes approximately 90 species of woody climbers from tropical Southeast Asia, India, and Indomalaysia to Australia. Flowers are funnel-shaped, bell-shaped, or tubular. Leaves and stems are covered with woolly hairs (lanate). Fruits are woody capsules.

Argyreia nervosa

WOOLLY MORNING-GLORY, ELEPHANT-CREEPER

Eastern India; widely naturalized. Evergreen woody climber to 40 ft.+; zones 10–11. Blooms warm months. Moderate moisture. Average, well-drained soil. Full to part sun. Flowers: vase-shaped, lobes flaring, lavender-pink, throat darker red-violet, covered with white, felty hairs; sepals 5, greenish with white pubescent hairs; capsule brown resembling a small version of the wood-rose, *Merremia tuberosa.* Leaves: cordate, to 12 in. wide, soft, with pinnate venation, dark green above, white woolly below. Stems: covered with woolly white hairs. *An aggressive, twining vine. Pollinated by hawkmoths at night. A potential pest and not recommended.*

Evolvulus

Evolvulus includes approximately 100 species of annual and perennial herbs or subshrubs, which are widely distributed primarily in the American tropics and temperate zones. They are shrubby or creeping plants but never climbing. The genus name means "not twining." Flowers are rotate to funnel-shaped. *Evolvulus* differs from *Convolvulus* by the 5-lobed stigma and nontwining habit.

Evolvulus glomeratus

BLUE-DAZE, DWARF MORNING-GLORY

Synonym: *E. pilosus* (misapplied). Brazil. Perennial subshrub, 10–15 in.; zones 8–10. Blooms warm months. Regular moisture, tolerates brief dry spells. Fertile, well-drained soil. Full sun to bright filtered light. Flowers: rotate, petals fused, blue; in small clusters. Leaves: oblanceolate to oblong, 1–2 in. long, downy. *Usually grown as seasonal ground cover. Subject to mildew in hot, moist conditions. Evolvulus pilosus has smooth gray-green leaves and solitary flowers. Both species are commonly referred to as blue-daze. Moderately salt tolerant.*

Ipomoea

Ipomoea includes approximately 600 species of mostly twining annual and perennial herbs, occasionally shrubs or rarely trees, which are widely distributed in mild temperate and tropical regions. Some, including yam or sweet potato (*batata* in Spanish), *I. batatas*, have tuberous roots. *Ipomoea batatas* should not be confused with *Dioscorea alata*, white yam (*ñame* in Spanish). Some ipomoeas thrive in arid regions or on sandy beaches. Certain species produce hallucinogenic compounds that can be toxic. Petals are united, salverform, trumpet-, funnel-, or bell-shaped, with or without lobes. The sap is often milky. *Ipomoea aquatica*, water spinach, water cabbage, or pond morning-glory, is a highly invasive beach and aquatic species which is prohibited in Florida. It is sometimes sold illegally in Asian markets or cultivated in waterways. Control could involve harvesting as fresh table greens and animal feed (Howard, pers. comm.). *Ipomoea cairica*, with palmately lobed leaves, is also highly invasive and prohibited. This species is sometimes confused with *I. carnea*, a benign ornamental shrub.

Tradescantia pallida 'Purple Heart'

Tradescantia spathacea

Argyreia nervosa

Evolvulus glomeratus

Ipomoea carnea

SHRUB IPOMOEA

Synonyms: *I. carnea* subsp. *fistulosa, I. fistulosa.* Mexico to South America. Evergreen shrub, 8–10 ft.; zones 9–11. Blooms warm months. Moderate moisture. Average, well-drained soil. Full to part sun. Flowers: trumpet-shaped, petals fused, pink, throat red-violet; in clusters near the ends of the branches. Leaves: elongated cordate, to 6 in. long, gray-green. Stems: hollow. *Susceptible to nematodes. Not known to be self-propagating. Growers complain that inspectors sometimes mistake this species for* I. cairica, *a noxious pest.*

Ipomoea hederifolia

SCARLET CREEPER, TROMPILLO ("LITTLE TRUMPET")

North and South America; widely naturalized. Annual or perennial vine; zones 8–11. Blooms warm months. Moderate moisture. Average, well-drained soil. Full to part sun. Flowers: trumpet-shaped, tube to 2 in. long, orange to scarlet. Leaves: cordate, 3- to 5-lobed. *An herbaceous vine. Grows in disturbed locations and coastal areas.* Ipomoea coccinea, *another scarlet-flowered species, is also widely naturalized but can be distinguished by the unlobed leaves with toothed margins.*

Ipomoea horsfalliae

CARDINAL-CREEPER, CRIMSON IPOMOEA, PRINCE'S VINE, LADY DOORLY

Jamaica; naturalized in the Caribbean and tropics. Evergreen twining climber, 5–10 ft.; zones 9–11. Blooms winter, spring. Moderate moisture. Average, well-drained soil. Full sun. Flowers: trumpet-shaped, petal lobes pointed, ruby-red; in many-flowered clusters. Leaves: palmately and deeply 3- to 5-lobed to almost divided, to 6 in. long, glossy dark green; margins entire to toothed; undulate. *A tuberous vine with milky sap. Ideal for framing a door. Difficult to propagate vegetatively and sets seed only irregularly in cultivation. Pollinated by hummingbirds. Suitable for coastal but not seaside landscaping. Similar to but more robust than* I. microdactyla, *an endangered species.*

Ipomoea indica

DAWN-FLOWER, OCEAN-BLUE MORNING-GLORY, DON DIEGO DEL DÍA, GLORIA DE LA MAÑANA

Synonym: *I. cathartica.* Origin obscure (possibly Florida, West Indies); pantropically distributed. Perennial twining climber to 25 ft.; zones 8–11. Blooms warm months. Moderate moisture. Average, well-drained soil. Full to part sun. Flowers: funnel-shaped, pinkish violet. Leaves: ovate, entire to 3-lobed. *Widely naturalized in disturbed coastal areas.*

Ipomoea microdactyla

WILD POTATO

Bahamas, Florida, Cuba, endangered in the wild. Perennial twining climber to 5 ft.; zones 9–11. Blooms fall, winter, spring. Seasonally moist/dry. Average, well-drained soil. Full to part sun. Flowers: trumpet-shaped, petals fused to edge, not pointed, scarlet to magenta-pink; mostly solitary. Leaves: ovate to lanceolate, palmately veined, entire to 5- to 7-lobed; margins strongly undulate. *Of pinelands and fields. This small tuberous vine is a protected species. It somewhat resembles* I. horsfalliae, *but the flowers are solitary or in small clusters and the leaves are often entire or shallowly lobed.*

Ipomoea pauciflora

TREE MORNING-GLORY

Mexico to Peru. Deciduous tree to 15 ft.+; zones 10–11. Blooms fall, winter, spring. Moderate, seasonally dry. Average, well-drained soil. Full sun. Flowers: funnel-shaped, petals lobed, white. Leaves: lanceolate, base cordate, 6–7 in. long; margins slightly undulate. Bark: silver-gray. *A small tree of dry coastal forests to middle elevations. Unusual in cultivation. Blooms sparsely over a long period on leafless branches. Asymmetrical architecture of the limbs suitable for spare or Japanese landscape designs.*

Ipomoea quamoclit

STAR MORNING-GLORY, SWEET-WILLY, CYPRESS-VINE, REGADERO

Synonym: *Quamoclit pinnata.* Pantropical. Annual or perennial twining climber, 10–15 ft.; zones 9–11. Blooms summer, fall, winter. Moderate moisture. Average, well-drained soil. Full to part sun. Flowers: trumpet-shaped, lobes pointed, ruby-red, rarely white.

Leaves: pinnately dissected, lobes linear, appearing compound, feathery. *A lovely and lacy harmless weed with tuberous roots. Self-seeding. Tubers must be removed to control.*

Ipomoea carnea

Ipomoea hederifolia

Ipomoea horsfalliae

Ipomoea indica

Ipomoea microdactyla

Ipomoea pauciflora

Quamoclit is said to be derived from an Aztec name or a Greek word for "kidney bean." Shown growing on a variegated pineapple (Ananas).

Jacquemontia

Jacquemontia includes approximately 150 species of annual and perennial twining climbers primarily from the American tropics and subtropics, plus a few from the Old World. Flowers are funnel-shaped, fairly small, usually blue or white, and borne in clusters. Leaves are simple, margins usually entire.

Jacquemontia pentantha

Synonym: *Convolvulus pentantha*. Tropical and subtropical America. Annual creeper, 3–4 ft.; zones 10–11. Blooms late winter, spring. Regular moisture and humidity. Average, well-drained soil. Full to part sun. Flowers: funnel-shaped, not lobed, blue-violet, petal seams white, to 1 in. long. Leaves: cordate, to 1.5 in. *A low, sprawling creeper native to coastal areas. Moderately salt tolerant.*

Merremia

Merremia includes approximately 70 species of twining herbaceous and woody vines, which are widely distributed in the tropics. *Merremia tuberosa* is a serious pest in the United States. It is spread through the distribution of wood-rose seed capsules, which are popular in dry floral arrangements. Those who carelessly discard the arrangements or attempt to grow the seed soon learn to regret it, as do their neighbors. This species is very difficult and costly to control once it is turned loose in the garden, soon overwhelming the largest trees. It is included here to encourage gardeners to seek and destroy it before it becomes entrenched.

Merremia tuberosa

WOOD-ROSE, REGRET-VINE, ROSA DE MADERA
Synonym: *Ipomoea tuberosa*. South America; widely distributed. Deciduous vine to 100 ft.+; zones 8–11. Blooms late fall, winter. Moist to dry. Most well-drained soils. Full to part sun. Flowers: funnel-shaped, yellow or occasionally white; cap-

sule papery to woody, rosebud-shaped. Leaves: palmately 7-lobed, sometimes entire, to 8 in. long. *Prohibited in South Florida. Prompt removal before pods are produced is strongly advised. It may take several seasons to eliminate these vines entirely. Use strongly discouraged for dry floral arrangement because of potential for escape. Woody, tulip-shaped Lagerstroemia speciosa capsules suggested as an alternative.*

Poranopsis

Poranopsis includes approximately 3 species of woody twining climbers from tropical Asia. Flowers are small, funnel-shaped, white, in large panicles. Leaves are simple.

Poranopsis paniculata

BRIDAL BOUQUET, SNOW-IN-THE-JUNGLE, CORALITA BLANCA
Synonym: *Porana paniculata*. Northern India and Myanmar (Burma). Evergreen twining climber, 25–50 ft.+; zones 10–11. Blooms intermittently in fall, early winter. Seasonally moist/dry. Average, well-drained soil. Full to part sun. Flowers: small, funnel-shaped, white, honey-scented; in many-flowered panicles. Leaves: cordate, 4–6 in. wide, dull green. *Aggressive*

woody vine of seasonally moist forests. Needs a strong arbor isolated from trees. Blooms repeatedly for a week at a time. Prune back radically at the end of the bloom season to control. Self-rooting at nodes. A sentimental favorite of Cuban-Americans.

CRASSULACEAE

STONECROP FAMILY
Crassulaceae includes approximately 32 genera of perennial herbs and shrubs, which are widely distributed, excluding the Pacific Islands, with greatest diversity in dry tropical and subtropical regions, especially southern Africa. Leaves

Ipomoea quamoclit

Merremia tuberosa, capsule

Jacquemontia pentantha

Merremia tuberosa

Poranopsis paniculata

are fleshy to succulent, opposite or in rosettes, sometimes peltate. Flowers are bisexual and radially symmetrical and are arranged in cymes or corymbs. Interspecific and intergeneric hybridization are fairly common and make their identification difficult. Stonecrops are pollinated by insects and birds. The tiny seeds are wind-dispersed and, in favorable conditions, may become pests. Most species flourish in semiarid regions but also do well in moist, humid areas if provided exceptionally good drainage and air movement to prevent rot. They are suitable for containers and rock gardens.

Aeonium

Aeonium (pronounced a-OH-knee-um) includes approximately 30 species of succulent, cluster-forming perennial herbs and shrubs from the Mediterranean region and Africa. These species are closely related to *Sempervivum* but more arboreal in habit. Flowers are small but often in many-flowered inflorescences. Leaves are fleshy but fairly thin and lack petioles (sessile). They are arranged in rosettes, either basal or at the ends of branches. Some of these species will be placed in *Sempervivum*.

Aeonium arboreum

TREE AEONIUM
Morocco; naturalized in parts of California and South America. Succulent shrub or treelet to 3 ft.+; zones 9–11. Blooms winter, spring. Dry. Average, coarse, well-drained soil. Full sun. Flowers: small, yellow; in dense conical panicles. Leaves: elliptic to spathulate, fleshy, glossy green; in rosettes to 6 in. wide, in whorls at the ends of the branches. Branches thick, candelabra-form. *Thrives in hot, dry coastal areas but not salt tolerant. Produces aerial roots in arid situations. 'Atropurpureum' has green and purple variegated leaves; 'Albo-variegata' has yellow and green variegated leaves; 'Schwarzkopf' leaves are purple-black.*

Aeonium canariense

CANARY ISLANDS AEONIUM, VELVET ROSE

Synonym: *Sempervivum canariense.* Canary Islands. Succulent shrub, 2–3 ft.; zones 9–11. Blooms winter, spring. Dry. Average, well-drained soil. Full sun. Flowers: small, white; in open conical panicles on leafy stalks. Leaves: obovate, tip mucronate, downy (pubescent), light green; in basal rosettes to 1 ft. wide.

Aeonium holochrysum

CANARY ISLANDS AEONIUM, VELVET ROSE

Synonym: *Sempervivum holochrysum.* Canary Islands. Succulent shrub, 2–3 ft.; zones 9–11. Blooms winter. Dry. Average, well-drained soil. Full sun. Flowers: small, yellow; in dense conical panicles; on leafy stalks. Leaves: obovate, tip mucronate, green, older leaves red; in rosettes at ends of branches.

Crassula

Crassula includes 200–300 species of succulent herbs, shrubs, or shrubby trees, which are widely distributed, with greatest diversity in tropical and southern Africa. Leaves are fleshy and lack petioles (sessile). Flowers are small. Plants are suitable for containers, rock gardens, or clefts in stone walls. Fungal diseases and rot are common with too much humidity. Allow soil to dry between waterings. The genus name refers to the thick stems and leaves.

Crassula arborescens

SILVER JADE
South Africa (Cape provinces). Succulent shrub, 3–8 ft.; zones 9–11. Blooms fall, winter. Moderate moisture to dry. Average to poor, well-drained soil. Full sun. Flowers: small, creamy white; stamens red. Leaves: obovate, silver-blue; margins purple-pink. *Salt tolerant.*

Crassula ovata

JADE-PLANT, BABY JADE, JAPANESE RUBBER-TREE, KERKY-BUSH (SOUTH AFRICA)
Synonyms: *C. argentea, C. portulacea.* South Africa. Succulent shrub, 3–6 ft.; zones 9–11. Blooms fall, winter. Moderate moisture to dry. Average to poor, well-drained soil. Full sun. Flowers: petals pinkish white, stamens pink. Leaves:

obovate, to 2 in. long, green, fleshy, opposite; margins red; in whorls at ends of branches. *Branches thick and rubbery, easily broken. Prop heavy branches. Not salt tolerant. Sometimes confused with* C. arborescens. *Also confused with elephant jade,* Portulacaria afra, *an inconsistent bloomer in cultivation with smaller leaves and reddish branches.*

Crassula perfoliata

PAINTBRUSH, PROPELLER-PLANT, SICKLE-PLANT
Synonym: *C. falcata.* South Africa. Perennial subshrub to 3 ft.; zones 10–11. Blooms late summer, fall. Regular moisture to somewhat dry. Average to poor, gritty, well-drained soil. Full sun. Flowers: small, scarlet, in dense flat-topped heads (umbels), sweet-scented; anthers yellow, conspicuous. Leaves: slightly

curved (falcate), to 2 in. long, gray-green; sessile. Stems: thick, upright or trailing. *The bases of the sessile leaves encircle the stem so the stem appears to perforate the blades. Tolerates arid conditions but foliage is more fulsome with regular moisture.*

Kalanchoe

Kalanchoe includes approximately 125 species of succulent annual and biennial herbs, shrubs, climbers, and small trees from the tropics, with greatest concentration in tropical Africa and Madagascar, 1 from South America, plus a few Asian. No consensus exists on pronunciation of the genus name but cal-ANN-co-way is most common. The name is thought to be derived from either a corrupted Chinese name or *kalanka*, a Hindi word meaning "rusty" because leaves

Aeonium arboreum 'Schwarzkopf'

Aeonium holochrysum

Crassula arborescens

Crassula ovata

often develop rust-colored spots with age. A number of species are cultivated. Leaves are usually simple (*K. pinnata* is an exception) and fleshy, with or without petioles. Flowers are bell-shaped or tubular, sometimes inflated. The sepals and petals each have 5 partly fused lobes. There are 10 stamens. Some species produce viviparous plantlets in notches along the leaf margins. Many arid forms thrive in moist climates with excellent drainage. A group of species have been shuttled between *Bryophyllum* and *Kalanchoe* over the years, but the genus *Bryophyllum* has been retired in the latest treatment of Crassulaceae (Eggli, pers. comm.). *Kalanchoe pinnata* (syn. *Bryophyllum pinnatum*), life plant, is an invasive pest and restricted in South Florida.

Kalanchoe beharensis

FELT-BUSH, VELVET-LEAF
Madagascar. Succulent shrub or small tree to 12 ft.; zones 9–11. Blooms winter. Moderate, seasonally dry. Average to poor, well-drained soil. Full to part sun. Flowers: small, urn-shaped, tan-yellow, throat orange or purplish; in many-flowered, diffuse panicles to 18 in. high. Leaves: deltoid, 8–14 in. long, upper surface concave, felty; margins toothed, undulate; peltate. *Several leaf colors exist with silvery green, gray, or bronze hairs.*

Kalanchoe blossfeldiana

FLAMING KATIE, CHRISTMAS KALANCHOE, CALANCHOE
Synonym: *K. globulifera* var. *coccinea*. Madagascar. Succulent herb to 1 ft.; zones 10–11. Blooms winter, spring. Moderate moisture. Open, gritty, well-drained soil. Full to part sun. Flowers: small, salverform, in many-flowered panicles. Leaves: ovate to elliptic, 1–3 in. long; margins crenate (scalloped); petioles to 1 in. long. *Cold-sensitive. Cultivars are available in many shades of red, pink, orange, yellow, and white. Easily propagated from leaf cuttings or bulbils on leaf margins. The selection in the photo has brilliant scarlet flowers and abundant holiday bloom.*

Kalanchoe delagoensis

MOTHER-OF-THOUSANDS
Synonyms: *Bryophyllum tubiflorum*, *K. tubiflora*. Madagascar; widely distributed. Succulent herb, 2–4 ft.; zones 10–11. Blooms fall, winter, spring. Moderate moisture to seasonally dry. Sandy, well-drained soil. Full sun to bright filtered light. Flowers: corolla bell-shaped, pendent, pink to orange; calyx gray; on erect stalk. Leaves: narrowly lance-shaped, to 6 in.+ long, dark green to brownish gray, older leaves spotted; arranged in whorls around the stem. *Perhaps better described as mother-of-weeds, this species produces hundreds of plantlets (bulbils) on the distal margins of the leaves. A noxious weed in favorable conditions. Not recommended in moist habitat. Species name often misspelled delagonensis. A number of species hybridize with K. delagoensis including K. daigremontia, K. rosei, and certain other species (Descoings, pers. comm.).*

Kalanchoe gastonis-bonnieri

CHANDELIER PLANT, CALANCHOE
Madagascar. Succulent perennial herb to 2 ft.; zones 9–11. Blooms fall, winter, spring. Moderate moisture. Coarse, well-drained soil. Full

Aeonium canariense

Kalanchoe beharensis

Crassula perfoliata

Kalanchoe blossfeldiana cultivar

Kalanchoe delagoensis

Kalanchoe delagoensis × *K. daigremontia*

sun. Flowers: bell-shaped, pendent, corolla yellow tinged with red; calyx russet; inflorescence a flat-topped corymb; on candelabra-like branched stalks. Leaves: diamond-shaped, to 3–6 in. long, fleshy, blue-green, more or less streaked maroon, gray or pinkish in drier conditions, thickly covered with powdery scales; margins scalloped; petiole broad, flat.

Kalanchoe grandiflora

Southern India. Succulent herb to 2 ft.; zones 10–11. Blooms fall, winter, spring. Regular moisture. Open, gritty, well-drained soil. Full sun. Flowers: tubular, lobes flared, pointed, yellow; in terminal corymbs on short, erect stalks. Leaves: ovate to diamond-shaped, light green, fleshy, covered with powdery white wax, becoming gray or laven-

der with age or when dry; petioles flat, broad; margins scalloped (crenate).

Kalanchoe pinnata

AIR PLANT, CHANDELIER PLANT, LIFE PLANT, HOJA DEL AIRE
Synonym: *Bryophyllum pinnatum.* Madagascar. Succulent herb to 6 ft.; zones 10–11. Blooms fall, winter, spring. Seasonally moist to dry. Open, gritty, well-drained soil. Full sun. Flowers: pendent; corolla lobes purplish maroon, partly enclosed by the calyx; calyx tubular, inflated, apex pointed, green with purple streaks; in terminal corymbs on erect stalks. Leaves: 5-pinnate, becoming irregularly pinnate to simple where they merge with bracts on the flower stalk, leaflets ovate, light green, fleshy, becoming yellowish and spotted with age;

margins scalloped (crenate). *An invasive pest and a restricted species in Florida. Produces plantlets on leaf margins. Angular buds dangle like glass crystals from a chandelier.*

Kalanchoe thyrsiflora

South Africa. Succulent perennial herb, 2–4 ft.; zones 9–11. Blooms winter. Moderate moisture, seasonally dry. Average, well-drained soil. Full sun. Flowers: bell-shaped, yellow; inflorescence erect, a thyrse. Leaves: wedge-shaped, erect and crowded on the stem, tips broad, truncate; margins often purplish red; petioles absent (sessile). *Develops a stem with age. Leaves distinctive.*

Sedum

Sedum includes approximately 450 species of succulent, mostly peren-

nial herbs plus a few subshrubs and shrubs from northern temperate regions and cooler altitudes in the tropics. Leaves are fleshy, sessile, and flat, club-shaped, or cylindrical. Flowers are usually small, 5-petaled, yellow or white, and arranged in cymes. Sedums are grown as ground covers, in rock gardens, or in flat containers. Water plants once or twice a week in hot, dry weather. The genus name is thought to be derived from the Latin verb "to sit" (*sedere*) because of the plants' prostrate habit.

Sedum rubrotinctum

STONECROP, CHRISTMAS CHEER, ORPINE, SEDAS
Synonym: *S. guatemalensis* (hort.). Mexico. Succulent herb, 2–10 in.; zones 9–11. Blooms winter, early spring. Moderate moisture, frequent mist. Coarse, well-drained soil. Full sun. Flowers: star-shaped, yellow, small; inflorescences short-stemmed. Leaves: club-shaped, fleshy, jade green, tinged reddish at the tip. *Previously described as a natural hybrid. This mat-forming plant glistens like a jewel and is found typically growing where it receives cool morning mists and dry afternoon heat. The species name means "red-tinted."*

CUCURBITACEAE

CUCUMBER FAMILY, GOURD FAMILY
Cucurbitaceae includes approximately 118 genera of annual or perennial tendrilled climbers, which are widely distributed, with greatest diversity in tropical and subtropical regions. They usually produce coiling tendrils for climbing. Many are grown in temperate zones as annuals, including familiar "vegetables" (actually fruits) such as squashes, pumpkins, gourds and cucumbers, as well as melons and loofah, the vegetable-sponge. Leaves are usually simple, often deeply lobed. Flowers are rotate or bell-shaped, and unisexual with male and female on the same plant (monoecious) or on different plants (dioecious). They are solitary or in clusters. The fruit is most commonly a berry or pepo (a berry with a hard rind), often quite large, or sometimes a dry capsule.

Kalanchoe gastonis-bonnieri

Kalanchoe grandiflora

Kalanchoe pinnata

Kalanchoe thyrsiflora

Sedum rubrotinctum

Gurania

Gurania includes approximately 40 species of herbaceous twining climbers from the American tropics. They are a primitive group of cucurbits with unique floral clusters made up of showy bracts. Plants are monoecious: flowers on young vines are male, while those on mature vines at the top of the canopy are female where they are readily accessible to bats and other pollinators. Leaves are more characteristic of the family. These species are cultivated for study and as curiosities.

Gurania makoyana

Panama (Darién Province). Evergreen herbaceous climber to 50 ft.+; zones 10–11. Blooms spring, summer. Regular moisture and humidity. Average to fertile, well-drained soil. Part sun to bright broken light. Flowers: small, yellow; bracts spiky, orange; in globular heads, to 1.5 in. wide. Leaves: rectangular in general outline, 5- to 7-lobed. Leaves and stems coarsely hairy. *A vigorous, twining vine. Not in general cultivation. An interesting primitive cucurbit with flowers that differ from the more typical solitary trumpetlike yellow flowers of the genus. Photographed at Fairchild Tropical Garden.*

Luffa

Luffa includes 6 or 7 species of tendrilled climbers from tropical regions of the Old and New World. Female flowers are solitary, male flowers in racemes. The commonly cultivated species are annuals. The dried and bleached fibrous skeletons of the cucumber-like fruit are used as abrasive bath or dish scrubbers. Fruit and seed are used medicinally. These species are raised commercially in Latin America and elsewhere.

Luffa aegyptiaca

LOOFAH, VEGETABLE-SPONGE
Synonyms: *L. cylindrica, L. gigantea* (hort.). Tropical Asia and Africa; naturalized in tropical America. Annual climber to 40 ft.+; zones 9–11. Blooms late winter, spring. Regular moisture and humidity. Average, well-drained soil. Full to part sun. Flowers: unisexual, salverform, to 4 in. wide, petals yellow, crumpled, not overlapping; fruit oblong, slightly angular, to 2 ft. long. Leaves: lobed or sometimes entire; margins more or less toothed. Stems: covered with soft hairs.

Momordica

Momordica includes approximately 45 species of annual and perennial herbaceous tendrilled climbers from the Old World tropics. Flowers are unisexual, radially symmetrical, and with male and female on the same plant (monoecious) or rarely on separate plants (dioecious). Female flowers are solitary, male flowers in clusters. The fruit is a spongy yellow capsule that splits open, revealing seeds with bright red seedcoats (sarcotesta). Birds are attracted by the color and spread the seed. *Momordica charantia* is a seasonal minor garden pest but a source of food for birds. The red sarcotesta is eaten in China and said to be tasty, but the seed it surrounds is poisonous to humans.

Momordica charantia

BALSAM PEAR, BITTER GOURD, WILD CUCUMBER
Old World tropics; widely naturalized. Annual climber to 10 ft.+; zones 9–11. Blooms warm months. Moderate moisture. Most well-drained soils. Full to part sun. Flowers: unisexual, rotate, yellow; fruit a bumpy, spindle-shaped yellow capsule with pointed ends, splitting open when ripe; seedcoat (sarcotesta) fleshy, glossy red. Leaves: simple, deeply 5-lobed, 1–2 in. wide; margins coarsely toothed; pungently aromatic when crushed.

Seed distributed by birds. A seasonal pest but not considered disruptive of wild habitats.

CYCLANTHACEAE

CYCLANTHUS FAMILY
Cyclanthaceae includes approximately 11 genera of stemless or very short-stemmed herbs, shrubs, or occasionally climbers from tropical America. Though leaves are palmlike, they are more closely allied to pandanus than palms. Flowers are unisexual, with male and female flowers in spiral rows on a spadix (monoecious). The petals and sepals (perianth) are reduced to a cup with toothlike lobes or the perianth may be absent. Coarse staminode strands resemble dried spaghetti. Two to numerous spathes are attached below the spadix and surround the inflorescence until it reaches maturity.

Carludovica

Carludovica includes 3 species of palmlike herbs from tropical America. Leaves are palmately divided or lobed, palmlike, and the petioles are often twice as long as the blades. Flowers are unisexual, with male and female flowers arranged in alternate rows on a spadix (monoecious). Each inflorescence has 2–4 spathes. Male flowers produce long, spaghetti-like staminodes which cover the inflorescence temporarily. Fiber is separated from the petioles and used for weaving baskets and "Panama" hats—made primarily in Ecuador.

Carludovica drudei

PANAMA HAT PLANT
Synonym: *C. utilis.* Mexico to Ecuador. Evergreen shrub, 8–12 ft.; zones 10–11. Blooms warm months. Moist and humid. Fertile, well-drained soil. Part sun to filtered light. Flowers: unisexual; spirally arranged around a spadixlike inflorescence; 4 tepals of female (carpellate) flowers elongated; outer bracts green, inner bracts white; cordlike staminodes (on left in photo) envelop the spadix until mature; fruit red. Leaves: palmately divided; petiole 6–7 ft. long, red-violet at the base. *Of rainforest understory, riverbanks, and disturbed areas.*

Gurania makoyana

Luffa aegyptiaca, female flower

Momordica charantia, capsule and flower

Carludovica drudei, inflorescences

Carludovica palmata is distinguished by its short tepals and hastula-like protuberance (pseudohastula) where the petiole attaches to the blade (Hammel, pers. comm.).

Dicranopygium

Dicranopygium includes approximately 44 species of palmlike herbs from southern Mexico to Peru. They are small, short-stemmed or stemless plants of forest understory. The species are not easily differentiated. They are unusual in cultivation but sought by fanciers of intriguing species. Leaf blades are pleated and deeply divided in the center. Flowers are reduced, the male and female flowers spirally arranged on a spadix.

Dicranopygium atrovirens

DWARF PANAMA HAT PLANT
Synonym: *Carludovica atrovirens.*

Dicranopygium atrovirens

Dillenia suffruticosa

Tropical America. Evergreen stemless herb to 2 ft.; zones 10–11. Blooms warm months. Moist and humid. Fertile, well-drained soil. Filtered light. Flowers: unisexual, male and female in alternate whorls on a spadix; male flowers with conspicuous, Medusa-like staminodes; spathes several, erect, pointed. Leaves: blade divided in the center, pleated; petiole longer than blade. *Identification uncertain but likely. Cold-sensitive. Suitable for containers that can be brought indoors during cold spells. Good air circulation helps deter sucking insects.*

DILLENIACEAE

DILLENIA FAMILY
Dilleniaceae includes approximately 12 genera of shrubs, trees, and occasionally herbs or climbers from tropical Australia, Southeast Asia, Indomalaysia, and tropical

Dillenia indica, immature fruit

Hibbertia scandens

America. This is a fairly primitive plant family. A few species are cut for timber, some used as ornamentals. Leaves are simple, rarely lobed. Flowers are bisexual, radially symmetrical, and yellow or white, rarely red. Stamens are usually numerous, sometimes fused at the base. Flowers are solitary or arranged in clusters. The fruit is a berry or capsule.

Dillenia

Dillenia includes approximately 60 species of evergreen or deciduous shrubs and trees from Indomalaysia, Australia, and Madagascar. Leaves are simple and papery with parallel, recessed lateral veins ending in marginal teeth. Flowers are solitary and radially symmetrical. The yellow or white petals are ephemeral. Stamens are usually numerous. The buds are difficult to distinguish from the young fruits—the calyx opening briefly when the flowers are receptive and then closing up again and developing into the outer layers of the fruit. The crisp fleshy sepals and the fleshy arils of *D. indica* are edible.

Dillenia indica

ELEPHANT-APPLE, SIMPOH (MALAYSIA), CHULTA (INDIA)
India, Sri Lanka, Southeast Asia, southern China. Evergreen tree to 75 ft.; zones 10–11. Blooms intermittently in summer. Moist, humid. Fertile, well-drained soil; neutral to acid pH. Full to part sun. Flowers: large, to 8 in. wide, pendent, petals

Dioscorea bulbifera

5, oblong, white, ruffled, short-lived; stamens numerous, yellow; solitary at the ends of the branches; fruit ovoid, to 8 in. wide, enclosed by layers of leathery, fleshy sepals; seeds black, hairy, with a fleshy aril. Leaves: oblanceolate, 10–14 in. long, papery, downy below, lateral veins parallel ending in sharp marginal teeth. *Cold-sensitive. Of forest streambanks. The fleshy arils are used in curry. Wood red.*

Dillenia suffruticosa

Synonym: *Wormia suffruticosa.* Malaysia, Indonesia (Sumatra); naturalized in Java, Sri Lanka. Evergreen tree, 5–10 ft., or possibly to 30 ft. in the wild; zones 10–11. Blooms intermittently in warm months. Regular moisture and humidity. Fertile, well-drained soil; neutral to acid pH. Part sun, broken light. Flowers: butter-yellow, to 3 in. wide. Leaves: broadly elliptic, to 1 ft. long, stiff, secondary veins parallel, minutely hairy close to the margins, reddish when young. *Suffruticosa means "shrubby." Grows in coastal South Florida in understory locations. Foliage and flowers very attractive. Suitable for containers.*

Hibbertia

Hibbertia includes 60–115 species of evergreen trees, shrubs, and climbers from Australia, New Guinea, Fiji, New Caledonia, Malaysia, and Madagascar. A few species are cultivated for the showy flowers.

Hibbertia scandens

BUTTON FLOWER, GUINEA GOLD-VINE, CLIMBING GUINEA FLOWER
Synonym: *H. volubilis.* Eastern Australia (New South Wales). Evergreen shrubby climber, 6–15 ft.; zones 9–11. Blooms spring, summer. Regular moisture and humidity. Fertile, well-drained soil. Full to part sun. Flowers: corolla 2.5 in. wide, petals 5, golden-yellow, edges ruffled; stamens many, golden; sepals 5, hairy; solitary. Leaves: ovate, 2–3 in. long, dark green, underside with silky hairs; margin faintly toothed; blade extends down the petiole (decurrent). Stems: red, silky haired. *Suitable for training on fences or as a ground cover. Uncommon but highly recommended.*

DIOSCOREACEAE

YAM FAMILY

Dioscoreaceae includes approximately 5 genera of twining herbaceous climbers, which are widely distributed in the tropics. They are monocots with simple but atypical net-veined leaves. Many have subterranean tubers or rhizomes. Flowers are usually unisexual, small, and inconspicuous. Some species are cultivated for the production of steroids and contraceptive pharmaceuticals. This family is closely related to the bat-flower family, Taccaceae.

Dioscorea

Dioscorea includes approximately 600 species of twining herbaceous vines, which are widely distributed in the tropics. The tuber of white yam (*ñame* in Spanish, pronounced nYAH-may) is an important staple in Latin America and elsewhere but is not widely consumed outside Hispanic communities in the United States. The flesh is starchy, not sweet, grayish white, similar to a potato. The orange yam, *Ipomoea batatas*, is in the morning-glory family, Convolvulaceae. Other inedible species are cultivated for the production of pharmaceutical hormones. A few are cultivated for the tortoiselike aboveground caudex, primarily by botanical gardens and collectors of curiosities. The underground tubers of *D. bulbifera* are eaten in Asia, probably as a subsistence food. The plant also produces small, tuberlike, lumpy bulbils in the leaf axils, which take root wherever they fall. It is a highly invasive pest and extremely difficult to eradicate. It is prohibited in Florida. The vine is easily recognized by the large, quilted, heart-shaped leaves with heart-shaped venation.

Dioscorea bulbifera

AIR POTATO, WILD YAM

Old World tropics; naturalized in Florida. Annual twining climber to 30 ft.; zones 9–11. Blooms rarely. Moderate moisture. Average, well-drained soil. Full to part sun. Flowers: unisexual, small, tubular, greenish, rarely produced; in pendent spikes. Leaves: broadly cordate, 5–7 in. wide and long, glossy, conspicuously quilted. *Invasive pest.*

Self-propagating by the irregular gray bulbils produced in the leaf axils. Produces flowers on rare occasions as a reaction to stress such as hurricanes (Hammer, pers. comm.). To eradicate, fallen bulbils must be rigorously collected and sprouts destroyed before new bulbils develop.

Dioscorea mexicana

Synonym: *D. macrostachya*. Mexico to Costa Rica. Seasonally dormant perennial climber to 10 ft.+; zones 9–11. Blooms summer. Seasonally moist/dry. Average, well-drained soil. Full sun. Flowers: small, urn-shaped, green, under 1 in. long, throat maroon; in pendent racemes; shoots develop from the top of the tuber. Leaves: cordate, sinus spreading, to 6 in. long, 5 primary veins. Caudex, or semiemergent tuber, corky, with pyramidal, faceted segments, 3–4 ft.+ wide. *Identification tentative. Remarkable disparity between the slender vine and large caudex. The South African species,* D. elephantipes, *develops an enormous tuber shaped like an elephant foot and with deeply cleft, blocklike facets.*

EBENACEAE

EBONY FAMILY,
PERSIMMON FAMILY

Ebenaceae includes 2 genera of shrubs and trees mostly from tropical and mild temperate regions, with a few species from colder temperate zones. Among them are several species of true ebony with beautiful blackish brown heartwood and light sapwood. Some species with similar bicolored wood in other families are sometimes referred to as ebony (see *Caesalpinia* species, *Jacaranda* species). In the United States, a few species are cultivated for fruit or as shade trees. Leaves are simple with smooth margins. Flowers are nonshowy, radially symmetrical, and bisexual or unisexual with male and female flowers on separate plants (dioecious) or combined with bisexual flowers (polygamous).

Diospyros

Diospyros includes approximately 475 species of shrubs and trees, which are widely distributed in temperate and tropical regions. Some species are grown for their edible fruit including the persimmon, *D. kaki*, and black sapote, *D. digyna*. Several species are grown for the valuable ebony wood. Most make handsome shade trees. Male and female flowers are mostly segregated on separate trees (dioecious), but a few bisexual flowers are usually intermingled (polygamous). Fruit may, therefore, appear on either tree but is usually more abundant on individuals with mostly female flowers.

Diospyros blancoi

VELVET-APPLE, MABOLO

Synonym: *D. discolor* (incorrectly). Philippines, Taiwan, Indonesia. Evergreen tree to 45 ft.; zones 9–11. Blooms spring. Regular moisture and humidity. Average, well-drained soil. Full sun. Flowers: white, female flowers solitary, male flowers in 7-flowered cymes; fruit a slightly compressed sphere covered with golden-brown, felty hairs. Leaves: oblong, leathery, to 10 in. Fruit edible and ornamental. A handsome landscape tree.

Dioscorea mexicana

Diospyros blancoi, fruit

Diospyros digyna

BLACK SAPOTE, SAPOTE NEGRO
Southern Mexico to Colombia.
Evergreen tree to 45 ft.; zones
10–11. Blooms spring. Seasonally
moist, fairly dry. Average, well-
drained soil. Full sun. Flowers: unisexual, yellowish green, inconspicuous, female flowers solitary, male
flowers in small clusters; fruit
tomato-shaped, skin leathery green,
flesh dark brown; calyx persistent.
Leaves: simple, oblong, 4–6 in.
long. *The fruit has sweet flesh but is
bland tasting so it is commonly mixed
with tart fruit juices or spiced and
made into pumpkin-pie-like fillings.*

ERICACEAE

RHODODENDRON FAMILY,
HEATH FAMILY
Ericaceae includes approximately
130 genera of mostly trees and
shrubs and a few woody climbers
and epiphytes, which are distributed from tundra to equator, with
greatest diversity in the tropics.
Rhododendrons and azaleas are
very familiar in temperate areas,
but the magnificent tropical Vireya
Group is relatively unknown in the
continental United States. Leaves
are mostly simple, with smooth or
sometimes serrated margins. Flowers are urn-, bell-, or funnel-shaped,
the petals more or less united.

Rhododendron

Rhododendron includes approximately 800 species of shrubs from
temperate and tropical regions.
Tropical rhododendrons, the Vireya
Group, grow in mountainous regions. They are epiphytes or litho-
phytes, growing in rock crevices or
on rotting logs in moist woodlands.

Diospyros digyna, large green fruit

Rhododendron laetum

Rhododendron 'Simbu Sunset'

They can be distinguished from
temperate species by their open
habit and unwrinkled, funnel-
shaped corolla with rounded lobes.
They thrive in conditions similar to
temperate species: bright understory, open, humus-rich acid soil,
and regular moisture. They are sensitive to nematodes. Infected
plants may recover if moved to a
new location after cleaning the
roots of old soil and root-knots.
Otherwise, grow in large containers
with gritty, fast-draining soil
amended with coarse bark. Use dilute liquid or slow-release fertilizer.
Vireyas are much hybridized in
Asia, though not as well known in
the United States. Hybrids come in
dazzling shades of red, pink, and
yellow. Tropical rhododendrons are
suitable for containers on screened
patios or in understory locations.

Rhododendron Vireya Group

VIREYA, TROPICAL RHODODEN-
DRON, MALAYSIAN RHODODEN-
DRON, RODODENDRO TROPICO
Southeast Asia to New Guinea.
Evergreen semiepiphytic shrubs,
3–5 ft.+; zones 9–11. Blooms fall,
winter, spring. Regular moisture
and humidity. Open, humus-rich,
well-drained soil; acid pH. Part sun,
bright broken light. Flowers: corolla
funnel-shaped, lobes rounded.
Leaves: elliptic, 4–7 in. long, in
whorls. *The species R. laetum is light
yellow. Hybrids come in many colors.
These are mountain plants which
bloom intermittently to almost constantly in months with cooler
evenings.*

EUPHORBIACEAE

POINSETTIA FAMILY,
SPURGE FAMILY
Euphorbiaceae includes approximately 307 genera of trees, shrubs,
herbs, and climbers, which are
widely distributed in the tropics.
The family taxonomy is currently
being revised. The fruits are usually
3-celled capsules. Species with 1
ovule per cell (chamber, locule) and
a milky sap will remain in Euphorbiaceae. Species with 2 ovules per
cell and lacking a milky sap will be
segregated into Phyllanthaceae (for
example, *Antidesma, Bischofia, Phyllanthus*) and Picrodendraceae (for

example, *Oldfieldia, Picrodendron*).
Putranjiva and *Drypetes*, 2 mustard-
producing genera, will be placed in
Putranjivaceae (Judd, pers.
comm.). These genera are related
to Malpighiaceae. Many species are
succulents adapted for survival in
arid regions. The arid-growing eu-
phorbs are often pachycaulous with
scattered spines, never arranged in
areoles, and secrete a poisonous
milky latex—characteristics that
distinguish this group from cacti
(Cactaceae). Leaves may be well-
developed, rudimentary, or absent.
Many species lack true petals and
sepals (perianth). *Hevea brasiliensis*,
the Amazon, or Pará, rubber-tree, is
of great economic and environmental importance. Collecting latex
in the Amazon region is viewed as a
sustainable occupation that maintains rain forest rather than clear-
cutting it for crops and grazing.

Acalypha

Acalypha includes approximately
400 species of mostly shrubs and
subshrubs from the tropics and
subtropics. Leaves are simple,
lobed, and palmately veined. Flowers are greatly reduced and lack
petals. They are unisexual, with
male and female flowers on the
same plant (monoecious) or on
separate plants (dioecious). Only
female plants of *A. hispida* are cultivated and they must be propagated
from cuttings. The catkinlike inflorescences appear fluffy due to the
much-branched red styles of hundreds of tiny flowers. Cultivars of *A.
wilkesiana* are old-fashioned multicolored foliage plants. In mild temperate regions acalyphas are sometimes grown as root-hardy perennials though plants never reach
mature size in a single season.

Acalypha hispida

CHENILLE PLANT, RED HOT CAT'S
TAIL, CALIFA, COLA DE GATO
Synonym: *A. sanderi*. Exact origin
obscure (Malaysia to New Guinea).
Evergreen shrub, 8–15 ft.; zones
9–11. Blooms warm months.
Regular moisture and humidity.
Sandy, well-drained soil. Full to
part sun. Flowers: unisexual, only
females in cultivation; pistils
5-branched, red; on pendent catkin-

like spikes, 12–15 in. long. Leaves: ovate, 8–12 in. long; margins toothed. *Excess moisture causes the inflorescences to mildew. The common name chenille comes from the French word for "caterpillar," which, in turn, was derived from "little dog." 'Alba' is pinkish white in subdued winter light or shade but usually turns bright pink to red in spring then fades again in summer.*

Acalypha reptans var. pygmaea

TRAILING CHENILLE PLANT, STRAWBERRY FIRE-TAILS, COLA DE GATITO ("KITTEN TAIL") Synonym: *A. repens* (hort.). Hispaniola. Evergreen subshrub, under 1 ft.; zones 10–11. Blooms warm months. Regular moisture and humidity. Sandy, well-drained soil. Full to part sun. Flowers: unisexual, only female plants cultivated; stigmas red, branched; inflorescence a spike or catkin, 2–3 in. long. Leaves: ovate to cordate, 1–1.5 in. long; margins toothed. *A sprawling or scandent subshrub suitable for hanging baskets or ground cover.*

Acalypha wilkesiana

COPPERLEAF, JOSEPH'S COAT, HOJA DE COBRE Synonyms: *A. amentacea* var. *wilkesiana, A. godseffiana* (hort.). Only known in cultivation (probably originating in Oceania). Evergreen shrub, 6–15 ft.; zones 10–11. Blooms warm months. Moderate moisture, drought tolerant. Sandy, well-drained soil. Full sun. Flowers: dioecious, reduced, in spikes, 6–10 in. long. Leaves: ovate, cordate, lanceolate to linear, 6–10 in. long, often pleated, tip acuminate to rounded; margins undulate, toothed; petioles short or absent. *Probably a cultigen. An old-fashioned foliage plant with selections in diverse color combinations and patterns.*

Aleurites

Aleurites includes approximately 5 species of trees from Southeast Asia and Oceania. They are salt tolerant. The genus name comes from the Greek word for "flour," alluding to the dusty white foliage. *Aleurites fordii* is cultivated for tung oil, a fast-drying ingredient of paints and

varnish. Though the flowers are very ornamental, the species is invasive. *Aleurites moluccana* is a shade tree and the state tree of Hawaii, though probably introduced by early seafarers. It had many utilitarian uses for indigenous peoples of the Pacific. Oil was pressed from the seed and used in lamps or the dry kernels were strung on a coconut rachis wick and burned like candles. The seeds are sometimes made into elaborate leis. Authentic seed leis are expensive, so plastic is often substituted (Howard, pers. comm.).

Aleurites moluccana

CANDLENUT TREE, KUKUI (HAWAII) Polynesia to Southeast Asia; naturalized in tropics. Evergreen tree, 30–60 ft.; zones 9–11. Blooms spring, summer. Moderate moisture. Most well-drained soils. Full

sun. Flowers: unisexual, white; in clusters; fruit round, 4-celled, 2 in. wide, gray-green turning black. Leaves: ovate, to 8 in. long, entire or 3- to 5-lobed, covered with downy white hairs; petioles long. *Xeric. Salt tolerant. Nuts edible if roasted.*

Antidesma

Antidesma includes approximately 150 species of trees and shrubs from tropical Africa, India, Southeast Asia, Indomalaysia, the western Pacific Islands, and Australia. New revisions segregate this genus into Phyllanthaceae. Flowers are tiny and lack petals. They are arranged in spikes, which become pendent when weighted down by the fruits (drupes). Male and female flowers are on separate trees (dioecious). Unpollinated female trees produce sterile fruits. The fruit is eaten fresh or made into

jelly or wine. Large tree species are cut for timber. A curious phenomenon is associated with the fruit of *A. bunius*: it is sweet-tart to most people but bitter to approximately 1 out of 15 with a genetic sensitivity to a chemical component (Howard, pers. comm.). Other species apparently do not cause this reaction.

Antidesma bunius

BIGNAY, CHINESE LAUREL Synonyms: *A. collettii, Stelago bunius.* Malaysia, Southeast Asia. Evergreen tree to 25 ft.; zones 10–11. Blooms summer. Moderate moisture. Average, well-drained soil. Full sun. Flowers: unisexual, very small; calyx cup-shaped; on a glandular disk; female flowers are on pedicels and borne in racemes, male flowers are sessile, in spikes; fruit a one-seeded drupelet, to 0.5 in. diameter, yellow, turning red to

Acalypha hispida

Acalypha reptans var. *pygmaea*

Acalypha wilkesiana

Aleurites moluccana

Aleurites moluccana, fruit

Antidesma bunius, fruit

purple. Leaves: ovate to oblong, 6–8 in. long, glossy dark green, tip acuminate; margins smooth. Twigs and leaves hairless. *A handsome shade tree with a dense, rounded crown.*

Breynia

Breynia includes approximately 25 species of trees and shrubs from Australia and Melanesia. Flowers are unisexual, with male and female flowers on the same plant (monoecious). The flowers lack petals and are usually solitary, though male flowers may sometimes be in clusters. *Breynia disticha* is sometimes cultivated. The species has green leaves in the wild, but selections with variegated leaves provide color in the landscape throughout the year. If grown without enough sunlight, however, variegated cultivars often revert to the natural green state. Can be maintained with pruning as a bedding plant. Grown as an annual in colder climates.

Breynia disticha
SNOW-BUSH, LEAF-FLOWER
Synonyms: *B. nivosa*, *Phyllanthus nivosus.* New Caledonia, Vanuatu (New Hebrides). Evergreen shrub, 3–6 ft.; zones 10–11. Blooms summer. Regular moisture. Fertile, humus-rich, well-drained soil. Part sun or bright broken light. Flowers: greenish, fragrant, petals absent; fruit red; inflorescence pendent. Leaves: ovate, 1–1.5 in. long, usually green but cultivated forms variegated white and red, distichous. Zigzag branching (divaricate). *'Atropurpurea' has dark purple leaves. 'Roseapicta' has leaves with white, pink, and green variegation and has red stems and petioles.*

Cnidoscolus

Cnidoscolus (pronounced snid-OS-ko-lus) includes approximately 75 species of small trees, shrubs, and herbs from tropical and temperate America. Flowers are unisexual, with male and female flowers usually on the same plant (monoecious). Called nettles or tread-softly, these species often have stinging hairs on the leaves and stems. Certain species are a serious threat to grazing animals. Chaya (*C. chayamansa*) lacks stinging hairs and is eaten as a spinach-like vegetable, sautéed quickly or added to soups and stews (calalou).

Cnidoscolus chayamansa
CHAYA, SPINACH-TREE
Mexico, Central America to Brazil. Evergreen tree, 10–20 ft.; zones 10–11. Blooms spring. Moderate moisture. Average, well-drained soil. Full to part sun. Flowers: small, corolla absent; calyx petal-like, white; in flat-topped cymes. Leaves: large, dark green, deeply palmately lobed; margins coarsely toothed; petioles to 2 ft. long; stinging hairs absent. *A small, densely shady, rounded tree. Fast-growing but brittle.*

Codiaeum

Codiaeum (pronounced code-e-A-um) includes approximately 15 species of trees and shrubs from Southeast Asia, Indomalaysia, and the Pacific Islands. Flowers are small and unisexual, with both sexes on the same plant (monoecious). Though commonly referred to as croton, *Codiaeum* should not be confused with the genus *Croton*, which is unusual in cultivation.

Cultivated plants are a cultigen which has been hybridized for cen-

Cnidoscolus chayamansa

Breynia disticha 'Roseapicta'

Cnidoscolus chayamansa, flowers

Codiaeum variegatum

Dalechampia aristolochiifolia

turies, resulting in a wide array of vividly splashed or spotted, smooth, ruffled or twisted, entire or lobed leaves. Crotons were popular in the early part of the 20th century. They lost their appeal for a while because they were used improperly as sheared hedges and foundation plants in full sun without irrigation and soon became unattractive. Crotons do not do well in summer sun. They are not xeric and need regular irrigation when hot. Mites, active in hot weather, further stress the plants, causing leaf loss. They proved unsatisfactory for sheared hedges because they do not produce new leaves on old growth, leaving lower branches bare sticks.

New vivid forms and proper use in the landscape have revived popularity of crotons. They are especially attractive mixed with other plants with dark green foliage and taller trees that provide midday protection from sun and heat. Long

or unruly branches should be selectively removed close to the ground, the leafy tips nipped only lightly for bushiness. Mites can usually be vanquished with a strong spray of water weekly in hot weather. Cuttings are easily rooted. Sap may irritate the skin of sensitive individuals.

Codiaeum variegatum

CROTON

Synonym: *C. variegatum* var. *pictum*. Only in cultivation. Evergreen shrub, 2–20 ft.; zones 9–11. Blooms warm months. Regular moisture and humidity when hot, moderate when cool. Fertile, humus-rich, well-drained soil; preferably acid pH. Bright filtered or broken light at midday. Flowers: unisexual, inconspicuous, in pendent 6-in. spikes, or sterile. Leaves: blades entire to variously lobed, variously marked with red, purple, green, and yellow; margins smooth.

Elaeophorbia drupifera

Locate in bright understory or group with other plants that provide midday protection in summer. Susceptible to fungal diseases in shade. Tolerates periodic dry conditions in winter but requires regular moisture when hot. In alkaline soil provide plentiful mulch and acid fertilizer.

Dalechampia

Dalechampia includes approximately 115 species of woody climbers and a few shrubs from the tropics and subtropics, with greatest diversity in South America. The genus is noteworthy for having the only climbers in this family. Leaves are simple; some species have irritating hairs. The small flowers are fascinating in their complexity and interesting to examine with a magnifying glass. *Dalechampia aristolochiifolia* has 3 small red, funnel-shaped female flowers subtended by feathery green (fimbriate) bracts. The 9 or 10 much-branched male flowers produce cream-colored pollen and are surrounded by clusters of fimbriate purple bracts. A knob-like gland produces a clear, sticky resin. Flowers are grouped in a highly modified inflorescence, though not a cyathium as in *Euphorbia*. Two colorful, leaflike involucral bracts and 4 green tepals subtend the inflorescence. The flowers are pollinated in the wild by resin-seeking bees or ants (Armbruster, pers. comm.).

Dalechampia aristolochiifolia

WINGED BEAUTY, MANICILLO, ORTIGUILLA

Peru. Evergreen twining climber, 10–15 ft.; zones 9–11. Blooms warm months. Moderate moisture. Average to fertile, humus-rich, well-drained soil. Full to part sun. Flowers: highly modified, as described in genus introduction; involucral bracts paired, magenta. Leaves: elongated cordate, 3–4 in. long, sparsely hairy; margins smooth to serrulate; no stinging hairs. *The species name alludes to a resemblance of the leaves to certain* Aristolochia *species.*

Elaeophorbia

Elaeophorbia includes 4 species of trees from tropical and southern

Africa. They are woody and somewhat succulent. *Elaeophorbia drupifera* is unusual in cultivation. The milky sap is caustic, dangerous to the eyes. The genus name means "olive food," referring to the somewhat olivelike fruit.

Elaeophorbia drupifera

Tropical Africa. Evergreen tree to 50 ft.; zones 9–11. Blooms warm months. Seasonally moist/dry. Average, well-drained soil. Full sun. Flowers: unisexual; fruit a fleshy drupe. Leaves: simple, obovate; spines in pairs. *Young branches are 4- to 6-angled becoming round and woody with age.*

Euphorbia

Euphorbia includes approximately 2000 species of herbs, shrubs, and trees, which are widely distributed in the tropics and subtropics and well represented in arid regions. Many are succulent. Leaves are often absent, or reduced and ephemeral. Flowers lack a perianth and are arranged in specialized clusters called cyathia. Each cyathium consists of one female flower reduced to a single pistil and fused to several male flowers, each reduced to a single stamen and enclosed by a cuplike involucre of bracteoles with one or more, usually yellow glands. In some species the cyathia are unisexual. There are often 2 or more bracts (cyathophylls) subtending the cyathia. (In the familiar poinsettia, *E. pulcherrima*, the small structures with yellow glands at the center of the colorful bracts are the cyathia.) The fruit is a 3-celled capsule with a single seed in each cell. The sticky, milky sap may be irritating to sensitive individuals. All parts are toxic if ingested and seriously caustic to the eyes.

A commonly cultivated group of *Euphorbia* hybrids are often referred to as *E. milii* hybrids whether or not they actually involve *E. milii* in their ancestry. Many of these originated with the late commercial grower Ed Hummel in California. Hummel never revealed whether they were open-pollinated or deliberate crosses, and none of these hybrids were recorded or published by him.

Recent exciting introductions are incorrectly labeled *E. milii* Thai hybrids. These hybrids involve *E. lophogona* and *E. milii* and are referred to as *E. ×lomi*, though whether or not these are the only species involved is unclear. They are grouped horticulturally according to hybrid origin and physical characteristics (Jankalski 2000).

Euphorbia gymnonota
BAHAMAS POINSETTIA
Andros, Turks and Caicos Islands (Bahamas). Evergreen shrub, 6–12 ft.; zones 10–11. Blooms all year. Dry. Poor, sandy, well-drained soil.

Full sun. Flowers: reduced, in cyathia, glands 5, yellow; stamens red; bracts (cyathophylls) red. Leaves: oblong to oblanceolate, to 2 in. long, dull medium green; tips mucronate. Stems: terete. Unarmed. *A slow-growing coastal shrub or small tree. Very salt tolerant. Rare in cultivation outside the Bahamas. Protected.*

Euphorbia heptagona
MILK-BARREL
Southern Africa. Succulent shrub, 6–12 ft.; zones 7–11. Blooms spring, summer. Dry. Gritty, well-drained soil. Full sun. Flowers: re-

duced, in cyathia. Leaves: rudimentary, brown. Stems: slender, cylindrical, slightly 6- to 12-angled, heavily spined along ridges. *Clump-forming shrub, branching from the base like a candelabra. The similar* E. atrispina, *a smaller species, is suitable for containers.*

Euphorbia ingens
Kenya to southeastern Africa. Deciduous succulent tree, 15–30 ft.; zones 7–11. Blooms spring, summer. Dry. Gritty, well-drained soil. Full sun. Flowers: reduced, cyathia solitary, glands yellow, at the tips of the stems; fruit in dense clusters.

Leaves: rudimentary, ephemeral. Stems: 4-sided in elongated segments; margins lined with purple-black mostly spineless tufts. *Very heat tolerant medium tree for dry gardens. Sometimes confused with* E. cooperi, *a spiny species.*

Euphorbia leucocephala
SNOW-BUSH, LITTLE CHRISTMAS FLOWER, PASCUITA
Mexico, Central America. Evergreen shrub to 10 ft.; zones 9–11. Blooms late fall, winter. Moderate moisture. Average, well-drained soil. Full sun. Flowers: reduced, in cyathia; bracts white, becoming reddish with age, inflorescences 1–2 in. wide; seed dispersed explosively. Leaves: narrowly elliptic, 2–3 in. long, undersides light green. *Like a huge snowball when covered with thousands of miniature poinsettia flowers. Blooms from Thanksgiving through New Year's in Florida. Naturally round habit. Suitable for hedges. Prune sharply in spring and then lightly once or twice until mid summer. Then do not prune until after the next bloom. Widely cultivated in the West Indies.*

Euphorbia leucodendron subsp. oncoclada
PENCIL-TREE
Synonyms: *E. alluaudii, E. oncoclada.* Madagascar. Deciduous succulent shrub or small tree to 12 ft.; zones 10–11. Blooms spring, summer. Dry. Average to poor, well-drained soil. Full sun. Flowers: reduced, unisexual, in small cyathia at the ends of the branches; involucral bracts very small, yellow, in whorls. Leaves: reduced, ephemeral. Branches cylindrical (terete), 0.5–1 in. thick, jointed, waxy gray-green, attached to a short trunk. *Pencil-like branches. Irritating sap. Subsp.* leucodendron *has thinner, unjointed branches (Rauh 1995).*

Euphorbia ×lomi California Group
GIANT CROWN-OF-THORNS, GIANT CHRIST-THORN
Garden hybrid, *E. milii* var. *hislopii* × *E. lophogona.* Evergreen succulent shrub to 4 ft.; zones 9–11. Blooms most of the year. Regular moisture. Gritty, well-drained soil. Full to part sun. Flowers: cyathia in clusters of

Euphorbia gymnonota

Euphorbia ingens, fruiting

Euphorbia leucocephala

Euphorbia heptagona

8 or 16; peduncles to 8 in. long. Leaves: oblong, 4–5 in. long; margins entire, undulate; sessile. Stems: angled lengthwise, spines in comblike fasciated crests. *Thrives in coastal locations. Moderately salt, heat, and drought tolerant. Suitable for rock gardens. A group of hybrids from the late Ed Hummel.*

Euphorbia ×lomi Heidelberg Group 'Samona'

CROWN-OF-THORNS, CORONA DE CRISTO

Garden hybrid, *E. milii* var. *milii* × *E. lophogona*. Semideciduous succulent shrub to 2 ft.; zones 9–11. Blooms most of the year. Moderate moisture to seasonally dry. Gritty,

well-drained soil. Full to part sun. Flowers: bracts red, selections yellow or red and yellow-spotted, about 0.5 in. wide. Leaves: obovate, 2–3 in. long; margins entire; sessile. Stems: terete to slightly angled. *One of the most common Euphorbia hybrids in cultivation. Thrives in coastal situations. Moderately tolerant of salt*

and dry conditions. Derived from a wild hybrid. Commonly misspelled sonoma, *perhaps confused with the California wine country.*

Euphorbia ×lomi Poysean Group

THAI CROWN-OF-THORNS, HYDRANGEA-FLOWERED CROWN-OF-THORNS

Garden hybrids, *E. milii* × *E. lophogona* × ?. Evergreen succulent shrubs to 3 ft.+; zones 9–11. Blooms most of the year. Regular moisture. Gritty, well-drained soil. Full sun to filtered light. Flowers: cyathia paired, on short peduncles, bracts paired, 1–2 in. wide, sessile, bases overlapping, often in clusters of 8. Leaves: oblanceolate, 4–5 in. long; sessile; margins undulate; spines paired or fasciated.

Euphorbia leucocephala

Euphorbia leucodendron subsp. *oncoclada*

Euphorbia ×lomi California Group

Euphorbia ×lomi California Group

Euphorbia ×lomi 'Samona'

A group of large-bracted Thai hybrids with complex ancestry. Color selections in shades of red, yellow, and green vary with age and light intensity (Smoley 2000). The word poysean means "eight saints," good luck in Chinese.

Euphorbia milii var. bevilanensis

Synonyms: *E. bevilanensis, E. splendens* var. *bevilanensis.* Southern Madagascar. Semideciduous succulent shrub, 3–5 ft.; zones 10–11. Blooms most of the year. Moderate moisture. Gritty, well-drained soil. Full sun. Flowers: usually 4 cyathia on short peduncles; bracts 2-lobed, somewhat heart-shaped, to 0.5 in. wide, with a small point between the lobes, red. Leaves: spathulate to wedge-shaped, to 2 in. long; tip abruptly acute or sometimes emarginate; stems round; spines solitary.

Euphorbia milii var. hislopii

CROWN-OF-THORNS, CHRIST THORN
Madagascar. Semideciduous succulent shrub to 3 ft.; zones 9–11. Blooms most of the year. Moderate moisture. Gritty, well-drained soil. Full to part sun. Flowers: cyathia in clusters of 8; in pairs on once-forked peduncles to 8 in. long. Leaves: simple, oblanceolate; margins entire, undulate; sessile; spines more or less fasciated (crested) like combs in vertical interrupted rows along the stems. *Suitable for rock gardens. Moderately salt tolerant. Thrives in coastal situations. Tolerates heat. 'Breon' (syn. E. milii var. breonii) is a larger-flowered variant.*

Euphorbia milii var. imperatae f. lutea

Madagascar. Evergreen shrub, 1.5–2 ft.; zones 10–11. Blooms most of the year. Moderate moisture and humidity. Fertile, well-drained soil. Part sun. Flowers: cyathia in pairs on 1- or 2-forked stalks; bracts 2, red, or yellow in this form. Leaves: dark green, dimorphic; obovate on the branches, tips mucronate; broadly ovate in the leaf axils, tips emarginate. *Forma lutea is smaller-flowered, more slender and erect than the red-flowered form. Uncommon in cultivation. From tropical rain forest and adapted to humid climates. Should not be confused with E. milii var. tananarivae (syn. E. milii var. lutea [hort.]) (Jankalski 2000).*

Euphorbia milii 'Minibell'

MINIATURE CROWN-OF-THORNS
Garden hybrid. Evergreen succulent shrub, 6–10 in.; zones 9–11. Blooms all year. Moderate moisture. Gritty,

well-drained soil. Full to part sun. Flowers: inflorescences in clusters of 2 or 3; bracts red, tiny. Leaves: obovate, to 1 in. long; spines usually solitary. Stems: terete. *Thrives in*

Euphorbia ×*lomi* Poysean Group

Euphorbia milii var. *bevilanensis*

Euphorbia milii var. *hislopii*

Euphorbia milii var. *imperatae* f. *lutea*

Euphorbia milii 'Minibell'

Euphorbia pulcherrima, red cultivar

coastal situations. *Salt and heat tolerant. Very attractive tucked into rock crevices or as a ground cover. An intraspecific hybrid by the late Ed Hummel, whose wife was named Minnie Belle. Paul Hutchison of Tropic World reputedly applied the cultivar name (Jankalski 2000).*

Euphorbia pulcherrima

POINSETTIA, FLOR DE PASCUAS
Synonym: *Poinsettia pulcherrima.* Mexico. Evergreen shrub, 4–15 ft.; zones 10–11. Blooms winter. Regular moisture. Gritty, humus-rich, well-drained soil. Full sun. Flowers: cyathia with one yellow gland; bracts leaflike; cultivars single or double, creamy white, red to maroon. Leaves: lanceolate, to 8 in. long, shallowly lobed. Stems: hollow, brittle. *The wild form is rarely cultivated. Holiday plants are hybrids grown from cuttings with inadequate root systems, and are sensitive to drying. After flowering, cut back and repot or plant outdoors. Prune every 3 months until late summer. Grow in full sun once established and avoid artificial lighting. Fourteen hours of darkness are needed to initiate bloom. Susceptible to rust and scab fungus.*

Euphorbia punicea

FLAME-OF-JAMAICA
Jamaica, Cuba. Evergreen shrub to 6 ft.; zones 10–11. Blooms most of the year. Moderate, seasonally dry. Average, well-drained soil. Full sun. Flowers: cyathia with 5 yellow glands; bracts ovate, red, in whorls. Leaves: oblong to obovate, to 7 in. long, silky smooth, firm. *Somewhat salt tolerant. Unusual in cultivation in the United States but highly recommended. Cuttings difficult to root, but can be accomplished in sand with misting but not watering. Preferred selections have large bracts.*

Euphorbia viguieri var. viguieri

Madagascar. Deciduous pachycaulous shrub, 3–6 ft.; zones 10–11. Blooms most of the year. Dry. Gritty, sandy, well-drained soil. Full sun. Flowers: cyathia in pairs, enclosed by vase-shaped, pointed red bracts; peduncles 8–10 in. long; blooming with and without leaves. Leaves: elliptic to obovate, to 14 in.

long. Stems: usually unbranched, 5- to 6-angled; spines large, branched, along the vertical ribs. *Suitable for rock gardens. Thrives in moist climates with excellent drainage. Has 5 listed varieties partly distinguished by the lengths of the inflorescence stalks (peduncles) (Rauh 1995).*

Jatropha

Jatropha includes approximately 150 species of trees, shrubs, and perennial and annual herbs, which are widely distributed in the tropics and subtropics, with greatest diversity in Africa and the Americas. Flowers are unisexual, with male and female flowers on the same plant (monoecious) or on different plants (dioecious). Leaves are simple or lobed. Flowers have true petals and sepals and are not reduced in cyathia as in *Euphorbia.* Attractive to butterflies, especially zebra

broad-wings. The genus includes species with pharmaceutical properties. The sap has been investigated as an alternative source of fuel. All parts are poisonous.

Jatropha integerrima

PEREGRINA, JATROFA
Synonyms: *J. hastata, J. pandurifolia.* Cuba, West Indies. Evergreen tree or shrub, 6–8 ft.; zones 9–11. Blooms fall, winter, spring. Moderate moisture to dry. Average, well-drained soil. Full to part sun. Flowers: unisexual, petals red, 0.75–1.25 in. wide; cymes 3-flowered, the central flower carpellate (female), the lateral flowers staminate (male). Leaves: obovate to elliptic, tips cuspidate, sometimes 3-lobed, to 8 in. long. *Commonly cultivated. Compact, pest resistant, xeric, almost everblooming and salt tolerant. The lobed leaf form was formerly segregated as*

J. pandurifolia. *Pink and white cultivars do not appear to be as vigorous.*

Jatropha multifida

CORAL-PLANT, PHYSIC-NUT
Mexico to Brazil. Evergreen shrub to 20 ft.; zones 9–11. Blooms all year. Dry. Average, well-drained soil. Full sun. Flowers: small, petals red, stalk long, inflorescence a flat-topped cyme; fruit yellow, fleshy. Leaves: 7–11, round, to 10 in. diameter, cut almost to the petiole (palmatisect). *Of semiarid habitat but grows in moist climates with excellent drainage. Water only during periods of severe drought. Thrives in coastal locations and rock gardens. Attractive to butterflies.*

Jatropha ortegae

Mexico. Deciduous tree to 10–15 ft.+; zones 9–11. Blooms summer. Moderate moisture to fairly dry.

Euphorbia pulcherrima, white double cultivar

Euphorbia punicea

Euphorbia viguieri var. *viguieri*

Jatropha integerrima

Jatropha multifida

Jatropha ortegae

Average, well-drained soil. Full sun. Flowers: urn-shaped (urceolate), petals fused with a small opening at apex, pendent, red. Leaves: obovate, to 5 in., in whorls, gray-white (glaucous); margins entire except for a few teeth near petiole. Bark: papery white, peeling. *Of dry forests. A natural bonsai-shaped tree with striking bark. Unusual in cultivation. Thrives in dry areas, not arid desert. Also grows in moist climates with adequate drainage.*

Jatropha podagrica
GOUT-PLANT, BOTTLE-PLANT
Central America. Semideciduous pachycaulous tree to 8 ft.; zones 10–11. Blooms all year. Moderate moisture to dry. Average, well-drained soil. Full sun. Flowers: petals small, red; inflorescence a flat-topped cyme, on a long peduncle; fruit yellow, fleshy, explosively dehiscent. Leaves: ovate, 5-lobed; margins undulate; peltate. Trunk: bristly, base swollen. *Thrives in coastal areas. Xeric. Attractive to butterflies.*

Macaranga
Macaranga includes 250–280 species of trees and shrubs from the Old World tropics. Flowers are unisexual, male and female flowers usually on separate plants (dioecious), rarely on the same plant (monoecious). Some species harbor ants in hollows in the twigs and stipules in the wild. Ants perform reciprocal favors, cleaning the plants of aphids and encroaching herbs. Used in folk medicine. The name is derived from a Malagasy name for one species.

Macaranga grandifolia
CORAL-TREE
Synonym: *Croton grandifolius.* Philippines. Evergreen tree, 12–20 ft.; zones 10–11. Blooms almost all year. Moderate moisture. Average, well-drained soil. Full sun. Flowers: unisexual, lacking petals, sepals small, scarlet; male flowers stalkless, on branched inflorescences near the base of the branches, female flowers with branched styles near the ends of the branches. Leaves: large, broadly ovate, scaly, back of veins reddish; margins irregular; peltate; petioles to 2 ft. long. *Sparsely branching from the base. Thrives near the coast. Unusual in cultivation in the continental United States but common in Hawaii (Howard, pers. comm.).*

Manihot
Manihot includes approximately 150 species of trees, shrubs, and herbs from tropical America. Flowers are unisexual, with male and female flowers on the same plant (monoecious). The rhizome of *Manihot esculenta* is a staple food in South America, Africa, and Asia (known as cassava or manioc in English, but most commonly known by the Spanish name *yuca*). The epidermis of the rhizome contains cyanide compounds and is poisonous if not peeled (including the red underbark) and cooked. Bitter yuca, so called because it contains more cyanide than the sweet variety (formerly known as *M. dulcis*), is pounded, washed, and made into an excellent, crackerlike bread (*casabe*). Sweet yuca is peeled and boiled like potatoes. The powdered starch is used as a transparent thickening agent similar to arrowroot or as a silken baby powder. Tapioca consists of tasteless pellets of the starch. The starch is also used as postage glue or refined into sugar, alcohol, and acetone. The latex of *M. carthagenensis* subsp. *glaziovii* is processed into Ceará rubber or a fuel substitute.

Yuca is easy to grow and thrives in poor soil. It is resistant to chewing insect pests because of the high cyanide content. Ants live in the hollow stem and defend the plant from herbivores. The tuber is high in fiber but poor in nutrients and protein. A subsistence diet of the tuber sometimes leads to malnutrition but the leaves are rich in viatmins and minerals. Yuca should not to be confused with the genus *Yucca* (see Agavaceae).

Manihot esculenta
TAPIOCA-PLANT, MANIOC, YUCA, CASSAVA, MANDIOCA
Synonyms: *Jatropha dulcis, M. dulcis.* Northern South America. Perennial herb, 7–12 ft.; zones 10–11. Blooms intermittently in warm months. Regular moisture. Most well-drained soils. Full sun. Flowers: unisexual, calyx bell-shaped, white or red-streaked, petals absent; in axillary clusters; capsules small, winged. Leaves: palmatisect with 3–7 lobes, green or sometimes variegated dark green and cream, often with red primary veins, peltate; petiole red. *This species is hybridized with* M. carthagenensis *subsp.* glaziovii *for disease resistance to mosaic virus. Usually propagated from cuttings.*

Phyllanthus
Phyllanthus includes 500–600 species of trees, shrubs, and herbs from tropical and subtropical regions. The latest revision segregates this genus into Phyllanthaceae. Leaves are in opposite ranks (distichous). In some

Jatropha podagrica

Manihot esculenta 'Variegata'

Macaranga grandifolia

species, leaves are very small and ephemeral, replaced in function by modified leaflike twigs (cladophylls). Flowers may be borne on cladophyll margins or on the twigs. Fruits have 2 ovules per locule. Flowers are unisexual, with male and female flowers usually on the same plant (monoecious) or rarely on separate plants (dioecious). Some species have medicinal properties.

Phyllanthus acidus

GOOSEBERRY TREE, OTAHEITE GOOSEBERRY, CIRUELA COSTEÑA
Synonym: *P. distichus.* Origin obscure; widely naturalized. Deciduous tree to 30 ft.; zones 10–11. Blooms late winter, spring. Regular moisture and humidity. Average, well-drained soil. Full sun. Flowers: unisexual, male and female flowers mingled in many-flowered fascicles near the ends of deciduous branches; fruit to 1 in. wide, with pumpkinlike grooves. Leaves: ovate, lanceolate, 2–3 in. long; in opposite ranks, appearing pinnate. *The sour fruits are used in drinks and chutneys. The origin of this species is often listed as Brazil; however, plants are known to have been introduced into Jamaica by Bounty Captain Bligh on his second voyage in 1792 along with breadfruit,* Artocarpus altilis *(Howard, pers. comm.).*

Ricinus

Ricinus includes a single species of shrub or shrubby tree probably from eastern Africa and the Middle East. It has been naturalized throughout the tropics where castor bean has been cultivated for millennia. The male flowers are borne toward the ends of the inflorescence, the female flowers are generally concentrated toward the base. The raw seed contains ricin, the most deadly natural poison known. Processed castor oil is universally known as an infamous laxative. The oil is also refined into a highly stable lubricating oil used for watches, fine instruments, and engines and has numerous chemical, pharmaceutical, and industrial uses. Certain cultivars are grown for their colorful foliage. In temperate climates, they are grown as annuals. Castor-bean is fast-growing and invasive. It also causes serious allergenic reaction in sensitive individuals (Burch, pers. comm.).

Ricinus communis

CASTOR-BEAN, CASTOR-OIL PLANT, PALMA CHRISTI
Synonym: *R. africanus.* Origin obscure (probably eastern Africa, Middle East); naturalized pantropically. Evergreen shrub, 6–30 ft.; zones 9–11. Blooms warm months. Moderate moisture. Most well-drained soils. Full sun. Flowers: unisexual, petals absent; stigmas 5-branched, red; fruit covered with stiff, green or bluish outgrowths (tubercles), aging to brown. Leaves: palmately 5- to 11-lobed, 1–3 ft. wide; margins toothed; peltate. *Selections in various foliage colors. Raw seed highly toxic. Invasive. Strongly discouraged for cultivation. Prohibited in South Florida and Texas.*

FABACEAE

LEGUME FAMILY, BEAN FAMILY
Fabaceae (Leguminosae) includes approximately 665 genera of trees, shrubs, herbs, and climbers, sometimes spined, which are widely distributed. Many species are xerophytes. One of the largest plant families, legumes are divided into 3 subfamilies based on flower morphology, Caesalpinioideae, Mimosoideae, and Papilionoideae, the arrangement followed here. Some authors treat these groups as independent families.

Bacteria in root nodules convert or "fix" gaseous nitrogen into organic compounds that naturally enrich the soil. Farmers often till legumes into the soil as "green manure" between crops. This family includes protein-rich crops, such as beans, peas, and lentils. Some species provide animal forage, fiber, timber, gums, dyes, and pharmaceuticals. Together with grains, some legumes provide the basic food of humans and animals. Some species are poisonous.

Leaves are alternate and pinnately compound, often with even numbers of leaflets (paripinnate), which are oppositely arranged, or sometimes palmately compound, trifoliolate, or simple. The base of the petiole and/or petiolule is often swollen at the joint (pulvinus). Flowers are mostly bisexual, usually with 10 to numerous stamens, and either bilaterally or radially symmetrical. The fruit is a characteristic beanlike pod (legume) that splits along both sides (as distinguished from a follicle that splits along one side), or less commonly, a loment that splits crosswise between the seeds.

FABACEAE
Subfamily Caesalpinioideae

Caesalpinioideae includes approximately 150 genera of trees, shrubs, herbs, and climbers. Leaves are usually pinnately compound, sometimes twice pinnate (bipinnate). Flowers are bilaterally symmetrical sometimes appearing almost radially symmetrical. One petal is more or less differentiated into a lip or standard.

Amherstia

Amherstia includes a single species of tree from Southeast Asia. It is native to monsoon rain forest with a short dry season in winter. *Amherstia nobilis* has a weeping habit and orchidlike flowers in cauliflorous, pendent racemes. It is often described as one of the most beautiful tropical flowering trees. Temperatures below 55°F inhibit flower development. Though the tree is known to survive in protected locations of subtropical Florida, it is not known to bloom in the subtropics except in warm greenhouses. Flowering is initiated by a dry season, but trees in containers should never be allowed to become completely dry. The species is often cultivated in Hawaii, Southeast Asia,

Phyllanthus acidus

Ricinus communis, purple-leafed form

Ricinus communis, inflorescence

India, Sri Lanka, and the West Indies. Trees are self-sterile. Solitary trees rarely, if ever, produce viable seeds. They are difficult to propagate vegetatively.

Amherstia nobilis

AMHERSTIA, PRIDE-OF-BURMA, QUEEN-OF-FLOWERING-TREES
Myanmar (Burma). Extinct in wild. Evergreen tree, 20–40 ft.; zone 11. Blooms winter or dry season. Seasonally moist and humid, sparingly in winter. Fertile, sandy, humus-rich, well-drained soil. Part sun, with protection from midday sun. Flowers: standard with a clawed base, red and white with a golden eye at the end; 2 small lateral wings; 5 sepals, 3 small, 2 large; bracts petal-like, red; in pendent racemes; fruit a red, beaked pod. Leaves: bipinnate, 12–18 in. long; young leaves pink, lax, becoming light green and stiffening (pouring out); leaflets elliptic, tips caudate. Bark: light gray. *An ultra-tropical. Thrives outdoors only in warm climates. Photographed at Ernesto's Nursery in Miami, Florida.*

Bauhinia

Bauhinia includes approximately 350 species of trees, shrubs, and climbers from the tropics. Leaves are usually bilobed, some opening and closing like a book, a unique adaptation that helps control evaporation. The shape suggests the footprint of cloven-hoofed animals, alluded to by several common names. Bauhinias disperse seeds explosively (dehiscent).

The Hong Kong orchid-tree, *Bauhinia* ×*blakeana*, is often presumed to be a natural hybrid of *B. variegata* and *B. purpurea*, though such a cross has never been duplicated. It is distinguished by 5 stamens and blooms from fall to spring. It is sterile and must be propagated by grafting. The flowers are highly fragrant and attractive to hummingbirds. The most common seed-bearing orchid-trees, *B. purpurea* and *B. variegata*, can be weedy. *Bauhinia purpurea* blooms in the fall. It is distinguished by 3 stamens and open, upcurved petal tips, varying from pale lavender and pink to magenta. It is a short-

lived shrubby tree susceptible to thorn bugs, which open the trunk to rot. *Bauhinia variegata*, a late winter-to-spring bloomer, has 5 stamens, and the broad petals touch or overlap. It is semideciduous, blooming most spectacularly on bare limbs. The genus is named for 16th-century Swiss herbalist-botanists Caspar and Jean Johannes Bauhin. They were brothers but not twins, contrary to the popular legend (Howard, pers. comm.). The subgenus *Phanera* includes many climbing specis. It is relatively unknown in the U.S.

Bauhinia aculeata

SPINY WHITE ORCHID-TREE,
PATA DE VACA ("COW'S FOOT")
Synonym: *B. ungula*. Central and South America. Semideciduous tree, 10–15 ft.+; zones 9–11. Blooms spring, summer. Moderate moisture. Average, sandy, well-drained soil. Full sun. Flowers: petals open (valvate), clawed; margins irregularly notched; stamens 10; in clusters of 1–3. Leaves: broadly ovate or oblong, bilobed, 2–5 in. wide, finely downy; paired spines in leaf axils; petioles short. *Subsp. grandiflora, from southern South America, has 4- to 6-in.-wide white*

flowers; subsp. aculeata, *from the West Indies, northern South America, and Central America, has creamy, 3-in.-wide flowers (Wunderlin, pers. comm.). Self-seeding.*

Bauhinia acuminata

DWARF WHITE ORCHID-TREE,
MOUNTAIN EBONY
Indomalaysia to Philippines. Evergreen shrub, 6–10 ft.; zones 9–11. Blooms warm months. Regular moisture and humidity. Fertile, humus-rich, well-drained soil. Part sun to bright broken light. Flowers: somewhat variable, petals elliptic to ovate, not clawed, overlapping to

Amherstia nobilis

Bauhinia aculeata subsp. grandiflora

Bauhinia acuminata

Bauhinia ×blakeana

Bauhinia divaricata 'Rosea'

open, to 3 in. wide, translucent to opaque white, slightly cupped. Leaves: bilobed, lobes elliptic, 4–5 in. wide. *A dainty, understory shrub or small tree. Heavy feeder. Tolerates full sun but best with some midday shelter. Needs micronutrients in wet climates and poor soils.*

Bauhinia ×blakeana

HONG KONG ORCHID-TREE
Only known in cultivation (disseminated from a monastery in southern China); presumed hybrid of *B. purpurea* × *B. variegata*. Evergreen tree to 50 ft.; zones 9–11. Blooms fall to early spring. Seasonally moist/dry when cool. Fertile, open, well-drained soil. Full sun. Flowers: petals magenta with lavender markings, standard with red flare, to 7 in. wide; margins ruffled; stamens 5, sterile; very fragrant. Leaves: almost round in general

outline, bilobed, to 8 in. wide. Trunk: short, usually solitary. *Hybrid status uncertain. Sterile, no pods, noninvasive. Propagate by grafting. Pruning or wind damage may initiate multiple trunks. Very attractive to hummingbirds.*

Bauhinia divaricata

POMPOM ORCHID-TREE,
PATA DE CHIVO ("GOAT'S FOOT")
Synonyms: *B. caribaea, B. porrecta.* Mexico to Costa Rica, West Indies (Greater Antilles). Evergreen shrub or tree, 10–30 ft.; zones 9–11. Blooms intermittently all year. Moderate moisture and humidity. Fertile, well-drained soil. Full sun. Flowers: petals lance-shaped, base clawed, white turning pink; one fertile stamen; in many-flowered pendent clusters. Leaves: bilobed, lobes ovate, tips acuminate, 2–3 in. long, older leaves deeply cleft, di-

verging in a wide V. Bark: tan. *The type species is a shrub or small tree with small leaves; 'Rosea' is a more ornamental, robust tree with larger flower clusters of a deeper pink color. Leaves are at least twice as large as the type. It does not breed true from seed suggesting a possible hybrid.*

Bauhinia fassoglensis

Synonym: *B. kirkii.* Eastern Africa (Sudan to South Africa). Evergreen shrubby climber; zones 9–11. Blooms spring. Seasonally moist/dry. Well-drained soil. Full sun. Flowers: 5 petals, 4 yellow, the lower petal reduced to a pointed green stub. Leaves: suborbicular, to 4 in. wide, bilobed but often only slightly cleft. *Unusual in cultivation. Has a large tuberous root. Leaves used for forage.*

Bauhinia forficata

WHITE ORCHID-TREE, PATA DE VACA
Synonym: *B. candicans.* Peru, Brazil, Argentina, Paraguay, Uruguay. Evergreen shrub, 10–20 ft.; zones 9–10. Blooms summer. Moderate moisture to fairly dry. Fertile, well-drained soil. Full sun. Flowers: petals elliptic, clawed, pure white, erect. Leaves: bilobed, lobes cleft to the middle, elongated, spreading in a V, to 6 in. long, smooth, dark green. Spines forked (hence *forficata*). *Unusual in cultivation. A compact tree, the dark foliage setting off the white flowers. Thrives in southern California.*

Bauhinia galpinii

RED BAUHINIA,
NASTURTIUM-BAUHINIA,
PRIDE-OF-THE-KAAP ("CAPE")
Synonym: *B. punctata* (invalid). Southeastern Africa. Semideciduous scandent shrub to 25 ft.; zones 8–11. Blooms primarily spring, intermittently in summer. Seasonally moist/dry. Fertile, well-drained soil. Full sun. Flowers: petals clawed, scarlet to salmon pink, rarely yellow, to 3 in. wide; 3 fertile stamens; pods slender, to 5 in. long. Leaves: bilobed, smaller than the flowers, to 2 in. Spined. *Grows as far north as the U.S. Gulf Coast. Sheds leaves in colder regions. Fairly drought resistant. Very attractive trained over an arbor. Propagated from seed but does not set seed reliably. Perhaps self-sterile.*

Bauhinia grandidieri

Madagascar. Semideciduous shrub, 6–10 ft.; zones 9–11. Blooms intermittently in warm months. Seasonally moist/dry or moderate. Average, well-drained soil. Full sun to bright broken light. Flowers: pink-lavender, to 1.5 in. wide, in the leaf axils. Leaves: pinnate; leaflets 2, obovate, 0.5–1 in. long, in fascicles. Branches arching. *Unusual in cultivation. In dry/poor conditions the architecture is spare and arching; in moist/fertile conditions, dense and spreading. Suitable for rock gardens and Japanese-style landscaping. Propagated from cuttings.*

Bauhinia jenningsii

COW'S-TONGUE, LENGUA DE VACA
Belize, eastern Mexico, Guatemala. Evergreen shrub, 4–10 ft.; zones 10–11. Blooms intermittently in warm months. Moderate moisture. Average, well-drained soil. Full to part sun. Flowers: corolla tubular, 1.5 in. long, petals yellow, partly enclosed by the salmon-red calyx that is split on one side (spathiform); in pendent clusters. Leaves: simple, lanceolate, to 4 in. long, firm. *Unusual in cultivation. This species has simple, long leaves (hence the name cow's-tongue), not the typical bilobed or paired leaves of most Bauhinia species.*

Bauhinia fassoglensis

Bauhinia forficata

Bauhinia galpinii

Bauhinia grandidieri

Bauhinia jenningsii

Bauhinia monandra

NAPOLEON'S COCKED HAT,
PINK BUTTERFLY TREE,
PALO DE ORQUÍDEAS

Origin obscure (possibly tropical America); widely naturalized in the tropics. Semideciduous shrub or tree, 15–45 ft.; zones 9–11. Blooms spring, sporadically in summer. Seasonally moist/dry. Average, well-drained soil. Full sun. Flowers: petals 5, clawed, 2–3 in. wide, creamy white with small red spots, turning pink, standard yellow with burgundy-red spots; one stamen (hence *monandra*); in terminal panicles; fruit a flattened pod, to 9 in. long. Leaves: bilobed, each lobe ear-shaped (auricular), to 7 in. long, dull green, slightly rough. Bark: gray. *Has a spreading habit. The single stamen is a good field mark.*

Bauhinia purpurea

FALL ORCHID-TREE, PURPLE
ORCHID-TREE, PATA DE VACA

Southern China, Southeast Asia, Philippines. Deciduous shrubby tree, 15–25 ft.; zones 10–11. Blooms late summer, fall. Moderate moisture. Average to poor, well-drained soil. Full sun. Flowers: variable, petals narrowly ovate, open (valvate), spreading, 4–5 in. wide, lateral petals curved upward, pale pink to red-violet, streaked with red; stamens always 3; pods 6–9 in. long, splitting with a snap and forcefully ejecting seed. Leaves: suborbicular, bilobed, deeply cleft, 6 in. wide. *The 3 stamens are a good field mark. Multitrunked. Brittle. Prone to internal rot. Heavily self-seeding. A common volunteer around telephone poles and in empty lots.*

Not recommended. Restricted in Florida. Substitute sterile B. ×blakeana.

Bauhinia semla

SEMLA GUM

Synonyms: *B. emarginata, B. retusa, B. roxburghiana* (misapplied). India, Nepal. Evergreen tree to 45 ft.; zones 8–11. Blooms fall. Seasonally moist/dry. Average, well-drained soil. Full sun. Flowers: small, pale yellow, delicately spotted with purple; in clusters. Leaves: simple, orbicular to kidney-shaped (reniform), unlobed or sometimes slightly notched at distal end, 7 in. wide and long, dull green, smooth. Bark: dark brown, rough. *From mountain regions, fairly cold tolerant. Unusual in cultivation but an excellent shade tree. A recent study segregates* B. semla *and* B. roxburghiana

(syn. B. emarginata) *into distinct species (Wunderlin, pers. comm.).*

Bauhinia tomentosa

BELL-BAUHINIA, ST. THOMAS TREE

Synonym: *Alvesia tomentosa.* Eastern Africa; naturalized in West Indies. Evergreen shrub, 6–15 ft.; zones 9–11. Blooms warm months. Moderate moisture. Average, well-drained soil. Full sun. Flowers: corolla bell-shaped, nodding, petals not clawed, upper petal usually with a maroon spot at the base, softly downy; 2–3 in. long; in pairs; pods flat, 4–5 in. long, explosively ejecting seed (dehiscent) when ripe. Leaves: bilobed, smooth to pubescent, 2–3 in. long, musky-scented when crushed. *A variable species. One form has golden-yellow flowers, which turn salmon with age.*

Bauhinia monandra

Bauhinia purpurea

Bauhinia semla

Bauhinia tomentosa

Bauhinia tomentosa, pink form

Bauhinia vahlii

Bauhinia variegata

A more dainty selection has light yellow flowers, which are raspberry-pink on the edges, and smaller leaves. *Forma* concolor *has light yellow flowers which do not change color and lack the throat spot.*

Bauhinia vahlii

MALU CREEPER

Himalayan foothills (Pakistan, northern India, Bhutan). Semideciduous climber; zones 7–11. Blooms spring. Seasonally moist/dry. Fertile, well-drained soil. Full sun. Flowers: white, petals with ruffled margins, 2 in. wide; pistil hairy, pink; stamens 3; in compact, many-flowered racemes. Leaves: rounded, bilobed, to 10 in. wide, woolly (tomentose) on underside. *Unusual in cultivation. Aggressive, woody vine that climbs by tendrils. Needs a strong support or maintain as a sprawling shrub with regular pruning.*

Bauhinia variegata

SPRING ORCHID-TREE, BUDDHIST BAUHINIA, MOUNTAIN EBONY, ÁRBOL ORCHÍDEA

Synonym: *Phanera variegata*. Southeast Asia. Briefly deciduous tree to 40 ft.; zones 10–11. Blooms late winter, spring. Seasonally moist/dry. Average, well-drained soil. Full sun. Flowers: petals 5, broadly obovate, overlapping, pink, magenta to white, standard with magenta flame-shaped spot or streaked, fragrant; stamens 5; pod oblong, to 10 in. Leaves: round, to 7 in. long, bilobed. 'Candida' has white flowers and a greenish-yellow standard. *Stamens are often reduced to 4 in California form. Seeds sometimes eaten, high in protein. Restricted in Florida. Bauhinia purpurea has only 3 stamens and blooms in fall. Bauhinia ×blakeana always has valvate magenta petals and lacks pods.*

Bauhinia yunnanensis

YUNNAN BAUHINIA

Southern China, northern Thailand. Evergreen climber to 40 ft.+; zones 9–11. Blooms spring, summer. Seasonally moist/dry. Fertile, well-drained soil. Part sun to bright filtered light. Flowers: white with magenta veins, clawed, 1.5–2 in. across, in loose clusters. Leaves: bifoliolate, leaflets ovate, to 1.5 in. *A slender, canopy-top vine in Thailand, climbing by tendrils. Commonly misidentified as B. corymbosa (Wunderlin, pers. comm.).*

Brownea

Brownea includes approximately 12 species of trees from northern South America to Costa Rica and the West Indies. Most grow in tropical forest understory, some at moderate elevation. Leaves are pinnate. New leaves are softly pendent and pinkish, stiffening into horizontal position with age, a characteristic referred to as "pouring out." Twigs are cross-shaped or angular in cross section. Species included here are sensitive to temperatures below 45°F but should recover if not frozen. They prefer neutral to acid soil pH and regular moisture. Flowers are in compact heads, stamens long and exserted. The 2 stunning species shown here are evocative of flamenco skirts and setting suns. The inflorescences are stalkless and grow directly from the branches (cauliflorous). These are understory plants which grow in subdued light. In cul-

Bauhinia variegata

Bauhinia variegata, California variant

Bauhinia variegata 'Candida'

Bauhinia yunnanensis

tivation they are not known to set seed. They are difficult if not impossible to transplant. Browneas are attractive to nectar-feeding birds.

Brownea ariza
MOUNTAIN-ROSE, ARIZA, PALO DE CRUZ

Synonyms: *B. princeps, B. rosa-de-monte.* Fringes of Amazon basin in Colombia, Venezuela, Ecuador, Peru. Evergreen tree to 50 ft.; zones 10–11. Blooms primarily late winter, spring, or intermittently. Regular moisture and humidity. Fertile, deep, well-drained soil; acid pH. Part sun to bright filtered light. Flowers: tubular, petals red; bracts greenish; stamens long-exserted; in a pendent, skirtlike inflorescence; cauliflorous. Leaves: pinnate, to 18 in. long; leaflets 10–18, elliptic, pink and pendent when young.

Flowers grow from the underside of spreading branches that arch to the ground. Pruning lower branches and growing in an elevated location will help display the flowers to better advantage.

Brownea coccinea subsp. capitella
ROSE-OF-VENEZUELA, FLOR DE ROSA

Synonym: *B. capitella.* Brazil, Venezuela, Guyana, Trinidad, Tobago. Evergreen shrub or small tree to 15 ft.; zones 10–11. Blooms primarily late winter, spring, intermittently in warm months. Regular moisture and humidity. Fertile, well-drained soil; acid pH. Part sun, bright filtered light. Flowers: petals scarlet; stamens very long-exserted, red-orange, filaments fused at base like a comb; bracts pink, visible in half-opened inflorescence; in globular heads to 10 in. diameter; cauliflorous. Leaves: pinnate, to 18 in. long; leaflets 10–18, elliptic. *The subspecies name refers to the globular (capitate) floral heads.*

Caesalpinia

Caesalpinia (pronounced cess-al-PIN-e-ah) includes approximately 100 species of trees and shrubs from the New and Old World tropics and subtropics. They are sometimes referred to as poincianas because certain species were once placed in *Poinciana,* a genus that has been retired. Royal poinciana is in the genus *Delonix.* A number of species are difficult to distinguish. Many species come from dry habitat and are xeric in cultivation. The flowers are mostly yellow, often with red or orange markings. They are bisexual and bilaterally symmetrical. One petal is differentiated into a lip or standard. The 10 stamens are often long and showy. Leaves are twice pinnate (bipinnate), the leaflets generally ovate and frequently small. Spines are often located in the leaf axils. Seeds should be abraded and soaked overnight before planting. The wood of some species is very hard with light and dark colors (Lewis 1998). Woodworkers particularly admire the fine, ebonylike quality.

Caesalpinia cacalaco

Synonyms: *Poinciana horrida, Coulteria mexicana.* Mexico. Evergreen shrub or small tree, 10–25 ft.; zones 10–11. Blooms spring, summer. Dry. Average to poor, well-drained soil. Full sun. Flowers: yellow, lip turning red; in spirelike racemes. Leaves: bipinnate, leaflets usually 3–4 pairs, ovate, to 2 in. long, widely spaced, gray-green, tips emarginate; spines in leaf axils. *Xeric.*

Caesalpinia cassioides
CASSIA-LEAFED CAESALPINIA

Synonym: *C. bicolor.* Eastern Peru and Ecuador, Colombia. Evergreen shrub, 6–10 ft.; zones 10–11. Blooms spring, summer. Moderate moisture. Deep, sandy, well-drained soil. Full sun. Flowers: corolla folded, scarlet to dark red, lip yellow protruding as a yellow rim; calyx bell-shaped, red; lobes pointed; stamens slightly exserted. Leaves: bipinnate, leaflets broadly ovate, about 1 in. long, 4–7 pairs, tips emarginate (indented at the apex). *The inflorescences suggest schools of little red fish with golden-rimmed mouths.*

Caesalpinia echinata
BRAZIL REDWOOD, PEACH-WOOD, PERNAMBUCO WOOD, PAU BRASIL

Synonym: *C. vesicaria.* Eastern Brazil. Endangered in wild. Evergreen tree, 15–40 ft.; zones 10–11. Blooms winter. Moderate moisture. Average, well-drained soil. Full to part sun. Flowers: petals bright yellow, spreading, standard streaked red; pods half-moon shaped, prickled. Leaves: bipinnate; leaflets usually 3 pairs, oblong to broadly rhomboid, sides unequal, 0.5–2 in.

Brownea ariza

Brownea coccinea subsp. *capitella,* partially open inflorescence

Caesalpinia cacalaco

Caesalpinia cassioides

Caesalpinia echinata

Caesalpinia gilliesii

long, stiff, tip truncate, retuse. Prickles on young branches. Bark: dark gray, spotted with white lenticels, underbark red. *An erect, densely foliated tree. The heartwood is made into violin bows. A red fabric dye is extracted from the wood.*

Caesalpinia gilliesii
PARADISE-POINCIANA, BIRD-OF-PARADISE BUSH
Synonym: *Poinciana gilliesii.* Western Argentina, Chile; naturalized in Mexico, Arizona. Deciduous shrub to 6 ft.; zones 7–11. Blooms spring, summer. Dry. Deep, open, well-drained soil. Full sun. Flowers: petals small, greenish yellow; stamens long-exserted, crimson. Leaves: bipinnate; leaflets 9–11 pairs, ovate, under 0.5 in. long, black spotted on underside; petiole and rachis reddish brown; unarmed. *Leaves aromatic when crushed. Mod-*

erately salt tolerant and suitable for coastal planting. Thrives in dry climates. The somewhat similar Caesalpinia pulcherrima has spines in the leaf axils.

Caesalpinia pulcherrima
DWARF POINCIANA, PRIDE-OF-BARBADOS, PEACOCK-FLOWER, GUACAMAYO ("MACAW")
Exact origin obscure (Mexico, Central America); widely distributed. Evergreen shrub, 6–15 ft.; zones 10–11. Blooms warm months. Moderate, seasonally dry. Sandy, well-drained soil. Full sun. Flowers: petals crimson with yellow edges, or all yellow; margins ruffled; in conical racemes to 18 in. tall. Leaves: bipinnate, to 1 ft. long; leaflets 8–14 pairs, oblong, to about 1 in. Spines in leaf axils. *Salt tolerant. Prune before pods are set for repeat bloom. Susceptible to tip-borers,*

which invade hollow stems. Remove branches below infestation and destroy. Attractive to giant swallowtail butterflies. Parrots feed on pods in the wild (Meerow, pers. comm.). 'Compton' has crimson flowers with white margins.

Caesalpinia punctata
BROWN EBONY, PARTRIDGE-WOOD, EBANO
Synonyms: *C. ebano, C. granadillo.* Venezuela, Colombia. Evergreen tree, 20–30 ft.; zones 10–11. Blooms summer, fall. Moderate, seasonally dry. Average to poor, well-drained soil. Full to part sun. Flowers: corolla 0.5 in. wide, yellow, standard red specked; stamens 10; calyx brown-pubescent; in erect axillary racemes. Leaves: bipinnate; pinnae 5; leaflets 3–4 pairs, oblong, 0.5 in. long. Spineless. Bark: mottled brown, white and gray. Branches are arching. *Wood resembles ebony. This group is in the process of revision and this identification is tentative, though likely. If the genus Libidibia is revived, this species would then be L. punctata (Lewis, pers. comm.).*

Caesalpinia violacea
BRASILETTO, CHALTECOCO
Synonyms: *Brasilettia violacea, Peltophorum brasiliensis.* Mexico (Yucatan), Guatemala, Cuba, Belize, Jamaica. Evergreen erect tree to 50 ft.; zones 10–11. Blooms summer. Seasonally moist/dry. Average, deep, well-drained soil. Full sun. Flowers: yellow, standard yellow or red; stamens short; mildly fragrant; racemes to 8 in. long; pods flat, to 8 in. long. Leaves: pinnate, 8–10 in. long; leaflets 6–7 pairs, oblong, 2–3 in., tips rounded to acute, dull green, young leaves russet. Bark: gray, flaking. *Has reddish-brown heartwood. Suitable for coastal locations. When this genus is revised, this species will be placed in Coulteria (Lewis, pers. comm.).*

Caesalpinia yucatanensis
YUCATÁN CAESALPINIA
Southern Mexico, Guatemala, Nicaragua. Evergreen tree to 20 ft.; zones 10–11. Blooms intermittently all year. Moderate moisture to seasonally dry. Deep, sandy, well-

drained soil. Full sun. Flowers: petals spreading, overlapping, yellow, standard smaller, more or less orange streaked. Leaves: bipinnate, leaflets 4 pairs, ovate, to 1 in. long. Branches brittle. *Coastal. Commonly misidentified as C. mexicana, which has the upper petals and standard in a fan, well separated from the lower petals. Three subspecies vary in amount of orange on the standard and shape of the petals.*

Cassia
Cassia includes approximately 30 species of trees and shrubs from the Old and New World tropics. The genus includes several outstanding ornamental tropical trees. This group once included species now segregated into *Senna*. Cassias can be distinguished from sennas by the S-curved stamens, sometimes embellished with nodules, and leaves without glands. Leaves are pinnate. Flowers are yellow, pink, or red. All the species are hosts of sulfur butterflies. Young trees may be seriously weakened by repeatedly defoliation. Look for the tiny white eggs where the new leaves are unfurling. The caterpillars are green with black stripes when feeding on foliage or yellow and black when feeding on flowers. Since the butterfly is abundant, the caterpillars can be handpicked or a nontoxic BT (*Bacillus thuringiensis*) biological control can be applied until plants are established. Cuban May beetles nibble leaves but are only a cosmetic problem. Abrade seed and soak before planting. Add micronutrients in alkaline soils if leaves appear chlorotic (yellowish green).

Cassia afrofistula
DWARF GOLDEN SHOWER, AUTUMN GOLDEN SHOWER
Synonyms: *C. abbreviata, C. beareana* (incorrectly). Tropical eastern Africa. Evergreen tree, 15–20 ft.; zones 9–11. Blooms intermittently in warm months. Seasonally moist/dry. Average, well-drained soil. Full sun. Flowers: lemon-yellow, about 2 in. wide; 3 longest stamens have a nodule on the filament, in erect, terminal panicles, faintly fragrant; pods cylindrical, pulp corky, 15–20 in. long. Leaves:

Caesalpinia pulcherrima, scarlet and yellow forms

Caesalpinia punctata

Caesalpinia violacea

Caesalpinia yucatanensis

pinnate, to 10 in. long; leaflets 6–10 pairs, 2–3 in. long, oblanceolate to triangular, short stalked. Young branches downy. *Suitable for small gardens. Not as cold-sensitive as C. fistula. Highly recommended.*

Cassia fistula

GOLDEN SHOWER TREE, INDIAN LABURNUM, LLUVIA DE ORO, CAÑAFISTOLO

Southeast Asia; widely distributed. Briefly deciduous tree, 15–45 ft.; zones 10–11. Blooms spring, sporadically in summer, fall. Seasonally moist/dry. Fertile, well-drained soil. Full sun. Flowers: light yellow, stamen filaments not nodular; in pendent racemes to 18 in. long; pods cylindrical, seeds in sticky brown pulp. Leaves: pinnate, 10–18 in. long, dull green; leaflets asymmetrically ovate, 6–8 pairs, about 6 in. long; margins undulate. *Flowers in 3 years from seed. Leaves fall during bloom, the flowers more dramatic on* bare limbs. *Branches brittle. Species name alludes to the pipe-shaped pods.*

Cassia javanica

PINK AND WHITE SHOWER, APPLE-BLOSSOM CASSIA

Synonym: *C. javanica* var. *indochinensis*. India, southern China, Indonesia (Java), Southeast Asia, Philippines. Evergreen tree, 30–50 ft.; zones 9–11. Blooms late spring, summer. Seasonally moist/dry. Average, well-drained soil. Full sun. Flowers: pink, fading white, stamens bright yellow, 3 longer filaments with swollen nodules; in short racemes; pods cylindrical, 10–20 in. long, dark brown, irregularly produced in cultivation. Leaves: pinnate, to 1 ft.; leaflets 7–10 pairs, oblong, glabrous to downy, 1.5 in. long. Trunk: light gray, smooth. *A variable species, possibly including hybrids. Some individuals are sterile or at least self-sterile.*

Tentative varieties and subspecies have been described, but since they are all widely cultivated throughout Southeast Asia, it is not possible to associate forms with native ranges. Their taxonomy remains inconclusive (Luckow 1996).

Cassia ×nealiae

RAINBOW-SHOWER

Garden hybrid, *C. javanica* × *C. fistula*. Deciduous tree, 30–50 ft.; zones 9–11. Blooms spring, summer. Seasonally moist/dry. Average, well-drained soil. Full sun. Flowers: on long, pendent stalk. Leaves: pinnate, intergrading between the hybrid parents. *Planted as a street tree in Honolulu. Sterile. Named hybrids are 'Queen's Hospital White', light yellow fading to white; 'Lunalilo Yellow', all light yellow; and 'Wilhelmina Tenney', yellow flushed with watermelon pink (Staples, pers. comm.).*

Cassia roxburghii

CEYLON CASSIA, RED CASSIA

Synonym: *C. marginata*. Sri Lanka, southern India. Evergreen tree, 15–30 ft.; zones 9–11. Blooms late summer, fall. Seasonally moist/dry. Full to part sun. Flowers: dark pink, 1 in. wide; stamens in groups of 3 different sizes. Leaves: pinnate,

Cassia afrofistula

Cassia fistula

Cassia javanica

Cassia fistula, flowers

Cassia ×*nealiae* 'Wilhelmina Tenney'

Cassia roxburghii

Cassia javanica, flowers

Cassia roxburghii, flowers

5–16 in. long; leaflets 10–20 pairs, oblong to rhombic, 1–2 in. long, faintly downy, tips emarginate or mucronate; in opposite ranks (distichous). New leaves pinkish. *Rounded dense canopy. Limbs cascade to the ground displaying the flowers on the upper side. Somewhat cold tolerant. Unusual but highly recommended.*

Colvillea

Colvillea includes a single species of large tree from Madagascar. The racemes of orange and yellow flowers are borne mostly near the top of mature specimens and are visible from a distance. With all its attributes, this species would be more common in cultivation if seeds were not difficult to collect. They are small and dispersed from on high, getting lost in the grass. When pods are ripe, plastic or cloth sheets can be laid on the ground to catch falling seed. Especially suited for landscaping where a straight trunk, minimal spread, and minimal debris are desirable. *Colvillea* is xeric, pest resistant, and low maintenance. Unusual ornamental for fall, a season with relatively few large flowering trees. Highly recommended.

Colvillea racemosa

COLVILLE'S GLORY
Madagascar. Threatened in wild. Evergreen tree to 50 ft.+; zones 9–11. Blooms fall. Seasonally moist/dry. Full sun. Flowers: calyx and buds round, bright orange, splitting open on one side allowing the golden-yellow stamens to protrude through the slit; in dense, spirelike, terminal racemes; pods woody, flat, to 8 in., splitting open (dehiscent) when ripe. Leaves: bipinnate, fernlike, to 25 in. long; leaflets very small. Trunk: rust to maroon, rough. *Fairly unusual in cultivation. Pods attractive to parrots. Xeric.*

Delonix

Delonix includes 10 species of trees from Madagascar, Africa, and India. Only a single species is commonly grown. Royal poinciana, *D. regia*, is considered the quintessential tropical flowering tree. It thrives in moist, humid climates with dry, mild winters. It does not flourish in California's climate and it does not bloom well in constantly moist tropics such as Singapore (Tan, pers. comm.). In Florida, trees go dormant in winter. In late spring, flowers burst open on bare limbs quickly followed by the fernlike leaves. Fast-growing, royal poincianas begin blooming when 3–4 years old, developing a full umbrella canopy by age 10. Plant 30 ft. from roadways, power lines, and buildings. The spread will be wider than the height. The trees are ideally located in open areas where branches cascade fully. Drastic pruning is not recommended. Removal of lower branches results in a funnel-shaped tree with flowers facing up so only the undersides are visible below. Because roots are superficial, under-plant with aroids, ferns, and bromeliads.

Flowers are scarlet, orange or, rarely, yellow. The standard is normally white with magenta markings. It lasts only a day while the flower is receptive, probably acting as a flag for nectar-feeding birds. The pod is very large, flat, and woody. Propagated from abraded and soaked seed. Color selections must be grafted. Night illumination seems to diminish bloom. Do not irrigate while dormant.

Delonix regia

ROYAL POINCIANA, FLAMBOYÁN, ÁRBOL DEL FUEGO, GUL MOHUR (INDIA), 'OHAI-'ULA (HAWAII) Madagascar, endangered in the wild. Deciduous tree, 40–50 ft.; zones 10–11. Blooms late spring, summer. Seasonally moist/dry. Average, well-drained soil. Full sun.

Flowers: petals clawed, orange to scarlet, standard white with burgundy spots; pod woody, 18–24 in. long, 3 in. wide, splitting on both sides, seeds transverse. Leaves: bipinnate, 12–16 in. long; leaflets tiny, emerald green. Bark: smooth, gray. *'Kampong Yellow'*, a sterile selection from Guyana, has light yellow

Colvillea racemosa, inflorescence

Delonix regia, flowers

Delonix regia 'Kampong Yellow'

Delonix regia 'Smather's Gold' with normal red

petals, white standard, and pinkish anthers. 'Smather's Gold' has golden-yellow petals and orange streaked standard.

Moullava

Moullava includes a single species of climber from India. It is possibly a threatened species. It is rarely cultivated, doubtless because it is densely armed with small, curved prickles. The inflorescences, however, are quite spectacular. Flowers are small in elongated panicles. Leaves are twice pinnate (bipinnate).

Moullava spicata

FALSE THORN, RAT-BEAN

Synonym: *Wagatea spicata*. Southwestern India; introduced Mauritius, Tanzania. Evergreen shrub; zones 10–11. Blooms late fall, winter. Seasonally moist/dry. Average, well-drained soil. Full sun. Flowers: corolla fleshy, yellow, never fully opening; calyx orange; in long panicles, 12–16 in. long. Leaves: bipinnate; pinnae 6–9 in. long; leaflets 6–7 pairs, ovate to elliptic, 1–2 in. long, somewhat unequal halves. Small, curved prickles on vegetative parts. *Unusual in cultivation. Branches long and clambering by the prickles, not twining.*

Parkinsonia

Parkinsonia includes approximately 29 species of deciduous trees and shrubs from drier areas of the Americas and from northeastern and South Africa. Though often described as evergreen, the tiny leaflets are deciduous, leaving the flattened, almost needlelike green rachis, or cladophyll, as the primary photosynthesizing organ. This reduction of surface area decreases evaporation, allowing the plant to thrive in arid conditions. Several *Parkinsonia* species are referred to as palo verde, meaning "green plant." Some were formerly segregated into the genus *Cercidium*. These plants do well in moist climates if provided excellent drainage, but the signature green coloration will blacken with mold and the plants will fail to thrive if fertilized and overwatered. Xeric and heat tolerant. Suitable for coastal locations. Invasive in Australia.

Parkinsonia aculeata

MEXICAN PALO VERDE, JERUSALEM-THORN, ESPINILLO

Exact origin obscure (Texas, Arizona, Mexico to Argentina); widely naturalized. Deciduous tree to 30 ft.; zones 8–11. Blooms intermittently in warm months. Moderate moisture, seasonally dry. Poor, gritty, well-drained soil. Full sun. Flowers: petals yellow, standard streaked russet; in loose racemes in the leaf axils; pods to 6 in. long. Leaves: pinnate, leaflets tiny, deciduous; rachis a linear, flattened phyllode, to 12 in. long, apple-green. Spines in axils. Trunk: brown, young branches green, older branches brown. *A graceful airy tree.*

Peltophorum

Peltophorum includes approximately 8 species of trees from the Old and New World tropics. Leaves are twice pinnate. The American species have microscopic, peglike hairs on the leaves (Barneby 1996). Flowers are yellow, the petals crumpled, in many-flowered racemes. Pods are lance-shaped, flat, with broad wings around the edges, the source of the common name shield tree. The cultivated species are suitable for shade trees and are easy to grow and maintain. Cut for lumber in the wild. A yellow fabric dye is extracted from *P. pterocarpum*. These species are often referred to as yellow poincianas, leading to confusion with yellow forms of royal poinciana, *Delonix regia*, which bloom about the same time.

Peltophorum africanum

AFRICAN FLAME-TREE, AFRICAN WATTLE, WEEPING WATTLE

Synonym: *Brasilettia africana*. Central eastern to southern Africa. Evergreen tree to 40 ft.; zones 8–11. Blooms spring, early summer. Moderate moisture to fairly dry. Average, well-drained soil. Full sun. Flowers: petals yellow, crumpled; anthers orange-yellow; buds 5-ribbed, with fine, light-brown hairs when young; on short pedicels; racemes compact, unbranched, spirelike to 10 in. tall; pods to 2 in. long, seeds 1–2. Leaves: bipinnate; leaflets small, about 20 pairs, ovate, tips mucronate. *A large lumber tree. Distinguished by the compact, little branched, spirelike inflorescences. From moderate altitude. Needs irrigation in hot, arid conditions.*

Parkinsonia aculeata, flowers and cladophylls

Moullava spicata

Parkinsonia aculeata

Peltophorum africanum

Peltophorum dubium

BRAZILIAN FLAME-TREE,
FAVEIRO OU SOBRASIL (BRAZIL)
Synonyms: *Caesalpinia dubia, P. vogelianum*. Uruguay, Argentina, Bolivia, southern Brazil. Evergreen tree to 30 ft., rarely to 75 ft.; zones 8–11. Blooms summer. Moderate moisture to seasonally dry. Average, well-drained soil. Full sun. Flowers: petals crinkled, yellow, mildly fragrant; calyx greenish; in open, branched panicles; pods green, to 3 in. long, flat, attenuated at the ends, narrowly winged; seeds 1–3. Leaves: bipinnate, to 1 ft. long; about 20 leaflets per pinnae, 0.5 in. long, tips mucronate. Bark: smooth, light gray. *From moderate altitude. Tends to bloom alternate years. Weedy in central Florida. Var. berteroanum is native to the West Indies.*

Peltophorum pterocarpum

COPPERPOD, RUSTY-SHIELD TREE
Synonyms: *P. ferrugineum, P. inerme.* Sri Lanka, southern India, Southeast Asia, Malaysia to Australia; widely distributed. Evergreen tree, 30 ft.+; zones 10–11. Blooms primarily late spring, early summer, fall. Seasonally moist/dry. Average, well-drained soil. Full sun. Flowers: petals crinkled, golden-yellow, fragrant at night; in panicles to 1.5 ft.; buds covered with rust-colored hairs; pods dark copper-red, lance-shaped, to 4 in. long; margins broadly winged. Leaves: bipinnate, 18–24 in. long; leaflets ovate, to 1 in.; tip indented (retuse). Young twigs covered with rust-colored hairs. *Dense, rounded canopy. Coastal. Deciduous in very dry conditions. Individual trees may bloom at different times.*

Saraca

Saraca includes approximately 11 species of trees from Indomalaysia. Petals are reduced. Calyces and bracteoles are showy. The flowers are sometimes produced directly on the branches and/or trunk (cauliflorous). Leaves are pinnate. New leaves are initially limp and pink, gradually turning green and stiffening into the horizontal position with maturity, a phenomenon referred to as "pouring out." Somewhat cold-sensitive, young trees benefit from the cover of nearby trees. They may be slow getting established but then grow rapidly. Saracas grow along riverbanks in the native habitat but thrive in less moist situations with plenty of mulch. Considered sacred to Buddhists, this tree is often planted around temples. The Buddha is believed to have been born under a saraca tree. Asoka or asok (pronounced ah-SHO-ka or AH-shock) is named in honor of a third-century-B.C. king of Magadha (northern India), who converted to and disseminated Buddhism. Hindus also regard the tree as a symbol of love.

Saraca indica

SORROWLESS TREE, ASOKA, ASOK
Southeast Asia to Indonesia (Java). Evergreen tree, 50–75 ft.; zones 10–11. Blooms winter, spring. Seasonally moist/dry. Fertile, well-drained soil; acid pH. Full sun to bright filtered light. Flowers: calyces and bracteoles yellow and orange, fragrant at night; often cauliflorous; pods flat, 2 in. wide, 6 in. long, dark red. Leaves: pinnate, leaflets 10, to 8 in. long; young

Peltophorum pterocarpum

Peltophorum dubium var. *dubium*

Saraca indica

Peltophorum pterocarpum, flowers and pods

Schotia brachypetala

leaves pink, limply pendent. *Bloom initiated by a dry period. Starts blooming when young. Attractive to butterflies.* Saraca thaipingensis *has all-yellow flowers.*

Schotia

Schotia includes 4 or 5 species of trees and shrubs from South Africa. One species is occasionally cultivated in the western United States and elsewhere. *Schotia brachypetala* is a spreading tree producing red flowers in summer. It does well in coastal California but blooms meagerly in South Florida possibly due to summer moisture and/or alkaline soil pH. The dark wood takes on a walnutlike polish, and the sawdust is said to be irritating to the eyes. Seeds are eaten in Africa.

Schotia brachypetala
TREE FUCHSIA, AFRICAN WALNUT, WEEPING BOER-BOON ("BOER BEAN")
Synonyms: *S. latifolia, S. semireducta*. Southeastern Africa, South Africa. Deciduous tree to 40 ft.; zones 8–10. Blooms spring, summer. Moderate moisture to dry. Average to poor, well-drained soil. Full sun. Flowers: petals reduced; calyx 4-lobed, rubbery, crimson; terminal or in the leaf axils or on the trunk (pachycaulous); pods woody, to 4 in. long. Leaves: pinnate, leaflets ovate, 4–7 pairs, pink to coppery when young. *Found in protected valley scrublands in South Africa (KwaZulu-Natal) and high veldt woodlands of Zimbabwe. Tolerates drought. The species name means "short petals."*

Senna

Senna includes 250–350 species of trees, shrubs, and herbs mostly from the tropics and subtropics. Many former *Cassia* species have been segregated into this genus. The flowers are usually yellow, rarely white, and have 5 unequal petals. Stamens are curved but not S-shaped as in *Cassia*. Leaves are pinnate, usually with nectaries (glands) on the petiole or rachis (midrib). Identification is based on the minutia of the number and size of fertile stamens, the number of leaflets, and the type and location of the glands. Sennas have a number of pharmaceutical uses, best known as an ingredient of certain laxatives. The roots add nitrogen to the soil. Some species are used as "green manure" by plowing under before planting the main food crop. Sennas are attractive to sulfur butterflies and may be periodically defoliated by the caterpillars. This serves as a natural "pruning" which is not harmful to established plants. Since sulfurs are an abundant species and birds feed on the caterpillars, avoid toxic chemicals. A nontoxic BT (*Bacillus thuringiensis*) biological control can be used until plants are established.

Senna alata
CANDLESTICK SENNA, RINGWORM SENNA, CANDELILLO
Synonyms: *Cassia alata, S. bracteata*. Tropical America; widely naturalized. Perennial shrub, 3–7 ft.; zones 9–11. Blooms warm months. Moderate moisture. Average, well-drained soil. Full sun. Flowers: petals and sepals yellow, cup-shaped; yellow, petal-like shielding bracts cover buds; stamens 2 fertile plus 5 staminodes; in dense, spirelike racemes on erect stalks; pods 4-angled with 4 papery wings, 4–8 in. long. Leaves: dull green, 1.5–2.5 ft. long; leaflets 6–14 pairs, oblong, 3–6 in. long, tip retuse or rounded; nectaries absent. Stems: pithy center. *One common name alludes to use as a folk remedy of unknown value for ringworm.* Senna didymobotrya *is similar but has bronze bracts and smaller leaflets.*

Senna artemisioides
SILVER SENNA, WOODWORM SENNA, PUNTY
Synonym: *Cassia artemisioides*. Australia. Evergreen shrub, 3–8 ft.; zones 9–11. Blooms intermittently all year. Moderate, drought tolerant. Open, well-drained soil. Full to part sun. Flowers: cup-shaped, yellow, fragrant; fertile stamens 10, anthers dark brown; in axillary clusters; pods small, flat, brown. Leaves: pinnate; leaflets variable among subspecies, usually 2–8 pairs, flat or rolled into needles or replaced by phyllodes (flattened petioles), gray-green, downy, 2–3 in. long. Stems: covered with light gray hairs. *Suitable for hot, arid regions. Xeric. Several subspecies with quite variable foliage were previously considered to be a group of complex hybrids. Needle-leafed subsp.* filifolia *is sometimes cultivated.*

Senna bicapsularis
YELLOW CANDLE-WOOD, RAMBLING CASSIA, CHRISTMAS BUSH
Synonyms: *Cassia bicapsularis, S. pendula* (misapplied). West Indies, tropical America. Semideciduous scrambling shrub to 10 ft.; zones 9–11. Blooms intermittently in warm months. Moderate moisture, seasonally dry. Average, well-drained soil. Full to part sun. Flowers: yellow, 1–1.5 in. wide; stamens 6 fertile plus one staminode; pods cylindrical. Leaves: pinnate, 3–5 in. long; leaflets 3–5 pairs, obovate, tips obtuse or rounded, 2–3 in. long; one or more nectaries on rachis between lower leaflets. *Weedy in California. Name commonly misapplied to* S. pendula *in Florida.*

Senna corymbosa
ARGENTINE SENNA
South America; naturalized from Texas to South Carolina, Florida. Semideciduous shrub to 12 ft.; zones 8–11. Blooms warm months. Moderate moisture, seasonally dry. Average, well-drained soil. Full to part sun. Flowers: bright yellow, spreading; fertile stamens 7, in 2 lengths; pods cylindrical. Leaves: pinnate, leaflets 2–3 pairs, narrowly lanceolate-oblong, 1.5 in. long, tip acuminate; nectaries usually 1, cylindrical, between lower leaflets. *Leaflets are relatively small and narrow compared to other commonly grown species. Deciduous in cold or dry conditions.*

Senna alata

Senna artemisioides

Senna bicapsularis

Senna corymbosa

Senna didymobotrya

POPCORN SENNA, AFRICAN SENNA
Synonyms: *Cassia didymobotrya*, *Cassia nairobensis*. Central and eastern Africa; widely naturalized. Semideciduous shrub, 6–10 ft.; zones 8–11. Blooms warm months. Moderate moisture, seasonally dry. Average, well-drained soil. Full sun. Flowers: cupped to almost spreading, yellow; buds covered by bronze-black shielding bracts; in erect, dense, spirelike racemes; pods flat, not winged, to 3 in. long, seeds transverse. Leaves: pinnate, to 1 ft. long; leaflets 8–16 pairs, oblong, tips mucronate, downy, nectaries absent, musky-scented. *Fast-growing. Especially attractive stepped up a slope. Habit similar to* S. alata *but with bronze bracts, flat pods, and smaller, pointed leaflets.*

Senna ligustrina

WILD PRIVET SENNA
Synonym: *Cassia bahamensis*. Caribbean basin including Central and South Florida. Evergreen shrub, 6–10 ft.; zones 8–11. Blooms spring. Seasonally moist/dry. Average, well-drained soil. Full sun. Flowers: yellow, to 1 in. wide; pods flat. Leaves: pinnate, 4–10 in. long; leaflets 4–8 pairs, lanceolate, tips acuminate; nectaries cylindrical or conical, at base of petioles; somewhat musky-scented. *Spreading habit. Self-seeding. The species and common names allude to a slight resemblance to privet,* Ligustrum *species.*

Senna mexicana var. chapmanii

BAHAMA SENNA,
CHAPMAN'S SENNA
Synonyms: *Cassia bahamensis* (misapplied), *S. chapmanii*. Bahamas, Cuba, South Florida. Evergreen shrub, 4–10 ft.; rarely a tree to 25 ft.; zones 9–11. Blooms warm months. Seasonally moist/dry. Sandy, well-drained soil. Full sun. Flowers: yellow; stamens 7 fertile; in axillary or terminal panicles; pods flat, 3–4 in. long, slightly curved; seeds transverse. Leaves: pinnate, 3–5 in. long; leaflets 4–5 pairs, elliptic to lanceolate, 1–2 in. long, tips mucronate; nectaries round, on rachis between lower leaflets. *Of coastal scrub and pinelands (Correll, 1996).*

Senna pendula var. glabrata

GOLDEN SENNA, BUTTERCUP SENNA
Synonym: *S. coluteoides*. Southern and eastern Brazil. Semideciduous scrambling shrub, 10–15 ft.; zones 9–11. Blooms primarily late winter, spring, or intermittently. Moderate moisture, seasonally dry. Average, well-drained soil. Full sun. Flowers: corolla cupped, golden-yellow, somewhat nodding, 1 in. wide; calyx green; stamens 6 fertile plus 1 staminode, stigmas large, brown; pod cylindrical, filled with sticky pulp. Leaves: pinnate, 3–5 in.; leaflets usually 4 pairs but 2–5 possible, ovate, 1–2 in. long; one or more conspicuous round nectaries on rachis between lower leaflets. *Often incorrectly listed as S. bicapsularis in Florida. Weedy and invasive.*

Senna polyphylla

DESERT SENNA,
SMALL-LEAFED SENNA
Synonym: *Cassia microphylla*. Puerto Rico, Virgin Islands, Hispaniola. Evergreen tree, 8–15 ft.; zones 10–11. Blooms intermittently fall, winter, spring. Moderate moisture. Average, well-drained soil. Full sun. Flowers: yellow, in pairs or small clusters in the leaf

Senna didymobotrya

Senna mexicana var. *chapmanii*

Senna ligustrina

Senna polyphylla

axils. Leaves: dimorphic, primary leaves very small, deciduous; secondary leaves 2–3 in. long, leaflets 4–12 pairs, less than 0.5 in. long. *Xeric. Good for winter color. Distinguished by the very small leaflets and a spreading bonsai-like habit. The common name "twin flower" should be reserved for* S. pallida *(syn.* Cassia biflora*).*

Senna racemosa

Synonym: *Cassia ekmaniana.* Yucatan, southern Mexico, Guatemala to Costa Rica, Cuba. Briefly deciduous tree, 12–35 ft.; zones 10–11. Blooms warm months. Moderate, seasonally dry. Average, well-drained soil. Full sun. Flowers: small, yellow, to 1 in. wide, sweetly fragrant. Leaves: pinnate; leaflets usually 5 pairs but 4–12 possible, lanceolate, tips acuminate, downy below. Bark: gray-white. *Unusual in cultivation. Suitable for coastal and fairly dry locations.*

Senna spectabilis

SPECTACULAR SENNA, CANDELILLO
Synonym: *Cassia spectabilis.* Central and South America. Evergreen tree, 15–25 ft.; zones 10–11. Blooms fall, winter. Seasonally moist/dry. Average, well-drained soil. Full sun. Flowers: yellow, to 1.5 in. wide, petals sometimes unequal, curved; in erect terminal panicles; pod slender, subcylindrical, to 1 ft. long. Leaves: pinnate, 10–20 in.; leaflets 6–18 pairs, lanceolate to elliptic, tips acute, downy, brownish hairs on young shoots. *Variable forms were formerly segregated into numerous species. Used as a living fence and to control erosion. A form cultivated in Thailand is described with a single enlarged lateral petal (Gardner et al. 2000). Weedy in moist conditions.*

Senna sulfurea

Synonyms: *Cassia arborescens, S. surattensis* subsp. *sulfurea.* India, Indomalaysia, Southeast Asia, tropical Australia. Semideciduous tree, 15–20 ft.; zones 10–11. Blooms warm months. Moderate moisture to seasonally dry. Average, well-drained soil. Full sun. Flowers: yellow, to 2 in. wide; stamens 10, fertile, equal length filaments short; in erect terminal clusters; pods flat,

papery, 12–16 in. long. Leaves: pinnate; leaflets usually 4–8 pairs, obovate, dark green, to 3 in. long. *The taxonomy of this species is still unsettled. All parts larger than* S. surattensis. *The dense panicles are distinctive. Sometimes the species is incorrectly called* S. surattensis *"beareana type," possibly a confusion with* Cassia afrofistula *(syn.* C. beareana*).*

Senna surattensis

SCRAMBLED-EGG TREE, GLAUCOUS SENNA
Synonyms: *Cassia glauca, Cassia surattensis.* India, Indomalaysia, Southeast Asia, tropical Australia. Evergreen shrub or tree to 15 ft.; zones 9–11. Blooms intermittently fall, winter, spring. Moderate moisture to seasonally dry. Average, well-drained soil. Full sun. Flowers: yellow, 1–1.5 in. wide, sepals unequal; 10 fertile stamens, 1 long; in

semierect clusters; pods flat, papery, 4–8 in. long. Leaves: pinnate, 3–10 in. long; leaflets usually 6–9 pairs, obovate to oblong, to 2 in. long, tip rounded, bluish green; club-shaped nectaries on the rachis between lower 2 or all leaflets.

Tamarindus

Tamarindus includes a single species from the Old World tropics, a cultigen unknown in the wild. Leaves are evenly pinnate. Each flower has 2 bracteoles. The 3 upper petals are showy, the lower 2 reduced. All but 3 stamens are reduced to scalelike staminodes. Tamarind has been grown for generations for the tart-sweet brown pulp around the seeds. The pulp has a datelike consistency and imparts its distinctive flavor to Worcestershire and steak sauces. It is an important ingredient in Indian chutneys, as a

candy, and in Asian dishes and sauces. In the West Indies and Latin America, it is used to make refreshing drinks and sherbet. The tree grows along riverbanks as well as in areas with seasonally moist/dry climates. It is an excellent shade tree and wind resistant. Seed distributed by animals.

Tamarindus indica

TAMARIND, INDIAN DATE, TAMARINDO
Synonym: *T. occidentalis.* Tropical Africa; widely cultivated. Evergreen tree to 60 ft.; zones 10–11. Blooms intermittently, primarily in summer. Seasonally moist/dry. Average, well-drained soil. Full sun. Flowers: petals creamy white with brown veins; bracts and bracteoles orange; fertile stamens 3, partly united; in pendent racemes; pods curved, 4–6 in. long, brown, rough,

Senna pendula var. *glabrata*

Senna polyphylla, flowers

Senna racemosa

Senna spectabilis

Senna sulfurea

Senna surattensis

constricted between seeds. Leaves: pinnate, 4–5 in. long; leaflets small, 10–18 pairs, oblong, tip retuse. Bark: gray, wrinkled. *Fairly slow-growing with a spreading, rounded crown and pendent branches. Used as a street or shade tree. Sometimes used for bonsai.*

FABACEAE
Subfamily Mimosoideae

Mimosoideae includes approximately 40 genera of mostly trees and shrubs, which are widely distributed. Some members of this subfamily are referred to as mimosas though they should not be mistaken for the genus *Mimosa*. Leaves are bipinnate (twice-divided), often fine and featherlike. Flowers are bisexual and radially symmetrical. Petals and sepals are often small and well hidden by the stamens, which are numerous and showy.

Acacia

Acacia includes 1000–1200 species of spiny trees, shrubs, and herbs from the tropics and mild temperate regions, predominantly Australia and southern Africa where acacias are known as thorn-trees or wattles. A number of species come from America and a few from western Pacific Islands. Leaves are twice pinnate (bipinnate), the leaflets very small. The hard seedcoats are abraded, boiled, and soaked before planting.

This genus features a number of interesting adaptations. Certain, mainly arid, species lack true leaves. Instead, they have green bladelike phyllodes, which are actually flattened petioles. The reduction of surface area decreases evaporation. Another adaptation is a symbiotic relationship with ants. Some species lack the bitter alkaloids that protect most other acacias. Instead, the ant plants produce beltian bodies on young leaflets, which produce fatty proteins that attract stinging ants. The queen ant lays her eggs in the hollow thorns and, while the larvae develop, soldier ants provide protection to the plant against herbivores.

In Africa hoofed animals such as giraffes browse on acacias daintily avoiding the thorns with their supple lips. *Acacia confusa, A. farnesiana, A. mearnsii,* and *A. melanoxylon* are invasive in Hawaii.

Acacia auriculiformis
EAR-POD ACACIA, DARWIN BLACK WATTLE (AUSTRALIA)
New Guinea, northern Australia. Evergreen tree to 50 ft.; zones 10–11. Blooms primarily late summer, fall. Moist to dry. Poor, sandy, well-drained soil. Full sun. Flowers: tiny; stamens yellow; in catkinlike, drooping spikes; coiled pods vaguely resemble human ears; seeds black, attached to ovary wall by bright orange, threadlike funicles. Leaves: blades absent, sickle-shaped phyllodes, 5–7 in. long. Bark: shredding. *Fast growing and brittle in windstorms. Invasive. Prohibited in South Florida. Removal recommended. Harvesting for the fine-grained cabinet wood should be considered as a control.*

Acacia baileyana
BAILEY'S THORN-TREE, GOLDEN MIMOSA, COOTAMUNDRA WATTLE (AUSTRALIA)
Australia (New South Wales). Evergreen tree to 20 ft.+; zones 8–10. Blooms winter, spring. Moderate moisture, seasonally dry. Average to poor, well-drained soil. Full sun. Flowers: tiny, yellow; in globular heads, to 0.25 in. wide; in many-flowered clusters; pods blue-gray, to 4 in. long. Leaves: bipinnate, to 2 in. long, stiff; leaflets tiny, bluish gray. *A stunning, small tree for Medi-*

terranean-type or fairly dry climates. Tends to be short-lived. Borers may infect plants in decline but are not thought to cause the decline. 'Purpurea' has purplish-gray leaves.

Acacia sphaerocephala
BULLHORN ACACIA, CACHO DE TORO
Central Mexico. Deciduous shrub; zones 9–11. Blooms spring. Seasonally moist/dry. Average to poor, well-drained soil. Full sun. Flowers: small; stamens yellow; in ovoid heads, 0.5 in. diameter. Leaves: bipinnate, to 4 in. long; leaflets small, dark green. Pairs of hornlike hollow spines, to 4 in. long, in leaf axils. *Blooms on bare branches before new leaves. Ants in the wild are attracted by the beltian bodies. Species name alludes to the spherical heads of flowers.*

Acacia tortuosa
TWISTED ACACIA, PICA-PICA ("STICKER-BUSH")
Synonyms: *A. parvifolia, Mimosa tortuosa.* West Indies, northern South America. Evergreen shrub or tree, 10–20 ft.; zones 10–11. Blooms intermittently, primarily winter, spring. Seasonally moist/dry. Average to poor, well-drained soil. Full sun. Flowers: small, fragrant; stamens yellow; in round heads to 0.5 in. wide; on stalks to 2 in.; usually solitary; pods subcylindrical, 3–5 in. long, rough (coriaceous). Leaves: bipinnate with 4–10 pairs of pinnae; leaflets tiny, 10–20 pairs, oblong, more or less downy. Small spines in axils. *Coastal. The species name alludes to the twisting of the pods after they open and/or the convoluted branching habit.*

Tamarindus indica

Acacia auriculiformis

Acacia baileyana

Acacia sphaerocephala

Acacia sphaerocephala, leaves showing beltian bodies

Adenanthera

Adenanthera includes approximately 10 species of trees from Southeast Asia to Australia and the Pacific Islands. Harvested for timber, dye, and fine cabinet wood. The genus name is derived from a tiny deciduous gland on the anthers. The red seeds are so uniform in weight that they have been used as standards to measure gold in Arabia and India. The seed of *Adenanthera* is exactly twice the weight of *Abrus*, another standard used in the Far East.

Adenanthera pavonina

RED SANDALWOOD, CORAL-PEA, CORAL-WOOD, CIRCASSIAN BEAN
Southeast Asia to Australia; widely naturalized. Deciduous tree, 45–50 ft.; zones 10–11. Blooms late winter, spring, summer. Moderate moisture to dry. Most well-drained soils. Full sun. Flowers: small, unpleasantly scented, petals white, anthers yellow; in elongated spikes in the leaf axils or in terminal panicles; pods slender to 12 in. long, curling after splitting, seeds bright scarlet, lens-shaped (lenticular). Leaves: bipinnate, to 12 in. long, with 2–5 pairs of pinnae; leaflets ovate, 4–6 staggered pairs. Unarmed. *Invasive. Prohibited in South Florida. Harvesting for fine wood suggested as a control. One common name alludes to Circassia, an area around the Black Sea.*

Albizia

Albizia includes 130–150 species of trees, shrubs, and climbers, which are widely distributed in the tropics and mild temperate areas. Some are referred to as mimosas but should not be confused with the genus *Mimosa*. The leaves are twice pinnate (bipinnate). Flowers have long, often showy, stamens. Inflorescences are compact heads or spikes. Curiously, the common spelling "albizzia" is incorrect even though that is the way Filippo degli Albizzi, who introduced *A. julibrissin* to Europe, spelled his name.

Albizia julibrissin

SILK-TREE, MIMOSA, PINK SIRIS, PERSIAN ACACIA
Iran, Asia; naturalized in the United States. Deciduous tree, 20–30 ft.; zones 7–9. Blooms late winter, spring. Moderate moisture. Sandy, well-drained soil. Full sun. Flowers: petals inconspicuous; stamens white with pink tips, to 3 in. long; in many-flowered clusters. Leaves: bipinnate, dark green; leaflets small, pointed. *Spreading tree, often with more than one trunk. Thrives in coastal regions but not salt tolerant. Weedy in some areas. Short-lived in humid regions where it is susceptible to mimosa wilt. Some cultivars are more wilt resistant.*

Albizia lebbeck

LEBBECK TREE, WHISTLING BEAN, WOMAN'S TONGUE
Tropical Asia and Africa; widely naturalized. Deciduous tree, 25–75 ft.; zones 9–11. Blooms late winter, spring, early summer. Moderate moisture. Most well-drained soils. Full sun. Flowers: stamens greenish white, jasmine-scented at night; in heads; pods broad, flat, tan, in clusters. Leaves: bipinnate; pinnae 6–10 in. long; leaflets mostly 5–6 pairs, oblong, sides

Acacia tortuosa

Adenanthera pavonina, pods and seeds

Albizia julibrissin

unequal, 1.5–2 in. long; subsessile. *Dry pods rustle in the wind, accounting for some common names. Invasive. Widely naturalized in South Florida though prohibited from distribution. Controls include harvesting for forage and fuel.*

Albizia niopoides

CARIBBEAN ALBIZIA, GUANACASTE
Synonyms: *A. caribaea, A. richardiana*. Tropical America, southern Antilles. Briefly deciduous tree to 100 ft.+; zones 10–11. Blooms warm months. Seasonally moist/dry. Average, well-drained soil. Full sun. Flowers: white, inconspicuous. Leaves: bipinnate, dark green. Bark: gray-white. *A stately, erect tree, developing a strong trunk with buttresses and a high canopy. Sheds leaves gradually with minimal litter. Unusual in cultivation but an excellent tree for open areas, providing perfect light filtration for understory plants.*

Archidendron

Archidendron includes approximately 90 species from Indomalaysia to New Guinea and Australia. Unusual in cultivation in the United States. The name means "chief tree," alluding to the great size of some species. The curved, orange pods are tightly constricted around the coin-shaped seeds. The seeds are blue to blue-black and hang by orange threads (funiculi) when the pod opens.

Archidendron lucyi

TASSEL-TREE
Synonym: *Affonsea lucyi*. Papua New Guinea, Australia. Evergreen tree, 15–25 ft.; zones 10–11. Blooms fall. Seasonally moist/dry. Average, well-drained soil. Full to part sun. Flowers: white, fragrant; in clusters on green, pendent stalks growing directly from the branches (cauliflorous); pod curved like a C, orange, constricted around the seeds; seeds disk-shaped, blue-black. Leaves pinnate; leaflets ovate, 3–4 in. long. *Unusual in cultivation in the United States. Related to Ebenopsis.*

Albizia niopoides

Albizia lebbeck

Calliandra haematocephala

Archidendron lucyi

Archidendron lucyi, pod

Calliandra

Calliandra includes approximately 200 species of small trees and shrubs from tropical and subtropical America, tropical Africa, India, and Madagascar. Leaves are bipinnate, the pinnae often reduced to a single pair branching in a Y. The corolla is tubular, mostly hidden by showy stamen filaments. The genus name alludes to the beautiful stamens. The flattened pod is oblanceolate or linear with swollen edges, splitting and dispersing seed from the tip (Howard 1989). The flowers retain a fresh appearance longer with a little light filtration from high canopy at midday. Add microelements and mulch well in alkaline soil. Attractive to nectar-feeding birds and butterflies. A number of species are cultivated. Some are difficult to distinguish. The size and number of the leaflets are good field marks.

Calliandra haematocephala

POWDER-PUFF, BELLOTA, GRANOLINO, CALIANDRA

Synonym: *C. inaequilatera*. Bolivia; widely cultivated. Evergreen shrub, 6–20 ft.; zones 10–11. Blooms primarily winter, spring. Moderate moisture. Fertile, well-drained soil. Full sun to bright broken or filtered light. Flowers: petals small; stamens to 2 in. long, crimson-tipped, white at base. Leaves: bipinnate, with one pair of pinnae; leaflets 5–8 pairs, elliptic, to 2 in. long, curved, sides unequal (oblique). *The species name means "red head." 'Alba' is* pure white. *'Nana' is a dwarf form suitable for bonsai. It could be confused with young plants of* C. tergamina *except for the more numerous leaflets.*

Calliandra houstoniana

Synonym: *Mimosa houstoniana*. Mexico to El Salvador. Evergreen shrub or tree, 6–8 ft.; zones 10–11. Blooms variously late summer to spring. Seasonally moist or wet/dry. Average, well-drained soil. Full to part sun. Flowers: corolla inconspicuous; calyx and buds green; stamens long-exserted, pinkish red; in spirelike racemes; pods flat, edges ridged. Leaves: bipinnate, with 13–15 pairs of pinnae; leaflets very small, 40–100 pairs. *An open, spreading tree with slender, feathery compound leaves. Attractive to small birds. The spirelike inflorescence distinguishes this species from other more commonly cultivated species.*

Calliandra surinamensis

PINK TASSEL-FLOWER, SURINAM CALLIANDRA

Northern South America; naturalized West Indies. Evergreen shrub, 10–15 ft.; zones 10–11. Blooms late winter, spring. Seasonally moist/dry. Fertile, humus-rich, well-drained soil. Full sun to bright filtered light. Flowers: tubular, white; stamen tips pink, white at base; in upright tassels, to 2 in. long; pod edges ridged, 3–5 in. long. Leaves: bipinnate, with 1–3 pairs of pinnae; leaflets oblong, 8–10 pairs, less than 0.5 in. long. The stamens begin to shrivel by midday exposing the stigma. Tolerates dry conditions.

Calliandra tergamina

FAIRY-DUSTER, PINK POWDER-PUFF

Synonym: *C. emarginata*. Mexico, Honduras. Evergreen shrub, 2–6 ft.; zones 10–11. Blooms warm months. Regular moisture. Average to fertile, well-drained soil. Full sun to bright filtered light. Flowers: corolla tubular; stamens red to pink; in subglobular heads, 1–1.5 in. wide. Leaves: bipinnate, with one pair of pinnae; leaflets broadly obovate, falcate, usually one pair; downy below, tips rounded to pointed. *Var.* emarginata *leaf tips notched (emarginate).* Calliandra eriophylla *has much smaller leaflets.* Calliandra haematocephala *'Nana' has globular red floral heads and at least 5 pairs of leaflets. All suitable for bonsai.*

Calliandra tweediei

RED TASSEL-FLOWER, MEXICAN FLAME-BUSH, CUNURE

Synonyms: *Calliandra guildingii*, *Inga pulcherrima*. Argentina, Brazil, Paraguay; naturalized in Mexico, West Indies, southwestern United States. Evergreen shrub to 8 ft.; zones 9–11. Blooms winter, spring, intermittently at other times. Regular moisture. Humus-rich, well-drained soil. Full to part sun. Flowers: corolla tubular, small, white; stamens long, red; in subglobular heads, the stamens of each individual flower in discrete clumps. Leaves: pinnate, with 2–7 pairs of pinnae, to 2 in. long; leaflets very small, 30 or more pairs, light green. *The clumped stamens combined with very small leaflets are good field marks. Of streamside locations. Self-propagating in the southwestern United States. Named for James Tweedie but often misspelled* tweedii.

Ebenopsis

Ebenopsis includes 3 species of trees and shrubs from Mexico and Texas. They grow in dry regions with adequate drainage. Formerly included in *Pithecellobium*, a genus that has been revised. Leaves are bipinnate with spines in the leaf axils. Flowers are in globular, mimosa-like heads on short spurs. The perianth is small. The fruit is a large woody, dehiscent pod that opens into 2 canoe-shaped or contorted valves revealing round reddish seeds, each in an individual chamber.

Ebenopsis ebano

TEXAS EBONY

Synonym: *Pithecellobium flexicaule*. Northern Mexico, Texas. Evergreen tree to 60 ft.; zones 9–10. Blooms summer. Moderate moisture to dry. Average, well-drained soil. Full sun. Flowers: small; stamens creamy white; in globular heads to 0.5 in. wide; in clusters; pods straight or curved, to 5 in. long. Leaves: bipinnate, crowded on the stem, with 3–6 pairs of pinnae; leaflets asymmetrically oblong, 3–6 pairs, 0.5 in. long. Spines small, in leaf axils. Branches flexuous. *A xeric species of*

Calliandra houstoniana

Calliandra surinamensis

Calliandra tergamina

Calliandra tweediei

semidesert; grows in seasonally moist climates with excellent drainage.

Inga

Inga includes 250–350 species of trees and shrubs from tropical America. The species are adapted to a wide range of conditions. Leaves are pinnate. Flowers have conspicuous, usually white, stamens. The various *Inga* species have distinctively shaped, usually 4-angled pods. The pods of the common species, *I. edulis*, are long and slender. Used for firewood and to control erosion. Nitrogen-fixing bacteria in root nodules improve soil fertility. The immature bean is a source of high-protein food for humans as well as cattle. The frothy, sweet pulp surrounding the seed of some species somewhat resembles vanilla ice cream.

Inga, *Erythrina*, and *Gliricidia* have long been interplanted with coffee and cacao for shade and to improve soil fertility. This low-impact farming method sustains individual farmers. Recent conversion to high-intensity farming methods includes removal of shade trees from coffee plantations in favor of monocultures of sun-grown coffee. One of many detrimental effects of this type of agriculture is a loss of alternative habitat for migratory birds in regions that have already sustained the destruction of native woodlands. A precipitous loss of migratory birds is closely related to the loss of seasonal habitats in North and South America.

Inga jinicuil

ICE-CREAM BEAN, COFFEE-SHADE, MADRE DE CAFÉ, GUABO, CUAJINIQUIL, SHIMBILLO
Synonyms: *I. paterno*, *I. radians*. Southern Mexico to Costa Rica. Evergreen tree, 30–45 ft.+; zones 10–11. Blooms spring, summer, or intermittently. Regular moisture to wet. Most soils. Full sun. Flowers: stamens white; in loose, tassel-like heads; pod thick, 4-angled, curved, 5–9 in. long. Leaves: pinnate; cup-shaped glands between each pair of leaflets; rachis winged. Pronounced he-knee-KWEEL. *A spreading streamside tree from coastal forests to moderate elevations. Pollinated in the wild by bats. Suitable for areas subject to periodic flooding.*

Lysiloma

Lysiloma includes 30–35 species of unarmed trees from tropical and subtropical America. *Lysiloma latisiliquum* and *L. sabicu* are grown in Florida. They have very attractive wood somewhat resembling mahogany. Leaves are twice pinnate (bipinnate), the leaflets small. Flowers are greenish white, in small heads. The papery pods have a distinctive 180° twist at the base. The 2 species included here provide a light-filtering canopy in summer but allow warming sunlight through in cooler months when they shed their leaves. This provides excellent light conditions for most understory plants. Leaflets are small and disappear into grass. *Lysiloma sabicu* is used as a street landscaping tree in South Florida (erroneously promoted as a native). It is distinguished by only 1 or 2 seeds per pod. It is weedy in disturbed locations. *Lysiloma latisiliquum*, wild tamarind (native to the Florida Keys), is suitable where a high canopy is advantageous. It is distinguished from the smaller *L. sabicu* by pods with about 10 seeds. Leaves have 2 pairs of pinnae with 10–14 oblong leaflets about 0.25 in. long. *Lysiloma watsonii* thrives in California and arid regions.

Lysiloma sabicu

SABICU, BAHAMA LYSILOMA, HORSEFLESH MAHOGANY
Bahamas, Cuba, Hispaniola, Yucatan. Briefly deciduous tree, 20–30 ft.; zones 9–11. Blooms intermittently in warm months. Seasonally moist/dry. Average, well-drained soil. Full sun. Flowers: stamens greenish white; in small, subglobular heads less than 1 in. wide; pods 3–4 in. long, papery, white and brown, twisted 180° at base, seeds 1–2, flat. Leaves: bipinnate, with 2–4 pairs of pinnae; leaflets 3–7 pairs, broadly ovate; young leaves reddish. Bark: gray, rough. *A slow-growing, salt-, wind-, and drought-tolerant umbrella-shaped tree. Self-seeding and sometimes invasive.*

Lysiloma watsonii

Synonyms: *L. acapulcensis*, *L. microphylla* var. *thornberi*. Mexico, southern Arizona. Deciduous shrub or small tree, 6–10 ft.; zones 9–11. Blooms late spring, summer. Dry. Average, well-drained soil. Full sun. Flowers: perianth minute, brownish red; stamens white; in globular heads to 0.5 in. diameter; in clusters. Leaves: bipinnate, with 2 or more pairs of pinnae; leaflets ovate, 0.5–1 in. long. *Photographed at Balboa Park, San Diego.*

Mimosa

Mimosa includes approximately 400 species of subshrubs, shrubs, small trees, and vines, which are widespread in the tropics and subtropics. Stems often have prickles. Leaves are bipinnate with the subdivisions (pinnae) pinnately or palmately arranged. The leaves of some species fold at night or when touched, leading to the common name, sensitive plant. Flowers are in heads, spikes, or racemes.

Mimosa martin-delcampoi

Southern Mexico. Evergreen shrub to 5 ft.+; zones 9–11. Blooms warm months. Moderate moisture. Average, well-drained soil. Full to part sun. Flowers: stamens pink; heads to 0.5 in. diameter; in erect panicles. Leaves: bipinnate, with 2 pairs of pinnae; leaflets 1–2 pairs, kidney-shaped (reniform), to 2 in. long; margins undulate.

FABACEAE
Subfamily Papilionoideae

Papilionoideae (Faboideae) includes approximately 430 genera of trees, shrubs, perennial and annual herbs, and climbers, which are widely distributed. This legume

Ebenopsis ebano

Inga jinicuil, flowers

Inga jinicuil, pod

Lysiloma sabicu

subfamily includes cultivated beans and peas, crops which are rich in protein. It also includes many outstanding ornamental flowering species. Leaves are pinnate, palmate, often trifoliolate, or sometimes reduced to a single leaflet (unifoliolate), appearing simple.

Flowers are papilionaceous, "pealike," or more literally, "butterfly-like." They have 5 highly modified petals: 1 differentiated into a banner (standard) usually in the uppermost position, 2 form lateral wings, and the 2 lower petals are fused into a keel.

Brya

Brya includes approximately 12 species of armed shrubs and trees from the West Indies. *Brya ebenus* is grown in Jamaica for its wood that turns almost black when seasoned, leading to the local name "ebony" (true ebony is in Ebenaceae).

Leaves are unifoliolate or trifoliolate. Flowers are solitary.

Brya ebenus

JAMAICAN RAIN-TREE, WEST INDIAN EBONY, AMERICAN EBONY, COCOSWOOD

Synonym: *Aspalathus ebenus*. Cuba, Jamaica. Semideciduous shrub or tree, 15–30 ft.; zones 10–11. Blooms intermittently in warm months. Moderate moisture, drought tolerant. Average, well-drained soil. Full sun. Flowers: papilionaceous, golden to orange-yellow; solitary in the leaf axils. Leaves: trifoliolate; leaflets obovate, to 0.5 in. long; sessile. Spines in the leaf axils. *Limbs arching, little-branched. Tolerates heat and salt. Suitable for seaside planting. Sometimes used for bonsai. The name rain-tree alludes to the way the buds remain quiescent when dry and then burst forth suddenly after a rain. May become deciduous when dry. Species name often misspelled ebanus.*

Mimosa martin-delcampoi

Brya ebenus

Lysiloma watsonii

Butea

Butea includes 2–4 species of trees from Southeast Asia and India. *Butea monosperma* is only occasionally cultivated in the United States. It may be slow-growing until it becomes established. A spectacular landscape tree with an erect crown and attractive, large foliage. It is deciduous for a short time in winter. Relatively pest resistant. Propagated from seed (flowers usually must be hand-pollinated), cuttings, or air-layers.

Butea monosperma

FLAME-OF-THE-FOREST, BASTARD TEAK, PALAS

Synonyms: *B. frondosa*, *Erythrina monosperma*. India, Myanmar (Burma), Malaysia, Sri Lanka. Briefly deciduous tree to 50 ft.; zones 10–11. Blooms late winter, spring. Seasonally moist/dry. Fairly fertile, well-drained soil. Full sun.

Flowers: orange-pink with silky white hairs; keel large, sickle-shaped; standard small, pointed; wings small; sepals black; in oblique to ascending racemes. Leaves: trifoliolate, leaflets rhombic, 7–10 in. wide, rigid, tips rounded; petiole to 10 in. Sap red. *Typically blooms unevenly with more flowers on some branches than others. In forests, the branches may clamber through neighboring trees. Large-keeled flowers and trifoliolate leaves resemble* Erythrina. *A yellow Thai cultivar has been reported (Schokman, pers. comm.).*

Cajanus

Cajanus (pronounced ka-HAN-us) includes 22–37 species of perennials from Asia and Africa. *Cajanus cajan* is a cultigen evolving from ancestral species that have hybridized with local species over centuries of cultivation. It is not known in the wild. Easy to grow and care-free, it is not only ornamental but extremely versatile as food, fodder, and fuel, an excellent source of protein, particularly important attributes in impoverished countries. Plants provide frequent harvests of tasty beans while the nitrogen-fixing root nodules enrich the surrounding soil and nourish other food crops. Plants are sometimes tilled under as "green manure" in the same way as alfalfa. *Cajanus cajan* is grown as an annual in temperate climates.

Cajanus cajan

PIGEON PEA, CONGO PEA, DAHL, GANDULES, CHINCHONCHILLO, FRIJOL DE ÁRBOL

Synonyms: *C. bicolor*, *C. flavus*, *C. indicus*. Cultigen possibly originating in India or the Middle East. Annual or short-lived perennial shrub, 5–8 ft.; zones 7–11. Blooms intermittently. Moderate moisture to seasonally dry. Average to poor, well-drained soil. Full to part sun. Flowers: papilionaceous, fragrant, standard golden-yellow to orange or purplish; calyx mahogany red; pods oblong, 4 in. long, green to tan with maroon streaks, constricted between the lens-shaped tan seeds. Leaves: trifoliolate; leaflets elliptic, 3–4 in. long, downy. *An ornamental shrub or hedge with edible beans. Highly recommended.*

Chadsia

Chadsia includes a single species of shrub from Madagascar. It is rare in cultivation and possibly in its natural habitat. Leaves are palmately compound. The flowers are papilionaceous with very elongated standards and keels. An open, airy shrub with arching branches. Slow growing at first. From low elevations.

Butea monosperma

Butea monosperma, flowers

Chadsia gravei

Cajanus cajan

Clitoria ternatea 'Pleno'

Chadsia gravei

Synonyms: *C. grandidieri, C. grandifolia.* Madagascar. Evergreen shrub, 6–12 ft.; zones 10–11. Blooms warm months. Moderate moisture to dry. Average, well-drained soil; may prefer acid pH. Full sun. Flowers: standard, keel, and wings elongated, light orange. Leaves: palmate, leaflets 5, linear, whitish below, 2–3 in. long. *Little is known about this species. It was growing in the same conditions as bougainvilleas.*

Clitoria

Clitoria includes approximately 94 species of herbaceous climbers from the tropics, with greatest diversity in the Americas. Leaves are usually trifoliolate. The flowers are inverted by a twist in the floral stalk (peduncle), with the standard below and the keel above. The wings are relatively large. Flowers are usually blue. The somewhat similar *Centrosema* species never have blue flowers. Grown as annuals in temperate regions.

Clitoria ternatea

BLUE BUTTERFLY PEA, AZULEJO, BEJUCO DE CONCHITOS ("SHELL-VINE")

Tropical Africa, South Africa; widely distributed. Annual or short-lived twining herb to 12 ft.+; zones 10–11. Blooms warm months. Regular moisture. Average, well-drained soil. Full sun. Flowers: corolla cobalt-blue, inverted (resupinate). Leaves: pinnate, leaflets 5–7, ovate to elliptic, about 1 in. long. *Grown as an annual in temperate zones. Suitable for hanging baskets, on a small trellis or fence. Self-seeding. 'Pleno' has a double corolla and is more commonly cultivated. A white selection exists.*

Crotalaria

Crotalaria includes approximately 629 species of shrubs and herbs from tropical and mild temperate areas of the world. Many similar species are not well documented and are difficult to identify. They are often referred to as rattleboxes because ripe seeds rattle loosely in the inflated pods. Members of this genus are sometimes used for fodder and as a nitrogen-enriching ground cover. Leaves are unifoliolate to trifoliolate. Flowers are pealike with a relatively large, rounded standard with 2 teeth hidden at the base.

Crotalaria laburnifolia

RATTLE-BOX, BIRD-FLOWER

Old World tropics. Evergreen shrub to about 6 ft.; zones 9–11. Blooms summer, fall. Moderate moisture to fairly dry. Average, well-drained soil. Full sun. Flowers: keel light green, beaked, standard golden; calyx mauve. Leaves: yellowish green, trifoliolate; leaflets elliptic, 1–2 in. long. *One of many plants cultivated for hemp fiber. The chartreuse foliage can be set off by planting with contrasted purple flowers or foliage. Prune lightly for shape and to encourage repeat flowering. Thrives in southern California.*

Erythrina

Erythrina includes approximately 120 species of deciduous trees and shrubs widely distributed in the tropics. Flowers are scarlet or orange, occasionally pink, yellow, or white. New World species often have tubular or knife-shaped standards enclosing the other floral parts, and sweet nectar which attracts hummingbird pollinators. Old World species commonly have backward-facing flowers with an open standard and a low-sugar and high-protein content which attracts perching birds. The fruit is a loment which is constricted between the seeds and splits crosswise, rather than a pod which splits lengthwise. The common name coral bean refers to the red seed of most species and coral tree (*koraalboom* in South Africa) to the red flowers. Leaves are usually trifoliolate. Stems are often heavily armed. In Florida, twig borers are a nuisance attacking branch tips before they flower but causing no lasting harm. Most species are poisonous though some have medicinal value.

Plants such as these which bloom during the dry season provide moisture and food for small animals and birds, including parrots (Meerow, pers. comm.). Several species are grown as coffee and cacao shade (also see *Inga, Gliricidia*). A number of species are commonly grown in California. Waimea Arboretum in Oahu, Hawaii, boasts about 100 species. The National Tropical Botanical Garden on Kauai island, Hawaii, also has a large collection.

The name *Erythrina variegata* has caused considerable confusion in the literature. The variegated leaf form was the first to be named and was given the name *E. variegata*. The nonvariegated form was at first thought to be a distinct species and was named *E. indica*. When the two were determined to be varieties of the same species, the older name *E. variegata* took precedence, so the nonvariegated form was renamed *E. variegata* var. *indica* and the variegated form *E. variegata* var. *variegata* (Howard, pers. comm.).

Erythrina ×bidwillii

HYBRID CORAL-TREE

Garden hybrid, *E. crista-galli × E. herbacea.* Deciduous shrub or tree to 10 ft.; zones 8–11. Blooms intermittently late spring to late summer. Moderate moisture. Average, well-drained soil. Full sun. Flowers: standard knife-shaped, curved, blood red; in long spirelike ascending racemes. Leaves: trifoliolate; leaflets ovate, 3–4 in. long, tips acuminate. *Grown as a perennial in mild temperate climates if roots are protected from freezing. Suitable for coastal locations. Prune after flowering to encourage repeat blooming.*

Erythrina caffra

COAST CORAL-TREE, SOUTH AFRICAN CORAL-TREE, KORAALBOOM (SOUTH AFRICA)

Synonym: *E. insignis.* South Africa (East Cape, KwaZulu-Natal). Deciduous tree, 20–30 ft., occasionally to 50 ft.; zones 9–11. Blooms late spring, early summer. Moderate moisture in winter, dry in spring, summer. Average, well-drained soil. Full sun. Flowers: standard tongue-shaped, light orange, backward-facing; stamens exserted; in erect to ascending, dense racemes; pods constricted around seeds, to 4 in. long; seeds red. Leaves: trifoliolate; leaflets triangular, 4–6 in. long. Trunk and branches are covered with small hooked prickles. *A spreading tree suitable for coastal planting. 'Flavescens' has creamy yellow flowers.*

Crotalaria laburnifolia

Erythrina ×bidwillii

Erythrina caffra

Erythrina coralloides

NAKED CORAL-TREE, MADRE BRAVA, BUCARE

Synonym: *Corallodendron coralloides*. Mexico, Arizona. Deciduous tree to 30 ft.; zones 8–11. Blooms spring. Moderate moisture in winter, dry spring, summer. Average, well-drained soil. Full sun. Flowers: standard knife-shaped, calyx covered with brown hairs; in short, erect racemes twice as broad as tall, fragrance of bell peppers; loments to 6 in. long. Leaves: trifoliolate; leaflets ovate to triangular. Bark: with small prickles. *A spreading tree. Blooms on naked branches. Used extensively for landscaping in Mexico City and southern California. Suitable for coastal locations.*

Erythrina crista-galli

COCKSPUR CORAL-TREE, CRY-BABY TREE, COCK'S COMB, GALLITO

Synonyms: *Corallodendron crista-galli, E. pulcherrima*. South America (eastern slope of the Andes). Deciduous shrub or tree to 15 ft.; zones 8–11. Blooms spring, intermittently in warm months. Seasonally moist/dry. Average to fertile, well-drained soil. Full sun. Flowers: standard tongue-shaped, dark red, pink below, keel columnar; stamens exserted; calyx cup-shaped, orange-pink; inflorescences usually

Erythrina coralloides, flowers

Erythrina coralloides

Erythrina crista-galli

Erythrina falcata

Erythrina folkersii

descending, 12–18 in. long. Leaves: trifoliolate; leaflets elliptic, to 6 in. long; petioles prickled. *Blooms later in summer on the Gulf Coast or where grown as a perennial. Protect root from freezing. Called cry-baby because drops of nectar overflow the lip like tears.*

Erythrina falcata

CEIBO DE JUJUY, PISNAY, BUCARE
Argentina, Brazil, Bolivia, Paraguay, Peru. Semideciduous tree to 50 ft.; zones 9–11. Blooms spring, early summer. Moderate, dry in spring, summer. Average, well-drained soil. Full sun. Flowers: standard hooked

(falcate), somewhat inflated, scarlet; in pendent clusters. Leaves: trifoliolate; leaflets elliptic to ovate, to 5 in. long. *The flowers resemble garlands of red chili-peppers ("chili ristras" in the Southwest). The species name alludes to the curved standard that resembles a falcon's beak.*

Erythrina folkersii

CORAL-TREE, EQUELITE, PITO
Mexico, Belize, Guatemala, Honduras. Deciduous tree, 15–25 ft.; zones 10–11. Blooms spring. Moderate, seasonally dry. Average, well-drained soil. Full sun. Flowers: standard knife-shaped, pinkish

scarlet; in erect, spirelike racemes, lower flowers descending; fruit black; seeds red. Leaves: trifoliolate; leaflets hastate to broadly ovate, to 8 in. long, side leaflets smaller, asymmetrical, acuminate at base and tip. *Unusual in cultivation. Fast growing.*

Erythrina herbacea

CHEROKEE-BEAN, COLORÍN, PATOL
Synonym: *E. arborea.* Florida, Texas to the Carolinas. Deciduous shrub, 5–8 ft.; zones 8–11. Blooms winter, spring. Moderate moisture. Sandy, well-drained soil. Full sun. Flowers: standard knife-shaped, scarlet to

pink, rarely white; calyx cup-shaped, red; in ascending spires to 1 ft. long; seeds scarlet. Leaves: trifoliolate; leaflets ovate to hastate. *Prune back sharply in fall for compact growth. Mulch to protect root in mild temperate areas.*

Erythrina humeana

DWARF CORAL-TREE, NATAL CORAL-TREE, MONKEY-TREE, KLEINKORAALBOOM (SOUTH AFRICA)
Synonyms: *E. hastifolia, E. humei, E. princeps.* Southeastern Africa. Deciduous tree to 12 ft.; zones 9–11. Blooms primarily late summer, fall, sometimes spring. Seasonally moist/dry. Average, well-drained soil. Full sun. Flowers: standard knife-shaped, to 3 in. long, backward-facing in ascending to curved racemes, on long stalks to 15 in.; seeds red. Leaves: trifoliolate, 6–8 in. long; leaflets rhombic (diamond-shaped), 4–5 in. long. Bark: gray. Prickles on younger branches. *A small, spreading tree suitable for coastal planting. 'Raja' is a more shrublike selection with more slender, spirelike inflorescences.*

Erythrina lysistemon

COMMON CORAL-TREE, LUCKY BEAN CORAL-TREE, TRANSVAAL KORAALBOOM (SOUTH AFRICA)
Southeastern Africa. Deciduous tree to 30 ft.+; zones 9–11. Blooms spring, summer. Moderate, seasonally dry. Average, well-drained soil. Full sun. Flowers: standard knife-shaped, 4 in. long, red-orange, backward-facing; in compact racemes on short peduncles; seeds red. Leaves: trifoliolate; leaflets obovate. Bark: gray, covered with black thorns. *Blooms on naked branches in dry season.*

Erythrina speciosa

PINK CORAL TREE
Southern Brazil. Deciduous tree 10–20 ft.; zones 10–11. Blooms late winter. Seasonally moist/dry. Average, well-drained soil. Full sun. Flowers: standard red or pink in var. *rosea,* knife-shaped, 3 in. long, spreading and curved upward, in compact racemes; calyx blackish. Leaves: trifoliolate; leaflets triangular to rhombic. Stems: light gray, covered with thorns. *Blooms on mostly bare branches.*

Erythrina herbacea

Erythrina humeana

Erythrina speciosa var. *rosea*

Erythrina humeana 'Raja'

Erythrina lysistemon

Erythrina variegata

INDIAN CORAL-TREE, TIGER'S CLAW, FLAME-TREE, MANDARAM (INDIA) Synonyms: *E. indica* var. *orientalis*, *E. parcellii*. Madagascar, Tanzania, India, Southeast Asia, Indomalaysia to Australia. Briefly deciduous tree to 80 ft.; zones 9–11. Blooms spring. Seasonally moist/ dry. Average, well-drained soil. Full sun. Flowers: standard flared, backward-facing, scarlet; in oblique clusters, to 10 in. long; pods 6–12 in. long. Leaves: trifoliolate, leaflets broadly ovate to rhombic, 6–8 in. long; petiole to 8 in. Bark: gray, streaked green. New growth thorny. *Suitable for coastal planting. Roots from large cuttings (a "quick stick"). Var. variegata (syn. E. variegata f. picta [hort.]), the variegated coral-tree or sunshine-tree, has green-and-yellow variegated leaves which tend to revert to green with age. It was originally introduced into the United States by botanist-collector Monroe Birdsey.*

Gliricidia

Gliricidia includes 3 or 4 species of trees or shrubs from tropical America. Leaves are pinnate. Flowers are papilionaceous. Seeds are dispersed explosively. *Gliricidia* has been used to shade cacao since the time of the Aztecs. The Indians observed that crops and other plants prospered when planted in conjunction with legumes (beans were also planted with squash and corn). They did not understand that nitrogen-fixing bacteria in root-nodules of many legumes enrich the soil. Later when coffee was introduced from the Old World, *Gliricidia* was used as coffee shade. It is also used as a support for vanilla and black pepper vines. Small coffee plantations shaded with *Gliricidia* and other species are being replaced by high-intensity farming, destroying one of the last habitats for migratory birds. Because large branches take root directly in the ground, *G. sepium* is used as a "living fence" ("quick stick") around farms and for erosion control. Leaves are soaked and the water used as a fertilizer or young plants are plowed under as "green manure." Seeds, bark and roots used as rat poison. Easily confused with *Hebestigma cubense*.

Gliricidia sepium

MEXICAN LILAC, MADRE DE CAFÉ ("MOTHER-OF-COFFEE"), BIEN VESTIDO ("WELL-DRESSED") Synonym: *G. maculata*. Tropical America. Briefly deciduous tree to 30 ft.; zones 10–11. Blooms spring. Seasonally moist/dry. Average, well-drained soil. Full sun. Flowers: pealike, pink to almost white; in dense clusters. Leaves: pinnate, leaflets ovate to lanceolate, 7–17 pairs, to 2 in. long. Unarmed. *Strongly recommended as a substitute for the weedy and invasive Millettia pinnata (syn. Pongamia pinnata). Flowers are similar but much showier on briefly bare branches in spring. Rarely produces seed in cultivation.*

Hebestigma

Hebestigma includes a single tree species from Cuba. It is a common street tree in Havana and San Juan, Puerto Rico. Easily confused with *Gliricidia sepium*. The flowers are similar in color and shape to *Gliricidia* but half the size, and the leaflets are larger.

Hebestigma cubense

Synonym: *Gliricidia platycarpa*. Cuba; naturalized in Puerto Rico. Deciduous tree to 40 ft.; zones 10–11. Blooms late winter to early summer. Seasonally moist/dry. Average, well-drained soil. Full sun. Flowers: small, pealike, pink-lavender, standard reflexed; 10 stamens, 1 solitary and 9 united in a bundle (diadelphous); in loose clusters. Leaves: pinnate; leaflets ovate, 3–4 in. long. *Of seasonally dry forest.*

Kennedia

Kennedia includes approximately 15 species of perennial vines and woody climbers from Australia and

Erythrina variegata var. *indica*

Gliricidia sepium

Erythrina variegata var. *variegata*

Gliricidia sepium, flowers

Hebestigma cubense

New Guinea. Flowers are papilionaceous. Leaves are usually trifoliolate. These species are sometimes cultivated as ornamentals.

Kennedia nigricans

BLACK CORAL-PEA

Western Australia. Perennial herbaceous climber to 10 ft.; zones 9–11. Blooms warm months. Moderate moisture. Average, well-drained soil. Full to part sun. Flowers: glossy purplish black, standard with 2 oval yellow spots, to 1.5 in. long; in clusters. Leaves: unifoliolate or trifoliolate; leaflets ovate, to 5 in. long, tips retuse.

Lonchocarpus

Lonchocarpus includes approximately 130 species of trees and shrubs from the American tropics, plus 1 from western Africa. Leaves are pinnate. *Lonchocarpus violaceus* is a highly desirable fall-blooming species occasionally cultivated in the United States. Highly recommended. A leaf or bark decoction of 3 ppm is reportedly used to selectively poison piranha fish without harming desirable fish species. Some species are cultivated for the production of rotenone, a natural pesticide.

Lonchocarpus violaceus

LANCEPOD, TROPICAL LILAC

Trinidad, Venezuela, Colombia. Evergreen tree, 10–20 ft.; zones 9–11. Blooms fall. Moderate, seasonally dry. Humus-rich, well-drained soil; slightly acid pH. Full to part sun. Flowers: pealike, fragrant; in ascending clusters on opposite sides of the branches; pods twisted, 3–8 in. long. Leaves: pinnate, 8–10 in. long, decussate; leaflets ovate to elliptic, 6–8 pairs, to 3 in. long. Branches arching. *More robust in acid soil. Prepare a large planting hole with peat moss in alkaline soil. Highly recommended fall bloomer. Var.* violaceus *has pinkish-violet flowers. West Indian var.* alba *has violet and white flowers.*

Millettia

Millettia includes approximately 90 species of trees, shrubs, and climbers from the Old World tropics. Leaves are pinnately compound. Flowers are pealike. In Southeast Asia, a red oil or "tallow" is used for fuel. Rotenone is extracted as a pesticide and is used to kill fish by paralysis of the swim bladder. Though commonly distributed by landscaping companies as a fast-growing shade tree, pongam, *Millettia indica*, is a noxious pest in the garden and invasive in wild areas. It is heavily self-seeding and young seedlings require considerable hand-pulling to control. Flowers are in small clusters in the dense canopy. Strongly discouraged for landscaping. A controlled species in Florida. *Gliricidia sepium* is highly recommended as a much better substitute. It is fast-growing, has showy pink flowers on naked limbs in spring, and rarely sets seed in cultivation.

Millettia pinnata

PONGAM, TALLOW-TREE, PUNGA-OIL TREE, INDIAN BEECH, KARANJA

Synonyms: *Derris indica, Pongamia pinnata.* Indomalaysia to Australia and the western Pacific Islands; widely distributed. Evergreen tree, 25–40 ft.+; zones 9–11. Blooms spring. Moderate moisture. Most soils. Full sun. Flowers: pealike, small, lavender and pink, in loose, pendent racemes; pods triangular, to 2 in. long, each with one seed. Leaves: pinnate, unpleasantly scented; leaflets 5–9, ovate, 3–4 in. long. *From mangrove forests. Salt tolerant. Seeds poisonous. Invasive.*

Mucuna

Mucuna includes approximately 100 species of woody climbers from the Old and New World tropics. Leaves are trifoliolate. The flowers have a large falcate keel partly enclosed by the wings and a shorter, pointed standard. *Mucuna bennetti* is sometimes called red jade-vine (a non sequitur) because the flower clusters resemble those of jade vine, *Strongylodon macrobotrys.* In sturdy trees it drapes like a curtain of red. The vine is aggressive and difficult to control, often best restricted to an arbor where the flowers can hang freely below. It is unusual in cultivation in the continental United States. A number of nondescript species called cowitch, including *M. pruriens* and *M. sloanei*, are widely naturalized in disturbed areas and fields. The pods have extremely irritating hairs.

Mucuna bennetti

NEW GUINEA CREEPER, MUCUNA VINE, RED JADE-VINE

New Guinea. Evergreen woody climber to 100 ft.+; zones 10–11. Blooms spring, fall. Seasonally moist/dry. Humus-rich, well-drained soil. Full sun. Flowers: keel and lateral lobes clawlike, scarlet tinged with purple, 3–4 in. long; calyx cup-shaped with 3 teeth, yellowish orange, covered with fine golden hairs; in pendent racemes on a stalk to 18 in. long. Leaves: trifoliolate; leaflets leathery, center leaflet elliptic, to 4 in. long, lateral leaflets asymmetrical. *Unusual in cultivation. Aggressive vine needing strong support.*

Periandra

Periandra includes approximately 7 perennial climbers from tropical America. Leaves are trifoliolate. The flower stalk is twisted, inverting the flower (resupinate). The standard or banner is bilobed and winglike, the true wings are fused face to face with the keel forming a tube shorter than the standard. The 10 stamens include 1 free and 9 united at the base (diadelphous). *Periandra coccinea* somewhat resembles *Centrosema virginiana*, a pink-violet wildflower of the southeastern United States. *Periandra* is related to the blue-flowered butterfly pea, *Clitoria.* The plant in the photo, collected by Fairchild Tropical Garden, is flourishing in my Miami garden. It quickly fills a hanging basket or covers an arbor with soft emerald-green foliage. Runners root at the nodes if allowed to spread. Has not

Kennedia nigricans

Lonchocarpus violaceus var. *violaceus*

Millettia pinnata

Mucuna bennetti

produced seed in cultivation. Easily propagated from cuttings.

Periandra coccinea

RED BUTTERFLY PEA, HOT LIPS
Synonym: *Clitoria coccinea*. Panama (Darién Province), Brazil. Perennial twining climber, 8–20 ft.+; zones 10–11. Blooms late winter, spring. Regular moisture. Average to fertile, well-drained soil. Full sun. Flowers: inverted, red, standard bilobed, hairy outside, to 1.25 in. long, keel and lateral wings fused into a tube; stamens 10 (diadelphous); in clusters of 3 in the leaf axils, 1 flower opening at a time; bracts 2, small; on peduncle to 5 in. long. Leaves: trifoliolate; leaflets oblong-ovate, 1–3.5 in. long, tips mucronate, paired stipels at the base; petiole to 2 in. long. *Unusual in cultivation. All parts pubescent. Easy to grow. Excellent in hanging baskets or to cover an arbor or fence. Blooms best in full sun. Mix with blue and white* Clitoria *forms or white* Vigna *for a patriotic display.*

Poitea

Poitea includes approximately 12 species of shrubs from the West Indies. Leaves are pinnately compound. Flowers are pealike. *Poitea carinalis* is occasionally cultivated in the United States. The crimson flowers are striking, somewhat reminiscent of redbud (*Cercis canadensis*) in blossom. Blooms for a long time if irrigation is withheld during dry seasons. Frequently cultivated in the West Indies. Suitable for xeric and coastal but not seaside landscaping.

Poitea carinalis

CARIBWOOD
Synonym: *Sabinea carinalis*. Dominica (West Indies). Deciduous shrub, 6–10 ft.; zones 10–11. Blooms winter, spring. Seasonally moist/dry. Average, well-drained soil. Full to part sun. Flowers: pealike, crimson, tinged purplish; calyx bell- or cup-shaped, in opposite rows in the leaf axils. Leaves: pinnate; leaflets 13–23, oblong, to 1 in. long. *Long, arching branches. The species name alludes to the keel-shaped (carinate) lip. Highly recommended.*

Sesbania

Sesbania includes approximately 50 species of trees, shrubs, and herbs from the tropics and subtropics. The taxonomy on some species is unclear. Leaves are pinnate. Flowers are pealike with a large, falcate keel. A few species are cultivated for their often large, beautiful flowers. The plants are somewhat shapeless and should be worked into more robust landscaping. Relatively short-lived.

Sesbania grandiflora

HUMMINGBIRD TREE, SCARLET WISTERIA-TREE, BABY BOOTIES, VEGETABLE-HUMMINGBIRD
Synonym: *Agati grandiflora*. Origin obscure (possibly West Indies); widely distributed. Evergreen shrubby tree, 10–15 ft.+; zones 10–11. Blooms intermittently in warm months. Regular moisture and humidity. Average soil. Full sun. Flowers: 3–4 in. long, keel beaklike, enclosing the wings, standard lax, reflexed, scarlet, sometimes white or pink; calyx funnel-shaped, green, broadly lobed; in few-flowered lax clusters; pod slender, 12–15 in. long. Leaves: pinnate; leaflets 9–25, oblong, 0.5–1 in. long. *Fast-growing. Has brittle wood. Some authors describe the species as Indonesian in origin. The white-flowered form in the photo is not clearly distinguished from an Australian species,* S. formosa.

Sesbania punicea

SCARLET SESBANIA, BRAZILIAN GLORY PEA, RATTLE BOX
Synonyms: *Daubentonia tripettii*, *S. tripettii* (hort.). Brazil, northern Argentina, Uruguay, Paraguay; naturalized in southeastern United States. Short-lived shrubby tree to 10 ft.; zones 8–11. Blooms warm months. Moist. Average soil. Full sun. Flowers: pealike with a fan-shaped standard, red-orange; pods 4-winged. Leaves: pinnate; leaflets ovate, 12–15 pairs, to about 1 in. long, tips mucronate. *Current treatment favors the resurrection of the genus* Daubentonia *for this species. A drooping form with a yellow spot on the standard is sometimes incorrectly called* Sesbania tripettii. *Naturalized in tidal marshes of the southeastern United States. Salt tolerant.*

Sophora

Sophora includes 45–50 species of trees, shrubs, and herbs, which are widely distributed in the tropics and mild temperate areas. Leaves are pinnate. Flowers pealike. The pods are constricted between the seeds and often 4-winged.

Sophora tomentosa

NECKLACE-POD (FLORIDA), SILVER BUSH (AUSTRALIA), BEAD-TREE
Synonyms: *S. havanensis, S. littoralis, S. occidentalis*. Origin obscure; distributed throughout the tropics. Semideciduous shrub, 10–15 ft.; zones 8–10. Blooms intermittently in warm months. Moderate moisture or seasonally moist/dry. Average, well-drained soil. Full to part sun. Flowers: yellow; in clusters; pods slender, woolly, constricted between seeds.

Leaves: pinnate, leaflets 9–19, elliptic, 1–2 in. long, densely woolly (tomentose), gray-green. *Pods resemble strings of beads. Suitable for beach landscaping. Hardy in coastal strands in the southeastern United States. Salt tolerant and xeric.*

Spartium

Spartium includes a single species of shrub from the Mediterranean. It is naturalized in parts of California, the Andes, and elsewhere. Leaves are linear and fall soon after they are produced. The green branches are photosynthetic (phylloclads). The flowers are pealike. The species has long been cultivated in southern Europe for essential oils and chemicals. The branches and fibers are used for weaving. Potentially invasive in amenable climates.

Periandra coccinea

Poitea carinalis

Sesbania grandiflora

Sesbania punicea

Spartium junceum
SPANISH BROOM, RETAMA MACHO, BROOM ABSOLUTE
Southern Europe, Canary Islands; naturalized in California, Andes. Deciduous shrub, 6–10 ft.; zones 6–9. Blooms warm months. Dry. Most well-drained soils. Full sun. Flowers: pealike, yellow, in spikes. Leaves: very small, spear-shaped to almost needlelike, ephemeral. Stems: terete phyllodes, functioning as leaves. *Xeric. Suitable for dry gardens. Used to stabilize embankments. Prune for compactness in the fall. The species name alludes to the rushlike, green, leafless branches. Invasive in coastal scrub in California.*

Strongylodon
Strongylodon includes approximately 4 species of woody vines from Madagascar to the Philippines and Polynesia. One species, *S. macrobotrys*, is cultivated for its fascinating blue-green flowers. The leaves are trifoliolate. The flowers have a hoodlike standard and a falcate keel. The vine is aggressive and fast-growing. A substantial support is recommended. The species name means "grapelike," alluding to the way the blue-green flower clusters dangle under an arbor like under-ripe green grapes with a frosty bloom.

Strongylodon macrobotrys
JADE-VINE, EMERALD CREEPER, CASCADA DE JADE
Philippines. Evergreen woody climber to 50 ft.+; zones 10–11. Blooms late winter, spring. Seasonally moist/dry. Average to fertile, well-drained soil. Full to part sun. Flowers: keel falcate, clasped between 2 small wings, standard hoodlike, blue-green, like oxidized copper; in pendent clusters 1–2 ft. long; pod 3 in. wide, 7 in. long, sporadically produced in cultivation. Leaves: trifoliolate; leaflets 5–6 in. long, young leaves gray-green. *Cut back sharply after bloom to control.*

Tipuana
Tipuana includes a single species of fast-growing tree from southern South America. Leaves are pinnate; flowers papilionaceous. Handsome foliage, low-water requirements, and yellow blossoms make this species a favorite shade and street tree in California, Argentina, and elsewhere. It is considered the finest type of rosewood dating back to the ancient Incas. The natural asymmetrical shape lends itself to Japanese gardening styles. It is evergreen in warm areas or deciduous at colder limits of its range.

Tipuana tipu
ROSEWOOD, TIPU, PRIDE-OF-BOLIVIA
Synonym: *T. speciosa*. Southern Brazil, Argentina, Bolivia. Semideciduous tree, 30–60 ft.; zones 8–11. Blooms spring, summer. Moderate moisture to dry. Deep, well-drained soil. Full sun. Flowers: yellow to apricot-pink, crinkled, butterfly-shaped, throat ringed with russet; in few-flowered racemes; pods to 4 in. long, resembling a samara with one long wing; seeds 1–3. Leaves: pinnate; leaflets 5–15, oblong, 1–3 in. long, downy below. *Moderately salt tolerant. Self-seeding and somewhat weedy in favorable conditions.*

Uraria
Uraria includes approximately 6 species of shrubs from the Old World. The species listed was collected on the Malaccan coast of the Malay Peninsula by Fairchild Tropical Garden. The flowers are small and pealike on stiff hairy stalks. The one-seeded pods are very small and hidden among the hairs. Leaves are pinnate. New flower spikes develop at the base of the old ones so remove spent inflorescences carefully. Propagated from seed.

Uraria crinita
CATTAIL PEA
Synonyms: *Doodia crinita, Hedysarum crinitum*. Southern China, Taiwan, Ryukyu Islands, Philippines, Southeast Asia, Indomalaysia. Short-lived perennial, 3–6 ft.; zones 10–11. Blooms fall. Regular moisture. Fertile, well-drained soil. Full to part sun. Flowers: pealike, violet; on erect, stiffly bristled racemes to 10 in.+ tall; calyces, tan, persistent, bristly; tiny pods one-seeded, about 0.25 in. long. Leaves: pinnate, to 7 in. long, leaflets 7, elliptic, stiff hairs on underside of leaf, rachis, and petioles; stipules leaflike. *New inflorescences develop from the base of the old. Unusual to rare in cultivation.*

Vigna
Vigna includes approximately 118 species of shrubby or climbing herbs mostly from the Old World tropics. These species are closely related to culinary beans, *Phaseolus*. The genus includes the mung bean, which is commonly used for bean sprouts, as well as other beans common in Asian cuisines. *Vigna caracalla* is cultivated for its ornamental, fragrant flowers. The coiled, shell shape of the flowers is a special adaptation for pollination. When a bee lights on the lower petals, a leverlike action forces the stamens to protrude from the coiled floral tube, dusting the bee's head with pollen. Cultivate on trellises, fences, or as ground cover.

Sophora tomentosa

Spartium junceum

Strongylodon macrobotrys

Tipuana tipu

Uraria crinita

Vigna caracalla

SNAIL-FLOWER, CORKSCREW FLOWER, SNAIL-BEAN, BERTONI BEAN

Synonym: *Phaseolus bertonii*. Tropical South America. Short-lived perennial climber, 10–20 ft.; zones 10–11. Blooms warm months. Regular moisture when hot, less when cool. Most well-drained soils. Full sun. Flowers: keel flattened, coiled snail-like, violet to white, fragrant; pods also coiled; seeds multicolored. Leaves: trifoliolate; leaflets ovate, dull green. Stems: twining. *Suitable for coastal planting. The beans are edible.*

FLACOURTIACEAE

FLACOURTIA FAMILY

Flacourtiaceae includes approximately 85 genera of shrubs and occasionally trees primarily from tropical and subtropical regions. This unnatural group has recently been revised. Most of the commonly cultivated species have been transferred to Salicaceae or Achariaceae. This group is related to the passion-flower family, Passifloraceae. A few species are cut for timber and some have pharmaceutical properties. Governor's plum, *Flacourtia indica*, from Africa and Southeast Asia, bears a tart-sweet fruit. It is invasive and prohibited in South Florida. Leaves are always simple, often with tiny glands, and arranged in opposite ranks (distichous). They sometimes have spines in the leaf axils. The branches have a zigzag (divaricate) growth pattern. Flowers are often small, solitary, inconspicuous, and usually bisexual but if unisexual, then male and female flowers may be on the same plant (monoecious) or on different plants (dioecious). Petals are sometimes absent. Usually an enlarged, disklike peduncle supports numerous stamens. The fruit is a capsule or berry.

Banara

Banara includes approximately 31 species of small trees from tropical America, with greatest diversity in Chile. The leaves are simple with serrated margins and small punctate glands at the base of the blade. The petals are rudimentary and the sepals small. *Banara vanderbiltii* is a handsome tree with somewhat acacia-like flowers. It is nearly extinct in its native Puerto Rico.

Banara vanderbiltii

PALO DE RAMÓN

Puerto Rico, endangered in the wild. Evergreen shrub or tree, 15–18 ft.+; zones 10–11. Blooms spring or intermittently in warm months. Seasonally moist/dry. Average, well-drained soil. Full sun. Flowers: perianth reduced, green, 8-parted, fragrant; fertile and sterile stamens golden-yellow in a showy cluster about 0.75 in. wide, on short stalks in the leaf axils. Leaves: elliptic, asymmetrical, 4–6 in. long, softly downy; margins serrate. *Of rocky woodlands and coastal areas. Unusual to rare in cultivation. Fruit small. Blooms prolifically in several brief flushes.*

Casearia

Casearia (pronounced kays-air-EE-ah) includes approximately 175 species of small trees or shrubs from the tropics, about 75 in the New World and 100 in the Old World. The leaf axils sometimes have spines. Flowers are bisexual and borne in panicles. There are 8–20 stamens, fertile stamens alternating with staminodes. *Casearia nitida* is unusually ornamental for this group of mostly nondescript plants with inconspicuous flowers. It bursts forth with a multitude of dainty flowers in spring, giving an impression somewhat like apple blossoms. This delightful species is unusual in cultivation. Though normally an erect grower, one tree topped by a hurricane developed a spreading, bonsai-like habit. This suggests that it can be variously trained through pruning. The leaves are burnished (hence *nitida*) and have tiny translucent spots or streaks and the margins are finely serrated.

Casearia nitida

SMOOTH CASEARIA

Synonym: *C. bahamensis*. Bahamas, Cuba, Jamaica, Hispaniola. Briefly deciduous tree, 15–20 ft.; zones 10–11. Blooms late spring. Seasonally moist/dry. Sandy, well-drained soil. Full sun to bright broken light. Flowers: petal-like calyx white; tiny, ruby-red staminodes alternate with the stamens; in many-flowered cymes; fruit a berry, yellow; seeds with red-orange arils. Leaves: ovate to elliptic, 1.5–2 in. long, punctate, tip obtuse to acuminate, base rounded, glossy; margins faintly toothed. Zigzag branching. *An erect, conical tree of scrub and coastal woodlands. Salt tolerant. Highly recommended. Top when young for a spreading shape.*

Oncoba

Oncoba includes approximately 4 species of shrubs or trees from Africa. *Oncoba spinosa* is sometimes cultivated and has become naturalized in Texas rangeland. The leaves are simple with serrated margins. The flowers are solitary with numerous stamens and staminodes. The fruit is sometimes made into trinket boxes or rattles in the native region.

Oncoba spinosa

FRIED-EGG TREE, SNUFFBOX TREE

Arabia, eastern Africa to northeastern South Africa. Semideciduous shrub or tree, 15–25 ft.; zones 7–11. Blooms early spring. Moderate moisture/seasonally dry. Average, well-drained soil. Full to part sun. Flowers: petals 5, white, 3–4 in. wide, ruffled; stamens yellow, numerous; fruit smooth, hard-shelled, green to red, to 2 in. long. Leaves: elliptic, 4–6 in. long; margins serrate. Spines to 1.5 in. long in leaf axils. Bark: patchy gray and green. *Bark used as a folk remedy for fever. A pest in southeastern Texas rangelands. Slow-growing. Deciduous in cooler part of range.*

Vigna caracalla

Banara vanderbiltii

Casearia nitida

Oncoba spinosa

Samyda

Samyda includes 9–30 species of shrubs from Mexico, the West Indies, and Central America. Leaves are in opposite ranks (distichous). Flowers are perfect and radially symmetrical. Petals are absent. Five petal-like sepals are fused at the base. Twelve flattened filaments are fused into a crownlike structure and mounted on the sepals, and staminodes are lacking. The fruit is a spongy capsule, the numerous seeds have colored arils. Flowers are borne in small clusters in the leaf axils in 2 rows along the branches, opening a few at a time. The 2 species described here are unusual in cultivation but highly recommended. These are open shrubs with zigzag branching and begin to flower when quite small. Both species are salt tolerant and excellent for seaside landscaping. They are pest resistant and easily propagated from seed or cuttings.

Samyda dodecandra

WILD GUAVA, MON REVE ROSE, BANSO

Synonyms: *S. serrulata*, *S. rosea*. West Indies. Evergreen shrub, 6–12 ft.; zones 10–11. Blooms repeatedly in warm months. Moderate moisture. Average, well-drained soil. Full sun. Flowers: sepals pink, on short peduncles in leaf axils; fertile stamens 12, staminodes absent; fruit ovoid, seeds arillate. Leaves: elliptic, 4–5 in. long, reddish or yellowish hairs below, mostly smooth above; margins coarsely toothed; distichous. Twigs with fine rust-colored hairs. *Species name alludes to the 12 stamens. Salt tolerant.*

Samyda dodecandra

Samyda velutina, fruit

Samyda velutina

CAFECITO ("LITTLE COFFEE")

West Indies. Spreading shrub to 6 ft.; zones 10–11. Blooms repeatedly in warm months. Moderate moisture. Average, well-drained soil. Full sun. Flowers: sepals white or pink inside, green outside, felty, in few-flowered clusters in the leaf axils, coconut-scented; fertile stamens 12, staminodes absent; capsule ovoid, raspberry-red, hairy, splitting into 4 sections, seeds with sticky orange arils. Leaves: oblong to oblanceolate, tips cuspidate, dark green, lighter below, felty; margins serrulate; distichous. *Identification uncertain but likely. Flowers repeatedly during warm months. Salt tolerant to the shoreline.*

GELSEMIACEAE

GELSEMIUM FAMILY

Gelsemiaceae includes 2 genera of woody vines (lianas) from tropical and mild temperate regions of Africa, Southeast Asia, Central America, South America, and the southeastern United States. This family was formerly included in Loganiaceae. Leaves are simple. Flowers are trumpet-shaped, the 5 petals fused at the base and the lobes flaring. There are 5 sepals and 5 stamens. The fruit is a 2-valved capsule. The seeds are flattened.

Gelsemium

Gelsemium includes 3 species of shrubs and climbers from the United States and Central America and 1 species from China, Southeast Asia, and Indomalaysia. *Gelsemium sempervirens* is cultivated for its fragrant flowers and is sometimes used to prevent erosion. Leaves are simple. Flowers are bisexual, trumpet-shaped, solitary or in few-flowered terminal or axillary clusters. Bracts are present. Fruit a capsule. All parts are toxic. Produces alkaloids that are important pharmaceutically.

Gelsemium sempervirens

CAROLINA JESSAMINE, EVENING TRUMPET-FLOWER

Southeastern United States to Texas and Guatemala. Semideciduous shrubby climber, 10–20 ft.;

Gelsemium sempervirens

zones 7–10. Blooms spring. Regular moisture. Average, well-drained soil; acid pH. Full sun. Flowers: trumpet-shaped, fragrant, petals 5, lobes flaring, golden to pale yellow, throat orange or yellow; jagged corona around throat. Leaves: lanceolate, to 4 in. long; glossy dark green, leathery. Stems: twining counterclockwise. *Suitable for arbors.*

GENTIANACEAE

GENTIAN FAMILY

Gentianaceae includes approximately 84 genera of mostly herbs and a few shrubs or small trees primarily from temperate regions with some from montane tropical regions. The family is related to the coffee family, Rubiaceae, and to the oleander family, Apocynaceae. Leaves are simple, mostly in opposite pairs, each pair at right angles to the pair above and below (decussate) or sometimes reduced, margins entire. The 4 or 5 petals are fused into a tube at the base, often ridged or folded along the seams. Flowers are usually bisexual, solitary or in clusters. The fruit is a dry capsule or rarely a berry.

Fagraea

Fagraea includes approximately 35 species of shrubs and trees from Sri Lanka, India, Southeast Asia, the southwestern Pacific Islands (Melanesia), and Australia. This genus was formerly included in the family Loganiaceae. Flowers are trumpet-shaped, sometimes large and/or fragrant. Leaves are simple. Uncommon in cultivation on the U.S. mainland. *Fagraea berteriana*, called pua wood in Hawaii, is sacred in Tahiti.

Fagraea ceilanica

CEYLON FAGRAEA

India, Sri Lanka, Southeast Asia. Evergreen climbing shrub, 10–30 ft.; zones 10–11. Blooms warm months. Regular moisture and humidity. Average, well-drained soil. Full sun. Flowers: large, funnel-shaped, with short lobes, greenish or creamy white, 6 in. long, 3 in. wide, thickly covered with felty hairs, fragrant at night. Leaves: elliptic to obovate, 6–10 in. long, glossy dark green, rubbery. Young shoots dark green. *A rambling, suckering shrub or climber with adhesive aerial roots. The species name refers to Ceylon, now known as Sri Lanka.*

GERANIACEAE

GERANIUM FAMILY

Geraniaceae includes approximately 7 genera of herbs and shrubs, which are widely distributed in temperate, subtropical, and montane tropical regions. This group includes familiar houseplants such as cranesbills and storksbills, whose names allude to the beaklike attachments of the fruits that are made up of 5 one-seeded schizocarps. Leaves generally are palmately veined, often lobed or divided. Some produce fragrant oils. The stem nodes are jointed. Flowers are showy with 5 petals. They are solitary or in clusters.

Geranium

Geranium includes approximately 300 species of mostly annual and perennial herbs plus a few shrubs of mild temperate regions and a few from montane regions of the tropics. Leaves are often deeply lobed. Geraniums are predominantly hardy species with radially symmetrical flowers that are usually solitary. They have 10 fertile stamens. Many species are cultivated. *Geranium maderense* is occasionally grown in southern California.

Geranium maderense

MADEIRA GERANIUM, MADEIRA CRANESBILL, GERANIO
Madeira Island. Short-lived perennial herb to 3 ft.; zones 8–9. Blooms late winter, spring, early summer. Moderate moisture. Fertile, gritty, well-drained soil; neutral pH. Part sun to bright broken light.

Flowers: pink, darker in the center with purple nectar guides in the throat; stalks covered with purple glandular hairs. Leaves: deeply lobed, 3–4 in. long; in basal rosettes on short, woody stalks. *The leaves are almost hidden by the tangle of hairy flower stalks in dry climates. Appearance is greener in cool, misty locations or greenhouses.*

Pelargonium

Pelargonium includes approximately 250 species of annual or perennial herbs, succulents, and shrubs primarily from South Africa, as well as the Mediterranean, Near East, and Arabia, plus a few from Australia and New Zealand. The myriad hybrids are of complex ancestry frequently involving *P. cucullatum* and *P. grandiflorum*. They are ubiquitous in southern California landscaping. Hybrids are grouped horticulturally according to leaf characteristics including the concentric-ringed "zoned" (*P.* ×*hortorum*), "scented-leaved," "ivy-leaved," and "regal" (*P.* ×*domesti- cum*) among others. Though commonly, but incorrectly, referred to as geraniums or florist's geraniums, pelargoniums are easily distinguished from true geraniums, *Geranium*, by the bilaterally symmetrical flowers, which are always in clusters, never solitary. They have 10 stamens but 3 or 5 are sterile. Pelargoniums are commonly grown as bedding plants or cascading down slopes or from baskets. They are cultivated as annuals in mild temperate climates or indoors in winter. Cuttings are propagated directly in the ground. Pelargoniums should be watered early in the day to allow foliage to dry before dark to diminish the chance of mildew.

Pelargonium cucullatum

PELARGONIUM
South Africa (Cape Province). Evergreen shrub to 6 ft.; zones 9–10. Blooms warm months. Moderate moisture. Fertile, gritty, well-drained soil; neutral pH. Full sun. Flowers: petals 5, pinkish purple, the upper 2 marked with dark purple veins; stamens dark purple; calyx and buds covered with long silky hairs. Leaves: almost round in general outline, to 4 in. wide, cupped (cucullate), shallowly lobed, covered with silky hairs; margins shallow-toothed, becoming red with age. *This erect species is an ancestor of many regal pelargonium hybrids. This group prefers moderate to low humidity and cool night temperatures but tolerates warm daytime temperatures.*

Pelargonium ×domesticum

REGAL PELARGONIUM, MARTHA WASHINGTON PELARGONIUM, SHOW PELARGONIUM, GERANIO
Garden origin. Evergreen perennial subshrub to 2 ft.; zones 9–10. Blooms late winter, spring, early summer. Moderate moisture, drier when cool. Fertile, gritty, well-drained soil; neutral pH. Full sun. Flowers: large, 2–3 in. wide, petals overlapping. Leaves: kidney-shaped to nearly round, to 4 in. wide, felty,

Fagraea ceilanica

Geranium maderense

Geranium maderense, flowers

Pelargonium cucullatum

Pelargonium ×*domesticum* 'Cha Cha'

Pelargonium peltatum

faintly zoned; margins lobed, toothed or scalloped. *Semitrailing to shrubby habit, variously colored and marked. Prefer cool nights. These hybrids may involve* P. angulosum, P. cucullatum, *and* P. grandiflorum. *'Cha Cha' has strawberry-pink-and-white petals, with red-violet nectar guides and splashes.*

Pelargonium peltatum

HANGING PELARGONIUM, IVY-LEAFED GERANIUM, GERANIO
South Africa. Evergreen perennial creeping herb, 1–2 ft.; zones 9–10. Blooms warm months. Moderate moisture, drier when cool. Fertile, gritty, well-drained soil; neutral pH. Full sun. Flowers: about 1 in. wide, petals not overlapping. Leaves: round in general outline, lobes pointed like English ivy, felty. *Trailing or pendent habit. Suitable for baskets, beds, and slopes. Prefers cool night temperatures.*

GESNERIACEAE

GESNERIAD FAMILY
Gesneriaceae includes approximately 126 genera of terrestrial and epiphytic herbs, or rarely shrubs from tropical regions worldwide. They are characteristic herbs of the rain forests of the American tropics. The family includes houseplants such as gloxinias and African violets. Leaves are simple, often fleshy, and hairy, often with purple coloration. Flowers are bell-shaped or tubular, with 5 fused petals, the lower 2 lobes more or less differentiated into a lip. Flowers are bisexual, with floral parts mounted on a nectar-producing disk (receptacle). They are commonly arranged in flat-topped clusters (cymes) or sometimes solitary. The fruit is a dry capsule or occasionally a berry.

Episcia

Episcia includes 9 species of stoloniferous herbs from South America. Cultivars come in a variety of foliage and floral colors. Leaves are softly hairy often with silvery or purplish markings. New plantlets develop at the ends of stolons, unique in this family. Culture is similar to African violets. Episcias are ultra-tropical, very sensitive to temperatures below 60°F and low humidity. They die back outdoors in subtropical areas but usually come back if protected by mulch and neighboring plants. Propagate by division. Suitable for hanging baskets and small areas of ground cover. Episcias need bright filtered light to bloom well but will burn in direct sunlight. Pests include sucking and chewing insects, nematodes, and snails.

Episcia cupreata

CARPET-PLANT, FLAME-VIOLET, STRAWBERRY BEGONIA
Brazil, Colombia, Venezuela, Peru. Evergreen succulent herb; zone 11. Blooms warm months. Even moisture and humidity. Fertile, humus-rich, well-drained soil. Bright filtered light. Flowers: trumpet-shaped, lobes toothed, orange to scarlet, throat yellow. Leaves: ovate, to 2 in. long, blade green and silvery scaled with green veins, hairy; margins crenate. 'Check Mate' is a prolific bloomer. Its leaves are chocolate brown.

Gloxinia

Gloxinia includes approximately 15 species of herbs from tropical America. Commonly grown as houseplants, they can be grown outdoors in mild weather. Their showy flowers are pollinated by birds and bees. Leaves are succulent and hairy. Generally, these tender rainforest species are intolerant of high night temperatures, low humidity, alkaline pH, and cold. *Gloxinia sylvatica* has a greater tolerance for heat and cold and thrives outdoors year-round in South Florida. It is highly recommended. *Sinningia speciosa*, one of the more commonly cultivated gesneriads, is usually, though incorrectly, referred to as gloxinia because it was once included in this genus.

Gloxinia sylvatica

BOLIVIAN SUNSET
Synonyms: *G. sylvatica* 'Bolivian Sunset' (hort.), *Seemania sylvatica*. Bolivia (eastern slope of the Andes), southwestern Brazil. Perennial rhizomatous herb to 2 ft.; zones 10–11. Blooms primarily winter, spring. Regular moisture and humidity. Fertile, well-drained soil. Bright filtered light. Flowers: inflated tubes, lobes tiny, outside scarlet, inside red and yellow-spotted, ridged; sepals 5-pointed, ridged; on 3- to 4-in. peduncles. Leaves: elliptic, 3–4 in. long, dark green, roughly hairy; petioles and stems reddish. *Fairly tolerant of winter chills and warm summer nights. Highly recommended. A cultivar name is often used inappropriately for this species. Cultivar names are not applicable when only one form exists. Tops die back in hot, dry conditions and new growth starts at the base.*

Streptocarpus

Streptocarpus includes approximately 130 species of annual and perennial herbs from tropical Africa, Madagascar, southern China, Southeast Asia, and Indo-malaysia. *Streptocarpus* species are stemless; *Streptocarpella* species have stems. Some *Streptocarpus* species come from tropical rain forests where many species grow epiphytically. Others come from grasslands. Leaves are in dense basal rosettes, lack petioles (sessile), and are more or less hairy. Flowers are trumpet-shaped and brightly colored. Culture is similar to African violets. Cold-sensitive.

Streptocarpus ×hybridus

CAPE PRIMROSE, ESTREPTOCARPO
Garden origin. Perennial herbs under 1 ft.; zone 11. Bloom in mild months. Evenly moist when warm, less when cool. Fertile, humus-rich, well-drained soil. Bright filtered light. Flowers: trumpet-shaped, outside more or less hairy. Leaves: lanceolate, in dense basal rosettes, quilted; sessile. *These multicolored rhizomatous hybrids involve South African* S. rexii *and other species in their ancestry.*

GOODENIACEAE

GOODENIA FAMILY
Goodeniaceae includes approximately 12 genera of herbs and shrubs, which are widely distributed in tropical and subtropical coastal regions, with greatest diversity in Australia. A few species are cultivated. Leaves are simple, usually spirally arranged, or sometimes in basal whorls. Flowers are bisexual and bilaterally symmetrical. The 5 petals are united at the base, the lobes flared to one side fanlike. This is the origin of the name half-flower. The flowers are solitary or are arranged in various types of inflores-

Episcia cupreata 'Check Mate'

Gloxinia sylvatica

Streptocarpus ×*hybridus*

cences: cymes, racemes, panicles, or heads. The fruit is a dry capsule, nut, or sometimes a fleshy drupe.

Scaevola

Scaevola (pronounced skay-VO-la) includes approximately 96 species of herbs and shrubs primarily from Australia and the South Pacific region. Their seeds can drift great distances in the ocean and finally germinate on beaches after the salt is washed away by rain. For this reason, their natural habitat is seaside dunes and forests. They are well suited to coastal landscaping but do well inland as well. *Scaevola taccada* (syn. *S. sericea*), a name that is apparently resolved after being batted back and forth for many years, is invasive in shore communities and should not be planted near the coast. Propagate by cuttings or division. Few pests. The genus name means "little hand," a reference to the shape of the flowers.

Scaevola aemula

FAN-FLOWER, BLUE FAN
Synonym: *S. humilis*. Southern and southeastern coasts of Australia. Perennial subshrub to 1 ft.; zones 8–11. Blooms warm months. Moderate moisture, tolerates dry periods. Sandy, well-drained soil. Full sun. Flowers: fan-shaped, blue-violet, center yellow and white. Leaves: obovate, 1–2 in. long; margins toothed. *Salt tolerant to the dunes. Suitable as a ground cover or in hanging baskets. Selections include 'Blue Fandango', more erect and shrublike*

than 'Blue Wonder'; 'Mauve Clusters' with mauve-violet flowers; and 'New Wonder' with smaller flowers.

Scaevola taccada

HALF-FLOWER, HAILSTONES, BEACH-BERRY
Synonym: *S. sericea*. Indian Ocean, tropical Asia to Pacific Islands. Evergreen shrub, 6–10 ft.; zones 10–11. Blooms almost all year. Moderate moisture. Sandy, well-drained soil. Full sun. Flowers: tubular with fan-shaped lobes, white, veins pale violet; clustered in the leaf axils; fruit white (hence the name hailstones). Leaves: obovate, 3–4 in. long; clustered at ends of branches. *The leaves of var. sericea are covered with gray hairs (sericeous); var. taccada leaves are glossy. An invasive pest of tropical shorelines. A controlled species in Florida. Inkberry, Scaevola plumieri, a smaller shrub with black fruit, is native to South Florida coastlines.*

HAEMODORACEAE

BLOODWORT FAMILY, KANGAROO-PAW FAMILY
Haemodoraceae includes approximately 14 genera of subtropical and temperate herbs primarily from southwestern Australia, New Guinea, South Africa, and North America. They are tuberous or rhizomatous plants of coastal woodlands. The family name as well as the common name bloodwort allude to the red sap in the rhizomes and *wort* is an Old English word for "plant." Leaves are sword-shaped

and basal, arranged in equitant fans that resemble irises. Flowers are bisexual and bilaterally symmetrical. The 6 petals are united into a tube at the base, the 6 lobes asymmetrically grouped to one side. The perianth is densely woolly (tomentose). The fruit is a dry capsule.

Anigozanthos

Anigozanthos includes approximately 11 species of herbs from southwestern Australia. Many become dormant in the dry season. They thrive in Mediterranean-type climates such as southern California. Flowers are very attractive to hummingbirds. Propagate by seed, or selections by division. Dwarf Bush Gem Series cultivars are more resistant to "ink spot," and are more floriferous than the type species. They are grown for the Australian cut-flower trade and are sometimes available in the United States.

Anigozanthos flavidus

KANGAROO-PAW
Southwestern Australia. Perennial herb, 1–2 ft.; zones 9–11. Blooms spring, early summer. Regular moisture. Gritty, well-drained soil, alkaline pH. Full sun. Flowers: tubular, lobes pointed, not reflexed, throat light green, covered with red or green hairs; stalk 4–6 ft.+, with soft reddish hairs. Leaves: sword-shaped; in equitant fans. *Thrives in hot climates and coastal locations. May become dormant when cold or dry.*

HAMAMELIDACEAE

WITCH HAZEL FAMILY
Hamamelidaceae includes approximately 25 genera of deciduous and evergreen trees and shrubs from mild temperate and subtropical regions, especially eastern Asia. Only a few species are cultivated in the United States. Leaves are simple or occasionally palmately lobed with toothed margins, alternately or spirally arranged, and sometimes aromatic. Flowers are bisexual, or unisexual with male and female flowers on the same plant (monoecious) or sometimes polygamous. Petals are sometimes absent. The inflorescence is a spike, raceme, panicle, or head. The fruit is a woody capsule.

Loropetalum

Loropetalum includes a single species of evergreen shrub or small tree from Japan, southern China, and the foothills of the Himalayas. *Loropetalum chinense* is an old favorite in mild coastal areas as far north as the Carolinas and Oregon as well as in subtropical areas of California and Florida. Leaves are simple with toothed margins and arranged in opposite ranks. Flowers are white, yellow, or pink. More intensely hued selections are enjoying a revival. The name alludes to the strap-shaped petals. Flowers are in small clusters at the ends of the branches. Bracts are present. Culture is similar to azaleas. Prune lightly after flowering for shape.

Scaevola aemula 'Blue Wonder'

Scaevola taccada var. *sericea*

Anigozanthos flavidus

Loropetalum chinense var. *rubrum*

The natural horizontal branching invites espaliering. Propagate from cuttings.

Loropetalum chinense

Synonym: *L. indicum.* China, Himalayan foothills, Japan. Evergreen shrub or small tree, 6–12 ft.; zones 7–10. Blooms most of the year. Moderate moisture, tolerates dry periods. Fertile, humus-rich, well-drained soil; acid pH. Full to part sun or bright broken light. Flowers: petals strap-shaped, creamy white, pink to magenta; in small clusters. Leaves: ovate, with bristly, stellate hairs; sometimes with a metallic sheen. *Slow-growing and xeric. Suitable for understory planting. Var. rubrum has magenta flowers. Leaves of 'Hines Purple-leaf Plum Delight' are deep purple below; 'Copper Glow' leaves are coppery.*

HELICONIACEAE

HELICONIA FAMILY

Heliconiaceae includes a single genus of herbs primarily from tropical America with a few species from South Pacific islands. Closely related to bananas (Musaceae), heliconias are rhizomatous herbs with erect, unbranched stalks. Growth is sympodial. Leaves are in opposite ranks (distichous) and paddle-shaped. Secondary veins are parallel and almost perpendicular to the midvein. The petiole bases sheath the stem in overlapping layers. Flowers are bisexual, often inconspicuous, and have 5 stamens plus one staminode. Each lasts for a day, but up to 50 flowers open in succession. The inflorescence is protected and often partly hidden by a brightly colored primary bract, which is canoe-shaped, beaked (bent like a parrot's beak), or spathelike. The secondary floral bracts (bracteoles) are often colorful. The inflorescence may be erect, pendent, and/or spirally arranged, and usually develops from the end of the leafy stalk, or rarely on a separate, leafless stalk. The fruit is a drupe. Water that collects in the upright bracts, the nectar, and fruit attract birds and other animals. American species are pollinated by hummingbirds. Pacific species have relatively inconspicuous inflorescences but ornamental leaves with reddish veins or red margins and are pollinated by bats.

Heliconia

Heliconia includes 200–250 species of clump-forming perennial herbs mainly from tropical America, plus 6 from the Pacific island region from Samoa to Sulawesi. They are grouped according to their habit as banana-like (musoid) with upright, spirally arranged leaves and long petioles; gingerlike (zingiberoid) with ladderlike (distichous) leaves; or cannalike (cannoid) with upright leaves and short petioles. They are also grouped by erect, pendent, or spirally arranged inflorescences. In the wild, a number of species may exist in the same habitat without hybridizing although they share the same pollinators. Other than a few isolated natural hybrids, *Heliconia* species strongly resist hybridization. Rather, the variability within the species is a result of their extensive ranges, accounting for named selections (Berry, pers. comm.).

Rainforest species are cold-sensitive, but those from higher elevations tolerate cooler temperatures. In full sun they need more moisture than in shaded spots. Mulch well to protect the rhizomes and maintain even moisture. After flowering, the stalk dies back and new shoots develop from the rhizome (polycarpic). Plants that "walk" too far from their preferred location need to be reset occasionally. Cut old stalks when they turn yellow. Heliconias like even moisture and some will grow in shallow water. They are heavy feeders. Use slow-release, high-potassium fertilizers. Small species are suitable for containers. Heliconias fail to flower in inadequate light. They make striking, long-lasting arrangements. Remove all or most of the leaves. Combine erect and pendent inflorescences or match them with aroid or palm foliage in tall, heavy containers.

Heliconia angusta 'Holiday'

Synonyms: *H. angustifolia, H. bicolor.* Southeastern Brazil. Rhizomatous herb, 2–3 ft.; zone 11. Blooms late fall, winter. Moist and humid. Fertile, humus-rich soil. Bright to medium filtered light. Flowers: sepals white; stalk and bracts red to pink; inflorescence erect, distichous. Leaves: narrowly lanceolate to oblong, 2–4 ft. long. *Other selections have orange to yellow bracts. Blooms for the winter holidays in northern latitudes. Protect from wind and cold. The species name means "narrow," alluding to the relatively narrow leaves. Species name often misspelled augusta.*

Heliconia aurantiaca

Mexico, Central America. Rhizomatous herb, 2–5 ft.; zones 10–11. Blooms winter, spring. Moist and humid. Fertile, humus-rich soil. Broken sun to medium filtered light. Flowers: sepals yellow; bracts orange turning green; inflorescence erect, distichous. Leaves: paddle-shaped; zingiberoid.

Heliconia bihai 'Lobster-claw One'

LOBSTER-CLAW HELICONIA, WILD PLANTAIN

Northern South America. Rhizomatous herb to 16 ft.; zones 9–11. Blooms spring, summer. Moist and humid. Fertile, humus-rich soil. Full sun to bright broken light. Flowers: sepals mostly hidden, green and white; bracts scarlet, green along the margins with a thin white edge, widely spaced; inflorescence erect, distichous. Leaves: musoid. *A commonly cultivated large heliconia. Root-hardy in zone 8 or 9 if rhizome is protected from freezing.*

Heliconia bourgaeana

Central eastern Mexico. Rhizomatous herb to 18 ft.; zone 11. Blooms warm months. Moist and humid. Fertile, humus-rich soil. Full sun to bright filtered light. Flowers: sepals yellow and green, mostly hidden inside bracts; primary bract maroon-pink, red, or crimson, with a greenish lip; inflorescence erect, distichous. Leaves: musoid.

Heliconia caribaea

WILD PLANTAIN, PLATANILLO, RIQUI-RIQUI

Lesser Antilles; widely distributed. Rhizomatous herb, 10–18 ft.; zones 10–11. Blooms warm months.

Heliconia angusta 'Holiday'

Heliconia aurantiaca

Heliconia bihai 'Lobster-claw One'

Moist and humid. Fertile, humus-rich soil. Full to part sun. Flowers: white to green, hidden inside bracts; bract bases imbricate, yellow, yellow-green to dark red or crimson or combinations, waxy; inflorescence erect, distichous. Leaves: musoid, waxy below. Stems: waxy. *'Purpurea' commonly cultivated. Fairly cold tolerant but leaves turn brown when exposed to near-freezing temperatures. Considerable variability due to isolation of populations in various Caribbean islands.*

Heliconia champneiana 'Splash'

Belize, Guatemala, Honduras. Rhizomatous herb to 13 ft.; zones 10–11. Blooms warm months. Moist and humid. Fertile, humus-rich soil. Full sun to bright broken light. Flowers: sepals green and yellow, hidden inside bracts; bracts golden-yellow with red speckles; stalk red; inflorescence erect, distichous. Leaves: musoid. *'Maya Gold' has little or no red markings.*

Heliconia chartacea 'Sexy Pink'

Guiana to Amazon. Rhizomatous herb, 10–16 ft.; zone 11. Blooms warm months. Moist and humid. Fertile, humus-rich soil. Full sun to medium filtered light. Flowers: sepals green; bracts bright pink with wide green margins; inflorescence pendent spirals on twisted rachis. Leaves: musoid, blades tend to split. Stems: more or less waxy. *A popular species but cold-sensitive. Can be grown in containers and brought indoors on chilly nights.*

Heliconia collinsiana

Rhizomatous herb to 10 ft.; zones 10–11. Blooms late spring, early summer. Moist and humid. Fertile, humus-rich soil. Bright filtered light. Flowers: prominent, sepals yellow to white; bracts red, broad at the base, narrowing to a long, curved point, widely spaced; rachis red; inflorescence pendent, distichous; fruit yellow. Leaves: musoid. *A tender rainforest species. Fred Berry, authority on heliconias, considered this species a variation of H. pendula, but did not publish that information before his death.*

Heliconia episcopalis

AMAZON BASIN

Rhizomatous herb to 8 ft.; zone 11. Blooms warm months. Moist and humid. Fertile, humus-rich soil. Full sun to medium filtered light. Flowers: sepals orange and yellow; bracts yellow and orange, tightly imbricate; inflorescence erect, distichous. Leaves: musoid. *A distinctive species. Name alludes to the resemblance of the tightly interlocked bracts to a priest's miter.*

Heliconia 'Golden Torch'

PARROT-FLOWER, YELLOW BIRD, PLÁTANO

Natural hybrid (Guyana), *H. psittacorum* × *H. spathocircinata*. Rhizomatous herb, 2–8 ft.; zones 10–11. Blooms spring, early summer to all year. Moist and humid. Fertile, humus-rich soil. Full sun to medium filtered light. Flowers: golden-yellow; bracts golden-yellow, tip and keel greenish. Leaves: musoid, erect. *A natural hybrid with several selections. Suitable for containers.*

Heliconia griggsiana 'Angry Moon'

WESTERN ECUADOR

Rhizomatous herb to 20 ft.+; zone 11. Blooms fall, winter, spring.

Heliconia bourgaeana

Heliconia caribaea 'Birdsey's Amarillo'

Heliconia caribaea 'Flash'

Heliconia caribaea 'Purpurea'

Heliconia caribaea 'Purpurea' color variant

Heliconia champneiana 'Splash'

Heliconia chartacea 'Sexy Pink'

Heliconia collinsiana

Moist and humid. Fertile, humus-rich soil. Full sun to bright filtered light. Flowers: yellow, hidden inside bracts; bracts pink to red with a blue-gray, waxy keel; inflorescence pendent, spirals on twisted red rachis. Leaves: musoid, waxy below. Stems: more or less waxy. *Potentially a very large plant. Of mild regions at moderate altitude. Cold- and heat-sensitive. For protected locations. Other selections yellow-green and lack the blue-gray coloration. Photographed in an arrangement with bluish palm leaves by the International Heliconia Society.*

Heliconia indica 'Spectabilis'
SOUTH PACIFIC HELICONIA

Only known in cultivation (possibly Papua New Guinea, South Pacific islands). Rhizomatous herb, 10–20 ft.; zone 11. Blooms fall, winter. Moist and humid. Fertile, humus-rich soil. Full sun to medium filtered light. Flowers: sepals green and red; bracts green and purple, hairy; inflorescence erect, distichous. Leaves: light green and coppery or green and red with white secondary veins. *Grown primarily as a foliage plant. Species has 6 varieties, all with reddish leaves and inconspicuous greenish inflorescences.*

Heliconia latispatha

Mexico to northern South America; widely distributed. Rhizomatous herb, 6–16 ft.; zones 10–11. Blooms warm months. Moist and humid. Fertile, humus-rich soil. Full sun to medium filtered light. Flowers: sepals yellow and green; bracts red and yellow; inflorescence erect, spirals on twisted rachis. Leaves: musoid. *Fairly tolerant of cold weather and dry conditions though leaves may brown. When 'Red-Yellow Gyro' blooms outside my window, color-coordinated spotted-breasted orioles visit for drinks and perhaps some nectar or a snack of whatever lurks in the bract basin.*

Heliconia lingulata

Peru, Bolivia. Rhizomatous herb, 10–15 ft.; zones 10–11. Blooms warm months. Moist and humid. Fertile, humus-rich soil. Full sun to bright filtered light. Flowers: greenish yellow, bract tips broad and rounded; erect, distichous or spiral arrangement. Leaves: musoid. *'Kampong' was introduced from cultivation in Belize. Its yellow and red bracts are more brightly colored than are those of the type species.*

Heliconia mariae
BEEFSTEAK HELICONIA

Central America, Colombia. Rhizomatous herb, 10–20 ft.; zone 11. Blooms summer. Moist and humid. Fertile, humus-rich soil. Full sun to part shade. Flowers: red, secrete a sticky mucous that turns

Heliconia episcopalis

Heliconia 'Golden Torch'

Heliconia indica 'Spectabilis'

Heliconia latispatha 'Red-Yellow Gyro'

Heliconia griggsiana 'Angry Moon'

Heliconia mariae

Heliconia lingulata 'Kampong'

black on the bract rims; bracts tightly overlapping (imbricate), blood red; inflorescence pendent. Leaves: musoid. *Cold-sensitive. Photographed in an arrangement with palm leaves and other heliconias by the International Heliconia Society.*

Heliconia metallica

Honduras to Bolivia. Rhizomatous herb, 3–8 ft.; zones 10–11. Blooms warm months. Moist and humid. Fertile, well-drained soil. Full sun to medium filtered light. Flowers: large and exposed, red to pink; bracts maroon to greenish; inflorescence erect, distichous to slightly twisted; on a leafless scape. Leaves: cannoid, dull maroon-purple below; midrib sometimes white. *The inflorescence on a leafless stalk is distinctive. The flowers are more conspicuous than the bracts in this species.*

Heliconia mutisiana
PINK PANTHER

Colombia. Rhizomatous herb, 7–20 ft.; zone 11. Blooms warm months. Moist and humid. Fertile, humus-rich soil. Bright to medium filtered light. Flowers: sepals yellow and green; bracts red covered with long white hairs, appearing pink when dry, red when wet; rachis pink to yellow, deeply sinuous, covered with long white hairs; inflorescence pendent, distichous. Leaves: musoid. *An unusual and tender rainforest species.*

Heliconia orthotrica

Ecuador. Rhizomatous herb to 6 ft.; zone 11. Blooms warm months. Moist and humid. Fertile, humus-rich soil. Full sun to bright filtered light. Flowers: dark green and white; bract pink with dark green margins,

keel pale yellow; rachis yellow; inflorescence erect, distichous. Leaves: musoid. *Highly regarded but cold-sensitive. Suitable for large containers, which can be brought indoors in cold weather. A variable species with many selections. 'Eden Pink' has pink bracts with a white base; 'Garden of Eden' is tricolored.*

Heliconia pogonantha

Costa Rica, Nicaragua. Rhizomatous herb to 25 ft.; zone 11. Blooms warm months. Moist and humid. Fertile, humus-rich soil. Bright filtered light to part shade. Flowers: sepals yellow and cream; bracts deep orange-red, yellow at base, covered with silky hairs; inflorescence pendent, distichous to slightly spiraled, densely ranked when young. Leaves: musoid. *Unusual in cultivation. Potentially very*

large. *Very cold-sensitive. Photographed in an arrangement by the International Heliconia Society.*

Heliconia psittacorum
PARROT-FLOWER, PARAKEET HELICONIA, PERIQUITOS

Lesser Antilles (West Indies) to eastern Brazil. Rhizomatous semi-aquatic herb, 3–5 ft.; zone 11. Blooms warm months. Moist to wet, humid. Fertile, humus-rich soil. Full to part sun. Flowers: orange to pale yellow; inflorescence erect, distichous. Leaves: musoid. *Suitable for containers. Thrives in low, wet areas. Can be grown with the rhizome submerged. The species name alludes to parrots for the colors and shape of the bracts. A number of natural hybrids involve this species. 'Strawberries and Cream' has pink bracts.*

Heliconia metallica

Heliconia mutisiana

Heliconia orthotrica 'Eden Pink'

Heliconia orthotrica 'Garden of Eden'

Heliconia pogonantha 'Barnum Bailey'

Heliconia psittacorum 'Strawberries and Cream'

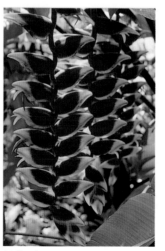

Heliconia rostrata

Heliconia sarapiquensis

Heliconia rostrata

HANGING LOBSTER-CLAW,
PAINTED LOBSTER-CLAW
Eastern Amazon region of Ecuador
and Peru; widely cultivated. Rhizomatous herb, 6–20 ft.; zones
10–11. Blooms warm months.
Moist and humid. Fertile, humus-rich, well-drained soil. Full to part
sun. Flowers: sepals yellow; bracts
scarlet and yellow with a green margin, covered with stiff short hairs;
inflorescence pendent, distichous.
Leaves: musoid, blade prone to
splitting in windy conditions. Underside of midrib often tinged red.
*Protect from wind damage. Blooms
on second-year growth. The species
name alludes to the beaklike shape of
the bracts. One of the more cold-tolerant species. Should not be confused
with the erect-flowered H. bihai 'Lobster-claw One'.*

Heliconia sarapiquensis

Panama, Costa Rica. Rhizomatous
herb, 3–9 ft.; zone 11. Blooms late
spring, early summer. Moist and
humid. Fertile, humus-rich, well-drained soil. Bright filtered light.
Flowers: sepals yellow; bracts pinkish red, golden-yellow at the base;
inflorescence erect, spiral on a
twisting yellow rachis. Leaves:
musoid, midrib spotted with red.
*A rather dainty, cold-sensitive species.
Unusual in cultivation. Suitable for
containers.*

Heliconia spissa

Southern Mexico. Rhizomatous
herb to 8 ft.; zones 10–11. Blooms
spring, summer. Moist and humid.
Fertile, humus-rich, well-drained
soil. Full sun to bright filtered light.
Flowers: sepals pale yellow, tips
green; bracts red, yellow base and

lip; inflorescence erect, spiraling on
twisted rachis. Leaves: musoid.

Heliconia stricta

Amazon River headwaters. Rhizomatous herb, 3–5 ft.; zone 11.
Blooms late spring to midsummer.
Moist and humid. Fertile, humus-rich, well-drained soil. Full sun to
bright filtered light. Flowers: sepals
green with a white tip; bracts 3–5,
cheeks red, pink or orange, yellow
or greenish near keel, margin
green; inflorescence erect, distichous. Leaves: musoid, ovate, midvein red-striped. *A variable species
recognized by the relatively few
bracts. Cold-sensitive.*

Heliconia vellerigera

Colombia, Ecuador, Peru. Rhizomatous herb, 10–20 ft.; zone 11. Blooms
warm months. Moist and humid.

Fertile, humus-rich, well-drained
soil. Full sun to part shade. Flowers: sepals yellow, bracts burgundy,
thickly covered with long hair; inflorescence pendent, distichous and
slightly spiraled. Leaves: musoid.
*Cold-sensitive. Potentially very large.
Smaller plants suitable for containers
that can be brought indoors when cool.*

Heliconia wagneriana

Central America to Colombia.
Rhizomatous herb, 4–15 ft.; zones
11. Blooms warm months, primarily spring. Moist and humid. Fertile, humus-rich, well-drained soil.
Full sun to bright filtered light.
Flowers: sepals dark green; bract
green and yellow with pink cheek,
lip bright green; inflorescence
erect, distichous. Leaves: musoid,
midrib reddish; margins undulate.
Cold-sensitive. The leaf blades split

Heliconia spissa 'Mexico Red'

Heliconia stricta 'Sharonii'

Heliconia stricta 'Tangerine Dream'

Heliconia vellerigera

Heliconia wagneriana

in windy conditions. *Suitable for containers.*

Heliconia xanthovillosa 'Shogun Jade'

Panama. Rhizomatous herb, 10–20 ft.; zone 11. Blooms spring, summer. Moist and humid. Fertile, humus-rich, well-drained soil. Full sun to bright filtered light. Flowers: yellow and white; bract green covered with yellow hairs; rachis yellow, sinuous; inflorescence pendent, distichous, somewhat twisted. All parts covered with yellowish hairs. Leaves: musoid. *Cold-sensitive. Smaller plants are suitable for containers that can be brought indoors when cool. Photographed in an arrangement with a Monstera leaf by the International Heliconia Society.*

HEMEROCALLIDACEAE

DAYLILY FAMILY

Hemerocallidaceae includes a single genus of perennial herbs from temperate areas from China and Japan to Europe. The family is related to and resembles lilies, Liliaceae, and was formerly included in that family. *Hemerocallis* species are rhizomatous or have tuberous roots. Leaves are simple and in opposite ranks (distichous). Flowers are bisexual and radially symmetrical. The perianth consists of 6 petal-like tepals in 2 whorls, commonly yellow, orange, and burnt-orange to brick-red. There are 6 fertile stamens. The flowers are arranged in cymes. The fruit is a capsule with black seeds.

Hemerocallis

Hemerocallis includes approximately 16 species of perennial herbs from temperate China and Japan to Europe. Plants in cultivation are mostly complex hybrids. A number of hybrids have been produced that thrive in the subtropics. Plants are fibrous-rooted or tuberous. The leaves are basal, strap-shaped, often keeled, or grasslike. The flowers are large and funnel-shaped. The genus name means "day-beautiful," alluding to the one-day life of the individual flowers. Buds open successively over a span of several weeks in spring. Some forms are fragrant. Propagate se-

lections by division. Seed is infrequently produced in cultivation, and hybrid seed, if viable, does not breed true. Thinning overgrown plants for good air circulation inhibits sucking insects. The flowers often orient themselves toward the morning sun. There are a number of dwarf cultivars.

Hemerocallis hybrids

DAYLILY

Garden origin. Seasonally dormant or evergreen perennial herbs, 2–3 ft.; zones 5–10. Blooms spring, early summer. Regular moisture during active growth, little when dormant. Fertile, well-drained soil. Full sun. Flowers: funnel-shaped, tepals 6, selections in many colors; scapes taller than leaves. Leaves: strap-shaped to linear. *Heat-tolerant hybrids such as 'Aztec Gold' will grow in the subtropics.*

HYACINTHACEAE

HYACINTH FAMILY

Hyacinthaceae includes approximately 67 genera of rhizomatous and bulbous herbs, which are widely distributed, with greatest diversity in the Mediterranean region and South Africa. Leaves are arranged in basal rosettes, but some species are leafless. Flowers are terminal on a central shoot in a compact spike or raceme.

Eucomis

Eucomis includes approximately 10 species of herbs from subtropical regions. This genus was formerly included in Liliaceae. A few species are occasionally cultivated. They have large bulbs, which need plenty of room to expand. Leaves are basal. The flowers are in clusters on a central stalk and topped by a tuft of sterile bracts (coma), somewhat resembling a pineapple. The bulbs should be mulched in winter to protect from cool temperatures or are wintered over in a dry spot indoors in colder regions. Suitable for containers.

Eucomis bicolor

PINEAPPLE-LILY

South Africa. Seasonally dormant herb to 18 in.; zones 8–10. Blooms summer. Seasonally moist/dry. Fer-

tile, well-drained soil. Full sun. Flowers: nodding, tepals greenish, more or less marked with purple; stamens purple-tipped; in a compact spike on a leafless, purple-spotted stalk, topped with a coma of sterile green bracts. Leaves: sword-shaped, in basal rosettes, glossy, purple-spotted; margins undulate.

HYPOXIDACEAE

HYPOXIS FAMILY

Hypoxidaceae includes approximately 9 genera of perennial herbs primarily from the Southern Hemisphere, with greatest diversity in southern Africa. The family is related to Velloziaceae. Plants have enlarged corms, mostly subterranean stems with just the apex above ground, which are covered with the fibrous leaf bases. Leaves are slender, linear to lanceolate, or sometimes in pleated fans and ar-

ranged in basal rosettes. Flowers are bisexual and radially symmetrical. The 6 tepals are usually yellow, sometimes tinged red. Three of the 6 stamens may be modified into staminodes. The fruit is a capsule or berry.

Molineria

Molineria includes approximately 7 species of herbs from Southeast Asia to Australia. These species were formerly placed in Liliaceae or Amaryllidaceae. They are clump-forming plants. The foliage is pleated, resembling slightly open fans, the overall effect resembles a young palm. Flowers are borne at the base of the leaves in whorls of coarse bracts at ground level. The flowers of *Hypoxis* species are similar but are on long stalks. The otherwise tasteless *Molineria* berries contain an artificial sweetening agent, which is used locally in

Heliconia xanthovillosa 'Shogun Jade'

Hemerocallis 'Aztec Gold'

Eucomis bicolor

Molineria capitulata

drinks but has not proven durable enough for commercial use. Leaf fibers are used to make fishnets.

Molineria capitulata

PALM-GRASS, STAR-GRASS

Synonyms: *Curculigo capitulata, M. recurvata*. Tropical Asia to Australia. Evergreen perennial herb, 2–3 ft.; zones 10–11. Blooms spring or in warm months. Moist and humid. Average, well-drained soil. Full sun. Flowers: tepals yellow, to 1 in. wide; filaments yellow, fused into a cup; stalkless; bracts, green with brown hairs, in compact whorls (involucres), at the base of the leaves. Leaves: basal, elliptic in general outline, 2–3 ft. tall, pleated, palm-like. *Species name sometimes misspelled capitata.*

IRIDACEAE

IRIS FAMILY

Iridaceae includes approximately 78 genera of herbs, which are widely distributed, with cultivated species primarily from southern Africa and the eastern Mediterranean region. They have fibrous roots and bulbs or corms. The tropical genera included here were formerly included in the genus *Iris. Iris* was the Greek goddess of the rainbow. Leaves are generally basal, sword-like, and arranged in fans with overlapping bases (equitant). Flowers are radially symmetrical with 3 sepals and 3 petals. The 3 stamens distinguish irises from lilies and amaryllis, which have 6 stamens. Horticulturally, the sepals are referred to as "falls" and the petals as "standards." The anthers are sometimes attached to the midline of the petals in bearded and crested forms. The fruit is a capsule.

Saffron is a condiment made from stamens of the Spanish *Crocus sativus*. This costly spice is a flavoring as well as yellow coloring in dishes of Iberian origin such as *paella*. The yellow coloring of traditional Latin American dishes comes from native annatto (achiote), *Bixa orellana*, which is flavorless. The saffron-colored robes of certain sects of Buddhist monks derive their color from much less costly turmeric, *Curcuma longa*, an Asian condiment and fabric dye.

Aristea

Aristea includes approximately 50 species of herbs from tropical Africa to South Africa and Madagascar. They have fibrous roots. Leaves are usually basal, arranged in opposite, fanlike ranks (equitant). Flowers are small, usually blue, and are arranged in many-flowered panicles. *Aristea ecklonii* is sometimes cultivated. Roots are sensitive to disturbance. Divide overgrown clumps, but do not separate individual plants. Can be grown from seed.

Aristea ecklonii

BLUE STARS

Southeastern Africa, Madagascar. Evergreen perennial herb, 1–2 ft.; zones 9–11. Blooms late spring, early summer. Regular moisture when hot, sparingly when cool. Sandy, humus-rich, well-drained soil. Full to part sun. Flowers: star-shaped, blue; in open panicles above the foliage; stalk 2–2.5 ft. tall. Leaves: basal, linear, grasslike, 12–18 in. tall, bases overlapping, fanlike (equitant); small leaflike bracts develop at the joints of the scape. *Develops large clumps. Flowers last only a day but others follow sequentially. A salt-tolerant plant suitable for the coastal garden.* Aristea major *is distinguished by spirelike inflorescences.*

Chasmanthe

Chasmanthe includes 3 species of cormous herbs from tropical and southern Africa. They are occasionally grown in the United States.

Leaves are sword-shaped, spreading like a fan with overlapping bases (equitant). The flowers are arranged in opposite rows on an erect stalk (distichous). The name means "yawning flower," referring to the long upper petal, or lip, which is extended forward—sometimes referred to as hooded. Cut back in late winter. Overwinter corms indoors in colder regions.

Chasmanthe floribunda

South Africa. Perennial cormous herb, 2–3 ft.; zones 9–10. Blooms late winter, spring. Moist to moderate. Fertile, well-drained soil. Full to part sun. Flowers: trumpet-shaped, upper petal elongated, red-orange to yellow; arranged compactly in opposite ranks; scape 2–3 ft. tall. Leaves: sword-shaped, equitant, to 2 ft. long. *Clump-forming. Usually grown in moist conditions but fairly tolerant. Shown here growing with agaves in the desert collection at Balboa Park.*

Crocosmia

Crocosmia includes 7–9 species of perennial herbs from tropical to southern Africa. Funnel-shaped flowers are arranged in opposite ranks (distichous). Leaves are slender, grasslike. The capsules are round. The name alludes to the saffronlike (*Crocus sativus*) aroma of the dried flowers. In cooler climates protect corms from freezing or store indoors. Cut back in fall for upright new growth. Divide in spring and avoid disturbing once active growth begins.

Crocosmia ×crocosmiiflora

MONTBRETIA

Garden hybrid (South Africa), *C. pottsii* × *C. aurea*. Seasonally dormant cormous herb, 2–3 ft.; zones 7–9. Blooms summer. Regular moisture during active growth, little when dormant. Fertile, well-drained soil. Full to part sun. Flowers: funnel-shaped, orange to yellow; on arching stalks. Leaves: narrowly sword-shaped, pleated, to 2 ft. long, arching; arranged in fans. *The most commonly cultivated* Crocosmia. *Develops large clumps.*

Dietes

Dietes includes approximately 6 species of rhizomatous herbs from tropical eastern and South Africa. Leaves are sword-shaped, arranged in fans (equitant). The flowers are bisexual, radially symmetrical with 6 tepals and a spreading 3-parted petal-like (petaloid) pistil. They last a single day but more flowers follow in succession. Difficult to eliminate once established. *Dietes* species thrive in Mediterranean-type climates with hot, dry summers. Blooms less profusely in moist conditions. A good companion for planting around ornamental flowering trees that require a dry dormant period in spring. Tough and pest resistant. Moderate-sized bedding plants.

Dietes bicolor

WILD IRIS, SPANISH IRIS, FORTNIGHT IRIS

Synonyms: *Iris bicolor, Moraea bicolor*. South Africa (East Cape).

Aristea ecklonii

Chasmanthe floribunda

Crocosmia ×crocosmiiflora

Evergreen perennial herb to 2.5 ft.; zones 9–10. Blooms intermittently in warm months. Moderate moisture. Average, well-drained soil. Full sun. Flowers: tepals obovate, light yellow with a maroon spot at the base, pistil petaloid, pale yellow; on long, wiry stalks. Leaves: sword-shaped, 2–3 ft. long, pale green. *Thrives in Mediterranean-type climates. Blooms less vigorously in moist conditions or where evening temperatures are warm. Self-seeding.*

Dietes iridioides

AFRICAN IRIS, FORTNIGHT IRIS
Synonyms: *D. vegeta, Moraea vegeta.* Tropical Kenya, Uganda to South Africa. Evergreen perennial herb to 3 ft.; zones 9–10. Blooms intermittently in dry months. Moderate moisture. Average, well-drained soil. Full sun. Flowers: tepals white with yellow streaks at the base; pistil petal-like, violet. Leaves: in basal fans, sword-shaped, to 3 ft. long. *Thrives in hot, dry climates such as southern California. Blooms more freely if irrigation is kept to a minimum in the dry season. Freely self-seeding and may become weedy.*

Neomarica

Neomarica includes approximately 12 species of rhizomatous evergreen herbs from tropical America. Each flower lasts only a day. Seeds are orange (*Iris* seeds are usually brown). Easy to grow and pest resistant. Plants are evergreen but growth slows in cool or dry weather. Leaves are spear-shaped and arranged in fans (equitant). The inflorescence develops from the midrib of a leaf—a distinctive characteristic (visible in photograph). Propagate by division, removing some of the older, outer leaves.

Neomarica caerulea

APOSTLE PLANT, MARICA IRIS, LIRIO
Synonyms: *Cypella caerulea, Marica caerulea.* Southern Brazil. Evergreen perennial herb to 3 ft.; zones 10–11. Blooms intermittently from midsummer to early winter. Seasonally moist and humid, drier when cool. Average, well-drained soil. Bright broken light or morning sun. Flowers: sepals spreading, vio-

let, streaked brown at base, petals smaller, purple with white and brown streaks, opening a few at a time, lightly fragrant; bract boatlike, green; inflorescence emerging from the leaf midvein. Leaves: basal, equitant, swordlike to 3 ft. long, notched near the base and above an inflorescence. *Flowers last a day, new flowers open every few days over several weeks. Stake the flowering leaf if necessary.* Neomarica gracilis *is similar but with white sepals.*

Trimezia

Trimezia includes 10–20 species of evergreen bulbous herbs from the American tropics. Leaves basal, arranged in fans and overlapping at the base (equitant). Flowers are usually yellow. The name refers to the 3 sepals, which are larger than the petals. *Trimezia martinicensis* is commonly grown in the West Indies and South Florida and is widely naturalized. It is xeric in seasonally moist/dry conditions. Viviparous plantlets develop at the joints of the stoloniferous scapes, taking root wherever the scape touches down (hence the name walking iris). Thin regularly to prevent weediness. Fruit, a dry capsule, is rarely produced in cultivation.

Trimezia martinicensis

WALKING IRIS
Synonyms: *Iris martinicensis, T. lurida.* Tropical America; widely naturalized. Perennial cormous herb to 2 ft.; zones 10–11. Blooms warm months. Seasonally moist and humid, fairly dry when cool. Average, well-drained soil. Full sun to bright filtered light. Flowers: petals smaller than the sepals, reflexed, 1.5 in. wide, cupped in center, yellow with brown spots. Leaves: basal, equitant, lanceolate, light green. *Flowers last only a day.*

Watsonia

Watsonia includes approximately 50 species of cormous perennial herbs from South Africa. They are seasonally dormant herbs with irislike, equitant leaves. They are closely related to *Gladiolus* but differ by having a branched style. Flowers are borne in opposite ranks on the stalk (distichous). Some species

are invasive weeds in Australia, especially the bulbil-producing *W. meriana.*

Watsonia borbonica

PINK WATSONIA, WILD GLADIOLUS
Synonym: *W. pyramidata.* South Africa (Southwest Cape, KwaZulu-Natal). Seasonally dormant perennial herb, 2–3 ft.; zones 9–10. Blooms spring. Moist during active growth, dry when dormant. Sandy, humus-rich, well-drained soil. Full sun. Flowers: funnel-shaped, pink, sometimes white, lightly scented; in opposite ranks on an erect spike to 3 ft. tall. Leaves: sword-shaped, to 2 ft. long, shorter than the flower spike. *A cormous, clump-forming herb of grassland habitat subject to dry season fires. In mild temperate areas, protect corms with mulch in winter. Divide in early spring.*

LAMIACEAE

MINT FAMILY
Lamiaceae (Labiatae) includes approximately 250 genera of herbs and subshrubs, or occasionally trees and woody climbers, which are widely distributed, with greatest diversity in the Mediterranean region. The family is currently undergoing intensive reorganization. Many species traditionally in the family Verbenaceae have been transferred to Lamiaceae. For the convenience of readers more familiar with the former arrangement, those species are kept together here as an informal subsection of the Lamiaceae. The family includes many culinary herbs such as sage, thyme, mint, spearmint, rosemary, basil, marjoram, the medicinal oils menthol and mint, and the fragrance lavender. Leaves are usually simple, aromatic, and opposite.

Dietes bicolor

Dietes iridioides

Neomarica caerulea

Trimezia martinicensis

The stems are frequently square in cross section. Flowers are bisexual and bilaterally symmetrical. Individual flowers are usually small, the 5 petals and 5 sepals fused into a tube at the base, the upper and lower lobes modified into lips. Clusters of flowers are often arranged opposite each other in the leaf axils in a pseudowhorl (verticillaster) around the stems, with the appearance of a single inflorescence. Occasionally flowers are solitary. Bracts may be large and leaflike. The fruit is a 4-seeded nutlet or a drupe.

Leonotis

Leonotis includes approximately 40 species of semiwoody herbs or shrubs from tropical and South Africa. Woolly flowers are tubular with a 3-lobed lower lip. Stamens are grouped in 2 pairs. They are borne in congested, opposite cymes (verticillasters), which surround the erect stalks at the nodes. The tubular calyces have 10 needle-like teeth and are joined at the base as a persistent disk. *Leonotis* is used locally as a folk medicine in infusions for colds, in animal drinking water to treat or prevent diseases, or smoked as a weak narcotic. These species thrive in dry, hot climates. Soil should almost dry between waterings. Prune back after blooming to keep tidy. Suitable for containers.

Leonotis leonurus

LION'S EAR, WILD DAGGA
South Africa. Perennial semiwoody herb or shrub, 4–8 ft.; zones 9–11. Blooms spring, summer. Moderate moisture to fairly dry in cool season. Average, well-drained soil. Full sun. Flowers: tubular, downy (pubescent), orange, arranged in verticillasters around the leafless terminal section of the stems at the nodes. Leaves: linear to narrowly ovate, to 5 in. long; margins slightly scalloped (crenulate); aromatic when crushed. *Thrives in southern California. A weed in Australia. 'Harrismith White' has white flowers.*

Leonotis nepetifolia

LION'S TAIL, BALD HEAD
Synonym: *Phlomis nepetifolia*. Tropical Africa; widely naturalized. Annual herb, 3–5 ft.; zones 7–10. Blooms winter, spring, various. Moderate moisture to fairly dry. Average, well-drained soil. Full sun. Flowers: tubular, orange, downy; calyx tubular, green, teeth 10, sharply pointed; in congested verticillasters. Leaves: ovate; margins toothed, 1–3 in. long. Stems: grooved, 4-angled. *Distributed as an annual by seed companies and now a weed in amenable conditions pantropically (Iwarsson, pers. comm.).*

Orthosiphon

Orthosiphon includes approximately 40 species of herbs from the Old World tropics. No authoritative study has been published on the listed species. The name remains tentative though based on the advice of experts familiar with the group. Grown as a bedding plant in Singapore (Tan, pers. comm.), which has a fairly uniform year-round climate.

Orthosiphon aristatus

CAT'S WHISKERS, CAT'S MOUSTACHE, JAVA-TEA
Synonyms: *Clerodendranthus spicatus, O. stamineus* (hort.). Southeast Asia, Indonesia to Australia, New Guinea. Perennial subshrub, 2–3 ft.; zones 9–11. Blooms fall, winter, spring. Regular moisture and humidity, less when cool. Fertile, well-drained soil. Part sun to bright filtered light. Flowers: violet to white, stamens long-exserted; in terminal spikes. Leaves: ovate, 3–4 in. long; margins deeply toothed. *A fast-growing plant suitable for the tropical perennial garden. Trim occasionally for compact growth. Highly recommended.*

Plectranthus

Plectranthus includes at least 350 species (probably closer to 500 with recent combinations) of shrubs and perennial and annual herbs, which are widely distributed in the Old World tropics. Many species previously segregated into numerous genera have been combined into *Plectranthus*. The familiar houseplant coleus, formerly in *Solenostemon*, is now placed in this genus. Other genera that have been merged with *Plectranthus* include *Englerastrum, Geniosporum, Isodyctyophorus, Mesona, Neohyptis, Nosema, Octomeron, Rabdosiella, Solenostemon,* and *Symphostemon*. Under consideration are *Aeollanthus, Anisochilus, Capatanopsis, Dauphinea, Holostylon, Leocus, Madlabium,* and *Pycnostachys* (Olmstead et al. 2000). The leaves are simple, softly to roughly hairy, aromatic, and often ornately patterned. Flowers are tubular, 2-lipped, the upper lip 3- or 4-lobed, arranged in terminal, spikelike panicles. The 2 pairs of stamens are of different lengths (didynamous). Giant white fly is a pest of these species where extant.

Plectranthus ecklonii

South Africa. Perennial subshrub to 6 ft.; zones 9–11. Blooms late summer, fall. Regular moisture when hot, less when cool. Moderately fertile, well-drained soil. Full to part sun. Flowers: tubular, 2-lipped, blue-violet; in branched terminal

Watsonia borbonica

Leonotis leonurus

Leonotis nepetifolia

Orthosiphon aristatus

Plectranthus ecklonii

spikes. Leaves: simple, broadly ovate, rough; margin toothed; aromatic. *A fall bloomer and suitable for containers. Prune in early spring for heavy bloom in fall. Color selections from pale sky-blue to white are attractive combined in the tropical perennial garden.*

Plectranthus scutellarioides hybrids

COLEUS, PAINTED NETTLE, CÓLEO
Synonyms: *Coleus blumei, Coleus verschaffeltii, Solenostemon scutellarioides*. Southern China, Southeast Asia, Indomalaysia to New Guinea and northern Australia. Short-lived perennial herbs, 1–3 ft.; zones 10–11. Bloom primarily spring or intermittently. Regular moisture. Average to fertile, well-drained soil. Full sun to bright filtered light. *Many color forms. Commonly grown as annuals and houseplants. Many new hybrids tolerate full sun.*

Salvia

Salvia includes approximately 900 species of annual, biennial, and perennial herbs and shrubs, which are widely distributed. Leaves are simple, often lacking petioles (sessile), and aromatic. Flowers are bisexual, tubular to bell-shaped, 2-lipped, the upper lip elongated forward, or hoodlike. There are 2 stamens. Flowers are arranged in spikes. Dark leaf color or hairs are typical of species that tolerate heat and drier conditions. Selections of scarlet sage, *S. splendens*, are commonly cultivated as annual bedding plants. Salvias are attractive to butterflies. In the West, hummingbirds and monarch butterflies are dependent on fall-blooming species such as salvias to fortify their energy reserves before long migrations. *Salvia officinalis* is culinary sage. Some species are used in perfumes and medicinally. Many unrelated aromatic plants are referred to as sages.

Salvia leucantha

MEXICAN BUSH-SAGE
Mexico to Colombia. Perennial herb, 3–5 ft.; zones 7–11. Blooms warm months. Moderate moisture to fairly dry. Sandy, well-drained soil. Full sun. Flowers: corolla tubular, white, 2-lipped, upper lip hooded; calyx magenta, downy; in spikelike, terminal verticillasters. Leaves: lanceolate, to 4 in. long. Foliage and arching stems covered with silvery hairs. *Thrives in dry or coastal locations but not seaside. Suitable for the tropical perennial garden.*

Scutellaria

Scutellaria includes approximately 350 species of herbs, which are widely distributed. Flowers are tubular, ascending, often clustered in terminal spikes or panicles. Scientific and common names allude to the helmet-shaped upper lip. There are 4 stamens. The leaves are simple, nonaromatic.

Scutellaria costaricana

HELMET-FLOWER, SKULLCAP, DRAGON'S TEARS, ESCUTELARIA
Synonyms: *S. argentata, Salvia* 'Red Fountain' (hort.). Costa Rica, Panama. Perennial subshrub, 2–6 ft.; zones 9–11. Blooms intermittently all year. Regular moisture. Fertile, humus-rich, well-drained soil. Full to part sun. Flowers: corolla tubular, red-orange, lower lip golden-yellow, upper lip helmet-shaped (galeate); calyx 2-lipped with a deciduous, hairy protuberance (scutellum). Leaves: ovate, to 4 in. long, dark green with recessed veins; margins minutely toothed. Stems: purple. *Color selections variable. Of understory and streamside locations, often to considerable altitude. Heat tolerant. Suitable for perennial beds or containers. Grown as an annual in colder regions.*

LAMIACEAE

Formerly Verbenaceae

This group of species, now included in Lamiaceae, were traditionally circumscribed by Verbenaceae. They are kept together here for the convenience of those familiar with the older arrangement. Inflorescences are often terminal.

Clerodendrum

Clerodendrum includes approximately 400 species of shrubs primarily from warm temperate and tropical regions of the Old World. Leaves are simple, often large. Flowers are tubular with spreading lobes in many-flowered panicles or cymes. The stamens are often long and showy. A number of species spread rapidly by suckers and some are also heavily self-seeding. *Clerodendrum bungei* and *C. chinense* are not recommended because they are particularly aggressive and difficult to control. *Clerodendrum japonicum* is listed as invasive in Hawaii.

Plectranthus scutellarioides hybrid

Clerodendrum aculeatum

Salvia leucantha

Clerodendrum bungei

Scutellaria costaricana

Clerodendrum chinense

Most species need firm control. Cut back in winter and dig up suckers. Because of their tendency to grow eastward toward the morning sun, they can be partially confined by planting on the west side of a barrier such as a driveway. They are attractive to butterflies.

Clerodendrum aculeatum

WEST INDIAN PRIVET

West Indies. Evergreen sprawling shrub to 6 ft.; zones 10–11. Blooms winter, spring. Moderate moisture. Average, well-drained soil. Full to part sun. Flowers: trumpet-shaped, tube about 1 in. long, lobes flaring, somewhat revolute, white; stamens white to violet, long-exserted; calyx green, strongly reflexed; in axillary cymes. Leaves: lanceolate, 2–3 in. long, dull-green; margins entire to faintly toothed, small spines in the axils. *Suitable as a barrier hedge. Habit spreading but can be pruned to shape.*

Clerodendrum bungei

GLORY-BOWER

Synonym: *C. foetidum*. China. Semideciduous shrub, 4–6 ft.; zones 8–11. Blooms late winter, spring. Moderate moisture. Average, well-drained soil. Full to part sun. Flowers: trumpet-shaped, petals light to dark pink; buds and calyx magenta; in dense cymes. Leaves: broadly ovate, to 1 ft. wide, reddish and red-veined, hairy below; margins toothed; musky-scented when crushed. *Aggressively suckering. Invasive. Marginally hardy but deciduous with frost. Not recommended.*

Clerodendrum chinense

CHINESE GLORY-BOWER, HONOLULU ROSE

Synonyms: *C. fragrans* (hort.), *C. philippinum*. China, Japan. Evergreen clambering shrub, 5–8 ft.; zones 10–11. Blooms spring, summer. Moderate moisture. Average, well-drained soil. Full sun to filtered light. Flowers: roselike, white; calyx red; in compact heads; dry flowers persistent. Leaves: broadly ovate, to 10 in. long, softly hairy; margins widely toothed; musky-scented when crushed. *The nose-gay clusters of roselike flowers are attractive, but this invasive, suckering clerodendrum* quickly loses its charm. Strongly discouraged.

Clerodendrum indicum

INDIAN GLORY-BOWER, TUBE-FLOWER, TURK'S TURBAN, GUARDIA CIVIL

Synonym: *C. siphonanthus*. Indonesia, India, Myanmar (Burma), often naturalized. Semideciduous shrub to 8 ft.; zones 8–11. Blooms warm months. Moderate moisture. Average, well-drained soil. Full to part sun. Flowers: trumpet-shaped, tubes long, slender, lobes revolute, creamy white, to 4 in. long, in terminal panicles; calyx thickens into a fleshy, star-shaped, red-orange fruit, to 1 in. wide (much smaller than *C. minahassae*). Leaves: lanceolate, to 6 in. long. *Aggressively suckering and self-seeding. Not recommended. An apparent hybrid of* C. speciosissimum, *with red flowers in dense cylindrical inflorescences, is rather unappealing, and is a prolific seeder.*

Clerodendrum minahassae

FAIRCHILD'S CLERODENDRUM, STARFISH CLERODENDRUM

Sulawesi (Celebes). Evergreen shrub to 8 ft.; zones 10–11. Blooms intermittently in warm months. Moderate moisture. Average, well-drained soil. Full to part sun. Flowers: trumpet-shaped, base tubular, to 6 in. long, lobes white, linear; in clusters in the leaf axils; calyx fleshy, glossy, red, 3–4 in. wide; seed-covering (sarcotesta) blue-green. Leaves: ovate, to 6 in. long, glossy, quilted; margins entire. *A very attractive shrub, flowering off and on throughout the year. The vividly exotic calyces provide a dramatic metamorphosis. Suitable for hedges. Self-seeding.*

Clerodendrum paniculatum

PAGODA-FLOWER

China, Southeast Asia, Malaysia. Evergreen shrub to 6 ft.; zones 10–11. Blooms warm months. Moderate moisture. Average, well-drained soil. Full to part sun. Flowers: trumpet-shaped, small, tube orange, lobes white, occasionally scarlet; buds and calyx scarlet, in many-flowered, erect terminal panicles to 18 in. above foliage. Leaves: subcordate, to 10 in. long; margins undulate. *Attractive to butterflies and hummingbirds. Aggressive. Cut back sharply after bloom and remove suckers.*

Clerodendrum quadriloculare

STARBURST CLERODENDRUM

Philippines. Evergreen shrub to 12 ft.; zones 10–11. Blooms winter, early spring. Moderate moisture. Average, well-drained soil. Full sun

Clerodendrum indicum

Clerodendrum indicum, fruit

Clerodendrum minahassae

Clerodendrum minahassae, fruit

Clerodendrum paniculatum

Clerodendrum quadriloculare

to bright filtered light. Flowers: tubular, tubes long, mauve-pink, lobes white, revolute; in many-flowered cymes. Leaves: lanceolate, 6–8 in. long, dark blue-green, glaucous above with silvery hairs, eggplant-purple below. Stems: distinctly 4-sided. *Adaptable and spectacular winter bloomer starting its fireworks display around the new year. Becomes top heavy in bloom and may topple if too tall. Prune back by half after bloom. Remove suckers at base. Pest resistant. Attractive to butterflies and hummingbirds. A selection has variegated leaves.*

Clerodendrum speciosissimum
JAVA GLORY-BOWER
Synonym: *C. fallax*. Indonesia (Java), Sri Lanka. Evergreen shrub, 4–8 ft.; zones 10–11. Blooms warm

months. Moderate moisture. Average, well-drained soil. Full sun. Flowers: trumpet-shaped, scarlet; stamens long-exserted, scarlet; seed covering (sarcotesta) aquamarine; inflorescence broadly cone-shaped. Leaves: broadly cordate, 6–10 in. wide, softly downy; margins undulate, crenulate; petioles and veins reddish. *Very large, downy leaves are distinctive. Attractive to swallowtail butterflies. Aggressive. Prune to 1 or 2 ft. after bloom and dig suckers. 'Bronze Prince' has purple to bronze leaves. See C. indicum for details on an apparent hybrid.*

Clerodendrum ×speciosum
HYBRID GLORY-BOWER-VINE
Garden (tropical Africa), *C. thomsoniae* × *C. splendens*. Evergreen climber to 20 ft.+; zones 10–11. Blooms fall, winter, spring. Moder-

ate moisture. Average, well-drained soil. Full to part sun. Flowers: corolla red-orange; stamens long-exserted; calyx cup-shaped with pointed lobes, purple, persistent. Leaves: ovate to cordate, 4–5 in. long, glabrous. *This hybrid is sterile and does not set seed. It is commonly confused with C. splendens, one of its parents. The purple calyx and lack of fruit are good field marks.*

Clerodendrum splendens
GLORY-BOWER-VINE
Synonym: *C. superbum* (hort.). Tropical Africa. Evergreen climber to 20 ft.+; zones 10–11. Blooms winter, spring. Moderate moisture. Average, well-drained soil. Full sun. Flowers: scarlet; stamens scarlet, not exserted; in dense cymes. Leaves: heart-shaped, to 6 in. long, glossy. *A twining vine which needs*

support and pruning for control. *An excellent fence or wall covering. Few pests. 'Copperleaf' has reddish leaves.*

Clerodendrum thomsoniae
BLEEDING-HEART, BAG-FLOWER
Central western Africa. Evergreen climber to 12 ft.; zones 10–11. Blooms spring, summer. Regular moisture. Average, well-drained soil. Full to part sun, bright filtered light. Flowers: corolla red, tubular; calyx white, rarely red, inflated, enclosing the tube of the corolla, heart-shaped. Leaves: ovate, to 7 in. long. *A small twining climber suitable for an arbor. Not invasive. Pest resistant. Often misspelled thomsonii.*

Clerodendrum ugandense
BUTTERFLY CLERODENDRUM
Synonym: *C. myricoides* 'Ugandense' (hort.). Tropical to southern

Clerodendrum speciosissimum

Clerodendrum ×speciosum

Clerodendrum splendens

Clerodendrum wallichii

Clerodendrum thomsoniae

Clerodendrum ugandense

Africa. Evergreen shrub, 5–10 ft.; zones 10–11. Blooms warm months. Moderate moisture. Fertile, humus-rich, well-drained soil. Full sun to bright filtered light. Flowers: petals pale blue-violet to white, lip violet; stamens long-exserted; in loose panicles. Leaves: elliptic to obovate, 4–6 in. long, glossy; margins finely toothed; aromatic. *Flowers dance like little butterflies with long antennae at the ends of long, arching branches. Not invasive. Sensitive to nematodes, but healthy plants are more resistant. Keep well mulched. Attractive to hummingbirds.*

Clerodendrum wallichii
Synonym: *C. nutans* (hort.). Southern China, Bhutan, Bangladesh, India, Southeast Asia. Evergreen shrub to 6 ft.; zones 9–11. Blooms late fall. Moderate moisture. Fertile, well-drained soil. Full sun to bright filtered light. Flowers: petals white, sepals green turning dark red; stamens long-exserted; in lax panicles. Leaves: lanceolate, glossy, to 6 in. long. *Spreading understory plant. Can be maintained as an informal hedge with light trimming. Suspend pruning after midsummer for fall bloom. Pest resistant.*

Congea
Congea includes approximately 7 species of clambering shrubs from Southeast Asia and India. *Congea tomentosa* is occasionally cultivated. The flowers are inconspicuous. The softly woolly bracts are showy, completely enveloping this shrubby climber like a pink cloud in late winter.

Congea tomentosa
SHOWER-OF-ORCHIDS, LLUVIA DE ORQUÍDEAS
Myanmar (Burma), Thailand. Evergreen clambering shrub, 10–15 ft.; zones 10–11. Blooms late winter. Seasonally moist, fairly dry. Humus-rich, well-drained soil; neutral to acid pH. Full sun. Flowers: tiny, white; stamens red; bracts showy, softly woolly, pink to mauve-lavender with age. Leaves: elliptic to oblong, to 8 in. long, more or less pubescent below. Young branches covered with soft hairs.

Does well in alkaline soil with added organics and occasional applications of microelements. Prune after bloom for a shrubby plant or train on a sturdy support. Pest resistant.

Cornutia
Cornutia includes approximately 15 species of trees and shrubs from the West Indies and tropical America. Leaves are large, the base of the blade often decurrent (tapering down the petiole), and highly aromatic when crushed. Flowers are small, blue to violet, with a 3-lobed upper lip, and are borne in many-flowered, erect or ascending panicles.

Cornutia grandifolia
PAVILLA ("LITTLE TURKEY HEN")
Mexico, Central America. Evergreen shrub or tree, 15–25 ft.; zones 10–11. Blooms late spring to early fall. Seasonally moist/dry. Average, well-drained soil. Full to part sun. Flowers: corolla violet, upper lip 3-lobed; buds and calyx downy, lavender; 2 fertile stamens; in erect terminal panicles. Leaves: broadly ovate to elliptic, to 10 in. long, tip tapering (acuminate), base decurrent, downy; margins widely toothed, undulate; tobacco-scented. *Uncommon and underutilized. Suitable as a privacy hedge. Of seasonally moist/dry forests. Pest resistant.*

Cornutia obovata
PALO DE NIGUA, CAPELO JUGÜERILLO ("JESTER'S CAP")
Puerto Rico, endangered in the wild. Evergreen tree or shrub, 10–20 ft.; zones 10–11. Blooms spring, early summer. Moist to moderate. Average, well-drained soil. Full to part sun. Flowers: small, upper lip 3-lobed, lower lip spreading at tip, pale violet, in many-flowered, ascending to erect panicles. Leaves: elliptic, 4–8 in. long, finely downy. *Wood used for shipbuilding and woodworking. Rare in cultivation in the United States.*

Congea tomentosa

Congea tomentosa, flowers and bracts

Cornutia grandifolia

Cornutia obovata

Gmelina

Gmelina includes approximately 35 species of trees and shrubs from Africa to Australasia. The floral parts are fused into a cup at the base. The corolla has a 2- to 4-lobed upper lip and a 2-lobed lower lip. Leaves are simple. Often armed with small spines in the leaf axils. Wood harvested for timber.

Gmelina arborea

GRAY TEAK, WHITE TEAK, SNAPDRAGON-TREE, INDIAN BULANG
India. Deciduous tree, 60–75 ft.+; zones 10–11. Blooms late winter, spring. Seasonally moist/dry. Average, well-drained soil. Full sun. Flowers: cup-shaped at base with 2 large spreading lips, upper lip 4-lobed, lower lip 2-lobed, rust-brown, throat golden-yellow. Leaves: cordate to broadly ovate, 4–8 in. long, dark, dull green, leathery, hairy below; margins shallowly lobed. Trunk: large, bark creamy white to light tan. *A large tree of seasonally moist/dry forest. Begins flowering when tree is leafless and continues after leafing out. One of several species referred to as teak.*

Gmelina philippensis

HEDGEHOG, WILD SAGE
Synonym: *G. hystrix.* Philippines. Evergreen scandent or clambering shrub to 10 ft.+; zones 10–11. Blooms warm months. Seasonally moist, moderate. Average, well-drained soil. Full to part sun. Flowers: cup-shaped, petal lobes pointed (1 large, 3 small), bright yellow, opening in pairs; bracts scalelike, tan, imbricate; inflorescence pendent, 6–12 in. long. Leaves: elliptic, 4–5 in. long; margins entire. Branches long, arching, pendent or climbing. Spines in leaf axils. *Fast-growing shrub. Unusual but attractive. Few significant pests.*

Holmskioldia

Holmskioldia (pronounced holm-she-OLD-ee-ah) includes approximately 10 species of scandent shrubs from tropical Africa and Asia. The name honors Danish botanist Theodor Holmskiold. The flowers, with a saucerlike calyx and narrowly tubular corolla, are very attractive to hummingbirds and butterflies. They are suitable for coastal planting and tolerant of poor soil. Shoots root where they touch ground and need to be thinned regularly. The species here are not known to produce seed in cultivation so are unlikely to become invasive. Very pest resistant and easy to grow.

Holmskioldia sanguinea

MANDARIN HAT, CHINESE HAT, PARASOL FLOWER
Sub-Himalayan Bangladesh, India, Bhutan, Nepal. Evergreen scandent shrub, 8–12 ft.; zones 9–11. Blooms warm months. Moderate moisture. Average, well-drained soil. Full to part sun. Flowers: corolla tubular, lobes minute, orange to greenish orange, red, or yellow; calyx fused, disk-shaped, of similar color; stamens 4, exserted; in axillary racemes. Leaves: ovate, 2–3 in. long, tips acuminate; margins faintly toothed. *'Mandarin Rouge' is a red selection reminiscent of the tasseled red hats worn by pre-revolutionary Mandarin Chinese. 'Citrina' is a yellow cultivar. Highly attractive to hummingbirds and butterflies.*

Holmskioldia tettensis

CUP-AND-SAUCER FLOWER
Synonym: *H. speciosa.* Tropical Africa, Asia. Evergreen shrub to 6 ft.; zones 9–11. Blooms primarily summer. Moderate moisture. Average, well-drained soil. Full to part sun. Flowers: corolla tubular, purple, lobes 5, flared; calyx disk-shaped, pink; stamens long-exserted, filaments purple, anthers white. Leaves: obovate, 1–2 in. long, slightly pubescent; margins faintly toothed. *Tolerates heat and brief dry periods. Suitable for coastal planting. Uncommon in cultivation.*

Excellent for attracting hummingbirds and butterflies.

Oxera

Oxera includes approximately 20 genera of shrubs or climbers from New Caledonia and Vanuatu (New Hebrides). Flowers are 4-lobed with 2 elongated, pointed lips. They have 2 long stamens. *Oxera pulchella* is unusual in cultivation. The species name means "beautiful," for the delicate flowers borne in pendent clusters from the leaf axils. Though little known, *O. pulchella* would be excellent in bridal bouquets.

Oxera pulchella

ROYAL CLIMBER
New Caledonia. Clambering shrub to 10 ft.; zones 10–11. Blooms late winter. Seasonally moist and humid, drier when cool. Fertile, well-drained soil. Full to part sun.

Gmelina arborea

Gmelina philippensis

Holmskioldia sanguinea

Holmskioldia sanguinea 'Mandarin Rouge'

Holmskioldia tettensis

Oxera pulchella

Flowers: corolla funnel-shaped, white, 4-lobed, 2-lipped, laterally compressed; calyx cup-shaped with 4 pointed greenish-yellow lobes, persistent; stamens long-exserted; in pendent cymes; peduncles short. Leaves: lanceolate, 4–5 in. long, leathery, glossy; margins entire. Bark: brown with raised black lenticels.

Vitex

Vitex includes approximately 250 species of trees and shrubs, which are widely distributed in the tropics, subtropics, and mild temperate regions. No authority is known to have made a definitive study of the species and firm identification of the variable forms is problematic. The leaves are resinously aromatic. This genus can be distinguished from close relatives by the palmately compound leaves with 3–9 leaflets. Flowers are tubular, 2-lipped, the upper lip 3-lobed, lower lip 2-lobed, in erect panicles or racemes.

Vitex agnus-castus

CHASTE TREE,
FIVE-LEAF CHASTE TREE
India, southeastern China, Philippines. Deciduous shrub or tree, 10–15 ft.; zones 8–10. Blooms late spring, early summer. Moderate moisture. Average, well-drained soil. Full sun. Flowers: tubular with flaring lips, deep blue-violet; in terminal racemes to 10 in. tall, densely gray pubescent; fruit a drupe. Leaves: palmate; leaflets 4–6, elliptic, 1–4 in. long, quite

irregular in size, whitish below; margins smooth. *The inflorescence is more compact than usually depicted for this species, making this identification somewhat tentative; however, this is an extremely variable species over its range (Atkins, pers. comm.). The foliage is resinously aromatic, a delicious, somewhat conifer-like scent.*

Vitex parviflora

THREE-LEAFED CHASTE TREE,
MOLAVE
Philippines. Briefly deciduous tree to 45 ft.; zones 10–11. Blooms summer. Moderate moisture. Average, well-drained soil. Full sun. Flowers: small, 2-lipped, pale blue-violet, in open panicles. Leaves: palmate; leaflets 3, lanceolate; margins smooth. *The species name means "small flowers." Foliage aromatic.*

LAURACEAE

LAUREL FAMILY
Lauraceae includes approximately 52 genera of mostly trees and shrubs, which are widely distributed in the tropics, plus some from mild temperate regions. They are typical species of Southeast Asian and Amazon rain forests. The family is considered evolutionarily primitive. Leaves are often aromatic, mostly simple, rarely lobed, and usually in spirally arranged. Flowers are small, bisexual or sometimes unisexual with male and female flowers on separate trees (dioecious), on the same tree (monoecious), or combined with bisexual flowers (polygamous). *Laurus no-*

bilis, bay-leaf, is a culinary herb from the Mediterranean region. A laurel-wreath crown made of the fragrant leaves was the original Olympic award. The spice cinnamon comes from the bark of *Cinnamomum verum*, an ultra-tropical tree. Strongly aromatic camphor oil, *C. camphora*, is commonly used in preparations to relieve respiratory congestion. Avocado, *Persea americana*, is an important commercial and door-yard fruit.

Persea

Persea includes approximately 200 species of shrubs and trees from tropical regions of Asia and the Americas. The Indians of Central America and West Indies have enjoyed the highly nutritious fruit of *P. americana* for millennia. The small, bumpy-skinned green to purple or black cultivars from Mexico and the U.S. Southwest include 'Fuerte', 'Gwen', and 'Haas'. Florida grows smooth-skinned Guatemalan and West Indian cultivars, which are medium to large, ovoid, round or long-necked, sometimes reddish, moister, and lower (though not low) in fat.

Flowers are polygamous. Some varieties open the first day with receptive pistils (type A) or fertile stamens (type B). On the second day the stamens are fertile (type A) or pistils (type B) receptive. In cultivation it is a common practice to plant type A cultivars close to type B to assure good fruit set ("every 'Pollock' needs a 'Lulu'"). Time-

lapse photography, however, has shown that the timing of the flower opening does not correspond with better pollination and fruit set. Other factors apparently control compatibility and fertility.

Avocados must ripen on the tree and are insipid if picked prematurely, often the case with shipped fruit. When ripe, avocados soften slightly within 3–4 days after picking and have a rich nutty flavor. The only way to tell when they are ready is to pick one every week or so.

Persea americana

AVOCADO, ALLIGATOR PEAR
(CALIFORNIA), AGUACATE
Synonyms: *Laurus persea, P. gratissima*. Mexico, Central America, West Indies; widely cultivated. Evergreen or briefly deciduous tree, 35–60 ft.; zones 10–11. Blooms late winter, spring. Seasonally moist/moderate. Average to fertile, well-drained soil. Full sun. Flowers: small, yellow-green, in axillary panicles; fruit a one-seeded drupe on a long stalk. Leaves: elliptic, 6–8 in. long, russet when young, not aromatic; margins smooth. *Trees take 10 or more years to fruit from seed and seedlings do not breed true. Select cultivars are grafted. Best kept pruned to 15–20 ft. for good production.*

LECYTHIDACEAE

BRAZIL-NUT FAMILY
Lecythidaceae includes approximately 20 genera of trees and shrubs from the Old and New World tropics, with greatest diversity in the Amazon rain forest. Genera formerly segregated into Barringtoniaceae are now included in this family. A few species are grown in the United States, principally in botanical gardens. Leaves are simple and alternately arranged. Flowers are bisexual, solitary or in terminal racemes, sometimes on specialized branches or growing directly from the branches (cauliflorous). Stamens are numerous, mounted on a disk that is supported by a stalk (androphore). The fruit is a woody capsule or berry. Certain species, known as monkey-pots, have a dry fruit that disperses its seed through an operculum (pixidium). Brazil-nuts, *Bertholletia*, are

Vitex agnus-castus

Vitex parviflora

Persea americana

commonly sold in nut mixes in the United States. In the wild, they are important food for primates, parrots, and other animal species. Harvesting nuts has been promoted as an economic alternative to cutting these large rainforest trees for timber. *Gustavia* and *Couroupita* have indehiscent fruit (seeds not dispersed).

Barringtonia

Barringtonia includes approximately 39 species of trees from coastal regions of the Old World tropics from eastern Africa to the Pacific Islands. This genus was formerly segregated into its own family, Barringtoniaceae, because it lacks the specialized androphore of the more typical genera. Several species are occasionally cultivated. The leaves are simple and clustered at the ends of the branches. Flowers are bisexual, usually 4-petaled, rarely 5-petaled, or sometimes petals are absent. Stamens are numerous and showy. Flowers of *B. racemosa* are on pendent racemes that resemble the feather boas women wore in the Roaring Twenties. Flowers open at night and fall shortly after dawn. Many emit a musky fragrance that attracts fruit bats in the wild. *Barringtonia racemosa*, however, has one of the most ethereally delicate fragrances in the plant world—an extraordinary visual and olfactory delight for the early riser. The flowers usually must be hand-pollinated in cultivation. The fruits are 3-sided capsules resembling a bishop's miter. Barringtonias grow around the mouths of rivers and tolerate seasonal flooding and brackish water. The seed is dispersed by ocean currents. Seeds contain a toxin that native peoples use to catch fish by paralysis of the swim bladder.

Barringtonia racemosa

Tropical Asia, Oceania, Australia. Evergreen tree to 50 ft.; zones 10–11. Blooms spring, early summer. Moist, tolerates periodic flooding. Fertile, well-drained soil. Full sun. Flowers: petals 4, pink; calyx dark red; stamens numerous, long-exserted, pink; clustered on pendent racemes, to 18 in. long;

fragrant. Leaves: elliptic to oblanceolate, 6–12 in. long, base acuminate; margins toothed. *The stunning flowers with their exquisite fragrance open at night and last only a short time after sunrise. Salt tolerant.*

Couroupita

Couroupita includes 4 species of trees and shrubby trees from the American tropics. The leaves are simple with serrate margins, clustered near the ends of the nonflowering branches. Flowers are on specialized, leafless branches near the base of the trunk. They are asymmetrical with 6 unequal-sized petals. Stamens and staminodes are on the inner surfaces of a clamshell-like androphore. The pistil is located in the center of the basal disk. *Couroupita guianensis*, infrequently found in cultivation, is a signature tree at Fairchild Tropical Garden. It perfumes the air for

Barringtonia racemosa

Couroupita guianensis, flowers.

many months of the year. *Couroupita* is pollinated by bats in its wild habitat but must be hand-pollinated in cultivation to produce its cannonball-like fruits. It is somewhat cold-sensitive.

Couroupita guianensis

CANNONBALL TREE, BALA DE CAÑÓN, COCO DE MONO

Northern South America, Panama to Honduras. Briefly deciduous tree, 35–125 ft.; zones 10–11. Blooms warm months. Seasonally moist/dry. Fertile, humus-rich, well-drained soil. Full sun. Flowers: irregular, 3–4 in. wide, petals unequal, orange-red, tinged purple; stamens numerous, on inner surfaces of a clamshell-like disk (androphore), filaments red-violet, staminodes white; fragrant; on leafless serpentine lower branches; fruit round, shell woody, scaly brown, 6–8 in. diameter, malodorous when ripe. Leaves: oblanceolate, 6–10 in. long, clustered near branch tips. *A canopy tree of tropical rain forests. Flowers borne on specialized lower branches. Note the clamshell-like androphore in the photo.*

Gustavia

Gustavia includes approximately 40 species of trees from tropical America. They are from seasonally moist inland forest at mid-elevations. The very long leaves have serrated margins and are arranged like fleur-de-lis at the ends of the branches. The exotically attractive flowers are borne directly on the branches (cauliflorous) often in the branch axils. They are radially symmetrical, often large and showy with 6–8 or more petals. The numerous stamens and staminodes are arranged in crownlike concentric circles. Floral parts are mounted on a conspicuous disk

Couroupita guianensis

(androphore). The scent is sweet but fetid. Plant at a prudent distance from habitation. Cold damage to the canopy may result in multiple shoots from the base. Add microelements in alkaline soils.

Gustavia superba

STINKWOOD, MANTECO, MEMBRILLO, CHOPÉ

Synonyms: *G. marcgraaviana, Pirigara superba.* Northwestern Colombia, Ecuador, Panama, Costa Rica. Evergreen tree, 15–35 ft.+; zones 10–11. Blooms warm months. Seasonally moist/dry. Fertile, humusrich, well-drained soil; acid pH. Full sun. Flowers: corolla 4–5 in. wide, magenta speckled and cream; staminodes yellow with burgundy tips; on short stalks; cauliflorous. Leaves: lanceolate, 18–24 in. long; margins entire, undulate; young leaves pinkish, the central leaves erect and the outer leaves arching—like a fleur-de-lis. *Fleetingly sweet-fetid aroma. Cold-sensitive.*

LEEACEAE

LEEA FAMILY

Leeaceae includes a single genus of herbs and shrubs from tropical Africa to India, Malaysia, and New Guinea. It is closely related to the grape family, Vitaceae, but is distinguished by its shrubby or herb habit, terminal inflorescences, and fused stamen filaments. Leaves are pinnately compound or sometimes simple. Flowers are very small, with 4, occasionally 5, petals united into a tube at the base. The fruit is a berry.

Leea

Leea includes approximately 40 species of herbs, shrubs, and small trees from the Old World tropics. Leeas are often cultivated in European greenhouses and the West Indies though less frequently in the United States. They are undemanding foliage plants that will bloom most of the year in understory locations. Leaves are simple to pinnately or bipinnately compound. Flowers are small, in many-flowered, flat-topped clusters (cymes). The stamen filaments are fused into a tube at the base. Fruits are berries.

Leea guineensis

Synonym: *L. coccinea.* Tropical Africa, Southeast Asia, Philippines, Taiwan. Evergreen shrub, 12–15 ft.; zones 10–11. Blooms warm months. Moderate moisture and humidity. Moderately fertile, well-drained soil. Part sun to bright broken light. Flowers: small, corolla pink; calyx and buds scarlet to red; in flat-topped cymes; fruit a brown, 4-seeded drupe, to 0.5 in. Leaves: bipinnate, leaflets 5–9, unevenly elliptic to oblong, 3–5 in. long, glossy, secondary veins faint; margins sparsely toothed mostly at the tip.

Leea rubra

INDIAN HOLLY

Synonyms: *L. brunoninan, L. linearifolia, L. polyphylla.* Southeast Asia, Philippines. Evergreen shrub, 6–8 ft.; zones 10–11. Blooms late summer, fall. Moderate moisture and humidity. Moderately fertile, well-drained soil. Morning sun to broken or filtered light. Flowers: small, corolla ruby-red; calyx and buds ruby-red; in flat-topped cymes. Leaves: bipinnate, leaflets 3–5, oblong, dull green, to 5 in. long; veins impressed; margins coarsely serrated. *Suitable for understory planting and hedges.*

LINACEAE

FLAX FAMILY

Linaceae includes approximately 14 genera of herbs, shrubs, and a few climbers and trees, which are widely distributed. Flax, *Linum,* is cultivated for linen fiber and linseed oil. Leaves are simple and often spirally arranged. Flowers are bisexual and radially symmetrical. They usually have 5 partially fused petals and 5–10 stamens. The fruit is a one-seeded drupe or capsule.

Reinwardtia

Reinwardtia includes a single species of shrub from sub-Himalayan regions of northeastern India and southwestern China. It can be distinguished from related genera by the presence of 3 pistils, 3 stamens, and 3 staminodes. The flowers are solitary or are arranged in few-flowered axillary or terminal clusters. The genus name should not be confused with the palm genus *Reinhardtia.*

Reinwardtia indica

YELLOW FLAX

Synonyms: *Linum trigynum, R. trigyna.* Southwestern China to northeastern India. Evergreen shrub, 2–3 ft.; zones 9–11. Blooms winter. Moist and humid. Fertile, well-drained soil. Full to part sun. Flowers: funnel-shaped, petals 5, united at base, lobes spreading, 1.5–2 in. wide, bright yellow; pistils 3. Leaves: elliptic, 1–2 in. long, dark green, tip mucronate, base decurrent; margin minutely toothed (serrulate); clustered near ends of branches. *A winter-flowering species but needs warm daytime temperatures to bloom. Frequently confused with* Linum flavum, *a hardy European flax, which has narrower, lanceolate leaves.*

Gustavia superba

Leea guineensis

Leea rubra

Reinwardtia indica

LOMANDRACEAE
CORDYLINE FAMILY

Lomandraceae includes approximately 14 genera of herbs, shrubs, and small trees from Southeast Asia, Australasia to New Zealand, New Guinea, and Polynesia as well as tropical America. This family name has recently been corrected to Laxmanniaceae (Judd, pers. comm.). The genera were formerly placed in the agave family, Agavaceae, or the dracaena family, Dracaenaceae, but their embryology distinguishes them from both. In the field, *Cordyline* is distinguished from *Agave* and *Beaucarnea* by its fleshy berries, and from *Dracaena* by its black seeds. Cordylines usually are rhizomatous. Numerous selections and hybrids of *Cordyline* are grown in the tropics for their colorful leaves. *Lomandra* is commonly grown along freeways in Australia (Judd, pers. comm.). Leaves are usually in whorls at the ends of unbranched stalks (tufted). Flowers are small, bisexual, with 6 tepals and 6 stamens.

Cordyline

Cordyline includes approximately 15 or more species of tufted herbs or treelike plants from Southeast Asia to the Pacific Islands. The species number is dependent on any reclassification of the forms currently clumped together as varieties of *C. fruticosa*. The little-branched stems are fibrous and ringed with leaf scars. Leaves are lanceolate, spineless, and lack petioles (sessile), in opposite rows clasping the stem and spiraling around it in a double helix. The unforked leaf bases help distinguish *Cordyline* from *Dracaena*. Flowers are white or red-violet, small, in branched terminal panicles. The fruit is a berry.

Cordyline cuttings can be rooted directly in the ground. A caution, however, is that this ease of propagation often leads to haphazard landscaping. Plants quickly become leggy, dull, and parched in hot sun and/or with inadequate moisture. Best in a group of several plants of varying heights sheltered among foliage where they add months of color to the landscape. To prevent plants from become leggy, cut back overly long stems a few at a time. Native peoples of New Guinea use the colorful leaves as clothing, hats, fiber, thatching, and in folk medicine. Throughout the Pacific region, leaves are used to wrap food before pit-cooking. Leaves are very festive on a tropical buffet as placemats.

Cordyline fruticosa
TI, PALM-LILY, CROTO

Synonym: *C. terminalis* (hort.). Papua New Guinea; widely distributed in Pacific Asia and Oceania. Evergreen shrub, 6–10 ft.; zones 10–11. Blooms intermittently in warm months. Regular moisture and humidity. Humus-rich, well-drained soil. Bright filtered light, bright shade in summer. Flowers: small, red-violet to white, more or less fragrant; in branched terminal panicles. Leaves: lanceolate to oblong, arranged in a double helix, spineless. *Common name ti pronounced TEA. Numerous selections. New leaves are variously streaked red, pink, green, and white, becoming greener with age. Suitable for coastal but not seaside landscaping.*

LYTHRACEAE
CRAPE MYRTLE FAMILY, LOOSESTRIFE FAMILY

Lythraceae includes approximately 30 species of mostly herbs and subshrubs, or occasionally shrubs or trees, which are widely distributed in the tropics. Both the pomegranate family, Punicaceae, and the duabanga family, Sonneratiaceae, are now included in this family. Stems are often 4-angled. Leaves are simple with smooth margins. Flowers are bisexual and radially or bilaterally symmetrical. The 6 petals are crumpled in bud and remain crinkled after they open (hence the name crape myrtle), or petals may be absent. The bases of the stamens and perianth are fused into a floral tube or cup (hypanthium). The fruit is a dry capsule or berry.

Cuphea

Cuphea includes approximately 260 species of annual and perennial herbs and shrubs from the American tropics. A number of species and hybrids are cultivated, some as annuals in temperate climates. They are suitable for the tropical perennial garden. Species with long red, yellow, or orange floral tubes (hypanthia) are often referred to as firecracker plants. Leaves are simple, on a very short stalk (subsessile). Flowers are solitary or in few-flowered clusters mostly in the leaf axils. The petals, usually small to minute, are attached to the rim of the elongated floral tube.

Cuphea hyssopifolia
FALSE HEATHER

Southern Mexico, Guatemala, Honduras. Evergreen shrub, 10–20 in.; zones 9–11. Blooms warm months. Regular moisture. Fertile, well-drained soil. Full sun. Flowers: petals violet or white, anthers coming just to the rim of the floral tube. Leaves: lanceolate, to 1 in. long; sessile. *A low, rounded plant often used as a ground cover. 'Mad Hatter' is a compact form and 'Aurea' has golden leaves. Cuphea calophylla is sometimes confused with this species. It can be distinguished by leaves that graduate in size from larger near the base of the branches to smaller toward the tips and by anthers that are hidden inside the floral tube (Graham, pers. comm.).*

Cuphea ignea
FIRECRACKER BUSH, CIGAR-FLOWER

Synonym: *C. platycentra*. Southern Mexico. Evergreen shrub, 3–5 ft.; zones 9–11. Blooms warm months. Regular moisture. Fertile, well-drained soil. Full sun. Flowers: floral tube red-orange to yellow-tipped, 1–1.5 in. long. Leaves: ovate, 1–1.5 in. long. Stems: usually dark red. *Used as a border or as a bedding plant. In Hawaii, thousands of the small flowers are strung together to produce very fine leis (Howard, pers. comm.). Trim occasionally for compact growth.*

Cuphea llavea
BAT-FACED CUPHEA

Synonyms: *C. barbigera, C. miniata, Parsonsia llavea*. Mexico. Evergreen shrub, 2–3 ft.; zones 9–11. Blooms summer. Moderate moisture to fairly dry. Average, well-drained soil. Full sun. Flowers: tube purple, petals resemble small red ears at the end of the floral tube; anthers white. Leaves: ovate; margins finely serrate (serrulate). *Stems and leaves turn reddish when cold. Suitable for*

Cordyline fruticosa cultivar

Cuphea hyssopifolia

Cuphea ignea

dry gardens. *The species name is pronounced ya-VEY-ah.*

Cuphea schumannii
FIRECRACKER BUSH, CIGAR FLOWER
Mexico. Evergreen shrub, 4–6 ft.; zones 9–11. Blooms warm months. Regular moisture. Fertile, well-drained soil. Full sun. Flowers: floral tube red-orange, streaked green, 1–1.5 in. long; petals minute, like tiny purple ears at the rim of the floral tube. Leaves: ovate, to 3 in. long. *Open habit with long arching branches. Suitable for the tropical perennial garden.*

Duabanga
Duabanga includes approximately 8 species of trees from India to the western Pacific Islands. This genus was formerly in its own family, Sonneratiaceae. The species are generally large, buttressed trees of moist upland rain forest and coastal mangrove. The musky-scented flowers are pollinated by bats. Ants protect the fruit from herbivores in the wild. The wood is used to make tea chests. Leaves are simple and arranged in opposite ranks along the stem (distichous). The 4–8 petals or petal-like sepals are attached to a conspicuous floral cup (hypanthium). Flowers are surrounded by a whorl of involucral bracts (epicalyx). The fruit is a capsule with tiny seeds.

Duabanga grandiflora
Synonyms: *D. sonneratioides, Lagerstroemia grandiflora.* India to Malaysia. Evergreen tree, 50–125 ft.; zones 10–11. Blooms late winter, early spring. Moderate moisture to seasonally wet. Fertile, well-drained soil; acid pH. Full sun. Flowers: pale yellow, musky-scented; in clusters at the ends of long, pendent branches; calyx toothed, persistent on the disk-shaped berry; seeds very small. Leaves: oblong, to 12 in. *A fast-growing tree with distinctive long branches that sweep from the crown to the ground in open locations. Somewhat cold-sensitive. Suitable for planting in areas that flood periodically. Unusual in cultivation.*

Ginoria
Ginoria includes approximately 14 species of shrubs from Mexico and the West Indies. Leaves are simple, sometimes with spines in the axils. Flowers are crinkled, abruptly narrowing (clawed) at the base, solitary or borne in clusters in the leaf axils. In Spanish, *clavel* or *clavelina* specifically translates to "carnation," but is also loosely applied, like rose or lily in English, to other species.

Ginoria glabra
CLAVELINA
Cuba. Evergreen shrub to 6 ft.; zones 10–11. Blooms late winter, spring, sporadically in warm months. Regular moisture. Average to fertile, well-drained soil. Full to part sun. Flowers: petals crinkled, base clawed, magenta; sepals orange, visible between the petal bases; in clusters in the leaf axils. Leaves: elliptic to lanceolate, 2–3 in. long; petiole red. Bark: reddish. *Unusual in cultivation in the United States.* Ginoria nudiflora *has small white flowers to 0.5 in. wide.*

Lagerstroemia
Lagerstroemia includes approximately 53 species of deciduous trees and shrubs from Asia to Australia. Leaves are simple, with very short petioles or sessile, often copper-colored when young. Flowers are bisexual and radially symmetrical. The 6 petals are crumpled in bud and remain crinkled; they narrow abruptly at the base (clawed), leaving openings ("windows") in the center through which the sepals are visible. Stamens are numerous. Fruits are ovoid woody capsules with a persistent calyx.

Selections and hybrids of crape myrtle, *Lagerstroemia indica,* are frequently cultivated in mild temperate regions. Hybrids involving *L. fauriei* are mildew resistant and recommended for growing in the

Cuphea schumannii

Duabanga grandiflora

Cuphea llavea

Duabanga grandiflora, flowers

Ginoria glabra

tropics. Flowers are produced on new growth. Drastic yearly pruning, though formerly recommended, stresses the plants. The latest advice is to nip out spent flowers and thin and shape lightly after flowering. Micronutrients may be needed in alkaline soils.

Queen's crape myrtle, *Lagerstroemia speciosa*, is a medium to large tree from Southeast Asia and is often grown in tropical regions. The classification of the variable forms of this species and that of several closely related species is still unresolved (Graham, pers. comm.). In the forest trees grow tall and erect, competing for sunlight, developing a high canopy and buttressed trunk. In open areas they do not grow as tall and develop a rounded canopy. This variability has resulted in multiple names, a number of which probably are not valid. Iden-

tification is partly based on grooves and other minutia of the capsules. The capsules are round to turbinate, woody and somewhat tulip-shaped after opening, attractive in dry floral arrangements. They are recommended as an alternative to the capsules of the highly invasive wood-rose, *Merremia tuberosa*.

Lagerstroemia floribunda

Synonym: *L. turbinata*. Southeast Asia. Deciduous tree, 20–40 ft.+; zones 10–11. Blooms late spring, summer. Seasonally moist/dry. Moderately fertile, well-drained soil. Full sun. Flowers: petals obovate to clawed at the base, valvate; pink-lavender, fading to white; capsules elongated ovoid. Leaves: elliptic, 8–10 in. long, with reddish, star-shaped hairs becoming greener with age, base rounded. *The open (valvate), not overlapping*

petals and the more branched inflorescences help distinguish this species *from* L. speciosa.

Lagerstroemia indica and hybrids

CRAPE MYRTLE

Garden hybrids (southern China to Southeast Asia). Deciduous shrubs or trees, 10–25 ft.; zones 7–10. Bloom late spring, summer, early fall. Regular moisture during active growth. Fertile, well-drained soil; acid pH. Full sun. Flowers: 1–2 in. wide; petals 6, crinkled, in shades of red, blue, purple, and white; calyx green, bell-shaped, 6-lobed; in terminal panicles; capsule ovoid, seeds winged. Leaves: ovate to oblong, to 2 in. long, dark green; petiole short or sessile; margins entire. Bark: flaking, cinnamon-brown and gray. Stems: 4-angled. *This group involves selections of* L. indica *as well*

as hybrids such as 'Centennial Red' though ancestry is often unclear.

Lagerstroemia macrocarpa

GIANT CRAPE MYRTLE, ROSE-OF-INDIA, BUNGOR (MALAYSIA)

Southeast Asia. Deciduous tree, 30–40 ft.+; zones 10–11. Blooms late spring. Seasonally moist/dry. Average, well-drained soil. Full sun. Flowers: petals crinkled, clawed, lavender-pink, 3–4 in. wide; sepals 5–6, hairs reddish brown, grooved; in dense, short clusters; capsule round, ends blunt, calyx persistent, reflexed. Leaves: oblong, 3–6 in. long, leathery. Bark: light gray, scaly, deeply furrowed. *Of dry forest and open areas. The relatively short leaves and large, densely clustered flowers help distinguish this species. Reddish lumber is similar to teak in quality.*

Lagerstroemia floribunda

Lagerstroemia 'Centennial Red'

Lagerstroemia macrocarpa

Lagerstroemia speciosa

Lagerstroemia speciosa

QUEEN'S CRAPE MYRTLE, FLOR DE LA REINA, JARUL (INDIA), BUNGOR (MALAYSIA)

Synonym: *L. flos-reginae*. Southern China, Southeast Asia. Deciduous tree, 30–60 ft.; zones 10–11. Blooms late spring, summer. Seasonally moist/dry. Moderately fertile, well-drained soil. Full sun. Flowers: corolla 2–3 in. wide, magenta to pink or lavender, fading to white, petals 5, crinkled, bases clawed; calyx 5- to 7-lobed, the cup with 10–14 ridges, hairs reddish brown; in mostly unbranched erect panicles to 10 in.+ tall; capsules round-ovoid, woody, to 1 in. diameter. Leaves: oblong, 6–10 in. long, leathery; midvein reddish; petiole, buds, and twigs with reddish hairs. Bark: light tan-gray, shredding in strips. *A variable species. In* L. loudonii *the inside of the calyx is tomentose.*

Lawsonia

Lawsonia includes a single species of shrub or small tree probably from eastern Africa or Asia. Leaves are simple. Twigs are more or less sharp. The rust-red sap, or henna, is used to dye hair, fabrics, horse manes, and fingernails; as body-paint; or as a folk remedy for skin diseases.

Lawsonia inermis

HENNA, MIGNONETTE TREE, ALHEÑA

Synonym: *L. alba*. Exact origin obscure (Old World tropics); widely naturalized. Evergreen shrub, 6–20 ft.; zones 9–11. Blooms spring, summer. Moderate moisture to seasonally dry. Average, well-drained soil. Full to part sun. Flowers: small, petals crinkled, clawed, cream or reddish in var. *rubra*; in many-flowered panicles; delicately

fragrant. Leaves: obovate to elliptic, to 2 in. long, glossy; margins entire. Unarmed. *Grown as a foliage plant and for the mignonette-like fragrance. Branches arching, open. Pest resistant, heat tolerant. The species name means "spineless."*

Punica

Punica includes 2 species of shrubs or small trees of mild temperate regions from southeastern Europe to the Himalayas. This genus was formerly segregated in its own family, Punicaceae. Pomegranates are known to have been cultivated in the Middle East since at least the Bronze Age. They thrive in arid climates with cool winter temperatures. Though most selections do not set fruit well in humid tropical areas, a green-fruited cultivar, 'Francis', is productive in Jamaica (Kong, pers. comm.). Twigs are often sharply pointed. Leaves are simple. Flowers are bisexual and radially symmetrical. Stamens are numerous. The fruit is a segmented berry with a hard, leathery rind (hesperidium). The mildly astringent juice is used as a folk remedy for tapeworm. Tannins extracted from the bark are used in tanning leather.

Punica granatum

POMEGRANATE, GRANADO

Middle East to Himalayan foothills. Deciduous shrub or tree, 10–20 ft.; zones 7–10. Blooms spring, summer. Dry. Average to fertile, well-drained soil; neutral to acid pH. Full sun. Flowers: funnel-shaped, red-orange; fruit red to green, leathery skinned, with short-toothed perianth tube persistent at the distal end. Leaves: narrowly elliptic to lanceolate, 2–4 in. long, tip usually mucronate; petioles often red. *Hardy. Suitable for coastal planting. Forma* plena *has double flowers.* 'Nana', *a dwarf form with small fruits, is suitable for containers.* 'Variegata' *has green and white foliage.*

MAGNOLIACEAE

MAGNOLIA FAMILY

Magnoliaceae includes 2 genera of shrubs and trees from eastern Asia and eastern North America as well as tropical South America. The order to which this family belongs

has traditionally been considered the ancestral prototype of other flowering plant families (angiosperms), though current science challenges that position, including the classification system followed by Judd et al. (1999). All the genera in this family, except *Liriodendron*, the temperate tulip-tree genus, are now included within the genus *Magnolia*, but have not been officially transferred at the time of writing.

Magnolia

Magnolia includes approximately 210 species of trees and shrubs from eastern Asia and eastern North America as well as tropical South America. Leaves are simple and arranged in whorls. Flowers are solitary, bisexual, radially symmetrical, and highly fragrant. The showy, mostly undifferentiated tepals are in whorls of 3, 6, or numerous and are spirally arranged on an elongated receptacle. The stamens are flattened (laminar), the filament and anther poorly differentiated. The superior ovary is prominent in the center of the flower. The compound fruits are in a conelike aggregate or in clusters. The seeds are covered with a fleshy red, pink, or orange coat (sarcotesta). Trees are cut for timber and the aromatic oils are used to flavor teas and in fragrances. The species and many hybrids are grown as ornamentals.

Magnolia grandiflora

SOUTHERN MAGNOLIA, BULL-BAY MAGNOLIA

Coastal Delaware to Central Florida. Evergreen tree, 45–80 ft.; zones 6–10. Blooms primarily spring, summer, or sporadically. Seasonally wet to moderate. Deep, sandy, humus-rich, fast-draining soil; acid pH. Full sun. Flowers: lemon-scented, tepals 12 in 3 whorls, 6–8 in. wide, creamy white to tan with age; stamens flat; terminal; fruit conelike with rust-colored hairs; seeds red. Leaves: elliptic, 6–10 in. long, glossy dark green, leathery; rust-colored scales below when young; margins entire. *Cultivated throughout native range. Also thrives in dry southern California and Latin America at moderate altitude. Trees*

Lagerstroemia speciosa, flowers

Lawsonia inermis var. *rubra*

Punica granatum

Punica granatum f. *plena*

often lack vigor in alkaline soils in South Florida unless a large acidified hole is prepared when planting. Water to root depth weekly in dry climates.

Magnolia virginiana

SWEET-BAY MAGNOLIA, SWAMP-BAY, LAUREL-BAY
Coastal southeastern United States. Semideciduous tree, 30–45 ft.; zones 5–10. Blooms spring. Seasonally wet to moderate. Deep, richly organic soil; acid pH. Full sun. Flowers: tepals 8 in 2 whorls, obovate, not overlapping (valvate), 4–5 in. wide, fragrant; terminal; fruit conelike; seeds red. Leaves: broadly ovate, 4–6 in. long, glossy above, chalky below, leathery; margins entire. *Of coastal wetlands. Add acidifying humus to a large planting hole in alkaline soils. Grows as far north as the southern New England coast where it is deciduous and remains shrub size (Howard, pers. comm.).*

Michelia

Michelia includes approximately 30 species of trees from China, Southeast Asia, the Malacca islands, and Japan. As noted above, *Michelia* will soon be included in the genus *Magnolia*. Distinguishing characteristics of this subgroup include the axillary rather than terminal flowers and clustered fruits rather than conelike aggregates. The species are threatened in the wild due to cutting for timber. They are cultivated in Asia for the fragrant oils, which are used in perfumery. Established trees may be marginally hardy.

Michelia ×alba

HYBRID CHAMPACA, WHITE CHAMPACA
Synonym: *Magnolia ×alba*. Garden hybrid, *M. champaca* × *M. montana*; only known in cultivation. Evergreen tree, 25–70 ft.+; zones 9–11. Blooms warm months. Seasonally moist to moderate. Fertile, well-drained soil; neutral to slightly acid pH. Full sun. Flowers: tepals cupped, in 2 whorls, not overlapping (valvate), white, fragrant; in the leaf axils. Leaves: ovate to lanceolate, 5–8 in. long. *The parents of this natural hybrid are uncertain. Reputedly longer-blooming than Miche-*

lia champaca. Habit conical with horizontal branches. Sensitive to root disturbance.

Michelia champaca

CHAMPACA, CHAMPAK
Synonym: *Magnolia champaca*. Lower elevations of the Himalayas, India, China to Southeast Asia. Evergreen tree, 20–25 ft., to 100 ft. in native habitat; zones 9–11. Blooms warm months. Seasonally moist to moderate. Fertile, humusrich, well-drained soil; neutral to slightly acid pH. Full to part sun. Flowers: tepals erect, slightly cupped, in 2 whorls, 2–3 in. wide, yellow-orange; very fragrant; in the leaf axils; fruit in clusters. Leaves: lanceolate to elliptic, 6–8 in. long, glossy, tip acuminate; margins undulate. Bark: gray. *Marginally hardy. Flowers tucked into pockets for fra-grance and used to adorn Buddhist temples in Southeast Asia. Wood used for carving. Does not tolerate root disturbance.*

MALPIGHIACEAE

BARBADOS CHERRY FAMILY, MALPIGHIA FAMILY
Malpighiaceae includes approximately 66 genera of woody climbers (lianas), trees, and shrubs from the tropics, with greatest diversity in tropical America. Leaves are simple, opposite, usually with paired glands on the petioles or near the base of the blade. They characteristically have T-shaped, occasionally irritating hairs. Flowers are usually bisexual, bilaterally to almost radially symmetrical, and in racemes. The 5 petals are often fringed and usually clawed. The sepals often have oil glands. There is one inconspicuous bract and 2 bracteoles. The fruit is a fleshy drupe, schizocarp, nut, or samara. The juicy fruits of *Malpighia emarginata* have high concentrations of vitamin C.

Bunchosia

Bunchosia includes approximately 60 species of shrubs and small trees from tropical America. These are plants of the forest understory. The leaves are simple, leathery, and often hairy, with 2 large glands at the base of the leaf blade on opposite sides of the midvein. Flowers are always yellow with 8–10 glands on the calyx. The 10 fertile stamens have fused bases. The one-seeded fruit (drupe) of *B. armeniaca* is very tasty and a nourishing source of food for wildlife.

Magnolia grandiflora

Magnolia virginiana

Magnolia virginiana, fruit

Michelia ×alba

Michelia champaca, flower and fruit

Bunchosia armeniaca
PEANUT-BUTTER PLANT, CEREZO, CIRUELA SILVESTRE ("FOREST CHERRY")
Synonym: *Malpighia armeniaca.* Northern and western South America. Evergreen shrub or tree, 10–30 ft.; zones 9–11. Blooms late spring, summer. Moderate moisture. Average, well-drained soil. Full to part sun. Flowers: small, yellow, clawed, in dense clusters; fruit plum-sized, orange. Leaves: ovate, 4–6 in. *Fruit has a sticky, sweet-textured pulp, a tasty fat-free combination of peanut butter with a touch of honey.*

Byrsonima
Byrsonima (pronounced buy-er-so-NEE-ma) includes approximately 150 species of shrubs and trees from tropical America. These are common plants of hillsides, savannas, or sometimes rain forest. The flowers are yellow, pink, or orange with hairy receptacles. The leaves lack glands but are usually hairy. The stamen filaments are hairy at the base. Fruits are fleshy and 3-seeded, often edible, and provide food for wildlife. The name is often misspelled brysonima.

Byrsonima crassifolia
CRABOO, NANCE
Synonyms: *B. lanceolata, Malpighia crassifolia.* Mexico, Central America, West Indies, northern South America. Evergreen tree, 15–30 ft.; zones 9–11. Blooms late spring, early summer. Moderate moisture. Average, well-drained soil. Full to part sun. Flowers: small, petals clawed, edges ruffled, yellow when young turning deep orange with age; in racemes to 6 in. long; fruit round, yellow, edible. Leaves: elliptic to oblanceolate, 3–5 in. long, leathery; clustered near the ends of the branches. *Coastal to seaside. Moderately salt tolerant. An ornamental flowering shade tree. Unusual but highly recommended. The species name alludes to the thick leaves.*

Byrsonima lucida
LOCUST-BERRY, MURICI
Synonym: *B. cuneata.* Florida, West Indies. Evergreen shrub, 6–15 ft.; zones 9–11. Blooms late spring, early summer. Seasonally moist/dry. Average, well-drained soil. Full to part sun. Flowers: small, white, turning pink, clawed; margins smooth. Leaves: obovate, 2–3 in. long, stiff, tapering toward the base. *A shrub of rocky pinelands and coastal scrub in South Florida and the Caribbean. Moderately salt tolerant.*

Callaeum
Callaeum includes approximately 10 species of shrubs and woody climbers from tropical America. The petals are yellow. Leaves are simple with glands at the base of the blade. The fruits are 3-winged samaras, one wing modified into a dorsal crest, with corky wing bases. Differs from *Mascagnia* by microscopic technicalities of the flowers.

Callaeum macropterum
GALLINITA ("LITTLE HEN")
Synonym: *Mascagnia macroptera.* Northern Mexico. Evergreen climber; zones 9–11. Blooms warm months. Moderate moisture. Average, well-drained soil. Full to part sun. Flowers: petals clawed; margins fringed, yellow; calyx with large glands; fruit a 3-winged samara, one wing reduced to a crest, tinted red. Leaves: elliptic, tip acuminate. *Coastal to inland forests. Poisonous to livestock. Stigmaphyllon differs by having glands on the petiole, not the calyx.*

Bunchosia armeniaca

Byrsonima crassifolia, flowers

Byrsonima lucida

Callaeum macropterum

Byrsonima crassifolia, habit

Galphimia

Galphimia includes approximately 10 species of shrubs and small trees from tropical and subtropical America. The flowers are small, the petals yellow and sharply narrowing at the base (clawed). The 10 stamens are alternately long and short. The calyx lacks glands. Flowers are borne in many-flowered racemes or panicles. Leaves are simple. The genus name is an anagram of *Malpighia*, a genus in which it was once incorrectly included.

Galphimia gracilis

SPRAY-OF-GOLD, THRYALLIS
Synonyms: *G. glauca* (misapplied), *Thryallis gracilis*. Mexico, Guatemala. Evergreen shrub, 3–6 ft.; zones 10–11. Blooms warm months. Regular moisture. Average, well-drained soil. Full sun to bright broken light. Flowers: petals clawed, 0.5 in. wide, yellow, faintly fragrant; in terminal racemes, 4–6 in. tall. Leaves: ovate to lanceolate, 2–3 in. long, glaucous, with 2 glands at base; petioles short. Young stems: russet-haired. *Coastal. Cold-sensitive. Brittle. Prune lightly. Does not like shearing. Often listed as* G. glauca, *a Brazilian species unknown in cultivation.*

Hiptage

Hiptage includes 20–25 species of shrubs and climbers from tropical Asia and Indomalaysia. Leaves have 2 glands at base of blade. Flowers are bilaterally symmetrical. The sepals are unequal in length and they have 2 linear glands attached at their bases. The fruit is a 3-winged samara.

Hiptage benghalensis

Synonym: *H. madablota*. India, Sri Lanka, Southeast Asia, Philippines, southern China, Taiwan. Evergreen shrub to woody climber; zones 10–11. Blooms late winter, spring. Moderate or seasonally moist/dry. Average, well-drained soil. Full to part sun. Flowers: fragrant, petals white, tinged yellow or pink, reflexed, clawed, edges fringed; sepals unequal in size, pinkish, red linear glands at base; in congested panicles. Leaves: ovate to lanceolate, to 6 in. long, young leaves hairy becoming leathery; margin glandular near the base. *Aggressive. Potentially invasive. Restricted in Florida. Not recommended.*

Malpighia

Malpighia includes approximately 40 species of trees and shrubs from tropical America, well represented in the West Indies and around the Caribbean basin. They are typically found in dry, deciduous forests. Leaves are generally small with small glands near the base of the blade. Flowers are pink or white, never yellow, and borne in the leaf axils. The fruits are fleshy.

Malpighia coccigera

MINIATURE HOLLY, BARBADOS HOLLY
West Indies. Evergreen shrub, 2–3 ft.; zones 9–11. Blooms intermittently in warm months. Moderate moisture. Average, well-drained soil. Part sun. Flowers: petals pinkish to white, bases long clawed. Leaves: ovate, 0.5–1 in. long, dark green, with hollylike, sharply pointed lobes; fruit red. Bark: light-colored, slightly shaggy. *Mounding to sprawling. Can be pruned to shape. Bloom brief, followed by red hollylike berries. Suitable for containers and bonsai. "Singapore holly" is a misleading name, though many West Indian species are grown in East Indian gardens.*

Galphimia gracilis

Galphimia gracilis, flowers

Hiptage benghalensis

Malpighia coccigera

Malpighia emarginata

Malpighia emarginata

BARBADOS CHERRY, WEST INDIAN CHERRY, ACEROLA

Synonyms: *M. glabra* (hort.), *M. punicifolia* (hort.). Mexico, West Indies, Central America. Evergreen shrub or tree to 15 ft.; zones 10–11. Blooms spring, summer. Regular moisture. Average, well-drained soil. Full to part sun. Flowers: petals pink, clawed, edges ruffled; fruit red, like a slightly lumpy cherry, rose-scented. Leaves: oblong to oblanceolate, 2–3 in. long, dark glossy green, tip emarginate to pointed; margins undulate. *The fruit has the most concentrated natural source of vitamin C known. It is fragrant and sweet, subacid, excellent fresh or in jellies. Attractive to birds.*

Stigmaphyllon

Stigmaphyllon includes approximately 100 species of woody vines (lianas) from tropical America. The leaves are simple, entire or occasionally lobed, and usually have a heart-shaped (cordate) base. There is a characteristic pair of glands on the petiole just below the leaf blade. Older stems often split into 2 strands, a unique characteristic (A. Gentry 1993). The flowers have 4–6 fertile stamens. The fruits are winged samaras, the wings thickened along the outer edges.

Stigmaphyllon ciliatum

AMAZON VINE, BUTTERFLY VINE, BRAZILIAN GOLDEN VINE

Central and South America, West Indies. Evergreen climber to 12 ft.; zones 10–11. Blooms winter, spring. Seasonally moist, moderate. Average, well-drained soil. Full to part sun. Flowers: petals clawed, edges fringed (fimbriate), yellow; sepals glandular; fruit a 3- or 4-winged samara; in clusters of 3–6. Leaves: ovate, base cordate; petioles with 2 glands; margins distinctly ciliate. *Coastal. The long hairs (cilia) on the margins of the heart-shaped leaves are distinctive.*

Stigmaphyllon sagraeanum

West Indies, Costa Rica to Peru. Evergreen twining climber to 12 ft.; zones 10–11. Blooms winter, spring. Seasonally moist/dry. Average, well-drained soil. Full to part sun. Flowers: yellow, 0.5 in. wide, petals clawed; in many-flowered clusters; fruit a winged, reddish brown samara. Leaves: lanceolate, 3–5 in. long, leathery, russet when young. *Coastal. Blooms prolifically. Suitable on a fence or other support.*

Tristellateia

Tristellateia (pronounced try-stell-ah-TAY-ah) includes approximately 20 species of woody climbers from Madagascar to Southeast Asia, Indomalaysia, New Guinea, and Australia including 1 from Africa and 1 from New Caledonia. Leaves are simple. Petals are yellow, narrowing abruptly at the base (clawed). The sepals are more or less glandular. The name refers to the 3-lobed, star-shaped samaras.

Tristellateia australasiae

SHOWER-OF-GOLD VINE, BAGNÍT

Southeast Asia, Taiwan, Malaysia, New Guinea to Australia. Evergreen woody climber to 30 ft.+; zones 10–11. Blooms warm months. Regular moisture. Average to fertile, well-drained soil. Full to part sun. Flowers: petals 5, base squared like a spade and clawed, edges smooth; glands dark red; in few- to many-flowered racemes. Leaves: elliptic to ovate, 4–6 in. long, dark green, leathery. *Of riversides. This almost ever-blooming species is cultivated in tropical and maritime Asia. Suitable for a fence or arbor.*

MALVACEAE

HIBISCUS FAMILY, MALLOW FAMILY

Malvaceae includes approximately 204 genera of herbs, shrubs, and soft-wooded trees, which are widely distributed, with greatest diversity in tropical America. The genera traditionally placed in Bombacaceae, Sterculiaceae, and Tiliaceae are now circumscribed within this family. These former families are kept together as subsections here for the convenience of readers familiar with the older arrangements. Cotton, jute, kapok, balsa wood, and okra are important economic crops. Chinese hibiscus, the variable cultigen known as *Hibiscus rosa-sinensis*, has been grown as an ornamental for millennia, often appearing in ancient works of art. Leaves are alternate, simple, palmately veined, lobed or sometimes compound, and the margins are often serrated. Flowers are often showy, mostly bisexual, and radially symmetrical. An involucre of leafy bracts (epicalyx) often encloses the calyx. There are 5 to numerous stamens. The filaments are more or less fused, sometimes forming a partial or complete tube (column) around the styles. Flowers are solitary or in cymes. The fruit is a dry capsule, sometimes filled with fibers, or a berry. Stems, leaves, and/or bracts are sometimes hairy or spined. The sap is mucilaginous.

Abelmoschus

Abelmoschus includes approximately 6 species of annual and perennial herbs from the Old World tropics and mild temperate regions. The leaves are deeply 3-lobed to dissected, with 2 small secondary lobes or teeth near the petiole. Leaves low on the stem may be simple. Plants are frequently found in low wetland areas. The genus *Abelmoschus* can be distinguished from *Hibiscus* by a spathelike, asymmetrical calyx that falls at the same time as the corolla and by the 5 stigmas being bunched together. *Hibiscus* usually has a 5-lobed, persistent calyx, and the stigmas diverge near the ends (Fryxell, pers. comm.). *Abelmoschus esculentus*, okra or gumbo, is a staple of African, Cajun, and Southern cooking. It has yellow flowers with a purple-maroon spot in the center, mounted on a stout peduncle, and large, deeply dissected leaves.

Abelmoschus moschatus

MUSK-MALLOW

Synonym: *Hibiscus abelmoschus*. Southern China, Southeast Asia, Indomalaysia to Australia. Annual

Stigmaphyllon ciliatum

Stigmaphyllon sagraeanum

Tristellateia australasiae

Abelmoschus moschatus

or short-lived perennial subshrub, 2–3 ft.+; zones 9–11. Blooms warm months. Regular moisture. Fertile, well-drained soil. Full sun. Flowers: corolla spreading, 3–4 in. wide, yellow, throat purple, solitary; involucral bracts 9; fruit a 5-sided inflated papery capsule; seed musky-scented. Leaves: palmate, 5- to 7-lobed or divided, 4–5 in. long; margins toothed. All parts hairy. *Self-seeding. Often escaped in wetlands. Flowers resemble okra, Abelmoschus esculentus. The red musk-mallow, subsp. tuberosus, sometimes misidentified as Abelmoscus rugosus (Fryxell, pers. comm.), has red and white flowers. Note that Hibiscus moscheutos is a distinct species.*

Abutilon

Abutilon includes 100–150 species of herbs and shrubs primarily of mild temperate regions plus a number from the tropics. Many complex hybrids are in cultivation. The flowers lack the epicalyx (an involucre of bracts or pseudocalyx) typical of many *Hibiscus* relatives. Flowers are solitary or in clusters and borne in the leaf axils. Petals are stalked (clawed).

Abutilon chittendenii

FLOWERING MAPLE
Honduras, Guatemala. Evergreen shrub, 10–15 ft.; zones 10–11. Blooms late winter, spring, early summer. Seasonally moist, moderate in cool weather. Average, well-drained soil. Full sun. Flowers: corolla lemon-yellow with orange streaks in the throat, petals spreading; staminal column short. Leaves: cordate, to 5 in. long, tip acute, silky; margins entire to shallowly lobed, serrate; veins reddish near the petiole. *Suitable for hedges or specimen plants with a sunny disposition. Species name is often misspelled.*

Abutilon ×hybridum

FLOWERING MAPLE, CHINESE LANTERN, BELLFLOWER
Garden hybrids. Evergreen shrubs, 1–5 ft.; zones 9–11. Bloom warm months. Regular moisture. Fertile, well-drained soil. Full to part sun. Flowers: corolla bell-shaped to spreading, 2–3 in. wide, often nodding, bases clawed; calyx green, visible through the openings ("windows") between the petal stalks. Leaves: ovate, to 4 in. long, more or less lobed; margins toothed or serrate. *Nodding flowers display well in hanging baskets. Should never be allowed to dry completely. Hybrids in many colors.*

Abutilon megapotamicum

TRAILING ABUTILON
Southern Brazil. Evergreen shrub to 6 ft.; zones 8–10. Bloom warm months. Regular moisture. Fertile, well-drained soil. Full to part sun. Flowers: bell-shaped, nodding, corolla yellow; calyx inflated bell-shaped, lobes pointed, russet to scarlet; solitary in the leaf axils. Leaves: lanceolate, to 3 in. long, bases cordate, entire to faintly lobed; margins serrate. *'Variegatum' has yellow-spotted leaves.*

Abutilon palmeri

PALMER'S ABUTILON, INDIAN MALLOW, VELVET-LEAF
Synonyms: *A. aurantiacum, A. macdougalii.* Baja California, Sonoran Desert of Mexico and Arizona. Evergreen shrub, 3–4 ft.; zones 9–10. Blooms spring. Moderate moisture to dry. Gritty, well-drained soil. Full to part sun. Flowers: corolla slightly cupped, yellow. Leaves: ovate, covered with blue-gray down; margins irregularly toothed. *Suitable for drier regions.*

Alyogyne

Alyogyne includes approximately 4 species of shrubs from southern and western Australia. The leaves are entire to deeply lobed or dissected. Flowers are solitary in the upper leaf axils. The 4–12 involucre bracts are usually united at the base. The stamen filaments are united in a column.

Alyogyne huegelii

BLUE HIBISCUS, LILAC HIBISCUS
Synonym: *Hibiscus huegelii.* Western Australia. Evergreen shrub, 4–6 ft.; zones 9–11. Blooms late spring, early summer. Moderate moisture, drier when cool. Fertile, well-drained soil. Full to part sun. Flowers: corolla spreading, to 3 in. wide, translucent pink-violet to bluish. Leaves: deeply 3- to 5-lobed, 1.5–3 in. long, with somewhat sticky hairs; margins toothed. *Erect to spreading, fast-growing shrub from dry habitat. Xeric. Prune after flowering for compact shape.*

Anisodontea

Anisodontea includes approximately 19 species of shrubs and sub-

Abelmoschus moschatus subsp. *tuberosus*

Abutilon chittendenii

Abutilon ×*hybridum* 'Vesuvius Red'

Abutilon megapotamicum

Abutilon palmeri

Alyogyne huegelii

shrubs from South Africa. The name refers to the irregularly toothed, 3- to 7-lobed or divided leaves. Petals narrow abruptly at the base (clawed). They are solitary or in small clusters. The 3-parted epicalyx (or involucre of bracts) is sometimes united to the calyx at the base.

Anisodontea capensis

SOUTH AFRICAN MALLOW
Synonyms: *Malva capensis, Malvastrum capense.* South Africa. Evergreen shrub, 3–4 ft.; zones 9–11. Blooms warm months. Seasonally moist, drier when cool. Fertile, well-drained soil. Full sun. Flowers: corolla 1–1.5 in. wide, petals clawed, pink with magenta streaks in the throat. Leaves: deeply but unevenly 3- to 5-lobed, 1–2 in. long, downy; margins toothed. Stems: downy. *Some plants in cultivation by this name may be* Anisodontea scabrosa. *'African Queen' is reputedly a cross between* A. capensis *and* A. ×hypomandarum.

Gossypium

Gossypium includes approximately 35 species of annual and perennial herbs and shrubs from mild temperate and tropical regions. Several species have been grown for millennia for cotton, a valuable commercial crop. The long fibers attached to the seed are used as cotton wool or spun into thread and woven into fabric. The seed is pressed for cottonseed oil and the leftover cake is used as a high-protein animal feed. The leaves are palmately 3- to 5-lobed and coarsely textured, more or less spotted with black oil glands. Flowers are hibiscus-like with 3 large, conspicuous, clasping involucral bracts. Commercially grown cotton requires high amounts of pesticides. Organically grown cotton is becoming more available, sometimes in natural blue, green, and khaki colors.

Gossypium barbadense

PIMA COTTON, EGYPTIAN COTTON, SEA ISLAND COTTON, CARIBBEAN COTTON, ALGODÓN
Synonym: *G. peruvianum.* Ecuador, Peru; widely cultivated. Annual or short-lived perennial shrub, 6–8 ft.; zones 9–11. Blooms late winter, spring. Seasonally moist/dry. Average, well-drained soil. Full sun. Flowers: corolla bell-shaped, never fully spreading, yellow; bracts (epicalyx) leaflike, clasping, edges toothed, maroon; capsules (bolls) round, papery; seeds with cotton lint attached. Leaves: coarse, ovate, to 6 in. long, lobed; margins toothed. Leaves and stems become reddish with age. *Pima cotton is a long staple fiber. Grown as a summer crop in mild temperate areas. First introduced at Sea Island, Georgia, and now a major cotton-producing species.*

Gossypium hirsutum

UPLAND COTTON, ALGODÓN
Synonym: *G. mexicanum.* Tropical America; widely cultivated. Annual or short-lived perennial shrub, 5–6 ft.; zones 9–11. Blooms late winter, spring. Moist during active growth, then dry. Average, well-drained soil. Full sun. Flowers: white to yellow, becoming pinkish; bracts 3, leafy, edges toothed; capsule (boll) ovoid, papery; cotton lint and fuzz attached to seed. Leaves: entire or 3- to 5-lobed, coarse. *Short staple cotton.*

Hibiscus

Hibiscus includes approximately 300 species of trees, shrubs, and herbs from warm temperate and tropical regions. The leaves are simple, palmately 3- to 5-lobed or dissected. Sap is mucilaginous. Flowers have 5 petals, are usually solitary, and last only a day. Few to many sepal-like bracts (a pseudocalyx) enclose the true sepals in an involucre. The stamen filaments are fused into a usually long and conspicuous column.

Hibiscus rosa-sinensis is a cultigen of unknown ancestry. Though it does not exist in the wild, depictions in ancient Oriental art suggest ancestors may have sprung from one or more species from the Indian Ocean region to China. The wood fibers are used to make fish nets in the Pacific. A purple-black dye made from crushed flowers has been used to blacken shoes and dye hair. Cut flowers will last a day out of water. Hybrid hibiscus are the horticultural counterpart of roses in tropical regions. They have been cultivated for millennia and have a deep cultural association with Hawaii and the Pacific Islands. *Hibiscus* species are also beautiful and less demanding than the hybrids.

Hybrids are complex and do not breed true from seed. They are propagated from cuttings in sandy loam or by grafting. New fancy hybrids tend to be shorter lived than old standards. Though prized, pampered, and easy to cross, hibiscus hybrids are fussy. Plants are easily stressed by too much or too little water and fertilizer, often responding by dropping buds. A generous application of mulch will help stabilize moisture. Use dilute, low-phosphate fertilizer with added microelements and apply monthly. Fancy hybrids are especially vulnerable to attack from pests, including nematodes, thrips, and scale insects. A recently introduced pest, gall midge, destroys the buds from inside. Infestations are difficult to treat because hibiscus are sensitive to oil-based sprays and pesticides such as Malathion™ which cause the leaves to drop.

Hibiscus arnottianus

HAWAIIAN WHITE HIBISCUS, KOKI'O-KE'OKE'O (HAWAII)
Hawaii. Evergreen shrub or tree, 15–25 ft.; zones 10–11. Blooms warm months. Regular moisture. Fertile, well-drained soil; slightly acid pH. Full sun. Flowers: white; stamens fused into a red, orange, or purple column to 6 in. long; bracts 5–7; scented; capsule papery, seed covered with brown down. Leaves: ovate, to 4 in. long, veins and petioles often red; mar-

Anisodontea capensis

Gossypium barbadense

Gossypium hirsutum, bolls

Hibiscus arnottianus 'Ruth Wilcox'

gins more or less toothed. *Trunks erect, with descending branches. Heavy pruning destroys the graceful habit. An ancestor of many hybrids. Subsp.* immaculatus *is endangered in the wild.*

Hibiscus brackenridgei
HAWAIIAN YELLOW HIBISCUS, MA'O-HAU-HELE (HAWAII)
Hawaii. Evergreen shrub or tree, 3–30 ft.; zones 10–11. Blooms winter, spring. Seasonally moist. Fertile, well-drained soil. Full sun. Flowers: corolla spreading, to 3 in. wide, bright yellow, sometimes with a purple spot at the base. Leaves: ovate, to 4 in. long, entire to irregularly 4- or 5-lobed, glossy dark green; margins toothed or scalloped. Branch tips more or less woolly or prickled. *Several varieties of various sizes exist on different islands. Subsp.* molokaianus *from*

Molokai *is 4–5 ft. tall and endangered in the wild.*

Hibiscus calyphyllus
PONDOLAND HIBISCUS
Synonym: *H. calycinus.* Tropical southern Africa, Madagascar, Mascarene Islands; naturalized in Hawaii. Evergreen shrub, 3–6 ft.; zones 10–11. Blooms late summer, fall. Seasonally moist/dry. Average, well-drained soil. Full sun. Flowers: corolla to 4 in. wide, petals crinkled, yellow with a maroon spot at the base. Leaves: broadly ovate to cordate, 2–4 in. long, mostly entire to somewhat angular or slightly lobed, downy (pubescent), tips rounded or obtuse; margins serrate to crenate (scalloped). *Flowers resemble okra,* Abelmoschus esculentus, *and musk mallow,* A. moschatus, *but the 5-lobed calyx and unlobed leaves are distinctive.*

Hibiscus coccineus
MARSH-MALLOW, SCARLET ROSE-MALLOW
Florida, Georgia. Perennial shrub to 6 ft.; zones 7–10. Blooms summer. Seasonally wet/moderate. Fertile soil. Full sun. Flowers: corolla spreading, to 4 in. wide, petals oblanceolate to somewhat rhombic, not overlapping, red, darker toward the center. Leaves: palmatisect, veins red. Stems: red. *Of wetlands. Suitable for damp locations and pond margins. Sugar was once extracted from the mucilaginous root and used to make a precursor of marshmallows.*

Hibiscus indicus
Synonym: *Alcaea indica.* Southern China. Evergreen shrub or small tree to 15 ft.; zones 9–11. Blooms fall, winter. Moderate moisture. Average, well-drained soil. Full sun. Flowers: corolla 3–4 in. wide, petals

spreading, pink, magenta spot at the base; involucral bracts 5–9. Leaves: lanceolate, 5–7 in. long, lobed, hairy, medium green. *An underutilized, pest-resistant hibiscus, noteworthy for its late season bloom when fewer plants are in flower. Much more forgiving and carefree than hibiscus hybrids.*

Hibiscus moscheutos hybrid
SWAMP ROSE-MALLOW HYBRID
Garden hybrid (*H. moscheutos* x ?). Semideciduous shrub to 8 ft.; zones 6–10. Blooms warm months. Regular moisture to wet. Sandy soil to wetlands. Full sun. Flowers: corolla 6–10 in. wide, petals spreading; involucral bracts 10–14. Leaves: ovate to cordate, to 7 in. long, shallow lobed, under sides tomentose; margins coarsely toothed. *The flowers of the type species are yellow with a red eye,*

Hibiscus brackenridgei subsp. *molokaianus*

Hibiscus calyphyllus

Hibiscus coccineus

Hibiscus indicus

Hibiscus moscheutos hybrid

Hibiscus mutabilis, double pink

Hibiscus 'All Aglow'

Hibiscus 'Brilliant'

about 4–5 in. wide. Plants in cultivation are probable hybrids possibly involving H. lasiocarpos and/or H.
grandiflora and selected for size
(Fryxell, pers. comm.).

Hibiscus mutabilis

COTTON-ROSE, CONFEDERATE
ROSE-MALLOW
China, Japan, Taiwan. Semideciduous shrub to 10 ft.; zones 7–10.
Blooms warm months. Regular
moisture. Average, well-drained
soil. Full sun. Flowers: open in the
morning either white turning pink
as the day progresses or pink turning darker pink; corolla single or
double. Leaves: ovate, to 5 in. long,
3- to 7-lobed. Stems: downy. *The
species name alludes to the change-
able floral color. A favorite of the Old
South. Not a true tropical. Little care
once established. Deciduous in areas
subject to frost.*

Hibiscus rosa-sinensis hybrids

CHINESE HIBISCUS, SHOE-BLACK
FLOWER, HIBISCO, ALOALO (HAWAII)
Garden origin. Evergreen shrubs,
5–15 ft.; zones 10–11. Bloom primarily spring, fall, or all year. Moderate but regular moisture, never
dry. Fertile, sandy, well-drained soil;
slightly acid pH. Full to part sun.
Flowers: corolla funnel-shaped or
spreading, 6–10 in. wide; sometimes crested, single or double.
Leaves: ovate, 3–6 in. long, 3- to 5-
lobed; margins usually toothed.
*Red flowers are considered sacred to
Polynesians. 'All Aglow', by Estelle
Kanzler, Homestead, Florida, received Hibiscus of the Year Award in
1974. 'Brilliant' is an old standard.
'Tubize', by Luc Vannoorbeeck,
Homestead, Florida, was named for
his hometown in Belgium.*

Hibiscus rosa-sinensis var. kermessinus

Exact origin obscure. Evergreen
shrub to 8 ft.; zones 10–11. Blooms
intermittently in warm months.
Moderate but regular moisture,
never dry. Fertile, sandy, well-
drained soil; slightly acid pH. Part
sun. Flowers: corolla red, reflexed,
pendent; margins toothed. Leaves:
ovate, toothed. *A parent of certain
hybrids. A variegated selection has
white-splashed leaves.*

Hibiscus sabdariffa

SORREL, ROSELLE,
TROPICAL CRANBERRY
Origin obscure (probably tropical
Africa). Annual to 8 ft.; zones 9–11.
Blooms late summer, fall. Regular
moisture. Sandy, well-drained soil.
Full sun. Flowers: corolla to 2 in.
wide, petals yellow, throat dark red;
solitary; capsule surrounded by

fleshy red calyx. Leaves: palmate;
leaflets 3–5, ovate; margins serrate;
gland at base of blade. Stems: red,
sparsely prickled. *In Jamaica, a red
beverage rich in vitamin C is served at
Christmas. The epicalyces are steeped
in hot water with pureed ginger. The
mixture is strained; sugar, wine, and
white rum are added to it and the
drink is served on ice. Cultivated by
Florida settlers as substitute for cran-
berries.*

Hibiscus schizopetalus

FRINGED HIBISCUS, PARASOL
HIBISCUS, JAPANESE LANTERN
HIBISCUS, FAROLITO CHINO,
KO'AKO'A (HAWAII)
Tropical eastern Africa. Evergreen
shrub to 12 ft.; zones 10–11.
Blooms warm months. Regular
moisture. Average, well-drained
soil; slightly acid pH. Full sun.
Flowers: corolla reflexed, deeply
lobed and fringed, red, sometimes
streaked pink; pendent, on a long
stalk. Leaves: ovate, to 4 in. long;
margins toothed. *This species is involved in the background of certain
fancy hybrids. The species name
means "cut petals."*

Hibiscus tiliaceus

MAHOE, SEA HIBISCUS, MAJAGUA,
HAU (HAWAII)
Exact origin obscure (tropical Asia);
widely distributed. Evergreen tree
to 15 ft.; zones 10–11. Blooms
warm months. Moist to moderate.
Average soil. Full sun. Flowers: funnel-shaped, petal margins reflexed,
yellow with purple-maroon spot in
center, becoming splotched orange

Hibiscus 'Tubize'

Hibiscus rosa-sinensis var. *kermessinus*

Hibiscus sabdariffa

Hibiscus schizopetalus

Hibiscus tiliaceus

Hibiscus tiliaceus subsp. *hastatus*

to dark red by afternoon. Leaves: broadly ovate, to 10 in. long, densely hairy below; margins serrate. *Salt tolerant. Many utilitarian uses by indigenous peoples of the Pacific. Forms impenetrable thickets. Restricted in Florida. Subsp.* hastatus *(syn.* H. hastatus*) flowers lack reflexed margins and are more or less pendent; leaves lanceolate to hastate or more or less 3-lobed; margins serrate.* Thespesia populnea *is found in the same areas but is distinguished by its large, heart-shaped leaves.*

Kosteletzkya

Kosteletzkya includes approximately 30 species of herbs and shrubs primarily from Madagascar, tropical and South Africa, plus a few from the Americas. Leaves are simple or palmately lobed or hastate with serrated margins. The round capsule is distinctive.

Kosteletzkya virginica

SALT-MARSH MALLOW
Southeastern United States. Perennial herb or subshrub, 3–4 ft.; zones 5–10. Blooms warm months. Moist to wet. Average soil. Full sun. Flowers: corolla spreading, 2–3 in. wide, pink; solitary; capsules round, hairy. Leaves: lanceolate, 4–5 in. long, usually 3-lobed, coarsely hairy; margins serrate. *Not a true tropical. A salt-tolerant native of brackish and freshwater marshes but can be grown in upland locations with adequate moisture. Roots sensitive to disturbance. Cut back in winter.*

Malva

Malva includes approximately 25 species of annual and perennial herbs and subshrubs from North America, the Mediterranean, and temperate Europe and Asia. Related genera, including Lavatera *and* Abelmoschus, *are in the process of revision, which may alter the names and numbers in this genus. Leaves are palmately lobed or dissected. Flowers are solitary or in small clusters in the leaf axils. Flowers present the fertile stamens first. Then the pistil extends through the center of the column and the stigmas are unfurled. The fruits are sometimes described as "cheeses" for their appearance.*

Malva assurgentiflora

ISLAND-ROSE, MALVA ROSA
Synonym: *Lavatera assurgentiflora.* Channel Islands, Southern California, Baja California. Evergreen shrub to 12 ft.; zones 9–10. Blooms warm months. Dry. Average, well-drained soil. Full sun. Flowers: petal margins reflexed, magenta with purple streaks; calyx cup-shaped with 5 pointed lobes, downy. Leaves: ovate, to 4 in. long, deeply and unevenly lobed; margins coarsely toothed. *Salt tolerant. Used for coastal windbreaks in California.*

Malvaviscus

Malvaviscus includes approximately 3 species of shrubs from tropical America. Leaves are simple, usually lobed. Petals remain spirally folded like a closed umbrella inviting pollination by hummingbirds. The fruit is a berry. Host species of painted-lady butterflies, Vanessa virginiensis. *The larvae sometimes dine on the foliage, but the plants quickly recover. They are otherwise fairly pest resistant. Excellent for the butterfly and hummingbird garden.*

Malvaviscus arboreus var. drummondii

WAX MALLOW, MINIATURE SLEEPING HIBISCUS
Synonym: *M. drummondii.* Mexico. Semideciduous shrub, 8–12 ft.; zones 8–10. Blooms warm months. Moderate moisture to fairly dry. Average to poor, well-drained soil. Full sun. Flowers: corolla remains spirally folded like an umbrella, red, ascending, 1.5–2 in. long. Leaves ovate, 2–3 in. long, not lobed, pubescent below; margins toothed. *A*

sprawling, adaptable shrub that can be trained as an informal hedge. Naturalized in disturbed areas of Texas and the Florida panhandle. Deciduous in areas subject to frost.

Malvaviscus penduliflorus

TURK'S CAP MALLOW, SLEEPING HIBISCUS, MAZAPAN
Tropical America. Evergreen shrub to 12 ft.; zones 9–11. Blooms warm months. Moderate moisture and humidity. Average to poor, well-drained soil. Full to part sun. Flowers: corolla remains spirally folded like an umbrella, to 4 in. long, pendent, red; epicalyx and calyx green. Leaves: ovate to cordate, 3–4 in. long, tip acuminate, smooth below; margins serrate. Branches arching. *Red form appears to be more vigorous than pink and white cultivars. Suitable as privacy hedges in moist*

Kosteletzkya virginica

Malvaviscus arboreus var. *drummondii*

Malva assurgentiflora

Malvaviscus penduliflorus, red and white forms

Pavonia bahamensis

areas. *Sometimes trained as a standard. Species name alludes to the pendent flowers.*

Pavonia

Pavonia includes approximately 180 species of herbs and shrubs from tropical and mild temperate regions. Leaves are entire or slightly 3-lobed with serrate margins. Flowers are solitary or clustered in the leaf axils. Involucral bracts are 5 to many. The fruit is often barbed, dispersed in the hair of animals.

Pavonia bahamensis

Bahamas, Florida Keys. Evergreen shrub to 12 ft.; zones 10–11. Blooms all year. Seasonally moderate, dry. Sandy, well-drained soil. Full to part sun. Flowers: corolla bell-shaped, calyx and epicalyx dark green, to about 1 in. long. Leaves: cordate, to 2.5 in. long; margins smooth. *Flowers dainty. Though not strikingly ornamental, this is one of the best plants for attracting hummingbirds, a valuable asset in areas where hummers usually cannot be lured to feeders such as South Florida. Also attracts warblers and butterflies (Hammer, pers. comm.).*

Pavonia ×gledhillii

Synonym: *P. multiflora* (misapplied). Garden hybrid, *P. makoyana* × *P. multiflora.* Evergreen shrub, 4–5 ft.; zones 10–11. Blooms warm months. Regular moisture during active growth. Fertile, well-drained soil. Part sun, especially morning sun. Flowers: petals maroon-black, folded, enclosed by maroon-black calyx and red epicalyx; anthers light blue, stigma 5-lobed, red, exserted at maturity. Leaves: lanceolate to narrowly oblong, 4–6 in. long; margins smooth to widely toothed, slightly recurved. *A sterile hybrid commonly but incorrectly referred to as* Pavonia multiflora. *Should receive several hours of morning sun to bloom well, but needs some protection from hot midday sun for freshest appearance.*

Pavonia strictiflora

Synonyms: *Goethea cauliflora, Goethea strictiflora.* Brazil. Evergreen shrub, 6–8 ft.; zones 10–11.

Blooms warm months. Regular moisture. Fertile, well-drained soil. Full to part sun. Flowers: petals ephemeral; stamens and styles white; bracts longer-lasting, dark red and white; cauliflorous. Leaves: broadly ovate, to 8 in. long, tips acuminate, medium green becoming reddish. *The erect, unbranched habit is suitable for small gardens and narrow passageways. May require micro-elements in alkaline soils.*

Sida

Sida includes 150–200 species of annual and perennial herbs and shrubs from tropical and mild temperate regions. Large-flowered species are cultivated for their mallowlike flowers. Many small-flowered sidas are common weeds. Leaves are entire or slightly lobed.

Flowers are usually yellow and lack involucral bracts.

Sida eggersii

British Virgin Islands, endangered in the wild. Evergreen shrub, 6–10 ft.+; zones 10–11. Blooms winter, spring. Moderate moisture, seasonally dry. Average, well-drained soil. Full to part sun. Flowers: pale yellow, in axillary clusters. Leaves: rhombic, sides unequal, base tapering, waxy gray, felty; margins undulate. *An endangered species of dry island valleys. Photographed in the Plant Conservation Collection at Fairchild Tropical Garden.*

Thespesia

Thespesia includes approximately 14 species of trees, primarily from the Old World, plus 1 from tropical

America. *Thespesia populnea* is a salt-tolerant tree of tropical coastlines. The large heart-shaped (cordate) leaves with smooth margins distinguish this species from *Hibiscus tiliaceus*, which is found in similar coastal areas.

Thespesia populnea

SEASIDE-MAHOE, PORTEA-TREE, PORTEA OIL-NUT, INDIAN TULIP-TREE, UMBRELLA-TREE

Pantropical. Evergreen tree to 40 ft.; zones 10–11. Blooms warm months. Moist to wet. Average soil. Full sun. Flowers: funnel-shaped, corolla lemon-yellow, turning pink to purplish, purple spot at the base, crinkled; calyx a shallow bell-shaped disk; usually solitary; capsule a compressed sphere. Leaves: cordate, surface rough, rarely variegated. *Of brackish marshes and*

Pavonia ×*gledhillii*

Pavonia strictiflora

Pavonia strictiflora, flowers

Sida eggersii

Thespesia populnea

beaches. Salt tolerant. Moderately soft, durable wood used for wheel rims, carving, and marine applications. Planted as a street tree especially in areas subject to flooding. Invasive. Restricted in Florida.

Wercklea

Wercklea includes approximately 12 species of shrubs or shrubby trees from tropical America. They come from montane cloud-forest. Leaves are large and palmately lobed. The trunks, petioles, and inflorescences are armed with prickles. The calyx is fused into a cup surrounded by 5 involucral bracts.

Wercklea ferox

Costa Rica to Ecuador. Evergreen shrub to 15 ft.; zones 10–11. Blooms warm months. Seasonally moist. Average, well-drained soil. Part sun to bright broken light. Flowers: golden-yellow; calyx and epicalyx dark red; in the leaf axils near the ends of the branches. Leaves: large, palmately lobed; veins and petioles red. Heavily armed with prickles. *Little-branched, soft-wooded. Tends to fall over from its own weight and root from nodes, producing impenetrable briar-patches in the wild. Grown as a curiosity, primarily in botanical gardens.*

MALVACEAE

Formerly Bombacaceae

KAPOK FAMILY

Bombacaceae, traditionally recognized as a distinct family, is now included within Malvaceae. It consists of approximately 25 genera of mostly trees, which are distributed pantropically and are well represented in the Americas. Several species are cultivated for their imposing architecture and large flowers. Certain tree species attain massive height and girth. Leaves are usually palmately compound, occasionally simple. Flowers are bisexual and radially symmetrical. The stamen filaments are partially fused at the base or sometimes completely united into a column. The calyx is cup-shaped, serving to attract perching birds for nectar and water. An epicalyx (involucre of bracts) is sometimes present. The fruit is a dry capsule or rarely fleshy.

Seeds are often imbedded in long fibers known as kapok.

Ceiba species have been cultivated for centuries for kapok and have become widely distributed in the tropics. Kapok was widely used as stuffing before the advent of synthetic fibers. Even now, where synthetics are unavailable, it is used in cushions and mattresses. Life jackets were stuffed with kapok until the 1950s. They were bulky, however, and had the misfortune of eventually becoming waterlogged. Balsa, *Ochroma*, is grown in plantations for its soft, extremely lightweight wood.

Adansonia

Adansonia includes 6 species of very large trees from Madagascar, plus 1 each from Africa and Australia. These giants are only suitable for large gardens.

Adansonia digitata, the baobab, is revered in Africa. It develops a massive, pachycaulous trunk. Some of the oldest trees are estimated to be 1000–2000 years old and have a girth of 75 ft. or more. Large numbers of these grotesquely majestic trees once marched across the African plain. Elephants punch holes in the trunks during droughts to obtain water stored inside.

Leaves are palmate. Flowers are solitary. In *Adansonia digitata*, they dangle at the end of a long stalk. Flowers open at night emitting a feta-cheese aroma attractive to bat pollinators. Animals, including primates, consume the capsules. Adansonias from Madagascar have upright flowers. The trunks resemble enormous wine bottles, standing upright on the savanna like giant sentinels. The stubby, gnarled branches of *A. grandidieri*, *A. madagascariensis*, and *A. za* gave rise to a legend about angry gods pulling up the trees by their roots and sticking them back head-first into the earth.

Adansonia gibbosa (syn. *A. gregorii*), native in parts of Australia, is called gourd tree or dead-rat tree because the fuzzy gray fruits suggest rats hanging by their tails.

Adansonia digitata

BAOBAB, MONKEY-BREAD TREE, UPSIDE-DOWN-TREE

Tropical eastern Africa; widely distributed. Deciduous tree, 75–100 ft.; zones 9–11. Blooms summer, fall. Seasonally moist/dry. Average, well-drained soil. Full sun. Flowers: petals white, reflexed; filaments

united into a column at base, spreading into a sphere terminally; on long pendent stalks; capsule ovoid, 8–10 in. long, woody, covered with golden-brown hairs, the pulp in cottony, sour-tasting chunks. Leaves: palmate; leaflets 5–7; margins toothed when young, then smooth, pubescent below. Bark is light gray, smooth. *Fast growing. Night blooming; flowers lasting until noon. The tree in the photo is 60–70 years old and 5–6 ft. in diameter, still only a baby.*

Bombax

Bombax includes approximately 20 species of trees from the Old World tropics. *Rhodognaphalon* is now a subgenus of *Bombax*. Trunks and branches are covered with large conical thorns. Leaves are palmate, the leaflets articulated (jointed) where they meet in the center and will snap off if bent. (*Pseudobombax* leaves are not articulated. Flowers are solitary. Numerous stamens are arranged in 2 concentric rings, the outer whorl in 5 clumps (fascicles). The filaments of the inner whorl are adherent—but not fused—to the style. Rain or irrigation during the dry season interrupts dormancy

Wercklea ferox

Adansonia digitata, flower

often resulting in less than spectacular bloom, though some individuals just seem to be poor bloomers. The seeds are surrounded by floss, but the kapok is of poorer quality than in *Ceiba*. Petals are added to curry in the Far East.

Bombax ceiba

RED KAPOK, RED COTTON-TREE, MALABAR SIMAL (INDIA)
Synonyms: *B. malabaricum*, *Salmalia malabarica*. Exact origin obscure (southern China, Indomalaysia). Deciduous tree to 80 ft.; zones 9–11. Blooms late winter. Moist to wet, seasonally dry. Average, well-drained soil. Full sun. Flowers: large, 6–9 in. wide, petals fleshy, glossy red, orange, or rarely golden, reflexing strongly after opening, then gradually relaxing; calyx cup-shaped, to 2 in. wide, shallowly lobed. Leaves: palmate, leaflets 5–7, elliptic, 8–10 in. long;

petioles to 12 in. long. Bark: gray, wrinkled horizontally, with conical thorns. *Withhold water in winter for bountiful bloom. Selections that formerly evolved from the same parent (Bombacaceae) will not hybridize.*

Ceiba

Ceiba (pronounced SAY-ba) includes approximately 15 species of large trees from tropical America. This genus now includes the species formerly in *Chorisia* (Ravenna 1998). Leaves are palmately compound, rarely simple. Flowers are funnel-shaped to spreading, borne in clusters or solitary. The 5 stamen filaments are fused into a tube or column at least at the base. Trunks are usually covered with thorns especially when young, becoming buttressed with age. Fruits are large, ovoid woody capsules, filled with silky hairs.

Ceiba pentandra was the tree-of-

life to the ancient Indians of Central America. The thorns were portrayed on their pottery as spiky surface ornamentation. Trees were distributed throughout the tropics for production of kapok shortly after the conquest of Mexico.

The *Ceiba insignis* aggregate includes 6 species that were traditionally in the genus *Chorisia*: *C. speciosa*, *C. pubiflora*, *C. chodatii*, *C. insignis*, *C. crispiflora*, *C. ventricosa*, and a new species, *C. lupuna*. Flowers have mostly fused staminal columns except in *Ceiba pubiflora*, though this is an unreliable characteristic. This group is highly regarded for the very large, colorful flowers which are distinguished from traditional *Ceiba* species by the corona of five 2-lobed staminodes surrounding the base of the stamens. This is a very similar, taxonomically unresolved aggregate which may include varieties, subspecies, or distinct species (Gibbs, pers. comm.).

Indigenous peoples throughout South America are known to have cultivated beautiful and useful species long before the arrival of Europeans. The species all readily hybridize but individuals are self-sterile. Thus, plants collected from one area might have easily integrated with local wild populations prehistorically. Parrots probably also contribute to seed distribution. Now, even wild-collected plants might involve hybrids or cultigens. Species identifications

here of plants in cultivation are highly subjective.

Ceiba chodatii

YELLOW SILK-FLOSS TREE, PALO BORRACHO, PAINA DE SEDA AMARILLA, PAINEIRA
Synonym: *Chorisia chodatii*. Northwestern Argentina, Paraguay, Bolivia. Deciduous tree, 20–30 ft.+; zones 9–11. Blooms late summer, fall. Moderate moisture, seasonally dry. Average, well-drained soil. Full sun. Flowers: funnel-shaped, light yellow, pubescent, slightly streaked magenta, throat yellow turning brown when old; margins smooth; stigma red; filaments united or free distally; calyx cup 2-lobed. Leaves: palmate; leaflets 5, narrowly elliptic, 6–7 in. long, dull; margins serrate at distal end; petiole 6 in. long. *The lilylike shape and yellow color are distinctive. This species has long been confused with* Ceiba insignis *(syn.* Chorisia insignis*), both in scientific and popular references. Note their different wild ranges.*

Ceiba crispiflora

SILK-FLOSS TREE, PAINA DE SEDA
Synonym: *Chorisia crispiflora*. Brazil (Rio State). Deciduous tree to 50 ft.; zones 9–11. Blooms midsummer through fall. Seasonally moist/dry. Average, well-drained soil. Full sun. Flowers: petals narrowly oblong, spreading, edges strongly undulate, pink distally, cream to light yellow centrally, streaked magenta; staminodes

Adansonia digitata

Bombax ceiba, orange form

Ceiba chodatii

dark red, white pubescent. Leaves: palmate. *These selections have characteristics similar to those defined for Ceiba crispiflora: 'LASCA Beauty' is a summer bloomer from the Los Angeles State and County Arboretum. 'Sugar Loaf' was introduced at the Kampong in Coconut Grove, Florida, from Rio de Janeiro.*

Ceiba insignis

WHITE SILK-FLOSS TREE, LUPUNA
Synonym: *Chorisia insignis.* Northern Peru, Ecuador. Deciduous tree to 50 ft.+; zones 9–11. Blooms fall, early winter. Seasonally moist/dry. Average, well-drained soil. Full sun.

Flowers: petals strongly reflexed, then spreading, creamy white, sometimes streaked with magenta, edges undulate, throat light yellow, turning brown when old, pubescent, faintly vanilla-scented; filaments fused or partly free near the ends; staminodes cream; calyx cup green, unequally 3-lobed. Leaves: palmate; leaflets 5–6; obovate, 4–6 in. long, articulated, dull green; margins serrate distally; petiole 4–6 in. long. Trunk: bottle-shaped, streaked green, more or less with cone-shaped thorns. *This possible hybrid has more lily-shaped flowers than the type.*

Ceiba Kampong Series Hybrids

SILK-FLOSS TREE, CHORISIA, PAINA DE SEDA
Garden hybrids. Deciduous trees, 20–50 ft.+; zones 9–11. Bloom fall. Seasonally moist/dry. Average, well-drained soil. Full sun. Flowers: petals white to pink, often streaked magenta; stamens partly free to fused. Leaves: palmate, leaflets 5–7; margins partly serrated to smooth. *Complex hybrids involving the C. insignis aggregate and possibly C. schottii. First- and second-generation hybrids exhibit characteristics similar to the various members of the C. insignis aggregate.*

Ceiba pentandra

GIANT KAPOK, SILK-COTTON TREE, LUPUNA, CEIBO, CEIBOTE
Synonyms: *Bombax pentandrum, C. caribeae, C. casearia.* Tropical America, widely distributed in the tropics. Deciduous tree, 100–200 ft.; zones 9–11. Blooms late winter, spring. Seasonally moist or wet, dry. Average, well-drained soil. Full sun. Flowers: petals 5, 2 in. wide, creamy white to reddish; in pendent oblique terminal clusters; capsules banana-shaped, leathery, to 10 in. long; filled with balls of silky fibers. Leaves: palmate, leaflets 5–7, obovate, 3–6 in. long. Trunk: green or brown, with or without conical thorns, heavily buttressed with age, to 30 ft. girth. *Branches horizontal. Brittle in wind. One form has brown, heavily thorned bark and dense clus-*

Ceiba crispiflora 'LASCA Beauty'

Ceiba crispiflora 'Sugar Loaf', flowers

Ceiba crispiflora 'LASCA Beauty', flowers

Ceiba Kampong Series Hybrids

ters of reddish flowers; another is mostly spineless with green bark and creamy white flowers. 'Pancoastal', introduced by Lester Pancoast from cultivation in Madagascar, has smooth green bark and diffuse floral clusters. Ceiba pentandra *is an alternate host for cacao swollen-shoot virus (badnavirus).*

Ceiba pubiflora
SILK-FLOSS TREE, PAINA DE SEDA
Synonym: *Chorisia pubiflora.* Paraguay, Brazil (Goiás, Mato Grosso). Deciduous tree to 50 ft.+; zones 9–11. Blooms fall. Seasonally moist/dry. Average, well-drained soil. Full sun. Flowers: spreading to slightly funnel-shaped, petals obovate to spathulate, pink to white, throat white or light yellow, with thin magenta streaks, edges undu-

late; stamens often free at the ends; staminodes white, smooth, not hairy.

Ceiba schottii
POCHOTE
Synonym: *Bombax schottii.* Mexico (Yucatan peninsula), Guatemala. Deciduous tree, 40–100 ft.; zones 9–11. Blooms late summer, fall. Seasonally moist/dry. Average, well-drained soil. Full sun. Flowers: funnel-shaped, erect, petals slender, creamy white turning tan, hairy; calyx tubular, 2-lobed; stamens 5, anthers red, filaments fused into a column at base. Leaves: palmate, 4–5 in. long; leaflets ovate, to 3 in. long, tips mucronate or retuse; petiole 2–3 in. long; margins smooth. *A tree of seasonally dry forests. Less common than* C. aesculifolia, *which*

ranges from Sonora to the Yucatan peninsula in Mexico and is distinguished by toothed leaflet margins.

Ceiba speciosa
CHORISIA, SILK-FLOSS TREE, PAINEIRA ROSA
Synonym: *Chorisia speciosa.* Southeastern Brazil (extending into Rondônia and Acre), Bolivia, Peru. Deciduous tree to 50 ft.+; zones 10–11. Blooms primarily fall. Seasonally moist/dry. Average, well-drained soil. Full sun. Flowers: petals ovate to spathulate; zoned pink distally, white in the center, streaked magenta; stamens fused or free at the ends; staminodes pink, not hairy. Leaves: palmate, leaflets 5–7, elliptic; margins serrate toward tips. Bark: conical thorns at least on young growth.

Highly recommended landscape tree, providing late-season color. Cuttings can be started directly in the ground in moist locations.

Ochroma
Ochroma (pronounced ahk-ROAM-ah) includes a single species of tree from tropical America. *Ochroma pyramidale* is characteristic of wet lowland forests. It is plantation grown for its soft, ultra-lightweight wood and for paper pulp and is also grown to control erosion. Balsa logs were used to build the raft Kon-Tiki sailed by Thor Heyerdahl and his crew from Peru to Tahiti. Heyerdahl wrote a popular book about this trip to support the hypothesis that Polynesia might have been populated from the east rather than the west.

Ceiba pentandra 'Pancoastal'

Ceiba schottii

Ceiba speciosa

Ceiba speciosa, trunk

Ceiba insignis

Ceiba pubiflora

Leaves are large and simple, slightly 3- to 5-lobed. The flowers are large and solitary with a long, thick column and partly fused, twisted filaments. The corolla is tightly folded around the column in the morning, becoming lax by nightfall. Flowers are pollinated by bats and flies. Allow plenty of space for a large, buttressed trunk. The tree is shallow-rooted and easily toppled by windstorms. Balsa should not be confused with balsam, a resinous oil as well as a common name for a number of unrelated plants. Seeds need heat to germinate. The seed floss is a type of kapok used for stuffing.

Ochroma pyramidale

BALSA, DOWN-TREE, BALSO REAL, LANO, TAMBOR

Synonyms: *O. bicolor*, *O. lagopus*. Tropical America. Evergreen tree to 45 ft.; zones 10–11. Blooms late winter, early spring. Seasonally moist/dry. Moderately fertile, well-drained soil. Full sun. Flowers: vase-shaped, 5–6 in. long, corolla white, musky-scented, almost enclosing the thick column; capsule cylindrical, 5-furrowed; seeds round with abundant silk. Leaves: broadly ovate, weakly 3- to 5-lobed, bases cordate, dark green, roughly hairy below, to 15 in. long. Unarmed. *Flowers open to a funnel shape, becoming limp, and fall later in the day.*

Pachira

Pachira (pronounced pah-KEY-ra) includes 10–20 or more species of large trees from tropical America. Leaves are palmately compound with 5–9 articulated leaflets that will snap off if bent. This distinguishes these species from *Pseudobombax*, which has unarticulated leaves. *Pachira* is distinguished from *Bombax* by the longer stamens, the large, woody fruit, and flossless seeds. The trunk may be armed or unarmed. The solitary flowers are large and funnel-shaped. The numerous stamens are fused at the base and divided into clumps (fascicles), which are arranged in 2 concentric whorls. *Pachira aquatica* has purple-tipped stamens. Another uncommonly cultivated species, *P. insignis*, has white-tipped stamens and reddish petals. Flowers are night blooming and pollinated by bats or insects. The fruit is a large, ovoid woody capsule. The seeds are eaten roasted or raw. In the wild, they grow along streambanks as well as in upland forests.

Pachira aquatica

GUIANA CHESTNUT, PROVISION-TREE, CASTAÑÓN

Synonyms: *Bombax aquatica*, *P. macrocarpa*. Tropical America.

Semideciduous tree, 35–75 ft.; zones 9–11. Blooms warm months. Seasonally moist/dry. Average, well-drained soil. Full sun. Flowers: corolla trumpet-shaped, cream, vanilla-scented; stamens numerous, fused at the base, ends free, magenta-purple turning ruddy red; calyx cup unlobed; capsule heart-shaped, to 10 in. long, woody, covered with rough brown hairs; seeds in a spongy pulp. Leaves: palmate, leaflets 6–8, obovate 6–8 in. long, tips pointed, petiolules articulated at the petiole. Trunk: buttressed, never thorned. *Flowers open at night, wilt by midmorning. Somewhat salt tolerant.*

Pachira quinata

WILD CHESTNUT, PACHOTE, CEDRO ESPINO, CASTAÑA

Synonyms: *Bombax fendleri*, *Bombacopsis quinatum*. Nicaragua to Colombia, Venezuela. Deciduous tree to 45 ft.; zones 9–11. Blooms late winter, early spring. Seasonally moist/dry. Average, well-drained soil. Full sun. Flowers: funnel-shaped, petals 5, bronze scales on

Ochroma pyramidale, flower and capsule

Pachira aquatica, flower

Pachira quinata

Pachira aquatica, buttressed trunk

Pachira quinata, leaves and trunk

the outside, white inside, 3–4 in. wide; stamens white, in clusters (fascicles). Leaves: palmate, leaflets 5–6, articulated at the petiole. Trunk: reddish brown, densely armed with long conical thorns. *Of coasts and inland. Salt tolerant. Selectively harvested for its valuable hard wood, which is used to make furniture. Night-blooming. Flowers fall by midday.*

Pseudobombax

Pseudobombax includes approximately 20 species of large trees from tropical America. Leaves are palmately compound, rarely simple (*P. simplifolium*). The leaflet petiolules are unarticulated (not jointed) where they join the petiole—a distinctive characteristic—and flex, but do not snap, when

bent. The stamens are long and showy. *Pseudobombax ellipticum*, shaving-brush tree, is frequently cultivated. The flowers open on bare branches shortly before the foliage. The cigarlike buds open with a pop in the evening. The petals curl back tightly, then gradually relax until the flower falls by midday. The calyx cup, filled with sweet nectar, attracts perching birds.

Pseudobombax ellipticum

SHAVING-BRUSH TREE, BROCHA DE AFEITAR
Synonyms: *Bombax ellipticum, Carolinea fastuosa*. Mexico, Guatemala; widely cultivated. Deciduous tree to 35 ft.; zones 9–11. Blooms late winter, early spring. Seasonally moist/dry. Average, well-drained soil. Full sun. Flowers: petals 5, reflexed, tan

hairs on outer side, greenish inside, 5–6 in. long; stamens many, pink or white, united into 10 clusters (fascicles) only at the base; calyx cup brown with basal glands. Leaves: palmate; leaflets 5–7, elliptic, tips pointed; petiolule wedge-shaped. Trunk: unarmed, bark gray, streaked green, developing a bottle shape. *Spread greater than height. 'Album' is thought to be a natural white variation.*

Pseudobombax grandiflorum

BRAZILIAN SHAVING-BRUSH TREE
Synonym: *Bombax grandiflorum*. Brazil. Deciduous tree to 100 ft.; zones 9–11. Blooms mid to late winter. Seasonally moist/dry. Average, well-drained soil. Full sun. Flowers: petals snow-white inside, purplish brown outside with silver

hairs; stamens 5–6, not as numerous as in *Pseudobombax ellipticum*. Leaves: palmate; leaflets 7–9, obovate, to 6 in. long, not articulated. Bark: gray with vertical ridges. *Potentially a very tall tree. Often confused with P. ellipticum 'Album' but distinguished by its earlier blooming season, the pure white inner surface of the petals, and fewer stamens.*

Quararibea

Quararibea (pronounced kwa-rah-ree-BAY-ah) includes 50 or more species of trees from tropical America. It is the largest genus in this group and one of the most prevalent genera of canopy trees in the rain forest. Leaves are simple and in opposite ranks. Trunks are unarmed. Branches are horizontal, radiating like spokes from the trunk. The flowers are borne singly or in small clusters in the leaf axils or directly on the branches and trunk (cauliflorous). The staminal column is 5-lobed. These species are pollinated by small climbing mammals, not bats. A traditional chocolate drink in Mexico is flavored with dry, ground flowers of *Quararibea funebris*. The genus name is derived from a native word for a species in Guyana. *Quararibea cordata* has an edible fruit and broadly cordate leaves.

Quararibea funebris

PALANCO (COSTA RICA), PATASTE (NICARAGUA)
Synonym: *Lexarza funebris*. Mexico, Central America. Evergreen tree, 35–100 ft.; zones 10–11. Blooms spring, early summer. Seasonally wet. Fertile, well-drained soil. Full to part sun. Flowers: pure white, 2 in. wide, dripping with lemon-scented nectar; stamen filaments fused into a column; fruit ovoid, 2–2.5 in. long, green with brown hairs and a persistent calyx. Leaves: simple, obovate, sides unequal, 10–12 in. long. Bark: smooth, gray, unarmed. *Branches radiate in whorls like spokes of a wheel, the ends drooping obliquely. Of riversides and tropical rain forests. Unusual in cultivation. The name relates to its use as a shade tree around cemeteries.*

Pseudobombax ellipticum

Pseudobombax ellipticum 'Album'

Pseudobombax grandiflorum

Pseudobombax grandiflorum, leaves

Quararibea funebris

MALVACEAE
Formerly Sterculiaceae
COCOA FAMILY

Sterculiaceae, traditionally recognized as a distinct family, is now included within Malvaceae. It consists of approximately 67 genera of shrubs and trees, rarely herbs or climbers, from the tropics, plus a few from mild temperate regions. Cacao, *Theobroma cacao*, is important economically for chocolate and cocoa. Cola-nut, *Cola*, once used to flavor carbonated beverages, is now largely replaced by synthetics. Some larger trees are harvested for timber. Several are grown as ornamentals.

Leaves are simple, palmately lobed to compound, with smooth margins. Flowers are usually bisexual, either radially or bilaterally symmetrical. Petals are sometimes reduced or absent, the sepals are then often petal-like (petaloid). The 10 stamens are in 2 concentric whorls, the outer 5 often reduced to staminodes, the inner 5 with filaments fused in a column. Flowers are solitary or in clusters (cymes, panicles, or racemes). The fruit is usually a dry capsule or schizocarp. Sometimes the schizocarps split into boat-shaped follicles with persistent fibers holding the spreading follicles together like basket handles. Seeds often have irritating hairs attached.

Abroma

Abroma includes approximately 10 species of shrub from Asia to Australia. The dry capsules split into 5 boatlike follicles lined with irritating hairs (hence the name devil's cotton). A jutelike fiber is made from the bark.

Abroma augusta
DEVIL'S COTTON

Synonym: *A. fastuosa*. India, Southeast Asia, Indomalaysia to Australia. Evergreen shrub to tree; zones 10–11. Blooms late winter. Seasonally moist/dry. Average, well-drained soil. Part sun to bright understory. Flowers: petals drooping, reddish brown, narrowly stalked; calyx bell-shaped, green, ridged, temporarily enclosing the petals (lower left in photo); epicalyx green, reflexed; dry capsules resemble an open umbrella, composed of 5 keeled segments lined with irritating hairs. Leaves: cordate, 3–12 in. long, shallowly lobed; margins serrate. *Attractive to butterflies. Also spelled* Ambroma *in older references.*

Brachychiton

Brachychiton includes 20–30 species of trees from Australia, plus 2 from Papua New Guinea. It is closely related to *Sterculia*, differing mainly by the anatomy of the fruits. The stems are often pachycaulous, bottle forms or sometimes with massive, partly subterranean caudices. Flowers lack true petals. The petal-like (petaloid) calyx is bell-shaped. Leaves are entire, palmately lobed or compound. Fruits are follicles with seeds in boatlike compartments. The species thrive in arid climates and in neutral to acid soil.

Brachychiton discolor
QUEENSLAND LACEBARK,
SCRUB BOTTLE-TREE,
KURRAJONG (AUSTRALIA)

Northern Australia, Queensland, New South Wales. Deciduous tree to 100 ft.; zones 10–11. Blooms late spring, summer. Seasonally moist/ dry. Average, well-drained soil; acid pH. Full sun. Flowers: corolla absent; calyx petal-like, 1–2 in. long, bell-shaped with pointed lobes, pink, velvety; in compact clusters; capsule 5-parted, woody, segments boatlike, black, containing large yellow seeds and irritating hairs. Leaves: ovate, 3- to 7-lobed; 6–8 in. diameter; dark, dull green, silvery wool below. Bark: with lacey green and white markings. Trunk: pachycaulous, more or less bottle-shaped. *Massive trees of seasonally moist/dry tropical forest, very drought tolerant. Young plants need protection and moisture.*

Brachychiton ×hybridus
HYBRID FLAME BOTTLE-TREE

Synonyms: *B. ×fordii* (hort.), *B. ×roseus* (hort.). Garden hybrid (Australia), *B. acerifolius* × *B. populneus*. Briefly deciduous tree, 15–20 ft.; zones 9–11. Blooms late spring, early summer. Dry. Average, well-drained soil; acid pH. Full sun. Flowers: corolla absent; calyx petal-like, bell-shaped, pink; in pendent masses to 4 ft. long. Leaves: elliptic, 6–8 in. long, more or less lobed. Trunk: short, caudex large, branches short, pendent. *A sterile hybrid. Avoid planting closer than 15 ft. from structures or pavement, which could eventually heave from the swelling caudex. Highly recommended for dry*

Abroma augusta

Brachychiton ×hybridus

Brachychiton rupestris

Brachychiton discolor

regions. Photographed in the carousel parking lot of Balboa Park.

Brachychiton rupestris

QUEENSLAND BOTTLE-TREE, NARROW LEAFED BOTTLE-TREE
Australia (Queensland). Deciduous tree to 25 ft.+; zones 9–11. Blooms late spring, early summer. Seasonally moist/dry. Average, well-drained soil; acid pH. Full sun. Flowers: corolla absent; calyx petal-like, bell-shaped, pinkish yellow with rounded lobes. Leaves: lanceolate, to 6 in. long. Develops a massive aboveground caudex or bottle

shape. Drought tolerant. Young plants need protection and moisture. Photographed at Balboa Park.

Dombeya

Dombeya includes approximately 250 species of shrubs and trees from Africa, Madagascar, and the Mascarene Islands. Dombeyas are highly prized for their profuse winter bloom. Leaves are broadly ovate to heart-shaped and more or less palmately lobed. The flowers have 5 petals which are usually persistent, turning tan with age. The calyx is 5-lobed and there are 3

bracts. Stamens are more or less fused and the pollen is microscopically spiny. Those species included here are xeric and suitable for public landscaping. The dense foliage shades out weeds around the base. Standing water may cause root rot. *Dombeya burgessiae* 'Seminole' is a cross made at the USDA Subtropical Horticulture Research Station at Chapman Field, Miami, Florida, between *D. burgessiae* 'Rosemound', a wild-collected pink selection, and a locally cultivated *D. burgessiae*. USDA records show 'Rosemound' was never distrib-

uted and was destroyed during Hurricane Andrew in 1992. Therefore, no plants in cultivation can legitimately be 'D. 'Rosemound' as sometimes labeled. 'Seminole' is in cultivation and has a compact habit and a long flowering season. It makes an outstanding flowering hedge. It must be propagated vegetatively.

Dombeya burgessiae 'Seminole'

SEMINOLE DOMBEYA, TROPICAL HYDRANGEA, ZULU CHERRY, PINK WILD PEAR
Synonyms: *D. elegans, D. rosea, D. ×seminole* (hort.). Garden hybrid (species from southeastern Africa), *D. burgessiae* × *D. burgessiae* 'Rosemound' . Evergreen shrub to 6–12 ft.; zones 9–11. Blooms late fall, winter, spring. Seasonally moist/dry. Gritty, well-drained soil. Full to part sun. Flowers: cup-shaped, petals deep pink, persistent; in clusters (umbels), on 3-in. stalks in the leaf axils. Leaves: ovate, 3–6 in. long, base cordate, often shallowly lobed, roughly hairy; margins irregularly toothed, undulate (wavy). *The type form has white or pink flowers. Highly recommended. See history in the genus heading.*

Brachychiton rupestris, flowers

Dombeya burgessiae 'Seminole'

Dombeya cacuminum

RED TREE DOMBEYA, STRAWBERRY SNOWBALL
Madagascar. Evergreen tree, 35–50 ft.; zones 9–11. Blooms winter. Moderate moisture. Gritty, well-drained soil. Full sun. Flowers: red; in pendent terminal clusters just below the canopy; capsules papery. Leaves: broadly ovate, to 6 in. long, with 3–5 pointed lobes, downy. *Of montane forests. Thrives in southern California. A good shade tree with a rounded canopy. Be cautioned: when in bloom, the flowers shed a musky-scented yellow nectar. Trees are pollinated by bats in the wild. Some pollination takes place in cultivation, possibly by bats, birds, or insects.*

Dombeya pulchra

RED AND WHITE DOMBEYA
Northeastern South Africa . Evergreen shrub; zones 9–11. Blooms fall. Seasonally moist/dry. Average, well-drained soil; acid pH. Full sun.

Dombeya cacuminum

Dombeya pulchra

Flowers: petals white, red at base. Leaves: cordate, slightly lobed, rough; margins irregularly toothed. *Unusual in cultivation but recommended.*

Dombeya spectabilis

WILD PEAR, UMBIHANYAKA ("SPRING'S HERALD" IN MALAGASY) Madagascar. Briefly deciduous tree, 25–45 ft.; zones 9–11. Blooms early spring. Seasonally moist in winter, dry in summer. Gritty, well-drained soil. Full sun. Flowers: open creamy white to pinkish, persistent. Leaves: broadly ovate, to 7 in. long; margins irregularly toothed. Stems: covered with reddish pubescence. *Reminiscent of pears in blossom. In California trees bloom profusely in April just before the new leaves appear.*

Dombeya wallichii

PINK BALL DOMBEYA, TASSEL-TREE, CHRISTMAS ROSE
Tropical eastern Africa, Madagascar. Evergreen shrub or tree to 20 ft.; zones 10–11. Blooms winter. Seasonally moist/dry. Average, well-drained soil. Full to part sun. Flowers: petals 5, pink, persistent; 5 sterile stamens plus 15 fertile, fused into a tube at the base; in compact heads, on pendent stalks to 10 in. long; capsule hairy. Leaves: cordate, 8–12 in. long, more or less lobed, covered with soft hairs; margins toothed. *A holiday bloomer in the Northern Hemisphere.* Dombeya ×cayeuxii *is a hybrid of* D. wallichii *with smaller bracts and bristly stems.*

Helicteres

Helicteres includes 40–60 species of shrubs and trees from tropical America and Asia. All parts are softly downy (pubescent). The stamens are fused into a column. The fruit is composed of 5 spirally twisted follicles, leading to the common name of screw-nuts. In Central America these species are aptly referred to as *cabo chancho,* loosely meaning "frayed rope-end."

Helicteres guazumifolia

SCREW-NUT TREE, CABO CHANCHO
Synonym: *H. mexicanus.* Mexico, Central and South America. Evergreen shrub, 6–15 ft.; zones 10–11. Blooms spring, early summer.

Moderate moisture to seasonally moist/dry. Average, well-drained soil. Full to part sun. Flowers: petals clawed, red; calyx tubular, red, 2-lobed, stem in column long-exserted; in pairs or small clusters; fruit composed of 5 spirally twisted follicles that unwind with age. Leaves: ovate, 2–4 in. long; margins toothed. *Flowers resemble miniature* Malvaviscus. *Very attractive to butterflies and hummingbirds.*

Kleinhovia

Kleinhovia includes a single species from tropical Asia, eastern Africa, and northern Australia. It is a large shade tree with rounded crown, suitable for landscaping in open parks. Flowers are small but in large, many-flowered panicles. The 5 petals are unequal, the upper petals clawed. The 5 sepals are larger than the petals.

Kleinhovia hospita

GUEST-TREE
China, India, Southeast Asia, northeastern Australia, Polynesia. Evergreen tree to 60 ft.; zones 9–11. Blooms late summer, early fall. Moderate moisture or seasonally moist/dry. Average, well-drained soil. Full sun. Flowers: petals unequal, pink to reddish; calyx petal-like; stamens 15 in 5 clusters; in large panicles; capsule inflated, 5-ribbed, to about 1 in. wide, light green (2 in upper middle of photo). Leaves: broadly ovate to cordate, to 1 ft. long; margins undulate. *A potentially large shade tree that needs room to spread. Set back a minimum of 25 ft. Underutilized but recommended for park landscaping and erosion control.*

Pterospermum

Pterospermum includes approximately 25 species of trees from tropical Asia. *Pterospermum acerifolium* is a large tree harvested for its durable, teaklike lumber. Leaves are in opposite ranks (distichous). Flowers are asymmetrical, petals spirally twisted. They open at night, lasting into the morning. Seeds are winged. An excellent shade tree if lower branches are pruned. Suitable for public landscaping.

Pterospermum acerifolium

MAPLE-LEAFED BAYUR
India, sub-Himalayan Asia to Indonesia (Java). Evergreen tree to 80 ft.; zones 8–11. Blooms late summer. Seasonally moist/dry. Average, well-drained soil. Full sun. Flowers: corolla tubular at base, to 7 in. long, white, split along one side, the lobes fanned asymmetri-

Dombeya spectabilis

Dombeya wallichii

Helicteres guazumifolia

Kleinhovia hospita

Pterospermum acerifolium

Sterculia ceramica, fruit

cally and spirally twisted; calyx lobes linear, free; capsule oblong, to 6 in. long, hairy; solitary. Leaves: broadly ovate, oblique, 8–14 in. long, irregularly and shallowly lobed, dark green above, light, woolly below, distichous; margins undulate. Petioles, fruits, buds, and twigs covered with rough, rust-colored hairs. Older trunks buttressed. *A large tree of forest streambanks. Not known to set seed in cultivation.*

Sterculia

Sterculia includes approximately 250 species of trees from the Old and New World tropics with greatest diversity in Asia. The genus name comes from Sterculius, the Greek god of cultivation and, by association, to the manure pile, alluding to the fetid odor of some species. The leaves are simple, more or less palmately lobed to compound, and typically clustered at the ends of the branches. The leaves and petioles are often quite variable in size. Flowers lack petals and the sepals are often petal-like and bell-shaped (similar to *Brachychiton*). They bear bisexual flowers or male and female flowers on the same plant (monoecious) or a combination of unisexual and bisexual flowers on the same plant (polygamous). The stamens and carpels are sometimes mounted on a stalk (androgynophore).

Sterculia ceramica

FAIRCHILD'S STERCULIA
Synonym: *S. luzonica*. Indonesia (Sulawesi, Moluccas, Ceram), Philippines, rare in the wild. Evergreen tree to 35 ft.+; zones 10–11. Blooms warm months. Seasonally moist/dry. Average, well-drained soil. Full sun. Flowers: inconspicuous; stamens white, numerous, unscented; capsule ovoid with a short neck, red-orange, on pendent stalk to 10 in. long; seeds black, glossy. Leaves: oblong-elliptic, to 10 in. long. *This species was collected by David Fairchild for whom it acquired its common name. It is rare in the wild as well as cultivation. The species name refers to the island of Ceram in the Moluccas.*

Sterculia foetida

GIANT STERCULIA, INDIAN ALMOND, JAVA-OLIVE, SKUNK TREE
Southeast Asia, India to Australia. Deciduous tree to 120 ft.+; zones 10–11. Blooms intermittently, primarily winter, spring. Seasonally moist/dry. Average, well-drained soil. Full sun. Flowers: unisexual; petals absent; calyx bell-shaped, dark red with yellow edges; in loose clusters; fetid aroma; capsule fist-sized, lobed, scarlet, woody; seeds black. Leaves: palmate, leaflets elliptic, 4–9, tips pointed, reddish when young. Bark: smooth, gray. *A potentially giant tree with buttressed trunk. Seeds edible but reportedly purgative.*

Sterculia tragacantha

Tropical western Africa. Deciduous tree, 30–60 ft.+; zones 10–11. Blooms spring. Wet to moderate moisture. Average, well-drained soil. Full sun. Flowers: lack corolla; calyx light green with reddish brown hairs; borne in dense panicles, from the leaf axils; fruit a reddish follicle. Leaves: simple, broadly oblong, 6–10 in. long, roughly hairy below; petiole to 3 in. long with an enlarged pulvinus at base; margins smooth. Trunk: buttressed with age. *The species name means "goat-scented," though the scent, while musky, is not unpleasant.*

Theobroma

Theobroma includes approximately 20 species of trees from tropical America. The small flowers grow directly from the stem (cauliflorous). *Theobroma cacao* is widely cultivated. The seeds are the source of cacao, which, after fermentation, becomes chocolate, cocoa (fat removed), and cocoa butter. Chocolate was first introduced to European explorers by the Aztec and Mayan civilizations, which used the sweet pulp to make a drink. The seeds were used as currency and as a flavoring. Chocolate contains several stimulants and can be addictive to some individuals. Hot chocolate was fashionable in Europe before the introduction of coffee. Like coffee, it is grown beneath shade trees such as *Syzygium*, *Inga*, and *Gliricidia* or in the rain forest.

Shade plantations are a sustainable farming method with low impact on the environment. Plantations provide alternative habitat for migratory birds.

Theobroma cacao

CACAO, CHOCOLATE TREE, KAKAW
Mexico to Central and South America; widely cultivated. Evergreen tree, 10–25 ft.; zone 11. Blooms warm months. Even moisture. Fertile, well-drained soil. Bright filtered light. Flowers: small, pink to white; solitary on short stalks growing directly from the trunk (cauliflorous); capsules are hard-shelled, light green to sky-blue, turning yellow, then reddish brown, 6–10 in. long. Leaves oblong; petioles short. *An ultra-tropical, heat-loving species. Subject to a number of diseases in plantations in Brazil and Africa. Resistant forms under development.*

Sterculia foetida

Theobroma cacao, flowers

MALVACEAE
Formerly Tiliaceae
LINDEN FAMILY
Tiliaceae, traditionally recognized as a distinct family, is now included within Malvaceae. It includes approximately 46 genera of mostly small to medium trees and shrubs plus a few herbs from the tropics and northern temperate regions. Genera formerly in Elaeocarpaceae are now included in this group. Several species are cultivated in the tropics as ornamentals as well as for timber, fruit, or jute fiber but, with the exception of *Grewia*, are infrequently cultivated in the United States. Leaves are simple, often in opposite ranks (distichous), with palmate or pinnate veins. Some are shallowly lobed and the leaf bases are often asymmetrical. Stems and leaves are covered with downy, microscopically star-shaped (stellate)

Sterculia tragacantha

Theobroma cacao, pods

hairs. The flowers are bisexual, sometimes functioning as male or female, or unisexual. They are radially symmetrical. The 5 petals often have large glands at the base, or petals are sometimes absent. Stamens are often numerous, sometimes showy, and usually fused at the base. The stamens and carpels are sometimes mounted on a stalk (androgynophore). Inflorescences are few- to many-flowered cymes or panicles. The fruit is a capsule, berry, or drupe.

Berrya

Berrya includes 3–5 species of trees from southern India, Sri Lanka, and Indomalaysia to the Pacific Islands, plus 2 from the Caribbean. This genus includes species formerly placed in *Carpodiptera*, now a subgenus of *Berrya*. They are distinguished by variations in the number of wings on the fruits and number of seeds per carpel. Leaves exhibit palmipinnate venation (palmate at base becoming pinnate toward tip). The American and African species have unisexual flowers with male and female on different plants (dioecious) while the Asian species have bisexual flowers. There are 2 American species, *B. cubensis* with 4-winged fruits and *B. hexaptera* with 6-winged fruits. *Berrya cubensis*, a variable species in isolated populations, was formerly divided among 3 species based on leaf size alone (Meijer, unpublished).

Berrya cubensis

MOUNTAIN-PEAR, TELCON
Synonyms: *Carpodiptera ameliae*, *Carpodiptera floribunda*, *Carpodiptera simonis*. Mexico, Guatemala, Belize, Caribbean. Evergreen tree, 30–75 ft.; zones 10–11. Blooms early summer. Moderate moisture. Average, well-drained soil. Full sun. Flowers: unisexual, lavender-pink, in many-flowered terminal and axillary panicles; calyx 2-lobed; capsule round, 4-winged. Leaves: ovate, 6–8 in. long, base cordate, dark green, glossy, sparsely hairy; margins undulate; petiole 2–3 in. long, reddish. Bark: smooth. *Of seasonally moist forests and riversides. A very attractive shade tree with a rounded crown and abundant flowers. Pest resistant. Underutilized but highly recommended. Only male flowers are known in the Miami area. Grow from cuttings.*

Grewia

Grewia includes approximately 150 species of shrubs and trees from the Old World tropics. *Grewia occidentalis* is occasionally cultivated in both humid and dry regions. It is a xeric, long-flowering shrub. It is very attractive as an informal privacy hedge or can be pruned to shape or espaliered. Leaves are small with toothed margins. Flowers are attractive to nectar-feeding birds. The fruits are used in drinks and refreshments.

Grewia occidentalis

STAR-FLOWER, FOUR-CORNERS, CROSS-BERRY
Southern Africa. Evergreen shrub, 6–8 ft.; zones 9–11. Blooms warm months. Moderate moisture. Fertile, well-drained soil. Full sun to bright broken light. Flowers: corolla to 1.5 in. wide, petals oblong, lavender-pink; sepals oblong, pink inside, greenish outside; stamen filaments red-violet with conspicuous golden anthers; opening one at a time, appearing solitary; in axillary fascicles; fruit 4-angled, orange, turning purple. Leaves: elliptic, 2 in. long; margins toothed. Young stems: hairy. *Commonly misidentified as G. caffra, which has rounded yellow petals and rounded fruits and is not known to be cultivated in the United States.*

Luehea

Luehea includes approximately 15 trees and shrubs from seasonally moist/dry forests of tropical America. Leaves are simple, more or less downy below. Flowers are usually white or pink, often showy. The petals are stalked at the base (clawed). *Luehea seemannii* is grown as a shade tree in Central America and the West Indies. Uncommon to rare in the United States but recommended. Possibly more suited to acid soil.

Luehea seemannii

GUÁCIMO, BOLAINA, ACOITA
Central America, Colombia, West Indies. Deciduous tree to 90 ft.; zones 10–11. Blooms late spring, early summer. Seasonally moist/dry. Fertile, well-drained soil; possibly acid pH. Full sun. Flowers: white, 4–5 in. wide, petals 5, obovate, valvate, clawed; sepals greenish white, reflexed; stigma buttonlike, style short; stamens numerous, white; involucre of bracts round with crenulate (scalloped) margin; capsule woody, 5-sided; seeds winged. Leaves: broadly ovate to oblong, 6–7 in. long, underside softly hairy; margins serrulate. Trunk: buttressed with age, bark light gray. *Large white flowers are very ornamental.*

MARANTACEAE

ARROWROOT FAMILY, PRAYER-PLANT FAMILY
Marantaceae includes approximately 30 genera of perennial herbs primarily from the tropics plus a few from subtropical and mild temperate regions. They are tuberous or rhizomatous plants of moist forest and wetlands. Many are grown as houseplants chiefly for their attractive foliage. Several have ornamental inflorescences as well. Leaves are simple, often marked with regular patterns. The petiole has a joint (pulvinus) just below the blade that allows the blade to fold lengthwise. Winged sheaths are on either side of the base of the petiole. These characteristics help distinguish these genera from gingers and heliconias. Flowers are small. They have 3 petals of unequal length, 3 sepals, one partially fertile stamen, and 3 or 4 sterile stamens (staminodes). One petal-like staminode covers the style and is usually longer than the true petals. Flowers are in cymes or cone-

Berrya cubensis

Grewia occidentalis

Luehea seemannii

Calathea burle-marxii

like bracteate heads (strobili) in the leaf axils, or on leafless scapes. The fruit is a capsule or berry.

Calathea

Calathea includes approximately 300 species of tuberous or rhizomatous herbs from the American tropics. They grow in moist forest and along streams. Most are cultivated as foliage plants, but a few have stunning, gingerlike inflorescences. The genus name comes from a Greek word meaning "basket," which refers to the interwoven (imbricate) bracts. Leaves are mostly paddle-shaped. Plants like regular moisture and humidity and dilute or slow-release fertilizer. Calatheas are suitable for containers. Most need protection from chills. Mist the foliage when dry. Propagate by division. The tubers of Guiana arrowroot, or toupinambour, *C. allouia*, and certain other species are made into a starch or eaten as a vegetable.

Calathea burle-marxii

ICE-BLUE CALATHEA, PLATANILLO ("LITTLE PLANTAIN")
Southeastern Brazil. Semideciduous rhizomatous herb, 3–4 ft.; zones 10–11. Blooms warm months. Regular moisture and humidity. Fertile, sandy, humus-rich, well-drained soil. Bright filtered light. Flowers: light red-violet; bracts cupped, spirally arranged, translucent white. Leaves: broadly ovate, to 15–20 in. long, dark green with faint featherlike markings; petioles long. *Of moist lowland tropical forest. Root-hardy in areas subject to light frost. Named for the late Brazilian landscape architect and plant collector, Roberto Burle Marx.*

Calathea crotalifera

RATTLESNAKE-PLANT, BIJAO
Mexico, Central America to Peru and Venezuela. Semideciduous rhizomatous herb, 3–8 ft.; zones 10–11. Blooms warm months. Regular moisture and humidity. Fertile, sandy, humus-rich, well-drained soil. Bright filtered light. Flowers: small, long-stalked; bracts 2-ranked, imbricate, greenish yellow with orange or yellow edges, selections pale yellow; inflorescence 6–8

in. tall, bracts distichous. Leaves: broadly ovate to elliptic. *Calatheas more typically have spirally arranged bracts. The species name alludes to the resemblance of the inflorescence to rattlesnake rattles. In coastal Colombia bijao leaves are used to wrap pasteles, a steamed, special-occasion chicken-and-rice dish.*

Calathea cylindrica

ICE-GREEN CALATHEA, PLATANILLO ("LITTLE PLANTAIN")
Southeastern Brazil. Semideciduous rhizomatous herb, 3–4 ft.; zones 10–11. Blooms warm months. Regular moisture and humidity. Fertile, sandy, humus-rich, well-drained soil. Bright filtered light. Flowers: white or yellow; bracts green, cuplike, spirally arranged. Leaves: broadly ovate, 15–25 in. long, dark green with faint feather markings; petioles

long. *Of lowland moist tropical forest. Root-hardy in areas subject to light frost.*

Calathea loeseneri

TULIP CALATHEA
Amazon headwaters of Colombia, Ecuador, Peru, Bolivia. Evergreen perennial herb, 2–2.5 ft.; zones 10–11. Blooms warm months. Regular moisture and humidity. Fertile, sandy, humus-rich, well-drained soil. Bright filtered light. Flowers: small, white with a violet lip; bracts pointed, white tinted pinkish lavender, inflorescence stalk to 2 ft. Leaves: broadly ovate to elliptic, tips pointed, with light feather markings; petioles densely hairy. *Tolerates seasonal flooding. Floriferous. If too chilly, blooming pauses and minor leaf damage may occur. Said to be sensitive to fluoridated water but in my experience this is not*

true. *Vigorous, easy to grow, very ornamental, and highly recommended.*

Calathea warscewiczii

Costa Rica, Nicaragua. Evergreen herb to 3 ft.; zones 10–11. Blooms warm months. Regular moisture. Fertile, sandy, humus-rich, well-drained soil. Bright filtered light. Flowers: white and yellow; bracts cup-shaped with revolute lips, creamy white becoming yellow with pink lips, spirally arranged, conelike; on a stalk 12–18 in. tall. Leaves: ovate to elliptic, green with variegated fishtail patterns in shades of green, covered with silvery hairs.

Maranta

Maranta includes approximately 20 species of perennial herbs from tropical America. A number of species are grown for their colorful

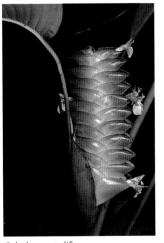
Calathea crotalifera

Calathea cylindrica

Calathea loeseneri

Calathea loeseneri, inflorescence

Calathea warscewiczii

Calathea warscewiczii, inflorescence

foliage. *Maranta* species are distinguished from calatheas by their branching stems. Culinary arrowroot comes from the rhizome of *M. arundinacea*, a Central American species widely cultivated in the tropics. Arrowroot, a transparent thickener similar to cornstarch, is used in cooking, for specialized paper coatings, and in biodegradable plastics. The fermented starch also has potential as an alternative source of alcohol fuels.

Maranta leuconeura
PRAYER-PLANT, HERRINGBONE-PLANT
Brazil. Perennial trailing herb under 1 ft.; zones 10–11. Blooms warm months. Regular moisture. Fertile, sandy, humus-rich, well-drained soil. Filtered light. Flowers: small, white, streaked violet, on short spikes. Leaves: broadly oblong, 3–6

in. long, feather patterned. *Flat, spreading leaves hug the ground. Called prayer-plant because the leaves may fold after dark or when dry. Cold-sensitive but grows back from rhizome if not frozen.* 'Erythroneura' leaves are boldly marked with red veins, dark and light green patterns, and maroon-red below. 'Kerchoviana' leaves are patterned in shades of green, underside pattern faintly outlined in red.

MELASTOMATACEAE
TIBOUCHINA FAMILY, MELASTOMA FAMILY
Melastomataceae includes approximately 200 genera of herbs, shrubs, and trees from the tropics and subtropics, with greatest diversity in South America. Leaves are simple, usually hairy. Instead of one midvein, they usually have 3–7 primary veins arching from base to apex.

Maranta leuconeura 'Erythroneura'

Dissotis rotundifolia

Heterocentron elegans

Stems are more or less 4-angled or 4-winged when young, often square in cross section, or sometimes round. Flowers are bisexual and slightly bilaterally symmetrical. Twice as many stamens as petals are mounted on a staminal cup (hypanthium). Stamens often come in 2 sizes or shapes (dimorphic), often with eyelashlike appendages. Flowers are in clusters or occasionally solitary, either in the leaf axils or terminal. The fruit is a capsule or berry with numerous twisted (cochleate) seeds. Although "Melastomataceae" is the common spelling, the *International Code of Botanical Nomenclature* also accepts "Melastomaceae" to agree with the type genus, *Melastoma*.

Dissotis
Dissotis includes approximately 100 species of shrubs and herbs from tropical and South Africa. Leaves are simple, with 3–7 primary veins, and are more or less hairy. Petioles are short. Flowers are solitary or in terminal clusters. The corolla consists of 4 or 5 petals. The sepals have hairy appendages. The name alludes to the unequal stamens (dimorphic). *Dissotis* is not known to be invasive, but it is sometimes so listed. In some cases, at least, this genus seems to have been mistaken for certain weedy species of *Heterocentron*.

Dissotis rotundifolia
TRAILING GLORY-FLOWER
Tropical Africa. Evergreen creeper; zones 10–11. Blooms warm months. Regular moisture to wet. Fertile, humus-rich, well-drained soil; acid pH. Full sun to bright filtered light. Flowers: petals 5, violet-pink, 1–1.5 in. wide; not known to set fruit in cultivation; solitary. Leaves: ovate, 0.5 in. long; 3 primary veins; petiole red. *Note the 5 petals* (Heterocentron elegans has 4). *Thrives in fountain or waterfall spray or as a ground cover.*

Heterocentron
Heterocentron includes approximately 6 species of herbs and shrubs from Mexico and Central America. Leaves are small with 3–9 or more primary veins. Flowers

have 4 petals. The anthers are dimorphic (in 2 forms). The genus name means "different," in the sense of unusual, for the bristlelike appendages on the anthers. Pearl flower, *H. subtriplinervium*, from Veracruz, Mexico, has clusters of white or sometimes pink flowers. It is widely naturalized in the tropics and is a pest in Hawaii.

Heterocentron elegans
SPANISH SHAWL
Synonyms: *Heeria elegans, Heterocentron sessilis, Monochaetum guatemalensis.* Southern Mexico to El Salvador. Evergreen creeper or subshrub, 1–3 ft.; zones 10–11. Blooms warm months. Regular moisture. Fertile, humus-rich, well-drained soil; acid pH. Bright filtered light. Flowers: solitary, petals 4, magenta. Leaves: ovate, dark green, sparsely hairy, to 1 in. long; margins serrulate, to 1 in. long. *Of montane regions. Sometimes apparently confused with* Dissotis rotundifolia, *which has 5 petals.*

Medinilla
Medinilla includes approximately 400 species from Africa to maritime Southeast Asia, particularly abundant in the Philippines and Borneo. In the wild, they grow in moist montane forest and along streambanks, often epiphytically and on rocks and fallen logs. Stems are 4-angled to 4-winged. Leaves are simple, often large. The conspicuous midvein forks into 3–5 main veins part way into the blade. Tufts of stiff nodular bristles at the base of the leaves are not stipules. Their function is unknown, but it has been suggested that they may serve for water and/or nutrient absorption (Almeda, pers. comm.). Flowers are small with 4 or 5 petals, borne in large clusters. Bracts and bracteoles are sometimes showy. The fruits are berries. Medinillas are suitable for containers or baskets with plenty of humus, bark, and grit for drainage. Less tender species thrive in open soil in bright understory locations. Use dilute liquid or slow-release fertilizers. The use of fungicide on cuts has been recommended. Flowers and fruits are attractive to birds.

Medinilla magnifica

PINK MEDINILLA,
UVA ROSA ("PINK GRAPE")
Philippines. Epiphytic or semiterrestrial shrub to 6 ft.; zone 11. Blooms warm months. Regular moisture and humidity. Coarse organic medium; acid pH. Bright filtered light. Flowers: small in grapelike panicles; bracts large, pink; berries pink turning bluish black. Leaves: broadly ovate to elliptic, 14–15 in. long, glossy dark green; midvein forks halfway through the blade into 5–7 primary veins; purple when young; sessile. Young stems: winged, corky. *Distinguished from M. myriantha by the conspicuous pink bracts.*

Medinilla miniata

CRIMSON MEDINILLA
Philippines (Luzon and Leyte islands). Semiterrestrial to epiphytic shrub, 3–4 ft.; zones 10–11. Blooms warm months. Regular moisture and humidity. Coarse organic medium; acid pH. Bright filtered light. Flowers: glossy ruby-red; in compact clusters; bracts obovate, purplish red to 2 in. long. Leaves: ovate to elliptic, 12–14 in. long, glossy dark green; midvein forking halfway through the blade into 5–7 veins; sessile. Young stems: winged, corky. *This unusual species was distributed by Lyon's Arboretum in Honolulu, which has a diverse collection of medinillas.*

Medinilla myriantha

ROSE-GRAPE MEDINILLA
Philippines, Indonesia, Southeast Asia. Semiterrestrial or epiphytic shrub, 3–4 ft.+; zones 10–11. Blooms summer. Regular moisture and humidity. Coarse organic medium or well-drained soil; acid pH. Full sun to bright filtered light. Flowers: small, pink; bracts small, inconspicuous, green and pink; berries pink-purple. Leaves: ovate, 7–9 in. long; midvein forking about 1 in. inside the blade into 7 main veins. Stems: round, not winged. *This species is forgiving and relatively tolerant of alkaline soil, chilly nights, and bright sunlight. Easy to grow. Distinguished from M. magnifica by nonshowy bracts. Highly recommended.*

Medinilla scortechinii

CORAL MEDINILLA
Malay Peninsula, Sumatra. Semiterrestrial or epiphytic shrub, 1–2 ft.; zone 11. Blooms warm months. Regular moisture and humidity. Humus-rich, well-drained soil; acid pH; or epiphytic. Bright filtered light. Flowers: orange; in panicles; flower stalks orange; resembling precious coral. Leaves: ovate, tips acuminate, 8–10 in. long; 5–7 main veins, leathery dark green, ascending. *Tends to be low and spreading. Photographed at Ernesto's Nursery in Miami, Florida.*

Melastoma

Melastoma includes approximately 70 species from Indomalaysia and the southeastern Pacific Islands. These species are in the process of revision and some species will likely be combined (Almeda, pers. comm.). Leaves and young stems are covered with short, stiff hairs. Plants thrive in fertile, neutral or slightly acid, well-drained soil. Asian *Melastoma* species are distinguished from South American *Tibouchina* species by the pink flowers, not purple or violet; round stems, not 4-angled; and fleshy fruits, not dry. The fruit is edible though seedy. *Melastoma malabathricum* is invasive and listed as a pest in Singapore, Florida, and Hawaii. *Melastoma candidum* is also invasive in Hawaii. These species do not thrive in alkaline soil such as in South Florida and are sensitive to nematodes. Under those conditions there is no threat of their becoming invasive and they can be grown in acidified holes or large containers.

Melastoma malabathricum

MELASTOMA, SINGAPORE RHODODENDRON, INDIAN RHODODENDRON
India, Southeast Asia . Evergreen

Medinilla magnifica

Medinilla miniata

Medinilla myriantha

Medinilla scortechinii

shrub or tree to 6 ft.; zones 10–11. Blooms warm months. Regular moisture and humidity. Fertile, well-drained soil; acid pH. Full sun to broken light. Flowers: pink; fruit a red berry. Leaves: simple, softly hairy; 3- to 5-veined. Stems: scaly, round. *Prune after bloom for compact growth.* Melastoma affine *(syns. M. denticulatum, M. polyanthum) is distinguished by stiff leaf hairs and purple berries. Sometimes incorrectly referred to as pink lasiandra, a synonym associated with Tibouchina,* not *Melastoma.*

Sonerila

Sonerila includes 100–150 species of herbs and subshrubs from Southeast Asia and southern China. Leaves are simple, with usually 3–5 main veins. Flowers are 3-parted, a characteristic unique to this genus, generally pink, in spikes or racemes.

Sonerila picta

Myanmar (Burma), Sumatra. Perennial trailing herb; zones 10–11. Blooms warm months. Regular moisture and humidity. Fertile, well-drained soil. Bright filtered light. Flowers: petals 3, pinkish violet. Leaves: obovate or ovate, to 2 in. long; midvein pinnately branched; margins serrulate. Stems: succulent. *Rare in cultivation.*

Tetrazygia

Tetrazygia includes approximately 25 species of shrubs and trees from Florida and the West Indies. *Tetrazygia bicolor* is sometimes cultivated. In Florida, it grows on the rocky ridge south of Miami both in pinelands, where its growth is limited by natural fires, or along the fringes of hammocks (hardwood forest "islands" surrounded by everglades), where it may reach tree stature. A 41-ft. tree in Castellow Hammock Park in this area was nominated for National Champion before it was destroyed by Hurricane Andrew in 1992 (Hammer, pers. comm.). *Tetrazygia* is native to oolite limestone pinelands and hammocks and does not thrive in sandy soils in nearby areas of the same region. This demonstrates the shortcomings of the common but unfortunate use of the word *native* when it is loosely applied to regional species without regard to their particular habitat.

Tetrazygia bicolor

WEST INDIAN LILAC, FLORIDA CLOVER-ASH
West Indies, South Florida. Evergreen shrub, 10–20 ft., rarely a tree to 40 ft.; zones 9–11. Blooms late spring, early summer. Seasonally moist/dry. Poor, well-drained, limestone soil; alkaline pH. Part sun to bright broken light. Flowers: petals 4–6, white; stamens bright yellow; in dense branched clusters (thyrses); fruit a berry. Leaves: lanceolate, 4–6 in. long, with 3 primary veins, glossy dark green above, white scaly/pubescent below. *Grows naturally on rocky limestone outcroppings.*

Tibouchina

Tibouchina includes 250–300 species of shrubs or small trees from tropical America, with greatest diversity in Brazil. This genus is currently in the process of revision and it is likely that a number of species will be combined. The labeling of species in the trade is unreliable. A number have acquired names of no known authority and hybrids are misrepresented as species. Leaves are simple with 3–7 primary veins, often densely hairy. The flowers are usually purple, violet, or white. The fruit is a dry capsule. Stems are usually 4-angled or 4-winged. (*Melastoma* is distinguished by its Asian origin, fleshy berries, and round stems.) Some *Tibouchina* species have become pests in areas with acid soil including Hawaii and the Far East but are no threat in alkaline conditions. They are also sensitive to nematodes. In those circumstances they may be grown in large containers or in holes acidified with humus or peat. Tibouchinas bloom on new, soft growth. Protect plants from wind and stake weak young shoots. For compact, sturdier growth and more flowers, cut back to woody stems after flowering and then nip out the tips of new shoots after they produce 2 or 3 pairs of leaves.

Tibouchina clavata

GLORY-BUSH, LASIANDRA
Synonym: *T. elegans.* Brazil. Evergreen shrub, 3–7 ft.+; zones 9–11. Blooms spring, summer. Regular moisture and humidity. Sandy, humus-rich, well-drained soil; acid pH. Full sun to bright filtered light. Flowers: blue-violet, occasionally white, valvate, 1.25 in. wide; stamens with long, eyelashlike appendages; calyx and buds white; in terminal clusters. Leaves: elliptic to

Melastoma malabathricum

Sonerila picta

Tetrazygia bicolor

Tibouchina clavata

Tibouchina 'Edward II'

slightly obovate, 5–7 in. long, with stiff, silvery, short hairs. Twigs faintly 4-winged, older stems round (terete). *Unusual in cultivation. Young growth lax, prune after bloom. Needs plenty of light to bloom.*

Tibouchina 'Edward II'

LARGE-FLOWERED GLORY-BUSH, PRINCESS-FLOWER
Origin unknown; hybrid?. Evergreen tree, 4–6 ft.; zones 10–11. Blooms warm months. Regular moisture and humidity. Sandy, humus-rich, well-drained soil; acid pH. Full sun to bright broken light. Flowers: petals vivid purple, to 3 in. wide; margins reflexed, often nodding; sepals and bracts red; in few-flowered terminal clusters; buds red-haired. Leaves: broadly ovate, to 7 in. long, tips apiculate, 5 primary veins, silky haired. Stems: red-haired. *An unrecognized species, possibly a hybrid (Almeda, pers. comm.). Sometimes labeled* T. urvilleana *'Edwardsii', the Latin form for a selection being illegal. Other plants commonly listed as selections of* T. urvilleana *but of unknown ancestry include* T. *'Athens Blue' and* T. *'Jules', a dwarf cultivar.*

Tibouchina granulosa

PURPLE GLORY-TREE, LASIANDRA, ARANHAS (BRAZIL)
Synonym: *Lasiandra granulosa.* Brazil, Bolivia. Evergreen shrub or tree to 10 ft., to 20 ft. in native habitat; zones 10–11. Blooms warm months. Regular moisture and humidity. Sandy, humus-rich, well-

drained soil; acid pH. Full sun to bright broken light. Flowers: petals vivid deep purple, 2 in. wide. Leaves: elliptic to lanceolate, 5–6 in. long, glossy dark green, 5 primary veins. Stems: 4-angled, young wood 4-winged. *Of moist tropical forest.*

Tibouchina heteromalla

LARGE-LEAFED GLORY-BUSH, LASIANDRA
Synonyms: *T. grandifolia, T. multiflora.* Brazil. Evergreen shrub, 3–6 ft.; zones 10–11. Blooms intermittently in warm months. Regular moisture and humidity. Fertile, sandy, humus-rich, well-drained soil; acid pH. Full sun to bright broken light. Flowers: petals vivid purple with white or red eyes, about 1 in. wide; in erect, branched terminal panicles. Leaves: large, broadly ovate to cordate, to 7 in. long, primary veins 3–5, impressed; cov-

Tibouchina granulosa

ered with long silvery, flat hairs. Young stems: vaguely 4-winged, peeling along the angles, weak, becoming woody. *Commonly but incorrectly listed as* T. grandiflora *even though flowers are relatively small.*

Tibouchina hybrid

HYBRID GLORY-BUSH, LASIANDRA, TRES CUEROS ("THREE VEINS")
Garden origin, *T. pilosa* × *T. fothergilae.* Evergreen shrub or small tree to 15 ft.; zones 10–11. Blooms warm months. Regular moisture and humidity. Sandy, humus-rich, well-drained soil; acid pH. Full sun to bright filtered light. Flowers: petals 5, purple with a white eye; buds and calyx red, hairy. Leaves: lanceolate, 3–5 in. long, silky haired, primary veins usually 3; petioles hairy. Stems, veins, and petioles reddish. *This hybrid is commonly sold in the trade as* T. urvilleana, *but the latter*

has broader ovate leaves, 5–7 primary veins, and the flowers lack the white eye.

Tibouchina urvilleana

GLORY-BUSH, LASIANDRA, SIETE CUEROS ("SEVEN VEINS")
Synonym: *Lasiandra semidecandra* (hort.). Brazil. Evergreen shrub or tree to 10 ft., larger in wild; zones 10–11. Blooms intermittently in warm months. Regular moisture and humidity. Sandy, humus-rich, well-drained soil; acid pH. Full sun to bright broken light. Flowers: petals deep vivid purple, to 2 in. wide; buds, calyx, and new growth red, hairy. Leaves: broadly ovate, silky haired, with 5–7 primary veins. *Commonly confused with hybrids in cultivation. Photographed at Longwood Gardens, Kennett Square, Pennsylvania.*

Tibouchina heteromalla

Tibouchina hybrid

Tibouchina urvilleana

MELIACEAE

MAHOGANY FAMILY

Meliaceae includes approximately 50 genera of trees and shrubs from tropical and mild temperate areas. Leaves are usually pinnately compound. Flowers are mostly bisexual with the filaments united in a column. They are arranged in panicles in the leaf axils. The fruit is a berry or capsule with sometimes winged seeds.

Melia

Melia includes 10–37 species of trees plus a few shrubs from Asia to Australia. *Melia azederach* is widely cultivated in mild temperate and tropical areas; however, because of proven invasive tendencies, cultivation is discouraged in moist tropical areas. Leaves are pinnate or bipinnate. Petals and calyx are free and 5- to 6-lobed. The 12 stamen filaments are united in a column. Fruit is a berry.

Melia azederach

CHINABERRY, PRIDE-OF-INDIA, TEXAS UMBRELLA-TREE, BEAD-TREE, MÉLIA, PARAÍSO

Synonym: *M. japonica* var. *semperflorens*. China to Australia, western Pacific Islands; naturalized in United States and Mediterranean region. Deciduous tree, 20–40 ft.; zones 7–10. Blooms spring, summer. Moist to fairly dry. Most well-drained soils. Full to part sun. Flowers: petals and sepals pink to white; filaments dark purple, fused; berries yellow, poisonous. Leaves: bipinnate, 2–3 ft.; leaflets lanceolate; margins toothed. *Timber tree in Far East. Familiar ornamental in the Old South. Invasive pest in Florida and Hawaii. Not recommended. 'Umbraculiformis' is an umbrella-shaped selection.*

MENYANTHACEAE

WATER-SNOWFLAKE FAMILY

Menyanthaceae includes 5 genera of freshwater aquatic and wetland herbs, which are widely distributed. This group is closely related to the aster family, Asteraceae, not the waterlily family, Nymphaeaceae. Leaves are usually simple, sometimes trifoliolate, dimorphic, and broad when floating or linear when submerged. Flowers are mostly bisexual and radially symmetrical, solitary or in clusters. Petals are sometimes fringed. The fruit is a capsule or berry. Some species are invasive in wetlands.

Nymphoides

Nymphoides includes approximately 20 species of aquatic herbs, which are widely distributed. Floating leaves are simple and suborbicular with cordate or sagittate bases. The short petioles may be attached to the margin or underside of the blade (peltate). The leaf bases sheathe the underwater stem. Male, female, and bisexual flowers are on the same plant (polygamous). The corolla is white or yellow with more or less fringed or ruffled margins. Flowers are emergent, not floating.

Nymphoides cristata

FLOATING HEART, FAIRY WATER-LILY

Synonym: *Menyanthes cristata*. Australia. Free-floating aquatic herb; zones 8–11 . Blooms warm months. Wet. Soil-less. Full sun. Flowers: emergent, petals 5, white; margins undulate, not fringed; stamens and nectar cup yellow; clustered in leaf axils. Leaves: ovate, 4–6 in. wide, sinus V-shaped, lobes pointed, green, mottled reddish; floating; petioles short, with sheathing bases. *Hardy American species N. cordata also has unfringed white petals. Nymphoides peltata, from Asia and Europe, is naturalized in the United States. It has yellow flowers and peltate leaves.*

Nymphoides indica

WATER-SNOWFLAKE, BANANA-PLANT

Pantropical. Free-floating aquatic herb; zones 10–11. Blooms warm months. Wet. Soil-less. Full sun. Flowers: emergent, polygamous, petals 7, white, yellow in center; margins deeply fringed; clustered in leaf axils. Leaves: round, base cordate with rounded lobes, green, to 8 in.; floating; petioles short, sheathing. *The common name banana-plant, used by the aquarium industry, alludes to the clusters of thickened roots attached to the flowering nodes just below the water surface.*

MORACEAE

FIG FAMILY

Moraceae includes approximately 53 genera of trees, shrubs, climbers, and a few herbs, primarily from mild temperate and tropical regions. Most produce a milky latex sap. Some are grown for their edible fruit including breadfruit, *Artocarpus altilis*; jakfruit, *Artocarpus heterophyllus*; figs, *Ficus* species; and mulberries, *Morus* species. Some *Ficus* species are also cultivated in the tropics as large to very large shade trees or for rubber. Some *Ficus* species are potentially invasive. Leaves are simple, sometimes deeply lobed. Flowers are reduced, often unisexual with male and female flowers on the same plant (monoecious) or on different plants (dioecious). Fruits are compound. Some tree species start out as epiphytes from seeds deposited by birds in crevices of trees or palms.

Melia azederach

Nymphoides indica

Artocarpus heterophyllus

As they grow, they send down roots that eventually strangle the host tree. Certain species produce adventitious roots from the branches, which, when they contact the ground, develop into multiple trunks. An individual banyan may become a colony by spreading laterally. One banyan in India covers several acres.

Artocarpus

Artocarpus includes approximately 50 species of trees from Southeast Asia and Indomalaysia. Leaves are lobed or unlobed. Flowers are unisexual with male and female flowers on the same tree (monoecious) or different trees (dioecious). Female flowers are in dense heads, male flowers in spikes. The fruits are syncarps. Several species are cultivated for timber or the fruits. Jackfruit, *A. heterophyllus*, is cultivated for the very large (up to 40 pound) fruit with tasty arils which is also quite ornamental and a curiosity in the garden. Breadfruit, *A. altilis*, is extremely cold-sensitive and only grown in warm tropics and greenhouses. It was one of the fruit trees that Captain Bligh of the H.M.S. *Bounty* transported from Tahiti to the West Indies on his second trip in 1792, to feed the slaves. A number of other edible species have recently been introduced to South Florida by Richard Campbell in the ultra-tropical collection at Fairchild Tropical Garden.

Artocarpus heterophyllus
JACKFRUIT, JAKFRUIT, JACA
Synonyms: *A. integrifolius* (incorrectly), *A. integer*. India to Peninsular Malaysia; widely cultivated. Evergreen tree to 50 ft.; zones 10–11. Blooms spring. Regular moisture. Average, well-drained soil. Full to part sun. Flowers: unisexual; fruit a syncarp, irregularly oblong to round, 1.5–2 ft. long, green to tan, surface covered with hard hexagonal projections, caulescent; seeds to 2 in. long. Leaves: elliptic to 8 in. long, unlobed.

Dorstenia

Dorstenia includes approximately 170 species of rhizomatous or tuberous herbs from tropical parts of Africa, India, the West Indies, and tropical America. They are primitive relatives of *Ficus*. Leaves are basal or cauline, simple, lobed or toothed. Flowers are reduced, unisexual. They are not enclosed by the peduncle like a fig, but are mounted on a fleshy disk or goblet-shaped receptacle which has a peltate stalk. When ripe, seeds are dispersed explosively. Some species are pachycaulous plants adapted to seasonally arid conditions and are treated as succulents. Suitable for containers.

Dorstenia bahiensis
Eastern Brazil. Semideciduous tuberous herb to about 1 ft.; zones 10–11. Blooms all year. Moderate to seasonally moist/dry. Fertile, well-drained soil. Filtered light. Flowers: unisexual, minute; on the surface of a fleshy disk-shaped receptacle with orange to mauve, undulate margins. Leaves: lanceolate, base cordate, glossy dark green; margins toothed. *Suitable as an understory bedding plant. May become deciduous in dry conditions.*

Ficus

Ficus includes 500–800 species of deciduous or evergreen trees, shrubs, and climbers widely distributed in the tropics, with great diversity in India, Southeast Asia, and Africa. Flowers are reduced, unisexual, enclosed inside a fleshy receptacle (syconium) more commonly known as a fig. Tiny, species-specific gall-wasp pollinators enter the figs through a porelike opening at the end. The fruits are often cauliflorous, or rarely, subterranean. The sap is a white latex. Ficus fruits are an important source of food for animals. At one time a number of *Ficus* species were grown for rubber latex, principally *F. elastica*, India or Assam rubber, and *F. lutea*, Congo rubber. These species have been largely replaced by Pará rubber *Hevea brasiliensis* (Euphorbiaceae).

Leaves are entire or occasionally lobed. Some trees have adventitious aerial or adhering roots. Many are fast-growing with aggressive, superficial root systems that can heave pavement and foundations and invade septic systems. They are top-heavy and inclined to top-ple in windstorms. Large species are unsuitable for the average garden or street landscaping. Some, including the Florida native *Ficus aurea*, are invasive. Indian laurel, *F. microcarpa*, is prohibited in Florida.

Boundary hedges of ficus and other potentially massive plants do not make good neighbors and are strongly discouraged. These plants require frequent and costly maintenance, and the roots are invasive. Between homes they put an uninvited burden on neighbors who did not ask for the considerable expense of maintaining their side of the hedge. For privacy, plant shrubs of moderate height such as *Ligustrum* species, *Megaskepasma erythrochlamys*, or *Thunbergia erecta*. To disguise a fence, cover it with flowering vines (mutual agreement strongly suggested). Otherwise set hedges away from property lines where the owner can maintain both sides.

Ficus aspera 'Parcell'
CLOWN-FIG, MOSAIC-FIG
Vanuatu (New Hebrides). Briefly deciduous tree, 25–50 ft.; zones 10–11. Blooms spring. Regular moisture. Average, well-drained soil. Full to part sun. Flowers: reduced, fruit spherical, 1–1.5 in. diameter, red with maroon stripes, downy; cauliflorous. Leaves: broadly ovate to elliptic, to 15 in. long, downy below; margins crenulate, toothed or lobed. *'Parcell' leaves are variegated in shades of*

Nymphoides cristata

Artocarpus heterophyllus, cut fruit

Dorstenia bahiensis

Ficus aspera 'Parcell'

green and cream. *Erect and noninvasive. An ornamental shade tree with ornamental fruit the size of Ping-Pong balls. 'Canon' has bronze leaves with reddish undersides.*

Ficus carica
COMMON FIG, HIGO, HIGUERA COMÚN
Turkey to Pakistan; widely distributed around the Mediterranean. Deciduous shrub or tree, 25–30 ft.; zones 8–11. Blooms warm months. Moderate moisture. Fertile, well-drained soil; neutral pH. Full to part sun. Flowers: reduced, in a syconium; fruits top-shaped (turbinate). Leaves: broadly ovate, 3- to 5-lobed; margins toothed. *Most commercial figs prefer dry climates. Several varieties are grown in California. 'Brown Turkey' is the best selection for moist climates. It is more resistant to nematodes, rusts, and anthracnose. Moderately salt tolerant.*

Ficus pumila
CREEPING FIG
Synonym: *F. repens* (hort.). Southeastern China to Vietnam. Evergreen shrub or climber to 40 ft.+; zones 9–11. Blooms rarely in cultivation. Moderate moisture. Most well-drained soils. Full to part sun. Flowers: minute, solitary; fruit pear-shaped to cylindrical, purple, rarely produced in cultivation. Leaves: ovate to elliptic, 1.5–2 in. long, clinging aerial roots in the axils. *Juvenile leaf form clinging, adult shrubby. 'Minima' tends to retain the juvenile form. Commonly used as a wall cover and as a highly effective deterrent to graffiti. Trim off nonclinging branches for flush growth.*

Ficus racemosa
CLUSTER FIG, RED RIVER FIG (AUSTRALIA), GULAR (INDIA)
Southern China, Southeast Asia to Australia. Semideciduous tree to 75 ft.+; zones 9–11. Blooms warm months. Seasonally moist/dry. Most well-drained soils. Full to part sun. Flowers: reduced; figs round, on short, leafless branches on the trunk. Leaves: elliptic to ovate, to 7 in. long; margins more or less toothed near tip; petiole to 4 in. long. *Potentially a massive, spreading*

shade tree. Cut for timber. Develops a deeply buttressed trunk with age.*

Ficus religiosa
BO TREE, SACRED FIG, BODHI TREE (THAILAND), PEEPUL (INDIA)
India, Southeast Asia to the Himalayan foothills. Semideciduous tree to 60 ft.; zones 9–11. Blooms warm months. Seasonally moist/dry. Most well-drained soils. Full to part sun. Flowers: reduced; figs ovoid, reddish, on short stalks. Leaves: deltoid to cordate with a very long drip-tip (aristate), glossy, reddish when young; margins smooth, slightly undulate. Trunk becomes buttressed but does not develop prop roots. *A handsome tree which often starts life as an epiphyte in the branches of other trees. Buddha is said to have received enlightenment while resting under a bo tree. Commonly cultivated near Buddhist and Hindu temples.*

Morus
Morus includes approximately 12 species of shrubs and trees, which are widely distributed in mild temperate and tropical areas. Leaves are simple, usually toothed. Flowers are reduced, unisexual, borne in catkinlike spikes. Fruits are small aggregates that resemble blackberries.

Morus nigra
BLACK MULBERRY, MORERA NEGRA
Origin obscure (probably southern Asia); widely naturalized. Deciduous shrub or tree to 20 ft.+; zones 5–11. Blooms spring. Moderate moisture. Most well-drained soils. Full to part sun. Flowers: reduced, greenish; fruit an elongated aggregate, 1–2 in. long, orange, ripening to black. Leaves: ovate, 2–3 in.

Ficus carica 'Brown Turkey'

Ficus pumila 'Minima'

Morus nigra

Ficus racemosa

Ficus religiosa

long, slightly lobed; margins coarsely toothed. *Often grown for the sweet, blackberry-like fruit, which is excellent in jam and attractive to birds and small animals. Self-seeding. May become weedy.*

MORINGACEAE

HORSERADISH TREE FAMILY

Moringaceae includes a single genus of trees from tropical Africa and Asia. The plants grow in seasonally moist/dry or semiarid habitats. The trunks have a pithy interior with a mucilaginous canal in the center. Some are pachycaulous. Leaves are irregularly 2–3 times pinnate and glandular. Mustard oils impart a mustard or horseradish aroma. Flowers are bisexual and asymmetrical. The 5 unequal, overlapping petals and 5 sepals are mounted on a cuplike receptacle. The 5 fertile stamens are interspersed with 5 staminodes. The inflorescence is a panicle or thyrse. The fruit is an elongated, 3- to 12-angled, 3-valved capsule that opens explosively (dehiscent). Seeds are usually 3-winged.

Moringa

Moringa includes approximately 10 species of trees or shrubs from mild temperate and tropical areas of Asia and Africa. *Moringa oleifera* has so many uses it is called a provision-tree. A condiment similar to horseradish is made from the roots. Immature pods, called drum-sticks, are used in Indian cur-

ries like string beans. The seeds are eaten roasted. Oil is used as a lighting fuel, in paints, and soap. Leaves are used as animal fodder. The wood is cut for fuel and processed into rayon fiber. An emulsion of the flowers is reportedly used to purify water. The ben-oil tree, *M. aptera*, produces a fine oil used as a watch lubricant.

Moringa oleifera

HORSERADISH TREE, DRUMSTICK-CURRY, PALO GARINGA

Arabia, India; naturalized in West Indies. Drought deciduous or evergreen tree to 20 ft.; zones 9–11. Blooms intermittently in warm months. Moist to dry. Average, well-drained soil. Full sun. Flowers: small, white, in many-flowered panicles; capsule 4-angled, to 18 in. long, black-brown when mature. Leaves: irregularly bipinnate to tripinnate, to 12 in. long; leaflets elliptic, tips rounded, odd-numbered (one terminal), 0.5–2 in. long; rachis reddish. Bark: corky. *Though legumelike in general appearance, the flowers are distinctive. Best kept pruned for compact form and wind resistance. Can be propagated from cuttings stuck directly in the ground ("quick-sticks"). Xeric.*

MUNTINGIACEAE

MUNTINGIA FAMILY

Muntingiaceae includes 3 genera of trees and shrubs from tropical America. These genera were previously associated with Elaeo-

carpaceae or Tiliaceae. The family is allied to the hibiscus family, Malvaceae, but lacks that family's mucilaginous sap. Leaves are simple, in opposite ranks (distichous). Flowers are bisexual and radially symmetrical. The 5 petals are free and may be pink, yellow, or white. The usually 5 sepals are united at the base. Stamens are numerous and united at the base. The fruit is a many-seeded berry.

Dicraspidia

Dicraspidia includes a single species of small evergreen tree from southern Central America and Colombia. It is distinguished by the unique, leaflike, peltate stipules. Flowers are bisexual and radially symmetrical. They have 5 overlapping petals and numerous stamens. Leaves are simple, downy below, and arranged in opposite ranks on either side of the branches (distichous).

Dicraspidia donnell-smithii

Northern Colombia, Panama, Costa Rica, Honduras. Evergreen shrub or small tree, 15–20 ft.; zones 10–11. Blooms spring. Regular moisture. Fertile, well-drained soil. Bright filtered light. Flowers: yellow, 2.5 in. wide; stamens many; borne in the leaf axils. Leaves: large, lanceolate to elliptic, dark green, downy white, distichous; margins toothed; on arching branches. *Rare in cultivation but fairly common in disturbed areas of southern Central America.*

Muntingia

Muntingia includes a single species of tree from tropical America. It is a weedy species of secondary growth forest, the seed widely dispersed by birds and bats (A. Gentry 1993). The tasty fruit is made into jams or steeped as a tea. Introduced into Sri Lanka where it is favored as a shade tree for its attractive symmetrical branching (Schokman, pers. comm.). Before the branches become heavy, they should be pruned back to prevent breaking in the wind. Bark fiber is used to make a jutelike twine. Should not be confused with the North American species *Prunus serotina* (Rosaceae) or *Trema micranthum* (Ulmaceae), which are also called capulin (Mabberley 1997).

Muntingia calabura

CALABURA, STRAWBERRY-TREE, JAMAICAN CHERRY, JAM-TREE, CAPULIN

West Indies, tropical America; widely naturalized. Evergreen tree to 30 ft.; zones 10–11. Blooms spring. Seasonally moist/dry. Average, well-drained soil. Full sun. Flowers: petals 5, clawed, white, crinkled; sepals 6, yellow, persistent; stamens many; stigma sessile; solitary or in small clusters; fruit a berry, yellow turning red, seeds numerous. Leaves: oblong to lanceolate, 3–5 in. long, base oblique, sticky white tomentose hairs below; margins serrate.
The broad, umbrella-like crown provides pleasant shade. Arbutus unedo is also called strawberry-tree.

MUSACEAE

BANANA FAMILY

Musaceae includes 2 genera of herbs from tropical Asia. *Ensete ventricosum*, Abyssinian banana, is a thick-stemmed provision plant often cultivated in Ethiopia but little known in the United States. *Musa textilis* is grown for its fiber, which is made into Manila hemp. The best-known species in the United States are the edible bananas and plantains, a group of sterile cultigens. Plants are often treelike with unbranched pseudostems composed of overlapping, sheathing petiole bases. Leaves are simple and spi-

Dicraspidia donnell-smithii

Muntingia calabura

Moringa oleifera

rally arranged, paddle-shaped with fleshy petioles. At maturity, the stems produce a terminal flowering spike, rarely two. Flowers are unisexual, with male and female flowers on the same plant (monoecious). Female flowers open first, male flowers develop later at the end of the stalk. Flowers are tubular and bilaterally symmetrical, with 6 petal-like tepals, 5 stamens, and one staminode or the perianth may be absent. Spathelike bracts protect the buds, and bracteoles separate the rows of flowers. The fruit is a berry. The seeds of commercial bananas never develop. Bananas are propagated from offsets.

Musa

Musa includes approximately 35 species of succulent herbs from tropical Asia. Leaves are paddle-shaped, often large. Petiole bases overlap creating a trunklike stalk or pseudostem. Flowers are unisexual. (The flowers of cannas, gingers, and calatheas are bisexual.) After a banana bears fruit, it dies and 1 or 2 new shoots are produced from the corm (sympodial growth).

Dessert bananas are selections of *Musa acuminata*. Plantains, selections of *M. paradisiaca*, are more starchy and glutinous, and are usually eaten fried or cooked in stews. Though a variety of excellent bananas exists, supermarkets usually carry only the commercial 'Grand Nain' or 'Cavendish' selections.

Shoots of established plants take 10–15 months to reach fruiting size. Bananas are heavy feeders. They thrive in a bed of mulch with watering once or twice weekly. The mulch conserves moisture in dry periods, adds fertility, and protects corms from cold. Bananas are occasionally grown in mild temperate areas though most require too long a growing period to reach fruiting size in a single season.

A fungal disease causes fruit tips to turn black and can be detected by the musty odor. Washing off dried flowers with a jet of water when fruits are young may help prevent infection. Panama disease is deadly. Buy plants from reliable sources. Clean up dry leaves for good air circulation in hot/humid conditions. Bananas take about 3 months to develop. Cut fruiting stalk when the bananas are full or when 1 or 2 show signs of ripening. Caution: banana sap leaves permanent black stains on clothing.

'Mysore', a 3- to 5-in. lady-finger banana, is highly recommended for its firm, sweet white flesh, even when very ripe, and its relative disease resistance.

Musa acuminata

DWARF CAVENDISH, CHINESE BANANA, GUINEO, BANANO
Synonyms: *M. cavendishii, M. nana*. Garden origin. Perennial herbs, 6–8 ft.; zones 10–11. Blooms warm months. Regular moisture and humidity. Fertile, well-drained soil. Full to part sun. Flowers: tubular; fruit sterile; bracts maroon; in pendent spikes. Leaves: paddle-shaped. Pseudostem: short. *A commercial banana. Average flavor.*

Musa balbisiana

WILD BANANA, BANANO SILVESTRE
China, India, Myanmar (Burma). Perennial herb to 20 ft.+; zones 9–11. Blooms warm months. Regular moisture and humidity. Fertile, well-drained soil. Full to part sun. Flowers: tubular; bracts maroon; in pendent spikes. Leaves: paddle-shaped. *An ornamental banana. Fruit edible but seeds are hard and round like* Canna. *Used as animal feed. Pollinated by bats in native habitat.*

Musa 'Koae'

AE-AE, A'AE'E (HAWAII)
Garden origin. Perennial herb to 25 ft.; zone 11. Blooms warm months. Evenly moist. Fertile, well-drained, sandy soil; acid pH. Full sun to medium filtered light. Flowers: tubular; fruit variegated green and white, to 7 in. long. Leaves: 2–3 ft. long, variegated with white, light and dark green markings. *Common name ae-ae pronounced EYE-eye. Sacred to early Hawaiians. An unstable mutation, producing degrees of variegation; mostly white leafed shoots don't survive (Whitman 2001). Fruit usually eaten cooked. Plants are sometimes grown in a container or lower light to maintain small size. Protect from wind and chills.*

Musa lasiocarpa

CHINESE BANANA, BANANO CHINO
Synonym: *Musella lasiocarpa*. South China (Yunnan Province). Perennial herb, 4–5 ft.; zones 7–11. Blooms warm months. Regular moisture and humidity. Fertile, well-drained soil. Full to part sun. Flowers: unisexual; bracts yellow, waxy; fruit to 1 in. long, jade green, covered with downy white hairs; hidden between bracts; inflorescence erect, compact. Leaves: short, broad, paddle-shaped, waxy below. *DNA studies show that this species is more closely related to* Ensete *than* Musa *and should be in its own genus,* Musella *(Kiew, pers. comm.), though the transfer has not been made at the time of writing. The species name means "woolly fruit." Locally common in China where used as animal fodder. A hardy mountain plant which dies to the ground after frost. Flowering spike long-lasting. Seed slow to germinate.*

Musa ornata

FLOWERING BANANA, BANANO DECORATIVO
Origin obscure (probably Bangladesh, Myanmar [Burma]). Perennial herb, 4–8 ft.; zones 9–11. Blooms warm months. Regular moisture and humidity. Fertile, well-drained soil. Full to part sun. Flowers: unisexual, tubular, bracts orange, pink, lavender, or white; fruit yellow-green, seedy, often not produced; inflorescence erect. Leaves: paddle-shaped, sometimes reddish below. *Size can be restricted by confining corm in tight container or growing in shade. Grown outdoors in mild regions.*

Musa acuminata, flowers

Musa balbisiana

Musa 'Koae', fruit

Musa lasiocarpa

Musa uranoscopus

RED TORCH BANANA,
RED FLOWERING THAI BANANA
Synonym: *M. coccinea*. Southern
China, Southeast Asia. Perennial
herb, 5–8 ft.; zones 9–11. Blooms
warm months. Regular moisture
and humidity. Fertile, well-drained
soil; acid pH. Full to part sun. Flowers: unisexual; bracts scarlet; spike
erect. Leaves paddle-shaped. *An ornamental banana with showy scarlet
bracts. Suitable for containers. Inflorescences may last up to 6 months.
Rarely fruits in cultivation.*

Musa velutina

PINK VELVET BANANA
Northeastern India, Assam. Perennial herb to 6 ft.; zones 8–11.
Blooms warm months. Regular
moisture and humidity. Fertile,
well-drained soil; acid pH. Full to
part sun. Flowers: unisexual; bracts
pink; fruit pink, downy; inflorescence erect. Leaves: paddle-shaped.
*Suitable for containers. Fruit edible
but with hard, round seeds like Canna.*

MYRSINACEAE

MYRSINE FAMILY
Myrsinaceae includes approximately 33 genera of trees, shrubs,
and climbers from tropical and
mild temperate regions, with greatest diversity in the Old World. They
are common, usually inconspicu-
ously flowered species of evergreen
forests. Leaves are simple, often
dotted with glands. Flowers are
small, radially symmetrical, and
mostly bisexual, but if unisexual,
then male and female flowers are
on different plants (dioecious).
The 4 or 5 sepals are fused at the
base. The 4 or 5 greenish white to
pink petals are fused into a tube at
the base. The 5 stamen filaments
are mounted on the corolla tube
(epipetalous). The inflorescence
is a cyme or panicle. The fruit is
a small one-seeded drupe. The
genera are closely related to
Theophrastaceae, which is distinguished, in part, by having
many-seeded berries.

Ardisia

Ardisia includes approximately 300
species of shrubs and small trees
primarily from tropical Asia and
America. Leaves are simple. Flowers are small and borne in few to
many-flowered cymes. Some are
cultivated as ornamentals. They
can be pruned to size and are suitable for hedges. *Ardisia elliptica* is
highly invasive in South Florida,
and *A. crenata* is invasive in Central
and North Florida.

Ardisia crenata

CORAL-BERRY
Synonym: *A. crenulata* (hort.).
Southern China, Southeast Asia,
southern Japan, Malaysia, Philippines. Evergreen shrub to 6 ft.;
zones 7–10. Blooms spring, summer. Moist to moderate. Average,
well-drained soil. Full sun to part
shade. Flowers: small, white to
pink. Leaves: elliptic to oblanceolate, 4–6 in. long, glossy dark
green; margins crenulate; clustered
at ends of branches. *Cultivated
for the dark foliage and bright red
berries. Weedy in Central and North
Florida.*

Ardisia elliptica

SHOE-BUTTON ARDISIA
Synonym: *A. humilis*. India, Southeast Asia, Japan, Philippines, Taiwan. Evergreen shrub to 15 ft.;
zones 9–11. Blooms warm months.
Seasonally moist/dry. Average,
well-drained soil. Full sun to part
shade. Flowers: pinkish green, in
small, pendent clusters in the leaf
axils; fruit a berry, subglobular.
Leaves: oblanceolate to 5 in. long;
young leaves and stem tips reddish; petioles short, red. *Sometimes
the names* A. solanacea *or* A. poly-
cephala *are misapplied in the literature (Long and Lakela 1971). Invasive in Hawaii and South Florida
(Hammer, pers. comm.).*

Musa ornata

Musa uranoscopus

Musa velutina

Ardisia crenata

Ardisia elliptica

Ardisia escallonioides

MARLBERRY

Synonym: *Icacorea paniculata*. Mexico, Bahamas, Florida Keys, West Indies. Evergreen shrub to 20 ft.; zones 10–11. Blooms spring. Moist to moderate. Average, well-drained soil. Full sun to part shade. Flowers: white in dense, terminal clusters; fruit a berry, purplish black, subglobular, dimpled at the distal end. Leaves: lanceolate to elliptic, 5–6 in. long, young leaves not reddish as in *A. elliptica*. *The common name is a corruption of marble-berry (Hammer, pers. comm.).*

Ardisia nigrescens

Synonym: *A. hirtella*. Belize. Evergreen shrub to 5 ft.; zones 9–11. Blooms spring. Moist to moderate. Average, well-drained soil. Full sun to part shade. Flowers: pink; fruit a berry, red. Leaves: lanceolate, tips acuminate, to 6 in.; margins undulate. *Unusual in cultivation.*

Ardisia revoluta

Central America. Evergreen shrub to 8 ft.; zones 10–11. Blooms spring. Moist to moderate. Average, well-drained soil. Full sun to part shade. Flowers: small, trumpet-shaped, white, petals strongly revolute (rolled back), in many-flowered panicles, 6–8 in. wide. Leaves: elliptic to obovate, 3–4 in. long, tip acute, leathery, dotted with resinous glands. *Unusual in cultivation.*

MYRTACEAE

MYRTLE FAMILY,
EUCALYPTUS FAMILY

Myrtaceae includes approximately 144 genera of evergreen trees and shrubs, which are widely distributed in tropical and mild temperate regions. Most of the genera are divided between 2 subgroups: the primarily New World group (Myrtoideae) has fleshy berries or drupes and opposite leaves, while the primarily Australian group (Leptospermoideae) produces dry nuts or capsules and has alternate or opposite leaves. Many ornamental tropical plants come from this family. Some are sources of culinary spices, aromatic and medicinal oils, fruit, and timber. Leaves are simple, usually leathery or firm,

often spotted with oil glands, and resinously aromatic. Flowers are mostly bisexual, radially symmetrical, and often scented. Sepals and petals are similar, usually numbering 4 or 5 each, free to more or less fused, or sometimes reduced or absent. Stamens are usually numerous and showy. Floral parts are mounted on a nectar-producing disk (hypanthium). The inflorescence is a cyme sometimes resembling a raceme or panicle. Many species have bark that sheds in thin irregular sheets revealing varicolored inner layers.

Acca

Acca includes 2 species of shrubs or small trees from South America. Leaves are simple with gray down below. Flowers have long, brightly colored stamens. *Acca sellowiana* is commonly cultivated for its edible fruit, which is eaten raw and in pre-

serves. Warm temperature is necessary to set fruit. The fleshy petals are also edible and sometimes added to salads. Choose cultivars such as 'Pineapple Gem' for good eating. 'Nazemetz' is hardy.

Acca sellowiana

PINEAPPLE-GUAVA, GUAYABA FEIJOA

Synonym: *Feijoa sellowiana*. Southern Brazil, Paraguay, Uruguay, northern Argentina. Evergreen shrub, 10–20 ft.; zones 8–9. Blooms spring, summer. Moderate, seasonally dry. Humus-rich, well-drained soil. Full sun. Flowers: petals white below, red above, to 1.5 in. wide, fleshy, curling up (involute); stamens long-exserted, red; in the leaf axils; solitary. Leaves: elliptic to oblong, dark green above, gray downy below, to 3 in. long. *Of dry mountainous regions. Xeric.*

Agonis

Agonis includes approximately 12 species of shrubs and small trees from western Australia. Leaves are simple, narrow, and willowlike. Flowers are cauliflorous, in clusters near the ends of the branches. The 10–20 stamens are shorter than the petals.

Agonis flexuosa

SWEET WILLOW-MYRTLE,
PEPPERMINT WILLOW

Western Australia. Evergreen tree, 25–35 ft.; zones 9–10. Blooms late spring. Moderate moisture, dry once established. Poor, sandy, well-drained soil. Full to part sun. Flowers: small, white, petals 5, round; stamens shorter than petals; sessile in leaf axils. Leaves: dimorphic, narrowly lanceolate, slightly curved, to 7 in. long, leathery; short and stiff when immature; peppermint-scented. Bark: reddish. *Graceful,*

Ardisia escallonioides

Ardisia nigrescens

Ardisia revoluta

Acca sellowiana

Agonis flexuosa

Callistemon 'Mauve Mist'

weeping habit. *Disease and pest resistant. Suitable for coastal planting. Stake and water regularly until established to encourage deep roots, then xeric. Cultivated in California. A number of selections are available.*

Callistemon

Callistemon includes 20–30 species of shrubs and small trees from Australia. The genus name means "beautiful stamens." Leaves are long, slender, and aromatic when crushed. Flowers are cauliflorous, in bottlebrush-like clusters near the branch tips. The sepals and petals are inconspicuous. The stamens are free or only slightly united at their bases. The filaments are long, flamboyantly colored, tipped with gleaming gold pollen when fresh. They are very attractive to nectar-feeding birds. After flowering, the branch continues to grow from the end of the inflorescence. Small woody persistent seed capsules are arranged in rows near the ends of the branches. Tip pruning in winter encourages a strong bloom and compactness. Thin for a bonsai effect. Most species prefer dry climates though a few thrive in moist climates with excellent drainage. *Callistemon viminalis* is suitable for wet locations. The species are difficult to identify with certainty. Bottlebrushes readily hybridize in the wild and cultivars probably involve hybrids. Selections do not come true from seed.

Callistemon 'Little John'

Callistemon citrinus

LEMON-SCENTED BOTTLEBRUSH
Synonym: *C. lanceolatus.* Eastern Australia. Evergreen tree, 5–25 ft.; zones 8–11. Blooms warm months. Moderate moisture to fairly dry. Average to poor, well-drained soil. Full sun. Flowers: perianth inconspicuous, stamens long, magenta to crimson; inflorescence ascending. Leaves: linear, 2–3 in. long, lemon-scented when crushed; young leaf tips reddish. *Suitable for coastal planting. 'Little John', a dwarf selection, 2–5 ft. high, makes a stunning hedge. It and 'Mauve Mist' are probable hybrids involving this species. Australians produce a wide range of color forms. Propagate by tip-cuttings. Attractive to hummingbirds.*

Callistemon viminalis

WEEPING BOTTLEBRUSH
Eastern Australia. Evergreen tree to 25 ft.; zones 9–11. Blooms intermittently in warm months. Moist to fairly dry. Average to poor soil. Full sun. Flowers: perianth inconspicuous; stamens showy; in clusters near the ends of pendent branches. Leaves: lanceolate to linear, to 3 in. long; aromatic. *An erect tree with weeping branches or sometimes sprawling. For a more treelike shape, look for plants with a vertical lead. For bonsai effects, look for lateral branching. Salt tolerant. The only bottlebrush that tolerates wet conditions. For street landscaping,* C. citrinus *or* C. rigidus *are preferable for their upright habits.*

Calyptranthes

Calyptranthes includes approximately 100 species of trees and shrubs from tropical America. Leaves are simple and stiff. Flowers are white and borne in many-flowered panicles. The calyx is cuplike with a lidlike cap (calyptrate). Petals are absent. Stamens are numerous, radiating from the rim of the floral cup (hypanthium). The fruit is a 3-seeded berry.

Calyptranthes zuzygium

MYRTLE-OF-THE-RIVER
Synonym: *Myrtus zuzygium.* Caribbean, Florida Keys, tropical America. Evergreen tree to 30 ft.; zones 10–11. Blooms late spring, early summer. Seasonally moist/dry. Average, well-drained soil. Full to part sun. Flowers: stamens white, arranged in a ring on the floral cup, fragrant; panicles branching in clusters of 3; fruit a red berry, becoming blue-black, waxy. Leaves: obovate to elliptic, 2–3 in. long, tips acute, glossy, aromatic; petiole short. Bark: roughly furrowed. *Calyptranthes thomasiana, from Puerto Rico and St. Thomas, is an endangered species.*

Chamelaucium

Chamelaucium includes approximately 23 species of heathlike shrubs from Western Australia. Suitable for Mediterranean-type climates. Leaves are simple, needlelike, and sessile. Flowers are small with spreading petals and short stamens. They are borne in panicles.

Callistemon viminalis

Calyptranthes zuzygium

Chamelaucium uncinatum

WAX FLOWER

Western Australia. Evergreen shrub to 10 ft.; zones 9–11. Blooms late winter, spring, early summer. Semiarid. Poor, sandy, well-drained soil; neutral to slightly acid pH. Full sun. Flowers: small, bell-shaped, petals spreading, white, waxy, aging pink to purplish; stamens fused into a tiny corona around the floral cup. Leaves: needlelike, about 1 in. long, minutely 3-sided, aromatic. *A spreading shrub of hot, dry regions. Thrives in California. Overwatering promotes root rot. Do not overfertilize or disturb root system. Prune after flowering. Used in cut-flower arrangements. Many selections.*

Corymbia

Corymbia includes approximately 110 species of trees from Australia and New Guinea. This group, known as bloodwoods, was formerly included in the genus *Eucalyptus*. Bark is rough and scaly, persistent, not peeling. Leaves are simple, exhibiting juvenile and adult forms (dimorphic). Flowers are bisexual and radially symmetrical. Sepals are small, the petals reduced or absent. The stamens are showy, arranged around the rim of the floral cup (hypanthium). They are borne in panicles at the ends of the branches. The fruit is an urn-shaped (urceolate) woody capsule.

Corymbia ficifolia

RED-FLOWERING GUM, FLAME BLOODWOOD, EUCALYPTO

Synonym: *Eucalyptus ficifolia.* Western Australia. Evergreen tree to 75 ft.; zones 9–11. Blooms summer, fall. Dry. Average, well-drained soil. Full sun. Flowers: stamens red; calyx cup creamy white; inflorescence at the ends of branches. Leaves: lanceolate, juvenile and adult forms similar except for size, dark green above, gray-green below, midvein reddish. Bark: red-brown. *Used for landscaping in southern California. The natural hybrid* (Corymbia ficifolia × C. calophylla) *has pink to red flowers. Floral color does not breed true from seed. Grafted plants are the only way to guarantee a particular color.*

Eucalyptus

Eucalyptus includes approximately 500 species of trees and shrubs from Australia. They are fast-growing and some old trees reach 200–300 ft. Leaves are usually dimorphic with juvenile and adult forms. Inflorescences are unbranched umbels. Each species has a distinctive, lidded capsule which is usually important for identification. Eucalyptus have myriad uses including hard and soft timbers, fuel, menthol, citronella, tannins, fiber, and oils. Koalas are dependent on certain *Eucalyptus* species.

They are divided horticulturally into several groups. Those called gum trees have smooth bark which is shed in thin flakes. They secrete gum (known commercially as kino), which seals the wounds after the bark peels away. Ironbarks, boxes, and peppermint barks have rough, persistent bark. Stringy barks are rough-barked but peel in long strands. Scrubby species are called *mallees*. Desert mallees store water in underground lignotubers, an adaptation which allows for regrowth after seasonal fires.

At the beginning of the 20th century, 4 fast-growing species, including *Eucalyptus camaldulensis*, were planted in California in hopes they would quickly produce timber for railroad ties and lumber for the burgeoning population. Unfortunately, the wood of young trees split and warped when dried and the industry failed, but the trees became widely naturalized and no one can imagine the California landscape now without them. Landscaping with *Eucalyptus* has been greatly reduced partly because accumulations of shed bark and leaves present a fire hazard due to their

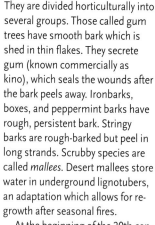

Chamelaucium uncinatum

Corymbia ficifolia

Corymbia ficifolia × *C. calophylla*

Eucalyptus camaldulensis

volatile oils and also because of recent invasions of pests.

Eucalyptus have been planted in many regions, sometimes to drain mosquito-infested swamps or for timber, but often at the expense of native habitat. Blue gum, *Eucalyptus globulus*, is invasive in Hawaii.

Eucalyptus camaldulensis
RIVER RED GUM, MURRAY RED GUM, EUCALYPTO ROJO

Synonym: *E. rostratus*. Australia; widely naturalized. Evergreen tree to 150 ft.; zones 9–11. Blooms spring, summer. Dry. Poor, well-drained soil. Full sun. Flowers: stamens white; in small clusters (umbels), on short stalks, 1–2 flowers opening at a time; capsule small, turbinate, hemispherical at the base with an almost flat cap which comes to an acute point in the center. Leaves: narrowly lanceolate, slightly curved, gray-green. Bark: smooth, shedding, light gray or reddish brown. Twigs reddish. *Currently the most commonly cultivated species worldwide. The distinctive capsules resemble little tops.*

Eucalyptus deglupta
RAINBOW GUM, MINDANAO GUM, BAGRAS (PHILIPPINES), KAMARERE (NEW GUINEA)

Synonym: *E. multiflora*. Philippines, Indonesia, Papua New Guinea. Evergreen tree to 200 ft.; zones 9–11. Blooms summer, fall. Seasonally moist/dry. Poor, well-drained soil. Full sun. Flowers: stamens white; in many-flowered clusters (umbels); capsules ovoid. Leaves: lanceolate to elliptic, glossy dark green above, dull below; opposite when young to slightly alternate with maturity. Bark: smooth, thin, peeling to reveal gray, pink, russet, and blue-green underbark. *Grown as a street or shade tree for the erect habit and ornamental bark. Thrives in seasonally moist/humid climate as well as dry.*

Eugenia
Eugenia includes 500–550 species of shrubs and trees principally from the American tropics, plus a number from mild regions of the Old World. Plants are usually pubescent. Species now segregated into *Syzygium* were previously included in this genus. Leaves are simple. Flowers have 4 or 5 showy petals. The sepals are fused at the base and have 4 lobes, which are persistent at the end of the fruits. The numerous stamens are about the same length as the petals. Flowers are solitary or in few-flowered racemes in the leaf axils. *Eugenia* fruits are fleshy or woody berries with long individual stalks (pedicels). This distinguishes *Eugenia* from *Syzygium*, which has sessile or very short-stalked flowers and fruits attached directly to the peduncle (primary inflorescence stalk). *Eugenia* species are sometimes called stoppers, a name purportedly derived from a tea, or infusion, used to treat diarrhea. *Eugenia uniflora* has long been used for hedges. It is invasive and prohibited in Florida.

Eugenia brasiliensis
BRAZIL CHERRY, GRUMIXAMA (BRAZIL)

Synonym: *Myrtus dombeyi*. Southern Brazil. Evergreen tree to 50 ft.; zones 10–11. Blooms spring. Moderate moisture. Average, well-drained soil. Full sun. Flowers: white, 4 petals, 4 sepals; fruit round, red to black like Bing cherries. Leaves: obovate, 2–5 in. long, smooth, tips attenuate; new leaves reddish. *Fruit edible. Resembles* E. luschnathiana. *Note differing leaf shapes and color of fruit.*

Eugenia luschnathiana
PITOMBA (BRAZIL)

Synonym: *E. lucescens*. Brazil. Evergreen shrub or tree, 20–25 ft.; zones 9–11. Blooms spring. Moderate moisture. Average, well-drained soil. Full sun. Flowers: white, to 1 in. wide, scented; fruit yellow-orange. Leaves: oblong, to 3 in. long, tips cuspidate. Bark: gray and rust, peeling. *Aromatic fruit is eaten raw and used to make jellies. The name pitomba is applied to a number of species with edible fruits.*

Eugenia uniflora
SURINAM CHERRY, PITANGA

Synonym: *E. brasiliana* (not *E. brasiliensis*). Tropical America. Evergreen shrub, 10–15 ft.; zones 10–11. Blooms late winter. Moist to moderate. Average, well-drained soil. Full to part sun. Flowers: small, 0.5 in. wide, white, stamens numerous; fruit ribbed, to 1 in.

Eucalyptus deglupta, flowers

Eugenia luschnathiana

Eucalyptus deglupta, bark

Eugenia brasiliensis

wide, red-orange to dark red. Leaves: ovate, 1.5–2 in. long, base cordate, tip acuminate, glossy, reddish when young, aromatic. *A common hedge plant. Fruit rich in vitamin C; used to make jellies. More common selections have a somewhat bitter but not unpleasant after-taste. Sweetest when dark red. Aromatic leaves are used as insect repellant. Invasive. Seed distributed by birds. Prohibited in Florida.*

Leptospermum

Leptospermum includes approximately 80 species of shrubs and from southeastern Australia and New Zealand. Leaves are simple, downy, and resinously fragrant. The 5 sepals are fused at the base. The 5 petals have rounded lobes with clawed bases. Stamens are numerous. Capsules are woody and persistent. *Leptospermum laevigatum*, a very salt-tolerant species, is sometimes used to stabilize dunes. *Leptospermum petersonii* is cultivated for its lemon-scented oil. Tea oil is important commercially as an ingredient in shampoos, astringents, and skin creams. *Leptospermum scoparium* and its many cultivars are commonly grown ornamentals in mild temperate and subtropical regions. They thrive in poor, dry conditions and are occasionally used for bonsai. Adaptable and relatively pest resistant.

Leptospermum scoparium

NEW ZEALAND TEA-TREE, MANUKA (MAORI)
Synonym: *L. nichollsii*. New Zealand, eastern Australia. Evergreen shrub, 3–6 ft.+; zones 8–10. Blooms spring, summer. Moderate moisture to dry. Poor, sandy, well-drained soil. Full sun. Flowers: spreading, to 1 in. wide, white, pink, or red, cultivars single or double; solitary or in small clusters in the leaf axils. Leaves: small, narrowly lanceolate, to 0.5 in. long, downy, aromatic. Branches arching to erect, downy when young. *Invasive in Hawaii.*

Lophostemon

Lophostemon includes 4–6 species of trees or shrubs from eastern Australia and southern New Guinea. Leaves are simple, in dense whorls at the ends of the branches. Flowers are borne in 3s, a simple inflorescence called a dichasium. The petals are clawed. The genus name alludes to the distinctive stamens, which are united into 5 crest-like columns. Trees are cut for timber and sometimes used in public landscaping.

Lophostemon confertus

BRUSH-BOX, BRISBANE BOX
Synonym: *Tristania conferta*. Eastern Australia. Evergreen tree, 50–100 ft.; zones 9–11. Blooms late spring, early summer. Seasonally moist/dry. Fertile, gritty, well-drained soil; neutral to slightly acid pH. Full sun. Flowers: petals white; stamens segregated into 5 brush-like white columns or fascicles; capsules top-shaped (turbinate), woody. Leaves: elliptic to lanceolate, dark green, in whorls near the ends of the branches. Bark: green and pink, shedding on upper branches. *Of rain forests or streamsides. Erect with rounded crown. Suitable as a street or shade tree. The 5 stamen crests are distinctive.*

Melaleuca

Melaleuca includes approximately 100 species of evergreen trees and shrubs from Australia plus a few from Indomalaysia. Leaves are simple, firm, the petioles very short (subsessile). The 5 petals are reduced. The sepals are united at the base into a tube. The branches continue to grow from the tip of the inflorescence. Some are called paper-barks for their dense papery layers of white bark. *Melaleuca quinquenervia* is the most serious pest species in South Florida. It was first introduced to support

Eugenia uniflora

Lophostemon confertus

Melaleuca bracteata, inflorescences

Leptospermum scoparium

Melaleuca linariifolia, inflorescences

everglades canal banks and levees and to absorb excess water. It has now overtaken vast acreage as an impenetrable monoculture. It is extremely difficult to eradicate. The thick bark insulates it from fire and heat opens the seed capsules dispersing billions of seed. It grows back from the roots if cut. The pollen is a major cause of seasonal respiratory allergies. A prohibited species in Florida. Removal from private property is strongly recommended. Commercial harvesting for fuel and essential oils should be more thoroughly explored as a means of control.

Melaleuca bracteata

BLACK TEA-TREE
Synonym: *M. monticola.* Australia. Evergreen tree to 25 ft.+; zones 9–10. Blooms late winter. Moderate moisture to dry. Average to poor, well-drained soil. Full sun. Flowers:

perianth green, stamens white, united at base; clustered near the ends of the branches. Leaves: narrowly lanceolate, to 1 in. long. Bark: furrowed, brown. *Conifer-like habit. Grows in both California and Florida climates.*

Melaleuca lateritia

ROBIN RED-BREAST BUSH
Western Australia. Evergreen shrub or small tree, 3–8 ft.; zones 9–11. Blooms late spring, summer. Dry. Average to poor, well-drained soil. Full to part sun. Flowers: stamens long, orange. Leaves: linear, flat, 1–2 in. long. *Resembles a small bottlebrush tree,* Callistemon *species. Attractive shrub for dry locations.*

Melaleuca linariifolia

SNOW-IN-SUMMER,
FLAX-LEAFED PAPER-BARK
Eastern Australia. Evergreen tree to 30 ft.; zones 7–11. Blooms late

spring, early summer. Dry. Average to poor, well-drained soil. Full sun. Flowers: stamens feathery, white; densely covering the branch tips. Leaves: linear, flattened, to 1 in. long. Bark: white, peeling in papery layers. *The species name alludes to the linear leaves. The asymmetrical crown, conifer-like leaves, and attractive papery bark lend this tree to Japanese-style landscapes. 'Snowstorm' is a dwarf selection.*

Melaleuca nesophila

PINK MELALEUCA,
WESTERN TEA-MYRTLE
Western Australia. Evergreen tree, 10–15 ft.; zones 9–11. Blooms summer. Dry, but tolerates seasonal moisture. Average to poor, well-drained soil. Full sun. Flowers: stamens lavender-pink to violet, tipped with golden pollen when fresh; inflorescences globular, on ascending branches. Leaves: nar-

rowly elliptic, 1–1.5 in. long, stiff, gray-green. Bark: light, peeling. *The species name means "loves islands." This xeric, salt-tolerant tree is used in areas with salt contamination from excess fertilizer. In coastal landscap-*

Melaleuca lateritia

Melaleuca bracteata

Melaleuca linariifolia

ing it often develops a windswept look. Very attractive to hummingbirds and butterflies. Species name often misspelled nesophylla.

Melaleuca quinquenervia

PUNK-TREE,
BROADLEAF PAPER-BARK
Synonym: *M. leucodendron* (misapplied). Eastern Australia, Melanesia, Papua New Guinea. Evergreen tree to 100 ft.+; zones 9–11. Blooms spring, summer. Wet to dry. Most soils. Full sun. Flowers: perianth reduced, purplish; stamens creamy white; in clusters near ends of branches; capsules woody, sessile; persistent. Leaves: narrowly elliptic, 4–9 in. long, aromatic, gray-green, 5 parallel veins (hence *quinquenervia*). Bark: white, in soft papery layers several inches deep. *Oil extracts used in cough syrups. Salt tolerant. Primary invasive pest of South and Central Florida and the Pacific Islands. Prohibited in Florida.*

Metrosideros

Metrosideros includes approximately 50 species of trees and shrubs from New Zealand and Melanesia, plus 1 from South Africa. The genus is currently being revised and some species will probably be transferred to *Callistemon* or *Melaleuca* to which the genus is closely allied.

Metrosideros excelsa

NEW ZEALAND CHRISTMAS TREE,
PAHUTUKAWA, RATA (MAORI)
Synonym: *M. tomentosa*. New Zealand. Evergreen tree to 35 ft.; zones 9–11. Blooms summer. Dry. Sandy, well-drained soil; neutral to acid pH. Full sun. Flowers: calyces woolly, white; stamens red. Leaves: elliptic to oblanceolate, 2–4 in. long, firm, dark green; undersides woolly; midveins light; sometimes variegated. Young growth white woolly. *Of coastal cliffs but does not tolerate salt-saturated soil. Trees become twisted and gnarled in windswept areas. Indigenous Maoris use rata wood for carving. Blooms at Christmas (summer time) in New Zealand.*

Myrcianthes

Myrcianthes includes approximately 50 species of shrubs and trees from tropical America. This genus is closely related to *Eugenia*. *Myrcianthes* differs primarily by flowers borne in 3- to 7-flowered dichasia. A dichasium is a simple inflorescence with a terminal flower and 2 lateral flowers, the lateral branches may themselves be divided into 3 flowers. Aromatic.

Myrcianthes fragrans

TWINBERRY, PALE STOPPER,
SIMPSON STOPPER
Synonym: *M. fragrans* var. *simpsonii*. Florida, West Indies. Evergreen shrub or tree to 15 ft.; zones 9–11. Blooms primarily spring or intermittently. Seasonally moist/dry. Average to poor, well-drained soil. Full to part sun. Flowers: small, white; inflorescences 3- to 7-flowered dichasia; fruit a berry, red to black. Leaves: small, elliptic to obovate, to 2 in. long, glossy light green with glandular, sometimes translucent (pellucid) dots. *Highly recommended for privacy hedges. 'Compacta' is a good selection for low hedges.*

Melaleuca nesophila

Melaleuca quinquenervia

Myrcianthes fragrans

Myrciaria cauliflora

Myrciaria

Myrciaria includes approximately 40 species of shrubs from tropical America. Jaboticaba, *M. cauliflora*, is an edible grapelike tropical fruit. The tree bears its flowers and round fruits directly on the trunk (cauliflorous). The genus is closely related to *Eugenia* but differs by its long calyx tube. Aromatic.

Myrciaria cauliflora

JABOTICABA, BRAZILIAN GRAPE TREE
Synonym: *Plinia cauliflora*. Bolivia, southern Brazil. Evergreen shrub or tree, 15–20 ft.; zones 9–11. Blooms late summer. Seasonally moist/dry. Average, well-drained soil. Full to part sun. Flowers: creamy white, caulescent; fruit globular, purple-black. Leaves: ovate to lanceolate, to 4 in. long; with translucent dots. Bark: reddish brown, peeling to re-veal cream to gray underbark. *A tasty tropical fruit.*

Myrciaria vexator

Costa Rica, Panama, Venezuela. Evergreen tree to 60 ft.; zones 10–11. Blooms late summer. Seasonally moist/dry. Average, well-drained soil. Full to part sun. Flowers: petals small, white; calyx cup greenish; stamens white; solitary, on short pedicels, cauliflorous, clustered near the ends of the weeping branches; fruit orange, edible. Leaves: oblong to lanceolate, 6 in. long, dark green. Bark: smooth, tan, peeling to reveal white underbark. Suitable as a shade tree.

Pimenta

Pimenta includes approximately 15 species of trees from tropical America. Two are widely cultivated for spice and scented oils and have become naturalized in some areas. Leaves are simple. Flowers are small with numerous stamens, borne in many-flowered panicles. Fruits are small drupes. They are attractive to birds, especially blue-jays. *Pimenta dioica* is cultivated in Jamaica and other regions of the Caribbean for culinary allspice. The aromatic scent suggests a blend of cinnamon and cloves. Allspice is an important spice in Latin American and Middle Eastern dishes. Bay-rum, an old-fashioned men's fragrance, is extracted from the leaves of *P. racemosa* by distillation in rum. Both species are handsome, pleasantly aromatic shade trees.

Pimenta dioica

ALLSPICE, JAMAICAN SWEET PEPPER, PIMIENTA DULCE
Synonym: *P. officinalis*. Eastern Mexico, Central America, Jamaica. Evergreen tree to 50 ft.; zones 10–11. Blooms spring. Seasonally moist/dry. Average, well-drained soil. Full sun. Flowers: sepals 4; stamens tan; in cymes in the leaf axils. Leaves: elliptic to oblong, to 5 in. long, tip rounded, papery, glossy dark green; clustered at the ends of the branches. Bark: tan, peeling in long strips. *A handsome, adaptable tree with a pleasantly spicy fragrance. Tolerates heat and drought. The species name is based on an early misconception that the species was dioecious.*

Pimenta racemosa

BAY-RUM TREE
West Indies, Surinam. Evergreen tree, 10–40 ft.; zones 10–11. Blooms spring. Seasonally moist/dry. Average, well-drained soil. Full sun. Flowers: small, white, short-lived; in panicles. Leaves: leathery, oblong to obovate, 3–4 in. long. *A pleasantly aromatic tree.*

Psidium

Psidium includes approximately 100 species of shrubs and trees from tropical and subtropical America. The aromatic fruits of certain species are eaten throughout tropical America. Guava, *P. gua-java*, is made into a fragrant paste or jelly or the fresh or preserved fruits are customarily eaten with a slice of cream cheese. The juice is used in drinks, pastry fillings, and other sweets. Leaves are simple. Flowers are usually solitary in the leaf axils. The petals are showy with numerous stamens attached to an elongated calyx tube (hypanthium). The handsome bark is smooth, reddish brown, shedding in large flakes to reveal contrasting gray, green, and white underbark layers. Guavas have temperature requirements similar to those of citrus, tolerating brief freezing temperatures when mature.

Psidium cattleianum

STRAWBERRY-GUAVA, GUAYABO
Synonym: *P. littorale*. Probably from southeastern Brazil, widely distributed. Evergreen shrub or tree to 20 ft.; zones 8–11. Blooms early summer. Moist to moderate. Average soil. Full to part sun. Flowers: white, petals spreading, about 1 in. wide; stamens yellow; solitary; fruit yellow and acid to purple and sweet. Leaves: elliptic to obovate, glossy, to 3 in. long; aromatic. *Yellow-fruited variety used primarily in preserves. Highly invasive in North and Central Florida but uncommon in South Florida (Hammer, pers. comm.). Invasive in Hawaii.*

Psidium guajava

YELLOW GUAVA, GUAYABO
Tropical America, native range obscure. Evergreen tree to 30 ft.; zones 9–11. Blooms spring. Moist to moderate. Average, well-drained soil. Full to part sun. Flowers: petals white, spreading, to about 1.5

Metrosideros excelsa

Pimenta dioica

Myrciaria vexator

Pimenta racemosa

Psidium cattleianum

in. wide; solitary; fruit ovoid, to 3 in. long, yellow, flesh pink, seedy. Leaves: ovate to elliptic, to 6 in. long. *A pest in Hawaii and Central Florida wetlands. Not naturalized in South Florida except in isolated wet areas (Hammer, pers. comm.). Where extant, the Caribbean fruit-fly lays its eggs in the young fruit, spoiling it. Leaves of 'José Jiménez' are deeply lobed.*

Syzygium

Syzygium includes 700–800 species of trees and shrubs from the Old World tropics. These species were formerly included in *Eugenia*. A distinguishing characteristic is the sessile or short-stalked fruits. Leaves are simple. Flowers have long, showy stamens. The species listed here have been cultivated for millennia. They are difficult to distinguish and the fruits are sometimes sterile. This suggests that they may involve cultigens (Ochse and van den Brink 1951). Fruits are crisp and sweet, sour or bland and often rose-scented. They are good in salads with oil and vinegar, cooked, or candied. In the Far East, they are eaten as a snack with a dash of soy sauce. In Central America, *Syzygium* species are sometimes used for shade and windbreaks on coffee plantations. They are important as a source of food for primates, habitat for migratory birds, and nectar for birds and bees. Propagate selections by air-layering or grafting. Culinary cloves are the unopened buds of *S. aromaticum*.

Syzygium cumini
JAVA-PLUM, JAMBOLAN, GUAYABO PESGUA
Synonym: *Eugenia jambolana*. Exact origin obscure (India, Southeast Asia, Indomalaysia); widely distributed. Semideciduous tree to 75 ft.; zones 10–11. Blooms spring. Seasonally moist/dry. Average, well-drained soil. Full sun. Flowers: small, creamy white, sessile; on many-flowered, pendent branches; fruit ovoid, purple to black, acid. Leaves: broadly oblong, 6–7 in. long, tip acuminate. *Invasive in North and Central Florida. A restricted species. May be deciduous*

in seasonally dry regions. The fruit varies from sweet to sour. The wood is used, like hickory or mesquite, to flavor grilled meat. Harvesting for barbecue fuel could be a profitable means of control.

Syzygium jambos
ROSE-APPLE, WAX JAMBU, MALABAR PLUM, MANZANA ROSA
Synonym: *Eugenia jambos*. Exact origin obscure (Indomalaysia); widely cultivated. Evergreen shrubby tree, 15–30 ft.; zones 10–11. Blooms late winter, spring. Seasonally moist/dry. Fertile, well-drained soil. Full to part sun. Flowers: petals small; stamens many, long, creamy white; in clusters; fruit globose, crisp, white, pink, or yellowish, waxy. Leaves: narrowly elliptic to lanceolate, 6–8 in. long, tapering at both ends. *Invasive in some areas. Canopy dense. Established*

trees marginally hardy. Somewhat salt tolerant.

Syzygium malaccense
MALAY APPLE, POMERAC, CASHEW (JAMAICA)
Synonym: *Eugenia malaccensis*. Malay Peninsula, Indonesia (Java, Sumatra). Evergreen tree, 20–60 ft.; zones 10–11. Blooms spring. Seasonally moist/dry. Fertile, well-drained soil. Full to part sun. Flowers: petals small; stamen filaments long, vibrant magenta; fruit red, flesh white, oblong, to 2 in. long, longitudinally furrowed; subsessile; in leaf axils and cauliflorous. Leaves: oblong, 8–10 in. long, base rounded or subcordate, tip cuspidate or obtuse; margins undulate. *'Kingston Pride' has large fruit, small seeds, and superior favor (Kong, pers. comm.).*

Syzygium samarangense
JAVA-APPLE, JAMBOSA, PERA DE AGUA
Synonym: *Eugenia javanica*. Southeast Asia, Malaysia, Indonesia, Philippines. Evergreen tree to 20 ft.+; zones 10–11. Blooms spring. Seasonally moist/dry. Fertile, humus-rich, well-drained soil. Full to part sun. Flowers: petals small; stamens cream; fruit pear-shaped with a flattened bottom, to 2 in. long, waxy, greenish white to pink-cheeked; sometimes seedless. Leaves: oblong, to 10 in. long, base rounded to subcordate, tip obtuse to abruptly cuspidate. *The flavor of the fruit resembles a bland, crisp apple.*

Syzygium wilsonii
LILLY-PILLY, GLOSSY POWDER-PUFF
Synonym: *Eugenia wilsonii*. Northeastern Australia. Evergreen shrub

Psidium guajava 'José Jiménez'

Syzygium cumini

Syzygium jambos 'Taiwan Pink'

Syzygium malaccense

Syzygium samarangense

Syzygium wilsonii

to 6 ft.; zone 11. Blooms spring. Regular moisture. Fertile, well-drained soil. Bright filtered light. Flowers: petals white, inconspicuous; stamens glossy red-violet; on a long pendent stalk; berries whitish. Leaves: elliptic, to 6 in. long, reddish when young. *Stamens are curled initially, exposing the long pistil ensuring cross-pollination. Cold-sensitive. Rare in cultivation. Suitable for containers. Handsome foliage with glistening flowers dangling like Christmas-tree baubles. Acquired by Fairchild Tropical Garden from Las Cruces Botanical Garden in Costa Rica.*

NELUMBONACEAE
LOTUS FAMILY
Nelumbonaceae includes a single genus of aquatic herbs from North America and southern Asia to Australia. It was formerly included in the water-lily family, Nymphaea-ceae. Leaves are held above the water (emergent), never floating, and have circular blades with a slightly concave surface. The long petioles are attached to the center of the blade (peltate). Flowers are bisexual and radially symmetrical. They have 4 tepals and numerous petal-like staminodes. The flowers are solitary on a separate, emergent scape. The fruit is a hard-shelled nut embedded in a spongy disk-shaped receptacle that supports the floral parts. The mature receptacles are woody and perforated, sometimes used in dry floral arrangements.

Nelumbo
Nelumbo includes 2 species of tuberous aquatic herbs from the tropics and mild temperate regions. American lotus, *N. lutea*, has yellow flowers and grows from temperate northeastern North America to the West Indies and eastern Mexico. The sacred lotus, *N. nucifera*, is grown throughout southeastern Asia, India, Oceania, and Australia. It is cultivated for the edible tubers, which can be recognized in Asian markets by the Swiss-cheeselike air channels. The species was distributed throughout the Old World tropics in ancient times and introduced into Egypt sometime after 500 B.C. The so-called Egyptian lotus, seen in the much earlier glyphs of the ancient pharaohs, is not a true lotus but a water-lily, *Nymphaea lotus* or *N. caerulea*. Revered by Buddhists, *Nelumbo* is grown in shallow, still-water ponds or large tubs submerged about a foot below the water surface. A gravel topping is used to keep the soil from floating. Slow-release fertilizer pellets are buried around the rhizomes. *Nelumbo* should not be confused with *Lotus*, a genus in the legume family, Fabaceae.

Nelumbo nucifera
SACRED LOTUS, LOTO
Synonyms: *Nelumbium speciosum, Nymphaea nelumbo*. Southern Asia to Australia; widely cultivated. Tuberous aquatic herb to 6 ft.; zones 9–11 . Blooms warm months. Wet. Pond muck. Full sun. Flowers: petals numerous, dark pink to white; sepals 4–5; stamens numerous; on a disk-shaped recep-tacle, fragrant. Leaves: round, dished in the center, peltate, glaucous, 1–2 ft. wide; petiole long; held above the water.

NYCTAGINACEAE
BOUGAINVILLEA FAMILY, FOUR-O'CLOCK FAMILY
Nyctaginaceae includes approximately 30 genera of trees, shrubs, herbs, and climbers widespread in tropical regions, plus a few in mild temperate areas, with greatest diversity in the New World tropics. Leaves are simple. Petals are absent. The calyx is urn-shaped (urceolate) and tubular, or petal-like. Petal-like bracts or a whorl (involucre) of bracts sometimes subtend the flowers. The fruit is a dry, one-seeded achene. Stems are often spined. *Bougainvillea* is one of the archetypical and most beloved tropical plants. The flowers are attractive to hummingbirds.

Bougainvillea
Bougainvillea includes approximately 18 species of shrubs and woody climbers from tropical South and Central America. Cultivated bougainvilleas are mostly hybrids and sports that involve *B. glabra*, *B. peruviana*, and *B. spectabilis*. Their ancestors came mostly from dry coastal areas or dry intermountain valleys. Leaves are simple, in whorls, usually with spines in the axils. Flowers are small, urn-shaped (urceolate), bisexual, and radially symmetrical. The 3 colorful bracts are commonly mistaken for flowers. Cultivated bougainvilleas resembling species are grouped here as *B. spectabilis* types with longer, duller leaves and *B. glabra* types with shorter shiny leaves. Species names are invalid when applied to hybrids.

Bougainvilleas bloom during the dry season and are at their finest in Mexico, California, and the Florida Keys, where they shed most of their leaves during the blooming season. In constantly moist conditions bloom can be induced by keeping bougainvilleas rootbound in containers. Container plants need water 2–3 times a week and dilute fertililzer once a month. Garden

Nelumbo nucifera

Nelumbo nucifera 'Momo Botán'

plants benefit from 2 or 3 applications of low-nitrogen fertilizer, such as 6–8–10, with added micronutrients during active green growth in the rainy season. Prune at the end of the rainy season and stop fertilizing and watering—unless exceptionally dry—until the next bloom is finished. Nitrogen fertilizer or partial shade inhibits bloom. Propagate from cuttings or suckers.

Bougainvillea glabra type
BOUGAINVILLEA, BUGANVÍLEA, PAPELILLO ("PAPER-FLOWER"), TRINITÁRIA

Brazil. Evergreen shrub, 6–10 ft.; zones 9–11. Blooms late winter, spring, early summer, or dry season. Moderate moisture to seasonally dry. Gritty, well-drained soil. Full sun. Flowers: ovoid, with short hairs; bracts 1.5 in. long, purple, tip acute. Leaves: ovate, 2–3 in. long, tip apiculate, glossy, minute hairs. *A compact shrub but sends out long shoots. Trim for shape. Suitable for hedges.*

Bougainvillea hybrids
BOUGAINVILLEA, BUGANVÍLEA, PAPELILLO ("PAPER-FLOWER"), TRINITÁRIA

Garden origin. Evergreen shrubs or climbers, 3–25 ft.; zones 9–11. Blooms winter, spring, summer, or dry season. Moderate moisture, seasonally dry. Gritty, sandy, well-drained soil. Full sun. Flowers: small, tubular to urn-shaped, greenish; bracts leaf-shaped, variously colored; in clusters of 3. Leaves: ovate, 2–5 in. long, usually dull green, minutely hairy, sometimes variegated; margins undulate, tips acuminate to aristate; spines in the leaf axils. *'Imperial Delight' is shrubby with white bracts*

Bougainvillea glabra type

Bougainvillea 'Imperial Delight'

Bougainvillea 'Miss Alice' and 'Silhouette'

Bougainvillea species, flowers

Bougainvillea hybrids

that develop a magenta-pink blush. 'Miss Alice' and 'Silhouette' are very large climbers with bracts.

Bougainvillea species

TREE BOUGAINVILLEA
Synonym: *B. arborea* (hort.). Origin uncertain. Semideciduous tree to 25 ft.+; zones 10–11. Blooms intermittently in warm months. Moderate moisture. Average, well-drained soil. Full sun. Flowers: urn-shaped, green and white; bracts about 1 in. long, always lavender-violet, persistent. Leaves: ovate, tip caudate (elongated and slender), 4–5 in. long, dark glossy green, minutely hairy. Spineless. *An arboreal species of unknown origin. Commonly listed as* B. arborea, *an invalid name (Howard, pers. comm.). Unique in its profuse bloom in spring and throughout the rainy season. Tends to become top-heavy. Reduce crown occasionally.*

Bougainvillea spectabilis type

BOUGAINVILLEA, BUGANVÍLEA, PAPELILLO ("PAPER-FLOWER"), TRINITÁRIA
Brazil. Evergreen clambering shrub to 25 ft.+; zones 9–11. Blooms spring. Moderate moisture to seasonally dry. Gritty, well-drained soil. Full sun. Flowers: urn-shaped, hairy; bracts 2–3 in. long. Leaves: broadly ovate, 4–5 in. long, tip acuminate, dull green. *Attractive to swallowtail butterflies. Suitable for training or espaliering on walls and fences. Photographed at Balboa Park.*

NYMPHAEACEAE

WATER-LILY FAMILY
Nymphaeaceae includes 8 genera of tuberous aquatic herbs, which are widely distributed in temperate and tropical regions. These genera are now classified as paleoherbs, neither monocot nor dicot. Leaves are large, cordate to circular, generally floating on the water surface. The petioles are attached to the bottom of the blade (peltate). Flowers are solitary, bisexual, radially symmetrical, with numerous tepals and intergraded staminodes, either emergent or floating. *Nelumbo* (in the Nelumbonaceae) and *Nymphaea* and *Victoria* (in the Nymphaeaceae) are large, ornamental aquatic species distinguished as follows: lotus, *Nelumbo*, have emergent leaves and emergent flowers; water-lilies, *Nymphaea*, have floating leaves and emergent or floating flowers; and giant water-lilies, *Victoria*, have very large floating leaves and floating flowers.

Nymphaea

Nymphaea includes approximately 40 species of rooted aquatic herbs, which are widely distributed. The ancestry of cultivated hybrids is generally obscure. Leaves are ovate to round, with a deep sinus almost to the petiole attachment. Petioles are attached to the bottom of the leaf (peltate). Flowers develop from the nodes of the submerged rhizomes or tubers. Numerous tepals intergrade with petal-like staminodes and the stamens in numerous whorls. The stamens are flattened (laminar). The fruit is a berry that develops underwater. Water-lilies are grouped horticulturally as hardy or tropical as well as day- or night-blooming. Night-bloomers open at night, but usually remain open until midday. Water-lilies are grown in shallow ponds or tubs submerged about 1.5 ft. below the water surface allowing the leaves to spread naturally. In deeper water, raise tubs on blocks. Plant in a mixture of loam, sand, and manure. Topdress with gravel to keep soil from floating. Feed 4 times a year with fertilizer tablets. Full sun is essen-

Bougainvillea species

Bougainvillea spectabilis type

tial for bloom. Adding small fish to the water helps control mosquito larvae. Plants will need to be thinned and debris cleared from the pond several times a season (Birdsey, pers. comm.).

Nymphaea capensis
CAPE BLUE WATER-LILY
Synonyms: *N. capensis* var. *zanzibariensis*, *N. zanzibariensis*. Tropical eastern Africa to South Africa, Madagascar. Rooted aquatic herb; zones 10–11. Blooms summer, fall. Wet. Pond muck. Full sun. Flowers: tepals to 6 in. wide, blue-violet to deep red-violet: stamens golden; day-blooming, fragrant. Leaves: almost round, 6–10 in. wide; margins dentate, undulate; purple below.

Nymphaea hybrids
WATER-LILY
Garden hybrids. Rooted aquatic herbs; zones 10–11. Bloom warm months. Wet. Pond muck. Full sun. Flowers: tepals and petal-like staminodes numerous, multihued; stamens golden; emergent or floating; solitary. Leaves: orbicular to ovate, 6–10 in. wide, peltate, with a deep sinus almost to the petiole, green to reddish or spotted; mostly floating on the surface of the water unless crowded; margins often undulate or toothed. *'James Birdsey'* is a day-bloomer. 'Wood's White Knight', a night-bloomer, is a hybrid of *'Sir Galahad'* × *'Missouri'*. Night-bloomers have large, emergent flowers which usually close by midday.

Victoria
Victoria includes 2 species of rooted aquatic herbs, 1 each from the Amazon and Paraná river basins. Leaves are round, to several feet wide, floating. The margins are upturned and red-bristled below in *V. amazonica*. Leaves of *V. cruziana*, from the Paraná basin in Uruguay, southern Brazil, and Argentina, have green upturned margins, are densely hairy below, and tolerates cooler water temperatures than *V. amazonica*. Petioles are attached to the center of the bottom of the leaves (peltate). Very dramatic and only suitable for large water gardens.

Nymphaea capensis

Nymphaea 'James Birdsey'

Nymphaea 'Wood's White Knight'

Victoria amazonica with *Nymphaea*

Victoria amazonica

GIANT WATER-LILY, WATER-PLATTER
South America (Amazon basin). Rooted aquatic herb; zones 10–11. Blooms warm months. Wet. Pond muck. Full sun. Flowers: cup-shaped, petals and stamens numerous, white on first day becoming pink; sepals prickled; floating. Leaves: orbicular, 3–6 ft. wide, underside red, bristled and corrugated along the veins; margins sharply upturned 2–6 in., red; floating. *Needs warm water temperature to thrive. The similar 'Longwood' (Victoria cruziana × V. amazonica) tolerates somewhat cooler water. Photographed at Fairchild Tropical Garden.*

OCHNACEAE

BIRD'S-EYE FAMILY, OCHNA FAMILY
Ochnaceae includes 20 genera of trees, shrubs, and a few herbs from the tropics, with greatest diversity in Brazil. Leaves are usually simple and leathery. Flowers are bisexual and radially symmetrical. They have 5 petals, 5 sepals, and 5 to numerous stamens mounted on a disklike receptacle. The fruit is a capsule or a berrylike aggregate, splitting into one-seeded, drupelike segments.

Ochna

Ochna includes approximately 600 species of mostly shrubs plus a few trees and herbs, which are widely distributed in the tropics and subtropics. A few species are cultivated for their bright yellow flowers and the whimsical appearance of the black seeds sticking out like Mickey Mouse ears from the red receptacles and sepals. Leaves are usually simple, with mostly serrate margins. Flowers are bisexual and radially symmetrical. Petals are usually 5, yellow, and short-lived. Sepals are usually 5, turning bright red, persistent. Stamens are numerous. The fruits are berrylike aggregates, which separate into one-seeded drupelets as the fleshy receptacle expands. Propagated from cuttings or seed. Relatively pest free. Though they tolerate dry conditions, plants maintain a fresher appearance when given adequate moisture during active growth.

Ochna kirkii

BIRD'S-EYE BUSH,
MICKEY MOUSE PLANT
Southeastern Africa. Evergreen shrub to 6 ft.; zones 10–11. Blooms late winter, early spring. Regular moisture, seasonally dry. Average, well-drained soil. Full to part sun. Flowers: petals 5, spreading, to 2 in. wide, bases clawed, bright yellow, short-lived; sepals green turning red, to 0.5 in. long, visible through the "windows" at the base of the petals, persistent; receptacle fleshy, red; seeds blue-green turning black, glossy. Leaves: obovate, 2–3 in. long; margins serrate.

Ochna mossambicensis

BIRD'S-EYE-BUSH,
MICKEY MOUSE PLANT
Mozambique. Evergreen shrub to 10 ft.; zones 10–11. Blooms late winter, early spring. Regular moisture, seasonally dry. Average, well-drained soil. Full to part sun. Flowers: petals 5, spreading, to 1 in. wide, bright yellow, bases clawed, short-lived; calyx green, turning bright red, persistent; receptacle red, fleshy; seeds blue-green turning black. Leaves: obovate, to 6 in. long, firm; margins serrate. *Flowers are smaller and the leaves are twice as large as O. kirkii.*

Ochna serrulata

BIRD'S-EYE BUSH
Synonyms: *O. atropurpurea, O. multiflora, O. serratifolia* (hort.). South Africa. Evergreen shrub to 6 ft.; zones 9–11. Blooms late spring, early summer. Regular moisture, seasonally dry. Average, well-drained soil. Full to part sun. Flowers: petals 5, bright yellow, bases clawed. to 1 in. wide, short-lived; calyx green, persistent, turning bright red; receptacle fleshy; fruit a berrylike aggregate splitting into drupelets, olive-green turning black. Leaves: lanceolate, to 2 in. long; margins serrate. *Photographed at Quail Botanical Garden.*

Ouratea

Ouratea includes approximately 200 species of trees and shrubs from the New World tropics and tropical Africa. Leaves are simple and smooth, with serrated margins and short petioles. Flowers are small and yellow, on long stalks, in many-flowered panicles. Fruits are aggregates that separate into 3 or 4 drupelets as the fleshy receptacle swells.

Ouratea tuerckheimii

Southern Mexico, Guatemala. Evergreen tree to 6 ft.+; zones 10–11. Blooms spring, summer. Season-

Victoria amazonica

Ochna kirkii

Ochna mossambicensis

Ochna serrulata

Ouratea tuerckheimii

ally moist/dry. Average, well-drained soil. Full to part sun. Flowers: small, yellow; calyx and receptacle red; in many-flowered panicles. Leaves: oblong to lanceolate, to 12 in. long; margins serrate. *Identification tentative. Unusual to rare in cultivation.*

OLEACEAE
OLIVE FAMILY, JASMINE FAMILY

Oleaceae includes approximately 29 genera of trees, shrubs, and woody climbers, which are widely distributed in tropical and mild temperate regions. *Olea europaea* is grown in Mediterranean-type climates for olives and olive oil as well as its beautiful light tan wood. Leaves are simple or compound, often aromatic. Flowers are mostly bisexual and radially symmetrical. The corolla is united at the base into a tube, usually with 4–8 free lobes, or is sometimes absent. There are 2 stamens, the filaments attached to the inside of the petal tube at their bases (epipetalous). Flowers are solitary or in many-flowered cymes or panicles. The fruit is a berry or capsule.

Jasminum

Jasminum includes approximately 230 species of trees, shrubs, and woody climbers, which are widely distributed in the tropics and mild temperate regions. Leaves are simple, trifoliolate or pinnate. Flowers are bisexual or unisexual and radially symmetrical; sepals 4, petals 4, or multiples of 4; stamens 2. The name "jessamine" was intentionally introduced by Julia Morton to help distinguish many fragrant flowers incorrectly referred to as jasmines from the true, but often invasive, cultivated jasmines (Morton 1971). Unfortunately, in some references these names are used interchangeably. True jasmines can be distinguished in part by their spreading, rotate petal lobes (the lobes are twisted like little propellers in pinwheel jessamines, *Tabernaemontana*). Gold Coast jasmine, *Jasminum dichotomum*, and *J. fluminense*, are invasive pests and prohibited in Florida. *Tabernaemontana* species are recommended as substitutes. *Gardenia* species are also suitable substitutes in acid soil.

Jasminum laurifolium

WINDMILL JASMINE, STAR JASMINE, ANGEL-WING JASMINE

Synonym: *J. nitidum*. Admiralty Islands (South Pacific), Papua New Guinea. Evergreen scandent shrub; zones 10–11. Blooms almost all year. Moderate moisture. Average, well-drained soil. Full sun. Flowers: petals narrow, white, undersides purplish, fragrant; buds and calyx red; stalks purplish red. Leaves: unifoliolate; leaflet ovate to lanceolate, glossy dark green, 3–5 in. long; margins smooth. *Coastal. Self-seeding and potentially weedy.*

Jasminum sambac

ARABIAN JASMINE, SAMBAC JASMINE, JASMÍN DE ARABIA

India, Myanmar, (Burma), Bangladesh; widely cultivated. Evergreen scandent shrub; zones 9–11. Blooms warm months. Regular moisture. Average, well-drained soil. Full sun. Flowers: corolla white, 1–1.5 in. wide, aging pinkish, single or double; solitary or in small clusters. Leaves: simple, ovate 3–4 in. long, dull or glossy. *Strongly fragrant. Moderately salt tolerant. Listed as invasive and a controlled species in Florida.*

Ligustrum

Ligustrum includes approximately 50 species of shrubs and trees from the Old World tropics and mild temperate regions. They are very commonly used as privacy hedges or pruned into small trees in landscaping. Leaves are simple, sometimes downy when young. Flowers are small, funnel-shaped, usually white or creamy, and fragrant, and are borne in many-flowered panicles. The fruits are small, fleshy drupes. Withhold pruning in spring for flowers. Use mulch to protect shallow roots. Mild temperate species

Jasminum laurifolium

Jasminum laurifolium, flowers

Jasminum sambac 'Grand Duke of Tuscany'

Jasminum sambac 'Maid of Orleans'

L. lucidum and *L. sinense* are invasive pests in Central and North Florida but do not thrive on the southern peninsula. *Ligustrum japonicum* is commonly grown in warmer regions of the United States.

Ligustrum japonicum
JAPANESE PRIVET

Synonyms: *L. coriaceum, L. japonicum* var. *rotundifolium*. Eastern Asia. Evergreen shrub to 10 ft.; zones 8–10. Blooms spring, early summer. Regular moisture. Most well-drained soils. Full to part sun. Flowers: small, white, trumpet-shaped, fragrant; in many-flowered panicles. Leaves: ovate, 2–3 in. long, tips bluntly acuminate to obtuse or somewhat rounded, dark glossy green, firm; margins smooth; petiole to 0.25 in. Stems: with conspicuous white lenticels. *Easily mistaken for* Ficus *and recommend as a lower maintenance substitute for tall hedges. Ligustrum can be distinguished by the lack of latex sap when a leaf is broken.*

ONAGRACEAE
EVENING PRIMROSE FAMILY,
FUCHSIA FAMILY

Onagraceae includes approximately 16 genera of perennial herbs, sometimes aquatic shrubs, and occasionally trees, which are widely distributed in tropical and temperate regions. Leaves are simple, entire or lobed, the margins often serrated. Flowers are usually bisexual and radially symmetrical with 4 petals and 4 sepals. The petals are often clawed (abruptly narrowing into a stalk at the base), and the floral parts are mounted on a floral cup (hypanthium). Flowers are solitary or in panicles, spikes, or racemes. The fruit is a capsule, nutlet, or berry.

Fuchsia

Fuchsia includes approximately 100 species of herbs and shrubs from Central and South America as well as New Zealand. They come from cool mountainous regions. Fuchsias are often grown as houseplants. Innumerable cultivars of uncertain ancestry exist. Flowers are usually pendent. They are divided horticulturally by single, semidouble, or double corollas. Hybrids of *F. triphylla* have long tubes and short lobes and are referred to horticulturally as the Triphylla Group. Trailing fuchsias are commonly grown in baskets or containers to allow the flowers to hang freely. Fuchsias prefer moderate temperatures and do not thrive in hot moist conditions. Old flowers should be nipped out regularly to encourage branching and more flowers. Pests include bud-mite, sucking insects, nematodes, and fungal diseases.

Fuchsia hybrids
FUCHSIA

Garden hybrids. Evergreen or deciduous herbs and shrubs, 0.5–5 ft.; zones 8–10. Bloom mild months. Part moisture. Fertile, humus-rich, well-drained soil. Full sun to bright filtered light. Flowers:

corolla pendent, sepal lobes erect. Leaves: ovate, obovate to lanceolate, to about 2 in. long, light to dark green, sometimes purplish; margins serrate to entire. *Sensitive to heat and cold. Grown outdoors in mild areas of California. Fuchsias do not thrive in climates with warm night temperatures. The Triphylla Group is more resistant to bud-mites. Attractive to hummingbirds.*

Hauya

Hauya includes approximately 20 species of trees and shrubs from Mexico and Central America. *Hauya heydeana* is a handsome tree which is unusual in cultivation. It grows at Waimea Botanical Garden, Hawaii, and at the Missouri Botanical Garden, Missouri. Leaves are simple with smooth margins. The calyx is 4-parted, fused at the base into an elongated floral tube (hypanthium). Flowers have 4 short-lived petals. The 8 stamens with long filaments are mounted on the rim of the hypanthium. The stigma is globular. Flowers are solitary in the leaf axils.

Hauya heydeana

Southern Mexico, Guatemala. Evergreen tree to 30 ft.; zones 10–11. Blooms warm months. Seasonally moist/dry. Average to fertile, well-drained soil. Full to part sun. Flowers: corolla tube green, lobes white, 2–2.5 in. wide, short-lived; stamens 8, filaments pink; calyx sharply reflexed, white, red with age; stigma globular. Leaves: ovate, 4–6 in. long, glossy; petioles reddish with

age; clustered near ends of slender branches. Bark: flaky. From tropical highlands to coastal. Difficult to propagate (Orr, pers. comm.). Unusual to rare in cultivation.

Ludwigia

Ludwigia includes approximately 80 species of herbs and shrubs, which are widely distributed, with greatest diversity in the Americas. Leaves, stems, and capsules are covered with short hairs. Leaves are simple. Flowers are bisexual and radially symmetrical. The calyx is 4-parted, fused at the base into a long floral tube (hypanthium). There are 4 petals and 8 stamens, with short filaments, mounted on the rim of the hypanthium. The stigma is globular. The flowers are solitary in the leaf axils. *Ludwigia peruviana* is a native of U.S. and Mexican wetlands despite its name, though it is widely distributed. It grows in shallow ponds or in low areas that are regularly flooded. It is heavily self-seeding and weedy.

Ludwigia peruviana
PRIMROSE-WILLOW

Mexico, southern United States; widely naturalized. Semiaquatic perennial shrub or subshrub, 3–4 ft.; zones 9–11. Blooms most of the year. Regular moisture to aquatic Bottom muck or average soil. Full to part sun. Flowers: spreading, 1.5 in. wide, petals 4, subtriangular, tips notched, lemon-yellow; calyx persistent on the capsule; in the leaf axils; capsule slender, to 2 in.

Ligustrum japonicum

Fuchsia 'Mrs. Marshall'

Fuchsia Triphylla Group

Hauya heydeana

long, 4-lobed, covered with stiff hairs; seeds numerous. Leaves: lanceolate, 3–4 in. long, tip acuminate. *Self-seeding. A common but attractive weed in wetlands and around nurseries. Note the 4 petals. Suitable for low wet areas and shallow pond margins.*

Oenothera

Oenothera includes approximately 120 species of perennial, biennial, and annual herbs. Leaves are simple, often lobed. Flowers have 4 petals and 8 stamens and are rotate to cupped, pink, yellow, or white. The name "evening primrose" is applied horticulturally to species with flowers that open in the late afternoon and sundrops refers to day-bloomers, but evening primrose is the name applied to the group as a whole.

Oenothera speciosa 'Rosea'

SUNDROPS, EVENING PRIMROSE
Synonyms: *Hartmannia speciosa, O.* 'Childsii' (hort.). Mexico, southern United States. Short-lived perennial or annual herb, 1–1.5 ft.; zones 6–10. Blooms warm months. Moderate moisture when hot, less when cool. Sandy to rocky, well-drained soil. Full sun. Flowers: saucer-shaped, 1–2 in. wide, white with pink veins and margins, center yellow. Leaves: basal leaves lanceolate, 3–4 in. long, leaves on stems smaller; margins undulate, irregularly lobed or toothed. *Commonly cultivated. Produces clump-forming runners. Suitable for rock gardens.*

ORCHIDACEAE

ORCHID FAMILY
Orchidaceae includes approximately 775 genera of epiphytic and terrestrial herbs plus a few climbers, which are widely distributed, with greatest diversity in tropical regions. Orchids belong to one of the largest, most advanced plant families. Thousands of intrageneric and intergeneric hybrids have been produced. Much has been written on the orchid family, and the sampling here can only hint at its diversity. Registration of orchid hybrids is well organized by the American Orchid Society and the Royal Botanic Gardens, Kew. Leaves are simple.

Those of epiphytes are generally stiff and leathery, sometimes arising from a thickened water-storing organ (pseudobulb). Terrestrials have mostly thin or grasslike leaves that develop from rhizomes or tubers. Flowers are bisexual with 3 similar, sometimes fused sepals and 3 petals, one of which is modified into a lip (labellum). The anthers and carpels are fused into a thick column. Pollen is clumped into usually 1 or 2, sometimes 3 or 4, pollinia. The stigma is recessed on the underside of the column. Flowers are sometimes equipped with elaborate devices to attract specific pollinators. The fruit is a dry capsule holding thousands of minute seeds that lack endosperm. In cultivation, seedlings are grown in tissue culture for about 2 years. Orchids are grouped into monopodial or sympodial growth types. Epiphytes are grown on tree limbs or in baskets or containers with coarse bark or special mixes. Their aerial roots are covered with a white, moisture-absorbing velamen and must be exposed to air, not planted in earth. Terrestrial orchids are grown in light, humus-rich soil or special mixes. Vanilla "beans" are the capsules of climbing orchids, *Vanilla* species.

×Ascocenda

×*Ascocenda* is the aggregate name of intergeneric hybrids of *Ascocentrum* and *Vanda* species. Growth is monopodial. *Ascocentrum*, typically of small size, lends compactness to hybrids. The yellow, orange, and red flowers transmit warm color variations to the normally purple, pink, and blue shades of *Vanda* species. Leaves are alternate, arranged in opposite ranks (distichous).

×Ascocenda hybrid

Garden origin, *Vanda* 'Josephine van Brero' × ×*Ascocenda* 'Yip Sum Wah'. Evergreen epiphytic herb; zones 10–11. Blooms spring, intermittently in warm months. Regular moisture and humidity. Mount on tree-fern slab or pot in orchid mix. Bright filtered light. Flowers: red-orange; in many-flowered, erect spikes. Leaves: linear, 4–6 in. long, distichous.

×Brassocattleya

×*Brassocattleya* is the aggregate name of intergeneric hybrids of *Brassavola* and *Cattleya* species. Commonly abbreviated BC.

×Brassocattleya Binosa 'Matasa'

Garden hybrid, *Brassavola nodosa* × *Cattleya bicolor*. Epiphytic herb; zones 10–11. Blooms intermittently from late spring to fall. Seasonally moist/dry. Mount on tree-fern slab or limb, pot in orchid mix. Part sun to bright broken light. Flowers: tepals linear, olive-green; lip 3-lobed, side lobes enclose the column, white and magenta-pink around the edges and on the veins. Leaves: linear, fleshy, 6–10 in. long.

An intergeneric hybrid I made for its ability to thrive outdoors in South Florida.

Calanthe

Calanthe includes approximately 150 species of mostly terrestrial herbs from South Africa, Madagascar, Southeast Asia, Indomalaysia to Australia, Japan, and Tahiti. They have sympodial growth and are evergreen with reduced pseudobulbs or deciduous with large pseudobulbs. Leaves are pleated, attached to the top of the pseudobulb. The flowers have 5 equal tepals and a 3-lobed lip with a long slender spur. Inflorescences are generally on a long and arching stalk. Flowers open over a period of several months. Grow in a cactus or succulent medium in a shallow dish or pot with good drainage or in a bed of humus and sand. Fertilize with a slow-release, balanced fertilizer during active growth. Separate pseudobulbs yearly and repot after bloom. Overcrowded bulbs will rot.

Calanthe vestita

Southeast Asia, Malaysia, Indonesia. Deciduous terrestrial herb; zones 10–11. Blooms late fall, winter. Regular moisture when in leaf, sparingly after leaves begin to yellow. Gritty, humus-rich, well-drained soil. Bright filtered light. Flowers: corolla white or mottled with pink, dark magenta near center; lip 3-lobed, fiddle-shaped; inflorescence stalk 3–4 ft. long, emerging from

Ludwigia peruviana

Oenothera speciosa 'Rosea'

×*Ascocenda* hybrid

base of pseudobulb. Leaves: elliptic to broadly obovate, pleated, 15–20 in. long; pseudobulbs ovoid, sides vertically grooved. *Leaves fall as flowering shoots initiate. Inflorescence lasts about 2 months.*

Cattleya

Cattleya includes 40–65 species of epiphytic herbs from Central and South America. They are found from high-altitude cloud-forests to coastal woodlands. The genus is closely allied to *Epidendrum*. Cattleyas are the quintessential orchids to most people, commonly used in corsages. Leaves are usually oblong and stiff, attached to the ends of stalked pseudobulbs. Pseudobulbs are short, swollen stems that store water; they are typical of orchids that grow in seasonally moist/dry climates. New growth arises from the base of the previous pseudobulb (sympodial). Flowers have spreading tepals and a simple or lobed, often fringed or ruffled lip.

Cattleyas are divided horticulturally into 2 groups. Those in the bifoliate group have 2, or occasionally 3, leaves at the end of slender pseudobulbs. Flowers are small to medium, born in clusters. The unifoliate, or labiate cattleyas, have a single leaf at the end of a stout pseudobulb and 1–3 large flowers with showy lips. This latter group is the basis of most hybrids. In Costa Rica, certain orchids are sometimes so prolific, even growing between roof tiles, that they are considered pests. Cattleyas readily hybridize with a number of related genera. Intergeneric hybrid names are usually abbreviated; for example, LC is an abbreviation for the group ×*Laeliocattleya* (*Laelia* × *Cattleya*).

Cattleya bowringiana

Synonym: *C. skinneri* var. *bowringiana.* Belize, Guatemala, Honduras. Epiphytic herb; zones 10–11. Blooms fall. Regular moisture and humidity, dry when cool. Mount on tree-fern slab or limb, pot in orchid mix. Bright broken light. Flowers: to 3 in. wide, magenta, throat with white spot. Leaves: bifoliate, oblong, to 8 in.; pseudobulb elongated, stemlike, to about 1 ft. long. Produces massive clumps. *This species is similar but more prolific and with smaller flowers than* C. skinneri, *which blooms in late winter and spring. Spectacular when massed on stumps or sturdy limbs. Forgiving and pest resistant.*

Cattleya ×guatemalensis

Natural hybrid (Central America), *C. aurantiaca* × *C. skinneri*. Epiphytic herb; zones 10–11. Blooms late fall, winter. Regular moisture and humidity; dry when cool. Mount on tree-fern slab or limb, pot in orchid mix. Bright broken light. Flowers: pinkish lavender to pinkish orange, lip tubular at base, tip red, throat orange; in many-flowered clusters. Leaves: bifoliate, oblong, to 6 in.; pseudobulb cylindrical, stemlike. *A natural hybrid resembling the* C. skinneri *parent vegetatively.*

Cattleya percivaliana

CHRISTMAS CATTLEYA

Synonym: *C. labiata* var. *percivaliana.* Venezuela. Epiphytic or lithophytic herb; zones 10–11. Blooms winter. Moist and humid, dry when cool. Mount on tree-fern slab or limb, pot in orchid mix. Full sun to bright broken light. Flowers: tepals pink-lavender, to 5 in. wide, lip deep magenta at tip, throat streaked with violet and orange; margins ruffled,

×*Brassocattleya* Binosa 'Matasa'

Calanthe vestita, 2 color forms

Cattleya ×*guatemalensis*

Cattleya bowringiana

pinkish; column white; scent musky. Leaves: unifoliate, medium green to 10 in. long. *The musky scent is a distinctive characteristic.*

Cymbidium

Cymbidium includes 50–70 species of terrestrial, lithophytic, and epiphytic herbs from mountainous regions of China, Southeast Asia, and India. There are myriad hybrids. Grown extensively for the florist trade. Growth is sympodial, developing large clumps. Leaves are strap-shaped, thin to leathery, on long pseudobulbs. Cymbidiums are grown extensively in the San Francisco area and other areas with mild temperatures and at moderate altitude in the tropics. In winter, they need full sun and protection from freezing; in summer, filtered light and cooling mist. They are usually grown as semiterrestrials in large beds or containers to accommodate the extensive root systems. Plants need a pre-flowering rest without fertilizer or irrigation.

Cymbidium hybrids

Garden origin. Evergreen epiphytic and semiterrestrial herbs; zones 8–9. Bloom winter, spring. Regular moisture and humidity; dry before flowering. Pot in chopped tree-fern, humus and grit, or specialized mixes. Bright filtered light in summer, full sun in winter. Flowers: many colors; lip contrasting with tepals. Leaves: strap-shaped; pseudobulbs large. *Green-flowered cymbidiums usually involve C. hookerianum.*

Dendrobium

Dendrobium includes approximately 900 species of epiphytic and terrestrial herbs from the Himalayas, China, Southeast Asia, Indonesia, Korea, and Japan to New Guinea and parts of Oceania. It is one of the largest orchid genera, and the extremely variable species are adapted to a diverse range of altitude and climate. The group is distinguished primarily by having 4 pollinia. Their taxonomy is complex and still unsettled. Leaves range from thick to papery, flat to terete. Growth is sympodial. Plants may be evergreen, semideciduous, or deciduous. Dendrobiums produce either fleshy, canelike stalks or pseudobulbs. The multiflowered inflorescences are terminal or arise from a subterminal node. Dendrobiums are so variable that for successful growing it is especially important to understand the conditions to which each species is adapted.

Dendrobium bigibbum

BUTTERFLY DENDROBIUM
Synonym: *D. phalaenopsis.* Australia, New Guinea, Indonesia. Evergreen epiphytic herb; zones 10–11. Blooms late summer, fall. Seasonally moist and humid, dry. Mount on tree-fern slab or limb, or pot in orchid mix. Part sun to bright broken light. Flowers: lateral petals larger than sepals and lip, in many-flowered clusters arising from a node near the end of the canelike pseudobulb. Leaves: elliptic, 6–7 in. long, leathery; deciduous after the

second season. *A variable and commonly grown species. Grows carefree in my garden except for water during extended drought. Plantlets develop at the nodes of old canes.*

Dendrobium lindleyi

Synonym: *D. aggregatum* (hort.). Southern China, India, Southeast Asia. Evergreen epiphytic herb; zones 9–11. Blooms late winter,

Dendrobium bigibbum

Cattleya percivaliana

Cymbidium 'Via Fiesta Verde'

Dendrobium lindleyi

early spring. Seasonally moist and humid/dry. Coarse organic orchid mix or epiphytic. Part sun to bright broken light. Flowers: tepals small, lip almost round, bright yellow, edges undulate; in many-flowered pendent racemes, 5–8 in. long, from a node on the pseudobulbs. Leaves: unifoliate, oblong, 2–3 in. long, pseudobulbs ovoid, compressed against the tree bark. *Floriferous. The 30-year-old specimen shown here welcomes visitors at the door of my home in South Florida. It encircles a live oak tree. Carefree other than needing water during extended drought. It has survived freezing nighttime temperatures.*

×*Doritaenopsis*

×*Doritaenopsis* is the aggregate name of intergeneric hybrids of *Doritis* and *Phalaenopsis*.

×*Doritaenopsis* hybrid

Epidendrum ibaguense

×*Doritaenopsis* hybrid
MOTH-ORCHID HYBRID

Garden hybrids. Evergreen epiphytic herb; zones 10–11. Blooms intermittently all year. Regular moisture and humidity. Mount on tree-fern slab or limb, pot in orchid mix. Bright filtered light. Flowers: tepals spreading, flat, white with magenta markings; lip 3-lobed, magenta, throat yellow with magenta spots; on arching stalk to 2 ft. Leaves: broadly obovate, closely set on a short stem. *Many of these hybrids are distributed through the florist and nursery trades. They are quite lovely but represent seconds that are not quite up to the breeders' standards and are often unnamed.*

Encyclia

Encyclia includes 150–235 species of epiphytic and lithophytic herbs

Encyclia radiata

Haemaria discolor

from tropical America and the West Indies. These species were formerly included in *Epidendrum*. The 1–4 strap-shaped, oblong, or linear leaves are attached to the end of the pseudobulb. Flowers have 5 fairly similar tepals, a simple or lobed lip, and are sometimes inverted (resupinate) with the lip uppermost.

Encyclia radiata
CLAMSHELL ORCHID

Central Mexico to Costa Rica. Evergreen epiphytic herb; zones 10–11. Blooms summer, or intermittently. Seasonally moist and humid, dry. Mount on tree-fern slab or limb, pot in orchid mix. Bright broken light. Flowers: inverted (resupinate), fragrant, tepals light yellow-green, lip-uppermost, shell-shaped, striped purple-maroon. Leaves: strap-shaped, 12–15 in. long; pseudobulbs ovoid.

Epidendrum

Epidendrum includes approximately 800 species of epiphytic or terrestrial herbs from mild temperate and tropical America. Leaves are usually borne at the ends of reed-like stalks or occasionally from the tips or bases of pseudobulbs. Flowers are often small, in umbel-like clusters. Cultural requirements vary greatly depending on origin.

Epidendrum ibaguense
REED-ORCHID

Synonym: *E. radicans*. Tropical America. Semiterrestrial herb, 3–4 ft.; zones 10–11. Blooms warm months. Regular moisture when hot, less when cool. Gritty, humus-rich, well-drained soil. Full to part sun. Flowers: small, yellow turning scarlet, lip fringed; in many-flowered clusters on a long stalk. Leaves: elliptic, to 4 in. long, base clasping stem. Stems: reed-like, erect to reclining, rooting at nodes. *Commonly cultivated terrestrial species. Becomes untidy unless the rambling canes are redirected with bamboo stakes. Suitable for baskets. Will produce new growth at nodes if pruned. Cut stems laid on moist humus in a shady spot will produce plantlets.*

Haemaria

Haemaria includes a single species of terrestrial herb from southern China, Malaysia, Indonesia (Sumatra), and Southeast Asia. It is quite variable over its extensive range. The leaves are simple and plants lack pseudobulbs. They are grouped horticulturally based primarily on leaf coloration. The black-leafed form is common in cultivation. Stems are succulent, erect, or scrambling and taking root at the nodes. The small, white flowers are borne in erect racemes. Suitable for beds of humus in warm, humid locations with broken light. Also suitable for container growing indoors.

Haemaria discolor
JEWEL-ORCHID

Synonyms: *Goodyera discolor*, *Ludisia discolor*. Southern China, Southeast Asia, Indonesia. Terrestrial herb to 1 ft.; zones 9–11. Blooms fall, winter, early spring. Evenly moist and humid. Fertile, humus-rich, well-drained soil. Bright to moderate filtered light. Flowers: small, white, fragrant; anther cap yellow; in erect, many-flowered terminal racemes. Leaves: ovate to elliptic, 2–3 in. long, black to maroon, veins reddish or silver, underside maroon; on a short stalk.

Lycaste

Lycaste includes approximately 35 species of mostly epiphytic, occasionally lithophytic or semiterrestrial herbs from tropical America and the West Indies. They grow from humid sea-level woodlands to cool cloud-forests at moderate to fairly high elevation. Leaves are pleated (plicate) on ovoid, compressed pseudobulbs. Thin basal bracts cover the pseudobulbs. Flowers are solitary, on leafless stalks that emerge from the base of the pseudobulb. A number of flowering stalks may be produced at once. The 3 pointed sepals are larger than the petals resulting in a triangular outline. The lip is 3-lobed. Culture varies depending upon origin. Seasonal temperature fluctuations are necessary to initiate flowering.

Lycaste dowiana

Costa Rica to Bolivia. Evergreen semiepiphytic herb; zones 10–11. Blooms late spring, summer. Seasonally moist/dry. Coarse organic orchid mix. Bright filtered light. Flowers: petals yellow, lip 3-lobed, lower lobe fringed and tinged pink-violet; sepals larger than petals, greenish brown. Leaves: pleated, to 15 in.+ long.

Miltonia

Miltonia includes approximately 15 species of epiphytic herbs primarily from moist forests of Brazil. Leaves are linear to oblong, a pair developing at the ends of the pseudobulbs. Flowers have narrow tepals and fiddle-shaped lips. The flower stalk develops from the base of the pseudobulb. Grow in baskets. Rhizomes are fairly long and quickly outgrow pots. Some former *Miltonia* species are now segregated into *Miltoniopsis*. They are primarily cool-growing mountain species from Ecuador to Costa Rica. This group is known as pansy-orchids and are distinguished by their broad tepals. The numerous hybrids of *Miltonia* and *Miltoniopsis* named before the separation of these groups are now intergeneric crosses. The original names are currently being retained to avoid the confusion of renaming all the hybrids.

Miltonia 'May Moir' × *M. spectabilis* 'Bicolor'

Garden hybrid. Evergreen epiphytic herb; zones 9–10. Blooms fall. Even moisture and humidity. Coarse organic orchid mix. Bright filtered light. Flowers: tepals pink-magenta with white reticulated markings, lip pink-magenta with a central white area and dark magenta spots. Leaves: oblong.

Oncidium

Oncidium includes approximately 420 species of primarily epiphytic, sometimes lithophytic or terrestrial herbs from tropical America with greatest diversity in the Andes and Brazil. Species are variable, found from sea level to fairly high altitude. The taxonomy is complex and still unsettled. One or 2 leaves develop from a pseudobulb, or pseudobulbs may be reduced or absent. Flowers are characteristically yellow with brown markings. Tepals are relatively small, the lip well developed and frilly. The general outline suggests a figure in a wide skirt resulting in the common name "dancing-lady" orchids. Oncidiums with long sprays of small flowers are extremely effective mounted in masses on lattice screens.

Oncidium sphacelatum

Mexico to El Salvador. Evergreen, semiepiphytic herb; zones 10–11. Blooms spring. Seasonally moist/dry. Mount on tree-fern slabs or limbs or grow in baskets, hanging or placed on the ground. Bright broken light. Flowers: tepals yellow and brown, lip yellow; on a branched stalk from top of pseudobulb, 3–6 ft. long. Leaves: sword-shaped, to 18 in., folded lengthwise into a V at base, on an ovoid, flattened pseudobulb. *Produces large clumps on beds of mulch. Particularly elegant when grown in baskets or on lathe screens where they can arch to the ground.*

Paphiopedilum

Paphiopedilum includes approximately 60 species of mostly terrestrial herbs from Southeast Asia, India to Papua New Guinea. Many in cultivation are cool-growing mountain plants that prefer moderately cool temperatures. Growth is sympodial. Leaves are strap-shaped to elliptic or ovate and plants lack pseudobulbs. Flowers range from delicate to plastic in appearance. The lip is bucket- or slipper-shaped. Venus-slippers, or "paphs," are often incorrectly referred to as cypripediums, a distinct genus of mostly north-temperate lady's-slipper orchids. They may also be confused with another slipper-lipped genus, *Phragmipedium*, from tropical America. Leaves and flowers are borne at the end of a short stalk. The absence of water-storing pseudobulbs indicates that these plants need regular moisture. Avoid misting the flowers. Grow in bark orchid mixes with dolomite added for alkalinity.

Paphiopedilum 'Gold Luna' × *P.* 'Mach 1'

VENUS-SLIPPER ORCHID
Garden hybrid. Evergreen terrestrial herb; zones 10–11. Blooms cooler months. Evenly moist, reduce when cool. Coarse organic orchid mix. Bright filtered light. Flowers: glossy, plastic appearance, to 5 in. wide, solitary on a stalk; pet-

Lycaste dowiana

Miltonia 'May Moir' × *M. spectabilis* 'Bicolor'

Oncidium sphacelatum

Paphiopedilum 'Gold Luna' × *P.* 'Mach 1'

Paphiopedilum haynaldianum × *P. glaucophyllum*

Phaius tankervilliae

als green with brown markings; lip cup-shaped; sepals green, spotted maroon, upper sepal larger than laterals. Leaves: broadly strap-shaped, keeled.

Phalaenopsis 'Bamboo Baby' × *P.* 'Coquí'

Phalaenopsis violacea var. *murtoniana*

Psychopsis 'Mendenhall Papilio' × *P.* 'Butterfly'

Paphiopedilum haynaldianum × *P. glaucophyllum*

VENUS-SLIPPER ORCHID

Garden hybrid (Southeast Asia). Evergreen terrestrial herb; zones 10–11. Blooms fall, winter. Evenly moist, reduce when cool. Coarse organic orchid mix. Medium filtered light. Flowers: green and pink with brown spots, solitary on an erect stalk. Leaves: straplike, leathery.

Phaius

Phaius includes approximately 30 species of often large, mostly terrestrial herbs from eastern Africa, Madagascar, Sri Lanka, India, and Southeast Asia to the South Pacific and Australia. Leaves are usually large and pleated (plicate) in groups of 3–10; pseudobulbs ovoid to stemlike. The floral lip is tubular. Grown in the ground in open, gritty, humus- and bark-enriched loam. Keep moist in summer. Reduce water to a minimum in winter.

Phaius tankervilliae

NUN'S ORCHID

China, Southeast Asia, Indomalaysia to Fuji, New Guinea, and Australia. Deciduous terrestrial herb, 3–4 ft.; zones 10–11. Blooms late winter, early spring. Seasonally moist/dry. Fertile, coarse, organic, well-drained soil. Broken light in summer, full sun in winter. Flowers: nodding, chocolate brown, white on underside, lip tubular, red to pink, fragrant; bracts large; in racemes, flowering stalk 4–6 ft. tall, emerges near the base of the pseudobulb. Leaves: elliptic, 3–4, pleated, to 3 ft. tall, from the base of an ovoid pseudobulb. *Allow space for a large root system and tall flowering spikes. Suitable for planting in bright understory locations.*

Phalaenopsis

Phalaenopsis includes approximately 50 species of mostly epiphytic, evergreen herbs from the Himalayan foothills, Southeast Asia, Indomalaysia, Philippines, Taiwan, and northeastern Australia. Growth is monopodial. The leaves are broad and fleshy, usually broadly obovate, tongue-shaped, sometimes mottled purplish. Leaves, flower stalks, and aerial roots develop from the nodes of a very short stem. Cultivated species and hybrids commonly have white, pink, or occasionally yellow flowers. The lateral petals are larger than the sepals. The lip is very short, 3-lobed, adorned with 2 antennae-like appendages at the tip of the center lobe, which is attached to the base of the column. The moth-like flowers are often numerous, arranged in opposite ranks (distichous) on one or more gracefully arching stalks, or sometimes a single or a few flowers are on short stalks. Flowers open successively, often over many months. If the old flowering stalk is cut back to about 12 in., leaving several nodes, new flowering shoots or plantlets often develop at the nodes.

Phalaenopsis 'Bamboo Baby' × *P.* 'Coquí'

MOTH-ORCHID

Garden hybrid. Evergreen epiphytic herb; zones 10–11. Blooms late winter, spring, summer. Regular moisture when hot, less when cool. Bark orchid mix. Bright filtered light. Flowers: tepals overlapping, light yellow grading to white in the center, specked with magenta, lip 3-lobed, central lobe triangular, yellow with an orange crest, lateral lobes horn-shaped; on an arching stalk. Leaves: thick, broadly obovate. Phalaenopsis 'Coquí' (P. 'Honeydew × P. amboinensis) *is from the onomatopoetic name of a ubiquitous chirping tree-frog in Puerto Rico.*

Phalaenopsis violacea var. *murtoniana*

Indonesia (Sumatra), Borneo, Malaysia. Evergreen epiphytic herb; zones 10–11. Blooms spring, summer. Regular moisture and humidity, reduce when cool. Bark orchid mix. Bright filtered light. Flowers: waxy, tepals greenish, vivid magenta radiating from lip; flowers open a few at a time, on a short stalk. Leaves: obovate, to 10 in. long, glossy dark green.

Psychopsis

Psychopsis includes approximately 5 species of epiphytic herbs from tropical America. The species were formerly included in *Oncidium*. Leaves are oblong, mottled reddish, arising from the tips of laterally compressed pseudobulbs. Fantastic, insectlike flowers dance at the end of long stalks like bait on a hook, opening 1 or 2 at a time over an extended period.

Psychopsis 'Mendenhall Papilio' × *P.* 'Butterfly'

Synonym: *Oncidium* 'Mendenhall Papilio' × *O.* 'Butterfly'. Garden origin (tropical America). Evergreen epiphytic herb; zones 10–11. Blooms spring, summer. Seasonally moist/dry. Bark orchid mixture. Bright broken light. Flowers: lip large, orbicular, lateral petals falcate, curving down around the lip, russet-brown and yellow; margins ruffled; sepals linear, slightly wider at ends, dark brown, reddish below. *Suitable for baskets.*

Renanthera

Renanthera includes approximately 15 species of mostly epiphytic herbs from the Himalayan foothills, Southeast Asia, Malaysia, and Indonesia to New Guinea. Growth is monopodial. The species may have short stems like *Vanda* or long, canelike clambering stems that may grow into the tree canopy. Leaves are mostly oblong and relatively short. Flowers are mostly scarlet and crimson, produced in many-flowered racemes on long stalks. They are somewhat cold-sensitive. Tall-growing monopodial orchids quickly outgrow containers. They do not like to be cut in short sections or have their roots damaged. A tall, movable stand is ideal. The late Marinus "Dick" Dijkmann, my botany advisor and a much-awarded orchidist, mounted monopodial orchids on stands he created out of hardware cloth rolled into 4- to 6-ft. cylinders with one end set in a concrete square 12 × 12 × 2 in. The cylinders were filled with tree-fern fiber or wrapped in a piece of reed screening. Plants could then be moved into the show area when in bloom or moved under protection during cold snaps.

Renanthera 'Kilauea'

Garden origin (Indomalaysia), *R. storiei* × *R.* 'Brookie Chandler'. Evergreen epiphytic herb; zone 11. Blooms spring, early summer. Regular moisture and humidity. Soil-less. Bright filtered light. Flowers: petals oblong, bases clawed, scarlet with raised maroon spots, edges wavy, lip tiny under the column; sepals linear. Leaves: straplike, keeled, bases clasping the stem; distichous. *Flowers resemble little clowns in polka-dot pants. Cold-sensitive. Needs frequent misting.*

Sobralia

Sobralia includes 100 or more species of terrestrial and epiphytic herbs from tropical America. Leaves are thin or leathery, on reed-like stalks. Flowers are often large, usually solitary, at the ends of the stalks, lasting 1 or 2 days but followed in succession by other flowers over a period of weeks. Most species prefer mild temperatures. Unusual in cultivation but highly recommended.

Sobralia decora

REED-ORCHID

Mexico to Costa Rica. Evergreen terrestrial herb to 3 ft.; zones 10–11. Blooms warm months. Evenly moist and humid, moderate in winter. Well-drained peat, grit, and bark. Bright filtered light. Flowers: petals red-violet, lavender, and white, lip tubular, throat yellow-orange; lower sepals long, spreading horizontally, white to lavender; sweetly fragrant, solitary, terminal, opening successively. Leaves: elliptic, leathery, to 10 in. long, on erect canes. *Flowers resemble bows tied to the ends of the reedlike stems. A clump-forming orchid of tropical mountain regions. Thrives in South Florida.*

×Sophrolaeliocattleya

×Sophrolaeliocattleya (SLC) is the aggregate name of trigeneric hybrids of *Sophronitis*, *Laelia*, and *Cattleya*. *Sophronitis coccinea* lends scarlet coloration to cattleya hybrids.

×Sophrolaeliocattleya 'Jewel Box'

Garden hybrid (tropical America). Evergreen epiphytic herb; zones 10–11. Blooms fall, early winter. Seasonally moist, fairly dry. Orchid mix or mount on tree limb. Bright broken light. Flowers: in clusters of 6–10; tepals scarlet with a sheen of crimson, 3–4 in. wide, fragrant. Leaves: bifoliate, oblong, to 7 in. long; pseudobulbs slender, to 10 in. *'Jewel Box' has greeted holiday visitors at my front door for 30 years. It has survived brief frosty nights growing naturally on the trunk of an oak. Its only care is an occasional spritz of water during extended dry periods. A hybrid by the late George Wakasuki of Miami.*

×Sophrolaeliocattleya 'Ocelot'

Garden hybrid, *Cattleya* 'Brabantine' × ×*SLC* 'Precious Stones'. Evergreen epiphytic herb; zones 10–11. Blooms spring. Seasonally moist, fairly dry. Orchid mix. Bright filtered light. Flowers: tepals red-orange and yellow with dark red spots, throat yellow, column violet, lip 3-lobed, lateral lobes white, central lobe red. Leaves: bifoliate, oblong.

Spathoglottis

Spathoglottis includes approximately 30 species of terrestrial herbs from tropical Asia and Australia, with greatest diversity in New Guinea. Leaves are sword-shaped or pleated (plicate). Flowers are borne at the end of a stalk, which is taller than the leaves. The center lobe of the 3-lobed lip has a slender clawed base and side appendages. The name means "spathelike tongue." Nursery plants are usually labeled *S. plicata*. However, hybridizing these species is an industry in Southeast Asia and it is likely that most plants in cultivation are complex hybrids for which a species name is inappropriate. Species are self-pollinating and self-seeding, while the hybrids are usually sterile.

Spathoglottis hybrids

Garden hybrids (India, Southeast Asia, Malaysia, Philippines). Evergreen terrestrial herbs, 1.5–2 ft.; zones 10–11. Bloom most of the year. Regular moisture, moderate in cool weather. Sandy, gritty, humus-rich, well-drained soil. Part sun. Flowers: about 1 in. wide, tepals various colors, central lobe of lip long-stalked; in upright clusters at the end of a long stalk. Leaves: elliptic, pleated, 1–1.5 ft. long. *Clump-forming. Appearance is fresher with a little protection from hot midday sun in summer.*

Stanhopea

Stanhopea includes 30–55 species of epiphytic, rarely lithophytic herbs from Mexico to Peru and Brazil. Growth is sympodial. Leaves are unifoliate or bifoliate, elliptic to lanceolate, up to 20 in. long, developing from the ends of small, ovoid pseudobulbs. Flowers are large, contorted, fragrant, and fairly short-lived. Buds open with an explosive pop. The sepals are often curled backwards (revolute). The flowering stalk develops from the base of the pseudobulb. Because the flower stalks grow downward stanhopeas are usually grown in shallow baskets or on tree-fern slabs or with the container hung on its side (see photo).

Renanthera 'Kilauea'

×*Sophrolaeliocattleya* 'Ocelot'

×*Sophrolaeliocattleya* 'Jewel Box'

Sobralia decora

Stanhopea tigrina

Mexico to Brazil. Evergreen epiphytic herb; zones 10–11. Blooms spring. Seasonally moist/dry. Open orchid mix. Medium filtered light. Flowers: lateral petals oblong, spreading, maroon and cream splashed, lip 3-lobed, cream with purplish speckles; sepals narrow, spotted, edges revolute; very fragrant. Leaves: pleated, 15–20 in. long.

Vanda

Vanda includes 35–45 species of epiphytic herbs from the foothills of the Himalayas to Malaysia. Growth is monopodial. Leaves are strap-shaped, keeled; bases are overlapping (imbricate) and clasp the stem. Leaves are arranged in opposite ranks (distichous). Species with terete or semiterete leaves are now segregated into *Papilionanthe*. The tepals are similar, some narrow with revolute margins, others large and spreading. The lip is smaller than the tepals, 3-lobed, and fused at the base to the short column. Flower spikes develop from the nodes. Vandas are stressed by cold, often dropping leaves below 50°F. Long aerial roots grow from the nodes and should be protected from breakage by hanging the pot or basket high. The plants need daily misting when hot. Vandas thrive outdoors under an open canopy in warm humid seasons, but most need protection on cool evenings. They can be grow on a stand (see description under *Renanthera*).

Vanda 'First and Last'

Garden hybrid. Evergreen epiphytic herb; zone 11. Blooms spring. Regular moisture and humidity. Support only or bark mix. Bright filtered light. Flowers: tepals clawed, lateral petals twisted slightly, white background densely spotted with magenta. Leaves: strap-shaped. *Cold-sensitive.*

Vanda luzonica

Philippines. Evergreen epiphytic herb; zone 11. Blooms fall. Regular moisture and humidity Support only or bark mix. Bright filtered light. Flowers: tepals narrow, revolute at base, spreading at tips, not-overlapping, white with maroon spots, to 3 in. wide. Leaves: strap-shaped, keeled to about 1 ft. long, in opposite ranks. *Of tropical rain forests. Cold-sensitive.*

Zeuxine

Zeuxine (pronounced ZOO-scene) includes approximately 25 species of perennial and 1 of annual terrestrial herbs from Africa, Madagascar, China, and Southeast Asia. Leaves are narrowly lanceolate or linear, sometimes reddish, on a short stalk. Flowers are small, the lip partly fused to the short column. There are 4 pollinia. Sepals form a hood over the column. *Zeuxine strateumatica* is difficult to propagate intentionally but has been widely distributed in topsoil, and has become naturalized throughout Florida and southern Georgia. It pops up as a dainty, if uninvited, guest only to disappear after flowering.

Zeuxine strateumatica

China, Southeast Asia, Sri Lanka, Malaysia; naturalized in Florida, southeastern Georgia. Annual herb, 6–8 in.; zones 8–11. Blooms midwinter. Evenly moist. Humus-rich, well-drained soil. Full sun to part shade. Flowers: tiny, white, lip

Spathoglottis hybrids

Stanhopea tigrina

Vanda 'First and Last'

Vanda luzonica

yellow; in erect, spirelike terminal spikes, flowers interspersed by leaflike bracts. Leaves: linear to sword-shaped, 2–3 in. long, olive-green. *The only known annual orchid. Self-seeding but difficult to propagate or transplant. The species name alludes to columns of tin soldiers with plumed hats and leaf-blade swords.*

OXALIDACEAE

CARAMBOLA FAMILY, OXALIS FAMILY
Oxalidaceae includes approximately 8 genera of perennial herbs and shrubs plus a few trees primarily from tropical and subtropical regions. Leaves are trifoliolate or pinnately or palmately compound. Some have a joint (pulvinus) at the base of the leaf blade that allows the leaves to fold. Flowers are bisexual and radially symmetrical. The fruit is usually a capsule.

Averrhoa

Averrhoa includes 2 species of trees from Indonesia. This genus is segregated into its own family, Averrhoaceae, by some authorities. Leaves are pinnately compound, the leaflets uneven in number (imparipinnate). The flowers have 10 alternately long and short stamens. Inflorescences are borne in the leaf axils as well as directly from the branches and trunk (cauliflorous). Fruits are fleshy, often produced in profusion. They contain oxalate (as do eggplant and spinach), which is harmless to most people but may be contraindicated for people with a history of kidney stones.

Averrhoa bilimbi

CUCUMBER-TREE, BILIMBI
Exact origin obscure (probably Indonesia); widely naturalized in tropics. Evergreen tree, 20–45 ft.; zones 10–11. Blooms spring, summer. Seasonally moist/dry. Fertile, well-drained soil. Full sun. Flowers: petals purple to blood red, more or less revolute; calyx cuplike with small, toothlike lobes; inflorescences in the leaf axils and cauliflorous; fruit oblong, acid, green, usually speckled with white spots. Leaves: pinnate; leaflets about 25–31, oblong, 3–4 in. long, tips caudate. *Edible fruits look very much like gherkin pickles hanging on short stalks from the limbs.*

Averrhoa carambola

CARAMBOLA, STAR-FRUIT
Exact origin obscure (probably Indonesia). Evergreen tree, 20–30 ft.; zones 10–11. Blooms warm months. Seasonally moist/dry. Moderately fertile, sandy soil. Full sun. Flowers: small, pink, throat magenta; in many-flowered panicles, stalks red; fruit generally ovoid with 5 wedge-shaped wings, waxy, greenish yellow to golden. Leaves: pinnate; leaflets 7–9, lanceolate. *Fruit pleasantly fragrant, texture crisp. Cultivar flavors vary from bland to tart or sweet. 'B10' is recommended. Sweetest when edges start to turn brown. Cross-cut, star-shaped slices are used to adorn dinner or fruit salads.*

Zeuxine strateumatica

Averrhoa carambola

Oxalis

Oxalis includes approximately 800 species of herbs and subshrubs, which are widely distributed in the tropics and mild temperate regions, most abundant in South Africa and South America. A number are common weeds. They have fibrous roots or tubers. Leaves are palmate, with 3 or sometimes 4 often heart-shaped leaflets. They contain oxalate, which gives them an astringent taste. Flowers are bisexual and radially symmetrical. The 5 free petals and sepals are pink, purple, yellow, or occasionally white. The fruit is a capsule. As the capsule ripens, the aril squeezes the seed until it spurts forcibly from the capsule (dehiscent) accounting for its wide dispersal (Howard, pers. comm.).

Oxalis tetraphylla

IRON-CROSS OXALIS, WOOD-SORREL, GOOD-LUCK PLANT
Synonym: *O. deppei*. Mexico, Panama. Perennial bulbous herb under 1 ft.; zones 8–10. Blooms warm months. Moderate but regular moisture. Fertile, humus-rich, well-drained soil. Part sun, bright filtered light. Flowers: pink or white; borne in umbels on stalks that are longer than the leaves. Leaves: basal, palmate; leaflets 4, purple near the bases. *A stemless herb with distinctive purple markings in the center of the leaves.*

PANDANACEAE

PANDANUS FAMILY, SCREW-PINE FAMILY
Pandanaceae includes 3 genera of mostly fibrous trunked trees plus a few climbers from the Old World

Averrhoa bilimbi

tropics, maritime Southeast Asia, and Australia. Most species are salt-tolerant trees of coastal areas and islands with stilt roots that give stability in shifting sands. Leaves are linear to sword-shaped, often with sharply toothed margins, sessile, in 2–4 ranks, and often arranged in spirals around a twisting trunklike stem (hence the name screw-pine). The flowers are reduced or the perianth is in 2 whorls of 5. They are bisexual but functionally unisexual, with male and female on different plants (dioecious) or combined with bisexual flowers (polygamous). Flowers are free, axillary or cauliflorous, or in indistinct panicle-like or racemelike inflorescences, or arranged on a spadixlike structure, either axillary, terminal, or in fascicles. Bracts are often petal- or spathelike. The fruit is a drupe, berry, or rarely a capsule, often in an aggregate or syncarp.

Freycinetia

Freycinetia includes approximately 175 species of climbing shrubs from Sri Lanka, Southeast Asia, and Oceania. Adherent aerial roots are produced at the nodes. Leaves are lanceolate, keeled, in opposite ranks (distichous). Flowers are reduced, arranged on a spadixlike structure. The inflorescences are each subtended by 3 petal-like bracts and clusters of 3 inflorescences are subtended by 3 spathes. The fruits are berries, partly fused into a syncarp. The habit is somewhat palmlike or bamboolike in appearance, the stems limber.

Freycinetia cumingiana
FLOWERING PANDANUS
Philippines. Evergreen climber; zone 11. Blooms late winter, spring. Regular moisture. Fast-draining mixture of sand, grit, and bark. Bright filtered light. Flowers: unisexual, perianth absent; on small green spadix; bracts triangular, pinkish orange, to 2 in. long. Leaves: lanceolate, 8–10 in. long; margins sharply serrulate. *Palm- or bamboolike with striking inflorescences. Grow in protected locations outside or in containers. Stake or tie errant shoots. Can be pruned occasionally.*

Pandanus

Pandanus includes approximately 750 species of trees and shrubs from the Old World tropics. Most of these species have not been studied. A few are cultivated for their striking architectural branching. They are very salt tolerant and develop large prop roots for support on beaches. Some produce impenetrable clumps suitable for large barrier hedges and windbreaks. Leaves are sword-shaped, often pleated, usually with sharply toothed margins and a row of sharp teeth along the back of the midrib. They spiral in 3 ranks around the ends of twisting branches. Flowers are unisexual, with male and female inflorescences on different plants (dioecious) or sometimes asexual (apomictic). The perianth is absent. Female flowers are densely arranged on a spadixlike inflorescence, male flowers in panicle-like clusters. The stamens are large and branched. Inflorescences are protected by numerous spathelike bracts. The fruits are fibrous syncarps, somewhat resembling pineapples, sometimes with edible but difficult-to-reach soft parts. As they age, the fruits partially divide into "keys" (segments).

Leaves are used for thatch and woven into rope, baskets, hats, mats, and whimsical toys such as grasshoppers. Though *Pandanus* grow naturally on beaches and coastal woodlands, cultivated species are xeric inland and drought tolerant. They are important on Pacific Islands for beach erosion control—the counterpart of mangrove species elsewhere. Many species are endangered and some are already extinct. Native species are protected in Australia.

Pandanus species
VARIEGATED PANDANUS,
VARIEGATED SCREW-PINE
Origin unknown. Evergreen shrub or tree to 10 ft.+; zones 10–11. Bloom unknown . Moderate moisture. Sandy, well-drained soil or beach sand. Full sun. Flowers: unisexual. Leaves: sword-shaped, to 5 in. wide and 4 ft. long, green near the margins with a pale yellow stripe toward the midrib, flat; margins not sharply toothed; in spiral clusters. *Identification uncertain. The common variegated pandanus in cultivation is usually identified as P. tectorius var. sinensis (syn. P. veitchii); however, the pictured species has much broader, longer, flat leaves, with unarmed margins.*

Pandanus tectorius
SCREW-PINE, WALKING TREE,
HALA (HAWAII), PANDAN (ASIA)
Synonym: *P. odoratissimus*. Indonesia, Australia (Queensland), Micronesia to Hawaii. Evergreen tree, 15–30 ft.+; zones 10–11. Blooms winter or intermittently. Moderate moisture. Sandy, well-drained soil or beach sand. Full sun. Flowers: unisexual; fruit partially fused, segments separate into small clusters of several keys, ripening orange. Leaves: sword-shaped, to 3 ft. long, drooping, pleated lengthwise into an M in cross section; margins with green spines. *Fleshy base of fruit edible. Male flowers fragrant. Suitable for coastal planting and for beach erosion control. The species name means "of roofs," perhaps alluding to its use for thatch.*

Pandanus utilis
SCREW-PINE, PANDANO,
PALMA DE CINTA
Origin obscure (perhaps Madagascar); widely distributed. Evergreen tree, 30–60 ft.; zones 10–11. Blooms winter or intermittently. Moderate moisture. Sandy, well-drained soil or beach sand. Full sun. Flowers: unisexual; fruit a syncarp separating into individual segments (keys)

Oxalis tetraphylla

Freycinetia cumingiana

Pandanus species

Pandanus tectorius

at the ends, not in clusters. Leaves: sword-shaped, green, flat; margins red-spined; in stiffly erect spiral clusters at branch tips. *Used to control beach erosion. Slow growing. Clean out old leaves to expose branching. Fruit is food for small island animals.*

PAPAVERACEAE
POPPY FAMILY

Papaveraceae includes approximately 23 genera of mostly annual and perennial herbs or subshrubs and a few small pachycaulous trees, primarily from northern temperate regions but with a few from the tropics. They usually have milky, yellow or orange sap. Some are cultivated as ornamentals, for poppy seeds, or for pain-killing pharmaceuticals such as morphine as well as illegal opiates. Leaves are simple, entire, or sometimes lobed. Flowers are bisexual and radially symmetrical or slightly asymmetrical. The 2 or 3 sepals are free or united. The petals are crumpled, usually large and showy, twice as numerous as the sepals, and in 2 whorls. Stamens are usually numerous. Flowers are mostly solitary, occasionally in panicles. The fruit is usually a capsule, dispersing seeds through pores or sometimes explosively (dehiscent).

Argemone

Argemone includes approximately 23 species of herbs and shrubs from North and South America, the West Indies, and 1 from Hawaii. The leaves are bluish gray (glaucous), usually deeply lobed, with sharply toothed margins and prickles along the back of the midrib. Flowers are solitary, often sessile in the leaf axils.

Argemone mexicana
PRICKLY POPPY, CHICALOTE

Mexico; widely naturalized. Perennial herb to 2 ft.; zones 8–11. Blooms warm months. Moderate moisture to seasonally dry. Poor, well-drained soil. Full sun. Flowers: petals 6, yellow, sometimes creamy white; solitary in the leaf axils. Leaves: deeply lobed, green or bluish; margins sharply toothed and spined. *A common weedy species of disturbed areas.*

Pandanus utilis, male flowers

Pandanus utilis, fruit

Pandanus utilis, trunks

Argemone mexicana

Argemone rosea

Argemone rosea

PINK ARGEMONE,
PINK PRICKLY POPPY

Chile, Argentina. Perennial herb; zones 9–11. Blooms warm months. Moderate moisture to fairly dry. Average to poor, well-drained soil. Full sun. Flowers: petals 6, white and pink toward the margins; solitary on a stalk. Leaves: deeply lobed, blue-gray; margins spiny-toothed. *Identification tentative but likely (Schwartz, pers. comm.). Acquired through the* Index Seminum *by Quail Botanical Garden. Rare, probably endangered. Most argemones have white or yellow flowers.*

Eschscholzia

Eschscholzia includes 8–10 species of annual or short-lived perennial herbs from the western United States and Mexico. They have clear sap. The leaves are basal, gray, and dissected, not spined. Flowers have 4–6 petals and are on long stalks.

Eschscholzia californica

CALIFORNIA POPPY

Western United States; naturalized in Europe. Annual herb, 1–2 ft.; zones 6–10. Blooms spring, early summer. Moderate moisture to fairly dry. Average to poor, well-drained soil. Full sun. Flowers: rotate, petals usually 4, orange-yellow. Leaves: basal, deeply dissected, gray-green, somewhat parsleylike. *A cultivated western wild flower often seen in open meadows from Oregon to southern California. Does not thrive in moist/humid regions. Many cultivars are available in-cluding doubles in reds, orange-pinks, and whites. Flowers do not open on overcast days.*

Romneya

Romneya includes a single species, a semiwoody perennial shrub from California and Baja California. This spreading shrub is cultivated throughout the southwestern United States. Leaves are deeply and irregularly lobed and gray-green (glaucous). Flowers are white, scented, and solitary at the ends of the branches. Said to be difficult to establish, but once started it can become a pest in warmer areas.

Romneya coulteri

MATILIJA POPPY,
CALIFORNIA TREE-POPPY

California, Mexico (Baja California). Perennial shrub to 8 ft.; zones 7–10. Blooms warm months. Moderate moisture to dry. Average to poor, sandy, well-drained soil. Full sun. Flowers: petals 6; solitary opening in succession over an extended period. Leaves: deeply lobed, glaucous. *Protect roots from freezing. Salt tolerant. Can be controlled somewhat by limiting water and fertilizer. After flowering, prune to 1 or 2 ft.*

PASSIFLORACEAE

PASSION-FLOWER FAMILY

Passifloraceae includes approximately 18 genera of climbers and a few shrubs from mild temperate and tropical regions, with greatest diversity in moist South American woodlands. Vines climb by tendrils. Leaves are simple or compound, palmately lobed or bilobed, often with pairs of yellow glands on the petioles. The flowers are usually bisexual and radially symmetrical. They have 5 petal-like sepals and 5 petals. The distinctive, fringelike corona, in one or more rings, is an outgrowth of the rim of the floral cup (hypanthium). The stamen filaments are fused into a prominent column, and a stalk (gynophore) supports the ovary. There are 3–5 anthers surrounding 1–3 stigmas. The flowers are solitary. The fruit is a berry or sometimes a capsule. These species are pollinated by birds, insects, and bats.

Passiflora

Passiflora includes approximately 480 species of herbaceous and woody climbers primarily from South America. Commonly called passion-flowers, these species are often cultivated for their elaborate flowers and a few for their aromatic, edible fruits. The juice is often used in commercial fruit punches. Self-sterile, most cultivated passion-flowers must be cross-pollinated by hand. Many are somewhat salt tolerant and suitable for seaside fences and balcony railings. Growth can be restricted somewhat by confining the roots in small containers and pruning. Passion-flowers attract butterflies including Julia, postman, zebra, queen, and the Gulf fritillary and serve as host to their larvae. Flowers are said to have been used by priests to illustrate the Passion of Christ to South American natives.

Passiflora 'Amethyst'

AMETHYST PASSION-FLOWER,
PASIONARIA

Synonyms: *P. amethystina* (misapplied), *P.* 'Lavender Lady', *P. violacea* (hort.). Garden hybrid. Evergreen perennial climber; zones 9–11. Blooms warm months. Regular moisture when hot, less when cool. Average to fertile, well-drained soil. Full to part sun. Flowers: pinkish violet, to 5 in. wide; corona deep purple with a white band; stamens greenish; fruit orange. Leaves: deeply 3-lobed, 3–4 in. long, dull green. *Ancestry uncertain, possibly a hybrid of* P. caerulea *and/or* P. amethystina. *Often misidentified as* P. amethystina *(Vanderplank 1991). Fruit not good eating. Tolerates near-freezing temperatures. Coastal. Suitable for containers.*

Passiflora ×belotii

PINK AND PURPLE PASSION-FLOWER

Synonyms: *P.* ×*alato-caerulea* (hort.), *P.* 'Empress Eugenie' (hort.). Garden hybrid, *P. alata* × *P. caerulea*. Evergreen climber to 50 ft.; zones 9–11. Blooms winter, spring. Regular moisture when hot, less when cool. Average to fertile, well-drained soil. Full to part sun. Flowers: petals pink; sepals white, edges smooth; outer corona ring purple with white bands, 2 inner rings short. Leaves: ovate, entire to 3-lobed. *Commonly cultivated. Marginally hardy and somewhat salt tol-*

Eschscholzia californica

Romneya coulteri

Passiflora 'Amethyst'

Passiflora ×*belotii*

erant. Often listed as P. caerulea, *an unusual species in the United States which has bluish white flowers and 5-lobed leaves.*

Passiflora coccinea

RED PASSION-FLOWER, GRANADILLA ROJA

Synonyms: *P. fulgens, P. toxicaria, P. velutina*. South America (Amazon basin). Evergreen climber; zones 9–11. Blooms warm months. Regular moisture when hot, less when cool. Average to fertile, well-drained soil. Full to part sun. Flowers: tepals often strongly reflexed, to 2 in. wide, cardinal red; coronas 2, short, erect, outer whorl blood red, inner whorl white. Leaves: entire, ovate, to 6 in. long, glossy; margins dentate. *Plants in cultivation may be hybrids. Orange or yellow fruit good eating quality. Distinguish from P. vitifolia by the unlobed leaves and absence of awns on the sepal tips.*

Passiflora edulis

PASSION-FRUIT VINE, GRANADILLA MORADA, MARACUYÁ

Synonym: *P. pallidiflora*. Brazil, Paraguay, northern Argentina; widely naturalized. Evergreen climber; zones 8–10. Blooms warm months. Seasonally moist, less when cool. Moderately fertile, well-drained soil. Full to part sun. Flowers: tepals white inside, corona purple with crinkled white tips, as long as the tepals. Leaves: 3-lobed, to 8 in. long. *This is the principal commercial species. Forma edulis has purple fruit; forma flavicarpa has yellow fruit. In Australia, the yellow and purple forms are cross-pollinated for disease resistance. Carpenter bees, where present, pollinate flowers. Invasive pest in Hawaii.*

Passiflora foetida

GOAT-SCENTED PASSION-FLOWER, PARCHITA DE CULEBRA, MARACUYÁ DE COBRA

Synonym: *P. gossipiifolia*. Central and South America, West Indies; widely naturalized. Perennial climber; zones 10–11. Blooms warm months. Seasonally moist, less when cool. Average, well-drained soil. Full to part sun. Flowers: tepals small, pink, corona purple and white, 1–2 in. wide; bracts much dissected, filamentous;

sweet-musky fragrance. Leaves: entire, ovate, or 3-lobed, to 4 in. long, dull green. *Extremely variable with more than 50 named varieties. The finely dissected bracts are a distinctive field mark. Coastal. Self-propagating and sometimes weedy.*

Passiflora 'Incense'

PURPLE PASSION-FLOWER, PASIONARIA

Garden hybrid, *P. incarnata × P. cincinnata*. Evergreen perennial climber; zones 8–11. Blooms warm months. Regular moisture when hot, less when cool. Average to fertile, well-drained soil. Full to part sun. Flowers: tepals purple; corona purple and violet, ends crinkled, as long as the petals. Leaves: palmate; leaflets 5, elliptic. *Developed experimentally at the Subtropical Horticulture Research Station (USDA), Chapman Field, in Dade County,*

Florida, for cold hardiness. Fruit edible, slightly acid.

Passiflora phoenicea

FRAGRANT PASSION-FLOWER

Synonym: *P. alata* 'Ruby Glow' (hort.). Brazil. Perennial climber to 50 ft.; zones 10–11. Blooms warm months. Seasonally moist, moderate moisture when cool. Average, well-drained soil. Full to part sun. Flowers: tepals to 6 in. wide, deep pink inside; corona cup-shaped, purple with white bands; bracts 3, green; intensely fragrant. Leaves: entire, broadly ovate, 6–8 in. long, 5–6 in. wide; one pair of yellow glands on petiole below blade. *Vigorous vine. Visited by Heliconius butterflies in my garden but not used as a host plant or eaten by larvae. Previously thought to be a form of P. alata. Flowers are more substantial and corona larger (Vanderplank 1991).*

Passiflora quadrangularis

GIANT PASSION-FLOWER, MARACUYÁ, SANDIA DE LA PASIÓN, TUMBO

Synonyms: *P. macrocarpa, P. tetragona*. West Indies, Central America; widely naturalized. Perennial climber; zones 10–11. Blooms warm months. Seasonally moist, moderate moisture when cool. Moderately fertile, well-drained soil. Full to part sun. Flowers: tepals purple and red; corona crinkled, purple- and white-banded; fruit ovoid, ð 10 in. long, orange to yellowish when ripe. Leaves: entire; petiole with 2 pairs of yellow glands. *Fruit large and good quality (hence the Spanish name meaning watermelon passion-fruit). It is pleasantly aromatic. Hybrids are easily confused with the species. Passiflora ×decaisneana (P. alata × P. quadrangularis) has red tepals.*

Passiflora coccinea

Passiflora edulis

Passiflora edulis, fruit

Passiflora foetida

Passiflora 'Incense'

Passiflora quadrangularis

Passiflora vitifolia

SCARLET PASSION-FLOWER
Synonyms: *P. punicea, P. sanguinea.*
Nicaragua to Peru. Perennial
climber; zones 10–11. Blooms
warm months. Moderate moisture.
Average, well-drained soil. Full to
part sun. Flowers: petals scarlet,
pointed, sepals with awns (needlelike appendages at tips). Leaves:
deeply 3-lobed, 5–7 in. long; margins serrate. Stems: with rust-colored hairs. *The species name alludes
to the lobed, somewhat grapelike
leaves. Not attractive to butterflies in
the United States. Passiflora coccinea is distinguished by its entire
leaves and the sepals are not awned.*

Passiflora xiikzodz

BAT-WINGED PASSION-FLOWER
Belize, eastern Guatemala, southeastern Mexico. Perennial climber;
zones 10–11. Blooms warm
months. Moderate moisture to dry.
Average, sandy, well-drained soil;
alkaline pH. Full to part sun. Flowers: petals absent; sepals 5, green,
petal-like, 1–1.5 wide; corona black
with white tips. Leaves: 2-lobed,
winglike, to 5 in. wide, peltate, mottled dark green, rubbery. Xiikzodz
*(pronounced ZIK-shots) means "bat-
wing" in Tzotzil, the language of the
Mayan Indians. Of coastal limestone
ridge. The unusual leaves lie flat
against walls or fences. Xeric. Suitable as ground cover in dry areas.*

PAULOWNIACEAE

PAULOWNIA FAMILY
Paulowniaceae includes a single
genus of trees from mild temperate
to subtropical Asia. These species
have intermediate characteristics
between the figwort family, Scrophulariaceae, and the tabebuia
family, Bignoniaceae. Leaves are
simple. Flowers are bilaterally symmetrical. The petals are fused at the
base and the lower petal is slightly
enlarged into a lip. The fruit is an
ovoid woody, 4-chambered capsule
with many small, winged seeds.

Paulownia

Paulownia includes 6 species of deciduous trees from mild temperate
to subtropical Asia. Some are
grown as timber trees for their fine
cabinetry wood. Leaves are simple,
large, and covered with slightly
sticky, glandular hairs. Flowers are
bisexual and bilaterally symmetrical. The corolla is trumpet- or bell-
shaped, the 5 petals fused at the
base with spreading lobes. The
lower lobes are slightly enlarged
into a lip. The inflorescence is a
large terminal panicle. Princess
tree, *P. tomentosa*, has large cordate, shallowly lobed leaves. It is
heavily self-seeding and highly invasive in temperate areas of the
southeastern United States. Harvesting for fine wood is recommended as a control.

Paulownia kawakamii

EMPRESS-TREE, FOXGLOVE-TREE,
ROYAL PAULOWNIA
Synonyms: *P. thyrsoidea, P. viscosa.*
Southern China, Taiwan. Deciduous
tree to 35 ft.+; zones 8–10. Blooms
late spring, early summer. Moderate moisture. Average to poor, well-
drained soil. Full sun. Flowers: corolla bell-shaped, lobes 5, the lower
2 somewhat enlarged into a lip,
light violet, throat pale yellow; in
erect terminal panicles. Leaves: cordate, to 12 in. long, 10 in. wide, with
3–5 shallow lobes, dark green; with
sticky, glandular hairs. *Tender when
young, hardy once established. Fast-
growing. Wood used in fine cabinetry.*

Passiflora phoenicea

Passiflora vitifolia

Passiflora xiikzodz

Paulownia kawakamii 'Sapphire Dragon'

PEDALIACEAE

SESAME FAMILY

Pedaliaceae includes approximately 17 genera of mostly herbs, occasionally shrubs or small trees, from mild temperate and tropical regions, primarily in coastal or arid locations. This family is related to the trumpet-creeper family, Bignoniaceae, as evidenced by the flower shape, but it differs by having mucilaginous glands and simple leaves. Leaves are simple, entire or dissected and oppositely arranged at least on lower branches. Flowers are bisexual and bilaterally symmetrical. The 5 sepals are partly united. The 5 petals are partly united and spurred. The flowers are usually solitary. The fruit is a barbed or winged capsule. Sesame, *Sesamum indicum*, has been cultivated in the Middle East since ancient times for nutritious seeds and oil.

Uncarina

Uncarina includes approximately 9 species of shrubs or small trees from Madagascar. Trunks and branches are pachycaulous and there is sometimes an underground caudex. The corolla is trumpet-shaped with spreading lobes, the lower 2 lobes slightly enlarged into a lip. *Uncarina* species are popular with succulent hobbyists and are becoming more widely appreciated. Trees have cultural requirements similar to *Adenium obesum*.

Uncarina grandidieri

Madagascar. Briefly deciduous shrub or small tree to 10 ft.; zones 9–11. Blooms warm months. Moderate moisture to fairly dry. Average, sandy, well-drained soil; alkaline pH. Full sun. Flowers: trumpet-shaped, golden-yellow, throat usually maroon/purple; solitary; capsules are winged and have stalked, glandular protuberances. Leaves: cordate, shallowly lobed, surface undulate and covered with velvety glandular hairs; petiole long, red with white hairs. Trunk and branches are pachycaulous. *Thrives in moist climates with excellent drainage. Yellow-flowered* U. decaryi *has 3-lobed leaves cut nearly to the midvein.* Uncarina abbreviata *has violet-pink flowers and lanceolate leaves.*

PHYTOLACCACEAE

POKEWEED FAMILY

Phytolaccaceae includes approximately 17 genera of mostly herbs, occasionally shrubs or trees, primarily from tropical America with a number from North America and South Africa. Anticancer pharmaceuticals and pesticides are derived from some species. Many species are toxic. Leaves are simple and alternately or spirally arranged. Flowers are reduced, usually bisexual, radially symmetrical, and borne in catkinlike racemes. They lack petals and the sepals are petal-like. Bracts are usually present.

Phytolacca

Phytolacca includes approximately 25 species of herbs, plus a few shrubs and trees from the tropics and temperate regions. *Phytolacca dioica* has unisexual flowers, male and female flowers are on separate individuals (dioecious). It is grown as a shade tree in southern Europe and Latin America. Pokeweed, *P. americana*, is a common weedy species in the eastern United States.

Phytolacca dioica

BELLA SOMBRA, BELLA UMBRA (SPANISH AND ITALIAN FOR "BEAUTIFUL SHADE")

Synonyms: *P. arborea*, *P. populifolia*. South America. Evergreen tree, 20–60 ft.; zones 9–10. Blooms spring, early summer. Moderate moisture to fairly dry. Average, well-drained soil. Full sun. Flowers: unisexual, petals absent; male flowers greenish white, to 0.5 in. wide, in 6- to 8-in. catkinlike racemes; female inflorescence short; fruit purple. Leaves: ovate to 8 in. long, leathery; veins and petiole yellowish. *Fast growing, somewhat pachycaulous tree. Grows in moist regions with excellent drainage. Develops buttresses with age. The species name means "dioecious."*

PIPERACEAE

Piperaceae includes 5–8 genera of herbs, some climbers, shrubs, or trees, which are widely distributed in the tropics. It belongs to a primitive group of paleoherbs, neither monocot nor dicot. *Peperomia* includes more than 1000 species, some grown as houseplants. Leaves are simple, entire, often fleshy. Flowers are usually unisexual with male and female flowers on the same plant (monoecious), on different plants (dioecious), or combined with bisexual flowers (polygamous). They are reduced, lack a perianth, and are densely arranged on slender spadixlike spikes. Bracts are present, often peltate.

Uncarina grandidieri

Uncarina grandidieri, flowers

Phytolacca dioica

Piper

Piper includes approximately 2000 species of herbs, some woody climbers and a few shrubs. Black pepper, *P. nigrum*, is the most widely consumed spice. It is cultivated in the tropics and has become naturalized in many areas, sometimes becoming invasive. Pipers have scattered vascular bundles and swollen or jointed stem nodes.

Piper auritum

EAR-LEAFED PEPPER, CORDONCILLO
Mexico, Central America, Colombia. Perennial herb, 6–15 ft.; zones 10–11. Blooms warm months. Seasonally moist, moderate. Average, well-drained soil. Full sun to medium filtered light. Flowers: white, rudimentary; on erect, slender spikes with drooping ends, 6–11 in. long; inflorescence borne opposite a leaf; fruit a small drupe. Leaves: simple, cordate, to 12 in. long, sides of base unequal, tip acuminate, softly hairy; petiole winged, often reddish. Stems: swollen nodes, long internodes. *A semi-woody species that produces large stands through suckering. Seeds are bat-dispersed. An invasive pest in Micronesia and other areas. Not recommended.*

Piper nigrum

BLACK PEPPER, PIMIENTA
India, Sri Lanka, Peninsular Malaysia. Perennial climber to 10 ft.+; zones 10–11. Blooms warm months. Regular moisture. Average, well-drained soil. Filtered light. Flowers: rudimentary, bisexual or unisexual, perianth absent, greenish; on pendent, slender spikes, inflorescences borne opposite a leaf, 4–6 in. long; fruit a small yellow to red drupe, drying black. Leaves: ovate, 4–6 in. long, tip acute, base cordate; palmate venation; petioles to 1 in. *White pepper is the same species with the black outer seedcoat removed, sometimes preferred for a more aesthetic appearance in light-colored dishes.*

PITTOSPORACEAE

PITTOSPORUM FAMILY
Pittosporaceae includes approximately 11 genera of trees, shrubs, and occasionally woody climbers (lianas), primarily from the Old World tropics and mild temperate regions, with greatest diversity in Australia. Leaves are simple, usually firm to leathery, with a resinous, conifer-like aroma when crushed. Flowers are usually radially symmetrical, bisexual or unisexual with male and female flowers on separate plants (dioecious) or combined with bisexual flowers (polygamous). They have 5 partly fused sepals, 5 partly fused petals, and 5 stamens. Flowers are solitary or in cymes or panicles. Bracts are present. The fruit is a capsule or berry.

Hymenosporum

Hymenosporum includes a single species of evergreen tree from eastern Australia and New Guinea. It is distinguished by its winged arillate seeds. *Hymenosporum flavum* thrives in southern California and is cultivated in other dry, subtropical climates as well as in mountainous regions of South America.

Hymenosporum flavum

SWEET-SHADE,
AUSTRALIAN FRANGIPANI
Synonym: *Pittosporum flavum*. Eastern Australia, New Guinea. Evergreen tree, 20–40 ft.+; zones 9–11. Blooms spring, early summer. Moderate moisture in winter, dry in summer. Average to fertile, well-

Piper auritum

Piper nigrum, with flower spikes

Hymenosporum flavum, flowers

Hymenosporum flavum

drained soil. Full to part sun. Flowers: trumpet-shaped, tube to 2 in. long, lobes spreading, twisted, creamy yellow to golden with age, throat reddish brown, fragrant; in dense terminal panicles, small capsules contain a single winged seed. Leaves: oblanceolate, tip apiculate, 4–6 in. long. *Fast-growing. Protect from harsh midday sun while young. Thrives in Mediterranean-type climate. Highly recommended.*

Pittosporum

Pittosporum includes 100–150 species of trees and shrubs from warm temperate and tropical areas of the Old World. Tropical species are generally from montane regions and somewhat cold tolerant. A number of species are cultivated, often as hedge plants. Leaves are simple, leathery. Flowers are creamy white, scented and borne in clusters. Fruits are usually bright orange. Cultivated species are often maintained as shrubs or hedges by pruning. Some species are potentially weedy. *Pittosporum pentandrum* is naturalized in disturbed areas and the edges of woodland hammocks in extreme southern Florida (Hammer, pers. comm.).

Pittosporum tobira

MOCK ORANGE,
JAPANESE PITTOSPORUM
China, Japan, Korea. Evergreen shrub or tree, 10–15 ft.; zones 8–10. Blooms spring, early summer. Regular moisture when hot, drier when cool. Sandy, well-drained soil. Full to part sun, bright broken light. Flowers: bell-shaped, creamy white turning yellow, citruslike fragrance; in rounded, terminal umbels; fruit round, yellow; seeds red. Leaves: obovate, 2–4 in. long, tips rounded, firm, glossy; margins recurved; in terminal whorls. *From subtropical coastal forest. Moderately salt tolerant. Used for dense hedges or screening.* 'Variegata' *has gray-green and white leaves.* 'Wheeler's Dwarf' *is suitable for low hedges.*

PLANTAGINACEAE

DIGITALIS FAMILY
Plantaginaceae includes approximately 114 genera of herbs or occasionally shrubs, which are widely distributed primarily in temperate regions, with some in subtropical and tropical regions. Some authorities prefer the name Veronicaceae (Olmstead, pers. comm.), but this name has not yet been recognized. Recent revisions place the family Globulariaceae and many former genera of Scrophulariaceae in this family. Leaves are simple, basal or cauline (on a stem). Flowers are usually bisexual and bilaterally symmetrical. They have usually 5, sometimes 4, fused sepals. The petals are fused at the base and the lobes are grouped into 2 lips. There are usually 4 stamens of 2 different lengths (didynamous).

Angelonia

Angelonia includes approximately 25 species of herbs and subshrubs from tropical America. Leaves are simple, with slightly sticky, glandular hairs. Flowers are bell-shaped with relatively large, spreading lobes. They may sometimes appear solitary but are in terminal racemes separated by leaflike bracts. Plants in cultivation are variously described as *A. salicariifolia* or *A. angustifolia*. The ancestry of the cultivated forms is uncertain, possibly involving hybrids.

Angelonia species

NARROW-LEAF ANGELON
Garden origin (tropical America). Evergreen short-lived perennial subshrub, 1.5–2.5 ft.; zones 9–10. Blooms warm months. Regular moisture. Fertile, well-drained soil.

Full sun. Flowers: bell-shaped with rounded, slightly cupped, spreading lobes, white and purple or indigo splashes; racemes terminal with leaflike bracts. Leaves: lanceolate, 2–4 in. long; margins serrulate; sessile. *Ancestry of cultivated forms uncertain. Prune after bloom for compact growth.*

Digitalis

Digitalis includes approximately 20 species of herbs and subshrubs from the Mediterranean to Central Asia. These are hardy plants of mild temperate climates, but they also thrive as winter bloomers in California and at higher altitudes in the tropics. They do not do well in hot, humid conditions with high nighttime temperatures. The pharmaceutical drug digitalis, a heart stimulant, is extracted from the dried leaves of *D. purpurea*. Removing spent floral spikes may encourage a second bloom.

Digitalis purpurea

DIGITALIS, COMMON FOXGLOVE
Western Mediterranean region, especially Spain and Portugal. Biennial or short-lived perennial herb, 3–4 ft.; zones 5–10. Blooms winter, spring, early summer. Regular moisture. Fertile, humus-rich, well-drained soil. Full sun to bright broken light. Flowers: bell-shaped, white, lavender to pink, throat with white-ringed purple spots; in spirelike racemes. Leaves: basal leaves broadly ovate, to 12 in. long, graduating into lanceolate cauline leaves, 2–3 in. long, rough; margins toothed. *Numerous color selections and hybrids. All parts are poisonous. Forma* albiflora *is known as white foxglove.*

Globularia

Globularia includes approximately 22 species of perennial herbs from the Canary and Cape Verde Islands to Europe and Asia Minor. This genus was formerly segregated in its own family, Globulariaceae. Leaves are simple, spirally arranged, with glandular hairs. Flowers are small, arranged in heads, spikes, or corymbs.

Globularia indubia

CANARY ISLAND GLOBE DAISY
Canary Islands, Cape Verde Islands, threatened in the wild. Evergreen perennial subshrub, 2–3 ft.; zones 7–10. Blooms spring. Moderate moisture. Average, well-drained soil. Part sun to bright broken light. Flowers: small, tubular, violet and white, in globular heads. Leaves: oblanceolate, to 6 in. long, glossy; margins smooth. *Mat-forming. Suitable for rock gardens.*

Isoplexis

Isoplexis includes approximately 3 species of subshrubs from Madeira and the Canary Islands. Leaves are simple with toothed margins and are hairy below. Stalks are also hairy. Flowers are tubular and 2-lipped, on spirelike racemes. Pollinated by birds. These species are threatened or endangered in the

Pittosporum tobira

Angelonia 'Pacific Princess'

Digitalis purpurea

wild. Several species can be seen at Quail Botanical Garden.

Isoplexis canariensis

CRESTA DE GALLO ("COCK'S CREST")
Synonym: *Digitalis canariensis.*
Grand Canary Island, endangered in the wild. Perennial herb to 6 ft.; zones 9–10. Blooms late spring, early summer. Moderate moisture. Average, well-drained soil. Part sun to bright broken light. Flowers: tubular, orange; in terminal, spirelike racemes. Leaves: lanceolate to elliptic, 6–12 in. long, dark green, stiff, felty below; margins sharply toothed; in whorls on erect stalks.

Otacanthus

Otacanthus includes approximately 4 species of subshrubs or herbs from Brazil. The name means "ear-like acanthus." These species were once mistakenly thought to belong in the acanthus family, Acanthaceae. Leaves are simple, ovate, with faintly scalloped (crenulate) margins. The petals are united at the base into a slender tube with 2 relatively large, flaring lips. Propagated from cuttings.

Otacanthus caeruleus

BRAZILIAN SNAPDRAGON,
LITTLE BLUE-BOY
Brazil. Perennial herb or subshrub to 3 ft.; zones 10–11. Blooms warm months. Moist and humid. Moderately fertile, well-drained soil. Part sun to bright filtered light. Flowers: base tubular, to 2 in. long, lips rounded, deep violet, white spot on lower lip below throat. Leaves: ovate, 1–3 in. long, dark green; margins slightly scalloped (crenulate). *Of moist tropical forests. Used as a bedding plant in protected areas. Suitable for containers.*

Russelia

Russelia includes approximately 52 species from Mexico to Colombia and Cuba. Leaves are simple, sometimes reduced or scalelike. Flowers are tubular with short lobes. Attractive to butterflies and hummingbirds.

Russelia equisetiformis

FOUNTAIN-PLANT,
HORSETAIL FIRECRACKER PLANT
Synonym: *R. juncea.* Mexico, Central America. Deciduous subshrub; zones 9–11. Blooms warm months. Moderate moisture to dry. Average to poor, well-drained soil. Full sun. Flowers: trumpet-shaped, 1–2 in. long, lobes short, flaring, scarlet, rarely yellow; in leaf axils. Leaves: elliptic, spurlike, 0.25 in. long. Stems: rushlike, arching, green. *Produces large suckering clumps that can be difficult to control. Best con-*fined with deep-set edging. Salt tolerant. Used in xeriscape and rock gardens. Cut to ground in winter to clean out dead stalks. Flowers attractive in arrangements. The species name alludes to the resemblance of the stems to horse-tail rushes, Equisetum.*

Russelia lilacina

Synonym: *R. campechiana* var. *lilacina.* Southern Mexico, Guatemala, Honduras. Spreading herb or subshrub, 2–3 ft.; zones 10–11. Blooms intermittently all year. Moderate moisture. Average, well-drained soil. Full to part sun. Flowers: trumpet-shaped, to 1 in. long, with 2 small spreading lips, light violet. Leaves: broadly ovate to cordate; margins serrate. *An unusual, low spreading plant with arching branches. Suitable for perennial beds.*

Russelia sarmentosa

CORAL-PLANT
Mexico, Central America, Cuba. Evergreen shrub to 6 ft.; zones 9–11. Blooms intermittently most of the year. Moderate moisture. Average, well-drained soil. Full to part sun. Flowers: tubular, red; in clusters. Leaves: ovate, dark green, surface glandular; margins shallow-toothed. *Almost ever-blooming. Suitable for hedges and coastal landscaping. Attractive to hummingbirds and butterflies.*

PLUMBAGINACEAE

PLUMBAGO FAMILY,
LEADWORT FAMILY
Plumbaginaceae includes approximately 27 genera of mostly perennial herbs plus a few shrubs and climbers, which are widely distributed, primarily in dry or coastal regions. Leaves are simple, usually entire or sometimes lobed, in whorls or fascicles, or sometimes basal. Chalk or water glands sometimes cover the leaf surface. Flowers are bisexual and radially symmetrical. They have 5 sepals and 5 petals which are tubular or cup-shaped at the base with free lobes. Bracts are small and leaflike. The inflorescence is a panicle, spike, raceme, or cyme. The fruit is an achene or nutlet.

Globularia indubia

Isoplexis canariensis

Otacanthus caeruleus

Russelia equisetiformis

Russelia lilacina

Russelia sarmentosa

Limonium

Limonium includes approximately 350 species of annual, biennial, and perennial herbs, which are widely distributed in coastal and arid regions. Often dried for "everlastings" in floral arrangements. Leaves are simple. The calyx persists around the dry capsule. *Limonium ramosissima* is an invasive pest of southern California coastal wetlands.

Limonium perezii

SEA-STATICE, SEA-LAVENDER, SEA-ROSEMARY

Synonym: *Statice perezii.* Canary Islands. Perennial herb or subshrub to 3 ft.; zones 8–9. Blooms late spring, summer. Moderately moist to fairly dry. Sandy, well-drained soil. Full sun. Flowers: tubular, calyx violet, corolla white; bracts rough; on long stalks. Leaves: blades broad; margins undulate. *Xeric over a broad range. Salt tolerant. Pollinated by flies.*

Plumbago

Plumbago includes 15–24 species of perennial and annual herbs and shrubs primarily from subtropical and tropical regions. Leaves are in whorls or fascicles on alternate sides of the stem. The buds have conspicuous sticky hairs. *Plumbago auriculata* is an old-fashioned landscape plant. Older selections are pale blue or white. 'Imperial Blue', a cerulean selection, has revitalized interest in the species. Plumbagos tolerate hot, dry conditions and thrive in coastal gardens. They need full sun to bloom well. The sprawling habit is put to advantage as a hillside soil retainer and cover in California. Plumbagos also thrive in humid climates in well-drained soil. Suitable as an informal hedge with light trimming but avoid drastic pruning in hot, dry weather. The name leadwort is reputedly derived from the plant's use as a folk rem-edy for infections and is said to impart a leaden hue to the skin. *Wort* is an Old English word for an herb. The sticky haired buds and calyces are a good field mark.

Plumbago auriculata

PLUMBAGO, CAPE LEADWORT

Synonym: *P. capensis.* South Africa. Evergreen shrub, 3–6 ft.; zones 9–11. Blooms warm months. Moderate moisture to seasonally dry. Moderately fertile, sandy, well-drained soil. Full sun. Flowers: corolla tubular, lobes spreading, blue or white; calyx and buds with sticky, glandular hairs; in many-flowered cymes. Leaves: oblanceolate to spathulate, to 2 in. long, base tapering down the petiole; in fascicles in alternating clusters on the stem; stipules ear-shaped; margins undulate. *A sprawling, suckering shrub. Xeric. Species name alludes to the ear-shaped, leaflike stipules at the* base of the leaves—a distinctive char-acteristic. 'Imperial Blue' is a ceru-lean selection; forma alba has white flowers.

Plumbago indica

CRIMSON LEADWORT

Synonym: *P. rosea.* Southeast Asia, southern China, Philippines, Indonesia. Evergreen shrub to 6 ft.; zones 10–11. Blooms primarily winter, or sporadically at any time. Regular moisture when hot, less when cool. Moderately fertile, sandy, well-drained soil; slightly acid pH. Full sun. Flowers: tubular, raspberry red; calyx with sticky hairs; on long arching spikes; not known to set fruit in cultivation. Leaves: ovate, to 4 in. long, gray-green; margins undulate. *Salt tolerant to the dunes. Blooms most heavily around the winter holidays. Allow to dry between waterings.*

POLYGALACEAE

POLYGALA FAMILY, MILKWORT FAMILY

Polygalaceae includes approximately 154 genera of herbs, shrubs, and climbers from the tropics and subtropics, predominantly South America, South Africa, and Australia. Though referred to as milkworts, these plants do not have a milky sap but were once thought to stimulate lactation. Leaves are simple, sometimes scalelike. Flowers are bisexual and bilaterally symmetrical or asymmetrical. The 5 sepals are often partly united or reduced, the 2 lateral sepals winglike. The 5 petals, sometimes reduced to 3, are often modified into a tube and keel. There is one bract and 2 bracteoles. Flowers are solitary or in heads, panicles, racemes, or spikes. The fruit is a capsule, nut, drupe, or samara.

Polygala

Polygala includes approximately 500 species of annual and perennial herbs, shrubs, and rarely trees. Flowers are butterfly-like (papilionaceous). The lower petal is often keeled and fringed or crested. The flowers may vaguely resemble those of certain legumes, but the simple leaves are distinctive.

Plumbago auriculata 'Imperial Blue'

Plumbago indica

Limonium perezii

Polygala apopetala

BAJA MILKWORT

Mexico (Baja California). Evergreen shrub or tree, 8–15 ft.; zones 6–10. Blooms spring, summer. Dry. Average to poor, gritty, well-drained soil. Full sun. Flowers: sepals 5 with 2 modified into petal-like wings, petals small, mostly united, lip keeled, magenta to pink. Leaves: lanceolate, 2–4 in. long, leathery, glaucous. *Cultivated in the U.S. Southwest.*

Polygala ×dalmasiana

Garden hybrid, *P. myrtifolia* × *P. oppositifolia.* Evergreen shrub, 3–8 ft.; zones 7–10. Blooms almost all year. Moderate moisture to fairly dry. Average to poor, gritty, well-drained soil. Full sun. Flowers: winged, red-violet, lip keeled, with a conspicuous white crest. Leaves: oblong, ovate to obovate, to 1 in. long; opposite and alternate arrangement on the same plant. *Grown as an ever-blooming shrub or hedge. Photographed at the Balboa Park Conservatory.*

Securidaca

Securidaca includes approximately 80 species of shrubs and scrambling climbers, which are widely distributed in the tropics, excluding Australia. They are distinguished by the fruits, which are samaras with a single wing. The genus name alludes to the hatchetlike shape of the samaras.

Securidaca diversifolia

EASTER VIOLET,
GALLITO ("LITTLE ROOSTER")

Mexico, Central America to Ecuador, West Indies. Evergreen scandent shrub to 10 ft.; zones 10–11. Blooms late winter, spring. Moderate moisture. Average to poor, well-drained soil. Full sun. Flowers: scented; magenta; lateral sepals winged; petals 4, united, 1 a keeled lip; in terminal racemes; fruit a single-winged, wedge-shaped samara. Leaves: simple, ovate, 3–4 in. long, dull green; young leaves chocolate brown, pubescent; petioles short; stipular glands in the axils. *Of open fields and savannas. Grow on an arbor, fence, or other support.*

POLYGONACEAE

BUCKWHEAT FAMILY,
CORAL-VINE FAMILY

Polygonaceae includes approximately 49 genera of herbs, shrubs, trees, and climbers, which are widely distributed and most common in northern temperate regions. The family includes grains, fruits, and vegetables such as buckwheat (kasha), rhubarb, sorrel, and sea-grape. Plants are characterized by stems with swollen nodes, sheathing stipules (ocreae), and winged seeds. Leaves are usually simple with smooth margins, sometimes greatly reduced. Flowers are often reduced, slightly bilaterally symmetrical, and bisexual or sometimes unisexual with male and female flowers on different plants (dioecious). Sepals and petals are similar, often in 2 whorls, sometimes with a tepal from the inner whorl more or less united to one in the outer whorl. The fruit is a 3-winged achene or nut.

Antigonon

Antigonon includes approximately 8 species of tendril-climbing woody climbers (lianas) from Mexico and Central America. Vines trained over a wall lend an old-fashioned Victorian charm. Roots are tuberous. Flowers are bisexual and bilaterally symmetrical. Tepals are petal-like, better developed than those of many species in the family. The inflorescence is a raceme or panicle. Fruits are 3-sided achenes (a dry fruit with a single seed). Tendrils develop from the ends of the inflorescences. Xeric. Tender but grown as a perennial in colder parts of its range if root protected from freezing. Sometimes weedy in warmer parts of range.

Antigonon guatemalense

CHAIN-OF-LOVE, CORALILLO
GRANDE, ROSA DE MONTAÑA

Synonym: *A. macrocarpa.* Mexico, Central America. Semideciduous climber to 40 ft.; zones 8–11. Blooms intermittently in warm months. Moderate moisture and humid, seasonally dry. Average to poor, well-drained soil. Full sun. Flowers: tepal lobes spreading, edges ruffled, white or pink; achene faintly 3-angled. Leaves: broadly cordate, 3–4 in. wide, pubescent; margins irregularly toothed, undulate; petioles less than 0.5 in. long

(subsessile). *Sometimes listed as a selection of* A. leptopus.

Antigonon leptopus

CORAL-VINE, MEXICAN CREEPER,
CHAIN-OF-LOVE, CORALITA,
ROSA DE MONTAÑA

Mexico, Central America; widely naturalized. Semideciduous climber to 40 ft.; zones 8–11. Blooms intermittently all year. Moderate moisture and humid/seasonally dry. Average to poor, well-drained soil. Full sun. Flowers: tepals cupped, edges smooth, pink to white; achene strongly 3-angled. Leaves: ovate to deltoid, to 5 in. long, somewhat downy; margins irregularly toothed; petioles greater than 0.5 in. *'Album' is an all-white selection. Listed as potentially invasive in Florida, though apparently does not set seed in South Florida.*

Polygala apopetala

Polygala ×dalmasiana

Securidaca diversifolia

Antigonon guatemalense

Antigonon leptopus

Coccoloba

Coccoloba includes approximately 400 species of trees, shrubs, and climbers primarily from the Atlantic coast of tropical and subtropical America. Leaves are simple, often large and stiff, with smooth margins. The stipules form a membranous sheath (ocreae) around the stem. Flowers are small, united at the base into a floral cup (hypanthium). They are arranged in spikes or racemes. Male and female flowers are on different trees (dioecious). Sea-grape, *C. uvifera*, a typical coastal tree in Florida and the Caribbean, is widely cultivated. It readily hybridizes with other *Coccoloba* species, producing an assortment of sterile offspring (Howard 1989). The fruits, purple when ripe, have a thin layer of sweet, juicy flesh between the thick skin and large seed. They are eaten fresh or made into a grapelike jelly. The tree has a strongly branched architecture and large, rounded leaves that turn reddish in winter. It is wind resistant.

Coccoloba uvifera

SEA-GRAPE, JAMAICAN KINO, UVERO
Synonym: *Polygonum uvifera*. Tropical America, primarily coastal Caribbean. Briefly deciduous tree to 30–50 ft.; zones 9–11. Blooms spring, summer. Seasonally moist/dry. Sandy, well-drained soil. Full sun. Flowers: unisexual, white, fragrant; in dense racemes to 12 in. long. Leaves: suborbicular, to 7 in. wide, thick and rigid; margins smooth; turning yellow and red in winter. Modified stipules (an ocreae) form a band of green tissue around the nodes. *Xeric. Salt tolerant to the dunes. Attractive to birds and butterflies. A spreading shade tree ideally suited to coastal locations. Though a potentially large tree, if vertical leads are removed when young, trees will never develop full size.*

Muehlenbeckia

Muehlenbeckia includes 15–20 species of clambering or creeping shrubs from Australasia and South America. Leaves are simple, usually small. The flattened green stems (phylloclads) of *M. platyclada* perform the function of leaves. Stems are initially wiry and erect, becoming lax and tangled. Flowers are minute.

Muehlenbeckia platyclada

RIBBON-BUSH, TAPEWORM PLANT
Synonym: *Homalocladium platycladum*. Solomon Islands. Deciduous clambering shrub to 10 ft.; zones 10–11. Blooms late winter, spring. Seasonally moist/dry. Average, well-drained soil. Bright filtered light. Flowers: tiny, petals greenish white; calyx red; clusters sessile in leaf axils; fruit a small, 3 sided red to black achene surrounded by the white perianth cup. Leaves: lanceolate, to 2 in. long; falling before flowering. Stems: green, flattened phylloclads, jointed at the nodes. *Also produces wiry round clambering shoots to 10 ft. or more. Grown primarily as a curiosity. Photographed in the private collection of Monroe Birdsey.*

Ruprechtia

Ruprechtia includes approximately 30 species of shrubs and trees from Mexico to South America. Leaves are simple. Flowers are unisexual, with male and female flowers on separate trees (dioecious). Female flowers are pink to magenta, in groups of 2–3 on branched peduncles and clustered in short inflorescences. The 3-winged calyx is persistent on the fruit, an achene. Male flowers are white, solitary, on short individual pedicles in elongated racemes. Plant several seedlings or propagate from cuttings or grafts to ensure male and/or female flowers. Distinguish from *Triplaris* by solid, not hollow, branches; short female inflorescences; and stalked male flowers.

Ruprechtia coriacea

SANGRE DE TORO, BISCOCHITO
Venezuela. Evergreen tree to 20 ft.; zones 10–11. Blooms late fall, winter. Seasonally moist/dry. Average, well-drained soil. Full to part sun. Flowers: unisexual, calyx of male flowers white, in long racemes, calyx of female flowers maroon to magenta, persistent on the developing fruit; in branching clusters. Leaves: elliptic, 6–8 in. long, dark green; secondary veins almost perpendicular to the midrib. Bark: gray, scaly. *Stems not hollow, and female flowers in short clusters, not long racemes as in Triplaris. Somewhat drought tolerant when mature.*

Triplaris

Triplaris includes approximately 17 species from South and Central America. They are fast-growing small to large erect trees of seasonally moist/dry forests and riverbanks. In the wild, hollow branches are usually inhabited by stinging ants, which protect the trees from herbivores. Leaves are simple. Flowers are unisexual, with male and female flowers on separate trees (dioecious). Male flowers are sessile on a congested spike. Female flowers are borne in racemes. The showy red, pink, or white calyces of the female flowers are persistent, the characteristic 3 wings remaining attached to the fruit. Mature fruits are dispersed, twirling like little helicopters to the ground. *Triplaris* species are underutilized as ornamentals but highly desirable. They are fast-growing from seed. Plant several seedlings or propagate from cuttings or grafts to ensure female and/or male flowers.

Triplaris cumingiana

LONG-JOHN, VOLADOR ("FLYER"), PAU FORMIGA ("ANT TREE" IN BRAZIL)
Colombia, Panama, northern Peru. Evergreen tree, 60–80 ft.; zones 9–11. Blooms late winter, early spring. Seasonally moist/dry. Fertile, well-drained soil. Full to part sun. Flowers: unisexual; male flowers white, in long spikes; female flower with 3-winged downy calyx, magenta, persistent on fruit; in

Coccoloba uvifera

Ruprechtia coriacea

Muehlenbeckia platyclada

Triplaris cumingiana, male and female flowers

long racemes, rachis bronze-haired. Leaves: oblong to elliptic, 10–14 in. long, midrib light green, sparsely haired below. Bark: thin, peeling in layers of gray, brown, and green. *An erect tree of riversides and seasonally moist forest. Somewhat drought tolerant. Long-John seems to be a corruption of long-johns for the bright red underwear. Trees in cultivation are difficult to distinguish from T. weigeltiana (Brandbyge 1986).*

PONTEDERIACEAE
WATER-HYACINTH FAMILY
Pontederiaceae includes approximately 6 genera of perennial aquatic herbs from mostly tropical and mild temperate regions. Some species are common free-floating or rooted plants of U.S. wetlands and are also grown in water gardens and ponds. Leaves are basal and spirally arranged, or cauline

(on a stalk) in opposite ranks (distichous), and sometimes fleshy or inflated, acting as floats. Flowers are bisexual and radially or bilaterally symmetrical. They are solitary or are arranged in racemes, spikes, or panicles. A spathelike bract is located at the base of the inflorescence. The 6 tepals are petaloid, one sometimes modified into a standard. The stamens are usually 6. The fruit is a capsule or nutlet.

Eichhornia
Eichhornia includes 7 species of aquatic herbs from tropical America. *Eichhornia crassipes* is a serious pest of waterways and wetlands and is prohibited from distribution in Florida. It reproduces at an incredible rate. On the positive side, the plants provide a nursery for fish fry, which in turn are eaten by wading birds. Natural controls include

forage for endangered manatees in Florida and rhinos in India. In Thailand, dried plant fibers are woven into baskets and attractive furniture, like a soft, flat rattan, and are now available in the United States. The roots do a prodigious job of filtering heavy metals and organic matter from water and are used in natural water purification systems in Indonesia.

Eichhornia crassipes
WATER-HYACINTH
South America; widely naturalized throughout the tropics and subtropics. Free-floating or rooted aquatic herb; zones 9–11 . Blooms warm months. Full sun. Flowers: tepals light violet, standard with a darker violet and golden flame-shaped spot; pistils of different flowers have long, medium, or short styles (heterostylous); in

Eichhornia crassipes

Triplaris cumingiana

Pontederia cordata

erect, emergent spikes. Leaves: broadly ovate, glossy, fleshy; petioles with bulging nodules full of air-filled cells. Roots fibrous. Floating or anchored. *Introduced for its attractive flowers. Rapidly spreading mats block waterways and crowd out less aggressive species. Leaves act as sails, spreading the mats.*

Pontederia
Pontederia includes approximately 5 species of rooted aquatic herbs from North and South America and the Caribbean. Leaves are fleshy and emergent. Flowers are small and arranged in spikes. The fruit is a one-seeded achene. Grow in shallow pond margins or in raised tubs just below the water surface.

Pontederia cordata
PICKEREL-WEED, WAMPEE
Synonym: *P. lanceolata*. Eastern North America, Caribbean. Rooted aquatic herb, 3–4 ft.; zones 3–11. Blooms warm months. Full sun. Flowers: blue-violet or rarely white or pink, with a white spot on the upper petal; on erect spikes subtended by a spathelike bract. Leaves: cordate to lanceolate; petioles and blades erect. *A rooted herb of temperate and tropical wetlands. Leaves and flowers emergent. Var. alba has white flowers.*

PORTULACACEAE
PORTULACA FAMILY, PURSLANE FAMILY
Portulacaceae includes 20–100 genera of annual and perennial herbs and shrubs, which are widely distributed, with considerable diversity in the western United States. Leaves are simple, often succulent. Flowers are bisexual and radially symmetrical. Authorities disagree whether the outer whorl of the perianth comprises 2 bracts or 2 sepals. There are 5 petals (or petaloid sepals), a branched style, and 3, 5, or numerous stamens. Flowers are solitary or are arranged in cymes.

Portulaca
Portulaca includes approximately 100 species of primarily annual herbs, which are widely distributed in the tropics and subtropics.

Leaves are simple with hairs in the axils. Flowers are often colorful, usually with 5 petals (or petaloid sepals) and 8 to numerous stamens. The fruit is a circumscissile (opening around the vertical axis) capsule. Species identification is difficult and many names remain unresolved because many species are self-pollinating. *Portulaca oleracea* is a weedy, nonornamental species in its wild form, sometimes eaten as cooked greens or in salads.

Portulaca oleracea 'Wildfire'

MOSS-ROSE, ROCK-ROSE, SUN-PLANT, PURSLANE

Cultigen; widely naturalized. Annual herb; zones 10–11. Blooms hot months. Moderate moisture to somewhat dry. Sandy, poor, well-drained soil. Full sun. Flowers: perianth fringed, red, yellow, white; stalkless (sessile), closing at night; fruit a circumscissile capsule. Leaves: obovate, to about 1 in. long, fleshy; petiole short (subsessile). Stems: fleshy, reddish in some cultivars. *Ornamental forms of the species are polyploid cultigens. A creeping to erect herb suitable for rock gardens. Does not thrive in moist conditions. Grown as a spring annual in Florida.* Portulaca grandiflora *has needlelike leaves.*

PROTEACEAE

PROTEA FAMILY

Proteaceae includes approximately 77 genera of shrubs and trees from tropical and subtropical regions of the Southern Hemisphere, with greatest diversity in Australia followed by South Africa, and a few in New Zealand and South America. It is an ancient family whose ancestors go back to the geologic epoch when Australia, South Africa, and South America were united as one continent, Gondwanaland. The species are found in habitats from arid, sandy coasts to cool, montane regions, usually in poor, acid soil. Some of the larger species are cut for timber or fire wood. *Macadamia* species are grown, primarily in Hawaii, for the edible nuts. Many species exhibit special adaptations. Short lateral roots are produced seasonally and are unique in their

ability to convert meager nutrients for absorption in poor soil. Some species have woody, subterranean tubers (lignotubers), an adaptation to frequent fires in the dry season. New shoots develop from the lignotuber in the wet season.

Leaves are simple, irregularly dissected, or pinnate. Flowers are usually bisexual, or, if unisexual, then male and female flowers are on the same plant (monoecious) or rarely on different plants (dioecious). The 4 tepals are highly modified, fused, often tubelike. Flowers are single or in pairs, usually arranged in terminal heads or racemes. Bracts are sometimes present. The fruit is often a conelike aggregate of drupes, follicles, achenes, or nuts. Many species are cultivated in southern California and dry parts of Hawaii. Relatively few are suitable for moist, humid climates or for alkaline soil. Attention to moisture requirements, excellent drainage, sparing amounts of low-nitrogen and low-phosphorus fertilizers, and proper soil pH are vital to successful growing.

Alloxylon

Alloxylon includes 2 or 3 species of trees from eastern Australia and New Guinea. The genus names *Oreocallis* and *Embothrium*, synonyms of the listed species, are now reserved for species of neotropical origin. Leaves are simple or pinnate. Flowers are bisexual, borne in pairs in many-flowered racemes or corymbs. Of seasonally

moist rain forest, these erect trees are cultivated for their fine timber as well as for shade. Trees seem to be on fire when in full bloom.

Alloxylon pinnatum

FIRE-TREE, SATIN-OAK, TREE-WARATAH

Synonyms: *Embothrium wickhamii*, *Oreocallis pinnatum*. Northeastern Australia, New Guinea. Evergreen tree to 50 ft.; zones 9–11. Blooms spring, early summer. Seasonally moist/dry. Sandy, humus-riched, well-drained soil; slightly acid pH. Full sun. Flowers: 4 petals fused into a long lip, scarlet; style scarlet; paired, in clusters in leaf axils near the branch ends. Leaves: simple, lance-shaped to narrowly oblong, 6–8 in. long. *Winged seeds flutter to the ground when the capsules open. Plants are adapted to seasonally moist climates unlike most members of this family. Cut broken branches cleanly to prevent internal rot.*

Banksia

Banksia includes approximately 72 species of shrubs and trees from Australia plus 1 from New Guinea. Leaves are simple, oblong to linear, leathery, often toothed or deeply lobed. Flowers are arranged in long spikes. Fruits are conelike aggregates (strobili). Banksias usually have large woody subterranean tubers (lignotubers). After fires, new shoots are produced from the trunk or lignotubers. Banksias with lignotubers produce more flowers if sharply pruned after flowering.

Leaves are used in dry arrangements. Fertilize no more than twice a year, using a very dilute, low-nitrogen, low-phosphate fertilizer. Propagate from cuttings or from seed after first burning the "cones" (Matthews 1993). Excellent for bird shelter and attractive to nectar-feeders.

Banksia hookeriana

HOOKER'S BANKSIA

Australia. Evergreen shrub to 5 ft.; zones 9–11. Blooms fall, winter. Moderate moisture when hot, less when cool. Poor, sandy, well-drained soil; neutral to slightly acid pH. Full sun. Flowers: white, woolly; seeds winged; spirally arranged on a flat-topped, cylindrical cone, to 12 in. tall. Leaves: linear, to 8 in. long, ribbony, rough, midvein yellow; margins coarsely saw-toothed. Lignotuber present. *Of semiarid areas. An important cut flower. Prune sharply after bloom.*

Banksia integrifolia

COAST BANKSIA, AUSTRALIAN HONEYSUCKLE

Northeastern Australia. Evergreen shrub or tree to 75 ft.; zones 8–11. Blooms summer, fall. Moderate moisture when hot, less when cool. Poor, sandy, well-drained soil; neutral to slightly acid pH. Full sun. Flowers: cream to greenish, aging bronze; inflorescence oblong, to about 6 in. tall, on branches or directly from the trunk (cauliflorous). Leaves: oblanceolate, to 8 in. long, dark dull green, silvery below; mar-

Portulaca oleracea 'Wildfire'

Alloxylon pinnatum

Banksia hookeriana

gins smooth or irregularly toothed when young. *One of the most variable* Banksia *species, distributed from coastal to inland regions. Fast-growing. Cultivated for shade and provides wildlife habitat. Used as rootstock for difficult-to-cultivate species. Salt tolerant.*

Banksia menziesii
MENZIES'S BANKSIA, FIREWOOD BANKSIA

Western Australia. Evergreen shrub or tree, 10–30 ft.; zones 9–11. Blooms fall. Moderate moisture when hot, less when cool. Poor, sandy, well-drained soil; neutral to slightly acid pH. Full sun. Flowers: pink and silver; stigmas yellow; inflorescence to 6 in. high, tightly cylindrical at first, flowers opening from bottom in vertical rows; capsules few-seeded. Leaves: oblong,

straplike, to 10 in. long, gray-green; margins broadly toothed. Lignotuber present. Grown for cut flowers. Has a reputation as difficult to cultivate. For compact growth and more flowers, prune sharply in late winter.

Banksia prionotes
ACORN BANKSIA, ORANGE BANKSIA

Western Australian. Evergreen shrub to wide-crowned tree, 20–30 ft.; zones 9–11. Blooms fall, winter. Moderate moisture when hot, less when cool. Poor, gritty, well-drained soil; slightly alkaline to acid pH. Full sun. Flowers: styles peach-orange, exserted; bracts felty, white; inflorescence unfurls into an acorn-like shape, to 6 in. tall, pointed at the top; fruit a woody cone. Leaves: strap-shaped, to 12 in. long, gray-green; margins large saw-toothed, cut almost to the midrib. *An adapt-*

able species which tolerates slightly alkaline to acid conditions. The species name alludes to the deeply toothed leaves. Flowers and leaves used in arrangements.

Banksia spinulosa
HAIRPIN BANKSIA

Eastern Australia. Evergreen shrub to 12 ft.; zones 8–10. Blooms fall, winter. Moderate moisture when hot, less when cool. Gritty to heavy, well-drained soil; slightly alkaline to acid pH. Full sun to bright shade. Flowers: yellow to honey brown; styles reddish brown, hooked ends resemble hairpins; inflorescence cylindrical, 6–8 in. tall. Leaves: linear, almost needlelike. Lignotuber often present. *Adaptable and common in native areas near coast. Sometimes grown as a hedge. Conifer-like appearance. Var.* collina *has*

broader leaves; var. cunninghammii *lacks a lignotuber.* 'Birthday Candles' *is a dwarf cultivar.*

Grevillea
Grevillea includes approximately 260 species of shrubs and trees primarily from Australia plus a few from nearby islands. Leaves are alternate, unevenly bipinnatesect, or simple and more or less lobed. Flowers are bisexual, borne in pairs on many-flowered racemes. The styles are usually long and coiled. These plants are attractive to nectar-feeding birds. In Australia, silky oak, *G. robusta*, is cultivated for its hard, smooth, oaklike wood, which is used to make fine furniture and cabinetry. Self-seeding and naturalized in California and Central Florida. Listed as an invasive pest in Hawaii. Prune after flowering to promote more bloom and compact shape. Relatively pest-free. Hybrids are usually grafted.

Grevillea juniperina
Australia (New South Wales). Evergreen shrub to 6 ft.; zones 9–10. Blooms spring, summer. Moderate moisture when hot, dry when cool. Poor, sandy to clay soil; neutral to slightly acid pH. Full sun. Flowers: perianth coiled like a snail shell, red, unfolds to expose the style; in pairs arranged in small clusters. Leaves: linear, to 1.5 in. long, needlelike. *Sprawling to erect. A variable and relatively adaptable species. Does not like root disturbance. Prune after flowering to promote good bloom and compact form. Propagated from cuttings. Hybrids must be grafted. Forma* sulphurea *has yellow flowers.*

Grevillea robusta
SILKY-OAK

Northeastern Australia. Evergreen tree, 40–120 ft.; zones 7–11. Blooms late winter, spring. Moderate moisture when hot, dry when cool. Poor, sandy to clay soil; acid pH. Full sun. Flowers: tepals flattened, golden with red spot; styles golden, hooked at the tip; in one-sided racemes, to 1 ft. or more long, near the ends of branches; capsules black, to 0.5 in. long, splitting open on one side; one-seeded. Leaves: pinnate, 12–18 in. long,

Banksia integrifolia, flowers

Banksia integrifolia, cones

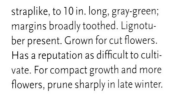

Banksia menziesii

Banksia prionotes

Banksia spinulosa var. *spinulosa*

Grevillea juniperina 'Rosea'

pinnae irregularly pinnatisect and forked, gray below. Trunk: gray, rough, smoother on branches. *Of subtropical rain forest. Brittle in wind. Thrives in both moist and dry climates. Naturalized in disturbed areas of California and Central Florida. Does not bloom well in alkaline soils of South Florida.*

Grevillea 'Robyn Gordon'

Garden hybrid (*G. banksii* × *G. bipinnatifida*). Evergreen shrub, 4–5 ft.; zones 9–10. Blooms summer. Moderate moisture when hot, dry when cool. Poor, sandy to clay soil; neutral to slightly acid pH. Full Sun. Flowers: perianth pink and red, coiled like a snail shell, unfolds to expose the style, paired, in small clusters. Leaves: bipinnatifid. *The first Grevillea hybrid. Sterile. Habit low and spreading. Prune after flowering for many blooms and compact form. Propagated from cuttings. Several other hybrids from the same parents (grexes).*

Leucadendron

Leucadendron includes approximately 79 species of shrubs and trees from South Africa. Leaves are simple, leathery. Flowers are unisexual, with male and female flowers on separate individuals (dioecious). Female flowers are in aggregate, conelike heads. Male flowers are in open heads. Though finicky and endangered in the wild, *L. argenteum* is among the more commonly cultivated species, prized for its silvery inflorescence and silvery blue-green foliage.

Leucadendron argenteum

SILVER TREE, CAPE SILVER TREE
South Africa (Table Mountain, West Cape), endangered in the wild.

Evergreen tree, 10–30 ft.; zones 9–10. Blooms spring or intermittently. Moderate moisture when hot, less when cool. Gritty, sandy, exceptionally fast-draining soil; acid pH. Full sun. Flowers: unisexual; bracts silvery haired; male flowers in open heads, to 2 in. wide; female flowers in compact, conelike heads, 2–5 in. long; terminal. Leaves: lanceolate, to 6 in. long, tips pointed; covered with long silvery hairs; sessile. *Adapted to frequent winds and cool mists of a limited montane region. Requires precise culture to thrive. Roots sensitive to disturbance. Protected in native habitat.*

Leucadendron galpinii

GALPIN'S LEUCADENDRON
South Africa. Evergreen tree to 10 ft.+; zones 9–10. Blooms spring, intermittent. Moderate moisture when hot, less when cool. Gritty, fast-draining soil; acid pH. Full sun. Flowers: unisexual; bracts silvery gray; male flowers in open heads; female flowers in spherical, conelike heads, 2–3 in. wide; terminal. Leaves: spathulate, 2–6 in. long, green, tips rounded; sessile.

Leucospermum

Leucospermum includes approximately 46 species of shrubs from South Africa and Zimbabwe. Leaves are simple with a few large teeth at the tip. Flowers are bisexual and arranged in heads. They are called pincushions for the numerous long curved styles (the pins) emerging from the cushionlike tepals. Much cultivated and hybridized. Species are endangered and protected in their native habitat.

Leucospermum hybrids

PINCUSHION-FLOWER
Garden hybrids (South Africa). Evergreen shrubs, 3–10 ft., zones 8–11. Bloom spring, summer. Moderate moisture when hot, dry when cool. Gritty, fast-draining soil; acid pH. Full sun. Flowers: tepals fused, curled inward; styles long. Leaves: straplike, firm; several large teeth at the tip. *These hybrids involve* L. cordifolium, *a species of mountain habitat. Usually somewhat hardy. Grown for cut-flowers. Will grow rapidly from seed but short-lived in culti-*

Grevillea 'Robyn Gordon'

Grevillea robusta, flowers

Leucadendron argenteum, female cone

Grevillea robusta

Leucadendron argenteum

vation. *Avoid root disturbance. Often kept pruned.*

Protea

Protea includes approximately 100 species from South Africa. It is perhaps the best-known genus in this family. Many selections are grown for cut flowers. They are full of sweet nectar so are referred to as "sugar bushes" in their native region. Leaves are simple, often straplike and firm. Flowers are borne in large, many-flowered heads surrounded by an involucre of bracts. Proteas need precise conditions to thrive. Plants are usually pruned sharply. The name "protea" is loosely applied to the whole family. Proteus was the sea god of Greek mythology who was able to change his form at will. *Protea* flower heads change appearance as they mature, unfolding somewhat

like an umbrella. Early botanists sometimes mistook various stages for different species.

Protea cynaroides

KING-PROTEA, GIANT PROTEA
South Africa (South Cape Province). Evergreen shrub to 6 ft.; zones 8–10. Blooms late winter, spring, or intermittently. Moderate moisture when hot, less when cool. Sandy, well-drained soil; slightly acid pH. Full sun. Flowers: slender; bracts lanceolate, green, pink, scarlet, crimson in many-flowered funnel-shaped or spreading heads, to 10 in. wide. Leaves: variable, broadly ovate to lanceolate, leathery; margins usually red; petiole 4–12 in. long. Branches stout, red. *National flower of South Africa. Extremely variable spreading shrub. Bloom season depends on individual origin, from coasts or mountains.*

Usually sharply pruned. An important cut flower.

Protea eximia

RAY-FLOWERED PROTEA, DUCHESS PROTEA
Synonym: *P. latifolia*. South Africa (South Cape Province). Evergreen shrub or tree, 6–10 ft.; zones 8–10. Blooms late winter, spring or intermittently. Moderate moisture when hot, dry when cool. Poor, sandy, well-drained soil; acid to somewhat alkaline pH. Full sun. Flowers: slender, cream with dark purple tips; bracts violet-pink to orange-pink, outer bracts with purple-black margins; inflorescence to 8 in. wide. Leaves: broadly ovate to 6 in. long, glossy green to gray; margins usually reddish, sometimes bluish. *Adaptable. Grows from moist lowland to montane regions. Marginally hardy, heat and wind tolerant. Con-*

sidered the least finicky protea to grow. Usually sharply pruned.

Stenocarpus

Stenocarpus includes approximately 25 species of shrubs and trees from Malaysia to Australasia. Leaves are entire to deeply lobed, often on the same individual. Flowers are bisexual, tubular, asymmetrical, yellow or scarlet, arranged in whorls. Nectar feeders are attracted to the large, jewel-like nectar droplets exuding from the base of each flower. *Stenocarpus sinuatus* is used for street landscaping in California and Australia. It is tender when young, becoming marginally hardy with age. Rooted woody cuttings begin to bloom while quite small. Can be maintained as a shrub with pruning or grown in containers. Reefwood, *S. salignus*, is grown in Indomalaysia for its fine timber.

Leucadendron galpinii, cones

Leucospermum 'African Red'

Leucospermum 'California Sunrise'

Protea cynaroides, fully opened floral head

Protea eximia, partly opened floral head

Stenocarpus sinuatus

FIRE-WHEEL TREE, WHITE SILKY-OAK
Eastern Australia, Papua New
Guinea. Evergreen tree, 40–90 ft.;
zones 9–11. Blooms fall, winter.
Seasonally moist, drier when cool.
Average, well-drained soil; neutral
pH. Full to part sun. Flowers: tubular, orange to scarlet; in whorls;
stigmas yellow; fruit a woody, boat-shaped follicle; seeds winged.
Leaves: highly variable on the same
tree, broadly ovate to oblong, often
pinnately lobed, to 1 ft. long, glossy
dark green, firm; margins sinuous.
*Adaptable, erect tree of coastal rain
forests. Grows in Mediterranean-type
climates as well as seasonally moist,
humid climates.*

ROSACEAE

ROSE FAMILY
Rosaceae includes approximately
85 genera of herbs, shrubs, and trees,
which are widely distributed and
most abundant in Northern Hemisphere temperate regions. In addition to roses, familiar temperate
members of this family include almonds, apples, apricots, cherries,
peaches, plums, quinces, raspberries, and strawberries. Loquat, *Eriobotrya japonica*, is a tasty tropical
fruit in the family. Leaves are simple to pinnately or palmately compound, sometimes in basal rosettes. The margins are serrated.
Flowers are usually bisexual and
radially symmetrical. They usually
have 5 petals, which are showy and
often narrowing into a stalk at the
base (clawed). They also have 5
sepals and sometimes 5 sepal-like
bracts (epicalyx). Stamens are 5 to
numerous, mounted on a floral cup
(hypanthium). Flowers are solitary
or are arranged in racemes or
cymes. The fruit is a drupe, pome,
or aggregate. Strawberries are the
fleshy receptacles.

Osteomeles

Osteomeles includes approximately
3 species from southern China,
New Zealand, and the Pacific islands. Leaves are pinnately compound. Flowers have 5 petals, 5
sepals, and numerous stamens.
The fruit is a small, applelike pome.

Osteomeles anthyllidifolia

'ULEI (HAWAII)
Hawaii, Polynesia to Ryukyu Islands. Semideciduous spreading
shrub or tree to 6 ft.; zones 8–10.
Blooms late summer, fall. Moderate moisture to fairly dry. Average,
well-drained soil. Full sun. Flowers:
spreading to revolute, to 0.5 in.
wide, white; in branching clusters
(corymbs); fruit white, flesh purple.
Leaves: pinnate, to 2 in. long, leaflets 11–15, oblong, to 0.33 in. *A
spreading, open shrub with fernlike
leaves and long, arching shoots.
Shoots covered with white hairs,
spineless. Wood is used to make fishnet hoops in the Pacific.*

Rhaphiolepis

Rhaphiolepis includes approximately 9 species of shrubs from
Southeast Asia. The genus name is
frequently misspelled. Leaves are
simple with toothed margins. Flowers are small, roselike, white or
pink, and fragrant and are borne in
terminal clusters. The fruit is a
small, purple to black pome. *Rhaphiolepis indica* is commonly grown
as a formal hedge in California. Unfortunately regular pruning eliminates the roselike flowers. A more
natural hedge, set back 3 or 4 ft.
from walks and windows, is more
attractive and can be maintained
with a yearly pruning after flowering. *Crataegus* species, temperate
members of this family are also
referred to as hawthorn.

Rhaphiolepis ×delacourii

ENCHANTRESS HAWTHORN
Garden hybrid, *R. indica* × *R. umbellata*. Evergreen shrub to 8 ft.; zones
8–10. Blooms late winter, spring.
Moderate moisture when hot, less
when cool. Moderately fertile, well-drained soil. Full sun. Flowers: petals pink. Leaves: simple, ovate to
obovate, 2–3 in. long, stiff, dark
green, pinkish when young; margins toothed. *Several grexes have
been made from the same parents,
some with double flowers. Suitable
for coastal planting. Naturally
rounded, erect shrubs.*

Rhaphiolepis indica

INDIAN HAWTHORN
Southeast China, Japan. Evergreen
shrub to 6 ft.; zones 8–10. Blooms
winter, spring. Regular moisture
when hot, less when cool. Moderately fertile, well-drained soil. Full
sun. Flowers: small, roselike, selections pink or white; stamens white
or ruddy pink; in branched clusters;
fruit bluish black. Leaves: ovate, to
2 in. long, firm, dark green, tips
pointed; margins faintly toothed.
Young stems: covered with russet
hairs. *A variable species with numerous cultivars and/or hybrids, some
more fragrant than others. Suitable
for coastal locations. Common hedge
plant in California. Withhold pruning
in winter and be rewarded with a prolific spring bloom.*

RUBIACEAE

COFFEE FAMILY, GARDENIA FAMILY
Rubiaceae includes approximately
650 genera of herbs, shrubs, trees,
or woody climbers (lianas), which
are widely distributed and a predominant group in tropical regions.
The family is best known for coffee,
Coffea species, and gardenias, *Gardenia* species. It includes several
commonly cultivated ornamentals,
notably *Ixora*, *Mussaenda*, and *Pentas* species. Quinine, a drug from
the bark of *Cinchona*, was the first
effective treatment for malaria, a
disease spread by mosquitoes.

Leaves are simple, usually
entire, rarely lobed, in opposite
pairs, often at right angles to the
pair above and below (decussate).
The stipules, variable and distinctive for each species, are sometimes leaflike or sometimes deciduous. They are located between the
bases of the leaf petioles (interpetiolar) rather than in the axils, sometimes giving the appearance of
whorls of 4 leaves. Flowers are bisexual and radially symmetrical.
The 4 or 5 petals are at least partly
fused, tubular, rotate, or trumpet-shaped. Some flowers have prominent seams where the petals are

Stenocarpus sinuatus

Osteomeles anthyllidifolia

Rhaphiolepis ×delacourii

Rhaphiolepis indica

joined. Sepals are also 4 or 5 and partly fused. Stamens are as numerous as petals, the filaments mounted on the petals (epipetalous). Flowers are solitary or arranged in cymes. The fruit is a berry, capsule, or schizocarp. Many species are attractive to nectar-feeding birds and butterflies.

Burchellia

Burchellia includes a single species of shrub from South Africa. It is unusual in cultivation. It has extremely hard wood, but with few uses because of the small size of the plant. Leaves are simple. Stipules are leaflike, interspersed between the leaves. Flowers are arranged in terminal clusters.

Burchellia bubalina

BUFFALO-WOOD, BUFFALO-HORN, WILD POMEGRANATE
Synonym: *B. capensis.* South Africa, Swaziland. Evergreen shrub to 10 ft.; zones 8–10. Blooms spring, summer. Dry. Average, well-drained soil; acid pH. Full sun. Flowers: tubular, slightly inflated, lobes small, pointed, red or scarlet; fruit a berry, reddish. Leaves: lanceolate, to 5 in. long, pubescent below; margins slightly revolute. *Photo of small plant at Quail Botanical Garden.*

Catesbaea

Catesbaea includes 16–20 species of shrubs or small trees from the West Indies, the Bahamas, and the Florida Keys. Leaves are simple, usually with small spines in the axils. Flowers are trumpet-shaped. The small-flowered lily-thorn, *C. parviflora,* is native to the extreme southern tip of Florida and the Florida Keys.

Catesbaea spinosa

LILY-THORN, SPANISH GUAVA
Cuba, Bahamas. Spiny evergreen shrub to 12 ft.; zones 9–11. Blooms intermittently all year. Seasonally moist/dry. Average, sandy, well-drained soil. Full to part sun. Flowers: trumpet-shaped, to 6 in. long, pendent; fruit yellow-orange, edible but insipid, with many small seeds. Leaves: obovate, to 2 in. long, dark green; in fascicles along the upper sides of the arching branches; with small spines in leaf axils. *Thrives in coastal locations. Unusual in cultivation in the United States but common in parts of the West Indies and Bahamas. An effective barrier hedge.*

Coffea

Coffea includes approximately 90 species of shrubs from tropical Africa and Madagascar. A number of selections are grown in the tropics for the production of coffee. In the United States, coffee is only grown commercially in Hawaii. Leaves are simple. Flowers are borne in the leaf axils. The fruit is an ovoid drupe with 2 pyrenes commonly known as coffee beans. The fleshy pulp is removed before roasting. Coffee is traditionally grown under shade trees known as *madre de café* (mother-of-coffee), including genera such as *Inga, Erythrina,* or *Gliricidia.* These legume species filter the hot sunlight and enrich the soil with nitrogen. Traditional farms are being replaced with sun-tolerant selections in high-intensity, unshaded coffee plantations. This is contributing to the dramatic loss of habitat for migrating birds. High-intensity farming has resulted in the overproduction of low-grade coffee, low economic return, and the loss of jobs for individual farmers.

Coffea arabica

ARABIAN COFFEE, CAFETO ARÁBICO
Ethiopia. Evergreen shrub to 10–15 ft.; zones 10–11. Blooms spring. Seasonally moist, less when cool. Fertile, well-drained soil. Part sun to bright filtered light. Flowers: rotate, white, lobes pointed; in leaf axils; fruit red, 2-seeded. Leaves: elliptic, to 6 in. long, glossy dark green, smooth. *Fine grade coffee. Heat- and cold-sensitive so commonly grown at milder altitudes, "mountain coffee."*

Coffea canephora

ROBUSTA COFFEE, CONGO COFFEE, CAFETO ROBUSTO
Tropical western Africa. Evergreen shrub, 8–12 ft.; zones 10–11. Blooms spring. Seasonally moist, less when cool. Fertile, well-drained soil. Full sun to bright filtered light. Flowers: rotate, white, petal lobes rounded; in many-flowered clusters, in leaf axils; fruit red, 2-seeded. Leaves: broadly obovate, to 12 in. long, glossy dark green, quilted. *Robusta coffee is less sensitive to extremes of heat and cold than Arabian and is more resistant to coffee rust, a fungal disease, but is lower quality.*

Gardenia

Gardenia includes approximately 60 species of shrubs from mild temperate and tropical regions of the Old World and the Pacific Islands. Leaves are simple. Flowers are trumpet-shaped or rotate. Numerous selections of *G. jasminoides* are cultivated. The fancy varieties are grown in acid soil in the subtropics. They are fussy, susceptible to sucking pests and nematodes. Look for selections grafted onto nematode-resistant rootstock, usually *G. thunbergia.* Nutrients are less soluble in alkaline soils and unavailable for absorption. Yellow leaves or falling buds indicate lack of microelements, too much or irregular moisture, or root problems. A large planting hole can be acidified with peat. In less than ideal conditions gardenias can be successfully grown in large containers. Do not disturb roots or containers when plants are in bud or they will drop the buds. *Gardenia taitensis* is more adaptable and pest resistant and recommended for alkaline soils.

Gardenia coronaria

ORANGE GARDENIA
Southeast Asia. Evergreen shrub, 10–15 ft.; zones 9–11. Blooms warm months. Regular moisture and humidity, moderate moisture when cool. Fertile, well-drained

Burchellia bubalina

Catesbaea spinosa, flowers and fruit

Coffea arabica

Coffea canephora

soil; neutral to acid pH. Full to part sun. Flowers: trumpet-shaped, tube to 4 in. long, creamy white turning yellow-orange, slightly fragrant. Leaves: elliptic, to 5 in. long; margins undulate.

Gardenia jasminoides

GARDENIA, CAPE JESSAMINE
Synonym: *G. augusta* (hort.). Southern China, Taiwan, Japan. Evergreen shrub, 5–10 ft.; zones 10–11. Blooms late winter, spring. Regular moisture and humidity, less when cool. Fertile, sandy, humus-rich, well-drained soil; neu-

tral to acid pH. Full sun. Flowers: rotate, white, turning cream, fragrant; cultivated selections usually have double corollas. Leaves: elliptic, 3–5 in. long, glossy dark green. *Oils used in perfumery. Highly sensitive to root disturbance and irregular irrigation. Pests include scale insects and thrips. 'Miami Supreme' has large flowers. 'Veitchii' blooms several times a season. 'Belmont' is large leafed and marginally hardy. The dwarf single-flowered form, sold as 'Radicans' or 'Little Gem', is G. jasminoides f. radicans.*

Gardenia taitensis

TAHITIAN GARDENIA, SYMBOL-FLOWER, TIARE
Society Islands, Polynesia. Evergreen shrub, 5–10 ft.; zones 10–11. Blooms warm months. Regular moisture and humidity, less when cool. Fertile, well-drained soil; neutral to acid pH. Full sun. Flowers: rotate, petals 8, lobes irregularly twisted, white, mildly fragrant. Leaves: broadly ovate, to 6 in. long. *A spreading to upright shrub. Prefers slightly acid soil but does well in limestone soils with added humus. Relatively pest resistant. Suitable for containers.*

Gardenia ternifolia subsp. jovis-tonantis

Synonym: *G. jovis-tonantis.* Central Africa. Evergreen shrub, 10–20 ft.; zones 10–11. Blooms spring. Moderate moisture. Average to fertile, well-drained soil. Full to part sun. Flowers: trumpet-shaped, to 4 in. long, tube slender, greenish, lobes creamy white to yellowish; calyx lobes linear; solitary; fruit yellow, rarely produced in cultivation. Leaves: obovate, 1–3 in. long, smaller in more sun, base tapering; petioles short. *This is a tentative but likely identification (Puttock, pers. comm.). A variable species. Unusual in cultivation. Hard wood used for knife handles.*

Gardenia thunbergia

WILD GARDENIA, FOREST GARDENIA
South Africa. Evergreen shrub to 15 ft.; zones 10–11. Blooms most of the year. Moderate moisture when hot, less when cool. Fertile, humus-rich, well-drained soil; neutral to acid pH. Full sun. Flowers: rotate, petals 8, lobes spreading, twisted, overlapping, white, fragrant; fruit round, to 4 in. wide, woody, rough-skinned. Leaves: elliptic, to 4 in. long, rumpled, glossy dark green; margins somewhat undulate. *Thrives in hot inland areas of southern California. Rootstock used for grafting fancy gardenia hybrids but well worth growing on its own.*

Hamelia

Hamelia includes approximately 16 species of shrubs from tropical America. *Hamelia patens* is often cultivated. It is a highly variable species with an extensive range. Self-seeding, it often appears in disturbed locations. Sometimes other species and probable hybrids are sold as *H. patens* cultivars. Leaves are simple. Flowers are tubular with small lobes, which are straight to only slightly flaring. A close examination of the arrangement of flowers on the inflorescence is needed to help distinguish plants in cultivation. Attractive to butterflies and hummingbirds. Caterpillars may partly defoliate plants periodically. Do not spray. Healthy trees will recover. They are xeric, but a thick layer of mulch will improve appearance.

Gardenia coronaria

Gardenia jasminoides

Gardenia taitensis, flowers

Gardenia taitensis

Hamelia cuprea

BELL FIRE-BUSH,
WEST INDIAN FIRE-BUSH

Cuba, Grand Cayman, Hispaniola, Jamaica. Evergreen shrub, 6–10 ft.; zones 10–11. Blooms intermittently in warm months. Seasonally moist/dry. Average to poor, well-drained soil. Full to part sun. Flowers: bell-shaped, to 1.5 in. long, golden-yellow, turning orange. Leaves: elliptic, to 4 in. long, tips acuminate; in small terminal clusters. *This shrub is uncommon in cultivation but highly recommended as a natural or pruned hedge. Not self-seeding like* H. patens *and a denser shrub. Suitable for poor and coastal locations.*

Hamelia longipes

Mexico, Central America. Evergreen tree to 15 ft.+; zones 9–11. Blooms warm months. Moderate moisture when hot, less when cool. Average, well-drained soil. Full to part sun. Flowers: tubular, about 1 in. long, yellow to orange, lobes small, barely flaring; on short stalks (pedicels); calyx red, scalelike; inflorescence a terminal panicle or thyrse. Leaves: elliptic, to 6 in. long; petiole red (but not midvein). *Confused when young with* H. patens *but becomes a sturdy tree. Few pests. Chills or butterfly larvae may temporarily defoliate plants. Avoid pesticides. Unusual but recommended as a small shade tree.*

Hamelia patens

FIRE-BUSH, BUTTERFLY BUSH,
COLORADILLO

Synonym: *H. erecta*. Mexico to South America, West Indies, Florida. Evergreen short-lived shrub or tree, 8–15 ft.; zones 9–11. Blooms intermittently in warm months. Seasonally moist/dry. Average, well-drained soil. Full to part sun. Flowers: small, tubular, lobes pointed, yellow, orange to scarlet; sessile and arranged along one side of the curved branches of the inflorescence (helicoid cyme); fruit red to black. Leaves: elliptic to obovate, to 8 in. long, dull, rough-haired, often splotched with red after cold; petiole and midvein red. *A sparse, open shrub. Somewhat weedy, seed distributed by birds. Cultivated selections may include hybrids. Attractive to zebra broad-wing butterflies, but in my garden its appeal to butterflies is overrated.*

Hamelia patens var. *glabra*

FIRE-BUSH, COLORADILLO

Synonym: *H. nodosa*. Mexico, Nicaragua to northern South America, Trinidad. Evergreen shrub, 6–12 ft.; zones 9–11. Blooms intermittently in warm months. Seasonally moist/dry. Average, well-drained soil. Full to part sun. Flowers: small, tubular, lobes 4, pointed, yellow-orange; sessile, along upper side of curving inflorescence branches (helicoid cyme); fruit black. Leaves: elliptic, glossy green, 2–3 in. long; petiole slightly reddish or not. *The identity of variety* glabra *was recently resolved (Elias, pers. comm.). Denser, stiffer habit than* H. patens. *Incorrectly referred to as African fire-bush. All hamelias are American, but the variety was introduced by way of Pretoria Botanical Garden (Hammer, pers. comm.).*

Hoffmannia

Hoffmannia includes approximately 45 species of shrubs from Mexico to South America. Leaves are simple. Stems are somewhat 4-angled. Flowers are small, 5-petaled, and borne in the leaf axils or on the lower, leafless nodes. Fruits are many-seeded small berries. *Hoffmannia ghiesbreghtii* and a hybrid are grown as understory plants for their attractive foliage. They are referred to as taffeta-plants for a crisp, iridescent fabric that aptly describes the leaf color.

Hoffmannia ghiesbreghtii

TAFFETA-PLANT

Mexico. Evergreen shrub, 3–4 ft.; zones 10–11. Blooms winter. Regular moisture. Fertile, well-drained soil. Bright filtered light. Flowers: small, rotate, light green; in small

Gardenia ternifolia subsp. *jovis-tonantis*

Gardenia thunbergia

Hamelia cuprea

Hamelia longipes

Hamelia patens var. *glabra*

Hamelia patens

axillary cymes in the leaf axils and on the leafless lower part of the stems. Leaves: elliptic to lanceolate, 6–10 in. long, iridescent red-green, purple below, quilted. *An erect, little-branched shrub. Stems 4-angled.* Hoffmannia ghiesbreghtii × *H. refulgens has bronze leaves.*

Ixora

Ixora includes approximately 300 species of shrubs, which are widely distributed in the tropics, with great diversity in Africa and Asia. Leaves are simple, opposite, with leaflike stipules alternating with the leaves, appearing to be whorls of 4 leaves. Flowers are trumpet-shaped, the base a slender tube with 4 spreading lobes (salverform), arranged in many-flowered umbels. Several species and numerous selections and hybrids are in cultivation. Cultivars are often listed under the species names *I. coccinea* or *I. chinensis*, based upon differences in the shapes of the petals and leaves. Species identification of highly manipulated cultivated plants is a reckless undertaking. For many years ixoras have been commonly grown as formal property-line hedges. With heavy pruning, lack of irrigation, and poor fertility, the hedges become rectangles of sticks with yellowish leaves and chopped flowers. Ixoras are not xeric, though they will tolerate brief dry periods when temperatures are cool. They require even moisture, filtered or broken light, regular fertilizer including chelated iron in alkaline soil, and a thick bed of mulch. They are most elegant in their natural rounded form with only occasional light shaping.

Ixora casei
GIANT IXORA

Synonyms: *I. duffii, I.* 'Super King' (hort.). Caroline Islands, Pohnpei Island (Micronesia). Evergreen shrub, 6–10 ft.; zones 10–11. Blooms warm months. Regular moisture and humidity when hot, less when cool. Fertile, humus-rich, well-drained soil; neutral to acid pH. Full sun to bright broken light. Flowers: salverform, lobes 4, pointed, scarlet; in rounded umbels, 5–6 in. wide. Leaves: elliptic to lanceolate, 6–8 in. long, smooth; margins serrate; petiole short. *Of South Pacific island woodlands. Natural rounded shape. Suitable for a* moderate-sized privacy screen. Well-mulched mature plants tolerate alkaline soil better than hybrid ixoras.*

Ixora findlaysoniana
SIAMESE WHITE IXORA

Myanmar (Burma), Thailand. Evergreen shrub, 6–10 ft.; zones 10–11. Blooms warm months. Regular moisture and humidity when hot, less when cool. Fertile, humus-rich, well-drained soil; neutral to acid pH. Part sun to bright filtered light. Flowers: salverform, tube to 2 in. long, lobes narrow, white, night fragrant; in flat-topped umbels. Leaves: elliptic, to 6 in. long, dull green. *Relatively uncommon. The pure white flowers are luminous on a moonlit patio. Excellent for a butterfly garden.*

Ixora hybrids
HYBRID IXORA, CRUZ DE MALTA, SANTA RITA

Garden hybrids (Southeast Asia, India). Evergreen shrubs, 2–6 ft.; zones 9–11. Bloom warm months. Regular moisture and humidity when hot, less when cool. Fertile, humus-rich, well-drained soil; neutral to acid pH. Part sun to bright filtered light. Flowers: salverform, tube long, slender, lobes 4, rounded to pointed, yellow, orange, scarlet, or white; in many-flowered clusters. Leaves: elliptic, obovate to oblanceolate, sessile to subsessile depending on heredity. *Cultivars range from dwarf ground covers to medium shrubs. 'Nora Grant' is more tolerant of alkaline soils. Choose a hybrid of appropriate mature size for the location to limit any need of excess pruning. Distinguish from Pentas by the 4 petal lobes.*

Ixora pavetta
TORCH-TREE

Synonym: *I. parviflora*. India, Sri Lanka. Evergreen shrub to 10 ft.; zones 10–11. Blooms late winter, spring. Regular moisture and humidity when hot, less when cool. Moderately fertile, well-drained soil; neutral to acid pH. Full to part sun. Flowers: salverform, small, cream-colored; buds ruddy; in dense, many-flowered clusters; sticky with nectar; sweet-musky fragrance. Leaves: oblong to elliptic, 3–8 in. long, dark green, ending in

Hoffmannia ghiesbreghtii

Hoffmannia ghiesbreghtii, flowers

Hoffmannia ghiesbreghtii × *H. refulgens*

Ixora casei

Ixora findlaysoniana, with ruddy daggerwing butterfly

an abrupt point (cuspidate). *The heavy fragrance is very attractive to nectar feeders, probably fruit bats, in the wild. The sap is volatile, and branches are used as torches in India.*

Manettia

Manettia includes approximately 80 species of slender twining climbers from tropical America. Leaves are simple with leaflike stipules. Flowers are tubular or funnel-shaped, solitary, in pairs or racemes. Pollinated by hummingbirds. The fruit is a capsule with winged seeds.

Manettia luteorubra

FIRECRACKER VINE,
BRAZILIAN FIRECRACKER
Synonyms: *M. bicolor, M. inflata.*
Southern Brazil, Paraguay, Uruguay. Evergreen climber, 10–15 ft.;

zones 10–11. Blooms warm months. Regular moisture. Fertile, well-drained soil. Part sun to bright filtered light. Flowers: tubular, slightly inflated, 1–1.5 in. long, red with short hairs, lobes and throat yellow; sepals 4, leaflike; in pairs on a stalk. Leaves: ovate, 3–4 in. long, dark green, firm. All parts covered with soft, slightly sticky hairs. *Of tropical woodlands and rain forests. Cold-sensitive. This moderate-sized vine is suitable for growing in trees in protected locations, on a trellis, or in hanging baskets.*

Mussaenda

Mussaenda includes 100–200 species of shrubs from tropical Asia, Africa, and some Pacific Islands. The name may be derived from a Malay word *nusenda* mean-

ing "beautiful." A few species and several hybrids are cultivated in the United States. Older hybrids were made in the Philippines and Southeast Asia. They were named for well-known women of the region. Leaves are simple. The corolla is trumpet-shaped and relatively inconspicuous. One or more of the 5 sepals are greatly enlarged and petal-like. These sepals are commonly mistaken for bracts. The flowers have styles in 2 lengths (heterostylous). Though the flowers are technically bisexual, they function unisexually, and breeders refer to seed-producing plants with long styles as "female" and those with short styles as "male" (Lantin-Rosario 1984). Mussaendas are somewhat cold-sensitive and prone to spotting. A thick layer of mulch

will protect roots and help maintain even moisture. Suitable for containers.

Mussaenda philippica 'Doña Aurorae'

PHILIPPINE MUSSAENDA,
WHITE FLAG, BUDDHA'S LAMP
Synonym: *M. philippica* var. *aurorae.*
Garden hybrid. Evergreen shrub, 6–20 ft.; zones 10–11. Blooms warm months. Regular moisture. Fertile, sandy, humus-rich, well-drained soil, acid pH. Full sun. Flowers: trumpet-shaped, golden-yellow; 5 enlarged, flat white sepals, lobes suborbicular, clawed at the base; margins smooth. Leaves: elliptical to ovate, 4–6 in. long. *A sport of M.* philippica *with enlarged white sepals was discovered in 1834 on Luzon Island in the Philippines. It was a functionally male plant. The plant was crossed with the normal* M. philippica, *which has 1 enlarged white sepal, and back-crossed to the sport, resulting in this hybrid.*

Mussaenda erythrophylla

RED FLAG MUSSAENDA,
ASHANTI BLOOD
Congo, tropical western Africa. Evergreen clambering or erect shrub, 6–10 ft.+; zones 10–11. Blooms warm months. Regular moisture. Fertile, sandy, humus-rich, well-drained soil. Full sun. Flowers: corolla trumpet-shaped, white, red in throat; one enlarged, velvety red sepal. Leaves: ovate, to 6 in. long, quilted. Stems: covered with red hairs. *A probable parent of the pink-flowered hybrid mussaendas. Ashanti refers to the former British protectorate, now Ghana.*

Mussaenda frondosa

WHITE MUSSAENDA
Southeast Asia, Indomalaysia. Evergreen shrub, 4–8 ft.; zones 10–11. Blooms warm months. Regular moisture. Fertile, sandy, humus-rich, well-drained soil. Full sun. Flowers: corolla trumpet-shaped, orange; calyx with one enlarged white sepal, downy, base long-stalked (clawed). Leaves: elliptic, to 6 in. long.

Ixora 'Nora Grant'

Ixora pavetta

Manettia luteorubra

Mussaenda philippica 'Doña Aurorae'

Mussaenda erythrophylla

Mussaenda hybrids
MUSSAENDA

Garden hybrids. Evergreen shrubs, 6–20 ft.; zones 10–11. Bloom warm months. Regular moisture. Fertile, sandy, humus-rich, well-drained soil; acid pH. Full to part sun. Flowers: corolla small, trumpet-shaped, yellow; sepals 1–5, usually white to pink, smooth or edges more or less revolute. Leaves: oblong to ovate, to 6 in. long. *Pink hybrids are often assumed to involve M. 'Doña Aurorae' and M. erythrophylla. Smooth sepals are usually considered more desirable.*

Mussaenda flava
YELLOW MUSSAENDA

Eastern Africa. Evergreen shrub, 4–8 ft.; zones 9–11. Blooms primarily spring or warm months. Regular moisture. Fertile, sandy, humus-rich, well-drained soil. Full sun. Flowers: corolla trumpet-shaped, yellow; calyx with one enlarged white or yellow sepal, 2–3 in. long, base clawed, smaller than *M. frondosa.* Leaves: ovate, 2–3 in. long. *More cold tolerant than hybrids. Used for hedges. Transferred recently to Pseudomussaenda flava.*

Nauclea

Nauclea includes 10 to numerous species of trees and shrubs from Old World tropical rain forests and Pacific Islands. Leaves are simple. The flowers are small, crowded into a compact globular head. The fruit is a round syncarp composed of numerous fused berries. *Nauclea orientalis* is unusual in the United States, but it is often grown as a wayside shade tree in Asia and Australia. It is highly suitable for periodically wet locations and can be used to stabilize embankments. The timber of some species is resistant to marine-borers. Related to and flowers resemble common buttonbush, *Cephalanthus occidentalis,* a Florida native.

Nauclea orientalis
LEICHHARDT TREE, CHEESE-WOOD, KANLUANG (SOUTHEAST ASIA)

Synonyms: *Cephalanthus orientalis, N. cordata.* Philippines, Indomalaysia. Evergreen tree to 45 ft.; zones 10–11. Blooms spring. Moderate moisture to wet, seasonally dry. Average, well-drained soil. Full sun. Flowers: small, tubular, yellow; stigma exserted, white; in a globular (capitate) head to 2 in. wide; compound fruit ovoid, fleshy, tan with a bumpy surface, 1–2 in. diameter. Leaves: broadly oblong to ovate, to 12 in., smooth; margins undulate. Branches drooping. Bark: yellowish tan, fissured. *A very pleasing tree of moderate size. Tolerates periodic flooding. Recommended as a shade tree.*

Pentas

Pentas includes approximately 34 species of herbs and shrubs from Africa, Madagascar, and Arabia. Leaves are simple, interspersed with smaller, leaflike stipules, arranged with successive leaf pairs at right angles (decussate). Flowers are salverform, arranged in umbels. Styles are long or short in different flowers (heterostylous). Fruits are capsules. One species, *P. lanceolata,* is commonly cultivated and selections are available in myriad floral hues. Prune only during active growth. Pentas are stressed and may die if pruned in winter. Overwatering makes them susceptible to fungal diseases of the root. Thin to allow air to circulate. Plants are fairly xeric but need moisture in extended dry spells. Pentas, especially dwarf selections, are susceptible to nematodes. Propagate selections from cuttings. Often grown as annuals.

Pentas lanceolata
PENTAS, EGYPTIAN STAR-CLUSTER

Yemen to tropical eastern Africa. Evergreen, short-lived shrub, 2–3 ft.; zones 10–11. Blooms warm months. Moderate moisture when hot, less when cool. Fertile, well-drained soil. Full sun. Flowers: tubular, with 5 pointed lobes, bluish white hairs around throat; in many-flowered corymbs. Leaves: lanceolate, 2–4 in. long, with minute, stiff hairs; margins toothed. *Attractive to butterflies including the endangered Schaus swallowtail (in the Florida Keys), malachites, zebra broadwings as well as hummingbirds. Suitable for containers. Nip out spent inflorescences.*

Pogonopus

Pogonopus includes 3 species of small trees from seasonally moist/dry forests of Central and South America. Leaves are thin and softly downy, gradually tapering to the petiole. Stipules are leaflike with a triangular base. Flowers are trumpet-shaped. One calyx lobe is greatly enlarged. Flowers are borne in drooping, many-flowered panicles at the ends of the branches.

Mussaenda frondosa

Mussaenda 'Doña Luz'

Mussaenda 'Lakambini'

Mussaenda 'Queen Sirikit'

Mussaenda flava

Nauclea orientalis

Flowers are red to purple, which distinguishes them from *Warszewiczia*, which has yellow flowers (but red calyces). One species, *P. speciosus*, which suggests a miniature-flowered mussaenda, is highly recommended.

Pogonopus speciosus

AMERICAN MUSSAENDA, COCK'S WATTLES, CRESTA DE GALLO ("COCK'S CREST")
Panama, Colombia, Venezuela. Evergreen shrub or tree, 10–20 ft.; zones 10–11. Blooms summer, fall. Moderate moisture. Moderately fertile, well-drained soil. Part sun to bright broken light. Flowers: trumpet-shaped, purplish red; calyx with 1 or 2 enlarged lobes, red; in drooping panicles. Leaves: elliptic to obovate, to 7 in. long, glossy. Handsome peeling bark. *Mulch well. Suitable for understory planting. Un-common in cultivation but highly recommended. Attractive to hummingbirds. Slightly cold-sensitive.*

Portlandia

Portlandia includes approximately 6 species of shrubs from the West Indies. A number are handsome with very ornamental, funnel- or bell-shaped flowers. *Portlandia grandiflora* flowers resemble Easter lilies. The seams where the petals are fused are prominent. Leaves are simple and glossy. The wild habitat is threatened. Fairly unusual in cultivation in the United States probably because they may be somewhat difficult to propagate. They produce seed in cultivation only irregularly and are generally propagated by air-layering. For seed production it has been suggested that plants might be self-sterile and need to be cross-pollinated.

Portlandia coccinea

Synonym: *P. coriacea*. Jamaica, threatened in the wild. Evergreen shrub, 5–10 ft.; zones 10–11. Blooms warm months. Regular moisture when hot, less when cool. Fertile, well-drained soil; alkaline pH. Bright broken sunlight. Flowers: corolla trumpet-shaped, 3–4 in. long, scarlet with white seams, lobes 5, revolute; calyx tubular. Leaves: ovate to elliptic, 3–4 in. long, glossy dark blue-green, leathery, tips cuspidate. *Rare in cultivation but highly recommended. Propagate from cuttings or air-layers. Var. proctorii has dark red flowers with yellow seams.*

Portlandia domingensis

CAMPANITA
Synonym: *Cubanola domingensis*. Dominican Republic. Evergreen shrub to 6 ft.+; zones 10–11. Blooms warm months. Regular moisture when hot, less when cool. Fertile, well-drained soil; alkaline pH. Bright broken sunlight. Flowers: corolla fully funnel-shaped, pendent, greenish yellow, buds strongly 5-angled, to 8 in. long. Leaves: ovate, to 6 in. long, glossy dark green, lighter below. *A spreading shrub or small tree of woodland understory on limestone outcroppings.*

Portlandia grandiflora

BELLFLOWER, CAMPANA GRANDE
Jamaica, Virgin Islands. Evergreen shrub or small tree, 6–10 ft.; zones 10–11. Blooms intermittently in warm months. Regular moisture when hot, less when cool. Fertile, well-drained soil; alkaline pH. Part sun to broken light. Flowers: corolla funnel-shaped, greenish at base grading to white, 6–7 in. long, fragrant, 5-angled, lobes pointed;

Pentas lanceolata

Pogonopus speciosus

Portlandia coccinea var. *proctorii*

Portlandia domingensis

Portlandia grandiflora

solitary, obliquely pendent. Leaves: elliptic, to 6 in. long, glossy dark green. *Large white flowers are striking against the glossy, dark foliage. Understory plants. Full sun tends to burn the flowers. Reminiscent of Easter lilies. Usually propagated by cuttings or air-layers.*

Posoqueria

Posoqueria includes approximately 12 species of trees from tropical America. Some species are large trees of the forest canopy. Leaves are simple. Flowers have long, slender tubes and short lobes, and are often referred to as needle-flowers. They are arranged in umbels.

Posoqueria latifolia

NEEDLE-FLOWER, PERFUME-TREE, BRAZILIAN OAK

Synonyms: *P. coriacea, Solena latifolia.* Central America, northern South America. Evergreen tree, 30–60 ft.; zones 10–11. Blooms primarily late summer, various. Seasonally moist/dry. Average, well-drained soil. Full to part sun. Flowers: trumpet-shaped, obliquely pendent, white, slender tubes to 7 in. long, lobes short, revolute, sweetly fragrant; in many-flowered umbels; fruit round, orange-yellow, to 2 in. wide. Leaves: oblong to broadly ovate, to 6 in. long. *Of rainforest margins, savannas, and riversides. Pollinated by hawkmoths. Branches take root where they reach the ground. Species name alludes to the relatively broad leaf blades.*

Psychotria

Psychotria includes approximately 1500 species of trees and shrubs plus a few epiphytes, which are widely distributed in the tropics. Leaves are simple, pairs arranged at right angles to the ones above and below (decussate). Flowers are small, in many-flowered corymbs. Fruits are 2-seeded drupes. Ipecac, a pharmaceutical drug used as an emetic in first aid for poisoning, is derived from *P. ipecacuanha.*

Psychotria nervosa

WILD COFFEE

Synonym: *P. undata.* Florida, West Indies. Evergreen shrub, 8–12 ft.; zones 9–11. Blooms intermittently in spring, summer. Seasonally moist/dry. Average, well-drained soil; alkaline pH. Full to part sun. Flowers: trumpet-shaped, white, petals 5; in umbels, 2–3 in. wide; in leaf axils; fruit red, 2-seeded (pyrenes). Leaves: lanceolate, 3–5 in. long, glossy, quilted. *Native of southern Florida and West Indies woodlands on limestone soil. Suitable for hedges. Xeric in seasonally moist/dry climates. Cardinals like the fruit and build nests in this shrub. Recommended as a medium hedge alternative to* Eugenia uniflora *and* Ficus *species.*

Psychotria viridis

Synonyms: *Palicourea viridis, Uragoga viridis.* Costa Rica to Bolivia. Evergreen shrub, 6–10 ft.; zones 10–11. Blooms spring. Seasonally moist/dry. Average, well-drained soil; alkaline pH. Full to part sun. Flowers: tiny, trumpet-shaped, white to greenish; in many-flowered clusters (corymbs); fruit purplish red. Leaves: quilted, glossy green. *Of forest understory on limestone. Used as a folk medicine combined with hallucinogenic plants.*

Richardia

Richardia includes approximately 15 species of annual and perennial herbs from tropical and subtropical America. Not intentionally cultivated, *R. grandiflora* is a pretty, harmless, and temporary little weed which springs up in lawns from the southeastern United States to Texas.

Richardia grandiflora

MEXICAN CLOVER

Tropical and subtropical America; widely naturalized. Perennial creeping herb; zones 8–10. Blooms intermittently, commonly after rain. Moist, seasonally dry. Average, well-drained soil. Full to part sun. Flowers: funnel-shaped, white with lavender-pink lobes. Leaves: ovate, under 1 in. long. *A common lawn weed. Produces sudden pink patches in the lawn after rain, then just as quickly disappears. The species name is only relative, a bit of botanical hyperbole.*

Rondeletia

Rondeletia includes approximately 130 species of shrubs and herbs from South America, the West Indies, and Panama. Leaves are simple. Flowers are funnel-shaped to salverform, often with tiny coronas around the throat, usually in clusters in the leaf axils. Uncommon but recommended.

Posoqueria latifolia

Psychotria nervosa, fruit

Psychotria viridis

Richardia grandiflora

Rondeletia leucophylla

Rondeletia odorata

Rondeletia leucophylla
PANAMA ROSE
Synonyms: *Arachnothryx leucophylla, Bouvardia discolor.* Mexico to Panama. Evergreen shrub, 3–5 ft.; zones 9–11. Blooms warm months. Regular moisture. Fairly fertile, well-drained soil. Full to part sun. Flowers: small, salverform, lobes 4–5, rose-pink; in compact heads; fragrant at night. Leaves: linear-lanceolate, 3–6 in. long, more or less silver-haired on the underside. *Attractive to nectar-feeding birds and butterflies. Suitable for the tropical perennial garden. Sometimes used as a bedding plant but not dense enough to shade out weeds. Trim lightly after bloom to compact. Propagate from cuttings or air-layers.*

Rondeletia odorata
PANAMA ROSE
Synonym: *R. speciosa.* West Indies, Panama. Evergreen shrub, 5–8 ft.; zones 10–11. Blooms warm months. Moderate moisture to seasonally dry. Average to fairly fertile, well-drained soil; alkaline pH. Full to part sun. Flowers: small, trumpet-shaped, orange-red, golden corona around throat; in tight clusters. Leaves: broadly ovate, 1–2 in. long, tips rounded, dark green, stiff, roughly hairy, quilted; margins reflexed. Stems: with woolly bronze hairs. *Of lowlands to mid-elevation montane forests on limestone. The overall appearance resembles a calico quilt. Adaptable and underutilized. Despite the species name, the flowers are not scented. It has been alleged that a fragrant tea is made from the root.*

Rondeletia strigosa
Mexico to Nicaragua. Evergreen subshrub or climber, 3–7 ft.; zones 10–11. Blooms most of the year. Seasonally moist/dry. Average to fairly fertile, well-drained soil; alkaline pH. Full to part sun. Flowers: small, trumpet-shaped, tiny corona around throat, magenta; in clusters. Leaves: ovate, to 1 in. long, glossy dark green, leathery. Stems: green. *Unusual in cultivation.*

Warszewiczia
Warszewiczia includes approximately 4 species from tropical America. These are understory trees of seasonally wet forest. Leaves are papery with slender, twisted, deciduous stipules.

Warszewiczia coccinea
WILD POINSETTIA, FLAG-TREE, CRESTA DE GALLO ("ROOSTER'S CREST")
Synonyms: *Mussaenda coccinea, W. pulcherrima.* West Indies, Central America, northwestern South America to Amazon basin. Evergreen tree to 20 ft.; zone 11. Blooms intermittently, primarily fall, winter. Seasonally moist, less when cool. Fertile, well-drained soil. Part sun to bright broken light. Flowers: corolla yellow, sessile; in cymes; calyx with one enlarged scarlet sepal; in terminal panicles. Leaves: elliptic, 1.5–2 ft. long, rough, clustered near ends of arching branches; margins undulate. *Of seasonally wet/dry forests. Cold-sensitive. 'David Auyong' is a spectacular selection from Trinidad with all 5 sepals enlarged. Photographed in the shadehouse at Tropical Paradise Nursery, Davie, Florida.*

RUSCACEAE
DRACAENA FAMILY, LILY-OF-THE-VALLEY FAMILY
Ruscaceae includes approximately 28 genera of herbs, shrubs, and trees, which are widely distributed in temperate and tropical regions. These species were transferred to Convallariaceae (Judd 1999) but are correctly circumscribed by Ruscaceae, a conserved name—a name in frequent use that is kept even when an older name is discovered (Judd 2002). Ruscaceae also circumscribes the species formerly distributed in Nolinaceae and Dracaenaceae. Flowers are small, bisexual or unisexual, and radially symmetrical. They are arranged in panicles, umbels, or racemes. The fruit is a red triangular nut.

Beaucarnea
Beaucarnea includes approximately 6 species of trees from southern Mexico to Honduras. The genus has been placed in a succession of families over the years including Agavaceae, Convallariaceae, Nolinaceae, and Dracaenaceae. Flowers are small, cream-colored, unisexual, and radially symmetrical. They are borne in large panicles of thousands of flowers. The fruit is nut-like, 3-sided, and red when fresh.

Leaves are sword-shaped, with smooth or minutely toothed margins, and taper to a threadlike tip. They can be distinguished from *Yucca* by the lack of a terminal leaf

Rondeletia strigosa

Warszewiczia coccinea 'David Auyong'

Beaucarnea guatemalensis

spine and from *Dracaena* by the lack of forked leaf bases. Beaucarneas, adapted to living in seasonally dry forests, develop water-storing pachycaulous trunks and often massive caudices. They are slow-growing and the trunks of some species do not begin to branch for many years. Locally these trees are drolly referred to as *palma culona* (palm-with-the-big-behind). In the wild, beaucarneas typically grow on fast-draining rocky hillsides.

Beaucarnea guatemalensis

PONYTAIL TREE, PALMA CULONA, IZOTE (MAYAN)
Synonym: *Nolina guatemalensis.* Guatemala, Honduras. Evergreen pachycaulous tree to 35 ft.; zones 10–11. Blooms summer. Moderate moisture. Gritty, well-drained soil. Full to part sun. Flowers: small,

cream; in terminal panicles, to 3 ft. tall. Leaves: sword-shaped, 2 ft. long, 1 in. wide, wider at the base, drooping against the branches, in terminal clusters; margins almost imperceptibly toothed; old leaves only briefly persistent. Trunk: short or flared into a caudex at the base, bark shallowly fissured, branches irregularly from the trunk. *Often sold as B. recurvata but distinguished by the limply drooping leaves with long tapering, twisted tips.*

Beaucarnea pliables

PONYTAIL TREE, ELEPHANT-FOOT TREE
Synonyms: *B. ameliae, Dasylirion pliables.* Southeastern Mexico. Evergreen pachycaulous tree to 25 ft.; zones 10–11. Blooms spring. Moderate moisture. Gritty, very well-drained soil. Full sun. Flowers: small, white; in stiffly erect pani-

cles. Leaves: sword-shaped, to 4 ft. long, 1 in. wide, tapering to a very long slender thread at the tip, arching at the base, ends drooping, in terminal clusters; old leaves briefly persistent. Trunk: cone-shaped to flaring at the base, bark coarsely fissured, branches from the caudex. *Distinguished from* B. guatemalensis *by arching leaves and from B. recurvata by basal branching and more erect inflorescences.*

Beaucarnea recurvata

PONYTAIL TREE, ELEPHANT-FOOT TREE, PATA DE ELEFANTE, PALMA CULONA
Synonym: *Nolina recurvata.* Southeastern Mexico. Evergreen pachycaulous tree to 25 ft.; zones 10–11. Blooms summer, fall. Moderate moisture to dry. Open, well-drained soil. Full sun. Flowers: small, cream; in oblique ascending pani-

cles. Leaves: sword-shaped, 3–4 ft. long, 1 in. wide, tapering into a long thread at the tip, arching; old leaves briefly persistent. Trunk: greatly swollen, 5 ft.+ wide at the base when mature, bark cracked in angular plates. *Distinctive features include the rounded caudex and branching from the top of the erect trunk, not from the caudex.*

Beaucarnea stricta

PONYTAIL TREE, ESTRELLAS ("STARS")
Synonyms: *B. glauca, Dasylirion strictum.* Southern Mexico. Evergreen pachycaulous tree to about 20 ft.; zones 9–11. Blooms spring, summer. Moderate moisture to dry. Open, very well-drained soil. Full to part sun. Flowers: small, white; in terminal panicles. Leaves: sword-shaped, 2–2.5 ft. long, 1 in. wide, stiff, bluish green, in stiffly radiat-

Beaucarnea pliables

Beaucarnea recurvata

ing clusters; margins finely toothed; old leaves persistent. Trunk: stiffly erect, tapering uniformly, 4–6 ft. wide at the base when mature, bark deeply fissured. *Distinctive features include stiffly radiating leaves and persistent dry leaves. Mature trees develop short branches.*

Dasylirion

Dasylirion includes approximately 15 species of stemless or short-stemmed shrubs and small pachycaulous trees from the southwestern United States and Mexico. Leaves are long, sword-shaped to linear with hooked, sharp teeth on the margins. The tips are dry and twisted, not spined (*Agave* and *Yucca* generally have spined leaf tips). The flowers are small, clustered in fascicles on tall, spikelike inflorescences. Some species thrive in moist climates with excellent drainage. Heat tolerant. Irrigate cultivated plants deeply once a week in hot, arid conditions. Used for fiber, thatch, and animal feed. Pulp said to be distilled into alcoholic beverage called *sotol* by local Indians. Dasylirions are seen by hikers in the Grand Canyon.

Dasylirion wheeleri

DESERT-SPOON, BEAR-GRASS, SOTOL

Arizona to northern Mexico. Evergreen pachycaulous tree, 6–8 ft.; zones 7–11. Blooms spring, summer. Arid. Average to poor, well-drained soil. Full to part sun. Flowers: tiny, cream; in fascicles on spikelike inflorescence, 10–20 ft. tall. Leaves: narrowly sword-shaped, gray-green, tips somewhat twisted and dry; stiffly and symmetrically radiating; margins armed with hooked teeth. Trunk: unbranched, erect, to 5 ft. *Striking globular symmetry.*

Dracaena

Dracaena includes approximately 80 species of perennial herbs, shrubs, and trees from the Old World tropics, the Canary Islands, and 1 each from Cuba and Central America. These are commonly used as xeric foliage plants. Leaves are narrow and linear to broadly sword-shaped, old leaves briefly persistent, arranged around straight or sinuous stalks, often variegated with cream or red stripes. The clasping leaf bases are generally fishtail- or wedge-shaped. The flowers are small, short-lived in many-flowered panicles. Relatively slow-growing in poor/dry conditions, but moisture and fertilizer encourage faster growth. Cuttings are used as container plants. Some cultivars probably involve hybrids.

Dracaena americana

Mexico, Central America, northwestern South America. Evergreen shrub or tree, 10–35 ft.; zones 8–11. Blooms spring. Seasonally moist/dry. Average, well-drained soil. Full to part sun. Flowers: small, yellowish white, fragrant; in many-flowered panicles; fruit yellow. Leaves: lanceolate, to 1 ft. long, green, clustered near the end of the limbs. Stems: canelike, ringed with leaf scars, branching from the base. *Wild habitat along rivers or seasonally moist/dry forests, at low to medium elevations.*

Dracaena draco

DRAGON-TREE, DRAGON'S BLOOD
Synonyms: *Asparagus draco, Yucca draconis.* Canary Islands. Evergreen

Beaucarnea stricta, a young, unbranched tree

Dasylirion wheeleri, with flower spike

pachycaulous tree, 20–50 ft.; zones 8–10. Blooms late winter, spring. Moderate moisture to dry. Gritty, well-drained soil. Full sun. Flowers: greenish white, tiny, in large panicles; fruit red-orange. Leaves: lanceolate, 1.5–2 ft. long, leathery, forked base orange; in terminal clusters; margins smooth. Trunk erect, branches radiate spokelike from the top. *Orange sap used in varnish for Stradivarius violins imparted a distinctive color. A few ancient massive trees are left in the Canary Islands. Orange leaf bases attractive in dry arrangements.*

Dracaena fragrans

FRAGRANT DRACAENA, CORN-PLANT, PALMILLO
Synonyms: *Cordyline fragrans, D. deremensis, Pleomele fragrans.* Tropical Africa. Evergreen tree, 6–15 ft.; zones 10–11. Blooms winter. Moderate moisture. Sandy, humus-rich, well-drained soil. Part sun to bright shade. Flowers: small, white, short-lived; in round clusters on a pendent stalk; sweetly fragrant. Leaves: lanceolate, to 2 ft. long, 3–4 in. wide, arching, young leaves striped yellow in the center aging green; sessile, bases clasp the stem; margins smooth. *Cuttings can be rooted directly in the ground. Nurseries sell large sprouting stem cuttings as "corn-plants," which quickly revert to the normal form. Protect from midday sun for fresh appearance and good coloration. 'Lemon Lime' is a hybrid with narrower leaves and yellow margins.*

Dracaena marginata

Synonym: *D. cincta.* Madagascar. Evergreen tree to 10 ft.; zones 10–11. Blooms inconsistently in cultivation. Seasonally moist/dry. Average, well-drained soil. Full sun to bright filtered light. Flowers: uncommon; in clusters, branches spirelike. Leaves: sword-shaped, to 18 in. long, 0.5 in. wide, green with thin red margins. Young stems slender, flexible; older stalks thick and stiff. *Suitable for coastal locations. Slow growing, little branched. Propagate cuttings directly in the ground. 'Tricolor' is pink and cream striped; margins red; in terminal whorls. Selections available with varying degrees of red or white variegation. For an unusual bedding plant, set out short cuttings and maintain by cutting back a few at a time to 6 in. when they become too tall and replant the tops.*

Dracaena reflexa

Madagascar, Mauritius. Evergreen shrub or tree, 10–15 ft.; zones 10–11. Blooms fall. Regular moisture. Average, well-drained soil; alkaline pH. Part sun to bright filtered light. Flowers: small, greenish yellow, white inside, in panicles. Leaves: lanceolate, 8–10 in. long, base sheathing stem, green, compactly arranged. Stems: flexible, sinuous, little-branched. *'Honoriae' has longer leaves with cream-colored margins. 'Song of India' and 'Song of Jamaica' have shorter variegated leaves.*

Liriope

Liriope includes 5 species of perennial, stemless herbs from Vietnam, China, and Japan. These are clump-forming, rhizomatous plants of mild temperate and tropical regions. The leaves are straplike or linear, sometimes variegated with white stripes. Flowers are small, white or violet, and clustered at the end of a scape. They are often grown as a ground cover or border, and are useful in place of grass around superficial tree roots or other areas that are difficult to

Dracaena americana

Dracaena draco

Dracaena draco, infructescence

Dracaena fragrans, inflorescences

Dracaena marginata 'Tricolor'

Dracaena reflexa 'Song of India'

Liriope muscari 'Variegata'

mow. Most commercial plants are mass produced for foliage and have nonshowy, usually white flowers, of uncertain ancestry. Select known species for ornamental flowers.

Liriope muscari
LILY-TURF
Synonyms: *L. graminifolia*, *L. platyphylla*. China, Taiwan, Japan. Evergreen or seasonally dormant herb to 18 in.; zones 7–10. Blooms intermittently in warm months. Regular moisture and humidity. Sandy, humus-rich, well-drained soil. Full sun to bright filtered light. Flowers: small, violet; on slender spikes. Leaves: narrowly strap-shaped, grasslike, dark green; margins of variegated forms white. *Suitable for ground cover and as a border plant. Blooms better in bright locations with plenty of humidity. Mondo grass, Ophiopogon species, are smaller plants with dark green, linear leaves.*

Sansevieria
Sansevieria includes approximately 70 species of evergreen rhizomatous herbs or shrubs from Africa, Madagascar, and India to Indomalaysia. These are mostly xeric plants of dry climates and rough terrain. They also thrive in moist conditions. Leaves are thick, fibrous, sword-shaped to cylindrical (terete). Flowers are small, borne on a scape. Rhizomes can become very aggressive outdoors, especially in moist conditions, and invade the garden becoming almost impossible to eradicate. Confining plants to containers is strongly recommended.

Sansevieria cylindrica
ST. GEORGE'S LANCE
Angola, Zambia. Perennial herb, 4–5 ft.; zones 10–11. Blooms winter. Moderate moisture to dry. Average, well-drained soil. Full sun to bright filtered light. Flowers: small, greenish white; on tall, spikelike raceme from the rhizome. Leaves: cylindrical, 3–4 ft.+ tall, with a lengthwise groove on one side, mottled green and gray, purplish in dry conditions, tip pointed.

Sansevieria hyacinthoides

BOWSTRING HEMP, SNAKE-PLANT, LENGUA DE SUEGRA ("MOTHER-IN-LAW TONGUE")

Synonyms: *S. guineensis, S. thyrsi-flora.* Southeastern Africa; widely naturalized. Perennial herb, 3–6 ft.; zones 10–11. Blooms winter, spring. Wet to dry. Average to poor, well-drained soil. Full sun to shade. Flowers: funnel-shaped, small, pinkish white; in spikelike racemes, 2–3 ft. tall. Leaves: basal, 1.5–3 ft.+ tall, sword-shaped, stiffly erect, fibrous, green, mottled gray-white; margins straight, reddish brown; petiole channeled; in whorls of 2–8. *Moderately salt tolerant. Invasive. A controlled species in Florida. Often listed as* S. trifasciata, *a distinct species with horizontal chevron stripes and often broad white leaf margins. It is also invasive.*

Sansevieria kirkii

Zanzibar, Tanzania. Perennial herb, 2–3 ft.; zones 10–11. Blooms winter. Moist to dry. Average to poor, well-drained soil. Full sun to shade. Flowers: tubular, tube pinkish, lobes cream; in floppy heads. Leaves: sword-shaped, in spreading clusters of 1–4, dark green or gray-green, with mottled cream spots and a metallic sheen; margins deeply undulate, edge purplish, to about 1 ft. Rhizomes red. *Leaves resemble* S. metallica *which has erect racemes of white flowers.*

RUTACEAE

CITRUS FAMILY

Rutaceae includes approximately 155 genera of mostly shrubs and trees, which are widely distributed but primarily tropical and subtropical. *Citrus* is the most commonly cultivated genus and includes oranges and grapefruits. Rind oils are used in medicines, cosmetics, fragrances, flavorings, and cleaning products. Other species are grown for their ornamental and/or fragrant flowers or as foliage plants. Leaves are simple or compound with smooth margins, sometimes modified into spines. Tiny translucent glandular cavities (pellucid dots) secrete aromatic oils and can be seen if the blade is held to the light. Flowers are bisexual, or unisexual with male and female flowers on the same plant (monoecious) or on different plants (dioecious), and are usually radially symmetrical. The corolla consists of 4 or 5 free or sometimes fused, white, yellow, or pink petals. The calyx consists of 4 or 5 sepals, sometimes reduced. There are usually twice the number of stamens as petals, or numerous stamens. Flowers are solitary or arranged in panicles, umbels, or racemes. Fruits are quite variable. *Citrus* fruits are segmented berries with leathery rinds (hesperidia). Other types of fruits include aggregates, capsules, drupes, samaras, and schizocarps.

Calodendrum

Calodendrum includes 2 species of evergreen trees from tropical Africa and coastal South Africa. The name means "beautiful tree." *Calodendrum capense* is doubtless one of the most spectacular trees of the subtropics. The pink and red flowers have the serendipitously appropriate fragrance of a strawberry milkshake. The leaves are simple and glossy dark green, which sets

Sansevieria cylindrica

Sansevieria hyacinthoides

Sansevieria kirkii

Calodendrum capense, flowers

Calodendrum capense

off the pink flowers. The crown is round and dense. This species is used as a wayside or shade tree in the Southern Hemisphere. *Calodendrum* is tender when young, becoming marginally hardy. Trees may take up to 12 years to bloom from seed, less when grafted. In flower they vaguely resemble a chestnut (*Castanea*) in blossom.

Calodendrum capense

CAPE CHESTNUT
Southern Africa. Semideciduous tree, 25–50 ft.+; zones 9–10. Blooms late spring or sporadically in summer. Regular moisture when hot, less when cool. Fertile, light, well-drained soil. Full sun. Flowers: petals linear, pink, burgundy at the base; 5 stamens interspersed with 5 petal-like staminodes, white with burgundy spots, fragrant; in dense terminal panicles; capsules 5-lobed, to 2 in. wide, wrinkled; seeds large, black. Leaves: simple, elliptic, to 7 in. long, at first woolly, turning glossy dark green; margins undulate. Bark: smooth, gray, young twigs hairy. *In California it blooms for about 4 weeks in late spring and is briefly deciduous. Highly recommended. Photographed at Quail Botanical Garden.*

Citrus

Citrus includes approximately 16 species of trees and shrubs from southern China to Southeast Asia and Polynesia. Leaves are simple, evolved from compound-leaf ancestors (technically unifoliolate) with glandular pellucid dots. The petioles are often winged and the axils usually have spines. Flowers are bisexual, radially symmetrical, and fragrant. Citrus fruits are the primary source of vitamin C in the typical American diet, but only a few varieties are marketed widely. Some cultivated citrus are probably ancient cultigens with obscure ancestry often producing seed asexually. Cultivation goes back millennia in India and China.

Citrus medica is probably one ancestor of contemporary citrus varieties. It has relatively large, sweet-scented flowers and curious, ridged, thick-skinned fruit. The peel is cut into thin slices and candied. Orange marmalade is a bittersweet preserve made from the rind of sour Seville oranges, *C. aurantium*. In the Caribbean, the juice is mixed with garlic to make mojo (pronounced MO-ho) sauce, a marinade. Flavoring and oils extracted from seed and rind are used in shampoos and biodegradable cleaning agents. Lemon, *C. limon*, is the most cold tolerant of commercially grown citrus.

Citrus is subject to numerous pests, some of serious commercial consequence. It is also a host of giant swallowtail butterfly larvae, which occasionally nibble the leaves. Fancy varieties are grafted. Pollinated by bees (see accompanying photo).

Citrus medica

CITRON, BUDDHA'S HAND, CEDRAT
India. Evergreen tree to 8 ft.; zones 9–11. Blooms late winter. Moderate but regular moisture. Fertile, humus-rich, well-drained soil; slightly acid pH. Full sun. Flowers: petals white inside, purplish outside, sweetly fragrant; calyx cup-shaped; fruit shaped like a baseball glove, thick-skinned with little juice. Leaves: simple, ovate, to 6 in. long, blade with pellucid dots, fragrant when crushed. *Marginally hardy when mature. Pellucid dots visible on fruit. Slightly salt tolerant. The common name citron is also applied to a candied melon rind used in fruitcakes.*

Correa

Correa includes approximately 11 species of shrubs and trees from tropical and temperate Australia. Leaves are simple and stiff. The petals are fused into a tube. The calyx is cup-shaped.

Correa reflexa

COMMON CORREA, CANDY-CORN CORREA, AUSTRALIAN FUCHSIA
Australia. Evergreen shrub to 10 ft.; zones 9–10. Blooms late summer, fall, winter. Moderate moisture. Fertile, well-drained soil. Full sun to bright broken light. Flowers: tubular, corolla red, with few long hairs, tip green with purple stripes; stamens 12, exserted. Leaves: entire, ovate, 2–3 in. long; midvein reddish. *Spreading or erect. The ends of the corolla tube are yellow in var.* pulchella.

Erythrochiton

Erythrochiton includes approximately 7 species of shrubs or trees from tropical America. Leaves are simple, clustered at the ends of the branches. The flowers are long and trumpet-shaped, the largest flowers in the citrus family. The calyx is usually brightly colored. Inflorescences are few- to many-flowered cymes. Fruits are fleshy at first, then dry, capsules separating into 5 follicles, each with one seed (visible in lower left in photo).

Erythrochiton brasiliensis

Venezuela, Brazil, Peru, Bolivia. Evergreen shrub, 5–15 ft.; zones 10–11. Blooms intermittently. Moderate moisture, less when cool. Fertile, humus-rich, well-drained soil; neutral pH. Part sun to bright broken light. Flowers: corolla trumpet-shaped, white; tube enclosed by the slightly inflated red calyx; fruit

Citrus medica, flower

Citrus medica, fruit

Correa reflexa

Erythrochiton brasiliensis

fleshy, red, becoming dry, splitting into 5 follicles. Leaves: simple, obovate to lanceolate, 8–14 in. long, stiff, dark green, aromatic; margins undulate. *Of tropical forest understory. Unusual in cultivation. Branches from the base. Erect habit is suitable for small gardens or narrow passageways. Acidify planting hole in alkaline soil and top-dress with copious mulch.*

Limonia

Limonia includes a single species of tree from southeastern Asia. Other species formerly placed in this genus have now been redistributed. Leaves are pinnate. Flowers are small. Used as a stock for grafting *Citrus* and as a source of India gum, which is used in glues and paints. Inner bark of *L. acidissima* is said to be used to smooth the skin in Southeast Asia (Schokman, pers. comm.). It should be noted, however, that some people develop a photochemical reaction to citrus oils, especially limes, causing a severe itching, blistering rash, and long-lasting skin discoloration. Caution is advised when using any product containing citrus oil. Note spelling: *Lemonia* is a synonym for *Ravenia*. The common lemon is *Citrus limon.*

Limonia acidissima

WOOD-APPLE, ELEPHANT-APPLE
Synonyms: *Feronia limonia, Feronia elephantum.* Southern China, Southeast Asia, India, Sri Lanka. Evergreen tree to 20 ft.; zones 9–11. Blooms late spring. Seasonally moist/dry. Fertile, well-drained soil. Full sun. Flowers: small, petals 5, greenish; anthers relatively large, rust-brown; fruit red. Leaves: pinnate, 2–3 in. long; leaflets 5, glossy, rachis winged. Spines needlelike, 1–3 in. long. *Note: the common name elephant-apple is also applied to Dillenia indica.*

Murraya

Murraya includes 4 or 5 species of shrubs or trees from China, India, Indomalaysia to Australia and the Pacific Islands. Leaves are odd-numbered pinnate (imparipinnate). Flowers are small with 10 free stamens. Fruits are small berries.

Murraya koenigii

CURRY-LEAF, KARAPINCHA
India, Sri Lanka. Evergreen tree, 10–20 ft.; zones 9–11. Blooms spring, summer, or intermittently. Seasonally moist/dry. Average, well-drained soil. Full sun to filtered light. Flowers: small, greenish, in compact clusters (corymbs); fruit ovoid, bluish black. Leaves: pinnate, leaflets 11–15+, oblique, strongly aromatic; margins serrulate. *Used as a curry seasoning in tropical India and Sri Lanka. Heavily self-seeding and weedy. The aroma permeates the surrounding area. Sometimes pruned as a hedge.*

Murraya paniculata

ORANGE JESSAMINE, MOCK ORANGE, CHINESE BOXWOOD, MIRTO, CHALCAS
Synonym: *M. exotica.* China, India to Australia; widely distributed and sometimes naturalized. Evergreen shrub or tree, 10–15 ft.; zones 10–11. Blooms intermittently in warm months. Moderate moisture. Average, well-drained soil. Full to part sun. Flowers: small, 5 petals white, citrus-scented; in compact corymbs; fruit a berry, ovoid, red-orange, to 0.5 in. long. Leaves: pinnate; leaflets 5–7, obovate, glossy dark green, to 1 in. long. *Very attractive small tree but more commonly pruned as a hedge. Fruit distributed by birds and a potential pest. Restricted in Florida.* 'Lakeview' has slightly larger leaves.

Pamburus

Pamburus includes a single species of tree from southern India and Sri Lanka. Leaves are simple. The leaf axils have spines. This citruslike tree is unusual in cultivation.

Pamburus missionis

Synonyms: *Atalantia missionis,*

Limonia missionis. Southern India, Sri Lanka. Evergreen tree to 15 ft.+; zones 10–11. Blooms late winter, early spring. Seasonally moist, moderate. Fertile, well-drained soil. Full to part sun. Flowers: small, petals 4, greenish cream; stamens 8; fruit seedy. Leaves: simple, oblong, 2–4 in. long, somewhat folded, glossy, tip acute; margins undulate; petiole short, 0.25 in. long, not winged. Spines in leaf axils, to 0.25 in. long. *Habit resembles Citrus species. Used as a shade tree in Sri Lanka (Schokman, pers. comm.).*

Ravenia

Ravenia includes approximately 14 species of shrubs and trees from tropical America. *Ravenia spectabilis* is unusual in cultivation but very desirable. Leaves are trifoliolate. Flowers are deep pink, bilaterally symmetrical (unusual in this family) with relatively broad, overlap-

Limonia acidissima

Murraya koenigii

Murraya paniculata

Pamburus missionis

Ravenia spectabilis

Swinglea glutinosa

ping petals. The stamens are triangular, mounted on the corolla around the throat. Note spelling: *Ravenea* is a genus of palms.

Ravenia spectabilis

TORTUGO

Synonym: *Lemonia spectabilis*. Cuba, Hispaniola. Evergreen shrub or tree to 12 ft.; zones 10–11. Blooms intermittently in warm months. Moist when hot, less when cool. Fertile, well-drained soil; alkaline pH. Full to part sun. Flowers: raspberry pink, to 1.5 in. wide, petals overlapping, surface glandular; stamens triangular attached to the edge of the throat; sepals 2, small, green; solitary in the leaf axils; fruit splits into 5 woody follicles. Leaves: trifoliolate; leaflets oblong to elliptic, glossy dark green with sheathing bases. *Attractive to swallowtail butterflies, skippers, and hummingbirds. Unusual in cultivation but highly recommended. Suitable for flowering hedges.*

Swinglea

Swinglea includes a single species of tree from the Philippines. It is grown in Asia for its fragrance. Leaves are trifoliolate, glossy, and strongly citrus-scented. Flowers have 5 petals and 10 stamens and are arranged in axillary clusters near the ends of the branches.

Swinglea glutinosa

TABOG

Philippines (Luzon). Evergreen tree, 15–30 ft.; zones 10–11.

Blooms warm months, primarily summer. Moderate moisture and humidity. Average, well-drained soil. Full to part sun. Flowers: petals 5, white; stamens 10; in small clusters near the ends of the branches. Leaves: trifoliolate; leaflets elliptic to ovate, glossy, to 2 in. long; citrus-scented. *Branches spiny. Suitable as a fragrant barrier hedge.*

SAPINDACEAE

LYCHEE FAMILY, SOAPBERRY FAMILY
Sapindaceae includes approximately 147 genera of shrubs, trees, and woody climbers (lianas), which are widely distributed most commonly in the tropics and subtropics though some genera are temperate. This family now includes the genera traditionally included in the horse-chestnut family, Hippocastanaceae, and the maple family, Aceraceae. Several species are cultivated. Lychee, *Litchi chinensis*, is an outstanding fruit eaten fresh, cooked, or dried. It has aromatic, translucent white flesh encased in a papery red shell. Dried fruits are commonly sold in Asian markets as a sweet snack. Longan or momón, *Dimocarpus longana*, somewhat similar to lychee, is eaten in Latin America and Asia but is not as well known in the United States.

Leaves are simple or palmately or pinnately compound. Flowers are bisexual, or unisexual with male and female flowers usually on the same plant (monoecious), occasionally on different plants (dioecious), or polygamous. They are ra-

dially or bilaterally symmetrical. Petals are 4 or 5, usually small, free, or sometimes absent. Sepals are 4 or 5, sometimes fused at the base. The inflorescences are sometimes showy, occasionally modified into tendrils in climbing species. The fruit is a capsule, nut, berry, often with a fleshy aril, or a schizocarp.

Aesculus

Aesculus includes approximately 13 species of deciduous shrubs and trees mostly from temperate Asia, Europe, and North America. Horsechestnuts were formerly segregated in their own family, Hippocastanaceae. *Aesculus indica* comes from temperate and subtropical forests south of the Himalayas and thrives in California. Leaves are palmately compound. Flowers are in spirelike panicles.

Aesculus indica

INDIAN HORSE-CHESTNUT, NARU, PANGAR

Synonym: *Pavia indica*. Sub-Himalayan region, northern India. Deciduous tree, 50–100 ft.; zones 7–10. Blooms late spring. Moderate moisture. Average, well-drained soil. Full to part sun. Flowers: light pink, red in center, upper petals spotted yellow; in ascending to erect spirelike panicles, 12–16 in. tall. Leaves: palmate, leaflets 5–7, oblong to oblanceolate, 8–12 in. long, on short stalks, pinkish when young; margins serrulate; petioles long, reddish. *Potentially a very large shade tree with a rounded crown.*

Blighia

Blighia includes 4 species of evergreen trees from tropical Africa. Leaves are pinnate. Flowers are unisexual, borne in racemes from the leaf axils. Seeds are arillate. The yellow arils of akee, *B. sapida*, are commonly eaten in Jamaica. The popularity of akee is severely limited by its high toxicity except during a very brief period immediately after opening naturally. Underripe or overripe arils are toxic. Even in experienced hands akee sometimes results in severe poisoning.

Blighia sapida

AKEE, SESO VEGETAL

Tropical western Africa. Evergreen tree, 20–40 ft.; zones 10–11. Blooms warm months. Seasonally moist and humid, dry. Average, well-drained soil. Full to part sun. Flowers: small, petals 5, greenish; fruit ovoid, skin leathery, 3- to 4-valved, tan turning red; splitting opening when ripe exposing cream-yellow arils, a red funicle, and glossy black seeds. Leaves: pinnate; leaflets 6–10, obovate, 4–6 in. long. *Arils are toxic except immediately after the fruit opens naturally. The funicle and seeds are always poisonous.*

Dimocarpus

Dimocarpus includes approximately 5 species from Southeast Asia to Australia. Leaves are pinnate, sometimes reduced to one leaflet (unifoliolate). Flowers are small, the corolla hairy. Called longan, *D. longan* 'Kohala' is considered the best selection and was introduced from Hawaii into South Florida by well-known pomologist Bill Whitman. It has a large fruit and a small seed. The rind is leathery and easily peeled.

Dimocarpus longan

LONGAN, DRAGON'S EYES, MAMÓN, LONGYEN (CHINA)

Synonym: *Euphoria longana*. India, Sri Lanka, Southeast Asia. Evergreen tree, 40–120 ft.; zones 10–11. Blooms late spring. Seasonally moist/dry. Average, well-drained soil. Full sun. Flowers: small, yellowish; fruit ripens in early summer, rind rough, greenish to yellowish tan, in large clusters. Leaves:

Aesculus indica

Blighia sapida, fruits

Dimocarpus longan 'Kohala'

pinnate, to 15 in. long; leaflets 7, lanceolate, midvein light. *Potentially large, buttressed tree but usually kept at moderate size in cultivation. The edible part of the fruit is the sweet, white aril. The rind is leathery and easily peeled.*

Dodonaea

Dodonaea includes approximately 68 species of shrubs and trees from mild temperate and tropical regions, with great diversity in Australia. *Dodonaea viscosa* is grown as a foliage plant and for the ornamental, papery 3-winged capsules. The flowers are inconspicuous. Leaves are simple or pinnate, covered with glandular dots, and secrete a sticky resin sometimes used to stop bleeding.

Dodonaea viscosa

VARNISH-LEAF, HOP-SEED BUSH
Pantropical. Evergreen shrub or small tree, 6–10 ft.+; zones 9–11. Blooms spring, summer. Moderate moisture, less in winter. Average to poor, well-drained soil; alkaline pH. Full sun. Flowers: reduced, lacking petals; capsules flat with 2–3 papery wings, green to tan or pinkish purple. Leaves: simple, obovate, elliptic to lanceolate, 3–5 in. long, blade decurrent; veins light; margins undulate. *Variable over its large range. 'Purpurea' is an especially showy selection with pinkish-purple capsules. Salt tolerant. Suitable for coastal landscaping.*

Harpullia

Harpullia includes approximately 37 species of trees from Madagascar, India, Indomalaysia to Australia. Male and female flowers are on different trees (dioecious) or sometimes polygamous. *Harpullia pendula* is rounded with pendent branches hanging to the ground. Leaves are pinnate. Flowers are white and inconspicuous, on pendent racemes beneath the canopy. The fruit is a 2-valved red-orange to yellow-orange leathery capsule that splits at maturity revealing 2 glossy black seeds. An excellent shade tree if lower branches are pruned. The sapwood is yellow with black heartwood and is highly prized for cabinetry in Australia.

Harpullia pendula

MORETON BAY TULIPWOOD
Eastern Australia. Evergreen tree, 20–50 ft.; zones 9–11. Blooms intermittently in warm months. Moderate moisture to somewhat dry. Average, well-drained soil. Full sun. Flowers: small, petals 5, greenish; in pendent racemes; capsules orange, splitting into 2 cuplike valves exposing 2 glossy black seeds. Leaves: pinnate; leaflets 4–8, oblong to lanceolate, glossy green. Branches drooping. Harpullia arborea *from India and Southeast Asia to the Philippines and New Guinea is*

Dodonaea viscosa 'Purpurea'

Koelreuteria elegans

Harpullia pendula

Koelreuteria elegans subsp. *formosana*, flowers

distinguished by the 8–10 leaflets on inclined branches and clawed petals.

Koelreuteria

Koelreuteria includes 3 or 4 species of trees from China, Korea, and Taiwan. Leaves are pinnate or bipinnate with uneven-numbered leaflets (imparipinnate), pinnae and leaflets are alternate. Flowers are small with a glandular red callus at the base of the yellow petals. The reddish fruits are inflated papery capsules with 3 longitudinal lobes. Some are listed as invasive. Varnish tree, *K. paniculata*, is a deciduous temperate species from northern China and Korea with a columnar habit and mostly once-pinnate leaves. Golden rain tree *Koelreuteria bipinnata*, from mild temperate regions of China, is deciduous and has bipinnate leaves. *Koelreuteria elegans*, the only subtropical species, is evergreen with bipinnate leaves.

Koelreuteria elegans
FLAMEGOLD TREE
Taiwan. Evergreen tree, 25–50 ft.; zones 9–11. Blooms late summer, fall. Moderate moisture, less when cool. Average, well-drained soil. Full sun. Flowers: petals usually 5, yellow with a red glandular callus; in panicles, about 1 ft. long or 2–3 ft. long in subsp. *formosana*; capsules ovoid, inflated, 3-lobed, pink, turning tan. Leaves: bipinnate, to 2 ft. long, or longer in subsp. *formosana*; pinnae 5–6, leaflets 11–13, asymmetrically lanceolate, 3–4 in. long; margins mostly smooth or irregularly toothed. *Subsp.* formo-

sana *(syn. K. formosana) produces billowing yellow clouds of flowers that last for a week or two. Flowers are followed by pink to red capsules resembling little Japanese lanterns.*

Litchi

Litchi includes a single species of tree that originated in southern China but no longer exists in the wild. Leaves are pinnately compound. Flowers are unisexual, in terminal panicles. The fruit is outstanding with a limited distribution in U.S. supermarkets but can be found in Asian markets. It is a one-seeded berry with a translucent, juicy white aril covering the large black seed. Asians prefer fleshier selections with shrunken, sterile seeds. The bumpy, leathery red husk is a perfect package and easily peeled away. In Asian markets, the fruit is also sold semidried as a lychee "nut." Dried fruits have a raisinlike consistency but a distinctive flavor and sandalwood scent.

Litchi chinensis
LYCHEE
Garden origin (China). Semideciduous tree, 25–50 ft.; zones 9–11. Blooms spring. Seasonally moist/dry. Fertile, well-drained soil. Full sun. Flowers: unisexual, inconspicuous, white; fruit ovoid, pink to red when ripe, to 1.5 in. long. Leaves: pinnate; leaflets 2–3 pairs, lanceolate, 3–6 in. long. *Larger fruits are produced on trees which are allowed to go dormant in winter. Withhold irrigation until new growth begins in spring.*

Majidea

Majidea includes a single species of tree from Madagascar and tropical Africa. Leaves are pinnate. Flowers have 4 petals and 5 sepals. This genus is rare in cultivation.

Majidea zanguebarica
Tropical Africa, Madagascar, possibly Zanzibar. Semideciduous tree, 35–60 ft.; zones 10–11. Blooms late summer. Moderate moisture to seasonally dry. Average, well-drained soil. Full sun. Flowers: petals 3 or 4, red; sepals 5, gray-green, downy; stamens 8; capsules inflated, papery, 3-lobed, red. Leaves: pinnate; leaflets 9–17, lanceolate, stiff. Bark: gray. *An erect, open tree which may shed its leaves in dry conditions. Photographed at Fairchild Tropical Garden.*

SAPOTACEAE
SAPODILLA FAMILY
Sapotaceae includes approximately 53 genera of trees and shrubs primarily from tropical regions. Several species are cultivated for their handsome foliage or edible fruit. All the species produce a latex sap. A characteristic field mark is the brown hairs on leaves and shoots. Leaves are simple, often spirally arranged in clusters at the ends of the branches. Flowers are bisexual and radially symmetrical. They have 4 or 8 sepals and petals, the petals fused at the base and overlapping, sometimes with appendages. Stamen filaments are mounted on the inside of the petals (epipetalous), sometimes alternating with sterile,

petal-like stamens (staminodes). The fruit is a berry. The seed has a conspicuous large oval scar (hilum) where the funicle was attached. *Sapote* is a Spanish name applied loosely (and variously in different countries) to several fleshy fruits in different families: *Pouteria sapota* and *Manilkara zapota* in Sapotaceae; *Diospyros digyna* in Ebenaceae; and *Casimiroa edulis* in Rutaceae. The fruit of *Mammea americana* is also called *sapote* in Cuba.

Manilkara

Manilkara includes approximately 65 species of trees and shrubs from the tropics. Leaves are simple. Flowers are inconspicuous, greenish white, solitary or in clusters. Chicle is made from the latex sap of *M. zapota*, the original chewing gum. It was used by the Mayan Indians but is now largely replaced by synthetics. The same tree produces a tasty fruit, sapodilla or sapote, with the flavor and slightly gritty texture of a pear sprinkled with brown sugar.

Manilkara zapota
SAPODILLA, NÍSPERO, SAPOTE, CHICLE
Synonyms: *Achras mammosa, Sapota zapotilla*. Mexico, Central America; widely distributed. Evergreen tree, 50–100 ft.; zones 10–11. Blooms spring or intermittently. Seasonally moist/dry. Average, well-drained soil. Full sun. Flowers: bell-shaped, petals white, sepals brown; fruit a slightly com-

Koelreuteria elegans, capsules

Litchi chinensis 'Kwai Mai Pink'

Majidea zanguebarica

Manilkara zapota

pressed orb with a rough, brown skin. Leaves: elliptic, to 6 in. long, in whorls at the ends of the branches. *Often grown as a large, spreading shade tree as well as for the fruits.*

Mimusops

Mimusops includes approximately 10 species of trees from the Old World tropics. Leaves are simple, often rigid and obovate. Flowers are inconspicuous and white. The petals are fused and each has a petal-like appendage.

Mimusops balata

cherry mahogany
Madagascar, possibly Indomalaysia. Evergreen tree, 60–100 ft.; zones 10–11. Blooms intermittently in warm months. Seasonally moist/dry. Average, well-drained soil. Full sun. Flowers: inconspicuous, funnel-shaped, about 1 in. long, greenish white, petals 5, with fringelike appendages; solitary or few-flowered on a long pedicel; fruit round, light yellow, pulp buttery, to 2 in. diameter. Leaves: obovate or spathulate, to 7 in. long, glossy light green, rigid; tip slightly indented (emarginate). *The milky latex is collected to make nonelastic rubber products. Sometimes grown as a wayside tree. Manilkara bidentata has much longer leaves, with flowers and fruits in clusters.*

Pouteria

Pouteria includes 200–325 species of trees and shrubs, which are widely distributed in the tropics. Leaves are simple. Flowers are cup-shaped to tubular. Fruits are berries with 1 or 2 large, glossy seeds. The common names of *Pouteria* fruits vary in different countries and regions. Mamey, *P. sapota*, is considered a delicacy in Latin America. It is often made into sherbets. It should not be confused with *Mammea americana*, in the family Clusiaceae, which has a more globular fruit with a wrinkled seed.

Pouteria campechiana

EGGFRUIT, CANISTEL, SAPOTE
AMARILLO, SAPOTE BORRACHO
Mexico to Panama; widely distributed. Evergreen tree, 20–60 ft.;

zones 10–11. Blooms winter. Seasonally moist/dry. Average, well-drained soil. Full sun. Flowers: small, cylindrical; in 2- to 3-flowered fascicles; fruit ovoid, end pointed, 5–7 in. long, skin smooth, yellow, pulp dense, golden, seeds 2, large, glossy black with a conspicuous hilum. Leaves: elliptic, to 6 in. long. *A rich, highly nutritious fruit, an important food for indigenous peoples and animals. The sweet flesh resembles a hard-boiled egg yolk in texture. Made into pies, cheesecakes, and shakes. Locally invasive in Florida where raccoons drag seeds into natural habitat (Hammer, pers. comm.).*

Pouteria sapota

MAMEY, MAMEY COLORADO,
MAMEY SAPOTE
Synonym: *Sideroxylon sapota*. Mexico to Nicaragua. Evergreen tree, 20–60 ft.; zone 11. Blooms late winter, spring. Regular moisture. Average, well-drained soil. Full sun. Flowers: tubular, in cauliflorous fascicles, fruit 5–7 in. long, rounded when young, becoming pointed at both ends like a small football, skin scaly brown, flesh deep orange, 1–4 glossy brown seeds. Leaves: oblanceolate to elliptic, 8–12 in. long; secondary veins parallel. *Cold-sensitive when young. Apply microelements in alkaline soil. Fruits weighing 1–5 lbs.*

take almost a year to ripen. 'Magana' is a preferred large selection.

Synsepalum

Synsepalum includes approximately 8 shrubs and trees from tropical Africa. *Synsepalum dulcificum* is an attractive shrub, often grown as a curiosity. The grape-size fruits trick the taste buds, causing anything consumed afterward to taste sweet. Owners of "miracle-fruits" enjoy the surprise of visitors who taste the fruit followed by a lime. Leaves are simple. The genus name alludes to the fused sepals of the tubular flowers.

Mimusops balata, flower upper left

Pouteria sapota, young fruit

Pouteria campechiana

Synsepalum dulcificum, fruit

Schlegelia parasitica

Synsepalum dulcificum

MIRACLE-FRUIT

Central and western tropical Africa. Evergreen shrub, 6–12 ft.; zones 10–11. Blooms intermittently in warm months. Regular moisture and humidity. Fertile, well-drained soil; slightly acid pH. Bright broken light. Flowers: small, corolla funnel-shaped; buds red; in many-flowered clusters; fruit a berry, ovoid, glossy red, one-seeded. Leaves: elliptic to oblanceolate, 3–6 in. long, firm. *Not a commercial artificial sweetener because the sweetening effect cannot be preserved.*

SCHLEGELIACEAE

SCHLEGELIA FAMILY

Schlegeliaceae includes approximately 12 genera of shrubs and climbers from tropical America. These genera were formerly included in the tabebuia family, Bignoniaceae. They are also related to the foxglove family, Plantaginaceae, and the figwort family, Scrophulariaceae. Leaves are simple and leathery. The petals are fused at the base with spreading lobes. The calyx is cup-shaped.

Schlegelia

Schlegelia includes approximately 12 species of climbers, some semiepiphytic, from tropical America. The species differ from most members of the Bignoniaceae by the simple, leathery leaves and fleshy, small berries rather than capsules. The glossy, trumpet-shaped flowers grow on short stalks in the leaf axils on older branches.

Schlegelia parasitica

Synonym: *Tanaeceum parasiticum*. Jamaica, Cuba, Lesser Antilles. Woody, semiepiphytic climber, 30–45 ft.+; zones 10–11. Blooms intermittently in warm months. Moderate moisture. Fertile, well-drained soil; alkaline pH. Full to part sun. Flowers: bell-shaped, fleshy, burgundy, throat streaked white; in clusters in the leaf axils; lip folded into the throat until the flower is mature as if "biting its lip." Leaves: ovate, 4–6 in. long, leathery, glossy dark green; margins smooth. *From moist forests, from low to medium elevations in limestone soil. Unusual in cultivation in the United States, but the dark foliage offers exceptional contrast and is an excellent screen on fences. Epiphytic, not parasitic as the species name implies.*

SCROPHULARIACEAE

FIGWORT FAMILY

Scrophulariaceae includes approximately 52 genera of herbs and subshrubs, rarely trees and climbers, which are widely distributed. This family is in the process of major revision. A few genera traditionally in Loganiaceae are now included in this family. Certain genera formerly included in this family have been moved to the revised digitalis family, Plantaginaceae. Leaves are simple with smooth or toothed margins. Flowers are bisexual and bilaterally symmetrical, sometimes nearly radially symmetrical. The calyx is composed of 3–5 fused sepals. The corolla consists of 4 or 5 partly fused petals with flaring lobes or sometimes with 2 lips. There are usually 4 stamens in 2 lengths (didynamous), sometimes 2, or occasionally 5 with 1 modified into a staminode. Stamens are mounted on the inside of the petals (epipetalous). The fruit is a capsule or schizocarp.

Buddleja

Buddleja includes approximately 100 species of shrubs and a few herbs from mild temperate and subtropical regions of North and South America, Africa, and Asia. These species were formerly included in Loganiaceae (Olmstead et al. 2001). Until further studies are completed, some authors lean toward segregating *Buddleja* in its own family, Buddlejaceae (Judd, pers. comm.). Though often written with the spelling variation *Buddleia* in the literature, *Buddleja* (pronounced bud-LAY-uh) is the older, preferred spelling. Leaves and stems are often hairy or scaly. The species listed remain evergreen in the subtropics but are grown as root-hardy perennials in mild temperate regions and cut back at the end of the growing season. Protect roots from freezing with a thick bed of mulch. Flowers are tubular with 4 small lobes. They are bisexual but functionally unisexual (self-sterile) and must be cross-pollinated. Butterflies enthusiastically perform this service. Hummingbirds are also frequent visitors.

Buddleja davidii

BUTTERFLY BUSH, SUMMER-LILAC, ORANGE-EYE

Synonym: *Buddleia davidii*. Southern China. Semideciduous shrub, 3–10 ft.; zones 6–10. Blooms warm months. Regular moisture when hot, less when cool. Fertile, well-drained soil; neutral to slightly acid pH. Full sun. Flowers: small, trumpet-shaped, more or less fragrant, selections white, pink, lavender to purple; throat orange; in oblique spirelike racemes at the ends of long, arching branches. Leaves: lanceolate, 2–3 in. long, undersides gray-green. *There are many selections. Highly attractive to butterflies and hummingbirds. Susceptible to nematodes, often declining in frost free areas, but invasive in the U.S. Northwest and certain other regions. Suitable for containers.*

Buddleja lindleyana

LINDLEY BUTTERFLY BUSH

Synonym: *Adenoplea lindleyana*. Southern China. Semideciduous shrub to 4 ft.+; zones 6–10. Blooms spring, summer. Moderate moisture. Average, well-drained soil. Full to part sun. Flowers: tubular, tube curved, lavender, lobes not spreading, red-violet; in lax or oblique racemes. Leaves: elliptic, dark green, 3–6 in. long, tip acuminate; stipules leaflike, ovate. *A spreading shrub with arching branches. The leaflike stipules are characteristic. Often performs better in South Florida than B. davidii (perhaps more resistant to nematodes).*

Buddleja madagascariensis

MADAGASCAR BUTTERFLY BUSH, SMOKE-BUSH

Synonyms: *B. nicodemia, Nicodemia madagascariensis*. Madagascar. Evergreen shrub to 10 ft.; zones 10–11. Blooms late winter, spring. Moderate moisture when hot, dry when cool. Average, well-drained soil. Full sun. Flowers: tubular, greenish gray, lobes 4, orange; in oblique panicles. Leaves: lanceolate, 4–8 in. long, dark green on upper side, white felty hairs below. Stems: covered with white felt. *A spreading xeric shrub. Very attractive to butterflies. Thrives in coastal locations. Heat tolerant. Invasive in Hawaii.*

Buddleja davidii

Buddleja lindleyana

Buddleja madagascariensis

Buddleja ×weyeriana

HYBRID ORANGE-BALL TREE
Garden hybrid, B. davidii × B. globosa. Deciduous shrub to 12 ft.; zones 6–9. Blooms warm months. Moderate moisture. Fertile, well-drained soil. Full sun. Flowers: trumpet-shaped, apricot-orange to yellow, throat orange; in terminal and axillary globular heads, 1–1.5 in. wide, fragrant. Leaves: lanceolate, to 8 in. long, dark green above, white felty below. Stems: white felty. *Thrives in southern California. Suitable for seaside locations. Similar to one parent, B. globosa, from Chile, Peru, and Argentina, but in that species the flower heads are on branched stalks.*

Leucophyllum

Leucophyllum includes approximately 12 species of spreading shrubs from North America. Some authorities place this species in Plantaginaceae. The genus name alludes to the white-woolly, blue-gray foliage. Leaves are simple. Flowers are bisexual, bilaterally symmetrical, and solitary in the leaf axils. The calyx is small and 5-lobed; the corolla 5-lobed and bell-shaped with 2 lips. Though native to semiarid regions, *L. frutescens* does well in humid climates with excellent drainage but is susceptible to mildew especially if mixed with moisture-loving plants. The gray foliage provides excellent color contrast in the landscape even when plants are not in bloom.

Leucophyllum frutescens

TEXAS SAGE, TEXAS RANGER,
SILVER LEAF, ASH-PLANT, CENIZO
Southwestern Texas, Mexico (Chihuahua desert). Evergreen shrub to 6 ft.; zones 8–11. Blooms intermittently in warm months. Moderate moisture to dry. Poor, sandy, well-drained soil. Full sun. Flowers: petals pink, magenta, or white. Leaves: oblanceolate, about 1 in. long, woolly, silvery-gray to gray-green; aromatic. *Xeric. Prefers sunny, dry locations. Marginally hardy. Suitable for coastal landscaping. Tolerates heat and salt. Drought resistant. Slow growing. Compact cultivars are available.*

SOLANACEAE

POTATO FAMILY, TOMATO FAMILY
Solanaceae includes approximately 147 genera of herbs, shrubs, trees, and climbers, which are widely distributed, with greatest diversity in the Americas. Though many species are highly poisonous, the family includes several common vegetables and fruits such as sweet and hot peppers, potatoes, eggplants, and tomatoes. Two American species, potatoes and tomatoes, play significant roles in European history and cuisine. Atropine, a drug derived from *Atropa*, is commonly used to dilate the pupils during eye examination. Capsaicin, the "heat" in chili peppers, *Capsicum* species, is used to treat certain painful disorders. Tobacco, *Nicotiana* species, is a more infamous member of the family. Leaves are simple, entire or lobed, rarely pinnately compound. They are sometimes grouped in pairs on alternating sides of the stem. Flowers are bisexual and usually radially symmetrical. The 5 sepals are fused. The corolla consists of 5 petals, tubular, funnel-shaped, or salverform, with spreading, pointed lobes. Buds are folded like an umbrella. The 5 stamen filaments are mounted on the inside of the petals (epipetalous). The anthers are often pressed together in a distinctive cone shape. Flowers are arranged in cymes though sometimes reduced to a single terminal flower. Plants are often hairy and frequently armed with spines and prickles. The fruit is a berry or a capsule, sometimes adorned with prickly spurs or enclosed by a calyx shaped like a paper lantern.

Acnistus

Acnistus includes a few to approximately 50 species of shrubs or trees from Central and South America. Common in fairly dry to cloud-forest understory. Leaves are simple. Flowers are clustered on stubby branches (fascicles) on the stems (A. Gentry 1993). In Costa Rica, epiphytic bromeliads and orchids are often grown on the limbs of *A. arborescens*. Birds are attracted to the fruit.

Acnistus arborescens

TREE-TOBACCO, COJOJO
Synonyms: *Atropa arborescens*, *Dunalia arborescens*. Mexico, Central America to Peru. Evergreen shrub or tree, 15–30 ft.; zones 10–11. Blooms spring. Moderate moisture. Average, well-drained soil. Bright broken light. Flowers: funnel-shaped, white, scented; in many-flowered fascicles on the branches; fruit tiny, round, pinkish orange when ripe. Leaves: elliptic to oblanceolate, to 6 in. long, pubescent. *A prolific bloomer. From misty cloud-forest at moderate altitude but thrives in humid coastal areas in cultivation.*

Brugmansia

Brugmansia includes approximately 14 species of soft-wooded shrubs or trees from tropical America. Leaves are simple. Flowers are large, trumpet-shaped, and pendent (*Datura* has inclined flowers). The calyx is green, long and tubular, closely or somewhat loosely fitted ("inflated") where it surrounds the base of the corolla. The calyx tube ends in several lobes ("toothed") or one large lobe ("spathelike"). The fruit is elongated and smooth. Most species produce scopolamine, a drug used to control motion sickness. In large quantities, it is hallucinogenic and highly toxic.

Brugmansias are primarily from Andean regions at moderate altitude. They thrive with cool night temperatures but are not hardy. A

Buddleja ×weyeriana

Leucophyllum frutescens

Acnistus arborescens

Brugmansia aurea

few species are from warm lowland climates. Though brugmansias do well in hot, dry climates, the flowers are more inclined to wilt early in the day. Ideal conditions include bright broken light with plenty of humidity and moderate moisture or evening mists.

Brugmansias are very easy to grow. They can be pruned into an umbrella shape that allows the flowers to hang freely like bells or as an informal hedge. They are easily propagated from large cuttings. Snails sometimes defoliate trees, but they recover quickly. Two important characteristics help distinguish the species: fully pendent or obliquely pendent flowers and toothed or spathelike calyces. Plants in cultivation are often hybrids and names are unreliable.

Brugmansia aurea
YELLOW ANGEL'S TRUMPET, CAMPANA
Synonyms: *Datura affinis*, *Datura aurea*, *Datura pittieri*. Andes of central Colombia to southern Ecuador. Evergreen shrub or tree, 8–12 ft.; zones 9–11. Blooms intermittently in warm months. Regular moisture and humidity when hot, less when cool. Average, well-drained soil. Part sun to bright filtered light. Flowers: corolla funnel-shaped, 12 in. long, fully pendent, lobe spurs strongly recurved, golden-yellow, darkening to peach-orange, rarely white; calyx 2- to 5-toothed, tight fitting around corolla neck. Leaves: smooth to minutely pubescent; margins toothed when young becoming entire.

Brugmansia ×candida
ANGEL'S TRUMPET, CAMPANA
Synonyms: *B. arborea* (hort.), *Datura candida*. Hybrid, *B. aurea × B. versicolor*. Evergreen tree, 8–12 ft.+; zones 10–11. Blooms intermittently in warm months. Regular moisture and humidity when hot, moderate moisture when cool. Average, well-drained soil. Part sun to bright filtered light. Flowers: corolla trumpet-shaped, fully pendent, white, pink or yellow, 8–12 in. long; fragrant; calyx, to 7 in. long, tight fitting around the narrow neck of the corolla, spathelike or few-toothed. Leaves: elliptic to oblong, dull green. *Possibly a natural hybrid. 'Grand Marnier' is a yellow selection. 'Knightii' has double flowers. This is the only brugmansia that produces double-flowered sports (Tristram 1998).*

Brugmansia ×insignis
PINK ANGEL'S TRUMPET, CAMPANA
Garden hybrid, (*B. suaveolens × B. versicolor*) × *B. suaveolens*. Evergreen tree, 8–12 ft.; zones 9–11. Blooms intermittently all year, almost continuously when hot. Regular moisture and humidity when hot, less when cool. Average, well-drained soil. Part sun to bright filtered light. Flowers: corolla loosely funnel-shaped, 12–15 in. long, obliquely pendent, downy, cream with green veins, lobes pink, spurs strongly recurved, to 8 in. wide; calyx 6–7 in. long, lobes 3- to 5-toothed, loose-fitting around the corolla neck which extends well beyond the calyx. Leaves: ovate to elliptic, 6–14 in. long, dull green. *A backcross. Very fragrant at night, like scented soap. 'Frosty Pink' is very prolific, large-flowered, and fast-growing.*

Brugmansia ×insignis 'Frosty Pink'

Flowers almost continuously at the beginning of the summer rainy season, then about twice a month. Especially attractive coinciding with the full moon. Requires minimal care. Highly recommended.

Brugmansia suaveolens
WHITE ANGEL'S TRUMPET
Synonym: *Datura gardneri*, *Datura suaveolens*. Southeastern Brazil; widely naturalized. Evergreen shrub or tree, 8–12 ft.; zones 10–11. Blooms intermittently in warm months. Regular moisture and humidity when hot, less when cool. Average, well-drained soil. Part sun to bright filtered light. Flowers:

Brugmansia ×candida

Brugmansia suaveolens

white to peach, funnel-shaped, to 10 in. long, obliquely pendent, lobe spurs short; mildly fragrant (hence *suaveolens*); calyx 3- to 5-toothed, loose-fitting, the corolla neck extends beyond the end of the calyx. Leaves: lanceolate, 8–10 in. long, glabrous to minutely pubescent. *Of coastal rain forest. Does not produce double flowers (see ×candida) (Tristram 1998). Flowers shorter than B. versicolor and not fully pendent.*

Brugmansia versicolor
PEACH ANGEL'S TRUMPET, CAMPANA

Synonyms: *B. arborea* (misapplied), *Datura mollis*. Ecuador (Guayaquil basin). Evergreen tree, 8–12 ft.; zones 8–11. Blooms intermittently in warm months. Regular moisture and humidity when hot, less when cool. Average, well-drained soil. Part sun to bright filtered light. Flowers: corolla funnel-shaped, 12–20 in. long, fully pendent, open white, turning peach (hence *versicolor*), lobe spurs recurved; fragrant at night; calyx spathelike with one long lobe, loose-fitting, corolla neck extending beyond the calyx. Leaves: smooth to downy. *Of high-elevation cloud-forest. Root-hardy in mild temperate regions. The leaves of 'Peaches and Cream' are variegated white and green. Sometimes misnamed B. arborea, a small-flowered species that is rarely cultivated in the United States.*

Brunfelsia

Brunfelsia includes approximately 40 species of shrubs or small trees from tropical America. A number of these species are cultivated and a few are difficult to distinguish. Most bloom when nights are cool and prefer acid soil. In alkaline soil, considerable organic matter should be added to a large, prepared hole and micronutrients should be applied on a regular basis. Leaves are simple. Flowers are salverform to rotate, the floral tubes short to very long, the lobes spreading. They are white to cream-colored, or purple to blue-violet fading to light blue or white. Stamens are in 2 pairs. Flowers are often strongly scented, usually at night.

Brunfelsia americana
LADY-OF-THE-NIGHT, FRANCISCAN RAIN-TREE, DAMA-DE-LA-NOCHE

Synonyms: *B. fallax, Brunfelsiopsis americana*. West Indies (Lesser Antilles). Evergreen shrub or tree, 12–20 ft.; zones 10–11. Blooms spring. Seasonally moist/dry. Humus-rich, well-drained soil; neutral pH. Full to part sun. Flowers: salverform, tube 2–2.5 in. long, lobes spreading, white, turning honey-colored with age; fragrant, more strongly at night; calyx cup-shaped; solitary in the leaf axils but appearing clustered at the ends of branches; fruit orange. Leaves: elliptic to oblanceolate, 3–5 in. long, firm. *Of open tropical woodlands. Blooms when nights are cool. Resembles Brunfelsia nitida, but the cup-shaped calyx is distinctive.*

Brunfelsia australis
YESTERDAY-TODAY-TOMORROW, PARAGUAY JESSAMINE

Argentina, Paraguay, southern Brazil. Evergreen shrub, 6–12 ft.; zones 9–11. Blooms late winter, spring. Seasonally moist/dry. Fertile, humus-rich, well-drained soil; acid pH. Full to part sun. Flowers: corolla tube 1–1.5 in. long, lobes spreading, purple with white eye, fading to white; solitary and set well apart; fragrant in the daytime. Leaves: obovate to elliptic, 3–4 in. long, tips bluntly pointed. *The flowers are solitary and set well apart. Distinguish from B. uniflora which also has solitary flowers but they are set close together so they appear clustered.*

Brunfelsia densifolia
SERPENTINE HILL RAIN-TREE

Puerto Rico, endangered in the wild. Evergreen shrub to 5 ft.+; zones 10–11. Blooms primarily spring, summer. Seasonally moist/dry. Fertile, humus-rich, well-drained soil. Full to part sun. Flow-

Brugmansia versicolor

Brunfelsia americana

Brunfelsia australis

Brunfelsia grandiflora

ers: corolla tube 6–7 in. long, lobes reflexed, creamy white, sweetly fragrant; fruit orange. Leaves: linear, to 3 in. long. *Unusual in cultivation. The long floral tubes and slender leaves are distinctive.*

Brunfelsia grandiflora
YESTERDAY-TODAY-TOMORROW, AYER-HOY-MAÑANA
Colombia to Bolivia (eastern slope of the Andes). Evergreen shrub, 8–12 ft.; zones 9–11. Blooms cool months. Moderate moisture when hot, less when cool. Fertile, sandy, humus-rich, well-drained soil; neutral pH. Full to part sun. Flowers: corolla tube 1–1.5 in. long, lobes spreading, to 2 in. wide, blue-violet with white eye around throat, fading to blue then white over several days; night fragrant; in many-flowered clusters. Leaves: 5–7 in. long, somewhat dull. *Of cool mountain woodlands. The most tolerant blue-and-white Brunfelsia for alkaline soil. Subsp. schultesii has somewhat smaller flowers and leaves.*

Brunfelsia lactea
Puerto Rico. Evergreen shrub or tree to 20 ft.; zones 9–11. Blooms cool months. Moderate moisture, less when cool. Fertile, well-drained soil; neutral to acid pH. Bright filtered light to part sun. Flowers: trumpet-shaped, tube slender, 2–3 in. long, lobes large, overlapping, white, scented; usually solitary. Leaves: elliptic to lanceolate, 4–5 in. long in filtered light, smaller in sun, dark green. Of cooler mountain regions. The largest flowered *Brunfelsia* in cultivation. Water drops in bright sunlight tend to cause brown spots on the flowers.

Brunfelsia nitida
LADY-OF-THE-NIGHT, DAMA-DE-LA-NOCHE
Synonym: *B. parvifolia.* Cuba. Evergreen shrub to 6 ft.; zones 10–11. Blooms intermittently in late spring, summer. Moderate moisture. Fertile, humus-rich, well-drained soil; neutral to acid pH. Full to part sun. Flowers: slender trumpet-shaped, tube 3–4 in. long, cream aging to honey-colored; calyx deeply lobed; fragrant primarily at night. Leaves: ovate, 2–3 in. long, glossy dark green. *Blooms when nights start to turn warm. Calyx distinctive. Cold-sensitive. An old favorite in Key West. The species name means "shiny." This brunfelsia has somewhat larger flowers than B. americana but is a smaller shrub.*

Brunfelsia pauciflora
MORNING-NOON-AND-NIGHT
Synonym: *Franciscea pauciflora.* Brazil. Evergreen shrub, 3–8 ft.; zones 9–11. Blooms spring. Regular moisture. Fertile, humus-rich, well-drained soil; acid pH. Full to part sun. Flowers: tube to 1.5 in. long, lobes spreading, 2–2.5 in. wide, purple fading to pale violet, white eye with a hairy halo around throat; calyx to 1 in., hairy; usually solitary in the leaf axils. Leaves: elliptic, 4–5 in. long; margins smooth, slightly undulate. *Low tolerance for alkaline conditions. Thrives*

Brunfelsia grandiflora

Brunfelsia nitida

Brunfelsia densifolia

Brunfelsia lactea

Brunfelsia nitida, flowers

Brunfelsia pauciflora

in southern California. 'Floribunda' (syn. B. eximia) has clusters of flowers in the leaf axils. 'Compacta' is a dwarf selection used as a medium bedding shrub.

Brunfelsia plicata
LADY-OF-THE-NIGHT, DAMA-DE-LA-NOCHE
Cuba. Evergreen shrub to 6 ft.; zones 10–11. Blooms late winter, spring. Moderate moisture when hot, less when cool. Fertile, sandy, humus-rich, well-drained soil; neutral to slightly acid pH. Part sun. Flowers: slender trumpet-shaped, tube to 4 in. long, lobes to 2 in. wide, ruffled, white aging to honey; calyx cup-shaped, toothed; clove-

scented at night. Leaves: elliptic to 6 in. long, glossy, leathery. *Of tropical woodlands. Should never dry out completely. Blooms when nights are cool. The most tolerant white-flowered brunfelsia for alkaline soils.*

Brunfelsia uniflora
YESTERDAY-TODAY-TOMORROW, VEGETABLE-MERCURY, MANACÁ
Synonym: *B. hopeana*. Bolivia, Argentina, Paraguay. Evergreen shrub to 6 ft.+; zones 10–11. Blooms cool months. Regular moisture when hot, less when cool. Fertile, well-drained soil; slightly acid pH. Full to part sun. Flowers: trumpet-shaped, tube to 1.5 in. long, purple fading to white, throat eye cream-

colored; solitary but set close together near ends of branches, appearing clustered; sweet-musky scent day and night. Leaves: elliptic, 2–3 in. long, more or less folded lengthwise; margins undulate. *The cloyingly sweet-musky scent is distinctive. Has smaller flowers than B. grandiflora and is a smaller shrub.*

Cestrum
Cestrum includes approximately 175 species of shrubs and trees from tropical America. Leaves are simple. Flowers are tubular or trumpet-shaped, often in many-flowered clusters, and sometimes scented. They are very attractive to butterflies and hummingbirds. Ces-

trum is preferred as the common name rather than jasmine to prevent confusion with true jasmines (family Oleaceae). Day-blooming cestrum, *C. diurnum*, is listed as invasive and is restricted in Florida though it is an important food for butterflies in winter. Night-blooming cestrum, *C. nocturnum*, is invasive in Hawaii.

Cestrum aurantiacum
ORANGE CESTRUM, HIERBA SANTA ANARANJADA
Synonyms: *C. chaculanum, C. paucinervium*. Mexico to Costa Rica. Evergreen shrub to 15 ft.; zones 9–11. Blooms intermittently in warm months. Moderate moisture to seasonally dry. Average, well-drained soil. Full sun. Flowers: trumpet-shaped, to about 1 in. long, yellow-orange, lobes small, pointed, revolute; in dense terminal clusters. Leaves: lanceolate, to 6 in. long, glossy dark green, aromatic when crushed. *Thrives in southern California, less floriferous in humid climates. Not known to set seed in Florida. Suitable for medium to tall privacy hedges in full sun.*

Cestrum diurnum
DAY-BLOOMING CESTRUM, DAY-BLOOMING JESSAMINE, HIERBA SANTA
West Indies; widely naturalized. Evergreen shrub to 20 ft.; zones 9–11. Blooms intermittently all year. Seasonally moist/dry. Most well-drained soils. Full to part sun. Flowers: small, trumpet-shaped, about 1 in. long, lobes recurved, white, weakly scented; in loose clusters; fruit purplish black. Leaves: oblong, to 4 in. long. *Fruit is toxic to humans but relished by birds. Though somewhat invasive in Florida, it is extremely attractive to native butterflies. Cestrum nocturnum has smaller flowers in dense clusters and is strongly scented at night.*

Cestrum elegans
PURPLE CESTRUM
Synonym: *C. purpureum*. Mexico. Evergreen shrub, 4–10 ft.; zones 9–11. Blooms intermittently, primarily cool months. Moderate moisture when hot, less when cool. Moderately fertile, well-drained

Brunfelsia plicata

Cestrum diurnum, with zebra broad-wing butterfly

Brunfelsia uniflora

Cestrum aurantiacum

Cestrum elegans 'Rosea'

soil. Full to part sun. Flowers: tubular, constricted just below the small, unexpanded lobes, selections mauve, pink, and violet. Leaves ovate, to 3 in. long; aromatic when crushed. *Very attractive to hummingbirds and butterflies. Compact selections are available.*

Datura

Datura includes 8 or 9 species of annual or perennial herbs and shrubs from North and South America. Leaves are simple, often with toothed margins. Known as devil's trumpets, the large, trumpet-shaped flowers are ascending, pollinated at night by sphinx moths. Fruits are round with irritating spurs. All contain the drug scopolamine and are highly toxic. Angel's trumpets, *Brugmansia* species, formerly included in this genus, are soft-wooded trees and shrubs with pendent flowers. Remember the adage: "Devil's trumpets look up toward heaven, angel's trumpets look down toward hell." Jimson weed, *D. stramonium*, is a temperate species.

Datura metel
DEVIL'S TRUMPET, HORN-OF-PLENTY, THORN-APPLE
Southern China; widely naturalized. Evergreen herb or shrub, 4–6 ft.; zones 9–11. Blooms intermittently, especially when nights are cool. Seasonally moist/dry. Average, well-drained soil. Full sun to bright broken light. Flowers: trumpet-shaped, lobes fluted, edges more or less spurred, ascending, white to eggplant-purple outside, white inside, 8–10 in. long. Leaves: ovate, to 8 in. long, dull; petioles and stems purple in purple-flowered forms. *This species is evergreen in the subtropics though grown as an annual in temperate regions. All parts poisonous. 'Cornucopia' and 'Flore Pleno' have 2–4 inserted, "double" corollas, 8–10 in. long.*

Goetzea

Goetzea includes 2 species from Puerto Rico and Hispaniola. They are seriously endangered, reduced to a few individuals in the wild. Leaves are simple. Flowers are funnel-shaped, pendent, bisexual but self-sterile, and cross-pollinated by birds.

Goetzea elegans
MATABUEY
Puerto Rico, almost extinct in the wild. Evergreen shrub or small tree; zones 10–11. Blooms late spring, early summer. Seasonally moist/dry. Average, well-drained soil; alkaline pH. Part sun. Flowers: funnel-shaped, light orange; fruit round, bright orange. Leaves: elliptic to lanceolate, to 3 in. long. *Of forest understory. Blooms near end of dry season. Photographed in the Plant Conservation Collection at Fairchild Tropical Garden.*

Iochroma

Iochroma includes approximately 10 species of shrubs and trees from tropical South America. Leaves are simple. Flowers are tubular or bell-shaped. Very attractive to hummingbirds, which serve as pollinators. The genus name alludes to the violet color of the flowers.

Iochroma warscewiczii
VIOLET TUBE-FLOWER
Colombia, Ecuador. Evergreen shrub or small tree, 4–10 ft.; zones 10–11. Blooms most of the year. Regular moisture and humidity. Fertile, well-drained soil. Bright filtered light. Flowers: tubular, 2–2.5 in. long, violet, toothlike lobes only slightly spreading; calyx cup-shaped. Leaves: obovate to oblanceolate, to 6 in. long, blade decurrent, downy; margins undulate. *Of tropical cloud-forests. Small spreading tree for protected locations or suitable for containers.* Iochroma cyaneum *has deep purple, more funnel-shaped flowers.*

Lycianthes

Lycianthes includes approximately 200 species of shrubs and climbers from tropical America and eastern Asia. Leaves are entire (not lobed) with blunt points. The 10-toothed calyces help distinguish this genus from closely related *Solanum*, which has 5-toothed calyces and lobed leaves.

Lycianthes rantonnei
BLUE POTATO-BUSH, PARAGUAYAN NIGHT-SHADE
Synonym: *Solanum rantonnetii* (incorrectly). Paraguay, Argentina. Evergreen scandent shrub, 5–8 ft.; zones 9–11. Blooms warm months. Moderate moisture. Fertile, well-drained soil. Full sun. Flowers: funnel-shaped, lobes fused, blue-vio-

Datura metel

Datura metel 'Cornucopia'

Goetzea elegans

Iochroma warscewiczii

let, rumpled; stamens prominent, golden. Leaves: ovate to lanceolate, to 4 in. long, slightly hairy; opposing leaves often of unequal length; margins undulate. *Cold-sensitive. Fast-growing. Suitable for coastal locations. Sometimes trained as a standard or espaliered. Grown as an annual in colder regions. Pruning encourages branching and more flowers. 'Royal Robe' has purple flowers.*

Solandra

Solandra includes approximately 10 species of shrubs and woody climbers from tropical America. They grow from tropical coastal forest to montane cloud-forest. Leaves are simple, entire, usually leathery or rubbery. Flowers are solitary, the corolla large, goblet-shaped, the cup tapering into a long, slender neck at the base. Flowers are fragrant primarily at night and pollinated by bats. The species commonly cultivated are aggressive heavy vines that require strong support. Prune back to woody branches after flowering. In California, *Solandra* species are often grown on the west side of houses for afternoon shade, especially along the Pacific coast, and receive their moisture through morning mist. They also thrive in humid climates that have a distinct dry season. Variegated forms have green-and-white leaves.

Solandra longiflora

CHALICE-VINE, CUP-OF-GOLD, COPA DE ORO, CÁLIZ DE ORO

Synonym: *Swartzia longiflora*. Cuba, Hispaniola, Jamaica. Evergreen woody climber to 30 ft.+; zones 9–11. Blooms cool months. Moderate moisture, seasonally dry. Fertile, well-drained soil. Full sun. Flowers: goblet-shaped, 10–12 in. long, cup constricted below the rim, lobes recurved, fringed, neck tubular at base, pale yellow, aging gold, with 10 radiating purple lines inside cup, night fragrant; calyx spathe-like, to 4 in. long, surrounding base of the corolla neck. Leaves: elliptic to ovate, to 6 in. long, base of the blade tapering down the short petiole (decurrent).

Solandra maxima

GOLDEN CHALICE-VINE, CUP-OF-GOLD, COPA DE ORO

Synonym: *Datura maxima*. Mexico to Peru, Venezuela. Evergreen woody climber to 40 ft.+; zones 9–11. Blooms cool months . Moderate moisture, seasonally dry. Fertile, well-drained soil. Full sun. Flowers: goblet-shaped, 10 in. long, cup spreading, rim not constricted, to 8 in. wide, lobes recurved; margins smooth, tubular at the base, yellow, aging gold, 5 radiating purple lines inside cup; coconut-scented; calyx tubular, slightly inflated, toothed, surrounding lower half of the corolla neck. Leaves: broadly elliptic to oblong, to 7 in. long, glossy; petiole to 6 in. *Photo of a plant growing at Balboa Park.*

Solanum

Solanum includes approximately 1400 species of herbs, shrubs, and climbers, rarely trees, which are widely distributed, with greatest diversity in the tropics and subtropics. It is a large, diverse group. Leaves are simple, lobed or compound. The flowers are rotate, sometimes bell-shaped, with fused or pointed, star-shaped lobes. The 5 stamen anthers are often fitted together like a cone. A number of species are grown as ornamentals. Many have prickles or spines. The fruit is a berry. The common white potato, *S. tuberosum*, is a cultigen that evolved through thousands of years in cultivation by the ancient peoples of the Andes. The potato was introduced into Europe where it became a staple. A devastating potato blight resulted in famine throughout Europe but most severely in Ireland and contributed to a historic migration of Europeans to the New World. Many wild species of potato, including such oddities as blue potatoes, are still eaten in the Andean countries.

Lycianthes rantonnei 'Royal Robe'

Solandra longiflora

Solandra maxima

While some members of this genus are edible, others are poisonous.

Solanum erianthum

POTATO-TREE, MULLEIN NIGHTSHADE, LAVA-PLATO ("PLATE-WASHER")

Synonym: *S. verbascifolium*. Tropical and subtropical Americas; widely naturalized. Evergreen shrub or tree, 6–25 ft.; zones 9–11. Blooms winter, spring. Seasonally moist/ dry. Average to poor, well-drained soil. Full to part sun. Flowers: rotate, lobes star-shaped, white or greenish, calyx and stalks densely woolly; fruit round, orange when ripe, to 1.5 in. Leaves: ovate to elliptic, woolly, 6–12 in. long. Stems: woolly. *In the Andes, people reportedly use a handful of the leaves to scrub dishes.*

Solanum quitoense

NARANJILLA ("LITTLE ORANGE"), LULO

Andes of Ecuador, Colombia, Central America; widely cultivated. Perennial to 6 ft.; zones 9–11. Blooms warm months. Moderate moisture. Average, well-drained soil. Full sun to bright shade. Flowers: rotate, lobes star-shaped, creamy white; calyx woolly; in axillary clusters near ends of branches; fruit round, yellow to orange, to 1 in. diameter, flesh greenish. Leaves: ovate, 8–15 in. long; margins coarsely toothed or lobed; petioles and veins often with reddish purple hairs. Prickles and down cover leaf blade, petioles, and stems. *Seedy fruit is grown commercially for juice and preserves. The pulpy citruslike juice is available frozen in U.S. markets with Latin American clientele. The residue is fed to animals.*

Solanum seaforthianum

PURPLE POTATO-VINE, ST. VINCENT'S LILAC

Tropical America, widely distributed. Evergreen climber or shrub to 20 ft.; zones 10–11. Blooms summer, fall. Moderate moisture. Average to fertile, well-drained soil. Full sun to bright broken light. Flowers: star-shaped, light blue-violet, lavender, pink, or white, 1 in. wide; in many-flowered clusters (cymes); fruit orange. Leaves: irregularly pinnatifid to pinnate, or sometimes simple, 4–8 in. long; leaflets or lobes 3–9. *Attractive to butterflies. Needs support of a fence or arbor.*

Solanum wendlandii

GIANT POTATO-VINE, PARADISE-FLOWER, WENDLAND'S NIGHTSHADE

Mexico to Colombia, widely naturalized. Evergreen twining climber to 20 ft.+; zones 10–11. Blooms spring. Moderate moisture. Average to fertile, well-drained soil. Full, part sun. Flowers: rotate, violet, to 2 in. wide, petals fused to edges, more or less notched with short spurs at junctions. Leaves: simple, entire, to irregularly pinnate or unevenly 3- to 5-lobed to dissected, to 10 in. long. Small hooked prickles on leaves and stems. *Vigorous vine. Frequently cultivated in the tropics. Needs sturdy support.*

Solanum wrightii

BRAZILIAN POTATO-TREE

Synonym: *S. macranthum*. Brazil, Bolivia. Evergreen tree, 8–20 ft.; zones 9–11. Blooms most of year, especially in warm months. Moderate moisture. Fertile, well-drained soil. Full sun. Flowers: star-shaped, to 2 in. wide, opening purple, fading white, lobes pointed; anthers long and conspicuous. Leaves: ovate to obovate, to 10 in.+ long, usually irregularly lobed or dissected, commonly prickled. Stems: commonly prickled. *'Thornless' has mostly long hairs instead of prickles. Propagate selection from cuttings or air-layering. The conspicuous long anthers help distinguish this species from* S. wendlandii.

Streptosolen

Streptosolen includes a single species of shrub from northwestern South America. The genus name refers to a twist in the corolla tube. Plants bloom when nights are cool. They are attractive to birds and butterflies and are pollinated by hummingbirds.

Streptosolen jamesonii

MARMALADE-BUSH, ORANGE BROWALLIA, MERMELADA

Synonym: *Browallia jamesonii*. Colombia, Ecuador, Peru. Evergreen sprawling shrub to 6 ft.; zones 10–11. Blooms late fall, winter, spring. Regular moisture when hot, less when cool. Average to fertile, well-drained soil. Full to part sun. Flowers: trumpet-shaped, tube twisted, lobes slightly revolute, open yellow, turning orange; in dense clusters (corymbs). Leaves: elliptic to obovate, 1–1.5 in. long, downy. *Of mountain woodlands. Cold-sensitive. A dense sprawl-*

Solanum erianthum

Solanum quitoense

Solanum seaforthianum

Solanum wendlandii

Solanum wrightii

ing shrub suitable for ground cover, containers, and hanging baskets. Provides excellent cover for birds. Trim lightly or stake for more shrubby shape. Underutilized but recommended for winter color.

STRELITZIACEAE

BIRD-OF-PARADISE FAMILY
Strelitziaceae includes 3 genera of rhizomatous and treelike herbs from Madagascar, southern Africa, and South America. They are frequently cultivated in the tropics. Leaves are large and usually paddle-shaped, resembling bananas, *Musa*, to which they are closely related. Flowers are bisexual and asymmetrical, produced in the leaf axils at the overlapping (imbricate) bases of the long petioles. They have 3 free, petal-like sepals and 3 petals; 1 petal is free and 2 are united, sometimes resembling a barbed arrow. There are 6 stamens, 1 sometimes modified into

a petal-like staminode. The fruit is a woody capsule.

Ravenala

Ravenala includes a single species of treelike herb from Madagascar. Leaves are paddle-shaped, arranged in a fan with overlapping (imbricate) bases at the top of the stem. In older plants, the lower leaves fall exposing the fibrous, palmlike trunk. They are slow-growing but may become very tall in favorable locations. The flowers and inflorescences are produced consecutively in the leaf axils. New shoots are produced at the base of the trunk; they are often removed to maintain the solitary form of the mother plant. Though often arranged in the landscape for their striking symmetry, off-shoots have no respect for landscape design and must be reset. It is a myth that they orient themselves toward the sun.

Ravenala madagascariensis

TRAVELERS' TREE,
PALMA DE VIAJERO
Madagascar. Evergreen treelike herb, 20–30 ft.+; zones 10–11. Blooms warm months. Regular moisture to seasonally dry. Fertile, sandy, humus-rich, well-drained

Streptosolen jamesonii

Ravenala madagascariensis, inflorescence

soil. Full sun. Flowers: inconspicuous, greenish white, secrete a mucilaginous fluid; bracts boatlike, greenish, imbricate; inflorescences produced sequentially from between the petiole bases. Leaves: oblong, paddle-shaped, 6–10 ft.+, in opposite ranks (distichous) on a

Ravenala madagascariensis

Strelitzia nicolai

single plane; petioles long, bases clasping stem, imbricate; blades arranged in a distinctive fan at the top of a stout, fibrous stem. *One common name refers to the water that collects in the leaf bases, presumably a source of drinking water.* Strelitzia nicolai *somewhat resembles young* Ravenala, *but its leaves spiral around the stem instead of being in a fanlike plane.*

Strelitzia

Strelitzia includes 4 species of stemless (acaulescent) and treelike herbs from South Africa. Leaves are paddle-shaped, spirally arranged in opposite ranks (spirally distichous). The species resemble and are sometimes confused with banana (*Musa*) or travelers' tree (*Ravenala*). Flowers are showy, one to several produced at a time in a large, canoelike bract (spathe). The 3 fused petals are blue, dart-shaped. Bird-of-paradise, *S. reginae*, is much used for landscaping along the coast highway in California, with morning mists as its principal irrigation. These plants also thrive in moist climates with excellent drainage. Small divisions or seed take several years to reach blooming size.

Strelitzia nicolai

WHITE BIRD-OF-PARADISE, TREE BIRD-OF-PARADISE
South Africa (Cape Provinces, KwaZulu-Natal). Evergreen tree-like herb, 15–30 ft.; zones 9–11. Blooms almost all year. Moderate moisture, seasonally dry. Fertile, humus-rich, well-drained soil. Full sun. Flowers: petals blue; calyx white; bracts canoe-shaped, waxy blue-green with a reddish edge; at the bases of the leaves. Leaves: paddle-shaped, in 2 ranks (spirally distichous); petioles to 3 ft. long; spirally arranged on a fibrous stem. *Produces dense clumps that benefit from periodic thinning. The spiral arrangement of the leaves helps distinguish this species from bananas* (Musa) *and travelers' tree* (Ravenala). *Suitable for coastal planting.*

Strelitzia reginae

BIRD-OF-PARADISE, CRANE-FLOWER, AVE DE PARAÍSO
South Africa (Cape Provinces, KwaZulu-Natal). Perennial herb, 4–7 ft.; zones 9–11. Blooms intermittently most of the year. Moderate moisture. Fertile, organically rich, well-drained soil; acid pH. Full sun. Flowers: petals blue, arrow-shaped; sepals orange; one to several, opening sequentially; one bract, canoe-shaped, waxy blue-green; on a long stalk. Leaves: oblong or lanceolate, glaucous; petiole stiffly erect. *Produces large clumps. Attractive to birds for the nectar as well as water captured in the bracts. Stemless (acaulescent). The leaf blade is greatly reduced in* S. parvifolia *(syn.* S. juncea*).*

TACCACEAE

BAT-FLOWER FAMILY
Taccaceae includes a single genus of rhizomatous or tuberous perennial herbs from tropical Asia, the Pacific Islands, Australia, Africa, and South America. A few species are cultivated for their attractive foliage as well as their other-worldly flowers. They are fascinating to children as well as adults. Indian arrowroot, *Tacca leontopetaloides*, is cultivated in tropical Asia and the Pacific for its starchy tubers. Leaves are basal, entire or lobed, with long petioles. Flowers are bisexual and radially symmetrical. They have 3 sepals, 3 petals, and 6 stamens, which are often black or purple-black, sometimes partly white and greenish. The 2–4 often winglike primary bracts are blackish, purple, green, or white and the secondary bracts are often numerous and threadlike. Flowers are clustered in umbels on a hollow scape The fruit is a berry.

Tacca

Tacca includes 10 species of rhizomatous or tuberous perennial herbs from Southeast Asia, Malaysia, Australasia, Africa, and South America. They are mostly plants of shady forest understory. These lily allies have handsome, glossy foliage and often black or white flowers, more or less tinged green or purple. Most are cold-sensitive tropicals but are grown outdoors in the subtropics as bedding plants with plentiful mulch in protected locations. They are suitable for containers. The inflorescence stalks are sometimes hidden beneath the foliage and may be staked for display. Most taccas are suitable for moderately shady locations. Though the taccas listed may become dormant in the wild in dry seasons, they may remain evergreen with regular moisture.

Tacca chantrieri

BAT-FLOWER, DRACULA-FLOWER, FLOR DE MURCIÉLAGO
Thailand. Evergreen tuberous herb to 2 ft.; zones 10–11. Blooms late winter to summer. Regular moisture. Fertile, humus-rich, well-drained soil. Filtered light to medium shade. Flowers: black to purplish white, nodding on long pedicels; 2 bracts broadly ovate and winglike, 2 smaller bracts perpendicular to the others, black, greenish, or reddish; bracteoles threadlike, 6–8 in. long, lax. Leaves: basal, lanceolate, glossy dark green, blade tapering down the petiole (decurrent).

Tacca integrifolia

CAT'S WHISKERS, BAT-FLOWER, BARBA DEL GATO
Eastern India, southern China, Southeast Asia, Indomalaysia. Seasonally dormant tuberous herb to 2.5 ft.; zones 10–11. Blooms intermittently in fall, winter, spring. Seasonally moist/dry. Fertile, organically rich, well-drained soil; neutral to acid pH. Filtered light to medium shade. Flowers: purplish black, on short peduncles; 2 broad and spreading bracts, white to purple, 2 narrower bracts below; bracteoles threadlike, 8–10 in. long, lax; scape to 40 in. long. Leaves:

Strelitzia nicolai, inflorescence

Strelitzia reginae

Tacca chantrieri

basal, lanceolate to broadly ovate, to 2 ft. long, glossy dark green; petioles purple. *Of monsoon forest.*

Tacca leontopetaloides

INDIAN ARROWROOT,
LION'S WHISKERS
Synonym: *T. pinnatifida.* Old World tropics. Seasonally dormant tuberous herb, 2–5 ft.; zones 10–11. Blooms spring, summer. Seasonally moist/dry. Fertile, organically rich, well-drained soil; neutral to acid pH. Part sun to bright filtered light. Flowers: green and black; primary bracts leaflike; secondary bracts threadlike, arching. Leaves: cauline (on a stem), to 10 in. long, irregularly and deeply lobed and forked.

Tacca palmata

Indonesia (Java). Seasonally dormant tuberous herb to 15 in.; zones 10–11. Blooms summer, fall. Seasonally moist/dry. Fertile, organically rich, well-drained soil; neutral to acid pH. Bright filtered light to medium shade. Flowers: black to purplish, nodding; 2 primary bracts erect, 2 smaller bracts below; threadlike bracteoles absent. Leaves: basal, palmatifid, 5-lobed, blade 6–8 in. long; petiole to 12 in.

Tacca palmatafida

Sulawesi (Celebes). Seasonally dormant tuberous herb to 2 ft.; zones 10–11. Blooms warm months. Seasonally moist/dry. Fertile, organically rich, well-drained soil; neutral to acid pH. Bright filtered light to part shade. Flowers: blackish purple, nodding; 2 primary bracts erect, 2 smaller bracts below; threadlike bracteoles absent. Leaves: basal, blade broadly ovate in general outline, to 12 in. long, with 5–7 large lobes at apex of the blade.

THEOPHRASTACEAE

JACQUINIA FAMILY
Theophrastaceae includes approximately 4 genera of trees and shrubs from tropical America and the West Indies. Leaves are simple and spirally arranged, sometimes with sharply toothed margins or spined tips. The blades contain fibers, which are visible when a leaf is bro-

ken—a good field mark. Flowers are mostly bisexual and radially symmetrical. The 4 or 5 sepals are fused as are the 4 or 5 petals. The 5 stamens alternate with 5 scalelike staminodes. The filaments are mounted on the inside of the corolla tube (epipetalous). The fruit is usually a many-seeded berry. The staminodes, fruits, and fibrous leaves help distinguish this family from Myrsinaceae (Judd, pers. comm.).

Clavija

Clavija (pronounced cla-V-ha) includes 50–55 species of evergreen shrubs or small trees from Nicaragua to Brazil and Hispaniola. Stems are unbranched, somewhat pachycaulous, and fibrous. Leaves are simple, in spirally arranged clusters at the ends of the stems. Flowers are unisexual, with male and female flowers on different

plants (dioecious), or if bisexual, then functionally unisexual, or sometimes polygamous.

Clavija nutans

Synonym: *C. integrifolia.* Brazil, Bolivia, Paraguay. Evergreen pachycaulous tree, 5–10 ft.; zones 10–11. Blooms fall, winter. Seasonally moist, less when cool. Average, well-drained soil. Part sun to bright broken light. Flowers: unisexual, orange to scarlet; in racemes clustered in the leaf axils near the ends of the branches; berries red-orange. Leaves: obovate to elliptic, to 1 ft.+ long; margins smooth; petioles short. *An erect, little-branched small tree suitable for small gardens or large containers.*

Jacquinia

Jacquinia includes 30–35 species of shrubs and trees from Central

America and the West Indies. Leaves are simple, the margins smooth or sharply toothed. Petal-like stamens (staminodes) alternate with the petals. These species are underutilized and recommended, especially for coastal locations. They are said to be fire resistant.

Jacquinia aurantiaca

Mexico, Central and South America. Evergreen shrub, 6–15 ft.; zones 9–11. Blooms spring, summer. Seasonally moist/dry. Poor, sandy, well-drained soil; alkaline pH. Full to part sun. Flowers: small, orange; in racemes near the ends of the branches; fruit ovoid, tangerine orange. Leaves: lanceolate, 3–4 in. long, stiff, tips spined; margins smooth; clustered near ends of short, stiff branches. *A xeric, salt-tolerant shrub suitable for coastal*

Tacca integrifolia

Tacca leontopetaloides

Tacca palmata

Tacca palmatafida

Clavija nutans

Jacquinia aurantiaca

areas. *Long-lasting ornamental fruit. Slow growing. Joewood, J. keyensis (syn. J. aurantiaca var. albiflora), from the Florida Keys, Bahamas, and West Indies, has white flowers.*

THYMELAEACEAE
MEZEREUM FAMILY

Thymelaeaceae includes approximately 53 genera of shrubs and trees, rarely climbers and herbs, which are widely distributed, with greatest diversity in tropical Africa and Australia. Leaves are simple, often spirally arranged. Flowers are usually bisexual and radially or almost radially symmetrical. The corolla is scalelike or absent. The calyx is petal-like (petaloid) and mounted on a tubular floral cup (hypanthium). Bracts are sometimes present. Flowers are solitary or are arranged in compact heads or racemes. The fruit is a berry or

drupe, sometimes an achene. The stems have a fibrous inner bark that comes off in strips when twigs are broken (Howard, pers. comm.). The fiber is sometimes used to make paper.

Dais

Dais includes 2 species of shrubs from Madagascar and southern Africa. Leaves are simple. The petal-like (petaloid) sepals are mounted on a tubular floral cup (hypanthium). The flowers are arranged in a loose head subtended by 2 woody bracts.

Dais cotinifolia
POMPOM TREE

Southeast Africa, Madagascar. Deciduous or evergreen shrub or small tree, 5–15 ft.; zones 10–11. Blooms late spring, summer. Seasonally moist/dry. Fertile, well-

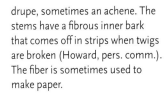

Dais cotinifolia

Gnidia madagascariensis

drained soil. Full to part sun. Flowers: floral tube greenish to pink, sepals petal-like, pink; in lax heads, fragrant; bracts 4, pink, becoming woody; in loose umbels to 3 in. wide. Leaves: oblanceolate to oblong, to 3 in. long, dull dark green. *Of moist woodland margins. An attractive summer-blooming shrub. String or thread is made from bark fibers. The species name alludes to a resemblance of the leaves to* Cotinus *(Anacardiaceae), smoke tree.*

Drimyspermum

Drimyspermum includes approximately 10 species of shrubs or trees from New Guinea, Fiji, the Solomon Islands, and Indonesia. Leaves are simple. The petal-like calyx is mounted on a slender floral tube. Flowers are clustered at the nodes near the ends of the branches. The name alludes to pungent-scented seeds. These species are unusual to rare in cultivation.

Drimyspermum macro-carpum

Synonym: *Phaleria macrocarpa.* New Guinea. Evergreen shrub to 10 ft.+; zones 10–11. Blooms spring. Seasonally moist/moderate. Fertile, well-drained soil. Full to part sun. Flowers: white, in loose clusters in the leaf axils. Leaves: lanceolate, to 4 in. long, glossy dark green. *Unusual to rare in cultivation. Photographed at Fairchild Tropical Garden.*

Gnidia

Gnidia includes approximately 140 species of shrubs and trees from Africa, Arabia, Madagascar, and Sri Lanka. Leaves are simple, opposite. Flowers have long floral tubes. Petal-like sepals are mounted on the rim of the tube. Woody fibers of *G. glauca* are used to make high-quality paper.

Gnidia madagascariensis

Synonym: *Lasiosiphon madagascariensis.* Madagascar. Evergreen shrub to 4 ft.+; zones 9–11. Blooms warm months. Seasonally moist, moderate. Fertile, well-drained soil. Part sun to bright filtered light. Flowers: small, orange; in compact, headlike (capitate) umbels, to 1.5

in. across. Leaves: elliptic to obovate, to 3 in. long, silky pubescent. Bark: smooth, reddish brown. *Heat tolerant. This colorful shrub is unusual to rare in cultivation in the United States.*

Phaleria

Phaleria includes approximately 20 species from Indomalaysia to New Guinea and Australia. Leaves are simple. Flowers have long, slender floral tubes. The petal-like sepals are small and attached to the tube rim.

Phaleria perrottetiana

Philippines. Evergreen spreading shrub to 5 ft.+; zones 10–11. Blooms spring. Seasonally moist/dry. Fertile, well-drained soil. Full to part sun. Flowers: white, in dense heads; fruit red. Leaves: lanceolate, to 6 in. long, glossy.

TURNERACEAE
TURNERA FAMILY

Turneraceae includes approximately 10 genera of annual and perennial herbs and shrubs primarily from tropical and subtropical America, Africa, Madagascar, and the Mascarene Islands. Leaves are simple usually with serrated margins. Flowers are bisexual and radially symmetrical. They have 5 sepals, 5 petals, and 5 stamens mounted on a floral disk (hypanthium). Flowers are usually solitary in the leaf axils but occasionally are arranged in racemes. The fruit is a small capsule.

Turnera

Turnera includes approximately 70 species of herbs and subshrubs from the Gulf Coast to Mexico and South America. *Turnera diffusa* and, to a lesser extent, *T. ulmifolia*, have been cultivated in Mexico and Central America since Mayan times for use as a stimulant tea, beverage flavoring, and a purported aphrodisiac. Leaves are simple, often with serrate, rarely lobed, margins, with a pair of nectaries at the base of the blade. They contain thymol, which gives them a resinous aroma when crushed. The pistils are either long or short in different flowers (heterostylous). Flowers arise from

Drimyspermum macrocarpum

Phaleria perrottetiana

a slit in the petioles of the upper leaves and their vascular tissue is connected through the petiole as well (Howard 1989). The common names politician's flower and banker's flower hold that the flowers open at 10 and close by 2. This is often true for plants that receive shade during the day. In fact, the flowers open as soon as they are touched by the first rays of the sun and may stay open as long as they receive direct sunlight. *Turnera* species are self-seeding and sometimes weedy. Trim to keep compact. Attractive to butterflies.

Turnera diffusa
BUTTERCUP BUSH, DAMIANA
Texas, Mexico, West Indies, Central America, Brazil. Perennial herb or subshrub, 2–6 ft.; zones 9–11. Blooms warm months. Moderate moisture to seasonally dry. Average, well-drained soil. Full to part sun. Flowers: corolla spreading, 1–1.5 in. wide, petals obovate with an acute point, yellow to almost white. Leaves: lanceolate; margins serrulate. *Quite variable over its extensive range. Habit open.*

Turnera subulata
POLITICIAN'S FLOWER
Synonyms: *T. elegans, T. trioniflora, T. ulmifolia* var. *elegans.* Panama to Bolivia and Brazil, West Indies; widely naturalized. Perennial herb or subshrub, 2–3 ft.; zones 9–11. Blooms warm months. Moderate moisture. Average, well-drained soil. Full to part sun. Flowers: fun-nel-shaped, petals cream, bright yellow near the base with a purple-brown eye; solitary. Leaves: ovate, oblong to oblanceolate, 1–3 in. long, pubescent, glands near the base; margins serrate; clustered at ends of the branches. *Of coastal to inland meadows and disturbed areas.*

Turnera ulmifolia
YELLOW ALDER, BUTTERCUP BUSH, BANKER'S FLOWER, MARILÓPEZ
West Indies, South Florida, Mexico and tropical America; widely naturalized. Evergreen perennial subshrub to 3 ft.+; zones 10–11. Blooms warm months. Moderate moisture. Average, well-drained soil. Full sun. Flowers: funnel-shaped, to 2 in. wide, petals yellow, edges toothed; style long or short (heterostylous), stigma bristled. Leaves: ovate, to 4 in. long, glossy dark green, pubescent; margins usually toothed. *Widely distributed and variable over its range. Of coastal and inland meadows and woodlands. Self-seeding and inclined to be weedy in favorable conditions.*

VELLOZIACEAE
TREE-LILY FAMILY
Velloziaceae includes approximately 8 genera of shrubby succulent herbs from dry areas of South America, Madagascar, eastern Africa, and Yemen. The taxonomy of this monocot family of treelets with lilylike flowers is unsettled. They grow in seasonally arid regions. It is surprising that these remarkable plants are not seen more often in succulent collections. Leaves are linear to sword-shaped with parallel veins, arranged in whorls at the ends of the branches. Stems are more or less pachycaulous and produce moisture-absorbing adventitious roots in dry conditions. Plants begin to bloom when quite small. Flowers are bisexual and radially symmetrical. They have 6 tepals, 3 fertile stamens, and 3 staminodes. Flowers are solitary in the leaf axils. The fruit is a capsule.

Vellozia
Vellozia includes approximately 124 species of pachycaulous herbs from Brazil. Tree-lilies are slow-growing plants from seasonally dry inland and coastal regions. Bloom typically follows a dry, cool season. Flowers are pollinated by hummingbirds. Adventitious roots near the base of the stem absorb scarce moisture unable to penetrate to the underground roots. The leaves are deciduous during the dry season, the persistent leaf sheaths leaving an attractive braided pattern on the stalks. These treelets are usually grown in containers.

Vellozia bahiana
TREE-LILY
Brazil (Bahia). Seasonally dormant pachycaulous tree, 1–6 ft.; zones 10–11. Blooms spring. Moderate moisture, seasonally dry. Sandy, gritty, well-drained soil. Full sun. Flowers: tepals lavender; ovary ovoid, covered with tubercles (soft projections). Leaves: sword-shaped, to 8 in. long; in whorls near ends of the branches. *Suitable for coastal planting. Water deeply but let dry before watering again. Taper off water in the fall and keep dry in winter when dormant. Suitable for containers. The vellozia in the photo was blooming when it was less than 1 ft. tall.*

VERBENACEAE
LANTANA FAMILY, PETREA FAMILY
Verbenaceae includes approximately 36 genera primarily of shrubs and trees, plus a few herbs and climbers, which are widely distributed but more abundant in tropical regions. Current revisions have transferred many genera traditionally included in this family to Lamiaceae. Leaves are simple, entire or occasionally lobed, the margins serrate. They are aromatic when crushed. The leaf axils sometimes have spines. Stems are often 4-angled. Flowers are bisexual and bilaterally symmetrical. The calyx consists of 5 partly fused sepals. There are 5 petals, the 2 upper lobes sometimes fused into a lip, the lower lobe may also be slightly liplike. The 4 stamens are in 2 lengths (didynamous). The inflorescence is a raceme or cyme. The fruit is a one-seeded drupe, capsule, or schizocarp.

Duranta
Duranta includes approximately 17 species of shrubs and trees from tropical and subtropical America. Leaves are simple, with toothed margins, and commonly with short spines in the axils. Flowers are

Turnera diffusa

Turnera subulata

Turnera ulmifolia

Vellozia bahiana

small, arranged in racemes or panicles. *Duranta erecta* is commonly cultivated. Though it is often described as a Florida native, there is no wild population in the United States (Scurlock 1992) indicating that early settlers introduced this species into the Keys. It is suitable for coastal planting but not directly on the beach. *Duranta erecta* exhibits 2 fruit types: one round and golden, the other greenish yellow and shriveled (Burch, pers. comm.). Spineless forms, color selections, and those with attractive fruit must be propagated from cuttings.

Duranta erecta
GOLDEN DEWDROP, SKY-FLOWER
Synonyms: *D. plumieri*, *D. repens*. Mexico to South America, West Indies; widely naturalized. Evergreen shrub, 10–15 ft.; zones 9–11.

Blooms intermittently in spring, fall. Moderate but regular moisture. Average to fertile, well-drained soil. Full to part sun. Flowers: corolla to 0.5 in. wide, violet with dark violet streaks and a white throat, or sometimes all white; in oblique or pendent racemes; fruit a yellow drupe, to 0.5 in. diameter. Leaves: ovate, 2–3 in. long; margins serrate. Spines in leaf axils to 1 in. long, occasionally spineless. Stems: 4-angled. *Attractive to butterflies. A variegated selection has green-and-white leaves. The highly ornamental 'Sapphire Shower' has purple flowers.*

Lantana
Lantana includes approximately 150 species of herbs and shrubs primarily from tropical America with a few from southern Africa.

Stems are often 4-angled, sometimes prickled or spined. Leaves are simple. Flowers are bisexual, slightly bilaterally symmetrical, aromatic, in spikes or heads. The fruits are small, black drupes. *Lantana camara* is commonly cultivated and sometimes marketed as a "native" (Hammer, pers. comm.). Lantanas are widely naturalized and have become invasive pests in many areas of the tropics, rooting at the nodes where they touch ground and forming dense thickets. The type species is not recommended for cultivation. The sterile dwarf hybrids, however, are suitable for cultivation. Lantanas are heat and salt tolerant. In temperate regions, they are grown as annuals. They are toxic to foraging animals but attractive to butterflies and hummingbirds.

Lantana camara
RED AND YELLOW LANTANA, RED AND YELLOW SAGE
Exact origin obscure (tropical America); widely naturalized. Evergreen shrub, 1–6 ft.+; zones 9–11. Blooms warm months. Moist to dry. Most well-drained soils. Full to part sun. Flowers: small, trumpet-shaped, yellow turning red-orange; in compact heads. Leaves: simple, ovate to lanceolate, 1.5–2.5 in. long, coarsely hairy, aromatic; margins serrate. *Sprawling or mounding, sometimes prickly. Invasive and restricted in Florida. Sterile hybrids may be cultivated. Cultivars have pink, yellow, or white flowers, and*

leaves of some selections are variegated with white or yellow.

Lantana montevidensis
PURPLE LANTANA, TRAILING LANTANA
Synonym: *L. sellowiana*. Argentina, Uruguay, southern Brazil. Perennial herb or subshrub to 3 ft.; zones 9–11. Blooms warm months. Moderate moisture to dry. Most well-drained soils. Full to part sun. Flowers: small, funnel-shaped, red-violet to white with yellow or white eyes; in compact clusters. Leaves: ovate to lanceolate, 1–2 in. long, coarse, aromatic, purple in bright sun; margins serrate. *Commonly grown, mounding, spreading ground cover. Heat and salt tolerant. Invasive in some areas.*

Petrea
Petrea includes 30–40 species of trees, shrubs, and shrubby climbers from tropical America. The clambering species common in cultivation is *P. volubilis*. *Petrea arborea*, a tree, is rarely cultivated in the United States. Petrea leaves are simple and sandpapery (asperous). They make serviceable nail files or finishing sandpaper. Often described as deciduous, the leaves are never shed all at once though many may fall when cold. Floral color selections are quite variable, the calyx and corolla often contrasting. The corolla is ephemeral. The blue, violet, or white petal-like calyx is persistent. The fruit is a 5-winged samara.

Petrea volubilis
PETREA, QUEEN'S WREATH, SANDPAPER-LEAF, FLEUR DE DIEU
Mexico, Central America to Brazil, West Indies. Semideciduous twiner to 30 ft.+; zones 10–11. Blooms late winter, spring. Seasonally moist/dry. Fertile, well-drained soil. Full sun. Flowers: corolla purple, pale violet, or white, white spot on upper petal, ephemeral; calyx pale blue-violet to white, persistent. Leaves: elliptic to obovate, to 10 in. long, dull, rough. *Of lowland forests. Vigorous climber that needs a sturdy support. Cut back after flowering. Can be kept pruned as a sprawling shrub. Moderately self-seeding. 'Albiflora' is*

Duranta erecta

Duranta erecta, fruit

Lantana camara

Lantana camara 'Drap d' Or'

Lantana montevidensis

all white. *Color selections propagated from cuttings. Habit photo taken at Fairchild Tropical Garden.*

Stachytarpheta

Stachytarpheta includes approximately 60 species of herbs and subshrubs, which are widely distributed, with greatest diversity in mild temperate and tropical America. Leaves are simple, aromatic, with toothed margins. Flowers are small, with 5 spreading corolla lobes. They are sessile or partly imbedded in a long, whiplike, terminal spike (Howard 1989). Bracts are present. These species are attractive to butterflies and hummingbirds. The species are variable and readily hybridize, often making identification difficult. They are heavily self-seeding and weedy in favorable conditions.

Stachytarpheta jamaicensis

BLUE PORTERWEED, JAMAICAN VERVAIN, DEVIL'S COACHWHIP
Synonym: *Verbena jamaicensis.*
Tropical and subtropical America. Perennial herb or subshrub, 2–6 ft.; zones 9–11. Blooms warm months. Regular moisture to fairly dry. Average to fertile, well-drained soil. Full to part sun. Flowers: small, blue-violet to magenta, throat white, short-lived but opening sequentially over a long period; on thin whiplike spikes, 6–20 in. long; bracts scalelike on spike; fruit imbedded in the spike tissue. Leaves: quilted; margins serrate. *This is an extremely variable species over its extensive range, but it is possible that more than one blue-violet species or hybrid are in cultivation. Regular moisture and full sun ensure almost constant bloom. Tolerant of poor conditions but appearance suf-* fers. *Attractive to monarch butterflies and host plant of Gulf fritillaries.*

Stachytarpheta mutabilis

PINK PORTERWEED, SNAKEWEED
Synonym: *Verbena mutabilis.* Tropical America. Perennial herb or subshrub, 2–4 ft.; zones 9–11. Blooms warm months. Regular moisture to fairly dry. Average, well-drained soil. Full to part sun. Flowers: small, pink to magenta, throat cream or pink with red border, short-lived, opening sequentially; on whiplike spike, 6–15 in. long; bracts scalelike. Leaves: ovate, 1–2 in. long, stiff, veins depressed; margins serrate. *Adaptable. Weedy. Spike is thicker than* S. jamaicensis.

VIOLACEAE

VIOLET FAMILY
Violaceae includes approximately 21 genera of herbs, shrubs, climbers, and rarely trees, which are widely distributed. *Viola* is the largest genus and the only one found in temperate regions (violets and pansies). In the tropics, *Viola* species grow primarily at higher altitudes. These hardy perennials with their whorls of basal leaves differ considerably from the shrubs, trees, or even vines characteristic of tropical woodlands. Many nondescript species are difficult to distinguish from members of the flacourtia family, Flacourtiaceae, unless in flower (A. Gentry 1993). Leaves are entire or lobed, usually alternate or sometimes oppositely arranged, with serrated margins. Flowers are bisexual, strongly to weakly bilaterally symmetrical or uncommonly radially symmetrical, and often subtended by bracts. The corolla is 5-parted, commonly with an enlarged, often pouched or

Petrea volubilis

Petrea volubilis

Petrea volubilis, lavender form

Stachytarpheta jamaicensis

Stachytarpheta mutabilis

spurred lip, which is more or less united at the base. There are 5, sometimes reduced sepals and 5 stamens. Flowers are usually solitary or sometimes in racemes. The fruit is a berry or capsule.

Hybanthus

Hybanthus includes approximately 150 species of mostly subshrubs or herbs, rarely shrubs, which are widely distributed in the tropics and well represented in the Americas. Flowers have a pouched lip. *Hybanthus prunifolius* is among the showier species that bloom in a "big bang" in the spring throughout the American tropics. Do not confuse the genus name with *Habranthus* in the amaryllis family, Amaryllidaceae.

Hybanthus prunifolius

Synonym: *Viola prunifolia*. Costa

Hybanthus prunifolius

Alpinia formosana

Rica to northern South America. Evergreen shrub, 6–15 ft.; zones 10–11. Blooms late winter, spring. Seasonally moist/dry. Average, well-drained soil. Part sun. Flowers: lip white with a yellow spot in the throat, short nectar pouch at the base, lateral petals reduced; pendent; calyx 5-parted, small, green; capsule 3-sided. Leaves: elliptic, 4–6 in. long, glabrous; margins serrate. Bark: light gray. *An understory shrub of tropical woodlands and seaside forests. The flowers dangle from the arching branches like medallions. They bloom in mass after a dry season.*

ZINGIBERACEAE

GINGER FAMILY

Zingiberaceae includes approximately 52 genera of rhizomatous herbs primarily from Southeast Asia and tropical America. *Costus* and related genera are segregated

Alpinia calcarata

by some authors into Costaceae. Cardamom, *Elettaria cardamomum*; turmeric, *Curcuma longa* (syn. *C. domestica*); ginger, *Zingiber officinale*; and galangal, *Alpinia galanga* are used as spices and herbal medicines. The starchy roots of *Curcuma angustifolia* are ground into East Indian arrowroot. Perfume oils are extracted from *Hedychium* flowers.

Gingers have sympodial growth: a new shoot is produced from the rhizome each season, flowers, and dies back. Some gingers produce reedlike pseudostems composed of the overlapping leaf bases. Ground-hugging species have no vertical stalk. Leaves are alternate, in opposite ranks (distichous), and paddle-shaped. Petioles are often long. A ligule (a flange) on either side of the base of the petiole clasps the stalk. There are 3 sepals and 3 petals, which are fused and usually small. The showy part of the flower consists of 2 lateral staminodes (reduced in *Alpinia*) and a lip (labellum). Only one stamen is fertile. Secondary bracts often subtend the flowers. The inflorescence is usually a terminal spike or panicle, sometimes on a separate, leafless scape (radical stalk). A primary bract sometimes subtends the inflorescence. The fruit is a dry or fleshy capsule.

Seasonally dormant species usually tolerate light frost if the rhizome is protected from freezing. Otherwise, the rhizome is overwintered indoors in a dry place. Gingers are propagated by division of the rhizome, seed, or bulbils (bulblike growths or viviparous plantlets that develop in the bracts of certain species). Most are excellent for cut flowers.

Alpinia

Alpinia includes approximately 200 species of evergreen herbs from Southeast Asia and the Pacific. Rhizomes and sometimes leaves and stalks are resinously aromatic. Alpinias have reedlike pseudostems. The largest species, *A. boia*, may reach 35 ft. tall. Alpinias differ from other gingers by the absence of arillate seeds. Flowers sometimes have shell-shaped lips. The inflorescences are terminal. Alpi-

nias produce large clumps that spread outward and may need to be reset occasionally. Cut back old stalks after flowering. Alpinias are best grown as understory plants. Hot sun parches leaves and flowers. A deep layer of mulch greatly reduces moisture and fertilizer requirements. Because they bloom on second-year growth, alpinias usually do not flower where the tops are killed back in winter. In zone 7 or 8, species that are root-hardy are sometimes grown for foliage. In colder areas, alpinias may be overwintered indoors in a container in a sunny location.

Alpinia calcarata

INDIAN GINGER, SNAP GINGER
India, China. Evergreen rhizomatous herb, 3–4 ft.; zones 8–10. Blooms late winter, spring. Regular moisture. Fertile, organically rich, well-drained soil. Morning sun or bright broken light. Flowers: lip shell-shaped, greenish white with maroon-brown markings; bract pointed, erect, persistent, at base of inflorescence. Leaves: narrowly lanceolate, to 12 in. long, 2 in. wide; glossy dark green; margins prickly. *Aromatic. Grown as a foliage plant to zone 8. The flowers are not particularly ornamental. This species and* A. nutans *are incorrectly sold as cardamom. Cardamom spice comes from* Elettaria cardamomum.

Alpinia formosana

PINSTRIPE GINGER,
WAIMANOLO (HAWAII)
Synonym: *A. kumatake*. Southern Japan, Taiwan. Evergreen rhizomatous herb to 6 ft.; zones 8–11. Blooms spring. Regular moisture. Fertile, organically rich, well-drained soil; slightly acid pH. Bright filtered light. Flowers: lip white with crimson markings, yellow near tip; bracts lanceolate, curved. Leaves: aromatic, to 24 in. long, 5 in. wide, green. *Cultivated forms have variegated leaves with narrow green and pure white stripes. Long cultivated in Japan. Rice is wrapped in the aromatic leaves for steaming. Distinguished from A.* zerumbet 'Variegata' *by the semi-erect inflorescence and green and white narrowly striped leaves.*

Alpinia galanga

THAI GINGER, GREATER GALANGAL
Synonym: *Maranta galanga*. Southeast Asia; widely cultivated. Semideciduous rhizomatous herb, 5–7 ft.; zones 7–11. Blooms spring. Regular moisture. Fertile, organically rich, well-drained soil. Full to part sun. Flowers: small, greenish white, throat with pinkish stripes, lip edges rolled up (involute); in many-flowered spirelike spikes to 10 in.; bracts large, shed before flowers open. Leaves: oblong to ovate, 16–20 in. long, 2–4 in. wide, puckered near midrib; margins undulate; petiole short. *Aromatic rhizomes a common ingredient in Thai cooking. One of the hardiest alpinias and the only one to flower the next season after being killed to the ground by frost.*

Alpinia Ginosa Series

Garden hybrids. Evergreen rhizomatous herbs, 8–12 ft.; zones 10–11. Bloom warm months. Regular moisture. Fertile, organically rich, well-drained soil. Morning sun or bright broken light. Flowers: small; bracts red, pink, or white; inflorescence ovoid. Leaves: oblanceolate, tip acuminate, to 28 in. long, 7 in. wide; petiole short. *A related group of Hawaiian hybrids with fuller, more rounded inflorescences than A. purpurata. All parts aromatic. Grown for cut flowers. 'Jungle King' and 'Jungle Queen' do well in the subtropics in protected locations. 'Kimi' and 'Kazu' are very tender ultra-tropicals.*

Alpinia katsumadai

China (Guangdong Province), Hainan Island. Evergreen rhizoma-
tous herb, 3–6 ft.; zones 8–11. Blooms late winter, spring, summer. Regular moisture. Fertile, organically rich, well-drained soil. Full sun to bright filtered light. Flowers: lip deeply shell-shaped, dark red spot inside lip and a few radiating lines, rim yellow with 3 projecting yellow tabs on the lower margin; inflorescence erect with a large, persistent bract at the base. Leaves: paddle-shaped, 20–24 in. long, 4–5 in. wide, glossy dark green; margins undulate. *Root-hardy to zone 8. Bloom short-lived but flowers several times a year. Crushed seeds are used in herbal medicine. Though named in honor of a Japanese botanist, the species is Chinese.*

Alpinia oxyphylla

Synonym: *Languas oxyphylla*. Southern China. Evergreen rhizomatous
herb, 6–8 ft.; zones 9–11. Blooms spring. Regular moisture. Fertile, organically rich, well-drained soil. Full to part sun. Flowers: white, lip striped pink with toothed edge, about 1 in. wide. Leaves: lanceolate, to 14 in. long, 3 in. wide, flat and ladderlike. Stalks stiffly upright. *The species name refers to a silvery-gray cast of the foliage. Ground seed used in Chinese herbal medicine. Marginally hardy alpinias such as this one are among the first gingers to bloom in the spring.*

Alpinia purpurata

RED GINGER
South Pacific (Moluccas, Yap to New Caledonia). Evergreen rhizomatous herb, 5–7 ft.+; zones 10–11. Blooms all year. Regular moisture. Fertile, organically rich, well-drained soil. Full sun to bright

Alpinia galanga

Alpinia 'Jungle King'

Alpinia 'Jungle Queen'

Alpinia 'Kimi'

Alpinia katsumadai

Alpinia oxyphylla

Alpinia purpurata

Alpinia purpurata 'Eileen McDonald'

broken light. Flowers: white, open a few at a time; bracts burgundy-red; inflorescence spirelike, to 12 in. tall. Leaves: oblong, 18–22 in. long, 4–6 in. wide, smooth. Rhizomes and stalks aromatic. *Of moist streambanks and lakebanks. Multiple flower spikes and viviparous plantlets commonly develop from the base of older inflorescences. They will take root if they touch the ground or can be cut for propagation. 'Eileen Mc-Donald', pink ginger, is somewhat smaller. It is not known if this form is a cultivar or a natural variation collected in the wild.*

Alpinia zerumbet
SHELL GINGER
Synonyms: *A. nutans* (misapplied), *A. speciosa*. Southeast Asia, India. Evergreen rhizomatous herb, 6–10 ft.+; zones 8–11. Blooms spring.

Regular moisture and humidity. Fertile, organically rich, well-drained soil. Bright understory. Flowers: buds and petals pearly pink to white, lip scoop-shaped, golden with magenta veins; spike pendent. Leaves: broadly oblong to lanceolate to 2 ft. long. *All parts fragrant. Fiber a good paper substitute. Freshest appearance with protection from midday sun. Grows to great height in the "gumbo" soil of New Orleans. Rhizome sometimes used as a substitute for galangal, A. galanga. 'Variegata' with yellow and green striped leaves is mass produced in tissue culture for foliage, usually with poor, contorted flowers. Distinguish from A. formosana with thin, white stripes and from A. sanderae which has erect inflorescences and broad white stripes.*

Alpinia zerumbet

Alpinia zerumbet 'Variegata'

Burbidgea schizocheila

Costus afer

Costus barbatus

Burbidgea
Burbidgea includes 5 species of rhizomatous evergreen herbs from Borneo. The floral lip is much reduced in this genus, but the petals are well developed. These are cold-sensitive plants of deep forest understory. They are suitable for container growing indoors.

Burbidgea schizocheila
GOLD BIRDS
Borneo. Evergreen rhizomatous herb to about 1 ft.; zones 10–11. Blooms spring, fall. Regular moisture. Fertile, organically rich, well-drained soil. Medium filtered light to medium shade. Flowers: petals well-developed, orange-yellow, to 2 in. long, 0.5 in. wide; spike to 6 in. Leaves: ovate to oblong, 4–6 in. long, purplish below, slightly puckered, fleshy. Stalks and petioles purple-maroon. *Best tightly potted in undersize containers. Suitable for shady locations. Does not tolerate direct sun.*

Costus
Costus includes approximately 42 genera of mostly evergreen perennial herbs, which are widely distributed in the tropics and well represented in tropical America and the West Indies. Some authorities prefer to segregate *Costus, Dimerocostus, Monocostus,* and *Tapeinochilos* into the family Costaceae based primarily upon the lack of aromatic oils in leaves and stalks and the spiral arrangement of the leaves. No preference is implied here other

than the strictly practical one of keeping these related genera together for comparison. Inflorescences are often in compact, bracteate, conelike heads (strobili) at the ends of the leafy stalks. Some species produce inflorescences on separate, leafless scapes. The leaves of most *Costus* species are burned by direct sunlight. They prefer understory locations with bright filtered light, regular moisture and humidity but never wet. A horticultural rule-of-thumb is that hairy-leafed costus are usually more cold-sensitive.

Costus afer
West Africa. Evergreen rhizomatous herb, 4–8 ft.; zones 9–11. Blooms spring, early summer. Regular moisture. Fertile, organically rich, well-drained soil. Part sun to bright filtered light. Flowers: bell-shaped, lip pink in the center and white with yellow edges, fragrant. Leaves: spirally arranged on reed-like stems. *Marginally hardy. Protect rhizomes from freezing. An excellent cut flower.*

Costus barbatus
RED TOWER SPIRAL GINGER
Costa Rica. Evergreen rhizomatous herb, 5–8 ft.; zones 9–11. Blooms spring. Regular moisture. Fertile, organically rich, well-drained soil. Part sun to bright filtered light. Flowers: golden-yellow; bracts bright red, scoop-shaped, curved outward; spike gradually extending to 1 ft. Leaves: narrowly elliptic, spirally arranged on a reedlike stalk, hairy below. *Widely cultivated. Fairly tolerant of cool temperatures but not frost. Of moist rain forest from low to moderate elevation. Thin old stems regularly. Good air circulation deters rot. The brighter the light, the more water required.*

Costus curvibracteatus
Central America. Evergreen rhizomatous herb to 2 ft.; zones 10–11. Blooms warm months. Regular moisture. Fertile, organically rich, well-drained soil. Bright filtered light. Flowers: lip red, vase-shaped, enclosed by the orange perianth; bracts pink. Leaves: broadly obovate, to 12 in. long, smooth, light

green with darker markings. *A low-growing species suitable for moist understory locations or containers.*

Costus cuspidatus

FIERY COSTUS

Synonym: *C. igneus.* Southeastern Brazil. Evergreen rhizomatous herb to 18 in.; zones 10–11. Blooms most of the year. Regular moisture. Fertile, organically rich, well-drained soil. Bright filtered light to medium shade. Flowers: yellow-orange, to 2 in. wide, flared, slightly hairy; bracts light green. Leaves: narrowly elliptic to lanceolate, to 8 in. long, tips acuminate, undersides and stem sheaths reddish violet, faintly hairy. *Reclining habit. Of rainforest understory. Tender. Almost ever-blooming, 2 or more flowers at a time. Propagated from brown-haired bulbils in leaf axils. Avoid spraying delicate flowers. Widely cultivated as a container plant.*

Costus lucanusianus

AFRICAN SPIRAL FLAG

Synonym: *C. dussii.* Cameroon, tropical western Africa. Evergreen rhizomatous herb, 5–10 ft.; zones 9–11. Blooms most of the year. Regular moisture. Fertile, organically rich, well-drained soil. Part sun to bright filtered light. Flowers: lip funnel-shaped, margin rolled (revolute), white, striped red with a golden-yellow spot in center. Leaves: elliptic. *Mildly fragrant. Weedy in favorable conditions. Often confused with C. afer, which has similarly marked but bell-shaped flowers.*

Costus malortieanus

Synonyms: *C. elegans, C. zebrinus.* Nicaragua, Costa Rica. Evergreen rhizomatous herb, 2–6 ft.; zones 10–11. Blooms warm months. Regular moisture. Fertile, organically rich, well-drained soil. Bright filtered light. Flowers: vase-shaped, 2–3 in. long, white, lip yellow, lobes russet-striped; bracts in a tight cone, green, flowers open 1 or 2 at a time. Leaves: broadly obovate, 10–12 in. long, to 8 in. wide, light green faintly marked with darker green, stiff silky hairs on both sides; sheaths reddish. *Foliage exceptionally attractive. Of low to middle elevation rainforest understory. Produces*

shoots in the axils of old inflorescences. *Prune to base after bloom to control. Thrives outdoors in South Florida. Cold produces tan spots on leaves. Cut back damaged shoots.*

Costus pulverulentus

Mexico. Evergreen rhizomatous herb, 3–8 ft.; zones 9–11. Blooms summer. Regular moisture. Fertile, organically rich, well-drained soil. Bright filtered light. Flowers: red-orange; bracts red-orange with a yellow callus, to greenish near base; spike cigar-shaped, pointed. Leaves: narrowly elliptic, to 8 in. long, maroon-striped, slightly hairy beneath. *Often confused with the West Indian species C. spicatus, which has oblanceolate leaves and a spike with a rounded apex. Costus woodsonii has elliptical leaves and a short, thick ovoid spike with a rounded apex.*

Costus speciosus

CRAPE GINGER, MALAY GINGER

Indomalaysia, Southeast Asia to the Himalayas; naturalized Central America, West Indies. Evergreen rhizomatous herb, 5–10 ft.; zones 9–11. Blooms summer, fall. Regular moisture. Fertile, organically rich, well-drained soil. Part sun to bright filtered light. Flowers: funnel-shaped, lip white to pink, ruffled; bracts pointed, purple-maroon with silky white hairs; spike compact. Leaves: broadly elliptic, to 1 ft. long, tip acuminate, reddish below, silky haired to minutely hairy; stalk tinged red. *Of low elevation forests. Rhizome used medicinally. Avoid spraying the delicate flowers if possible. 'Variegatus' has white-streaked leaves.*

Costus talbotii

Southern Nigeria, Cameroon, tropical western Africa. Evergreen rhizomatous herb to 2 ft.; zones 10–11. Blooms spring, summer. Regular moisture. Fertile, organically rich, well-drained soil. Bright filtered light. Flowers: lip spreading, pearly white, pinkish petals below with yellow spot at base; bracts pink. Leaves: elliptic, smooth. *A rare costus. Suitable for containers. Tender. Differs from C. speciosus by small size and flower not funnel-shaped.*

Costus varzearum

Brazil. Evergreen rhizomatous herb, 4–6 ft.; zones 10–11. Blooms fall. Regular moisture. Fertile, organically rich, well-drained soil.

Bright filtered light. Flowers: tubular, lip orange- and red-striped, enclosed by ovate, pink to orange perianth; bracts, dark green, streaked red at base. Leaves:

Costus curvibracteatus

Costus cuspidatus

Costus lucanusianus

Costus malortieanus

Costus pulverulentus

Costus speciosus

broadly obovate, purple below. *Species name means "of flooded forest."*

Costus woodsonii

INDIAN-HEAD GINGER

Panama, Costa Rica, Nicaragua. Evergreen rhizomatous herb, 7–9 ft.; zones 9–11. Blooms late winter, spring. Regular moisture. Fertile, organically rich, well-drained soil. Bright broken light. Flowers, tubular, orange, sticking out at an angle from the red-orange bracts, broadly ovate; head compact, ovoid, to 4 in. tall. Leaves: obovate to elliptic, base heart-shaped, glossy. *An understory plant. Nectar glands around the outside of the inflorescence attract ants, which aid in pollination. Somewhat resembles* C. spicatus, *which has cigar-shaped spikes.*

Curcuma

Curcuma includes approximately 40 species of deciduous rhizomatous herbs from Southeast Asia, India, and Malaysia. These species are referred to as hidden lilies because the inflorescences are often partly hidden among the leaves. All curcumas are referred to as *olena* in Hawaiian which has led to the occasional application of the name *C. olena*—a name that does not exist botanically. Leaves are basal, usually with long petioles. The flower spikes are on individual leafless scapes (radicals) or on the leafy stem. The fertile flowers are in usually shorter, less colorful scoop-shaped bracts at the base of the inflorescence with an ornamental coma of sterile bracts on top. Curcumas are stunning jewels of the tropics and rapidly catching on as houseplants and cut-flowers. Many are suitable for container growing and thrive outdoors where it is moist and humid in summer and dry in winter. Because they die back to the ground in winter, curcumas withstand brief freezing temperatures as long as the rhizome is protected. A thick bed of mulch is generally adequate to zone 8 or sometimes even to zone 7. Mark well to prevent disturbance during dormant period. In colder areas, rhizomes can be dug up and overwintered indoors in a dry spot. Grow in sandy loam with added peat. Keep dry when dormant and begin regular watering when shoots appear. Raise potted plants for good display.

Curcuma alismatifolia

SIAM TULIP

Thailand. Seasonally dormant rhizomatous herb to 2 ft.; zones 9–11. Blooms summer, fall. Seasonally moist/dry. Fertile, organically rich, well-drained soil; alkaline pH. Part sun to bright filtered light. Flowers: white with a purple lip, in lower greenish bracts; sterile coma bracts very large, to 3 in. long, petal-like, pink, white, or dark pink, erect. Leaves: narrowly spear-shaped, midvein purple. *Of limestone soils. Rare in cultivation until recently. Suitable as a container plant. Very attractive cut flowers. The species name alludes to the distinctive foliage, which resembles leaves of the water plantain family, Alismataceae. Stake flower stalks.*

Curcuma australasica

AUSSIE PLUME

Australia (northern Queensland). Seasonally dormant rhizomatous herb to 2 ft.; zones 8–11. Blooms late spring, summer. Seasonally moist/dry. Fertile, organically rich,

Costus talbotii

Costus varzearum

Costus woodsonii

Curcuma alismatifolia

Curcuma alismatifolia, inflorescences

well-drained soil; alkaline pH. Part sun to bright filtered light. Flowers: yellow, lip has smooth edge, in green, scoop-shaped bracts; coma bracts pinkish burgundy. Leaves: broadly ovate, to 2 ft. long, ribbed. *One of the more commonly grown curcumas.*

Curcuma elata

GIANT PLUME

India. Seasonally dormant rhizomatous herb to 6 ft.; zones 7–11. Blooms spring. Seasonally moist/dry. Fertile, organically rich, well-drained soil. Slightly filtered light. Flowers: white to pale yellow, lip golden, in green bracts; coma bracts pink, flattened and spreading; inflorescence 10–14 in. high, emerges before leaves. Leaves: 30 in. long, 10 in. wide, slightly rough; first leaves to emerge have light purple-maroon stripe on midvein, later leaves green. *A dependable grower but blooms better after a long dormant period, as in zones 8 and 9. Blooms inconsistently in zones 10 and 11. Grown as far north as eastern North Carolina.* Curcuma zedoaria *has shorter inflorescences and erect, scooped, maroon coma bracts.*

Curcuma flaviflora

FIERY CURCUMA, FIERY HIDDEN-LILY, RED FIRE-BALL

Northern Thailand, southern China. Seasonally dormant rhizomatous herb to 2 ft.; zones 8–11. Blooms summer. Seasonally moist/dry. Fertile, organically rich, well-drained soil. Bright filtered light. Flowers: golden; bracts tomato-red; on a very short stalk at ground level; inflorescence breaks out of the base of the leaf sheaths. Leaves: elliptic, 1–2 ft. long, light green. *Stunning, but ground-level inflorescence needs consideration for display. Containers can be raised on a stand when plant is in bloom. In the ground, a raised bed or bank would be ideal.*

Curcuma harmandii

EMERALD PAGODA, SIAM DIAMOND

Thailand, Myanmar (Burma). Seasonally dormant rhizomatous herb to 2 ft.; zones 9–11. Blooms summer, fall. Seasonally moist/dry. Fertile, organically rich, well-drained soil. Bright filtered light. Flowers:

greenish white, exserted from bract, lip white with 2 reddish stripes, edge toothed, under 1 in. wide, lateral staminodes threadlike; all bracts green, leathery, leaflike. Leaves: broadly ovate. *An unusual curcuma with completely exposed flowers and relatively long distance between the bracts. One flower opens at a time from several buds within each bract. Fairly new in cultivation. Probably not hardy.*

Curcuma petiolata

PINK TOWER CURCUMA, JEWEL OF THAILAND

Synonym: *C. cordata* (incorrectly). Thailand. Seasonally dormant rhizomatous herb to 2 ft.; zones 8–11. Blooms summer. Seasonally moist/dry. Fertile, organically rich, well-drained soil. Bright shade. Flowers: lip tubular, golden almost enclosed by white perianth; fertile

bracts green with pink edges; coma bracts deep pink, pointed; inflorescence cylindrical. Leaves: very broadly ovate, 8–10 in. wide, 14 in. long. *Suitable for areas with indirect light, never direct sun.* Curcuma petiolata, C. sumatrana, C. australasica, *and* C. phaeocaulis *are difficult to distinguish without close comparison of the flowers (see species descriptions). These species have been cultivated for centuries and wild collections may actually represent naturalized variations of the same species (Wood, pers. comm.). 'Emperor', a white-bracted curcuma, is often incorrectly listed as a cultivar of* C. petiolata *(see* Curcuma *species entry).*

Curcuma phaeocaulis

Indonesia (Java). Seasonally dormant rhizomatous herb, 3–4 ft.; zones 8–11. Blooms spring. Seasonally moist/dry. Fertile, organi-

cally rich, well-drained soil. Bright filtered light. Flowers: tubular, yellow lip enclosed by pink perianth, fertile bracts green; inflorescence low among the petiole stalks below the blades. Leaves: paddle-shaped, to 30 in. long, 7 in. wide, midvein dark maroon; petioles long. *Resembles a large* C. zedoaria, *which also has leaves with maroon midveins.* Curcuma elata *has light purple-maroon midvein on first leaves only. Very closely related (Wood, pers. comm.).*

Curcuma rabdota

STRIPED CURCUMA

Synonym: *C. gracillima.* Thailand. Seasonally dormant rhizomatous herb to 2 ft.; zones 9–11. Blooms summer. Seasonally moist/dry. Fertile, organically rich, well-drained soil. Bright filtered light. Flowers: rose-pink in brown-maroon bracts with green stripes and pink cheeks;

Curcuma australasica

Curcuma elata

Curcuma flaviflora

Curcuma harmandii

Curcuma petiolata

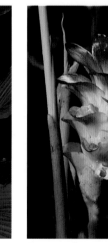

Curcuma phaeocaulis

coma bracts rosy pink with a touch of brown. Leaves: broadly ovate, pleated. *A variable species, the various natural forms often given cultivar names. Divide in fall after leaves dry. Suitable for containers.*

Curcuma roscoeana

JEWEL-OF-BURMA, BURMESE HIDDEN-LILY
India, Southeast Asia, Malaysia; wild habitat threatened. Seasonally dormant rhizomatous herb to 3 ft.; zones 9–11. Blooms summer, fall. Seasonally moist/dry. Fertile, organically rich, well-drained soil. Bright filtered light. Flowers: tubular, yellow; bracts all fertile, peach-orange to dark red-orange. Leaves: broadly ovate to elliptic, light green with darker veins, to 12 in. long. *One of the most popular curcumas. Choice selections have deep color and orderly rows of bracts. Suitable for*

containers on patios and balconies with filtered midday sun. Cut flowers last about 2 weeks. Wait until some flowers open before cutting.

Curcuma species

QUEEN-LILY
Synonym: *C. petiolata* (misapplied). Malaysia. Seasonally dormant rhizomatous herb to 3 ft.; zones 7–11. Blooms summer. Seasonally moist/dry. Fertile, organically rich, well-drained soil. Bright filtered light. Flowers: golden-yellow, fertile bracts green; coma bracts pinkish white. Leaves: glossy with raised veins, 14 in. long, 5 in. wide; petioles 4–6 in. long. *Unnamed species, usually misrepresented as* C. petiolata, *a distinct species (see). This curcuma has larger inflorescences. A variegated form,* C. 'Emperor', *is grown for its striped foliage as well as its flowers (Wood, pers. comm.).*

Curcuma sumatrana

SUMATRA HIDDEN-LILY
Indonesia. Seasonally dormant rhizomatous herb, 1.5–2 ft.; zones 9–11. Blooms summer, fall. Seasonally moist/dry. Fertile, organically rich, well-drained soil. Bright filtered light. Flowers: tubular, yellow, lip fringed; fertile bracts flattened, spoon-shaped, not deeply scooped, streaked green and burgundy; coma bracts pointed, bright pink. Leaves: oblong to elliptic, light green with darker veins, to 1 ft. long. *The inflorescence is thicker, shorter, and more ovoid than* C. petiolata. *The floral lip is larger than* C. australasica *and fringed. This curcuma has a compact growth habit, very suitable for containers.*

Curcuma zedoaria

ZEDOARY
Synonym: *C. inodora.* India. Sea-

sonally dormant rhizomatous herb, 2–2.5 ft.; zones 8–11. Blooms spring. Seasonally moist/dry. Fertile, organically rich, well-drained soil. Morning sun to bright filtered light. Flowers: yellow, bracts scoop-shaped, reddish-tipped, coma bracts burgundy, scooped, upright; inflorescence emerges before leaves in spring; spike 6–8 in. Leaves: lanceolate, to 18 in. long, 4 in. wide, midvein blackish maroon. *Prefers the longer dormancy period at the cooler end of its range. Zedoary root is a condiment and stimulant used in folk medicine. Curcuma elata has purplish midribs on first leaves only and a flattened coma.*

Dimerocostus

Dimerocostus includes 2 species of rhizomatous herbs from tropical America. This genus is included in Costaceae by some authors. Leaves are slender, elliptic, and spirally arranged on reedlike stalks. Flowers have an enlarged lip and large lateral lobes. They are arranged in spirally twisting terminal spikes. Stems are erect or reclining.

Dimerocostus strobilaceus

CREPE GINGER
Synonym: *D. elongatus.* Honduras to Panama, Venezuela, Surinam. Evergreen rhizomatous herb to 8 ft.; zones 10–11. Blooms warm months. Regular moisture. Fertile, organically rich, well-drained soil. Morning sun to bright filtered light. Flowers: yellow, lip broad, lateral lobes oblong, edges revolute;

Curcuma rabdota

Curcuma roscoeana

Curcuma species

Curcuma sumatrana

Curcuma zedoaria

Dimerocostus strobilaceus

Dimerocostus strobilaceus subsp. *gutierrezii*

bracts triangular to ovate, green, sheathing; spike spirally twisted, 1–2 ft. tall, terminal. Leaves: narrowly elliptic; margins undulate; spirally arranged, widely spaced on the stalk. *Of moist lowland forest margins and open areas with erect to reclining stems. Subsp.* gutierrezii, *from Peru, Bolivia (eastern slope of the Andes), Venezuela, and Surinam, is a smaller plant with narrower leaves than the type and a lighter yellow lip. Avoid spraying delicate flowers if possible. Direct sunlight causes flowers to wilt quickly.*

Etlingera

Etlingera includes approximately 60 species of rhizomatous herbs from Indomalaysia. Only *E. elatior*, the large and stunning torch ginger, is widely cultivated. It is sometimes grown commercially for cut flowers. Leaves are on reedy stalks. Inflorescences are usually produced on short leafless scapes or at ground level. Flowers are located in whorls of ornamental bracts. They bloom almost all year in warm climates. Protect from freezing and wind. The rhizome is extensive and etlingeras are generally not suitable for average containers.

Etlingera elatior

TORCH GINGER, WAX FLOWER, PORCELAIN-FLOWER
Synonyms: *Nicolaia elatior, Phaeomeria magnifica*. Malay Peninsula, Indonesia (Java), Sulawesi (Celebes); naturalized throughout tropical Asia. Evergreen rhizomatous herb, 6–15 ft.; zones 10–11. Blooms intermittently in warm months. Seasonally moist/dry to regular moisture in warm climates. Fertile, organically rich, well-drained soil. Morning sun to bright filtered light. Flowers: tubular with white or gold margins; bracts waxy, red, pink, or purple with white margins, in whorls around a subglobular head; sterile outer bracts enclose the inner fertile bracts until head is fully expanded, then reflex downward; on a leafless scape to 4 ft. Leaves: lanceolate 2–3 ft. long, purplish below, on erect, reedlike stalks, 5–15 ft. tall. *All parts aromatic. Tender. Protect rhizome from freezing. In warm moist conditions plants remain evergreen.*

Globba

Globba includes approximately 35 species of rhizomatous or tuberous herbs from Southeast Asia and Indomalaysia. These are small plants of woodland understory. Leaves are elliptic, on short stalks usually less than 2 ft. high. Bulbils, aboveground bulblike, asexual reproductive structures, sometimes replace some of the flowers. Globbas are distinguished by long, fishhooklike stamens with toothlike appendages. The stamens are mounted on the floral lip. Inflorescences are produced at the end of the leafy stalk. Suitable for containers. Grown outdoors in shaded locations. Propagate by division of the rhizomes, seed, or bulbils.

Globba atrosanguinea

Borneo. Perennial rhizomatous herb, 1–2 ft.; zones 10–11. Blooms summer. Seasonally moist/dry. Fertile, organically rich, well-drained soil. Bright filtered light. Flowers: yellow; bracts red-orange; inflorescence erect. Leaves: purplish below. *Globba variabilis* subsp. *pusilla* from Peninsular Malaysia is similar.

Globba leucantha subsp. tricolor

Southern Thailand, Borneo, Malaysia. Seasonally dormant rhizomatous herb to 1 ft.; zones 10–11. Blooms spring, early summer. Seasonally moist/dry. Fertile, organically rich, well-drained soil. Bright filtered light. Flowers: tiny, white, yellow, and violet; bracts and rachis white, pendent. Leaves: elliptic, to 3 in. long, tips acuminate, downy. *A dainty plant suitable for containers.*

Globba schomburgkii

Thailand. Seasonally dormant rhi-

zomatous herb, 1–1.5 ft.; zones 8–11. Blooms summer. Seasonally moist/dry. Fertile, organically rich, well-drained soil. Bright filtered light. Flowers: yellow with a red-orange spot on lip; fertile flowers at the distal end of the pendent inflorescence; bulbils at the base. Leaves: lanceolate, to 6 in. long, with shallow ridges. *Self-propagating by bulbils. This species shares a pot with a Hemerocallis on my patio, alternating bloom seasons. Globba marantina is a similar but smaller species without a spot on the lip.*

Globba winitii

DANCING LADY GINGER, DANCING GIRL
Thailand. Seasonally dormant rhizomatous herb to 1.5 ft.; zones 8–11. Blooms summer. Seasonally moist/dry. Fertile, organically rich,

Etlingera elatior, pink form

Etlingera elatior, red form

Globba atrosanguinea

Globba leucantha subsp. *tricolor*

Globba schomburgkii

Globba winitii

well-drained soil. Bright filtered light. Flowers: yellow; bracts reflexed, mauve-violet or white; one fertile stamen on a very long filament; on pendent floral stalk. Leaves: lanceolate, base cordate, lobes overlapping, to 10 in. long. *Does not produce bulbils. Long-lasting cut flowers. Suitable for containers. 'White Dragon' could possibly be a distinct species (Wood, pers. comm.).*

Hedychium

Hedychium includes approximately 50 species of rhizomatous herbs and a few epiphytes, from Southeast Asia and Indomalaysia. This group, commonly referred to as ginger-lilies, includes many splendid cultivated ornamentals. Unfortunately, some have become invasive in Hawaii and in other areas. Sterile hybrids recommended. Hedychiums are erect, reedy

stemmed plants with terminal inflorescences. The inflorescence is cylindrical or cone-shaped. Flowers are often highly fragrant, the essential oils used in perfumery. The floral tubes are long and slender and frequently extend well beyond the bracts. The perianth is 3-lobed. There are 2 distinctive linear pendent staminodes. The single fertile stamen is held perpendicular to the staminodes. The outer edge of the lip is often lobed and the base is clawed. The 3-valved fruit splits open revealing bright orange arils and dark red seeds which are attractive to birds. Species from higher altitudes and their hybrids have greatest cold resistance. Though most tolerate full sun with sufficient moisture, the flowers remain fresher longer in somewhat filtered light. Cut back old canes when they start to yellow.

Hedychium coccineum

SCARLET GINGER-LILY,
SCARLET BUTTERFLY GINGER
Himalayan foothills, Myanmar (Burma), southern China, Thailand. Perennial rhizomatous herb, 4–8 ft.; zones 8–11. Blooms intermittently in summer, fall. Seasonally moist/dry. Fertile, organically rich, well-drained soil. Part sun to bright filtered light. Flowers: lip funnel-shaped, pale orange to deep scarlet; bracts tubular, green in orderly ranks; 2–4 flowers in each bract; inflorescence cylindrical. Leaves: lanceolate, 1–1.5 ft. long. *Of low-elevation mountainous regions. Evergreen in warm climates. Blooms 3 or 4 times a year, the flowers opening successively over several weeks.*

Hedychium coronarium

BUTTERFLY GINGER, WHITE GINGER-LILY, GARLAND-FLOWER
Origin obscure (probably India, Myanmar [Burma]); cultivated for millennia. Perennial rhizomatous herb, 4–6 ft.; zones 7–11. Blooms warm months. Moist to wet, seasonally dry. Fertile, organically rich, well-drained soil. Morning sun to bright filtered light. Flowers: white with faintly yellow-green throat, lip projects downward, somewhat nodding, sweetly fragrant; filaments white; bracts tightly overlapping in cone-shaped heads, green. Leaves: lanceolate, 1–2 ft. long. *Of low-elevation mountainous regions. Tolerates boggy locations. Flowers often used in Hawaiian leis; the oils in*

perfumery. Var. chrysoleucum *has white flowers with yellow centers and orange filaments. Invasive in Hawaii, Jamaica, and New Zealand.*

Hedychium cylindricum

Indonesia (Sumatra), Borneo. Evergreen epiphytic rhizomatous herb, 24–30 in.; zones 10–11. Blooms fall, winter, spring, irregularly in summer. Seasonally moist/dry. Fertile, organically rich, well-drained soil. Morning sun to bright filtered light. Flowers: creamy white, lip fringed; spike elongated, cylindrical; bracts overlapping; fragrant at night. Leaves: lanceolate, to 14 in. long, 3 in. wide, glossy. *Produces dense clumps. A ginger for winter bloom in warm areas.*

Hedychium flavescens

YELLOW GINGER-LILY,
AWAPUHI MELEMELE (HAWAII)
Northeastern India, Nepal. Perennial rhizomatous herb, 6–10 ft.; zones 9–11. Blooms late summer, fall. Seasonally moist/dry. Fertile, organically rich, well-drained soil. Bright filtered light. Flowers: entirely pale yellow to creamy yellow; filaments yellow; lip elliptic, upright. Leaves: to 2 ft. long. *Blooms when nights begin to cool.*

Hedychium gardnerianum

KAHILI GINGER, SALMON BUTTERFLY GINGER, SALMON GINGER-LILY
India, Nepal near Katmandu. Perennial rhizomatous herb to 8 ft.; zones 7–11. Blooms summer, fall. Seasonally moist/dry. Fertile, organically rich, well-drained soil Morning sun to bright understory. Flowers: lip normally yellow, 'Tara' lip tangerine-orange; often producing 2 flowers per bract; capsules fleshy, orange; arils ruby-red; gardenia-like fragrance. Leaves: waxy bluish. *Of mountain regions. Hardy. Grows in regions of southwestern England warmed by the Gulf Stream. Invasive in Hawaii and a potential pest in other mild, moist areas.*

Hedychium gracile

Synonym: *H. glaucum.* India. Seasonally dormant rhizomatous herb; zones 8–11. Blooms summer. Seasonally moist/dry. Fertile, organically rich, well-drained soil. Bright

Globba winitii 'White dragon'

Hedychium coccineum

Hedychium coronarium

Hedychium cylindricum

Hedychium flavescens

filtered light to part shade. Flowers: pale greenish to yellowish white, petals narrow, twisted; stamens scarlet; in 6- to 8-in. oblique to erect spikes; fragrant at night. Leaves: lanceolate, green below. *Of mountainous woodlands. Rhizomes are very close to the surface. Mulch well to insulate from freezing. More suited to shade than most hedychiums. Leaves of var. glaucum are more oblong to broadly ovate and glaucous below.*

Hedychium horsfieldii

Indonesia (Java). Evergreen rhizomatous herb, 1.5–2 ft.; zones 10–11. Blooms spring. Seasonally moist/dry. Fertile, organically rich, well-drained soil. Bright filtered light to bright shade. Flowers: perianth lobes slender, creamy yellow, lip rudimentary; 2 lateral staminodes form a white hood over the short fertile stamen; bracts 5–9, overlapping (imbricate), each bearing 1 or 2 flowers. Leaves: 3–6, lance-shaped, blade to 1 ft. long, thick, glossy dark green, arching. *A spare bloomer but the white flowers are striking against the dark foliage.*

Hedychium 'Luna Moth'

Garden hybrid. Seasonally dormant rhizomatous herb to 4 ft.; zones 8–11. Blooms summer, fall. Seasonally moist/dry. Fertile, organically rich, well-drained soil. Bright filtered light to bright shade. Flowers: spreading, petals white with a pale yellow streak along the midline; stamen orange; sweetly fragrant. Leaves: oblanceolate, thick, glossy. *Hybrid parents from moist mountain woodlands. Marginally hardy with protection of dormant rhizome.*

Hedychium 'Pink V'

Garden origin. Perennial rhizomatous herb, 4–6 ft.; zones 8–11. Blooms summer, fall. Seasonally moist/dry. Fertile, organically rich, well-drained soil. Bright filtered light to bright shade. Flowers: white with deep peach-pink center, sweetly fragrant; in compact clusters opening over several weeks. Leaves: 16 in. long, 3 in. wide, glossy. *One of ginger expert Tom Wood's magnificent hybrids.*

Kaempferia

Kaempferia includes approximately 50 species of seasonally dormant small herbs from southern China, India, Southeast Asia, and Indomalaysia. Their wild habitat is seriously threatened by deforestation. The species often have ornamentally marked foliage somewhat resembling *Maranta* and *Calathea*.

Commonly cultivated species are prostrate with short rhizomes and tuberous roots. Flowers are borne singly or in pairs, opening over an extended period. Some deciduous species such as *Kaempferia rotunda* bloom at the end of a dry season before new leaves are produced. The petal-like parts consist of 2 staminodes (sterile stamens) and a lip, or labellum, which is subdivided into 2 lobes, giving the impression of a 4-lobed flower (Wood, pers. comm.). Kaempferias are shade-loving understory plants. Mark site to prevent disturbance during dormancy. *Kaempferia* and *Globba* are the most shade tolerant gingers. Suitable for container growing.

Kaempferia pulchra

PEACOCK GINGER-LILY
Thailand, Myanmar (Burma). Sea-

Hedychium gardnerianum 'Tara'

Hedychium gardnerianum, infructescence

Hedychium gracile

Hedychium horsfieldii

Hedychium 'Luna Moth'

Hedychium 'Pink V'

Kaempferia pulchra, peacock type

Kaempferia pulchra, silver-spotted type

sonally dormant rhizomatous or tuberous herb under 1 ft.; zones 8–11. Blooms warm months. Seasonally moist and humid, dry. Fertile, organically rich, well-drained soil; alkaline pH. Filtered light to bright shade. Flowers: always pink-lavender with a white spot in center, one to a few opening sequentially; on a short stalk. Leaves: basal, 2–3, broadly ovate to suborbicular, spreading, 6–8 in. long, dark green patterned with silver, waxy coating giving a frosted appearance. *A variably marked species of limestone hills. Cultivar names are often given to natural variations. The silver-spotted form blooms well into winter. One commonly cultivated form eventually looses its spots, becoming uniformly green.*

Kaempferia roscoeana

Thailand . Seasonally dormant rhi-

Kaempferia roscoeana

Monocostus uniflorus

zomatous or tuberous herb; zones 8–11. Blooms warm months. Moist and humid/seasonally dry. Fertile, organically rich, well-drained soil; alkaline pH. Filtered light to bright shade. Flowers: white with light yellow spot in center, to 2 in. wide. Leaves: ovate, to 14 in. long, 2 bands of variegation. *Flowers always white, larger than K. pulchra, lobes slightly overlapping. This species has the largest leaf among the prostrate kaempferias (Wood, pers. comm.).*

Kaempferia rotunda

Exact origin obscure, widely distributed throughout Southeast Asia. Seasonally dormant rhizomatous or tuberous herb; zones 10–11. Blooms spring. Seasonally moist and humid, dry. Fertile, organically rich, well-drained soil; alkaline pH. Filtered light to bright shade. Flowers: perianth with 3 slender white

Kaempferia rotunda

Riedelia species

lobes, staminode lobes pink, magenta spot at base and white in center, outer edges frilled. Leaves: basal, lance-shaped, purple below, ascending to erect, patterned. *Widely cultivated in tropical Asia for culinary and medicinal purposes. Identification unresolved. The leaves are more pointed than usual for this species (Wood, pers. comm.). Blooms before leaves emerge.*

Monocostus

Monocostus includes a single species of small herb from a limited area on the eastern side of the Andes in Peru. Some authors place this genus in Costaceae. The genus is distinguished from *Costus* and *Dimerocostus* by the solitary flowers which are borne in the leaf axils rather than at the end of the leafy stalk (terminal). The habit is creeping to decumbent (upturned at the ends of the stalks). The leaves spiral around a twisting stalk. The flowers are funnel-shaped with a long tube. Plants are suitable for containers in bright reflected light with plenty of humidity. They bloom continuously over many months. Protect them from chilly temperatures, drying wind, and bright sun.

Monocostus uniflorus

YELLOW SPIRAL GINGER
Synonyms: *Costus uniflorus, M. ulei.* Eastern Peru, endemic to a limited region. Seasonally dormant rhizomatous herb to 1 ft.; zones 10–11. Blooms intermittently all year. Regular moisture. Fertile, organically rich, well-drained soil. Filtered light to medium shade. Flowers: funnel-shaped with flaring bright yellow lobes, throat more or less streaked with red; calyx long, green; fruit 2-lobed, elongated. Leaves: ovate, to 2 in. long, thick with narrow red margins; spirally arranged around a trailing stem with upturned ends (decumbent). *Of tropical rain forest. Cold-sensitive.*

Riedelia

Riedelia includes approximately 60 species of rhizomatous herbs from the Moluccas to New Guinea. The fruit splits into 2, instead of 3, segments—a distinctive characteristic.

The plant included here is occasionally cultivated. It is striking especially when grown in groups. The showy buds are long-lasting, scarlet to pink, remaining several weeks before the flower opens but then quickly falling. The clusters of round, yellow-green fruits that follow are also attractive. Plants are tender and need protection on cold nights and filtered or indirect light. They are pollinated by birds. The unnamed species shown here is sometimes misidentified as *R. coralina.* That species of moderate altitude has a fan of oblong, 20-in. thick glossy leaves radiating from the base, its inflorescence is congested, and the plant is larger than this species (Wood, pers. comm.).

Riedelia species

New Guinea. Evergreen rhizomatous herb, 2–3 ft.; zones 10–11. Blooms late winter, spring. Regular moisture. Fertile, organically rich, well-drained soil. Bright filtered or indirect light. Flowers: tubular, dark pink, long-lasting, barely opening; in open, terminal spikes. Leaves: lanceolate, to 18 in. long, glossy dark green with lighter midveins. Stems: short. *Of low-altitude rain forest.*

Siphonochilus

Siphonochilus includes approximately 15 species of rhizomatous herbs from tropical Africa. They come primarily from seasonally dry savannas and woodlands. Leaves are broad, leathery, and somewhat pleated. Flowers are on a terminal spike. *Siphonochilus* is not closely related to *Kaempferia* as previously thought.

Siphonochilus decorus

Synonym: *Kaempferia decora.* Tropical Africa. Seasonally dormant herb to 2 ft.; zones 10–11. Blooms late spring, early summer. Seasonally moist/ dry. Fertile, organically rich, well-drained soil. Bright filtered light. Flowers: funnel-shaped, bright yellow, lip large with 2 lobes above; bracts tubular, green, each bearing a single flower; on a slender spike. Leaves: broadly ovate, somewhat folded, thick, dark green with impressed veins; on a short stem. *The yellow flowers somewhat resemble those of* Dimerocostus strobilaceus, *but the plant is much smaller. Suitable for containers.*

Tapeinochilos

Tapeinochilos includes 8–10 species of rhizomatous herbs from New Guinea, Australia, and the Moluccas Islands (Indonesia). The genus is included in Costaceae by some authors. *Tapeinochilos ananassae* is sometimes cultivated, primarily in botanical gardens. It is a variable species probably due to its distribution over a number of Pacific Islands. Flowers are usually borne on a separate leafless scape rising directly from the rhizome which is typical of plants from New Guinea and Australia; or sometimes on the leaf stalk (or both), typical of plants from the Moluccas. Plants are ten-

der, for warm or protected areas. Other ornamental species have bracts that vary from red and yellow to almost black. They are ultra-tropical and hence rare in cultivation in the continental United States.

Tapeinochilos ananassae

PINEAPPLE GINGER, GIANT SPIRAL GINGER, INDONESIAN WAX GINGER
Synonyms: *Costus ananassae, T. queenslandiae.* Ambon and Sulu islands (Moluccas), New Guinea, Ceram, northeastern Australia . Perennial rhizomatous herb, 4–8 ft.; zone 11. Blooms late spring, summer. Moist and humid. Fertile, organically rich, well-drained soil. Bright filtered light. Flowers: tubular, orange-yellow; bracts pointed, waxy red; on a separate scape or on the leafy stalk. Leaves: lanceolate. *Of moist forest understory. The species name alludes to the pineap-*

*ple-shaped inflorescence (*Ananas *is the pineapple genus). Var.* queenslandiae, *from northeastern Australia, is considered a distinct species by some authorities. Photo of a plant producing flowers on the leaf stalk.*

Zingiber

Zingiber includes approximately 60 species of seasonally dormant rhizomatous herbs from Southeast Asia and Indomalaysia to northeastern Australia. The aromatic rhizomes of Chinese ginger, *Z. officinale*, a rarely flowering cultigen, are sold fresh, candied, or as a powdered spice. This ginger is also commonly used as an herbal remedy for stomach upset and is reputed to have anticancer and antimalarial properties. Zingibers are grown for their ornamental, cone-like inflorescences (strobili), which consist of overlapping or scoop-shaped bracts that turn red or yellow after the flowers mature. *Zingiber* is distinguished from other gingers by a hornlike appendage on the stamen. Flowers are one per bract and short-lived. A foamy, fragrant nectar in the bracts attracts birds and small animals. The fruits develop under the water in the bracts which serve to protect them from insects. The inflorescence usually develops on a separate stalk (scape) directly from the rhizome after the leaves are fully developed. Leaves are in opposite ranks (distichous) on a canelike stalk. Propagate by division. Cut inflorescences last up to 2 weeks. Be-

cause inflorescences are low and partly hidden, they are ideally grown outdoors on a raised retaining wall or slope (Burch, pers. comm.).

Zingiber neglectum

Indonesia (Java). Seasonally dormant rhizomatous herb to 6 ft.; zones 8–11. Blooms summer. Seasonally moist/dry. Fertile, organically rich, well-drained soil. Part sun to bright filtered light. Flowers: translucent white with purple splotches; bracts green, turning glossy red, edges revolute, spikes 6–10 in. tall; on a scape to 18 in. high. Leaves: lanceolate, to 12 in. long, 3 in. wide. *The species name means "hidden," alluding to the inflorescence being partially hidden by the foliage.*

Zingiber spectabile

BEEHIVE GINGER, PINECONE GINGER
Malaysia, southern Thailand. Seasonally dormant rhizomatous herb to 12 ft.; zones 9–11. Blooms warm months. Seasonally moist/dry. Fertile, organically rich, well-drained soil. Part sun to bright filtered light. Flowers: lip purple-brown with yellow spots enclosed by whitish side lobes; bracts waxy, scoop-shaped, greenish, turning light yellow then red as they mature, edges revolute; spike cylindrical, to 1 ft. high. Leaves: lanceolate, to 20 in. long, softly downy below. *Of moist tropical lowland forests and streamsides.*

Zingiber zerumbet

WILD GINGER, RED PINECONE GINGER, BITTER GINGER, SHAMPOO GINGER, AWAPUHI
Possibly southern India, Sri Lanka; widely cultivated. Seasonally dormant rhizomatous herb to 4 ft.; zones 8–11. Blooms summer. Seasonally moist/dry. Fertile, organically rich, well-drained soil. Part sun to bright filtered light. Flowers: light yellow; bracts green, turning bright red after flowering; in dense spikes. Leaves: lanceolate, distichous. *Much used in folk medicine. Liquid in cone has a ginger/pine essence. 'Darcy' (incorrectly 'Darceyi') is grown for its white-margined foliage and burnished, mahogany-red bracts.*

Siphonochilus decorus

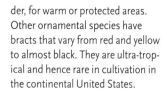

Tapeinochilos ananassae

Zingiber neglectum

Zingiber spectabile

Zingiber zerumbet, in flower

ZYGOPHYLLACEAE
LIGNUM VITAE FAMILY

Zygophyllaceae includes approximately 27 genera of shrubs, trees, and annual or perennial herbs, primarily from arid tropical and warm temperate regions. Some species

Zingiber zerumbet 'Darcy'

Bulnesia arborea, flowers

have very durable hard wood. The resinous sap has pharmaceutical properties. Leaves are evenly pinnate (paripinnate), the leaflets entire, usually sessile, with unequal sides, often falcate (curved), in opposite pairs, occasionally one of

each leaflet pair being greatly reduced and appearing alternate. Stems are often jointed at the nodes. Flowers are bisexual and usually radially symmetrical. They have 5 mostly free sepals, 5 clawed petals, and 10–15 stamens. Flowers are solitary or arranged in cymes. The fruit is a 5-, 4-, or 2-winged capsule or schizocarp. Seeds are often covered with a brightly colored sarcotesta (fleshy outer seedcoat). The Spanish name *guayacán* is applied to several trees with hard wood including *Bulnesia*, *Guaiacum*, and certain *Tabebuia* species.

Bulnesia

Bulnesia includes approximately 9 species of shrubs and trees from South America. It is a primary tree of dry tropical forests. The wood is very hard and durable, similar to that of *Guaiacum* species. Leaves are pinnate with even numbers of falcate, sometimes minute leaflets. *Bulnesia* species have more than twice as many leaflets as *Guaiacum* species. The opposite leaf arrangement helps distinguish this family from legumes (Fabaceae). Flowers are yellow, bisexual, and radially symmetrical. Capsules are 5-winged, usually producing small, sterile seeds. It is unknown why an occasional tree produces the larger fertile seeds (self-sterile?). Harvest seed as soon as the capsules turn yellow. Dry the seeds, peel off the red sarcotesta and soak in water for 24 hours before planting. Keep evenly moist until germination. *Bulnesia arborea* has many virtues for cultivation. It is an excellent shade tree and blooms 3 or 4 times a year. It can be used to control erosion. Trees are xeric and have a moderate growth rate. They are low maintenance because the small leaflets shed gradually and disappear into the grass. Conversely, avoid planting over walks and drives where steady shedding might be a nuisance.

Bulnesia arborea
BULNESIA, VERA WOOD, GUAYACÁN

Colombia, Venezuela. Evergreen tree to 60 ft.; zones 10–11. Blooms intermittently in warm months. Moderate moisture to seasonally

dry. Average, well-drained soil. Full sun. Flowers: golden-yellow, petals clawed, in pairs, on short forked branchlets; capsule 5-winged, one-seeded. Leaves: pinnate,; leaflets 8–9 pairs, oblong, 1–2 in. long, oblique; sessile. Bark: reddish brown, flaking. *Rounded canopy. Blooms 2–4 times in summer. Suitable for coastal planting. Highly recommended.*

Guaiacum

Guaiacum includes approximately 6 species of shrubs and trees from tropical America. The impervious, self-lubricating timber was used for the hinges of the Panama Canal locks as well as ships' pulleys and bearings. The wood is heavier than water and does not float. *Guaiacum sanctum* was almost decimated for the resin guaiac, which was mixed with other compounds to treat syphilis before the advent of antibiotics. Leaves have even numbers of leaflets (paripinnate), only a few pairs per leaf. Flowers are pale blue-violet to purple, bisexual, and radially symmetrical. These species are highly desirable for landscaping. Propagate only from seed or air-layers of cultivated plants. Score and soak the seed after removing all the red sarcotesta that inhibits germination. Tolerates moist conditions with excellent drainage. Growth is extremely slow in the natural habitat, but cultivated plants can be encouraged to grow more quickly with fertilizer. The species are rare and protected. Lignum Vitae Key in the Florida Keys is a sanctuary for *Guaiacum sanctum*.

Guaiacum officinale
COMMON LIGNUM VITAE, GUAIAC, PALO SANTO, GUAYACÁN

West Indies, Surinam, Venezuela, Colombia, endangered in the wild. Evergreen tree to 30 ft.; zones 10–11. Blooms late winter, spring, sporadically in summer. Moderate moisture, seasonally dry. Rocky, well-drained soil. Full to part sun. Flowers: blue-violet, to 0.75 in. wide, petals not clawed, downy; in clusters; capsules flat, 2-winged; seeds black, sarcotesta red. Leaves: paripinnate; leaflets usually 2 or 3 pairs,

Bulnesia arborea

Guaiacum officinale

Guaiacum sanctum, flowers and fruit

obovate, falcate, 1–1.5 in. long; petioles short. *Protected species. Suitable for seaside landscaping. Distinguish from* G. sanctum *by the unclawed petals, fewer stalked leaflets, and flat, penny-sized capsules.*

Guaiacum sanctum

LIGNUM VITAE, HOLY-WOOD, PALO SANTO, GUAIAC, GUAYACÁN
Synonyms: *G. guatemalense, Guajacum sanctum.* Florida Keys, Mexico to Costa Rica, West Indies, endangered in the wild. Evergreen tree, 10–30 ft.; zones 10–11. Blooms late winter, spring, sporadically in summer. Moderate moisture, seasonally dry. Rocky, well-drained soil. Full to part sun. Flowers: light blue-violet to purple, to 0.75 in. wide, petals clawed, somewhat twisted; solitary or in few-flowered clusters; capsule mostly 4-winged; seeds black with a red sarcotesta. Leaves: paripinnate, 3–4 in. long; leaflets usually 3–4 pairs, obovate to oblanceolate, 1–1.5 in. long, slightly falcate; sessile. *Protected species. Of dry islands and coastal regions. Suitable for seaside planting. Slow growing.*

APPENDIX 1

Invasive and Potentially Invasive Species

This list includes only pest species listed in this volume. Many are ornamental and common in cultivation. They have been included so that they may be recognized by gardeners and removed from sale by responsible nurseries (see details on specific species in the text).

The species in this list are in public records as being invasive or potentially invasive in particular areas of the United States. Please note that such species may be weedy or invasive in some regions or climates and harmless in others. Species may be widely or only locally invasive. Some spread more aggressively than others and are more likely to take over wild habitat. In addition, invasive characteristics may change, such as with the introduction of a pollinator, predator, or disease.

Any plant species that produces wind- or animal-dispersed seeds or other propagules, even "cultivated native" species, has the potential to become invasive or weedy outside the biological balance and controls of its undisturbed natural habitat.

This list is derived from the Florida Exotic Pest Plant Council's list of invasive and potentially invasive species; the Exotic Pest Council of Miami-Dade County Park and Recreation Department's Natural Areas Management Program and the Department of Environmental Resources Management (DERM); and on-line lists from the University of Hawaii and the California Pest Plant Council. These lists are available on the Web (see addresses at the end of this book).

Of the 3 states named above only Florida is known to restrict or prohibit pest species at this time (2002). A prohibited species may not be grown or distributed in the state. It must be removed from property before development. Controlled species may not be grown within 500 feet of wild plant communities that they are known to invade.

Certain species not listed here may be invasive outside the United States. These are mentioned, when known, in the text.

Acacia auriculiformis (Florida prohibited; Hawaii)
Acacia farnesiana (Hawaii)
Adenanthera pavonina (Florida prohibited)
Agave sisalana (Florida)
Albizia julibrissin (North Florida)
Albizia lebbeck (Florida prohibited)
Antigonon leptopus (Florida)
Ardisia crenata (North Florida)
Ardisia elliptica (Florida prohibited; Hawaii)
Aristolochia elegans (Florida)
Asystasia gangetica (Florida; Hawaii)
Bauhinia purpurea (Florida controlled)
Bauhinia variegata (Florida controlled)
Buddleja madagascariensis (Hawaii)
Carpobrotus edulis (California)
Casuarina spp. (Florida prohibited; Hawaii)
Catharanthus roseus (California; Florida controlled)
Cereus hildmannianus (Hawaii)
Cestrum diurnum (Florida prohibited)

Clerodendrum bungei (Florida)
Clerodendrum japonicum (Hawaii)
Colocasia esculenta (Florida)
Dioscorea bulbifera (Florida prohibited)
Eichhornia crassipes (California; Florida prohibited)
Epipremnum aureum (Florida controlled)
Eucalyptus camaldulensis (California)
Eugenia uniflora (Florida controlled)
Grevillea robusta (California; Hawaii)
Hedychium coronarium (Hawaii)
Hedychium flavescens (Hawaii)
Hedychium gardnerianum (Hawaii)
Hibiscus tiliaceus (Florida prohibited)
Hiptage benghalensis (Florida)
Hylocereus undatus (Florida)
Jasminum dichotomum (Florida prohibited)
Jasminum fluminense (Florida prohibited)
Jasminum sambac (Florida)
Kalanchoe delagoensis
Kalanchoe pinnata (California; Florida; Hawaii)

Lantana camara (Hawaii)
Leptospermum scoparium (Hawaii)
Ligustrum lucidum (Florida)
Ligustrum sinense (Florida)
Melaleuca quinquenervia (California; Florida prohibited; Hawaii)
Melastoma spp. (Hawaii)
Melia azederach (Florida; Hawaii)
Merremia tuberosa (Florida prohibited; Hawaii)
Millettia pinnata (Florida controlled)
Montanoa hibiscifolia (Hawaii)
Murraya paniculata (Florida controlled)
Nandina domestica (North Florida, Texas)
Passiflora edulis (Hawaii)
Passiflora foetida (Florida)
Phoenix reclinata (Florida)
Pistia stratiotes (California; Florida prohibited)
Pouteria campechiana (Florida controlled)
Psidium cattleianum (Florida prohibited; Hawaii)

Psidium guajava (Florida prohibited; Hawaii)

Ricinus communis (California; Florida prohibited; Hawaii, Texas)

Russelia equisetiformis (Florida)

Sansevieria hyacinthoides (Florida controlled)

Scaevola taccada (Florida controlled; Hawaii)

Schefflera actinophylla (Florida prohibited; Hawaii)

Schinus terebinthifolius (California; Florida prohibited; Hawaii)

Senna pendula var. *glabrata* (Florida)

Spartium junceum (California; Hawaii)

Spathodea campanulata (Hawaii)

Sphagneticola trilobata (Florida controlled; Hawaii)

Syngonium podophyllum (Florida controlled)

Syzygium cumini (Florida controlled)

Syzygium jambos (Florida controlled)

Thespesia populnea (Florida prohibited)

Thunbergia alata (Hawaii)

Thunbergia grandiflora (Hawaii)

Tibouchina spp. (Hawaii)

Tithonia diversifolia (Hawaii)

Tradescantia spathacea (Florida controlled; Hawaii)

Washingtonia robusta (Florida controlled)

APPENDIX 2

Rare, Endangered, and Threatened Species

The species in this list represent only those species that appear in this volume. Unfortunately tens of thousands more are endangered or threatened, and many more are already extinct. The rate of species extinction and loss of biodiversity is increasing at an alarming rate. The primary cause is the accelerating destruction of wild habitats worldwide.

An endangered species is one with critically low numbers in the wild and is in danger of extinction if the conditions that threaten it continue to deteriorate. A threatened species may or may not be relatively abundant but is rapidly decreasing in number and is likely to become endangered if deterioration of its habitat continues. The status of the listed species at the time of publication is noted in the text though that status may change.

Many of these species survive (sometimes abundantly) only through cultivation. The loss of any species, whether locally native or distant, is a loss to biodiversity and a loss of valuable, often yet unstudied, resources.

Agave spp.

Agave victoriae-reginae

Aiphanes minima

Aloe spp.

Argemone rosea

Banara vanderbiltii

Beccariophoenix madagascariensis

Borassus aethiopium

Brunfelsia densifolia

Calopyxis grandidieri

Calyptranthes thomasiana

Chamaedorea metallica

Chamaedorea seifrizii

Cheirolophus canariensis

Coccothrinax crinita

Cornutia obovata

Cryptanthus zonatus

Curcuma roscoeana

Delonix regia

Dictyosperma album

Globularia indubia

Goetzea elegans

Guaiacum officinale

Guaiacum sanctum

Hibiscus arnottianus

Hibiscus brackenridgei

Hyophorbe lagenicaulis

Hyophorbe verschaffeltii

Ipomoea microdactyla

Isoplexis canariensis

Kaempferia spp.

Latania loddigesii

Leucadendron argenteum

Lodoicea maldivica

Michelia spp.

Moullava spicata

Pachypodium spp.

Pericallis webbii

Portlandia coccinea

Pritchardia aylmer-robinsonii

Protea cynaroides

Protea eximia

Pseudophoenix sargentii

Roystonea spp.

Sabal causiarum

Sida eggersii

Sterculia ceramica

Tabebuia spp.

APPENDIX 3

Plants for Coastal Landscaping

Flowering plants have varying degrees of tolerance for salt. Those listed here are grouped into two sections. The first section includes species with moderate to excellent tolerance for salt. They thrive in exposed areas near the shoreline, some right up to the dunes. The second section lists species that thrive in the open, sandy soil and windy conditions typical of coastal areas. They are slightly to moderately salt tolerant but may not tolerate heavy amounts of salt spray produced by storms. Immediately drenching leaves and soil with fresh water after a salt-laden windstorm may reduce serious effects. For details on individual species, see text.

Species with Moderate to Excellent Salt Tolerance

Aleurites moluccana
Allagoptera arenaria
Aloe arborescens
Aloe maculata
Anigozanthos flavidus
Aptenia cordifolia
Aristea ecklonii
Asystasia gangetica
Asystasia travancorica
Banksia integrifolia
Barleria lupulina
Barringtonia racemosa
Bismarckia nobilis
Borassus aethiopium
Bougainvillea spp.
Brya ebenus
Bucida spinosa
Butia capitata
Byrsonima crassifolia
Byrsonima lucida
Caesalpinia gilliesii
Caesalpinia pulcherrima
Caesalpinia yucatanensis
Callistemon viminalis
Calotropis gigantea
Carpobrotus spp.
Casearia nitida
Catesbaea spinosa
Cereus hildmannianus
Clusia lanceolata
Clusia rosea

Coccoloba uvifera
Coccothrinax argentata
Coccothrinax barbadensis
Cocos nucifera
Combretum coccineum
Consolea spp.
Cordia sebestena
Crassula arborescens
Crinum asiaticum
Crinum kirkii
Cryptostegia grandiflora
Cryptostegia madagascariensis
Dodonaea viscosa
Dolichandrone spathacea
Dracaena marginata
Duabanga grandiflora
Eucalyptus spp.
Euphorbia gymnonota
Euphorbia ×lomi
Euphorbia milii var. hislopii
Euphorbia milii 'Minibell'
Euphorbia punicea
Evolvulus glomeratus
Ficus carica
Freycinetia cumingiana
Gloriosa superba
Glottiphyllum spp.
Guaiacum officinale
Guaiacum sanctum
Hibiscus tiliaceus
Hylocereus spp.
Hymenocallis littoralis
Hyophorbe lagenicaulis

Hyophorbe verschaffeltii
Hyphaene compressa
Ilex cassine
Ipomoea indica
Jacquemontia pentantha
Jacquinia aurantiaca
Jacquinia keyensis
Jasminum sambac
Jatropha integerrima
Kosteletzkya virginica
Lampranthus spp.
Lantana camara
Lantana montevidensis
Latania loddigesii
Leptospermum scoparium
Leucophyllum frutescens
Limonium perezii
Livistona chinensis
Lodoicea maldivica
Lysiloma sabicu
Magnolia virginiana
Malva assurgentiflora
Melaleuca nesophila
Nerium oleander
Ochrosia elliptica
Pachira aquatica
Pachira quinata
Pandanus spp.
Parkinsonia aculeata
Passiflora xiikzodz
Peltophorum pterocarpum
Pentalinon luteum
Pereskia aculeata

Pereskia bleo
Phoenix canariensis
Phoenix reclinata
Pittosporum tobira
Plumbago indica
Plumeria obtusa
Pritchardia aylmer-robinsonii
Pseuderanthemum carruthersii
Pyrostegia venusta
Russelia equisetiformis
Sabal bermudana
Salvia leucantha
Samyda dodecandra
Samyda velutina
Sansevieria spp.
Scaevola aemula
Schotia brachypetala
Senna mexicana
Senna racemosa
Serenoa repens
Sesbania punicea
Solandra longiflora
Solandra maxima
Sophora tomentosa
Spartium junceum
Spathodea campanulata
Syagrus sancona
Syzygium jambos
Tabebuia bahamensis
Tabebuia lepidota
Thespesia populnea
Thevetia thevetioides
Thrinax radiata

Tipuana tipu
Tristellateia australasiae
Washingtonia filifera
Washingtonia robusta
Yucca aloifolia

Species with Slight to Moderate Salt Tolerance

Abutilon spp.
Acacia tortuosa
Acalypha spp.
Adenium obesum
Adonidia merrillii
Aechmea blanchetiana
Aechmea dichlamydea
Aechmea spp.
Aeonium arboreum
Aeonium canariense
Aeonium holochrysum
Agapanthus spp.
Agave neglecta
Agave spp.
Agonis flexuosa
Albizia julibrissin
Allamanda spp.
Aloe distans
Aloe spp.
Ananas bracteatus
Annona muricata
Annona squamosa
Antigonon spp.
Archontophoenix alexandrae
Aristea ecklonii
Aristolochia spp.
Asclepias curassavica
Asclepias physocarpa
Banara vanderbiltii
Beaucarnea spp.
Beaumontia grandiflora
Brachychiton spp.

Brugmansia spp.
Brugmansia suaveolens
Brunfelsia spp.
Buddleja davidii
Buddleja madagascariensis
Buddleja ×weyeriana
Bulnesia arborea
Caesalpinia spp.
Callistemon spp.
Calodendrum capense
Capparis cynophallophora
Carissa macrocarpa
Carpentaria acuminata
Catharanthus roseus
Cestrum spp.
Ceiba spp.
Cistus spp.
Citrus spp.
Cordia lutea
Cordyline fruticosa
Crassula spp.
Crateva spp.
Crinum spp.
Delonix regia
Dictyosperma album
Dillenia suffruticosa
Distictis buccinatoria
Distictis ×rivers
Duranta erecta
Echium candicans
Echium decaisnei
Echium judaicum
Echium nervosum
Echium wildpretii
Eranthemum spp.
Erythrina ×bidwillii
Erythrina caffra
Erythrina coralloides
Erythrina humeana
Erythrina variegata

Eugenia spp.
Galphimia gracilis
Grevillea spp.
Hamelia spp.
Hauya heydeana
Hibiscus rosa-sinensis
Holmskioldia sanguinea
Holmskioldia tettensis
Hymenocallis spp.
Inga jinicuil
Ipomoea hederifolia
Ipomoea pauciflora
Ipomoea quamoclit
Ixora spp.
Jacaranda arborea
Jacaranda caerulea
Jasminum laurifolium
Jatropha podagrica
Kalanchoe spp.
Koelreuteria bipinnata
Koelreuteria elegans
Leonotis spp.
Lycianthes rantonnei
Macaranga grandifolia
Magnolia grandiflora
Malpighia spp.
Malvaviscus spp.
Metrosideros excelsa
Muehlenbeckia platyclada
Opuntia spp.
Osmoxylon lineare
Passiflora spp.
Pentalinon luteum
Pereskia grandifolia
Petrea volubilis
Plumbago auriculata
Podranea ricasoliana
Protea cynaroides
Protea eximia

Pseudogynoxys chenopodioides
Punica granatum
Quisqualis indica
Rhaphiolepis ×delacourii
Rhaphiolepis indica
Romneya coulteri
Ruellia spp.
Russelia sarmentosa
Saritaea magnifica
Sedum spp.
Senecio cineraria
Stapelia spp.
Stenocarpus sinuatus
Sterculia spp.
Stigmaphyllon ciliatum
Stigmaphyllon sagraeanum
Strelitzia nicolai
Strelitzia reginae
Tabebuia aurea
Tabebuia 'Carib Queen'
Tabebuia guayacan
Tecoma capensis
Tecoma castanifolia
Tecoma ×smithii
Tecoma stans
Tecomanthe venusta
Thevetia spp.
Thunbergia spp.
Tillandsia usneoides
Trachelospermum jasminoides
Turnera diffusa
Turnera subulata
Turnera ulmifolia
Uncarina grandidieri
Uraria crinita
Vellozia bahiana
Vigna caracalla
Vitex spp.
Wigandia urens

APPENDIX 4

Xerophytic Plants

Some species listed in this volume are more adaptable to dry conditions than others. They might tolerate a few weeks without irrigation or even drought without appreciable harm. Some will behave as xeric in certain climates but not in others. Some are adapted to arid conditions. The list is intended as a general guide. It applies to plants growing in climates where they are known to thrive and are well established in the ground.

Every plant is xeric in its native habitat. This definition is a bit arbitrary for plants in cultivation and is generally applied to plants that do not need irrigation beyond the local rainfall.

Beyond the natural adaptability of any particular species, a number of environmental factors contribute to the length of time a species will tolerate dry conditions. Large trees with roots that reach the water table may not be technically xeric but do not require irrigation. Refer to the text for details.

Abutilon palmeri
Acacia spp.
Acca sellowiana
Adansonia spp.
Adenium obesum
Aechmea spp.
Aeonium spp.
Agave spp.
Albizia spp.
Aleurites moluccana
Allagoptera arenaria
Aloe spp.
Alstonia scholaris
Alyogyne huegelii
Amaryllis belladonna
Ananas spp.
Anigozanthos spp.
Antidesma bunius
Antigonon spp.
Aptenia cordifolia
Ardisia spp.
Aristea ecklonii
Asclepias spp.
Asystasia gangetica
Attalea spp.
Barleria lupulina
Barleria oenotheroides
Bauhinia spp.
Beaucarnea spp.
Berrya spp.
Bismarckia nobilis

Bixa orellana
Bombax ceiba
Bougainvillea spp.
Brachychiton spp.
Brahea armata
Bromelia spp.
Brya ebenus
Bucida spinosa
Buddleja madagascariensis
Bulbine frutescens
Bulnesia arborea
Bunchosia armeniaca
Butia capitata
Byrsonima spp.
Caesalpinia spp.
Callaeum macropterum
Calliandra spp.
Callistemon spp.
Calotropis gigantea
Canella winterana
Capparis cynophallophora
Carissa macrocarpa
Carpobrotus spp.
Casearia nitida
Cassia spp.
Catalpa longissima
Catesbaea spinosa
Catharanthus roseus
Cecropia spp.
Ceiba spp.
Cereus spp.

Chamaedorea seifrizii
Cheirolophus canariensis
×Chitalpa tashkentensis
Cistus spp.
Clerodendrum spp.
Clusia lanceolata
Clusia rosea
Coccoloba uvifera
Coccothrinax spp.
Cochlospermum vitifolium
Cocos nucifera
Colvillea racemosa
Combretum spp.
Congea tomentosa
Consolea spp.
Copernicia baileyana
Cordia spp.
Coreopsis leavenworthii
Corymbia ficifolia
Couroupita guianensis
Crassula spp.
Crateva religiosa
Crescentia spp.
Crinum asiaticum
Delonix regia
Delostoma lobbii
Dicraspidia donnell-smithii
Dietes bicolor
Dietes iridioides
Diospyros spp.
Distictis spp.

Dombeya spp.
Dypsis decaryi
Dypsis lutescens
Ebenopsis ebano
Echium spp.
Eucalyptus spp.
Eugenia spp.
Ficus spp.
Furcraea spp.
Geranium maderense
Gliricidia sepium
Gloriosa superba
Glottiphyllum spp.
Gmelina arborea
Grevillea robusta
Grewia occidentalis
Hamelia spp.
Harpullia pendula
Hebestigma cubense
Hohenbergia spp.
Hoya spp.
Hylocereus spp.
Hyophorbe spp.
Hyphaene spp.
Ilex cassine
Ipomoea spp.
Jacaranda spp.
Jacquinia aurantiaca
Jatropha spp.
Kalanchoe spp.
Kigelia africana

Kleinhovia hospita
Koelreuteria spp.
Kopsia fruticosa
Kopsia pruniformis
Lampranthus spp.
Lantana spp.
Leea spp.
Leonotis spp.
Leptospermum scoparium
Leucophyllum frutescens
Ligustrum japonicum
Limonium perezii
Lonchocarpus violaceus
Lonicera spp.
Lophostemon confertus
Loropetalum chinense
Lysiloma spp.
Macfadyena unguis-cati
Malpighia coccigera
Malpighia emarginata
Malvaviscus penduliflorus
Mammea americana
Mangifera indica
Melaleuca lateritia
Melaleuca nesophila
Mesua ferrea
Metrosideros excelsa
Molineria capitulata

Monstera deliciosa
Montanoa spp.
Moringa oleifera
Murraya spp.
Nandina domestica
Nerium oleander
Newbouldia laevis
Ochroma pyramidale
Ochrosia elliptica
Oncoba spinosa
Opuntia
Orbea
Pachira spp.
Pachypodium spp.
Pandanus spp.
Parkinsonia aculeata
Parmentiera spp.
Passiflora xiikzodz
Pelargonium spp.
Peltophorum spp.
Pereskia spp.
Pericallis webbii
Persea americana
Phoenix spp.
Phymaspermum acerosa
Pimenta spp.
Pittosporum flavum
Plectranthus ecklonii

Plumbago spp.
Plumeria spp.
Podachaenium eminens
Poitea carinalis
Polygala apopetala
Pouteria campechiana
Pseudobombax spp.
Pseudogynoxys chenopodioides
Pseudophoenix spp.
Psychotria nervosa
Pterospermum acerifolium
Ptychosperma elegans
Punica granatum
Pyrostegia venusta
Quararibea funebris
Roystonea regia
Russelia equisetiformis
Sabal spp.
Samyda spp.
Sansevieria spp.
Schinus molle
Schotia brachypetala
Sedum spp.
Senecio cineraria
Senecio tamoides
Senna spp.
Serenoa repens
Sophora tomentosa

Spartium junceum
Spathodea campanulata
Spondias purpurea
Stapelia spp.
Sterculia spp.
Strongylodon macrobotrys
Strophanthus spp.
Syagrus spp.
Tabebuia spp.
Tagetes lucida
Tecoma spp.
Tecomanthe dendrophila
Thevetia spp.
Thrinax radiata
Thunbergia kirkii
Tillandsia spp.
Tipuana tipu
Tithonia diversifolia
Trichodiadema spp.
Trimezia martinicensis
Tulbaghia violacea
Turnera spp.
Vitex spp.
Washingtonia spp.
Wodyetia bifurcata
Yucca spp.
Zombia antillarum

Glossary

acaulescent lacking a stem.

achene a small fruit with one seed and a thin, dry outer coat (pericarp).

acicular needlelike.

actinomorphic radially symmetrical, pertaining to a flower that can be divided into equal halves along more than one plane.

aculeate with a sharp point or prickle.

acuminate of an elongated, gradually tapering leaf tip.

acute of leaf tips or other organs that taper sharply to a point.

adventitious of plant parts, usually roots, in an atypical location.

aerial roots roots that originate and are primarily above ground.

aggregate fruit fruit of one flower with separate carpels developing in close contact on one receptacle but not fused as in a syncarp (for example, a raspberry).

air-layering also known as mossing, or marcotting, a propagation technique whereby a short section of young branch is stripped of its outer layers of bark, including the cambium layer, and wrapped with sphagnum moss and covered tightly with plastic. After roots develop in the moss, the branch is removed and potted.

alternate leaf arrangement having only one leaf at each node, generally alternating on either side of the stem.

androecium the male parts of a flower collectively, all the filaments and anthers.

androgynophore a stalk or disk supporting the stamens and carpels.

androphore a stalk or disk supporting the stamens.

annual a plant that completes its life cycle in one season and then dies.

annulus corona (see photos of *Nerium*, p. 66).

anther the pollen-bearing part of the stamen, often borne on a filament.

apex the distal or free end of a stem, root, or leaf.

apiculate with a sharply tapering point and somewhat concave sides.

appendix the sterile tip of the spadix in the aroid family, Araceae (see photo of *Amorphophallus titanum*, p. 79).

aquatic growing partly or wholly in water.

arboreal of trees.

arborescent treelike.

areole of cacti, a raised or recessed circular area from which spines and bristles arise, evolved from a modified branch tip.

aril a fleshy covering of certain seeds arising from the funiculus (seed attachment point). Compare sarcotesta.

arillate having an aril.

aristate having a leaf tip with a long, slender extension of the midvein, sometimes referred to as a drip-tip.

asperous rough.

asymmetrical having a shape that cannot be divided into equal halves.

attenuate having a long, gradually tapering point with concave sides.

auricular ear-shaped.

awn a needlelike appendage or bristle.

axil, axillary the angle between a leaf and the stem.

backcross a cross between a hybrid and one of its parents.

basal of a leaf arising from a rhizome, root, bulb, or corm.

beaked in the shape of a parrot's beak.

beltian bodies glands on the leaves of certain species that provide food for symbiotic ants (see photo of *Acacia sphaerocephala*, p. 210).

berry a fleshy fruit developing from one carpel with one or more seeds.

biennial a plant that completes its life cycle in 2 years, fruiting the second year.

bifoliate having paired leaves, of orchids bearing 2 leaves per pseudobulb.

bifoliolate having a compound leaf with 2 leaflets (one pair), often the result of reduction of one or more leaflets into other structures.

bifurcate forked twice.

bilabiate enlarged or otherwise differentiated floral parts forming 2 lips.

bilaterally symmetrical zygomorphic, of a flower that can be divided into equal, mirror-image halves on only one plane.

binomial the combined genus and species names.

bipinnate a twice compound leaf, the blade divided into leaflets arranged along a common axis (rachis), the primary divisions (pinnae) themselves divided into leaflets (pinnules).

bipinnatifid twice pinnately lobed, as for bipinnate but the blade not completely divided to the axes (rachis).

bisexual of flowers bearing both male (stamens) and female (carpels) structures.

blade lamina, the expanded part of the leaf, not including the petiole if present.

boss a mound of aboveground roots at the base of the trunk.

bract an ornamental and/or protective, modified leaf subtending a flower or inflorescence, technically not a part of the flower though it may function as a perianth and may develop color during flowering.

bracteole a secondary bract, usually smaller or shaped differently than the primary bract.

bud an undeveloped flower or growing point of a stem or leaf.

bud imprint bud printing, an impression left by surrounding leaves on younger leaves while in bud, strongly evident in many *Agave* species.

bulb a thick, generally subterranean, undeveloped stem bud.

bulbil an asexually produced bulblike structure arising from a bract, inflorescence, or leaf axil.

bulbous bulbiferous, bearing bulbs.

buttress bracing outgrowths at the base of the trunk of some large trees (see photo of *Pachira aquatica*, p. 264).

caducous falling shortly after maturing.

calceolate pouched like the toe of a slipper.

callus a thickened or raised tissue, sometimes ornamental.

calyx the sepals collectively, the outer whorl of the perianth.

calyx tube a tube composed of partially or wholly fused sepals.

cambium a layer of secondary growing tissue encircling woody plants between the bark and wood, which increases girth and lays down new vascular tissue as the stem expands.

campanulate bell-shaped, gobletlike in the upright position.

cannoid having a cannalike habit with ascending leaves and short petioles, applied to certain heliconias. Compare musoid and zingiberoid.

canopy crown, the leafy upper part of a tree.

capitate an inflorescence with flowers in a tight, rounded head.

capsule a dry, dehiscent fruit.

carinate boat-shaped.

carnivorous of a plant that traps and derives some of its nutrients from insects or other small animals.

carpel a simple pistil or one ovule-bearing part of a compound pistil.

carpellate pistillate, bearing carpels but not stamens, a female flower.

cataphyll a modified leaf appearing before the production of new leaves or an inflorescence.

caudate tail-like, ending in an elongated appendage.

caudex (pl. **caudices**) a swollen trunk-root intersection that serves as a water-storing organ, located aboveground or partly or wholly underground.

caulescent possessing a trunk or stem.

cauliflorous flowers developing directly from the trunk or branches.

cauline of a stem, or associated with a stem.

cespitose of a plant that produces a cluster of offspring from suckers. Sometimes spelled *caespitose*.

chartaceous thin, papery.

ciliate having a fringe of hairs as on a leaf or petal margin.

circumscissile splitting around the narrow axis, or opening like a lid, as in capsules of *Portulaca*.

cirrose of a tendril developing from the tip of a leaf, as an extension of the midvein, as in *Gloriosa superba*.

cladophyll a flattened leaflike branchlet that functions like a true leaf.

clambering scandent, of a plant that climbs without specialized devices such as twining, adhesive pads, or tendrils. Compare scrambling and climber.

clawed of a petal or sepal that narrows abruptly into a stalk at the base.

cleft of an organ such as a leaf that is divided almost to its axis.

climber a plant that climbs by various devices, such as by twining, tendrils, or adhesive pads. Compare clambering.

cochleate coiled like a snail shell.

column a tube consisting of fused stamen filaments that surround the style, a characteristic of the hibiscus family, Malvaceae; also the knoblike fused pistil and stamens in orchids.

coma a whorl of sterile bracts or leaves above the fertile bracts, or a tuft of hairs attached to a seed.

common name a vernacular plant name, often varying from region to region and sometimes applied to more than one species at different times or places.

complete of a flower possessing all 4 floral whorls: calyx, corolla, stamens, and carpels.

compound leaf a leaf blade that is divided into leaflets, which are arranged either palmately (like a fan) and usually attached to the end of a petiole, or pinnately (like a feather) and attached to the leaf midvein or rachis.

conduplicate folded once lengthwise like a book.

cone a strobilus, of flowering plants with compact inflorescences including bracts that resemble the cones of conifers.

connate fused.

cordate heart-shaped, applied to the whole leaf or just the base.

coriaceous firm but flexible.

corm an annual, subterranean bulblike stem.

corolla the petals collectively, usually the second whorl of the perianth inside the calyx.

corona annulus; a crownlike ring of modified floral tissue, often the stamen filaments.

corrugated wrinkled or ridged.

corymb, corymbose an indeterminate flat- or round-topped inflorescence with the flowers opening from the outside inward. Compare cyme.

costapalmate a type of palm leaf with the leaflet bases congested on a short rachis, ends spreading in a fan, sides often arching like a rooster's tail (see photo of *Bismarckia nobilis*, p. 95).

creeping of plants with horizontally spreading stems that produce roots and shoots from the nodes. Compare trailing.

crenate scalloped or round-toothed.

crenulate finely crenate.

crest ridgelike, a fascicle.

cross a hybrid produced by the sexual propagation of plants with different physical characteristics.

crown the branches and leafy canopy of a tree, the principal feature of a plant's habit.

crownshaft pertaining to certain pinnate-leafed palms, an expanded petiole base that sheaths the top of the trunk.

cucullate hooded, hoodlike.

cultigen a plant that has been in cultivation for so long that its origins are obscure. Hybridization and selection are likely to have occurred over many centuries of cultivation. Wild populations are unknown or are derived from cultivated plants.

cultivar a selection of a cultivated species with special characteristics that differ in some significant way from the wild species or variety, growing true to type or propagated vegetatively. A cultivar name is capitalized and in roman type and enclosed by single quotes. Cultivar names are invalid unless registered with the International Society of Horticultural Science and published. Sometimes abbreviated as cv. (pl. cvs.) but no longer accepted.

cuneate triangular; of a leaf with the petiole attached to one angle, not to a side.

cuspidate narrowing abruptly with convex sides.

cv. (pl. **cvs.**) cultivar. No longer accepted.

cyathium (pl. **cyathia**) the highly specialized inflorescence of *Euphorbia* species, with flowers reduced to clusters of carpels and stamens, often including glands and usually lacking a perianth.

cyathophyll a bract associated with the cyathia of *Euphorbia* species.

cyme a determinate, flat- or round-topped inflorescence with flowers opening from the center outwards. Compare corymb.

deciduous not evergreen, shedding leaves or other plant parts naturally.

decumbent of a reclining branch or stem with an upturned tip. Compare creeping and trailing.

decurrent of a leaf blade that tapers along the sides of the petiole.

decussate having pairs of opposite leaves arranged perpendicularly to the pairs immediately above and below.

deflexed bent downward and tilted forward. Compare reflexed.

defoliate an unnatural loss of leaves. Compare deciduous.

dehiscent having a seed capsule that splits open, often explosively, when ripe, releasing its seed. Compare indehiscent.

deltoid broadly triangular in outline.

dentate of margins with triangular teeth.

determinate of an inflorescence where flowers open from the top to the bottom. This type of inflorescence is not capable of further growth. Compare indeterminate.

diadelphous having stamens in 2 bundles or rings, or one stamen segregated from the others.

dichasium (pl. **dichasia**) a simple inflorescence with a terminal flower and 2 lateral branches, each either with one flower (total of 3 flowers) or themselves dichasia (total of 7 flowers).

dichotomous forking repeatedly by 2s in a regular pattern.

dicot formerly one of the primary divisions of flowering plants (angiosperms) but now considered an arbitrary classification because they are not monophyletic. Most are now included within eudicots (Judd et al. 1999).

didynamous having 2 pairs of stamens of unequal length.

digitate spreading like the fingers of the hand.

dimorphic occurring in 2 distinct forms or shapes (also trimorphic, polymorphic).

dioecious having male (staminate) and female (carpellate) flowers on separate plants.

disk of the floral disk, an enlargement of the receptacle and/or the bases of the calyx, corolla, and stamens.

disk flower disk floret, a specialized flower with a tubular corolla often found in the aster family, Asteraceae, with or without surrounding ray flowers.

dissected having a cleft leaf or other organ.

distichous having leaves or other parts arranged in ranks on opposite sides of a stem or stalk.

distinct free, not fused or united.

divaricate branching at wide angles, giving a zigzag appearance.

double of a flower with more than the normal complement of petals or other floral parts.

drupe an indehiscent fruit with one or more seeds surrounded by a hard inner layer (the pit or endocarp), a fleshy middle layer (mesocarp), and a thin skin (exocarp), as in a peach or mango.

elliptic, elliptical broadest in the middle, tapering uniformly toward the ends.

emarginate of a leaf apex with a small notch at the tip where the midvein meets the margin.

emergent rising above the water.

endemic native to a limited region.

endocarp the inner layer of fruit surrounding the seed, such as the hard pit of a peach.

endosperm starchy, oily tissue surrounding the embryo of a seed.

ensiform narrowly sword-shaped with straight, parallel margins and an acute tip.

entire having smooth leaf margins, not toothed or lobed.

ephemeral very short lived.

epicalyx a pseudocalyx, a calyxlike involucre of bracts that surrounds the true calyx.

epilithic of a plant that grows on rocks, a lithophyte.

epipetalous on or attached to the petals, usually applied to stamens mounted at their bases on the petals.

epiphyte, epiphytic a plant that grows upon another plant and uses it for support but does not derive nourishment from the host plant. Compare parasite.

epitasis the production of asexual plantlets or bulbils from an aboveground part of the plant, commonly from an inflorescence or bract.

epithet any part of the scientific name that qualifies the genus (species, subspecies, variety, form).

equitant fanned leaves whose folded bases enclose the base of the leaf above, common in the iris family, Iridaceae.

eudicot, tricolpate one of the major divisions of flowering plants (angiosperms), a new classification which includes most of the species formerly known as dicots. They have more than one cotyledon (seed leaf) and have woody or herbaceous stems. The term "tricolpate" indicates the presence of 3 grooves on the pollen.

evergreen a plant that normally retains most of its foliage throughout the year.

exocarp the outside wall of the pericarp, the outside layer or the skin of a fleshy fruit.

exotic any species outside its natural ecosystem, including those from local or regional but dissimilar habitats.

exserted protruding beyond the surrounding organs, often applied to stamens. Compare included.

eye a contrasting spot around the center or throat of a flower.

falcate curved, like a falcon's beak (see photo of *Erythrina falcata*, p. 218).

family a related collection of genera with defined characteristics.

fan-leafed palmate, leaflet bases congested at the end of a petiole, with tips spreading like a fan.

fascicle a crest, an inflorescence or vegetative part in a compact, raised cluster.

felted having densely matted hairs.

fetid malodorous, having a foul odor.

filament the stalk of a stamen bearing the anther, not always present.

filiferous threadlike.

filiform filament-like.

fimbriate fringed.

flabellate pleated and spreading like a fan or wedge.

flaccid limp, lax.

fleshy juicy, moisture storing.

flexuous zigzag.

floral cup hypanthium, cup, or ringlike structure composed of the fused bases of the stamens, perianth (compare disk).

floral tube a tubular floral cup, composed of fused floral parts, an androperianth tube.

floriferous flowering in profusion, or bearing flowers over an extended period.

flower the reproductive structures and accessory parts in angiosperms composed of at least one or more stamens and/or carpels, with or without a perianth.

foliage a collective term for leaves.

follicle a dry, dehiscent fruit with one to many seeds derived from one carpel and splitting open only along one side (legumes split on both sides).

form, forma a taxon below variety, a relatively minor variation rarely used anymore, commonly replaced by a cultivar name. Sometimes abbreviated as f.

free not united, not fused.

frond the leaflike structure in ferns, colloquially applied to palms or pinnately compound leaves.

fruit the ripened ovary of a flower and any attached floral remnants.

fruticose shrublike.

funiculus (pl. **funiculi**) funicle, a threadlike stalk that sometimes connects a seed to the placenta of the ovary.

furcate forked.

fuscous dark.

fused connate, wholly or partially joined.

fusiform spindle-shaped.

galeate helmet-shaped.

gall an abnormal swelling with an external cause, usually insects.

geniculate bent, as a knee.

genus (pl. **genera**) the first part of the scientific name, the principal rank below family and above species. Genus names are italicized (or underlined) and begin with a capital letter.

glabrous, glabrate smooth, glossy.

gland a secretory organ.

glaucous covered with a fine dust or bloom.

globular, globose globe-shaped, a sphere.

glochid of cacti, a barbed spine or tuft arising from an areole.

graft a scion, a bud or twig spliced to a rootstock.

grex a group of hybrids that are the offspring of independent lines of the same parent species.

group cultivars with unspecified similarities or relationships. Group names begin with a capital letter and are written in roman type.

gum kino, a sticky resinous secretion that becomes hard when dry.

guttered channeled, concave with upturned edges, serving to guide water toward the stem and root.

gynoecium the female parts of the flower collectively, the stigmas, styles, and ovaries.

gynophore a stalk or disk supporting the gynoecium in some species.

habit the overall shape or appearance of a species.

halophyte a plant that grows in saline conditions.

hastate arrow-shaped, pointed at the apex with 2 spreading, pointed basal lobes (see photo of *Anthurium* 'Obake', p. 81). Compare sagittate.

hastula of palms, a raised area at the end of a petiole to which palmate leaflets are attached (see photo of *Coccothrinax barbadensis*, p. 100).

head capitulum, a compact, rounded inflorescence, with usually sessile flowers on a short axis or disk (see photo of *Cheirolophus canariensis*, p. 128).

helicoid spirally coiled.

hemiepiphyte semiepiphyte, a climber that may eventually lose contact with the ground.

herb a nonwoody plant. Used colloquially for fragrant culinary annuals and perennials and their leaves, flowers, or roots.

herbaceous herblike, nonwoody.

hesperidium a berry with a leathery skin and partitioned flesh, such as an orange.

heterostylous, heterostyly of plants with flowers having styles in 2 or more lengths.

hirsute coarsely hairy.

hispid having bristly hairs.

hort. of garden origin, a name mistakenly adopted in horticulture but without botanical merit.

hybrid a cross, a plant or animal resulting from the breeding of individuals with differing characteristics.

hybrid vigor having characteristics that are more robust or desirable than those of either parent.

hypanthium (pl. **hypanthia**) a floral cup, disk, or tube composed of the fused bases of the calyx, corolla, and/or stamens.

hypogynous of a flower with perianth inserted (attached) below the ovary, the ovary superior.

imbricate of leaves or bracts overlapping in a regular pattern, appearing braided (see photo of *Ravenala madagascariensis*, p. 354).

imparipinnate of a pinnately compound leaf with an odd number of leaflets, terminating in a single leaflet. Compare paripinnate.

imperfect a unisexual flower, one that bears either stamens or carpels, not both.

impressed sunken into the surface.

included enclosed within, applied to stamens that do not extend beyond the edges of a tubular or funnel-shaped perianth. Compare exserted.

incomplete flower a flower lacking one or more of the 4 floral whorls: calyx, corolla, stamens, or carpels.

indehiscent of a fruit that does not split open to release its seed. Compare dehiscent.

indeterminate of an inflorescence with flowers opening from bottom to top, the stalk continuing to lengthen as the buds mature toward the tip, as in a panicle or raceme.

indigenous native.

indumentum a general term for hairs, small glands, scales, and other surface adornment.

induplicate folded upward in cross section, V-shaped. Compare reduplicate.

inermous unarmed, spineless.

inferior with the ovary located below the attachment of the perianth and stamens (compare superior); also the lower surface or underside of an organ such as a leaf.

inflated loose-fitting or appearing filled with air (see photo of *Asclepias physocarpa*, p. 73).

inflorescence a cluster of flowers and their arrangement on a specialized stalk (rachis).

infructescence a cluster of fruits and their arrangement on a specialized stalk (rachis).

infundibular funnel-shaped.

inserted attached to or mounted upon.

intergeneric hybrid a hybrid resulting from parents of 2 different genera, indicated by the symbol × preceding the genus name.

internode the area of stem between 2 nodes.

introduction an introduced species, any plant from outside its specific native habitat.

invalid name a name that does not conform to the International Code of Botanical Nomenclature, lacking valid description or publication. Invalid names appear as synonyms and in technical works are followed by the Latin *nom illegal*.

involucre a whorl of bracts subtending a flower, inflorescence, or fruit as at the base of a strawberry.

involute rolled inward. Compare revolute.

keel carinate, somewhat resembling the keel of a boat, a prominent midrib down the underside of a leaf or flower, the sides forming a trough.

labellum the upper or lower petal or petals of a flower that differ from the lateral petals in shape or markings, a lip.

laminar flattened.

lanate woolly, the hairs matted.

lanceolate lance-shaped, of a narrow, elongated leaf that is widest near the base and tapers gradually to the tip. Compare oblanceolate.

lateral on either side of an axis.

latex a sticky white, clear, or yellow sap characteristic of certain plant groups such as the poinsettia family, Euphorbiaceae; fig family, Moraceae; and oleander family, Apocynaceae.

lax lacking rigidity, limp.

leaf a vegetative organ found in flowering plants (angiosperms), developing from a stem or rhizome, composed of a variously modified blade and often having a leaf stalk (petiole). Leaves are usually green, containing chlorophyll necessary for photosynthesis. They are variously adapted for absorbing light while also performing the functions of respiration and transpiration.

leaflet a pinnule, one leaflike member of a compound leaf.

legume a pod, a fruit of the legume family, Fabaceae, consisting of 2 valves derived from a modified leaf that opens along 2 seams, such as a pea pod.

lenticel a pore with raised edges in the bark, through which gases are exchanged.

lenticular lens-shaped.

lepidote having a rough surface due to the presence of peltate scales, a distinguishing characteristic of the leaves of certain *Tabebuia* and other species.

liana a woody climber (not herbaceous), often very large.

lignotuber a woody subterranean tuber found in some plants subject to seasonal fires, producing new shoots after a burn, as in some species of the protea family, Proteaceae.

ligule a slender sheath at the base of ginger or some palm leaves that clasps the stem.

linear slender with parallel margins.

lingulate tonguelike, as in the fused petals in a ray flower of the aster family, Asteraceae.

lip, labellum upper or lower petal(s) of a flower that differ from the lateral petals in shape or markings.

lithophyte, lithophytic a plant that grows on rocks.

littoral of the seashore.

lobe the free, often flaring edges of a funnel- or tube-shaped calyx or corolla.

lobed leaf a leaf with the edges divided into pointed or rounded sections, the sinuses not cutting more than halfway to the midvein. Compare entire.

locule a chamber within a fruit or ovary.

loment a legume that splits crosswise (rather than lengthwise) into one-seeded segments.

lorate strap-shaped, not rigid.

lunate crescent-shaped.

mammillate having raised nipplelike projections, found in certain *Agave* and cacti species, usually tipped with sharp teeth or spines.

margin the edge of a leaf, petal, or other organ.

mealy granular.

Mediterranean-type climate hot, dry summer and fall days with cool nights and cooler, moist winters, found in southern California, South Africa, Australia, and Chile.

meristem the areas of tissue where cell division takes place; a growing point, generally at the apex of stems and the cambium. Also used as a generic term for plants growing in tissue culture.

mesocarp the middle layer of the fruit wall surrounding the seed(s), as in the fleshy part of an apple or mango.

midrib the primary vein of a leaf, an extension of the petiole, usually along the midline of the leaf.

misapplied a valid scientific name applied to the wrong species, a homonym.

monocarpic, hapaxanthic blooming once before dying.

monocot one of the primary divisions of flowering plants (angiosperms) characterized by a single seed leaf or cotyledon.

monoculture a species that grows, or is cultivated, to the exclusion of other species, at the expense of diversity.

monoecious having male (staminate) and female (carpellate) flowers on the same plant.

monopodial a growth pattern that is continuous from the terminal bud without secondary branching, typical of palms and certain orchids. Flowers are produced at the nodes. Compare sympodial.

mucronate of leaves with a small spur at the tip, an extension of the midrib.

multi-annual a plant that lives for 3 or more years before blooming and then dies, such as most *Agave* species.

musoid having a banana-like habit with ascending whorls of leaves and long petioles, applied to certain heliconias. Compare zingiberoid and cannoid.

native an organism in association with its natural habitat.

nectar guides colored veins in the throat of a flower, thought to direct pollinators toward the nectar source, bringing the pollinator into close contact with the pollen and/or stigma.

nectary a glandular region involved in the production of nectar.

nerve a plant vein.

node a joint along a stalk from which leaves, stipules, lateral branches, and flowers may develop.

oblanceolate of a narrow lance-shaped leaf that is widest toward the tip. Compare lanceolate.

oblique having unequal sides. Also used of a plant part inclined at an angle.

oblong having parallel or nearly parallel margins and rounded or blunt ends.

obovate ovate with the widest area near the tip.

obtuse having a broadly rounded, wide-angled or rather blunt end.

ocreae a tubular sheath composed of 2 stipules encircling the stem at the base of the petiole, a characteristic of the buckwheat family, Polygonaceae.

offset shoot, pup, a plantlet developing from the base of the parent plant, a vegetative form of reproduction.

open valvate, of petals or sepals that do not overlap.

open-pollinated pollinated without human intervention.

opposite leaf arrangement having 2 leaves per node, generally on opposite sides of the stem.

orbicular circular.

ovary the seed-bearing organ of a flower at the base of the pistil.

ovate oval, widest at the base and narrowing toward the apex.

ovoid egg-shaped.

ovule the megasporangium, the body in the ovary containing the female gametes.

pachycaulous having a thickened, moisture-conserving stem (see photo of *Pachypodium lamerei*, p. 67).

palmate of a compound leaf with leaflets attached by their bases to a common point, usually the end of the petiole (see photo of *Pachira quinata*, p. 264).

palmatifid of a leaf blade palmately lobed no more than halfway to the petiole.

palmatisect of a leaf blade palmately divided almost to the petiole.

palmipinnate of leaf veins arranged palmately at the base, becoming pinnate toward the tip (see photo of *Berrya cubensis*, p. 270).

panicle a branched indeterminate inflorescence, the branches racemes or corymbs.

papilionaceous butterfly-like, as in flowers of the legume subfamily Papilionoideae, or resembling those flowers and usually composed of a standard, 2 lateral wings, and 2 lower petals united along their central edges into a keel.

papillae glandular hairs.

papillose bumpy.

pappus the modified calyx of a flower in the composite family, Asteraceae, either bristly or scaly.

parallel veined having primary leaf veins running more or less parallel to the midvein or secondary veins parallel to each other but perpendicular to the midvein.

parasite an organism that derives all or part of its nourishment from another organism, the host.

paripinnate evenly pinnate, of a pinnately compound leaf with an even number of leaflets, usually paired, and lacking a leaflet at the tip. Compare imparipinnate.

parthenogenesis asexual reproduction.

pedatifid of a leaf with lobes perpendicular to the primary rachis to which the petiole is attached centrally (see photo of *Philodendron goeldii*, p. 85).

pedatisect as for pedatifid except the lobes, or some lobes, are cut to the rachis (see photo of *Syngonium podophyllum*, p. 87).

pedicel the stalk of an individual flower.

peduncle the main stalk of an inflorescence to which the stalked or stalkless flowers are attached, a rachis.

pellucid spot a translucent glandular spot, as on the skin of an orange.

peltate having the petiole attached to the undersurface of a leaf rather than at the margin.

pepo an indehiscent capsule with a pulpy interior and a hard or leathery shell.

perennial a plant with a life cycle of more than 2 years, usually blooming annually.

perfect, hermaphroditic a bisexual flower having both stamens and carpels.

perforate with perforations or openings.

perianth the calyx and corolla collectively, literally "around the anthers."

pericarp the outer layers of a fruit enclosing the seeds.

persistent of leaves, bracts, or flower parts that remain attached, not deciduous.

petal a unit of the corolla, usually the second whorl from the outside of a flower.

petaloid petal-like, of another organ that resembles a petal.

petiole the stalk of a leaf, not always present. Compare sessile.

petiolule the stalk of a leaflet, not always present.

phylloclad a flattened stem or branch that functions like a leaf.

phyllode a flattened petiole that functions as a leaf, usually thick and leathery, the leaf blade often reduced, deciduous, or absent, an adaptation that reduces surface area and evaporation.

pilose sparsely covered with long soft hairs.

pinna (pl. **pinnae**) a leaflet of a pinnate leaf, or the first division of a bipinnate leaf.

pinnate of a compound leaf with leaflets arranged along an axis (rachis).

pinnatifid of a leaf blade with pinnately arranged lobes, the leaf margins cut less than halfway to the rachis.

pinnatisect as pinnatifid but with the leaf margins cut almost to the rachis.

pinnule the leaflets of a bipinnate leaf.

pistil the female reproductive parts (gynoecium) of a flower consisting of one carpel, one stigma and style; a compound pistil is composed of multiple carpels and one or more stigmas and styles.

pistillate of a female flower bearing one or more carpels but no fertile stamens.

plicate pleated, folded like a fan (see photo of *Coccothrinax barbadensis*, p. 100).

plumose featherlike.

pod a colloquial name for the fruit of a legume or, a general term for any nonfleshy fruit.

pollen the grains containing spores, the male gametes, often bright yellow, orange, or red, produced on an anther in flowering plants.

pollinator a bird, bat, insect, mammal, or other agent that transmits pollen to a receptive stigma, often involving highly specialized mechanisms. Wind and water are inanimate means of pollination.

pollinia a sticky mass of pollen grains, typical in orchids and certain other groups.

polycarpic blooming repeatedly throughout the life of the plant.

polygamous bearing both unisexual and bisexual flowers on the same plant.

polymorphic having more than one distinct form.

polyploid having more than the normal set of chromosomes (2n) in each cell, usually sterile.

pome a firm but fleshy fruit with seeds enclosed by a thin, papery endocarp, such as an apple.

posterior lobes lobes at the base of a leaf, as in sagittate or hastate leaves.

precocious developing early, often applied to flowers of deciduous plants that open before the new leaves are fully developed.

prickle a sharp outgrowth from the epidermis.

procumbent trailing along the ground without taking root.

propagule a general term for any plant part, sexual or asexual, that may be used for propagation.

pruinose, frosted, having a refractive or sparkly surface created by scales or fluid-filled cells.

pseudobulb a bulb-shaped, swollen stem that functions as a water-storing organ, found in certain orchids usually from seasonally dry climates.

pseudocalyx an epicalyx, an involucre of calyxlike bracts.

pseudostem a stemlike structure, such as the overlapping leaf bases of banana, *Musa*, or the aboveground neck of the bulb in *Crinum*.

pubescent covered with soft, short hairs like a peach, downy, often used as a general term for soft hairs.

pulvinus a swelling or joint at the base of a petiole or petiolule (legume family, Fabaceae) or base of the blade (arrowroot family, Marantaceae), often associated with leaves that fold when dry or in response to touch, stress, or darkness.

punctate dotted with small pits.

pup a plantlet developing from the base of the parent plant, a vegetative form of reproduction. Also known as offset or shoot.

pyrene a nutlet, a seed surrounded by a hard endocarp, such as in *Coffea*.

pyxidium a circumscissile capsule that releases seed through an operculum, as in the Brazil-nut family, Lecythidaceae.

quick stick a living fence, a large cutting that will root directly in the ground.

raceme an indeterminate inflorescence with stalked flowers arranged along one axis (see photo of *Barringtonia racemosa*, p. 244). Compare spike.

rachis (pl. **rachises**) the main stalk of an inflorescence or axis of a compound leaf.

radially symmetrical actinomorphic, of a flower that can be divided into equal halves along more than one plane.

ramiflorous of flowers borne directly on the branches.

rank one column of alternate or opposite leaves; one level of nomenclature.

ray flower the radiating flowers around the periphery of the floral heads of some members of the aster family, Asteraceae, having a tubular corolla with a flattened lobe (ligule).

receptacle the thickened end of a stalk (pedicel) on which a flower is mounted.

reclining leaning backwards.

recurved curved backwards.

reduplicate having an inverted fold in cross section, as in certain palm leaflets. Compare induplicate.

reflexed bent down sharply.

regular actinomorphic, of a radially symmetrical flower.

rein a long, slender leafy extension from certain palm petioles or dangling fibers remaining after the leaflets divide.

reniform kidney-shaped.

resupinate of a leaf or flower inverted by a twist of the stalk (as in *Alstroemeria*).

reticulate netted or netlike.

revolute rolled under or back. Compare involute.

rhizome a thick, prostrate stem running along or just below the ground surface with roots and stalks developing at the nodes.

rhombic diamond-shaped.

ring scar a ring around the trunk, typically of palms, where a leaf has separated.

rosette a whorl of leaves around a common point, either at ground level or at the apex of a stem (as in *Aechmea* species).

rotate wheel-shaped, of a flower with a very short tube and spreading lobes.

rugose uneven, bumpy, wrinkled, corrugated.

sagittate arrowhead-shaped, with a triangular blade and backward-pointing, not spreading, basal lobes, alluding to the head shape and horns of Sagittarius the Goat (see photo of *Alocasia micholitziana*, p. 78). Compare hastate.

salverform a corolla with a slender, tubular base and spreading lobes shaped like a salver (a pedestal-type serving dish).

sarcotesta a fleshly outer seed coat, often brightly colored (see photo of *Guaiacum sanctum*, p. 374).

scabrous roughly scaly.

scandent clambering, climbing without the aid of tendrils, twining, or other devices. Compare scrambling.

scape a leafless stalk arising directly from a rhizome, bearing a flower or inflorescence, found in monocots.

scrambling of a plant that climbs with the aid of tendrils or prickles. Compare clambering and scandent.

scurfy gritty.

seasonally dormant of herbs that die back to a subterranean rhizome during cold or dry seasons, or plants that remain evergreen but stop all growth seasonally.

secund arranged along one side of an axis.

selection a distinctive form, clone, or cultivar that remains constant when propagated.

semideciduous a plant which normally is evergreen but may become deciduous during unusually dry or cold periods.

semiepiphytic a mostly epiphytic plant with aerial roots but also able to grow on (but not in) the ground.

semiterete subterete (which see).

semiterrestrial a mostly terrestrial plant with the ability to thrive as an epiphyte in certain circumstances.

sepal a unit of the outer floral whorl collectively referred to as the calyx, often protecting the flower in bud, sometimes petal-like (petaloid) or absent.

serrate saw-toothed, having leaf margins with teeth angled toward the apex.

serrulate finely serrate.

sessile lacking a stalk or petiole.

setose bristly or bristlelike.

shrub a woody plant lacking a main trunk or axis, branching near the base.

silique a flattened capsule that splits into 2 halves longitudinally with seeds mounted on a papery septum.

simple an undivided leaf, not compound.

sinuous having a 2-dimensional wavy outline. Compare undulate.

sinus a gap, space, or opening.

sp. (pl. **spp.**) species.

spathe a specialized bract that surrounds a spadix or inflorescence, opening on one side, characteristic of the aroid family, Araceae (see photo of *Monstera deliciosa*, p. 84), and the palm family, Arecaceae.

spathiform spathelike.

spathulate like a spatula, spoon-shaped.

species the lowest basic division of plants and other organisms, a group of closely related individuals with similar characteristics. The species name is the second word of a scientific name and is never capitalized but always italicized (or underlined). Sometimes abbreviated as sp. (pl. spp.).

spike an unbranched indeterminate inflorescence with stalkless flowers, colloquially used for any slender inflorescence. Compare raceme.

spindle-shaped swollen in the center, tapering toward both ends, fusiform.

spine a modified stipule or sharp branchlet found in a leaf axil or a sharp point at the tip of a leaf as in *Agave*. Compare thorn.

spur a usually backward-pointing projection at the base of a flower containing nectar.

stamen the male reproductive organ of flowering plants, typically comprising a filament and pollen-bearing anther.

staminate having stamens but lacking carpels, a male flower.

staminode a sterile, often highly modified stamen, often resembling the petals (see photos of *Lampranthus* species, p. 50).

standard an enlarged or otherwise distinctive erect petal often found in irises, orchids, and legumes. In horticulture, a shrub pruned to resemble a small tree.

stellate starlike, having multiple branched microscopic scales, a characteristic of certain groups.

sterile infertile, lacking fruit and/or viable seed.

stigma the sticky part of the pistil, usually the apex, that receives the pollen.

stipe a small stalk supporting a flower part or spathe of an aroid.

stipel, stipellate resembling stipules of the leaflets.

stipule a usually small, highly modified leafy structure in the axil of the petiole or sometimes alternating with the petioles of opposite leaves, deciduous or absent in certain plant groups, their presence or form characteristic of different groups of plants.

stolon, stoloniferous a runner or horizontal stem from which offsets develop.

striate striped or streaked.

strobilus (pl. **strobili**) a cone or conelike structure, as the inflorescences of *Costus* and *Zingiber* species.

style the stalk of a pistil bearing the stigma, not always present.

subshrub a small shrubby perennial that is at least partly woody.

subsp. subspecies, also written ssp.

subspecies a taxon or division of a species, above variety, that has distinctive characteristics unique to plants from a specific range. Sometimes abbreviated as subsp. (pl. subspp.).

subterete cylindrical, with a groove down one side, somewhat C-shaped in cross section.

succulent partially or wholly fleshy or juicy; moisture storing stems, leaves or roots.

sucker an auxiliary shoot from the root.

superior with the ovary located above the attachment of the perianth and stamens. Compare inferior.

syconium a fruit composed of a flask-shaped fleshy receptacle with reduced flowers enclosed on the inner surface, a fig (*Ficus* species).

symbiosis, symbiotic having a mutually beneficial association with another organism.

sympodial a growth pattern where a plant develops from the terminal bud eventually culminating in an inflorescence. Successive growth starts from lateral buds from the stem or rhizome. A characteristic of many herbaceous perennials, such as bananas, heliconias, gingers, and certain orchids. Compare monopodial.

syncarp a compound fruit, coalescent fruits developing from fused floral parts (see photo of *Artocarpus*, p. 277).

synonym a name applied to a plant that is later found to have been previously named or the name rejected for technical reasons. Sometimes abbreviated as syn. (pl. syns.).

taxon (pl. **taxa**) a general term for any taxonomic rank. Compare epithet.

tendril a modified branch, leaf, or other structure that coils around, sticks to, or hooks onto a support.

tepals sepals and petals, often numerous, which are similar in color, form, and size, sometimes only distinguishable as an inner and outer whorl (see photo of *Hemerocallis* 'Aztec Gold', p. 234).

terete cylindrical, round in cross section or slightly angled.

terminal at the distal end of a branch or stalk, at the apex.

terrestrial growing with the roots anchored in the ground.

thorn a sharp outgrowth from the stem other than at a node (see photo of *Pachira quinata*, p. 264). Compare spine, prickle.

thyrse an inflorescence with a central axis consisting of an indeterminate raceme or panicle with lateral branches ending in determinate cymes or dichasia.

tomentose of short, densely matted, stiff hairs that are rough to the touch.

trailing procumbent, of horizontal stems that do not take root. Compare creeping.

tree a woody plant with one or several well-developed trunks.

trichome a hairlike, glandular outgrowth of the epidermis.

trifoliate of orchids bearing 3 leaves per pseudobulb.

trifoliolate a compound leaf with 3 leaflets, as is typical of certain groups such as *Erythrina* species.

tripinnate of a compound leaf subdivided 3 times.

triquetrous succulent cylindrical leaves with 3 flattened sides, triangular in cross section (see photos of *Carpobrotus* species, p. 48).

trunk a woody, bark-covered or thick fibrous stem (as in palms) that supports the leafy canopy.

tuber a thickened underground stem that serves as a storage organ.

tubercle a soft projection.

tubular of a flower with at least partly fused petals and/or sepals, more or less cylindrical to narrowly funnel-shaped, often with free or fused lobes.

tufted a general term to describe plants with leaves clustered at the ends of a stalk rather than evenly distributed.

turbinate top-shaped.

twining climbing by encircling a support such as a tree limb.

type species the typical form of a plant, not a variant or cultivar, a species as originally defined by the author.

ultra-tropical of very cold-sensitive species that thrive only in year-round tropical conditions. These species are generally too cold-sensitive to be grown outdoors in the subtropics.

umbel a determinate, flat-topped inflorescence with individual flowers arising from a common point.

undulate having a 3-dimensionally wavy margin. Compare sinuous.

unifoliate of orchids bearing one leaf per pseudobulb.

unifoliolate of a compound leaf reduced to a single leaflet, other leaflets sometimes reduced to tendrils, spines, or other structures.

unisexual of flowers that are either male (staminate) or female (pistillate) (see photo of *Begonia* 'Merry Christmas', p. 133).

united of flower parts, fused, connate.

urceolate, urn-shaped, swollen at the base with a narrow neck (see photo of *Jatropha ortegae*, p. 193).

valvate open, of petals or sepals that do not overlap.

valve a section of a fruit or capsule corresponding to a carpel, sometimes splitting at the intersections at maturity.

var. (pl. **vars.**) variety.

variety a taxon or division of a species below subspecies, which has distinctive characteristics that are not necessarily unique to plants from a specific range. Sometimes abbreviated as var. (pl. vars.).

vascular bundle scars broken ends of the xylem and phloem tubes that transport water and nutrients in plants, sometimes visible where leaves have fallen, particularly evident on palm trunks.

vellum a spongy, moisture-absorbing covering of certain aerial roots, often found in orchids and aroids.

verticillaster a pseudo-whorl of paired cymes in opposite leaf axils appearing to be one inflorescence, common in the mint family, Lamiaceae (see photo of *Leonotis leonurus*, p. 237).

vine a generic term for a climbing plant.

viscid sticky.

viviparous of seeds or asexual propagules that sprout while still attached to the parent plant.

wheel-shaped rotate, arranged like the spokes of a wheel.

whorl a cluster of leaves or other organs densely arranged around a point or short stalk.

whorled leaf arrangement having 3 or more leaves at a node.

wing a lateral organ, appendage, or membrane sometimes found on stems, petioles, capsules, or seeds.

xeric, xerophytic thriving in arid conditions; in horticulture: growing without irrigation when established in favorable conditions. This does not imply that these plants will thrive with complete neglect or in any set of conditions.

zingiberoid having a gingerlike habit with horizontal alternate leaves and short petioles, applied to certain heliconias. Compare cannoid and musoid.

zygomorphic bilaterally symmetrical, of a flower that can be divided into equal halves on only one plane, the halves are mirror images.

Bibliography

Adema, F. 2000. Notes on Malesian Fabaceae (Leguminosae-Papilionoideae) 7. The Genus *Millettia*. *Blumea* 45 (411): 403–425.

Allen, E. W. 1981. *Leguminosae (Peltophorum)*. University of Wisconsin.

Almeda, F. 1990. Melastomataceae. *Manual of the Flowering Plants of Hawai'i*. Vol. 1. Bishop Museum Special Publication 83. University of Hawaii Press.

Alverson, W. S., and J. A. Steyermark. 1997. Bombacaceae. In: J. A. Steyermark et al., eds., *Flora of the Venezuelan Guayana* 3: 496–527.

Anderson, E. F. 2001. *The Cactus Family*. Timber Press.

Armstrong, W. P. 1998. The truth about cauliflory. *Zoonooz* (February). Zoological Society of San Diego.

Armstrong, W. P. 1999a. The gums that changed the California landscape. *Zoonooz* (January). Zoological Society of San Diego.

Armstrong, W. P. 1999b. The yucca and its moth. *Zoonooz* (April). Zoological Society of San Diego.

Arnold, T. H., and B. C. De Wet, eds. 1993. Plants of southern Africa: names and distribution. *Memoirs of the Botanical Survey of South Africa*.

Baensch, U., and U. Baensch. 1994. *Blooming Bromeliads*. Hagen Book Division.

Bailey, L. H., and E. Zoe. 1976. *Hortus Third*. Revised by the staff of the Bailey Hortorium, Cornell University. Macmillan Publishing Company.

Barneby, R. C. 1996. Neotropical Fabales at New York: asides and oversights, key to American taxa of *Peltophorum*. *Brittonia* 48 (2): 174–187.

Barneby, R. C., and J. W. Grimes. 1996. Silk tree, guanacaste, monkey's earring: a generic system for the synandrous Mimosaceae of the Americas. Part I. *Abarema, Albizia*, and allies. *Memoirs of the New York Botanical Garden* 74: 173–178.

Bartholomäus, A., A. De la Rosa Cortés, J. O. Santos Gutiérrez, L. E. Acero Duarte, and W. Moosbrugger. 1998. *El Manto de la Tierra, Flora de Los Andes*. CAR, GTZ, KFW, Colombia.

Bar-Zvi, D. 1996. *Tropical Gardening*. Pantheon Books.

Berry, F., and W. J. Kress. 1991. *Heliconia, An Identification Guide*. Smithsonian Institute Press.

Birdsey, M. 1951. *The Cultivated Aroids*. Gillick Press.

Brandbyge, J. 1986. A revision of the genus *Triplaris* (Polygonaceae). *Nordic Journal of Botany* 6: 545–570.

Breedlove, D. E., P. E. Berry, and P. H. Raven. 1982. The Mexican and Central American species of *Fuchsia* (Onagraceae) except for section *Encliandra*. *Annals of the Missouri Botanical Garden* 69 (1): 209–234.

Brickell, C., and J. D. Zud, eds. 1997. *The American Horticulture Society A–Z Encyclopedia of Garden Plants*. DK Publishing.

Brown, B. F. 1994a. *Cordyline, Ti Plant, King of Tropical Foliage*. Valkaria Gardens.

Brown, B. F. 1994b. *Crotons of the World*. Valkaria Gardens.

Burch, D. 2001. Key to the cassias and sennas in cultivation in Florida. *Proceedings of the Menninger Flowering Tree Conference*.

Campbell, R. J., ed. 1992. *A Guide to Mangos in Florida*. Fairchild Tropical Garden.

Chandler, P. 1990. Coral-trees in California. *Pacific Horticulture* 51 (3).

Chevallier, A. 1996. *The Encyclopedia of Medicinal Plants*. DK Press.

Condon, M. 1996. "Hanging loose" with *Gurania* and *Psiguria*. *The Cucurbit Network News* 3 (1).

Coombes, A. J. 1994. *Dictionary of Plant Names*. Timber Press.

Correll, D. S., and H. B. Correll. 1996. *Flora of the Bahama Archipelago*. A.R.G. Gantner Press.

Diniz, M. A. 1988. Bignoniaceae. In: E. A. Bell, E. Launert, and M. L. Gonçalves, eds., *Flora Zambesiaca*. Managing Committee Publication 8 (3): 61–85.

Eggli, U., ed. 2001. *Illustrated Handbook of Succulent Plants: Monocotyledons*. Springer Press.

Eggli, U., ed. 2002. *Illustrated Handbook of Succulent Plants: Dicotyledons*. Springer Press.

Elias, T. 1991. Chitalpas. *Pacific Horticulture* 52 (4):16–18.

Eliovson, S. 1991. *The Gardens of Roberto Burle Marx*. Sagapress/Timber Press.

Ellison, D. 1995. *Cultivated Plants of the World; Trees, Shrubs, Climbers*. Flora Publications International, Australia

Epple, A. O., and L. E. Epple. 1995. *A Field Guide to the Plants of Arizona*. Falcon Press.

Fernald, M. L. 1950. *Gray's Manual of Botany*. American Book Company.

Gardner, S., P. Sidisunthorn, and V. Anusarnsunthorn. 2000. *A Field Guide to Forest Trees of Northern Thailand*. Chiang Mai University. Kobfai Publishing Project, Thailand.

Gentry, A. H. 1973. Flora of Panama, Part 4, Family 172. Bignoniaceae. *Annals of the Missouri Botanical Garden* 60: 781–977.

Gentry, A. H. 1982. The cultivated species of *Tabebuia* with notes on other cultivated Bignoniaceae. *Proceedings of the Menninger Flowering Tree Conference.*

Gentry, A. H. 1992. Bignoniaceae. *Flora Neotropica.* New York Botanical Garden.

Gentry, A. H. 1993. *A Field Guide to the Families and Genera of Woody Plants of Northwest South America (Colombia, Ecuador, Peru) with Supplementary Notes on Herbaceous Taxa.* Chicago Press.

Gentry, H. S. 1982. *Agaves of Continental North America.* University of Arizona Press.

Gibbs, P. E., J. Semir, and N. D. Da Cruz. 1988. A proposal to unite the genera *Chorisia* Kunth and *Ceiba* Miller (Bombacaceae). *Notes of the Royal Botanical Garden, Edinburgh* 45 (1): 125–136.

Graf, A. B. 1992. *Tropica, Color Encyclopedia of Exotic Plants and Trees.* 4th ed. Roehrs.

Greuter, W., F. R. Barrie, H. M. Burdet, W. G. Chaloner, V. Demoulin, D. L. Hawksworth, P. M. Jørgensen, D. H. Nicolson, P. C. Silva, P. Trehane, and J. McNeill, eds. 1994. *International Code of Botanical Nomenclature* (Tokyo). Koeltz Scientific Books.

Griffiths, M. 1992. *Index of Garden Plants, The New Royal Horticulture Society Dictionary.* Timber Press.

Haehle, R. G., and J. Brookwell. 1999. *Native Florida Plants, Low-Maintenance Landscaping and Gardening.* Gulf Publishing Company.

Hammer, R. L. 1999. *Prohibited Plant Species.* Department of Natural Resources Management (DERM), Miami, Florida.

Hammer, R. L. 2002. *Everglades Wildflowers.* Globe-Pequot Press.

Hawkes, A. D. 1965. *Encyclopedia of Cultivated Orchids.* Faber.

Heywood, V. H., ed. 1993. *Flowering Plants of the World.* Oxford University Press.

Hooker, J. D. 1893. *Thunbergia kirkii*, native of east tropical Africa. *Curtis's Botanical Magazine* 109: 66–77.

Howard, R. A. 1989. *Flora of the Lesser Antilles, Dicotyledoneae-Part 3*, vol. 6. Arnold Arboretum, Harvard University.

Howard, R. A., with A. J. Bornstein. 1989. *Flora of the Lesser Antilles, Dicotyledoneae-Part 2*, vol. 5. Arnold Arboretum, Harvard University.

Howard, R. A., with E. S. Kellogg and G. Staples. 1988a. *Flora of the Lesser Antilles, Monocotyledoneae.* Arnold Arboretum, Harvard University.

Howard, R. A., with E. S. Kellogg, and G. Staples. 1988b. *Flora of the Lesser Antilles, Dicotyledoneae-Part 1*, vol. 4. Arnold Arboretum, Harvard University.

Hulme, M. M. 1954. *Wild Flowers of Natal.* Shuter and Shooter.

Hutchinson, J., and J. M. Dalziel. 1954. *Flora of West Tropical Africa*, vol. 1. Crown Agent for the Colonies, London.

Iredell, J. 1994. *Growing Bougainvilleas.* Simon and Schuster.

Irish, M., and G. Irish. 2000. *Agaves, Yuccas, and Related Plants.* Timber Press.

Jacobs, M. 1965. The genus *Capparis* (Capparidaceae) from the Indus to the Pacific. *Blumea* 12 (3): 385–541.

Jankalski, S. 2000. Crown of thorns hybrids—past and present. *Cactus and Succulent Journal* (U.S.) 72 (4): 202–204.

Judd, W. 1996. The Pittosporaceae in the southeastern United States. *Harvard Papers in Botany* 8: 15–26.

Judd, W. 1997. The Asphodelaceae in the southeastern United States. *Harvard Papers in Botany* 11: 109–123.

Judd, W. 2000. The Hypoxidaceae in the southeastern United States. *Harvard Papers in Botany* 5: 79–98.

Judd, W. S., C. S. Campbell, E. A. Kellogg, and P. F. Stevens. 1999. *Plant Systematics, A Phylogenetic Approach.* 1st. ed. Sinauer Associates.

Judd, W. S., C. S. Campbell, E. A. Kellogg, P. F. Stevens, and M. J. Donoghue. 2002. *Plant Systematics, A Phylogenetic Approach.* Rev. ed. Sinauer Associates.

Kimnach, M. 1964. *Epiphyllum phyllanthus. Cactus and Succulent Journal* (U.S.) 36 (4). Huntington Botanical Garden.

Kimnach, M. 1984. *Hylocereus escuintlensis*, a new series from Guatemala. *Cactus and Succulent Journal* (U.S.) 56: 177–180.

Krempin, J. 1990. *Palms and Cycads Around the World.* Krempin Books.

Krukoff, B. A., and R. C. Barneby. 1974. Conspectus of species of the genus *Erythrina. Lloydia* 37 (3): 332–459.

Lantin-Rosario, T. 1984. *The Ornamental Mussaendas of the Philippines.* Institute of Plant Breeding Bulletin 6,. College of Agriculture, University of the Philippines.

Larsen, K., H. Ibrahim, S. H. Khaw, and L. G. Saw. 1999. *Gingers of Peninsular Malaysia and Singapore.* Natural History Publications, Borneo.

Leeuwenberg, A. J. M. 1991. A revision of *Tabernaemontana*, the Old World species. Part 1. *Revis.*

Leeuwenberg, A. J. M. 1994. A revision of *Tabernaemontana*, the New World species. Part 2. *Revis.*

Leme, E. M. C. 1999. Contribution to the study of genus *Alcantarea. Bulletin of the Brazilian Society of Bromeliads* 7.

Letty, C. 1962. *Wild Flowers of the Transvaal.* Department of Agriculture, Pretoria.

Lewis, G. P. 1998. Caesalpinia, *a Revision of the Poincianella-Erythrostemon Group.* Royal Botanic Gardens, Kew.

Lock, J. M. 1988. *Cassia* sensu lato (Leguminosae-Caesalpinioideae) in Africa. *Kew Bulletin* 43 (2): 333–342.

Long, R. W., and O. Lakela. 1971. *A Flora of Tropical Florida.* University of Miami Press.

Lorenzi, H. 2000. *Árvores Brasileiras.* 2 vols. 3d ed. Instituto Plantarum de Estudos da Flora. Nova Odessa, SP, Brazil.

Lorenzi, H., and H. Moreira de Souza. 2001. *Plantas Ornamentais no Brasil.* 3d ed. Instituto Plantarum de Estudos da Flora. Nova Odessa, SP, Brazil.

Luckow, M. 1996. The cultivated species of *Cassia, Senna*, and *Chamaecrista* (Leguminosae). *Baileya* 23: 195–241.

Luer, C. A. 1972. *The Native Orchids of Florida*, vol. 1. New York Botanical Garden.

Luther, H. E. 1995. Notes on the genus *Pepinia. Bromélia* 2 (4).

Luther, H. E. 1997. A new *Pepinia* from eastern Colombia. *Bromélia* 4 (3).

Luther, H. E. 2000. *An Alphabetical List of Bromeliad Binomials.* 7th ed. Selby Botanical Gardens and the Bromeliad Society International.

Maas, P. J. M. 1972. Costoideae (Zingiberaceae). *Flora Neotropica* 8: 1–140.

Mabberley, D. J. 1997. *The Plant Book, A Portable Dictionary of the Vascular Plants.* 2nd ed. Cambridge University Press.

Mathias, M. E., ed. 1982. *Flowering Plants in the Landscape.* California Press.

Matthews, L., with paintings by Z. Carter. 1993. *Proteas of the World.* Timber Press.

Mayo, S. J., J. Bogner, and P. Boyce. 1997. *Araceae.* Continental Printing, Belgium.

McCubbins, T., and G. B. Tasker. 2002. *Florida Gardener's Guide.* Rev. ed. Cool Springs Press.

McLennan, R. 1995. *Growing Proteas*. Kangaroo Press.

Meijer, Willem. Unpublished monograph on *Berrya/Carpodyptera*.

Menninger, E. A. 1962. *Flowering Trees of the World*. Hearthside Press.

Menninger, E. A. 1975. *Color in the Sky, Flowering Trees in Our Landscape*. Stuart.

Morton, J. 1971. *Exotic Plants. Golden Nature Guide*. Western Publishing Company.

Morton, J. 1974. *500 Plants of South Florida*. Seemann Publishing Company.

Morton, J. 1976. The pigeon pea (*Cajanus cajan* Millsp.)—a high protein tropical bush legume. *HortScience* 11 (1): 11–19.

Muller, K. K., T. E. Broder, and W. Beittel. 1974. *Trees of Santa Barbara*. Santa Barbara Botanic Garden.

Munz, P. A. 1974. *A Flora of Southern California*. Berkeley, California.

Neal, B. 1992. *Gardener's Latin*. Algonquin Books of Chapel Hill.

Neal, M. C. 1965. *In Gardens of Hawaii*. Bishop Museum Press.

Ochse, J. J., with R. C. Bakhuizen van den Brink. 1951. *Fruits and Fruit Culture in the Dutch East Indies*. G. Kolff and Company.

Olkowski, W., S. Daar, and H. Olkowski. 1995. *The Gardener's Guide to Common-Sense Pest Control*. Taunton Press.

Olmstead, R., and collaborators. 2000– . *A Synoptical Classification of the Lamiales*. Web ed. Department of Botany, University of Washington, Seattle.

Pennington, T. D. 1997. The genus *Inga. Botany*, pp. 1–844.

Puplava, K., and P. Sirois. 2001. *Trees and Gardens of Balboa Park*. Tecolote Press.

Quattrocchi, U. 2000. *CRC World Dictionary of Plant Names, Common Names, Eponyms, Synonyms, and Etymology*. 4 vols. CRC Press.

Rauh, W. 1995. *Succulent and Xerophytic Plants of Madagascar*. 2 vols. Strawberry Press.

Ravenna, P. 1998. On the identity, validity, and actual placement in *Ceiba* of several *Chorisia* species (Bombacaceae) and description of two New South American species. *Onira Botanical Leaflets* (Santiago, Chile) 3 (15).

Sajeva, M., and M. Costanzo. 2000. *Succulents II, The New Illustrated Dictionary*. Timber Press.

Santos, E. 1964. New combinations of the genera *Chorisia. Sellowia* 16 (16): 163–172.

Schokman, L. In press. *Plants of the Kampong*. 2nd ed. Harvard University Printing Office.

Scurlock, J. P. 1992. *Native Trees and Shrubs of the Florida Keys: A Field Guide*. Laurel Press.

Smoley, B. 2000. Giant-flowered *Euphorbia milii* hybrids. *Cactus and Succulent Journal* (U.S.) 72 (4): 198–201.

Sohmer, S. H., and R. Gustafson. 1987. *Plants and Flowers of Hawai'i*. University of Hawaii Press.

Standley, P. C. 1961. *Trees and Shrubs of Mexico*. National Herbarium, Smithsonian Museum.

Standley, P. C., and S. J. Record. 1936. The forests and flora of British Honduras. *Field Museum of Natural History*, Botany Series, vol. 12

Standley, P. C., and L. O. Williams. 1961a. Flacourtiaceae. *Flora of Guatemala*. Fieldiana, Botany 24 (7): 82–109.

Standley, P. C., and L. O. Williams. 1961b. Turneraceae. *Flora of Guatemala*. Fieldiana, Botany 24 (7): 109–115.

Stearn, W. T. 1992a. *Botanical Latin*. Timber Press

Stearn, W. T. 1992b. *Stearn's Dictionary of Plant Names for Gardeners*. Cassel Publishers.

Stebbins, M. 1999. *Flowering Trees of Florida*. Pineapple Press.

Sunset Books. 1995. *Sunset Western Garden Book*. Sunset Publishing Corporation.

Tasker, G. B. 1994. *Enchanted Ground*. University Press Syndicate Company.

Tenenbaum, F., ed. 1996. *Taylor's Guide to Seashore Gardening*. Houghton Mifflin Company.

Todzia, C. A., and F. Almeda. 1991. A revision of *Tibouchina* section *Lepidotae* (Melastomataceae: Tibouchineae). *Proceeding of the California Academy of Sciences* 4 (6): 175–206.

Trehane, P., C. D. Brickell, B. R. Baum, W. L. A. Hetterscheid, A. C. Leslie, J. McNeill, S. A. Spongberg, and F. Vrugtman, eds. 1995. *International Code of Nomenclature for Cultivated Plants*. Quarterjack Publishing.

Tristram, M. 1998. Notes on *Brugmansia* species. Drawn from Ph.D. thesis, T. E. Lockwood, 1973. Harvard University.

Turner Jr., R. J., and E. Wassen, eds. 1997. *Botanica*. Mynah, Random House Australia.

Van Wyk, B., and G. Smith. 1996. *Guide to the Aloes of South Africa*. Briza Publications.

Vanderplank, J. 1991. *Passion-Flowers*. MIT Press.

Wasshausen, D. C. 1995. Acanthaceae. In: J. A. Steyermark et al., eds., *Flora of Venezuelan Guayana* 2: 335–374.

Whistler, W. A. 2000. *Tropical Ornamentals, A Guide*. Timber Press.

Whitman, William F. 2001. *Five Decades with Tropical Fruit*. Quisqualis Books with Fairchild Tropical Garden.

Whitmore, B., and T. C. Whitmore, eds. 1983. Lythraceae (*Lagerstroemia*). *Tree Flora of Malaya*, vol. 2. Longman Publishing Company.

Whitson, T. D., L. C. Burrill, S. A. Dewey, D. W. Cudney, B. E. Nelson, R. D. Lee, and R. Parker. 1996. *Weeds of the West*. Pioneer of Jackson Hole.

Wiggins, I. 1980. *Flora of Baja California*. Stanford University

Wilson, R. G., and C. Wilson. 1964. *Bromeliads in Cultivation*. Hurricane Press.

Women's Club of Havana. 1958. *Flowering Plants from Cuban Gardens*. Criterion Books.

Woodson, R. E., Jr. 1938. An evaluation of the genera *Plumeria* and *Himatanthus* Willd. *Annals of the Missouri Botanical Garden* 25: 189–224.

Wunderlin, R. P. 1983. Revision of the arborescent bauhinias (Fabaceae: Caesalpinioideae: Cercideae) native to Middle America. *Annals of the Missouri Botanical Garden* 70: 95–127.

Wunderlin, R. P. 1997. *Guide to the Vascular Plants of Florida*. University Press of Florida.

Wunderlin, R. P. In press. *Guide to the Vascular Plants of Florida*. Rev. ed. University Press of Florida.

Wurdack, J. J. 1967. The cultivated glorybushes, *Tibouchina* (Melastomataceae). *Baileya* 15 (1): 1–6.

Yong, H. 1981 *Magnificent Plants, Malaysian Natural Heritage*. Tropical Press.

Zomlefer, W. B. 1994. *Guide to Flowering Plant Families*. Chapel Hill.

List of Web Sites

American Association of Botanical Gardens and Arboreta
 http://www.aabga.org
Australian Plants, Botany, Horticulture Home Page.
 http://www.anbg.gov.au.
Balboa Park and Gardens, San Diego, California.
 http://www1.sddt.com/features/balboapark/gardens.html.
Betrock's PlantFinder. Betrock Information Systems.
 www.hortworld.com.
Botanical Garden links.
 http://www.rbge.org.uk/forms/multisite2.html.
California Exotic Pest Plant Council (CalEPPC).
 http://www.caleppc.org/info/plantlist.html.
Desert Botanical Garden, Phoenix, Arizona.
 http://www.desertbotanicalgarden.org.
Directory of International Cultivar Registration Authorities (ICRAs).
 http://www.ishs.org/sci/icra.htm.
Fairchild Tropical Garden, Coral Gables, Florida.
 www.fairchildgarden.org.
The Families of Flowering Plants: Descriptions, Illustrations,
Identification, and Information Retrieval. 2000. 14th ed. by L. Watson and M. J. Dallwitz. Published on the Internet:
 http://biodiversity.uno.edu/delta.
Florida Exotic Pest Council (FLEPPC).
 http://www.fleppc.org.
Huntington Botanical Gardens, San Marino, California.
 http://www.huntington.org/BotanicalDiv/
 HEHBotanicalHome. html.
International Code of Botanical Nomenclature (Tokyo). Botanical Code or ICBN.
 http://www.bgbm.fu-berlin.de/iapt/nomenclature/code/
 tokyo-e/contents.htm.
International Code of Nomenclature for Cultivated Plants. Cultivated Plant Code or ICNCP.
 http://www.ishs.org/sci/icra/htm.
International Legume Database and Information Service. World Database of Legumes. University of Southampton, United Kingdom, School of Biological Sciences.
 http://www.ildis.org.
International Plant Names Index (IPNI). Database of plant names and bibliography. The Royal Botanic Gardens, Kew, the Harvard University Herbaria, and the Australian National Herbarium.
 http://www.us.ipni.org.
Invasive and Noxious Plants. PLANTS Database, U.S. Department of Agriculture, Natural Resources Conservation Service.
 http://plants.usda.gov.

Longwood Gardens, Kennett Square, Pennsylvania.
 http://www.longwoodgardens.org.
Miami-Dade County Fruit and Spice Park, Homestead, Florida.
 www.co.miami-dade.fl.us/parks/fruitandspice.htm.
National Botanical Institute, South Africa.
 http://www.nbi.ac.za.
National Genetic Resources Program. Germplasm Resources Information Network (GRIN). Database of the National Germplasm Resources Laboratory, Beltsville, Maryland. U.S. Department of Agriculture, Agriculture Research Service.
 http://www.ars-grin.gov/var/apache/cgi-bin/npgs/html/
 tax_search.pl.
National Tropical Botanical Garden, Hawaii and Florida.
 http://www.ntbg.org.
Parrot Jungle, Miami, Florida.
 www.parrotjungle.com.
Plant Scientific Names Glossary. American Society for Horticultural Science (ASHS).
 http://www.ashs.org/resources/plantnames/
 nomenclatureinfo.
Quail Botanical Garden, Encinitas, California.
 http://qbgardens.com.
Royal Botanic Gardens, Kew.
 http://www.kew.org.
San Diego Zoo and Wild Animal Parks.
 www.sandiegozoo.com.
South African Botanical Diversity Network (SABONET).
 http://www.sabonet.org/reddatalist/database.html.
Threatened and Endangered Plants. PLANTS Database, U.S. Department of Agriculture, Natural Resources Conservation Service.
 http://plants.usda.gov.
Threatened and Endangered Species System (TESS). U.S. Fish and Wildlife Service.
 http://ecos.fws.gov.
University of Hawaii, Home Page including lists of native and alien plants.
 www.botany.hawaii.edu.
University of Miami, Gifford Arboretum, Coral Gables, Florida.
 http://fig.cox.miami.edu/Arboretum/flowers.html.
Vascular Tropicos. VAST Nomenclature Database, W3Tropicos. Missouri Botanical Garden.
 http://mobot.mobot.org/w3t/search/vast.html.

Index of Scientific & Common Names

Abelmoschus 253
Abelmoschus esculentus 253
Abelmoschus moschatus 253
Abelmoschus rugosus 253
abey, see *Jacaranda*
Abroma 266
Abroma augusta 266
Abroma fastuosa, see *A. augusta*
Abutilon 254
Abutilon aurantiacum, see *A. palmeri*
Abutilon chittendenii 254
Abutilon macdougalii, see *A. palmeri*
Abutilon megapotamicum 254
Abutilon palmeri 254
Acacia 210
Acacia auriculiformis 210
Acacia baileyana 210
Acacia parvifolia, see *A. tortuosa*
Acacia sphaerocephala 210
Acacia tortuosa 210
Acalypha 186
Acalypha amentacea, see *A. wilkesiana*
Acalypha godseffiana, see *A. wilkesiana*
Acalypha hispida 186
Acalypha pendula, see *A. reptans* var. *pygmaea*
Acalypha repens, see *A. reptans* var. *pygmaea*
Acalypha reptans var. *pygmaea* 187
Acalypha sanderi, see *A. hispida*
Acalypha wilkesiana 187
Acanthaceae 28
Acanthus 28
Acanthus mollis 28

Acanthus montanus 28
Acanthus spinosus 28
Acca 282
Acca sellowiana 282
acerola, see *Malpighia emarginata*
achiote, see *Bixa orellana*
Achras mammosa, see *Manilkara zapota*
Acnistus 346
Acnistus arborescens 346
Acoelorrhaphe 90
Acoelorrhaphe wrightii 90
acoita, see *Luehea seemannii*
Adansonia 260
Adansonia digitata 260
Adansonia gibbosa 260
Adansonia grandidieri 260
Adansonia madagascariensis 260
Adansonia za 260
adelfa, see *Nerium*, see also *Thevetia peruviana*
Adenanthera 211
Adenanthera pavonina 211
Adenium 62
Adenium arabicum, see *A. obesum*
Adenium multiflorum, see *A. obesum*
Adenium obesum 62
Adenocalymna 134
Adenocalymna comosum 134
Adenoplea lindleyana, see *Buddleja lindleyana*
Adonidia 90
Adonidia merrillii 90
Adoxaceae 41
ae-ae, see *Musa* 'Koae'
Aechmea 152

Aechmea 'Blue Tango' 152
Aechmea blanchetiana 152
Aechmea burle-marxii 152
Aechmea chantinii 152
Aechmea dichlamydea 152
Aechmea distichantha 152
Aechmea fasciata 153
Aechmea fendleri 153
Aechmea fulgens 153
Aechmea fulgens × *A. ramosa* 153
Aechmea gamosepala 153
Aechmea luddemanniana 153
Aechmea mariae-reginae 153
Aechmea nudicaulis 154
Aechmea pineliana 154
Aechmea roberto-seidelii, see *A. pineliana*
Aechmea thyrsigera, see *A. gamosepala*
Aechmea victoriana 154
Aechmea weilbachii 154
Aechmea woronowii 154
Aechmea zebrina 155
Aeonium 180
Aeonium arboreum 180
Aeonium canariense 180
Aeonium holochrysum 180
Aesculus 341
Aesculus indica 341
Affonsea lucyi, see *Archidendron lucyi*
African fan-palm, see *Borassus aethiopium*
African flame-tree, see *Peltophorum africanum*
African lily, see *Agapanthus praecox*
African tulip-tree, see *Spathodea campanulata*

African walnut, see *Schotia brachypetala*
African wattle, see *Peltophorum africanum*
Agallostachys pinguin, see *Bromelia pinguin*
Agapanthaceae 42
Agapanthus 42
Agapanthus africanus 42
Agapanthus minor 42
Agapanthus praecox 42
agapanto, see *Agapanthus*
Agati grandiflora, see *Sesbania grandiflora*
Agavaceae 42
Agave 42
Agave americana 43
Agave angustifolia 43
Agave attenuata 43
Agave complicata, see *A. americana*
Agave consideranti, see *A. victoriae-reginae*
Agave decipiens 44
Agave desmettiana 44
Agave echinoides, see *A. stricta*
Agave expansa, see *A. americana*
Agave ferdinandi-regis, see *A. victoriae-reginae*
Agave filifera 44
Agave ghiesbreghtii 44
Agave glaucescens, see *A. attenuata*
Agave heteracantha, see *A. lechuguilla*
Agave huehueteca, see *A. ghiesbreghtii*
Agave laxifolia, see *A. decipiens*
Agave lechuguilla 44

Agave miradorensis, see *A. desmettiana*

Agave morrisii, see *A. sobolifera*

Agave multilineata, see *A. lechuguilla*

Agave neglecta 45

Agave parryi 45

Agave patonii, see *A. parryi*

Agave picta, see *A. americana*

Agave poselgeri, see *A. lechuguilla*

Agave purpusorum, see *A. ghiesbreghtii*

Agave pygmae 46

Agave roezliana, see *A. ghiesbreghtii*

Agave seemanniana 46

Agave sisalana 46

Agave sobolifera 46

Agave striata, see *A. stricta*

Agave stricta 46

Agave tequilana 46

Agave victoriae-reginae 47

Agave vivipara, see *A. angustifolia*

Aglaonema 76

Aglaonema commutatum 76

Aglaonema costatum 76

Aglaonema 'Peacock' 76

Agonis 282

Agonis flexuosa 282

aguacate, see *Persea*

Aiphanes 90

Aiphanes corallina, see *A. minima*

Aiphanes minima 91

air plant, see *Kalanchoe pinnata*; *Tillandsia*

air potato, see *Dioscorea bulbifera*

Aizoaceae 48

ajo ornamental, see *Tulbaghia violacea*

ajo-ajo, see *Cordia alliodora*

akee, see *Blighia sapida*

alamanda, see *Allamanda*

Albizia 211

Albizia caribaea, see *A. niopoides*

Albizia julibrissin 211

Albizia lebbeck 211

Albizia niopoides 212

Albizia richardiana, see *A. niopoides*

Alcaea indica, see *Hibiscus indicus*

Alcantarea 155

Alcantarea glaziouana 155

Alcantarea imperialis 155

alder, yellow, see *Turnera ulmifolia*

Aleurites 187

Aleurites fordii 187

Aleurites moluccana 187

alexandra palm, see *Archontophoenix alexandrae*

algodón, see *Gossypium*

algodonillo, see *Cochlospermum*

alheña, see *Lawsonia*

Alismataceae 50

Allagoptera 91

Allagoptera arenaria 91

Allamanda 63

Allamanda blanchetii 63

Allamanda cathartica 63

Allamanda cathartica var. *schottii*, see *A. schottii*

Allamanda 'Cherries Jubilee' 63

Allamanda neriifolia, see *A. schottii*

Allamanda schottii 64

Allamanda violacea, see *A. blanchetii*

Alliaceae 51

alligator pear, see *Persea americana*

Alloxylon 320

Alloxylon pinnatum 320

allspice, see *Pimenta dioica*

aloalo, see *Hibiscus rosa-sinensis*

Alocasia 77

Alocasia ×*amazonica* 77

Alocasia alba, see *A. macrorrhizos*

Alocasia cuprea 77

Alocasia 'Green Velvet', see *A. micholitziana*

Alocasia indica var. *metallica*, see *A. plumbea*

Alocasia longiloba 77

Alocasia lowii, see *A. longiloba*

Alocasia macrorrhizos 77

Alocasia macrorrhizos var. *rubra*, see *A. plumbea*

Alocasia micholitziana 78

Alocasia plumbea 78

Alocasia portei 78

Alocasia zebrina 78

Aloe 124

Aloe arborescens 125

Aloe barbadensis, see *A. vera*

Aloe camperi 125

Aloe capitata 125

Aloe cernua, see *A. capitata*

Aloe ciliaris 125

Aloe cryptopoda var. *wickensii* 125

Aloe distans 126

Aloe eru, see *A. camperi*

Aloe ferox 126

Aloe frutescens, see *A. arborescens*

Aloe kedongensis 126

Aloe latifolia, see *A. maculata*

Aloe maculata 127

Aloe marlothii 127

Aloe mudenensis 127

Aloe natalensis, see *A. arborescens*

Aloe perfoliata, see *A. maculata*

Aloe pienaarii, see *A. cryptopoda* var. *wickensii*

Aloe plicatilis 127

Aloe rubroviolacea 127

Aloe saponaria, see *A. maculata*

Aloe speciosa 127

Aloe spectabilis, see *A. marlothii*

Aloe supralaevis, see *A. ferox*

Aloe tidmarshi, see *A. ciliaris*

Aloe vera 127

Aloe wickensii, see *A. cryptopoda* var. *wickensii*

aloe, American, see *Agave americana*

Alpinia 361

Alpinia calcarata 361

Alpinia formosana 361

Alpinia galanga 362

Alpinia Ginosa Series 362

Alpinia katsumadai 362

Alpinia kumatake, see *A. formosana*

Alpinia nutans, see *A. zerumbet*

Alpinia oxyphylla 362

Alpinia purpurata 362

Alpinia sanderae 363

Alpinia speciosa, see *A. zerumbet*

Alpinia zerumbet 363

Alstonia 64

Alstonia scholaris 64

Alstonia venenata 64

Alstroemeria 51

Alstroemeria caryophyllaea 51

Alstroemeria hybrids 51

Alstroemeria inodora, see *A. psittacina*

Alstroemeria psittacina 52

Alstroemeria pulchella, see *A. psittacina*

Alstroemeriaceae 51

Alternanthera 52

Alternanthera brasiliana 52

Alvesia tomentosa, see *Bauhinia tomentosa*

Alyogyne 254

Alyogyne huegelii 254

amapola, see *Plumeria*

Amaranthaceae 52

Amaranthus caudatus 52

×*Amarcrinum* 53

×*Amarcrinum howardii*, see ×*A. memoria-corsii*

×*Amarcrinum memoria-corsii* 53

Amaryllidaceae 53

Amaryllis 53

Amaryllis belladonna 53

amaryllis, see *Amaryllis*; *Hippeastrum*

Amazon lily, see *Eucharis*

Amazon vine, see *Stigmaphyllon ciliatum*

Ambroma, see *Abroma*

American mussaenda, see *Pogonopus speciosus*

American oil-palm, see *Attalea cohune*

Amherstia 195

Amherstia nobilis 196

Amorphophallus 78

Amorphophallus bulbifer 78

Amorphophallus campanulatus, see *A. paeoniifolius*

Amorphophallus gigas 79

Amorphophallus lambii 79

Amorphophallus paeoniifolius 79

Amorphophallus selebicus, see *A. titanum*

Amorphophallus tinekeae 79

Amorphophallus titanum 79

Anacardiaceae 58

anaconda, see *Cordia sebestena*

Anamomus dicrana, see *Myrcianthes fragrans*

Ananas 155

Ananas bracteatus 155

Ananas comosus 155

Ananas nanus 156

ancahuita, see *Cordia boissieri*

Androlepis 156

Androlepis donnell-smithii, see *A. skinneri*

Androlepis skinneri 156

angelon, narrow-leafed, see *Angelonia* sp.

Angelonia 314

Angelonia angustifolia 314

Angelonia salicariifolia 314

Angelonia sp. 314

angel's trumpet, see *Brugmansia*

angel-wings, see *Caladium*

Anigozanthos 228

Anigozanthos flavidus 228

Anisodontea 254

Anisodontea capensis 255
annatto, see *Bixa orellana*
Annona 60
Annona deliciosa, see *Rollinia deliciosa*
Annona montana 'Fairchild' 60
Annona muricata 61
Annona odoratissimus, see *Artabotrys hexapetalus*
Annona squamosa 61
Annona uncinatus, see *Artabotrys hexapetalus*
Annonaceae 60
anón, see *Annona squamosa*
Anthurium 80
Anthurium andraeanum, see *A.* ×*cultorum*
Anthurium bakeri 80
Anthurium bonplandii var. *guayanum* 80
Anthurium clarinervium 80
Anthurium ×*cultorum* 80
Anthurium ×*ferrierense*, see *A.* ×*cultorum*
Anthurium floribundum, see *Spathiphyllum floribundum*
Anthurium ×*hortulanum* 80
Anthurium hybrids 81
Anthurium scherzerianum, see *A.* ×*hortulanum*
Antidesma 187
Antidesma bunius 187
Antidesma collettii, see *A. bunius*
Antigonon 317
Antigonon guatemalense 317
Antigonon leptopus 317
Antigonon macrocarpa, see *A. guatemalense*
anturio, see *Anthurium* 80
Aphelandra 28
Aphelandra colorata, see *Ruellia chartacea*
Aphelandra hartwegiana 28
Aphelandra sinclairiana 29
Aphelandra squarrosa 28
Apocynaceae 62
Apocynaceae (formerly Asclepiadaceae) 72
apostle plant, see *Neomarica caerulea*
apple-blossom cassia, see *Cassia javanica*
apple, velvet, see *Diospyros blancoi*
Aptenia 49
Aptenia cordifolia 49
Aquifoliaceae 75
Arabian coffee, see *Coffea arabica*

Arabian jasmine, see *Jasminum sambac*
Araceae 76
Arachnothryx leucophylla, see *Rondeletia leucophylla*
Aralia elegantissima, see *Schefflera elegantissima*
aralia, false, see *Schefflera elegantissima*
Araliaceae 88
aranhas, see *Tibouchina*
árbol del fuego, see *Delonix regia*
árbol orchídea, see *Bauhinia*
arboricola, see *Schefflera arboricola*
Archidendron 212
Archidendron lucyi 212
Archontophoenix 91
Archontophoenix alexandrae 91
Ardisia 281
Ardisia crenata 281
Ardisia crenulata, see *A. crenata*
Ardisia elliptica 281
Ardisia escallonioides 282
Ardisia hirtella, see *A. nigrescens*
Ardisia humilis, see *A. elliptica*
Ardisia nigrescens 282
Ardisia revoluta 282
Areca 92
Areca alba, see *Dictyosperma album*
Areca catechu 92
Areca lutescens, see *Dypsis lutescens*
Areca oleracea, see *Roystonea oleracea*
areca palm, see *Dypsis lutescens*
Arecaceae 89
Arecastrum romanzoffianum, see *Syagrus romanzoffiana*
areira, see *Schinus terebinthifolius*
Argemone 308
Argemone mexicana 308
Argemone rosea 309
Argentine trumpet-vine, see *Clytostoma callistegioides*
Argyreia 177
Argyreia nervosa 177
Aristea 235
Aristea ecklonii 235
Aristolochia 123
Aristolochia elegans 124
Aristolochia gigantea 124
Aristolochia gigas, see *A. grandiflora*
Aristolochia globiflora, see *A. ringens*
Aristolochia grandiflora 124

Aristolochia littoralis, see *A. elegans*
Aristolochia ringens 124
Aristolochia sylvicola, see *A. gigantea*
Aristolochiaceae 123
aristoloquia, see *Aristolochia*
ariza, see *Brownea ariza*
Arrabidaea magnifica, see *Saritaea magnifica*
arrowhead, see *Philodendron*; *Sagittaria*
arrowhead vine, see *Syngonium podophyllum*
arrowroot, culinary, see *Maranta*
arrowroot, East Indian, see *Curcuma*
arrowroot, Guiana, see *Calathea allouia*
arrowroot, Indian, see *Tacca leontopetaloides*
arrowroot, Queensland, see *Canna indica*
Artabotrys 61
Artabotrys hexapetalus 61
Artocarpus 277
Artocarpus altilis 277
Artocarpus heterophyllus 277
Artocarpus integer, see *A. heterophyllus*
Artocarpus integrifolius, see *A. heterophyllus*
Arum bulbiferum, see *Amorphophallus bulbifer*
arum, giant, see *Amorphophallus gigas*
arum-lily, see *Zantedeschia*
Asclepiadaceae, see Apocynaceae (formerly Asclepiadaceae)
Asclepias 73
Asclepias curassavica 73
Asclepias gigantea, see *Calotropis gigantea*
Asclepias physocarpa 73
×*Ascocenda* 298
Ashanti blood, see *Mussaenda erythrophylla*
ash-plant, see *Leucophyllum frutescens*
Asok, see *Polyalthia*; *Saraca*
Asoka, see *Polyalthia*; *Saraca*
Aspalathus ebenus, see *Brya ebenus*
Asparagus draco, see *Dracaena draco*
Asphodelaceae 124
Asteraceae 128
Astrocaryum 92

Astrocaryum mexicanum 92
Asystasia 29
Asystasia bella, see *Mackaya bella*
Asystasia coromandeliana, see *A. gangetica*
Asystasia gangetica 29
Asystasia travancorica 29
Atalantia missionis, see *Pamburus missionis*
atapaima, see *Plumeria*
Athanasia acerosa, see *Phymaspermum acerosa*
Atropa arborescens, see *Acnistus arborescens*
Attalea 92
Attalea butyracea 93
Attalea cohune 93
Attalea zonensis, see *A. butyracea*
Aussie plume, see *Curcuma australasica*
Australian fuchsia, see *Correa reflexa*
Australian pine, see *Casuarina*
autograph tree, see *Clusia rosea*
ave de paraíso, see *Strelitzia reginae*
Averrhoa 306
Averrhoa bilimbi 306
Averrhoa carambola 306
avocado, see *Persea americana*
awapuhi, see *Zingiber zerumbet*
awapuhi melemele, see *Hedychium flavescens*
azucena, see *Amaryllis*; *Crinum*; *Eucharis*; *Hippeastrum*
azulejo, see *Clitoria*

baby booties, see *Sesbania grandiflora*
baby jade, see *Crassula ovata*
bag-flower, see *Clerodendrum thomsoniae*
bagnít, see *Tristellateia australasiae*
bagras, see *Eucalyptus deglupta*
Bahama whitewood, see *Canella winterana*
Bailey palm, see *Copernicia baileyana*
Bailey's thorn-tree, see *Acacia baileyana*
bala de cañón, see *Couroupita guianensis*
balazos, see *Monstera deliciosa*
bald head, see *Leonotis nepetifolia*
balloon cotton-bush, see *Asclepias physocarpa*

balsa, see *Ochroma pyramidale*
balsam, see *Impatiens*
balsam apple, see *Clusia rosea*
balsam pear, see *Momordica charantia*
Balsaminaceae 132
balsemkopiva, see *Bulbine frutescens*
balso real, see *Ochroma pyramidale*
bamboo, heavenly, see *Nandina domestica*
bamboo palm, see *Chamaedorea seifrizii*; *Dypsis lutescens*
banana, see *Musa*
banana-plant, see *Nymphoides indica*
banano, see *Musa*
Banara 224
Banara vanderbiltii 224
Banksia 320
Banksia hookeriana 320
Banksia integrifolia 320
Banksia menziesii 321
Banksia prionotes 321
Banksia spinulosa 321
banso, see *Samyda dodecandra*
baobab, see *Adansonia digitata*
barba de capuchino, see *Tillandsia usneoides*
barba de gato, see *Tacca integrifolia*
Barbados cherry, see *Malpighia emarginata*
Barbados gooseberry, see *Pereskia aculeata*
Barbados holly, see *Malpighia coccigera*
Barbados lily, see *Hippeastrum puniceum*
barbed-wire fence, see *Bromelia pinguin*
Barleria 29
Barleria albostellata 29
Barleria cristata 30
Barleria lupulina 30
Barleria micans, see *B. oenotheroides*
Barleria oenotheroides 30
Barleria querimbensis, see *B. repens*
Barleria repens 30
Barringtonia 244
Barringtonia racemosa 244
bat-flower, see *Tacca chantrieri*
Bauhinia 196
Bauhinia aculeata 196
Bauhinia acuminata 196
Bauhinia ×blakeana 197
Bauhinia candicans, see *B. forficata*

cata
Bauhinia caribaea, see *B. divaricata*
Bauhinia corymbosa 199
Bauhinia divaricata 197
bauhinia emarginata, see *B. semla*
Bauhinia fassoglensis 197
Bauhinia forficata 197
Bauhinia galpinii 197
Bauhinia grandidieri 197
Bauhinia jenningsii 197
Bauhinia kirkii, see *B. fassoglensis*
Bauhinia monandra 198
Bauhinia porrecta, see *B. divaricata*
Bauhinia punctata, see *B. galpinii*
Bauhinia purpurea 198
Bauhinia retusa, see *B. semla*
Bauhinia roxburghiana, see *B. semla*
Bauhinia semla 198
Bauhinia tomentosa 198
Bauhinia ungula, see *B. aculeata*
Bauhinia vahlii 199
Bauhinia variegata 199
Bauhinia yunnanensis 199
bay-rum tree, see *Pimenta racemosa*
bead-tree, see *Melia*; *Sophora*
beaked yucca, see *Yucca rostrata*
bear-grass, see *Dasylirion wheeleri*
Beaucarnia 333
Beaucarnia ameliae, see *B. pliables*
Beaucarnia glauca, see *B. stricta*
Beaucarnia guatemalensis 334
Beaucarnia pliables 334
Beaucarnia recurvata 334
Beaucarnia stricta 334
Beaumontia 64
Beaumontia grandiflora 64
Beaumontia multiflora 64
Beccariophoenix 93
Beccariophoenix madagascariensis 93
beefwood, see *Casuarina equisetifolia*
Begonia 133
Begonia hybrids 133
Begonia nelumbiifolia 134
Begoniaceae 133
bejuco colorado, see *Cydista*
bejuco de ajo, see *Mansoa*
bejuco de conchitos, see *Clitoria*

bejuco de murciélago, see *Macfadyena*
bella sombra, see *Phytolacca dioica*
belladonna, see *Amaryllis belladonna*
bell fire-bush, see *Hamelia cuprea*
bell-bean tree, see *Markhamia zanzibarica*
bell-bush, forest, see *Mackaya bella*
bellflower, see *Abutilon* hybrids; *Portlandia grandiflora*
bellota, see *Calliandra haematocephala*
bells, yellow, see *Tecoma stans*
Beloperone flavicoma, see *Justicia fulvicoma*
Beloperone guttata, see *Justicia brandegeana*
Beloperone 'Super Goldy', see *Pachystachys lutea*
Bengal clock-vine, see *Thunbergia grandiflora*
ben-oil, see *Moringa*
Bentinckia 94
Bentinckia nicobarica 94
Berberidaceae 134
Bermuda palmetto, see *Sabal bermudana*
Berrya 270
Berrya ameliae, see *B. cubensis*
Berrya cubensis 270
Bertoni bean, see *Vigna caracalla*
be-still tree, see *Thevetia peruviana*
betel-nut palm, see *Areca catechu*
bien vestido, see *Gliricidia sepium*
bignay, see *Antidesma bunius*
Bignonia aequinoctialis, see *Cydista aequinoctialis*
Bignonia argyreo-vilescens, see *Macfadyena unguis-cati*
Bignonia callistegioides, see *Clytostoma callistegioides*
Bignonia capreolata 134
Bignonia cherere, see *Distictis buccinatoria*
Bignonia chinensis, see *Campsis grandiflora*
Bignonia comosa, see *Adenocalymna comosum*
Bignonia hymenaea, see *Mansoa hymenaea*
Bignonia magnifica, see *Saritaea magnifica*

Bignonia spathacea, see *Dolichandrone spathacea*
Bignonia tulipifera, see *Spathodea campanulata*
Bignoniaceae 134, 345
bijao, see *Calathea crotalifera*
bilimbi, see *Averrhoa bilimbi*
Billbergia 156
Billbergia bicolor, see *B. pyramidalis*
Billbergia 'Catherine Wilson' 156
Billbergia distachia var. *maculata* 156
Billbergia kuhlmannii 156
Billbergia nudicaulis, see *A. nudicaulis*
Billbergia pyramidalis 157
Billbergia viridiflora 157
bird-flower, see *Crotalaria laburnifolia*
bird-of-paradise, see *Strelitzia*
bird-of-paradise bush, see *Caesalpinia gilliesii*
bird's-eye bush, see *Ochna*
bird's-nest anthurium, see *Anthurium bonplandii*
biribá, see *Rollinia deliciosa*
biscochito, see *Ruprechtia coriacea*
Bismarck palm, see *Bismarckia nobilis*
Bismarckia 94
Bismarckia nobilis 94
bitter gourd, see *Momordica charantia*
Bixa 146
Bixa orellana 147
Bixaceae 146
black olive, spiny, see *Bucida spinosa*
black-eyed Susan, see *Thunbergia alata*
bleeding-heart, see *Clerodendrum thomsoniae*
bleo, see *Pereskia bleo*
Blighia 341
Blighia sapida 341
bloodleaf, see *Iresine diffusa*
blood-lily, see *Scadoxus multiflorus*
bloodwood, see *Corymbia*
blue-bell, see *Barleria cristata*
blue-bells, Mexican, see *Ruellia tweediana*
blue-daze, see *Evolvulus glomeratus*
blue ginger, see *Dichorisandra thyrsiflora*
blue sage, see *Eranthemum pul-*

chellum

blue stars, see *Aristea ecklonii*

blue weed, see *Echium judaicum*

blushing bromeliad, see *Neoregelia carolinae*

bo tree, see *Ficus religiosa*

bodhi tree, see *Ficus religiosa*

Boer-boon, weeping, see *Schotia brachypetala*

Boerlagiodendron lineare, see *Osmoxylon lineare*

bois cannelle, see *Canella winterana*

bolaina, see *Luehea seemannii*

Bolivian sunset, see *Gloxinia sylvatica*

Bombacaceae, see Malvaceae (formerly Bombacaceae)

Bombacopsis quinatum, see *Pachira quinata*

Bombax 260

Bombax aquatica, see *Pachira aquatica*

Bombax ceiba 261

Bombax ellipticum, see *Pseudobombax ellipticum*

Bombax fendleri, see *Pachira quinata*

Bombax grandiflorum, see *Pseudobombax grandiflorum*

Bombax malabaricum, see *B. ceiba*

Bombax pentandrum, see *Ceiba pentandra*

Bombax schottii, see *Ceiba schottii*

Bombax vitifolium, see *Cochlospermum vitifolium*

bonga, see *Areca catechu*

Boraginaceae 147

Borassus 94

Borassus aethiopium 94

Borassus flabellifer 94

bottlebrush, lemon-scented, see *Callistemon citrinus*

bottlebrush, weeping, see *Callistemon viminalis*

bottle-palm, see *Hyophorbe lagenicaulis*

bottle-plant, see *Jatropha podagrica*

bottle-tree, hybrid flame, see *Brachychiton ×hybridus*

bottle-tree, narrow leafed, see *Brachychiton rupestris*

bottle-tree, Queensland, see *Brachychiton rupestris*

bottle-tree, scrub, see *Brachychiton discolor*

Bougainvillea 291

Bougainvillea arborea, see *Bougainvillea* sp.

Bougainvillea glabra 292

Bougainvillea hybrids 292

Bougainvillea sp. 293

Bougainvillea spectabilis 293

boundary tree, see *Newbouldia laevis*

bouton blanc, see *Alternanthera brasiliana*

Bouvardia discolor, see *Rondeletia leucophylla*

bower-vine, see *Pandorea jasminoides*

bowstring hemp, see *Calotropis*; *Sansevieria*

boxwood, see *Jacaranda caerulea*

Brachychiton 266

Brachychiton discolor 266

Brachychiton ×fordii, see *B. ×hybridus*

Brachychiton ×hybridus 266

Brachychiton ×roseus, see *B. ×hybridus*

Brachychiton rupestris 267

Brahea 95

Brahea armata 95

Brahea filamentosa, see *Washingtonia filifera*

brarna, see *Crateva religiosa*

Brasilettia africana, see *Peltophorum africanum*

Brasilettia violacea, see *Caesalpinia violacea*

Brasiletto, see *Caesalpinia violacea*

Brassaia actinophylla, see *Schefflera actinophylla*

Brassicaceae 150

×*Brassocattleya* 298

Brazil redwood, see *Caesalpinia echinata*

Brazilian flame-tree, see *Peltophorum dubium*

Brazilian oak, see *Posoqueria latifolia*

Brazilian plume, see *Justicia carnea*

Brazilian rose, see *Cochlospermum vitifolium*

Brazilian snapdragon, see *Otacanthus caeruleus*

Brazilian torch, see *Ruellia rosea*

breadfruit, see *Artocarpus atilis*

Breynia 188

Breynia disticha 188

Breynia nivosa, see *B. disticha*

briar-tree, see *Bucida spinosa*

bridal bouquet, see *Poranopsis paniculata*

bridal-flower, see *Dyschoriste hygrophyllodes*

bridal-wreath, see *Stephanotis floribunda*

Brisbane box, see *Lophostemon confertus*

brocha de afeitar, see *Pseudobombax ellipticum*

Bromelia 157

Bromelia balansae 157

Bromelia humilis 157

Bromelia pinguin 157

Bromelia pyramidalis, see *Billbergia pyramidalis*

Bromeliaceae 151

Browallia jamesonii, see *Streptosolen jamesonii*

Brownea 199

Brownea ariza 200

Brownea capitella, see *B. coccinea* subsp. *capitella*

Brownea coccinea subsp. *capitella* 200

Brownea princeps, see *B. ariza*

Brownea rosa-de-monte, see *B. ariza*

brown-turkey fig, see *Ficus carica*

Brugmansia 346

Brugmansia arborea 348

Brugmansia aurea 347

Brugmansia ×candida 347

Brugmansia ×insignis 347

Brugmansia suaveolens 347

Brugmansia versicolor 348

Brunfelsia 348

Brunfelsia americana 348

Brunfelsia australis 348

Brunfelsia densifolia 348

Brunfelsia fallax, see *B. americana*

Brunfelsia grandiflora 349

Brunfelsia hopeana, see *B. uniflora*

Brunfelsia lactea 349

Brunfelsia nitida 349

Brunfelsia parvifolia, see *B. nitida*

Brunfelsia pauciflora 349

Brunfelsia plicata 350

Brunfelsia uniflora 350

Brunfelsiopsis americana, see *Brunfelsia americana*

Brunsvigia rosea, see *Amaryllis belladonna*

brush-box, see *Lophostemon confertus*

Brya 215

Brya ebenus 215

Bryophyllum pinnatum, see *Kalanchoe pinnata*

bubble-gum vine, see *Podranea ricasoliana*

bucare, see *Erythrina*

buccaneer palm, see *Pseudophoenix sargentii*

Bucida 174

Bucida spinosa 174

Buddha's hand, see *Citrus medica*

Buddha's lamp, see *Mussaenda philippica*

Buddleia, see *Buddleja*

Buddleja 345

Buddleja davidii 345

Buddleja lindleyana 345

Buddleja madagascariensis 345

Buddleja nicodemia, see *B. madagascariensis*

Buddleja ×weyeriana 346

buffalo-horn, see *Burchellia bubalina*

buganvílea, see *Bougainvillea*

bulang, see *Gmelina arborea*

Bulbine 128

Bulbine caulescens, see *B. frutescens*

Bulbine frutescens 128

bull-bay magnolia, see *Magnolia grandiflora*

bullhorn acacia, see *Acacia sphaerocephala*

Bulnesia 373

Bulnesia arborea 373

Bunchosia 250

Bunchosia armeniaca 251

bungor, see *Lagerstroemia macrocarpa*

Burbidgea 363

Burbidgea schizocheila 363

Burchellia 325

Burchellia bubalina 325

Burchellia capensis, see *B. bubalina*

bush-lily, see *Clivia miniata*

busy Lizzie, see *Impatiens*

Butea 216

Butea frondosa, see *B. monosperma*

Butea monosperma 216

Butia 96

Butia bonnetii, see *B. capitata*

Butia capitata 96

buttercup bush, see *Turnera ulmifolia*

buttercup tree, see *Cochlospermum vitifolium*

butterfly bush, see *Buddleja; Hamelia*

butterfly dendrobium, see *Dendrobium bigibbum*

butterfly gardenia, see *Tabernaemontana divaricata*

butterfly ginger, see *Hedychium*

butterfly palm, see *Dypsis lutescens*

butterfly tree, see *Bauhinia monandra*

butterfly vine, see *Stigmaphyllon ciliatum*

butterfly weed, see *Asclepias curassavica*

button flower, see *Hibbertia scandens*

Byrsonima 251

Byrsonima crassifolia 251

Byrsonima cuneata, see *B. lucida*

Byrsonima lanceolata, see *B. crassifolia*

Byrsonima lucida 251

cabbage palm, see *Sabal palmetto*

cabo chancho, see *Helicteres guazumifolia*

cacao, see *Theobroma cacao*

cacho de toro, see *Acacia sphaerocephala*

Cactaceae 163

cacto de Pascua, see *Schlumbergera*

cactus intergeneric hybrids 163

Cactus microdasys, see *Opuntia microdasys*

Cactus pereskia, see *Pereskia aculeata*

Caesalpinia 200

Caesalpinia bicolor, see *C. cassioides*

Caesalpinia cacalaco 200

Caesalpinia cassioides 200

Caesalpinia dubia, see *Peltophorum dubium*

Caesalpinia ebano, see *C. punctata*

Caesalpinia echinata 200

Caesalpinia gilliesii 201

Caesalpinia granadillo, see *C. punctata*

Caesalpinia mexicana 201

Caesalpinia pulcherrima 201

Caesalpinia punctata 201

Caesalpinia vesicaria, see *C. echinata*

Caesalpinia violacea 201

Caesalpinia yucatanensis 201

cafecito, see *Samyda velutina*

cafeto, see *Coffea*

Cajanus 216

Cajanus bicolor, see *C. cajan*

Cajanus cajan 216

Cajanus flavus, see *C. cajan*

Cajanus indicus, see *C. cajan*

cala, see *Zantedeschia*

calabash, see *Crescentia*

calabura, see *Muntingia calabura*

Caladium 81

Caladium bicolor, see *C. ×hortulanum*

Caladium esculentum, see *Colocasia esculenta*

Caladium ×hortulanum 81

Caladium lindenii 81

caladium, giant, see *Alocasia cuprea*

calalou, see *Amaranthaceae; Xanthosoma*

calanchoe, see *Kalanchoe*

Calanthe 298

Calanthe vestita 298

Calathea 271

Calathea allouia 271

Calathea burle-marxii 271

Calathea crotalifera 271

Calathea cylindrica 271

Calathea loeseneri 271

Calathea warscewiczii 271

caliandra, see *Calliandra*

calico flower, see *Aristolochia elegans*

califa, see *Acalypha*

California poppy, see *Eschscholzia californica*

California tree-poppy, see *Romneya coulteri*

cáliz de oro, see *Solandra*

Calla aethiopica, see *Zantedeschia aethiopica*

calla, see *Zantedeschia*

Callaeum 251

Callaeum macropterum 251

Calliandra 213

Calliandra emarginata, see *C. tergamina*

Calliandra guildingii, see *C. tweediei*

Calliandra haematocephala 213

Calliandra inaequilatera, see *C. haematocephala*

Calliandra surinamensis 213

Calliandra tergamina 213

Calliandra tweediei 213

Callipsyche aurantiaca, see *Eucrosia aurantiaca*

Callistemon 283

Callistemon citrinus 283

Callistemon lanceolatus, see *C. citrinus*

Callistemon viminalis 283

Calodendrum 338

Calodendrum capense 338

Calophanes hygrophyllodes, see *Dyschoriste hygrophyllodes*

Calopyxis 175

Calopyxis grandidieri 175

Calotropis 73

Calotropis gigantea 73

Calotropis procera 73

Calyptranthes 283

Calyptranthes zuzygium 283

campana, see *Brugmansia; Portlandia*

campanas, see *Tecoma*

campanilla, see *Saritaea magnifica*

Campsis 134

Campsis grandiflora 135

caña comestible, see *Canna indica*

cañafistolo, see *Cassia fistula*

canang odorant, see *Cananga odorata*

Cananga 61

Cananga odorata 61

canario, see *Allamanda cathartica*

Canary Island date-palm, see *Phoenix canariensis*

candelillo, see *Senna alata*

candlenut tree, see *Aleurites moluccana*

candle-tree, see *Parmentiera cereifera*

candy-corn correa, see *Correa reflexa*

canela, see *Canella*

Canella 167

Canella alba, see *C. winterana*

Canella winterana 167

Canellaceae 167

canistel, see *Pouteria campechiana*

Canna 168

Canna edulis, see *C. indica*

Canna hybrids 168

Canna indica 168

Cannaceae 167

cannonball tree, see *Couroupita guianensis*

Cape chestnut, see *Calodendrum capense*

Cape honeysuckle, see *Tecoma capensis*

Cape leadwort, see *Plumbago auriculata*

Cape primrose, see *Streptocarpus ×hybridus*

Cape silver tree, see *Leucadendron argenteum*

capelo jugüerillo, see *Cornutia obovata*

Capparidaceae, see Brassicaceae

Capparis 150

Capparis cynophallophora 150

Capparis erythrocarpus 150

Capparis henryi, see *C. micracantha*

Capparis jamaicensis, see *C. cynophallophora*

Capparis micracantha 150

Caprifoliaceae 168

capulín, see *Muntingia calabura*

Caracas big-leaf, see *Wigandia urens*

carambola, see *Averrhoa carambola*

cardamom, see *Elettaria cardamomum*

cardinal-creeper, see *Ipomoea horsfalliae*

cardinal's crest, see *Odontonema cuspidatus*

cardinal's guard, see *Pachystachys coccinea*

Cardwell lily, see *Proiphys amboinensis*

Caribbean royal palm, see *Roystonea oleracea*

Caribbean thatch-palm, see *Thrinax radiata*

caribwood, see *Poitea carinalis*

caricature plant, see *Graptophyllum pictum*

Carissa 65

Carissa grandiflora, see *C. macrocarpa*

Carissa macrocarpa 65

Carludovica 183

Carludovica atrovirens, see *Dicranopygium atrovirens*

Carludovica drudei 183

Carludovica utilis 183i

Carolina jessamine, see *Gelsemium sempervirens*

Carolinea fastuosa, see *Pseudobombax ellipticum*

Carpentaria 96

Carpentaria acuminata 97

carpet-plant, see *Episcia*

carpet-weed, see Aizoaceae

Carpobrotus 49

Carpobrotus deliciosus 49
Carpobrotus edulis 49
Carpodiptera ameliae, see *Berrya cubensis*
Carpodiptera floribunda, see *Berrya cubensis*
Carpodiptera simonis, see *Berrya cubensis*
carrion-flower, see *Stapelia*; *Orbea*
Caryota 97
Caryota cumingii 97
Caryota mitis 97
Caryota monostachya 98
Caryota no 97
Caryota nymphiana 97
Caryota obtusa 97
Caryota sobolifera, see *C. mitis*
Caryota urens 97
cascabel, see *Thevetia*
Cascabela thevetia, see *Thevetia peruviana*
Cascabela thevetioides, see *Thevetia thevetioides*
cascada de jade, see *Strongylodon macrobotrys*
Casearia 224
Casearia bahamensis, see *C. nitida*
Casearia nitida 224
cassava, see *Manihot esculenta*
Cassia 201
Cassia abbreviata, see *C. afrofistula*
Cassia afrofistula 201
Cassia alata, see *Senna alata*
Cassia arborescens, see *Senna sulfurea*
Cassia artemisioides, see *Senna artemisioides*
Cassia bahamensis, see *Senna ligustrina*; *S. mexicana*
Cassia beareana, see *C. afrofistula*
Cassia bicapsularis, see *Senna bicapsularis*
Cassia didymobotrya, see *Senna didymobotrya*
Cassia ekmaniana, see *Senna racemosa*
Cassia fistula 202
Cassia glauca, see *Senna surattensis*
Cassia javanica 202
Cassia marginata, see *C. roxburghii*
Cassia microphylla, see *Senna polyphylla*
Cassia nairobensis, see *Senna didymobotrya*

Cassia ×nealiae 202
Cassia roxburghii 202
Cassia spectabilis, see *Senna spectabilis*
Cassia surattensis, see *Senna surattensis*
castañón, see *Pachira*
castor-oil plant, see *Ricinus communis*
Casuarina 169
Casuarina equisetifolia 169
Casuarina glauca 169
Casuarinaceae 169
cat's moustache, see *Orthosiphon aristatus*
Catalpa 135
Catalpa longissima 135
catawba, see *Catalpa longissima*
Catesbaea 325
Catesbaea spinosa 325
Catharanthus 65
Catharanthus roseus 65
Catherine's wheel, see *Scadoxus multiflorus*
cat's claw, see *Macfadyena unguis-cati*
cat's tail, see *Bulbine frutescens*
cat's whiskers, see *Capparis micracantha*; *Orthosiphon*; *Tacca*
Cattleya 299
Cattleya bowringiana 299
Cattleya ×guatemalensis 299
Cattleya labiata var. *percivaliana*, see *C. percivaliana*
Cattleya percivaliana 299
Cattleya skinneri var. *bowringiana*, see *C. bowringiana*
catuche, see *Annona muricata*
Cecropia 170
Cecropia adenopus, see *C. pachystachya*
Cecropia pachystachya 170
Cecropia peltata 170
Cecropiaceae 170
cedrat, see *Citrus medica*
cedro espino, see *Pachira quinata*
cegador, see *Opuntia*
Ceiba 261
Ceiba caribeae, see *C. pentandra*
Ceiba casearia, see *C. pentandra*
Ceiba chodatii 261
Ceiba crispiflora 261
Ceiba insignis 262
Ceiba insignis aggregate, see *Ceiba*
Ceiba Kampong Series 262

Ceiba pentandra 262
Ceiba pubiflora 263
Ceiba schottii 263
Ceiba speciosa 263
ceibo, see *Ceiba pentandra*
ceibo de jujuy, see *Erythrina falcata*
Celosia 52
Celosia argentea 52
Celosia cristata, see *C. argentea*
cenizo, see *Leucophyllum*
Centaurea canariensis, see *Cheirolophus canariensis*
Centrostemma multiflorum, see *Hoya multiflora*
century-plant, see *Agave*
Cephalanthus orientalis, see *Nauclea orientalis*
Cerbera ahouai, see *Thevetia ahouai*
Cerbera fruticosa, see *Kopsia fruticosa*
Cerbera peruviana, see *Thevetia peruviana*
Cerbera thevetioides, see *Thevetia thevetioides*
Cercidium 205
Cerdana alliodora, see *Cordia alliodora*
Cereus 164
Cereus hildmannianus 164
Cereus peruvianus, see *C. hildmannianus*
Cereus undatus, see *Hylocereus undatus*
Cereus uruguayensis, see *C. hildmannianus*
cerezo, see *Bunchosia*
ceriman, see *Monstera deliciosa*
Cestrum 350
Cestrum aurantiacum 350
Cestrum chaculanum, see *C. aurantiacum*
Cestrum diurnum 350
Cestrum elegans 350
Cestrum nocturnum 350
Cestrum paucinervium, see *C. aurantiacum*
Cestrum purpureum, see *C. elegans*
Chadsia 216
Chadsia grandidieri, see *C. gravei*
Chadsia grandifolia, see *C. gravei*
Chadsia gravei 217
Chaetothylax rothschuhii, see *Schaueria flavicoma*
chaff-flower, see *Alternanthera*
chaguaramo, see *Roystonea*

chain-of-love, see *Antigonon*
chalcas, see *Murraya paniculata*
chalice-vine, see *Solandra*
chaltecoco, see *Caesalpinia violacea*
Chamaedorea 98
Chamaedorea donnell-smithii, see *C. seifrizii*
Chamaedorea erumpens, see *C. seifrizii*
Chamaedorea metallica 98
Chamaedorea seifrizii 98
Chambeyronia 98
Chambeyronia macrocarpa 98
Chamelaucium 283
Chamelaucium uncinatum 283
champaca, see *Michelia champaca*
champak, see *Michelia champaca*
chandelier plant, see *Kalanchoe*
Chasmanthe 235
Chasmanthe floribunda 235
chaste tree, see *Vitex agnus-castus*
chaya, see *Cnidoscolus chayamansa*
cheese-wood, see *Nauclea orientalis*
cheflera, see *Schefflera*
Cheirolophus 128
Cheirolophus canariensis 128
chenille plant, see *Acalypha hispida*
chenille plant, trailing, see *Acalypha reptans*
cherere, see *Distictis buccinatoria*
Cherokee-bean, see *Erythrina herbacea*
cherry, Barbados, see *Malpighia emarginata*
cherry, Brazil, see *Eugenia brasiliensis*
cherry, Surinam, see *Eugenia uniflora*
cherry mahogany, see *Mimusops balata*
cherry palm, see *Pseudophoenix vinifera*
chestnut, Cape, see *Calodendrum capense*
chestnut, Indian horse, see *Aesculus indica*
chestnut, wild, see *Pachira quinata*
chestnut-leafed elder, see *Tecoma castanifolia*
chicalote, see *Argemone mexicana*

chicle, see *Manilkara zapota*

chinaberry, see *Melia azedarach*

chinchonchillo, see *Cajanus cajan*

Chinese boxwood, see *Murraya paniculata*

Chinese evergreen, see *Aglaonema*

Chinese fan-palm, see *Livistona chinensis*

Chinese fringe-flower, see *Loropetalum chinense*

Chinese hat, see *Holmskioldia sanguinea*

Chinese lantern, see *Abutilon*

Chinese laurel, see *Antidesma bunius*

Chinese trumpet-creeper, see *Campsis grandiflora*

chirlobirlo, see *Tecoma stans*

×*Chitalpa* 135

×*Chitalpa tashkentensis* 135

chocolate tree, see *Theobroma cacao*

Chonemorpha 65

Chonemorpha fragrans 65

Chonemorpha macrophylla, see *C. fragrans*

chopé, see *Gustavia superba*

Chorisia 261

Chorisia chodatii, see *Ceiba chodatii*

Chorisia crispiflora, see *Ceiba crispiflora*

Chorisia insignis, see *Ceiba insignis*

Chorisia speciosa, see *Ceiba speciosa*

Christmas berry, see *Schinus terebinthifolius*

Christmas bush, see *Senna bicapsularis*

Christmas cactus, see *Schlumbergera*

Christmas cattleya, see *Cattleya percivaliana*

Christmas cheer, see *Sedum rubrotinctum*

Christmas flower, little, see *Euphorbia leucocephala*

Christmas kalanchoe, see *Kalanchoe blossfeldiana*

Christmas palm, see *Adonidia merrillii*

Christmas pride, see *Ruellia macrantha*

Christmas rose, see *Dombeya wallichii*

Chrysalidocarpus lutescens, see

Dypsis lutescens

chulta, see *Dillenia indica*

cigar-flower, see *Cuphea ignea*

Cineraria ×*hybrida* 129

Cineraria maritima, see *Senecio cineraria*

cineraria, wild, see *Pericallis webbii*

cinnamon, wild, see *Canella winterana*

Circassian bean, see *Adenanthera pavonina*

ciruela costeña, see *Phyllanthus acidus*

ciruela Española, see *Spondias purpurea*

ciruela silvestre, see *Bunchosia armeniaca*

Cistaceae 170

Cistus 171

Cistus ×*corbariensis* 171

Cistus creticus 171

Cistus ×*dansereaui* 171

Cistus incanus subsp. *creticus*, see *C. creticus*

Cistus ×*lusitanicus*, see *C.* ×*dansereaui*

Cistus ×*purpureus* 171

citron, see *Citrus medica*

Citrus 339

Citrus medica 339

clamshell orchid, see *Encyclia radiata*

clavelina, see *Ginoria glabra*

Clavija 356

Clavija integrifolia, see *C. nutans*

Clavija nutans 356

Cleome 150

Cleome hassleriana 151

Cleome spinosa, see *C. hassleriana*

Clerodendranthus spicatus, see *Orthosiphon aristatus*

Clerodendrum 238

Clerodendrum aculeatum 239

Clerodendrum bungei 239

Clerodendrum chinense 239

Clerodendrum fallax, see *C. speciosissimum*

Clerodendrum foetidum, see *C. bungei*

Clerodendrum fragrans, see *C. chinense*

Clerodendrum indicum 239

Clerodendrum minahassae 239

Clerodendrum myricoides, see *C. ugandense*

Clerodendrum nutans, see *C. wallichii*

Clerodendrum paniculatum 239

Clerodendrum philippinum, see *C. chinense*

Clerodendrum quadriloculare 239

Clerodendrum siphonanthus, see *C. indicum*

Clerodendrum speciosissimum 240

Clerodendrum ×*speciosum* 240

Clerodendrum splendens 240

Clerodendrum superbum, see *C. splendens*

Clerodendrum thomsoniae 240

Clerodendrum ugandense 240

Clerodendrum wallichii 241

climbing ylang-ylang, see *Artabotrys hexapetalus*

Clitoria 217

Clitoria coccinea, see *Periandra coccinea*

Clitoria ternatea 217

Clivia 53

Clivia miniata 53

clock-vine, Bengal, see *Thunbergia grandiflora*

clock-vine, bush, see *Thunbergia erecta*

clock-vine, orange, see *Thunbergia gregorii*

clover, Mexican, see *Richardia grandiflora*

clown-fig, see *Ficus aspera*

clubfoot, see *Pachypodium lamerei*

Clusia 172

Clusia lanceolata 172

Clusia rosea 172

Clusiaceae 171

Clytostoma 135

Clytostoma callistegioides 135

Cnidoscolus 188

Cnidoscolus chayamansa 188

Coccoloba 318

Coccoloba uvifera 318

Coccothrinax 99

Coccothrinax argentata 99

Coccothrinax argentea 99

Coccothrinax barbadensis 99

Coccothrinax crinita 100

Coccothrinax dussiana, see *C. barbadensis*

Cochliostema 176

Cochliostema odoratissimum 176

Cochliostema velutinum 176

Cochlospermaceae 173

Cochlospermum 173

Cochlospermum orinocense 173

Cochlospermum vitifolium 173

cock-a-doodle-doo, see *Tecoma capensis*

cock's comb, see *Erythrina crista-galli*

cock's wattles, see *Pogonopus speciosus*

coco-de-mer, see *Lodoicea maldivica*

coco de mono, see *Couroupita guianensis*

coconut, double, see *Lodoicea maldivica*

coconut palm, see *Cocos nucifera*

Cocos 100

Cocos arenaria, see *Allagoptera arenaria*

Cocos capitata, see *Butia capitata*

Cocos nucifera 100

Cocos romanzoffiana, see *Syagrus romanzoffiana*

cocoswood, see *Brya ebenus*

cocotero, see *Cocos*

cocotero doble, see *Lodoicea maldivica*

cocoyam, see *Xanthosoma maffafa*

Codiaeum 188

Codiaeum variegatum 189

Coffea 325

Coffea arabica 325

Coffea canephora 325

coffee, see *Coffea* 325

coffee, wild, see *Psychotria nervosa*

coffee-shade, see *Inga*; *Gliricidia*; *Erythrina*

cohune palm, see *Attalea cohune*

cojojo, see *Acnistus arborescens*

cojón, see *Stemmadenia litoralis*

cola de camarón, see *Justicia brandegeana*

cola de gatito, see *Acalypha reptans*

cola de gato, see *Acalypha hispida*

Colchicaceae 173

cóleo, see *Plectranthus scutellarioides*

Coleus blumei, see *Plectranthus scutellarioides*

Coleus verschaffeltii, see *Plectranthus scutellarioides*

coleus, see *Plectranthus scutellarioides*

Colocasia 81

Colocasia antiquorum, see *C. es-*

culenta

Colocasia esculenta 81

Colocasia indica, see *Alocasia macrorrhizos*

coloradillo, see *Hamelia*

colorín, see *Erythrina herbacea*

Colvillea 203

Colvillea racemosa 203

Colville's glory, see *Colvillea racemosa*

Combretaceae 174

Combretum 175

Combretum aubletii, see *C. rotundifolium*

Combretum coccineum 175

Combretum grandidieri, see *Calopyxis grandidieri*

Combretum grandiflorum 175

Combretum indicum, see *Quisqualis indica*

Combretum rotundifolium 175

Commelinaceae 176

Complaya trilobata, see *Sphagneticola trilobata*

Compositae, see Asteraceae

Congea 241

Congea tomentosa 241

Congo coffee, see *Coffea canephora*

Congo pea, see *Cajanus cajan*

Conopharyngia pachysiphon, see *Tabernaemontana pachysiphon*

Consolea 164

Consolea corallicola 164

Consolea moniliformis 164

Consolea spinosissima 164

Convallariaceae, see Ruscaceae

Convolvulaceae 177

Convolvulus pentantha, see *Jacquemontia pentantha*

copa de oro, see *Solandra*

Copernicia 101

Copernicia baileyana 101

Copernicia hospita 101

Copernicia macroglossa 102

Copernicia torreana, see *C. macroglossa*

Copernicia wrightii, see *Acoelorrhaphe wrightii*

copey, see *Clusia rosea*

copperleaf, see *Acalypha wilkesiana*

copperpod, see *Peltophorum pterocarpum*

coq du levant, see *Artabotrys hexapetalus*

coral-berry, see *Aechmea fulgens; Ardisia crenata*

coral-creeper, see *Barleria*

repens

coralillo, see *Antigonon*

coralita blanca, see *Poranopsis*

Corallodendron coralloides, see *Erythrina coralloides*

Corallodendron crista-galli, see *Erythrina crista-galli*

coral-pea, see *Adenanthera pavonina*

coral-plant, *Jatropha multifida; Russelia sarmentosa*

coral-tree, see *Erythrina*

coral-vine, see *Antigonon*

coral-wood, see *Adenanthera pavonina*

corazón de fuego, see *Bromelia pinguin*

Cordia 147

Cordia alliodora 147

Cordia boissieri 147

Cordia goeldiana 148

Cordia lutea 148

Cordia nitida 148

Cordia sebestena 148

Cordia superba 148

cordoncillo, see *Piper auritum*

Cordyline 246

Cordyline fragrans, see *Dracaena fragrans*

Cordyline fruticosa 246

Cordyline terminalis, see *C. fruticosa*

Coreopsis 128

Coreopsis leavenworthii 128

corkscrew flower, see *Vigna caracalla*

corn-plant, see *Dracaena fragrans*

Cornutia 241

Cornutia grandifolia 241

Cornutia obovata 241

coroba, see *Jacaranda cuspidifolia*

Coromandel, see *Asystasia gangetica*

corona de Cristo, see *Euphorbia milii*

Correa 339

Correa reflexa 339

corteza, see *Tabebuia guayacan*

Corymbia 284

Corymbia ficifolia 284

Corymbia ficifolia × *C. calophylla* 284

Corypha 102

Corypha umbraculifera 102

Corypha utan 102

Costaceae 361, 363, 367, 371, 372

Costus 363

Costus afer 363

Costus ananassae, see *Tapeinochilos ananassae*

Costus barbatus 363

Costus curvibracteatus 363

Costus cuspidatus 364

Costus dussii, see *C. lucanusianus*

Costus elegans, see *C. malortieanus*

Costus igneus, see *C. cuspidatus*

Costus lucanusianus 364

Costus malortieanus 364

Costus pulverulentus 364

Costus speciosus 364

Costus spicatus 265

Costus talbotii 364

Costus uniflorus, see *Monocostus uniflorus*

Costus varzearum 364

Costus woodsonii 365

Costus zebrinus, see *C. malortieanus*

cotton, see *Gossypium* 255

cotton-bush, balloon, see *Asclepias physocarpa*

cotton-palm, see *Washingtonia filifera*

cotton-rose, see *Hibiscus mutabilis*

cotton-tree, red, see *Bombax ceiba*

Coulteria mexicana, see *Caesalpinia cacalaco*

Couroupita 244

Couroupita guianensis 244

cow-okra, see *Parmentiera aculeata*

cow's-tongue, see *Bauhinia jenningsii*

coyure, see *Aiphanes minima*

craboo, see *Byrsonima crassifolia*

cranberry, tropical, see *Hibiscus sabdariffa*

crane-flower, see *Strelitzia reginae*

crape myrtle, see *Lagerstroemia*

Crassula 180

Crassula arborescens 180

Crassula argentea, see *C. ovata*

Crassula falcata, see *C. perfoliata*

Crassula ovata 180

Crassula perfoliata 180

Crassula portulacea, see *C. ovata*

Crassulaceae 179

Crateva 151

Crateva hygrophylla, see *C. magna*

Crateva lophosperma, see *C. magna*

Crateva macrocarpa, see *C. religiosa*

Crateva magna 151

Crateva membranifolia, see *C. religiosa*

Crateva nurvala, see *C. magna*

Crateva religiosa 151

Crateva roxburghii, see *C. religiosa*

Crateva tapia 151

creeper, cardinal, see *Ipomoea horsfalliae*

creeper, coral, see *Barleria repens*

creeper, emerald, see *Strongylodon macrobotrys*

creeper, malu, see *Bauhinia vahlii*

creeper, Munzerabad, see *Thunbergia mysorensis*

creeper, New Guinea, see *Mucuna bennetti*

creeper, scarlet, see *Ipomoea hederifolia*

crepe jessamine, see *Tabernaemontana divaricata*

Crescentia 135

Crescentia acuminata, see *C. cujete*

Crescentia alata 136

Crescentia arborea, see *C. cujete*

Crescentia cereifera, see *Parmentiera cereifera*

Crescentia cujete 136

Crescentia pinnata, see *Kigelia africana*

Crescentia trifolia, see *C. alata*

cresta de gallo, see *Isoplexis; Pogonopus; Warszewiczia*

crinodonna, see ×*Amarcrinum*

Crinum 54

Crinum asiaticum 54

Crinum asiaticum var. *sinicum* 54

Crinum bulbispermum 54

Crinum 'Ellen Bosanquet' 54

Crinum giganteum, see *C. jagus*

Crinum jagus 54

Crinum kirkii 54

Crinum pedunculatum 54

Crinum procerum, see *C. asiaticum*

Crinum 'Queen Emma' 54

Crinum scabrum 54

Crinum zeylanicum, see *C. scabrum*

Crocosmia 235

Crocosmia ×*crocosmiiflora* 235

Crossandra 30
Crossandra infundibuliformis 30
Crossandra nilotica 31
Crossandra undulifolia, see *C. infundibuliformis*
cross-berry, see *Grewia occidentalis*
Crotalaria 217
Crotalaria laburnifolia 217
croto, see *Codiaeum*; *Cordyline*
Croton grandifolius, see *Macaranga grandifolia*
croton, see *Codiaeum variegatum*
crown, king's, see *Justicia carnea*
crown-flower, see *Calotropis gigantea*
crown-of-thorns, see *Euphorbia milii*
Cruciferae, see Brassicaceae
cruz de Malta, see *Ixora*
cry-baby tree, see *Erythrina crista-galli*
Cryptanthus 157
Cryptanthus zonatus 158
Cryptostegia 73
Cryptostegia grandiflora 73
Cryptostegia madagascariensis 74
cuajiniquil, see *Inga jinicuil*
Cubanola domingensis, see *Portlandia domingensis*
cucumber, wild, see *Momordica charantia*
cucumber-tree, see *Averrhoa bilimbi*
Cucurbitaceae 182
cunure, see *Calliandra tweediei*
cup-and-saucer flower, see *Holmskioldia tettensis*
Cuphea 246
Cuphea barbigera, see *C. llavea*
Cuphea hyssopifolia 246
Cuphea ignea 246
Cuphea llavea 246
Cuphea miniata, see *C. llavea*
Cuphea platycentra, see *C. ignea*
Cuphea schumannii 247
cup-of-gold, see *Solandra*
Curculigo capitulata, see *Molineria capitulata*
Curcuma 365
Curcuma alismatifolia 365
Curcuma australasica 365
Curcuma cordata, see *C. petiolata*
Curcuma elata 366
Curcuma flaviflora 366
Curcuma gracillima, see *C. rab-*

dota
Curcuma harmandii 366
Curcuma inodora, see *C. zedoaria*
Curcuma petiolata 366
Curcuma phaeocaulis 366
Curcuma rabdota 366
Curcuma roscoeana 367
Curcuma sp. 367
Curcuma sumatrana 367
Curcuma zedoaria 367
curry-leaf, see *Murraya koenigii*
Cuspidaria callistegioides, see *Clytostoma callistegioides*
custard-apple, see *Annona squamosa*
Cyclanthaceae 183
Cydista 136
Cydista aequinoctialis 136
Cymbidium 300
Cypella caerulea, see *Neomarica caerulea*
cypress-vine, see *Ipomoea quamoclit*
Cyrtosperma 82
Cyrtosperma johnstonii 82
Cyrtostachys 102
Cyrtostachys glauca 103
Cyrtostachys lakka, see *C. renda*
Cyrtostachys renda 103

dagga, wild, see *Leonotis leonurus*
dagger-plant, see *Yucca aloifolia*
dahl, see *Cajanus cajan*
Dahlia 128
Dahlia arborea, see *D. imperialis*
Dahlia imperialis 129
Dais 357
Dais cotinifolia 357
daisy, Canary Island globe, see *Globularia indubia*
daisy, Mexican bush, see *Tithonia diversifolia*
daisy, oxeye, see *Sphagneticola trilobata*
daisy, tree, see *Montanoa*
daisy-tree, see *Podachaenium eminens*
Dalechampia 189
Dalechampia aristolochiifolia 189
dalur, Burmese, see *Crateva magna*
dalur, marsh, see *Crateva religiosa*
dama-de-la-noche, see *Brunfelsia*
damiana, see *Turnera diffusa*

dancing-girl, see *Globba winitii*
dancing-ladies, see *Ruellia tweediana*
dasheen, see *Colocasia esculenta*
Dasylirion 335
Dasylirion pliables, see *Beaucarnia pliables*
Dasylirion strictum, see *Beaucarnia stricta*
Dasylirion wheeleri 335
date-palm, see *Phoenix dactylifera*
date-palm, Canary Island, see *Phoenix canariensis*
date-palm, dwarf, see *Phoenix roebelinii*
date-palm, Senegal, see *Phoenix reclinata*
datilera, see *Phoenix dactylifera*
Datura 351
Datura affinis, see *Brugmansia aurea*
Datura aurea, see *Brugmansia aurea*
Datura candida, see *Brugmansia ×candida*
Datura gardneri, see *Brugmansia suaveolens*
Datura maxima, see *Solandra maxima*
Datura metel 351
Datura mollis, see *Brugmansia versicolor*
Datura pittieri, see *Brugmansia aurea*
Datura suaveolens, see *Brugmansia suaveolens*
Daubentonia tripettii, see *Sesbania punicea*
dawn-flower, see *Ipomoea indica*
day-lily, see *Hemerocallis*
dead-rat tree, see *Adansonia gibbosa*
Delonix 203
Delonix regia 204
Delostoma 136
Delostoma integrifolium 136
Delostoma lobbii 136
Delostoma vargasii, see *D. lobbii*
Dendrobium 300
Dendrobium aggregatum, see *D. lindleyi*
Dendrobium bigibbum 300
Dendrobium lindleyi 300
Dendrobium phalaenopsis, see *D. bigibbum*
Derris indica, see *Millettia pinnata*

desert-rose, see *Adenium obesum*
desert-spoon, see *Dasylirion wheeleri*
devil's coachwhip, see *Stachytarpheta*
devil's cotton, see *Abroma augusta*
devil's ivy, see *Epipremnum*
devil's trumpet, see *Datura metel*
devil-tree, see *Alstonia scholaris*
Dichorisandra 176
Dichorisandra thyrsiflora 176
Dicranopygium 184
Dicranopygium atrovirens 184
Dicraspidia 279
Dicraspidia donnell-smithii 279
Dictyosperma 103
Dictyosperma album 103
Dieffenbachia 82
Dieffenbachia cultivars 82
Dietes 235
Dietes bicolor 235
Dietes iridioides 236
Dietes vegeta, see *D. iridioides*
Digitalis 314
Digitalis canariensis, see *Isoplexis canariensis*
Digitalis purpurea 314
Dillenia 184
Dillenia indica 184
Dillenia suffruticosa 184
Dilleniaceae 184
Dimerocostus 367
Dimerocostus elongatus, see *D. strobilaceus*
Dimerocostus strobilaceus 367
Dimocarpus 341
Dimocarpus longan 341
Dioscorea 185
Dioscorea bulbifera 185
Dioscorea macrostachya, see *D. mexicana*
Dioscorea mexicana 185
Dioscoreaceae 185
Diospyros 185
Diospyros blancoi 185
Diospyros digyna 186
Diospyros discolor, see *D. blancoi*
Dipladenia boliviensis, see *Mandevilla boliviensis*
Dipteracanthus squarrosus, see *Ruellia squarrosa*
Dissotis 272
Dissotis rotundifolia 272
Distictis 136
Distictis buccinatoria 137
Distictis ×rivers 137

Dizygotheca elegantissima, see *Schefflera elegantissima*
Dodonaea 342
Dodonaea viscosa 342
Dolichandrone 137
Dolichandrone spathacea 137
Dombeya 267
Dombeya burgessiae 'Seminole' 267
Dombeya cacuminum 267
Dombeya elegans, see *D. burgessiae* 'Seminole'
Dombeya pulchra 267
Dombeya rosea, see *D. burgessiae* 'Seminole'
Dombeya ×seminole, see *D. burgessiae* 'Seminole'
Dombeya spectabilis 268
Dombeya wallichii 268
Don Diego del día, see *Ipomoea indica*
Doodia crinita, see *Uraria crinita*
×*Doritaenopsis* 301
Dorstenia 277
Dorstenia bahiensis 277
doum, see *Hyphaene compressa*
down-tree, see *Ochroma pyramidale*
Doxantha unguis-cati, see *Macfadyena unguis-cati*
Dracaena 335
Dracaena americana 335
Dracaena cinta, see *D. marginata*
Dracaena deremensis, see *D. fragrans*
Dracaena draco 338
Dracaena fragrans 336
Dracaena marginata 336
Dracaena reflexa 336
Dracaenaceae, see Ruscaceae
Dracontium 82
Dracontium dressleri, see *D. soconuscum*
Dracontium soconuscum 82
Dracula-flower, see *Tacca chantrieri*
dragon's eyes, see *Dimocarpus longan*
dragon's blood, see *Dracaena draco*
dragon's tears, see *Scutellaria costaricana*
dragon-tree, see *Dracaena draco*
Drimyspermum 357
Drimyspermum macrocarpum 357
drumstick-curry, see *Moringa*

oleifera
Duabanga 247
Duabanga grandiflora 247
Duabanga sonneratioides, see *D. grandiflora*
duchess protea, see *Protea eximia*
duck-flower, see *Aristolochia gigantea*
dumb-cane, see *Dieffenbachia*
Dunalia arborescens, see *Acnistus arborescens*
Duranta 358
Duranta erecta 359
Duranta plumieri, see *D. erecta*
Duranta repens, see *D. erecta*
dusty miller, see *Senecio cineraria*
Dutchman's pipe, see *Aristolochia grandiflora*
dwarf date-palm, see *Phoenix roebelinii*
dwarf poinciana, see *Caesalpinia pulcherrima*
Dypsis 104
Dypsis decaryi 104
Dypsis leptocheilos 104
Dypsis lutescens 105
Dyschoriste 31
Dyschoriste hygrophyllodes 31
Dyschoriste sp. 31

ear-pod acacia, see *Acacia auriculiformis*
earth star, see *Cryptanthus zonatus*
Easter lily vine, see *Beaumontia grandiflora*
Easter violet, see *Securidaca diversifolia*
ébano, see ebony
Ebenaceae 185
Ebenopsis 213
Ebenopsis ebano 213
ebony, American, see *Brya ebenus*
ebony, brown, *Caesalpinia punctata*
ebony, green, see *Jacaranda caerulea*
ebony, mountain, see *Bauhinia acuminata*; *B. variegata*
ebony, Texas, see *Ebenopsis ebano*
ebony, West Indian, see *Brya ebenus*
Echites grandiflorus, see *Beaumontia grandiflora*
Echites scholaris, see *Alstonia scholaris*

Echium 148
Echium bourgaeanum, see *E. wildpretii*
Echium candicans 149
Echium decaisnei 149
Echium fastuosum, see *E. candicans*
Echium judaicum 149
Echium nervosum 149
Echium wildpretii 149
Ecuador laurel, see *Cordia alliodora*
eggfruit, see *Pouteria campechiana*
Egyptian star-cluster, see *Pentas lanceolata*
Eichhornia 319
Eichhornia crassipes 319
Elaeis 105
Elaeis guineensis 105
Elaeis madagascariensis, see *E. guineensis*
Elaeis melanococca, see *E. guineensis*
Elaeis oleifera, 105
Elaeophorbia 189
Elaeophorbia drupifera 189
elder, see *Sambucus canadensis*
elder, yellow, see *Tecoma stans*
elderberry, see *Sambucus canadensis*
elephant-apple, see *Dillenia*; *Limonia*
elephant-creeper, see *Argyreia nervosa*
elephant-ear, see *Alocasia*; *Caladium*; *Colocasia*
elephant-foot tree, see *Beaucarnia*
elephant-yam, see *Amorphophallus paeoniifolius*
Elettaria cardamomum 361
Embothrium wickhamii, see *Alloxylon pinnatum*
emerald pagoda, see *Curcuma harmandii*
empress-tree, see *Paulownia kawakamii*
Encyclia 301
Encyclia radiata 301
Epidendrum 301
Epidendrum ibaguense 301
Epidendrum radicans, see *E. ibaguense*
Epiphyllanthus 167
Epiphyllum 165
Epiphyllum hookeri, see *E. phyllanthus*
Epiphyllum oxypetalum 165
Epiphyllum phyllanthus var.

hookeri 165
Epiphyllum stenopetalum, see *E. phyllanthus*
Epipremnum 82
Epipremnum aureum 83
Epipremnum pinnatum 83
Episcia 227
Episcia cupreata 227
equelite, see *Erythrina folkersii*
Eranthemum 31
Eranthemum nervosum, see *E. pulchellum*
Eranthemum nigrum 31
Eranthemum pulchellum 31
Eranthemum 'Twilight', see *Ruspolia* 'Twilight'
Eranthemum wattii 31
eranthemum, false, see *Pseuderanthemum carruthersii*
Ericaceae 186
Ervatamia, see *Tabernaemontana*
Erythea armata, see *Brahea armata*
Erythrina 217
Erythrina arborea, see *E. herbacea*
Erythrina ×bidwillii 217
Erythrina caffra 217
Erythrina constantiana, see *E. caffra*
Erythrina coralloides 218
Erythrina crista-galli 218
Erythrina falcata 219
Erythrina folkersii 219
Erythrina hastifolia, see *E. humeana*
Erythrina herbacea 219
Erythrina humeana 219
Erythrina humeana 'Raja', see *E. humeana*
Erythrina humei, see *E. humeana*
Erythrina indica var. *orientalis*, see *E. variegata*
Erythrina insignis, see *E. caffra*
Erythrina lysistemon 219
Erythrina monosperma, see *Butea monosperma*
Erythrina parcellii, see *E. variegata*
Erythrina princeps, see *E. humeana*
Erythrina pulcherrima, see *E. crista-galli*
Erythrina speciosa 219
Erythrina variegata 220
Erythrina variegata f. *picta*, see *E. variegata*
Erythrochiton 339

Erythrochiton brasiliensis 339
Eschscholzia 309
Eschscholzia californica 309
escobilla, see *Combretum rotundifolium*
escutelaria, see *Scutellaria*
espatifilo, see *Spathiphyllum*
espatodea, see *Spathodea*
espinillo, see *Parkinsonia*
estefanote, see *Stephanotis*
estrellas, see *Beaucarnia stricta*
estreptocarpo, see *Streptocarpus*
estrofanto, see *Strophanthus*
Etlingera 368
Etlingera elatior 368
eucalypto, see *Eucalyptus*; *Corymbia*
Eucalyptus 284
Eucalyptus camaldulensis 285
Eucalyptus deglupta 285
Eucalyptus ficifolia, see *Corymbia ficifolia*
Eucalyptus multiflora, see *E. deglupta*
Eucalyptus rostratus, see *E. camaldulensis*
Eucharis 55
Eucharis amazonica 55
Eucharis moorei, see *E. amazonica*
Eucharis ulei 56
Eucomis 234
Eucomis bicolor 234
Eucrosia 56
Eucrosia aurantiaca 56
Eugenia 285
Eugenia brasiliana, see *E. uniflora*
Eugenia brasiliensis 285
Eugenia jambolana, see *Syzygium cumini*
Eugenia jambos, see *Syzygium jambos*
Eugenia javanica, see *Syzygium samarangense*
Eugenia lucescens, see *E. luschnathiana*
Eugenia luschnathiana 285
Eugenia malaccensis, see *Syzygium malaccense*
Eugenia uniflora 285
Eugenia wilsonii, see *Syzygium wilsonii*
Euphorbia 189
Euphorbia alluaudii, see *E. leucodendron*
Euphorbia bevilanensis, see *E. milii* var. *bevilanensis*
Euphorbia gymnonota 190

Euphorbia heptagona 190
Euphorbia ingens 190
Euphorbia leucocephala 190
Euphorbia leucodendron 190
Euphorbia ×*lomi* 190
Euphorbia milii var. *bevilanensis* 192
Euphorbia milii var. *hislopii* 192
Euphorbia milii var. *imperatae* f. *lutea* 192
Euphorbia milii 'Minibell' 192
Euphorbia oncoclada, see *E. leucodendron*
Euphorbia pulcherrima 193
Euphorbia punicea 193
Euphorbia splendens, see *E. milii*
Euphorbia viguieri 193
Euphorbiaceae 186
Euphoria longana, see *Dimocarpus longan*
Eurycles sylvestris, see *Proiphys amboinensis*
evening primrose, see Onagraceae
Everglades palm, see *Acoelorrhaphe wrightii*
Evolvulus 177
Evolvulus glomeratus 177
Evolvulus pilosus 177

Fabaceae 195
Fabaceae (Caesalpinioideae) 195
Fabaceae (Mimosoideae) 210
Fabaceae (Papilionoideae/ Faboideae) 214
Fagraea 225
Fagraea berteriana 225
Fagraea ceilanica 225
fairy-duster, see *Calliandra tergamina*
fairy water-lily, see *Nymphoides cristata*
false aralia, see *Schefflera elegantissima*
false heather, see *Cuphea hyssopifolia*
false hops, see *Justicia brandegeana*
false sisal, see *Agave decipiens*
fan-flower, see *Scaevola aemula*
fan-palm, African, see *Borassus aethiopium*
fan-palm, Chinese, see *Livistona chinensis*
fan-palm, desert, see *Washingtonia filifera*
fan-palm, Hawaiian, see *Pritchardia aylmer-robinsonii*

fan-palm, Mexican, see *Brahea armata*; *Washingtonia robusta*
fan-palm, ruffled, see *Licuala grandis*
farolito Chino, see *Hibiscus schizopetalus*
Fausto, see *Thunbergia grandiflora*
faveiro ou Sobrasil, see *Peltophorum dubium*
Feijoa sellowiana, see *Acca sellowiana*
felt-bush, see *Kalanchoe beharensis*
Ferdinanda eminens, see *Podachaenium eminens*
fern-tree, see *Jacaranda mimosifolia* 139
Feronia elephantum, see *Limonia acidissima* 340
Feronia limonia, see *Limonia acidissima* 340
Ficus 277
Ficus aspera 'Parcell' 277
Ficus carica 278
Ficus pumila 278
Ficus racemosa 278
Ficus religiosa 278
Ficus repens, see *F. pumila*
fig, see *Ficus*
fig, cluster, see *Ficus racemosa*
fig, common, see *Ficus carica*
fig, creeping, see *Ficus pumila*
fig, Red River, see *Ficus racemosa*
fig, sacred, see *Ficus religiosa*
filodendro, see *Philodendron*
fire-bush, see *Hamelia*
firecracker, see *Cuphea*
firecracker plant, see *Crossandra*
firecracker plant, horsetail, see *Russelia equisetiformis*
firecracker vine, see *Manettia luteorubra*
fire-lily, see *Clivia miniata*
fire-spike, see *Odontonema*
fire-tree, see *Alloxylon pinnatum*
fire-wheel tree, see *Stenocarpus sinuatus*
fishtail palm, see *Caryota*
Fittonia 32
Fittonia verschaffeltii 32
Flacourtiaceae 224
flag-tree, see *Warszewiczia coccinea*
flamboyán, see *Delonix regia*
flamboyán azul, see *Jacaranda*

mimosifolia
flamegold tree, see *Koelreuteria elegans*
flame-of-Jamaica, see *Euphorbia punicea*
flame-of-the-forest, see *Butea monosperma*
flame-tree, see *Erythrina variegata*
flame-vine, see *Pyrostegia venusta*
flame-violet, see *Episcia*
flaming Katie, see *Kalanchoe blossfeldiana*
flaming sword, see *Vriesea ensiformis*
flamingo-flower, see *Anthurium* ×*cultorum*; *Justicia carnea*
flax, yellow, see *Reinwardtia indica*
fleur d'amour, see *Tabernaemontana divaricata*
fleur de Dieu, see *Petrea volubilis*
floating heart, see *Nymphoides*
floradora, see *Stephanotis floribunda*
flor de cáliz, see *Hylocereus undatus*
flor de ilán, see *Cananga odorata*
flor de la reina, see *Lagerstroemia speciosa*
flor de Mayo, see *Plumeria*
flor de murciélago, see *Tacca chantrieri*
flor de novia, see *Stephanotis*
flor de Pascuas, see *Euphorbia pulcherrima*
flor de rosa, see *Brownea coccinea* subsp. *capitella*
flor de seda, see *Asclepias curassavica*
Florida clover-ash, see *Tetrazygia bicolor*
Florida holly, see *Schinus terebinthifolius*
flowering maple, see *Abutilon*
forest bell-bush, see *Mackaya bella*
fortnight iris, see *Dietes bicolor*
fountain-plant, see *Russelia equisetiformis*
four-corners, see *Grewia occidentalis*
foxglove, see *Digitalis purpurea*
foxglove-tree, see *Paulownia kawakamii*
foxtail-palm, see *Wodyetia bi-*

furcata

foxtail-violet, see *Dyschoriste* sp.

franchipán, see *Plumeria*

Franciscea pauciflora, see *Brunfelsia pauciflora*

frangipani, see *Plumeria*

frangipani, Australian, see *Hymenosporum flavum*

frangipani-vine, see *Chonemorpha fragrans*

freckle-face, see *Hypoestes phyllostachya*

freijo, see *Cordia goeldiana*

French oak, see *Catalpa longissima*

Freycinetia 307

Freycinetia cumingiana 307

fried-egg tree, see *Oncoba spinosa*

frijol de árbol, see *Cajanus*

fringe-flower, see *Loropetalum chinense*

fruta de condessa, see *Rollinia deliciosa*

Fuchsia 297

Fuchsia hybrids 297

fuchsia, Australian, see *Correa reflexa*

fuchsia, tree, see *Schotia brachypetala*

Furcraea 47

Furcraea macdougalii 47

galangal, see *Alpinia galanga*

gallinita, see *Callaeum macropterum*

gallito, see *Erythrina cristagalli, Securidaca diversifolia*

Galphimia 252

Galphimia glauca 252

Galphimia gracilis 252

Galpin's leucadendron, see *Leucadendron galpinii*

gandules, see *Cajanus*

Ganges primrose, see *Asystasia gangetica*

Gardenia 325

Gardenia augusta, see *G. jasminoides*

Gardenia coronaria 325

Gardenia jasminoides 326

Gardenia jovis-tonantis, see *G. ternifolia*

Gardenia taitensis 326

Gardenia ternifolia subsp. *jovis-tonantis* 326

Gardenia thunbergia 326

gardenia, see *Gardenia*

gardenia, butterfly, see *Tabernaemontana divaricata*

garland-flower, see *Hedychium coronarium*

garlic, society, see *Tulbaghia violacea*

garlic-pear, see *Crateva religiosa*

garlic-vine, see *Mansoa hymenaea*

gebang palm, see *Corypha utan*

Geiger tree, see *Cordia sebestena*

Gelsemiaceae 225

Gelsemium 225

Gelsemium sempervirens 225

Gentianaceae 225

Geraniaceae 226

geranio, see *Geranium; Pelargonium*

Geranium 226

Geranium maderense 226

geranium, cranesbill, see *Geranium*

geranium, ivy-leafed, see *Pelargonium peltatum*

geranium, storksbill, see *Pelargonium*

Gesneriaceae 227

ginger, see Zingiberaceae

ginger, beehive, see *Zingiber spectabile*

ginger, bitter, see *Zingiber zerumbet*

ginger, blue, see *Dichorisandra thyrsiflora*

ginger, butterfly, see *Hedychium*

ginger, Chinese, see *Zingiber officinale*

ginger, crape, see *Costus speciosus; Dimerocostus strobilaceus*

ginger, culinary, see under *Zingiber*

ginger, dancing lady, see *Globba winitii*

ginger, Indian, see *Alpinia calcarata*

ginger, Indian-head, see *Costus woodsonii*

ginger, Indonesian wax, see *Tapeinochilos ananassae*

ginger, Malay, see *Costus speciosus*

ginger, pineapple, see *Tapeinochilos ananassae*

ginger, pinecone, see *Zingiber spectabile*

ginger, pink, see *Alpinia purpurata* 'Eileen McDonald'

ginger, pinstripe, see *Alpinia formosana*

ginger, red, see *Alpinia purpurata*

ginger, red pinecone, see *Zingiber zerumbet*

ginger, shampoo, see *Zingiber zerumbet*

ginger, shell, see *Alpinia zerumbet*

ginger, snap, see *Alpinia calcarata*

ginger, spiral, see *Costus*

ginger, Thai, see *Alpinia galanga*

ginger, torch, see *Etlingera elatior*

ginger, wild, see *Zingiber zerumbet*

gingerbread palm, see *Hyphaene compressa*

ginger-lily, see *Hedychium; Kaempferia*

Ginoria 247

Ginoria glabra 247

gladiolus, wild, see *Watsonia borbonica*

Gliricidia 220

Gliricidia maculata, see *G. sepium*

Gliricidia platycarpa, see *Hebestigma cubense*

Gliricidia robinia var. *sepium*, see *G. sepium*

Gliricidia sepium 220

Globba 368

Globba atrosanguinea 368

Globba leucantha subsp *tricolor* 368

Globba schomburgkii 368

Globba winitii 368

Globularia 314

Globularia indubia 314

gloria de la mañana, see *Ipomoea indica*

Gloriosa 174

gloriosa lily, see *Gloriosa superba*

Gloriosa superba 174

glory-bower, see *Clerodendrum*

glory-bush, see *Tibouchina*

glory-flower, trailing, see *Dissotis rotundifolia*

glory-tree, purple, see *Tibouchina granulosa*

Glottiphyllum 49

Glottiphyllum linguiforme 49

Gloxinia 227

Gloxinia sylvatica 227

Gmelina 242

Gmelina arborea 242

Gmelina hystrix, see *G. philippensis*

Gmelina philippensis 242

Gnidia 357

Gnidia madagascariensis 357

Goethea cauliflora, see *Pavonia strictiflora*

Goethea strictiflora, see *Pavonia strictiflora*

Goetzea 351

Goetzea elegans 351

gold birds, see *Burbidgea schizocheila*

golden dewdrop, see *Duranta erecta*

golden glory-climber, see *Thunbergia gregorii*

golden net-bush, see *Pseuderanthemum carruthersii*

golden shower, see *Cassia fistula*

golden shower, autumn, see *Cassia afrofistula*

golden shower, dwarf, see *Cassia afrofistula*

golden vine, Brazilian, see *Stigmaphyllon ciliatum*

Gomphocarpus physocarpus, see *Asclepias physocarpa*

Gonatopus 83

Gonatopus boivinii 83

Goodeniaceae 227

good-luck plant, see *Oxalis tetraphylla*

Goodyera discolor, see *Haemaria discolor*

gooseberry tree, see *Phyllanthus acidus*

Gossypium 255

Gossypium barbadense 255

Gossypium hirsutum 255

Gossypium mexicanum, see *G. hirsutum*

Gossypium peruvianum, see *G. barbadense*

gout-plant, see *Jatropha podagrica*

granadilla, see *Passiflora*

granado, see *Punica*

granolino, see *Calliandra*

graptofilo, see *Graptophyllum*

Graptophyllum 32

Graptophyllum pictum 32

green-goddess anthurium, see *Anthurium* hybrids

green-velvet alocasia, see *Alocasia micholitziana*

Grevillea 321

Grevillea juniperina 321

Grevillea robusta 321

Grevillea 'Robyn Gordon' 322

Grewia 270
Grewia caffra 270
Grewia occidentalis 270
grigri, see *Aiphanes minima*
grumixama, see *Eugenia brasiliensis*
guabo, see *Inga jinicuil*
guacamayo, see *Caesalpinia pulcherrima*
guácimo, see *Luehea*
guaiac, see *Guaiacum*
Guaiacum 373
Guaiacum guatemalense, see *G. sanctum*
Guaiacum officinale 373
Guaiacum sanctum 374
Guajacum, see *Guaiacum*
guajalote, see *Parmentiera aculeata*
guamacho, see *Pereskia*
guanábana, see *Annona muricata*
guanacaste, see *Albizia niopoides*
guardia civil, see *Clerodendrum indicum*
guarumo, see *Cecropia peltata*
guarupa, see *Jacaranda mimosifolia*
guava, pineapple, see *Acca sellowiana*
guava, Spanish, see *Catesbaea spinosa*
guava, strawberry, see *Psidium cattleianum*
guava, wild, see *Samyda dodecandra*
guava, yellow, see *Psidium guajava*
guayaba feijoa, see *Acca sellowiana*
guayabo, see *Psidium guajava*
guayabo pesgua, see *Syzygium cumini*
guayacán, see *Bulnesia*; *Guaiacum*; *Tabebuia*
guest-tree, see *Kleinhovia hospita*
Guiana chestnut, see *Pachira aquatica*
Guinea gold-vine, see *Hibbertia scandens*
guineo, see *Musa acuminata*
gul mohur, see *Delonix regia*
gular, see *Ficus racemosa*
gum tree, see *Eucalyptus*; *Corymbia*
Gurania 183
Gurania makoyana 183
Gustavia 244

Gustavia marcgraaviana, see *G. superba*
Gustavia superba 245
Guttiferae, see Clusiaceae
Guzmania 158
Guzmania lingulata 158
Guzmania sanguinea 158
Guzmania wittmackii 158

Habranthus 56
Habranthus ×floryi 56
Habranthus robustus 56
Haemanthus 56
Haemanthus albiflos 56
Haemanthus albomaculatus, see *H. albiflos*
Haemanthus katherinae, see *Scadoxus multiflorus*
Haemanthus natalensis, see *Scadoxus puniceus*
Haemanthus puniceus, see *Scadoxus puniceus*
Haemaria 301
Haemaria discolor 301
Haemodoraceae 228
hala, see *Pandanus*
Hamamelidaceae 228
Hamelia 326
Hamelia cuprea 327
Hamelia erecta, see *H. patens*
Hamelia longipes 327
Hamelia nodosa, see *H. patens* var. *glabra*
Hamelia patens 327
Hamelia patens var. *glabra* 327
Harpullia 342
Harpullia arborea, see *Harpullia*
Harpullia pendula 342
Hartmannia speciosa, see *Oenothera speciosa*
hat plant, Mandarin, see *Holmskioldia sanguinea*
hat-palm, Puerto Rican, see *Sabal causiarum*
hau, see *Hibiscus tiliaceus*
Hauya 297
Hauya heydeana 297
hawthorn, enchantress, see *Rhaphiolepis ×delacourii*
hawthorn, Indian, see *Rhaphiolepis indica*
hazelberry, see *Loropetalum chinense*
heather, false, see *Cuphea hyssopifolia*
heavenly bamboo, see *Nandina domestica*
Hebestigma 220
Hebestigma cubense 220

hedge-cactus, see *Cereus hildmannianus*
hedgehog, see *Gmelina philippensis*
Hedychium 369
Hedychium coccineum 369
Hedychium coronarium 369
Hedychium cylindricum 369
Hedychium flavescens 369
Hedychium gardnerianum 369
Hedychium glaucum, see *H. gracile*
Hedychium gracile 369
Hedychium horsfieldii 370
Hedychium 'Luna Moth' 370
Hedychium 'Pink V' 370
Hedysarum crinitum, see *Uraria crinita*
Heeria elegans, see *Heterocentron elegans*
Heliconia 229
Heliconia angusta 229
Heliconia angustifolia, see *H. angusta*
Heliconia aurantiaca 229
Heliconia bicolor, see *H. angusta*
Heliconia bihai 229
Heliconia bourgaeana 229
Heliconia caribaea 229
Heliconia champneiana 230
Heliconia chartacea 230
Heliconia collinsiana 230
Heliconia episcopalis 230
Heliconia 'Golden Torch' 230
Heliconia griggsiana 230
Heliconia indica 'Spectabilis' 231
Heliconia latispatha 231
Heliconia lingulata 231
Heliconia mariae 231
Heliconia metallica 232
Heliconia mutisiana 232
Heliconia orthotrica 232
Heliconia pogonantha 232
Heliconia psittacorum 232
Heliconia rostrata 233
Heliconia sarapiquensis 233
Heliconia spissa 233
Heliconia stricta 233
Heliconia vellerigera 233
Heliconia wagneriana 233
Heliconia xanthovillosa 234
Heliconiaceae 229
Helicteres 268
Helicteres guazumifolia 268
Helicteres mexicanus, see *H. guazumifolia*
helmet-flower, see *Scutellaria costaricana*

Hemerocallidaceae 234
Hemerocallis 234
Hemerocallis hybrids 234
hemp, see *Agave sisalana*
hemp, bowstring, see *Calotropis*; *Sansevieria*
henna, see *Lawsonia inermis*
Heptapleurum arboricolum, see *Schefflera arboricola*
herald's trumpet, see *Beaumontia grandiflora*
herringbone-plant, see *Maranta leuconeura*
hesper-palm, blue, see *Brahea armata*
Heterocentron 272
Heterocentron elegans 272
Heterocentron sessilis, see *H. elegans*
Hevea 73
Hibbertia 184
Hibbertia scandens 184
Hibbertia volubilis, see *H. scandens*
hibisco, see *Hibiscus*
Hibiscus 255
Hibiscus abelmoschus, see *Abelmoschus moschatus*
Hibiscus arnottianus 255
Hibiscus brackenridgei 256
Hibiscus calycinus, see *H. calyphyllus*
Hibiscus calyphyllus 256
Hibiscus coccineus 256
Hibiscus huegelii, see *Alyogyne huegelii*
Hibiscus incanus, see *H. moscheutos*
Hibiscus indicus 256
Hibiscus moscheutos 256
Hibiscus mutabilis 257
Hibiscus palustris, see *H. moscheutos*
Hibiscus rosa-sinensis 257
Hibiscus rosa-sinensis var. *kermessinus* 257
Hibiscus rugosus, see *Abelmoschus moschatus*
Hibiscus sabdariffa 257
Hibiscus schizopetalus 257
Hibiscus tiliaceus 257
hibiscus, blue, see *Alyogyne huegelii*
hibiscus, Chinese, see *Hibiscus rosa-sinensis*
hibiscus, fringed, see *Hibiscus schizopetalus*
hibiscus, Hawaiian white, see *Hibiscus arnottianus*
hibiscus, Hawaiian yellow, see

Hibiscus brackenridgei

hibiscus, Japanese lantern, see *Hibiscus schizopetalus*

hibiscus, lilac, see *Alyogyne huegelii*

hibiscus, miniature sleeping, see *Malvaviscus arboreus* var. *drummondii*

hibiscus, parasol, see *Hibiscus schizopetalus*

hibiscus, sea, see *Hibiscus tiliaceus*

hibiscus, sleeping, see *Malvaviscus penduliflorus*

hidden-lily, see *Curcuma*

hierba santa, see *Cestrum*

higo, see *Ficus*

higo marino, see *Carpobrotus*

higuera común, see *Ficus carica*

Hippeastrum 56

Hippeastrum bifidum, see *Rhodophiala bifida*

Hippeastrum equestre, see *H. puniceum*

Hippeastrum evansiae 57

Hippeastrum hybrids 57

Hippeastrum puniceum 57

Hippocastanaceae, see Sapindaceae

Hiptage 252

Hiptage benghalensis 252

Hiptage madablota, see *H. benghalensis*

Hoffmannia 327

Hoffmannia ghiesbreghtii 327

hog-palm, see *Pseudophoenix sargentii*

Hohenbergia 158

Hohenbergia nudicaulis, see *Aechmea nudicaulis*

Hohenbergia rosea 159

Hohenbergia stellata 159

hoja de cobre, see *Acalypha wilkesiana*

hoja del aire, see *Kalanchoe pinnata*

Holarrhena tomentosa, see *Wrightia arborea*

holiday-cactus, see *Schlumbergera*

holly, dahoon, see *Ilex cassine*

holly, Florida, see *Schinus terebinthifolius*

holly, Indian, see *Leea rubra*

holly, miniature, see *Malpighia coccigera*

Holmskioldia 242

Holmskioldia sanguinea 242

Holmskioldia speciosa, see *H. tettensis*

Holmskioldia tettensis 242

holy-wood, see *Guaiacum sanctum*

Homalocladium platycladum, see *Muehlenbeckia platyclada*

Homalomena 83

Homalomena rubescens 84

honeysuckle, see *Lonicera*

honeysuckle, Australian, see *Banksia integrifolia*

Hong Kong orchid-tree, see *Bauhinia* ×*blakeana*

Honolulu rose, see *Clerodendrum chinense*

hop-headed barleria, see *Barleria lupulina*

hop-seed bush, see *Dodonaea viscosa*

hops, false, see *Justicia brandegeana*

horn-of-plenty, see *Datura metel*

horseflesh mahogany, see *Lysiloma sabicu*

horseradish tree, see *Moringa oleifera*

horse-tail tree, see *Casuarina*

Hottentot fig, see *Carpobrotus edulis*

Hoya 74

Hoya angustifolia, see *Hoya pottsii*

Hoya multiflora 74

Hoya obscurinervia, see *Hoya pottsii*

Hoya pottsii 74

Hoya purpureofusca 74

hummingbird tree, see *Sesbania grandiflora*

hunter's robe, see *Epipremnum aureum*

hurricane palm, see *Dictyosperma album*; *Ptychosperma macarthurii*

Hyacinthaceae 234

Hybanthus 361

Hybanthus prunifolius 361

Hydrocleys 50

Hydrocleys nymphoides 50

Hydrosme gigantiflorus, see *Amorphophallus paeoniifolius*

Hylocereus 165

Hylocereus escuintlensis 165

Hylocereus tricostatus, see *H. undatus*

Hylocereus undatus 165

Hymenocallis 57

Hymenocallis caribaea 57

Hymenocallis littoralis 57

Hymenocallis tubiflora 57

Hymenosporum 313

Hymenosporum flavum 313

Hyophorbe 106

Hyophorbe lagenicaulis 106

Hyophorbe verschaffeltii 106

Hyphaene 106

Hyphaene compressa 107

Hyphaene coriacea 107

Hypoestes 32

Hypoestes phyllostachya 32

Hypoestes sanguinolenta 32

Hypoxidaceae 234

Icacorea paniculata, see *Ardisia escallonioides*

ice-cream bean, see *Inga*

ice-plant, see Aizoaceae

ice-plant, tongue-leaf, see *Glottiphyllum linguiforme*

ilang-ilang, see *Cananga odorata*

Ilex 75

Ilex cassine 76

Ilex paraguariensis 75

impala-lily, see *Adenium obesum*

Impatiens 132

Impatiens auricoma 132

Impatiens pseudoviola hybrids 132

Impatiens New Guinea Group 'Rosetta' 132

Impatiens oliveri, see *I. sodenii*

Impatiens sodenii 132

imperial philodendron, see *Philodendron* ×*evansii*

Indian almond, see *Sterculia foetida*

Indian arrowroot, see *Tacca leontopetaloides*

Indian bean, see *Catalpa longissima*

Indian beech, see *Millettia pinnata*

Indian date, see *Tamarindus indica*

Indian horse-chestnut, see *Aesculus indica*

Indian mallow, see *Abutilon palmeri*

Indian shot, see *Canna indica*

Indian tulip-tree, see *Thespesia populnea*

indigo, Mexican, see *Justicia spicigera*

Inga 214

Inga edulis, see *Inga*

Inga jinicuil 214

Inga paterno, see *I. jinicuil*

Inga pulcherrima, see *Calliandra tweediei*

Inga radians, see *I. jinicuil*

Iochroma 351

Iochroma cyaneum 351

Iochroma warscewiczii 351

ipe, see *Tabebuia impetiginosa*

Ipomoea 177

Ipomoea aquatica, see *Ipomoea*

Ipomoea batatas, see *Ipomoea*

Ipomoea cairica, see *Ipomoea*

Ipomoea carnea 178

Ipomoea cathartica, see *I. indica*

Ipomoea coccinea 178

Ipomoea fistulosa, see *I. carnea*

Ipomoea hederifolia 178

Ipomoea horsfalliae 178

Ipomoea indica 178

Ipomoea microdactyla 178

Ipomoea pauciflora 178

Ipomoea quamoclit 178

Ipomoea tuberosa, see *Merremia tuberosa*

Iresine 52

Iresine diffusa 52

Iresine herbstii 53

Iresine lindenii, see *I. diffusa*

Iridaceae 235

Iris bicolor, see *Dietes bicolor*

Iris martinicensis, see *Trimezia martinicensis*

iris, African, see *Dietes iridioides*

iris, marica, see *Neomarica caerulea*

iris, Spanish, see *Dietes bicolor*

iris, walking, see *Trimezia martinicensis*

iris, wild, see *Dietes bicolor*

iron-cross, see *Oxalis tetraphylla*

ironwood, see *Casuarina*; *Mesua*

island-rose, see *Malva assurgentiflora*

Isoplexis 314

Isoplexis canariensis 315

Ixora 328

Ixora casei 328

Ixora duffii, see *I. casei*

Ixora findlaysoniana 328

Ixora hybrids 328

Ixora parviflora, see *I. pavetta*

Ixora pavetta 328

Ixora 'Super King', see *I. casei*

ixora, giant, see *Ixora casei*

ixora, Siamese white, see *Ixora findlaysoniana*

izote, see *Beaucarnia guatemalensis*

jaboticaba, see *Myrciaria cauliflora*
jaca, see *Artocarpus heterophyllus*
Jacaranda 137
Jacaranda acutifolia, see *J. mimosifolia*
Jacaranda arborea 137
Jacaranda caerulea 137
Jacaranda cuspidifolia 138
Jacaranda jasminoides 138
Jacaranda mimosifolia 139
Jacaranda ovalifolia, see *J. mimosifolia*
Jacaranda sagraeana, see *J. caerulea*
Jacaranda tomentosa, see *J. jasminoides*
jackfruit, see *Artocarpus heterophyllus*
Jacobinia aurea, see *Justicia aurea*
Jacobinia candicans, see *Justicia candicans*
Jacobinia carnea, see *Justicia carnea*
Jacobinia coccinea, see *Pachystachys coccinea*
Jacobinia mohintli, see *Justicia spicigera*
Jacobinia spicigera, see *Justicia spicigera*
Jacquemontia 179
Jacquemontia pentantha 179
Jacquinia 356
Jacquinia aurantiaca 356
Jacquinia keyensis 357
jade-plant, see *Crassula ovata*
jade-vine, see *Strongylodon macrobotrys*
jade-vine, red, see *Mucuna bennetti*
jakfruit, see *Artocarpus heterophyllus*
Jamaica caper, see *Capparis cynophallophora*
Jamaican cherry, see *Muntingia calabura*
Jamaican kino, see *Coccoloba uvifera*
Jamaican rain-tree, see *Brya ebenus*
Jamaican sweet pepper, see *Pimenta dioica*
Jamaican vervain, see *Stachytarpheta jamaicensis*
jambolan, see *Syzygium cumini*
jambosa, see *Syzygium samarangense*
jam-tree, see *Muntingia cala-*

bura
Japanese privet, see *Ligustrum japonicum*
Japanese rubber-tree, see *Crassula ovata*
jaras, see *Cistus*
jarul, see *Lagerstroemia speciosa*
jasmín de Arabia, see *Jasminum sambac*
jasmine, see *Jasminum*
jasmine, angel-wing, see *Jasminum laurifolium*
jasmine, star, see *Jasminum laurifolium*
jasmine, windmill, see *Jasminum laurifolium*
Jasminum 296
Jasminum laurifolium 296
Jasminum nitidum, see *J. laurifolium*
Jasminum sambac 296
Jatropha 194
Jatropha dulcis, see *Manihot esculenta*
Jatropha hastata, see *J. integerrima*
Jatropha integerrima 193
Jatropha multifida 193
Jatropha ortegae 193
Jatropha pandurifolia, see *J. integerrima*
Jatropha podagrica 194
Java-apple, see *Syzygium samarangense*
Java-olive, see *Sterculia foetida*
Java-plum, see *Syzygium cumini*
Java-tea, see *Orthosiphon aristatus*
jelly-palm, see *Butia capitata*
Jerusalem-thorn, see *Parkinsonia aculeata*
jessamine, Cape, see *Gardenia jasminoides*
jessamine, Carolina, see *Gelsemium sempervirens*
jessamine, Ceylon, see *Tabernaemontana divaricata*
jessamine, Chinese star, see *Trachelospermum jasminoides*
jessamine, Confederate, see *Trachelospermum jasminoides*
jessamine, crape, see *Tabernaemontana divaricata*
jessamine, day-blooming, see *Cestrum diurnum*
jessamine, Indian, see *Quisqualis indica*
jessamine, Madagascar, see *Stephanotis floribunda*

jessamine, night-blooming, see *Cestrum nocturnum*
jessamine, orange, see *Murraya paniculata*
jessamine, Paraguay, see *Brunfelsia australis*
jessamine, pinwheel, see *Tabernaemontana australis*
jessamine, wild orange, see *Tabernaemontana arborea*
jewel-of-Burma, see *Curcuma roscoeana*
jewel-of-Thailand, see *Curcuma petiolata*
jewel-orchid, see *Haemaria discolor*
jicara, see *Crescentia alata*
Joaquin, see *Cordia sebestena*
jocote, see *Spondias purpurea*
Joewood, see *Jacquinia keyensis*
Joseph's coat, see *Acalypha wilkesiana*
Justicia 32
Justicia aurea 33
Justicia betonica 33
Justicia brandegeana 33
Justicia callistachya, see *Odontonema callistachyum*
Justicia candicans 33
Justicia carnea 33
Justicia coccinea, see *Pachystachys coccinea*
Justicia comosa, see *Justicia fulvicoma*
Justicia fulvicoma 33
Justicia lutea, see *Pachystachys lutea*
Justicia spicigera 34

Kaempferia 370
Kaempferia decora, see *Siphonochilus decorus*
Kaempferia pulchra 370
Kaempferia roscoeana 371
Kaempferia rotunda 371
kahili ginger, see *Hedychium gardnerianum*
kakaw, see *Theobroma cacao*
Kalanchoe 180
Kalanchoe beharensis 181
Kalanchoe blossfeldiana 181
Kalanchoe daigremontia 181
Kalanchoe delagoensis 181
Kalanchoe gastonis-bonnieri 181
Kalanchoe globulifera, see *K. blossfeldiana*
Kalanchoe grandiflora 182
Kalanchoe pinnata 182
Kalanchoe rosei 181
Kalanchoe thyrsiflora 182

Kalanchoe tubiflora, see *K. delagoensis*
kangaroo-paw, see *Anigozanthos flavidus*
kanluang, see *Nauclea orientalis*
kapok, giant, see *Ceiba pentandra*
kapok, red, see *Bombax ceiba*
karanja, see *Millettia pinnata*
karapincha, see *Murraya koenigii*
Kennedia 221
Kennedia nigricans 221
kerky-bush, see *Crassula ovata*
Kigelia 139
Kigelia africana 139
Kigelia pinnata, see *K. africana*
king-palm, see *Archontophoenix alexandrae*
king-protea, see *Protea cynaroides*
king's crown, see *Justicia carnea*
king's mantle, see *Thunbergia erecta*
Kleinhovia 268
Kleinhovia hospita 268
knight's star, see *Hippeastrum*
ko'ako'a, see *Hibiscus schizopetalus*
Koelreuteria 343
Koelreuteria bipinnata 343
Koelreuteria elegans 343
Koelreuteria elegans subsp. *formosana* 343
Koelreuteria formosana, see *K. elegans*
koki'o-ke'oke'o, see *Hibiscus arnottianus*
Kopsia 65
Kopsia fruticosa 65
Kopsia pruniformis 65
Kopsia vinciflora, see *Kopsia fruticosa*
kopsia, see *Kopsia*; *Ochrosia*
koraalboom, see *Erythrina*
Kosteletzkya 258
Kosteletzkya virginica 258
kudu-lily, see *Adenium obesum*
kukui, see *Aleurites moluccana* 187
kurrajong, see *Brachychiton*

Labiatae, see Lamiaceae
laburnum, Indian, see *Cassia fistula*
lacebark, Queensland, see *Brachychiton discolor*
Lady Doorly, see *Ipomoea hors-*

falliae
lady-of-the-night, see *Brunfelsia*
lady-palm, see *Rhapis excelsa*
Lagerstroemia 247
Lagerstroemia elegans, see *L. indica*
Lagerstroemia floribunda 248
Lagerstroemia flos-reginae, see *L. speciosa*
Lagerstroemia grandiflora, see *Duabanga grandiflora*
Lagerstroemia indica 248
Lagerstroemia loudonii 249
Lagerstroemia macrocarpa 249
Lagerstroemia speciosa 249
Lagerstroemia turbinata, see *L. floribunda*
Lagos spinach, see *Celosia argentea*
Lamiaceae 236
Lamiaceae (formerly Verbenaceae) 238
Lampranthus 49
Lampranthus aureus 49
Lampranthus deltoids 49
Lampranthus zeyheri 50
Lamprococcus victorianus, see *Aechmea victoriana*
lancepod, see *Lonchocarpus violaceus*
Languas oxyphylla, see *Alpinia oxyphylla*
lano, see *Ochroma*
Lantana 359
Lantana camara 359
Lantana montevidensis 359
Lantana sellowiana, see *L. montevidensis*
lapacho, see *Tabebuia guayacan*
Lasiandra granulosa, see *Tibouchina granulosa*
Lasiandra semidecandra, see *Tibouchina urvilleana*
lasiandra, see *Tibouchina*
Lasiosiphon madagascariensis, see *Gnidia madagascariensis*
Latania 107
Latania loddigesii 107
latanier balai, see *Coccothrinax argentea*
latan-palm, blue, see *Latania loddigesii*
Lauraceae 243
laurel, Chinese, see *Antidesma bunius*
laurel negro, see *Cordia alliodora*
laurel-bay magnolia, see *Magnolia virginiana*
Laurus persea, see *Persea ameri-*

cana
Laurus winterana, see *Canella winterana*
lava-plato, see *Solanum erianthum*
Lavatera assurgentiflora, see *Malva assurgentiflora*
Lawsonia 249
Lawsonia alba, see *L. inermis*
Lawsonia inermis 249
Laxmanniaceae 246
leadwort, Cape, *Plumbago auriculata*
leadwort, crimson, *Plumbago indica*
leaf-flower, see *Breynia disticha*
Leavenworth's tickseed, see *Coreopsis leavenworthii*
Lebbeck tree, see *Albizia lebbeck*
lechoso, see *Calotropis*; *Stemmadenia*
lechuga de agua, see *Pistia*
lechuguilla, see *Agave lechuguilla*
Lecythidaceae 243
Leea 245
Leea brunoninan, see *L. rubra*
Leea coccinea, see *L. guineensis*
Leea guineensis 245
Leea linearifolia, see *L. rubra*
Leea polyphylla, see *L. rubra*
Leea rubra 245
Leeaceae 245
Leguminosae, see Fabaceae
Leichhardt tree, see *Nauclea orientalis*
Lemonia spectabilis, see *Ravenia spectabilis*
lemon-vine, see *Pereskia aculeata*
lengua de suegra, see *Sansevieria hyacinthoides*
lengua de vaca, see *Bauhinia jenningsii*
Leonotis 237
Leonotis leonurus 237
Leonotis nepetifolia 237
leopard-palm, see *Amorphophallus gigas*
Leptospermum 286
Leptospermum nichollsii, see *L. scoparium*
Leptospermum scoparium 286
Leucadendron 322
Leucadendron argenteum 322
Leucadendron galpinii 322
Leucophyllum 346
Leucophyllum frutescens 346
Leucospermum 322

Leucospermum hybrids 322
Lexarza funebris, see *Quararibea funebris*
Libidibia punctata, see *Caesalpinia punctata*
Licuala 107
Licuala grandis 108
Licuala peltata 108
Licuala peltata subsp. *sumawongii* 108
licuri palm, see *Syagrus coronata*
lignum vitae, see *Guaiacum*
Ligustrum 296
Ligustrum coriaceum, see *L. japonicum*
Ligustrum japonicum 297
lilac, Mexican, see *Gliricidia sepium*
lilac, tropical, see *Lonchocarpus violaceus*
lilly-pilly, see *Syzygium wilsonii*
lily, queen, see *Curcuma* sp.
lily, tree, see *Vellozia bahiana*
lily-of-the-Incas, see *Alstroemeria*
lily-of-the-Nile, see *Agapanthus praecox*; *Zantedeschia aethiopica*
lily-pad begonia, see *Begonia nelumbiifolia*
lily-thorn, see *Catesbaea spinosa*
lily-turf, see *Liriope muscari*
Limnocharis humboldtii, see *Hydrocleys nymphoides*
Limonia 340
Limonia acidissima 340
Limonia missionis, see *Pamburus missionis*
Limonium 316
Limonium perezii 316
Linaceae 245
Linum trigynum, see *Reinwardtia indica*
lion's ear, see *Leonotis leonurus*
lion's tail, see *Leonotis nepetifolia*
lion's whiskers, see *Tacca leontopetaloides*
lipstick-tree, see *Bixa orellana*
lirio de cinta, see *Hymenocallis*
lirio, see *Neomarica caerulea*
Liriope 336
Liriope graminifolia, see *L. muscari*
Liriope muscari 337
Liriope platyphylla, see *L. muscari*
lis rouge, see *Hippeastrum puniceum*

Litchi 343
Litchi chinensis 343
little blue-boy, see *Otacanthus caeruleus*
little Christmas flower, see *Euphorbia leucocephala*
Livistona 108
Livistona chinensis 108
lluvia de oro, see *Cassia fistula* 202
lluvia de orquídeas, see *Congea tomentosa*
lobster-claw, see *Heliconia bihai*
lobster-claw, painted, see *Heliconia rostrata*
Lochnera rosea, see *Catharanthus roseus*
locust-berry, see *Byrsonima lucida*
Lodoicea 108
Lodoicea maldivica 109
Loganiaceae 345
Lomandraceae 246
Lonchocarpus 221
Lonchocarpus violaceus 221
longan, see *Dimocarpus longan*
long-john, see *Triplaris cumingiana*
longyen, see *Dimocarpus longan*
Lonicera 169
Lonicera hildebrandiana 169
Lonicera japonica 169
loofah, see *Luffa aegyptiaca*
Lophostemon 286
Lophostemon confertus 286
Loropetalum 228
Loropetalum chinense 229
Loropetalum indicum, see *L. chinense*
loto, see *Nelumbo*
lotus, see *Nelumbo*; see under *Nymphaea*
lotus-leafed begonia, see *Begonia nelumbiifolia*
loulu, see *Pritchardia aylmerrobinsonii*
love-charm, see *Clytostoma callistegioides*
Lucita Wait's palm, see *Ptychosperma waitianum*
lucky-nut, see *Thevetia peruviana*
Ludisia discolor, see *Haemaria discolor*
Ludwigia 297
Ludwigia peruviana 297
Luehea 270
Luehea seemannii 270
Luffa 183

Luffa aegyptiaca 183

Luffa cylindrica, see *L. aegyptiaca*

Luffa gigantea, see *L. aegyptiaca*

lulo, see *Solanum quitoense*

lupuna, see *Ceiba insignis*

Lycaste 301

Lycaste dowiana 302

lychee, see *Litchi chinensis*

Lycianthes 351

Lycianthes rantonnei 351

Lysiloma 214

Lysiloma acapulcense, see *L. watsonii*

Lysiloma latisiliquum 214

Lysiloma microphylla, see *L. watsonii*

Lysiloma sabicu 214

Lysiloma watsonii 214

Lythraceae 246

ma'o-hau-hele, see *Hibiscus brackenridgei*

mabolo, see *Diospyros blancoi*

Macaranga 194

Macaranga grandifolia 194

Macarthur palm 114

Macfadyena 139

Macfadyena dentate 139

Macfadyena unguis-cati 139

Mackaya 34

Mackaya bella 34

Madeira geranium, see *Geranium maderense*

madre brava, see *Erythrina coralloides*

madre de café, see *Gliricidia; Inga; Erythrina*

Magnolia 249

Magnolia ×*alba,* see *Michelia* ×*alba*

Magnolia champaca, see *Michelia champaca*

Magnolia grandiflora 249

Magnolia virginiana 250

magnolia, southern, see *Magnolia grandiflora*

magnolia, sweet-bay, see *Magnolia virginiana*

Magnoliaceae 249

maguey, see *Agave americana*

maharajah palm, see *Cyrtostachys renda*

mahoe, see *Hibiscus tiliaceus*

mahogany, cherry, see *Mimusops balata*

majagua, see *Hibiscus tiliaceus*

Majidea 343

Majidea zanguebarica 343

Malabar simal, see *Bombax*

ceiba

malanga, see *Xanthosoma maffafa*

Malay apple, see *Syzygium malaccense*

mallow, salt-marsh, see *Kosteletzkya virginica*

mallow, South African, see *Anisodontea capensis*

mallow, wax, see *Malvaviscus arboreus*

Malpighia 252

Malpighia armeniaca, see *Bunchosia armeniaca*

Malpighia coccigera 252

Malpighia crassifolia, see *Byrsonima crassifolia*

Malpighia emarginata 253

Malpighia glabra, see *M. emarginata*

Malpighia punicifolia, see *M. emarginata*

Malpighiaceae 250

malu creeper, see *Bauhinia vahlii*

Malva 258

Malva assurgentiflora 258

Malva capensis, see *Anisodontea capensis*

malva rosa, see *Malva assurgentiflora*

Malvaceae 253

Malvaceae (formerly Bombacaceae) 260

Malvaceae (formerly Sterculiaceae) 266

Malvaceae (formerly Tiliaceae) 269

Malvastrum capense, see *Anisodontea capensis*

Malvaviscus 258

Malvaviscus arboreus 258

Malvaviscus drummondii, see *M. arboreus*

Malvaviscus penduliflorus 258

mamey colorado, see *Pouteria sapota*

mamey sapote, see *Mammea americana*

Mammea 172

Mammea americana 173

mammee apple, see *Mammea americana*

mamón, see *Dimocarpus longan*

manacá, see *Brunfelsia uniflora*

mandaram, see *Erythrina variegata*

Mandevilla 65

Mandevilla boliviensis 66

Mandevilla cereola, see *M. boliviensis*

Mandevilla hybrids 66

mandioca, see *Manihot esculenta*

Manettia 329

Manettia bicolor, see *M. luteorubra*

Manettia inflata, see *M. luteorubra*

Manettia luteorubra 329

Mangifera 58

Mangifera indica 59

mango, see *Mangifera indica*

manicillo, see *Dalechampia aristolochiifolia*

Manihot 194

Manihot carthagenensis subsp. *esculenta* 194

Manihot dulcis, see *M. esculenta*

Manihot glaziovii 194

Manila palm, see *Adonidia merrillii*

Manilkara 343

Manilkara zapota 343

mánioc, see *Manihot esculenta*

Mansoa 139

Mansoa alboviolaceum, see *M. hymenaea*

Mansoa alliacea 139

Mansoa hymenaea 139

Mansoa verrucifera 139

manteco, see *Gustavia superba*

manto de rey, see *Thunbergia erecta*

manzana rosa, see *Syzygium jambos*

maple-leafed bayur, see *Pterospermum acerifolium*

maracuyá, see *Passiflora edulis*

Maranta 271

Maranta arundinacea 271

Maranta galanga, see *Alpinia galanga*

Maranta leuconeura 271

Marantaceae 270

margarita, see *Tagetes lucida*

marigold, see *Tagetes lucida*

marilópez, see *Turnera ulmifolia*

Markhamia 140

Markhamia hildebrandtii, see *M. lutea*

Markhamia lutea 140

Markhamia platycalyx, see *M. lutea*

Markhamia zanzibarica 140

marlberry, see *Ardisia escallonioides*

marmalade-bush, see *Strepto-*

solen jamesonii

Marsdenia floribunda, see *Stephanotis floribunda*

marsh-mallow, see *Hibiscus coccineus*

Martha Washington pelargonium, see *Pelargonium* ×*domesticum*

masarocco, see *Echium candicans*

Mascagnia macroptera, see *Callaeum macropterum*

mast-tree, see *Polyalthia longifolia*

matabuey, see *Goetzea elegans*

matál, see *Asclepias curassavica*

mataratón, see *Gliricidia sepium*

matilija poppy, see *Romneya coulteri*

Maximiliana, see *Attalea*

maypan coconut, see *Cocos*

mazapan, see *Malvaviscus penduliflorus*

Medinilla 272

Medinilla magnifica 273

Medinilla miniata 273

Medinilla myriantha 273

Medinilla scortechinii 273

Megaskepasma 34

Megaskepasma erythrochlamys 34

Melaleuca 286

Melaleuca bracteata 287

Melaleuca lateritia 287

Melaleuca leucodendron, see *M. quinquenervia*

Melaleuca linariifolia 287

Melaleuca monticola, see *M. bracteata*

Melaleuca nesophila 287

Melaleuca quinquenervia 288

Melastoma 273

Melastoma malabathricum 273

Melastomataceae 272

Melia 276

Melia azedarach 276

Melia japonica, see *M. azedarach*

Meliaceae 276

membrillo, see *Gustavia superba*

Menyanthaceae 276

Menyanthes cristata, see *Nymphoides cristata*

mermelada, see *Streptosolen jamesonii*

Merremia 179

Merremia tuberosa 179

Mesembryanthemum, see *Lampranthus aureus*

Mesembryanthemum bulbosum, see *Trichodiadema bulbosum*

Mesembryanthemum cordifolium, see *Aptenia cordifolia*

Mesembryanthemum deliciosus, see *Carpobrotus deliciosus*

Mesembryanthemum deltoides, see *Lampranthus deltoids*

Mesembryanthemum edulis, see *Carpobrotus edulis*

Mesembryanthemum zeyheri, see *Lampranthus zeyheri*

Mesua 173

Mesua ferrea 173

Metrosideros 288

Metrosideros excelsa 288

Metrosideros tomentosa, see *M. excelsa*

Mexican blue-bells, see *Ruellia tweediana*

Mexican bush-sage, see *Salvia leucantha*

Mexican creeper, see *Antigonon leptopus*

Mexican fan-palm, see *Brahea armata*

Mexican flame-bush, see *Calliandra tweediei*

Mexican flame-vine, see *Pseudogynoxys chenopodioides*

Mexican indigo, see *Justicia spicigera*

Mexican marigold, see *Tagetes lucida*

Mexican milkweed, see *Asclepias curassavica*

Mexican sunflower, see *Tithonia diversifolia*

Mexican tree-daisy, see *Montanoa hibiscifolia*

Michelia 250

Michelia ×*alba* 250

Michelia champaca 250

Mickey Mouse plant, see *Ochna*

mignonette tree, see *Lawsonia inermis*

milk-barrel, see *Euphorbia heptagona*

milkweed, Mexican, see *Asclepias curassavica*

milkweed, swan, see *Asclepias physocarpa*

milk-wood, see *Alstonia scholaris*

milkwort, see *Polygala*

milky-way tree, see *Stemmadenia litoralis*

Millettia 221

Millettia pinnata 221

Miltonia 302

Miltoniopsis, see *Miltonia*

Mimosa 214

Mimosa martin-delcampoi 214

Mimosa tortuosa, see *Acacia tortuosa*

mimosa, see *Albizia julibrissin*

mimosa, golden, see *Acacia baileyana*

Mimusops 344

Mimusops balata 344

Ming tree, see *Bucida spinosa*

miracle-fruit, see *Synsepalum dulcificum*

mirasol, see *Tithonia*

mirto, see *Murraya*; Myrtaceae

mock orange, see *Murraya paniculata*, *Pittosporum tobira*

mohintli, see *Justicia spicigera*

molave, see *Vitex parviflora*

Molineria 234

Molineria capitulata 235

Molineria recurvata, see *M. capitulata*

mombin, purple, see *Spondias purpurea*

Momordica 183

Momordica charantia 183

mon reve rose, see *Samyda dodecandra*

mondo grass, see *Ophiopogon*

monkey-bread tree, see *Adansonia digitata*

monkey-brush, see *Combretum rotundifolium*

monkey-plant, see *Ruellia makoyana*

monkey-pot, see Lecythidaceae

monkey-tree, see *Erythrina humeana*

Monochaetum guatemalensis, see *Heterocentron elegans*

Monocostus 371

Monocostus ulei, see *M. uniflorus*

Monocostus uniflorus 371

Monstera 84

Monstera adansonii 84

Monstera deliciosa 84

Monstera pertusa, see *M. adansonii*

Monstera tuberculatum 84

Montanoa 129

Montanoa grandiflora 129

Montanoa guatemalensis 129

Montanoa hibiscifolia 129

montbretia, see *Crocosmia*

Moraceae 276

Moraea bicolor, see *Dietes bicolor*

Moraea vegeta, see *Dietes iridioides*

morera negra, see *Morus nigra*

Moreton Bay tulipwood, see *Harpullia pendula*

Moringa 279

Moringa oleifera 279

Moringaceae 279

morning-glory, dwarf, see *Evolvulus glomeratus*

morning-glory, ocean-blue, see *Ipomoea indica*

morning-glory, star, see *Ipomoea quamoclit*

morning-glory, tree, see *Ipomoea pauciflora*

morning-glory, woolly, see *Argyreia nervosa*

morning-noon-and-night, see *Brunfelsia*

morro, see *Crescentia alata*

Morus 278

Morus nigra 278

mosaic-fig, see *Ficus aspera* 'Parcell'

mosaic-plant, see *Fittonia verschaffeltii*

Moses-in-the-bulrushes, see *Tradescantia spathacea*

moss-rose, see *Portulaca*

mother-of-thousands, see *Kalanchoe delagoensis*

moth-orchid, see *Phalaenopsis*; ×*Doritaenopsis*

Moullava 205

Moullava spicata 205

mountain-pear, see *Berrya cubensis*

mountain-rose, see *Brownea ariza*

mountain thistle, see *Acanthus montanus*

Mucuna 221

Mucuna bennetti 221

mucuna vine, see *Mucuna bennetti*

Muehlenbeckia 318

Muehlenbeckia platyclada 318

muelle, see *Schinus molle*

mulberry, black, see *Morus nigra*

Muntingia 279

Muntingia calabura 279

Muntingiaceae 279

Munzerabad creeper, see *Thunbergia mysorensis*

murici, see *Byrsonima lucida*

Murraya 340

Murraya exotica, see *M. paniculata*

Murraya koenigii 340

Murraya paniculata 340

Musa 280

Musa acuminata 280

Musa balbisiana 280

Musa cavendishii, see *M. acuminata*

Musa coccinea, see *M. uranoscopus*

Musa 'Koae' 280

Musa lasiocarpa 280

Musa nana, see *M. acuminata*

Musa ornata 280

Musa uranoscopus 281

Musa velutina 281

Musaceae 279

Musella lasiocarpa, see *Musa lasiocarpa*

musk-mallow, see *Abelmoschus moschatus*

Mussaenda 239

Mussaenda coccinea, see *Warszewiczia coccinea*

Mussaenda erythrophylla 329

Mussaenda flava 329

Mussaenda frondosa 329

Mussaenda hybrids 330

Mussaenda philippica 'Doña Aurorae' 330

mussaenda, American, see *Pogonopus speciosus*

Myrcianthes 288

Myrcianthes fragrans 288

Myrcianthes fragrans var. *simpsonii*, see *M. fragrans*

Myrciaria 289

Myrciaria cauliflora 289

Myrciaria vexator 289

Myrsinaceae 281

Myrtaceae 282

myrtle, crape, see *Lagerstroemia indica*

myrtle, giant crape, see *Lagerstroemia macrocarpa*

myrtle, queen's crape, see *Lagerstroemia speciosa*

myrtle, western tea, see *Melaleuca nesophila*

myrtle-of-the-river, see *Calyptranthes zuzygium*

Myrtus dombeyi, see *Eugenia brasiliensis*

Myrtus zuzygium, see *Calyptranthes zuzygium*

na, see *Mesua ferrea*

naked ladies, see *Amaryllis belladonna*

nance, see *Byrsonima crassifolia*

Nandina 134

Nandina domestica 134

Napoleon's cocked hat, see *Bauhinia monandra*

naranjilla, see *Solanum quito-ense*

narrow leafed bottle-tree, see *Brachychiton rupestris*

naru, see *Aesculus indica*

nasturtium-bauhinia, see *Bauhinia galpinii*

Natal plum, see *Carissa macrocarpa*

Nauclea 330

Nauclea cordata, see *N. orientalis*

Nauclea orientalis 330

Navia 159

Navia arida 159

necklace-pod, see *Sophora tomentosa*

needle-flower, see *Posoqueria latifolia*

Nelumbium speciosum, see *Nelumbo nucifera*

Nelumbo 291

Nelumbo nucifera 291

Nelumbonaceae 291

Neodypsis, see *Dypsis*

Neomarica 236

Neomarica caerulea 236

Neophloga, see *Dypsis* 104

Neoregelia 159

Neoregelia carolinae 159

Neoregelia concentrica 159

Neoregelia cruenta 160

Neoregelia hybrids 160

Nerium 66

Nerium divaricatum, see *Tabernaemontana divaricata*

Nerium indicum, see *N. oleander*

Nerium odoratum, see *N. oleander*

Nerium oleander 66

nerve-plant, see *Fittonia verschaffeltii*

net-bush, golden, see *Pseuderanthemum carruthersii*

New Zealand Christmas tree, see *Metrosideros excelsa*

New Zealand tea-tree, see *Leptospermum scoparium*

Newbouldia 140

Newbouldia laevis 140

Nicodemia madagascariensis, see *B. madagascariensis*

Nicolaia elatior, see *Etlingera elatior*

Nidularium

Nidularium innocentii

night-blooming cereus, see *Hylocereus undatus*

nightshade, mullein, see

Solanum erianthum

night-shade, Paraguayan, see *Lycianthes rantonnei*

nightshade, Wendland's, see *Solanum wendlandii*

Nile cabbage, see *Pistia stratiotes*

Nile trumpet, see *Markhamia lutea*

níspero, see *Manilkara zapota*

Nolina guatemalensis, see *Beaucarnia guatemalensis*

Nolina recurvata, see *Beaucarnia recurvata*

Nolinaceae, see Ruscaceae

no-me-toques, see *Impatiens*

nopal, see *Opuntia*

nopal cegador, see *Opuntia microdasys*

nun's orchid, see *Phaius tankervilliae*

Nyctaginaceae 291

Nymphaea 293

Nymphaea capensis 294

Nymphaea hybrids 294

Nymphaea nelumbo, see *Nelumbo nucifera*

Nymphaea zanzibariensis, see *N. capensis*

Nymphaeaceae 293

Nymphoides 276

Nymphoides cordata 276

Nymphoides cristata 276

Nymphoides indica 276

Nymphoides peltata 276

oak, Brazilian, see *Posoqueria latifolia*

oak, satin, see *Alloxylon pinnatum*

oak-leafed bear's breeches, see *Acanthus mollis*

Ochna 295

Ochna atropurpurea, see *O. serrulata*

Ochna kirkii 295

Ochna mossambicensis 295

Ochna multiflora, see *O. serrulata*

Ochna serratifolia, see *O. serrulata*

Ochna serrulata 295

Ochnaceae 295

Ochroma 263

Ochroma bicolor, see *O. pyramidale*

Ochroma lagopus, see *O. pyramidale*

Ochroma pyramidale 264

Ochrosia 66

Ochrosia elliptica 66

Ochrosia parviflora, see *O. elliptic*

octopus-tree, see *Schefflera actinophylla*

Odontadenia 67

Odontadenia grandiflora, see *O. macrantha*

Odontadenia macrantha 67

Odontadenia speciosa, see *O. macrantha*

Odontonema 34

Odontonema callistachyum 35

Odontonema cuspidatum 35

Odontonema geminatum, see *O. callistachyum*

Odontonema strictum 35

Odontonema tubaeforme, see *O. strictum*

Oenothera 298

Oenothera 'Childsii', see *O. speciosa*

Oenothera speciosa 298

'ohai-'ula, see *Delonix regia*

oil-palm, African, see *Elaeis guineensis*

oil-palm, American, see *Attalea cohune*

okra, see *Abelmoschus esculentus*

old maid, see *Catharanthus roseus*

old man palm, see *Coccothrinax crinita*

Oleaceae 296

oleander, see *Nerium oleander*

oleander, climbing, see *Strophanthus gratus*

oleander, yellow, see *Nerium*; *Thevetia peruviana*

Onagraceae 297

Oncidium 302

Oncidium sphacelatum 302

Oncidium, see also *Psychopsis*

Oncoba 224

Oncoba spinosa 224

Ophiopogon 337

Opuntia 165

Opuntia engelmannii var. *lindheimeri* 166

Opuntia herfeldtii, see *Opuntia rufida*

Opuntia lindheimeri, see *O. engelmannii*

Opuntia linguiformis, see *O. engelmannii*

Opuntia lubrica, see *O. rufida*

Opuntia macrocalyx, see *O. microdasys*

Opuntia microdasys 166

Opuntia moniliformis, see *Consolea moniliformis*

Opuntia rufida 166

Opuntia spinosissima, see *Consolea corallicola*

orange-ball tree, see *Buddleja ×weyeriana*

orange-eye, see *Buddleja davidii*

Orania nicobarica, see *Bentinckia nicobarica*

Orbea 74

Orbea variegata 74

Orbignya, see *Attalea*

Orchidaceae 298

orchid-cactus, see Cactus intergeneric hybrids; *Epiphyllum*

orchid-tree, see *Bauhinia*

Oreocallis pinnatum, see *Alloxylon pinnatum*

orpine, see *Sedum*

Orthophytum 160

Orthophytum gurkenii 160

Orthosiphon 237

Orthosiphon aristatus 237

Orthosiphon stamineus, see *O. aristatus*

ortiguilla, see *Dalechampia aristolochiifolia*

Oscularia caulescens, see *Lampranthus deltoids*

Oscularia deltoides, see *Lampranthus deltoids*

Osmoxylon 88

Osmoxylon lineare 88

Osteomeles 324

Osteomeles anthyllidifolia 324

Otacanthus 315

Otacanthus caeruleus 315

otaheite gooseberry, see *Phyllanthus acidus*

Ouratea 295

Ouratea tuerckheimii 295

Oxalidaceae 306

Oxalis 306

Oxalis deppei, see *O. tetraphylla*

Oxalis tetraphylla 306

Oxera 242

Oxera pulchella 242

oxeye daisy, see *Sphagneticola trilobata*

oyster-plant, see *Tradescantia spathacea*

Pachira 264

Pachira aquatica 264

Pachira macrocarpa, see *P. aquatica*

Pachira quinata 264

pachote, see *Pachira quinata*

Pachypodium 67

Pachypodium baronii 67

Pachypodium cactipes, see *P. rosulatum*

Pachypodium lamerei 67

Pachypodium lealii 67

Pachypodium rosulatum 68

Pachypodium rutenbergianum 68

Pachypodium saundersii, see *P. lealii*

Pachystachys 35

Pachystachys coccinea 35

Pachystachys lutea 35

pagoda-flower, see *Clerodendrum paniculatum*

pahutukawa, see *Metrosideros excelsa*

paina de seda, see *Ceiba chodatii*

paineira, see *Ceiba chodatii*

paintbrush, see *Crassula perfoliata*

paintbrush, red, see *Scadoxus puniceus*

paintbrush, royal, see *Scadoxus puniceus*

paintbrush, white, see *Haemanthus albiflos*

painted fingernails, see *Neoregelia cruenta*

painted nettle, see *Plectranthus scutellarioides*

palanco, see *Quararibea funebris*

palas, see *Butea monosperma*

pale stopper, see *Myrcianthes fragrans*

Palicourea viridis, see *Psychotria viridis*

palma Africana, see *Elaeis guineensis*

palma Christi, see *Ricinus communis*

palma culona, see *Beaucarnia*

palma datilera, see *Phoenix dactylifera*

palma de cinta, see *Pandanus*

palma de viajero, see *Ravenala madagascariensis*

palma real, see *Roystonea regia*

Palmae, see Arecaceae

Palmer's abutilon, see *Abutilon palmeri*

palmetto, saw, see *Serenoa repens*

palm-grass, see *Molineria capitulata*

palmier royal, see *Roystonea regia*

palmillo, see *Dracaena fragrans*

palm-lily, see *Cordyline fruticosa*

palmyra palm, see *Borassus flabellifer*

palo borracho, see *Ceiba chodatii*

palo de cruz, see *Brownea ariza*

palo de nigua, see *Cornutia obovata*

palo de orquídeas, see *Bauhinia*

palo de Ramón, see *Banara vanderbiltii*

palo de velas, see *Parmentiera cereifera*

palo garinga, see *Moringa oleifera*

palo hormiga, see *Triplaris cumingiana*

palo santo, see *Guaiacum*

palo verde, see *Parkinsonia aculeata*

Pamburus 340

Pamburus missionis 340

Panama hat plant, see *Carludovica drudei*

Panama hat plant, dwarf, see *Dicranopygium atrovirens*

Panama rose, see *Rondeletia*

Pancratium amboinense, see *Proiphys amboinensis*

Pancratium caribaeum, see *Hymenocallis caribaea*

pandan, see *Pandanus*

Pandanaceae 306

pandano, see *Pandanus*

Pandanus 307

Pandanus odoratissimus, see *P. tectorius*

Pandanus tectorius 307

Pandanus tectorius var. *sinensis* 307

Pandanus utilis 307

Pandanus veitchii 307

pandanus, flowering, see *Freycinetia cumingiana*

Pandorea 140

Pandorea jasminoides 140

Pandorea ricasoliana, see *Podranea ricasoliana*

pangar, see *Aesculus indica*

Papaveraceae 308

papelillo, see *Bougainvillea*

paper-bark, see *Melaleuca quinquenervia*

paper-bark, flax-leafed, see *Melaleuca linariifolia*

Paphiopedilum 302

paradise-flower, see *Solanum wendlandii*

paradise-poinciana, see *Caesalpinia gilliesii*

paraíso, see *Melia azedarach*

parakeet heliconia, see *Heliconia psittacorum*

parasol flower, see *Holmskioldia sanguinea*

parchita de culebra, see *Passiflora foetida*

Parkinsonia 205

Parkinsonia aculeata 205

parlor-ivy, see *Senecio tamoides*

Parmentiera 140

Parmentiera aculeata 141

Parmentiera alata, see *Crescentia alata*

Parmentiera cereifera 141

Parmentiera edulis, see *P. aculeata*

parrot-flower, see *Heliconia* 'Golden Torch'; *H. psittacorum*

Parsonsia llavea, see *Cuphea llavea*

partridge-wood, *Caesalpinia punctata*

Pascuita, see *Euphorbia leucocephala*

Passiflora 309

Passiflora alata 'Ruby Glow', see *P. phoenicea*

Passiflora 'Amethyst' 309

Passiflora amethystina 309

Passiflora ×*belotii* 309

Passiflora coccinea 310

Passiflora edulis 310

Passiflora foetida 310

Passiflora fulgens, see *P. coccinea*

Passiflora 'Incense' 310

Passiflora 'Lavender Lady', see *P.* 'Amethyst'

Passiflora macrocarpa, see *P. quadrangularis*

Passiflora pallidiflora, see *P. edulis*

Passiflora phoenicea 310

Passiflora punicea, see *P. vitifolia*

Passiflora quadrangularis 310

Passiflora sanguinea, see *P. vitifolia*

Passiflora tetragona, see *P. quadrangularis*

Passiflora toxicaria, see *P. coccinea*

Passiflora velutina, see *P. coccinea*

Passiflora violacea 309

Passiflora vitifolia 311

Passiflora xiikzodz 311

Passifloraceae 309

passion-flower, see *Passiflora*

passion-fruit vine, see *Passiflora edulis*

pata de chivo, see *Bauhinia divaricata*

pata de elefante, see *Beaucarnia*

pata de vaca, see *Bauhinia*

pataste, see *Quararibea funebris*

patol, see *Erythrina herbacea*

pau Brasil, see *Caesalpinia echinata*

pau d'arco, see *Tabebuia impetiginosa*

pau formiga, see *Triplaris cumingiana*

pau santo, see *Guaiacum sanctum*

Paulownia 311

Paulownia kawakamii 311

Paulownia thyrsoidea, see *P. kawakamii*

Paulownia tomentosa 311

Paulownia viscosa, see *P. kawakamii*

Paulowniaceae 311

Paurotis wrightii, see *Acoelorrhaphe wrightii*

paurotis-palm, see *Acoelorrhaphe wrightii*

Pavia indica, see *Aesculus indica*

pavilla, see *Cornutia grandifolia*

Pavonia 259

Pavonia bahamensis 259

Pavonia ×*gledhillii* 259

Pavonia multiflora 259

Pavonia strictiflora 259

pea, black coral, see *Kennedia nigricans*

pea, blue butterfly, see *Clitoria ternatea*

pea, Brazilian glory, see *Sesbania punicea*

pea, cattail, see *Uraria crinita*

pea, pigeon, see *Cajanus cajan*

pea, red butterfly, see *Periandra coccinea*

peace-lily, see *Spathiphyllum*

peach-wood, see *Caesalpinia echinata*

peacock-flower, see *Caesalpinia pulcherrima*

peanut-butter plant, see *Bunchosia armeniaca*

Pedaliaceae 312

peepul, see *Ficus religiosa*

Pelargonium 226

Pelargonium cucullatum 226
Pelargonium ×domesticum 226
Pelargonium peltatum 227
pelican-flower, see *Aristolochia ringens*
Peltophorum 205
Peltophorum africanum 205
Peltophorum brasiliensis, see *Caesalpinia violacea*
Peltophorum dubium 206
Peltophorum ferrugineum, see *P. pterocarpum*
Peltophorum inerme, see *P. pterocarpum*
Peltophorum pterocarpum 206
Peltophorum vogelianum, see *P. dubium*
pencil-tree, see *Euphorbia leucodendron*
Pentalinon 68
Pentalinon luteum 68
Pentas 330
Pentas lanceolata 330
Pepinia 160
Pepinia sanguinea 160
pepper, black, see *Piper nigrum*
pepper, Brazilian, see *Schinus terebinthifolius*
pepper, California, see *Schinus molle*
pepper, ear-leafed, see *Piper auritum*
pepper-berry, see *Schinus terebinthifolius*
peppermint willow, see *Agonis flexuosa*
pepper-tree, see *Schinus molle*
pera de agua, see *Syzygium*
peregrina, see *Jatropha integerrima*
Pereskia 166
Pereskia aculeata 166
Pereskia bleo 167
Pereskia corrugata, see *P. bleo*
Pereskia grandifolia 167
perfume-tree, see *Posoqueria latifolia*
Periandra 221
Periandra coccinea 222
Pericallis 129
Pericallis ×hybrida 129
Pericallis webbii 129
periquitos, see *Heliconia psittacorum*
periwinkle, Madagascar, see *Catharanthus roseus*
Pernambuco wood, see *Caesalpinia echinata*
Persea 243
Persea americana 243

Persea gratissima, see *P. americana*
Persian acacia, see *Albizia julibrissin*
Persian shield, see *Strobilanthes dyerianus*
Peruvian lily, see *Alstroemeria psittacina*
Peruvian mastic, see *Schinus molle*
Peschiera arborea, see *Tabernaemontana arborea*
Peschiera australis, see *Tabernaemontana australis*
Petrea 359
Petrea arborea 359
Petrea volubilis 359
petticoat palm, see *Copernicia macroglossa*; *Washingtonia filifera*
Phaedranthus buccinatorius, see *Distictis buccinatoria*
Phaeomeria magnifica, see *Etlingera elatior*
Phaius 303
Phaius tankervilliae 303
Phalaenopsis 303
Phalaenopsis violacea 303
Phaleria 357
Phaleria macrocarpa, see *Drimyspermum macrocarpum*
Phaleria perrottetiana 357
Phaseolus bertonii, see *Vigna caracalla*
Phenera variegata, see *Bauhinia variegata*
Philippine violet, see *Barleria cristata*
Philodendron 84
Philodendron 'Autumn' 85
Philodendron bipinnatifidum 85
Philodendron ×evansii 85
Philodendron glaucophyllum, see *P. hastatum*
Philodendron goeldii 85
Philodendron hastatum 85
Philodendron hybrid 85
Philodendron lundii, see *P. bipinnatifidum*
Philodendron selloum, see *P. bipinnatifidum*
Philodendron speciosum 85
Philodendron williamsii, see *P.* hybrid
Phloga, see *Dypsis*
Phlomis nepetifolia, see *Leonotis nepetifolia*
Phoenix 109
Phoenix canariensis 110
Phoenix dactylifera 110

Phoenix reclinata 110
Phoenix roebelinii 110
Phyllanthus 194
Phyllanthus acidus 195
Phyllanthus distichus, see *P. acidus*
Phyllanthus nivosus, see *Breynia disticha*
Phymaspermum 129
Phymaspermum acerosa 129
physic-nut, see *Jatropha multifida*
Phytolacca 312
Phytolacca arborea, see *P. dioica*
Phytolacca dioica 312
Phytolacca populifolia, see *P. dioica*
Phytolaccaceae 312
pica-pica, see *Acacia tortuosa*
pickerel-weed, see *Pontederia cordata*
pigtail-anthurium, see *Anthurium ×hortulanum*
Pimenta 289
Pimenta dioica 289
Pimenta officinalis, see *P. dioica*
Pimenta racemosa 289
pimienta, see *Piper nigrum*
pimienta dulce, see *Pimenta dioica*
pimiento falso, see *Schinus molle*
pinang, see *Areca catechu*
pincushion-flower, see *Leucospermum*
pindo palm, see *Butia capitata*
pine, Australian, see *Casuarina*
pineapple, see *Ananas comosus*
pineapple, miniature, see *Ananas nanus*
pineapple, variegated, see *Ananas bracteatus*
pineapple-guava, see *Acca sellowiana*
pineapple-lily, see *Eucomis bicolor*
pink ball, see *Dombeya wallichii*
pink panther, see *Heliconia mutisiana*
pink siris, see *Albizia julibrissin*
pinwheel jessamine, see *Tabernaemontana australis*
piña, see *Ananas*
Piper 313
Piper auritum 313
Piper nigrum 313
Piperaceae 312
Pirigara superba, see *Gustavia superba*
pisnay, see *Erythrina falcata*

Pistia 85
Pistia stratiotes 86
pita, see *Agave americana*
pitanga, see *Eugenia uniflora*
pitaya, see *Hylocereus undatus*
Pitcairnia 161
Pitcairnia grafii 161
Pitcairnia sanguinea, see *Pepinia sanguinea*
pitch-apple, see *Clusia rosea*
Pithecellobium flexicaule, see *Ebenopsis ebano*
pito, see *Erythrina folkersii*
pitomba, see *Eugenia luschnathiana*
Pittosporaceae 313
Pittosporum 314
Pittosporum flavum, see *Hymenosporum flavum*
Pittosporum tobira 314
Plantaginaceae 314
plantain, see *Heliconia*; *Musa*
plantanillo, see *Heliconia*; *Calathea*
Platyaechmea distichantha, see *Aechmea distichantha*
Platyaechmea zebrina, see *Aechmea zebrina*
Plectranthus 237
Plectranthus ecklonii 238
Plectranthus scutellarioides 238
Pleomele fragrans, see *Dracaena fragrans*
Pleroma splendens, see *Tibouchina urvilleana*
plum, Natal, see *Carissa macrocarpa*
plum, Spanish, see *Spondias purpurea*
Plumbaginaceae 315
Plumbago 316
Plumbago auriculata 316
Plumbago capensis, see *P. auriculata*
Plumbago indica 316
Plumbago rosea, see *P. indica*
plume, giant, see *Curcuma elata*
Plumeria 68
Plumeria alba 69
Plumeria bahamensis, see *P. obtusa*
Plumeria hybrids 69
Plumeria inaguensis, see *P. obtusa*
Plumeria obtusa 69
Plumeria pudica 69
Plumeria rubra 69
Plumeria stenopetala 69
pochote, see *Ceiba schottii* 263

Podachaenium 130
Podachaenium eminens 130
Podranea 141
Podranea brycei, see *P. ricasoliana*
Podranea ricasoliana 141
Pogonopus 330
Pogonopus speciosus 331
Poinciana gilliesii, see *Caesalpinia gilliesii*
Poinciana horrida, see *Caesalpinia cacalaco*
poinciana, dwarf, see *Caesalpinia pulcherrima*
poinciana, royal, see *Delonix regia*
poinciana, yellow, see *Peltophorum*
Poinsettia pulcherrima, see *Euphorbia pulcherrima*
poinsettia, see *Euphorbia pulcherrima*
poinsettia, Bahamas, see *Euphorbia gymnonota*
poinsettia, wild, see *Warszewiczia coccinea*
poison-bulb, see *Crinum asiaticum*
Poitea 222
Poitea carinalis 222
pokosola, see *Ochrosia elliptica*
politician's flower, see *Turnera subulata*
polka-dot plant, see *Hypoestes phyllostachya*
Polyalthia 61
Polyalthia longifolia 61
Polygala 316
Polygala apopetala 317
Polygala ×*dalmasiana* 317
Polygalaceae 316
Polygonaceae 317
Polygonum uvifera, see *Coccoloba uvifera*
pomegranate, see *Punica granatum*
pomegranate, wild, see *Burchellia bubalina*
pomerac, see *Syzygium malaccense*
pompom bauhinia, see *Bauhinia divaricata* 'Rosea'
pompom tree, see *Dais cotinifolia*
Pondoland hibiscus, see *Hibiscus calyphyllus*
pongam, see *Millettia pinnata*
Pongamia pinnata, see *Millettia pinnata*
Pontederia 319
Pontederia cordata 319

Pontederia lanceolata, see *P. cordata*
Pontederiaceae 319
ponytail tree, see *Beaucarnia*
poppy, see Papaveraceae
Porana paniculata, see *Poranopsis paniculata*
Poranopsis 179
Poranopsis paniculata 179
porcelain-flower, see *Etlingera elatior*
Port St. John's creeper, see *Podranea ricasoliana*
Portea 161
Portea petropolitana 161
Portea-tree, see *Thespesia populnea*
porterweed, blue, see *Stachytarpheta jamaicensis*
Portlandia 331
Portlandia coccinea 331
Portlandia coriacea, see *P. coccinea*
Portlandia domingensis 331
Portlandia grandiflora 331
Portulaca 319
Portulaca oleracea 320
Portulacaceae 319
Posoqueria 332
Posoqueria latifolia 332
potato, air, see *Dioscorea bulbifera*
potato, talingo, see *Amorphophallus paeoniifolius*
potato, wild, see *Ipomoea microdactyla*
potato-bush, blue, see *Lycianthes rantonnei*
potato-tree, see *Solanum erianthum*
potato-tree, Brazilian, see *Solanum wrightii*
potato-vine, giant, see *Solanum wendlandii*
potato-vine, purple, see *Solanum seaforthianum*
Pothoidium 86
Pothoidium lobbianum 86
Pothos aureus, see *Epipremnum aureum*
pothos, see *Epipremnum*
Pothuava mariae-reginae, see *Aechmea mariae-reginae*
Pothuava nudicaulis, see *Aechmea nudicaulis*
Pothuava pineliana var. *minuta*, see *Aechmea pineliana*
poui, see *Tabebuia*
Pouteria 344
Pouteria campechiana 344

Pouteria sapota 344
powder-puff, see *Calliandra*
powder-puff, glossy, see *Syzygium wilsonii*
prayer-plant, see *Maranta leuconeura*
Prestonia 69
Prestonia glabrata, see *P. mollis*
Prestonia mollis 69
prickly pear, bunny-ear, see *Opuntia microdasys*
prickly pear, cow-tongue, see *Opuntia engelmannii*
prickly poppy, see *Argemone*
pride-of-Barbados, see *Caesalpinia pulcherrima*
pride-of-Bolivia, see *Tipuana tipu*
pride-of-Burma, see *Amherstia nobilis*
pride-of-India, see *Melia azedarach*
pride-of-Madeira, see *Echium candicans*
pride-of-the-Kaap, see *Bauhinia galpinii*
primrose, evening, see *Oenothera*
primrose-willow, see *Ludwigia peruviana*
prince's vine, see *Ipomoea horsfalliae*
princess-flower, see *Tibouchina*
princess-palm, see *Dictyosperma album*
Pritchardia 112
Pritchardia aylmer-robinsonii 112
privet, Japanese, see *Ligustrum japonicum*
privet, West Indian, see *Clerodendrum aculeatum*
privet, wild, see *Senna ligustrina*
Proiphys 57
Proiphys amboinensis 57
propeller-plant, *Crassula perfoliata*
Protea 323
Protea cynaroides 323
Protea eximia 323
Protea latifolia, see *P. eximia*
protea, giant, see *Protea cynaroides*
Proteaceae 320
provision-tree, see *Moringa*; *Pachira*
Pseuderanthemum 35
Pseuderanthemum carruthersii 36
Pseuderanthemum pulchellum,

see *Eranthemum pulchellum*
Pseuderanthemum sinuatum 36
Pseudobombax 265
Pseudobombax ellipticum 265
Pseudobombax grandiflorum 265
Pseudogynoxys 130
Pseudogynoxys chenopodioides 130
Pseudomussaenda flava, see *Mussaenda flava*
Pseudophoenix 113
Pseudophoenix lediniana 113
Pseudophoenix sargentii 113
Pseudophoenix vinifera 113
Psidium 289
Psidium cattleianum 289
Psidium guajava 289
Psidium littorale, see *P. cattleianum*
Psychopsis 303
Psychotria 332
Psychotria nervosa 332
Psychotria undata, see *P. nervosa*
Psychotria viridis 332
Pterospermum 268
Pterospermum acerifolium 268
Ptychosperma 114
Ptychosperma alexandrae, see *Archontophoenix alexandrae*
Ptychosperma elegans 114
Ptychosperma macarthurii 114
Ptychosperma waitianum 114
pua wood, see *Fagraea*
Puerto Rican hat-palm, see *Sabal causiarum*
pulai, see *Alstonia scholaris*
punga-oil tree, see *Millettia pinnata*
Punica 249
Punica granatum 249
punk-tree, see *Melaleuca quinquenervia*
punty, see *Senna artemisioides*
purple bignonia, see *Saritaea magnifica*
purple queen, see *Tradescantia pallida* 'Purple Heart'
purslane, see *Portulaca*
Pyrostegia 141
Pyrostegia ignea, see *P. venusta*
Pyrostegia venusta 141

Quamoclit pinnata, see *Ipomoea quamoclit*
Quararibea 265
Quararibea funebris 265
quebracho, see *Tabebuia impetiginosa*

queen-lily, see *Eucrosia auranti-aca*

queen-of-flowering-trees, see *Amherstia nobilis*

queen-palm, see *Syagrus romanzoffiana*

queen's wreath, see *Petrea volubilis*

Queensland bottle-tree, see *Brachychiton rupestris*

Queensland lacebark, see *Brachychiton discolor*

queen-spiderwort, see *Dichorisandra thyrsiflora*

Quesnelia 161

Quesnelia arvensis 161

Quesnelia marmorata 161

Quesnelia quesneliana 161

quiche, see *Guzmania lingulata*

quisqual, see *Quisqualis indica*

Quisqualis 175

Quisqualis indica 175

rabo de león, see *Agave stricta*

rainbow bark, see *Eucalyptus deglupta*

rainbow-shower, see *Cassia ×nealiae*

rain-tree, Franciscan, see *Brunfelsia americana*

rain-tree, Jamaican, see *Brya ebenus*

rain-tree, Serpentine Hill, see *Brunfelsia densifolia*

Rangoon creeper, see *Quisqualis indica*

Raphia 114

Raphia farinifera 114

Raphia pedunculata, see *R. farinifera*

Raphia regalis 114

raphia, see *Raphia farinifera*

rata, see *Metrosideros excelsa*

rat-bean, see *Moullava spicata*

rattle-box, see *Crotalaria laburnifolia*

rattlesnake-plant, see *Calathea crotalifera*

Ravenala 354

Ravenala madagascariensis 354

Ravenea 115

Ravenea rivularis 115

Ravenia 340

Ravenia spectabilis 341

ray-flowered protea, see *Protea eximia*

red cloak, see *Megaskepasma erythrochlamys*

red hot cat's tail, see *Acalypha hispida*

reed-orchid, see *Epidendrum ibaguense*, *Sobralia decora*

reed-palm, see *Chamaedorea seifrizii*

regadero, see *Ipomoea quamoclit*

regret-vine, see *Merremia tuberosa*

reina de la noche, see *Hylocereus undatus*

Reinhardtia 115

Reinhardtia latisecta 115

Reinwardtia 245

Reinwardtia indica 245

Reinwardtia trigyna, see *R. indica*

Renanthera 303

retama macho, see *Spartium junceum*

Rhaphidophora pinnata, see *Epipremnum pinnatum*

Rhaphiolepis 324

Rhaphiolepis ×delacourii 324

Rhaphiolepis indica 324

Rhapis 115

Rhapis 'Akatsuki', see *R. excelsa*

Rhapis excelsa 115

Rhodocactus bleo, see *Pereskia bleo*

Rhododendron 186

Rhododendron laetum 186

Rhododendron Vireya Group 186

rhododendron, Singapore, see *Melastoma*

Rhodognaphalon 260

Rhodophiala 58

Rhodophiala bifida 58

Rhoeo discolor, see *Tradescantia spathacea*

Rhynchospermum jasminoides, see *Trachelospermum jasminoides*

ribbon-bush, see *Muehlenbeckia platyclada*

Richardia 332

Richardia grandiflora 332

Ricinus 195

Ricinus africanus, see *R. communis*

Ricinus communis 195

Riedelia 371

Riedelia sp. 371

riqui-riqui, see *Heliconia caribaea*

robin red-breast bush, see *Melaleuca lateritia*

roble blanco, see *Tabebuia rosea*

roble cimarrón, see *Tabebuia haemantha*

rock-rose, see *Cistus*; *Portulaca*

rododendro, see *Rhododendron*

Rollinia 62

Rollinia deliciosa 62

Romneya 309

Romneya coulteri 309

Rondeletia 332

Rondeletia leucophylla 333

Rondeletia odorata 333

Rondeletia speciosa, see *R. odorata*

Rondeletia strigosa 333

rooster-flower, see *Aristolochia ringens*

rosa amarilla, see *Cochlospermum*

rosa de madera, see *Merremia*

rosa de montaña, see *Antigonon*

rosa del sol, see *Aptenia*

Rosaceae 324

rose-apple, see *Syzygium jambos*

rose-bay, see *Nerium oleander*

rose-cactus, see *Pereskia*

rose-dipladenia, see *Mandevilla* hybrids

rose-grape, see *Medinilla myriantha*

rose, Panama, see *Rondeletia*

roselle, see *Hibiscus sabdariffa*

rose-mallow, see *Hibiscus moscheutos*

rose-mallow, Confederate, see *Hibiscus mutabilis*

rose-mallow, scarlet, see *Hibiscus coccineus*

rose-mallow, swamp, see *Hibiscus moscheutos*

rose-of-Venezuela, see *Brownea coccinea*

rose-of-India, see *Lagerstroemia macrocarpa*

rosewood, see *Tipuana tipu*

Roupellia boivinii, see *Strophanthus boivinii*

Roupellia grata, see *Strophanthus gratus*

royal climber, see *Oxera pulchella*

royal palm, see *Roystonea regia*

royal palm, Caribbean, see *Roystonea oleracea*

royal paulownia, see *Paulownia kawakamii*

royal poinciana, see *Delonix regia*

Roystonea 116

Roystonea elata, see *R. regia*

Roystonea oleracea 116

Roystonea regia 117

rubber, Ceará, see *Manihot*

rubber, Pará, see *Hevea*

rubber-vine, see *Cryptostegia*

Rubiaceae 324

Ruellia 36

Ruellia affinis, see *R. speciosa*

Ruellia amoena, see *R. brevifolia*

Ruellia brevifolia 36

Ruellia brittoniana, see *R. tweediana*

Ruellia chartacea 36

Ruellia coerulea, see *R. tweediana*

Ruellia colorata, see *R. chartacea*

Ruellia elegans, see *R. rosea*

Ruellia graecizans, see *R. brevifolia*

Ruellia macrantha 36

Ruellia makoyana 36

Ruellia malacosperma 37–38

Ruellia multisetosa 37

Ruellia pereducta 37

Ruellia rosea 37

Ruellia speciosa 37

Ruellia squarrosa 37

Ruellia tweediana 37

Ruprechtia 318

Ruprechtia coriacea 318

Ruscaceae 333

Ruspolia 38

Ruspolia 'Twilight' 38

Russelia 315

Russelia campechiana, see *R. lilacina*

Russelia equisetiformis 315

Russelia juncea, see *R. equisetiformis*

Russelia lilacina 315

Russelia sarmentosa 315

rusty-shield tree, see *Peltophorum pterocarpum*

Rutaceae 338

Ruttya 38

Ruttya fruticosa 38

×*Ruttyruspolia* 38

×*Ruttyruspolia* 'Phyllis van Heeden' 38

Sabal 117

Sabal bermudana 117

Sabal causiarum 117

Sabal palmetto 117

sabal palm, see *Sabal palmetto*

sabicu, see *Lysiloma sabicu*

Sabinea carinalis, see *Poitea carinalis*

sacred lotus, see *Nelumbo nucifera*

sage, Mexican bush, see *Salvia leucantha*

sage, purple, see *Lantana montevidensis*

sage, red and yellow, see *Lantana camara*

sage, Texas, see *Leucophyllum frutescens*

sage, wild, see *Gmelina philippensis*

Sagittaria 50

Sagittaria lancifolia 51

Sagittaria montevidensis 51

Sagus farinifera, see *Raphia farinifera*

Sagus ruffia, see *Raphia farinifera*

Salicaceae 224

Salmalia malabarica, see *Bombax ceiba*

salmwood, see *Cordia alliodora*

salt-marsh mallow, see *Kosteletzkya virginica*

Salvia 238

Salvia leucantha 238

Salvia 'Red Fountain', see *Scutellaria costaricana*

Sambucus 41

Sambucus canadensis 41

Samyda 225

Samyda decandra, see *S. dodecandra*

Samyda dodecandra 225

Samyda rosea, see *S. dodecandra*

Samyda serrulata, see *S. dodecandra*

Samyda velutina 225

Sanchezia 38

Sanchezia glaucophylla, see *S. parvibracteata*

Sanchezia nobilis, see *S. parvibracteata*

Sanchezia parvibracteata 38

Sanchezia speciosa 39

Sanchezia spectabilis, see *S. speciosa*

sandalwood, red, see *Adenanthera pavonina*

sandía de la passión, see *Passiflora quadrangularis*

sandpaper-leaf, see *Petrea*; *Cordia*

sangre de toro, see *Ruprechtia coriacea*

Sansevieria 337

Sansevieria cylindrica 337

Sansevieria guineensis, see *S. hyacinthoides*

Sansevieria hyacinthoides 338

Sansevieria kirkii 338

Sansevieria metallica 338

Sansevieria thyrsiflora, see *S. hyacinthoides*

Sansevieria trifasciata 338

Santa Rita, see *Ixora*

Sapindaceae 341

sapodilla, see *Manilkara zapota*

Sapota zapotilla, see *Manilkara zapota*

Sapotaceae 343

sapote 343

sapote, black, see *Diospyros digyna*

sapote, mamey, see *Pouteria sapota*

sapote amarillo, see *Pouteria campechiana*

Saraca 206

Saraca indica 206

Sargent's cherry palm, see *Pseudophoenix sargentii*

Saritaea 142

Saritaea magnifica 142

satin-oak, see *Alloxylon pinnatum*

sauco, see *Sambucus canadensis*

sausage-tree, see *Kigelia africana*

sávila, see *Aloe vera*

Scadoxus 58

Scadoxus multiflorus subsp. *katherinae* 58

Scadoxus puniceus 58

Scaevola 228

Scaevola aemula 228

Scaevola humilis, see *S. aemula*

Scaevola sericea, see *S. taccada*

Scaevola taccada 228

scarlet comb, see *Combretum coccineum*

scarlet ipomoea, see *Ipomoea hederifolia*

Schaueria 39

Schaueria calicotricha, see *S. flavicoma*

Schaueria flavicoma 39

Scheelea, see *Attalea*

Schefflera 88

Schefflera actinophylla 89

Schefflera arboricola 89

Schefflera elegantissima 89

Schinus 59

Schinus molle 59

Schinus terebinthifolius 60

Schippia 118

Schippia concolor 118

Schizocasia portei, see *Alocasia portei*

Schlegelia 345

Schlegelia parasitica 345

Schlegeliaceae 345

Schlumbergera 167

Schlumbergera hybrids 167

scholar-tree, see *Alstonia scholaris*

Schotia 207

Schotia brachypetala 207

Schotia latifolia, see *S. brachypetala*

Schotia semireducta, see *S. brachypetala*

schwarzkopf, see *Aeonium arboreum*

Scindapsus aureus, see *Epipremnum aureum*

Scotch attorney, see *Clusia rosea*

scrambled-egg tree, see *Senna surattensis*

screw-nut tree, see *Helicteres guazumifolia*

screw-pine, see *Pandanus*

Scrophulariaceae 345, also see Plantaginaceae

Scutellaria 238

Scutellaria argentata, see *S. costaricana*

Scutellaria costaricana 238

sea-grape, see *Coccoloba uvifera*

sea-lavender, see *Limonium perezii*

sea statice, see *Limonium perezii*

sealing-wax palm, see *Cyrtostachys renda*

sea-rosemary, see *Limonium perezii*

seashore-palm, see *Allagoptera arenaria*

seaside-mahoe, see *Thespesia populnea*

Securidaca 317

Securidaca diversifolia 317

sedas, see *Sedum*

Sedum 182

Sedum guatemalensis, see *S. rubrotinctum*

Sedum rubrotinctum 182

Seemania sylvatica, see *Gloxinia sylvatica*

selloum, see *Philodendron bipinnatifidum*

semaphore-cactus, see *Consolea corallicola*

Seminole dombeya, see *Dombeya burgessiae* 'Seminole'

semla, see *Bauhinia semla*

Sempervivum canariense, see *Aeonium canariense*

Sempervivum holochrysum, see *Aeonium holochrysum*

Senecio 130

Senecio candicans, see *S. cineraria*

Senecio cineraria 130

Senecio confusus, see *Pseudogynoxys chenopodioides*

Senecio tamoides 131

Senecio webbii, see *Pericallis webbii*

Senegal date-palm, see *Phoenix reclinata*

Senna 207; see also *Cassia*

Senna alata 207

Senna artemisioides 207

Senna bicapsularis 207

Senna bracteata, see *S. alata*

Senna chapmanii, see *S. mexicana*

Senna coluteoides, see *S. pendula*

Senna corymbosa 207

Senna didymobotrya 208

Senna ligustrina 208

Senna mexicana var. *chapmanii* 208

Senna pendula var. *glabrata* 208

Senna polyphylla 208

Senna racemosa 209

Senna spectabilis 209

Senna sulfurea 209

Senna surattensis 209

Serenoa 118

Serenoa arborescens, see *Acoelorrhaphe wrightii*

Serenoa repens 119

Sesbania 222

Sesbania formosa 222

Sesbania grandiflora 222

Sesbania punicea 222

Sesbania tripettii, see *S. punicea*

seso vegetal, see *Blighia sapida*

Setcreasea pallida, see *Tradescantia pallida*

shaving-brush tree, see *Pseudobombax*

shell-flower, see *Pistia stratiotes*

she-oak, see *Casuarina*

shimbillo, see *Inga*

shin-dagger, see *Agave lechuguilla*

shoe-black flower, see *Hibiscus rosa-sinensis*

shower, golden, see *Cassia fistula*

shower, pink and white, see *Cassia javanica*

shower, rainbow, see *Cassia* ×*nealiae*

shower-of-gold vine, see *Tristellateia australasiae*
shower-of-orchids, see *Congea tomentosa*
shrimp-plant, see *Justicia; Pachystachys*
shrimp-plant, red, see *Ruellia chartacea*
Siam diamond, see *Curcuma harmandii*
Siam tulip, see *Curcuma alismatifolia*
sickle-plant, see *Crassula perfoliata*
Sida 259
Sida eggersii 259
Sideroxylon sapota, see *Pouteria sapota*
siete cueros, see *Tibouchina urvilleana*
silk-cotton tree, see *Ceiba pentandra*
silk-floss tree, see *Ceiba speciosa*
silk-tree, see *Albizia julibrissin*
silky-oak, see *Grevillea robusta*
silky-oak, white, see *Stenocarpus sinuatus*
silver and red foxtail, see *Celosia argentea*
silver bush, see *Sophora tomentosa*
silver jade, see *Crassula arborescens*
silver leaf, see *Leucophyllum frutescens*
silver palm, see *Coccothrinax argentea*
silver palm, Florida, see *Coccothrinax argentata*
silver pimento-palm, see *Schippia concolor*
silver-top, see *Coccothrinax argentata*
silver tree, see *Leucadendron argenteum*
silver trumpet-tree, see *Tabebuia aurea*
silver vase, see *Aechmea fasciata*
simpoh, see *Dillenia indica*
Simpson stopper, see *Myrcianthes fragrans*
Singapore holly, see *Malpighia coccigera*
Sinningia speciosa 227
Siphonochilus 371
Siphonochilus decorus 371
sisal, see *Agave sisalana*
sisal, false, see *Agave decipiens*

skullcap, see *Scutellaria costaricana*
skunk tree, see *Sterculia foetida*
sky-flower, see *Duranta erecta*
sky-vine, see *Thunbergia grandiflora*
smoke-bush, see *Buddleja madagascariensis*
snail-flower, see *Vigna caracalla*
snake-plant, see *Sansevieria hyacinthoides*
snakeweed, see *Stachytarpheta*
snapdragon-tree, see *Gmelina arborea*
snow-bush, see *Breynia disticha, Euphorbia leucocephala*
snow-flower, see *Spathiphyllum floribundum*
snow-in-summer, see *Melaleuca linariifolia*
snow-in-the-jungle, see *Poranopsis paniculata*
snuffbox tree, see *Oncoba spinosa*
Sobralia 304
Sobralia decora 304
Solanaceae 346
Solandra 352
Solandra longiflora 352
Solandra maxima 352
Solanum 352
Solanum erianthum 353
Solanum macranthum, see *S. wrightii*
Solanum quitoense 353
Solanum rantonnetii, see *Lycianthes rantonnei*
Solanum seaforthianum 353
Solanum verbascifolium, see *S. erianthum*
Solanum wendlandii 353
Solanum wrightii 353
Solena latifolia, see *Posoqueria latifolia*
Solenostemon scutellarioides, see *Plectranthus scutellarioides*
solitaire palm, see *Ptychosperma elegans*
Sonerila 274
Sonerila picta 274
Sophora 222
Sophora havanensis, see *S. tomentosa*
Sophora littoralis, see *S. tomentosa*
Sophora occidentalis, see *S. tomentosa*
Sophora tomentosa 222

×*Sophrolaeliocattleya* 304
sorrel, see *Hibiscus sabdariffa*
sorrel, wood, see *Oxalis tetraphylla*
sorrowless tree, see *Saraca indica*
sotol, see *Dasylirion wheeleri*
sour fig, see *Carpobrotus deliciosus*
soursop, see *Annona muricata*
soursop, mountain, see *Annona montana*
Spanish bayonet, see *Yucca aloifolia*
Spanish broom, see *Spartium junceum*
Spanish guava, see *Catesbaea spinosa*
Spanish ladies, see *Ruellia tweediana*
Spanish moss, see *Tillandsia usneoides*
Spanish shawl, see *Heterocentron elegans*
Spartium 222
Spartium junceum 223
Spathicarpa 86
Spathicarpa sagittifolia 86
Spathiphyllum 86
Spathiphyllum floribundum 87
Spathodea 142
Spathodea campanulata 142
Spathodea laevis, see *Newbouldia laevis*
Spathodea longiflora, see *Dolichandrone spathacea*
Spathodea lutea, see *Markhamia lutea*
Spathodea nilotica, see *S. campanulata*
Spathoglottis 304
Sphagneticola 131
Sphagneticola trilobata 131
spider-flower, see *Cleome hassleriana*
spider-flower tree, see *Crateva tapia*
spider-lily, see *Hymenocallis*
spiderwort, see *Tradescantia*
spinach-tree, see *Cnidoscolus chayamansa*
spindle palm, see *Hyophorbe verschaffeltii*
spiral flag, African, see *Costus lucanusianus*
spiral ginger, see *Costus*
spiral ginger, giant, see *Tapeinochilos ananassae*
spiral ginger, yellow, see *Monocostus uniflorus*

split-leaf philodendron, see *Philodendron bipinnatifidum*
Spondias 60
Spondias cirouella, see *S. purpurea*
Spondias mexicana, see *S. purpurea*
Spondias purpurea 60
spray-of-gold, see *Galphimia gracilis*
spurge, see Euphorbiaceae
St. George's lance, see *Sansevieria cylindrica*
St. Thomas tree, see *Bauhinia tomentosa*
St. Vincent's lilac, see *Solanum seaforthianum*
Stachytarpheta 360
Stachytarpheta jamaicensis 360
Stachytarpheta mutabilis 360
Stanhopea 304
Stanhopea tigrina 305
Stapelia 75
Stapelia ambigua, see *S. grandiflora*
Stapelia gigantea 75
Stapelia grandiflora 75
Stapelia leendertziae 75
Stapelia nobilis, see *S. gigantea*
Stapelia variegata, see *Orbea variegata*
Stapelia wilmaniae, see *S. leendertziae*
starfish flower, see *Stapelia; Orbea*
star-flower, see *Grewia occidentalis*
star-fruit, see *Averrhoa carambola*
star-grass, see *Molineria capitulata*
star-nut palm, see *Astrocaryum mexicanum*
Statice perezii, see *Limonium perezii*
Stelago bunius, see *Antidesma bunius*
Stemmadenia 70
Stemmadenia bella, see *S. litoralis*
Stemmadenia litoralis 70
Stenocarpus 323
Stenocarpus sinuatus 324
Stenolobium stans, see *Tecoma stans*
Stephanotis 75
Stephanotis floribunda 75
Sterculia 269
Sterculia ceramica 269
Sterculia foetida 269

Sterculia luzonica, see *S. ceramica*

Sterculia tragacantha 269

Sterculiaceae, see Malvaceae (formerly Sterculiaceae)

Stigmaphyllon 253

Stigmaphyllon ciliatum 253

Stigmaphyllon sagraeanum 253

stinkwood, see *Gustavia superba*

stonecrop, see *Sedum*

strawberry begonia, see *Episcia*

strawberry fire-tails, see *Acalypha reptans*

strawberry-guava, see *Psidium cattleianum*

strawberry snowball, see *Dombeya cacuminum*

strawberry-tree, see *Muntingia calabura*

Strelitzia 355

Strelitzia juncea, see *S. parvifolia*

Strelitzia nicolai 355

Strelitzia parvifolia 355

Strelitzia reginae 355

Strelitziaceae 354

Streptocalyx subnuda, see *Aechmea woronowii*

Streptocarpus 227

Streptocarpus ×*hybridus* 227

Streptocarpus rexii 227

Streptosolen 353

Streptosolen jamesonii 353

Strobilanthes 39

Strobilanthes dyerianus 39

Strongylodon 223

Strongylodon macrobotrys 223

Strophanthus 70

Strophanthus boivinii 70

Strophanthus divaricatus 70

Strophanthus gratus 70

Strophanthus preussii 70

Suessenguthia multisetosa, see *Ruellia multisetosa*

sugar-apple, see *Annona squamosa*

sultana, see *Impatiens*

summer-lilac, see *Buddleja davidii*

summer-torch, see *Billbergia pyramidalis*

sundial, see *Pentalinon luteum*

sundrops, see *Oenothera*

sunflower, see *Tithonia diversifolia*

sun-plant, see *Portulaca*

sun-rose, baby, see *Aptenia cordifolia*

sunshine-tree, *Erythrina variegata*

Surinam cherry, see *Eugenia uniflora*

Swartzia longiflora, see *Solandra longiflora*

sweet mace, see *Tagetes lucida*

sweet potato, see *Ipomoea*

sweet-scented marigold, see *Tagetes lucida*

sweet-shade, see *Hymenosporum flavum*

sweetsop, see *Annona squamosa*

sweet-Willy, see *Ipomoea quamoclit*

Swinglea 341

Swinglea glutinosa 341

Swiss cheese plant, see *Monstera adansonii*; *M. deliciosa*

Syagrus 119

Syagrus coronata 119

Syagrus romanzoffiana 119

Syagrus sancona 120

Syagrus tessmanii, see *S. sancona*

symbol-flower, see *Gardenia taitensis*

Syngonium 87

Syngonium auritum, see *S. neglectum*

Syngonium neglectum 87

Syngonium podophyllum 87

Synsepalum 344

Synsepalum dulcificum 345

Syzygium 290

Syzygium cumini 290

Syzygium jambos 290

Syzygium malaccense 290

Syzygium samarangense 290

Syzygium wilsonii 291

Tabebuia 142

Tabebuia argentea, see *T. aurea*

Tabebuia aurea 143

Tabebuia avellanedae, see *T. impetiginosa*

Tabebuia bahamensis 143

Tabebuia caraiba, see *T. aurea*

Tabebuia 'Carib Queen' 143

Tabebuia chrysantha, see *T. ochracea*

Tabebuia chrysotricha 143

Tabebuia dugandii, see *T. impetiginosa*

Tabebuia eximia, see *T. umbellata*

Tabebuia gaudichaudii, see *Tecoma castanifolia*

Tabebuia guayacan 144

Tabebuia haemantha 144

Tabebuia heptaphylla, see *T. impetiginosa*

Tabebuia heterophylla 144

Tabebuia impetiginosa 144

Tabebuia ipe, see *T. impetiginosa*

Tabebuia lepidota 144

Tabebuia ochracea 144

Tabebuia pallida 144

Tabebuia palmeri, see *T. impetiginosa*

Tabebuia pentaphylla, see *T. heterophylla*

Tabebuia rosea 145

Tabebuia umbellata 145

Tabernaemontana 70

Tabernaemontana arborea 71

Tabernaemontana australis 71

Tabernaemontana coronaria, see *T. divaricata*

Tabernaemontana corymbosa 71

Tabernaemontana divaricata 71

Tabernaemontana holstii, see *T. pachysiphon*

Tabernaemontana litoralis, see *Stemmadenia litoralis*

Tabernaemontana orientalis, see *T. pandacaqui*

Tabernaemontana pachysiphon 71

Tabernaemontana pandacaqui 71

Tabernaemontana schippii, see *T. arborea*

tabog, see *Swinglea glutinosa*

Tacca 355

Tacca chantrieri 355

Tacca integrifolia 355

Tacca leontopetaloides 356

Tacca palmata 356

Tacca palmatafida 356

Tacca pinnatifida, see *T. leontopetaloides*

Taccaceae 355

taffeta-plant, see *Hoffmannia ghiesbreghtii*

Tagetes 131

Tagetes lucida 131

tail-flower, see *Anthurium* ×*hortulanum*

tail-grape, see *Artabotrys hexapetalus*

talingo potato, see *Amorphophallus paeoniifolius*

talipot palm, see *Corypha umbraculifera*

talipote, see *Corypha umbraculifera*

tallow-tree, see *Millettia pinnata*

tamarind, see *Tamarindus indica*

tamarindo, see *Tamarindus indica*

Tamarindus 209

Tamarindus indica 209

Tamarindus occidentalis, see *T. indica*

tambor, see *Ochroma pyramidale*

Tanaeceum parasiticum, see *Schlegelia parasitica*

tania, see *Xanthosoma maffafa*

táparo, see *Crescentia cujete*

Tapeinochilos 372

Tapeinochilos ananassae 372

Tapeinochilos queenslandiae, see *T. ananassae*

tapeworm plant, see *Muehlenbeckia platyclada*

tapioca-plant, see *Manihot esculenta*

taro, see *Colocasia esculenta*

taro, giant, see *Alocasia macrorrhizos*

taro-vine, see *Monstera adansonii*

tassel-flower, see *Calliandra*

tassel-tree, see *Dombeya wallichii*

tassel-tree, white, see *Archidendron lucyi*

tea myrtle, see *Melaleuca nesophila*

teak, see *Gmelina arborea*

teak, bastard, see *Butea monosperma*

tea-tree, see *Leptospermum*

Tecoma 145

Tecoma augustatum, see *T. stans*

Tecoma bahamensis, see *Tabebuia bahamensis*

Tecoma capensis 145

Tecoma castanifolia 146

Tecoma guayacan, see *Tabebuia guayacan*

Tecoma incisa, see *T. stans*

Tecoma jasminoides, see *Pandorea jasminoides*

Tecoma mollis, see *T. stans*

Tecoma ricasoliana, see *Podranea ricasoliana*

Tecoma ×*smithii* 146

Tecoma stans 146

Tecomanthe 146

Tecomanthe dendrophila 146

Tecomanthe venusta, see *T. dendrophila*

Tecomaria capensis, see *Tecoma capensis*

tecomate, see *Crescentia alata*

teddy-bear palm, see *Dypsis leptocheilos*

telcón, see *Berrya cubensis*

temple-tree, see *Crateva religiosa*, *Plumeria*

teresita, see *Montanoa grandiflora*

Tetrazygia 274

Tetrazygia bicolor 274

Texas ebony, see *Ebenopsis ebano*

Texas ranger, see *Leucophyllum frutescens*

Texas umbrella-tree, see *Melia azedarach*

Texas wild olive, see *Cordia boissieri*

thatch-palm, Caribbean, see *Thrinax radiata*

thatch-palm, Florida, see *Thrinax radiata*

Theobroma 269

Theobroma cacao 269

Theophrastaceae 356

Thespesia 259

Thespesia populnea 259

Thevetia 72

Thevetia ahouai 72

Thevetia neriifolia, see *T. peruviana*

Thevetia nitida, see *T. ahouai*

Thevetia peruviana 72

Thevetia thevetioides 72

thevetia, broadleaf, see *Thevetia ahouai*

thevetia, giant, see *Thevetia thevetioides*

thistle, mountain, see *Acanthus montanus*

thorn, false, see *Moullava spicata*

thorn-apple, see *Datura metel*

thorn-tree, see *Acacia*

thorn-tree, Bailey's, see *Acacia baileyana*

thread-palm, see *Washingtonia robusta*

Thrinax 120

Thrinax barbadensis, see *Coccothrinax barbadensis*

Thrinax garberi, see *Coccothrinax argentata*

Thrinax radiata 120

Thryallis gracilis, see *Galphimia gracilis*

Thunbergia 39

Thunbergia alata 39

Thunbergia battiscombei 39

Thunbergia erecta 40

Thunbergia fragrans 40

Thunbergia gibsonii, see *T. gregorii*

Thunbergia grandiflora 40

Thunbergia gregorii 40

Thunbergia kirkii 40

Thunbergia laurifolia 40

Thunbergia mysorensis 41

Thunbergia togoensis 41

Thymelaeaceae 357

ti, see *Cordyline fruticosa*

tiare, see *Gardenia taitensis*

Tibouchina 274

Tibouchina clavata 274

Tibouchina 'Edward ll' 275

Tibouchina elegans, see *T. clavata*

Tibouchina grandifolia, see *T. heteromalla*

Tibouchina granulosa 275

Tibouchina heteromalla 275

Tibouchina hybrid 275

Tibouchina multiflora, see *T. heteromalla*

Tibouchina urvilleana 275

tiger's claw, see *Erythrina variegata*

Tiliaceae, see Malvaceae (formerly Tiliaceae)

Tillandsia 161

Tillandsia capitata 162

Tillandsia cyanea 162

Tillandsia dyeriana 162

Tillandsia filiformis, see *T. usneoides*

Tillandsia funckiana 162

Tillandsia ionantha 162

Tillandsia stricta 162

Tillandsia usneoides 162

tipu, see *Tipuana tipu* 223

Tipuana 223

Tipuana speciosa, see *T. tipu*

Tipuana tipu 223

titan-arum, see *Amorphophallus titanum*

Tithonia 131

Tithonia diversifolia 131

toa, see *Casuarina* 169

Togo thunbergia, see *Thunbergia togoensis*

torch-aloe, see *Aloe arborescens*

torch-tree, see *Ixora pavetta*

tortugo, see *Ravenia spectabilis*

totumo, see *Crescentia cujete*

toupinambour, see *Calathea allouia*

tower-of-jewels, see *Echium wildpretii*

Trachelospermum 72

Trachelospermum asiaticum 72

Trachelospermum grandiflorum, see *Chonemorpha fragrans*

Trachelospermum jasminoides 72

Tradescantia 176

Tradescantia ×*andersoniana*,

see *T.* Andersoniana Group

Tradescantia Andersoniana Group 176

Tradescantia pallida 'Purple Heart' 177

Tradescantia spathacea 177

travelers' tree, see *Ravenala madagascariensis*

tree-daisy, see *Montanoa*

tree-lily, see *Vellozia bahiana*

tree-tobacco, see *Acnistus arborescens*

tree-waratah, see *Alloxylon pinnatum*

tres cueros, see *Tibouchina* hybrid

triangle-palm, see *Dypsis decaryi*

Trichodiadema 50

Trichodiadema bulbosum 50

Trimezia 236

Trimezia lurida, see *T. martinicensis*

Trimezia martinicensis 236

trinitaria, see *Bougainvillea*

Triplaris 318

Triplaris cumingiana 318

Tristania conferta, see *Lophostemon confertus*

Tristellateia 253

Tristellateia australasiae 253

trompillo, see *Ipomoea hederifolia*

tropical hydrangea, see *Dombeya*

trumpet, golden, see *Allamanda cathartica*

trumpet, Nile, see *Markhamia lutea*

trumpet-bush, orange, see *Tecoma* ×*smithii*

trumpet-creeper, see *Campsis*; *Distictis*

trumpet-flower, evening, see *Gelsemium sempervirens*

trumpet-flower, Nepal, see *Beaumontia grandiflora*

trumpet-tree, see *Tabebuia*; *Dolichandrone*; *Cecropia*

trumpet-vine, see *Clytostoma*; *Podranea*

tube-flower, see *Clerodendrum indicum*; *C. minahassae*

tube-flower, violet, see *Iochroma warscewiczii*

Tulbaghia 51

Tulbaghia violacea 51

tulip, Siam, see *Curcuma alismatifolia* 365

tulipán Africano, see *Spathodea campanulata*

tulip-tree, African, see *Spathodea campanulata*

tulipwood, Moreton Bay, see *Harpullia pendula*

tumbo, see *Passiflora quadrangularis*

tuna, see *Opuntia*

Turk's cap mallow, see *Malvaviscus penduliflorus*

Turk's turban, see *Clerodendrum indicum*

Turnera 357

Turnera diffusa 358

Turnera elegans, see *T. subulata*

Turnera subulata 358

Turnera trioniflora, see *T. subulata*

Turnera ulmifolia 358

Turnera ulmifolia var. *elegans*, see *T. subulata*

Turneraceae 357

twin plum, see *Ochrosia elliptica*

twinberry, see *Myrcianthes fragrans*

'ulei, see *Osteomeles anthyllidifolia*

umbrella-tree, see *Schefflera*

umbrella-tree, Texas, see *Melia azedarach*

Uncarina 312

Uncarina grandidieri 312

Unona odorata, see *Cananga odorata*

uñitas, see *Macfadyena*

upside-down-tree, see *Adansonia*

Uragoga viridis, see *Psychotria viridis*

Uraria 223

Uraria crinita 223

Urceolina ulei, see *Eucharis ulei*

Urechites lutea, see *Pentalinon luteum*

Urechites pinetorum, see *Pentalinon luteum*

uva rosa, see *Medinilla magnifica*

Uvaria longifolia, see *Polyalthia longifolia*

Uvaria odorata, see *Cananga odorata*

uvero, see *Coccoloba uvifera*

Vaal River lily, see *Crinum bulbispermum*

Vanda 305

Vanda luzonica 305

vaquero blanco, see *Cydista aequinoctialis*

varnish-leaf, see *Dodonaea viscosa*

vegetable-hummingbird, see *Sesbania grandiflora*

vegetable-mercury, see *Brunfelsia uniflora*

vegetable-sponge, see *Luffa aegyptiaca*

Veitchia 120

Veitchia arecina 121

Veitchia macdanielsii, see *V. arecina*

Veitchia merrillii, see *Adonidia merrillii*

Veitchia montgomeryana, see *V. arecina*

Vellota miniata, see *Clivia miniata*

Vellozia 358

Vellozia bahiana 358

Velloziaceae 358

velvet-apple, see *Diospyros blancoi*

velvet-leaf, see *Abutilon palmeri*; *Kalanchoe beharensis*

velvet-plant, trailing, see *Ruellia makoyana*

Venus-slipper orchid, see *Paphiopedilum*

vera wood, see *Bulnesia arborea*

Verbena jamaicensis, see *Stachytarpheta jamaicensis*

Verbena mutabilis, see *Stachytarpheta mutabilis*

Verbenaceae 358, see also *Lamiaceae*

Victoria 294

Victoria amazonica 295

Victoria cruziana 294

Victoria hybrid 294

Vigna 223

Vigna caracalla 224

Vinca rosea, see *Catharanthus roseus*

vinca, see *Catharanthus roseus*

vinca, shrub, see *Kopsia fruticosa*

vine-lily, see *Gloriosa superba*

Viola prunifolia, see *Hybanthus prunifolius*

Violaceae 360

violet, Easter, see *Securidaca diversifolia*

violet, foxtail, see *Dyschoriste* sp.

violet, Philippine, see *Barleria cristata*

vireya, see *Rhododendron* Vireya Group

Vitex 243

Vitex agnus-castus 243

Vitex parviflora 243

volador, see *Triplaris*

voodoo lily, see *Amorphophallus paeoniifolius*

Vriesea 162

Vriesea conferta, see *V. ensiformis*

Vriesea ensiformis 163

Vriesea geniculata, see *Alcantarea glaziouana*

Vriesea glaziouana, see *Alcantarea glaziouana*

Vriesea imperialis, see *Alcantarea imperialis*

vriesea, giant, see *Alcantarea imperialis*

Wagatea spicata, see *Moullava spicata*

wahane, see *Pritchardia aylmer-robinsonii*

waimanolo, see *Alpinia formosana*

walking tree, see *Pandanus*

wampee, see *Pontederia cordata*

Warszewiczia 333

Warszewiczia coccinea 333

Warszewiczia pulcherrima, see *W. coccinea*

Washington palm, see *Washingtonia*

Washingtonia 121

Washingtonia filamentosa, see *W. filifera*

Washingtonia filifera 122

Washingtonia robusta 122

water-bonnet, see *Pistia stratiotes*

water-hyacinth, see *Eichhornia crassipes*

water-lettuce, see *Pistia stratiotes*

water-lily, see *Nymphaea*; see also *Nelumbo*

water-lily, fairy, see *Nymphoides*

water-lily, giant, see *Victoria*

water-platter, see *Victoria*

water-poppy, see *Hydrocleys nymphoides*

water-snowflake, see *Nymphoides*

water spinach, see *Ipomoea*

Watsonia 236

Watsonia borbonica 236

Watsonia pyramidata, see *W. borbonica*

watsonia, pink, see *Watsonia borbonica*

wattle, African, see *Peltophorum africanum*

wattle, Cootamundra, see *Acacia baileyana*

wattle, Darwin black, see *Acacia auriculiformis*

wax flower, see *Chamelaucium*; *Etlingera*

wax jambu, see *Syzygium jambos*

wax rose, see *Pereskia grandifolia*

wax-leafed ligustrum, see *Ligustrum japonicum*

Wedelia trilobata, see *Sphagneticola trilobata*

Wercklea 260

Wercklea ferox 260

West Indian cherry, see *Cordia nitida*; *Malpighia emarginata*

West Indian lilac, see *Tetrazygia bicolor*

whistling bean, see *Albizia lebbeck*

Wigandia 150

Wigandia caracasana, see *W. urens*

Wigandia urens 150

wild cucumber, see *Momordica charantia*

wild pear, see *Dombeya spectabilis*

willow-myrtle, sweet, see *Agonis flexuosa*

window-palm, see *Beccariophoenix*; *Reinhardtia*

wine-palm, see *Butia capitata*; *Pseudophoenix vinifera*

winged beauty, see *Dalechampia aristolochiifolia*

winged calabash, see *Crescentia alata*

wisteria-tree, scarlet, see *Sesbania grandiflora*

Wodyetia 122

Wodyetia bifurcata 123

woman's tongue, see *Albizia lebbeck*

wood-apple, see *Limonia acidissima*

wood-rose, see *Merremia tuberosa*

wood-sorrel, see *Oxalis tetraphylla*

Wormia suffruticosa, see *Dillenia suffruticosa*

Wrightia 72

Wrightia arborea 72

Wrightia tomentosa, see *W. arborea*

Xanthosoma 87

Xanthosoma maffafa 87

Xanthosoma sagittifolium 87

yam, see *Ipomoea*

yam, wild, see *Dioscorea bulbifera*

yautía, see *Xanthosoma maffafa*

yellow bird, see *Heliconia* 'Golden Torch'

yellow candles, see *Pachystachys lutea*

yellow candle-wood, see *Senna bicapsularis*

yellow elder, see *Tecoma stans*

yellow poinciana, see *Peltophorum*

yerba anis, see *Tagetes lucida*

yesterday-today-tomorrow, see *Brunfelsia grandiflora*

ylang-ylang, see *Cananga odorata*

yoke-wood, see *Catalpa longissima*

yuca, see *Manihot esculenta*

Yucca 47

Yucca aloifolia 48

Yucca draconis, see *Dracaena draco*

Yucca gloriosa, see *Y. aloifolia*

Yucca rostrata 48

Yucca thompsoniana 48

Yucca yucatana, see *Y. aloifolia*

yucca, beaked, see *Yucca rostrata*

yuquilla, see *Canna indica*

yuraguana, see *Coccothrinax argentea*

Zantedeschia 87

Zantedeschia aethiopica 88

Zantedeschia elliottiana 88

Zantedeschia pentlandii 88

zedoary, see *Curcuma zedoaria*

Zephyranthes 56

Zephyranthes grandiflora 56

Zephyranthes robusta, see *Habranthus robustus*

Zeuxine 305

Zeuxine strateumatica 305

Zingiber 372

Zingiber neglectum 372

Zingiber spectabile 372

Zingiber zerumbet 372

Zingiberaceae 361

Zombia 123

Zombia antillarum 123

zombie-palm, see *Zombia antillarum*

Zulu cherry, see *Dombeya burgessiae*

Zulu giant, see *Stapelia leendertziae*

Zygocactus, see *Schlumbergera*

Zygophyllaceae 373